Lecture Notes in Computer Science 8693

Commenced Publication in 1973
Founding and Former Series Editors:
Gerhard Goos, Juris Hartmanis, and Jan van Leeuwen

David Fleet   Tomas Pajdla   Bernt Schiele
Tinne Tuytelaars (Eds.)

Computer Vision – ECCV 2014

13th European Conference
Zurich, Switzerland, September 6-12, 2014
Proceedings, Part V

 Springer

Volume Editors

David Fleet
University of Toronto, Department of Computer Science
6 King's College Road, Toronto, ON M5H 3S5, Canada
E-mail: fleet@cs.toronto.edu

Tomas Pajdla
Czech Technical University in Prague, Department of Cybernetics
Technicka 2, 166 27 Prague 6, Czech Republic
E-mail: pajdla@cmp.felk.cvut.cz

Bernt Schiele
Max-Planck-Institut für Informatik
Campus E1 4, 66123 Saarbrücken, Germany
E-mail: schiele@mpi-inf.mpg.de

Tinne Tuytelaars
KU Leuven, ESAT - PSI, iMinds
Kasteelpark Arenberg 10, Bus 2441, 3001 Leuven, Belgium
E-mail: tinne.tuytelaars@esat.kuleuven.be

Videos to this book can be accessed at
http://www.springerimages.com/videos/978-3-319-10601-4

ISSN 0302-9743   e-ISSN 1611-3349
ISBN 978-3-319-10601-4   e-ISBN 978-3-319-10602-1
DOI 10.1007/978-3-319-10602-1
Springer Cham Heidelberg New York Dordrecht London

Library of Congress Control Number: 2014946360

LNCS Sublibrary: SL 6 – Image Processing, Computer Vision, Pattern Recognition,
and Graphics

Typesetting: Camera-ready by author, data conversion by Scientific Publishing Services, Chennai, India

Printed on acid-free paper

Springer is part of Springer Science+Business Media (www.springer.com)

Foreword

The European Conference on Computer Vision is one of the top conferences in computer vision. It was first held in 1990 in Antibes (France) with subsequent conferences in Santa Margherita Ligure (Italy) in 1992, Stockholm (Sweden) in 1994, Cambridge (UK) in 1996, Freiburg (Germany) in 1998, Dublin (Ireland) in 2000, Copenhagen (Denmark) in 2002, Prague (Czech Republic) in 2004, Graz (Austria) in 2006, Marseille (France) in 2008, Heraklion (Greece) in 2010, and Florence (Italy) in 2012. Many people have worked hard to turn the 2014 edition into as great a success. We hope you will find this a mission accomplished.

The chairs decided to adhere to the classic single-track scheme. In terms of the time ordering, we decided to largely follow the Florence example (typically starting with poster sessions, followed by oral sessions), which offers a lot of flexibility to network and is more forgiving for the not-so-early-birds and hard-core gourmets.

A large conference like ECCV requires the help of many. They made sure there was a full program including the main conference, tutorials, workshops, exhibits, demos, proceedings, video streaming/archive, and Web descriptions. We want to cordially thank all those volunteers! Please have a look at the conference website to see their names (http://eccv2014.org/people/). We also thank our generous sponsors. Their support was vital for keeping prices low and enriching the program. And it is good to see such a level of industrial interest in what our community is doing!

We hope you will enjoy the proceedings ECCV 2014.

Also, willkommen in Zürich!

September 2014

Marc Pollefeys
Luc Van Gool
General Chairs

Preface

Welcome to the proceedings of the 2014 European Conference on Computer Vision (ECCV 2014) that was in Zurich, Switzerland. We are delighted to present this volume reflecting a strong and exciting program, the result of an extensive review process. In total, we received 1,444 paper submissions. Of these, 85 violated the ECCV submission guidelines and were rejected without review. Of the remainder, 363 were accepted (26,7%): 325 as posters (23,9%) and 38 as oral presentations (2,8%). This selection process was a combined effort of four program co-chairs (PCs), 53 area chairs (ACs), 803 Program Committee members and 247 additional reviewers.

As PCs we were primarily responsible for the design and execution of the review process. Beyond administrative rejections, we were not directly involved in acceptance decisions. Because the general co-chairs were permitted to submit papers, they played no role in the review process and were treated as any other author.

Acceptance decisions were made by the AC Committee. There were 53 ACs in total, selected by the PCs to provide sufficient technical expertise, geographical diversity (21 from Europe, 7 from Asia, and 25 from North America) and a mix of AC experience (7 had no previous AC experience, 18 had served as AC of a major international vision conference once since 2010, 8 had served twice, 13 had served three times, and 7 had served 4 times).

ACs were aided by 803 Program Committee members to whom papers were assigned for reviewing. There were 247 additional reviewers, each supervised by a Program Committee member. The Program Committee was based on suggestions from ACs, and committees from previous conferences. Google Scholar profiles were collected for all candidate Program Committee members and vetted by PCs. Having a large pool of Program Committee members for reviewing allowed us to match expertise while bounding reviewer loads. No more than nine papers were assigned to any one Program Committee member, with a maximum of six to graduate students.

The ECCV 2014 review process was double blind. Authors did not know the reviewers' identities, nor the ACs handling their paper(s). We did our utmost to ensure that ACs and reviewers did not know authors' identities, even though anonymity becomes difficult to maintain as more and more submissions appear concurrently on arXiv.org.

Particular attention was paid to minimizing potential conflicts of interest. Conflicts of interest between ACs, Program Committee members, and papers were based on authorship of ECCV 2014 submissions, on their home institutions, and on previous collaborations. To find institutional conflicts, all authors,

Program Committee members, and ACs were asked to list the Internet domains of their current institutions. To find collaborators, the DBLP (www.dblp.org) database was used to find any co-authored papers in the period 2010–2014.

We initially assigned approximately 100 papers to each AC, based on affinity scores from the Toronto Paper Matching System and authors' AC suggestions. ACs then bid on these, indicating their level of expertise. Based on these bids, and conflicts of interest, approximately 27 papers were assigned to each AC, for which they would act as the primary AC. The primary AC then suggested seven reviewers from the pool of Program Committee members (in rank order) for each paper, from which three were chosen per paper, taking load balancing and conflicts of interest into account.

Many papers were also assigned a secondary AC, either directly by the PCs, or as a consequence of the primary AC requesting the aid of an AC with complementary expertise. Secondary ACs could be assigned at any stage in the process, but in most cases this occurred about two weeks before the final AC meeting. Hence, in addition to their initial load of approximately 27 papers, each AC was asked to handle three to five more papers as a secondary AC; they were expected to read and write a short assessment of such papers. In addition, two of the 53 ACs were not directly assigned papers. Rather, they were available throughout the process to aid other ACs at any stage (e.g., with decisions, evaluating technical issues, additional reviews, etc.).

The initial reviewing period was three weeks long, after which reviewers provided reviews with preliminary recommendations. Three weeks is somewhat shorter than normal, but this did not seem to cause any unusual problems. With the generous help of several last-minute reviewers, each paper received three reviews.

Authors were then given the opportunity to rebut the reviews, primarily to identify any factual errors. Following this, reviewers and ACs discussed papers at length, after which reviewers finalized their reviews and gave a final recommendation to the ACs. Many ACs requested help from secondary ACs at this time.

Papers, for which rejection was clear and certain, based on the reviews and the AC's assessment, were identified by their primary ACs and vetted by a shadow AC prior to rejection. (These shadow ACs were assigned by the PCs.) All papers with any chance of acceptance were further discussed at the AC meeting. Those deemed "strong" by primary ACs (about 140 in total) were also assigned a secondary AC.

The AC meeting, with all but two of the primary ACs present, took place in Zurich. ACs were divided into 17 triplets for each morning, and a different set of triplets for each afternoon. Given the content of the three (or more) reviews along with reviewer recommendations, rebuttals, online discussions among reviewers and primary ACs, written input from and discussions with secondary ACs, the

AC triplets then worked together to resolve questions, calibrate assessments, and make acceptance decisions.

To select oral presentations, all strong papers, along with any others put forward by triplets (about 155 in total), were then discussed in four panels, each comprising four or five triplets. Each panel ranked these oral candidates, using four categories. Papers in the two top categories provided the final set of 38 oral presentations.

We want to thank everyone involved in making the ECCV 2014 Program possible. First and foremost, the success of ECCV 2014 depended on the quality of papers submitted by authors, and on the very hard work of the reviewers, the Program Committee members and the ACs. We are particularly grateful to Kyros Kutulakos for his enormous software support before and during the AC meeting, to Laurent Charlin for the use of the Toronto Paper Matching System, and Chaohui Wang for help optimizing the assignment of papers to ACs. We also owe a debt of gratitude for the great support of Zurich local organizers, especially Susanne Keller and her team.

September 2014   David Fleet
                                                          Tomas Pajdla
                                                          Bernt Schiele
                                                       Tinne Tuytelaars

Organization

General Chairs

Luc Van Gool   ETH Zurich, Switzerland
Marc Pollefeys   ETH Zurich, Switzerland

Program Chairs

Tinne Tuytelaars   KU Leuven, Belgium
Bernt Schiele   MPI Informatics, Saarbrücken, Germany
Tomas Pajdla   CTU Prague, Czech Republic
David Fleet   University of Toronto, Canada

Local Arrangements Chairs

Konrad Schindler   ETH Zurich, Switzerland
Vittorio Ferrari   University of Edinburgh, UK

Workshop Chairs

Lourdes Agapito   University College London, UK
Carsten Rother   TU Dresden, Germany
Michael Bronstein   University of Lugano, Switzerland

Tutorial Chairs

Bastian Leibe   RWTH Aachen, Germany
Paolo Favaro   University of Bern, Switzerland
Christoph Lampert   IST Austria

Poster Chair

Helmut Grabner   ETH Zurich, Switzerland

Publication Chairs

Mario Fritz   MPI Informatics, Saarbrücken, Germany
Michael Stark   MPI Informatics, Saarbrücken, Germany

Demo Chairs

Davide Scaramuzza   University of Zurich, Switzerland
Jan-Michael Frahm   University of North Carolina at Chapel Hill,
                         USA

Exhibition Chair

Tamar Tolcachier   University of Zurich, Switzerland

Industrial Liaison Chairs

Alexander Sorkine-Hornung   Disney Research Zurich, Switzerland
Fatih Porikli   ANU, Australia

Student Grant Chair

Seon Joo Kim   Yonsei University, Korea

Air Shelters Accommodation Chair

Maros Blaha   ETH Zurich, Switzerland

Website Chairs

Lorenz Meier   ETH Zurich, Switzerland
Bastien Jacquet   ETH Zurich, Switzerland

Internet Chair

Thorsten Steenbock   ETH Zurich, Switzerland

Student Volunteer Chairs

Andrea Cohen   ETH Zurich, Switzerland
Ralf Dragon   ETH Zurich, Switzerland
Laura Leal-Taixé   ETH Zurich, Switzerland

Finance Chair

Amael Delaunoy   ETH Zurich, Switzerland

Conference Coordinator

Susanne H. Keller   ETH Zurich, Switzerland

Area Chairs

Lourdes Agapito	University College London, UK
Sameer Agarwal	Google Research, USA
Shai Avidan	Tel Aviv University, Israel
Alex Berg	UNC Chapel Hill, USA
Yuri Boykov	University of Western Ontario, Canada
Thomas Brox	University of Freiburg, Germany
Jason Corso	SUNY at Buffalo, USA
Trevor Darrell	UC Berkeley, USA
Fernando de la Torre	Carnegie Mellon University, USA
Frank Dellaert	Georgia Tech, USA
Alexei Efros	UC Berkeley, USA
Vittorio Ferrari	University of Edinburgh, UK
Andrew Fitzgibbon	Microsoft Research, Cambridge, UK
JanMichael Frahm	UNC Chapel Hill, USA
Bill Freeman	Massachusetts Institute of Technology, USA
Peter Gehler	Max Planck Institute for Intelligent Systems, Germany
Kristen Graumann	University of Texas at Austin, USA
Wolfgang Heidrich	University of British Columbia, Canada
Herve Jegou	Inria Rennes, France
Fredrik Kahl	Lund University, Sweden
Kyros Kutulakos	University of Toronto, Canada
Christoph Lampert	IST Austria
Ivan Laptev	Inria Paris, France
Kyuong Mu Lee	Seoul National University, South Korea
Bastian Leibe	RWTH Aachen, Germany
Vincent Lepetit	TU Graz, Austria
Hongdong Li	Australian National University
David Lowe	University of British Columbia, Canada
Greg Mori	Simon Fraser University, Canada
Srinivas Narasimhan	Carnegie Mellon University, PA, USA
Nassir Navab	TU Munich, Germany
Ko Nishino	Drexel University, USA
Maja Pantic	Imperial College London, UK
Patrick Perez	Technicolor Research, Rennes, France
Pietro Perona	California Institute of Technology, USA
Ian Reid	University of Adelaide, Australia
Stefan Roth	TU Darmstadt, Germany
Carsten Rother	TU Dresden, Germany
Sudeep Sarkar	University of South Florida, USA
Silvio Savarese	Stanford University, USA
Christoph Schnoerr	Heidelberg University, Germany
Jamie Shotton	Microsoft Research, Cambridge, UK

Kaleem Siddiqi	McGill, Canada
Leonid Sigal	Disney Research, Pittsburgh, PA, USA
Noah Snavely	Cornell, USA
Raquel Urtasun	University of Toronto, Canada
Andrea Vedaldi	University of Oxford, UK
Jakob Verbeek	Inria Rhone-Alpes, France
Xiaogang Wang	Chinese University of Hong Kong, SAR China
Ming-Hsuan Yang	UC Merced, CA, USA
Lihi Zelnik-Manor	Technion, Israel
Song-Chun Zhu	UCLA, USA
Todd Zickler	Harvard, USA

Program Committee

Gaurav Aggarwal	Joao Barreto	Kristin Branson
Amit Agrawal	Jonathan Barron	Steven Branson
Haizhou Ai	Adrien Bartoli	Francois Bremond
Ijaz Akhter	Arslan Basharat	Michael Bronstein
Karteek Alahari	Dhruv Batra	Gabriel Brostow
Alexandre Alahi	Luis Baumela	Michael Brown
Andrea Albarelli	Maximilian Baust	Matthew Brown
Saad Ali	Jean-Charles Bazin	Marcus Brubaker
Jose M. Alvarez	Loris Bazzani	Andres Bruhn
Juan Andrade-Cetto	Chris Beall	Joan Bruna
Bjoern Andres	Vasileios Belagiannis	Aurelie Bugeau
Mykhaylo Andriluka	Csaba Beleznai	Darius Burschka
Elli Angelopoulou	Moshe Ben-ezra	Ricardo Cabral
Roland Angst	Ohad Ben-Shahar	Jian-Feng Cai
Relja Arandjelovic	Ismail Ben Ayed	Neill D.F. Campbell
Ognjen Arandjelovic	Rodrigo Benenson	Yong Cao
Helder Araujo	Ryad Benosman	Barbara Caputo
Pablo Arbelez	Tamara Berg	Joao Carreira
Vasileios Argyriou	Margrit Betke	Jan Cech
Antonis Argyros	Ross Beveridge	Jinxiang Chai
Kalle Astroem	Bir Bhanu	Ayan Chakrabarti
Vassilis Athitsos	Horst Bischof	Tat-Jen Cham
Yannis Avrithis	Arijit Biswas	Antoni Chan
Yusuf Aytar	Andrew Blake	Manmohan Chandraker
Xiang Bai	Aaron Bobick	Vijay Chandrasekhar
Luca Ballan	Piotr Bojanowski	Hong Chang
Yingze Bao	Ali Borji	Ming-Ching Chang
Richard Baraniuk	Terrance Boult	Rama Chellappa
Adrian Barbu	Lubomir Bourdev	Chao-Yeh Chen
Kobus Barnard	Patrick Bouthemy	David Chen
Connelly Barnes	Edmond Boyer	Hwann-Tzong Chen

Roger Grosse
Matthias Grundmann
Chunhui Gu
Xianfeng Gu
Jinwei Gu
Sergio Guadarrama
Matthieu Guillaumin
Jean-Yves Guillemaut
Hatice Gunes
Ruiqi Guo
Guodong Guo
Abhinav Gupta
Abner Guzman Rivera
Gregory Hager
Ghassan Hamarneh
Bohyung Han
Tony Han
Jari Hannuksela
Tatsuya Harada
Mehrtash Harandi
Bharath Hariharan
Stefan Harmeling
Tal Hassner
Daniel Hauagge
Søren Hauberg
Michal Havlena
James Hays
Kaiming He
Xuming He
Martial Hebert
Felix Heide
Jared Heinly
Hagit Hel-Or
Lionel Heng
Philipp Hennig
Carlos Hernandez
Aaron Hertzmann
Adrian Hilton
David Hogg
Derek Hoiem
Byung-Woo Hong
Anthony Hoogs
Joachim Hornegger
Timothy Hospedales
Wenze Hu

Zhe Hu
Gang Hua
Xian-Sheng Hua
Dong Huang
Gary Huang
Heng Huang
Sung Ju Hwang
Wonjun Hwang
Ivo Ihrke
Nazli Ikizler-Cinbis
Slobodan Ilic
Horace Ip
Michal Irani
Hiroshi Ishikawa
Laurent Itti
Nathan Jacobs
Max Jaderberg
Omar Javed
C.V. Jawahar
Bruno Jedynak
Hueihan Jhuang
Qiang Ji
Hui Ji
Kui Jia
Yangqing Jia
Jiaya Jia
Hao Jiang
Zhuolin Jiang
Sam Johnson
Neel Joshi
Armand Joulin
Frederic Jurie
Ioannis Kakadiaris
Zdenek Kalal
Amit Kale
Joni-Kristian
    Kamarainen
George Kamberov
Kenichi Kanatani
Sing Bing Kang
Vadim Kantorov
Jörg Hendrik Kappes
Leonid Karlinsky
Zoltan Kato
Hiroshi Kawasaki

Verena Kaynig
Cem Keskin
Margret Keuper
Daniel Keysers
Sameh Khamis
Fahad Khan
Saad Khan
Aditya Khosla
Martin Kiefel
Gunhee Kim
Jaechul Kim
Seon Joo Kim
Tae-Kyun Kim
Byungsoo Kim
Benjamin Kimia
Kris Kitani
Hedvig Kjellstrom
Laurent Kneip
Reinhard Koch
Kevin Koeser
Ullrich Koethe
Effrosyni Kokiopoulou
Iasonas Kokkinos
Kalin Kolev
Vladimir Kolmogorov
Vladlen Koltun
Nikos Komodakis
Piotr Koniusz
Peter Kontschieder
Ender Konukoglu
Sanjeev Koppal
Hema Koppula
Andreas Koschan
Jana Kosecka
Adriana Kovashka
Adarsh Kowdle
Josip Krapac
Dilip Krishnan
Zuzana Kukelova
Brian Kulis
Neeraj Kumar
M. Pawan Kumar
Cheng-Hao Kuo
In So Kweon
Junghyun Kwon

Junseok Kwon	Xiaoming Liu	Hossein Mobahi
Simon Lacoste-Julien	Xiaobai Liu	Pranab Mohanty
Shang-Hong Lai	Ming-Yu Liu	Pascal Monasse
Jean-François Lalonde	Marcus Liwicki	Vlad Morariu
Tian Lan	Stephen Lombardi	Philippos Mordohai
Michael Langer	Roberto Lopez-Sastre	Francesc Moreno-Noguer
Doug Lanman	Manolis Lourakis	Luce Morin
Diane Larlus	Brian Lovell	Nigel Morris
Longin Jan Latecki	Chen Change Loy	Bryan Morse
Svetlana Lazebnik	Jiangbo Lu	Eric Mortensen
Laura Leal-Taixé	Jiwen Lu	Yasuhiro Mukaigawa
Erik Learned-Miller	Simon Lucey	Lopamudra Mukherjee
Honglak Lee	Jiebo Luo	Vittorio Murino
Yong Jae Lee	Ping Luo	David Murray
Ido Leichter	Marcus Magnor	Sobhan Naderi Parizi
Victor Lempitsky	Vijay Mahadevan	Hajime Nagahara
Frank Lenzen	Julien Mairal	Laurent Najman
Marius Leordeanu	Michael Maire	Karthik Nandakumar
Thomas Leung	Subhransu Maji	Fabian Nater
Maxime Lhuillier	Atsuto Maki	Jan Neumann
Chunming Li	Yasushi Makihara	Lukas Neumann
Fei-Fei Li	Roberto Manduchi	Ram Nevatia
Fuxin Li	Luca Marchesotti	Richard Newcombe
Rui Li	Aleix Martinez	Minh Hoai Nguyen
Li-Jia Li	Bogdan Matei	Bingbing Ni
Chia-Kai Liang	Diana Mateus	Feiping Nie
Shengcai Liao	Stefan Mathe	Juan Carlos Niebles
Joerg Liebelt	Yasuyuki Matsushita	Marc Niethammer
Jongwoo Lim	Iain Matthews	Claudia Nieuwenhuis
Joseph Lim	Kevin Matzen	Mark Nixon
Ruei-Sung Lin	Bruce Maxwell	Mohammad Norouzi
Yen-Yu Lin	Stephen Maybank	Sebastian Nowozin
Zhouchen Lin	Walterio Mayol-Cuevas	Matthew O'Toole
Liang Lin	David McAllester	Peter Ochs
Haibin Ling	Gerard Medioni	Jean-Marc Odobez
James Little	Christopher Mei	Francesca Odone
Baiyang Liu	Paulo Mendonca	Eyal Ofek
Ce Liu	Thomas Mensink	Sangmin Oh
Feng Liu	Domingo Mery	Takahiro Okabe
Guangcan Liu	Ajmal Mian	Takayuki Okatani
Jingen Liu	Branislav Micusik	Aude Oliva
Wei Liu	Ondrej Miksik	Carl Olsson
Zicheng Liu	Anton Milan	Bjorn Ommer
Zongyi Liu	Majid Mirmehdi	Magnus Oskarsson
Tyng-Luh Liu	Anurag Mittal	Wanli Ouyang

Geoffrey Oxholm
Mustafa Ozuysal
Nicolas Padoy
Caroline Pantofaru
Nicolas Papadakis
George Papandreou
Nikolaos
  Papanikolopoulos
Nikos Paragios
Devi Parikh
Dennis Park
Vishal Patel
Ioannis Patras
Vladimir Pavlovic
Kim Pedersen
Marco Pedersoli
Shmuel Peleg
Marcello Pelillo
Tingying Peng
A.G. Amitha Perera
Alessandro Perina
Federico Pernici
Florent Perronnin
Vladimir Petrovic
Tomas Pfister
Jonathon Phillips
Justus Piater
Massimo Piccardi
Hamed Pirsiavash
Leonid Pishchulin
Robert Pless
Thomas Pock
Jean Ponce
Gerard Pons-Moll
Ronald Poppe
Andrea Prati
Victor Prisacariu
Kari Pulli
Yu Qiao
Lei Qin
Novi Quadrianto
Rahul Raguram
Varun Ramakrishna
Srikumar Ramalingam
Narayanan Ramanathan

Konstantinos
  Rapantzikos
Michalis Raptis
Nalini Ratha
Avinash Ravichandran
Michael Reale
Dikpal Reddy
James Rehg
Jan Reininghaus
Xiaofeng Ren
Jerome Revaud
Morteza Rezanejad
Hayko Riemenschneider
Tammy Riklin Raviv
Antonio Robles-Kelly
Erik Rodner
Emanuele Rodola
Mikel Rodriguez
Marcus Rohrbach
Javier Romero
Charles Rosenberg
Bodo Rosenhahn
Arun Ross
Samuel Rota Bul
Peter Roth
Volker Roth
Anastasios Roussos
Sebastien Roy
Michael Rubinstein
Olga Russakovsky
Bryan Russell
Michael S. Ryoo
Mohammad Amin
  Sadeghi
Kate Saenko
Albert Ali Salah
Imran Saleemi
Mathieu Salzmann
Conrad Sanderson
Aswin
  Sankaranarayanan
Benjamin Sapp
Radim Sara
Scott Satkin
Imari Sato

Yoichi Sato
Bogdan Savchynskyy
Hanno Scharr
Daniel Scharstein
Yoav Y. Schechner
Walter Scheirer
Kevin Schelten
Frank Schmidt
Uwe Schmidt
Julia Schnabel
Alexander Schwing
Nicu Sebe
Shishir Shah
Mubarak Shah
Shiguang Shan
Qi Shan
Ling Shao
Abhishek Sharma
Viktoriia Sharmanska
Eli Shechtman
Yaser Sheikh
Alexander Shekhovtsov
Chunhua Shen
Li Shen
Yonggang Shi
Qinfeng Shi
Ilan Shimshoni
Takaaki Shiratori
Abhinav Shrivastava
Behjat Siddiquie
Nathan Silberman
Karen Simonyan
Richa Singh
Vikas Singh
Sudipta Sinha
Josef Sivic
Dirk Smeets
Arnold Smeulders
William Smith
Cees Snoek
Eric Sommerlade
Alexander
  Sorkine-Hornung
Alvaro Soto
Richard Souvenir

Anuj Srivastava
Ioannis Stamos
Michael Stark
Chris Stauffer
Bjorn Stenger
Charles Stewart
Rainer Stiefelhagen
Juergen Sturm
Yusuke Sugano
Josephine Sullivan
Deqing Sun
Min Sun
Hari Sundar
Ganesh Sundaramoorthi
Kalyan Sunkavalli
Sabine Süsstrunk
David Suter
Tomas Svoboda
Rahul Swaminathan
Tanveer
  Syeda-Mahmood
Rick Szeliski
Raphael Sznitman
Yuichi Taguchi
Yu-Wing Tai
Jun Takamatsu
Hugues Talbot
Ping Tan
Robby Tan
Kevin Tang
Huixuan Tang
Danhang Tang
Marshall Tappen
Jean-Philippe Tarel
Danny Tarlow
Gabriel Taubin
Camillo Taylor
Demetri Terzopoulos
Christian Theobalt
Yuandong Tian
Joseph Tighe
Radu Timofte
Massimo Tistarelli
George Toderici
Sinisa Todorovic

Giorgos Tolias
Federico Tombari
Tatiana Tommasi
Yan Tong
Akihiko Torii
Antonio Torralba
Lorenzo Torresani
Andrea Torsello
Tali Treibitz
Rudolph Triebel
Bill Triggs
Roberto Tron
Tomasz Trzcinski
Ivor Tsang
Yanghai Tsin
Zhuowen Tu
Tony Tung
Pavan Turaga
Engin Türetken
Oncel Tuzel
Georgios Tzimiropoulos
Norimichi Ukita
Martin Urschler
Arash Vahdat
Julien Valentin
Michel Valstar
Koen van de Sande
Joost van de Weijer
Anton van den Hengel
Jan van Gemert
Daniel Vaquero
Kiran Varanasi
Mayank Vatsa
Ashok Veeraraghavan
Olga Veksler
Alexander Vezhnevets
Rene Vidal
Sudheendra
  Vijayanarasimhan
Jordi Vitria
Christian Vogler
Carl Vondrick
Sven Wachsmuth
Stefan Walk
Chaohui Wang

Jingdong Wang
Jue Wang
Ruiping Wang
Kai Wang
Liang Wang
Xinggang Wang
Xin-Jing Wang
Yang Wang
Heng Wang
Yu-Chiang Frank Wang
Simon Warfield
Yichen Wei
Yair Weiss
Gordon Wetzstein
Oliver Whyte
Richard Wildes
Christopher Williams
Lior Wolf
Kwan-Yee Kenneth
  Wong
Oliver Woodford
John Wright
Changchang Wu
Xinxiao Wu
Ying Wu
Tianfu Wu
Yang Wu
Yingnian Wu
Jonas Wulff
Yu Xiang
Tao Xiang
Jianxiong Xiao
Dong Xu
Li Xu
Yong Xu
Kota Yamaguchi
Takayoshi Yamashita
Shuicheng Yan
Jie Yang
Qingxiong Yang
Ruigang Yang
Meng Yang
Yi Yang
Chih-Yuan Yang
Jimei Yang

Bangpeng Yao	Stefanos Zafeiriou	Weishi Zheng
Angela Yao	Hongbin Zha	Bo Zheng
Dit-Yan Yeung	Lei Zhang	Changyin Zhou
Alper Yilmaz	Junping Zhang	Huiyu Zhou
Lijun Yin	Shaoting Zhang	Kevin Zhou
Xianghua Ying	Xiaoqin Zhang	Bolei Zhou
Kuk-Jin Yoon	Guofeng Zhang	Feng Zhou
Shiqi Yu	Tianzhu Zhang	Jun Zhu
Stella Yu	Ning Zhang	Xiangxin Zhu
Jingyi Yu	Lei Zhang	Henning Zimmer
Junsong Yuan	Li Zhang	Karel Zimmermann
Lu Yuan	Bin Zhao	Andrew Zisserman
Alan Yuille	Guoying Zhao	Larry Zitnick
Ramin Zabih	Ming Zhao	Daniel Zoran
Christopher Zach	Yibiao Zhao	

Additional Reviewers

Austin Abrams	Lukas Bossard	Victor Escorcia
Hanno Ackermann	Katie Bouman	Sandro Esquivel
Daniel Adler	Hilton Bristow	Nicola Fioraio
Muhammed Zeshan	Daniel Canelhas	Michael Firman
Afzal	Olivier Canevet	Alex Fix
Pulkit Agrawal	Spencer Cappallo	Oliver Fleischmann
Edilson de Aguiar	Ivan Huerta Casado	Marco Fornoni
Unaiza Ahsan	Daniel Castro	David Fouhey
Amit Aides	Ishani Chakraborty	Vojtech Franc
Zeynep Akata	Chenyi Chen	Jorge Martinez G.
Jon Almazan	Sheng Chen	Silvano Galliani
David Altamar	Xinlei Chen	Pablo Garrido
Marina Alterman	Wei-Chen Chiu	Efstratios Gavves
Mohamed Rabie Amer	Hang Chu	Timnit Gebru
Manuel Amthor	Yang Cong	Georgios Giannoulis
Shawn Andrews	Sam Corbett-Davies	Clement Godard
Oisin Mac Aodha	Zhen Cui	Ankur Gupta
Federica Arrigoni	Maria A. Davila	Saurabh Gupta
Yuval Bahat	Oliver Demetz	Amirhossein Habibian
Luis Barrios	Meltem Demirkus	David Hafner
John Bastian	Chaitanya Desai	Tom S.F. Haines
Florian Becker	Pengfei Dou	Vladimir Haltakov
C. Fabian	Ralf Dragon	Christopher Ham
Benitez-Quiroz	Liang Du	Xufeng Han
Vinay Bettadapura	David Eigen	Stefan Heber
Brian G. Booth	Jakob Engel	Yacov Hel-Or

David Held
Benjamin Hell
Jan Heller
Anton van den Hengel
Robert Henschel
Steven Hickson
Michael Hirsch
Jan Hosang
Shell Hu
Zhiwu Huang
Daniel Huber
Ahmad Humayun
Corneliu Ilisescu
Zahra Iman
Thanapong Intharah
Phillip Isola
Hamid Izadinia
Edward Johns
Justin Johnson
Andreas Jordt
Anne Jordt
Cijo Jose
Daniel Jung
Meina Kan
Ben Kandel
Vasiliy Karasev
Andrej Karpathy
Jan Kautz
Changil Kim
Hyeongwoo Kim
Rolf Koehler
Daniel Kohlsdorf
Svetlana Kordumova
Jonathan Krause
Till Kroeger
Malte Kuhlmann
Ilja Kuzborskij
Alina Kuznetsova
Sam Kwak
Peihua Li
Michael Lam
Maksim Lapin
Gil Levi
Aviad Levis
Yan Li

Wenbin Li
Yin Li
Zhenyang Li
Pengpeng Liang
Jinna Lie
Qiguang Liu
Tianliang Liu
Alexander Loktyushin
Steven Lovegrove
Feng Lu
Jake Lussier
Xutao Lv
Luca Magri
Behrooz Mahasseni
Aravindh Mahendran
Siddharth Mahendran
Francesco Malapelle
Mateusz Malinowski
Santiago Manen
Timo von Marcard
Ricardo Martin-Brualla
Iacopo Masi
Roberto Mecca
Tomer Michaeli
Hengameh Mirzaalian
Kylia Miskell
Ishan Misra
Javier Montoya
Roozbeh Mottaghi
Panagiotis Moutafis
Oliver Mueller
Daniel Munoz
Rajitha Navarathna
James Newling
Mohamed Omran
Vicente Ordonez
Sobhan Naderi Parizi
Omkar Parkhi
Novi Patricia
Kuan-Chuan Peng
Bojan Pepikj
Federico Perazzi
Loic Peter
Alioscia Petrelli
Sebastian Polsterl

Alison Pouch
Vittal Premanchandran
James Pritts
Luis Puig
Julian Quiroga
Vignesh Ramanathan
Rene Ranftl
Mohammad Rastegari
S. Hussain Raza
Michael Reale
Malcolm Reynolds
Alimoor Reza
Christian Richardt
Marko Ristin
Beatrice Rossi
Rasmus Rothe
Nasa Rouf
Anirban Roy
Fereshteh Sadeghi
Zahra Sadeghipoor
Faraz Saedaar
Tanner Schmidt
Anna Senina
Lee Seversky
Yachna Sharma
Chen Shen
Javen Shi
Tomas Simon
Gautam Singh
Brandon M. Smith
Shuran Song
Mohamed Souiai
Srinath Sridhar
Abhilash Srikantha
Michael Stoll
Aparna Taneja
Lisa Tang
Moria Tau
J. Rafael Tena
Roberto Toldo
Manolis Tsakiris
Dimitrios Tzionas
Vladyslav Usenko
Danny Veikherman
Fabio Viola

Table of Contents

Segmentation and Saliency

Poster Session 6

Video Registration to SfM Models

Till Kroeger[1] and Luc Van Gool[1,2]

[1] Computer Vision Laboratory, ETH Zurich, Switzerland
[2] ESAT - PSI / IBBT, K.U. Leuven, Belgium
{kroegert,Bvangool}@vision.ee.ethz.ch

Abstract. Registering image data to Structure from Motion (SfM) point clouds is widely used to find precise camera location and orientation with respect to a world model. In case of videos one constraint has previously been unexploited: temporal smoothness. Without temporal smoothness the magnitude of the pose error in each frame of a video will often dominate the magnitude of frame-to-frame pose change. This hinders application of methods requiring stable poses estimates (e.g. tracking, augmented reality). We incorporate temporal constraints into the image-based registration setting and solve the problem by pose regularization with model fitting and smoothing methods. This leads to accurate, gap-free and smooth poses for all frames. We evaluate different methods on challenging synthetic and real street-view SfM data for varying scenarios of motion speed, outlier contamination, pose estimation failures and 2D-3D correspondence noise. For all test cases a 2 to 60-fold reduction in root mean squared (RMS) positional error is observed, depending on pose estimation difficulty. For varying scenarios, different methods perform best. We give guidance which methods should be preferred depending on circumstances and requirements.

1 Introduction

Due to recent advances in 3D range imaging highly accurate and large 3D models for real-world environments can easily be obtained [1,20,38] and are already available for many city areas. Given structural information about the world, many new opportunities for computer vision (CV) applications in scene understanding arise. Videos are a rich source for capturing and analyzing social activities, human/vehicular traffic and events. This allows for CV applications such as multi-view object tracking, vehicle and pedestrian trajectory analysis, video cutting, multi-video event and scene summarization. Registration of video data to a 3D world model using visual information is an essential requirement for many of these applications. They benefit from accuracy and robustness of pose estimations (6-DoF, position and orientation) for one or several videos at all frames, rather than live performance and efficiency. As processing for these higher level CV applications happens mostly offline (or in batches) global reasoning is sufficient and preferable over live or incremental pose tracking. Localization using visual information only has the advantage that only visual sensors are required and will work even in GPS-denied environments.

D. Fleet et al. (Eds.): ECCV 2014, Part V, LNCS 8693, pp. 1–16, 2014.

Fig. 1. Left & Top right: frame-wise registered hand-held video with 300 frames, The camera's path (red) is noisy due to PnP estimation errors: The average frame-to-frame position difference is 57cm while the ground truth camera moves with approximately 5cm/frame. Bottom right: refined camera path (with Kernel Regression).

The standard approach of image-based registration to SfM models ([34,35,16,26,25]) involves the following steps for each image/video frame: computing 2D image features, matching them to features associated with 3D points, finding the pose using a standard perspective-n-point (PnP) algorithm in a RANSAC loop with 2D-3D correspondences. Direct application of this technique to video data results in very noisy pose estimates, as illustrated in Fig. 1 (left & top right). The path of the camera is drawn in red and exhibits strong positional noise: the average positional difference between poses of successive frames is one order of magnitude larger than the ground truth motion. The true motion is completely *dominated by uncorrelated positional errors*. Using frame-wise PnP estimates we also have to deal with estimation failures (i.e. gaps) and pose outliers in addition to noisy poses. This is unsatisfactory since many tasks, such as multi-view tracking or augmented reality, require *accurate, gap-free* and *smooth* poses as input. This is why we explore several regression methods to exploit temporal smoothness for refining PnP camera poses, which were independently estimated for every video frame. Our aim is to bridge the gap between unreliable, noisy, incomplete, frame-wise pose estimates in SfM models to accurate and smooth pose trajectories to be used for higher-level CV applications.

Our main contribution is the reduction of pose errors for all frames of a video, for which approximate and possibly incomplete frame-wise estimated poses are available. In order to achieve this, we adapt several model fitting techniques (Splines Smoothing, Kernel Regression, Non-Linear Least-Squares optimization) to the problem. We propose a new pose parametrization to be able to use spline and kernel smoothing methods for camera poses. In Non-Linear Least-Squares optimization we introduce a novel bending energy minimization extension for camera pose smoothing. We discuss several combinations of the three methods. All methods are evaluated on real and synthetic data for various difficult scenarios. We give guidance on which method works best under which circumstances. Until now, no such comprehensive description and evaluation for global pose trajectory refinement exists. We are the first to contribute a carefully designed benchmark on synthetic and real data for this.

Paper Overview: Sec. 2, lists related work. The video pose registration methods (Spline Smoothing, **SP**, Kernel Regression **KR**, non-lin. least-squares optimization **LS**) and variants are proposed in Sec. 3, and evaluated in Sec. 4. Sec. 5 concludes the paper.

2   Related Work

Landmark recognition, localization of images are active fields of research: An image is to be positioned with respect to reference images with known localization (e.g. GPS) [40,17], at city scale, with efficient feature representation [36,21], using databases of building facades [32], and even larger world-wide approximate localization [14]. Other methods rely on localization by recognition of landmarks, e.g. [4]. These methods do not rely on 3D structure, but on localized reference images and 2D features. Generally, most of these techniques employ image retrieval techniques and 2D similarity measures based on feature matching. In contrast to this [11] relies on 3D features to recognize places.

Image-based registration to 3D SfM models is concerned with complete (6-DoF) pose estimation. Poses are computed with 2D-3D correspondences based on feature matching [37]. Poses retrieved in this way are more accurate and dependency on visually similar reference images is reduced. Scaling these techniques is difficult, due to the large amounts of features in the matching step. Perspective-n-Point (PnP) algorithms find the pose given a set of 2D-3D correspondences [43,42,23,24]. [25] improves the feature matching step by RANSAC co-occurrence-based sampling. Focus has been put on efficient feature storage and matching [5], with vocabulary trees [16], prioritized matching [26], efficient correspondence search [35,34], match pre-filtering using image retrieval [7], and discriminative visual element mining in challenging scenarios, such as registering paintings [3]. [12,9] address the problem of finding the (6-DoF) pose of observed objects. [31] estimates the pose using lines instead of point features.

Localization of image sequences and videos has received attention as well. [10] registers video frames by employing fundamental matrix constraints between a video frame and the two closest GPS-annotated reference images. GPS coordinates are extracted for all frames by Spline Smoothing. Similarly, [39] retrieves geolocalized images and uses Bayesian tracking for refinement. [18] coarsely localizes image sequences with large time-gaps, such as series of photographs of entire tourist trips on a world-wide grid. Visual odometry in car-mounted cameras is used for localization in a known road network [6]. [2] optimizes poses when no model but frame-to-frame pose changes and measurement uncertainties are available from essential matrices or inertial sensors.

Video registration to 3D SfM models received less attention than image-based registration. However, it is an integral part of SLAM [8,19,30,29]. There, the focus lies on jointly tracking features, and improving their and the camera's localization. In contrast to this the scene structure is predetermined in our task. We do not have a prior on the camera's location. Additionally, the reconstructed environments in SLAM are usually small controlled indoor environments. Imaging conditions for SfM and localization are the same in SLAM, which is generally not the case when a query video has to be registered to separately reconstructed 3D models. [37] localizes video sequences by matching and tracking SIFT features. Similarly, [27] estimates poses by matching and tracking DAISY features. Registration to high-quality CAD models has been worked on as well: ego-motion is tracked in [22] by edge matching in omnidirectional videos, in [15] by feature tracking and coarse-to-fine refinement of edge alignment. [16] finds poses for every frame of videos separately, simplifying the matching by computing virtual views. [41,33] rely on computing SfM from a query video first, and retrieve poses by alignment of the world model and the SfM model from the query video.

SLAM and feature-tracking based techniques work for small datasets or when features can be matched reliably. If matching is difficult (larger city scenes, strongly varying imaging conditions), tracking features will easily result in propagation of matching errors. Techniques that reconstruct the sequence first and match later suffer from typical SfM problems: model deformation and fragmentation, matching problems and the need for manual subsequent alignment with a world model. Because of these principled problems we want to match as many frames as possible directly to the world model and rely on global pose refinement.

3   Registration of Videos to SfM Models

Frame-wise registered videos can exhibit strong noise in individual poses, estimation gaps and pose outliers as illustrated in Fig. 1. Noise, outliers and estimation gaps can be dealt with when incorporating temporal smoothness. On approximately and incompletely registered poses for each frame, described in Sec. 3.1, we build the refinement methods proposed in Sec. 3.2, 3.3, and 3.4. The goal is to improve every frame's pose estimate while being robust towards outliers. We chose Spline Smoothing as a well-known representatives of regularization and basis expansion techniques, Kernel Regression as a representative for probabilistic kernel methods and Non-Linear Least-Squares optimization as representative for direct optimization of re-projection errors as also used in bundle adjustment.

3.1   Image-Based Registration

A SfM model is represented by 3D points and associated SIFT [28] feature descriptors from the views in which the 3D points were observed. We match a new query image by extracting SIFT features, matching them to all features associated with the 3D points, and thereby retrieve a putative set of 2D to 3D correspondences. For known internal parameters many recent pose estimation algorithms (EPnP[23], ASPnP[43], OPnP[42], RPnP[24]) can be used directly in a RANSAC-loop to retrieve (6-DoF) camera position and orientation [34,35,16,26,25]. In the remainder of the paper we assume given internal camera parameters (focal length, projection center, no radial distortion).

3.2 Spline Smoothing

In Spline Smoothing (**SP**) piece-wise polynomial functions $f(x_i)$ are fitted to N sites x_i with observations y_i by minimizing the residual sum of squares (RSS):

$$RSS(f, \lambda) = \lambda \sum_{i=1}^{N} w_i (y_i - f(x_i))^2 + (1 - \lambda) \int (f''(x))^2 dx. \tag{1}$$

The camera pose estimate at time x_i is denoted with y_i (observed), and $f(x_i)$ (smoothed). The N data sites correspond to the number of video frames. A camera pose is represented as a position t and rotation matrix R. We parametrize the pose as a 9-dimensional vector $y = [t^T \ r_1^T \ r_2^T]$ with unit vectors r_1 and r_2 as viewing direction and up-vector of the camera. The RSS is regularized by f's second derivative, i.e. to minimizing the bending energy. The data fidelity term is weighted by w_i, the inlier count after RANSAC, down-weighting poses with few 2D-3D correspondences. The regularization parameter $\lambda \in [0, 1]$ is found via leave-one-out cross-validation.

We propose a variant of a smoothing spline including the camera parameters' covariance Σ and the Mahalanobis distance in the data fidelity term (**SP+C**). Deviation from estimated poses are penalized stronger in the data fidelity term if the cameras' pose estimates are with low variance:

$$RSS(f, \lambda) = \lambda \sum_{i=1}^{N} w_i (y_i - f(x_i))^T \Sigma^{-1} (y_i - f(x_i)) + (1 - \lambda) \int (f''(x))^2 dx. \tag{2}$$

The solution for both spline variants is a weighted linear combination of the observations. The chosen pose parametrization is an approximation to rigid Euclidean motion which is part of the Special Euclidean Lie Group SE(3). Some constraints on orientation cannot be enforced by the spline formulation: orthogonality ($r_1 \cdot r_2 = 0$) and unit norm ($\|r_1\| = \|r_2\| = 1$). However, if the change in R is small, we can assume $\|r_1\| \approx 1 \approx \|r_2\|$ and $r_1 \cdot r_2 \approx 0$. This allows using this under-constrained approximation in smoothing. We can enforce constraints afterwards: For each $f(x_i)$ we re-normalize r_1, r_2 to unit norm and recover $R' = [r_3 \ r_1 \ r_2]^T$ with $r_3 = r_1 \times r_2$. To get a valid rotation matrix we enforce orthogonality by singular value decomposition $[U, S, V] = \text{svd}(R')$ and set $R' = U \cdot V^T$. This approximation is valid as long as the between-frame change in R is slow. See experiments in Sec. 4.1, 4.4 for an analysis of the limits of this parametrization. As alternative parametrization, we experimented with quaternions and an angle-axis representation, with less stable results.

3.3 Kernel Regression

A smoothing spline works well in cases of outlier-free data, perturbed by Gaussian noise. However, even after RANSAC a few pose outliers can remain. In order to avoid a hard inlier-outlier decision for poses, we can still use a RANSAC-inspired pose estimation approach. But instead of keeping only the best result (i.e. sample with highest inlier count) we keep the M best pose samples. This leads to M pose estimates for all N frames. Using the *best* RANSAC samples requires randomly distributed outliers. If outliers are systematic, M *random* samples have to be used to avoid biased estimates. A Nadaraya-Watson model, or Kernel Regression (**KR**), can represent poses over N data sites probabilistically:

$$p(y, x) = \frac{1}{W} \sum_{i=1}^{N} \sum_{j=1}^{M} w_{i,j} \ k(x - x_{i,j}, y - y_{i,j}) \tag{3}$$

where k is the density function, $w_{i,j}$ sample inlier count, $W = \sum_{i=1}^{N} \sum_{j=1}^{M} w_{i,j}$. The pose sample j at time x_i is denoted $y_{i,j}$. We use a Gaussian kernel

$$k(x, y) = \frac{1}{\sqrt{2\pi}} \exp\left(-\frac{1}{2}\left(\frac{x^2}{h_x} + \frac{y^2}{h_y}\right)\right) \tag{4}$$

with bandwidths h_y in parametric space for the camera pose and h_x in time. Both parameters are found in leave-one-out cross-validation. The regression function $f(x_i)$ corresponds to conditional averages of target y_i conditioned on time x_i:

$$f(x_i) = \mathbb{E}(y|x_i) = \int y \ p(y, x_i) dy. \tag{5}$$

This representation allows for a non-parametric probabilistic interpretation of the camera's pose at all times. Outliers can be filtered out effectively. However, it depends on integration over all kernel functions, which can be time consuming.

3.4   Non-linear Least-Squares Optimization

SP and KR (Sec. 3.2, 3.3) operate directly on estimated poses, and are therefore dependent on initial PnP pose quality. We propose a similar objective function as eq. (1) with data fidelity and smoothing term, but instead of using estimated poses in the data fidelity term, we can use the 2D-3D correspondences directly by measuring the 3D point re-projection error. The objective function can be minimized as a Non-Linear Least-Squares (**LS**) problem:

$$RSS(P_1, \dots, P_n) = \sum_{i=1}^{N} \sum_{j=1}^{J_i} (z_{i,j} - P_i \, Z_{i,j})^2 + \lambda \, T^T K T \tag{6}$$

where $P_i = C \cdot [R_i, \ -R_i \cdot t_i]$, with C known camera calibration, J_i the number of 2D-3D correspondences after RANSAC for pose P_i, and $z_{i,j}$, $Z_{i,j}$ the known 2D and 3D locations of correspondence j in pose P_i. K is the bending penalty matrix as in the Reinsch–form for SP[13, p.154]. $T = [t_1, \dots, t_n]$ is a matrix of camera locations. PnP poses are only required as initialization, reducing dependency on PnP methods. The additional advantage of this approach is that other constraints, such as planarity of camera movement (**LS+CP**), can be integrated:

$$RSS(P_1, \ldots, P_n, CP) = \sum_{i=1}^{N} \sum_{j=1}^{J_i} (z_{i,j} - P_i Z_{i,j})^2 + \lambda \, T^T K T + \theta \sum_{i=1}^{N} \mathrm{D}^2(CP, t_n)$$

$$\tag{7}$$

where D (3rd term) returns the distance of camera position t_n to camera plane CP. The camera plane is a free variable in the optimization. Because the regularization parameters λ and θ cannot easily be found automatically, we set them manually to balance the influence of all residuals. Starting the optimization with PnP poses and associated 2D-3D correspondences, we cannot easily remove the influence of incorrect 2D-3D correspondences. However, we can use a Cauchy loss for the re-projection error $\varDelta(x) = \log(1 + x)$ to mitigate the influence from outlying correspondences. The Ceres-Solver[1] is used to minimize eq. (6, 7).

3.5 Combinations and Variants

Besides the discussed methods SP, KR, LS and variants SP+C, LS+CP we include several combinations in our experiments when suitable. The estimated poses from PnP algorithms can be further refined by using Non-Linear Least-Squares optimization of the re-projection error, i.e. eq. (6) without smoothing ($\lambda = 0$) (**LSWS**). Based on LSWS we can again start Spline Smoothing (**LSWS+SP**) or Kernel Regression (**LSWS+KR**). When LS is started from PnP pose estimates, outliers are corrected due to the smoothing term. This correction is improved when LS is initialized from Spline Smoothing solutions (**SP+LS**), and may also be combined with the assumption of planarity of camera movement (**SP+LS+CP**). For some frames no pose estimates exist. This is due to RANSAC failures because of too many outliers or noisy correspondences. Gaps in PnP pose estimates can also be deliberate: Feature matching and RANSAC pose estimation is the main bottleneck for large SfM scenes. It may be necessary to consider only every nth camera pose and interpolate in between. Such gaps can be closed after pose refinement by using standard cubic interpolating splines with knots given by the output of our proposed methods.

4   Experiments

In three experiments we evaluate the performance of the proposed methods and variants, while assuming that unreliable PnP poses from an arbitrary source are available as input. We evaluate with exemplary state-of-the-art PnP methods as mentioned in Sec. 3.1. The first experiment (Sec. 4.1) on synthetic data shows the stability of the smoothing methods with respect to different degrees of pose changes, 2D observation noise, number of 2D-3D correspondences and outlier contamination. The second experiment (Sec 4.2,4.3) shows the performance of the methods on real SfM data of city environments. In the first two experiments

---

[1] http://code.google.com/p/ceres-solver/

we ignore any occurring gap in the PnP pose estimates. In the third experiment (Sec. 4.4) we compare the methods when interpolating over gaps following the smoothing. We focus on the positional (root mean squared, RMS) error to ground truth camera locations. The reasons are 1) space constraints, 2) the camera position is more sensitive to typical problems in feature-based pose estimation (noisy/incorrect 2D-3D correspondences) than orientation and 3) position and orientation errors are strongly correlated. See supplementary material for full results. We consider frame-wise PnP pose estimates, computed with ASPnP [43], as baseline. We chose ASPnP as best performing PnP method (See table 3 in Sec. 4.2). Results for further refined poses (LSWS) without smoothing, and simple Kalman Filtering (KF) are also included. The experimental setup remains the same in all experiments: regularization parameters for SP and KR are automatically determined via cross-validation. Regularization parameters for LS are set manually and are the same for all experiments: $\lambda = \theta = 10^5$. We scale the 3D model to real-world scale. All variants of LS run for 10 iterations. State and observation covariances for KF are computed in an EM-style algorithm. To limit memory-complexity in KR, we set $M = 20$ pose samples per frame.

4.1   Synthetic Video Sequence

The synthetic data consists of a camera (focal length 1000 px, 1280x720 resolution), viewing a simple 3D structure (2 walls at a 135 angle) with 800 3D-points at a distance of 10 meters. We create sequences of 300 frames by rotating the camera around the visible structure (Fig. 2, top left). For every frame we randomly sample 25 2D-3D correspondences and compute the pose. In different sequences with increasing speed of rotation (degrees/frame) we test the effect on smoothing and stability of the pose parametrization. All experiments are repeated 25 times and results averaged. Fig. 2 shows the positional error of our proposed methods against the ASPnP baseline. Increasing speed of rotation around the structure, shown in Fig. 2 (a), enlarges pose differences between successive frames. This shows how each method is affected by increasing pose differences and the sensitivity of the pose parametrization for SP and KR, outlined in Sec. 3.2. In Fig. 2 (b) we examine the performance if the number of 2D-3D correspondences before computing the PnP pose in each frame is decreased, (c) Gaussian noise is added to the 2D feature locations, and (d) the percentage of (uniformly distributed) pose outliers is increased. These plots show the reliability of each method with respect to typical challenges in feature-based pose estimates. We observe:

- KR and SP perform well for slow pose changes. The under-constrained pose parametrization leads to a rising performance loss for fast pose changes.
- LSWS and LS are unreliable (out of scope in plots) due to strong 2D, 3D noise, leading to local optima in optimization. SP+C is unreliable as well.
- The overall best performing and stable method is LS optimization initialized with the result of Spline Smoothing (SP+LS): The local optima problem of LS and LSWS are avoided by initializing the poses near the real optima. SP+LS is hardly affected by low feature count, noise, outliers and fast pose changes.

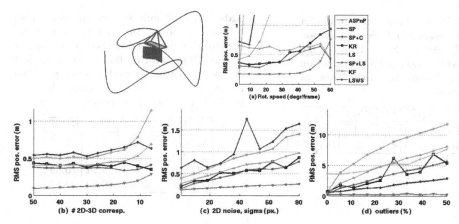

Fig. 2. Refinement results for synthetic video. Top Left: Synthetic sequence (300 frames) of camera (red) rotating around structure (green). Refinement result for (a) varying speed of movement around the structure (degrees/frame), (b) number of 2D-3D correspondences, (c) 2D Gaussian noise, (d) contamination with PnP pose outliers. The legend of (a) also applies to (b,c,d). In (a) LS,LSWS,SP+C,KF are partly out of scope.

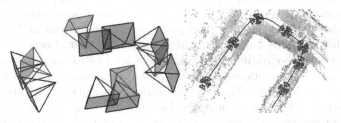

Fig. 3. Left: Rigid camera setup for street-view image capture. Blue camera: used in SfM, red: used only for evaluation. Right: Exemplary SfM Model from 300 frames. Path of van and mounted cameras in scene every 40 frames.

4.2 Street-View Video Sequence – Dataset and PnP Baseline

Since no public dataset for video registration is available we created our own: Street-view image data was captured with 8 cameras, rigidly mounted onto a van, in 1628x1236 resolution, at 10 fps for 30 seconds. The visible street scene was reconstructed with (on average) 400K 3D points. Additionally to the 8 cameras used for SfM, 2 or 4 additional cameras were mounted on the van for evaluation. SfM reconstruction with a rigid multi-camera installation on a moving van returns poses for all cameras and the van at all times. Using known rigid camera setup and van pose, precise pose ground truth can be inferred for the additional cameras as well. The rigid camera configuration and an example SfM Model can be seen in Fig. 3. Data was gathered in 4 locations, one of which is

Table 1. Time for parameter estimation via Cross Validation (SP, SP+C, KR), Expectation Maximization (KF), and solution (sec). Parameters in LS are set manually.

	KF	SP	SP+C	KR	LS
P.Estim.	< 1	7	81	637	NaN
Solution	< 1	< 1	2	164	52

Table 2. PnP failure rates (percent of all frames). A: pose estim. failure, no pose returned, B: failure to find good pose (pos.err < 1m), C: pose estim. failure when at least one other method found a good pose, D: failure to find good pose when all other methods returned good poses.

	OPnP	ASPnP	EPnP	RPnP
A	0.17	0.03	0.64	2.19
B	13.46	11.82	11.85	14.98
C	**0**	0	0.14	0.69
D	1.27	0.30	0.69	2.82

displayed in Fig. 3, resulting in 12 videos with each 300 frames. Typical problems for feature matching in this case are over/underexposure of the images, uneven distribution of feature locations, motion blur, lack of sufficient view overlap (the SfM cameras are looking down, the additional cameras are looking up). The additional cameras are (independently) registered to the SfM Model in our evaluation. PnP poses are obtained from OPnP, ASPnP, EPnP, RPnP. Table 2 compares (A) all methods in terms of percentages of failed pose estimates, (B) failure to find good (pos. err < 1m) poses, (C) failed pose estimates when at least one other method found a good pose, and (D) failure to find a good pose when all other methods found one. ASPnP offers the overall best performance.

Because strong pose outliers are still present for all PnP methods, we proceed to identify and remove outliers, and provide all refinement results for varying levels of removal. Ideally, outliers are identified automatically without the help of ground truth. This can be achieved by using positional differences between PnP poses of successive frames if outliers are randomly distributed and not systematic. For evaluation purposes we simplify the task and use the ground truth error for outlier removal: We define five positional error thresholds: $\rho_{1,...,5} = \{.54, .65, 8.7, 47, \infty\}$ representing meters of allowed error in camera position to ground truth position. They correspond to $\{80, 85, 90, 95, 100\}$ percent of the data as inliers. Poses with an error above a chosen threshold are removed from the PnP baseline and considered as gaps. For ρ_5 we do not remove any pose.

In table 3 all PnP methods are listed with RMS positional error to ground truth in meters (left) and error of viewing direction in degrees (right) for $\rho_{1,...,5}$. We note that the positional error increases significantly in all PnP methods once fewer outliers are removed. The same order of magnitude for positional errors for image-based registration in typical city scenarios is reported independently in [34,35,26,15]. Confirming [43], ASPnP offers the best results. EPnP is not as precise in easy pose estimation scenarios ($\rho_{1,2}$) but gains if outliers are present ($\rho_{3,4,5}$). Note how the orientational and positional errors compare: for pose errors around 5-6 meters, the error in orientation is still < 2 degrees. Average PnP runtimes (seconds) are: OPnP 1.31, ASPnP 0.22, EPnP, 0.25, RPnP: 0.13.

Table 3. PnP pose estimation errors. Left 4 col.: positional RMS error in meters, Right 4 col.: viewing direction errors in degrees (ignoring roll). Rows: Estimation error for outlier varying outlier threshold ρ. Thresholds are chosen such that $\{80, 85, 90, 95, 100\}$ percent of the data are inliers. See also table 4 (left) for median positional PnP errors.

	OPnP-t	ASPnP-t	EPnP-t	RPnP-t	OPnP-R	ASPnP-R	EPnP-R	RPnP-R
$\rho = \rho_1$	0.44	0.14	0.16	0.25	0.29	0.27	0.28	0.3
$\rho = \rho_2$	0.44	0.15	0.67	1.69	0.29	0.27	0.38	0.44
$\rho = \rho_3$	6.58	4.76	2.97	3.48	2.61	1.97	1.72	1.85
$\rho = \rho_4$	12.23	10.49	8.26	9.26	6.62	5.06	5.59	5.09
$\rho = \rho_5$	26.09	23.77	17.96	27.48	10.49	8.85	8.44	9.42

	OPnP-t	ASPnP-t	EPnP-t	RPnP-t
$\rho = \rho_1$	0.381 (K)	**0.065 (J)**	0.066 (J)	0.133 (J)
$\rho = \rho_2$	0.375 (K)	**0.064 (I)**	0.290 (E)	0.576 (I)
$\rho = \rho_3$	1.042 (L)	**0.599 (J)**	1.300 (L)	0.809 (J)
$\rho = \rho_4$	**1.479 (J)**	1.697 (L)	2.281 (L)	1.531 (L)
$\rho = \rho_5$	2.609 (J)	2.684 (L)	2.812 (J)	**2.267 (J)**

Fig. 4. Best refinement result (RMS position error) for all PnP methods. The letter (same as in table 5) indicates the method that gave best results. The graph (right) corresponds to the table (left) and plots best refinements for each PnP method over ρ.

In the remainder of the experiments ASPnP will be used as the preferred PnP baseline. We will report the results of *all* refinement methods based on ASPnP poses (Table 5). Additionally, we will provide the results of *only the best* refinement method based on all PnP baselines (Table 4 (right) & Fig. 4).

4.3 Street-View Video Sequence – Video Registration

We adopt the following shorthand notation. **A**: PnP baseline error, **B**: LSWS, **C**: KF, **D**: SP, **E**: SP+C, **F**: LSWS+SP, **G**: KR, **H**: LSWS+KR, **I**: LS, **J**: LS+CP, **K**: SP+LS, **L**: SP+LS+CP. Fig. 4 lists the best performing refinement method over all PnP methods with absolute positional RMS error. In table 5 the relative scores for all refinement methods in relation to the ASPnP baseline RMS positional error (Col. A) are listed (Col. B:L). Table 4 shows the best refinement results using median errors (right), and median PnP baseline error (left), to illustrate the performance when disregarding outliers. Table 1 lists runtimes for parameter estimation and solutions for the proposed methods. Comparing the best smoothing results for all PnP methods (Table 4 & Fig. 4) we observe:

- Refinement after ASPnP offers significantly better results with few outliers ($\rho_{1,2,3}$) than other PnP methods: the best method reduces the error of the

Table 4. Median PnP baseline positional error (left) and best median refinement error (right). This table shows the gain in positional accuracy from PnP baseline to best performing refinement method with respect to the median ground truth positional error. The letter (same as in table 5) indicates the used method.

	OPnP-t	ASPnP-t	EPnP-t	RPnP-t	OPnP-t	ASPnP-t	EPnP-t	RPnP-t
$\rho = \rho_1$	**.053 (A)**	.055 (A)	.074 (A)	.073 (A)	.042 (J)	**.041 (J)**	.043 (K)	.041 (F)
$\rho = \rho_2$	**.053 (A)**	.055 (A)	.075 (A)	.074 (A)	**.042 (K)**	.042 (K)	.043 (L)	.042 (I)
$\rho = \rho_3$	**.056 (A)**	.057 (A)	.079 (A)	.079 (A)	.044 (K)	**.043 (K)**	.044 (K)	.043 (J)
$\rho = \rho_4$	**.060 (A)**	.062 (A)	.086 (A)	.084 (A)	.046 (K)	**.045 (K)**	.047 (J)	.046 (J)
$\rho = \rho_5$	**.066 (A)**	.067 (A)	.092 (A)	.091 (A)	.053 (J)	.050 (J)	**.048 (L)**	.049 (J)

Table 5. Refinement results. Top 5 rows: positional RMS error (meters). Bottom 5 rows: orientation error (degrees). Col A: Baseline PnP error, Col B-L: avg. of *relative* improvement over baseline PnP pose error in all videos. Notation: **A**: PnP error, **B**: LSWS, **C**: KF, **D**: SP, **E**: SP+C, **F**: LSWS+SP, **G**: KR, **H**: LSWS+KR, **I**: LS, **J**: LS+CP, **K**: SP+LS, **L**: SP+LS+CP

	A	B	C	D	E	F	G	H	I	J	K	L
$\rho = \rho_1$	0.14	1.30	0.90	1.19	1.01	1.56	0.51	0.52	2.18	2.26	2.16	2.22
$\rho = \rho_2$	0.15	1.24	0.96	1.19	1.01	1.53	0.46	0.44	2.23	2.26	2.19	2.24
$\rho = \rho_3$	4.76	1.03	1.15	1.82	1	1.91	1.23	1.27	20.21	23.56	19.34	21.92
$\rho = \rho_4$	10.49	1	1.11	2.23	1.24	2.20	2.01	2.03	18.40	21.99	19.65	20.76
$\rho = \rho_5$	23.77	1	1.23	3.51	1.60	3.56	5.50	5.62	59.68	58.36	37.03	38.85
$\rho = \rho_1$	0.27	1.10	0.94	1.10	1.01	1.20	0.79	0.80	1.34	1.35	1.34	1.35
$\rho = \rho_2$	0.27	1.08	1.02	1.10	1.01	1.18	0.72	0.73	1.34	1.33	1.35	1.33
$\rho = \rho_3$	1.97	1.04	0.99	1.36	1	1.39	1.06	1.13	1.18	1.18	1.43	1.42
$\rho = \rho_4$	5.06	1.02	0.98	1.65	0.97	1.70	1.31	1.30	1.04	1.06	1.29	1.29
$\rho = \rho_5$	8.85	1.01	0.97	2.54	0.95	2.58	1.76	1.76	0.99	1	1.45	1.44

worst method by 83 percent. For $(\rho_{4,5})$ PnP dependency decreases: best method reduces the error of the worst method by only 19 percent.

- In general, least-squares techniques, LS (I), LS+CP (J), SP+LS (K), SP+LS+CP (L) offer the best performance for all outlier levels.
- For $\rho_{4,5}$ the introduction of the camera plane assumption and the initialization using splines SP+LS (K), SP+LS+CP (L) offer a small gain.
- For median errors (table 4) variants of LS (I,J,K,L) also perform best. CP inclusion gives no improvement. The results do not depend on the PnP method.

Comparing *relative* method accuracy for ASPnP as baseline (table 5) we observe:

- SP (D) is increasingly helpful with growing outlier contamination ($\rho_{3,4,5}$). Similar to results on synthetic data, SP+C (E) does not help much.
- In general, all LS variants (I,J,K,L) offer significantly better results than any other method. In contrast to our experiments on synthetic data, for real data

LSWS (B) and, as a consequence LS (I) / LS+CP (J) have similar scores in positional accuracy to SP+LS (K) / SP+LS+CP (L). Initialization using splines slightly improves orientation estimation. Inclusion of a CP in the optimization marginally improves the result, but leads to a slower convergence.

- KF (C) and KR (G,H) help primarily in case of many outliers ($\rho_{4,5}$), LSWS (B) helps for ($\rho_{1,2,3}$). Initializing SP (D) or KR (G) with LSWS (B) in LSWS+SP (F), LSWS+KR (H) leads to a marginal improvement.

As in our experiment on synthetic data, variants of LS perform best on real data as well. The influence of initial PnP poses is weak if few outliers are present.

Comparison with registration after reconstruction: An alternative way of video registration is SfM reconstruction of a query video, and alignment of the new model to the ground truth. We reconstructed every video with standard SfM tools. The camera poses were rigidly aligned to the ground truth by minimizing the RMS positional error. The resulting positional error of **9.051 meters** is significantly worse than our best refinement result with an error of **2.267 meters** (See fig. 4, ρ_5 for no outlier removal). This is mainly due to SfM model deformation and fragmentation. See supplementary material for more details.

4.4   Gap Interpolation

There are three scenarios where gaps, i.e. missing pose estimates for a consecutive number of frames, can occur: 1) Failure of the PnP algorithm to converge, 2) Removal of identified pose outliers, 3) deliberate speed-up by matching every nth frame to the SfM model. In our third experiment gaps are created deliberately in the synthetic dataset (Sec. 4.1, fast non-linear camera motion) and street-view dataset (Sec 4.2, mostly linear, slow camera motion). We keep every nth pose, leaving the remaining frames as gaps, and refine the camera path. We interpolate over the gaps with cubic interpolation splines by using the refined poses as knots,

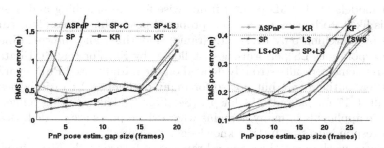

Fig. 5. Positional RMS pose error for refined poses after gap interpolation. Every nth PnP pose is kept, remaining frames are gaps, poses are smoothed, and result interpolated with cubic splines. Left: Synthetic dataset, Right: Street-view videos. Note: due to high, very volatile error LSWS, LS (left) and SP+C (right) were not plotted. KF and KR (right) exhibit high error and are out of scope.

and evaluate on all frames including gaps. Fig. 5 shows the positional RMS error for increasing gap sizes on real (right) and synthetic data (left). We observe:

- KR and KF are rarely helpful: For large gaps KF's linear dynamics assumption is violated, conditional averaging in KR is unstable. LS,LSWS,SP+C have the same problem as in Sec. 4.1.
- SP shows reliable refinement over gaps. The gain over the ASPnP baseline depends on the degree of non-linearity of camera motion: The camera motion eliminates any gain after 7,10 (synthetic,real) skipped frames.
- As in our previous experiments, SP+LS offers the overall best performance on both datasets. The inclusion of a CP as constraint offers an additional boost in real data. SP+LS (left) and LS+CP (right) lose their gain over the baseline only after 20 and 30 skipped frames, respectively.

5   Discussion and Conclusion

The three experiments show that in *all test cases* in synthetic and real data most proposed methods improve pose accuracy over frame-wise registered poses by including temporal smoothness. The best achieved improvement ranges from 2 to 60-fold reduction in RMS positional error depending on the outlier contamination and magnitude of pose changes between frames.

Generally, variants of LS provide the best results for positional, but not for orientational accuracy. The positional accuracy can be improved further by adding additional constraints, such as a planar motion assumption (LS+CP). Robust initialization (SP+LS) can help with convergence when strong noise in 2D and 3D is present. SP provides the fastest method with good results. Inclusion of camera parameter covariances (SP+C) did not improve accuracy due to many spurious feature matches. KR was able to handle outlying poses efficiently, but conditional averaging decreases accuracy when poses are already good. If speed is a constraint SP and LS scale linearly and are close to real-time performance. In case orientation is more important than position and the data is strongly contaminated with outliers, SP offers the best performance. Even for medium sized SfM models ($\sim 10^5$ 3D points) frame-wise feature matching and pose estimation is likely to be slower than our proposed pose refinements. This can be mitigated by matching only every nth frame, smoothing and interpolating. In case of interpolation, LS performs best, followed by SP. For real SfM data we note that refinement results strongly depend on the initially used PnP algorithm in case of few outliers (ρ_1) but not so for many outliers (ρ_5) : ratio of best to worst result: 0.17 for ρ_1, but 0.81 for ρ_5. (See Fig. 4). The resulting refinement methods are applicable in many domains where video poses are needed: Besides 2D-3D correspondences no further knowledge is required.

The present work opens three main branches of future work. First, from the large body of works on regularization, basis expansion, and probabilistic kernel methods, we adapted several techniques (SP, KR) to the problem of video registration. Different parametrizations and techniques, such as random regression forests can be examined. Second, combinations of this method with pose estimation through feature tracking [27,37] can be explored. Third, the LS refinement can naturally be combined with previous works on video pose estimation where SLAM is applied to a video first, and matched to a 3D world afterwards [41,33].

Acknowledgments. This work was supported by the European Research Council (ERC) under the project VarCity (#273940).

References

1. Agarwal, S., Snavely, N., Simon, I., Seitz, S., Szeliski, R.: Building Rome in a day. In: ICCV (2009)
2. Agrawal, M.: A Lie Algebraic Approach for Consistent Pose Registration for General Euclidean Motion. In: IEEE/RSJ IROS (2013)
3. Aubry, M., Russell, B.C., Sivic, J.: Painting-to-3D Model Alignment Via Discriminative Visual Elements. ACM TOG (2013)
4. Bergamo, A., Torresani, L.: Leveraging Structure from Motion to Learn Discriminative Codebooks for Scalable Landmark Classification. In: CVPR (2013)
5. Boix, X., Gygli, M., Roig, G., Van Gool, L.: Sparse Quantization for Patch Description. In: CVPR (2013)
6. Brubaker, M.A., Geiger, A., Urtasun, R.: Lost! Leveraging the Crowd for Probabilistic Visual Self-Localization. In: CVPR (2013)
7. Cao, S., Snavely, N.: Graph-Based Discriminative Learning for Location Recognition. In: CVPR (2013)
8. Davison, A.J., Reid, I.D., Molton, N.D., Stasse, O.: MonoSLAM: real-time single camera SLAM. PAMI (2007)
9. Gordon, I., Lowe, D.G.: What and Where: 3D Object Recognition with Accurate Pose. In: CLOR 2006 (2006)
10. Hakeem, A., Vezzani, R., Shah, M., Cucchiara, R.: Estimating Geospatial Trajectory of a Moving Camera. In: ICPR (2006)
11. Hao, Q., Cai, R., Li, Z., Zhang, L., Pang, Y., Wu, F.: 3D visual phrases for landmark recognition. In: CVPR (2012)
12. Hao, Q., Cai, R., Li, Z., Zhang, L., Pang, Y., Wu, F., Rui, Y.: Efficient 2D-to-3D Correspondence Filtering for Scalable 3D Object Recognition. In: CVPR (2013)
13. Hastie, T., Tibshirani, R., Friedman, J.: The Elements of Statistical Learning, Data Mining, Inference, and Prediction, 2nd edn. Springer (2009)
14. Hays, J., Efros, A.A.: IM 2 GPS: estimating geographic information from a single image. In: CVPR (2008)
15. Hsu, S., Samarasekera, S., Kumar, R., Sawhney, H.S.: Pose estimation, model refinement, and enhanced visualization using video. In: CVPR (2000)
16. Irschara, A., Zach, C., Frahm, J.M., Bischof, H.: From structure-from-motion point clouds to fast location recognition. In: CVPR (2009)
17. Kalantidis, Y., Tolias, G., Avrithis, Y.: Viral: Visual image retrieval and localization. Multimedia Tools and Applications (2011)
18. Kalogerakis, E., Vesselova, O., Hays, J., Efros, A.A., Hertzmann, A.: Image Sequence Geolocation with Human Travel Priors. In: ICCV (2009)
19. Klein, G., Murray, D.: Parallel Tracking and Mapping for Small AR Workspaces. In: ISMAR (2007)
20. Klingner, B., Martin, D., Roseborough, J.: Street View Motion-from-Structure-from-Motion. In: ICCV (2013)

21. Knopp, J., Sivic, J., Pajdla, T.: Avoiding confusing features in place recognition. In: Daniilidis, K., Maragos, P., Paragios, N. (eds.) ECCV 2010, Part I. LNCS, vol. 6311, pp. 748–761. Springer, Heidelberg (2010)
22. Koch, O., Teller, S.: Wide-Area Egomotion Estimation from Known 3D Structure. In: CVPR (2007)
23. Lepetit, V., Moreno-Noguer, F., Fua, P.: EPnP: An Accurate O(n) Solution to the PnP Problem. IJCV (2009)
24. Li, S., Xu, C., Xie, M.: A Robust O(n) Solution to the Perspective-n-Point Problem. PAMI (2012)
25. Li, Y., Snavely, N., Huttenlocher, D., Fua, P.: Worldwide pose estimation using 3D point clouds. In: Fitzgibbon, A., Lazebnik, S., Perona, P., Sato, Y., Schmid, C. (eds.) ECCV 2012, Part I. LNCS, vol. 7572, pp. 15–29. Springer, Heidelberg (2012)
26. Li, Y., Snavely, N., Huttenlocher, D.P.: Location Recognition using Prioritized Feature Matching. In: Daniilidis, K., Maragos, P., Paragios, N. (eds.) ECCV 2010, Part II. LNCS, vol. 6312, pp. 791–804. Springer, Heidelberg (2010)
27. Lim, H., Sinha, S.N., Cohen, M.F., Uyttendaele, M.: Real-time image-based 6-dof localization in large-scale environments. In: CVPR (2012)
28. Lowe, D.G.: Distinctive Image Features from Scale-Invariant Keypoints. IJCV (2004)
29. Newcombe, R.A., Davison, A.J.: Live dense reconstruction with a single moving camera. In: CVPR (2010)
30. Newcombe, R.A., Lovegrove, S.J., Davison, A.J.: DTAM: Dense tracking and mapping in real-time. In: ICCV (2011)
31. Ramalingam, S., Bouaziz, S., Sturm, P.: Pose Estimation Using Both Points and Lines for Geolocation. In: ICRA (2011)
32. Robertson, D., Cipolla, R.: An Image-Based System for Urban Navigation. In: BMVC (2004)
33. Rodriguez, J., Aggarwal, J.: Matching aerial images to 3-D terrain maps. PAMI (1990)
34. Sattler, T., Leibe, B., Kobbelt, L.: Fast image-based localization using direct 2D-to-3D matching. In: ICCV (2011)
35. Sattler, T., Leibe, B., Kobbelt, L.: Improving Image-Based Localization by Active Correspondence Search. In: Fitzgibbon, A., Lazebnik, S., Perona, P., Sato, Y., Schmid, C. (eds.) ECCV 2012, Part I. LNCS, vol. 7572, pp. 752–765. Springer, Heidelberg (2012)
36. Schindler, G., Brown, M., Szeliski, R.: City-Scale Location Recognition. In: CVPR (2007)
37. Se, S., Lowe, D., Little, J.: Vision-based mobile robot localization and mapping using scale-invariant features. In: ICRA (2001)
38. Tanskanen, P., Kolev, K., Meier, L., Camposeco, F., Saurer, O., Pollefeys, M.: Live Metric 3D Reconstruction on Mobile Phones. In: ICCV (2013)
39. Vaca-Castano, G., Zamir, A.R., Shah, M.: City scale geo-spatial trajectory estimation of a moving camera. In: CVPR (2012)
40. Zamir, A.R., Shah, M.: Accurate image localization based on google maps street view. In: Daniilidis, K., Maragos, P., Paragios, N. (eds.) ECCV 2010, Part IV. LNCS, vol. 6314, pp. 255–268. Springer, Heidelberg (2010)
41. Zhao, W., Nister, D., Hsu, S.: Alignment of continuous video onto 3D point clouds. In: CVPR (2004)
42. Zheng, Y., Kuang, Y., Sugimoto, S., Aström, K., Okutomi, M.: Revisiting the PnP Problem: A Fast, General and Optimal Solution. In: ICCV (2013)
43. Zheng, Y., Sugimoto, S., Okutomi, M.: ASPnP: An Accurate and Scalable Solution to the Perspective-n-Point Problem. IEICE TIS (2013)

Soft Cost Aggregation with Multi-resolution Fusion

Xiao Tan[1,2], Changming Sun[1], Dadong Wang[1], Yi Guo[1], and Tuan D. Pham[3]

[1] CSIRO Computational Informatics, North Ryde, NSW 1670, Australia
[2] The University of New South Wales, Canberra, ACT 2600, Australia
[3] The University of Aizu, Fukushima, Japan
tanxchong@gmail.com, tdpham@u-aizu.ac.jp,
{changming.sun,dadong.wang,yi.guo}@csiro.au

Abstract. This paper presents a simple and effective cost volume aggregation framework for addressing pixels labeling problem. Our idea is based on the observation that incorrect labelings are greatly reduced in cost volume aggregation results from low resolutions. However, image details may be lost in the low resolution results. To take advantage of the results from low resolution for reducing these incorrect labelings while preserving details, we propose a multi-resolution cost aggregation method (MultiAgg) by using a soft fusion scheme based on min-convolution. We implement our MultiAgg in applications on stereo matching and interactive image segmentation. Experimental results show that our method significantly outperforms conventional cost aggregation methods in labeling accuracy. Moreover, although MultiAgg is a simple and straight-forward method, it produces results which are close to or even better than those from iterative methods based on global optimization.

Keywords: Multi-resolution fusion, Cost aggregation, Stereo matching, Interactive segmentation.

1 Introduction

Many early vision problems, such as stereo matching and image segmentation, can be formulated as pixel-labeling problems. The labels represent some specified local quantities [13] such as disparity for stereo matching or background/object index for segmentation. Generally, a good labeling should be both locally smooth and edge-preserving while being consistent with the observed data. The labeling methods can be generally categorized into two classes. One is the local cost aggregation methods such as the recently developed cost volume filtering [11] and non-local aggregation [16]. In these methods, the cost volume is aggregated within a local region by implicitly making a spatial smoothness assumption. Another alternative to the local method is the global method. In global methods, the labeling problem is solved by minimizing an energy function which explicitly incorporates local smoothness constraints. In general, global methods produce more satisfactory results at a cost of running time. Conversely, local aggregation methods are more efficient but yield less accurate results.

D. Fleet et al. (Eds.): ECCV 2014, Part V, LNCS 8693, pp. 17–32, 2014.

Local cost aggregations typically use adaptive supports to achieve edge preserving aggregation. One good example of these methods is the bilateral filter [14] based supports as proposed in the adaptive window method [21]. However, due to the high computational complexity of the full kernel implementation to the bilateral filter, many methods [17,18] are proposed for speeding up the implementation with the cost of a lower accuracy. In addition to these bilateral filter based methods, various methods based on different types of adaptive support are developed for cost aggregation, such as those in [6], [8], and [11]. Recently, non-local cost aggregation methods are proposed based on tree structures [16]. Unlike the local aggregation methods as mentioned above, the non-local methods propagate the contribution of a pixel to all other pixels. These methods are robust in low texture regions.

Multi-resolution image processing is an old but still widely used scheme [15]. One of its important characteristics in solving pixel-labeling problem is that the incorrect labeling can be reduced in a lower resolution version of the original image, but the risk of losing important details increases as the resolution goes down. The balance between low resolution and high resolution is found by incorporating the multi-resolution or coarse-to-fine methods into an optimization framework [4,7,19]. Yang and Pollefeys propose a multi-resolution cost aggregation method by summing up the matching scores computed from several kernels in different resolutions [20]. Another method [22] uses the results from the lower resolution to guide the search range at a higher resolution. These methods are very efficient and can be easily implemented in hardware with parallel acceleration. However, they do not produce satisfactory results.

Despite the fact that current cost aggregation methods achieve great success by introducing edge-aware filtering methods into adaptive local cost aggregation or by using minimum spanning tree (MST) for non-local aggregation, all these methods are sensitive to the local property of the images. For example, unreliable results by local adaptive cost aggregation methods are usually observed in textureless regions. By aggregating cost on a MST, non-local methods perform well in textureless regions, but they are vulnerable in regions containing too much texture, particularly in regions containing repetitive patterns. Because the contribution of a pixel to another is measured by the distance of the path between two pixels on the tree, a pixel in highly textured regions can hardly receive any contribution from other pixels. Then a challenging question that follows is: whether the multi-resolution technique can be introduced to break the bottleneck of both local and non-local cost aggregation methods, providing comparable or even better results than global methods, while still maintaining the computational efficiency without using any iterative optimization methods.

In this paper, we present a multi-resolution cost aggregation method (Multi-Agg) to achieve this goal. In our method, a cost volume is computed at the original resolution. The guidance image (e.g., the reference image in stereo matching) and the cost volume are both down sampled from the original resolution to the lowest resolution. Then a soft aggregation is carried out from the lowest resolution. The aggregation results from the low resolution are passed to the next higher resolution and the results are fused with the cost volume there for the next round of soft aggregation. The final labeling is decided from the soft aggregation results at the original resolution by the winner-take-all (WTA) method.

A great advantage of our soft aggregation scheme is that it takes both the advantages of reducing incorrect labeling from low resolutions and preserving details from fine resolutions. The proposed method is a generic framework that works well with many current state-of-the-art cost aggregation methods including both local and non-local aggregation methods. The proposed method boosts the robustness of these methods against different local features, such as the lack of texture or too much texture. We implement our methods to address two vision tasks: stereo matching and interactive segmentations. Experimental results show that our method outperforms current state-of-the-art cost aggregation methods both quantitatively and visually.

Another advantage of our method is its computational efficiency which is inherited from the current well developed fast cost aggregation methods. In addition, our method is straightforward, without involving any iterative process, and the fusion process is carried out independently for each pixel, which means that it can be easily embedded into parallelized acceleration systems.

2   Method

2.1   Adaptive Cost Aggregation

In this section, we firstly review several adaptive cost aggregation (ACA) methods. Assuming that a cost volume have been computed and denoted by $C_l(p)$ for pixel p at label l. ACA methods compute the aggregation results by

$$\hat{C}_l(p) = \sum_{q \in \Omega_p} w_{q,p} C_l(q) \tag{1}$$

where $\hat{C}_l(p)$ is the aggregation results, $w_{q,p}$ is the weight between pixel p and q measured in the guidance image I, and Ω_p is the support region of p. Different methods are used in defining $w_{q,p}$ and Ω_p. For example, authors in [11] and [21] use the bilateral filtering weights and the guided filtering weights as $w_{q,p}$ respectively. In [8], Ω_p is delineated by the cross based skeleton, and all pixels are used as Ω_p for non-local aggregation [16].

2.2   Multi-resolution Aggregation and Soft Cost Fusion

Unlike conventional aggregation methods, we first build two pyramids by recursively half down-sampling the cost volume and the guidance image before carrying out cost aggregation (see Fig. 1). The down-sampling of the cost volume is performed at each individual label in the image space. Denote the pyramids of guidance images and cost volumes by $\left\{I^{(1)}, I^{(2)}, I^{(3)}, ..., I^{(N)}\right\}$ and $\left\{C^{(1)}, C^{(2)}, C^{(3)}, ..., C^{(N)}\right\}$ where N is the total number of level of the pyramids; $I^{(1)}$ and

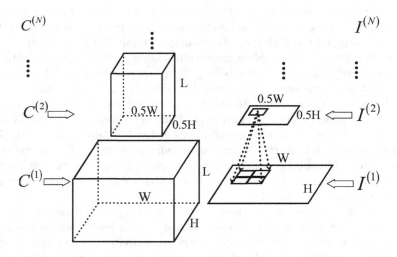

Fig. 1. Down-sampling is performed sequentially on both the guidance image and the cost volume. The size of the original image is $W \times H$, and the size of label space is L. The down-sampling of the cost volume is only carried out on image space. One pixel in a lower resolution corresponds four pixels in the next higher resolution

$C^{(1)}$ are the original guidance image and cost volume. The multi-resolution aggregation starts from the lowest resolution: aggregating $C^{(N)}$ under the guidance by $I^{(N)}$ using the ACA method in Eq. (1). The aggregation results in the nth level, $\hat{C}^{(n)}$, are passed to the next higher resolution and are fused with $C^{(n-1)}$. We expect that incorrect labelings are reduced while the details are preserved in the fused cost volume. Therefore, the fusion should hold some properties:

1. Fusion results encourage suggested labels from the results of lower resolution. The suggested labels are those where the value of $\hat{C}^{(n)}$ is low.
2. The extremely low value of $C^{(n-1)}$ should stay low in the fusion results.
3. Labels which are close to the suggested labels should also have low cost values in fusion results.

The functionality of the first requirement is obvious: it helps to reduce incorrect labelings in higher resolution by considering its lower resolution results. The second requirement is necessary for preserving details and boundaries in the higher resolution images. Generally, when a label l of a pixel p has an extremely low value in the cost function in the higher resolution but l does not have a low value in the aggregation results of its corresponding pixel p' at the lower resolution, it is very likely that p lies in regions containing details which are lost in the lower resolution results. The third requirement is useful in some applications, such as stereo matching and optical flow estimation, where the label of a pixel is close to those of its corresponding pixels in higher resolutions.

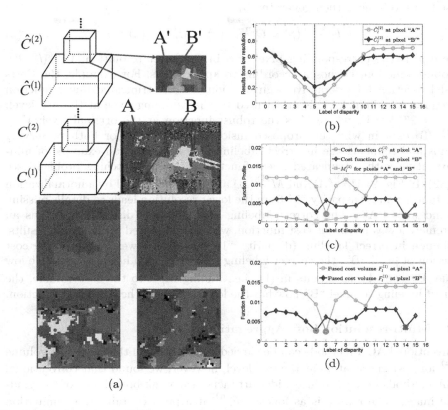

Fig. 2. (a) Applying a WTA method on the aggregation result at lower resolution: $\hat{C}_{l'}^{(2)}$, and the cost volume at higher resolution: $C^{(1)}$. (b) Aggregation result at pixels "A'" and "B'". Label which has the lowest cost is denoted by the vertical dash line. (c) Cost function of A and B in $C^{(1)}$ and min-convolution results between the aggregation results in (b) and a truncated linear function. Lowest cost values are denoted in "green", "red", and "yellow". (d) Correct labels (green points) have the lowest cost after fusion. Incorrect label (denoted by red cross) where the value of the original cost is the lowest does not stay to be the lowest after fusion

Even though the fusion method which satisfies the three points as mentioned above may not be unique, we found that the following method is very efficient and effective for applications at hand. In this method, $\hat{C}^{(n)}$ is firstly min-convoluted [5] with a robust function and then the results are added to $C^{(n-1)}$ to generate a fused cost volume $F^{(n-1)}$ at level $n-1$. The result of min-convolution [5] at pixel p is the lower envelop of functions by rooting the robust function at points of $\left(l', \hat{C}_{l'}^{(n)}(p')\right)$ for all l'. That is

$$M_l^{(n-1)}(p) = \min_{l'}\left(\widehat{C}_{l'}^{(n)}(p') + V^{(n)}(l-l')\right) \qquad (2)$$

Fused cost volume is then generated by

$$F_l^{(n-1)}(p) = C_l^{(n-1)}(p) + M_l^{(n-1)}(p) \tag{3}$$

where p' is the corresponding pixel of p in the lower resolution; $V^{(n)}(l - l')$, a robust function, is chosen according to applications. For example, the Potts model function for interactive segmentation and the truncated linear function for stereo matching. $V^{(n)}$ is augmented by the sampling scale at the nth level: $V^{(n)} = 2^{n-1} \times V$, where V is the robust function at the original level: $V = V^{(1)}$. To explain why the proposed fusion scheme works for both preserving details and reducing the incorrect labelings, we now show an example of min-convolution with a truncated linear function in stereo matching problem (see Fig. 2). In Fig. 2, $M_l^{(1)}(A)$ and $M_l^{(1)}(B)$ are both subtracted by a normalization constant for all l. Disparity "5" from the lower resolution leads to details missing around pixel "A'". The correct labeling to pixel "A" (disparity "6") has an extremely low value in the cost function, which is preserved in the fusion results. Although incorrect labeling (disparity "14") has the lowest value of the cost function of pixel "B", the correct labeling (disparity "5") has a comparable low value. By considering results in (b), i.e., adding $M_l^{(1)}$ to the cost volume, the correct labeling to pixel "B" now has the lowest value in the fused cost function.

2.3 Multi-resolution Soft Aggregation

Conventional ACA methods can be carried out directly on the fused cost volume $F_l^{(n)}$ for cost aggregation at the nth level; however, we found that conventional ACA methods may introduce wider artifacts near weak boundaries of the guidance image. The reason is as follows: $F_l^{(n)}$ at a pixel contains the summation of the cost values over all corresponding pixels at the original resolution, which leads to large value differences of $F_l^{(n)}$ for different labels. This large difference is likely to over-penalize the labeling discontinuity when using conventional ACA methods. Recall the scheme for soft cost fusion in the previous section, we propose a soft aggregation method: instead of directly using the cost volume in aggregation, the min-convolution [5] results between F and a robust function are aggregated (see Fig. 3). Empirically, $V^{(n)}(l - l')$, the robust function in the previous section, can be directly used here. That is

$$E_l^{(n)}(q) = \min_{l'}\left(F_l^{(n)}(q) + V^{(n)}(l - l')\right) \tag{4}$$

and

$$\hat{C}_l^{(n)}(p) = \sum_{q \in \Omega_p} w_{q,p} E_l^{(n)}(q) \tag{5}$$

2.4 Implementation Issues and Algorithm Steps

Being a generic framework, our method works very well with many advanced cost aggregation methods. Theoretically, different ACA methods or different

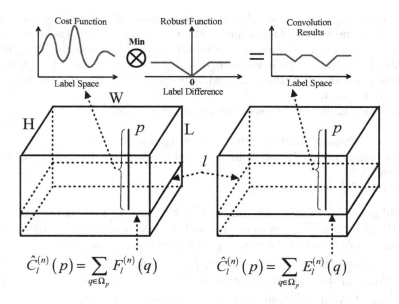

Fig. 3. Conventional ACA methods carried out the aggregation on the cubic of fused cost volume of the nth level. Soft aggregation is carried out on the cubic of min-convolution results

parameters can be used for cost aggregation in different levels. In this study, we use the same ACA method with constant parameters, such as window size and weighting parameters, in different levels for simplicity.

The first issue is the computational complexity. The complexity of our method is depended on the adopted ACA method and the robust function V. We focus on two types of V: truncated linear function and Potts model function. According to [4], the min-convolution requires 3 operations (add or minus) for each pixel at each label when using the truncated linear function and requires 2 operations when using the Potts model function. As the total number of pixels is reduced by 4 times in the next lower resolution, the operations for all resolutions is $\frac{4}{3}$ times of that in the original resolution. For an image being processed with size $W \times H$ and the label space size L, the total number of operations of min-convolution in cost fusion is $\left(\frac{4}{3} + \frac{1}{4}\left(3 \times \frac{4}{3}\right)\right) WHL$ (for truncated linear model) or $\left(\frac{4}{3} + \frac{1}{4}\left(2 \times \frac{4}{3}\right)\right) WHL$ (for Potts model). The total number of operations of min-convolution in soft aggregation is $\left(3 \times \frac{4}{3}\right)WHL$ (for truncated linear model) or $\left(2 \times \frac{4}{3}\right)WHL$ (for Potts model). As the guidance image is the same for all labels, guidance image down-sampling is performed only once and the overhead is negligible. The number of operations for building the cost volumes pyramid is $\frac{4}{3}WHL$. Assume that the ACA method being employed requires O operations for aggregating cost volume in the original resolution level, our method requires $\frac{4}{3}O + 8WHL$ (for truncated linear model) or $\frac{4}{3}O + 6WHL$ (for Potts model) operations in total.

Another issue to be discussed is how many levels of hierarchical images are needed. We found that for local aggregation methods, the larger the area covered by Ω_p in the lowest resolution is, the better the results become. Thus, we set the number of levels N to a value so that Ω_p just covers the whole image at the lowest resolution. For the non-local aggregation method [16], the level N is empirically set to 5.

Algorithm 1 shows the steps of the proposed method.

Algorithm 1. Steps of Multi-Resolution Soft Aggregation:

Inputs: Input image I, cost volume C, robust function V, number of multi-resolutions N.

Outputs: A labeling for all pixels in I.

1. Build pyramids of guidance images $I^{(1)}, I^{(2)}, ..., I^{(N)}$ and cost volumes $\{C^{(1)}, C^{(2)}, ..., C^{(N)}\}$. Set current level, $n = N$, and set $M_l^{(N)}$ to zeros.
2. From $n = N$ to $n = 1$ iteratively perform step (a) to step (d).
   a. Compute the fused cost volume, $F_l^{(n)}$, using Eq. (3).
   b. Compute the min-convolution results, $E_l^{(n)}$, using Eq. (4), then carry out ACA on $E_l^{(n)}$ and obtain $\hat{C}^{(n)}$ as given in Eq. (5).
   c. If $n = 1$, go to step (3). Otherwise, compute $M_l^{(n-1)}$ using Eq. (2).
   d. Set $n := n - 1$.
3. Output the labeling for all pixels in I by using the WTA method on $\hat{C}^{(1)}$.

3   Applications and Experiments

3.1   Stereo Matching

We evaluated our method combined with three popular ACA techniques: Cost-Filter [11], MST [16], and CLMF-0 [8], using the Middlebury stereo benchmark [1]. These methods are denoted by MultiAgg (GF), MultiAgg (MST), and MultiAgg (CLMF-0) respectively. All methods are implemented in C++ on a PC with 2.0 GHz CPU and 4 GB RAM using single-core implementation. The comparison between our method and the conventional ACA methods is conducted.

For comparison, the same method [11] is employed for calculating all cost volumes. The default parameters in [11] and [16] are used for guided filtering and MST based ACA in both the conventional ACA methods and those in the MultiAgg methods. As CLMF-0 uses a different cost volume calculation method in its original work [8], the parameters for CLMF-0 and MultiAgg (CLMF-0) are tuned with care so that the best results are presented. The truncated linear function is used as the robust function: $V(l_1, l_2) = \rho \min(|l - l'|, d)$. We set $\{\rho, d\} = \{2 \times 10^{-4}, 5\}$ in MultiAgg (GF) and MultiAgg (MST) and $\{\rho, d\} = \{1 \times 10^{-3}, 5\}$ in MultiAgg (CLMF-0). Results from different methods are shown in Fig. 4. We further applied the weighted median filter based occlusion handling method [11] to the results. With post-processing, the results from MultiAgg (GF)

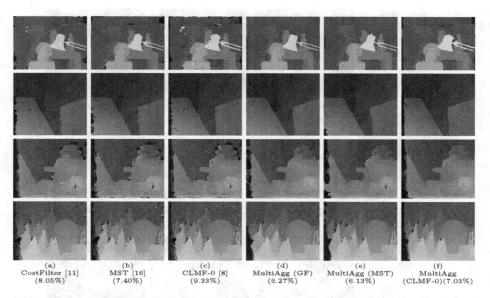

(a)	(b)	(c)	(d)	(e)	(f)
CostFilter [11]	MST [16]	CLMF-0 [8]	MultiAgg (GF)	MultiAgg (MST)	MultiAgg
(8.05%)	(7.40%)	(9.33%)	(6.27%)	(6.13%)	(CLMF-0)(7.03%)

Fig. 4. Experimental results on the Middlebury datasets. (a)-(c) are results from conventional aggregation methods: (d)-(f) are results from our MultiAgg methods. The average percentage of bad pixels over four images are given at the bottom of the results. Compared with conventional aggregation methods, the MultiAgg methods achieve globally better performance. For instance, see the highly textured regions around the top right corner of the "Tsukuba" dataset and the regions around the head of the teddy bear in the "Teddy" dataset

(see Fig. 6) are the best among the six methods. The quantitative evaluation is presented in Table 1 for the comparison with other methods (including global optimization based methods) on the Middlebury datasets. Table 1 and Fig. 4 show that our method outperforms the conventional ACA methods which use hard aggregation in a single resolution. Our method is also close to or even better than many iterative methods which are based on global optimization, such as [9] and [23]. For the four Middlebury datasets, the average running time (excluding occlusion handling) of CostFilter, MST, CLMF-0, MultiAgg (GF), MultiAgg (MST), MultiAgg (CLMF-0) are 1.5 s, 0.14 s, 0.42 s, 2.2 s, 0.31 s, and 0.71 s respectively. The running time of MultiAgg is about 1.5 to 2.2 times slower than corresponding ACA methods in the original resolution.

Since methods in [11] and [23] use local linear model for addressing stereo matching problem, we explicitly compared these two methods with our MultiAgg (GF) which also uses the local linear model. Table 1 shows that the ranking of our method is similar to the method in [23] (ranked 15 versus ranked 14) and both methods significantly outperform the method in [11] (ranked 35). More comparisons on the widely used stereo datasets are given in Fig. 5 where results without occlusion handling from MultiAgg (GF) and [11] are presented.

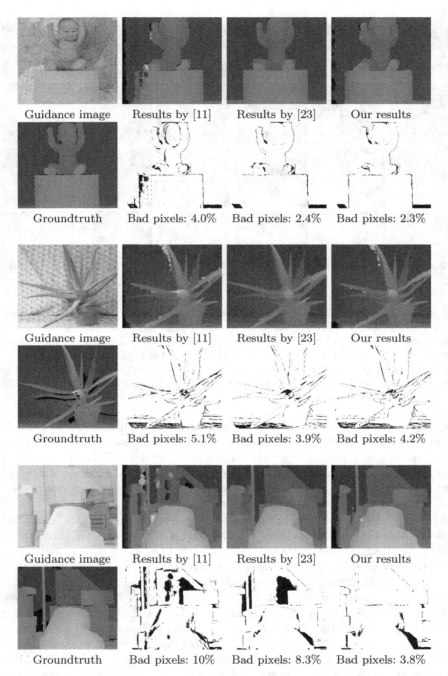

Fig. 5. Comparison among our method MultiAgg (GF), and methods in [11], and [23]. Ratio of bad pixels in non-occluded regions are given (error > 1 pixel). Our method preserves details and boundaries very well while reducing large mount of incorrect labelings in textureless regions

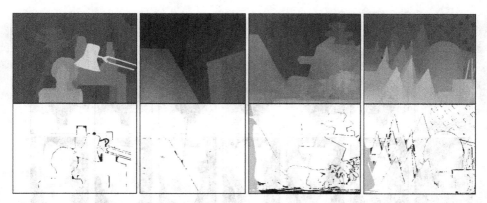

Fig. 6. Stereo matching results. First row: results from MultiAgg (GF) with occlusion handling. All results are obtained using constant parameters. Second row: error maps (error > 1 pixel). Errors in the occluded regions are colored in gray and errors in non-occluded regions are colored in black

Table 1. Evaluation on the Middlebury benchmarks

Methods	Total Rank	Average Rank	Tsukuba nocc	all	disc	Venus nocc	all	disc	Teddy nocc	all	disc	Cones nocc	all	disc
ADCensus [10]	1	10.9	1.07	1.48	5.73	0.09	0.25	1.15	4.10	6.22	10.9	2.42	7.25	6.95
LLR [23]	14	28.3	1.05	1.65	5.64	0.29	0.81	3.07	4.56	9.81	12.2	2.17	8.02	6.42
MultiAgg (GF)	15	30.0	1.52	1.82	8.20	0.16	0.39	2.03	5.09	10.5	13.8	2.27	7.49	6.71
PMF [9]	22	34.6	1.74	2.04	8.07	0.33	0.49	4.16	2.52	5.87	8.30	2.13	6.80	6.32
CostFilter [11]	35	42.1	1.51	1.85	7.61	0.20	0.39	2.42	6.16	11.8	16.0	2.71	8.24	7.66

3.2 Interactive Image Segmentation

In image segmentation, we evaluated MultiAgg (GF) and MultiAgg (MST). For comparison, we implement three other popular methods: CostFilter [11], Grabcut [12], and MST [16]. Although the non-local aggregation method in [16] is proposed typically for stereo matching, it can be naturally adopted for interactive image segmentation.

For pixels whose labels l' are given by the user we define the cost as

$$C_l(p) = \begin{cases} 0 & l = l', \\ K & \text{otherwise.} \end{cases} \tag{6}$$

where K is a very large value. To compute the cost value of pixels not labeled by the user, we build a color histogram ($8 \times 8 \times 8$ bins) for each label based on the provided strokes from users. The value in the histogram H_l is normalized so that the summation over all bins equals to 1. Then the cost of assigning label l_p to p is defined as

$$C_l(p) = (1 - H_l(B_p)) \tag{7}$$

where B_p is the index of the bin where p falls into. Unlike [12], where the image is segmented only into background and foreground, our implementation segments

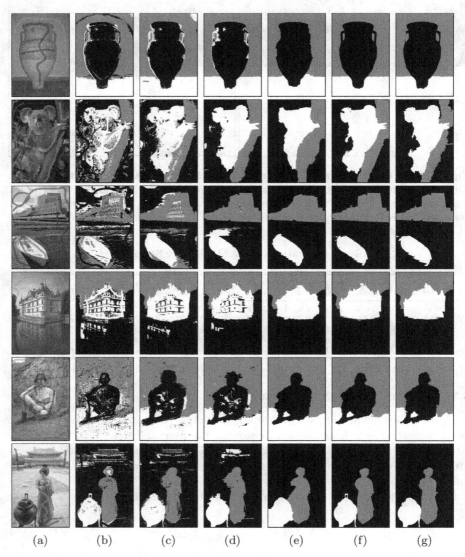

(a)   (b)   (c)   (d)   (e)   (f)   (g)

Fig. 7. Interactive segmentation results. Input images courtesy from [2]. From the left to the right are: (a) strokes by users, (b) cost volume, (c) results from CostFilter [11], (d) results from MST aggregation [16], (e) results from Graph Cuts (one iteration of [12]), (f) results from MultiAgg (GF), and (g) results from MultiAgg (MST). Note that the large amount of incorrect labeling disappear in our results and boundaries are also better preserved

image into multiple (three) parts. The robust function $V(l_1, l_2)$ is a Potts model function with value P if the two labels are not equal. Fig. 7 shows the results from different methods on the same cost volume. The parameters of the ACA methods in CostFilter [11] and MultiAgg (GF) are the same as those in [11]. The parameters of the ACA methods in MST [16] and MultiAgg (MST) are the same as those in [16]. We set $P = 0.25$ for MultiAgg (GF), and $P = 2.0$ for MultiAgg (MST).

Being a local aggregation method in a single resolution, method in [11] does not handle the large amount of incorrectly labeled pixels well. By using MST, method in [16] outperforms the method in [11] in textureless regions. Unfortunately it does not performs well in regions containing too much texture. Grab-Cut [12] does well in reducing incorrect labeling in both highly textured and textureless regions thank to the global optimization; however, its smoothness term which penalizes labeling inconsistency among 4 or 8 neighborhoods is prone to introducing boundary shrinking artifacts. Results show that our method produces the best results where the total number of incorrect labelings is minimum while boundaries are well preserved.

3.3 Discussions

The benefit of using MultiAgg is clearly demonstrated in our experiments. For a better understanding for the reason behind the good performance of MultiAgg, let us look at Fig. 8. A first observation is that the guidance image becomes smooth as the resolution goes low. This is very important for eliminating incorrect labeling in the textured regions. Since the value of a pixel in low resolution is the averaging value of all corresponding pixel in the original resolution, it is expected that regions with similar texture have a similar color in the low resolution image. As a result, pixels in highly textured regions are able to receive contributions from other pixels in regions with similar texture when carrying out ACA in low resolution. However, since pixel values of highly textured regions in original resolution change dramatically, a pixel in these regions can hardly receive contribution from other pixels even for non-local aggregation method [16]. Two other observations are as follows: (1) The low resolution cost volume contains less noises than that of high resolution. (2) Pixels become closer to each other in low resolution. In virtue of these three points, incorrect labelings caused by local characteristics can be greatly reduced in results of low resolution. The downside of carrying out ACA in low resolution is the ambiguity of boundaries and the missing of details owing to the averaging effect in the sampling process. Based on the fact that the cost function of pixels at object boundaries usually has an extremely low value at the correct label, our soft fusion strategy (in Section 2.2) takes into account low resolution results and fuse them into a new cost volume where the incorrect labelings are reduced while the details and boundaries are also well preserved.

The next question that follows is how the robust function influences the results. The robust function controls the strength of the results from low resolution fusing into the cost volume at the next higher resolution. When the strength of the robust function increases, the final results will therefore be biased towards

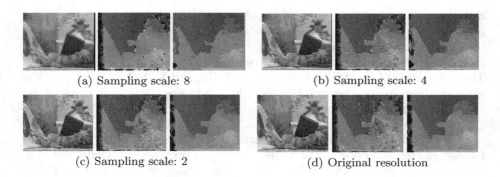

(a) Sampling scale: 8   (b) Sampling scale: 4

(c) Sampling scale: 2   (d) Original resolution

Fig. 8. Cost aggregation in multi-resolutions. From the left to the right for each sub-figure are guidance images, cost volumes, and soft aggregation results. Note that the highly textured region around the head of the teddy bear in the original guidance image is smoothed in the low resolution; and ACA in low resolution produces accurate results in these regions. Despite details are lost in the low resolution results, these details are recovered in high resolution results thanks to the soft cost fusion strategy

the low resolution results where the labeling is smooth but details may be lost. On the other hand, weak robust function will help preserve details, but may fail to eliminate the large amount of incorrect labelings.

3.4   Limitations

Our method has a common limitation as other cost aggregation methods on the application of stereo matching – it may produce incorrect disparity values for highly slant surfaces by smoothing the values. The smoothing is caused by the fronto-parallel surface model which is implicity used in cost aggregation methods. One example can be found at the bottom of the "Teddy" dataset where the disparity values of pixels on a highly slant plane are smoothed. This artifact is unavoidable for cost aggregation methods when piecewise smoothness is forced. Slant plane based methods (e.g., [3] and [9]) would be used for finding slant plane models at the cost of using a complex iterative optimization process.

4   Conclusions

This paper has presented MultiAgg, a generic cost volume aggregation framework for effectively addressing pixel-labeling problems. The key contribution is the idea of adaptively fusing the cost aggregation results from multi-resolutions in a coarse-to-fine manner. Experimental results have shown that MultiAgg produces more accurate results than current state-of-the-art methods both visually and quantitatively. In addition to its effectiveness, another advantage is its computational efficiency which is inherited from the fast cost aggregation methods.

In future, we will explore the implementation of MultiAgg in addressing a more challenging problem of approximate nearest-neighbor field where the size of the labels space is huge.

References

1. http://www.vision.middlebury.edu/stereo/ (2013)
2. Arbelaez, P., Maire, M., Fowlkes, C., Malik, J.: Contour detection and hierarchical image segmentation. PAMI 33(5), 898–916 (2011)
3. Bleyer, M., Rhemann, C., Rother, C.: Patchmatch stereo-stereo matching with slanted support windows. BMVC 11, 1–11 (2011)
4. Felzenszwalb, P.F., Huttenlocher, D.P.: Efficient belief propagation for early vision. IJCV 70(1), 41–54 (2006)
5. Felzenszwalb, P.F., Huttenlocher, D.P.: Distance transforms of sampled functions. Theory of Computing 8(1), 415–428 (2012)
6. Hosni, A., Bleyer, M., Gelautz, M., Rhemann, C.: Local stereo matching using geodesic support weights. In: ICIP, pp. 2093–2096 (2009)
7. Lei, C., Yang, Y.H.: Optical flow estimation on coarse-to-fine region-trees using discrete optimization. In: ICCV, pp. 1562–1569 (2009)
8. Lu, J., Shi, K., Min, D., Lin, L., Do, M.N.: Cross-based local multipoint filtering. In: CVPR, pp. 430–437 (2012)
9. Lu, J., Yang, H., Min, D., Do, M.: Patchmatch filter: Efficient edge-aware filtering meets randomized search for fast correspondence field estimation. In: CVPR, pp. 1854–1861 (2013)
10. Mei, X., Sun, X., Zhou, M., Jiao, S., Wang, H., Zhang, X.: On building an accurate stereo matching system on graphics hardware. In: ICCV, pp. 467–474 (2011)
11. Rhemann, C., Hosni, A., Bleyer, M., Rother, C., Gelautz, M.: Fast cost-volume filtering for visual correspondence and beyond. In: CVPR, pp. 3017–3024 (2011)
12. Rother, C., Kolmogorov, V., Blake, A.: GrabCut: Interactive foreground extraction using iterated graph cuts. ACM Transactions on Graphics (TOG) 23, 309–314 (2004)
13. Szeliski, R., Zabih, R., Scharstein, D., Veksler, O., Kolmogorov, V., Agarwala, A., Tappen, M., Rother, C.: A comparative study of energy minimization methods for Markov random fields with smoothness-based priors. PAMI 30(6), 1068–1080 (2008)
14. Tomasi, C., Manduchi, R.: Bilateral filtering for gray and color images. In: ICCV, pp. 839–846 (1998)
15. Willsky, A.S.: Multiresolution Markov models for signal and image processing. Proceedings of the IEEE 90(8), 1396–1458 (2002)
16. Yang, Q.: A non-local cost aggregation method for stereo matching. In: CVPR, pp. 1402–1409 (2012)
17. Yang, Q.: Recursive bilateral filtering. In: Fitzgibbon, A., Lazebnik, S., Perona, P., Sato, Y., Schmid, C. (eds.) ECCV 2012, Part I. LNCS, vol. 7572, pp. 399–413. Springer, Heidelberg (2012)
18. Yang, Q., Tan, K.H., Ahuja, N.: Real-time O(1) bilateral filtering. In: CVPR, pp. 557–564 (2009)
19. Yang, Q., Wang, L., Yang, R., Stewénius, H., Nistér, D.: Stereo matching with color-weighted correlation, hierarchical belief propagation, and occlusion handling. PAMI 31(3), 492–504 (2009)

20. Yang, R., Pollefeys, M.: Multi-resolution real-time stereo on commodity graphics hardware. In: CVPR, vol. 1, pp. I–211 (2003)
21. Yoon, K.J., Kweon, I.S.: Adaptive support-weight approach for correspondence search. PAMI 28(4), 650–656 (2006)
22. Zhao, Y., Taubin, G.: Real-time stereo on GPGPU using progressive multi-resolution adaptive windows. Image and Vision Computing 29(6), 420–432 (2011)
23. Zhu, S., Zhang, L., Jin, H.: A locally linear regression model for boundary preserving regularization in stereo matching. In: Fitzgibbon, A., Lazebnik, S., Perona, P., Sato, Y., Schmid, C. (eds.) ECCV 2012, Part V. LNCS, vol. 7576, pp. 101–115. Springer, Heidelberg (2012)

Inverse Kernels for Fast Spatial Deconvolution

Li Xu[1], Xin Tao[2], and Jiaya Jia[2]

[1] Image & Visual Computing Lab, Lenovo R&T
[2] The Chinese University of Hong Kong

Abstract. Deconvolution is an indispensable tool in image processing and computer vision. It commonly employs fast Fourier transform (FFT) to simplify computation. This operator, however, needs to transform from and to the frequency domain and loses spatial information when processing irregular regions. We propose an efficient spatial deconvolution method that can incorporate sparse priors to suppress noise and visual artifacts. It is based on estimating inverse kernels that are decomposed into a series of 1D kernels. An augmented Lagrangian method is adopted, making inverse kernel be estimated only once for each optimization process. Our method is fully parallelizable and its speed is comparable to or even faster than other strategies employing FFTs.

Keywords: deconvolution, inverse kernels, numerical analysis, optimization.

1 Introduction

Deconvolution has been an essential tool for solving many image/video restoration and computer vision problems. It was also used in astronomy imaging [24], medical imaging [9], signal decoding, etc. In recent years, it is extensively applied to systems in computational photography and image/video editing, including flutter shutter motion deblurring [19], general motion deblurring [6,30,22,4,14,10,28,25,29,21], coded aperture and depth [13,32], and image super-resolution [2,23,17], since many types of degradation can be partly modeled or approximated by convolution, where kernels are monotonically decaying low-pass filters.

While convolution is easy to apply, its inverse problem of properly deconvolving images is not that simple. Band-limited convolution kernels have incomplete coverage in the frequency domain, which makes inversion ill-conditioned, especially under the existence of unavoidable quantization errors and camera noise. Regularization can remedy this problem – see early work of Wiener filtering [27] and Tikhonov deconvolution [26]. Existing methods are in two streams, which have their respective characteristics.

Spatial Deconvolution. Very few deconvolution methods are performed in the spatial domain, owing to the high computational cost. Richardson-Lucy method [20] does not involve regularization and thus may suffer from the noise and ringing problems. Progressive approach [31] suppresses ringings by operations in

D. Fleet et al. (Eds.): ECCV 2014, Part V, LNCS 8693, pp. 33–48, 2014.

image pyramids. Good performance is yielded in sparse prior deconvolution [13], which requires to solve large linear systems. With the re-weighting numerical scheme, the coefficient matrix of the linear system is no-longer Toeplitz and cannot be accelerated using FFTs. This indicates that sparse-prior deconvolution, albeit useful for preserving structures and suppressing ringings, is not translation invariant.

Deconvolution in Frequency Domain. The convolution theorem states that spatial convolution can be computed by point-wise multiplication in frequency domain, which brings out pseudo-inversion in the frequency domain [16]. Shan et al. [22] fitted the gradient distribution using two convex functions. The half-quadratic implementation [11] mathematically links general α-norms to a family of hyper-Laplacian distributions. These iterative methods employ a few FFTs in each pass. Each FFT is with complexity $O(n \log n)$ where n is the pixel number in the image. Although frequency domain deconvolution is fast, it is non-trivial for further speedup by parallelization. Nor is it suitable to handle irregular regions, which however are common in object motion blur [3] and focal blur [13].

Our Contribution. In this paper, we analyze the main difficulty of spatial deconvolution and propose a new numerical scheme based on inverse kernels to fill the gap between recent frequency-domain fast deconvolution and spatial pseudo-inverse. They are inherently linked in our system by introducing kernels constructed according to regularized optimization. The new relationship enables empirical strategies to inherit the nice properties in these two streams of work and to significantly speed up spatial deconvolution.

Although several useful sparse gradient priors may not lead to translation invariant process for deconvolution. We found it is possible to approximate them with a series of operators that are indeed spatially translation invariant. Accordingly, we propose an effective numerical scheme based on the augmented Lagrangian multipliers [15,1] and kernel decomposition [18]. The resulting operations are no more than estimation of a set of 1D kernels that can be repeatedly applied to images in iterations.

Unlike all previous *fast* robust deconvolution techniques, our method works spatially and has a number of advantages. 1) It is easy to implement and parallelize. 2) It runs comparably with or even faster than FFT-based deconvolution for high-resolution images. 3) This method can deal with arbitrarily irregular regions without much computation overhead. 4) Visual artifacts are much reduced.

We apply our method to applications of extended depth of field [12], motion deblurring [29], and image upscaling using back projection [8].

2 Motivation and Analysis

To understand the inherent difference between spatial and frequency domain deconvolution, we begin with the discussion of convolution expressed in the form

$$y = x * k + \epsilon,$$

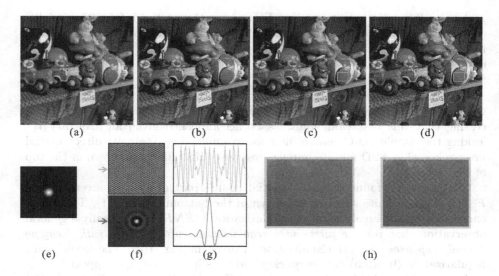

(a)   (b)   (c)   (d)

(e)   (f)   (g)   (h)

Fig. 1. Illustration of regularized inverse filters. (f). (a) is a Gaussian blurred image. (b)-(d) are the restored images by convolving the regularized inverse filter, Wiener deconvolution, and 1D separated Wiener deconvolution. (e) shows the Gaussian kernel. (f) shows the direct inverse filter, and regularized inverse filter from top down. (g) contains 1D scan lines of the two inverse filters in (f). (h) shows the close-ups of (c) and (d).

where k is the kernel, y is the degraded observation, x is the latent image, $*$ refers to the convolution operator, and ϵ indicates additive noise.

We first explain the inverse kernel problem using the simple Wiener deconvolution and then discuss the issues in designing a practical spatial solver using sparse gradient priors, which is effective to suppress noise and visual artifacts.

2.1   Spatial Inverse Kernels for Wiener Deconvolution

Wiener deconvolution introduces a pseudo-inverse filter in frequency domain, expressed as

$$W = \frac{\overline{F(k)}}{|F(k)|^2 + \frac{1}{SNR}},   (1)$$

where $F(\cdot)$ denotes Fourier transform and $\overline{F(\cdot)}$ is its complex conjugate. SNR represents the signal to noise ratio that helps suppress the high frequency part of the inverse filter. The restored image is thus

$$x = F^{-1}(W \cdot F(y)),   (2)$$

where F^{-1} is the inverse Fourier transform.

Albeit efficient, restoration using FFTs loses the spatial information as discussed above and could be less favored in several applications. This motivates us to approximate this process using pseudo-inverse w in the spatial domain, expressed as

$$x = F^{-1}(W) * y = w * y, \tag{3}$$

where w is the latent (pseudo) spatial inverse kernel. It is known in signal processing that this task cannot always be accomplished given an arbitrary W. Taking the simple 2D Gaussian filter for example (Fig. 1(e)), its direct spatial inverse kernel is a 2D infinite impulse response (IIR) filter, as shown in the top of Fig. 1(f).

Contrarily, we found that the spatial counterpart of Wiener inversion, i.e. $F^{-1}(W)$, has a finite support, as shown in the bottom of Fig. 1(f). The difference is due to the involvement of regularization $1/SNR$. It is actually a general observation that *inverse filters with regularization are typically with decaying spatial responses.* An 1D visualization is given in Fig. 1(g). The kernel with regularization (bottom) decays quickly and thus has a compact support.

An image degraded by a Gaussian kernel (Fig. 1(e)) is shown in Fig. 1(a). The restored image using the spatial inverse kernel with compact support is given in Fig. 1(d), with visual artifacts near image border, which can be ameliorated by padding. To further increase the sharpness and suppress artifacts, we turn to a more advanced sparse gradient regularization.

2.2   Sparse Gradient Regularized Deconvolution

State-of-the-art deconvolution makes use of sparse gradient priors [13,11], making the overall computation more complex than a Wiener one. In this paper, we propose a practical scheme to achieve spatial deconvolution even with these challenging highly non-convex sparse priors. We describe two issues in this process, which concern kernel size and non-separability of regularized deconvolution.

Kernel Size. Spatial inverse kernels could be of considerable sizes. For a Gaussian kernel with variance $\sigma = 3$, the corresponding regularized inverse filter using Eq. (1) has a finite support of 51×51. Although it is independent of the input image size, it still lays a large computational burden to 2D convolution.

Kernel Non-separability. Many kernels are inherently non-separable. Even for those that are separable, their inversions are not. For example, each Gaussian kernel can be decomposed into two 1D filters, applied in the horizontal and vertical directions respectively. However, its inversion is not separable due to regularization. The road to speeding up regularized deconvolution by simply performing 1D filtering is thus blocked.

The comparison in Fig. 1(c) and (d) illustrates the difference. There is a 2D inverse kernel of Gaussian created according to Eq. (1) and a separated approximation using outer product of two 1D filters, formed also following Eq. (1). The restoration result using the re-combined 1D filters is shown in (d). It contains obvious oblique-line artifacts (see the close-ups in (h)).

We address these two issues using kernel decomposition with SVD, presented below.

3   Sparse Prior Robust Spatial Deconvolution

Sparse gradient regularized deconvolution works very well with a hyper Laplacian prior [11]. It minimizes the function of

$$E(x) = \sum_{i=1}^{n} \left(\frac{\lambda}{2}(x * k - y)_i^2 + |c_1 * x|_i^\alpha + |c_2 * x|_i^\alpha \right), \tag{4}$$

where i indexes image pixels. c_1 and c_2 are finite differential kernels in horizontal and vertical directions to approximate the first-order derivatives. α controls the shape of the prior with $0.5 \le \alpha < 1$. A common way to solve this function is to employ a penalty decomposition

$$E(x; z_1, z_2) = \sum_{i=1}^{n} \left(\frac{\lambda}{2}(x * k - y)_i^2 + \sum_{j \in \{1,2\}} \frac{\beta}{2}(z_j - c_j * x)_i^2 + |z_j|_i^\alpha \right), \tag{5}$$

where z_1 and z_2 are auxiliary variables to approximate regularizers. The problem approaches the original one only if β is large enough. The solver is thus formed as iteratively updating variables as

$$z_j^{t+1} \leftarrow \operatorname{argmin}_z E(x^t, z_j, \beta^t), \tag{6}$$

$$x^{t+1} \leftarrow \operatorname{argmin}_x E(x, z_j^{t+1}, \beta^t), \tag{7}$$

$$\beta^{t+1} \leftarrow 2\beta^t. \tag{8}$$

t indexes iterations. Since z_j has an analytical solution (or can be found in look-up tables) [11], the main computation lies in the FFT inversion step to compute x, which gives

$$x = F^{-1} \left(\frac{\sum_j \overline{F(c_j)} F(z_j) + \frac{\lambda}{\beta} \overline{F(k)} F(y)}{\sum_j |F(c_j)|^2 + \frac{\lambda}{\beta} |F(k)|^2} \right). \tag{9}$$

It involves several FFTs. Basically, update of z_j is performed in spatial domain as it involves pixel-wise operations. So domain switch is unavoidable.

3.1   Penalty Decomposition Inverse Kernels

We expand Eq. (9) by decomposing the numerator and denominator and apply inverse FFT separately. It yields

$$x = F^{-1} \left(\frac{1}{\sum_j |F(c_j)|^2 + \frac{\lambda}{\beta} |F(k)|^2} \right) * \left(\sum_j c_j' * z_j + \frac{\lambda}{\beta} k' * y \right), \tag{10}$$

where c'_j and k' are adjoint kernels of c_j and k by rotating these kernels by 180 degree, and j indexes differential kernels c. The operations $c'_j * z_j$ and $k' * y$ are now in spatial domain. $k' * y$ is a constant independent of variables z and x.

$(\sum |F(c_j)|^2 + \frac{\lambda}{\beta}|F(k)|^2)^{-1}$ in Eq. (10) is the inversion in the frequency domain. Its domain switch to pixel values, in fact, corresponds to a spatial inverse kernel. The regularization makes its finite support exist. So it is possible to estimate spatial inverse kernels corresponding to this term, i.e.,

$$w_\beta = F^{-1}\left(\frac{1}{\sum_j |F(c_j)|^2 + \frac{\lambda}{\beta}|F(k)|^2}\right). \qquad (11)$$

This process raises a technical challenge. Because β varies in iterations, w_β needs to be re-estimated in each pass. A series of spatial inverse filters thus should be produced, which are not optimal and waste much time.

3.2 Augmented Lagrangian Inverse Kernels

To fit the spatial processing framework, we adopt the *augmented Lagrangian* (AL) method [15,5] to approximate deconvolution. AL was originally used to transform constrained optimization to an unconstrained one with the conventional *Lagrangian* and an additional augmented penalty term. Specifically, we transform Eq. (4) into

$$E(x; z_j, \gamma_j) = \sum_{i=1}^{n} \left(\frac{\lambda}{2}(x * k - y)_i^2 + \sum_{j \in \{1,2\}} |z_j|_i^\alpha \right.$$
$$\left. + \sum_{j \in \{1,2\}} \frac{\beta}{2}(z_j - c_j * x)_i^2 - \langle \gamma_j, (z_j - c_j * x)\rangle_i \right), \qquad (12)$$

where the term in the second row is the augmented Lagrangian multiplier specific for this problem. $\langle \cdot \rangle$ is the inner product of two vectors. The major difference from the original penalty decomposition optimization is that here the update of γ_j prevents β from varying while the optimization still proceeds nicely. The iterative solver is given by

$$z_j^{t+1} \leftarrow \operatorname{argmin}_z E(x^t, z_j, \gamma_j^t), \qquad (13)$$
$$x^{t+1} \leftarrow \operatorname{argmin}_x E(x, z_j^{t+1}, \gamma_j^t), \qquad (14)$$
$$\gamma_j^{t+1} \leftarrow \gamma_j^t - \beta(z_j^{t+1} - c_j * x^{t+1}). \qquad (15)$$

From the convergence point of view, the AL method has basically no difference with penalty decomposition. But it is much more suitable for our deconvolution framework, in which β can be fixed, resulting in the same inverse kernel in all iterations.

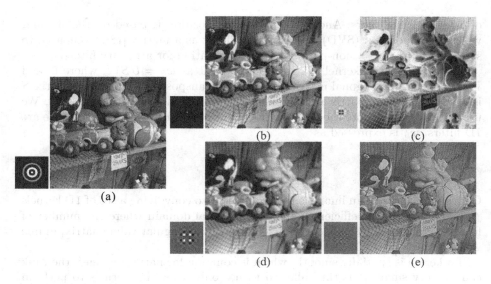

Fig. 2. Separating filters. A spatial inverse filter shown in (a) can be approximated as a linear combination of a few simpler ones as shown from (b)-(e). Each of them is separable. The finally restored image in (a) can be formed as a linear combination of images restored by these simple filters respectively.

By re-organizing the terms, we get an expression for the target image:

$$x = F^{-1} \left(\frac{1}{\sum_j |F(c_j)|^2 + \frac{\lambda}{\beta}|F(k)|^2} \right) *$$

$$F^{-1} \left(\sum_i \overline{F(c_j)}(F(z_j) - \frac{1}{\beta}F(\gamma_j)) + \frac{\lambda}{\beta}\overline{F(k)}F(y) \right),$$

$$= w_\beta * \left(\sum_{j \in \{1,2\}} c'_j * (z_j - \frac{1}{\beta}\gamma_j) + \frac{\lambda}{\beta}k' * y \right), \tag{16}$$

where w_β denotes the same spatial inverse filter defined in Eq. (11). The difference is that β in this form no longer varies during iterations. $c'_j * (z_j - \frac{1}{\beta}\gamma_j)$ can be efficiently computed using forward/backward difference. $k' * y$ is a constant and can be computed only once before the iteration. w_β is a spatial inverse kernel that can also be pre-computed and stored.

It seems now we successfully produce workable inverse kernel without heavy computation spent to re-estimating it in each iteration. But there are still two aforementioned *size* the *separability* issues that may influence deconvolution efficiency. We further propose a decomposition procedure to address them.

Inverse Kernel Decomposition. Kernel decomposition techniques have been widely explored. Steerable filters [7] decompose kernels into linear combination of a set of basis filters. Another kernel decomposition is based on the singular value decomposition (SVD) of w_β by treating it as a matrix [18]. Compared to steerable filter, it is a non-parametric decomposition for arbitrary filters.

Given our spatial kernel w_β, we decompose it as $w_\beta = USV'$, where U and V' are unitary orthogonal matrices, V' is the transpose of V, and the matrix S is a band-diagonal matrix with nonnegative real numbers in the diagonal. We use f_u^l and f_v^l to denote the lth column vectors of U and V, which in essence are 1D filters. w_β is expressed as

$$w_\beta = \sum_l s_l f_u^l f_v^{l'}. \tag{17}$$

Convolving w_β with an image is now equivalent to convolving a set of 1D kernels f_u^l and f_v^l. It can be efficiently applied in spatial domain where the number of filters is controlled by the non-zero elements in the singular value matrix, in line with the rank of the kernel.

If a kernel is spatially smooth, which is common for natural images, the rank can be very small. It is thus allowed to use only a few 1D kernels to perform deconvolution. Note that we can even lower the approximation precision by dropping small non-zeros singular values for further acceleration. One example of the kernel and its decomposition is shown in Fig. 2. The filtered images are shown together with their separable filters. In this examples, 7 separable filters are used to approximate the inverse regularized Gaussian, which verifies that most inverse kernels are not originally separable.

3.3 More Discussions

Our spatial deconvolution is an iterative process. For each deconvolution process, we only need to use SVD to estimate w_β as several 1D kernels once. If the kernel was decomposed before, w_β is stored in our files for quick lookup. In this regard, common kernels, such as Gaussians, can be pre-computed to save computation during deconvolution.

The spatial support of the 1D inverse kernels depends on the amount of regularization, i.e. the weight λ. For noisy images, λ is set small, corresponding to strong regularization. Accordingly, the size of inverse kernels is small. In practice, the support of 1D kernels is estimated by thresholding insignificant values in the kernel and removing boundary zero values, which are determined automatically once λ is given.

The pseudo-code for inverse kernel deconvolution is provided in Alg. 1.

4 Experimental Validation

We evaluate the system performance with regard to running time and result quality. Our main objective is to handle focal, Gaussian or even sparse motion blur. In our implementation, primary parameters in Eq. (12) are set as follows: $\lambda \in [500, 3000]$, depending on the image noise level; β is fixed to 10 for all

---

Algorithm 1. $x = \text{FastSpatialDeconvolution}(y, k)$

---

1 $w_\beta \leftarrow \text{real}\left(F^{-1}\left(\frac{1}{\sum_i |F(c_i)|^2 + \frac{\lambda}{\beta}|F(k)|^2} \right) \right)$

2 $\{s_l, f_u^l, f_v^l\} \leftarrow \text{svd}(w_\beta)$

3 Discard $\{s_l, f_u^l, f_v^l\}$ pairs with s_l below a threshold

4 $x^1 \leftarrow y, \gamma^1 \leftarrow 0$

5 **for** $t = 1$ **to** maxIters

6 　　**do** $z_i^{t+1} \leftarrow \text{argmin}_z E(x^t, z_i, \gamma_i^t)$

7 　　　$a \leftarrow \sum_{i \in \{1,2\}} c_i' * (z_i^{t+1} - \frac{1}{\beta}\gamma_i^t) + \frac{\lambda}{\beta}k' * y$

8 　　　$x^{t+1} \leftarrow 0$

9 　　　**for** $l = 1$ **to** $length(\{s_l\})$

10 　　　　**do** $x^{t+1} \leftarrow x^{t+1} + s_l \cdot a * f_u^l * f_v^{l'}$

11 　　　$\gamma_i^{t+1} \leftarrow \gamma_i^t - \beta(z_i^{t+1} - c_i * x^{t+1})$

Table 1. Running time (in seconds) and PSNRs for different methods

Image Size	RL	IRLS	TVL1	Fast PD	Ours
325x365	0.91	85.83	7.50	0.59	0.57
1064x694	2.28	241.34	22.20	2.00	3.27
1251x1251	6.19	537.89	54.30	4.61	7.30
PSNRs	20.2	24.3	22.7	23.3	23.7

images; totally 5 iterations are enough in practice. We compared our method with others, including the spatial-domain Richardson-Lucy (RL) deconvolution, IRLS [13] (short for the iterative re-weighted least squares) approach, TVL1 deconvolution [28] and the fast deconvolution [11], denoted as PD for "penalty decomposition". The TVL1 method is implemented in C language and all the other four methods are implemented in MATLAB. We run 20 iterations for the standard RL. All other methods are based on the authors' implementation with default parameters.

Running time is obtained on different sizes of images. In total, we collect 10 natural images with different resolutions. They are blurred with Gaussian filters with variance $\sigma \in \{1, 2, 3, 4, 5\}$ respectively. Small Gaussian noise is added to each image. Running time for three resolutions is reported in Table 1. Our method is similarly fast as PD employing FFTs and is a magnitude faster than IRLS and TVL1. Our method updates z with analytical solutions. It can be further sped up by using a look-up table. As w_β is pre-computed, we do not include its estimation time in the table. In our experiments, a 51×51 kernel is computed in 0.1 second. The final PSNRs of all the 10 examples are included in Table 1.

We show in Fig. 3 a visual comparison along with close-ups for different methods. Our result is comparable with the sharpest one while not containing extra visual artifacts.

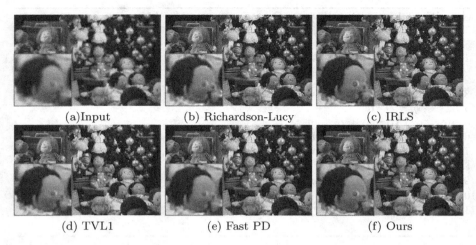

| (a)Input | (b) Richardson-Lucy | (c) IRLS |

| (d) TVL1 | (e) Fast PD | (f) Ours |

Fig. 3. Visual comparison. Similar quality results manifest that our method does not introduce additional visual artifacts

Fig. 4. Sample motion and focal blur kernels for validation

Statistics of Filters. We now present the statistics of the 1D filters w_β learned from different types of kernels. We collected a set of filters in real motion blur, representative Gaussian convolution, and natural out-of-focus. The 8 motion blur kernels are from [14]. The Gaussian blur kernels are with different scales, controlled by variance $\sigma \in \{1, 2, 3, 4, 5\}$. We also collect from internet the real focal blur kernels. We normalize all of them to size 35×35. A few examples are shown in Fig. 4.

The statistics in Table 2 indicate that motion deconvolution typically requires more 1D kernels to approximate the inverse filter than others, due primarily to large kernel variation and complex shapes. Convolving tens of kernels that approximate w_β is in fact a completely parallel process and can be easily accelerated using multiple-core CPU and GPU.

The number of 1D kernels is determined by thresholding the singular values and dropping out insignificant ones. Varying the threshold results in different numbers of 1D kernels and thus affects the performance. We show in Fig. 5 how the threshold affects the quality of restored images. One threshold can be applied to different types of kernels to generate reasonable results. We also note based

Table 2. Kernel decomposition statistics. "Average number" refers to the average number of non-zero singular values, i.e., the number of 1D filters used. "Average length" is the length of each 1D kernel.

Type	Avg. number	Avg. length
Motion	36.4	110.3
Gaussian	8.3	71.2
Out-of-focus	15.7	87.8

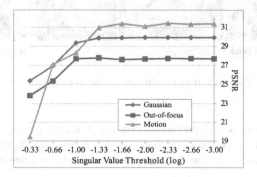

Fig. 5. PSNRs versus singular value thresholds for different types of kernels. The singular value thresholds are plotted in a logarithmic scale.

on Table 2 that one threshold may generate different numbers of 1D kernels depending on the structure and complexity of the original convolution kernels.

5 Applications

We apply our method to a few computer vision and computational photography applications.

5.1 Deconvolution-Intensive Super-Resolution

Iterative back-projection [8] is one effective scheme to upscale images and videos, and is fast in general. In this process, reconstruction errors are back projected into the high resolution image through interpolation and deconvolution, expressed as

$$h^{t+1} = h^t + (l - (h^t * G) \downarrow) \uparrow *p, \tag{18}$$

where G is a kernel that could be Gaussian [8] or non-Gaussian [17], h is the target high-resolution image and l is its low-resolution version. $\downarrow$ and $\uparrow$ are simple downscaling and upscaling with interpolation operations. p is the pseudo-inverse of the kernel. A good p positively influences high-quality image super-resolution.

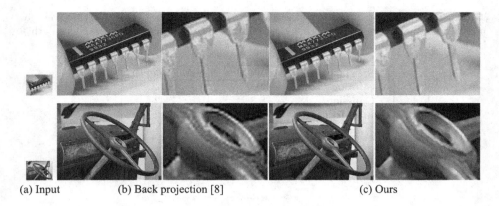

(a) Input   (b) Back projection [8]   (c) Ours

Fig. 6. Super-resolution by back-projection

So we substitute our spatial deconvolution for p, which counts in regularization in deconvolution. It produces the results shown in Fig. 6. They demonstrate the usefulness of our inverse kernel scheme, as visual artifacts are suppressed.

5.2   Extended Depth of Field

The proposed method can be applied to removal of part of focal blur. We employ it in the extended depth of field photography [12], which generates a blurry image for each depth layer and restores it using deconvolution. Blurry image generation is achieved by controlling the motion of the detector during image integration or rotating the focus ring. Since the resulting blur PSFs belong to the generalized Gaussian family, they can be efficiently computed using our spatial scheme. Fig. 7 shows two examples. It takes 1.7s by our method on a single CPU core to produce the results shown in (b) with resolution 681×1032. In comparison, the fast deconvolution method [11] takes 2s to produce the results in (c). Our method can be fully parallelized to much speed up computation.

5.3   Motion Deblurring

Motion blur kernels are in general asymmetric, corresponding to a larger number of 1D kernels in our decomposition step. It reveals the non-separable nature of motion kernels. Our inverse kernel scheme is still applicable here thanks to the independence of each 1D filtering pass. We show in Fig. 8 the IRLS deconvolution results of [13] and our inverse filter results. The ground truth clear images and motion blur kernels are presented in the original paper [14]. While both approaches work in spatial domain, ours takes 0.5s to process the 255×255 images, compared to the 70 seconds by the IRLS method.

(a) Input   (b) Ours   (c) PD [11]

Fig. 7. Reconstructed pictures from extended depth of field cameras

5.4   Real-Time Partial Blur Removal

Our method directly helps partial image deconvolution. Fourier transform requires square inputs and any error produced after domain switch will be propagated across pixels due to the lack of spatial consideration. Our method does not have these constraints. Our current implementation can achieve real-time performance on 130×130 patches on a single CPU core. It is notable that any shapes of regions can be handled in this system. Our empirically processed regions are slightly expanded from the user marked ones to include more pixels in optimization in order to avoid boundary visual artifacts.

One example is shown in Fig. 9, where a book is focal blurred. We restore a patch using our method, which does not introduce unexpected ringing artifacts. Our method takes only 0.07 second to process the content, compared with 0.4 second needed in the FFT-based method [11] to process all pixels within the tightest bounding box enclosing the selected region. The close-ups are shown in (c) and (d). The difference is caused by processing only the marked pixels by our method and processing all pixels in the rectangular bounding box by the FFT-involved method.

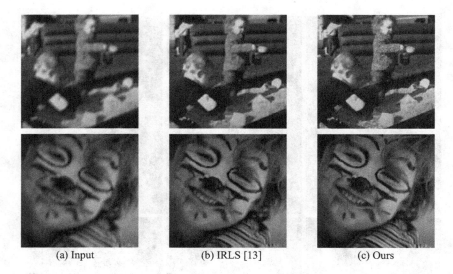

(a) Input   (b) IRLS [13]   (c) Ours

Fig. 8. Motion deblurring examples

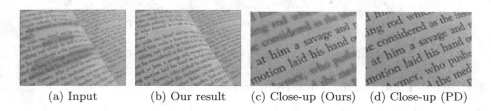

(a) Input   (b) Our result   (c) Close-up (Ours)   (d) Close-up (PD)

Fig. 9. Partial Blur Removal. In (a), we mark a few pixels for deconvolution. The result is shown in (b) with the close-up in (c). The FFT-based method (PD) yields the result shown in (d) by devolving all pixels in the bounding box.

6   Conclusion

We have presented a spatial deconvolution method leveraging the pseudo-inverse spatial kernels under regularization. Fixed kernel estimation is achieved using the augmented Lagrangian method. Our framework is general and finds many applications. Its impact is the numerical bridge to connect fast frequency-domain operations and robust local spatial deconvolution. Our method inherits the speed and location-sensitivity advantages in these two streams of work and opens up a new area for future exploration.

The method could be amazingly efficient if these 1D kernel bases involved in decomposition are handled by different threads in the parallel computing architecture. It works well for general Gaussian and other practical motion and focal blur kernels. One direction for future work is to investigate spatially varying inverse kernels for complex blur.

Acknowledgements. The work described in this paper was partially supported by a grant from the Research Grants Council of the Hong Kong Special Administrative Region (Project No. 413113). The authors would like to thank Shicheng Zheng for his help in implementing part of the algorithm.

References

1. Afonso, M.V., Bioucas-Dias, J.M., Figueiredo, M.A.: An augmented lagrangian approach to the constrained optimization formulation of imaging inverse problems. IEEE Transactions on Image Processing 20(3), 681–695 (2011)
2. Agrawal, A.K., Raskar, R.: Resolving objects at higher resolution from a single motion-blurred image. In: CVPR (2007)
3. Chakrabarti, A., Zickler, T., Freeman, W.T.: Analyzing spatially-varying blur. In: CVPR, pp. 2512–2519 (2010)
4. Cho, S., Lee, S.: Fast motion deblurring. ACM Trans. Graph. 28(5) (2009)
5. Danielyan, A., Katkovnik, V., Egiazarian, K.: Image deblurring by augmented lagrangian with bm3d frame prior. In: Workshop on Information Theoretic Methods in Science and Engineering, pp. 16–18 (2010)
6. Fergus, R., Singh, B., Hertzmann, A., Roweis, S.T., Freeman, W.T.: Removing camera shake from a single photograph. ACM Trans. Graph. 25(3), 787–794 (2006)
7. Freeman, W.T., Adelson, E.H.: The design and use of steerable filters. IEEE Trans. Pattern Anal. Mach. Intell. 13(9), 891–906 (1991)
8. Irani, M., Peleg, S.: Motion analysis for image enhancement: Resolution, occlusion, and transparency. Journal of Visual Communication and Image Representation 4(4) (1993)
9. Jerosch-Herold, M., Wilke, N., Stillman, A.E., Wilson, R.F.: Magnetic resonance quantification of the myocardial perfusion reserve with a fermi function model for constrained deconvolution. Medical physics 25, 73 (1998)
10. Joshi, N., Zitnick, C.L., Szeliski, R., Kriegman, D.J.: Image deblurring and denoising using color priors. In: CVPR, pp. 1550–1557 (2009)
11. Krishnan, D., Fergus, R.: Fast image deconvolution using hyper-laplacian priors. In: NIPS (2009)
12. Kuthirummal, S., Nagahara, H., Zhou, C., Nayar, S.K.: Flexible depth of field photography. IEEE Trans. Pattern Anal. Mach. Intell. 33(1), 58–71 (2011)
13. Levin, A., Fergus, R., Durand, F., Freeman, W.T.: Image and depth from a conventional camera with a coded aperture. ACM Trans. Graph. 26(3), 70 (2007)
14. Levin, A., Weiss, Y., Durand, F., Freeman, W.T.: Understanding and evaluating blind deconvolution algorithms. In: CVPR, pp. 1964–1971 (2009)
15. Lin, Z., Chen, M., Ma, Y.: The augmented lagrange multiplier method for exact recovery of corrupted low-rank matrices. UIUC Technical Report UILU-ENG-09-2215 (2010)
16. Mathews, J., Walker, R.L.: Mathematical methods of physics, vol. 271. WA Benjamin New York (1970)
17. Michaeli, T., Irani, M.: Nonparametric blind super-resolution. In: ICCV (2ss013)
18. Perona, P.: Deformable kernels for early vision. IEEE Trans. Pattern Anal. Mach. Intell. 17(5), 488–499 (1995)
19. Raskar, R., Agrawal, A.K., Tumblin, J.: Coded exposure photography: motion deblurring using fluttered shutter. ACM Trans. Graph. 25(3), 795–804 (2006)

20. Richardson, W.H.: Bayesian-based iterative method of image restoration. Journal of the Optical Society of America 62(1), 55–59 (1972)
21. Schmidt, U., Rother, C., Nowozin, S., Jancsary, J., Roth, S.: Discriminative non-blind deblurring. In: CVPR, pp. 604–611 (2013)
22. Shan, Q., Jia, J., Agarwala, A.: High-quality motion deblurring from a single image. ACM Trans. Graph. 27(3) (2008)
23. Shan, Q., Li, Z., Jia, J., Tang, C.-K.: Fast image/video upsampling. ACM Trans. Graph. 27(5), 153 (2008)
24. Starck, J.L., Pantin, E., Murtagh, F.: Deconvolution in astronomy: A review. Publications of the Astronomical Society of the Pacific 114(800), 1051–1069 (2002)
25. Tai, Y.-W., Lin, S.: Motion-aware noise filtering for deblurring of noisy and blurry images. In: CVPR, pp. 17–24 (2012)
26. Tikhonov, A., Arsenin, V., John, F.: Solutions of ill-posed problems (1977)
27. Wiener, N.: Extrapolation, interpolation, and smoothing of stationary time series: with engineering applications. Journal of the American Statistical Association 47(258) (1949)
28. Xu, L., Jia, J.: Two-phase kernel estimation for robust motion deblurring. In: Daniilidis, K., Maragos, P., Paragios, N. (eds.) ECCV 2010, Part I. LNCS, vol. 6311, pp. 157–170. Springer, Heidelberg (2010)
29. Xu, L., Zheng, S., Jia, J.: Unnatural l0 sparse representation for natural image deblurring. In: CVPR, pp. 1107–1114 (2013)
30. Yuan, L., Sun, J., Quan, L., Shum, H.-Y.: Image deblurring with blurred/noisy image pairs. ACM Trans. Graph. 26(3), 1 (2007)
31. Yuan, L., Sun, J., Quan, L., Shum, H.-Y.: Progressive inter-scale and intra-scale non-blind image deconvolution. ACM Trans. Graph. 27(3) (2008)
32. Zhou, C., Lin, S., Nayar, S.K.: Coded aperture pairs for depth from defocus and defocus deblurring. International Journal of Computer Vision 93(1), 53–72 (2011)

Deep Network Cascade for Image Super-resolution

Zhen Cui[1,2], Hong Chang[1], Shiguang Shan[1], Bineng Zhong[2], and Xilin Chen[1]

[1] Key Lab of Intelligent Information Processing of Chinese Academy of Sciences
(CAS), Institute of Computing Technology, CAS, Beijing, China
[2] School of Computer Science and Technology, Huaqiao University, Xiamen, China
{zhen.cui,hong.chang}@vipl.ict.ac.cn, {sgshan,xlchen}@ict.ac.cn,
bnzhong@hqu.edu.cn

Abstract. In this paper, we propose a new model called deep network cascade (DNC) to gradually upscale low-resolution images layer by layer, each layer with a small scale factor. DNC is a cascade of multiple stacked collaborative local auto-encoders. In each layer of the cascade, non-local self-similarity search is first performed to enhance high-frequency texture details of the partitioned patches in the input image. The enhanced image patches are then input into a collaborative local auto-encoder (CLA) to suppress the noises as well as collaborate the compatibility of the overlapping patches. By closing the loop on non-local self-similarity search and CLA in a cascade layer, we can refine the super-resolution result, which is further fed into next layer until the required image scale. Experiments on image super-resolution demonstrate that the proposed DNC can gradually upscale a low-resolution image with the increase of network layers and achieve more promising results in visual quality as well as quantitative performance.

Keywords: Super-resolution, Auto-encoder, Deep learning.

1 Introduction

In visual information processing, high-resolution (HR) images are still desired for more useful information [26]. However, due to the limitation of physical devices, we can only obtain low-resolution (LR) images of the specific object in some scenes such as a long-distance shooting. To handle this problem, the super-resolution (SR) technique is usually employed to recover the lost information in the source image. With increasing applications in video surveillance, medical, remote sensing images, etc., the SR technique has been attracting more and more attention in the computer vision community over the past decades [7,9,33,10,8].

The conventional super-resolution methods attempt to recover the source image by solving the ill-posed inverse problem, $y = Hx + v$, where x is the unknown HR image to be estimated, y is the observed LR image, H is the degradation matrix, and v is the additional noise vector. Under the scarcity of observed LR images, the inverse process is a underdetermined problem, thus

D. Fleet et al. (Eds.): ECCV 2014, Part V, LNCS 8693, pp. 49–64, 2014.

the solution is not unique. To find a reasonable solution, some sophisticated statistical priors of natural images are usually incorporated into the reconstruction process [7]. However, these reconstruction-based methods have a limit of magnification factor [1,21].

To address this problem, recently, example-based SR methods [33,10,5,8,32] have been proposed in succession. They use machine learning techniques to predict the missing frequency band of upsampled image from an external dataset [33] or the testing image itself [10,5,32]. Typically, in view of human visual mechanism, sparse representation (or sparse coding) is employed to super-resolution. They either emphasize on the construction of more representative dictionaries, such as learning coupled dictionaries of LR and HR counterpart patches [33] or multi-scale dictionaries [34], or focus on the robustness of sparse coefficients by integrating some priors, such as using centralized sparse constraints [5] and manifold structure constraints [22]. Generally, a huge training set is required to capture the rich characteristics of natural images for image super-resolution.

In contrary, some recent studies [3,10,32] indicate that local image structures tend to redundantly recur many times within and across different image scales, and super-resolution may be conducted on those self-similarity examples from the testing image itself. Specifically, Glasner et al. [10] utilized recurrence of patches to generate virtual LR image patches, which are fed into the classical reconstruction-based SR scheme. Yang et al. [32] further refined the self-similarity by in-place self-similarity. The self-similarity technique is empirically found to work well especially for a small upscaling factor. To robustly recover a LR image with a properly large scale, these few studies have also begun to more or less use an iterative strategy to upscale the LR image. Even so, more efficient gradual SR models still remain to be developed for image SR. Moreover, some crucial problems need to be studied in the gradual unscaling models, such as the propagation of estimated error, the collaboration of overlapping patches, etc.

In this paper, we propose a deep learning scheme called deep network cascade (DNC) to gradually upscale low-resolution images layer by layer, which is the first time to our knowledge. On one hand, to reasonably enhance high-frequency texture details, we employ non-local self-similarity (NLSS) search on the input image in multi-scale, which can bypass the assumption on the image degradation process. On the other hand, by taking the NLSS results as the input, the collaborative local auto-encoder (CLA) is proposed to suppress the noises and meanwhile collaborate the overlapping reconstructed patches. In CLA, to reduce the learnable parameters and make auto-encoder easily controllable, we adopt weight-tying on all patches and L_1 sparse constraint on hidden neurons. Closing the loop on the two steps forms a cascade layer, named stacked collaborative local auto-encoder (stacked CLA or SCLA), which refines the super-resolution image well.

Multiple SCLA models can be successively concatenated into the deep network cascade, where the higher layer takes the output SR image of the lower layer as input. With the increase of network layers, the magnification factor of the learned SR image can be enlarged gradually. Inevitably, in the deep network, the synthetic "error" textures (e.g., noises, artifacts, etc.) will propagate and even spread in next network layers, which leads to a large deviation from the source HR image. To reduce the effects, we use the back-projected technique [14] to contrain the super-resolved image in each layer. To train the DNC model, we adopt the greedy layer-wise optimization strategy. Extensive experiments on single image super-resolution demonstrate the effectiveness of the proposed method on visual quality as well as objective evaluation.

2   Related Work

Generally, existing super-resolution methods fall into three categories: interpolation-based [35], reconstruction-based [7,27] and example-based [9,11,4,33,10,5,8,34,25,32] methods. Interpolation-based methods are simple and effective for SR, such as bilinear, bicubic or other sampling methods [35]. However, with the increasing magnification factor, they are prone to generate overly smooth edges. Reconstruction-based methods usually borrow a certain prior to predict the SR image, but they are still limited to small magnification factors [21] or a scarcity of observed LR images.

Example-based methods break the limitation. They attempt to learn the high-frequency details from an external training dataset or the testing image itself. Freeman *et al.* [9] used the nearest neighbor (NN) to estimate the high-frequency information and a Markov network to handle the compatibility between patches. Later on, by assuming the similarity of manifold structures between LR and HR counterparts, Chang *et al.* [4] used locally linear embedding (LLE) to predict the HR patches. More recently, the sparse coding based methods [6,33] were proposed for image restoration. Typically, the coupled filters (or dictionaries) [33] are learnt to share sparse structures on HR and LR counterparts, but it requires a large amount of training pairs. Aimed at this problem, the non-local prior may be employed to enrich the textural information [10,5,22]. They used the non-local prior with a designed degradation process [5] or a shallow model [22]. Specifically, the self-similarity prior of the testing image itself is used to generate virtual observed LR examples [10,32]. Empirically, the self-similarity works better on small upscaling factors [36,32]. To address this problem, a few studies [10,32] start to gradually upscale the LR image, but they lack a more explicit layer-wise model. Different from previous works, here we develop a new layer-wise model, referred to deep network cascade, to upscale the input LR image layer by layer, each layer with a refined SR result.

Deep learning attempts to learn layered, hierarchical representations of high-dimensional data [12,13], and has been successfully applied in many computer vision problems. Classical unit learning models in deep architecture include sparse coding [17], restricted Boltzmann machine (RBM) [12], anto-encoder [13,2,29], etc. Specifically, the (stacked) denoising auto-encoder (DA) [28,31] has shown effectiveness in image inverse problems such as denoising and inpainting. Our method differs from DA in two ways: first, DA requires clean data (ground truth) in the training process, assuming that the degradation function is implicitly known, while the CLA relaxes the condition by feeding the model with NLSS search results; second, our method is imposed on local patches with tied weight, sparse and compatibility constraints, which can greatly reduce the number of the learnable parameters when suppressing the noises.

3   The Proposed Network Cascade

Below we denote a vector/matrix by a lowercase/uppercase letter in bold. The transposition of a vector or matrix is denoted by the superscript $^\mathsf{T}$. We denote the input LR image by $\mathbf{x} \in \mathbb{R}^N$, and denote the extracted i-th $(i = 1, 2, \cdots, n)$ patch from $\mathbf{x}$ by $\mathbf{x}_i = \mathcal{F}_i\mathbf{x} \in \mathbb{R}^d$, where $\mathcal{F}_i$ is the extracting patch operation (*i.e.*, a matrix in math). Given the LR image $\mathbf{x}$, the aim is to recover its HR image with a magnification factor s.

As shown in Fig.1(a), we upscale the LR image with the deep network of l cascade layers, each with a small scaling constant $s^{1/l}$. With the super-resolved image of the former layer as the input, we can successively stack l cascade layers to upscale the image. By doing this, we can obtain a stable SR solution for large scaling factors, while the reconstruction-based methods have a limit of a upscaling factor [21], and even the example-based methods usually work well on small upsampling factors [20,36,32]. However, as the mutuality only exists in two adjacent layers, minor distortions and estimation errors might propagate and accumulate from layer to layer, which easily leads to a large deviation from the source HR image for the final SR result. To reduce this effect, a global "back-projection" [14] constraint is used to make super-resolved images evolve along a proper direction. To do super-resolution more credibly in each network unit (or layer), we encapsulate two blocks: NLSS search and CLA. By iteratively stacking them as a cascade layer of DNC, referred to SCLA, the super-resolved image of each layer can be gradually refined. Below we further illustrate SCLA.

As discussed above, the image degradation process from the source image to the observed LR image often accompanies with complicated variations (*e.g.*, blur, downscaling, noise, etc.), and is always unknown in real-world problems. Therefore, it is intractable and impractical to learn the transformation format between HR and LR images, as many related methods do. To this end, we employ the NLSS prior on the input image itself to enhance textural high-frequency information. Since natural image patches recur many times within an image and even across different scales [10], we can always find some similar patches for a given patch. Concretely, in a network unit, we denote the input image by $\mathbf{x}$, which comes from the SR image of the former layer or the source LR image in the first layer. Before super-resolution, the bicubic interpolation is imposed on the input image to generate the initialized SR image (marked as $\mathbf{x}$ again for simplification). For a patch $\mathbf{x}_i$ extracted from $\mathbf{x}$, we perform the non-local self-similarity search in multi-scale images, which may come from blur and successive downscaling (*e.g.*, $s^{1/l}$ scaling factor) versions of $\mathbf{x}$. Given $\mathbf{x}_i$, suppose the

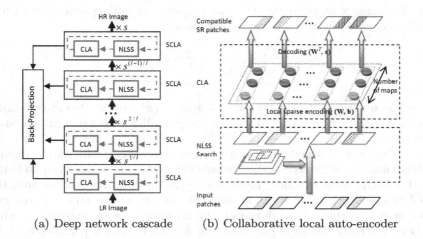

(a) Deep network cascade   (b) Collaborative local auto-encoder

Fig. 1. Illustration of the proposed deep network cascade for image SR. Note that we don't plot the back-projection step in the right figure for simplification.

top K nearest neighbors, $\mathbf{x}_i^1, \cdots, \mathbf{x}_i^K$, are chosen from these multi-scale images, we can roughly estimate a new enhanced patch $\widehat{\mathbf{x}}_i$ as

$$\widehat{\mathbf{x}}_i = \sum_{j=1}^{K} \varpi_i^j \mathbf{x}_i^j, \tag{1}$$

where the weight ϖ_i^j may be set to Gaussian kernel with normalization. The estimated patch $\widehat{\mathbf{x}}_i$ usually contains more abundant texture information than the input patch $\mathbf{x}_i$.

With the high-frequency details generated from the NLSS search, the structure distortions or estimation errors also often accompany in the enhanced patches, and might be further propagated and even magnified in next layers of the deep network cascade. To relieve this phenomenon, an extension of auto-encoder, called CLA, is proposed to suppress the noises as well as collaborate the overlapping patches.

The CLA is adopted on the patches $\widehat{\mathbf{x}}_i (i = 1, \cdots, n)$ with constraints coming from two sides. First, a weight-tying scheme like convolutional network [19] is used to reduce the parameter space as well as preserve a certain flexibility to other variances. Moreover, a few of hidden neurons should be activated for a given stimulus (*i.e.*, a patch here) in view of human visual mechanism, which refers to the sparsity of codes. Second, the compatibility constraint on overlapping patches is added into auto-encoder to induce more smooth and natural textures for the integrated SR image. Actually, the output patch $\mathbf{z}_i$ of CLA can be combined into a SR image $\tilde{\mathbf{x}}$ by averaging the overlapping part among patches, which is formally computed from the following equation,

$$\tilde{\mathbf{x}} = (\sum_{i=1}^{n} \mathcal{F}_i^\mathsf{T} \mathcal{F}_i)^{-1} \sum_{i=1}^{n} (\mathcal{F}_i^\mathsf{T} \mathbf{z}_i). \tag{2}$$

Due to the requirement of compatibility among patches, $\mathbf{z}_i$ should be ideally equal to $\mathcal{F}_i \tilde{\mathbf{x}}$, which is regarded as the compatibility constraint presented in Section 4.

In addition, a pre-learned (denoising) auto-encoder trained with a large amount of patches from other external images or only the testing image may be used to initialize CLA. Given the enhanced image patches as the output of NLSS search, the revised auto-encoder network can be adapted to suppress the noises or artifacts. Furthermore, to avoid a large deviation and accelerate the optimization, we implicitly regularize the network parameters by feeding the learnt parameters of the former layer into the next layer. As a whole, the collaborative local auto-encoder plays an important role in accomplishing a more natural SR image with milder texture structures.

4   Collaborative Local Auto-encoder

In this section, we will first give the formulation of collaborative local auto-encoder, then provide a gradient-based optimization algorithm for CLA.

4.1   Formulation

Given the patches $\mathbf{x}_i(i = 1, \cdots, n)$ sampled from the LR image $\mathbf{x}$, we compute $\hat{\mathbf{x}}_i \in \mathbb{R}^d$ through the NLSS search (Eqn. (1)), which are then input to CLA. As discussed in Section 3, CLA contains two constraints: the sparse constraint and the compatibility constraint. Concretely, CLA can be formulated into the following optimization problem,

$$\min_{\mathbf{W}, \mathbf{b}, \mathbf{c}} \quad l(\mathbf{x}, \mathbf{W}, \mathbf{b}, \mathbf{c}) + \gamma g(\mathbf{U}) + \eta h(\mathbf{Z}), \tag{3}$$

where $\mathbf{W} \in \mathbb{R}^{m \times d}$ is the tied weights of network (m is the number of maps/filters, $m \gg d$), $\mathbf{b}, \mathbf{c}$ are respectively the bias of the encoder and decoder, $\mathbf{U}, \mathbf{Z}$ are the hidden neurons on the encoder and decoder level (or $\mathbf{Z}$ can be considered as the output of auto-encoder), γ and η are the balance parameters. Below we discuss the three terms in detail.

The first term represents the reconstruct error of auto-encoder on local patches. Like convolutional networks [19], each filter is tied on all patches within the image to form one map during encoding, which sharply reduces the number of learnable parameters while maintaining a certain flexibility by the over-complete filter bank.

Formally, the loss function can be written as,

$$l(\mathbf{x}, \mathbf{W}, \mathbf{b}, \mathbf{c}) = \frac{1}{2n}\sum_{i=1}^{n} \|\mathbf{z}_i - \widehat{\mathbf{x}}_i\|^2, \tag{4}$$

$$\mathbf{y}_i = \sigma(\mathbf{W}\widehat{\mathbf{x}}_i + \mathbf{b}), \tag{5}$$

$$\mathbf{u}_i = \frac{\mathbf{y}_i}{\sqrt{\mathbf{y}_i^\mathsf{T}\mathbf{y}_i}}, \tag{6}$$

$$\mathbf{z}_i = \mathbf{W}^\mathsf{T}\mathbf{u}_i + \mathbf{c}. \tag{7}$$

Eqn.(5) represents a nonlinear encoder with a point-wise hyperbolic tangent function $\sigma(x) = \frac{e^{ax}-e^{-ax}}{e^{ax}+e^{-ax}}$ (the gain a), which is easy to implement sparsity because its values range from -1 to 1. Eqn.(7) represents a decoder with the bias $\mathbf{c}$. In order to reduce the effect of filter scale, the L_2-normalization is performed on all hidden nodes of the encoder level as expressed in Eqn.(6).

The second term is the sparse constraint on all hidden neurons of the encoder level. Previous sparse deep learning methods [23,18,28,31] usually employ the deviation of the expected activation (*i.e.*, K-L divergence) to regularize the sparsity. However, we have to painstakingly tune the activation rate and balance parameter to reach a certain sparsity. Differed from those works, we directly use the L_1 norm, *i.e.*,

$$g(\mathbf{U}) = \frac{1}{n}\sum_{i=1}^{n} \|\mathbf{u}_i\|_1, \tag{8}$$

where $\mathbf{U} = [\mathbf{u}_1, \mathbf{u}_2, \cdots, \mathbf{u}_n]$. The L_1 norm of the hyperbolic tangent operation can easily produce zero-value neurons and avoid tuning the extensive hyperparameters, which has been used in sparse filters with better effectiveness [24]. In addition, the L_1 norm on L_2 normalized features can be implemented through a few lines of MATLAB code.

The third term denotes the compatibility constraint on the reconstructed patches from the decoder. The compatibility on overlapping parts of the reconstructed patches is necessary for suppressing the artifacts. Ideally, the reconstructed patches and the corresponding patches extracted from the estimated image $\widetilde{\mathbf{x}}$ in Eqn. (2) should be as similar as possible. Formally, we can incorporate a regularization term into our model, *i.e.*,

$$h(\mathbf{Z}) = \frac{1}{2n}\sum_{i=1}^{n} \|\mathbf{z}_i - \mathcal{F}_i\widetilde{\mathbf{x}}\|^2, \tag{9}$$

where $\mathbf{Z} = [\mathbf{z}_1, \mathbf{z}_2, \cdots, \mathbf{z}_n]$.

4.2   Optimization

To optimize the objective function in Eqn.(3), we employ the limited-memory BFGS (L-BFGS) method [16], which is often used to solve nonlinear optimization problems without any constraints. L-BFGS is particularly suitable for the problems with a large amount of variables under the moderate memory requirement. To utilize L-BFGS, the gradients of the object function need to be derived.

Algorithm 1. Image Super-resolution with DNC

Input: LR image $\mathbf{x}$, patch size p, upscale factor s, stacked layer number l, neighbor
  number K, balance parameters γ, η.
Output: SR image $\widetilde{\mathbf{x}}, \mathbf{W}, \mathbf{b}, \mathbf{c}$.
  1. Set $t = 1$. Initialize $\mathbf{W}^t, \mathbf{b}^t, \mathbf{c}^t$ with (denoising) auto-encoder;
  2. **repeat**
  3.   Initialize $\mathbf{x}^{(t)}$ by interpolating $\mathbf{x}^{(t-1)}$ ($\mathbf{x}^{(0)} = \mathbf{x}$) with a scale factor $s^{1/l}$.
  4.   **repeat**
  5.   Sample overlapping patches $\mathbf{X}^{(t)} = [\mathcal{F}_1 \mathbf{x}^{(t)}, \cdots, \mathcal{F}_n \mathbf{x}^{(t)}]$ from $\mathbf{x}^{(t)}$.
  6.   Compute $\widehat{\mathbf{X}}^{(t)}$ in Eqn.(1) by using the NLSS search.
  7.   L-BFGS optimization for new $\mathbf{W}^{(t)}, \mathbf{b}^{(t)}, \mathbf{c}^{(t)}$ by using Eqn.(12).
  8.   Predict new SR image $\widetilde{\mathbf{x}}^{(t)}$ by using Eqn.(5), (6), (7) and (2).
  9.   Perform the back-projection operation for $\widetilde{\mathbf{x}}^{(t)}$.
  10. $\mathbf{W}^{(t+1)} = \mathbf{W}^{(t)}; \mathbf{b}^{(t+1)} = \mathbf{b}^{(t)}; \mathbf{c}^{(t+1)} = \mathbf{c}^{(t)}; \mathbf{x}^{(t+1)} = \widetilde{\mathbf{x}}^{(t)}$.
  11. $t = t + 1$.
  12.   **until** reach a satisfied solution.
  13. **until** reach l layers.
  14. **return** SR image $\mathbf{x}^{(t)}$.

However, the L_1 norm in Eqn. (8) is not first-order differentiable at zero value.
For this, we use the soft-absolute function $\|x\|_1 = \sqrt{x^2 + \epsilon}$, where ϵ is a small
constant (*e.g.*, $1.0E - 9$). So Eqn. (8) can be rewritten as,

$$g(\mathbf{U}) = \frac{1}{n} \sum_{i=1}^{n} \mathbf{1}_m^\intercal \sqrt{\mathbf{u}_i \otimes \mathbf{u}_i + \epsilon \mathbf{1}_m}, \qquad (10)$$

where $\otimes$ is an element-wise multiplication operation and $\mathbf{1}_m$ is a column vector
with m ones. Next we define some matrices to facilitate the derivation as listed
in the following,

  - $\widehat{\mathbf{X}} = [\widehat{\mathbf{x}}_1, \widehat{\mathbf{x}}_2, \cdots, \widehat{\mathbf{x}}_n]$, a matrix of n patches obtained from NLSS search.
  - $\widetilde{\mathbf{X}} = [\mathcal{F}_1 \widetilde{\mathbf{x}}, \mathcal{F}_2 \widetilde{\mathbf{x}}, \cdots, \mathcal{F}_n \widetilde{\mathbf{x}}]$, a matrix of n patches extracted from the recon-
    structed SR image in Eqn. (2).
  - $\mathbf{Y} = [\mathbf{y}_1, \mathbf{y}_2, \cdots, \mathbf{y}_n]$, a matrix of the encoding neurons before L_2 normal-
    ization.
  - $\mathbf{U} = [\mathbf{u}_1, \mathbf{u}_2, \cdots, \mathbf{u}_n]$, a matrix of the hidden neurons after L_2 normalization.
  - $\mathbf{Z} = [\mathbf{z}_1, \mathbf{z}_2, \cdots, \mathbf{z}_n]$, a matrix of the output units after decoding.

Thus the object function in Eqn.(3) can be reformulated as,

$$f(\mathbf{x}, \mathbf{W}, \mathbf{b}, \mathbf{c}) = \frac{1}{2n} \|\mathbf{Z} - \widehat{\mathbf{X}}\|_F^2 + \frac{\eta}{2n} \|\mathbf{Z} - \widetilde{\mathbf{X}}\|_F^2 + \frac{\gamma}{n} \mathbf{1}_m^\intercal (\sqrt{\mathbf{U} \otimes \mathbf{U} + \epsilon \mathbf{1}_{m \times n}}) \mathbf{1}_n \quad (11)$$

After a series of derivations, we can obtain the gradients of the function f with
respect to the variables $\mathbf{W}, \mathbf{b}, \mathbf{c}$ as follows:

$$\frac{\partial f}{\partial \mathbf{W}} = \frac{1}{n} \mathbf{U} \mathbf{A}^\intercal + \frac{1}{n} \mathbf{C} \widehat{\mathbf{X}}^\intercal, \qquad \frac{\partial f}{\partial \mathbf{b}} = \frac{1}{n} \mathbf{C} \mathbf{1}_n, \qquad \frac{\partial f}{\partial \mathbf{c}} = \frac{1}{n} \mathbf{A} \mathbf{1}_n, \qquad (12)$$

where

$$\mathbf{A} = (\mathbf{Z} - \widehat{\mathbf{X}}) + \eta(\mathbf{Z} - \widetilde{\mathbf{X}}), \quad \mathbf{B} = \mathbf{WA} + \gamma \mathbf{U} \oslash \sqrt{\mathbf{U} \otimes \mathbf{U} + \epsilon}, \tag{13}$$

$$\mathbf{R} = \mathbf{1}_{m \times n} \oslash \left(\mathbf{1}_m \sqrt{\mathbf{1}_m^\mathsf{T} (\mathbf{Y} \otimes \mathbf{Y} + \epsilon)} \right), \quad \mathbf{Q} = \mathbf{1}_{m \times n} - \mathbf{Y} \otimes \mathbf{Y}, \tag{14}$$

$$\mathbf{C} = (\mathbf{B} - (\mathbf{1}_m (\mathbf{1}_m^\mathsf{T} (\mathbf{U} \otimes \mathbf{B})))) \otimes \mathbf{Y} \otimes \mathbf{R}) \otimes \mathbf{R} \otimes \mathbf{Q}. \tag{15}$$

In the above equations, $\otimes$ and $\oslash$ are respectively the element-wise multiplication and division operation.

4.3 Stacked CLA

The collaborative local auto-encoder is then stacked to get a deep architecture, where the input of each layer is obtained from the output SR results of the former layer. The whole SR process with SCLA is concluded in Algorithm 1.

5 Experiments

In this section, we evaluate the performance of the proposed method on the examples frequently-used in those SR literatures. Here we also consider two classic evaluation criterions: human visual quality, objective performance on PSNR and SSIM [30]. The magnification factor is set to 3 or 4 used in most SR literatures. Empirically, we also find the SR images with a larger magnification factor (*e.g.*, 6~8) are satisfactory on visual performance. With an overlarge factor, the SR image will deviate from the ground-truth, which naturally leads to a worse quantitative performance. Due to space limitation, more SR results may be downloaded from the website: http://vipl.ict.ac.cn/paperpage/DNC/.

Experimental Configuration. We use patch size with 7×7 pixels, *i.e.*, the window size of the filter in CLA. The sampling step of patches is set to 2 pixels. The layer number of the network cascade is set to $l = 5$ as default. In the generation process of multi-scale images used for the NLSS search, we employ a low-pass Gaussian filter with a standard deviation of 0.55 as used in [32]. In the NLSS search, we choose the first nearest neighbor to predict the new patch. In CLA, the parameter a in the hyperbolic tangent function is set to 1, the number of filters (or maps) is set to 200, the sparse parameter γ and the collaborative parameter η are respectively set to 0.01 and 0.1. To suppress the noises in SR, we pre-train a denoising auto-encoder with Gaussian noises $\sigma = 1, 5, 10$ as the initial network of CLA, where the training data only contains the input image and its downscaled images. In addition, due to the sensibility to the luminance component, we transform RGB images into YCbCr images and then conduct super-resolution on the luminance channel of YCbCr, as most SR methods do.

5.1 Visual Performance

In the first experiment, we show the whole super-resolution process in visual performance with increasing layers. An example is shown in Fig.2. The input low-resolution image is very blur especially for those characters in the bottom lines.

Table 1. PSNR (dB) and SSIM results of the reconstructed high-resolution images on luminance components (3×). For each method, two columns are PSNR and SSIM respectively. The bold (*resp.* underlined) values denote the best (*resp.* second best.)

Images	Yang *et al.* [33]	Kim *et al.* [15]	Lu *et al.* [22]	DNC NSLL	DNC NSLL+CLA
Bike	24.01 / 0.773	<u>24.43</u> / <u>0.784</u>	23.78 / 0.767	24.29 / 0.782	**24.56 / 0.796**
Butterfly	26.16 / 0.877	<u>27.09</u> / <u>0.894</u>	25.48 / 0.857	26.64 / <u>0.894</u>	**27.83 / 0.914**
Flower	28.73 / 0.837	<u>28.91</u> / 0.832	28.30 / 0.829	28.89 / <u>0.840</u>	**29.15 / 0.849**
Girl	33.38 / <u>0.823</u>	33.00 / 0.807	33.13 / 0.819	<u>33.43</u> / <u>0.823</u>	**33.48 / 0.826**
Hat	30.45 / 0.858	30.67 / 0.847	30.29 / 0.854	<u>30.83</u> / <u>0.863</u>	**31.02 / 0.868**
Parrots	29.60 / <u>0.906</u>	<u>29.76</u> / 0.893	29.20 / 0.900	29.69 / <u>0.906</u>	**30.18 / 0.913**
Parthenon	27.07 / 0.795	27.14 / 0.790	26.44 / 0.729	<u>27.40</u> / <u>0.802</u>	**27.49 / 0.811**
Plants	32.72 / 0.903	32.90 / 0.891	32.33 / 0.899	<u>33.05</u> / <u>0.907</u>	**33.13 / 0.913**
Raccoon	<u>29.12</u> / **0.772**	29.03 / 0.760	28.81 / 0.758	29.05 / 0.767	**29.15 / 0.772**

We gradually upscale the LR image into a 3 factor HR image with five cascade layers, each with a equal scale factor[1] of $3^{1/5} \approx 1.25$. With the increase of layers, the characters become more and more clear. Compared with the state-of-the-art methods [10,15][2], DNC achieves comparable, even better visual performance for most SR characters, which have less noticeable artifacts. Note these result are best viewed in zoomed PDF.

In the next experiment, we compare our method with the recent state-of-the-art methods [33,10,15,8] in terms of visual quality. They either learn a transformation from LR patches to HR patches by external examples [33,15], or utilize the self-similarity of the input image itself to perform single image super-resolution [10,8]. We adopt those common testing examples in their literatures. Most results are quoted from the related literatures except [15] for which we use their released codes. Fig.3 shows the SR results of different methods on "child" by 4× and "cameraman" by 3×. The results of [10] appear to be overly sharp with some artifacts, *e.g.*, some ghost artifacts along the face contour in "child", and some jags in camera area of "cameraman". The SR images of [15] and [33] take on some smoothness on edges (*e.g.*, corner of mouth) and accompany with small artifacts along salient edges.

In addition, we also test our method on the images of natural landscapes, as shown in Fig.4. Those type of images usually contain diverse textures and rich fine structures. As shown in this figure, the textures super-resolved by [8] are a little blurry, as [32] does. In comparison, for our method, the restored edges are much sharper and clearer, and more textural structures are also recovered. As a whole, the SR images of our method look more natural.

---

[1] We also tried the setting where each layer magnifies the same number of pixels, which achieves a similar performance with the equal scaling setting.

[2] Since Kim's method [15] uses additional samples to pre-learn a model, here we use the general model released from their website for fair comparison.

(a) Input   (b) DNC-1   (c) DNC-2   (d) DNC-3

(e) DNC-4   (f) DNC-5

(g) Kim *et al.*[15]   (h) Glasner *et al.*[10]

Fig. 2. An example of gradual SR by 3×. The proposed network cascade magnifies the input LR image layer by layer in (b)-(f). Please zoom PDF with 324 × 405 pixels.

(a) Kim *et al.*[15]

(b) Yang *et al.*[33]

(c) Glasner *et al.*[10]

(d) DNC

Fig. 3. Super-resolution results on "child" (4×) and "cameraman" (3×). Please zoom PDF with 512×512 and 768×768 pixels respectively for "child" and "cameraman".

(a) Kim *et al.*[15]

(b) Freeman & Fattal[8]

(c) Yang *et al.*[32]

(d) DNC

Fig. 4. Super resolution results (3×). Results best viewed in zoomed PDF, at least 642 × 429 pixels for the former and 963 × 642 pixels for the latter.

5.2   Objective Evaluation

To evaluate the SR methods objectively, PSNR and SSIM [30] are used to measure their performance. Since the SR process is only imposed on the luminance
channel of the color image, we only consider the quantitative difference on the
luminance channel between the SR image and the original image. According to
the protocol in [5], we conduct super-resolution on 9 images by a scale factor
of 3. As shown in Tab.1, we also compare the other state-of-the art methods
[33,15,22]. For our method, NLSS actually works in a deep model mode, *i.e.*,
it stacks several NLSS even without auto-encoder, which we think accounts for
its competitive results over these related methods with single-layer model. In
addition, CLA also plays an important role in removing noises and artifacts especially for the deep network, though it doesn't bring a great improvement on
PSNR and SSIM in most cases [3]. That is, CLA may efficiently suppress those
noises and artifacts while NLSS produces rich textural details. As a whole, our
method is more efficient to perform super-resolution due to its elaborate design
in the production of texture structures and the suppression of noises.

Computational Efficiency. The computational cost of the proposed method
mainly spends on the NLSS search and the computation of CLA. In practice,
each cascade layer only needs to stack three CLAs (*i.e.*, loops), which can reach a
satisfying solution. Currently, for each image in our experiments, it takes about
several minutes without any optimized Matlab code on a general PC. However,
the algorithm can easily be parallelized with GPU for fast processing, as those
common deep learning algorithms do. In addition, we may speed up the NLSS
search process in a local neighbor area like in-place self-similarity in [32].

6   Conclusion

In this paper, we propose a deep network cascade to conduct the image super-
resolution problem layer by layer. In each layer, we elaborately integrate the
non-local self-similarity search and collaborative local auto-encoder. The CLA
can efficiently suppress artifacts and collaborate the compatibility among overlapping patches while the NLSS search enriches the textural detail of patches.
By iteratively stacking the NLSS search and the CLA with the back-projection
constraint, the super-resolution results can be refined, which also makes the SR
information properly propagate in the network cascade. After the concatenation
of multiple SCLA models, each with a small scale factor, the input LR image can
be gradually upscaled into a more natural-looking HR image. Extensive experiments demonstrate the proposed method is more effective and more promising
in the task of image super-resolution. In future work, we will consider how to
accelerate the algorithm.

---

[3] The quantitative score as well as visual performance is actually very subtle for the
competitive SR methods.

Acknowledgements. This work is partially supported by Natural Science Foundation of China under contracts Nos. 61025010, 61222211, 61202297, and 61272319.

References

1. Baker, S., Kanade, T.: Limits on super-resolution and how to break them. IEEE Transactions on Pattern Analysis and Machine Intelligence 24(9), 1167–1183 (2002)
2. Bengio, Y., Lamblin, P., Popovici, D., Larochelle, H.: Greedy layer-wise training of deep networks. In: Advances in Neural Information Processing Systems (NIPS), vol. 19, p. 153 (2007)
3. Buades, A., Coll, B., Morel, J.-M.: A non-local algorithm for image denoising. In: IEEE Conference on Computer Vision and Pattern Recognition, CVPR (2005)
4. Chang, H., Yeung, D.-Y., Xiong, Y.: Super-resolution through neighbor embedding. In: IEEE Computer Society Conference on Computer Vision and Pattern Recognition (CVPR), vol. 1, p. I–275 (2004)
5. Dong, W., Zhang, L., Shi, G.: Centralized sparse representation for image restoration. In: IEEE International Conference on Computer Vision (ICCV), pp. 1259–1266 (2011)
6. Elad, M., Aharon, M.: Image denoising via sparse and redundant representations over learned dictionaries. IEEE Transactions on Image Processing 15(12), 3736–3745 (2006)
7. Farsiu, S., Robinson, M.D., Elad, M., Milanfar, P.: Fast and robust multiframe super resolution. IEEE Transactions on Image Processing 13(10), 1327–1344 (2004)
8. Freedman, G., Fattal, R.: Image and video upscaling from local self-examples. ACM Transactions on Graphics 30(2), 12 (2011)
9. Freeman, W.T., Jones, T.R., Pasztor, E.C.: Example-based super-resolution. IEEE Computer Graphics and Applications 22(2), 56–65 (2002)
10. Glasner, D., Bagon, S., Irani, M.: Super-resolution from a single image. In: IEEE International Conference on Computer Vision (ICCV), pp. 349–356 (2009)
11. Gunturk, B.K., Batur, A.U., Altunbasak, Y., Hayes III, M.H., Mersereau, R.M.: Eigenface-domain super-resolution for face recognition. IEEE Transactions on Image Processing 12(5), 597–606 (2003)
12. Hinton, G.E., Osindero, S., Teh, Y.W.: A fast learning algorithm for deep belief nets. Neural Computation 18(7), 1527–1554 (2006)
13. Hinton, G.E., Salakhutdinov, R.R.: Reducing the dimensionality of data with neural networks. Science 313(5786), 504–507 (2006)
14. Irani, M., Peleg, S.: Improving resolution by image registration. Graphical Models and Image Processing 53(3), 231–239 (1991)
15. Kim, K.I., Kwon, Y.: Single-image super-resolution using sparse regression and natural image prior. IEEE Transactions on Pattern Analysis and Machine Intelligence 32(6), 1127–1133 (2010)
16. Le, Q.V., Ngiam, J., Coates, A., Lahiri, A., Prochnow, B., Ng, A.Y.: On optimization methods for deep learning. In: International Conference on Machine Learning, ICML (2011)
17. Lee, H., Battle, A., Raina, R., Ng, A.Y.: Efficient sparse coding algorithms. In: Advances in neural information processing systems (NIPS), vol. 19, p. 801 (2007)
18. Lee, H., Ekanadham, C., Ng, A.: Sparse deep belief net model for visual area v2. In: Advances in neural information processing systems (NIPS), vol. 20, pp. 873–880 (2008)

19. Lee, H., Grosse, R., Ranganath, R., Ng, A.Y.: Convolutional deep belief networks for scalable unsupervised learning of hierarchical representations. In: International Conference on Machine learning (ICML), pp. 609–616 (2009)
20. Lin, Z., He, J., Tang, X., Tang, C.-K.: Limits of learning-based superresolution algorithms. International Journal of Computer Vision 80(3), 406–420 (2008)
21. Lin, Z., Shum, H.-Y.: Fundamental limits of reconstruction-based superresolution algorithms under local translation. IEEE Transactions on Pattern Analysis and Machine Intelligence 26(1), 83–97 (2004)
22. Lu, X., Yuan, H., Yan, P., Yuan, Y., Li, X.: Geometry constrained sparse coding for single image super-resolution. In: IEEE Conference on Computer Vision and Pattern Recognition (CVPR), pp. 1648–1655 (2012)
23. Ranzato, M., Boureau, Y.L., LeCun, Y.: Sparse feature learning for deep belief networks. In: Advances in neural information processing systems (NIPS), vol. 20, pp. 1185–1192 (2007)
24. Ngiam, J., Koh, P.W., Chen, Z., Bhaskar, S., Ng, A.Y.: Sparse filtering. In: Advances in Neural Information Processing Systems (NIPS), vol. 24, pp. 1125–1133 (2011)
25. Nguyen, K., Sridharan, S., Denman, S., Fookes, C.: Feature-domain super-resolution framework for gabor-based face and iris recognition. In: IEEE Conference on Computer Vision and Pattern Recognition (CVPR), pp. 2642–2649 (2012)
26. Park, S.C., Park, M.K., Kang, M.G.: Super-resolution image reconstruction: a technical overview. Signal Processing Magazine 20(3), 21–36 (2003)
27. Tipping, M.E., Bishop, C.M.: Bayesian image super-resolution. In: Advances in Neural Information Processing Systems (NIPS), vol. 15, pp. 1279–1286 (2002)
28. Vincent, P., Larochelle, H., Bengio, Y., Manzagol, P.-A.: Extracting and composing robust features with denoising autoencoders. In: International Conference on Machine learning (ICML), pp. 1096–1103. ACM (2008)
29. Wang, W., Cui, Z., Chang, H., Shan, S., Chen, X.: Deeply coupled auto-encoder networks for cross-view classification. arXiv preprint arXiv:1402.2031 (2014)
30. Wang, Z., Bovik, A.C., Sheikh, H.R., Simoncelli, E.P.: Image quality assessment: from error measurement to structural similarity. IEEE Transactions on Image Processing 13(4), 600–612 (2004)
31. Xie, J., Xu, L., Chen, E.: Image denoising and inpainting with deep neural networks. In: Advances in Neural Information Processing Systems (NIPS), pp. 350–358 (2012)
32. Yang, J., Lin, Z., Cohen, S.: Fast image super-resolution based on in-place example regression. In: IEEE Conference on Computer Vision and Pattern Recognition, CVPR (2013)
33. Yang, J., Wright, J., Huang, T., Ma, Y.: Image super-resolution as sparse representation of raw image patches. In: IEEE Conference on Computer Vision and Pattern Recognition (CVPR), pp. 1–8 (2008)
34. Zhang, K., Gao, X., Tao, D., Li, X.: Multi-scale dictionary for single image super-resolution. In: IEEE Conference on Computer Vision and Pattern Recognition (CVPR), pp. 1114–1121 (2012)
35. Zhang, L., Wu, X.: An edge-guided image interpolation algorithm via directional filtering and data fusion. IEEE Transactions on Image Processing 15(8), 2226–2238 (2006)
36. Zontak, M., Irani, M.: Internal statistics of a single natural image. In: IEEE Conference on Computer Vision and Pattern Recognition, CVPR (2011)

Spectral Edge Image Fusion: Theory and Applications

David Connah[1], Mark Samuel Drew[2], and Graham David Finlayson[3]

[1] University of Bradford, UK
[2] Simon Fraser University, Vancouver, Canada
[3] University of East Anglia, Norwich, UK

Abstract. This paper describes a novel approach to the fusion of multidimensional images for colour displays. The goal of the method is to generate an output image whose gradient matches that of the input as closely as possible. It achieves this using a constrained contrast mapping paradigm in the gradient domain, where the structure tensor of a high-dimensional gradient representation is mapped *exactly* to that of a low-dimensional gradient field which is subsequently reintegrated to generate an output. Constraints on the output colours are provided by an initial RGB rendering to produce 'naturalistic' colours: we provide a theorem for projecting higher-D contrast onto the initial colour gradients such that they remain close to the original gradients whilst maintaining exact high-D contrast. The solution to this constrained optimisation is closed-form, allowing for a very simple and hence fast and efficient algorithm. Our approach is generic in that it can map any N-D image data to any M-D output, and can be used in a variety of applications using the same basic algorithm. In this paper we focus on the problem of mapping N-D inputs to 3-D colour outputs. We present results in three applications: hyperspectral remote sensing, fusion of colour and near-infrared images, and colour visualisation of MRI Diffusion-Tensor imaging.

Keywords: Image fusion, gradient-based, contrast, dimensional reduction, colour, colour display.

1 Introduction

As imaging technology has developed to solve a variety of problems, so the richness of imaging systems data has increased. Hyperspectral imaging systems used in remote sensing, for example, routinely capture > 200 channels of spectral data [5], while medical imaging systems capture multi-dimensional, and multi-modal image sets [19]. Ultimately these images are often interpreted by human observers for analysis or diagnosis, and it is therefore crucial that dimensionality is reduced such that the image can be displayed on an output device such as a colour monitor. This process is termed *image fusion*.

Thus, in the image fusion problem, there can be 10, or 20, or hundreds of values per pixel, and we are interested in reducing the number to 1 for a representative greyscale output or 3 for colour visualization. The simplest way to visualise

D. Fleet et al. (Eds.): ECCV 2014, Part V, LNCS 8693, pp. 65–80, 2014.

the information is to simply average the values to produce a greyscale. This approach preserves basic scene structure but suffers from *metamerism*, where different multi-valued inputs are assigned the same output value.

Where the input values correspond to radiances at different wavelengths, a colour output can be generated by mapping the visible part of the spectrum to display RGB via projection onto a set of colour matching functions, which represent human sensitivity to wavelength [20]. At least such an approach produces a 'naturalistic' RGB image, where we define 'natural' as the colours that would be seen by a human observer, but it begs the question of how to take into account the influence of spectral values beyond the human visual system's sensitivity. One idea is to simply stretch the colour matching functions over the full wavelength range of the data [20]; in this case the displayed output produces a false-colour RGB visualisation of the entire spectral range. In general false-colour visualisations can be hard to interpret when object colours are very different from their natural appearance. Furthermore, these spectral projection methods do not say how to fuse non-spectral multi-valued data, e.g. multi-modal medical data.

In order to incorporate non-spectral data a more general approach is required. Generic dimensionality techniques such as PCA [37] or ISOMAP [8] can be applied to map multi-valued data to a 3-D space that is then interpreted as colour values. These approaches maximise the separation of colours in the output image, i.e. minimise the incidence of metamerism, but again produce false colourings. Also, while the incidence of metamerism may be minimised relative to some global objective function, there often aren't enough degrees of freedom to remove it completely.

To get closer to the preservation of all the multi-valued information in the output image, spatial information must be taken into account [30]. This can be done, for example, by transforming images into a multiscale representation, merging information at each spatial scale, and then inverting the multiscale transformation to produce an output image [4,24]. Practically, while this has the potential to preserve more information, artefacts such as haloing and ghost images are common. Also, the outputs are rendered in greyscale, which is a disadvantage. One way around this is to retain the RGB colour information whilst swapping in the new greyscale to take the place of the original luminance (i.e., intensity) information [35,31]. However, while such an approach does produce colour output in the fused image, the 3-D nature of colour is not fully harnessed.

An alternative approach to incorporating spatial information is to work in the gradient domain, where edge information is represented. Gradient domain processing has attracted significant interest due to the importance of edges in human perception [7], and has been applied in a range of fields such as HDR processing [12], image editing [28], and computational photography [3] among others. In the area of image fusion a key paper is the contrast preserving variational algorithm of Socolinsky and Wolff [33] who generate a greyscale image such that its gradient matches that of a multi-channel image as closely as possible. This approach preserves key image information in the output, but still generates a greyscale output.

In this paper we present a gradient domain approach to image fusion that: generates colour outputs, incorporates constraints to allow a more 'natural' colour labelling, and can be applied to both spectral and non-spectral data. The approach is motivated by the work of Socolinsky and Wolff and the colorisation work of Drew and Finlayson [11], who use a gradient domain decomposition to apply the gradient from a greyscale image to a colour image, which they use to regulate the output of a colorization algorithm. The key contribution in the present paper is a theorem similarly yielding a gradient decomposition, but one which can be applied to the more general N-D to M-D mapping. This result allows us generalise Socolinsky and Wolff's work [33] to map N-D images to a colour, rather than just greyscale, output while also exactly matching contrast[1].

Our Spectral Edge (SpE) method is applicable to any domains where a) a transformation is required from an N-D space to an M-D space, b) the images in the individual channels are registered, and c) there is a a putative M-D image available with a viable colour scheme; this image may be captured by a separate device, or generated from the image data. The generality of the method makes it applicable to a wide range of problems, including: mapping multispectral / hyperspectral images to RGB; fusing RGB and NIR images; colour to greyscale; mapping 3D colour images to 2D to enhance images for colour-deficient observers; pan-sharpening; multi-exposure; dark flash; and visualisation of high-D medical image data such as MRI or time-activity curve data, to name a few. In this paper we report results for the applications of remote sensing, RGB / NIR fusion, and medical DTMRI data, with the output a colour image ($M = 3$) and $N > M$. Clearly for visualising medical data there is no concept of a 'natural' colour image; in these cases we can constrain the output colours using a putative false-colour labelling that is appropriate for the task.

The paper is organised as follows: in the next section we review related work in the application areas that we tackle in this paper; in §3 we describe the underlying mathematical formulation, and algorithmic details, of the method; in §4 we show the results of the method for three representative applications; and we conclude the paper in §5.

2   Related Work

The image fusion literature encompasses a wide range of applications and techniques. Different channels are typically treated as independent greyscale images and mapped to a single greyscale output, e.g. by averaging them. A popular framework is to decompose each channel into a multi-scale representation, fuse the images at each scale – e.g. by choosing the maximum wavelet coefficient over all images for that pixel / region – and inverting the decomposition step to recover a greyscale output. This approach has been followed using Laplacian

---

[1] U.S. patent granted March 2014 [6].

pyramids [4] and their variants [36], wavelets [24], complex wavelets [23], perceptual transforms using centre-surround filters [38], bilateral filtering [21], or multi-scale representations of the first fundamental form [32]. These methods are often complex and intensive to compute, as well as being prone to generating artefacts when conflicting information appears in different image channels, making them more suited to fusing pairs of images rather than multiple channels. Finally, the base layer of the pyramid, or wavelet decomposition, is often a low-pass average image, which can lead to poor colour separation at edges for low spatial scales.

Socolinsky and Wolff [33] cast image fusion as a variational problem, where the goal is to find a greyscale output with gradient information as similar as possible to the input image set. This approach solves the problem of greyscale separation at low spatial scales, but can also be prone to warping artefacts close to edges. These are exacerbated by the ambiguity of gradient ordering at each pixel [15]. Piella [29] uses a variational approach to generate an output that simultaneously preserves the underlying geometry of the multivalued image, similarly to Socolinsky and Wolff, and performs an edge enhancement to improve greyscale separation at object boundaries. The integration of gamut constraints means that potential for artefacts is greatly reduced using this method, but necessitates that the objective function is minimised using an iterative gradient descent scheme, which restricts the speed of the method. As with the wavelet-based approaches, the outputs are in greyscale only.

Several strategies exist for mapping high-dimensional images to RGB, rather than just greyscale. Jacobson et al. [20] investigate different fixed projections; these have an advantage over adaptive methods that colours remain fixed across different visualisations, but the disadvantage that they preserve less information. Adaptive approaches using standard decompositions such as PCA and ICA have also proved popular. Tyo et al. [37] use PCA to extract a 3-D subspace from the spectral data, and then rotate the basis of this space so that the final 3D co-ordinates form a plausible RGB image. While this approach is information preserving, the false coloured output can deviate from the 'natural' representation, and the global nature of the transform means that localised metamerism may still be common.

In particular applications greyscale fusion schemes can also be applied to generate colour outputs. Schaul et al. [31] employ fusion of near-infrared (NIR) and RGB images as part of a de-hazing scheme. They firstly decompose the RGB image into an opponent-based representation and then use an edge-aware multiscale representation to fuse the NIR and luminance channels into a single greyscale. This greyscale is then swapped into the original image as the luminance component. Our approach differs in that it maps the contrast of each of the R, G and B, channels as well as the NIR image, rather than just luminance and NIR. Fay et al. [13] use dual-band RGB / long-wave infrared (LWIR) to improve night-vision in low-light settings. This work, which results in fused colour imagery, is specifically focused on a low-light-sensitive visible-light CCD imager.

The approach we outline here is generic, in that it can be applied to a range of input and output dimensions. In this respect our work is closely related to that of Lau *et al.* [22] who proposed an optimisation based approach to colour mapping. They firstly cluster input colours into groups, and then maximise separation of those groups in a target colour space. They also include constraints on how far resulting colours can deviate from the colours in the target colour space such that the output remains 'naturalistic'. Although the goal and application of our technique is similar, our approach is markedly different in that we work on gradients, thus focusing the colour separation on spatial boundaries between objects or segments. The speed and low complexity of our method also makes it more suitable for visualising hyperspectral images.

In medical imaging, high-D information such as Time-Activity Curve multi-dimensional data is routinely reduced to RGB output, using various strategies such as false-colour renderings of the final sample or of the integral under the curve (cf. [19]). Our approach can be adapted to any application where a viable 3D colour output is available, whether one that is natural or colour obtained as a pseudocolour rendering. Our gradient domain approach focuses on separating colours at object boundaries, and can be used to improve colour visualisations derived from global mappings such as ICA or PCA.

3   Spectral Edge Image Fusion (SpE)

3.1   Definition of Gradient and Contrast

The goal of our method is to preserve the gradient of a high-dimensional image in a low-dimensional representation. The gradient of a multi-channel image C at a single pixel is given by the gradient matrix:

$$
\nabla C = \begin{bmatrix} C_{,x}^1 & C_{,y}^1 \\ \vdots & \vdots \\ C_{,x}^N & C_{,y}^N \end{bmatrix},
\tag{1}
$$

where the function C^i is the ith channel of an N-channel image C and subscripts x and y denote derivatives in the x- and y-directions. The gradient matrix ∇C contains the partial derivatives of C in the x and y directions; the gradient in direction $d = [\cos\theta, \sin\theta]^T$ is $\nabla C\, d$. Assuming a Euclidean metric, the squared magnitude of the gradient in direction d is given by:

$$
m^2 = d^T(\nabla C)^T \nabla C\, d.
\tag{2}
$$

The 2×2 matrix $Z_C = (\nabla C)^T \nabla C$ is known in differential geometry as the First Fundamental Form, and was introduced to the image processing literature by Di Zenzo [10] as the structure tensor.

The structure tensor representation is powerful because it encodes magnitude information for the N-dimensional matrix in 2 dimensions: given Z_C we can compute the gradient magnitude in any direction d.

A fundamental idea behind our method, therefore, is: *in order for a low-dimensional image (low-D) to have an identical contrast to a high-dimensional image (high-D), the structure tensor for both must be identical.*

3.2 Exact Contrast Mapping

In Socolinsky and Wolff [33], the authors have a similar goal in mapping high-D contrast, defined by the the structure tensor, to a scalar image, approximately. In the first stage of their algorithm they define a scalar gradient field ∇I by multiplying the first eigenvector of $\boldsymbol{Z}_C$ by the first eigenvalue of $\boldsymbol{Z}_C$; the resulting gradient field has the closest possible possible structure tensor – $\boldsymbol{Z}_I$ – that a scalar field can have to $\boldsymbol{Z}_C$ in the least squares sense.

In the novel approach presented here, instead of creating a scalar gradient-field we create M gradient fields, where M is the number of channels in our output image; we refer to this set of gradient fields as an M-D gradient-field. By doing this we can now generate an $M-D$ gradient field whose structure tensor matches the original structure tensor $\boldsymbol{Z}_C$ *exactly*.

In order to ensure that the output is coloured naturally, we suppose that we have access to a putative low-D version $\widetilde{\boldsymbol{R}}$ of the high-D image data which has naturalistic colours: this image may either be captured by a specific device (e.g. an RGB camera), or generated from the high-D using some algorithm (e.g. a true colour rendering of remote sensing data). We then use the contrast information from the high-D image, and the colour information from the putative low-D image, to generate a new low-D gradient field, which we finally reintegrate to generate a colour output. This idea motivates the following theorem:

SPECTRAL EDGE (SPE) PROJECTION THEOREM:
Given a multidimensional image $\boldsymbol{C}$ and a putative RGB "guiding" image $\widetilde{\boldsymbol{R}}$, we can generate a new RGB gradient matrix $\nabla \boldsymbol{R}$ that is as close as possible to the gradient of the RGB image, and whose contrast matches that of $\boldsymbol{C}$ exactly.

For the most common application of our method, we start with an N-D higher-dimensional input image $\boldsymbol{H}$, with the *goal* of generating a 3-band colour image $\boldsymbol{R} = (R, G, B)$. We denote the desired colour gradient at each pixel by $\nabla \boldsymbol{R}$, which is a 3×2 gradient matrix:

$$\nabla \boldsymbol{R} = \begin{pmatrix} R_{,x} & R_{,y} \\ G_{,x} & G_{,y} \\ B_{,x} & B_{,y} \end{pmatrix} \tag{3}$$

This is the output of our algorithm, which is subsequently to be reintegrated.

We also have a putative RGB colour image, generated by some initial algorithm or captured by a colour camera, which we denote $\widetilde{\boldsymbol{R}}$. We denote the gradient matrices of these images as $\nabla \boldsymbol{H}$, $\widehat{\nabla \boldsymbol{R}}$, and $\nabla \boldsymbol{R}$ for respectively the high-D image, putative RGB image, and output RGB image. We notate $\widehat{\nabla \boldsymbol{R}}$ carefully since it is in fact the putative colour gradient we wish to alter to create an output RGB gradient.

For our 3 gradient fields, the Di Zenzo matrices are defined as:

$$Z_H = (\nabla H)^T(\nabla H), \ Z_R = (\nabla R)^T(\nabla R), \ \widetilde{Z}_R = (\widetilde{\nabla R})^T(\widetilde{\nabla R}) \quad (4)$$

Now we aim to satisfy two conditions: **(1)** For a generated ∇R, i.e. the result of the theorem, we wish Z_R to equal Z_H, the structure tensor for the higher-D image, so that contrast is mapped exactly from high-D to low-D; and **(2)** the output gradient ∇R should approximate as closely as possible the putative gradient $\widetilde{\nabla R}$, so that no large colour shifts are obtained. That is, we desire an altered colour gradient $\nabla R \simeq \widetilde{\nabla R}$, subject to **(1)** and **(2)**.

A solution obeying **(1)** can be found easily if we keep only within the span of colour gradient $\widetilde{\nabla R}$, and seek a 2×2 linear matrix transform A such that

$$\nabla R = \widetilde{\nabla R} \, A \quad (5)$$

so that the colour gradient will not differ greatly from the approximation. In that case the desired relation between Di Zenzo matrices is as follows:

$$Z_R \equiv Z_H$$
$$\Rightarrow Z_R = \nabla R^T \nabla R = A^T \widetilde{\nabla R}^T \widetilde{\nabla R} \, A \equiv Z_H \quad (6)$$
$$\Rightarrow A^T \widetilde{Z}_R A \equiv Z_H$$

Given this relation, we satisfy **(1)** above provided matrix A is any solution of (6). For example, one solution is given by:

$$A = \left(\sqrt{\widetilde{Z}_R}\right)^+ \sqrt{Z_H} \quad (7)$$

where the matrix square root is the unique symmetric root [18] of the real positive semi-definite symmetric matrices $\widetilde{Z}_R$ and Z_H, and $^+$ indicates the Moore-Penrose pseudoinverse (even though $\sqrt{\widetilde{Z}_R}$ is square, nonetheless we guard against instability by using the pseudoinverse rather than the inverse).

To show that A is indeed a valid solution we can see that:

$$A^T \widetilde{Z}_R A = (\sqrt{Z_H}\sqrt{\widetilde{Z}_R}^+)\widetilde{Z}_R(\sqrt{\widetilde{Z}_R}^+\sqrt{Z_H}) = Z_H \quad (8)$$

since $\sqrt{Z_H}$ and $\sqrt{\widetilde{Z}_R}^+$ are symmetric.

The *complete* set of solutions solving (6) then consists of all matrices A that are any 2×2 orthogonal transform O away from (7):

$$A = \left(\sqrt{\widetilde{Z}_R}\right)^+ O \sqrt{Z_H}, \quad O^T O = I_2 \quad (9)$$

since any such solution satisfies (6):

$$A^T \widetilde{Z}_R A = (\sqrt{Z_H}O^T\sqrt{\widetilde{Z}_R}^+)\widetilde{Z}_R(\sqrt{\widetilde{Z}_R}^+ O \sqrt{Z_H}) = Z_H \quad (10)$$

To produce realistic colours we also wish to fulfil constraint **(2)** , that the adjusted gradient ∇R approximates as closely as possible the putative colour gradient $\widetilde{\nabla R}$. From (5), this implies a constraint on rotation O as follows:

$$
\begin{aligned}
\nabla R &\simeq \widetilde{\nabla R} \\
\Rightarrow \widetilde{\nabla R}\, A &\simeq \widetilde{\nabla R} \\
\Rightarrow A &\simeq I_2 \\
\Rightarrow \sqrt{\widetilde{Z}_R}^{+} O \sqrt{Z_H} &\simeq I_2 \\
\Rightarrow O \ \sqrt{Z_H} &\simeq \sqrt{\widetilde{Z}_R}
\end{aligned}
\tag{11}
$$

with I_2 the 2×2 identity matrix. The last line of (11) says that O should be chosen to rotate $\sqrt{Z_H}$ such that it is as close as possible to $\sqrt{\widetilde{Z}_R}$. This problem is known as the Orthogonal Procrustes Problem [18]; the solution in the least-squares sense is to firstly use a singular value decomposition to express the product of square roots of $\widetilde{Z}_R$ and Z_H:

$$
\sqrt{\widetilde{Z}_R}\left(\sqrt{Z_H}\right)^{T} = D\, \Gamma\, E^{T}
\tag{12}
$$

with Γ diagonal (the transpose on the second term above is actually unnecessary since $\sqrt{\widetilde{Z}_H}$ is symmetric but we include it to agree with the formulation in [18]). Then the solution O that minimises the last line of (11) in terms of Least Squares is given by:

$$
O = D\, E^{T}
\tag{13}
$$

We can now obtain A by substituting this solution for O into equation (9), and then directly derive a modified colour gradient ∇R using (5).   ∎

Importantly, we note that in this theorem Z_H is not in fact restricted to being derived from a higher-dimensional image — it can be any Di Zenzo matrix from an image of any dimension, e.g. that for a greyscale Near-Infra-Red (NIR) image, or alternatively that for a 4-D image generated by appending the NIR image to RGB. Similarly R could refer to an output of any dimension, provided a putative gradient $\widetilde{\nabla R}$ can be specified.

In summary, starting from a lower-D image containing a naturalistic rendering of the scene $\widetilde{R}$, at *each pixel* we find a transform A of the $M \times 2$ gradient matrix of the lower-D image such that (i) the altered gradient has an identical *contrast* as that for the higher-D image – i.e. we transfer the higher-D contrast to the lower-D image; and (ii) the altered lower-D gradient ∇R *remains in the span* of the unaltered gradient, at each pixel; i.e. the new $M \times 2$ gradient is a 2×2 linear transform away from the putative gradient.

3.3   Reintegration

The contrast mapping process results in an M-D gradient matrix ∇R at each pixel location. We would like to treat ∇R as a set of M gradient fields, one for each output channel, defined by the rows of ∇R. The final phase of the algorithm is to reintegrate each gradient field in turn to generate M new output channels. However, in general each of the approximate gradient fields will be *non-integrable*, i.e. will not in fact be the gradient for a scalar image. An output image must therefore be reconstructed by computing an image whose gradient matches that of the target field as closely as possible, by minimising some error function. Interestingly, however, we have more information available here than in the traditional reintegration problem of forming a greyscale image I from a gradient-approximation – we have the actual, N-D image dataset itself.

If we denote the approximate gradient field from the i-th channel of ∇R as $P^i = \left(R^i_{,x} R^i_{,y} \right)$, then we seek a scalar image I such that:

$$R^i = \arg\min_I \| P^i - \nabla I \|_n \tag{14}$$

where n defines the norm used in the error function. For $n = 2$ the solution could be given by the solution to Poisson's equation, and a number of approaches have been applied to do this, e.g. [16,1]. However since here we also have the N-D data H, we can use the look-up-table approach of Finlayson *et al.* in [15,14], which minimises the error function in (14) for $n = 2$ using a LUT mapping from the high-D image H to each R^i. This constraint means that the final image is guaranteed to be free of artefacts, and facilitates the operation of the algorithm in real time. Importantly, in [15] it was shown that if a multi scale gradient is approximately integrable across multiple scales then a LUT mapping is the correct reintegrating function.

3.4   Implementation Details

To compute the gradient matrices $\widetilde{\nabla R}$ and ∇H we use local finite differencing, i.e. for an image C at pixel (x, y) and channel i, $C^i_{,x}(x, y) = C^p(x-1, y) - C^i(x, y)$ and $C^p_{,y}(x, y) = C^p(x, y-1) - C^p(x, y)$, although other gradient operators, e.g. Sobel operators, would serve the purpose just as well. Furthermore, given the global nature of the reintegration approach in [15], the gradient operator could also be applied at different spatial scales, and reintegrated simultaneously. For other reintegration techniques the finest spatial scale is advised to reduce blurring in the output. There is a potentially large discrepancy in image dimensionalities between input and output, i.e. $N \gg M$ for input dimensionality N and output M, and as a result the total high-D contrast may not be displayable within the low-D gamut. Here, we mitigate this with a simple contrast scaling approach whereby 99% of pixel values are mapped within the image gamut, although more complex gamut mapping strategies could also be employed [25] as post-processing after applying the algorithm.

The complexity of the contrast projection algorithm is $O(P)$, where P is the number of pixels. The complexity of the reintegration is also $O(P)$ [15], although using other approaches, such as iterative Poisson solvers, can increase the complexity. Memory requirements are low, since most of the calculations are performed on 2×2 structure tensor matrices. In our case the chosen reintegration

[15] increases memory requirements since the high-dimensional image needs to be stored and used in the reintegration. But the chief advantage of this method is its ability to remove artefacts.

The method is general in the choice of output colour space. We represent images in sRGB for the applications here, but the putative low-D image could be represented in a different space, e.g. a perceptually uniform space such as CIELAB, and then mapped to sRGB for display. This would be a good approach in applications where Euclidean distances in sensor-space should correlate with the magnitude of perceived differences in the output.

4   Experiments

4.1   Experiment Paradigms

In this paper we show results of our method in three application areas: i) hyperspectral / multispectral remote sensing, ii) fusion of NIR / LWIR (thermal imaging) with RGB; and iii) medical MRI diffusion-tensor imaging. Each of the applications falls naturally within the same computational framework; we explain below how to adapt this framework for each application.

Remote Sensing Applications. Images captured for remote sensing applications, e.g. from satellite or airborne imaging systems, typically span the visible, near infra-red and far-infra red wavelength spectrum. Here we use data from two publicly available datasets: a) Landsat 7 [27], and b) AVIRIS [26]. The Landsat 7 satellite captures 8 separate images; 3 in the visible range, 4 IR images (including one thermal image) and a panchromatic detail image; these images are captured using a scanning radiometer. The three visible images are captured from 450-515nm (blue), 525-605 (green), and 630-690 nm (red), and we use these as the B, G and R channels respectively of $\widetilde{R}$; H then consists of the three RGB channels, and three IR images captured at: 750-900nm (NIR); 1550-1750nm (SWIR); and 2090-2350nm (SWIR). We omit the thermal and panchromatic channels as they have different spatial resolutions than the other images.

The AVIRIS data is captured from an airborne imaging system, and uses a "sweep-broom" hyperspectral camera with 224 adjacent spectral channels, which span a spectral range 380-2500 nm and are sampled at approximately 10nm intervals. To generate $\widetilde{R}$ in this case we project the visible wavelengths, 380-730nm, onto the sRGB colour matching functions [34], to generate a true-colour sRGB rendering; H is composed of all 224 channels.

Visualising NIR / LWIR Images. Pairs of RGB and NIR (or thermal) images can be captured using different methods, e.g. using a beamsplitter and two CCD arrays to capture registered NIR and RGB, or taking successive photographs with an IR filter ("hot mirror") present and absent.

To apply our technique to this problem we construct a 4-D image H by appending the NIR channel to the colour image. This 4D image is used to calculate the high-D gradient ∇H while the original RGB image is used to calculate the putative gradient $\widetilde{\nabla R}$.

We compare our technique with: (a) "alpha blending", where the RGB outputs, R_{out} G_{out}, and B_{out} are constructed as convex combinations of the RGB and NIR input images, e.g. $R_{out} = \alpha R + (1 - \alpha)NIR$ for $0 \geq \alpha \leq 1$; (b) "luminance replacement", where the RGB image is firstly mapped to YIQ space, and the luminance component, Y, is then replaced by the NIR image; (c) the colour-cluster optimisation method of Lau *et al.* [22].

Medical Applications. In some fusion applications there is no "true-colour" rendering of the input image available, but labelling the input data using colour still has value for interpreting the data. In medical imaging, for example, multimodal and multidimensional imaging devices such as PET, MRI and diffusion tensor imaging (DTI) systems are used to gather physiological data that is displayed as an image, and used by clinicians to aid diagnosis.

Here we apply our algorithm the problem of visualising MRI Diffusion-Tensor data. In this application the data consists of 3×3 symmetric positive semi-definite matrices at each spatial location, and is hence 6-D. To preserve its character, 6-D vectors are formed respecting a Log-Euclidean metric [2]. The most common method for visualising such data is to display loadings on the first 3 principal component vectors [37]. A more perceptually meaningful approach than PCA is to carry out multi-dimensional scaling (MDS) on the 6-vectors, descending to 3-D [19]; then the result is conceived as approximately perceptually uniform CIELAB colour and then mapped to standard gamma-corrected sRGB display space. To apply our algorithm we use both PCA and MDS approaches to generate different putative RGB outputs $\widetilde{\nabla R}$, and the 6-D tensor output to calculate ∇H .

4.2   Results

Results from the multispectral Landsat data are shown in Figs. 1 and 2, and a result from the hyperspectral AVIRIS data is shown in Fig. 3. Each example includes the RGB rendering, an example IR image, and the output of our method. For Fig. 3 we also show the result of using a stretched colour-matching function approach (cf. [20]). In each case the content of the output SpE image shares the same colour scheme as the putative true-colour RGB output, and as well integrates the information from the additional channels. In particular, because of the inclusion of IR data, the presence of bodies of water becomes more pronounced than in the original.

Figures 4 and 5 show results for the problem of merging RGB and NIR images. In Figs. 4(c,d) alpha-blending and luminance replacement outputs significantly alter the natural colouring. The method of Lau *et al.* Fig. 4(e) attempts to incorporate detail from the NIR image and does keep natural colours. Our approach

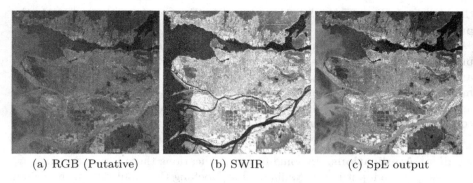

| (a) RGB (Putative) | (b) SWIR | (c) SpE output |

Fig. 1. A remote sensing example using images from Landsat [27] (see text for details)

| (a) RGB (putative) | (b) MWIR | (c) SpE output |

Fig. 2. A second image set taken from the Landsat database

focuses on preserving the information content in all four input image planes; as a result the presence of the NIR image is much more noticeable in regions of low contrast in the original RGB, e.g. around the trees. In Fig. 5 we succeed in keeping colour information intact while displaying NIR information more visibly. As in the non-gradient approach [17], age-spots are removed, along with freckles; but as well, more of the NIR content is displayed using the SpE method.

We also demonstrate that our method can be used to fuse RGB with longer-wave, even thermal, IR (wavelengths $> 10\mu$m). Figure 6 shows fusion results for an image from the OTCBVS dataset [9], which contains registered RGB and thermal images. The fusion is successful, with hidden structures made visible.

In Fig. 7 we show results for the medical, DTI, application. This data consists of 55 axial images of brain slices, each representing a different depth plane. In Fig. 7(a), we use PCA weightings to generate a putative RGB for a single axial slice, mapped to RGB and with each colour channel mapped to [0..1]. In Fig. 7(b) we show results of the SpE method for the same slice; the image clearly better incorporates full 6-D contrast information.

In Fig. 7(c) we show the same slice, where the putative RGB is generated from an MDS scaling; this image is taken from [19]. In Fig. 7(c) the output is already optimising information content as global data, but our SpE projection in Fig. 7(d) shows the substantive effect of SpE in including more of the higher-D information, and focusing colour separation on boundaries between regions.

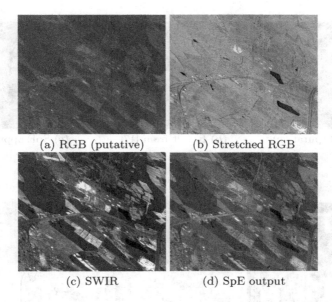

(a) RGB (putative)   (b) Stretched RGB

(c) SWIR   (d) SpE output

Fig. 3. Example of hyperspectral image fusion; images taken from AVIRIS dataset [26]. In (b), the largely blue output is due to most of the energy measured in each pixel spectrum residing in the visible band, which is on the small-wavelength end in the full measured spectrum extending from 370.5nm to 2507.6nm.

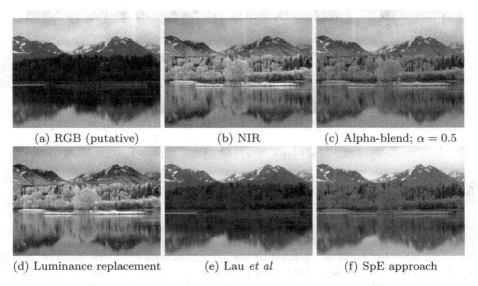

(a) RGB (putative)   (b) NIR   (c) Alpha-blend; $\alpha = 0.5$

(d) Luminance replacement   (e) Lau *et al*   (f) SpE approach

Fig. 4. Comparison of SpE with other methods for an RGB + NIR fusion application

(a) RGB (putative)   (b) Result from [17]   (c) SpE approach

Fig. 5. RGB + NIR fusion application

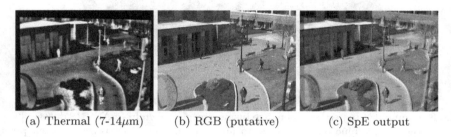

(a) Thermal (7-14μm)   (b) RGB (putative)   (c) SpE output

Fig. 6. Example of thermal + RGB fusion; images taken from OTCBVS dataset [9]

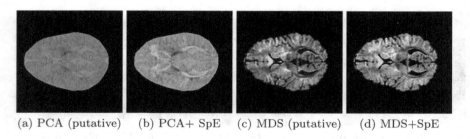

(a) PCA (putative)   (b) PCA+ SpE   (c) MDS (putative)   (d) MDS+SpE

Fig. 7. Visualization of 6-D DTMRI data: (a,b) PCA approach, (c,d) MDS method

5   Conclusion

In this work we have presented a novel, gradient-domain, approach for mapping images of any dimension to images of any other dimension. The method is based on mapping contrast, defined by the structure tensor matrix, exactly onto a low-dimensional gradient field, and incorporates constraints on the naturalness of output colours borrowed from a putative RGB rendering. The approach is formulated as a constrained optimisation with a closed-form solution, making the method both fast and efficient. We have demonstrated applications in mapping high-dimensional images to RGB outputs for display, and will expand the applicability to new areas in future work.

References

1. Agrawal, A., Chellappa, R., Raskar, R.: An algebraic approach to surface reconstruction from gradient fields. In: Int. Conf. on Comp. Vision, pp. 174–181 (2005)
2. Arsigny, V., Fillard, P., Pennec, X., Ayache, N.: Log-euclidean metrics for fast and simple calculus. Mag. Res. in Medicine 56, 411–421 (2006)
3. Bhat, P., Zitnick, C.L., Cohen, M., Curless, B.: Gradientshop: A gradient-domain optimization framework for image and video filtering. ACM Trans. Graph. 10, 10:1–10:14 (2010)
4. Burt, P.J., Adelson, E.H.: Merging images through pattern decomposition. In: Proc. SPIE 0575, Applications of Digital Image Processing VIII. pp. 173–181 (1985)
5. Campbell, J.B., Wynne, H.: Introduction to Remote Sensing, 5th edn. Guilford Press (2011)
6. Connah, D., Drew, M., Finlayson, G.: Method and system for generating accented image data. In: U.S. patent No. 8682093 and UK patent GB0914982.4 (March 25, 2014)
7. Cornsweet, T.: Visual Perception. Academic Press, New York (1970)
8. Cui, M., Hu, J., Razdan, A., Wonka, P.: Color to gray conversion using ISOMAP. Vis. Comput. 26, 1349–1360 (2010)
9. Davis, J., Sharma, V.: Background-subtraction using contour-based fusion of thermal and visible imagery. Comp. Vis. and Im. Und.; IEEE OTCBVS WS Series Bench 106 (2-3), 162–182 (2007)
10. Di Zenzo, S.: A note on the gradient of a multi-image. Comp. Vision, Graphics, and Image Proc. 33, 116–125 (1986)
11. Drew, M., Finlayson, G.: Improvement of colorization realism via the structure tensor. Int. J. Image and Graphics 11(4), 589–609 (2011)
12. Fattal, R., Lischinski, D., Werman, M.: Gradient domain high dynamic range compression. ACM Trans. on Graphics 21, 249–256 (2002)
13. Fay, D., Waxman, A.M., Aguilar, M., Ireland, D., Racamato, J., Ross, W., Streilein, W.W., Braun, M.I.: Fusion of multi-sensor imagery for night vision: Color visualization, target learning and search. In: 3rd Int. Conf. Information Fusion, pp. 215–219 (2000)
14. Finlayson, G., Connah, D., Drew, M.: Image reconstruction method and system, U.S. and U.K. filing, British Patent Office Application Number GB0914603.6 (August 20, 2009)
15. Finlayson, G.D., Connah, D., Drew, M.S.: Lookup-table-based gradient field reconstruction. IEEE Trans. Im. Proc. 20(10), 2827–2836 (2011)
16. Frankot, R.T., Chellappa, R.: A method for enforcing integrability in shape from shading algorithms. IEEE Trans. on Patt. Anal. and Mach. Intell. 10, 439–451 (1988)
17. Fredembach, C., Barbuscia, N., Süsstrunk, S.: Combining visible and near-infrared images for realistic skin smoothing. In: Color Imaging Conf. (2009)
18. Golub, G., van Loan, C.: Matrix Computations. John Hopkins U. Press (1983)
19. Hamarneh, G., McIntosh, C., Drew, M.S.: Perception-based visualization of manifold-valued medical images using distance-preserving dimensionality reduction. IEEE Trans. on Medical Imaging 30(7), 1314–1327 (2011)
20. Jacobson, N., Gupta, M., Cole, J.: Linear fusion of image sets for display. IEEE Trans. on Geosciences and Remote Sensing 45, 3277–3288 (2007)
21. Kotwal, K., Chaudhuri, S.: Visualization of hyperspectral images using bilateral filtering. IEEE Trans. Geosci. and Remote Sen. 48(5), 2308–2316 (2010)

22. Lau, C., Heidrich, W., Mantiuk, R.: Cluster-based color space optimizations. In: Int. Conf. on Comp. Vision, pp. 1172–1179 (2011)
23. Lewis, J., O'Callaghan, R., Nikolov, S., Bull, D., Canagarajah, C.: Region-based image fusion using complex wavelets. In: 7th Int. Conf. on Information Fusion, vol. 1, pp. 555–562 (2004)
24. Li, H., Manjunath, B., Mitra, S.: Multisensor image fusion using the wavelet transform. Graphical Models and Im. Proc. 57(3), 235–245 (1995)
25. Morovic, J.: Color Gamut Mapping. John Wiley & Sons (2008)
26. NASA: Aviris: Airborne visible / infrared imaging spectrphotometer (2013), http://aviris.jpl.nasa.gov/
27. NASA: Landsat imagery (2013), http://glcf.umd.edu/data/gls/
28. Pérez, P., Gangnet, M., Blake, A.: Poisson image editing. ACM Trans. Graph. 22(3), 313–318 (2005)
29. Piella, G.: Image fusion for enhanced visualization: a variational approach. Int. J. Comput. Vision 83(1), 1–11 (2009)
30. Pohl, C., Genderen, J.L.V.: Multisensor image fusion in remote sensing: concepts, methods and applications. Int. J. of Remote Sensing 19(5), 823–854 (1998)
31. Schaul, L., Fredembach, C., Süsstrunk, S.: Color image dehazing using the near-infrared. In: Int. Conf. on Im. Proc. (2009)
32. Scheunders, P.: A multivalued image wavelet representation based on multiscale fundamental forms. IEEE Trans. Im. Proc. 11(5), 568–575 (2002)
33. Socolinsky, D., Wolff, L.: Multispectral image visualization through first-order fusion. IEEE Trans. Im. Proc. 11, 923–931 (2002)
34. Stokes, M., Anderson, M., Chandrasekar, S., Motta, R.: A standard default color space for the internet – sRGB (1996), http://www.w3.org/Graphics/Color/sRGB
35. Toet, A.: Natural colour mapping for multiband nightvision imagery. Infor. Fusion 4, 155–166 (2003)
36. Toet, A., Ruyven, J.J.V., Valeton, J.M.: Merging thermal and visual images by a contrast pyramid. Optical Eng. 28(7), 789–792 (1989)
37. Tyo, J., Konsolakis, A., Diersen, D., Olsen, R.: Principal-components-based display strategy for spectral imagery. IEEE Trans. on Geosciences and Remote Sensing 41, 708–718 (2003)
38. Waxman, A., Gove, A., Fay, D., Racamoto, J., Carrick, J., Seibert, M., Savoye, E.: Color night vision: Opponent processing in the fusion of visible and ir imagery. Neural Networks 10, 1–6 (1997)

Spatio-chromatic Opponent Features

Ioannis Alexiou and Anil A. Bharath

BICV Group, Imperial College London, UK

Abstract. This work proposes colour opponent features that are based on low-level models of mammalian colour visual processing. A key step is the construction of opponent spatio-chromatic feature maps by filtering colour planes with Gaussians of unequal spreads. Weighted combination of these planes yields a spatial center-surround effect across chromatic channels. The resulting feature spaces – substantially different to CIELAB and other colour-opponent spaces obtained by colour-plane differencing – are further processed to assign local spatial orientations. The nature of the initial spatio-chromatic processing requires a customised approach to generating gradient-like fields, which is also described. The resulting direction-encoding responses are then pooled to form compact descriptors. The individual performance of the new descriptors was found to be substantially higher than those arising from spatial processing of standard opponent colour spaces, and these are the first chromatic descriptors that appear to achieve such performance levels individually. For all stages, parametrisations are suggested that allow successful optimisation using categorization performance as an objective. Classification benchmarks on Pascal VOC 2007 and Bird-200-2011 are presented to show the merits of these new features.

Keywords: Colour descriptors, image categorization, colour-opponency, biologically-inspired, pooling, Bird 200, Pascal VOC.

1 Introduction

In image classification, colour is often treated as an auxiliary feature that can be called on to boost classification rates. To be specific, a common approach to the incorporation of colour has been to fuse chromatic features with achromatic features such as SIFT [16]. Colour features on their own have, to date, not been shown *individually* to produce good classification performance. This might be attributed to the substantial information about image structure that is contained within achromatic gradients; it may also be that illumination variations and shadows can cause strong shifts in hue and saturation. Both of these factors may be important considerations. Clearly, with the exception of effects in perception that are induced by higher cognition, one would wish that, for two arbitrary image patches, descriptor similarities should follow perceptual similarity. It is, therefore, not unreasonable to explore how biological mechanisms of processing colour information might differ from existing techniques for generating colour descriptors. We first review the existing relevant literature on colour descriptors.

D. Fleet et al. (Eds.): ECCV 2014, Part V, LNCS 8693, pp. 81–95, 2014.

1.1 Related Work in Colour Description

Prior research on colour descriptors has included the effects of different colour representations on classification performance in standard datasets [18], [12]. This has led to four main variants of descriptor that are relevant to the work reported in this paper:

Colour SIFT. Previous work [18] has explored various colour-spaces in image classification, but used a common descriptor sampling approach: in essence, SIFT-based descriptors were applied on the channels of various colour spaces. The two feature types most relevant to the current paper may be described as "OpponentSIFT and "C-SIFT, and both are derived from opponent colour spaces. The difference between these two features is that C-SIFT makes use of C-invariants as suggested by [12] to provide confidence on the colour channels, whereas OpponentSIFT relies only on the raw colour-opponent channels.

HSV-SIFT. Another recent approach [2] computed SIFT descriptors over all three channels of the HSV color space, yielding one descriptor for each channel. HSV channels, however, produce a description which is not purely invariant to light intensity; different lighting conditions affect the colour encoding in the hue and saturation channels. This lighting sensitivity feeds into the descriptors produced by such an approach.

Hue-SIFT. The technique of [20] combines the achromatic SIFT descriptor with a hue histogram. The hue channel of HSV space is known to exhibit unstable behaviour for colour pixels that lie close to the grey axis of a bi-conical colour-space model. To address this, the implementation proposed in [20] uses the saturation values to weight the bins of the hue histogram. This weighting reduces the effect of low-confidence hue values, improving the reliability of the hue histogram over an unweighted version.

MS-SIFT. Multi-spectral SIFT [5] is an extension of SIFT into an opponent colour space. Four channels of information – the RGB and near infra-red channels – are decorrelated, producing a space that is closely related to the opponent-colour model. A SIFT-type feature is then constructed from the decorrelated data. The experiments discussed in [5] departed from the (currently) more widely used classification pipelines, in that sparse and scale-selective keypoints, rather than dense sampling, were used to assess the performance of the multi-spectral features.

SO-DO units. A biologically-inspired descriptor, proposed by Zhang *et al.* [22], imitates the colour processing thought to be found in the early stages of some mammalian visual systems. The SO-DO scheme employs colour opponent processing units that split the signed outputs of weakly oriented filters applied separately on colour channels; other authors [21,11] have used similar processing models. The single-opponency (SO) units were extended to double-opponency (DO) units by applying another set of oriented filters to each colour opponency channel obtained from the SO units. One critique of this system – at least from a biological perspective – is that *primate* vision applies opponent processing as early as the retina. Directionally-selective neuronal responses in primates only emerge (neglecting feedback) further in the feed-forward visual path, at the level of the primary visual cortex. Nevertheless, we consider this approach to be quite relevant, and its performance is discussed in Sec. 5.

Discriminative Colour Descriptors. A recent suggestion for incorporating colour information in classification is the approach of the so-called "discriminative color descriptors" [14], in which the spatial colour information is clustered according to criteria that minimize the mutual information of colour features obtained from the CIELAB colour space. The clusters are assigned to the original image using a bag-of-words approach to build up a classification pipeline.

2 Motivation

A digital image acquisition typically yields values in three channels of RGB colour space. Because of the broad wavelength sensitivity functions of pixel sensors and the spatial interpolation (for example, to compensate for Bayer pattern sampling) on many sensing devices, a change in the light falling at some point in the imaging plane will manifest itself on all three channels of nearby image pixels. Consequently, if gradient fields are computed for each of the three channels, the change introduced by illumination will be distributed across all bins of all gradient histograms. Decorrelating transformations, such as Principal Components Analysis (PCA) or Zero-Phase Components Analysis (ZCA) [6] can be used to remove this linear correlation, and it has been noted that the resulting transformed colour spaces appear quite similar to the so-called opponent colour space, which contain channels that explicitly encode *differences* in red-green and blue-yellow components.

Standard chromatic opponency is thought to encode spatial colour efficiently, and in simple colour grouping tasks leads to results that are more closely aligned with human

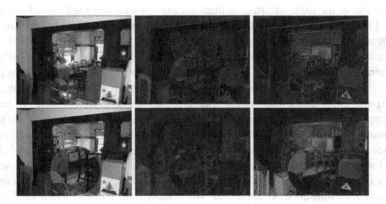

Fig. 1. A comparison illustrating the apparent loss of visual information from the raw $a*$ and $b*$ channels of CIELAB space relative to the equivalent Opponent Difference of Gaussians (OpDoG). The first image on the top row shows the original image and detail region. The top middle and top right images show the proposed opponent R-G and B-Y OpDoG channels. Both circled regions are at a zoomed scale so that detail can be seen. The leftmost image of the bottom row shows the detail of the original image at the zoomed scale; the middle bottom panel shows the R-G component of La^*b^* space (i.e. $a*$), and the right panel, the B-Y channel (b^*). Note (detail) the difference in responses near to edges.

perception than "raw" RGB space. A well-known opponent colour space is CIELAB, but there are related spaces, such as LUV. The CIELAB space is produced from the trichromatic colour space CIEXYZ. This trichromatic colour space is calculated by "projecting" raw RGB space to the perceptual colour triangle. The three main colour coordinates of the CIEXYZ descriptions are used in an antagonistic organisation in order to capture the two main colour opponencies of red-green, blue-yellow and a third channel which provides only luminance information.

Commonly used opponent colour spaces, such as CIELAB, bear some similarities to colour processing found in mammalian retinal physiology [13,7]. For example, an appropriate non-dynamic model to describe the mapping from photoreceptor activation through to the firing rates of retinal ganglion cells is a Difference-of-Gaussians applied to distinct colour channels. This model does indeed process colour channels in an antagonistic manner. However, the operation of smoothing with different spatial kernels and colour channel differencing is non-commutative. At this point, it is worth comparing biological spatial and wavelength colour opponency with CIELAB space to highlight the difference. Roughly, with CIELAB, or any other common opponent channel, pixel-wise differences are used to yield the opponent channels or planes. We have found that directional colour boundaries are visibly less distinctive in standard CIELAB space (see Fig. 1, bottom middle and right panels). On the other hand, by paying attention to the order of computation involving smoothing and channel differencing, we can preserve much chromatic boundary information (Fig. 1, detail, top middle and top right panels). By using a custom approach to building descriptors from a more biologically accurate colour opponent space, performance from chromatic channels is greatly improved. Descriptors can, of course still be constructed for CIELAB space, but the gradient information that would be captured is less likely to contain salient information. The evidence for this is also present in the literature in classification experiments reported elsewhere, see for example [18]. Often, low performance in colour space is addressed by the continued use of the achromatic channels in final classifiers.

Before detailing this "Opponent Difference of Gaussians" space, we will outline the main contributions of this paper. We first use a colour processing model with a center-surround (isotropic) structure in order to generate colour representation channels that capture spatio-chromatic opponencies. The approach taken to tune a series of parameters for opponency, gradient estimation and pooling is discussed in Sec. 4. Because of the introduction of this spatial filtering model which modifies the Fourier content of an image (see Sec. 3.1), a custom gradient-like field estimation method is required. A generalised form of transfer function, allowing more freedom than partial derivatives of a Gaussian, is used in place of gradient field calculations. New pooling patterns are then learned using an optimisation approach. We demonstrate the *individual* performance of these joint spatial and colour descriptors, then show that feature fusion adds further improvements to classification rates.

2.1 Modelling Biological Opponent Colour Channels

The peak firing rate of neurons with isotropic spatial receptive fields occurring early in the visual system can be roughly approximated in a variety of ways. Two common alternatives from computational neuroscience are *Difference*, (*not* "Derivative") of Gaussians (DoG) and the *Laplacian* of Gaussian (LoG), also known in computer vision. In an algorithmic implementation of a luminance-only retinotopic model, either DoG or LoG functions could be spatially sampled to produce a convolution mask. If modelling luminance-only receptive field responses, the difference between these two options is not substantial, though one has a larger number of parameters to play with in the DoG model. When one is attempting to model biological colour-opponent channel processing, the difference between an LoG and a DoG is crucial, as we shall next see. For a *single* achromatic channel, the opponent model can be understood in terms of the center-surround spatial weighting, D, described in Eq. (1), using a two-dimensional coordinate vector $\mathbf{r}$, with respect to a centre $\mathbf{r}_0$:

$$D(\mathbf{r}|\mathbf{r}_0, \sigma_{ce}, \sigma_{su}) = A_{ce} \exp\left(-\frac{|\mathbf{r} - \mathbf{r}_0|^2}{2\sigma_{ce}^2}\right) - A_{su} \exp\left(-\frac{|\mathbf{r} - \mathbf{r}_0|^2}{2\sigma_{su}^2}\right) \quad (1)$$

Because this Difference of Gaussians is isotropic, parameter subscripts "*ce*" and "*su*" refer to the centre and surrounding regions, respectively, around a central spatial location $\mathbf{r}_0$; $A_{..}$ refers to the amplitude scalings, $\sigma_{..}$ controlling spread, and $\sigma_{su} > \sigma_{ce}$.

In primates, biological colour-opponent processing has different colour channels contributing to the centre and surround regions of a single unit. This cannot be achieved by applying a single D (as in Eq. (1)) or LoG function to the *difference* of colour channels. This is because although convolution itself is commutative with addition (or subtraction), the fully distributive property of convolution suggests that, for most non-trivial functions, f, g, h_1, h_2 of one, two or a higher number of dimensions *in general*:

$$(f - g) * (h_1 \pm h_2) \neq f * h_1 \mp g * h_2 \quad (2)$$

In the context of two-dimensional colour planes, f and g are arbitrary real-valued chromatically selective channels and h_1 and h_2 are pairs of spatial convolution masks; $*$ denotes two-dimensional convolution. For the inequality expressed in (2), equality can only be reached iff $h_1 = h_2$ or $f = g$, or any of the 4 operands on the Left Hand Side (LHS) is identically 0. The net effect is that the Right Hand Side (RHS) of (2), in which two different blurring functions h_1 and h_2 are applied to channels f and g respectively, captures different information to either sum or difference of spatial blurring functions applied to an opponent $(f - g)$ channel (LHS of (2)). This appears to be important.

A first step in our colour-opponent DoG descriptor is therefore obtained by convolving the raw colour channels with the two Gaussian functions, denoted by G_{ce} and G_{su}, for the central and surrounding colour planes, respectively:

$$OpDoG = W_c \bar{\times}_3 (I * G_{ce}) - W_s \bar{\times}_3 (I * G_{su}) \quad (3)$$

The two Gaussian spatial kernels are applied through convolution across each of the three colour channels of an RGB image, denoted by I. The desired opponency channel is obtained by applying the two mixing vectors to the convolution outputs. In (3) we describe this with a tensor-vector product along mode 3, using the notation of Kolda [15], and treating both the $M \times N \times 3$ result of $I * G_{ce}$ and the $M \times N \times 3$ result of $I * G_{su}$ as order 3 tensors. The result of a tensor-vector product is one less than the order of the tensor, and so the terms to either side of the "-" sign are order-2 tensors, and may be treated as 2D scalar fields.

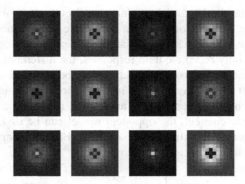

Fig. 2. This illustrates the opponent DoGs that have been used to encode chromatic contrast. The opponent colours were not restricted to Red-Green and Blue-Yellow, but allowed to vary in order to identify useful combinations. These are the actual kernel sizes used to generate the OpDoG results. Best viewed in colour; see text for details.

The terms W_c and W_s are both 3×1 mixing vectors containing the coefficients for the desired colour components of the opponency, and both take the form $[w_r, w_g, w_b]^\mathsf{T}$. For any pair of selected centre and surround mixing vectors, the output of Eq. (3) is therefore a single 2D array which incorporates a single opponency. There are, of course, many mixing combinations of these channels. A subset of all possible opponent DoGs was examined in this work, and these are presented in Fig. 2, which illustrates 12 opponent DoGs, organised into 4 columns. The first column has the red component as the surround characteristic. The central components on the first column use the remainder channels of green and blue, as well as their blend (cyan). In the second column, the green component is used in the surround, with the remaining channels (and their blends) forming the center components. The same approach was taken for the third and fourth columns.

3 From Opponency to Descriptors

The feature maps from the opponent DoGs were further processed to capture directional information. In most single-channel descriptor constructions, derivative estimators are applied directly to the intensity channel to yield a gradient field. However, given that spatial filtering has already been applied to generate the OpDoG feature planes, the estimation of directional information from the "modified" image data requires an appropriate operator to be designed.

3.1 Directional Responses

Because of the approximate similarity of the OpDoG operator to an isotropic Laplacian, one might expect that its effect on a single opponent channel would be similar to a bandpass filter. However, it turns out that in order to achieve an overall (net) response that is closer to that of a Gaussian derivative, expressed in 2D Fourier space (u_x, u_y) as:

$$\hat{T}_{GDD} \propto u_x \, \exp\left[-\left(\frac{u_x^2}{2\sigma_{u_x}^2} + \frac{u_y^2}{2\sigma_{u_y}^2}\right)\right] \tag{4}$$

(see Fig. 3(b)), a spatial kernel is required such that the cascade of operators – OpDoG followed by some direction selective operators – will yield a field that encodes something similar to gradient direction in the relevant opponent channel. This has an almost direct biological analogy in the computational structure of higher mammals, in which afferent projections of neurons with isotropic receptive fields in the Lateral Geniculate Nucleus (LGN), a thalamic structure, are collected and weighted to yield direction-sensitive responses in visual cortex. Recognising this, we opted to take a more general approach to designing the subsequent gradient-field operators, doing so in the Fourier domain (see Fig. 3).

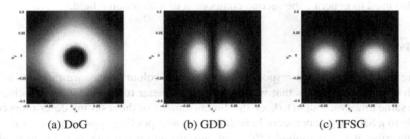

(a) DoG   (b) GDD   (c) TFSG

Fig. 3. This series of figures illustrates magnitude spectra in Fourier-domain (u_x, u_y). (a) The *approximate* effect of an OpDoG operator at a fixed slice in colour space; (b) a Gaussian Directional Derivative (GDD) imposes a spatial pattern that is clearly anisotropic. To build descriptors, (a) has to be processed to be direction selective, as in (b), and multiple directions must be synthesized. We found that the magnitude spectrum in (c) performs well, and is referred to as a *shifted gradient* (compare with (b)). Note that because opponency is applied across colour space, these illustrations are only approximate.

Fig. 3 (a) shows the effective range of frequencies that the OpDoG responses produce in Fourier space. Comparing Fig. 3 (a) with (b), it can be noted that a single-channel DoG Fourier response down-weights a large circular region in the middle (low frequencies); some of these frequency components are retained in a GDD operator. However, due to the combination of spectral bands in the OpDoG, it is unknown precisely which spatial frequency bands are modified, relative to a single-channel GDD. Thus, a flexible directional (i.e. tunable) transfer function (see Fig. 3 (c)) is proposed to produce a directional filter (Eq. (5)) when taken with the effect of the OpDoG. The new band pass selective filter (see Fig. 3 (c)) is applied on the output of OpDoG (Fig. 3 (a)), and falls inside the effective region of the OpDoG Fourier response; because it will have a frequency response quite different to a GDD, we refer to it as a *shifted* gradient operator.

We propose a Transfer Function of a generalised "Shifted Gradient", in the Fourier domain. The form of this function is:

$$\hat{T}_{TFSG} \propto \exp\left[-\left(\frac{|\log_\kappa u_x - \log_\kappa u_{x0}|^\gamma}{(\log_\kappa \sigma_{u_x})^\gamma} + \frac{|\log_\kappa u_y - \log_\kappa u_{y0}|^\gamma}{(\log_\kappa \sigma_{u_y})^\gamma}\right)\right] \tag{5}$$

The components of Fourier space of each OpDoG channel that correspond to anti-symmetry in image space were extracted from the magnitude spectrum illustrated in Fig. 3 (c). The form of $\hat{T}_{TFSG}$ is appropriate to introduce orientation selectivity into Fourier space following the application of OpDoG filtering. It also allows parameter optimisation to be applied to improve classification performance. In Sec. 4, we will describe the range of the parameter values of Eq. (5) in order to produce directional responses. We will also describe the method used to optimise performance. Briefly, the final directional channel design was found by optimising the effect of the five parameters of the TFSG function on classification performance: the $\log_{\kappa}$ term in Eq. (5) modulates the radial skewness of the function; real parameter γ modulates the shape of the pass-band, changing its spatial kurtosis; parameter pair of (u_{x_0}, u_{y_0}) translates the band-pass regions and the parameter pair of $(\sigma_{x_y}, \sigma_{u_y})$ controls the width and the aspect ratio of the transfer function. A $\pi/2$ rotation of the pattern shown in Fig. 3(c) was also used to generate the second component of a directional field.

3.2   Pooling Patterns

Having generated directed responses for opponent colour space, we pursued an approach to build descriptors that would enable parameter tuning to be easily achieved. At the same time, we sought to keep the dimensionality of the resulting descriptors comparable to a SIFT-type approach. In addition to a new pooling approach, which we will now describe, we also applied SIFT grid and histogram-binning methods to produce descriptors from the post-filtered (i.e. TFSG-processed) OpDoG fields. Comparisons of performance between both of these pooling approaches are presented in Sec. 5.

The directional responses from the shifted gradient operators can be captured over discrete image space by applying a descriptor pooling scheme similar to that used in SIFT features [16] or a Gaussian arrangement of pooling sectors [19,4]. The SIFT descriptor uses histograms to describe the gradient patterns in a local region of image space; there is no sub-patch weighting when producing the descriptor entries (though there is for the overall patch orientation estimate). Yet, two other studies [19,4] have shown that application of local spatial weighting during pooling can improve the performance of a descriptor. Both of these studies applied Gaussian pooling functions. We wished to explore whether non-Gaussian patterns could be applied successfully.

Using the two-dimensional form of:

$$\hat{\Phi} = \exp\left[-\alpha\left|\log_b\left(\frac{x^2+y^2}{d_n^2}\right)\right|^p - \beta|\theta - \theta_m|^p\right] \qquad (6)$$

we designed two-dimensional templates for use as pooling functions to encode the shifted spatial gradient outputs into the elements of colour patch descriptors. The terms on the RHS of Eq. (6) allow spatial kurtosis (p), skewness (log_b), spatial-scale (α and β) and translation (radial $\frac{(x^2+y^2)}{d_n^2}$ and angular $\theta - \theta_m$). The discrete indices (m, n) refer to pooling regions in angular ($m = 0, 1, ..., 7$) and radial ($n = 1, 2$) fashion. Fig. 4 illustrates the distributions after they have been tuned following the procedures to be described in Sec. 4.

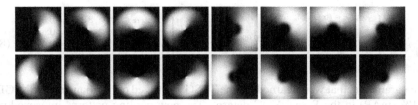

Fig. 4. These 16 spatial pooling patterns were learned from a set of training data. They are applied by Frobenius inner product to the outputs of eight directed channels of opponent colour, leading to comparable descriptor sizes to a "standard" SIFT descriptor. The borders of these patterns incorporate smooth weight decay. Novel factors of this design are the polar arrangement of these patterns, and their strong degree of spatial overlap. Each pooler produces 8 entries in the final descriptor for each OpDoG channel.

The poolers are applied over 16×16 patches spaced every 6 pixels, following TFSG filtering of each OpDoG channel. The operation between the pooling pattern and a channel patch of the same size as the pooler is a simple Frobenius inner product.

4 Optimisation

A classification pipeline was set up to use the Pascal VOC 2007 dataset in order to tune descriptor construction. A data selection process identified the minimum size of a subset of images from the training data that would lead to reliable performance increments through a classification module. This reduced the likelihood of overfitting, whilst removing the need to use all descriptors from all images during an intensive optimisation process. On the selected subset of images, the pooling arrangement was then tuned with the objective of maximizing classification performance, again on training data. The encoding of image to descriptor is described in the order of Sec. 2.1, 3 and 4, but the final design used the optimisation described in this Section.

The harvested features, each in the form of 128-dimensional vectors, are projected onto their 80 principal components to reduce dimensionality. The projected features are clustered by fitting 256 Gaussian models using a standard Gaussian Mixture Model. A diagonal covariance matrix structure was enforced. A spatial pyramid of two levels $(0,1)$ and three horizontal stripes, similar to the approach of Van de Sande *et al.*[18], was used to define the descriptor-codebook relationships using Fisher vector encoding [17]. There are two separate learning stages, with the first stage learning the parameters discussed in Sec. 2.1 (by seeking in Eq. (3) the σ_{ce} and σ_{su} of G_{ce} and G_{su} within $(0.1, 2)$ with a stride of $\delta_{ce,su} = 0.25$) and Sec. 3 for the directional OpDoG channels. The second stage uses the learned parameters of the OpDoGs with subsequent gradient field approximation to learn the pooling patterns.

We used the mAP to tune all parameters using Powells multidimensional direction set method within the bounds (and a stride of $\delta_{(.)}$) outlined in Eq. (7) and Eq. (8):

$$\hat{T}_{TFSG} = \begin{cases} \kappa & : \{\kappa \in (0.1, 4), \delta_\kappa = 0.5\} \\ \gamma & : \{\gamma \in (0.1, 4), \delta_\gamma = 0.5\} \\ u_{x_0} & : \{u_{x_0} \in (0.1, 0.4), \delta_{u_{x_0}} = 0.05\} \\ u_{y_0} & : \{u_{y_0} \in (0.1, 0.4), \delta_{u_{y_0}} = 0.05\} \\ \sigma_{u_x} & : \{\sigma_{u_x} \in (0.1, 5.5), \delta_{\sigma_{u_x}} = 0.05\} \\ \sigma_{u_y} & : \{\sigma_{u_y} \in (0.1, 5.5), \delta_{\sigma_{u_y}} = 0.05\} \end{cases} \quad (7) \qquad \hat{\Phi} = \begin{cases} \alpha & : \{\alpha \in (0.01, 8), \delta_\alpha = 0.5\} \\ \beta & : \{\alpha \in (0.01, 8), \delta_\beta = 0.5\} \\ p & : \{p \in (0.5, 4.5), \delta_p = 0.5\} \\ d_m & : \{d_m \in (0.1, 0.9), \delta_{d_m} = 0.1\} \\ \theta_m & : \{\theta_m \in [0, 2\pi), \delta_{\theta_m} = \pi/4\} \end{cases} \quad (8)$$

The parameters that were learned for the TFSG improved performance over the GDD by 1.1% (mAP) in the Pascal VOC dataset. The new pooling patterns improved performance over SIFT-type pooling schemes by 2.3% (mAP) and 3.4% (mAP) for the Gaussian based configuration as ("Daisy") in [18,4] using 17 pooling regions. In Sec. 5, individual OpDoG channel performance is reported, as are comparisons of different pooling techniques and colour spaces.

5   Classification Benchmarks

Classification performance was assessed using a series of experiments designed to identify consistent causes (e.g. parameter settings) of improvement in categorization performance. This included parameters of the OpDoGs, the gradients, and the pooling patterns found in Sec. 4. We built a standard categorization pipeline for both the Bird-200 [3] and Pascal VOC 2007 [10] datasets. The parameters found through optimisation (see Sec. 4) using a VOC2007 training subset were evaluated on the VOC2007 test set and on the Bird-200 dataset without further optimisation. This shows that the parameter tuning does generalise, leading to satisfactory performance on a completely different dataset. Although we performed comparisons using standard smoothed gradient estimators ("SIFT" in the Tables), we also built an independent, parallel path of processing that allowed us to vary the mixing of the basic colour channels. In the performance results, these are referred to by the opponent components involved "-RG", "-RB", "-RC", "-GB", "-GM" and "-BY" (red-green, red-blue, red-cyan, green-blue, green-magenta, blue-yellow), all being produced from Eq. (3) and sampled by the pooling patterns presented in Fig. 4. The experiments were separated into single scale and multiscale versions, leading to different sets of results. This approach was necessary in order to tease out the nature of any performance differences, particularly as the complexity of the encoding increases by a factor of approximately 4 in moving from single-scale to multi-scale methods. To enable performance comparisons, the nearest relevant opponent filtering system – the SO method – is included in the Pascal evaluation. The performance in this test did not warrant further evaluation in the Bird-200 dataset.

Single/Multiscale. The *single scale* classification rates were obtained using the following setup. The low-level feature spaces resulting from the OpDoG channels were sampled using the pooling patterns shown in Fig. 4. The number of pooling regions (16) was selected to be as comparable to the commonly-used 128-element SIFT descriptor [16] as practical. For all descriptors, 16×16 patches were sampled and these were spaced (dense grid) every 3 pixels, as described in the relevant experimental section (referred to using the suffix "SNG"). The multiscale classification setup is performed by following a previously described [9] arrangement of 4 scales. For these experiments, the descriptor sampling density was fixed at 3 pixels. Similar to the experiments of Chatfield *et al.*

[9], the spatial pooling size of the SIFT descriptor for the multiscale case (referred to with suffix "MLT") was set to 4, 6, 8 and 10 pixels.

Classification Pipeline. For the experiments on both datasets, a Gaussian Mixture Model was employed to produce 256 components for use in Fisher-vector encoding [17]. A spatial pyramid of two levels (0,1) and 3 horizontal stripes [18] was also applied to allow comparison with other recent work. Finally, an SVM employing a Hellinger kernel was used for the Fisher vectors, to maintain consistency with other recent work [17]. In order to accommodate the different pyramidal levels in the classifier, the kernels generated from each level of the pyramids were averaged and fed into an SVM for each class. The testing protocol of Pascal VOC was used to report class-specific average precision. The authors of the Bird-200 dataset provide the splits for the training and testing without a specific classification measure. Thus, the mAP and per- class classification accuracy are reported and discussed.

5.1 Experiments on Pascal VOC 2007

The mean average precision (mAP) is provided for the Pascal VOC 2007 dataset [10]. In Fig. 5, results from six combinations of possible colour opponencies are presented in order to assess individual OpDoG channel performance. The performance of the OpDoGs is compared with a state-of-the-art approach which is based on the implementation described in [9] and is denoted as "SIFT-MLT". Actually, using this particular classification pipeline, two scale sampling approaches were taken and compared: a multiscale (SIFT-MLT) and a single scale (SIFT-SNG). The proposed colour features were used only in single scale and are directly comparable to SIFT-SNG. However, the new colour opponent channels are not used in a multiscale fashion because of the computational cost that would be incurred in Fisher vector encoding when combining multiscale features with multi colour-opponency.

Despite the lower performance of single-scale OpDoG-based descriptors relative to an achromatic SIFT-MLT, a more direct comparison is facilitated by using a single scale of the basic pipeline. For example, OpDoGs that include green chromatic channels perform better than SIFT-SNG, even though in some cases the relative improvements are marginal. To our knowledge, this is the first *comparable* colour feature with a performance that surpasses achromatic SIFT-SNG. Instead of extending single-scale OpDoG features to multiscale versions, we opted to use late fusion to seek performance boosts. The OpDoGs-FUSED feature is created by merging all OpDoG flavours with SIFT-MLT. The resulting performance is indicative of a complementary effect between chromatic and achromatic channels of processing. Although not shown in Fig. 5, it was found that merging SIFT-MLT with OpDoG-SNG-RG and OpDoG-SNG-GM yielded rates as high as 62% mAP – suggesting that green spatial/chromatic opponent channels significantly enhance performance.

Specific improvements may be assessed by noting how much each processing stage affects the performance; to keep the results succinct (see Sec. 4), we used average performance of all colour opponent flavours (lower half of Fig. 5). The lowest performing descriptor is C-SIFT [1], which is a standard dense-SIFT implementation applied on the colour channels modulated by the C-invariant as described in [1,18]. SplitGrad-SD

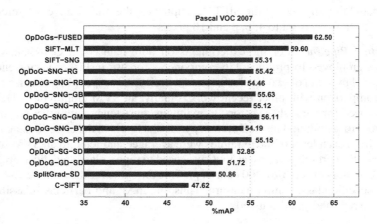

Fig. 5. The mAP is presented for each feature using the Pascal VOC 2007 dataset and protocol. This figure provides two sets of comparisons. The first presents the best performance of colour-opponent channels, including the use of feature fusion (from OpDoGs-FUSED to OpDoG-SNG-BY). The next set of results, starting from OpDoG-SG-PP and ending with C-SIFT [18] assesses changes in low-level processing modules, such as the gradient computation and the pooling schemes.

is quite similar to the SO units [22], but splits the positive and negative parts of gradient into two channels. Sampling is done with the SIFT approach i.e. a 16 × 16 grid and 128-bin histogram, "SD". The "OpDoG-GD-SD" feature represents the average of all colour opponent channels, Gaussian derivatives (referred to as "GD") and the SIFT descriptor (referred as "SD"). The feature "OpDoG-SG-SD" shows improved performance over "OpDoG-GD-SD" by replacing the gradient estimation with the shifted gradients (referred to as "SG"), described in Sec. 3. Finally, the "OpDoG-SG-PP" improves relative to "OpDoG-SG-SD" by replacing the SIFT descriptor with the pooling patterns (referred as "PP") from Fig. 4.

Comparing the rates of Fig. 5 with other recent results in the literature, we found the performance closest to ours was obtained by recent work of Khan *et al.* [14] (62% mAP); see also [18], which reports 56.6% mAP for C-SIFT. However, these approaches provide results of *fused* versions and not individual colour-channel performance; the proposed OpDoG features appear to stand out, significantly exceeding the individual channel performance of techniques such as the discriminative colour descriptors [14] (12% mAP).

5.2 Experiments on Bird-200-2011

The Bird-200 [3] dataset was selected for several reasons. First, it has a far larger number of sub-categories than Pascal VOC (200 species of bird - 11,788 images), and it is considered that colour and shape are equally important for fine-grained discrimination within this dataset. It is, thus, quite an appropriate challenge that is not overly dependent on either shape or colour features alone.

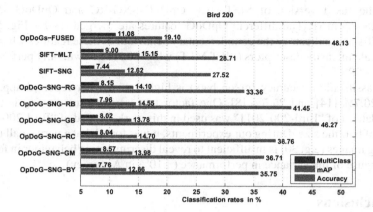

Fig. 6. Three different classification metrics were used to assess classification performance. The mAP rates are produced by using all of the training set, whilst the "Accuracy" and "Multiclass" measurements were obtained by randomly selecting 30 training examples for 10 iterations.

This dataset is also accompanied with suggested train-test splits, but the exact protocol for reporting the performance is optional. Thus, using the suggested data partitioning, three classification metrics are reported. In the red bars of Fig. 6, the mAP is reported as per the Pascal VOC protocol, using all of the training examples; classification accuracy (green bars) was calculated as per the Caltech 101 protocol (using 30 training examples), and Multiclass accuracy using 30 training examples, is displayed using blue bars. Baseline categorization performance is established with SIFT-MLT and SIFT-SNG to be able to identify relative improvements. In Fig. 6, all OpDoG features perform better than the SIFT-SNG. It is surprising that OpDoG-SNG-RB and OpDoG-SNG-RC perform closely to SIFT-MLT (comparing the mAPs), which is a feature with 4 times the computational effort of OpDoG and SIFT-SNG. Hence, this pair of features suggests that the OpDoG channels which capture red-opponent contrast are highly appropriate for this dataset. This claim is supported by noting that (not shown in

Table 1. Performance comparisons. Columns with (*) combine grey-scale and colour features, usually SIFT. Others are only colour. OpDoG is the fusion of all OpDoG channels, OpFused* combines these with SIFT-MLT. ALL uses all features in [18].

(a) VOC2007

Feature Type	OpFused*	OpDoG	ALL*[18]	C-SIFT*[18]	DCD*[14]	SODOSIFT[22]
mAP	62.5%	58.5%	60.5%	56.6%	12%-62%	46.5%

(b) Bird200

Feature Type	OpFused*	OpDoG	DCD*[14]	TriCos*[8]	C-SIFT[14]
Accuracy	48.1%	46.5%	26.7%	25.5%	21.1%

figures) the fused version of SIFT-MLT, OpDoG-SNG-RC and OpDoG-SNG-RB reached 18.4% mAP. The different OpDoG features are merged (as for Fig. 5) with SIFT-MLT so as to illustrate the complementary behaviour of these features when added to multiscale intensity descriptors (SIFT-MLT) which, on their own, only perform at an Accuracy of 28%.

The classification accuracy (green bars) is higher than other reported approaches such as 26.7% [14] and 25.5% [8]. One factor that is worth mentioning is that the updated dataset of "Bird-200-2011" was used in this work, instead of "Bird-200-2010", which is of half the size. During our experiments, it was found that a very small number of training images (e.g. 30) is insufficient to reveal discriminating behaviour in features, partly because of the variance in performance ($\pm 10\%$ in Accuracy).

6 Conclusions

This work suggests a new method for generating colour descriptors. Spatio-chromatic channels are created by differences between chromatic channel pairs that have been smoothed with Gaussians of different widths. Second, directional responses are created, using a customised filter design in the discrete Fourier domain. Pooling functions are then applied to create descriptors. In order to tune the process behind the OpDoG channels, a learning approach was introduced. This learning approach was sufficiently general to allow performance tuning by altering the mixing and center-surround parameters of the OpDoGs, the subsequent gradient estimators, and the design of the spatial pooling patterns. To our knowledge, the resulting descriptors are the first chromatic-sensitive descriptors, i.e. capturing both chromatic and structural information, that yield high performance when used on their own. They were also amenable to clustering and dictionary generation, and when tested alongside multiscale chromatic features, appear to provide additional performance gains, showing that they contain complementary information. Also, it is worth repeating that some of the OpDoG features – for example, containing green channel opponency – appear to exceed the performance of standard achromatic SIFT in single-scale comparisons with a minimal computational effort (10 ms per image). A more general observation is that differences in feature performance cannot be reliably found using a CalTech-like testing protocol: larger amounts of data are needed in training, along with a performance measure such as mean-Average Precision (mAP).

References

1. Abdel-Hakim, A.E., Farag, A.A.: CSIFT: A SIFT descriptor with color invariant characteristics. In: IEEE Computer Society Conference on Computer Vision and Pattern Recognition, vol. 2, pp. 1978–1983 (2006)
2. Bosch, A., Zisserman, A., Muoz, X.: Scene classification using a hybrid generative/discriminative approach. IEEE Transactions on Pattern Analysis and Machine Intelligence 30(4), 712–727 (2008)
3. Branson, S., Wah, C., Schroff, F., Babenko, B., Welinder, P., Perona, P., Belongie, S.: Visual recognition with humans in the loop. In: Daniilidis, K., Maragos, P., Paragios, N. (eds.) ECCV 2010, Part IV. LNCS, vol. 6314, pp. 438–451. Springer, Heidelberg (2010)
4. Brown, M., Hua, G., Winder, S.: Discriminative learning of local image descriptors. IEEE Transactions on Pattern Analysis and Machine Intelligence 33(1), 43–57 (2011)

5. Brown, M., Süsstrunk, S.: Multispectral SIFT for scene category recognition. In: Computer Vision and Pattern Recognition (CVPR), Colorado Springs, pp. 177–184 (June 2011)

6. Brown, M., Süsstrunk, S., Fua, P.: Spatio-chromatic decorrelation by shift invariant filtering. In: CVPR Workshop on Biologically Consistent Vision (WBCV 2011), Colorado Springs, pp. 9–16 (June 2011)

7. Buzás, P., Kóbor, P., Petykó, Z., Telkes, I., Martin, P.R., Lénárd, L.: Receptive field properties of color opponent neurons in the cat lateral geniculate nucleus. The Journal of Neuroscience 33(4), 1451–1461 (2013)

8. Chai, Y., Rahtu, E., Lempitsky, V., Van Gool, L., Zisserman, A.: TriCoS: A tri-level class-discriminative co-segmentation method for image classification. In: Fitzgibbon, A., Lazebnik, S., Perona, P., Sato, Y., Schmid, C. (eds.) ECCV 2012, Part I. LNCS, vol. 7572, pp. 794–807. Springer, Heidelberg (2012)

9. Chatfield, K., Lempitsky, V., Vedaldi, A., Zisserman, A.: The devil is in the details: an evaluation of recent feature encoding methods. In: Proceedings of the British Machine Vision Conference, BMVC (2011)

10. Everingham, M., Gool, L., Williams, C.I., Winn, J., Zisserman, A.: The Pascal Visual Object Classes (VOC) challenge. International Journal of Computer Vision 88(2), 303–338 (2010)

11. Gao, S., Yang, K., Li, C., Li, Y.: A color constancy model with double-opponency mechanisms. In: IEEE International Conference on Computer Vision (ICCV), pp. 929–936. IEEE (2013)

12. Geusebroek, J.-M., Van den Boomgaard, R., Smeulders, A.W.M., Geerts, H.: Color invariance. IEEE Transactions on Pattern Analysis and Machine Intelligence 23(12), 1338–1350 (2001)

13. Johnson, E.N., Hawken, M.J., Shapley, R.: The orientation selectivity of color-responsive neurons in macaque V1. The Journal of Neuroscience 28(32), 8096–8106 (2008), doi:10.1523/JNEUROSCI.1404-08.2008

14. Khan, R., Van de Weijer, J., Khan, F.S., Muselet, D., Ducottet, C., Barat, C.: Discriminative color descriptors. In: IEEE Conference on Computer Vision and Pattern Recognition (CVPR), pp. 2866–2873. IEEE (2013)

15. Kolda, T.G., Bader, B.W.: Tensor decompositions and applications. SIAM Review 51(3), 455–500 (2009)

16. Lowe, D.G.: Distinctive image features from scale-invariant keypoints. International Journal of Computer Vision 60(2), 91–110 (2004)

17. Sánchez, J., Perronnin, F., Mensink, T., Verbeek, J.: Image classification with the Fisher vector: Theory and practice. International Journal of Computer Vision 105(3), 222–245 (2013)

18. Van de Sande, K.E.A., Gevers, T., Snoek, C.G.M.: Evaluating color descriptors for object and scene recognition. IEEE Transactions on Pattern Analysis and Machine Intelligence 32(9), 1582–1596 (2010)

19. Simonyan, K., Vedaldi, A., Zisserman, A.: Descriptor learning using convex optimisation. In: Fitzgibbon, A., Lazebnik, S., Perona, P., Sato, Y., Schmid, C. (eds.) ECCV 2012, Part I. LNCS, vol. 7572, pp. 243–256. Springer, Heidelberg (2012), doi:10.1007/978-3-642-33718-5-18

20. van de Weijer, J., Gevers, T., Bagdanov, A.D.: Boosting color saliency in image feature detection. IEEE Transactions on Pattern Analysis and Machine Intelligence 28(1), 150–156 (2006)

21. Yang, K., Gao, S., Li, C., Li, Y.: Efficient color boundary detection with color-opponent mechanisms. In: IEEE Conference on Computer Vision and Pattern Recognition, CVPR (2013)

22. Zhang, J., Barhomi, Y., Serre, T.: A new biologically inspired color image descriptor. In: Fitzgibbon, A., Lazebnik, S., Perona, P., Sato, Y., Schmid, C. (eds.) ECCV 2012, Part V. LNCS, vol. 7576, pp. 312–324. Springer, Heidelberg (2012), doi:10.1007/978-3-642-33715-4-23

Modeling Perceptual Color Differences by Local Metric Learning

Michaël Perrot, Amaury Habrard, Damien Muselet, and Marc Sebban

LaHC, UMR CNRS 5516, Université Jean-Monnet, F-42000, Saint-Étienne, France
{michael.perrot,amaury.habrard,
damien.muselet,marc.sebban}@univ-st-etienne.fr

Abstract. Having perceptual differences between scene colors is key in many computer vision applications such as image segmentation or visual salient region detection. Nevertheless, most of the times, we only have access to the rendered image colors, without any means to go back to the true scene colors. The main existing approaches propose either to compute a perceptual distance between the rendered image colors, or to estimate the scene colors from the rendered image colors and then to evaluate perceptual distances. However the first approach provides distances that can be far from the scene color differences while the second requires the knowledge of the acquisition conditions that are unavailable for most of the applications. In this paper, we design a new local Mahalanobis-like metric learning algorithm that aims at approximating a perceptual scene color difference that is invariant to the acquisition conditions and computed only from rendered image colors. Using the theoretical framework of uniform stability, we provide consistency guarantees on the learned model. Moreover, our experimental evaluation shows its great ability (i) to generalize to new colors and devices and (ii) to deal with segmentation tasks.

Keywords: Color difference, Metric learning, Uniform color space.

1 Introduction

In computer vision, the evaluation of color differences is required for many applications. For example, in image segmentation, the basic idea is to merge two neighbor pixels in the same region if the difference between their colors is "small" and to split them into different regions otherwise [4]. Likewise, for visual salient region detection, the color difference between one pixel and its neighborhood is also the main used information [1], as well as for edge and corner detection [27,28]. On the other hand, in order to evaluate the quality of color images, Xue et al. have shown that the pixel-wise mean square difference between the original and distorted image provides very good results [36]. As a last example, the orientation of gradient which is the most widely used feature for image description (SIFT [16], HOG [7]) is evaluated as the ratio between vertical and horizontal differences.

D. Fleet et al. (Eds.): ECCV 2014, Part V, LNCS 8693, pp. 96–111, 2014.

Depending on the application requirement, the used color difference may have different properties. For material edge detection, it has to be robust to local photometric variations such as highlights or shadows [28]. For gradient-based color descriptors, it has to be robust to acquisition condition variations [6,20] or discriminative [27]. For most applications and especially for visual saliency detection [1], image segmentation [4] or image quality assessment [36], the color difference has to be above all perceptual, i.e. proportional to the color difference perceived by human observers. In the computer vision community, some color spaces such as CIELAB or CIELUV are known to be closer to the human perception of colors than RGB. It means that distances evaluated in these spaces are more perceptual than distances in the classical RGB spaces (which are known to be non uniform). Thus, by moving from RGB to one of these spaces with a default transformation [23,24], the results of many applications have improved [1,2,4,11,18]. Nevertheless, it is important to know that this default approach provides a perceptual distance between the colors in the rendered image (called image-wise color distance) and not between the colors as they appear to a human observer looking at the real scene (called scene-wise color distance). The transformation from the scene colors to the image rendered colors is a succession of non-linear transformations which are device specific (white balance, gamma correction, demosaicing, compression, ...). For some applications such as image quality assessment, it is required to use the image-wise color distances since only the rendered image colors need to be compared, whatever the scene colors. But for a lot of other applications such as image segmentation, saliency detection, ..., we claim that a scene-wise perceptual color distance should be used. Indeed, in these cases, the aim is to be able to evaluate distances as they would have been perceived by a human observing the scene and not after the camera transformations. Some solutions exist [12] to get back to scene colors from RGB camera outputs but they require calibrated acquisition conditions (known illumination, known sensor sensitivities, RAW data available,...).

In this paper we propose a method to estimate scene-wise color distances from non calibrated rendered image colors. Furthermore, we go a step further towards an invariant color distance. This invariance property means that, considering one image representing two color patches, the distance is predicting how much difference would have perceived a human observer looking at the two real patches under standard fixed viewing conditions, such as the ones recommended by the CIE (Commission Internationale de l'Eclairage) in the context of color difference assessment [22]. In other words, whatever the acquisition device or the illuminant, an invariant scene-wise distance should return stable values.

Since the acquisition condition variability is huge, rather than using models of invariance [6,20] and models of acquisition devices [13,34], we propose to automatically learn an invariant perceptual distance from training data. In this context, our objective is three-fold and takes the form of algorithmic, theoretical and practical contributions:

- First, we design a new metric learning algorithm [37] dedicated to approximate reference perceptual distances from the image rendered RGB space. It aims

at learning local Mahalanobis-like distances in order to capture the non linearity
required to get a scene-wise perceptual color distance.

- Second, modeling the regions as a multinomial distribution and making use
of the theoretical framework of uniform stability, we derive consistency guarantees on our algorithm that show how fast the empirical loss of our learned metric
converges to its true generalization value.

- Lastly, to learn generalizable distances, we create a dataset of color patches
that are acquired under a large range of acquisition conditions (different cameras, illuminations, viewpoints). We claim that this dataset [37] may play the
role of benchmark for the computer vision community.

The rest of this paper is organized as follows: Section 2 is devoted to the presentation of the related work in color distances and metric learning. In Section 3,
we present the experimental setup used to generate our dataset of images. Then,
we introduce our new metric learning algorithm and perform a theoretical analysis. Finally, Section 4 is dedicated to the empirical evaluation of our algorithm.
To tackle this task, we perform two kinds of experiments: first, we assess the
capability of the learned metrics to generalize to new colors and devices; second,
we evaluate their relevance in a segmentation application. We show that in both
settings, our learned metrics outperform the state of the art.

2   Related Work

2.1   Perceptually Uniform Color Distance

A large amount of work has been done by color scientists around perceptual
color differences [31,9,22], where the required inputs of the proposed distances
are either *reflectance spectra* or the *device-independent color components* CIE
XYZ [31]. These features are obtained with particular devices such as spectrophotometer or photoelectric colorimeter [31]. It is known that neither the
euclidean distance between reflectance spectra nor the euclidean distance between XYZ vectors are perceptual, i.e. these distances can be higher for two
colors that look similar than for two colors that look different. Consequently,
some color spaces such as CIELAB or CIELUV have been designed to be more
perceptually uniform. In those spaces, specific color difference equations have
been proposed to improve perceptual uniformity over the simple euclidean distance [9]. The ΔE_{00} [22] distance is one nice example of such a distance. It corresponds to the difference perceived by a human looking at the two considered
colors under standard viewing conditions recommended by the CIE (illuminant
D65, illuminance of 1000 lx, etc.).

However, it is worth noting that in most of the computer vision applications,
the available information does not take the form of a reflectance spectra or
some device-independent components, as assumed above. Indeed, the classical
acquisition devices are cameras that use iterative complex transforms from the
irradiance (amount of light) collected by each CCD sensor cell to the pixel intensity of the output image [13]. These device-dependent transforms are color
filtering, white-balancing, gamma correction, demosaicing, compression, etc. [34]

which are designed to provide pleasant images and not to accurately measure colors. Consequently, the available RGB components in color images do not allow us to get back to the original spectra or XYZ components. To overcome this limitation, two main strategies have been suggested in the literature: either by applying a default transformation from RGB components to $L^*a^*b^*$ (CIELAB space) or $L^*u^*v^*$ (CIELUV space) assuming a given configuration, or by learning a coordinate transform to actual $L^*a^*b^*$ components under particular conditions.

Using default transformations A classical strategy consists in using a default transformation from the available RGB components to XYZ and then to $L^*a^*b^*$ or $L^*u^*v^*$ [1,4,11,18]. This default transformation assumes an average gamma correction of 2.2 [23], color primaries close to ITU-R BT.709 [24] and D65 illuminant (Daylight). Finally, from the estimated $L^*a^*b^*$ or $L^*u^*v^*$ (denoted $\widehat{L^*a^*b^*}$ and $\widehat{L^*u^*v^*}$ respectively) of two pixels, one can make use of the euclidean distance. In the case of $L^*a^*b^*$, one can use $\widehat{L^*a^*b^*}$ to estimate more complex and accurate distances such as ΔE_{00} via its estimate $\widehat{\Delta E_{00}}$ ([22]), that will be used in our experimental study as a baseline. As discussed in the introduction, when using this approach, the provided color distance characterizes the difference between the colors in the rendered image after the camera transformations and is not related to the colors of the scene.

Learning coordinate transforms to $L^*a^*b^*$ For applications requiring the distances between the colors in the scene, the acquisition conditions are calibrated first and then the images are acquired under these particular conditions [14,15]. Therefore, the camera position and the light color, intensity and positions are fixed and a set of images of different color patches are acquired. Meanwhile, under the same exact conditions, a colorimeter measures the actual $L^*a^*b^*$ components (in the scene) for each of these patches. In [15], they learn then the best transform from camera RGB to actual $L^*a^*b^*$ components with a neural network. In [14], they first apply the default transform presented before from camera RGB to $\widehat{L^*a^*b^*}$ and then learn a polynomial regression (until quadratic term) from the $\widehat{L^*a^*b^*}$ to the true $L^*a^*b^*$. However, it is worth mentioning that in both cases the learned transforms are accurate only under these acquisition conditions. Thus, these approaches can not be applied on most of the computer vision applications where such an information is unavailable.

From our knowledge, no previous work has both underlined and answered the problem of the approximations that are made during the estimation of the $L^*a^*b^*$ components in the very frequent case of uncalibrated acquisitions. The standard principle consisting in applying a default transform leads to distances that are only coarsely perceptual with respect to the scene colors. We will see in the rest of this paper that rather than sequentially moving from space to space with inaccurate transforms, a better way consists in learning a perceptual metric directly in the image rendered RGB space. This is a matter of metric learning for which we present a short survey in the next section.

2.2 Metric Learning

Metric learning (see [3] for a survey) arises from the necessity for a lot of applications to accurately compare examples. The underlying idea is to define application dependent metrics which are able to capture the idiosyncrasies of the data at hand. Most of the existing work in metric learning is focused on learning a Mahalanobis-like distance of the form $d_{\mathbf{M}}(\mathbf{x}, \mathbf{x}') = \sqrt{(\mathbf{x} - \mathbf{x}')^T \mathbf{M}(\mathbf{x} - \mathbf{x}')}$, where $\mathbf{M}$ is a positive semi-definite (PSD) matrix to optimize. Note that using a Cholesky decomposition of $\mathbf{M}$, the Malahanobis distance can be seen as a Euclidean distance computed after applying a learned data linear projection.

The work of [32] where the authors maximize the distance between dissimilar points while maintaining a small distance between similar points has been pioneering in this field. Following this idea, Weinberger and Saul [29] propose to learn a PSD matrix dedicated to improve the k-nearest neighbors algorithm. To do so, they force their metric to respect local constraints. Given triplets (z_i, z_j, z_k) where z_j and z_k belong to the neighborhood of z_i, z_i and z_j being of the same class, and z_k being of opposite class, the constraints impose that z_i should be closer to z_j than to z_k with a margin ε. To overcome the PSD constraint, which requires a costly projection of $\mathbf{M}$ onto the cone of PSD matrices, Davis et al. [8] optimize a Bregman divergence under some proximity constraints between pairs of points. The underlying idea is to learn $\mathbf{M}$ such that it remains close to a matrix $\mathbf{M_0}$ defined a-priori. If the Bregman divergence is finite, the authors show that $\mathbf{M}$ is guaranteed to be PSD.

An important limitation of learning a unique global metric such as a Mahalanobis distance comes from the fact that no information about the structure of the input space is taken into account. Moreover, since a Mahalanobis distance boils down to projecting the data into a new space via a linear transformation, it does not allow us to capture non linearity. Learning local metrics is one possible way to deal with these two issues[1]. In [30], the authors propose a local version of [29], where a clustering is performed as a preprocess and then a metric is learned for each cluster. In [26], Wang et al. optimize a combination of metric bases that are learned for some anchor points defined as the means of clusters constructed, for example, by the K-Means algorithm. Other local metric learning algorithms have been recently proposed, only in a classification setting, such as [33] which makes use of random forests and absolute position of points to compute a local metric; in [10], a local metric is learned based on a conical combination of Mahalanobis metrics and pair-wise similarities between the data; a last example of this non exhaustive list comes from [21], where the authors learn a mixture of local Mahalanobis distances.

3   Learning a Perceptual Color Distance

In this section, we present a way to learn a perceptual distance that is invariant across acquisition conditions. First, we explain how we have created an image

---

[1] Note that kernel learning is another solution to consider non linearity in the data.

dataset designed for this purpose. Then, making use of the advantages of learning local metrics, we introduce our new algorithm that aims at accurately approximating a perceptual color distance in different parts of the RGB space. We end this section by a theoretical analysis of our algorithm.

3.1   Creating the Dataset

Given two color patches, we want to design a perceptual distance not disturbed by the acquisition conditions. So we propose to use pairs of patches for which we can measure the true perceptual distance under standard viewing conditions and to image them under different other conditions.

The choice of the patches is key in this work since all the distances will be learned from these pairs. Consequently, the colors of the patches have to be well distributed in the RGB cube in order to be able to well approximate the color distance between two new pairs that have not been seen in the training set. Moreover, as we would like to learn a local perceptual distance, we need pairs of patches whose colors are close from each other. According to [22], ΔE_{00} seems to be a good candidate for that because it is designed to compare similar colors. Finally, since hue, chroma and luminance differences impact the perceptual color difference [22], the patches have to be chosen so that all these three variations are represented among the pairs.

Given these three requirements, we propose to use two different well-known sets of patches, namely the Farnsworth-Munsell 100 hue test and the Munsell atlas (see Fig. 1). The Farnsworth-Munsell 100 hue test is one of the most famous color vision tests which consists in ordering 84 patches in the correct order and any misplacement can point to some sort of color vision deficiency. Since these 84 patches are well distributed on the hue wheel, their colors will cover a large area of the RGB cube when imaging them under an important range of acquisition conditions. Furthermore, consecutive patches are known to have very small color differences and then, learning perceptual distances from such pairs is a good purpose. This set is constituting the main part of our dataset. Nevertheless, the colors of these patches first, are not highly saturated and second, they mostly exhibit hue variations and relatively small luminance and chroma differences. In order to cope with these weaknesses, we add to this dataset the 238 patches constituting the Munsell Student Color Set [19]. These patches are characterized by more saturated colors and the pairs of similar patches mostly exhibit luminance and chroma variations (since only the 5 principal and 5 intermediate hues are provided in this student set).

To build the dataset, we first use a spectroradiometer (Minolta CS 1000) in order to measure the spectra of each color patch of the Farnsworth set, the spectra of the Munsell atlas patches being available online [2]. Five measurements have been done in our light cabinet and the final spectra are the average of each measurement. From these spectra, we evaluate the $L^*a^*b^*$ coordinates of each patch under D65 illuminant. Then, we evaluate the distance ΔE_{00} between all

---

[2] https://www.uef.fi/spectral/spectral-database

Fig. 1. Some images from our dataset showing (first row) the 84 used Farnsworth-Munsell patches or (second row) the 238 Munsell patches under different conditions.

the pairs of color patches [22]. Since we need patch pairs whose colors are similar, following the CIE recommendations (CIE Standard DS 014-6/E:2012), we select among the $C_{84}^2 + C_{238}^2$ available pairs only the 223 that are characterized by a Euclidean distance in the CIELAB space (denoted ΔE_{ab}) less than 5.

Note that the available ΔE_{00} have been evaluated in the standard viewing conditions recommended by the CIE for color difference assessment and we would like to obtain these reference distances whatever the acquisition conditions. Consequently, we propose to use 4 different cameras, namely Kodak DCS Pro 14n, Konica Minolta Dimage Z3, Nikon Coolpix S6150 and Sony DCR-SR32 and a large variety of lights, viewpoints and backgrounds (since background also perturbs the colors of the patches). For each camera, we acquire 50 images of each Farnsworth pair and 15 of each Munsell pair (overall, 41, 800 imaged pairs). Finally, after all these measurements and acquisitions, we have for each image of a pair, two image rendered RGB vectors and one reference distance ΔE_{00}.

3.2   Local Metric Learning algorithm

In this section, our objective is to approximate the reference distance ΔE_{00} by a metric learning approach in the RGB space which aims at optimizing K local metrics plus one global metric. For this task, we perform a preprocess by dividing the RGB space into K local parts thanks to a clustering step. From this, we deduce $K+1$ regions defining a partition $C_0, C_1, \ldots, C_K$ over the possible pairs of patches. A pair $p = (\mathbf{x}, \mathbf{x}')$ belongs to a region C_j, $1 \leq j \leq K$ if both $\mathbf{x}$ and $\mathbf{x}'$ belong to the same cluster j, otherwise p is assigned to region C_0. In other words, each region C_j corresponds to pairs related to cluster j, while C_0 contains the remaining pairs whose points do not belong to the same cluster. Then, we approximate ΔE_{00} by learning a Mahalanobis-like distance in every C_j ($j = 0, 1, \ldots, K$), represented by its associated PSD 3×3 matrix $\mathbf{M_j}$.

Each metric learning step is done from a finite-size training sample of n_j triplets $T_j = \{(\mathbf{x_i}, \mathbf{x_i'}, \Delta E_{00})\}_{i=1}^{n_j}$ where $\mathbf{x_i}$ and $\mathbf{x_i'}$ represent color patches belonging to the same region C_j and $\Delta E_{00}(\mathbf{x_i}, \mathbf{x_i'})$ (ΔE_{00} for the sake of simplicity) their associated perceptual distance value. We define a loss function l on any pair of patches $(\mathbf{x}, \mathbf{x}')$: $l(\mathbf{M_j}, (\mathbf{x}, \mathbf{x}', \Delta E_{00})) = \left| \Delta_{T_j}^2 - \Delta E_{00}(\mathbf{x}, \mathbf{x}')^2 \right|$ where

---

Algorithm 1. Local metric learning

---

input : A training set S of patches; a parameter $K \geq 2$
output: K local Mahalanobis distances and one global metric
begin

    Run K-means on S and deduce $K+1$ training subsets T_j $(j = 0, 1 \ldots, K)$ of triplets $T_j = \{(\mathbf{x_i}, \mathbf{x'_i}, \Delta E_{00})\}_{i=1}^{n_j}$ (where $\mathbf{x_i}, \mathbf{x'_i} \in C_j$ and $\Delta E_{ab}(\mathbf{x_i}, \mathbf{x'_i}) < 5$)

    for $j = 0 \to K$ **do**

        Learn $\mathbf{M_j}$ by solving the convex optimization Problem (1) using T_j

---

$\Delta_{T_j} = \sqrt{(\mathbf{x} - \mathbf{x'})^T \mathbf{M_j}(\mathbf{x} - \mathbf{x'})}$, l measures the error made by a learned distance $\mathbf{M_j}$. We denote the empirical error over T_j by $\hat{\varepsilon}_{T_j}(\mathbf{M_j}) = \frac{1}{n_j} \sum_{(\mathbf{x}, \mathbf{x'}, \Delta E_{00}) \in T_j} l(\mathbf{M_j}, (\mathbf{x}, \mathbf{x'}, \Delta E_{00}))$. We suggest to learn the matrix $\mathbf{M_j}$ that minimizes $\hat{\varepsilon}_{T_j}$ via the following regularized problem:

$$\arg\min_{\mathbf{M_j} \succeq 0} \hat{\varepsilon}_{T_j}(\mathbf{M_j}) + \lambda_j \|\mathbf{M_j}\|_{\mathcal{F}}^2, \tag{1}$$

where $\lambda_j > 0$ is a regularization parameter and $\| \cdot \|_{\mathcal{F}}$ denotes the Frobenius norm. To obtain a proper distance, $\mathbf{M_j}$ must be PSD (denoted by $\mathbf{M_j} \succeq 0$) and thus has to be projected onto the PSD cone as previously explained. Due to the simplicity of $\mathbf{M_j}$ (3×3 matrix), this operation is not costly [3]. It is worth noting that our optimization problem takes the form of a simple regularized least absolute deviation formulation. The interest of using the least absolute deviation, rather than a regularized least square, comes from the fact that it enables accurate estimates of small ΔE_{00} values.

The pseudo-code of our metric learning algorithm is presented in Alg. 1. Note that to solve the convex problem 1, we use a classical interior points approach. Moreover, parameter λ_j is tuned by cross-validation.

Discussion about Local versus Global Metric. Note that in our approach, the metrics learned in the K regions $C_1, \ldots, C_K$ are local metrics while the one learned for region C_0 is rather a global metric considering pairs that do not fall in the same region. Beyond the fact that such a setting will allow us to derive generalization guarantees on our algorithm, it constitutes a straightforward solution to deal with patches at test time that would not be concerned by the same local metric in the color space. In this case, we make use of the matrix $\mathbf{M_0}$ associated to partition C_0. Another possible solution may consist in resorting to a Gaussian embedding of the local metrics. However, because this solution would imply learning additional parameters, we suggest in this paper to make use of this simple and efficient (parameters-wise) strategy. In the segmentation experiments of this paper, we will notice that $\mathbf{M_0}$ is used in only ~20% of the cases. Finally, note that if $K = 1$, this boils down to learning only one global metric over the whole training sample. In the next section, we justify the consistency of this approach.

---

[3] We noticed during our experiments that $\mathbf{M_j}$ is, most of the time, PSD without requiring any projection on the cone.

3.3   Theoretical study

In this part, we provide a generalization bound justifying the consistency of our method. It is derived by considering (i) a multinomial distribution over the regions, and (ii) per region generalization guarantees that are obtained with the uniform stability framework [5].

We assume that the training sample $T = \cup_{j=0}^{K} T_j$ is drawn from an unknown distribution P such that for any $(\mathbf{x}, \mathbf{x}', \Delta E_{00}) \sim P$, $\Delta E_{00}(\mathbf{x}, \mathbf{x}') \le \Delta_{\max}$, with $\Delta_{\max}$ the maximum distance value used in our context. We assume any input instance $\mathbf{x}$ to be normalized such that $\|\mathbf{x}\| \le 1$, where $\| \cdot \|$ is the L2-norm[4].

The $K + 1$ regions $C_0, \ldots, C_K$ define a partition of the support of P. In partition C_j, let $D_j = \max_{(\mathbf{x}, \mathbf{x}', \Delta E_{00}) \sim P(C_j)} (\|\mathbf{x} - \mathbf{x}'\|)$ be the maximum distance between two elements and $P(C_j)$ be the marginal distribution.

Let $\mathbf{M} = \{\mathbf{M}_0, \mathbf{M}_1, \ldots, \mathbf{M}_K\}$ be the $K+1$ matrices learned by our Alg. 1. We define the true error associated to $\mathbf{M}$ by $\varepsilon(\mathbf{M}) = \sum_{j=0}^{K} \varepsilon_{P(C_j)}(\mathbf{M}_j) P(C_j)$ where $\varepsilon_{P(C_j)}(\mathbf{M}_j) = \mathbb{E}_{(\mathbf{x}, \mathbf{x}', \Delta E_{00}) \sim P(C_j)} l(\mathbf{M_j}, (\mathbf{x}, \mathbf{x}', \Delta E_{00}))$ is the local true risk for C_j. The empirical error over T of size n is defined as $\hat{\varepsilon}_T(\mathbf{M}) = \frac{1}{n} \sum_{j=0}^{K} n_j \hat{\varepsilon}_{T_j}(\mathbf{M}_j)$ where $\hat{\varepsilon}_{T_j}(\mathbf{M}_j) = \frac{1}{n_j} \sum_{(\mathbf{x}, \mathbf{x}', \Delta E_{00}) \in T_j} l(\mathbf{M_j}, (\mathbf{x}, \mathbf{x}', \Delta E_{00}))$ is the empirical risk of T_j.

Generalization Bound Per Region C_j. To begin with, for any learned local matrix $\mathbf{M}_j$, we provide a bound on its associated local **true risk** $\varepsilon_{P(C_j)}(\mathbf{M}_j)$ in function of the **empirical risk** $\hat{\varepsilon}_{T_j}(\mathbf{M}_j)$ over T_j.

Lemma 1 (Generalization bound per region). *With probability* $1 - \delta$, *for any matrix* $\mathbf{M}_j$ *related to a region* C_j, $0 \le j \le K$, *learned with Alg. 1, we have:*

$$|\varepsilon_{P(C_j)}(\mathbf{M_j}) - \hat{\varepsilon}_{T_j}(\mathbf{M_j})| \le \frac{2D_j^4}{\lambda_j n_j} + \left(\frac{4D_j^4}{\lambda_j} + \Delta_{\max}\left(\frac{2D_j^2}{\sqrt{\lambda_j}} + 2\Delta_{\max}\right)\right) \sqrt{\frac{\ln(\frac{2}{\delta})}{2n_j}}.$$

The proof of this lemma is provided in the supplementary material (Online Resource 1) and is based on the uniform stability framework. It shows that the consistency is achieved in each region with a convergence rate in $O(1/\sqrt{n})$. When the region is compact, the quantity D_j is rather small making the bound tighter.

Generalization Bound for Alg. 1. The generalization bound of our algorithm is based on the fact that the different marginals $P(C_j)$ can be interpreted as the parameters of a multinomial distribution. Thus, $(n_0, n_1, \ldots, n_K)$ is then a IID multinomial random variable with parameters $n = \sum_{j=0}^{n} n_j$ and $(P(C_0), P(C_1), \ldots, P(C_K))$. Our result makes use of the Bretagnolle-Huber-Carol concentration inequality for multinomial distributions [25] which is recalled in the supplementary material (Online Resource 1) for the sake of completeness (this result has also been used in [35] in another context).

We are now ready to introduce the main theorem of the paper.

---

[4] Since we work in the RGB cube, any patch belongs to $[0; 255]^3$ and it is easy to normalize each coordinate by $255\sqrt{3}$.

Theorem 1. *Let $C_0, C_1, \ldots, C_k$ be the regions considered, then for any set of metrics $\mathbf{M} = \{\mathbf{M_0}, \ldots, \mathbf{M}_K\}$ learned by Alg. 1 from a data sample T of n pairs, we have with probability at least $1 - \delta$ that*

$$\varepsilon(\mathbf{M}) \leq \hat{\varepsilon}_T(\mathbf{M}) + L_B \sqrt{\frac{2(K+1)\ln 2 + 2\ln 2/\delta}{n}} + \frac{2(KD^4 + 1)}{\lambda n}$$

$$+ \left(\frac{4(KD^4 + 1)}{\lambda} + \Delta_{\max}\big(\frac{2(KD^2 + 1)}{\sqrt{\lambda}} + 2(K+1)\Delta_{\max}\big)\right) \sqrt{\frac{\ln(\frac{4(K+1)}{\delta})}{2n}},$$

where $D = \max_{1 \leq j \leq K} D_j$, $L_B = \max\{\frac{\Delta_{max}}{\sqrt{\lambda}}, \Delta_{max}^2\}$ is the bound on the loss function and $\lambda = \min_{0 \leq j \leq K} \lambda_j$ is the minimum regularization parameter among the $K + 1$ learning problems used in Alg. 1.

The proof of this theorem is provided in the supplementary material (Online Resource 1). The first term after the empirical risk comes from the application of the Bretagnolle-Huber-Carol inequality with a confidence parameter $1 - \delta/2$. The last terms are derived by applying the per region consistency Lemma 1 to all the regions with a confidence parameter $1 - \delta/2(K + 1)$ and the final result is derived thanks to the union bound.

This result justifies the global consistency of our approach with a standard convergence rate in $O(1/\sqrt{n})$. We can remark that if the local regions $C_1, \ldots, C_n$ are rather small (*i.e.* D is significantly smaller than 1), then the last part of the bound will not suffer too much on the number of regions. On the other hand, there is also a trade-off between the number/size of regions considered and the number of instances falling in each region. It is important to have enough examples to learn good models.

4   Experiments

Evaluating the contribution of a metric learning algorithm can be done in two ways: (1) assessing the quality of the metric itself, and (2) measuring its impact once plugged in an application. In the following, we first evaluate the generalization ability of the learned metrics on our dataset. Then, we measure their contribution in a color segmentation application.

4.1   Evaluation on Our Dataset

To evaluate the generalization ability of the metrics, we conduct two experiments: We assess the behavior of our approach when it is applied (i) on new unseen colors and (ii) on new patches coming from a different unseen camera. In these experiments, we consider all the pairs of patches $(\mathbf{x}, \mathbf{x}')$ of our dataset characterized by a $\Delta E_{ab} < 5$, resulting in 41,800 pairs. Due to the large amount of data, combined with the relative simplicity of the 3×3 local metrics, we notice that the algorithm is rather insensible to the choice of λ. Therefore, we use $\lambda = 1$ in all our experiments. The displayed results are the average over 5 runs.

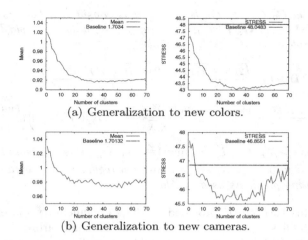

(a) Generalization to new colors.

(b) Generalization to new cameras.

Fig. 2. (a): Generalization of the learned metrics to new colors; (b) Generalization of the learned metrics to new cameras. For (a) and (b), we plotted the Mean and STRESS values as a function of the number of clusters. The horizontal dashed line represents the STRESS baseline of $\widehat{\Delta E_{00}}$. For the sake of readability, **we have not plotted** the mean baseline of $\widehat{\Delta E_{00}}$ at 1.70.

To estimate the performance of our metric we use two criteria we want to make as small as possible. The first one is the mean absolute difference, computed over a test set TS, between the learned metric Δ_T - *i.e.* the metric learned with Alg. 1 - w.r.t. a training set of pairs T and the reference ΔE_{00}. As a second criterion, we use the STRESS[5] measure [17]. Roughly speaking, it evaluates quadratic differences between the learned metric Δ_T and the reference ΔE_{00}. We compare our approach to the state of the art where Δ_T is replaced by $\widehat{\Delta E_{00}}$ [22] in both criteria, i.e. transforming from rendered image RGB to $\widehat{L^*a^*b^*}$ and computing the $\widehat{\Delta E_{00}}$ distance.

Generalization to Unseen Colors. In this experiment, we perform a 6-fold cross validation procedure over the set of *patches*. Thus we obtain, on average, 27927 training pairs and 13873 testing pairs. The results are shown on Fig. 2(a) according to an increasing number of clusters (from 1 to 70). We can see that using our learned metric Δ_T instead of the state of the art estimate $\widehat{\Delta E_{00}}$ [22] enables significant improvements according to both criteria (where the baselines are 1.70 for the mean and 48.05 for the STRESS). Note that from 50 clusters, the quality of the learned metric declines slightly while remaining much better than $\widehat{\Delta E_{00}}$. Figure 2(a) shows that $K = 20$ seems to be a good compromise between a high algorithmic complexity (the higher K, the larger the number of learned

---

[5] STandardized REsidual Sum of Squares.

metrics) and good performances of the models. When $K = 20$, using a Student's t test over the mean absolute differences and a Fisher test over the STRESS, our method is significantly better than the state of the art with a p-value $< 1^{-10}$. Figure 2(a) also emphasizes the interest of learning several local metrics. Indeed, optimizing 20 local metrics rather than only one is significantly better with a p-value smaller than 0.001 for both criteria.

Generalization to Unseen Cameras. In this experiment, our model is learned according to a 4-fold cross validation procedure such that each fold corresponds to the pairs coming from a given camera. Thus we learn the metric on a set of 31350 pairs and test it on a set of 10450 pairs. Therefore, this task is more complicated than before. The results are presented in Fig. 2(b). We can note that our approach always outperforms the state of the art for the mean criterion (of baseline 1.70). Regarding the STRESS, we are on average better when using between 5 to 60 clusters. Beyond 65 clusters, the performances decrease significantly. This behavior likely describes an overfitting phenomenon due to the fact that a lot of local metrics have been learned that are more and more specialized for 3 out of 4 cameras, and unable to generalize well to the fourth one. For this series of experiments, $K = 20$ is still a good value to deal with the trade-off between complexity and efficiency. Using a Student's t test over the mean absolute differences and a Fisher test over the STRESS, our method is significantly better with p-values respectively $< 1^{-10}$ and < 0.006. The interest of learning several local metrics rather than only one is still confirmed. Applying statistical comparison tests between $K = 20$ and $K = 1$ leads to small p-values < 0.001.

Thus for both series of experiments, $K = 20$ appears to be a good number of clusters and allows significant improvements. Therefore, we suggest to take this value in the next section to tackle a segmentation problem. Before that, let us finish this section by geometrically showing the interest of learning local metrics. Figure 3(a) shows ellipsoids uniformly distributed in the RGB space whose surface corresponds to the RGB colors lying at the corresponding learned local distance of 1 from the center of the ellipsoid. It is worth noting that the variability of the shapes and orientations of the ellipsoids is high, meaning that each local metric could capture local specificities of the color space. The experimental results presented in the next section will prove this claim.

4.2   Application to Image segmentation

In this experiment, we evaluate the performance of our approach in a color based image segmentation application. We propose to use the approach from [4] that suggests a nice extension of the classical mean-shift algorithm by accounting color information. Furthermore, the authors show that the more perceptual the used distance, the better the results. Especially, by using the default transform from the available camera RGB to the $\widehat{L^*u^*v^*}$, they significantly improve the segmentation results over the simple RGB coordinates. Our aim is not to propose a new segmentation algorithm but to use the exact algorithm proposed

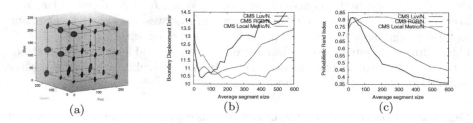

(a)   (b)   (c)

Fig. 3. (a) Interest of learning local metrics. We took 27 points uniformly distributed on the RGB cube. Around each point we plotted an ellipsoid where the surface corresponds to the RGB colors lying at a learned distance of 1. In this case we used the metric learned by our algorithm using $K = 20$. (b) Boundary Displacement Error (lower is better) versus the average segment size. (c) Probabilistic Rand Index (higher is better) versus the average segment size.

in [4] working in the RGB space and to replace in their code (publicly available) the distance between two colors with our learned color distance Δ_T. By this way, we can compare the perceptual property of our distance with this of the recommended default approach (euclidean distance in the $\widehat{L^*u^*v^*}$ space).

Therefore, we take exactly the same protocol as [4]. We use the same 200 images taken from the well-known Berkeley dataset and the associated ground-truth that is constituted by 1087 segmented images provided by humans. In order to assess the quality of the segmentation, as recommended by [4], we use the average Boundary Displacement Error (BDE) and the Probabilistic Rand Index (PRI). Note that the better the quality of the segmentation, the lower the BDE and the higher the PRI. The segmentation algorithm proposed in [4] has one main parameter which is the color distance threshold under which two neighbor pixels (or sets of pixels) have to be merged in the same segment. As in [4], we plot the evolution of the quality criteria versus the average segment size (see Figs. 3(b) and 3(c)). For comparison, we have run the code from [4] for the parameters providing the best results in their paper, namely "CMS Luv/N.", corresponding to their color mean-shift (CMS) applied in the $\widehat{L^*u^*v^*}$ color space. The results of CMS applied in the RGB color space with the classical euclidean distance are plotted as "CMS RGB/N." and those of CMS applied with our color distance in the RGB color space are plotted as "CMS Local Metric/N.".

For both criteria, we can see that our learned color distance significantly improves the quality of the results over the two other approaches, i.e. it provides a segmentation that is closer to the one computed by humans. This is truer when the segment size is increasing (right part of the plots). It is important to understand that increasing the average segment size (moving to the right on the plots) is like merging neighbor segments in the images. So by analyzing the curves, we can see that for the classical approaches ("CMS Luv/N." and "CMS RGB/N."), it seems that the segments that are merged together when moving

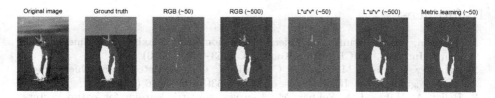

Fig. 4. Segmentation illustration. When the number of clusters is low (around 50), the segmentation provided by RGB or $\widehat{L^*u^*v^*}$ are far from the ground truth, unlike our approach which provides nice results. To get the same perceptual result, both methods require about 500 clusters.

to the right on the plot are not the ones that would be merged by humans. That is why both criteria are worst (BDE increases and PRI decreases) on the right for these methods. On the other hand, it seems that our distance is more accurate when merging neighbor segments since for high average segment sizes, our results are much better. This point can be observed in Fig. 4, where the segment size is high, i.e. when the number of clusters is low (50), the segmentation provided by RGB or $\widehat{L^*u^*v^*}$ are far from the ground truth, unlike our approach which provides nice results. To get the same perceptual result, both methods require about 500 clusters. We provide more segmentation comparisons in the supplementary material (Online Resource 1).

5 Conclusion

In this paper, we presented a new local metric learning approach for approximating perceptual distances directly in the rendered image RGB space. Our method outperforms the state of the art for generalizing to unseen colors and to unseen camera distortions and also in a color image segmentation task. The model is both efficient - for each pair one only needs to find the two clusters of the patches and to apply a 3×3 matrix - and expressive thanks to the local aspect allowing us to model different distortions in the RGB space. Moreover, we derived a generalization bound ensuring the consistency of the learning approach. Finally, we designed a dataset of color patches which can play the role of a benchmark for the computer vision community.

Future work will include the use of metric combination approaches together with more complex regularizers on the set of models (mixed and nuclear norms for example). Another perspective concerns the spatial continuity of the learned metrics. Even though Fig. 3(a) shows ellipsoids that tend to be locally regular leading to a certain spatial continuity, our model does not explicitly deal with this issue. One solution may consist in resorting to a Gaussian embedding of the local metrics. From a practical side, the development of transfer learning methods for improving the generalization to unknown devices could be an interesting direction. Another different perspective would be to learn photometric invariant distances.

References

1. Achanta, R., Susstrunk, S.: Saliency detection using maximum symmetric surround. In: Proc. of ICIP, Hong Kong, pp. 2653–2656 (2010)
2. Arbelaez, P., Maire, M., Fowlkes, C., Malik, J.: Contour detection and hierarchical image segmentation. IEEE Trans. on PAMI 33(5), 898–916 (2011)
3. Bellet, A., Habrard, A., Sebban, M.: A survey on metric learning for feature vectors and structured data (arxiv:1306.6709v3). Tech. rep. (August 2013)
4. Bitsakos, K., Fermüller, C., Aloimonos, Y.: An experimental study of color-based segmentation algorithms based on the mean-shift concept. In: Daniilidis, K., Maragos, P., Paragios, N. (eds.) ECCV 2010, Part II. LNCS, vol. 6312, pp. 506–519. Springer, Heidelberg (2010)
5. Bousquet, O.: Stability and generalization. JMLR 2, 499–526 (2002)
6. Burghouts, G.J., Geusebroek, J.-M.: Performance evaluation of local colour invariants. Computer Vision and Image Understanding 113 (1), 48–62 (2009)
7. Dalal, N., Triggs, B.: Histograms of oriented gradients for human detection. In: Proc. of CVPR, pp. 886–893 (2005)
8. Davis, J.V., Kulis, B., Jain, P., Sra, S., Dhillon, I.S.: Information-theoretic metric learning. In: Proc. of ICML, pp. 209–216 (2007)
9. Huang, M., Liu, H., Cui, G., Luo, M.R., Melgosa, M.: Evaluation of threshold color differences using printed samples. JOSA A 29(6), 883–891 (2012)
10. Huang, Y., Li, C., Georgiopoulos, M., Anagnostopoulos, G.C.: Reduced-rank local distance metric learning. In: Blockeel, H., Kersting, K., Nijssen, S., Železný, F. (eds.) ECML PKDD 2013, Part III. LNCS, vol. 8190, pp. 224–239. Springer, Heidelberg (2013)
11. Khan, R., van de Weijer, J., Khan, F., Muselet, D., Ducottet, C., Barat, C.: Discriminative color descriptor. In: Proc. of CVPR, Portland, USA (2013)
12. Kim, S.J., Lin, H.T., Lu, Z., Süsstrunk, S., Lin, S., Brown, M.S.: A new in-camera imaging model for color computer vision and its application. IEEE Trans. Pattern Anal. Mach. Intell. 34(12), 2289–2302 (2012)
13. Kim, S.J., Lin, H.T., Lu, Z., Susstrunk, S., Lin, S., Brown, M.S.: A new in-camera imaging model for color computer vision and its application. IEEE Trans. on PAMI 34(12), 2289–2302 (2012)
14. Larraín, R.E., Schaefer, D.M., Reed, J.D.: Use of digital images to estimate {CIE} color coordinates of beef. Food Research Int. 41(4), 380 (2008)
15. León, K., Mery, D., Pedreschi, F., León, J.: Color measurement in l*a*b* units from rgb digital images. Food Research Int. 39(10), 1084–1091 (2006)
16. Lowe, D.G.: Distinctive image features from scale-invariant keypoints. IJCV 60(2), 91–110 (2004)
17. Melgosa, M., Huertas, R., Berns, R.S.: Performance of recent advanced color-difference formulas using the standardized residual sum of squares index. JOSA A 25(7), 1828–1834 (2008)
18. Mojsilovic, A.: A computational model for color naming and describing color composition of images. IEEE Trans. on Image Processing 14(5), 690–699 (2005)
19. Munsell, A.H.: A pigment color system and notation. The American Journal of Psychology 23(2), 236–244 (1912)
20. van de Sande, K.E.A., Gevers, T., Snoek, C.G.M.: Evaluating color descriptors for object and scene recognition. IEEE Trans. on PAMI 32(9), 1582–1596 (2010)
21. Semerci, M., Alpaydın, E.: Mixtures of large margin nearest neighbor classifiers. In: Blockeel, H., Kersting, K., Nijssen, S., Železný, F. (eds.) ECML PKDD 2013, Part II. LNCS, vol. 8189, pp. 675–688. Springer, Heidelberg (2013)

22. Sharma, G., Wu, W., Dalal, E.N.: The ciede2000 color-difference formula: Implementation notes, supplementary test data, and mathematical observations. Color Research Applications 30, 21–30 (2005)
23. Stokes, M., Anderson, M., Chandrasekar, S., Motta, R.: A standard default color space for the internet: sRGB. Tech. rep., Hewlett-Packard and Microsoft (1996), http://www.w3.org/Graphics/Color/sRGB.html
24. Union, I.T.: Parameter values for the hdtv standards for production and international programme exchange, itu-r recommendation bt.709-4. Tech. rep (March 2000)
25. van der Vaart, A.W., Wellner, J.A.: Weak convergence and empirical processes. Springer, Heidelberg (2000)
26. Wang, J., Kalousis, A., Woznica, A.: Parametric local metric learning for nearest neighbor classification. In: Proc. of NIPS, pp. 1610–1618 (2012)
27. Gevers, T., van de Weijer, A.D.B.J.: Boosting color saliency in image feature detection. IEEE Trans. on PAMI 28(1), 150–156 (2006)
28. Gevers, T., van de Weijer, J.M.G.J.: Edge and corner detection by photometric quasi-invariants. IEEE Trans. on PAMI 27(4), 1520–1526 (2005)
29. Weinberger, K.Q., Blitzer, J., Saul, L.: Distance metric learning for large margin nearest neighbor classification. In: Proc. of NIPS (2006)
30. Weinberger, K.Q., Saul, L.K.: Distance metric learning for large margin nearest neighbor classification. JMLR 10, 207–244 (2009)
31. Wyszecki, G., Stiles, W.S.: Color Science: Concepts and Methods, Quantitative Data and Formulas, 2nd revised ed. John Wiley & Sons Inc. (2000)
32. Xing, E.P., Ng, A.Y., Jordan, M.I., Russell, S.: Distance metric learning, with application to clustering with side-information. In: Proc. NIPS, pp. 505–512 (2002)
33. Xiong, C., Johnson, D., Xu, R., Corso, J.J.: Random forests for metric learning with implicit pairwise position dependence. In: Proc. of KDD, pp. 958–966. ACM (2012)
34. Xiong, Y., Saenko, K., Darrell, T., Zickler, T.: From pixels to physics: Probabilistic color de-rendering. In: Proc. of CVPR, Providence, USA (2012)
35. Xu, H., Mannor, S.: Robustness and Generalization. Machine Learning 86(3), 391–423 (2012)
36. Xue, W., Mou, X., Zhang, L., Feng, X.: Perceptual fidelity aware mean squared error. In: Proc. of ICCV (2013)
37. Freely avaible on the authors' personal web pages

Online Graph-Based Tracking

Hyeonseob Nam, Seunghoon Hong, and Bohyung Han

Department of Computer Science and Engineering, POSTECH, Korea
{namhs09,maga33,bhhan}@postech.ac.kr

Abstract. Tracking by sequential Bayesian filtering relies on a graph-ical model with temporally ordered linear structure based on temporal smoothness assumption. This framework is convenient to propagate the posterior through the first-order Markov chain. However, density prop-agation from a single immediately preceding frame may be unreliable especially in challenging situations such as abrupt appearance changes, fast motion, occlusion, and so on. We propose a visual tracking algorithm based on more general graphical models, where multiple previous frames contribute to computing the posterior in the current frame and edges be-tween frames are created upon inter-frame trackability. Such data-driven graphical model reflects sequence structures as well as target character-istics, and is more desirable to implement a robust tracking algorithm. The proposed tracking algorithm runs online and achieves outstanding performance with respect to the state-of-the-art trackers. We illustrate quantitative and qualitative performance of our algorithm in all the sequences in tracking benchmark and other challenging videos.

Keywords: Online tracking, Bayesian model averaging, patch matching.

1 Introduction

Most of online probabilistic tracking algorithms employ graphical models with linear structure and estimate the target state sequentially, where the inference of the posterior is based only on the immediately preceding frame due to the first-order Markov assumption. These methods reduce search space for obser-vation by relying on temporal smoothness assumption between two consecutive frames. However, they underestimate other kinds of challenges—for example, radical appearance changes, fast motion, shot changes, and occlusion—and the potential benefit from the collaboration of multiple frames. Therefore, we claim that tracking algorithms should consider the characteristics of target and scene in addition to temporal smoothness and that more general graphical models can reduce tracking errors by propagating densities from multiple tracked frames.

We propose a novel online tracking algorithm beyond the first-order Markov chain, where a more general graph structure is obtained during tracking to adapt sequence structure and propagate the posterior over time. Multiple preceding frames propagate density functions to estimate the optimal target state in the current frame, and the choice of the frames depends on the characteristics of

D. Fleet et al. (Eds.): ECCV 2014, Part V, LNCS 8693, pp. 112–126, 2014.

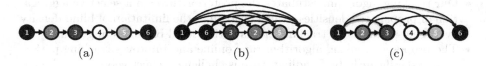

Fig. 1. Framework of our algorithm compared to existing methods. Nodes correspond to frames whose intensities encode the characteristics observed in individual frames. The numbers in the nodes indicate frame indices. (a) Chain model propagates densities sequentially regardless of the characteristics of frames. (b) Bayesian model averaging [1] tracks target in an increasing order of variations and makes a blind average of the posteriors from all previously tracked frames. (c) Our algorithm measures the tracking feasibility between frames, and the density functions are propagated from only relevant frames through a more flexible graphical model compared to (a) and (b).

target and scene. In other words, our framework learns a general directed graphical model actively and tracks a target under the identified graphical model. The proposed framework has some common properties with [1], which also employs a more complex graphical model and estimates the posterior using Bayesian model averaging, but has the following critical differences: 1) our algorithm runs online while [1] is an offline technique, 2) we actively identify appropriate frames for density propagation instead of blind model averaging, and 3) the proposed algorithm is more efficient due to the reduction of the number of posterior propagations. The main concept of our framework is illustrated in Figure 1; instead of using all the tracked frame for density propagation as shown in Figure 1(b), we adaptively determine appropriate frames to improve tracking performance and reduce computational complexity as shown in Figure 1(c). Note that we can avoid further density propagation from the frames with very different characteristics and isolate tracking errors in such frames naturally.

Given a graphical model constructed with tracked frames, we identify a set of nodes in the graph from which the new frame is connected based on tracking plausibility so that we obtain the updated graphical model. Finding the appropriate nodes to track from in the current graphical model is computationally expensive, so we maintain a small subset of representative frames to facilitate the procedure. Once the new graphical model is obtained, we propagate the posterior density to the new frame by an efficient patch matching technique [2]. Our approach has something common with the methods based on multiple target templates [3,4,5] but is clearly different from them because we propagate the posteriors to the current frame from multiple parents using the identified graphical model; it is more advantageous to preserve multi-modality in the posterior. Now, we have an online tracking algorithm that learns a graph structure and solves target tracking jointly. The main contributions of our tracking algorithm are summarized below:

- We propose an adaptive and active algorithm to identify a general graphical model for tracking based on the sequence structure characterized by target and scene.

- Our tracking algorithm estimates the posterior through a selective aggregation of propagated densities, which overcomes the limitation of blind density averaging and isolates tracking errors within local branches in graph.
- The proposed tracking algorithm runs online and improves tracking performance significantly by handling various challenges effectively.

This paper is organized as follows. We first review related work in Section 2, and describe the overall framework of our algorithm in Section 3. The detailed formulation and methodology are described in Section 4 and Section 5 illustrates experimental results.

2   Related Work

Visual tracking algorithms are composed of tracking control and observation, and each algorithm is typically constructed by a combination of two components. There are several options in tracking control, which include local optimization methods, sampling-based approaches and tracking-by-detection framework. Local optimization methods [6,7,8] are simple and easy to implement, but may be stuck at local optima. To avoid this limitation, many tracking algorithms employ sampling based density propagation techniques, which are based on either sequential Bayesian filtering [9,3,4,10,5] or MCMC [11]. Recently, thanks to the advance of object detection technique, tracking-by-detection approaches are used widely [12,13,14], which can also be regarded as dense sampling method.

All the tracking algorithms listed above depend on linear graphical model or sequential processing based on the first-order Markov assumption. They focus on the density propagation or the optimal search problem between two temporally adjacent frames. This framework is useful to exploit temporal smoothness between frames but has critical limitations in handling the challenges violating the property, *i.e.*, significant appearance changes, shot changes, and occlusion. To ameliorate these problems, [11] proposes an online tracking algorithm to propagate the posterior by MCMC sampling, [15] utilizes high-order Markov chain, and [16] models occlusion explicitly using a SVM-based classifier. However, note that these efforts are still limited to the optimization of target state given the information of target and tracker state in the a single or at most a few preceding frame(s). Recently, [1] proposes an offline algorithm to actively search a suitable order of frames for tracking, where the posterior of a new frame is estimated by propagating posteriors from all tracked frames and aggregating them through Bayesian model averaging. Although these methods do not rely on chain models any more, the graphical model for tracking is fixed and are not adaptive to the characteristics of the input video. Also, note that most of offline tracking algorithms still depend on linear graphical model [17,18,19,20,21].

Another main challenges in visual tracking is how to maintain the appearance of target in a robust manner. Many tracking algorithms have been investigating this problem and some promising solutions have been proposed such as template update [22,23,6], sparse representation [3,4,5], incremental subspace learning [9], multi-task learning [10], multiple instance learning [13], P-N learning [12], and

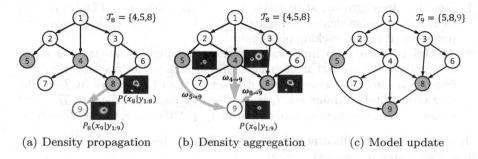

(a) Density propagation   (b) Density aggregation   (c) Model update

Fig. 2. Procedure of the proposed algorithm performed in a frame. (a) When a new frame (red hollow node) is given, each representative frame (shaded in pink) propagates the posterior to the new frame, creating a corresponding edge in the existing graphical model. (b) Propagated posteriors from all representative frames are weighted and aggregated to compute the final target posterior in the new frame. (c) The target state is estimated and the list of representative frames is updated if necessary.

so on. Although robust appearance models enable tracker to handle various appearance changes effectively, fundamental limitation of sequential approaches by linear graphical models—its weakness to temporal failures and multi-modal variations—still remain. This is partly because tracking control and observation are investigated separately even though joint optimization of the two problems is potentially helpful to improve overall performance.

Contrary to prior studies, our approach couples the two components more tightly. We employ preliminary observation to determine the structure of graphical model, and the adaptively identified graphical model facilitates robust observation. This procedure performs online, and we implement an online tracking algorithm based on the adaptively constructed graph structure.

3   Algorithm Overview

The main goal of this work is to progressively construct a graphical model that is appropriate for tracking but is not necessarily limited to chain models, and sequentially estimate the posterior of target state $\mathbf{x}_t$ at the tth frame given observation $\mathbf{y}_{1:t}$. When a new frame t arrives, our algorithm selectively propagates density functions to estimate the posterior $P(\mathbf{x}_t|\mathbf{y}_{1:t})$. To reduce the computational cost, we maintain the m most representative frames within the graph, $\mathcal{T}_{t-1} = \{t^{(1)}, ..., t^{(m)}\}$ ($m \ll t-1$), in an online manner and allow only the frames in $\mathcal{T}_{t-1}$ to propagate densities to frame t with relevant weights. Our algorithm performs the following procedures to track the target and update the graphical model at each frame:

1. **Density propagation step** propagates density functions from $P(\mathbf{x}_u|\mathbf{y}_{1:u})$ $\forall u \in \mathcal{T}_{t-1}$ to the frame t through a patch matching technique [2], and creates an edge from each frame in $\mathcal{T}_{t-1}$ to the frame t.

2. **Density aggregation step** estimates the target posterior $P(\mathbf{x}_t|\mathbf{y}_{1:t})$ by a weighted Bayesian model averaging, where the weight of each edge is computed based on its tracking plausibility.
3. **Model update step** first evaluates the reliability of the tracking result and updates the model if necessary. Specifically, if the tracking result at frame t is also more reliable and distinctive than the frames in $\mathcal{T}_{t-1}$, the new representative frame set $\mathcal{T}_t$ is obtained by adding frame t to $\mathcal{T}_{t-1}$ and removing the least appropriate one from $\mathcal{T}_{t-1}$. Otherwise, we set $\mathcal{T}_t = \mathcal{T}_{t-1}$.

These three steps are illustrated in Figure 2, and we discuss the detailed procedure of each step in the next section.

4   Main Algorithm

This section describes our main algorithm, which includes progressive graph construction technique and density propagation through weighted Bayesian model averaging [24]. We first present how the target posterior is estimated by the weighted Bayesian model averaging based on patch matching [2]. Then we discuss how to construct a general graphical model in a progressive fashion and how to maintain target models for persistent tracking.

4.1   Density Propagation by Patch Matching

In the sequential Bayesian filtering framework, the density function is propagated recursively and the posterior is estimated through prediction and update steps. In our scenario, density propagation does not necessarily happen between two temporally adjacent frames but can be performed via any frames tracked previously. The propagated density at frame t from frame u denoted by $P_u(\mathbf{x}_t|\mathbf{y}_{1:t})$ is defined as

$$P_u(\mathbf{x}_t|\mathbf{y}_{1:t}) = \alpha_{u \to t} P_u(\mathbf{y}_t|\mathbf{x}_t) \int P(\mathbf{x}_t|\mathbf{x}_u)P(\mathbf{x}_u|\mathbf{y}_{1:u})d\mathbf{x}_u, \qquad (1)$$

where $P(\mathbf{x}_t|\mathbf{x}_u)$ is the transition model from frame u to frame t, $P_u(\mathbf{y}_t|\mathbf{x}_t)$ is likelihood at frame t with respect to frame u, and $\alpha_{u \to t}$ is a normalization constant.

The recursive posterior estimation is implemented through patch matching with sampling [1], where the prediction and update steps in each Bayesian filter are handled jointly. Each patch inside a candidate bounding box defined by a sample in frame u are matched with a certain patch in frame t, and the patch votes for the target center using a Gaussian kernel. The voting map for each sample is obtained by aggregating the votes from all patches in the bounding box, and the further aggregation of the voting maps constructs the posterior of frame t. Mathematically, the posterior is approximated as

$$P_u(\mathbf{x}_t|\mathbf{y}_{1:t}) \approx \sum_{\mathbf{x}_u^i \in \mathbb{S}_u} P_u(\mathbf{y}_t|\mathbf{x}_t)P(\mathbf{x}_t|\mathbf{x}_u^i)$$

$$= \sum_{\mathbf{x}_u^i \in \mathbb{S}_u} \sum_{j=1}^{r_u^i} \mathcal{N}(\mathbf{x}_t; f_{u \to t}(\mathbf{c}_i^j) - \mathbf{a}_i^j, \boldsymbol{\Sigma}), \tag{2}$$

where $\mathbb{S}_u$ denotes a set of samples drawn from $P(\mathbf{x}_u|\mathbf{y}_{1:u})$, r_u^i is the number of patches within the bounding box defined by each sample $\mathbf{x}_u^i$. The patch match function $f_{u \to t}(\mathbf{c}_i^j)$ finds correspondence of the patch centered at $\mathbf{c}_i^j$, and $\mathbf{a}_i^j$ is the offset from $\mathbf{x}_u^i$ to $\mathbf{c}_i^j$. Each voting is smoothed using Gaussian kernel $\mathcal{N}(\cdot)$ with a variance $\boldsymbol{\Sigma}$. We maintain multiple posteriors in several different scales to handle the variation in size of the target. Note that each propagation creates a directed edge between two corresponding frames in the graphical model.

4.2 Density Aggregation by Weighted Bayesian Model Averaging

Our tracking algorithm employs a weighted Bayesian model averaging to propagate the posterior density functions similar to [1]. Since we do not rely on the first-order Markov chain any more, there are a number of options to propagate the posterior to the current frame from all the previous frames.

Let $\mathcal{T}_{t-1} = \{t^{(1)}, \ldots, t^{(m)}\}$, where t is the index of the current frame and $t^{(1)}, \ldots, t^{(m)} \leq t - 1$, be a set of representative frame indices that have outgoing edges to the tth frame in the graphical model. In other words, only the frames corresponding to the elements in $\mathcal{T}_{t-1}$ among all the tracked frames propagate densities to the tth frame. Then, the posterior at the current frame $P(\mathbf{x}_t|\mathbf{y}_{1:t})$ is estimated by a weighted sum of the propagated densities from $u \in \mathcal{T}_{t-1}$ denoted by $P_u(\mathbf{x}_t|\mathbf{y}_{1:t})$ as illustrated in Figure 2, which is formally given by

$$P(\mathbf{x}_t|\mathbf{y}_{1:t}) \propto \sum_{u \in \mathcal{T}_{t-1}} \omega_{u \to t} P_u(\mathbf{x}_t|\mathbf{y}_{1:t})$$

$$= \sum_{u \in \mathcal{T}_{t-1}} \omega_{u \to t} P_u(\mathbf{y}_t|\mathbf{x}_t) \int P(\mathbf{x}_t|\mathbf{x}_u)P(\mathbf{x}_u|\mathbf{y}_{1:u})d\mathbf{x}_u, \tag{3}$$

where $\omega_{u \to t}$ is the weight for each posterior. This formulation is similar to the one proposed in [1] and the detailed derivation is omitted due to space limitation. By integrating patch matching process in Eq. (2), the posterior at frame t is estimated approximately by the following equation:

$$P(\mathbf{x}_t|\mathbf{y}_{1:t}) = \sum_{u \in \mathcal{T}_{t-1}} \omega_{u \to t} \sum_{\mathbf{x}_u^i \in \mathbb{S}_u} \sum_{j=1}^{r_u^i} \mathcal{N}(\mathbf{x}_t; f_{u \to t}(\mathbf{c}_u^j) - \mathbf{a}_u^j, \boldsymbol{\Sigma}). \tag{4}$$

Propagating density from one frame to another means that there exists a directed edge between the two frames in the graphical model, where the weight for the edge is $\omega_{u \to t}$, where u is a parent frame of t. All nodes are supposed to have

$|\mathcal{T}_{t-1}|$ incoming edges, where $|\cdot|$ denotes the number of elements in a set. The remaining issue is how to determine the weight factor, $\omega_{u \to t}$.

The weight factor $\omega_{u \to t}$ is determined by the suitability of tracking along the edge from frame u to t, considering the path from the initial frame to frame u in the graph structure. For the purpose, we define a measure to estimate the potential risk resulting from tracking between frame u and t, which is given by

$$\delta_{u \to t} = \max\left(\delta_u, d_c(u, t)\right), \tag{5}$$

where $d_c(u, t)$ represents the estimated tracking error between two directly connected frames u and t, and δ_u represents the accumulated tracking error up to frame u. $d_c(u, t)$ measures the dissimilarity between target appearances in frame u and t, where the target at frame t is tentatively obtained based on the propagated posterior from frame u as

$$\mathbf{x}^*_{u \to t} = \arg\max_{\mathbf{x}_t} P_u(\mathbf{x}_t | \mathbf{y}_{1:t}). \tag{6}$$

Given the target templates τ_u and τ_t, which are obtained from the bounding boxes corresponding to $\mathbf{x}^*_u$ and $\mathbf{x}^*_{u \to t}$, respectively, we compute the deformation cost between τ_u and τ_t as follows:

$$d_c(u, t) \equiv \underset{j}{\text{median}}\left(||\mathbf{c}^j_u - f_{u \to t}(\mathbf{c}^j_u; \tau_t)||\right), \tag{7}$$

where $f_{u \to t}(\mathbf{c}^j_i; \tau_t)$ is a patch matching function from the jth patch centered at $\mathbf{c}^j_u$ inside template τ_u at frame u to template τ_t at frame t. The accumulated tracking error δ_u is obtained by the maximum tracking error in the minimax path from the initial frame to frame u, which is formally given by

$$\delta_u = \min_{v \in \mathcal{T}_{u-1}} \delta_{v \to u} = \min_{v \in \mathcal{T}_{u-1}} \left(\max\left(\delta_v, d_c(v, u)\right)\right), \tag{8}$$

where v denote the parent frames of u in the graph. Note that δ_u is computed when tracking at frame u is completed and hence given at frame t.

Based on tracking error $\delta_{u \to t}$, defined in Eq. (5), the normalized weight for each outgoing edge $\omega_{u \to t}, \forall u \in \mathcal{T}_{t-1}$ is given by,

$$\omega_{u \to t} = \frac{\exp(-\eta \cdot \delta_{u \to t})}{\sum_{s \in \mathcal{T}_{t-1}} \exp(-\eta \cdot \delta_{s \to t})}, \tag{9}$$

where η is a scale factor and set to $\eta = (\min_u \delta_{u \to t})^{-1}$. In this way, each propagated density $P_u(\mathbf{x}_t | \mathbf{y}_{1:t})$ along each directed edge from $\mathcal{T}_{t-1}$ is aggregated to obtain the posterior $P(\mathbf{x}_t | \mathbf{y}_{1:t})$ at frame t.

4.3   Model Update

When the density propagation and aggregation steps are completed, the optimal target state is given by the MAP solution as

$$\mathbf{x}^*_t = \arg\max_{\mathbf{x}_t} P(\mathbf{x}_t | \mathbf{y}_{1:t}). \tag{10}$$

After obtaining the tracking result $\mathbf{x}_t^*$ in a new frame and augmenting the graphical model including the new frame t, we update the list of representative frames, $\mathcal{T}_{t-1}$. Note that maintaining an appropriate set of frames $\mathcal{T}_t$ is important to track subsequent frames and avoid drift problem.

To achieve this goal, we apply an online classifier based on k-nearest neighbors and decide whether the tracking result corresponds to target object or background. If it turns out to be target, we update the representative frame set based on the predefined measure. We discuss these two issues next.

Template Classification. Suppose that we have collected a set of positive and negative templates, corresponding to target and background respectively, during tracking until frame $t-1$. The set is denoted by $\mathcal{D}_{t-1} = \{\boldsymbol{\tau}_1^+, ..., \boldsymbol{\tau}_{N_p}^+, \boldsymbol{\tau}_1^-, ..., \boldsymbol{\tau}_{N_n}^-\}$, where $\boldsymbol{\tau}^+$ and $\boldsymbol{\tau}^-$ represent positive and negative templates, respectively, and N_p and N_n denote the numbers of positive and negative examples, respectively. To classify the obtained target template $\boldsymbol{\tau}_t^*$ corresponding to $\mathbf{x}_t^*$, we use the following measure

$$S = \frac{S_p}{S_p + S_n} \tag{11}$$

where S_p is an average distance between $\boldsymbol{\tau}_t^*$ and k-nearest positive templates in $\mathcal{D}_{t-1}$ and S_n is the distance between $\boldsymbol{\tau}_t^*$ and the nearest negative template. The distance measure used to compute S_p and S_n is the Sum of Squared Distance (SSD)[1]. The estimated template $\boldsymbol{\tau}_t^*$ is determined as the target object if $S < \rho$, where ρ is a classifier threshold and typically set to 0.5. Note that S_n considers only a single nearest negative template while S_p considers k-nearest positive templates, which is useful to make the classifier robust to false positives. One may argue that this strategy may not be appropriate to handle radical target appearance changes, but there is a trade-off between avoiding drift problem and adapting new appearances; we found that the conservative method works better in practice.

Once $\boldsymbol{\tau}_t^*$ is classified as a target object, we construct $\mathcal{D}_t$ from $\mathcal{D}_{t-1}$ by replacing old templates in $\mathcal{D}_{t-1}$ with new positive and negative templates. The positive template is obtained from our MAP solution $\mathbf{x}_t^*$, and the negative templates are generated considering background context and distracting regions. The background context is captured by sampling background templates around the identified target $\mathbf{x}_t^*$. The distractors are regions that have similar appearance as target, therefore sampled from modes in $P(\mathbf{x}_t|\mathbf{y}_{1:t})$ except $\mathbf{x}_t^*$. Note that the number of elements in $\mathcal{D}$ remains same in each frame.

Maintaining Representative Frames. Maintaining a small subset of frames propagating densities, $\mathcal{T}_t$, is crucial to achieve good tracking performance with efficiency. We consider the following two properties to maintain a reasonable set of representative frames $\mathcal{T}_t$:

---

[1] We used SSD instead of patch matching here because SSD is more efficient and patch matching is not particularly better than SSD for this purpose.

- **Distinctiveness**: Frames in $\mathcal{T}_t$ should be unique in the set to effectively cover various aspects of target in the entire graph.
- **Usefulness**: Frames in $\mathcal{T}_t$ should potentially contribute to tracking subsequent frames.

We now discuss how we update $\mathcal{T}_t$ online by taking the both properties into account. Let $\kappa_{u,t}$ denote the weight of frame $u \in \mathcal{T}_t$ in terms of representativeness for further tracking. The weight depends on two factors, $\kappa_u^{(1)}$ and $\kappa_{u,t}^{(2)}$, which correspond to distinctiveness and usefulness, respectively.

To make the elements in $\mathcal{T}_t$ distinctive, frames with redundant target appearances need to be removed from the set. The weight for frame distinctiveness is computed by

$$\kappa_u^{(1)} = \min_{v \in \mathcal{T}_{t-1} \setminus \{u\}} \Delta(u, v), \tag{12}$$

which corresponds to the distance between the template in frame u and the most similar target template within other frames in $\mathcal{T}_{t-1}$. Specifically, $\Delta(u, v)$ is determined by the two factors as

$$\Delta(u, v) = d_c(u, v) \cdot d_p(u, v), \tag{13}$$

where d_c measures the degree of the target deformation, as defined in Eq. (7), and d_p measures the dissimilarity of target appearances based on average ℓ_2 distances between all matched patches within the target templates.

On the other hand, we claim that the frames having recently propagated densities with large weights are more useful to track subsequent frames, and such potential of frames are measured by

$$\kappa_{u,t}^{(2)} = (1 + \sigma y_t \omega_{u \to t}) \kappa_{u,t-1}^{(2)}, \tag{14}$$

where $\omega_{u \to t}$ is weight for density propagation from frame $u \in \mathcal{T}_{t-1}$ to frame t as defined in Eq. (9), $y_t \in \{+1, -1\}$ indicates whether tracking result at frame t is classified as foreground ($+1$) or background (-1) in the template classification step, and σ controls update rate set to 0.1.

By combining the weights for the two different aspects, the weight for each frame $u \in \mathcal{T}_t$ is given by

$$\kappa_{u,t} = \kappa_u^{(1)} \cdot \kappa_{u,t}^{(2)}. \tag{15}$$

The weight for the new frame t is computed by the same manner, except that $\kappa_{t,t-1}^{(2)}$ is computed by the median of $\kappa_{u,t-1}^{(2)}, \forall u \in \mathcal{T}_{t-1}$. Given these weights for frames in $\mathcal{T}_{t-1}$ and t, we update the $\mathcal{T}_t$ as follows:

$$\mathcal{T}_t = \begin{cases} (\mathcal{T}_{t-1} \setminus \{m\}) \cup \{t\}, & \text{if } \kappa_{t,t} > \kappa_{m,t} \\ \mathcal{T}_{t-1}, & \text{otherwise} \end{cases} \tag{16}$$

where

$$m = \underset{u \in \mathcal{T}_{t-1}}{\operatorname{argmin}} \kappa_{u,t}.$$

After $\mathcal{T}_t$ is obtained by Eq. (16), the weights $\kappa_{i,t}, \forall i \in \mathcal{T}_t$ are re-normalized such that all weights are summed up to one.

5   Experiment

Our tracking algorithm is tested in a variety of challenging sequences and compared with many state-of-the-art online tracking algorithms included in the tracking benchmark [25]. We present implementation details of the proposed algorithm and extensive experimental results.

5.1   Datasets and Compared Algorithms

To evaluate the performance of our tracking algorithm in various scenarios, we conducted experiments on all the 50 sequences in the tracking benchmark dataset [25] and added 10 more sequences publicly available, which are more challenging and difficult to be handled by online trackers. The sequences from the benchmark dataset contain various challenges such as illumination variation, background clutter, occlusion, etc. More challenges are included in the 10 additional sequences: heavy occlusion (*TUD, campus, accident*), abrupt target motion (*bike, tennis*) and shot changes (*boxing, youngki, skating, dance, psy*).

We compared our algorithm with top 10 trackers by one-pass evaluation (OPE) in the tracking benchmark [25], which include SCM [5], Struck [14], TLD [12], ASLA [26], CXT [27], VTD [28], VTS [29], CSK [30], LSK [7] and DFT [31]. In addition, the state-of-the-art offline tracking algorithm OMA [1] is also included in our evaluation. We used default parameters for all compared methods. Our method is denoted by OGT (Online Graph-based Tracking).

5.2   Implementation and Performance

Our algorithm employs patch matching technique across multiple scales for density propagation. Specifically, 4×4 patches are used for patch matching and 13

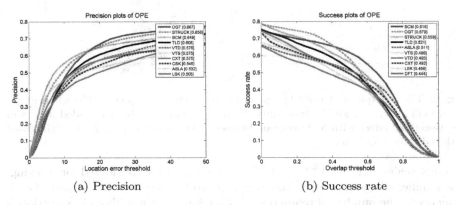

(a) Precision   (b) Success rate

Fig. 3.   Tracking performance in all the 50 sequences in the tracking benchmark dataset. Precision and success ratio are measured by center location errors and bounding box overlap ratios, respectively. The ranks are set with center location error 25 and overlap ratio 0.5.

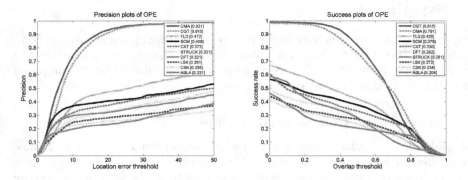

Fig. 4. Tracking performance in the additional 10 sequences with more challenging events. Precision and success ratio are measured by center location errors and bounding box overlap ratios, respectively. The ranks are set with center location error 25 and overlap ratio 0.5.

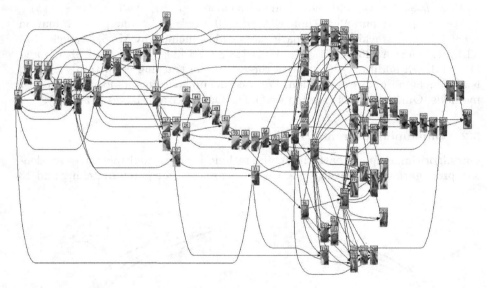

Fig. 5. The example of identified graph structure in *skating* sequence. The whole graph is very complex, and we illustrate only the frames that have been included in $\mathcal{T}$ and the associated edges with high weights. Frames included in the final $\mathcal{T}$ are highlighted with red bounding boxes.

different scales $(1.1^{-6}, 1.1^{-5}, \ldots, 1.1^0, \ldots, 1.1^5, 1.1^6)$ are considered for tracking. The number of representative frames in $\mathcal{T}$ set to 12 except the initial part of each sequence[2]. The number of templates in $\mathcal{D}$ for k-nearest neighbor classification is 600 with 300 positive and negative examples, and k is set to 10. All parameters

---

[2] At the beginning of sequences, the new frame is added to $\mathcal{T}$ without removing elements as long as the estimated target is classified as foreground and $|\mathcal{T}| < 12$.

Fig. 6. Qualitative performance evaluation for 10 additional sequences. From top to bottom, tracking results for *tennis, skating, accident, bike, boxing, campus, TUD, youngki, psy* and *dance* sequences are presented.

Table 1. Average center location error (in pixels). Red: best, blue: second best.

	LSK	ASLA	CXT	DFT	CSK	Struck	SCM	VTD	VTS	TLD	OMA	OGT
tennis	79.3	67.2	129.8	87.1	112.3	109.5	66.0	81.0	58.9	64.5	6.4	4.9
skating	85.9	45.2	41.5	83.3	61.1	23.8	49.0	37.1	42.9	35.3	7.9	6.4
accident	68.4	59.4	9.0	13.6	76.0	56.4	2.8	70.8	70.4	5.4	3.1	6.0
bike	70.4	88.6	22.2	131.1	103.3	8.4	13.6	85.7	82.1	16.9	17.4	7.2
boxing	97.1	137.3	137.3	73.2	108.8	122.7	95.9	82.9	80.4	73.3	10.3	11.1
campus	44.6	12.2	33.4	1.3	2.1	83.1	12.6	45.1	44.8	46.7	2.6	2.5
TUD	21.1	72.6	36.4	8.2	55.4	54.4	12.2	46.5	48.2	18.9	4.2	11.8
youngki	108.9	144.1	67.9	72.6	163.9	115.1	114.5	112.5	116.0	60.2	11.0	11.5
psy	153.9	188.8	143.7	205.3	1022.9	76.3	211.6	129.5	123.6	55.6	14.7	26.2
dance	163.9	117.5	176.8	157.1	147.0	107.1	208.5	188.4	201.1	105.0	14.9	23.7
Average	89.4	93.3	79.8	83.3	185.3	75.7	78.7	88.0	86.8	48.2	9.3	11.1

Table 2. Average bounding box overlap ratio. Red: best, blue: second best.

	LSK	ASLA	CXT	DFT	CSK	Struck	SCM	VTD	VTS	TLD	OMA	OGT
tennis	0.20	0.12	0.08	0.06	0.04	0.28	0.11	0.07	0.09	0.10	0.65	0.77
skating	0.04	0.13	0.25	0.11	0.09	0.40	0.20	0.25	0.21	0.33	0.45	0.54
accident	0.35	0.43	0.80	0.47	0.32	0.32	0.86	0.41	0.41	0.75	0.75	0.66
bike	0.20	0.16	0.39	0.02	0.15	0.54	0.49	0.16	0.17	0.45	0.43	0.57
boxing	0.07	0.03	0.01	0.17	0.05	0.04	0.13	0.14	0.16	0.21	0.70	0.66
campus	0.58	0.63	0.56	0.81	0.81	0.24	0.62	0.35	0.36	0.50	0.81	0.83
TUD	0.62	0.30	0.51	0.60	0.38	0.30	0.68	0.41	0.38	0.67	0.83	0.65
youngki	0.12	0.12	0.38	0.14	0.10	0.09	0.13	0.16	0.14	0.24	0.63	0.64
psy	0.11	0.11	0.10	0.07	0.09	0.34	0.07	0.20	0.25	0.38	0.64	0.56
dance	0.12	0.10	0.08	0.11	0.12	0.08	0.07	0.09	0.09	0.07	0.53	0.57
Average	0.24	0.21	0.32	0.26	0.22	0.26	0.34	0.22	0.23	0.37	0.64	0.65

are fixed throughout the experiment. Our algorithm runs at 1 frame/sec in average based on an unoptimized Matlab implementation except patch matching function [2], which is written in C/C++.

To evaluate performance of our algorithm, we followed the same protocols in [25], where precision and success rate are measured by using densely sampled thresholds on center location error and bounding box overlap ratio, respectively. Figure 3 illustrates quantitative evaluation for all the sequences in the tracking benchmark. Performance of our tracker in benchmark dataset is competitive with the state-of-the-art online trackers, which indicates that our tracker is suitable to handle general challenges for tracking.

In the additional sequences involving more challenges, on the other hand, our tracker outperforms all other trackers with large margin and even comparable the state-of-the-art offline tracker, OMA [1]. It is because existing techniques typically rely on the first-order Markov assumption for tracking a new frame while our algorithm relaxes the restriction and isolates temporal tracking failures within local branches in the graph structure. The results for this experiment are illustrated in Figure 4. Table 1 and 2 summarize the average scores of center location error and overlap ratio for the additional 10 sequences, respectively. The identified graph reflects the structure of an input sequence pretty well, which is illustrated in Figure 5. As shown in the figure, our algorithm maintains a reasonable representative frames $\mathcal{T}$ in each frame and propagates density function successfully to the new frame. The results for qualitative evaluation are presented in Figure 6.

6   Conclusion

We presented a novel online tracking algorithm, which progressively construct a graphical model beyond chain model, which is more appropriate for tracking. The target posterior of a new frame is estimated by propagating densities from previously tracked frames and making a weighted average of the densities based on the relevance of the existing frames with respect to the new frame. For computational efficiency, only a small number of frames is maintained for density propagation in an online manner, so that they capture important characteristics of input video and are potentially useful for tracking subsequent frames. Outstanding experimental results on 50 sequences in the tracking benchmark and 10 more challenging sequences show the benefit of our progressive graph construction algorithm for tracking.

Acknowledgments. This work was supported partly by MEST Basic Science Research Program through the NRF of Korea (NRF-2012R1A1A1043658), ICT R&D program of MSIP/IITP [14-824-09-006, Novel computer vision and machine learning technology with the ability to predict and forecast], and Samsung Electronics Co., Ltd.

References

1. Hong, S., Kwak, S., Han, B.: Orderless tracking through model-averaged posterior estimation. In: ICCV (2013)
2. Korman, S., Avidan, S.: Coherency sensitive hashing. In: ICCV (2011)
3. Bao, C., Wu, Y., Ling, H., Ji, H.: Real time robust l1 tracker using accelerated proximal gradient approach. In: CVPR (2012)
4. Mei, X., Ling, H.: Robust visual tracking using $l1$ minimization. In: ICCV (2009)
5. Zhong, W., Lu, H., Yang, M.-H.: Robust object tracking via sparsity-based collaborative model. In: CVPR (2012)
6. Han, B., Comaniciu, D., Zhu, Y., Davis, L.: Sequential kernel density approximation and its application to real-time visual tracking. TPAMI 30 (2008)
7. Liu, B., Huang, J., Yang, L., Kulikowski, C.A.: Robust tracking using local sparse appearance model and k-selection. In: CVPR, pp. 1313–1320 (2011)
8. Sevilla-Lara, L., Learned-Miller, E.G.: Distribution fields for tracking. In: CVPR, pp. 1910–1917 (2012)
9. Ross, D.A., Lim, J., Lin, R.-S., Yang, M.-H.: Incremental learning for robust visual tracking. IJCV 77 (2008)

10. Zhang, T., Ghanem, B., Liu, S., Ahuja, N.: Robust visual tracking via multi-task sparse learning. In: CVPR (2012)
11. Kwon, J., Lee, K.M.: Tracking of abrupt motion using wang-landau monte carlo estimation. In: Forsyth, D., Torr, P., Zisserman, A. (eds.) ECCV 2008, Part I. LNCS, vol. 5302, pp. 387–400. Springer, Heidelberg (2008)
12. Kalal, Z., Mikolajczyk, K., Matas, J.: Tracking-Learning-Detection. TPAMI (2012)
13. Babenko, B., Yang, M.-H., Belongie, S.: Robust object tracking with online multiple instance learning. TPAMI 33 (2011)
14. Hare, S., Saffari, A., Torr, P.H.S.: Struck: Structured output tracking with kernels. In: ICCV (2011)
15. Pan, P., Schonfeld, D.: Visual tracking using high-order particle filtering. Signal Processing Letters 18, 51–54 (2011)
16. Kwak, S., Nam, W., Han, B., Han, J.H.: Learning occlusion with likelihoods for visual tracking. In: ICCV (2011)
17. Buchanan, A.M., Fitzgibbon, A.W.: Interactive feature tracking using K-D trees and dynamic programming. In: CVPR (2006)
18. Gu, S., Zheng, Y., Tomasi, C.: Linear time offline tracking and lower envelope algorithms. In: ICCV (2011)
19. Uchida, S., Fujimura, I., Kawano, H., Feng, Y.: Analytical dynamic programming tracker. In: ACCV (2011)
20. Wei, Y., Sun, J., Tang, X., Shum, H.-Y.: Interactive offline tracking for color objects. In: ICCV (2007)
21. Sun, J., Zhang, W., Tang, X., Shum, H.-Y.: Bi-directional tracking using trajectory segment analysis. In: ICCV (2005)
22. Matthews, I., Ishikawa, T., Baker, S.: The template update problem. IEEE Trans. Pattern Anal. Mach. Intell. 26, 810–815 (2004)
23. Jepson, A.D., Fleet, D.J., El-Maraghi, T.F.: Robust online appearance models for visual tracking. IEEE Trans. Pattern Anal. Mach. Intell. 25, 1296–1311 (2003)
24. Hoeting, J.A., Madigan, D., Raftery, A.E., Volinsky, C.T.: Bayesian model averaging: A tutorial. Statistical Science 14 (1999)
25. Wu, Y., Lim, J., Yang, M.-H.: Online object tracking: A benchmark. In: CVPR (2013)
26. Jia, X., Lu, H., Yang, M.-H.: Visual tracking via adaptive structural local sparse appearance model. In: CVPR (2012)
27. Dinh, G.T.B., Vo, N., Medioni: Context tracker: Exploring supporters and distracters in unconstrained environments. In: CVPR (2011)
28. Kwon, J., Lee, K.-M.: Visual tracking decomposition. In: CVPR (2010)
29. Kwon, J., Lee, K.M.: Tracking by sampling trackers. In: ICCV (2011)
30. Henriques, J.F., Caseiro, R., Martins, P., Batista, J.: Exploiting the circulant structure of tracking-by-detection with kernels. In: Fitzgibbon, A., Lazebnik, S., Perona, P., Sato, Y., Schmid, C. (eds.) ECCV 2012, Part IV. LNCS, vol. 7575, pp. 702–715. Springer, Heidelberg (2012)
31. Sevilla-Lara, L., Learned-Miller, E.: Distribution fields for tracking. In: CVPR (2012)

Fast Visual Tracking via
Dense Spatio-temporal Context Learning

Kaihua Zhang[1], Lei Zhang[2], Qingshan Liu[1], David Zhang[2], and Ming-Hsuan Yang[3]

[1] S-mart Group, Nanjing University of Information Science & Technology
[2] Dept. of Computing, The Hong Kong Polytechnic University, HongKong
[3] Electrical Engineering and Computer Science, University of California at Merced, USA
`zhkhua@gmail.com`, {`cslzhang,csdzhang`}`@comp.polyu.edu.hk`,
`qsliu@nuist.edu.cn`, `mhyang@ucmerced.edu`

Abstract. In this paper, we present a simple yet fast and robust algorithm which exploits the dense spatio-temporal context for visual tracking. Our approach formulates the spatio-temporal relationships between the object of interest and its locally dense contexts in a Bayesian framework, which models the statistical correlation between the simple low-level features (i.e., image intensity and position) from the target and its surrounding regions. The tracking problem is then posed by computing a confidence map which takes into account the prior information of the target location and thereby alleviates target location ambiguity effectively. We further propose a novel explicit scale adaptation scheme, which is able to deal with target scale variations efficiently and effectively. The Fast Fourier Transform (FFT) is adopted for fast learning and detection in this work, which only needs 4 FFT operations. Implemented in MATLAB without code optimization, the proposed tracker runs at 350 frames per second on an i7 machine. Extensive experimental results show that the proposed algorithm performs favorably against state-of-the-art methods in terms of efficiency, accuracy and robustness.

1 Introduction

Visual tracking is one of the most active research topics due to its wide range of applications such as motion analysis, activity recognition, surveillance, and human-computer interaction, to name a few [29]. The main challenge for robust visual tracking is to handle large appearance changes of the target object and the background over time due to occlusion, illumination changes, and pose variation. Numerous algorithms have been proposed with focus on effective appearance models, which are based on the target appearance [8,1,28,22,17,18,19,23,21,31] or the difference between appearances of the target and its local background [11,16,14,2,30,15]. However, if the appearances are degraded severely, there does not exist enough information extracted for robustly tracking the target, whereas its existing scene can provide useful context information to help localizing it.

In visual tracking, a local context consists of a target object and its immediate surrounding background within a determined region (see the regions inside the red rectangles in Figure 1). Most of local contexts remain unchanged as changes between two consecutive frames can be reasonably assumed to be smooth as the time interval is usually small (30 frames per second (FPS)). Therefore, there exists a strong spatio-temporal

D. Fleet et al. (Eds.): ECCV 2014, Part V, LNCS 8693, pp. 127–141, 2014.

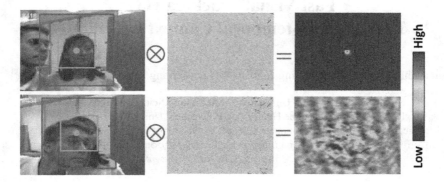

Fig. 1. The proposed method handles heavy occlusion well by learning dense spatio-temporal context information. Note that the region inside the red rectangle is the context region which includes the target and its surrounding background. Left: although the target appearance changes much due to heavy occlusion, the spatial relationship between the object center (denoted by solid yellow circle) and most of its surrounding locations in the context region is almost unchanged. Middle: the learned spatio-temporal context model (some regions have similar values which show the corresponding regions in the left frames have similar spatial relations to the target center.). Right: the learned confidence map.

relationship between the local scenes containing the object in consecutive frames. For instance, the target in Figure 1 undergoes heavy occlusion which makes the object appearance change significantly. However, the local context containing the object does not change much as the overall appearance remains similar and only a small part of the context region is occluded. Thus, the presence of local context in the current frame helps to predict the object location in the next frame. This temporally proximal information in consecutive frames is the temporal context which has been recently applied to object detection [10]. Furthermore, the spatial relation between an object and its local context provides specific information about the configuration of a scene (see middle column in Figure 1) which helps to discriminate the target from background when its appearance changes much.

2   Related Works

Most tracking algorithms can be categorized as either generative [22,17,18,19,23,21,31] or discriminative [11,16,14,2,30,15] based on their appearance models. A generative tracking method learns an appearance model to represent the target and searches for image regions with best matching scores as the results. While it is critical to construct an effective appearance model in order to handle various challenging factors in tracking, the involved computational complexity is often increased at the same time. Furthermore, generative methods discard useful information surrounding target regions that can be exploited to better separate objects from backgrounds. Discriminative methods treat tracking as a binary classification problem with local search which estimates decision boundary between an object image patch and the background. However, the objective

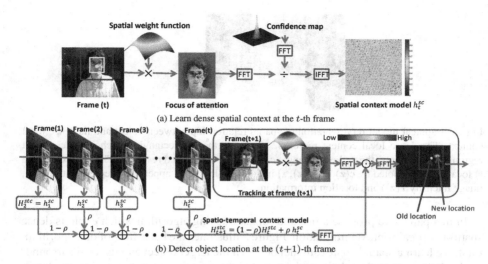

(a) Learn dense spatial context at the t-th frame

(b) Detect object location at the $(t+1)$-th frame

Fig. 2. Basic flow of our tracking algorithm. The local context regions are inside the red rectangles while the target locations are indicated by the yellow rectangles. FFT denotes the Fast Fourier Transform and IFFT is the inverse FFT.

of classification is to predict instance labels which is different from the goal of tracking to estimate object locations [14]. Moreover, while some efficient feature extraction techniques (e.g., integral image [11,16,14,2,30] and random projection [30]) have been proposed for visual tracking, there often exist a large number of samples from which features need to be extracted for classification, thereby entailing computationally expensive operations. Generally speaking, both generative and discriminative tracking algorithms make trade-offs between effectiveness and efficiency of an appearance model. Notwithstanding much progress has been made in recent years, it remains a challenging task to develop an efficient and robust tracking algorithm.

Recently, several methods [27,13,9,25] exploit context information to facilitate visual tracking via mining the information of regions with consistent motion correlations to the target object. In [27], a data mining method is used to extract segmented regions surrounding the object as auxiliary objects for collaborative tracking. To find consistent regions, key points surrounding the object are first extracted to help locating the object position in [13,9,25]. The SIFT or SURF descriptors are then used to represent these consistent regions. However, computationally expensive operations are required in representing and finding consistent regions. Furthermore, due to the sparsity natures of key points and auxiliary objects, some consistent regions that are useful for locating the object position may be discarded. In contrast, the proposed algorithm does not have these problems because all the local regions surrounding the object are considered as the potentially consistent regions, and the motion correlations between the objects and its local contexts in consecutive frames are learned by the spatio-temporal context model that is efficiently computed by FFT.

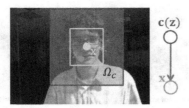

Fig. 3. Graphical model representation of spatial relationship between object and its dense local context. The dense local context region Ω_c is inside the red rectangle which includes object region surrounding by the yellow rectangle centering at the tracked result $\mathbf{x}^\star$. The context feature at location $\mathbf{z}$ is denoted by $\mathbf{c}(\mathbf{z}) = (I(\mathbf{z}), \mathbf{z})$ including a low-level appearance representation (i.e., image intensity $I(\mathbf{z})$) and location information.

In this paper, we propose a fast and robust tracking algorithm which exploits dense spatio-temporal context information. Figure 2 illustrates the basic flow of our algorithm. First, we learn a spatial context model between the target object and its local surrounding background based on their spatial correlations in a scene by solving a deconvolution problem. Next, the learned spatial context model is used to update a spatio-temporal context model for the next frame. Tracking in the next frame is formulated by computing a confidence map as a convolution problem that integrates the dense spatio-temporal context information, and the best object location can be estimated by maximizing the confidence map (See Figure 2 (b)). Finally, based on the estimated confidence map, a novel explicit scale adaptation scheme is presented, which renders an efficient and accurate tracking result.

The key contributions of the proposed algorithm are summarized as follows:

- To the best of our knowledge, it is the first work to use dense context information for visual tracking and achieves fast and robust results.
- We propose a novel explicit scale update scheme to deal with the scale variations of the target efficiently and effectively.
- The proposed algorithm is simple and fast that needs only 4 FFTs at 350 FPS in MATLAB.
- The proposed algorithm has the merits of both generative and discriminative methods. On the one hand, the context includes target and its neighbor background, thereby making our method have the merits of discriminative models. On the other hand, the context is a whole of target and background, rendering our method the merits of generative models.

3   Problem Formulation

The tracking problem is formulated by computing a confidence map which estimates the object location likelihood:

$$m(\mathbf{x}) = P(\mathbf{x}|o),\tag{1}$$

Fig. 4. Illustration of the characteristic of the non-radially symmetric function $h^{sc}(\cdot)$ in (3). Here, the left eye is the tracked target denoted by $\mathbf{x}_l$ whose context is inside the green rectangle while $\mathbf{x}_r$ represents the right eye which is a distractor with context inside the blue rectangle. Although $\mathbf{z}$ has similar distance to $\mathbf{x}_l$ and $\mathbf{x}_r$, their spatial relationships are different (i.e., $h^{sc}(\mathbf{x}_l - \mathbf{z}) \neq h^{sc}(\mathbf{x}_r - \mathbf{z})$), and this helps discriminating $\mathbf{x}_l$ from $\mathbf{x}_r$.

where $\mathbf{x} \in \mathbb{R}^2$ is an object location and o denotes the object present in the scene. (1) is equal to the posterior probability $P(o|\mathbf{x})$ because we use uniform prior $P(o)$ for the target presence for simplicity. In the following, the spatial context information is used to estimate (1) and Figure 3 shows its graphical model representation.

In Figure 3, the object location $\mathbf{x}^\star$ (i.e., coordinate of the tracked object center) is tracked. The context feature set is defined as $X^c = \{\mathbf{c}(\mathbf{z}) = (I(\mathbf{z}), \mathbf{z})|\mathbf{z} \in \Omega_c(\mathbf{x}^\star)\}$ where $I(\mathbf{z})$ denotes image intensity at location $\mathbf{z}$ and $\Omega_c(\mathbf{x}^\star)$ is the neighborhood of location $\mathbf{x}^\star$ that is twice the size of the target object. By marginalizing the joint probability $P(\mathbf{x}, \mathbf{c}(\mathbf{z})|o)$, the object location likelihood function in (1) can be computed by

$$\begin{aligned} m(\mathbf{x}) &= P(\mathbf{x}|o) \\ &= \textstyle\sum_{\mathbf{c}(\mathbf{z}) \in X^c} P(\mathbf{x}, \mathbf{c}(\mathbf{z})|o) \\ &= \textstyle\sum_{\mathbf{c}(\mathbf{z}) \in X^c} P(\mathbf{x}|\mathbf{c}(\mathbf{z}), o) P(\mathbf{c}(\mathbf{z})|o), \end{aligned} \tag{2}$$

where the conditional probability $P(\mathbf{x}|\mathbf{c}(\mathbf{z}), o)$ models the spatial relationship between the object location and its context information which helps to resolve ambiguities when the degraded image measurements allow different interpretations, and $P(\mathbf{c}(\mathbf{z})|o)$ is a context prior probability which models appearance of the local context. The main task in this work is to learn $P(\mathbf{x}|\mathbf{c}(\mathbf{z}), o)$ as it bridges the gap between object location and its spatial context.

3.1 Spatial Context Model

The conditional probability function $P(\mathbf{x}|\mathbf{c}(\mathbf{z}), o)$ in (2) is defined as

$$P(\mathbf{x}|\mathbf{c}(\mathbf{z}), o) = h^{sc}(\mathbf{x} - \mathbf{z}), \tag{3}$$

where $h^{sc}(\mathbf{x} - \mathbf{z})$ is a function (see Figure 4 and Section 3.4) with respect to the relative *distance* and *direction* between object location $\mathbf{x}$ and its local context location $\mathbf{z}$, thereby encoding the spatial relationship between an object and its spatial context.

Note that $h^{sc}(\mathbf{x} - \mathbf{z})$ is not a radially symmetric function (i.e., $h^{sc}(\mathbf{x} - \mathbf{z}) \neq h^{sc}(|\mathbf{x} - \mathbf{z}|)$), and takes into account different spatial relationships between an object and its local contexts. This helps to resolve ambiguities when similar objects appear in close proximity. For example, when a method tracks an eye based only on appearance (denoted by $\mathbf{x}_l$) in the *davidindoor* sequence shown in Figure 4, the tracker may be easily distracted to the right one (denoted by $\mathbf{x}_r$) because both eyes and their surrounding backgrounds have similar appearances (when the object moves fast and the search region is large). However, in the proposed method, while the locations of both eyes are at similar distances to location $\mathbf{z}$, their relative locations to $\mathbf{z}$ are different, resulting in different spatial relationships, i.e., $h^{sc}(\mathbf{x}_l - \mathbf{z}) \neq h^{sc}(\mathbf{x}_r - \mathbf{z})$. That is, the non-radially symmetric function h^{sc} helps to resolve ambiguities effectively.

3.2   Context Prior Model

In (2), the context prior probability is related to the context appearance which is simply modeled by

$$P(\mathbf{c}(\mathbf{z})|o) = I(\mathbf{z})w_\sigma(\mathbf{z} - \mathbf{x}^\star), \tag{4}$$

where $I(\cdot)$ is image intensity that represents appearance of context and $w_\sigma(\cdot)$ is a Gaussian weighted function defined by

$$w_\sigma(\mathbf{z} - \mathbf{x}^\star) = ae^{-\frac{|\mathbf{z} - \mathbf{x}^\star|^2}{\sigma^2}}, \tag{5}$$

where a is a normalization constant that restricts $P(\mathbf{c}(\mathbf{z})|o)$ in (4) to range from 0 to 1 that satisfies the definition of probability and σ is a scale parameter.

In (4), it models focus of attention that is motivated by the biological visual system which concentrates on certain image regions requiring detailed analysis [24]. The closer the context location $\mathbf{z}$ is to the currently tracked target location $\mathbf{x}^\star$, the more important it is to predict the object location in the coming frame, and larger weight should be set (please refer to Figure 2 (a)). Different from our algorithm that uses a spatially weighted function to indicate the importance of context at different locations, there exist other methods [3,26] in which spatial sampling techniques are used to focus more detailed contexts at the locations near the object center (i.e., the closer the location is to the object center, the more context locations are sampled).

3.3   Confidence Map

The confidence map of an object location is modeled as

$$m(\mathbf{x}) = P(\mathbf{x}|o) = be^{-|\frac{\mathbf{x} - \mathbf{x}^\star}{\alpha}|^\beta}, \tag{6}$$

where b is a normalization constant, α is a scale parameter and β is a shape parameter (please refer to Figure 5).

The confidence map $m(\mathbf{x})$ in (6) takes into account the prior information of the target location which is able to handle the location ambiguity problem effectively. The object location ambiguity problem often occurs in visual tracking which adversely affects tracking performance. In [2], a multiple instance learning technique is adopted to

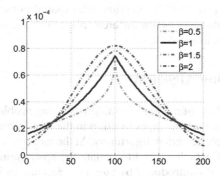

Fig. 5. Illustration of 1-D cross section of the confidence map $m(\mathbf{x})$ in (6) with different parameters β. Here, the object location $\mathbf{x}^\star = (100, 100)$.

handle the location ambiguity problem with favorable tracking results. The closer the location is to the currently tracked position, the larger probability that the ambiguity occurs with (e.g., predicted object locations that differ by a few pixels are all plausible solutions and thereby cause ambiguities). In our method, we resolve the location ambiguity problem by choosing a proper shape parameter β. As illustrated in Figure 5, a large β (e.g., $\beta = 2$) results in an oversmoothing effect for the confidence value at locations near to the object center, failing to effectively reduce location ambiguities. On the other hand, a small β (e.g., $\beta = 0.5$) yields a sharp peak near the object center, and activates much fewer positions when learning the spatial context model. This in turn may lead to overfitting in searching for the object location in the coming frame. We find that robust results can be obtained when $\beta = 1$ in our experiments.

3.4 Fast Learning Spatial Context Model

Based on the confidence map function (6) and the context prior model (4), our objective is to learn the spatial context model (3). Putting (6), (4) and (3) together, we formulate (2) as

$$
\begin{aligned}
m(\mathbf{x}) &= be^{-|\frac{\mathbf{x}-\mathbf{x}^\star}{\alpha}|^\beta} \\
&= \sum_{\mathbf{z}\in\Omega_c(\mathbf{x}^\star)} h^{sc}(\mathbf{x}-\mathbf{z})I(\mathbf{z})w_\sigma(\mathbf{z}-\mathbf{x}^\star) \\
&= h^{sc}(\mathbf{x}) \otimes (I(\mathbf{x})w_\sigma(\mathbf{x}-\mathbf{x}^\star)),
\end{aligned}
\tag{7}
$$

where $\otimes$ denotes the convolution operator.

We note (7) can be transformed to the frequency domain in which the Fast Fourier Transform (FFT) algorithm [20] can be used for fast convolution. That is,

$$
\mathcal{F}(be^{-|\frac{\mathbf{x}-\mathbf{x}^\star}{\alpha}|^\beta}) = \mathcal{F}(h^{sc}(\mathbf{x})) \odot \mathcal{F}(I(\mathbf{x})w_\sigma(\mathbf{x}-\mathbf{x}^\star)),
\tag{8}
$$

where $\mathcal{F}$ denotes the FFT function and $\odot$ is the element-wise product. Therefore, we have

$$
h^{sc}(\mathbf{x}) = \mathcal{F}^{-1}\left(\frac{\mathcal{F}(be^{-|\frac{\mathbf{x}-\mathbf{x}^\star}{\alpha}|^\beta})}{\mathcal{F}(I(\mathbf{x})w_\sigma(\mathbf{x}-\mathbf{x}^\star))}\right),
\tag{9}
$$

where $\mathcal{F}^{-1}$ denotes the inverse FFT function. The spatial context model h^{sc} learns the relatively spatial relations between different pixels (please refer to Figure 4 and Section 3.1) in a Bayesian framework.

4   Proposed Tracking Algorithm

Figure 2 shows the basic flow of our algorithm. The tracking problem is formulated as a detection task. We assume that the target location in the first frame has been initialized manually or by some object detection algorithms. At the t-th frame, we learn the spatial context model $h_t^{sc}(\mathbf{x})$ (9), which is used to update the spatio-temporal context model $H_{t+1}^{stc}(\mathbf{x})$ (12) to reduce noise introduced by target appearance variations. H_{t+1}^{stc} is then applied to detect the object location in the $(t+1)$-th frame. When the $(t+1)$-th frame arrives, we crop out the local context region $\Omega_c(\mathbf{x}_t^\star)$ based on the tracked location $\mathbf{x}_t^\star$ at the t-th frame and construct the corresponding context feature set $X_{t+1}^c = \{\mathbf{c}(\mathbf{z}) = (I_{t+1}(\mathbf{z}), \mathbf{z}) | \mathbf{z} \in \Omega_c(\mathbf{x}_t^\star)\}$. The object location $\mathbf{x}_{t+1}^\star$ in the $(t+1)$-th frame is determined by maximizing the new confidence map

$$\mathbf{x}_{t+1}^\star = \arg\max_{\mathbf{x} \in \Omega_c(\mathbf{x}_t^\star)} m_{t+1}(\mathbf{x}), \tag{10}$$

where $m_{t+1}(\mathbf{x})$ is represented as

$$m_{t+1}(\mathbf{x}) = H_{t+1}^{stc}(\mathbf{x}) \otimes (I_{t+1}(\mathbf{x})w_{\sigma_t}(\mathbf{x} - \mathbf{x}_t^\star)), \tag{11}$$

which is deduced from (7) and can use FFT for fast convolution. Here, H_{t+1}^{stc} derives from the spatial context model h_t^{sc} with a low-pass temporal filtering processing and hence is able to reduce the noise introduced by abrupt appearance changes of I_{t+1}.

4.1   Update of Spatio-temporal Context

The spatio-temporal context model is updated by

$$H_{t+1}^{stc} = (1 - \rho)H_t^{stc} + \rho h_t^{sc}, \tag{12}$$

where ρ is a learning parameter and h_t^{sc} is the spatial context model computed by (9) at the t-th frame. We note (12) is a temporal filtering procedure which can be easily observed in frequency domain

$$H_\omega^{stc} = F_\omega h_\omega^{sc}, \tag{13}$$

where $H_\omega^{stc} \triangleq \int H_t^{stc} e^{-j\omega t} dt$ is the temporal Fourier transform of H_t^{stc} and similar to h_ω^{sc}. The temporal filter F_ω is formulated as

$$F_\omega = \frac{\rho}{e^{j\omega} - (1 - \rho)}, \tag{14}$$

where j denotes imaginary unit. It is easy to validate that F_ω in (14) is a low-pass filter [20]. Therefore, our spatio-temporal context model is able to effectively filter out image noise introduced by appearance variations, leading to more stable results.

4.2 Update of Scale

According to (11), the target location in the current frame is found by maximizing the confidence map derived from the weighted context region surrounding the previous target location. However, the scale of the target often changes over time. Therefore, the scale parameter σ in the weight function w_σ (5) should be updated accordingly. We propose the scale update scheme as

$$
\begin{cases}
s'_t = \sqrt{\frac{m_t(\mathbf{x}^\star_t)}{m_{t-1}(\mathbf{x}^\star_{t-1})}}, \\
\bar{s}_t = \frac{1}{n}\sum_{i=1}^{n} s'_{t-i}, \\
s_{t+1} = (1-\lambda)s_t + \lambda\bar{s}_t, \\
\sigma_{t+1} = s_t\sigma_t,
\end{cases}
\tag{15}
$$

where $m_t(\cdot)$ is the confidence map at the t-th frame that is computed by (11), and s'_t is the estimated scale between two consecutive frames. To avoid over-sensitive adaptation and to reduce noise introduced by estimation error, the estimated target scale s_{t+1} is obtained through filtering in which $\bar{s}_t$ is the average of the estimated scales from n consecutive frames, and $\lambda > 0$ is a fixed filter parameter (similar to ρ in (12)). The derivation details of (15) can be found at http://www4.comp.polyu.edu.hk/~cslzhang/STC/STC.htm.

4.3 Analysis and Discussion

We note that the low computational complexity is one prime characteristic of the proposed algorithm. In learning the spatial context model (9), since the confidence map (11) and the scale updating (15) can be pre-computed only once before tracking, there are only 4 FFT operations involved for processing one frame. The computational complexity for computing each FFT is only $\mathcal{O}(MN\log(MN))$ for the local context region of $M \times N$ pixels, thereby resulting in a fast method (350 FPS in MATLAB on an i7 machine). More importantly, the proposed algorithm achieves robust results as discussed bellow.

Difference with Related Work. It should be noted that the proposed dense spatio-temporal context tracking algorithm is significantly different from recently proposed approaches that use FFT for efficient computation [5,4,15].

In [5,4], the formulations are based on correlation filters that are directly obtained by classic signal processing algorithms. At each frame, correlation filters are trained using a large number of samples, and then combined to find the most correlated position in the next frame. In [15], the filters proposed by [5,4] are kernelized and used to achieve more stable results. The proposed algorithm is significantly different from [5,4,15] in several aspects. First, our algorithm models the spatio-temporal relationships between the object and its local contexts which is motivated by the human visual system that exploits context to help resolving ambiguities in complex scenes efficiently and effectively. Second, our algorithm focuses on the regions which require detailed analysis, thereby effectively reducing the adverse effects of background clutters and leading to more robust results. Third, our algorithm handles the object location ambiguity problem using the confidence map with a proper prior distribution, thereby achieving more

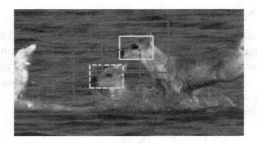

Fig. 6. Illustration of why the proposed model is equipped to handle distractor. The target inside the yellow dotted rectangle is the distractor. The different surrounding contexts can well discriminate target from distactor.

stable and accurate performance for visual tracking. Finally, our algorithm solves the scale adaptation problem while the other FFT-based tracking methods [5,4,15] only track objects with a fixed scale and achieve less accurate results than our method.

Robustness to Occlusion and Distractor. As shown in Figure 1, the proposed algorithm handles heavy occlusion well as most of context regions are not occluded which have similar relative spatial relations (see middle column of Figure 1) to the target center. This helps to determine the target center. Figure 6 illustrates that our method is robust to distractor (i.e., the bottom left object). If tracking the target only based on its appearance information, the tracker will be distracted to the top right one because of their similar appearances. Although the distractor has similar appearance to the target, most of their surrounding contexts have different appearances which are useful to discriminate target from distractor.

5   Experiments

We evaluate the proposed spatio-temporal context (STC) tracking algorithm using 18 video sequences with challenging factors including heavy occlusion, drastic illumination changes, pose and scale variation, non-rigid deformation, background cluster and motion blur. We compare the proposed STC tracker with 18 state-of-the-art methods in which the context tracker [9] and the FFT-based trackers [4,15] (i.e., ConT, MOS and CST in Table 1) are included. For other context-based tracking methods [27,13,25], their source codes are not available for evaluation and the implementations require some technical details and parameters not discussed therein. The parameters of the proposed algorithm are *fixed* for all the experiments. For other trackers, we use either the original source or binary codes provided in which parameters of each tracker are tuned for best results. The 18 trackers we compare with are: scale mean-shift (SMS) tracker [7], fragment tracker (Frag) [1], semi-supervised Boosting tracker (SSB) [12], local orderless tracker (LOT) [21], incremental visual tracking (IVT) method [22], online AdaBoost tracker (OAB) [11], multiple instance learning tracker (MIL) [2], visual tracking decomposition method (VTD) [17], L1 tracker (L1T) [19], tracking-learning-detection (TLD) method [16], distribution field tracker (DF) [23], multi-task tracker (MTT) [31],

Table 1. Success rate (SR)(%). Red fonts indicate the best performance while the **blue** fonts indicate the second best ones. The total number of evaluated frames is 7, 591.

Sequence	SMS	Frag	SSB	LOT	IVT	OAB	MIL	VTD	L1T	TLD	DF	MTT	Struck	ConT	MOS	CT	CST	LGT	STC
animal	13	3	51	15	4	17	83	96	6	37	6	87	93	58	3	92	94	7	94
bird	33	64	13	5	78	94	10	9	44	42	94	10	48	26	11	8	47	89	65
bolt	58	41	18	89	15	1	92	3	2	1	2	2	8	6	25	94	39	74	98
cliffbar	5	24	24	26	47	66	71	53	24	62	26	55	44	43	6	95	93	81	98
chasing	72	77	62	20	82	71	65	70	72	76	70	95	85	53	61	79	96	95	97
car4	10	34	22	1	97	30	37	35	94	88	26	22	96	90	28	36	44	33	98
car11	1	1	19	32	54	14	48	25	46	67	78	59	18	47	85	36	48	16	86
cokecan	1	3	38	4	3	53	18	7	16	17	13	85	94	20	2	30	86	18	87
downhill	81	89	53	6	87	82	33	98	66	13	94	54	87	71	28	82	72	73	99
dollar	55	41	38	40	21	16	46	39	39	39	100	39	100	100	89	87	100	100	100
davidindoor	6	1	36	20	7	24	30	38	18	96	64	94	71	82	43	46	2	95	100
girl	7	70	49	91	64	68	28	68	56	79	59	71	97	74	3	27	43	51	98
jumping	2	34	81	22	100	82	100	87	13	76	12	100	18	100	6	100	100	5	100
mountainbike	14	13	82	71	100	99	18	100	61	26	35	100	98	25	55	89	100	74	100
ski	22	5	65	55	16	58	33	6	5	36	6	9	76	43	1	60	1	71	68
shaking	2	25	30	14	1	39	83	98	3	15	84	2	48	12	4	84	36	48	96
sylvester	70	34	67	61	45	66	77	33	40	89	33	68	81	84	6	77	84	85	78
woman	52	27	30	16	21	18	21	35	8	31	93	19	96	28	2	19	21	66	100
Average SR	35	35	45	35	49	49	52	49	40	62	53	59	75	62	26	62	60	68	94

structured output tracker (Struck) [14], context tracker (ConT) [9], minimum output sum of square error (MOS) tracker [4], compressive tracker (CT) [30], circulant structure tracker (CST) [15] and local-global tracker (LGT) [6]. For the trackers involving randomness, we repeat the experiments 10 times on each sequence and report the averaged results. Implemented in MATLAB, our tracker runs at 350 FPS on an i7 3.40 GHz machine with 8 GB RAM. The MATLAB source codes are available at http://www4.comp.polyu.edu.hk/~cslzhang/STC/STC.htm.

5.1 Experimental Setup

The size of context region is initially set to twice the size of the target object. The parameter σ_t of (15) is initially set to $\sigma_1 = \frac{s_h + s_w}{2}$, where s_h and s_w are height and width of the initial tracking rectangle, respectively. The parameters of the map function are set to $\alpha = 2.25$ and $\beta = 1$. The learning parameter $\rho = 0.075$. We note that as illustrated by Figure 2 (b), the weights from other frames are smaller than that from the current observation no matter how small ρ is set. Thus, the current observation is the most important one. The scale parameter s_t is initialized to $s_1 = 1$, and the learning parameter $\lambda = 0.25$. The number of frames for updating the scale is set to $n = 5$. To reduce effects of illumination change, each intensity value in the context region is normalized by subtracting the average intensity of that region. Then, the intensity in the context region multiplies a Hamming window to reduce the frequency effect of image boundary when using FFT [20,5].

5.2 Experimental Results

We use two evaluation criteria to quantitatively evaluate the 19 trackers: the center location error (CLE) and success rate (SR), both computed based on the manually labeled ground truth results of each frame. The score of success rate is defined as $score = \frac{area(R_t \bigcap R_g)}{area(R_t \bigcup R_g)}$, where R_t is a tracked bounding box and R_g is the ground truth bounding box, and the result of one frame is considered as a

Table 2. Center location error (CLE)(in pixels) and average frame per second (FPS). Red fonts indicate the best performance while the **blue** fonts indicate the second best ones. The total number of evaluated frames is 7, 591.

Sequence	SMS	Frag	SSB	LOT	IVT	OAB	MIL	VTD	L1T	TLD	DF	MTT	Struck	ConT	MOS	CT	CST	LGT	STC
animal	78	100	25	70	146	62	32	17	122	125	252	17	19	76	281	18	16	166	15
bird	25	13	101	99	13	9	140	57	60	145	12	156	21	139	159	79	20	11	15
bolt	42	43	102	9	65	227	9	177	261	286	277	293	149	126	223	10	210	12	8
cliffbar	41	34	56	36	37	33	13	30	40	70	52	25	46	49	104	6	6	10	5
chasing	13	9	44	32	6	9	13	23	9	47	31	5	6	16	68	10	5	6	4
car4	144	56	104	177	14	109	63	127	16	13	92	158	9	11	117	63	44	47	11
car11	86	117	11	30	7	11	8	20	8	12	6	8	9	8	8	9	8	16	7
cokecan	60	70	15	46	64	11	18	68	40	29	30	10	7	36	53	16	9	32	6
downhill	14	11	102	226	22	12	117	9	35	255	10	77	10	62	116	12	129	12	8
dollar	55	56	66	66	23	28	23	65	65	72	3	71	18	5	12	20	5	4	2
davidindoor	176	103	45	100	281	43	33	40	86	13	27	11	20	22	78	28	149	12	8
girl	130	26	50	12	36	22	34	41	51	23	27	23	8	34	126	39	43	35	9
jumping	63	30	11	43	4	11	4	17	45	13	73	7	42	4	155	6	3	89	4
mountainbike	135	209	11	24	5	11	208	7	74	213	155	7	8	149	16	11	5	12	6
ski	91	134	10	12	51	11	15	179	161	222	147	33	8	78	386	11	237	13	12
shaking	224	55	133	90	134	22	11	5	72	232	11	115	23	191	194	11	21	33	10
sylvester	15	47	14	23	138	12	9	66	49	8	56	18	9	13	65	9	7	11	11
woman	49	118	86	131	112	120	119	110	148	108	12	169	4	55	176	122	160	23	5
Average CLE	79	63	54	70	84	43	43	58	62	78	52	80	19	42	103	29	54	22	8
Average FPS	12	7	11	0.7	33	22	38	5	1	28	13	1	20	15	200	90	120	8	350

success if $score > 0.5$. Table 1 and Table 2 show the quantitative results in which the proposed STC tracker achieves the best or second best performance in most sequences both in terms of center location error and success rate. Furthermore, the proposed tracker is the most efficient (350 FPS on average) algorithm among all evaluated methods. Although the CST [15] and MOS [4] methods also use FFT for fast computation, the CST method performs time-consuming kernel operations and the MOS tracker computes several correlation filters in each frame, making these two approaches less efficient than the proposed algorithm. Furthermore, both CST and MOS methods only track target with fixed scale, which achieve less accurate results than the proposed method with scale adaptation. Figure 7 shows some tracking results of different trackers. For presentation clarity, we only show the results of the top 7 trackers in terms of average success rates. More results can be found in the paper website http://www4.comp.polyu.edu.hk/~cslzhang/STC/STC.htm.

Illumination, Scale and Pose Variation. There are large illumination variations in the evaluated sequences. The appearance of the target object in the *car4* sequence changes significantly due to the cast shadows and ambient lights (see #200, #250 in the *car4* sequence shown in Figure 7). Only the models of IVT, L1T, Struck and STC adapt to these illumination variations well. Likewise, only the VTD and our STC methods perform favorably on the *shaking* sequence because the object appearance changes drastically due to the stage lights and sudden pose variations. The *davidindoor* sequence contain gradual pose and scale variations as well as illumination changes. Note that most reported results using this sequence are only on subsets of the available frames, i.e., not from the very beginning of the *davidindoor* video when the target face is in nearly complete darkness. In this work, the full sequence is used to better evaluate the performance of all algorithms. Only the proposed algorithm is able to achieve favorable tracking results on this sequence in terms of both accuracy and success rate. This can be attributed to the use of dense spatio-temporal context information which facilitates filtering out noisy observations (as discussed in Section 4.1), enabling the proposed STC algorithm

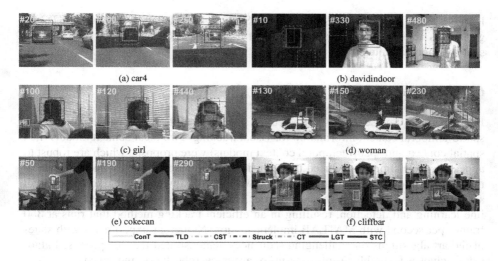

(a) car4

(b) davidindoor

(c) girl

(d) woman

(e) cokecan

(f) cliffbar

| ConT | TLD | CST | Struck | CT | LGT | STC |

Fig. 7. Screenshots of tracking results. More results and videos can be found in the supplementary material.

to relocate the target when object appearance changes drastically due to illumination, scale and pose variations.

Occlusion, Rotation, and Pose Variation. The target objects in the *woman*, *girl* and *bird* sequences are partially occluded at times. The object in the *girl* sequence also undergoes in-plane rotation (See #100, #120 of the *girl* sequence in Figure 7) which makes the tracking tasks difficult. Only the proposed algorithm is able to track the objects successfully in most frames of this sequence. The *woman* sequence has non-rigid deformation and heavy occlusion (see #130, #150, #230 of the *woman* sequence in Figure 7) at the same time. All the other trackers fail to successfully track the object except for the Struck and the proposed STC algorithms. As most of the local contexts surrounding the target objects are not occluded in these sequences, such information facilitates the proposed algorithm relocating the object even they are almost fully occluded (as discussed in Figure 1).

Background Clutter and Abrupt Motion. In the *animal*, *cokecan* and *cliffbar* sequences, the target objects undergo fast movements in the cluttered backgrounds. The target object in the *chasing* sequence undergoes abrupt motion with 360 degree out-of-plane rotation, and the proposed algorithm achieves the best performance in terms of both success rate and center location error. The *cokecan* video contains a specular object with in-plane rotation and heavy occlusion, which makes this tracking task difficult. Only the Struck and the proposed STC methods are able to successfully track most of the frames. In the *cliffbar* sequence, the texture in the background is very similar to that of the target object. Most trackers drift to background except for CT, CST, LGT and STC (see #300 of the *cliffbar* sequence in Figure 7). Although the target and its local background have very similar texture, their spatial relationships and appearances of local contexts are different which are used by the proposed algorithm when learning a confidence map (as discussed in Section 4.3). Hence, the proposed STC algorithm is able to separate the target object from the background based on the dense spatio-temporal context.

6   Conclusion

In this paper, we presented a simple yet fast and robust algorithm which exploits dense spatio-temporal context information for visual tracking. Two local context models (i.e., spatial context and spatio-temporal context models) were proposed which are robust to appearance variations introduced by occlusion, illumination changes, and pose variations. An explicit scale adaptation scheme was proposed which is able to adapt target scale variations effectively. The Fast Fourier Transform algorithm was used in both online learning and detection, resulting in an efficient tracking method that runs at 350 frames per second with MATLAB implementation. Numerous experiments with state-of-the-art algorithms on challenging sequences demonstrated that the proposed algorithm achieves favorable results in terms of accuracy, robustness, and speed.

Acknowledgements. Kaihua Zhang is supported in part by the NUIST Scientific Research Foundation under Grant S8113049001. Lei Zhang is supported in part by the Hong Kong Polytechnic University ICRG Grant (G-YK79). Ming-Hsuan Yang is supported in part by the NSF CAREER Grant #1149783 and NSF IIS Grant #1152576. Qingshan Liu is supported in part by NSFC under Grant 61272223 and NSF of Jiangsu Province under Grant BK2012045.

References

1. Adam, A., Rivlin, E., Shimshoni, I.: Robust fragments-based tracking using the integral histogram. In: CVPR, pp. 798–805 (2006)
2. Babenko, B., Yang, M.-H., Belongie, S.: Robust object tracking with online multiple instance learning. PAMI 33(8), 1619–1632 (2011)
3. Belongie, S., Malik, J., Puzicha, J.: Shape matching and object recognition using shape contexts. PAMI 24(4), 509–522 (2002)
4. Bolme, D.S., Beveridge, J.R., Draper, B.A., Lui, Y.M.: Visual object tracking using adaptive correlation filters. In: CVPR, pp. 2544–2550 (2010)
5. Bolme, D.S., Draper, B.A., Beveridge, J.R.: Average of synthetic exact filters. In: CVPR, pp. 2105–2112 (2009)
6. Cehovin, L., Kristan, M., Leonardis, A.: Robust visual tracking using an adaptive coupled-layer visual model. PAMI 35(4), 941–953 (2013)
7. Collins, R.T.: Mean-shift blob tracking through scale space. In: CVPR, vol. 2, pp. II–234 (2003)
8. Collins, R.T., Liu, Y., Leordeanu, M.: Online selection of discriminative tracking features. PAMI 27(10), 1631–1643 (2005)
9. Dinh, T.B., Vo, N., Medioni, G.: Context tracker: Exploring supporters and distracters in unconstrained environments. In: CVPR, pp. 1177–1184 (2011)
10. Divvala, S.K., Hoiem, D., Hays, J.H., Efros, A.A., Hebert, M.: An empirical study of context in object detection. In: CVPR, pp. 1271–1278 (2009)

11. Grabner, H., Grabner, M., Bischof, H.: Real-time tracking via on-line boosting. In: BMVC, pp. 47–56 (2006)
12. Grabner, H., Leistner, C., Bischof, H.: Semi-supervised on-line boosting for robust tracking. In: Forsyth, D., Torr, P., Zisserman, A. (eds.) ECCV 2008, Part I. LNCS, vol. 5302, pp. 234–247. Springer, Heidelberg (2008)
13. Grabner, H., Matas, J., Van Gool, L., Cattin, P.: Tracking the invisible: Learning where the object might be. In: CVPR, pp. 1285–1292 (2010)
14. Hare, S., Saffari, A., Torr, P.H.: Struck: Structured output tracking with kernels. In: ICCV, pp. 263–270 (2011)
15. Henriques, J.F., Caseiro, R., Martins, P., Batista, J.: Exploiting the circulant structure of tracking-by-detection with kernels. In: Fitzgibbon, A., Lazebnik, S., Perona, P., Sato, Y., Schmid, C. (eds.) ECCV 2012, Part IV. LNCS, vol. 7575, pp. 702–715. Springer, Heidelberg (2012)
16. Kalal, Z., Matas, J., Mikolajczyk, K.: Pn learning: Bootstrapping binary classifiers by structural constraints. In: CVPR, pp. 49–56 (2010)
17. Kwon, J., Lee, K.M.: Visual tracking decomposition. In: CVPR, pp. 1269–1276 (2010)
18. Kwon, J., Lee, K.M.: Tracking by sampling trackers. In: ICCV, pp. 1195–1202 (2011)
19. Mei, X., Ling, H.: Robust visual tracking and vehicle classification via sparse representation. PAMI 33(11), 2259–2272 (2011)
20. Oppenheim, A.V., Willsky, A.S., Nawab, S.H.: Signals and systems, vol. 2. Prentice-Hall, Englewood Cliffs (1983)
21. Oron, S., Bar-Hillel, A., Levi, D., Avidan, S.: Locally orderless tracking. In: CVPR, pp. 1940–1947 (2012)
22. Ross, D.A., Lim, J., Lin, R.S., Yang, M.-H.: Incremental learning for robust visual tracking. IJCV 77(1), 125–141 (2008)
23. Sevilla-Lara, L., Learned-Miller, E.: Distribution fields for tracking. In: CVPR, pp. 1910–1917 (2012)
24. Torralba, A.: Contextual priming for object detection. IJCV 53(2), 169–191 (2003)
25. Wen, L., Cai, Z., Lei, Z., Yi, D., Li, S.Z.: Online spatio-temporal structural context learning for visual tracking. In: Fitzgibbon, A., Lazebnik, S., Perona, P., Sato, Y., Schmid, C. (eds.) ECCV 2012, Part IV. LNCS, vol. 7575, pp. 716–729. Springer, Heidelberg (2012)
26. Wolf, L., Bileschi, S.: A critical view of context. IJCV 69(2), 251–261 (2006)
27. Yang, M., Wu, Y., Hua, G.: Context-aware visual tracking. PAMI 31(7), 1195–1209 (2009)
28. Yang, M., Yuan, J., Wu, Y.: Spatial selection for attentional visual tracking. In: CVPR, pp. 1–8 (2007)
29. Yilmaz, A., Javed, O., Shah, M.: Object tracking: A survey. ACM Computing Surveys 38(4) (2006)
30. Zhang, K., Zhang, L., Yang, M.-H.: Real-time compressive tracking. In: Fitzgibbon, A., Lazebnik, S., Perona, P., Sato, Y., Schmid, C. (eds.) ECCV 2012, Part III. LNCS, vol. 7574, pp. 864–877. Springer, Heidelberg (2012)
31. Zhang, T., Ghanem, B., Liu, S., Ahuja, N.: Robust visual tracking via multi-task sparse learning. In: CVPR, pp. 2042–2049 (2012)

Extended Lucas-Kanade Tracking

Shaul Oron[1], Aharon Bar-Hillel[2], and Shai Avidan[3]

[1] Tel Aviv University, Israel
shauloro@post.tau.ac.il
[2] Microsoft Research
aharonb@microsoft.com
[3] Tel Aviv University, Israel
avidan@eng.tau.ac.il

Abstract. The Lucas-Kanade (LK) method is a classic tracking algorithm exploiting target structural constraints thorough template matching. Extended Lucas Kanade or ELK casts the original LK algorithm as a maximum likelihood optimization and then extends it by considering pixel object / background likelihoods in the optimization. Template matching and pixel-based object / background segregation are tied together by a unified Bayesian framework. In this framework two log-likelihood terms related to pixel object / background affiliation are introduced in addition to the standard LK template matching term. Tracking is performed using an EM algorithm, in which the E-step corresponds to pixel object/background inference, and the M-step to parameter optimization. The final algorithm, implemented using a classifier for object / background modeling and equipped with simple template update and occlusion handling logic, is evaluated on two challenging data-sets containing 50 sequences each. The first is a recently published benchmark where ELK ranks 3rd among 30 tracking methods evaluated. On the second data-set of vehicles undergoing severe view point changes ELK ranks in 1st place outperforming state-of-the-art methods.

1 Introduction

The famous Lucas-Kanade (LK) algorithm[19] is an early, and well known, algorithm that takes advantage of object structural constraints by performing template based tracking.

Structure is a powerful cue which can be very beneficial for reliable tracking. Early methods performing template matching [19,21,20,7] later evolved and inspired the use of multiple templates and sparse representations to represent target appearance [30,5,14,24], and for known target classes a more complex use of structure can be made [27]. Learning based tracking methods can also use template matching, some examples are by target appearance mining [15] or exemplar based classification [4]. Some methods disregard target structure, for example by performing pixel-wise classification [3,11] or using histogram representations [6]. Although this can be beneficial in cases where targets are highly deformable, these methods are in most cases very pron to drift as they do not enforce any structural constraints.

Using structure, in the form of template matching, can help tracking algorithms avoid drift and maintain accurate tracking through target and scene appearance changes.

D. Fleet et al. (Eds.): ECCV 2014, Part V, LNCS 8693, pp. 142–156, 2014.

These changes can be related to in/out-of-plane rotation, illumination changes, motion blur, rapid camera movement, occlusions, target deformations and more. The drift problem is extremely difficult since tracking is performed without user intervention, apart from some initialization in the first frame, which is usually a rectangle bounding the target region.

One of the problems arising when using target templates, bounded by a rectangle, is the inclusion of background pixels in the target image. When matching the template, one is also required to match the included background pixels which can ultimately lead to drift. Our proposed method therefore attempts to perform template matching, using the structural cue, while requiring object / background consistencies between template and image pixels.

The contribution of this work is a novel template tracking algorithm we denote Extended Lucas Kande or ELK. Inspired by the famous LK algorithm our algorithm extends the original one to accounts for pixels object / background likelihood. We first cast the original LK problem is terms of probabilistic inference demonstrating the loss function minimizing the sum-of-square-difference (SSD) between image and template is equivalent to maximum likelihood estimation under Gaussian noise assumption. We then introduce hidden variables related to image and template pixels object / background likelihoods. We derive an extension of the original LK algorithm which includes 2 additional log-likelihood terms in the loss function. These terms enforce that object / background template pixels are matched to object / background image pixels respectively. In addition, from this derivation emerge pixel weights, used in the template matching term computation, as well as a factor regularizing between the template matching term and the object / background log-likelihood terms, which can be used to regularize between ordered template matching and disordered probability mode matching. We derive an estimation-maximization (EM) algorithm which enables maximizing the loss function and inferring the hidden variables.

We implement this new algorithm using a boosted stumps classifier for object / background modeling and equip it with a simple occlusion handling logic. The resulting algorithm achieves results comparable to state-of-the-art methods on a challenging tracking benchmark ranking in 3rd place among 30 trackers evaluated.

2   Extended Lukas Kanade Tracking

The Lucas-Kanade (LK) tracking algorithm works quite well when the template to be tracked consists entirely of pixels belonging to the object. Problems arise when background pixels are added to the template which cause the algorithm to drift.

To combat that we propose a Bayesian model that combines template matching (i.e., regular LK) with objecthood reasoning at the pixel level. Tracking is performed by finding a $2D$ transformation that maximizes the model likelihood.

We start in section 2.1 by introducing notation and casting traditional template matching, as done by the LK algorithm, in a probabilistic framework. In section 2.2 we extend the probabilistic framework to include pixel objecthood reasoning, by introducing a model including foreground/background hidden variables. In section 2.3 we derive an EM formulation for inferring the hidden objecthood variables and optimizing some of the model parameters, not including the tracking transformation. Finally, in section 2.4, we show how the tracking transformation can be found as part of the EM M-step, using an extension of the traditional LK algorithm.

2.1 Template Matching and Traditional LK

We wish to track template $\mathbf{T}$ with the set of pixels $\mathbf{P} = \{\mathbf{p}\}_{i=1}^{n}$, where $\mathbf{p} = (x, y)$ is the 2D pixel location, and $\mathbf{T}(\mathbf{p})$ denotes pixel $\mathbf{p}$ of template $\mathbf{T}$. Let $\mathbf{I}$ denote the image at time t. We say that image pixel $\mathbf{I}(W(\mathbf{p}; \omega))$ is mapped to template pixel $\mathbf{T}(\mathbf{p})$ by the transformation W with parameter vector ω. Examples are 2D translation or similarity transformation. The algorithm assumes an estimated position of $\mathbf{T}$ in the image at time $t - 1$ is known and given by ω^{t-1}, i.e the set of pixels $\mathbf{I}(W(\mathbf{P}; \omega^{t-1}))$ is a noisy replica of $\mathbf{T}$.

Given template $\mathbf{T}$, the estimated previous position ω^{t-1}, and a new image $\mathbf{I}$, LK looks for an update $\Delta\omega$ s.t. $\omega = \omega^{t-1} + \Delta\omega$ with $\Delta\omega$ minimizing:

$$\Delta\omega = \arg\min \sum_{\mathbf{p} \in \mathbf{P}} (\mathbf{I}(W(\mathbf{p}, \omega^{t-1} + \Delta\omega)) - \mathbf{T}(\mathbf{p}))^2 \qquad (1)$$

Using a Gauss-Newton method.

This algorithm has a natural probabilistic interpretation. Assuming a Gaussian independent pixel noise we look for the maximum likelihood pixel set $\mathbf{I}(W(\mathbf{P}; \omega^{t-1} + \Delta\omega))$:

$$\max_{\Delta\omega} logP(\mathbf{I}(W(\mathbf{P}; \omega^{t-1} + \Delta\omega))|\mathbf{T})$$

$$= \max_{\Delta\omega} \sum_{\mathbf{p} \in \mathbf{P}} logG(\mathbf{I}(W(\mathbf{p}, \omega^{t-1} + \Delta\omega)) - \mathbf{T}|0, \sigma) \qquad (2)$$

$$= -\tfrac{1}{2}|\mathbf{P}|log(2\pi\sigma^2) - \tfrac{1}{2\sigma^2} \min_{\Delta\omega}[\sum_{\mathbf{p} \in \mathbf{P}} (\mathbf{I}(W(\mathbf{p}, \omega^{t-1} + \Delta\omega)) - \mathbf{T}(\mathbf{p}))^2]$$

Where $G(x|\mu, \sigma) = \frac{1}{\sqrt{2\pi}\sigma}\exp(-\frac{1}{2\sigma^2}(x - \mu)^2)$ is the Gaussian density function. In words, we assume that the (log) probability of the image given the template is (log) Gaussian. Since the optimization in equations (1) and (2) are the same w.r.t the optimal $\Delta\omega$, we see that LK is equivalent to searching for a maximum likelihood pixel set.

Note that in an important sense, this is not a traditional ML formulation: usually the data to explain is *fixed* and we learn model parameters which makes it the most likely. Here the model has no 'traditional' parameters (it has σ, but it is not relevant to the optimization), and the data to explain is what we optimize over, by treating the transformation ω as a parameter and optimizing over it.

2.2 Template Matching with Objecthood Inference

In this section we present a graphical model that combines rigid template matching with pixel based foreground/background reasoning. The model is presented as a Bayesian network with an added event constraint. It is then simplified to a graphical model over 4 variables: the pixel values of template and image, and hidden variables determining their foreground/background affiliation.

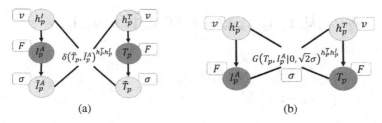

(a)   (b)

Fig. 1. Graphical Model: (a) before and (b) after simplification. (a) We observe image $\mathbf{I}$ and template $\mathbf{T}$ and wish to estimate the hidden variables: $h_p^{\mathbf{I}}$ (hidden binary variable, is the image pixel an object or background?), $\tilde{\mathbf{I}}_p$ (hidden image), $h_p^{\mathbf{T}}$ (hidden binary variable, is the template pixel an object or background?), $\tilde{\mathbf{T}}_p$ (hidden template). (b) After simplification, the hidden template $\tilde{\mathbf{T}}_p$ and image $\tilde{\mathbf{I}}_p$ vanish, and all we have to estimate are the binary variables $h_p^{\mathbf{I}}$ and $h_p^{\mathbf{T}}$. The match between $\mathbf{T}$ and $\mathbf{I}$ is assumed to come from a Gaussian distribution G with 0 mean and σ variance.

The Model. The image $\mathbf{I}$ and the template $\mathbf{T}$ we observe are assumed to be noisy measurements of some hidden and noisy source image $\tilde{\mathbf{I}}$ and template $\tilde{\mathbf{T}}$. We further know that pixels in the template and the image can belong to the object or the background. Clearly, we would like to make sure that when we match pixels in the template to pixels in the image we match object pixels and not background pixels.

To do that, let $h(\mathbf{p})$ be a binary variable that determines if the pixel belongs to the background (i.e., is 0) or object (i.e., is 1). This gives us four variables per pixel: the pixel in the hidden template $\tilde{\mathbf{T}}(\mathbf{p})$, its corresponding pixel in the hidden image $\tilde{\mathbf{I}}(W(\omega, \mathbf{p}))$, and their binary object/background binary variables $h_p^{\mathbf{T}} = h(\tilde{\mathbf{T}}(\mathbf{p}))$ and $h_p^{\mathbf{I}} = h(\tilde{\mathbf{I}}(W(\omega, \mathbf{p})))$, respectively. For brevity, from now on we will denote $\mathbf{T}_p = \mathbf{T}(\mathbf{p})$ and $\mathbf{I}_p = \mathbf{I}(W(\mathbf{p}, \omega))$.

The Connections between the hidden variables and the observables $\mathbf{T}_p$ and $\mathbf{I}_p$ are given by the graphical model in Figure 1(Left), which is replicated for each pixel $\mathbf{p} \in \mathbf{P}$. The prior probabilities of pixels (both template and image) to be foreground are Bernoulli distributed with a parameter v, i.e. $P(h = 1) = v$, $P(h = 0) = 1 - v$. The pixel appearance models, with parameters shared between template and image, are given by $P(\mathbf{I}_p | h_p^{\mathbf{I}}, F), P(\mathbf{T}_p | h_p^{\mathbf{T}}, F)$. We denote by F the parameters of this conditional probability. For example, we can implement F using two discrete histograms of pixel values, one for the object and one for the background, or we can use a discriminative model. Finally, we let $P(\tilde{\mathbf{T}}_p | \mathbf{T}_p) = G(\tilde{\mathbf{T}}_p | \mathbf{T}_p, \sigma), P(\tilde{\mathbf{I}}_p | \mathbf{I}_p) = G(\tilde{\mathbf{I}}_p | \mathbf{I}_p), \sigma)$ be Gaussian connections.

The model described up until now is a standard Bayesian network. However, in the space spanned by this network, we are interested in the subspace obeying the following condition: if both template $\mathbf{T}_p$ and image $\mathbf{I}_p$ are object pixels, than $\tilde{\mathbf{T}}_p$ and $\tilde{\mathbf{I}}_p$ are identical, i.e. $\mathbf{T}_p$ and $\mathbf{I}_p$ are noisy replica of the same source. Denoting this event by Ω, we are interested in:

$$P_\Omega(h_p^{\mathbf{T}}, h_p^{\mathbf{I}}, \mathbf{T}_p, \mathbf{I}_p, \tilde{\mathbf{T}}_p, \tilde{\mathbf{I}}_p) = P(h_p^{\mathbf{T}}, h_p^{\mathbf{I}}, \mathbf{T}_p, \mathbf{I}_p, \tilde{\mathbf{T}}_p, \tilde{\mathbf{I}}_p) 1_\Omega \tag{3}$$

where 1_Ω is given by :

$$1_\Omega = \begin{cases} 1, & h_p^{\mathbf{T}} = 0 \ or \ h_p^{\mathbf{I}} = 0 \\ \delta(\tilde{\mathbf{T}}_p - \tilde{\mathbf{I}}_p) & h_p^{\mathbf{T}} = 1 \ and \ h_p^{\mathbf{I}} = 1 \end{cases} = \delta(\tilde{\mathbf{T}}_p - \tilde{\mathbf{I}}_p)^{h_p^{\mathbf{T}} h_p^{\mathbf{I}}} \tag{4}$$

with $\delta(\cdot)$ denoting the Dirac delta. The event-restricted joint probability we consider is hence:

$$\begin{aligned} P_\Omega(h_p^{\mathbf{T}}, h_p^{\mathbf{I}}, \mathbf{T}_p, \mathbf{I}_p, \tilde{\mathbf{T}}_p, \tilde{\mathbf{I}}_p) = \\ P(h_p^{\mathbf{T}}) P(h_p^{\mathbf{I}}) P(\mathbf{T}_p | h_p^{\mathbf{T}}) P(\mathbf{I}_p | h_p^{\mathbf{I}}) G(\tilde{\mathbf{T}}_p | \mathbf{T}_p) G(\tilde{\mathbf{I}}_p | \mathbf{I}_p) \delta(\tilde{\mathbf{T}}_p - \tilde{\mathbf{I}}_p)^{h_p^{\mathbf{T}} h_p^{\mathbf{I}}} \end{aligned} \tag{5}$$

The model parameters are $\Theta = \{v, F, \sigma, \omega\}$. Like in the formalism presented for traditional LK, we optimize here not only over traditional model parameters $\{v, F, \sigma\}$, but also over the data we explain via the choice of ω.

Model Simplification. We can simplify the model by integrating $\tilde{\mathbf{T}}, \tilde{\mathbf{I}}$ out:

$$P_\Omega(h_p^{\mathbf{T}}, h_p^{\mathbf{I}}, \mathbf{T}_p, \mathbf{I}_p) = \int \int P_\Omega(h_p^{\mathbf{T}}, h_p^{\mathbf{I}}, \mathbf{T}_p, \mathbf{I}_p, \tilde{\mathbf{T}}_p, \tilde{\mathbf{I}}_p) d\tilde{\mathbf{T}} d\tilde{\mathbf{I}} = \tag{6}$$

$$P(h_p^{\mathbf{T}}) P(h_p^{\mathbf{I}}) P(\mathbf{T}_p | h_p^{\mathbf{T}}) P(\mathbf{I}_p | h^{\mathbf{I}})$$

$$\times \int \int G(\tilde{\mathbf{T}}_p | \mathbf{T}_p, \sigma) \cdot G(\tilde{\mathbf{I}}_p | \mathbf{I}_p, \sigma) \delta(\tilde{\mathbf{T}}_p - \tilde{\mathbf{I}}_p)^{h_p^{\mathbf{T}} h_p^{\mathbf{I}}} d\tilde{\mathbf{T}} d\tilde{\mathbf{I}}$$

If $h_p^{\mathbf{T}} = 0$ or $h_p^{\mathbf{I}} = 0$, the double integral decomposes into two independent integrals of Gaussian CDF, hence it is 1. If $h_p^{\mathbf{T}} = 1$, $h_p^{\mathbf{I}} = 1$ the double integral collapses into a single integral of a product of Gaussians. Such a product of two Gaussians is a scaled Gaussian, with the scaling factor itself a Gaussian $G(\mathbf{T}_p - \mathbf{I}_p | 0, \sqrt{2}\sigma)$ [8] in the means $\mathbf{T}_p, \mathbf{I}_p$. Therefore, the double integral at the end of the equation above simplifies to $G(\mathbf{T}_p - \mathbf{I}_p | 0, \sqrt{2}\sigma)^{h_p^{\mathbf{T}} h_p^{\mathbf{I}}}$. Following the elimination of $\tilde{\mathbf{T}}_p, \tilde{\mathbf{I}}_p$ we get a simpler model structure over 4 variables:

$$P_\Omega(h_p^{\mathbf{T}}, h_p^{\mathbf{I}}, \mathbf{T}_p, \mathbf{I}_p) = \tag{7}$$

$$P(h_p^{\mathbf{T}}) P(h_p^{\mathbf{I}}) P(\mathbf{T}_p | h_p^{\mathbf{T}}) P(\mathbf{I}_p | h_p^{\mathbf{I}}) G(\mathbf{T}_p - \mathbf{I}_p | 0, \sqrt{2}\sigma)^{h_p^{\mathbf{T}} h_p^{\mathbf{I}}}$$

This simplified model is described in the graphical model is Figure 1(Right)

2.3   An EM Formulation

As in traditional LK, we are given a template $\mathbf{T}$, the estimated position in the previous frame ω^{t-1}, and a new image $\mathbf{I}^t$ (we will omit the t super script for notation simplicity), and we look for an update $\omega = \omega^{t-1} + \Delta\omega$ giving us the maximum-likelihood pixel set:

$$\max_{\Theta} \log P(\mathbf{T}, \mathbf{I}_\omega | \Theta) = \max_{\Delta\omega} \max_{v,F,\sigma} \log P(\mathbf{T}, \mathbf{I}_{\omega^{t-1}+\Delta\omega} | v, F, \sigma) \tag{8}$$

Assuming pixel independence we have

$$\log P(\mathbf{T}, \mathbf{I}_\omega) = \sum_{\mathbf{p} \in \mathbf{P}} \log P(\mathbf{T}_p, \mathbf{I}_p) \tag{9}$$

$$= \sum_{\mathbf{p} \in \mathbf{P}} \sum_{h_p^{\mathbf{T}} \in \{0,1\}} \sum_{h_p^{\mathbf{I}} \in \{0,1\}} \log P(h_p^{\mathbf{T}}, h_p^{\mathbf{I}}, \mathbf{T}_p, \mathbf{I}_p)$$

With $P(h_p^{\mathbf{T}}, h_p^{\mathbf{I}}, \mathbf{T}_p, \mathbf{I}_p)$ given by Eq. 7. Expressions like this, containing a summation inside the log function are not optimization-friendly in a direct manner, so we resort to EM [9] optimization. In our case the parameters are $\Theta = \{v, F, \sigma, \omega\}$, the hidden variables are:

$$H = \{H^{\mathbf{T}}, H^{\mathbf{I}}\} = \{h_p^{\mathbf{T}}, h_p^{\mathbf{I}}\}_{\mathbf{p} \in \mathbf{P}}, \tag{10}$$

and the observables are

$$O = \{\mathbf{T}, \mathbf{I}\} = \{\mathbf{T}_p, \mathbf{I}_p\}_{\mathbf{p} \in \mathbf{P}}. \tag{11}$$

Following the EM approach, we will optimize Θ by

$$\Theta_{new} = \arg\max_{\Theta} E_{old} \log P(H^{\mathbf{T}}, H^{\mathbf{I}}, \mathbf{T}, \mathbf{I}) \tag{12}$$

where $E_{old} = E_{P(H^{\mathbf{T}}, H^{\mathbf{I}} | \mathbf{T}, \mathbf{I}, \Theta_{old})}$.

E-step: Given known $\mathbf{T}, \mathbf{I}, \Theta_{old}$, the distribution $P(H^{\mathbf{T}}, H^{\mathbf{I}} | \mathbf{T}, \mathbf{I}, \Theta_{old})$ over the hidden variables is easy to infer. $P(H^{\mathbf{T}}, H^{\mathbf{I}} | \mathbf{T}, \mathbf{I}, \Theta_{old})$ decomposes into a product of

$$P(h_p^{\mathbf{T}}, h_p^{\mathbf{I}} | \mathbf{T}_p, \mathbf{I}_p, \Theta_{old}) \tag{13}$$

for each pixel $\mathbf{p}$, using pixel independence assumption. Since $h_p^{\mathbf{T}}, h_p^{\mathbf{I}}$ are discrete binary variables, we can get the conditional probability for any pixel $\mathbf{p}$, hidden values $b_1, b_2 \in \{0, 1\}$, by:

$$P(h_p^{\mathbf{T}} = b_1, h_p^{\mathbf{I}} = b_2 | \mathbf{T}_p, \mathbf{I}_p) =$$

$$\frac{P(h_p^{\mathbf{T}}=b_1, h_p^{\mathbf{I}}=b_2, \mathbf{T}_p, \mathbf{I}_p)}{\sum_{a_1 \in \{0,1\}} \sum_{a_2 \in \{0,1\}} P(h_p^{\mathbf{T}}=a_1, h_p^{\mathbf{I}}=a_2, \mathbf{T}_p, \mathbf{I}_p)} \tag{14}$$

Computing the conditional distribution hence requires only evaluating Eq. 7 four times, for the four possible combinations of $h_p^{\mathbf{T}}, h_p^{\mathbf{I}}$ values. We will see below that the objecthood probability $P(h_p^{\mathbf{T}} = 1, h_p^{\mathbf{I}} = 1 | \mathbf{T}_p, \mathbf{I}_p)$ has the role of template-matching pixel weights in the optimization of ω and σ. For the optimization of other parameters, the probabilities $P(h_p^{\mathbf{I}} | \mathbf{T}_p, \mathbf{I}_p), P(h_p^{\mathbf{T}} | \mathbf{T}_p, \mathbf{I}_p)$ are used, and they are obtained from $P(h_p^{\mathbf{T}} = 1, h_p^{\mathbf{I}} = 1 | \mathbf{T}_p, \mathbf{I}_p)$ by simple marginalization.

M-step: For notation convenience, let $P_{old}(H^{\mathbf{T}}, H^{\mathbf{I}}) = P(H^{\mathbf{T}}, H^{\mathbf{I}}|\mathbf{T}, \mathbf{I}, \Theta_{old})$. For a single pixel we have to maximize the expectation of the log of Eq. 7 which, after some manipulation leads to the following update equations:

$$v^{new} = \frac{\sum_{\mathbf{p} \in \mathbf{P}} P_{old}(h_p^{\mathbf{I}}) + P_{old}(h_p^{\mathbf{T}})}{2|\mathbf{P}|} \tag{15}$$

$$\sigma^{new} = \sqrt{\frac{\sum_{\mathbf{p} \in \mathbf{P}} P_{old}(h_p^{\mathbf{I}} = 1, h_p^{\mathbf{T}} = 1)(\mathbf{T}_p - \mathbf{I}_p)^2}{\sum_{\mathbf{p} \in \mathbf{P}} P_{old}(h_p^{\mathbf{I}} = 1, h_p^{\mathbf{T}} = 1)}}$$

As stated before, F can be implemented using two histograms $F = (F^0, F^1)$, with $F^0(c)$, $F^1(c)$ keeping the frequency of pixel value c according to figure (F^0) and background (F^1) histogram respectively. In that case, the update rule would be

$$F^l(c) = \frac{\sum_{p:p=c} P_{old}(h_p^I = l) + P_{old}(h_p^T = l)}{2|\mathbf{P}|} \quad for \ l \in \{0, 1\} \tag{16}$$

However, we use instead a discriminative model. In this case we use the previous pixel weights $P_{old}(h_p^{\mathbf{I}})$, $P_{old}(h_p^{\mathbf{T}})$ as pixel weights when training the parameters F of the model. As for the transformation parameters ω, gathering the terms dependent on it from the expected log-likelihood gives the following optimization problem:

$$\max_{\omega} \sum_{b \in \{0,1\}} \sum_{\mathbf{p} \in \mathbf{P}} [P_{old}(h_p^{\mathbf{I}} = b) \log P(\mathbf{I}_p|h_p^{\mathbf{I}} = b)) \tag{17}$$

$$- \frac{1}{4\sigma^2} \sum_{\mathbf{p} \in \mathbf{P}} P_{old}(h_p^{\mathbf{I}} = 1, h_p^{\mathbf{T}} = 1)(\mathbf{T}_p - \mathbf{I}_p)^2]$$

We see that ω has to optimize a balance of two terms: The first is a foreground (and background) likelihood term, demanding that foreground pixels will correspond to the foreground appearance model (and similarly for background pixels). The second term requires rigid template matching and traditional LK, but only for pixels with high probability of being foreground. The relative weight of the two terms depends on σ, so adaptively changing this parameter moves the emphasis between appearance-based orderless matching and rigid template matching. We next see that the Gauss Newton optimization technique used in standard LK can be extended for the new objective function.

2.4   ELK Optimization Algorithm

maximizing Equation 17 in the context of a forward-additive LK algorithm is straightforward. Given image $\mathbf{I}$ taken at time t, we use F, the parameters of the conditional distribution, to obtain a log probability images for foreground $\mathbf{I}_1 = \log P(\mathbf{I}|h^{\mathbf{I}} = 1)$ and background $\mathbf{I}_0 = \log P(\mathbf{I}|h^{\mathbf{I}} = 0)$. Then, we use the standard first order Taylor expansion to approximate each of them and arrive at the following objective function that we wish to maximize:

$$L(\Delta\omega) = \sum_{\mathbf{p}\in\mathbf{P}} \{ \mathbf{Q_0}(\mathbf{p})[\mathbf{I_0}(\mathbf{p},\omega) + \nabla\mathbf{I_0}\frac{dW(\omega)}{d\omega}\Delta\omega] \tag{18}$$

$$+\mathbf{Q_1}(\mathbf{p})[\mathbf{I_1}(W(\mathbf{p},\omega)) + \nabla\mathbf{I_1}\frac{dW(\omega)}{d\omega}\Delta\omega]$$

$$-\mathbf{Q}(\mathbf{p})[\mathbf{T}(\mathbf{p}) - \mathbf{I}(W(\mathbf{p},\omega)) - \nabla\mathbf{I}\frac{dW(\omega)}{d\omega}\Delta\omega]^2 \}$$

where

$$\mathbf{Q_0}(\mathbf{p}) = P_{old}(h^{\mathbf{I}}(W(\mathbf{p},\omega)) = 0) \tag{19}$$

$$\mathbf{Q_1}(\mathbf{p}) = P_{old}(h^{\mathbf{I}}(W(\mathbf{p},\omega)) = 1)$$

$$\mathbf{Q}(\mathbf{p}) = \frac{1}{4\sigma^2}P_{old}(h^{\mathbf{I}}(W(\mathbf{p},\omega)) = 1, h^{\mathbf{T}}(\mathbf{p}) = 1)$$

Equation 18 is an extension of the standard LK objective function. The third row works on the input image $\mathbf{I}$ and is the regular LK objective function measuring the similarity between the template and the image, weighted by $\mathbf{Q}$. This term requires the pixels of the template and image to match each other, but only if both of them are likely to be object pixels. The first row works on the (log) likelihood background image $\mathbf{I_0}$ and requires the motion to match the prior assignment of pixels to foreground and background, as given by the weight function $\mathbf{Q_0}$. Similarly, the second row works on the (log) likelihood foreground image $\mathbf{I_1}$ and requires the motion to match the prior assignment of pixels to foreground and background, as given by the weight function $\mathbf{Q_1}$.

Taking the derivative of L with respect to $\Delta\omega$, setting it to 0 and rearranging into the following vector notation:

$$V_0 = \sum_{\mathbf{p}\in\mathbf{P}} \mathbf{Q_0}(\mathbf{p})\nabla\mathbf{I_0}\frac{dW(\omega)}{d\omega} \tag{20}$$

$$V_1 = \sum_{\mathbf{p}\in\mathbf{P}} \mathbf{Q_1}(\mathbf{p})\nabla\mathbf{I_1}\frac{dW(\omega)}{d\omega}$$

$$V = \sum_{\mathbf{p}\in\mathbf{P}} \mathbf{Q}(\mathbf{p})[\mathbf{T}(\mathbf{p}) - \mathbf{I}(W(\mathbf{p},\omega))]\nabla\mathbf{I}\frac{dW(\omega)}{d\omega}$$

$$M = \sum_{\mathbf{p}\in\mathbf{P}} \mathbf{Q}(\mathbf{p})[\nabla\mathbf{I}\frac{dW(\omega)}{d\omega}]^T[\nabla\mathbf{I}\frac{dW(\omega)}{d\omega}]$$

Leads to the following equation:

$$V_0 + V_1 - 2V + 2M\Delta\omega = 0 \tag{21}$$

And the solution is:

$$\Delta\omega = M^{-1}(V - \frac{V_0 + V_1}{2}) = M^{-1}V - M^{-1}(\frac{V_0 + V_1}{2}) \tag{22}$$

where the vectors V_0, V_1, V_2, V are in R^l (l is the number of parameters of the transformation, i.e., $l = 6$ for 2D affine transformation) and the matrix M is an invertible $l \times l$ matrix.

We obtained a simple extension of the standard LK solution which is $\Delta \omega = M^{-1}V$ in our current notation, by adding a term corresponding to the gradient of the foreground / background (log) likelihood. Like in standard LK this step should be iterated several times until convergence, and repeating the algorithm in multiple scales can enhance the convergence range.

Note that since $\mathbf{Q(p)}$ is inversely proportional to σ (see Eq. 19), so is the vector V and the matrix M, but not V_0, V_1. The term $M^{-1}V$ is invariant to σ, but the newly added term $M^{-1}\left(\frac{V_0+V_1}{2}\right)$ is proportional to σ. Small σ values hence lead to the traditional LK algorithm, and large σ emphasizes the new term. This is reasonable, as large σ corresponds to a weak demand for template matching.

Figure 2 illustrates the main components of ELK. When a new image arrives, we wish to maximize the expected log likelihood (Eq. 17) containing the two terms. In this case, trying to match the template, or the foreground/background images separately leads to wrong answer. Only the combined optimization function tracks the template correctly.

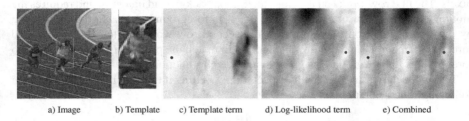

a) Image   b) Template   c) Template term   d) Log-likelihood term   e) Combined

Fig. 2. Contribution of new log-likelihood terms to combined optimization function. From left to right: a) Image with final target bounding box overlaid. b) Target template. c) optimization function template matching term (weighted SSD), maximum marked in blue (brighter is better). d) optimization function combined log-likelihood terms, maximum marked in red. e) Combined optimization function including both template and log-likelihood, maximum marked in green. On their own both template matching and log-likelihood terms do not point to the correct target position however the combined loss does point out the correct target position.

3   Experiments

We evaluate ELK tracking performance using two data-sets[1]. The first is a recently published tracking benchmark [26]. comparing 29 tracking algorithms on a challenging set of 50 sequences. The sequences include abrupt motion, object deformations, in/out-of-plane rotations, illumination changes, occlusions, blur and clutter. The second dataset [22], also containing 50 sequences, depicts road scenes captured from 3 backwards facing cameras mounted on a maneuvering vehicle. The data contains vehicle targets

---

[1] Code and data will be made available at
http://www.eng.tau.ac.il/~oron/ELK/ELK.html

undergoing severe view point changes related to turning, overtaking maneuvers and going around traffic circles, some examples are shown in figure 5. Results for 7 tracking algorithms have been reported on this data-set, among which are recently published algorithms which produce state-of-the-art results on the benchmark mentioned above.

We adopt the one-pass success criterion, suggested in the benchmark, which quantifies both centering accuracy and scale. We measure the overlap between predicted and ground truth bounding boxes, i.e. the intersection area of the boxes divided by the union area, for each frame. A success curve is then computed for each sequence by measuring the fraction of frames with $overlap \geq threshold$ for $threshold$ values in $[0, 1]$. The success is then averaged over all sequences producing a final curve showing overall performance of each method at every $threshold$ value. In addition the area-under-curve (AUC) is used as a figure of merit to compare between the different tracking methods.

3.1 Implementation Details

For each frame we run a single EM iteration: the transformation ω is optimized for $P_{old}(H^{\mathbf{T}}, H^{\mathbf{I}})$ computed in the previous frame, followed by an E-step to recompute $P(H^{\mathbf{T}}, H^{\mathbf{I}})$. Taking a region-of-interest (ROI) around the last target position, we use two scales, in the lower scale we search only for a 2D-translation in an exhaustive manner. We then use this as an initial guess for the full resolution level where we search for both location and scale using the Gauss-Newton iterations described in section 2.4. We limit the number of Gauss-Newton iterations to 5 per frame. In addition we always consider zero-order-hold (ZOH). This practice was found to help avoid singular scale errors induced by gradient decent. Choosing between these two states is done using a confidence measure as will be explained later.

The images processed are transformed into YCbCr representation, and photometrically scaled to have standard deviation of 1 in every channel. We use a discriminative classifier in order to obtain pixel foreground/background probabilities. The classifier is trained by boosting random decision stumps [1]. Our feature space consists of pixel YCbCr values in a 8x8 window around each pixel as well a histogram-of-oriented-gradients (HOG) feature of 8 bin histograms built in 4 spatial cells of size 2×2. The margins provided by the classifier are transformed into the range $[0, 1]$ using a sigmoid.

In order to cope with target deformations and appearance changes we regularly update both our target model and our foreground/background model every K frames (in our experiments $K = 5$). This is done only when tracking confidence is high meaning we are not occluded or drifting. We use two measures to establish tracking confidence. The first is the weighted mean-square-error (MSE), between the current target image and the predicted target location, normalized by mean weight value (punishing for overall low foreground likelihood). As a threshold for this measure we use twice its median value in a sliding temporal window. The second confidence measure is demanding that the median of the weight map exceeds a threshold (in our experiments we use threshold= 0.75, meaning we require at least 50% of pixels to have foreground likelihood greater than 0.75). The template and foreground/background model are updated only if both measures indicate high confidence. When updating the template we consider the current appearance, the previous appearance, or the initial appearance, taking the one producing the minimal normalized MSE. When updating the foreground/background model the image foreground/background weights are used as weights for classifier training.

We note that using a standard PC our non-optimized Matlab implementation runs at $\sim 1\,fps$, processing rate may vary according to target size.

3.2 Results

For the benchmark data-set [26], ELK produces results comparable to state-of-the-art methods as presented in figure 3. It is ranked in 3rd place for overall performance on this benchmark data-set (among 30 tracking methods evaluated), with AUC of 0.454 (following Struck 0.474 and SCM with 0.499). See table 2 for a full list of tracking methods appearing in all figures. Performance of simple LK tracking (without our extensions) are not presented since the simple LK tracker produces very poor results achieving an AUC score of 0.05. Table 1 presents AUC and ELK rank for different sequence attributes in the benchmark data-set. We observe that ELK ranks first or second for sequences exhibiting out-of-plane rotations or deformation. It also produces decent results for sequences with fast motion scale variations, occlusions and in-plane rotations ranking 4th in all categories. The lowest rank (7) is obtained for sequences with illumination variation. This is not surprising as both template appearance and object / background models suffer from abrupt illumination variations affecting all terms in the optimized.

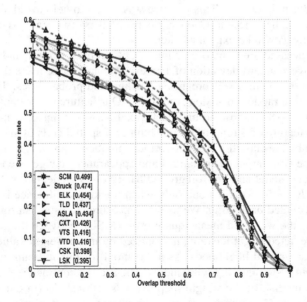

Fig. 3. Success plot for the benchmark data-set [26], showing top 10 methods (out of 30): ELK (in Green) is ranked 3rd in overall performance demonstrating results comparable to state-of-the-art methods (best viewed in color)

Table 1. ELK success and rank for different sequence attributes in the benchmark [26] data-set

Attribute	Number of Seq.	AUC	Rank
In-plane rotation	31	0.430	4
Out-of-plane rotation	39	0.462	2
Deformation	19	0.479	1
Scale variation	28	0.423	4
Occlusion	29	0.409	4
Illumination variation	25	0.390	7
Motion blur	12	0.336	5
Fast motion	17	0.387	4

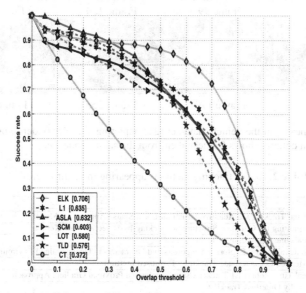

Fig. 4. Success plot for the vehicle data-set [22]: ELK (in Green) is ranked 1st in overall performance, with a large margin, among 8 tracking methods evaluated on this data (best viewed in color).

On the vehicles data set of [22], where template matching plays a more significant role, ELK outperforms all the other methods tested with a significant margin. The success plots are presented in figure 4. As can be seen in figure 5, this data set contains challenging scenarios with respect to viewpoint, scale change, and illumination. However, the fact that vehicles are rigid provide more opportunities for template matching, and makes ELK the clear winner. For this data simple LK achieved AUC of only 0.35.

Frame 1   Frame 1   Frame 1   Frame 1

Frame 101   Frame 99   Frame 154   Frame 74

Frame 220   Frame 170   Frame 255   Frame 130

Fig. 5. Sample frames from the vehicle data-set [22] depicting vehicles undergoing severe view point changes. Each column shows frames taken from the same sequence.

Table 2. List of tracking methods appearing in result figures

Method	Paper
ASLA[14]	Visual Tracking via Adaptive Structural Local Sparse Appearance Model
CSK[13]	Exploiting the Circulant Structure of Tracking-by-Detection with Kernels
CT[29]	Real-time Compressive Tracking
CXT[10]	Context Tracker: Exploring Supporters and Distracters in Unconstrained Environments.
ELK	Extended Lucas Kanade Tracking - **Proposed method**
L1[5]	Real Time Robust L1 Tracker Using Accelerated Proximal Gradient Approach
LOT[23]	Locally Orderless Tracking
LSK[18]	Robust Tracking using Local Sparse Appearance Model and K-Selection
SCM[30]	Robust Object Tracking via Sparsity-based Collaborative Model
Struck[12]	Struck: Structured Output Tracking with Kernels.
TLD[15]	Tracking-Learning-Detection
VTD[16]	Visual Tracking Decomposition
VTS[17]	Tracking by Sampling Trackers

4   Conclusions

ELK is a novel tracking algorithm combining template matching with pixel object / background segregation. This special combination allows ELK to be more resistive to drift as it can perform template matching while disregarding template background pixels. Additionally the new log-likelihood terms introduced into the optimization, can direct the algorithm when deformation, that cannot be accounted for by the template, occur. This allows the algorithm to maintain reliable tracking in the presence of severe deformations until the model is updated.

ELK was demonstrated to produce results comparable to state-of-the-art methods on a recently published tracking data-set ranking 3rd among 30 tracking methods. In addition, on a second challenging data-set, of vehicles undergoing severe view point changes, ELK came in first outperforming 7 other tracking methods.

ELKs performance can be further improved through better occlusion reasoning and explicit handling of illumination variations which is currently a weak spot for the algorithm.

References

1. Appel, R., Fuchs, T., Dollar, P., Perona, P.: Quickly boosting decision trees a pruning under-achieving features early. In: ICML (2013)
2. Avidan, S.: Support vector tracking. PAMI (2004)
3. Avidan, S.: Ensemble tracking. In: CVPR (2005)
4. Babenko, B., Yang, M.H., Belongie, S.: Visual tracking with online multiple instance learn-ing. In: CVPR (2009)
5. Bao, C., Wu, Y., Ling, H., Ji, H.: Real time robust l1 tracker using accelerated proximal gradient approach. In: CVPR (2012)
6. Comaniciu, D., Ramesh, V., Meer, P.: Real-time tracking of non-rigid objects using mean shift. In: CVPR (2000)
7. Cootes, T., Edwards, G., Taylor, C.: Active appearance models. TPAMI (2001)
8. DeGroot, M.: Optimal Statistical Decisions. McGraw-Hill, New York (1970)
9. Dempster, A.P., Laird, N.M., Rubin, D.B.: Maximum likelihood from incomplete data via the em algorithm. Journal of the Royal Statistical Society 39(1), 1–38 (1977)
10. Dinh, T.B., Vo, N., Medioni., G.: Context tracker: Exploring supporters and distracters in unconstrained environments. In: CVPR (2011)
11. Grabner, H., Grabner, M., Bischof, H.: Real-time tracking via online boosting. In: BMVC (2006)
12. Hare, S., Saffari, A., Torr., P.H.S.: Struck: Structured output tracking with kernels. In: ICCV (2011)
13. Henriques, J.F., Caseiro, R., Martins, P., Batista, J.: Exploiting the circulant structure of tracking-by-detection with kernels. In: Fitzgibbon, A., Lazebnik, S., Perona, P., Sato, Y., Schmid, C. (eds.) ECCV 2012, Part IV. LNCS, vol. 7575, pp. 702–715. Springer, Heidelberg (2012)
14. Jia, X., Lu, H., Yang, M.H.: Visual tracking via adaptive structural local sparse appearance model. In: CVPR (2012)
15. Kalal, Z., Mikolajczyk, K., Matas, J.: Tracking-learning-detection. TPAMI (2010)
16. Kwon, J., Lee, K.M.: Visual tracking decomposition. In: CVPR (2010)
17. Kwon, J., Lee, K.M.: Tracking by sampling trackers. In: ICCV (2011)
18. Liu, B., Huang, J., Yang, L., Kulikowsk, C.: Robust tracking using local sparse appearance model and k-selection. In: CVPR (2011)
19. Lucas, B.D., Kanade, T.: An iterative image registration technique with an application to stereo vision. In: Proccedings of Imageing Understanding Workshop (1981)
20. Matthews, I., Baker, S.: Lucas-kanade 20 years on: A unifying framework. IJCV (2004)
21. Matthews, I., Ishikawa, T., Baker, S.: The template update problem. TPAMI (2004)
22. Oron, S., Bar-Hillel, A., Avidan, S.: Real time tracking-with-detection. Submitted to Machine Vision and Applications (2014)
23. Oron, S., Hillel, A.B., Levi, D., Avidan, S.: Locally orderless tracking. In: CVPR (2012)

24. Ross, D., Lim, J., Lin, R.S., Yang, M.H.: Incremental learning for robust visual tracking. IJCV (2007)
25. Stauffer, C., Grimson, E.: Learning patterns of activity using real-time tracking. PAMI (2000)
26. Wu, Y., Lim, J., Yang, M.H.: Online object tracking: A benchmark. In: CVPR (2013)
27. Xiang, Y., Song, C., Mottaghi, R., Savarese, S.: Monocular multiview object tracking with 3d aspect parts. In: European Conference on Computer Vision, ECCV (2014)
28. Yilmaz, A., Javed, O., Shah, M.: Object tracking: A survey. ACM. Comp. Survey 38(4) (2006)
29. Zhang, K., Zhang, L., Yang, M.-H.: Real-time compressive tracking. In: Fitzgibbon, A., Lazebnik, S., Perona, P., Sato, Y., Schmid, C. (eds.) ECCV 2012, Part III. LNCS, vol. 7574, pp. 864–877. Springer, Heidelberg (2012)
30. Zhong, W., Lu, H., Yang, M.H.: Robust object tracking via sparsity-based collaborative model. In: CVPR (2012)

Appearances Can Be Deceiving: Learning Visual Tracking from Few Trajectory Annotations*

Santiago Manen[1], Junseok Kwon[1], Matthieu Guillaumin[1], and Luc Van Gool[1,2]

[1] Computer Vision Laboratory, ETH Zurich, Switzerland
[2] ESAT - PSI / IBBT, K.U. Leuven, Belgium
{smanenfr,kwonj,guillaumin,vangool}@vision.ee.ethz.ch

Abstract. Visual tracking is the task of estimating the trajectory of an object in a video given its initial location. This is usually done by combining at each step an appearance and a motion model. In this work, we learn from a small set of training trajectory annotations how the objects in the scene typically move. We learn the relative weight between the appearance and the motion model. We call this weight: *visual deceptiveness*. At test time, we transfer the deceptiveness and the displacement from the closest trajectory annotation to infer the next location of the object. Further, we condition the transference on an event model. On a set of 161 manually annotated test trajectories, we show in our experiments that learning from just 10 trajectory annotations *halves* the center location error and improves the success rate by about 10%.

Keywords: Visual tracking, Motion learning, Event modelling.

1 Introduction

Visual object tracking from static cameras is an important topic of computer vision with applications in video surveillance, traffic monitoring, and augmented reality [27]. Typically, visual tracking starts with the initial location of the object in an initial frame. Then, an appearance model which is continuously updated attempts to localize the object at each subsequent frame [20,18,16,19,8].

An aspect of tracking in surveillance video that is often disregarded is the possibility to generalize from a set of annotated trajectories of other objects, *i.e.* supervised learning of visual tracking. Using trajectories as training data poses two main challenges which have discouraged the tracking community. First, trajectories are sequential data and objects can adopt a wide variety of trajectories. Hence, predicting trajectories is very challenging and its functional form is much more complex than for recognition and detection [4]. Second, such annotations are more costly to obtain than bounding boxes or class labels. Despite these problems, we believe that trajectories are very informative for a given scene, such that a few may suffice to robustly learn visual tracking. As any learning

---

* Electronic supplementary material - Supplementary material is available in the online version of this chapter at http://dx.doi.org/10.1007/978-3-319-10602-1_11. Videos can also be accessed at http://www.springerimages.com/videos/978-3-319-10601-4

D. Fleet et al. (Eds.): ECCV 2014, Part V, LNCS 8693, pp. 157–172, 2014.
© Springer International Publishing Switzerland 2014

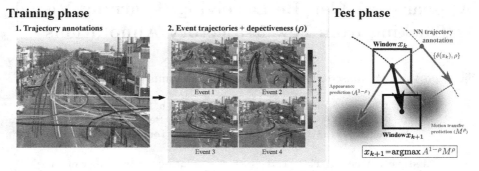

Fig. 1. At training time, we obtain trajectory annotations (1) we associate them to the events in the scene and we learn their *visual deceptiveness* ρ (2). At test time (right), we transfer displacement δ and deceptiveness ρ from the closest annotations in the same event and combine it with the appearance model to predict the next location of the object. (All our figures are best viewed in color)

scenario, our framework has two phases, as shown in Fig. 1. The first is a *training phase*, where annotated data is collected for a scene and a model for tracking is learnt. The second is to use this model to improve tracking in a *test* sequence of the same scene, where previously unseen objects are tracked from their initial bounding boxes. We run experiments on traffic surveillance videos and show that even a few trajectory annotations considerably improve tracking performance.

Similar to other visual tracking methods, we use a mixture of *appearance* (A) and *motion* (M) models [27]. Our motion model is based on transferring displacements observed in the training set and the mixture weight $\rho \in [0, 1]$ between A and M is determined at every step of tracking, also using transfer from annotated trajectories (*c.f.* Fig. 1). In essence, this mixture weight captures the situations in which the appearance of an object is not reliable for tracking. For this reason, we refer to ρ as *visual deceptiveness*. Importantly, in our framework, the user does not provide ρ for the ground-truth trajectories, but instead we propose an automatic way to learn it. As we show in this paper, the regions with high deceptiveness typically align with the failure cases of the appearance model: occlusions with static objects, tracking of small objects, bad lighting conditions.

Furthermore, we propose to associate the trajectories and their deceptiveness to the events discovered by [13]. In essence, [13] segments the video in consistent optical flow prototypes. This association improves the robustness of our deceptiveness estimation and removes ambiguities when transferring displacements. We show in our experiments that combining events and deceptiveness produces the best results in our datasets and improves over the state of the art [6,7,8].

In summary, our main contributions are: i) A framework to learn the visual deceptiveness of annotated trajectories, which are automatically selected; ii) A motion model based on transferring displacement and deceptiveness from trajectories; iii) The conditioning of this transfer on an event model; iv) The thorough evaluation of performance on two fully annotated test videos (with 161 trajectories in total, publicly available online). In the following, we first discuss related work in Sec. 2. We then present our tracking model in Sec. 3 and, in Sec. 4, the training procedure, *i.e.*, how visual deceptiveness is learnt and tracks selected for annotation. The conditioning on the event model is presented in Sec. 5 and our experimental validation in Sec. 6. We draw conclusions in Sec. 7.

2   Related Work

There are many works on single and multiple target tracking [3,10,24,15,23]. The most relevant ones are those based on motion prior and trajectory patterns.

Spatial Motion Prior. Several authors [1,30] have proposed tracking methods that uses static, space-dependent fields as a motion prior. These works simply encode the dominant direction of motion for each spatial region, limiting their use to simple videos. Rodriguez *et al.* [22] extended this idea with a set of motion directions, able to capture time-varying patterns. Further spatio-temporal dependencies between nearby motion patterns have been recently explored by Liu *et al.* [17] for tracking sport players. There, the authors exploit correlations between players and hand-designed motion rules for sport games.

We go beyond these works by conditioning our motion model spatially and temporally, without any further assumptions on the type of scene. We rely on a state-of-the-art unsupervised event discovery model [13] to capture, via optical flow prototypes, the dynamics of motion in a scene.

Analyzing Trajectory Patterns. In our work, we automatically select which trajectories should be annotated by a user. This relates to works, mostly on human tracking, that find typical trajectories patterns in videos. Zhou *et al.* [31] analyze the collective behavior of pedestrians in crowded scenes. They identify trajectory clusters and derive a generative model from which trajectories can be simulated. Similarly, when tracking in a simple physical environment, Kitani *et al.* [11] are able to predict plausible paths and destinations of people. These methods learn trajectory patterns in an unsupervised manner, hence assuming that automatic tracking succeeds. They are thus limited to scenarios where failures are relatively rare. In difficult tracking situations, [29] and [17] resort to a large amount of manually annotated trajectories. As this is very time-consuming, they have focused on a domain where tracks can be easily re-used: sport fields.

In our traffic scenes, automatic tracks fail rather often, so manual annotations are also necessary to correct them. To reduce the annotation cost as much as possible, our method automatically selects which trajectories shall be annotated.

Combining Motion and Appearance. Combining appearance and motion models has already been explored by various works. Yang and Nevatia [26] combined motion patterns and appearance models for multiple object tracking, but without assessing which component is more critical to the success of tracking. Cifuentes *et al.* [2] studies tracking with moving cameras and automatically chooses at each frame the most appropriate among six simple camera motion models (*e.g.*, "travelling", "forward", etc.). For single-object tracking, Kwon and Lee [14] proposed an MCMC sampling method to select, at each frame, the best tracker out of a pool of independent motion and appearance trackers.

In these works, the trackers are independent or naïvely combined. In contrast, we integrate motion and appearance in a single mixture model tracker, and we learn at training time how to adapt this weight dynamically to minimize tracking errors at test time. Notably, this weight (the *visual deceptiveness*) is not a fixed value: it depends on the time and the location of the object to track.

3 Tracking with Motion and Deceptiveness Transfer

In this section, we describe our tracking model. For now, we assume that a set $\mathcal{T}$ of trajectory annotations with their respective local deceptiveness is available. As explained in the introduction, the *visual deceptiveness* ρ is a mixture weight which has a high value when the appearance model is less reliable. Thus, it identifies image regions where tracking based on appearance is more difficult.

More formally, let x_k be the current estimated position of the tracked object at frame k and $y_{1:k}$ be the set of all previous observations until this step. Then, like most single object tracking methods [7,14], we compute the posterior distribution of the location at frame k based on the following Bayesian filtering:

$$p(x_{k+1}|y_{1:k+1}) \propto \underbrace{p(y_{k+1}|x_{k+1})}_{A(y_{k+1}|x_{k+1})^{1-\rho}} \underbrace{\int p(x_{k+1}|x_k)p(x_k|y_{1:k})\mathrm{d}x_k}_{M(x_{k+1}|y_{1:k})^{\rho}}, \tag{1}$$

where we have highlighted the definitions of A, M and ρ. In the equation above, we have abstracted the *appearance* model A, a *motion* model M and a weight ρ between the two. The value of ρ depends on x_k and determines the relative weight between the motion model and the appearance model.

As appearance model, we use the tracker of [7], which was shown to be the state of the art [25]. This model predicts the most likely location for the object in frame $k+1$ based on the appearance model trained up to frame k.

Displacement Transfer Motion Model. Our motion model, illustrated in Fig. 1, is based on *transferring* a displacement probability distribution from ground-truth trajectories, which we model as a Gaussian distribution:

$$M(x_{k+1}|y_{1:k}) = \mathcal{N}(x_k + \delta(x_k), \sigma_M), \tag{2}$$

where $\delta(x_k)$ is the displacement at x_k as estimated from $\mathcal{T}$, and σ_M is a fixed variance. Note that x_k is uniquely determined by $y_{1:k}$. From $\mathcal{T}$, we also estimate $\rho(x_k)$, which leads to the following expression for the probability of x_{k+1}:

$$p(x_{k+1}|y_{1:k+1}) \propto A(y_{k+1}|x_{k+1})^{1-\rho(x_k)}\mathcal{N}(x_k + \delta(x_k), \sigma_M)^{\rho(x_k)}. \tag{3}$$

Similarly to [7], the scale and aspect ratio of the windows are sampled.

Nearest Neighbor Displacement and Deceptiveness Estimation from $\mathcal{T}$. Let $\mathcal{T} = \{\bar{x}_{k'}^i, i \in [1, \cdots, N]\}$ be the set of annotated trajectories, where $\bar{x}_{k'}^i$ is the bounding box of trajectory $\bar{x}^i$ at time k'. Since $\mathcal{T}$ contains few annotations, we estimate the displacement $\delta(x_k)$ and deceptiveness $\rho(x_k)$ using the nearest neighbour bounding-box $\bar{x}_{k'}^i$ of x_k in $\mathcal{T}$ and use its deceptiveness $\rho(\bar{x}_{k'}^i)$, but only if $\bar{x}_{k'}^i$ is close enough. Formally, we use

$\bar{x}^i_{k'} = \operatorname{argmin}_{b \in \mathcal{T}} d(x_k, b) = \|c(x_k) - c(b)\| \cdot (1 - IoU(x_k, b))$, where $c(\cdot)$ is the center of a window, $\|\cdot\|$ is the Euclidean norm and $IoU(\cdot, \cdot)$ is the intersection over union of two windows, and:

$$\delta(x_k) = \begin{cases} \bar{x}^i_{k'+1} - \bar{x}^i_{k'} & \text{if } d(x_k, \bar{x}^i_{k'}) \leq \kappa \\ 0 & \text{otherwise} \end{cases} \quad \text{and} \quad \rho(x_k) = \begin{cases} \rho(\bar{x}^i_{k'}) & \text{if } d(x_k, \bar{x}^i_{k'}) \leq \kappa \\ 0 & \text{otherwise.} \end{cases}$$

$$(4)$$

That is, if $\bar{x}^i_{k'}$ is further than κ, our model falls back to the appearance model alone. This κ threshold avoids transferring from too distant neighbours. In our experiments, we use a σ_M of 2 pixels and a κ of 25.

4   Training Phase: Learning to Track

An important contribution of our work is to learn, from a set of trajectory annotations, the visual deceptiveness of the scene, *c.f.* Sec. 4.1. Annotating trajectories is a tedious task, so we want to limit their number. We present in Sec. 4.2 a method to automatically select which tracks the user should annotate.

4.1   Learning the Visual Deceptiveness of Tracks

The crux of our system is the visual deceptiveness $\rho \in [0, 1]$ of trajectories, *i.e.*, the relative weight between motion and appearance models to be used when tracking (*c.f.* Eq. (3)). We propose to learn it in 2 steps from a set of annotated trajectories $\mathcal{T}$. We first learn a *raw deceptiveness* $\widetilde{\rho}$ independently for each ground-truth trajectory. As $\widetilde{\rho}$ tends to overfit to its own track, in the second step we diffuse it across neighboring trajectories to obtain a more consistent deceptiveness ρ that generalizes better. We detail these steps below.

Learning Raw Deceptiveness from One Trajectory. In this section we want to learn the raw deceptiveness $\widetilde{\rho}$ of a single ground-truth trajectory. This is a vector of values $\widetilde{\rho}_k$ for each frame k in the trajectory. We learn it by tracking the object automatically and seeing where and how much ground-truth motion information is needed to reproduce the ground-truth object trajectory.

Problem formulation. We start with the important observation that $\widetilde{\rho}$ should be *sparse*, *i.e.*, rely on appearance as much as possible instead of motion. This prevents overfitting and ensures that unobserved or unexpected behavior of the objects will still be captured. In other words, we want $\widetilde{\rho} > 0$ only when strictly necessary. We encode this objective with the following optimization problem:

$$\begin{aligned} \underset{\widetilde{\rho}}{\text{minimize}} \quad & \sum_{k=1}^{T} \widetilde{\rho}_k \\ \text{subject to} \quad & \forall k \in [1, T], \quad 0 \leq \widetilde{\rho}_k \leq 1, \\ & \text{trackingError}(\widetilde{\rho}) \leq \theta, \end{aligned}$$

$$(5)$$

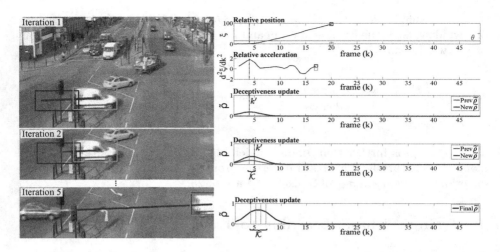

Fig. 2. We learn how to make the tracker reproduce a trajectory that is closer than trackingError to the ground-truth. We start by completely trusting appearance ($\widetilde{\rho}=0$) and we track with it. If trackingError goes over θ then an update is applied to $\widetilde{\rho}$ and we restart tracking. The process is repeated until $\widetilde{\rho}$ is high enough to fulfill the trackingError constraint. (NB: The original images have been flipped for clarity.)

where trackingError is a function that measures the overall error made by the tracker over the full trajectory and $\theta \geq 0$ is the threshold we use to decide whether the tracking was successful. In our experiments, we use the common *Center Location Error* (CLE) as trackingError. When tracking an object during T frames, trackingError $= \sum_{k=1}^{T} \xi_k / T$, where ξ_k is the distance at frame k between the center location of the automatic and the ground-truth trajectories.

Note that a solution always exists: setting $\widetilde{\rho}$ to **1**, the tracker is simply reproducing the ground-truth and the trackingError is 0. In practice, this never happens with the relatively loose error threshold θ of 15 pixels that we use.

Deceptiveness as a set of local Gaussian updates. The optimization problem in Eq. (5) is very general and complex to solve because the tracking error depends on the full trajectory and the full sequence of $\widetilde{\rho}$. Fortunately, we can exploit the cumulative nature of trackingError and the sequential properties of tracking (as detailed below and in the supplementary material) to derive an efficient algorithm that starts from $\widetilde{\rho} = \mathbf{0}$ and iteratively increments it until the trackError constraint is fulfilled. To do so, we propose to model $\widetilde{\rho}$ as the truncated sum of a set of *local spatial Gaussian updates* $\mathcal{G} = \{g(\cdot | k_i')\}_{i=1...N_c}$, where each Gaussian update g has a fixed standard deviation σ_{up} and is centered around a frame k_i':

$$\widetilde{\rho}_k = \min\left(1, \sum_{i=1}^{N_c} g(k|k_i')\right), \qquad g(k|k_i') = \widetilde{\mathcal{N}}(s(k)|s(k_i'), \sigma_{\mathrm{up}}), \qquad (6)$$

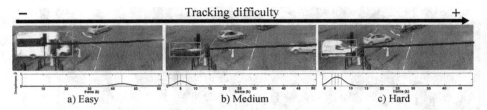

Fig. 3. Learning $\tilde{\rho}$ independently for each object can give different results. Compared to b), a) is easier to track because it is bigger and c) is harder to track because it contrasts more with the occluding traffic lights.

where $s(k)$ is the cumulative distance from the frame 1 to frame k. Since the values of $\tilde{\rho}$ are now sums over local Gaussian updates, learning $\tilde{\rho}$ becomes finding the (small) set $\mathcal{G}$ of frames k'_i where to apply those updates. Notably, multiple updates will accumulate near the most deceptive regions of a track.

In practice, we set σ_{up} to the size of the bounding box and g has a maximum response of 0.2 at the center of the Gaussian, hence the notation $\tilde{\mathcal{N}}$.

Optimization process. Using this new definition of $\tilde{\rho}$, we now describe our variation of backjumping [21] to optimize of Eq. (5), as illustrated in Fig. 2. We initialize $\mathcal{G} = \varnothing$, $\tilde{\rho} = 0$ and $k = 1$, and repeat the following steps:

1. We track the object using $\tilde{\rho}$ from frame k until failure or end of track.
   If we reached the end of the track, we return $\tilde{\rho}$ as the solution.
   Otherwise we continue with the following:
2. We find the frame k' where the relative acceleration between the track and the ground-truth is maximum, *i.e.*, we use the 2nd-order derivative of ξ_k.
   We add $g(\cdot|k')$ to the set of local updates $\mathcal{G}$ and remove from $\mathcal{G}$ all the updates on later frames, since they are now potentially irrelevant.
3. We recompute $\tilde{\rho}$ as for the new set of local Gaussians $\mathcal{G}$. Let $k'' < k'$ be the first frame for which the deceptiveness was impacted by this update.
4. We set $k = k''-1$ and go back to step 1.

In this algorithm, we have exploited many observations. First, trackingError is cumulative, hence we know that the tracking has failed as soon as the partial error reaches θ. Second, a failure at frame k can only be recovered with updates on earlier frames. Finally, an update at frame k invalidates all the later updates but does not affect earlier tracking.

To further prevent overfitting, we post-process as described below the deceptiveness of ground-truth tracks $\tilde{\rho}$ to ensure spatial consistency.

Spatial Diffusion of Raw Deceptiveness. Some objects, due to size and appearance, are harder to track than others, *c.f.* Fig. 3. Therefore, the learnt $\tilde{\rho}$ are not always good estimates of the deceptiveness for all tracks. We aim to learn an *underlying* deceptiveness ρ that is *consistent* for neighboring annotations, hence finding regions in the scene where appearance is deceiving, *c.f.* Fig. 4.

To this end, we propose diffusing the $\tilde{\rho}$ across the image pixels with [12], employing a grid-graph with 8-connected neighbourhoods. The graph has pairwise

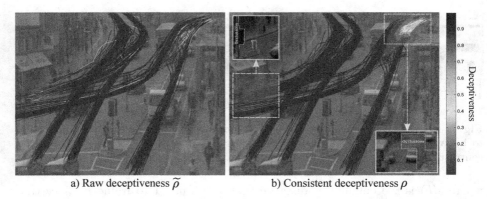

a) Raw deceptiveness $\widetilde{\rho}$ b) Consistent deceptiveness ρ

Fig. 4. Comparison of raw and consistent deceptiveness. Note the variability of $\widetilde{\rho}$ and how ρ manages to detect the underlying difficult zones, cropped occlusions in b). The intensity of ρ translates to the difficulty of the occlusions.

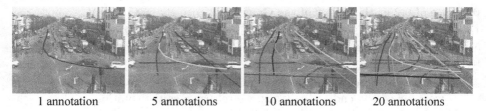

1 annotation   5 annotations   10 annotations   20 annotations

Fig. 5. Trajectory annotations we obtain with the IAP annotation selection method

potentials encouraging smoothness via l_2-norm between neighbouring ρ values and unaries trying to preserve the original $\widetilde{\rho}$. Specifically, we define N_{ij} as the number of trajectories that include pixel (i, j). For each pixel (i, j) with at least one observation ($N_{ij} > 0$), we assign it a representative observation $\widetilde{\rho}_{ij}$, which is the average of the observations in a spatial neighbourhood of radius of 25% of the average size of the windows. We then use $\widetilde{\rho}_{ij}$ to define unary potentials:

$$U_{ij}(\rho) = \begin{cases} \mathcal{N}(\rho|\widetilde{\rho}_{ij}, \sigma_D) & \text{if } N_{ij} > 0 \\ \text{Unif}(0, 1) & \text{otherwise,} \end{cases} \tag{7}$$

which we discretize uniformly in 11 values: $0, 0.1, \ldots, 1$. That is, for pixels with observations ($Nij > 0$) our unary is a Gaussian centered around $\widetilde{\rho}_{ij}$ with a fixed standard deviation $\sigma_D = 0.2$. Otherwise ($N_{ij} = 0$), the unary is uniform.

Our experiments show that this diffusion improves tracking at test time.

4.2   Automatic Annotation Selection

In our work, we aim at improving tracking performance by exploiting trajectory annotations. As already argued, we want to limit the number of annotations that the user has to provide. Thus, we propose to first automatically select the most *representative* and *diverse* trajectories using a variant of Affinity Propagation (AP, [5]), which we denote as *Incremental Affinity Propagation* (IAP).

Using AP is beneficial in our scenario. First, it is a clustering algorithm which is based on *data similarities*, which are more natural for sequential data such as tracks than data points. Second, AP is an *exemplar-based* clustering method that selects the data sample that is the most representative for each cluster.

However, AP has the drawback that the exemplars for K clusters need not be a superset of the exemplars for $K' < K$ clusters. Ideally, if the user has already annotated K' tracks, observes that the performance can still be improved and believes that annotating $K > K'$ could help, then only $K-K'$ new tracks should be needed, and not K. Thus, whether the user chooses to annotate tracks one-by-one or by batches has no influence on the final tracking performance.

To achieve this property, we use the so-called *data preference* value P_i to ensure that, when AP returns a set ψ_N of N exemplars, it is a superset of ψ_{N-1}. This is done in a incremental fashion by modifying P_i dynamically, using P_i^k at step k. We start with $P_i^1 = \lambda_1$, a constant value determined so that only one exemplar is chosen: $\psi_1 = \{t_{i_1}\}$. Then, at each subsequent step $k \geq 2$, we assign an infinite preference to the already selected trajectories ψ_{k-1}, *i.e.*, $P_i^k = \infty$ if $t_i \in \psi_{k-1}$, and λ_k otherwise. λ_k is found by bisection such as AP returns a set of k exemplars, ψ_k. In practice, the sequence of λ_k is progressively increasing. This process is repeated until N trajectories have been incrementally clustered.

To define track similarities, we first represent a track t_i by a set of $Q = 50$ trajectory centers interpolated uniformly in space: $t_i = \{c_j^i, j = 1 \ldots Q\}$. Interpolation in space is a very effective way to account for variation in time and speed, while avoiding to resort to more complex methods such as dynamic time warping. Then, for a pair of trajectories (t_i, t_j), we define their asymmetric similarity $\hat{s}(t_i, t_j)$ as $\hat{s}(t_i, t_j) = -\sum_{k=1}^{Q} \min_l \|c_k^i - c_l^j\|^2$. Finally, we symmetrize the similarities using $S(t_i, t_j) = \frac{1}{2} (\hat{s}(t_i, t_j) + \hat{s}(t_j, t_i))$.

Fig. 5 shows the trajectory annotations we obtain with this procedure. We show in the experiments that IAP yields more useful annotations than a random trajectory selection, especially for a small number of annotations.

5   Conditioning Transfer on an Event Model

The flow of objects in structured scenes typically presents patterns and spatio-temporal dependencies [13,1]. We build upon the model and code of [13] to exploit this idea and improve tracking performance. Put simply, [13] learns a Hidden Markov Model (HMM) temporal segmentation of the video by finding prototypical optical flows, (*c.f.* Fig. 6). The states of the HMM correspond to *events* and the transition probabilities between such events are also learnt. We can use this HMM to assign a global event to each frame in a video of the same scene. In our videos, it successfully detects high-level sequences in the scene, such as traffic light cycles. Among the benefits of [13], it is completely unsupervised, so we train it with sequences of 30 minutes without requiring any user interaction,

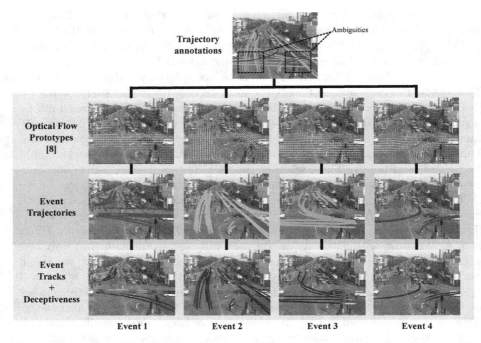

Fig. 6. Illustration of our full learning phase with 40 annotations for *Hospedales1*, with trajectories and deceptiveness conditioned on events. Ambiguous regions present in the original annotations (top) do not occur in event trajectories.

and it automatically finds the optimal number of events. To exploit the events, we adapt both the training and test phases as described below.

Training Phase. We use the HMM model to infer the event s_k of each frame k in the training set. Then, the bounding-boxes $\bar{x}_k^i$ of trajectories i in frame k are augmented with the event information. That is, a trajectory annotation i is now composed of a sequence of location, deceptiveness and event triplets $\left\{(\bar{x}_k^i, \rho_k^i, s_k^i)\right\}_k$. The event model does not impact how we learn the raw deceptiveness $\tilde{\rho}$, since it is learned individually for each trajectory, but we apply the spatial smoothing separately for each event and its associated (sub-)trajectories.

Test Phase. We also infer the most probable event segmentation of the test sequences using the HMM model. Thereby also obtaining an event s_k for each frame k. Then, we condition the nearest neighbour search described in Sec. 3 on s_k. We do this by simply restricting the search on the subset of the trajectory annotations that are also assigned to s_k: $\bar{x}_{k'}^i = \operatorname{argmin}_{(b,\cdot,s_k)\in\mathcal{T}} d(x_k, b)$. After $\bar{x}_{k'}^i$ is found, its displacement and deceptiveness are transferred as in Sec. 3.

Fig. 6 shows how associating the trajectory annotations to events prevents ambiguities that can appear when searching the nearest neighbor. This conditioning corresponds to grouping the trajectory annotations by event, so we refer to these groups as *event trajectories*. Note from Fig. 6 how the trajectory annotations are much more powerful than optical flow in regions where objects are small or occluded. We show in the experiments that this association has a considerable impact on the tracking performance at test time.

6   Experiments

We present in this section our experimental setup and results. In Sec. 6.1 we first describe our datasets and evaluation metrics. The remainder of the section is split in two parts: we first show in Sec. 6.2 a comparison with the state of the art and then, in Sec. 6.3, we evaluate the impact of the different components of our framework on the final results. We use the same parameters for all the experiments, as defined in the previous chapters. We also provide an analysis of the speed of our method in Sec. 6.4.

6.1   Dataset and Experimental Protocol

For our experiments, we have used two different scenarios from [13], denoted as *Hospedales1*, (*c.f.* Fig. 6), and *Hospedales3*, (*c.f.* Fig. 4). These two scenarios show two different crossings with heavy vehicle traffic and traffic light cycles. They are challenging due to occlusions, appearance changes (vehicles turning), low resolution and entry/exit points at the horizon.

We have used [28] to create 61 and 100 test track annotations, respectively, for a total length of 112,345 frames (74.5 minutes). For training, we collected 517 and 341 additional trajectory annotations, respectively. We have created them on a completely separate span of time of 10 minutes in each scene. In total we have 858 available training tracks.[1] However, our method only needs a small subset of them. This larger number of training tracks will help us evaluate important aspects of our method: (i) How does the tracking performance evolve as we use more trajectory annotations? (ii) Are our automatically selected tracks better than randomly selected tracks? We provide answers in Sec. 6.3.

Concerning the event discovery model of [13], since it is unsupervised, we trained it on a 30-minute clip for each sequence, without the need for human intervention or annotation. These training clips were chosen such that they do not contain any of the objects of the test sequences.

To measure performance, we use two popular tracking performance metrics [25]: the *Center Location Error* (CLE) and the *Success Plot* (SP). CLE averages for each target object and each frame the distance between the center of the estimated window and the center of the ground-truth window. The Success Plot measures the percentage of frames where the target object is successfully detected for a certain intersection-over-union (*IoU*) threshold [25], *i.e.* the detection rate. For one target object, detection rate is plotted as a function of *IoU*, as it is varied between 0 and 1. To summarize the plots for all target objects, we compute their areas-under-the-curve (*AuC*) and we refer to the average over tracks as SP. A high-performing tracker will have a low CLE and a high SP.

---

[1] This data is available on **www.vision.ee.ethz.ch/~smanenfr/deceptiveness**

Table 1. Comparison with the state of the art on 61 tracks in *Hospedales1* and 100 tracks in *Hospedales3*. The improvement of our approach with respect to the state of the art is shown in blue in parenthesis. In bold we show the best method between [7], [8], [6] and using 10 annotations in our method.

(a) Hospedales1 (61 tracks)

Metrics	[6]	[8][2]	[7]	[7] with Kalman	Proposed method with # annotations				
					0	10	20	30	40
CLE ↓	31.8	39.7	42.5	40.4	42.5	**9.6** (-70%)	10.6 (-67%)	9.6 (-70%)	10.4 (-67%)
SP ↑	0.35	0.41	0.48	0.49	0.48	**0.59** (+20%)	0.57 (+16%)	0.58 (+18%)	0.57 (+16%)

(b) Hospedales3 (100 tracks)

Metrics	[6]	[8][2]	[7]	[7] with Kalman	Proposed method with # annotations				
					0	10	20	30	40
CLE ↓	57.6	68.7	33.2	44.3	33.2	**23.9** (-28%)	28.4 (-14%)	17.7 (-47%)	16.0 (-52%)
SP ↑	0.15	0.21	0.43	0.39	0.43	**0.44** (+2%)	0.45 (+5%)	0.46 (+7%)	0.46 (+7%)

6.2 Comparison with the State of the Art

Tabs. 1a and 1b show the performance of the state of the art and our framework for *Hospedales1* and *Hospedales3*, respectively. Note that [6,7,8] rank within the 5 best single object trackers according to the recent exhaustive benchmark [25][3]. We show the performance of our framework for different number of annotations, a common theme that we adopt in the experimental section of this work. We obviously obtain the same result as [7] if we do not use any annotations, because in that case our model precisely falls back to the appearance model. As we are provided with trajectory annotations we obtain a considerable improvement with respect to the state of the art. For example, with as few as 10 trajectory annotations, we obtain a relative improvement of 70% and 28% CLE for *Hospedales1*

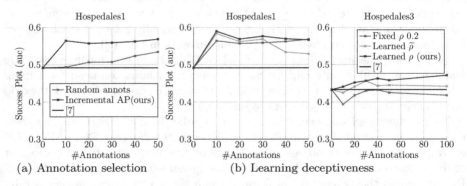

(a) Annotation selection   (b) Learning deceptiveness

Fig. 7. In a) we compare our IAP annotation selection method with a random ranking baseline using a fixed ρ of 0.2 and all events (over 10 different runs). b) compares the results of the proposed framework using different variants of deceptiveness (see text).

---

[2] We only evaluated [8] for the frames for which it provided a bounding box.
[3] We used the code of the authors publicly available in their webpage.

and *Hospedales3* respectively and 20% and 2% SP for these same scenarios. With 30 trajectory annotations, the improvement *Hospedales3* becomes 47% for CLE and 7% for SP. For comparison, we also extended [7] with a Kalman filter [9] (using a hand-tuned $\rho = 0.2$) and show that it brings a much lower improvement than our motion model. This occurs despite the use of the exact same fixed parameters for our motion model and the Kalman filter. The classical Kalman filter is simply not as powerful as our motion model since it does not learn from trajectory annotations. These results highlight the difficulty of tracking in our videos, and the huge benefits that our method is able to gain from a few manual annotations.

Note that our framework is not restricted to the use of the appearance model of [7]. It can easily accommodate future, better performing appearance models.

6.3 Baseline Comparison

In this section we perform some baseline comparisons for the three main components of our proposed framework: (i) Our selection annotation approach, (ii) learning the visual deceptiveness and (iii) conditioning the transfer on the event model of [13]. For space reasons, we only show the SP performance metric. We show all the results in the supplementary material.

Automatic Annotation Selection. We compare the IAP annotation selection method described in Sec. 4.2 with an incremental random selection baseline. Fig. 7a shows the performance of the framework with these two methods and a fixed ρ of 0.2. For the random sampling of annotations, we show the average of the curves obtained with 10 different random sets. Due to space constraints, Fig. 7a only shows the results for the scene *Hospedales1*. The results of *Hospedales3*, which have similar conclusions, can be found in the supplementary material. Our annotation selection approach shows a considerable improvement for few annotations, since we pick representative and diverse trajectories. This is especially important for practical applications, where obtaining trajectory annotations is costly. As expected, this difference between the two methods decreases as more annotations become available and vanishes when using all of them.

Learning Deceptiveness. Learning ρ is a major component of our framework and our contributions. We show in Fig. 7b the final tracking performance if we use a fixed deceptiveness of 0.2, if we learn it independently for each trajectory $(\tilde{\rho})$ and if we additionally diffuse it spatially to obtain a consistent deceptiveness ρ. We draw two conclusions: i) Diffusing the deceptiveness across trajectories improves the performance of our approach and considerably impacts its stability with respect to the annotation sets. As expected, the diffusion aggregates the independently learned deceptiveness, extracting an underlying and consistent one, *c.f.* Fig. 4. ii) Learning deceptiveness with the proposed algorithm improves the results with respect to fixing the deceptiveness to a hand-tuned value of 0.2, and consistently outperforms the baseline tracker on both datasets. The improvement is especially noticeable in *Hospedales3*, since this dataset has zones

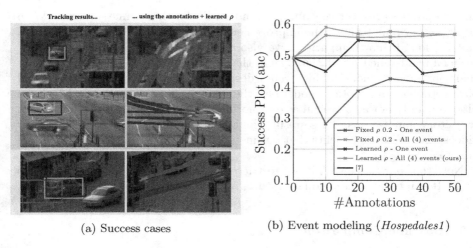

(a) Success cases   (b) Event modeling (*Hospedales1*)

Fig. 8. a) shows some cases in which our framework improves the tracking results. Ground truth in green, [7] in red and ours (40 annotations) in blue. Our method can track through deceiving zones by following previously learned trajectories in the regions where the original tracker failed at training time. b) shows a comparison of conditioning the transfer on one or all events with fixed and learned deceptiveness for *Hospedales1*.

with different degrees of difficulty to track. Fig. 4 shows how our framework is able to learn larger ρ values for regions with more difficult occlusions.

Fig. 8a shows some examples of especially difficult tracking regions with the corresponding deceptiveness that we have learned and how it helped to successfully track the objects at test time.

Conditioning Transfer on an Event Model. The last component of our framework, and one of our contributions, is the conditioning of the transfer on the events in the scene. We show in Fig. 8b how much this can improve tracking performance in *Hospedales1*. Again, the results of *Hospedales3* can be found in the supplementary material. Generally, using conditioning on events in the scene improves results, whether we learn the visual deceptiveness or not. Indeed, transferring from the event trajectories helps to solve ambiguities in the scene, *c.f.* Fig. 6. Importantly, even when using just one event the method we propose to learn ρ also gives better results than a fixed ρ. Overall, the best results are obtained with our full framework: learning deceptiveness and conditioning the transfer on the event model of the scene.

6.4   Speed

The proposed tracking framework is very efficient at test time. Computing the appearance model of [7] takes 175ms per frame on average. In contrast, computing our motion model comes at a cost of only 1.5ms with unoptimized code, excluding the real-time optical flow computation. This occurs because at test time the algorithm just has to do a nearest neighbor search and transfer the displacement and deceptiveness that was learned at training time.

7 Conclusion

In this paper, we have proposed a new visual tracking framework for a surveillance setup where we combine appearance and motion models in a single tracker. In this framework, we automatically learn from a small set of trajectory annotations how deceiving the appearance model is in different spatial and temporal regions of the scene. This leads to the concept of *visual deceptiveness*. At test time, we transfer the displacement and deceptiveness from the trajectory annotations. The framework is extended by conditioning the learning and transfer on an event model, which helps resolving ambiguities when searching for the closest trajectory from which to transfer. Moreover, we propose an incremental clustering approach to automatically select from the training sequence a small number of tracks which should be annotated by the user. We show in our experiments that those contributions are complementary and lead to state-of-the-art tracking results on 161 tracks that we publicly release.

One of the limitations of our current framework is that it disregards context, *i.e.* the position of the other vehicles, to learn deceptiveness. We plan to include such context modelling in future work. We also want to cast our framework in an active learning scenario, where the learned deceptiveness on the first few annotated tracks will guide the selection of new trajectory annotations so as to further improve tracking. Ideally, the system would also find the number of annotated tracks that are needed.

Acknowledgements. This work was supported by the European Research Council (ERC) under the project VarCity (#273940). The authors gratefully acknowledge support by Toyota.

References

1. Ali, S., Shah, M.: Floor fields for tracking in high density crowd scenes. In: Forsyth, D., Torr, P., Zisserman, A. (eds.) ECCV 2008, Part II. LNCS, vol. 5303, pp. 1–14. Springer, Heidelberg (2008)
2. Cifuentes, C.G., Sturzel, M., Jurie, F., Brostow, G.J.: Motion models that only work sometimes. In: BMVC (2012)
3. Collins, R.T., Liu, Y., Leordeanu, M.: Online selection of discriminative tracking features. PAMI 27(10), 1631–1643 (2005)
4. Everingham, M., Van Gool, L., Williams, C.K.I., Winn, J., Zisserman, A.: The PASCAL Visual Object Classes Challenge (VOC2012) Results (2012), http://www.pascal-network.org/challenges/ VOC/voc2012/workshop/index.html
5. Frey, B.J., Dueck, D.: Clustering by passing messages between data points. Science 315, 972–976 (2007)

6. Hare, S., Saffari, A., Torr, P.H.S.: Struck: Structured output tracking with kernels. In: ICCV (2011)
7. Jia, X., Lu, H., Yang, M.-H.: Visual tracking via adaptive structural local sparse appearance model. In: CVPR (2012)
8. Kalal, Z., Mikolajczyk, K., Matas, J.: Tracking-learning-detection. PAMI 34(7), 1409–1422 (2012)
9. Kalman, R.E.: A new approach to linear filtering and prediction problems. Transactions of the ASME–Journal of Basic Engineering (1960)
10. Khan, Z., Balch, T., Dellaert, F.: MCMC-based particle filtering for tracking a variable number of interacting targets. PAMI 27(11), 1805–1918 (2005)
11. Kitani, K.M., Ziebart, B.D., Bagnell, J.A., Hebert, M.: Activity forecasting. In: Fitzgibbon, A., Lazebnik, S., Perona, P., Sato, Y., Schmid, C. (eds.) ECCV 2012, Part IV. LNCS, vol. 7575, pp. 201–214. Springer, Heidelberg (2012)
12. Kolmogorov, V.: Convergent tree-reweighted message passing for energy minimization. PAMI (2006)
13. Kuettel, D., Breitenstein, M.D., Van Gool, L., Ferrari, V.: What's going on? Discovering spatio-temporal dependencies in dynamic scenes. In: CVPR (2010)
14. Kwon, J., Lee, K.M.: Tracking by sampling trackers. In: ICCV (2011)
15. Leibe, B., Schindler, K., Cornelis, N., Van Gool, L.J.: Coupled object detection and tracking from static cameras and moving vehicles. PAMI 30(10), 1683–1698 (2008)
16. Li, X., Dick, A., Wang, H., Shen, C., van den Hengel, A.: Graph mode-based contextual kernels for robust svm tracking. In: ICCV (2011)
17. Liu, J., Carr, P., Collins, R.T., Liu, Y.: Tracking sports players with context-conditioned motion models. In: CVPR (2013)
18. Mei, X., Ling, H.: Robust visual tracking using l1 minimization. In: ICCV (2009)
19. Oron, S., Bar-Hillel, A., Levi, D., Avidan, S.: Locally orderless tracking. In: CVPR (2012)
20. Pérez, P., Hue, C., Vermaak, J., Gangnet, M.: Color-based probabilistic tracking. In: Heyden, A., Sparr, G., Nielsen, M., Johansen, P. (eds.) ECCV 2002, Part I. LNCS, vol. 2350, pp. 661–675. Springer, Heidelberg (2002)
21. Prosser, P.: Hybrid algorithms for the constraint satisfaction problem. In: Computational Intelligence (1993)
22. Rodriguez, M., Ali, S., Kanade, T.: Tracking in unstructured crowded scenes. In: ICCV (2009)
23. Segal, A.V., Reid, I.D.: Latent data association: Bayesian model selection for multi-target tracking. In: ICCV (2013)
24. Smith, K., Carleton, A., Lepetit, V.: General constraints for batch multiple-target tracking applied to large-scale videomicroscopy. In: CVPR (2008)
25. Wu, Y., Lim, J., Yang, M.-H.: Online object tracking: A benchmark. In: CVPR (2013)
26. Yang, B., Nevatia, R.: Multi-target tracking by online learning of non-linear motion patterns and robust appearance models. In: CVPR (2012)
27. Yilmaz, A., Javed, O., Shah, M.: Object tracking: A survey. In: ICASSP (2006)
28. Yuen, J., Russell, B.C., Liu, C., Torralba, A.: Labelme video: Building a video database with human annotations. In: ICCV (2009)
29. Zhang, T., Ghanem, B., Ahuja, N.: Robust multi-object tracking via cross-domain contextual information for sports video analysis. In: ICASSP (2012)
30. Zhao, X., Medioni, G.: Robust unsupervised motion pattern inference from video and applications. In: ICCV (2011)
31. Zhou, B., Wang, X., Tang, X.: Understanding collective crowd behaviors:learning a mixture model of dynamic pedestrian-agents. In: CVPR (2012)

Generalized Background Subtraction Using Superpixels with Label Integrated Motion Estimation

Jongwoo Lim[1] and Bohyung Han[2]

[1] Division of Computer Science and Engineering, Hanyang University, Seoul, Korea
[2] Department of Computer Science and Engineering, POSTECH, Korea
jlim@hanyang.ac.kr, bhhan@postech.ac.kr

Abstract. We propose an online background subtraction algorithm with superpixel-based density estimation for videos captured by moving camera. Our algorithm maintains appearance and motion models of foreground and background for each superpixel, computes foreground and background likelihoods for each pixel based on the models, and determines pixelwise labels using binary belief propagation. The estimated labels trigger the update of appearance and motion models, and the above steps are performed iteratively in each frame. After convergence, appearance models are propagated through a sequential Bayesian filtering, where predictions rely on motion fields of both labels whose computation exploits the segmentation mask. Superpixel-based modeling and label integrated motion estimation make propagated appearance models more accurate compared to existing methods since the models are constructed on visually coherent regions and the quality of estimated motion is improved by avoiding motion smoothing across regions with different labels. We evaluate our algorithm with challenging video sequences and present significant performance improvement over the state-of-the-art techniques quantitatively and qualitatively.

Keywords: generalized background subtraction, superpixel segmentation, density propagation, layered optical flow estimation.

1 Introduction

Moving object detection in videos is a critical step to many computer vision problems such as visual tracking, scene understanding, human motion analysis, unmanned vehicle navigation, event detection and so on. One of the approaches for this task is background subtraction, also known as foreground/background segmentation, which is typically based on appearance modeling and update of foreground and background in local or global areas. Traditionally, background subtraction has been investigated in a stationary camera environment [1–6], but researchers recently started to study the problem with a moving camera. Background subtraction with a freely moving camera is obviously more challenging particularly due to unreliable motion estimation caused by fast motion,

D. Fleet et al. (Eds.): ECCV 2014, Part V, LNCS 8693, pp. 173–187, 2014.
© Springer International Publishing Switzerland 2014

occlusion, motion blur, etc. Consequently, a simple extension of background subtraction algorithms to a moving camera environment would fail easily because appearance models are prone to be contaminated by inaccurate image registration across frames. Our goal in this work is to tackle the more challenging foreground/background segmentation problem, where we propose a superpixel-based modeling of appearance and motion and a separate foreground/background motion estimation using segmentation mask.

There are several closely related works for background subtraction in videos captured by a moving camera. The most primitive algorithms are probably motion segmentation and its extensions [7–9], and they separate foreground from background based on homography or homography+parallax. However, they assume that the dominant motion is from background and only residual motions belong to foreground objects, which may not be true in practice. A few approaches to combine motion estimation and appearance modeling are recently proposed for online background subtraction [10, 11], but they rely on robust estimation of long term trajectories such as particle video [12]. In [13, 14], block-based density propagation techniques are proposed for generalized background subtraction[1], but their algorithms are complex and involve many free parameters; the performance in a general setting may not be consistent. On the other hand, [15] employs a matrix factorization technique with low rank and group sparsity constraints of long-term trajectories, and [16] proposes a multi-layer segmentation algorithm by label propagation from given sparse trajectories. However, both methods run offline and rely on robust trajectory estimation. None of previous works investigate the interaction between segmentation and motion estimation although they are tightly coupled since the quality of estimated motion can be improved by human annotated foreground and background boundaries as discussed in [17].

Contrary to existing techniques, our generalized background subtraction algorithm utilizes the segmentation mask to compute foreground and background motion fields and use them to maintain more accurate appearance and motion models. Given pixelwise motion vectors, the proposed algorithm propagates foreground and background appearance models of the previous frame, which are defined in each superpixel, through a sequential Bayesian filtering. It also builds motion models for each superpixel based on the motion vector observations. Pixelwise foreground/background likelihood is computed based on the appearance and motion models, and segmentation labels are determined by binary belief propagation. Label estimation in each pixel triggers update of motion and appearance models in each superpixel, and the final label of the frame is obtained after convergence via a few iterations.

The overview of our algorithm is illustrated in Figure 1. Our algorithm is differentiated from previous works such as [13, 14] in the sense that there is interaction between foreground/background segmentation and motion estimation, and appearance and motion modeling is performed on homogeneous regions

---

[1] This term means background subtraction in a moving camera environment, and is first used in [13].

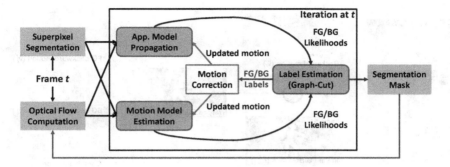

Fig. 1. Overview of our algorithm. Main contributions in our algorithm are highlighted with yellow boxes and a red line. Note that we compute separate foreground and background motion fields.

(superpixels) for more efficient and accurate estimation. The advantages and characteristics of the proposed algorithm are summarized below:

- Our algorithm employs segmentation mask to estimate foreground and background motion fields separately and avoids motion smoothing across regions with different labels. It improves segmentation quality by maintaining more accurate appearance and motion models.
- Instead of a regular grid-based modeling as in [13, 14], superpixel-based modeling is employed for reliable density estimation; the observations of color and motion in a superpixel are coherent, and simple density representations are sufficient for accurate modeling.
- The proposed algorithm is more efficient than [13] by using simple histograms in density representation and avoiding complex inference procedures in density propagation. The performance is improved significantly with fewer number of free parameters.

The organization of this paper is as follows. Section 2 summarizes superpixel segmentation method used in our algorithm and Section 3 describes our motion estimation technique based on segmentation mask. The main background subtraction algorithm is presented in Section 4, where model construction, density propagation, and label estimation with likelihood computation are discussed in detail. Section 5 illustrates experimental results with real videos.

2 Superpixel Segmentation

Contrary to [13, 14], where the frames are divided into regular rectangular grid blocks, we employ a superpixel segmentation for modeling appearance and motion. In a superpixel, appearance and motion are likely to be homogeneous hence estimated density functions are to be more reliable and accurate given a limited number of pixels.

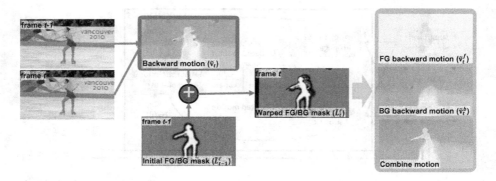

Fig. 2. Separate foreground and background motion estimation by segment mask propagation from the previous label. Note that [13, 14] use backward motion in green plate, but our algorithm employs a separate motion field for each label in orange plate. The combined motion shows clearer motion boundary. The motion images are color-coded to visualize the direction and magnitude, and the white, gray, and black areas in the mask images represent the foreground, background, and ambiguous regions respectively.

We use the ERS superpixel segmentation algorithm [18], due to its simplicity and perceptually good performance, which formulates the superpixel segmentation as a graph partitioning problem. Given a graph $G = (V, E)$ and the number of superpixels K, the goal is to find $A \subseteq E$ such that the resulting graph $\widetilde{G} = (V, A)$ contains K connected subgraphs. Note that a vertex corresponds to a pixel in image and edges are typically constructed by the 4-neighborhood system, where the weight of an edge is computed by the similarity between the features observed at the connected vertices. The objective function to solve the graph partitioning problem is given by

$$\max_{A} \quad \mathcal{H}(A) + \lambda\mathcal{B}(A) \tag{1}$$
$$\text{s.t} \ \ A \subseteq E \text{ and } N_A \geq K$$

where $\mathcal{H}$ and $\mathcal{B}$ denote entropy rate of random walk and balancing term respectively, and N_A is the number of connected components in $\widetilde{G}$. The entropy rate term encourages compact and homogeneous segments and the balancing function is to segment with similar sizes.

Although the exact optimization is difficult, it can be solved by a greedy algorithm efficiently and the solution by this approach always provides 0.5 approximation bound. We refer the reader to [18] for more details.

3   Motion Estimation with Segmentation Mask

Unlike existing approaches that use a single motion field, we propose to estimate two separate motion fields for foreground and background of the scene. Due to the smoothness assumption that most optical flow algorithms adopt, the motion field near motion boundary or depth discontinuity tend to be over-smoothed and blurred. For foreground/background segmentation, motion boundaries are the most important regions and inaccurate motions near the area often produce incorrect labels. It is because the erroneous motion vectors compromise the estimated motion models and corrupt the propagated appearance models.

Our idea is motivated by [17], where the accuracy of motion estimation is improved significantly with object boundary annotation by human. We compute separate motion fields for foreground and background using the corresponding segmentation masks estimated by our algorithm in the previous frame. To compute the backward motion field $\mathbf{v}_t^\ell$ for label $\ell \in \{f, b\}$ at frame t, we need the warped foreground/background segmentation mask $\tilde{L}_t^\ell$, which is estimated from the mask in the previous frame L_{t-1}^ℓ and the backward motion without segmentation mask $\mathbf{v}_t$ using [19], as

$$\tilde{L}_t^\ell(\mathbf{x}) = \hat{L}_{t-1}^\ell(\mathbf{x} + \mathbf{v}_t(\mathbf{x})), \tag{2}$$

where $\hat{L}_{t-1}^f = L_{t-1}^f$ and $\hat{L}_{t-1}^b = \xi(L_{t-1}^b, r)$. The morphological erosion function with label L and radius r denoted by $\xi(L, r)$ is performed to reduce the effect of occluded or uncovered background pixels.

Once the segmentation mask $\tilde{L}_t^\ell$ is given, we compute the backward motion field $\mathbf{v}_t^\ell$ for each foreground and background label using [19], which ignores the observations in the unset region and propagates motions spatially from the neighboring pixels. Figure 2 illustrates the procedure to compute backward foreground/background motion fields.

4   Background Subtraction Algorithm

Our foreground/background segmentation algorithm is composed of the following three steps: model construction, density propagation, and label estimation with likelihood computation. These procedures are repeated in each frame until convergence. We describe technical details of each of these three steps.

4.1   Appearance and Motion Models

We construct appearance and motion models for foreground and background in each superpixel. These models are two main factors to determine the label of each pixel, and accurate and efficient estimation of the models is crucial for the success of our algorithm. We employ simple histogram to represent appearance and motion models since basic operations on histogram(s) such as addition, product, and convolution can be implemented straightforwardly and performed with low computational cost. In addition, histogram is advantageous compared to continuous distributions such as kernel density estimation used in [13] especially when feature dimensionality is low.

Suppose that we have maintained the posterior of appearance corresponding to the ith superpixel at frame t, which is a normalized histogram denoted by

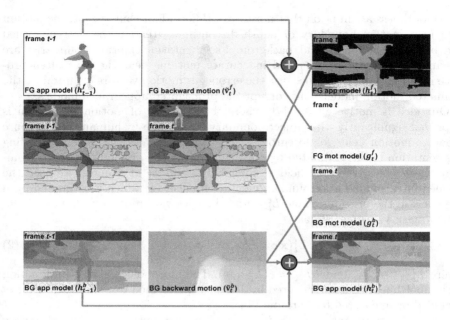

Fig. 3. Appearance model propagation by sequential Bayesian filtering. The models are constructed for individual superpixels. Note that we do not propagate motion models over time but compute them independently in each frame.

$h_t^\ell(\mathbf{c}; i)$, where $\mathbf{c}$ is a random variable for color and label $\ell \in \{f, b\}$ is a segment label. The motion histogram learned for the ith superpixel with label ℓ is also a normalized histogram denoted by $g_t^\ell(\mathbf{v}; i)$, where $\mathbf{v}$ is a random variable for motion. Since label information in the new frame is not available, we simply transfer labels from the previous frame using pixelwise motion $\mathbf{v}_t^\ell$ and set initial label to each pixel. Note that we need to maintain appearance and motion models for foreground and background separately in each superpixel.

4.2   Propagation of Appearance Models

Maintaining accurate appearance models of foreground and background is critical to obtain reliable likelihoods of both labels in each pixel. For the purpose, we propagate density function for appearance model by sequential Bayesian filtering, which is composed of prediction and update steps given by

$$p(x_t|z_{1:t-1}) = \int p(x_t|x_{t-1})\, p(x_{t-1}|z_{1:t-1})\, dx_{t-1} \qquad (3)$$

$$p(x_t|z_{1:t}) \propto p(z_t|x_t)\, p(x_t|z_{1:t-1}), \qquad (4)$$

where $p(x_t|z_{1:t-1})$ and $p(z_t|x_t)$ are prior and measurement density function, respectively. In our context, the histogram propagated from the previous frame

(a) FG/BG mask   (b) $\Gamma_t(\mathbf{x})$ (c) $\Delta_t(\mathbf{x})$

Fig. 4. Motion consistency mask for likelihood estimation. Given the foreground (white) and background (gray) mask in (a) and the backward motions, the uncovered region (colored as black) can be found as (b). The black pixels in (c) are those with large color inconsistency between the current frame and the warped frame by the motion field. Refer to the text for more detail.

corresponds to prior distribution, and the appearance histogram observed in the current frame is measurement distribution. We now describe how the two distributions are constructed in our algorithm.

The prior distribution at frame t is estimated by a weighted sum of appearance models in frame $t-1$. The temporally propagated histogram $h_{t-1|t}^{\ell}(\mathbf{c}; i)$ corresponding to label ℓ in the ith superpixel is obtained as follows:

$$h_{t-1|t}^{\ell}(\mathbf{c}; i) = \frac{1}{n^{\ell}(\mathcal{S}_i)} \sum_{\mathbf{x} \in \mathcal{S}_i, L(\mathbf{x})=\ell} h_{t-1}^{\ell}(\mathbf{c}; s_{t-1}(\mathbf{x} + \mathbf{v}_t^{\ell}(\mathbf{x}))), \qquad (5)$$

where $n^{\ell}(\mathcal{S}_i)$ is the number of pixels with label ℓ in the ith superpixel $\mathcal{S}_i$, $s_t(\mathbf{x})$ returns superpixel index of pixel located at $\mathbf{x}$ in frame t, and $\mathbf{v}_t^{\ell}(\mathbf{x})$ denotes backward motion vector for label ℓ observed at pixel $\mathbf{x}$. This procedure is illustrated in Figure 3.

For the measurement distribution denoted by $o_t^{\ell}(\mathbf{c}; i)$, we construct a normalized histogram for each label based on pixel colors in $\mathcal{S}_i$ at frame t. Note that each pixel whose label is not ℓ in the ith superpixel contributes to all bins in the histogram equally. Finally, the posterior of appearance in the current frame is obtained by the product of prior and measurement distributions as

$$h_t^{\ell}(\mathbf{c}; i) = o_t^{\ell}(\mathbf{c}; i) \cdot h_{t-1|t}^{\ell}(\mathbf{c}; i). \qquad (6)$$

Note that the posterior is normalized to sum to one after we compute likelihoods for foreground and background. Unlike the appearance model estimated by sequential Bayesian filtering, the motion model $g_t^{\ell}(\mathbf{v}; i)$ is not propagated, but built from the motion field of the current frame.

4.3 Likelihood Computation and Label Estimation

Each superpixel has two sets of appearance and motion models; one is for foreground and the other is for background. Given the models at frame t, we compute foreground and background likelihoods of each pixel $\mathbf{x}$, denoted by $p^{\ell}(\mathbf{x})$ for label $\ell \in \{f, b\}$, which are given by a weighted geometric mean of appearance likelihood $h_t^{\ell}(\mathbf{c}(\mathbf{x}); s_t(\mathbf{x}))$ and motion likelihood $g_t^{\ell}(\mathbf{v}(\mathbf{x}); s_t(\mathbf{x}))$ as

Fig. 5. Label update over iterations. **r0**: The initial label propagated from the previous frame. **r1-r2**: The updated label after the first and second iteration. The racket is recovered in *tennis* sequence, and the false foreground label on the ground in *NFL* sequence is removed.

$$p^\ell(\mathbf{x}) = h_t^\ell(\mathbf{c}(\mathbf{x}); s_t(\mathbf{x}))^\alpha \cdot g_t^\ell(\mathbf{v}(\mathbf{x}); s_t(\mathbf{x}))^{1-\alpha}, \qquad (7)$$

where likelihoods are computed with the models in superpixel $s_t(\mathbf{x})$, and α ($0 \leq \alpha \leq 1$) controls relative weights between appearance and motion. If there is no foreground (or background) in a superpixel, the corresponding likelihood is set to zero.

If a pixel in the current frame is in the background region but its projected position by the backward background motion $\mathbf{v}_t^b(\mathbf{x})$ was in the foreground region in the previous frame, the pixel is likely to be uncovered from occlusion. The uncovered region can be identified by

$$\Gamma_t(\mathbf{x}) = L_{t-1}^f(\mathbf{x} + \tilde{\mathbf{v}}_t^b(\mathbf{x})) \wedge \tilde{L}_t^b(\mathbf{x}), \qquad (8)$$

where $\tilde{L}_t^b(\mathbf{x})$ is the warped background mask at frame t and $L_{t-1}^f(\mathbf{x})$ is the foreground mask at frame $t-1$ as defined in Section 3. In motion likelihood estimation, the contribution of uncovered pixels for the foreground model is discarded.

Also, the pixel color consistency between the current frame and the warped image by the label's motion is checked, and pixels with large color inconsistency are ignored in the motion likelihood computation for the label, *i.e.*,

$$\Delta_t(\mathbf{x}) = \begin{cases} 1 \text{ if } \| \mathbf{c}_t(\mathbf{x}) - \mathbf{c}_{t-1}(\mathbf{x} + \mathbf{v}_t^\ell(\mathbf{x})) \|^2 > \theta \\ 0 \text{ otherwise} \end{cases}, \qquad (9)$$

where $\mathbf{c}_t(\mathbf{x})$ and $\mathbf{c}_{t-1}(\mathbf{x})$ are the color values at $\mathbf{x}$ in the current and the previous frame. Figure 4 shows the examples of the $\Gamma_t(\mathbf{x})$ and $\Delta_t(\mathbf{x})$ masks, in which the black pixels are not used in motion likelihood computation.

Once foreground and background likelihoods of each pixel is computed, we estimate the label of each pixel by inference in Markov Random Field. Let $G = (V, E)$ be a graph with a set of vertices and edges, which are denoted by V and E, respectively. Each pixel corresponds to a vertex in the graph and edges connect four neighborhood vertices. Our objective is to minimize an energy function, which is composed of two terms—data and smoothness terms, which are given by observation potentials of individual vertices, $\Phi(\mathbf{x})$, and compatibility potentials of individual edges, $\Psi(\mathbf{x}, \mathbf{x}')$, respectively.

Fig. 6. Visualization of the foreground/background appearance models. Note that the proposed temporal propagation scheme maintains accurate appearance models, even where the background scene is occluded by foreground objects. Gray areas in the images for background appearance denote the absence of appearance models, and our algorithm learns the models quickly using new observations.

The observation potentials for foreground and background of each pixel $\mathbf{x}$ are given by

$$\Phi^{\ell}(\mathbf{x}) = \frac{p^{\ell}(\mathbf{x})}{p^f(\mathbf{x}) + p^b(\mathbf{x})}, \tag{10}$$

where $p^f(\mathbf{x})$ and $p^b(\mathbf{x})$ are computed by Eq. (7). The compatibility potential for an edge is defined by color difference between two adjacent pixels, $\mathbf{x}$ and $\mathbf{x}'$, which is given by

$$\Psi(\mathbf{x}, \mathbf{x}') = \exp\left(\frac{-||\mathbf{c}(\mathbf{x}) - \mathbf{c}(\mathbf{x}')||^2}{2\sigma_c^2}\right), \tag{11}$$

where σ_c is the parameter to control the effect of color difference. The optimization problem can be solved efficiently by binary belief propagation, and the labels are determined by comparing the believes for foreground and background at each pixel.

4.4   Iterative Update of Models and Labels

If the label of each pixel is re-estimated, the propagated appearance models and the estimated motion models in each superpixel should also be updated. Then, model propagation and label estimation procedures in Section 4.2 and 4.3 need to be repeated until convergence to improve overall performance. The foreground/background label estimation result in each iteration is presented in Figure 5, which shows gradual improvement of labels in each iteration.

Figure 6 illustrates the learned and propagated foreground and background models. Note that the initially occluded background regions (visualized as gray) are filled with correct appearance models using the information propagated from the previous frames.

Table 1. The experimental setup for comparison.

Algorithms	Block	Motion	Density estimation
Proposed method	ERS (300),	FG/BG layered motions,	histogram
– with grid blocks	grid (300),	FG/BG layered motions,	histogram
– with a single motion	ERS(300),	single motion,	histogram
Kwak *et al.* [13]	grid,	single motion,	KDE
Lim *et al.* [14]	grid,	single motion,	histogram

5   Experiment

We tested the proposed algorithm extensively with many videos involving various challenges such as background clutter, fast motion, occlusion, complex foreground shape, etc. Also, our algorithm is compared with the state-of-the-art techniques qualitatively and quantitatively.

5.1   Experiment Setup

Our algorithm requires two important external components: motion estimation and superpixel segmentation. Dense optical flow maps are estimated by the algorithm in [19], and superpixel segmentation is obtained from [18]. Although their results may affect overall performance of our algorithm substantially, we do not investigate their performance in this paper.

We evaluated the proposed algorithm called Generalized Background Subtraction using Superpixels (GBSSP), and two state-of-the-art algorithms developed by Kwak *et al.* [13] and Lim *et al.* [14]. The two algorithms [13, 14] employ block-based modeling and propagation strategy, where a regular rectangular blocks are used without sophisticated estimation of region boundaries. Table 1 summarizes the similarities and differences between the compared algorithms. Trajectory-based online moving camera background subtraction technique [11] has different characteristics compared to density propagation-based algorithms including ours; it assumes a certain camera model to classify the trajectories into foreground or background while ours does not have any assumption about parametric motion model. Consequently, it may show completely different performance depending on the choice of input sequences[2].

Our algorithm involves several free parameters[3]. Note that we fixed the parameters for each algorithm in all experiments to make the our evaluation fair and realistic. The initializations of all compared algorithms could be computed by motion segmentation followed by a few iterations of individual algorithms, which requires substantial amount of efforts for parameter tuning. Instead, to focus on the performance of foreground/background model propagation in all algorithms, we used the ground-truth labels for the first frames.

---

[2] Thus direct comparison with [11] is not conducted in our experiment given the situation that the implementation is not available. Please refer to the paper for indirect performance evaluation for a few common sequences.

[3] In Section 3, $r = 7$, and in Section 4.3, $\alpha = 0.7$, $\theta = 0.025$, $\sigma_c = 5$.

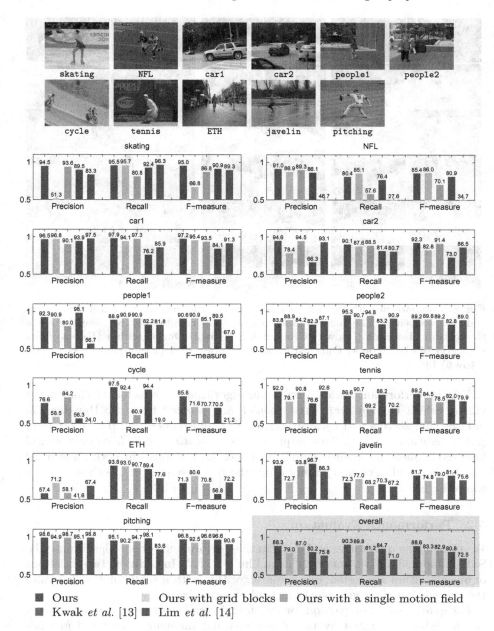

Fig. 7. Quantitative comparison results. The first frames of the tested sequences are illustrated at the top. The first 11 plots illustrate the precision and recall scores together with F-measure scores for the 5 different algorithms. Overall, the proposed algorithm outperforms [13] and [14] as illustrated in the highlighted graph. The benefit of superpixel segmentation and separate foreground/background motion are also supported by the results.

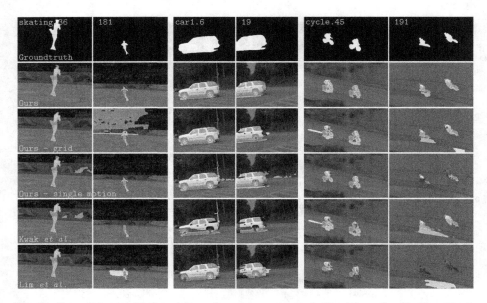

Fig. 8. Comparison with two internal and two external algorithms for *skating, car1*, and *cycle* sequences. The images in each row show the result of the five algorithms. See the text for discussion. **(Row1)** Groundtruth **(Row2)** Our algorithm **(Row3)** Ours with grid blocks **(Row4)** Ours with a single motion field **(Row5)** Kwak *et al.* [13] **(Row6)** Lim *et al.* [14]

For the performance evaluation of our algorithm, we selected 11 challenging videos, which include *car1, car2, people1* and *people2* from the Hopkins 155 dataset [20], *skating* and *cycle* from [13], *NFL* and *tennis* from [14], *ETH* from [21], *javelin* and *pitching*. Some sequences, *cycle, skating*, or *NFL*, contain several hundred frames and involve significant appearance changes in both foreground and background. The first frames of all the tested sequences are shown at the top of Figure 7.

5.2   Performance Evaluation

We present the qualitative and quantitative performance of our algorithm (GB-SSP) compared to Kwak *et al.* [13], and Lim *et al.* [14]. In addition, two variations of our algorithm are tested; one is our algorithm with a single motion field and the other is based on grid blocks instead of superpixels.

For quantitative comparison, precision and recall scores are computed based on the labels generated by the algorithms and manually annotated ground-truths. We used the precision and recall measures defined in [11]:

$$precision = \frac{TP}{TP + FP} \quad \text{and} \quad recall = \frac{TP}{TP + FN},$$

where TP, FP, TN, and FN denote the number of true-positive, false-positive, true-negative, and false-negative pixels, respectively. Note that the definition

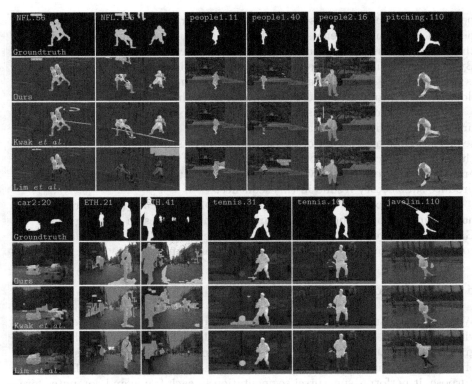

Fig. 9. Comparison with two external algorithms for *NFL, people1, people2, pitching, car2, ETH, tennis.* and *javelin* sequences. **(Row1)** Groundtruth **(Row2)** Our algorithm **(Row2)** Kwak *et al.* [13] **(Row3)** Lim *et al.* [14]

of precision is different from the one used in [13, 14], $\frac{TN}{FP+TN}$, which tends to exaggerate precision performance when background area is large. The precision used here is more discriminative especially when the foreground region is small, and it is more consistent with human perception.

Figure 7 illustrates the quantitative results from the five algorithms for all the eleven test sequences. F-measure, which is the harmonic mean of precision and recall, for each algorithm is shown together with the precision and recall value. GBSSP is particularly better than [13] and [14] in *cycle* and *tennis* sequence, and achieves considerable performance improvement over the other two methods in many cases. Overall, our algorithm outperforms [13] and [14] by about 8% and 16%, respectively, on average. The accuracy of [13] is relatively low in *car1*, *car2* and *cycle* sequences and the performance of [14] is even worse; it fails in *cycle* and *people1*. It is notable that both the construction of superpixels and the estimation of separate motion fields are helpful to improve performance and that the combination of two components even boosts performance.

Figure 8 shows the foreground/background segmentation results in *skating*, *car1*, and *cycle* sequences for all five algorithms. Although they involves severe motion blur, low contrast background, or non-planar geometry, our method performs very well on most sequences. It gets lower precision scores than human perception in some sequences since their ground-truth marking does not include the cast shadows by foreground objects, which are easily classified as foreground. By explicitly considering the uncovered region and the pixel consistency, which is made possible by the separate motion field estimation, the foreground mask does not bleed to nearby background areas with similar colors.

We provide more comparisons with the two state-of-the-art algorithms in Figure 9. Our algorithm illustrates visually better or at least similar results in all sequences compared to all other methods. *ETH* sequence is apparently most challenging, which is probably because foreground objects appear as tiny blobs and the facade color is very similar to the pedestrians. All algorithms fail to produce satisfactory results in this sequence.

Since our algorithm does not require complex inference procedures such as nonparametric belief propagation and sequential Bayesian filtering based on Gaussian mixture models, it is 6∼7 times faster than [13]. In a standard laptop computer, it approximately takes 6 seconds per frame.

6   Conclusion

We presented an online foreground/background segmentation algorithm for videos captured by a moving camera. Our algorithm maintains reliable foreground and background appearance models over time and obtains the label of each pixel based on the learned appearance and motion models. For the purpose, it performs superpixel segmentation in each frame and computes foreground/background motion fields by exploiting segmentation mask. The appearance models of each superpixel are propagated through a sequential Bayesian filtering and the motion models are also estimated for each superpixel. Pixelwise foreground and background likelihoods are computed by the appearance and motion models, and binary belief propagation is applied to infer the labels in each iteration. This procedure is performed multiple iterations in each frame, and the final labels are obtained upon convergence. Our algorithm is conceptually simple and presents significant performance gain compared to the state-of-the-art techniques.

Acknowledgements. We thank the reviewers for valuable comments and suggestions. The work is supported partly by the ICT R&D programs of MSIP/KEIT (No. 10047078), MKE/KEIT (No. 10040246), and MSIP/IITP [14-824-09-006, Novel computer vision and machine learning technology with the ability to predict and forecast; 14-824-09-014, Basic software research in human-level lifelong machine learning (Machine Learning Center)].

References

1. Elgammal, A., Harwood, D., Davis, L.: Non-parametric model for background subtraction. In: Vernon, D. (ed.) ECCV 2000. LNCS, vol. 1843, pp. 751–767. Springer, Heidelberg (2000)
2. Stauffer, C., Grimson, W.: Adaptive background mixture models for real-time tracking. In: CVPR, pp. 246–252 (1999)
3. Lee, D.: Effective gaussian mixture learning for video background subtraction. IEEE TPAMI 27, 827–832 (2005)
4. Sheikh, Y., Shah, M.: Bayesian object detection in dynamic scenes. In: CVPR (2005)
5. Wren, C., Azarbayejani, A., Darrell, T., Pentland, A.: Pfinder: Real-time tracking of the human body. IEEE TPAMI 19, 780–785 (1997)
6. Han, B., Davis, L.: Density-based multi-feature background subtraction with support vector machine. IEEE TPAMI 34, 1017–1023 (2012)
7. Hayman, E., Eklundh, J.O.: Statistical background subtraction for a mobile observer. In: ICCV (2003)
8. Mittal, A., Huttenlocher, D.: Scene modeling for wide area surveillance and image synthesis. In: CVPR (2000)
9. Yuan, C., Medioni, G., Kang, J., Cohen, I.: Detecting motion regions in the presence of a string parallax from a moving camera by multiview geometric constraints. IEEE TPAMI 20 (2007)
10. Sheikh, Y., Javed, O., Kanade, T.: Background subtraction for freely moving cameras. In: ICCV (2009)
11. Elqursh, A., Elgammal, A.: Online moving camera background subtraction. In: Fitzgibbon, A., Lazebnik, S., Perona, P., Sato, Y., Schmid, C. (eds.) ECCV 2012, Part VI. LNCS, vol. 7577, pp. 228–241. Springer, Heidelberg (2012)
12. Sand, P., Teller, S.: Particle video: Long-range motion estimation using point trajectories. In: CVPR, pp. 2195–2202 (2006)
13. Kwak, S., Lim, T., Nam, W., Han, B., Han, J.H.: Generalized background subtraction based on hybrid inference by belief propagation and bayesian filtering. In: ICCV, pp. 2174–2181 (2011)
14. Lim, T., Han, B., Han, J.H.: Modeling and segmentation of floating foreground and background in videos. Pattern Recognition 45, 1696–1706 (2012)
15. Cui, X., Huang, J., Zhang, S., Metaxas, D.N.: Background subtraction using low rank and group sparsity constraints. In: Fitzgibbon, A., Lazebnik, S., Perona, P., Sato, Y., Schmid, C. (eds.) ECCV 2012, Part I. LNCS, vol. 7572, pp. 612–625. Springer, Heidelberg (2012)
16. Ochs, P., Brox, T.: Object segmentation in video: A hierarchical variational approach for turning point trajectories into dense regions. In: ICCV, pp. 1583–1590 (2011)
17. Liu, C., Freeman, W., Adelson, E., Weiss, Y.: Human-assistied motion annotation. In: CVPR (2008)
18. Liu, M.Y., Tuzel, O., Ramalingam, S., Chellappa, R.: Entropy rate superpixel segmentation. In: CVPR, pp. 2097–2104 (2011)
19. Liu, C.: Beyond pixels: exploring new representations and applications for motion analysis. PhD thesis, Massachusetts Institute of Technology (2009)
20. Tron, R., Vidal, R.: A benchmark for the comparison of 3-d motion segmentation algorithms. In: CVPR (2007)
21. Ess, A., Leibe, B., Gool, L.V.: Depth and appearance for mobile scene analysis. In: ICCV 2007 (2007)

Spectra Estimation of Fluorescent and Reflective Scenes by Using Ordinary Illuminants

Yinqiang Zheng[1], Imari Sato[1], and Yoichi Sato[2]

[1] National Institute of Informatics, Japan
[2] The University of Tokyo, Japan
{yqzheng,imarik}@nii.ac.jp, ysato@iis.u-tokyo.ac.jp

Abstract. The spectrum behavior of a typical fluorescent object is regulated by its reflectance, absorption and emission spectra. It was shown that two high-frequency and complementary illuminations in the spectral domain can be used to simultaneously estimate reflectance and emission spectra. In spite of its accuracy, such specialized illuminations are not easily accessible. This motivates us to explore the feasibility of using ordinary illuminants to achieve this task with comparable accuracy. We show that three hyperspectral images under wideband and independent illuminants are both necessary and sufficient, and successfully develop a convex optimization method for solving. We also disclose the reason why using one or two images is inadequate, although embedding the linear low-dimensional models of reflectance and emission would lead to an apparently overconstrained equation system. In addition, we propose a novel four-parameter model to express absorption and emission spectra, which is more compact and discriminative than the linear model. Based on this model, we present an absorption spectra estimation method in the presence of three illuminations. The correctness and accuracy of our proposed model and methods have been verified.

Keywords: Fluorescence, reflectance, hyperspectral imaging.

1 Introduction

Recently, fluorescence has aroused much interest in the computer vision community, due to its quite special Stokes wavelength shift effect and its color invariance under varying spectra illuminations [23]. Specifically, as an inherent physical property, a pure fluorescent object would absorb energy in a certain wavelength range, and re-emit it in a longer (or more exactly, redder) wavelength range. Irrespective of the illumination spectra, the spectra distribution of emission keeps constant except its magnitude.

The necessity of accounting for fluorescence has been justified in computational color constancy [4] and accurate color relighting [9,11,13], when nontrivial fluorescent components are present in the scene. Its unique spectral properties have also facilitated some important applications. For example, the wavelength shift effect was utilized to suppress highlights and inter-reflections in photometric stereo [19,22], while the color invariance used in [10] for camera spectral sensitivity calibration. These applications and perhaps more in prospect warrant the ongoing endeavors of exploring fluorescence.

However, a typical fluorescent object is usually a composite of reflective and fluorescent components. The reflective component reflects back the irradiance at the same

D. Fleet et al. (Eds.): ECCV 2014, Part V, LNCS 8693, pp. 188–202, 2014.
© Springer International Publishing Switzerland 2014

(a) Illuminants   (b) Spectra   (c) Scene (LED)   (d) Reflectance   (e) Fluorescence

Fig. 1. Using ordinary illuminants for fluorescence and reflectance separation. (a) shows the three incandescent, LED and fluorescent bulbs used in the experiments on real images, whose spectra are presented in (b). The scene under LED is shown in (c), and its recovered reflective and fluorescent components are given in (d) and (e), respectively.

wavelength, thus interacting with the illuminant quite differently from the fluorescent component. It is therefore the prerequisite to segment the fluorescent from the reflective component (see Fig.1(c-e) for an example). Some existing works have achieved solid progress toward this end in RGB images. Zhang and Sato [23] separated these two components under two different illuminations by means of independent component analysis. In contrast, Han et al. [10] used a single RGB image with the assistance of a reflectance color checker.

As demonstrated in those works on reflectance-only scenes, like [7,12,17] and many others, multispectral or hyperspectral information is essential in scenarios where color accuracy takes precedence, such as high-definition color production and e-heritage archiving. Similarly, when dealing with a fluorescent-reflective scene, it would be more desirable to recover the full spectra information, rather than being satisfied with the RGB color only. In the following, we briefly review the most closely related works on fluorescence-reflectance spectra estimation.

1.1 Related Works on Fluorescence Spectra Estimation

Some researchers have tried to recover the spectra of fluorescence. For example, Tominaga et al. [21] adopted two different light sources to estimate the fluorescent emission spectra. Alterman et al. [1] tried to unmix multiplexed images and obtain the appearance of individual fluorescent dye, while Boyd et al. [5] estimated the reflectance and fluorescent emission spectra of coral, without recovering the absorption spectra. In all these works, only a portion of the spectra are recovered.

Actually, reflectance and fluorescent emission are naturally detached under narrowband illuminations. Rooted in this observation, the classical bispectral method for full spectra measurement is widely known, and has been well documented in the literature [14]. However, this bispectral method in its original form is very laborsome and thus appropriate to measure a single point only. Lam and Sato [13] successfully extended it to measure a whole scene by using a monochromatic camera and a programmable filter. Similar to reflectance [15,18], it was noted therein that the fluorescent emission and absorption can also be well represented by the linear subspace models, which are usually leaned from principle component analysis (PCA) of training data. Such PCA-based linear models were utilized in [13] to reduce the number of images. In spite of that, about 30 images are necessary to estimate the complete spectra of a fluorescence-reflectance scene.

The classical bispectral method also links directly to the latest bispectral coding scheme [20], which used multiplexed narrowband illuminations and images to recover the full spectra of a fluorescent-reflective scene.

Instead of capturing dozens of images, Fu et al. [9] proposed an appealing method to separate the reflective and fluorescent components of a scene by using two hyperspectral images taken under high-frequency and complementary illuminations in the spectral domain. Although it is highly accurate and convenient, to generate high-frequency illuminations requires some specialized devices, like a programmable lighting source, which are very expensive thus not widely available. As for absorption spectra estimation, they developed a data driven method under the assumption that the emission and absorption spectra have the same basis coefficients. As a result, the recovered absorption spectra assume nontrivial error, when the underlying assumption is violated.

In a similar spirit to our work, Fu et al. [8] tried to simplify the hardware setup of [9] by using instead multiple colored illuminations and a trichromatic camera. Compared with a hyperspectral camera, a RGB camera is definitely desirable in terms of cost reduction, yet tends to undermine the estimation accuracy of emission spectra due to the classical metamerism hurdle in recovering spectra from trichromatic values. In addition, the colored illumination spectra were still generated by a programmable lighting source therein.

1.2   Overview of This Work

Rather than relying on specialized narrowband or high-frequency illuminations, we aim to propose a new method for fluorescence and reflectance separation by using such ordinary illuminants as LED bulbs and fluorescent lamps (see Fig.1(a-b) for the three illuminants used in the experiments of this paper), without sacrificing accuracy nor increasing much human workload. We show that three hyperspectral images under arbitrarily independent illuminations are both necessary and sufficient to this task. Actually, due to linear dependence between the PCA-based linear model of reflectance and that of emission, using one or two images tends to be inaccurate, although embedding the linear models into the imaging equation would lead to an apparently overconstrained system. However, using three images would result in a nonconvex bilinear programming problem, which is challenging to solve in general. Fortunately, through proper transformation, we successfully reformulate it into an elegant linear system. On the basis of this system, we develop a convex optimization method, whose solution can be further polished via a few alternating iterations. Experiments on simulated data have verified that our proposed method is as accurate as the state-of-the-art method [9], although only ordinary illuminants are used. Our method has also been demonstrated to be effective by using real images.

Since the absorption can not be directly observed in the image, we have to estimate it in an indirect way. To facilitate this task, we propose instead a four-parameter nonlinear model to represent the emission and absorption spectra, which is much more compact than the well-known PCA-based linear model, yet assumes almost comparable representation power. Our inspiration is drawn from the observation that shapes of typical emission and absorption spectra are very similar to the density function of the skew Cauchy distribution [2, 3]. Relying on this model and the similarity between the emission and absorption spectra pair, we develop a new method for absorption spectra estimation in the presence of three images, which is clearly advantageous in accuracy over the heuristic method in [9].

To sum up, our major contributions are: (i). Revealing for the first time the linear dependence between the PCA-based linear models of reflectance and emission; (ii). Deriving an elegant linear system for the imaging equations in the presence of three hyperspectral images; (iii). Developing an effective method to separate fluorescent and reflective components by using ordinary illuminants; (iv). Proposing a novel four-parameter nonlinear model to parameterize emission and absorption spectra on the basis of the skew Cauchy distribution.

The remaining parts of this paper are organized as follows. In Sec.2, we show how to separate the reflectance and fluorescent emission by using ordinary spectra illuminations. Sec.3 includes the four-parameter nonlinear model for representing emission and absorption spectra as well as the absorption spectra estimation method. We present experiment results by using simulated data and real images in Sec.4, and briefly conclude this paper in Sec.5.

2   Reflectance and Emission Spectra Separation

As mentioned above, a typical fluorescent object exhibits the mixed spectrum behavior of reflectance and fluorescence. According to [9, 23], the radiance at wavelength λ of a pure reflective surface is computed as $l(\lambda)r(\lambda)$, in which $l(\lambda)$ is the illumination spectra and $r(\lambda)$ is the reflectance spectra. In contrast, due to the particular absorption-emission mechanism, the radiance of a pure fluorescent surface is regulated by $\left(\int l(\hat{\lambda})a(\hat{\lambda})d\hat{\lambda}\right)e(\lambda)$, in which $a(\lambda)$ and $e(\lambda)$ are the absorption and emission spectra, respectively. Therefore, the total radiance $p(\lambda)$ of a fluorescent-reflective surface can be calculated by the following imaging equation

$$p(\lambda) = l(\lambda)r(\lambda) + \left(\int l(\hat{\lambda})a(\hat{\lambda})d\hat{\lambda}\right)e(\lambda). \tag{1}$$

Note that the absorption spectra $a(\lambda)$ is merged into a scalar coefficient of emission, i.e. $\int l(\hat{\lambda})a(\hat{\lambda})d\hat{\lambda}$, thus it could not be directly observed in the radiance $p(\lambda)$. Therefore, the full spectra estimation problem is usually formulated as a separation problem of reflectance and fluorescent emission at the first stage.

Rather than using specialized narrowband or high-frequency illuminations, we aim at achieving this separation task by using ordinary illuminants. As shall be disclosed later, we have found that, by using three hyperspectral images, the separation is feasible under the mild assumption that the three illumination spectra are wideband and mutually independent. This mild condition allows us to use such ordinary illuminants in daily life as LED bulbs and fluorescent lamps.

2.1   Using Three Hyperspectral Images

Given three illumination spectra $l_j(\lambda)$ and their corresponding radiance $p_j(\lambda)$ recorded by a hypersepctral camera with n bands, the imaging equation in eq.(1) can be rewritten as

$$p_j(\lambda_i) = l_j(\lambda_i)r(\lambda_i) + a_j e(\lambda_i), i = 1, 2, \cdots, n, j = 1, 2, 3, \tag{2}$$

where the scalar a_j is introduced to represent the absorption coefficient $\int l_j(\lambda)a(\lambda)d\lambda$. Due to the scale ambiguity between a_j and e, without loss of generality, we can simply introduce a scale constraint such that $a_1 + a_2 + a_3 = 1$. It causes no problem since a_1, a_2 and a_3 are positive for an excited fluorescent-reflective object.

Apparently, the three equations in eq.(2) provide $3n + 1$ constraints, one of which is the scale constraint $a_1 + a_2 + a_3 = 1$ that we have introduced. The number of variables is $2n + 3$. It seems to tell that using three images would result in an overconstrained system, without involving any low-dimensional models of reflectance and emission. To obtain the reflectance and emission spectra, we need to solve the following bilinear programming problem

$$\min_{a_j, \mathbf{r}, \mathbf{e}} \left\| \begin{bmatrix} L_1 & A_1 \\ L_2 & A_2 \\ L_3 & A_3 \end{bmatrix} \begin{bmatrix} \mathbf{r} \\ \mathbf{e} \end{bmatrix} - \begin{bmatrix} \mathbf{p}_1 \\ \mathbf{p}_2 \\ \mathbf{p}_3 \end{bmatrix} \right\|_2^2 , \, s.t., \sum_{j=1}^{3} a_j = 1, a_j \geq 0, \mathbf{r} \geq \mathbf{0}, \mathbf{e} \geq \mathbf{0}, \tag{3}$$

in which L_j, $j = 1, 2, 3$, represents $diag\{l_j(\lambda_1), \cdots, l_j(\lambda_n)\}$, while A_j denotes the diagonal matrix of a_j. In addition, $\mathbf{p}_j = \begin{bmatrix} p_j(\lambda_1), \cdots, p_j(\lambda_n) \end{bmatrix}^T$, $\mathbf{r} = \begin{bmatrix} r(\lambda_1), \cdots, r(\lambda_n) \end{bmatrix}^T$ and $\mathbf{e} = \begin{bmatrix} e(\lambda_1), \cdots, e(\lambda_n) \end{bmatrix}^T$.

The optimization problem in eq.(3) is very challenging due to its nonconvexity, arising from the bilinear correlation between a_j and $\mathbf{e}$. We can retrieve its global minimum by using two-dimensional exhaustive search, which is extremely slow. In contrast, using certain local optimization method would require a reasonable initialization, which is unknown yet. In the following, we reformulate the imaging equations into a linear system, which in turn clearly reveals the condition on the illumination spectra for solution uniqueness.

2.2   Reformulation and Practical Algorithm

For the current time being, let us assume that the absorption scalars a_1, a_2 and a_3 are known. Then, the first two equations in eq.(2) happen to have the same number ($2n$) of constraints and variables, from which the reflectance $r(\lambda_i)$ and the emission $e(\lambda_i)$ can be solved in closed form as

$$r(\lambda_i) = \frac{a_2 p_1(\lambda_i) - a_1 p_2(\lambda_i)}{a_2 l_1(\lambda_i) - a_1 l_2(\lambda_i)}, e(\lambda_i) = \frac{p_2(\lambda_i)l_1(\lambda_i) - p_1(\lambda_i)l_2(\lambda_i)}{a_2 l_1(\lambda_i) - a_1 l_2(\lambda_i)}. \tag{4}$$

After plugging eq.(4) into the third equation of eq.(2), we obtain

$$p_3(\lambda_i) = \frac{l_3(\lambda_i)\left[a_2 p_1(\lambda_i) - a_1 p_2(\lambda_i)\right] + a_3 \left[p_2(\lambda_i)l_1(\lambda_i) - p_1(\lambda_i)l_2(\lambda_i)\right]}{a_2 l_1(\lambda_i) - a_1 l_2(\lambda_i)}. \tag{5}$$

By multiplying the denominator $a_2 l_1(\lambda_i) - a_1 l_2(\lambda_i)$ at both sides of eq.(5), a very compact linear equation can be obtained after some basic algebraic operations

$$\begin{bmatrix} p_2 l_3 - p_3 l_2 & p_3 l_1 - p_1 l_3 & p_1 l_2 - p_2 l_1 \end{bmatrix} \begin{bmatrix} a_1 & a_2 & a_3 \end{bmatrix}^T = 0, \tag{6}$$

in which the wavelength index λ_i has been omitted for brevity. Therefore, all n bands can be stacked into a matrix form

$$\left[\mathbf{p}_2 \odot \mathbf{l}_3 - \mathbf{p}_3 \odot \mathbf{l}_2 \quad \mathbf{p}_3 \odot \mathbf{l}_1 - \mathbf{p}_1 \odot \mathbf{l}_3 \quad \mathbf{p}_1 \odot \mathbf{l}_2 - \mathbf{p}_2 \odot \mathbf{l}_1\right] \begin{bmatrix} a_1 \\ a_2 \\ a_3 \end{bmatrix} = M \begin{bmatrix} a_1 \\ a_2 \\ a_3 \end{bmatrix} = \mathbf{0}, \qquad (7)$$

where the operator $\odot$ denotes element-wise multiplication of vectors. M is the $n \times 3$ data matrix constructed from the radiance vectors $\mathbf{p}_j$ and illumination spectra vectors $\mathbf{l}_j, j = 1, 2, 3$.

In the noise-free case, eq.(7) has a unique solution, as long as the rank of M is 2. This condition can be easily satisfied when the three illumination spectra are wideband and independent.

In presence of image noise, the rank of M is usually 3. Based on eq.(7), we can easily estimate the absorption scalars by solving the following convex quadratic program

$$\min_{a_1, a_2, a_3} \left\| M \begin{bmatrix} a_1 & a_2 & a_3 \end{bmatrix}^T \right\|_2^2, s.t., a_1 + a_2 + a_3 = 1, a_1 \geq 0, a_2 \geq 0, a_3 \geq 0. \qquad (8)$$

In the derivation process of eq.(6), the three images are not treated in a balanced manner, that is, to explicitly build the linear system on the third image, while using the first and second images to solve the reflectance and emission spectra. In addition, the nonnegative constraints of reflectance and emission spectra have been ignored. To further improve accuracy, we can start from the solution from eq.(8), and minimize eq.(3) via the standard alternating minimization scheme. Specifically, given a_1, a_2 and a_3, all n bands become independent, thus we can easily update $r(\lambda_i)$ and $e(\lambda_i), i = 1, 2, \cdots, n$, by solving n trivial quadratic programs

$$\min_{r(\lambda_i), e(\lambda_i)} \left\| \begin{bmatrix} l_1(\lambda_i) a_1 \\ l_2(\lambda_i) a_2 \\ l_3(\lambda_i) a_3 \end{bmatrix} \begin{bmatrix} r(\lambda_i) \\ e(\lambda_i) \end{bmatrix} - \begin{bmatrix} p_1(\lambda_i) \\ p_2(\lambda_i) \\ p_3(\lambda_i) \end{bmatrix} \right\|_2^2, s.t., r(\lambda_i) \geq 0, e(\lambda_i) \geq 0. \qquad (9)$$

When $r(\lambda_i)$ and $e(\lambda_i), i = 1, 2, \cdots, n$, are known, a_1, a_2 and a_3 can be updated by solving

$$\min_{a_1, a_2, a_3} \left\| \begin{bmatrix} \mathbf{e} & & \\ & \mathbf{e} & \\ & & \mathbf{e} \end{bmatrix} \begin{bmatrix} a_1 \\ a_2 \\ a_3 \end{bmatrix} - \begin{bmatrix} \mathbf{p}_1 - \mathbf{l}_1 \odot \mathbf{r} \\ \mathbf{p}_2 - \mathbf{l}_2 \odot \mathbf{r} \\ \mathbf{p}_3 - \mathbf{l}_3 \odot \mathbf{r} \end{bmatrix} \right\|_2^2, s.t., a_1 + a_2 + a_3 = 1, a_1 \geq 0, a_2 \geq 0, a_3 \geq 0.$$
$$(10)$$

Since the initialization from solving eq.(8) is already sufficiently accurate, the maximum iteration number of alternating minimization is chosen to be 10 in all the experiments. In addition, it is well known that a small convex quadratic program with simple bound constraints can be directly solved via the active set method. Therefore, we can solve all the programs in eq.(8), eq.(9) and eq.(10) efficiently by using linear algebraic operations in closed form, rather than resorting to the more complicated iterative interior point method [6].

To sum up, the procedures of our algorithm for reflectance and fluorescent emission separation are: (i). Constructing the data matrix M in eq.(7); (ii). Solving eq.(8) to obtain the absorption scalars a_1, a_2 and a_3; (iii). Solving eq.(9) and eq.(10) alternatively to

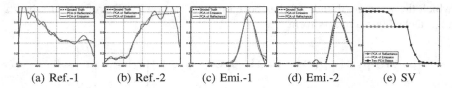

(a) Ref.-1   (b) Ref.-2   (c) Emi.-1   (d) Emi.-2   (e) SV

Fig. 2. Dependence between the reflectance and the emission PCA bases. (a) and (b) show that a reflectance spectra can be well approximated by the emission bases, while (c) and (d) illustrate that the reflectance bases can approximate the emission spectra as well. The reason lies in the linear dependence between these two bases, as verified by their singular values (SV) in (e).

refine the estimation of the reflectance $r(\lambda_i)$ and the emission $e(\lambda_i), i = 1, 2, \cdots, n$, until the maximum number of iterations (10 in our experiments) is reached. To deal with a fluorescent-reflective scene, one should repeat the above procedures for all pixels in the scene. Due to this pixel-wise independence, the whole algorithm can be easily parallelized for faster speed.

Until now, we have shown that using three hyperspectral images under mild restrictions on the illumination spectra is sufficient for fluorescent and reflective spectra separation. In the following, we explore the possibility of reducing the number of images further.

2.3   Using One or Two Images

Given a single hyperspectral image, we have only the first equation of eq.(2) at hand

$$p_1(\lambda_i) = l_1(\lambda_i)r(\lambda_i) + a_1e(\lambda_i), i = 1, 2, \cdots, n. \tag{11}$$

Here, to resolve the ambiguity between a_1 and e, we can assume that $a_1 = 1$. Therefore, eq.(11) has $2n$ variables and n constraints, and as a result infinitely many solutions.

It has long been known that practical reflectance can be well represented by a linear model with low dimensionality, e.g. 8, as verified in [15, 18]. Lam and Sato [13] observed that the fluorescent emission can also be accurately approximated by using a 12-D linear model leaned from PCA of training data. In order to reduce the number of variables, a straightforward idea is to embed the linear models into eq.(11) as follows

$$\mathbf{p}_1 = L_1\mathbf{r} + \mathbf{e} = L_1B_r\mathbf{c}_r + B_e\mathbf{c}_e. \tag{12}$$

At first glance, eq.(12) is overconstrained, since the number of constraints is n, which is usually much larger than the total number of bases (8+12=20). The coefficients $\mathbf{c}_r$ and $\mathbf{c}_e$ can be obtained by solving the following convex quadratic program

$$\min_{\mathbf{c}_r, \mathbf{c}_e} \left\| [L_1B_r\ B_e]\begin{bmatrix}\mathbf{c}_r\\\mathbf{c}_e\end{bmatrix} - \mathbf{p}_1 \right\|_2^2, s.t., B_r\mathbf{c}_r \geq \mathbf{0}, B_e\mathbf{c}_e \geq \mathbf{0}, \tag{13}$$

into which we have incorporated the nonnegative constraints of reflectance and emission.

However, our experiment results, as shall be shown in Fig.5, reveal that the estimation accuracy of reflectance and emission is very poor even in no presence of image noise. By closer investigation, we have found that the primary reason lies in the linear dependence of the bases of reflectance and emission. Specifically, as shown in Fig.2, although the PCA-based linear model of reflectance can express a reflectance spectra exactly, it can also approximate emission with reasonable accuracy, and vice versa. This dependence is more obvious when observing the singular values of these two bases in Fig.2(e). We have also observed that simply reducing the number of bases, surely at the cost of weakening expression power, would rarely remedy this dependence problem.

How about using two images? Given the second illumination spectra $l_2(\lambda)$ and its corresponding radiance $p_2(\lambda)$, the second equation in eq.(2) reads

$$p_2(\lambda_i) = l_2(\lambda_i)r(\lambda_i) + a_2 e(\lambda_i), i = 1, 2, \cdots, n. \tag{14}$$

To fix the scale ambiguity of a_1 and a_2, we add a scale constraint such that $a_1 + a_2 = 1$.

Again, eq.(11) and eq.(14) offer $2n + 1$ constraints, thus less than the number of variables $2n + 2$. One possible way is to introduce the linear models for reflectance and emission, which still suffers from the basis dependence problem, as shall be shown in Fig.5(b-c). Note that, in the solving process, we conduct one-dimensional search over a_1 to make sure that the globally optimal solution is retrieved, although eq.(11) and eq.(14) are bilinear in terms of a_1, a_2 and $e(\lambda_i)$.

Using high-frequency illuminations [9] can be interpreted as another remedy, since the absorption scalars a_1 and a_2 tend to be equal under high-frequency and comple-mentary illuminations. In effect, it adds another constraint $a_1 = a_2$, and makes eq.(11) and eq.(14) uniquely solvable. Unfortunately, this equality does not hold under ordinary illuminations.

One might consider to use RGB images, instead of hyperspectral images, so as to further reduce the cost. Unfortunately, when using RGB images, one illumination offers only three constraints, such a separation method would rely heavily on the subspace model to reduce the number of variables, and consequently, should be more likely to suffer from the aforementioned linear dependence problem.

One might also wonder why using the linear subspace models caused no problem in [13]. Let us recall that narrowband illuminations were used there. Under this condition, reflectance and fluorescence are almost detached, because of the wavelength shift effect. Therefore, the work [13] is more about spectra fitting of individual components than on spectra separation.

3 Absorption Spectra Estimation

In this section, we show how to estimate the absorption spectra $a(\lambda_i), i = 1, 2, \cdots, n$, by using the three absorption scalars a_1, a_2, a_3, as well as the estimated emission spectra $e(\lambda_i)$. Note that the aforementioned linear model in [13] is inapplicable to our setup, since its dimensionality is much larger than the number of constraints that we have at hand.

As shown in Fig.3(a), the absorption and emission spectra pair of a typical fluores-cent material have bell-like shapes, with a long tail toward the short-wavelength and the long-wavelength direction, respectively. This is very similar to the density function of the skew Cauchy distribution, as shown in Fig.3(b-d). This observation motivates us to develop a compact low-dimensional representation of absorption and emission spectra.

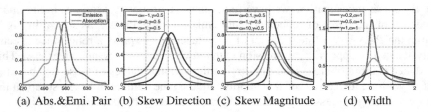

| (a) Abs.&Emi. Pair | (b) Skew Direction | (c) Skew Magnitude | (d) Width |

Fig. 3. The absorption and emission spectra pair of a typical fluorescent material (a) v.s. the density function of the skew Cauchy distribution, with varying tail direction (b), skewness magnitude (c) and width (d).

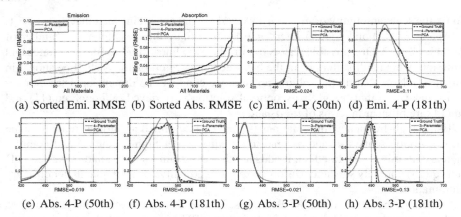

| (a) Sorted Emi. RMSE | (b) Sorted Abs. RMSE | (c) Emi. 4-P (50th) | (d) Emi. 4-P (181th) |

| (e) Abs. 4-P (50th) | (f) Abs. 4-P (181th) | (g) Abs. 3-P (50th) | (h) Abs. 3-P (181th) |

Fig. 4. Verification of the four-parameter (4-P) and three-parameter (3-P) nonlinear models. (a) and (b) show the sorted fitting error (RMSE) of all 181 materials for emission and absorption spectra, respectively. Some examples of reasonable fitting (50th) and worst fitting (181th) are shown in (c-h).

3.1 Four-Parameter Nonlinear Model

Being a variant of the standard Cauchy distribution, the skew Cauchy distribution has a skewness parameter to control the magnitude and direction of its skew tail. The analytic form of its density function reads [2, 3]

$$f(x|x_0, \gamma, \omega) = \frac{\gamma}{\pi\left[\gamma^2 + (x - x_0)^2\right]} \left\{\frac{1}{\pi}\arctan\left[\frac{\omega(x - x_0)}{\gamma}\right] + \frac{1}{2}\right\}, x \in \mathbb{R}, \quad (15)$$

where x_0, γ and ω are the location, width and skewness parameter, respectively. The skew Cauchy distribution is a special case of the skew t-distribution, when the number of degrees of freedom (DoF) is 1. When the DoF approaches infinity, the skew t-distribution reduces to the well-known skew normal distribution [3]. We prefer the skew Cauchy distribution because of its relatively simple analytical form.

An important property by observing Fig.3 is that the tail is toward to the left when $\omega < 0$, while to the right when $\omega > 0$. In addition, the skew magnitude is determined by the absolute value of ω. This property actually allows us to explicitly discriminate the absorption spectra from the emission spectra.

In order to express the fluorescent emission and absorption, we introduce a height parameter h and obtain the ultimate four-parameter model

$$f(x|x_0, \gamma, \omega, h) = \frac{h}{[\gamma^2 + (x - x_0)^2]} \left\{ \frac{1}{\pi} \arctan \left[\frac{\omega(x - x_0)}{\gamma} \right] + \frac{1}{2} \right\}. \tag{16}$$

To verify the validity of our proposed model, we have tried to fit it to the fluorescence spectra dataset [16] with 181 fluorescent materials in the visible range from 420 nm to 700 nm with an increment of 5nm. As shown in Fig.4, the four-parameter (4-P) model can represent both the emission and the absorption with reasonable accuracy, although it is slightly less accurate than the PCA-based linear model (with dimensionality 12).

Since there are only three images in our setup, it is impossible to estimate the four parameters of an absorption spectra. To resolve this problem, we further observe that the emission and absorption pair of a fluorescent material usually have almost the same length of tail, as illustrated by the representative pair in Fig.3(a). Thanks to the special property of a skew Cauchy distribution mentioned above, we can first fit the four pa- rameter model to the emission spectra so as to find its skewness parameter $\tilde{\omega}$, and then use $-\tilde{\omega}$ as the skewness parameter of its corresponding absorption spectra model. We have also verified that this three-parameter (3-P) model of absorption is of sufficient accuracy, as shown in Fig.4(b), (g) and (h). Admittedly, this low-dimensional model tends to smooth out some high-frequency details of the absorption spectra. However, it should be acceptable, since the absorption spectra is emerged into a scalar coefficient of emission, as shown in eq.(1).

3.2   Estimation Method

Based on the model in eq.(16) and the skewness parameter $-\tilde{\omega}$, the absorption spectra can be expressed as

$$a(\lambda|\bar{\lambda}_0, \bar{\gamma}, \bar{h}; -\tilde{\omega}) = \frac{\bar{h}}{[\bar{\gamma}^2 + (\lambda - \bar{\lambda}_0)^2]} \left\{ \frac{1}{\pi} \arctan \left[\frac{-\tilde{\omega}(\lambda - \bar{\lambda}_0)}{\bar{\gamma}} \right] + \frac{1}{2} \right\}, \tag{17}$$

in which $\bar{\lambda}_0$, $\bar{\gamma}$ and $\bar{h}$ are the three unknown parameters. To estimate these three param- eters, we can solve the following nonlinear minimization problem

$$\min_{\bar{\lambda}_0, \bar{\gamma}, \bar{h}} \left(\int l_1(\lambda)a(\lambda)d\lambda - a_1 \right)^2 + \left(\int l_2(\lambda)a(\lambda)d\lambda - a_2 \right)^2 + \left(\int l_3(\lambda)a(\lambda)d\lambda - a_3 \right)^2, \tag{18}$$

for which we use the standard Gauss-Newton method.

Considering that eq.(18) defines a minimal problem with three variables and three constraints, one might seek to find all the feasible solutions. However, due to the anti- trigonometric function in eq.(17), this is too challenging. By fitting the four-parameter model to the recovered emission spectra, we can find at the same time a reasonable initialization for $\bar{\lambda}_0$, $\bar{\gamma}$ and $\bar{h}$. This initialization is of tremendous benefit to the locally optimal Gauss-Newton method, and makes it work very well for solving eq.(18).

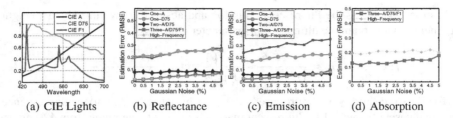

(a) CIE Lights   (b) Reflectance   (c) Emission   (d) Absorption

Fig. 5. Estimation accuracy w.r.t. varying noise levels by using synthetic data. (a) shows the three ordinary illumination spectra used in simulation. The estimation error (RMSE) for reflectance, emission and absorption are shown in (b), (c) and (d), respectively. The number (One, Two and Three) in the legend indicates the number of illuminants used.

4   Experiment Results

4.1   Synthetic Data

Here, we evaluate the accuracy of our proposed methods on synthetic data, and disclose how it compares with that of the state-of-the-art method [9] using specialized high-frequency illuminations.

The standard CIE A, D75 and F1 illumination spectra are used, as shown in Fig.5(a). We randomly select one color from the 18 color patches on the Macbeth color checker as the reflectance spectra. As for the absorption and emission pair, we randomly select one pair from the fluorescent spectra dataset [16] with 181 materials in all. All spectra are normalized such that the maximum value is 1. We add zero-mean Gaussian noise onto the synthesized hyperspectral signals, with standard deviations from 0 to 5% relative magnitude. At each deviation level, we measure the root mean square error (RMSE) of the estimated spectra, with respect to their corresponding ground truth.

By following [9], the period of the high-frequency illuminations is chosen to be 35 nm. We carefully adjust the phase to make sure that the two illuminations are as complementary as possible, while avoiding the singularities when they have the same value.

The average RMSE over 200 independent runs for reflectance and emission are respectively shown in Fig.5(b) and Fig.5(c), from which we can see that our separation method has the same accuracy as [9], although only ordinary illuminants are used. In addition, as illustrated in Fig.5(d), our absorption spectra estimation method is clearly better in accuracy than the heuristic method in [9].

To further validate our analysis on the risk of using one or two ordinary illuminants, we also include them into comparison, as shown in Fig.5(b-c). Even in no presence of noise, the estimation accuracy of using one or two illuminants is not satisfactory. Note that, in the solving process, we have used convex optimization or exhaustive one-dimensional search to preclude any potential influence of local minima. As analyzed in Sec.2.3, the estimation inaccuracy is indeed caused by the dependency between the linear subspace models of reflectance and fluorescent emission.

An interesting observation from Fig.5(b-c) is that, when using two illuminants, the estimation accuracy is higher than using three illuminants in the highly noisy cases, e.g., with 5% relative noise. This is due to that our algorithm for three illuminants does

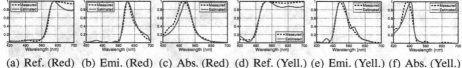

(a) Ref. (Red) (b) Emi. (Red) (c) Abs. (Red) (d) Ref. (Yell.) (e) Emi. (Yell.) (f) Abs. (Yell.)

Fig. 6. The estimated reflectance, emission and absorption spectra for the red (a-c) and yellow (d-f) patch in the scene of Fig.1, w.r.t. their respective measured ground truth.

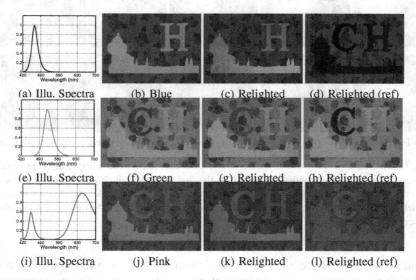

(a) Illu. Spectra   (b) Blue   (c) Relighted   (d) Relighted (ref)

(e) Illu. Spectra   (f) Green   (g) Relighted   (h) Relighted (ref)

(i) Illu. Spectra   (j) Pink   (k) Relighted   (l) Relighted (ref)

Fig. 7. Relighting the scene in Fig.1(c) under blue, green and pink color illuminations.

not involve the subspace models in the process of minimizing eq.(3), in order to be relatively fair when comparing with [9]. It is expected that, when the subspace models are embedded into our algorithm, the separation accuracy could be further improved, at the cost of longer running time.

4.2 Real Images

We use as lighting sources three ordinary illuminants, including an incandescent, a LED and a fluorescent bulb, as shown in Fig.1(a). Their spectra are presented in Fig.1(b). An EBA JAPAN NH-7 hyperspectral camera is used to capture images in the visible range from 420 nm to 700 nm with an interval of 5 nm. For visualization, all hyperspectral images are shown in RGB.

Given three hyperspectral images, we first separate the fluorescent and reflective components by following the procedures in Sec.2.2, and then estimate the absorption spectra by using the method in Sec.3.2.

As shown in Fig.1(c), we first design a scene with three fluorescent patches, whose reflectance, absorption and emission spectra have been measured. Fig.1(d) and Fig.1(e) show the rendered RGB images of our estimated reflectance and fluorescent emission

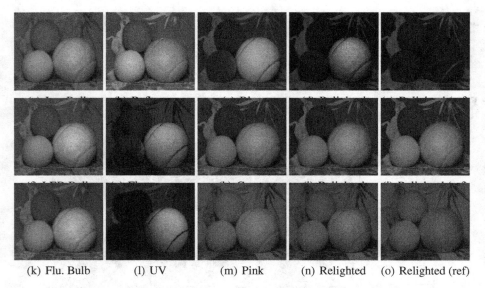

(k) Flu. Bulb   (l) UV   (m) Pink   (n) Relighted   (o) Relighted (ref)

Fig. 8. Tennis ball and sport shorts scene. The 1st column shows the scene under the three il-luminants. Our separation results are shown in the 2nd column, which also includes the scene under near UV light for reference. The 3rd column shows the scene under novel color illumina-tions, while the 4th and 5th columns include the relighting results with fluorescence and without fluorescence, respectively.

spectra, respectively. By referring to the quantitative comparison in Fig.6, we can see that the estimated spectra are sufficiently close to their corresponding measured ones. As for the estimated reflectance spectra in Fig.6(a) and (d), minor discrepancy occurs in the range from 630 nm to 700 nm. This is caused by low-irradiance of the fluores-cent bulb in that range, as shown in Fig.1(b). This low-irradiance problem causes some inaccuracy in the process of posterior white balancing.

Given the full spectra of a fluorescent-reflective scene, we can easily relight the scene under any illumination spectra on the basis of the imaging equation. The relighting results of the scene in Fig.1(c) under blue, green and pink illuminations are shown in Fig.7, from which we can see that accounting for reflectance only would cause poor relighting results, when nontrivial fluorescence is present in the scene.

We have also evaluated our methods on scenes with manmade objects, like the ten-nis ball and sport shorts scene in Fig.8 and the candle scene in Fig.9. The apparent advantages in relighting results not only reveal the effectiveness of our proposed meth-ods, but also underline the necessity of accounting for fluorescence. In Fig.8(d), the relighted tennis ball assumes nontrivial discrepancy from its ground truth in Fig.8(c). We are speculating that the felty surface of a tennis ball goes somehow beyond the dif-fuse imaging equation in eq.(1). To further identify the reason and the possible solution is our future work.

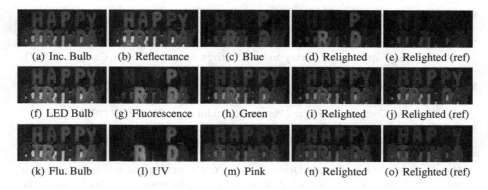

(a) Inc. Bulb	(b) Reflectance	(c) Blue	(d) Relighted	(e) Relighted (ref)
(f) LED Bulb	(g) Fluorescence	(h) Green	(i) Relighted	(j) Relighted (ref)
(k) Flu. Bulb	(l) UV	(m) Pink	(n) Relighted	(o) Relighted (ref)

Fig. 9. Candle scene. The scene under various illuminations, as well as the separation and relighting results, have the same layout as in Fig.8.

5   Conclusions

We have proposed accurate and effective methods to estimate the full spectra of a fluorescent-reflective scene by using hyperspectral images under ordinary illuminations. We disclosed the linear dependence between the PCA-based linear bases of reflectance and fluorescent emission, and showed that using one or two images is insufficient for accurate reflectance and emission separation. In the presence of three hyperspectral images, we have reformulated the imaging equations into a linear system, and revealed that three wideband and independent illuminants in general are sufficient for the separation task. An elegant convex optimization method was proposed for solving, whose solution can be further polished via a few alternating iterations. As for absorption estimation, we proposed a novel four-parameter nonlinear model to express absorption and emission spectra. Based on this model, an absorption spectra estimation method in the presence of three illuminations was proposed as well. Experiment results have verified the accuracy and effectiveness of our proposed methods.

Considering that the four-parameter model is more discriminative than the linear model, it might benefit the task of separating the fluorescent and reflective components in a single hyperspectral image. We plan to explore this possibility in the future.

References

1. Alterman, M., Schechner, Y., Weiss, A.: Multiplexed fluorescence unmixing. In: IEEE International Conference on Computational Photography pp. 1–8 (2010)
2. Arnold, B., Beaver, R.: The skew-Cauchy distribution. Statistics & Probability Letters 49(3), 285–290 (2000)
3. Azzalini, A.: The Skew-Normal and Related Families, 1st edn. Cambridge University Press (2014)
4. Barnard, K.: Color constancy with fluorescent surfaces. In: Proc. of the Color and Imaging Conference, pp. 257–261 (1999)
5. Boyd, S., Parikh, N., Chu, E., Peleato, B., Eckstein, J.: Separating the fluorescence and reflectance components of coral spectra. Applied Optics 40(21), 3614–3621 (2001)

6. Boyd, S., Vandenberghe, L.: Convex Optimization, 1st edn. Cambridge University Press (2004)
7. Chane, C., Mansouri, A., Marzani, F., Boochs, F.: Integration of 3D and multispectral data for cultural heritage applications: survey and perspectives. Image and Vision Computing 31(1), 91–102 (2013)
8. Fu, Y., Lam, A., Kobashi, Y., Sato, I., Okabe, T., Sato, Y.: Reflectance and fluorescent spectra recovery based on fluorescent chromaticity invariance under varying illumination. In: IEEE Conference on Computer Vision and Pattern Recognition, pp. 2163–2170 (2014)
9. Fu, Y., Lam, A., Sato, I., Okabe, T., Sato, Y.: Separating reflective and fluorescent components using high frequency illumination in the spectral domain. In: IEEE International Conference on Computer Vision, pp. 457–464 (2013)
10. Han, S., Matsushita, Y., Sato, I., Okabe, T., Sato, Y.: Camera spectral sensitivity estimation from a single image under unknown illumination by using fluorescence. In: IEEE Conference on Computer Vision and Pattern Recognition, pp. 805–812 (2012)
11. Johnson, G., Fairchild, M.: Full-spectral color calculations in realistic image synthesis. IEEE Computer Graphics and Applications 19(4), 47–53 (1999)
12. Kim, S., Zhuo, S., Deng, F., Fu, C., Brown, M.: Interactive visualization of hyperspectral images of historical documents. IEEE Trans. Visualization and Computer Graphics 16(6), 1441–1448 (2010)
13. Lam, A., Sato, I.: Spectral modeling and relighting of reflective-fluorescent scenes. In: IEEE Conference on Computer Vision and Pattern Recognition, pp. 1452–1459 (2013)
14. Leland, J., Johnson, N., Arecchi, A.: Principles of bispectral fluorescence colorimetry. In: Proc. SPIE, vol. 3140, pp. 76–87 (1997)
15. Maloney, L.: Evaluation of linear models of surface spectral reflectance with small numbers of parameters. J. Opt. Soc. Am. A 3(10), 1673–1683 (1986)
16. McNamara, G., Gupta, A., Reynaert, J., Coates, T., Boswell, C.: Spectral imaging microscopy web sites and data. Cytometry Part A 69(8), 863–871 (2006)
17. Park, J., Lee, M., Grossberg, M., Nayar, S.: Multispectral imaging using multiplexed illumination. In : IEEE International Conference on Computer Vision, pp. 1–8 (2007)
18. Parkkinen, J., Hallikainen, J., Jaaskelainen, T.: Characteristic spectra of munsell colors. J. Opt. Soc. Am. A 6(2), 318–322 (1989)
19. Sato, I., Okabe, T., Sato, Y.: Bispectral photometric stereo based on fluorescence. In: IEEE Conference on Computer Vision and Pattern Recognition, pp. 270–277 (2012)
20. Suo, J., Bian, L., Chen, F., Dai, Q.: Bispectral coding: compressive and high-quality acquisition of fluorescence and reflectance. Optics Express 22(2), 1697–1712 (2014)
21. Tominaga, S., Horiuchi, T., Kamiyama, T.: Spectral estimation of fluorescent objects using visible lights and an imaging device. In: Proc. of the Color and Imaging Conference, pp. 352–356 (2011)
22. Treibitz, T., Murez, Z., Mitchell, B.G., Kriegman, D.: Shape from fluorescence. In: Fitzgibbon, A., Lazebnik, S., Perona, P., Sato, Y., Schmid, C. (eds.) ECCV 2012, Part VII. LNCS, vol. 7578, pp. 292–306. Springer, Heidelberg (2012)
23. Zhang, C., Sato, I.: Separating reflective and fluorescent components of an image. In: IEEE Conference on Computer Vision and Pattern Recognition, pp. 185–192 (2011)

Interreflection Removal Using Fluorescence

Ying Fu[1], Antony Lam[2], Yasuyuki Matsushita[3],
Imari Sato[4], and Yoichi Sato[1]

[1] The University of Tokyo, Japan
[2] Saitama University
[3] Microsoft Research Asia
[4] National Institute of Informatics

Abstract. Interreflections exhibit a number of challenges for existing shape-from-intensity methods that only assume a direct lighting model. Removing the interreflections from scene observations is of broad interest since it enhances the accuracy of those methods. In this paper, we propose a method for removing interreflections from a single image using fluorescence. From a bispectral observation of reflective and fluorescent components recorded in distinct color channels, our method separates direct lighting from interreflections. Experimental results demonstrate the effectiveness of the proposed method on complex and dynamic scenes. In addition, we show how our method improves an existing photometric stereo method in shape recovery.

Keywords: Fluorescence, bispectral model, bispectral interreflection model, and interreflection removal.

1 Introduction

Interreflection is a global light transport process whereby light reflected from a surface point illuminates other points. In the presence of interreflections, an intensity observation of a scene consists of the directly reflected light rays after a single-bounce on a surface (direct component) and light rays that bounce off of the scene surface multiple times before they reach the camera (indirect component). Modeling and removing interreflections is of broad interest for making shape-from-intensity methods to work properly, because most of them are designed to take only the direct component as input.

Recent studies on this problem provide deeper understandings about the inverse light transport and show that the direct and indirect components can be separated for static scenes image [23,18,15]. In addition, some papers have tackled the problem for dynamic scenes but the capture process may require specialized masks [18,20] or motion compensation [1].

In this paper, we show that separation can be achieved for dynamic scenes by capturing only a single image using *fluorescence* (see Fig. 1). Fluorescent materials[1] not only reflect incident light but also absorb and emit light at longer

---

[1] In practice, fluorescent materials show both ordinary reflection and fluorescent emission.

D. Fleet et al. (Eds.): ECCV 2014, Part V, LNCS 8693, pp. 203–217, 2014.

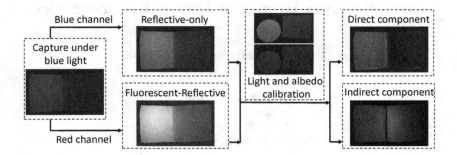

Fig. 1. Overview of the proposed method. A fluorescent object is captured under blue light, whose blue channel is a reflective-only image and red channel is a wavelength-shifted fluorescent-reflective image. The lighting and albedo are calibrated by images of the flat white target and fluorescent sheet captured under blue and red light. After calibration, direct and indirect components can be recovered.

wavelengths [13] (see Fig. 2) . This physical property allows us to obtain single-shot images that contain reflective-only images at the same wavelength as the illuminant and wavelength-shifted images that are a mixture of fluorescent emission and interreflections of those emissions. We call this wavelength-shifted image a fluorescent-reflective image. We illustrate these concepts with an example. If a scene is illuminated by a blue light source, the reflective-only image is recorded in the blue channel, and the fluorescent-reflective image could be captured in the red channel (see Fig. 1). Interreflections still exist in both channels but using this bispectral measurement, we develop a direct-indirect decomposition method by deriving a new interreflection model for fluorescence and extending Liao *et al.* [15] where they used varying light colors and multiple images. Unlike Liao *et al.*'s method, our method only requires a single image with an assumption of commonly available fluorescent materials, which enables interreflection removal from a dynamic scene.

In summary, our main contributions are that we

- derive a general interreflection model for fluorescent materials,
- develop a method to separate direct-indirect components from reflective-only and fluorescent-reflective measurements, and
- show that a single-shot measurement is sufficient for the decomposition using fluorescence.

2   Related Work

Fluorescence. Fluorescent analysis has received attention in recent years in computer vision. Examples of such work can be found in color rendering [11,25], reflectance and re-radiation modeling [10], camera spectral sensitivity estimation [8], 3D reconstruction [21,24], immersion range scanning [9], and color relighting of real scenes [4,14]. In many of these methods, a phenomenon of

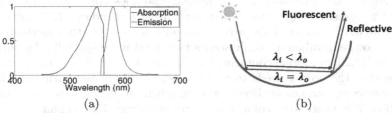

Fig. 2. (a) An example of absorption and emission spectra in the McNamara and Boswell fluorescence spectral dataset [16]. (b)When the fluorescent material is illuminated, it will reflect at the same wavelength and emit light at longer wavelengths.

fluorescence known as Stokes shift is exploited to achieve results. Specifically, Stokes shift can be described simply as the absorption of light at shorter wavelengths and emission of light at longer wavelengths [13]. The way this works is that when incident light hits a fluorescent surface, the surface's absorption spectrum will determine how much of the light is absorbed. Some of the absorbed energy is then released in the form of an emission spectrum at longer wavelengths than the incident light. The remainder of the absorbed energy is released as heat. In this paper, we take advantage of Stokes shift to assist with interreflection removal.

Interreflection. There have been a number of methods that analyze interreflection and demonstrate applications such as shape recovery. Koenderink and Doorn [12] presented a general model for diffuse interreflections. Forsyth *et al.* [3,2] studied how interreflections affect shape recovery. Later, Nayar *et al.* [19] addressed the interplay between interreflections and shape by iteratively refining the shape and reflectance of surfaces. They then extended their algorithm to colored and multi-colored surfaces [17].

Despite the effectiveness of past approaches such as [19] and [17], the modeling and separation of interreflections is of broader interest because most shape-from-intensity methods assume only direct lighting. Thus solving the problem of separating out interreflections would allow for improving an entire body of methods in the literature. An early example of such work was presented by Funt *et al.* [5,6] where the color different effect in interreflections was used to separate interreflections from direct lighting. Later, Seitz *et al.* [23] proved the existence of an inverse light transport operator capable of separating m-bounced light from scenes with uniform albedo and Lambertian surfaces. However, their method requires a laser and scene capture is very time consuming. In addition, their method is not robust to complex shapes. Nayar *et al.* [18] were able to separate direct and global lighting components for complex scenes using spatially high frequency illumination. In principle, their method would be very fast but in practice, they require additional images or reduced resolution.

More recently, Liao *et al.* [15] removed interreflections by using spectrum-dependent albedo in scenes but their method still needs two images captured under different illuminations. In this paper, we show that by exploiting properties of fluorescence, interreflections can be removed using only using one color image under one illumination. Our method also does not require a highly specialized setup and images can be captured using a standard RGB camera in a straightforward manner. This provides an advantage over other methods for interreflection removal on dynamic scenes that need more specialized setups such as masks [18,20] or motion compensation [1]. Like Liao *et al.* [15], our main drawback is that the object needs to be homogeneously colored with the reflective and fluorescent component. However, even when an object does not satisfy this condition, it is possible to color it using commonly available paint.

3   Bispectral Model for Interreflection Removal

In this section, we first introduce the bispectral model for fluorescent materials. We then briefly review the interreflection model for ordinary reflective materials with a uniform albedo and Lambertian surface and derive the interreflection model for fluorescence. After that, we present our model to separate direct and indirect lighting based on fluorescence. Finally, we describe the practical issues of lighting and albedo calibration.

3.1   Bispectral Model

In general, the appearance of fluorescent materials consists of both reflective and fluorescent components [22]. If we assume a Lambertian surface, the local reflection of the reflective component can be described as

$$E_r(x, \lambda) = \rho(x, \lambda)L(\lambda)\cos\theta, \tag{1}$$

where $\rho(x, \lambda)$ is the albedo of the surface point x at wavelength λ, $L(\lambda)$ is the incoming radiance from the light source, and θ is the angle between the surface normal and light source directions. We refer to $\rho(x, \lambda)$ as the *reflective albedo*.

Unlike the reflective component that reflects light rays at the same wavelength as the incident light, the fluorescent component absorbs and emits light at different wavelengths from the incident one [25,10,22]. Another interesting property is that, as shown by Glassner [7], fluorescence emissions have no directional characteristics and are uniformly radiated in all directions. In other words, fluorescence emissions behave like light reflected from a Lambertian diffuse surface. Therefore, the outgoing radiance E_f from a fluorescent material under the light $L(\lambda_i)$ can be written as

$$E_f(x, \lambda_i, \lambda_o) = \eta(x, \lambda_i, \lambda_o)L(\lambda_i)\cos\theta, \tag{2}$$

where λ_i and λ_o represent the incident and outgoing wavelengths, respectively, and $\eta(x, \lambda_i, \lambda_o)$ is a direction-invariant function that describes the re-radiation property of the fluorescence. According to the characteristics of fluorescence [22], $\eta(x, \lambda_i, \lambda_o)$ can be factored as

$$\eta(x, \lambda_i, \lambda_o) = \mu(x, \lambda_o)a(x, \lambda_i), \tag{3}$$

where $a(x, \lambda_i)$ and $\mu(x, \lambda_o)$ define the absorption and emission factors of the fluorescent material, respectively. In the following, we call $\mu(x, \lambda_o)$ the *fluorescent albedo*. The incoming radiance energy is absorbed by $a(x, \lambda_i)$ as $\int a(x, \lambda_i)L(\lambda_i)d\lambda_i$; therefore, Eq. (2) can be rewritten as

$$E_f(x, \lambda_o) = \mu(x, \lambda_o) \left(\int a(x, \lambda_i)L(\lambda_i)d\lambda_i \right) \cos\theta. \tag{4}$$

Finally, the observation $E(= E_r + E_f)$ becomes

$$E(x, \lambda_o) = \left[\rho(x, \lambda_o)L(\lambda_o)\delta(\lambda_i - \lambda_o) + \mu(x, \lambda_o) \int a(x, \lambda_i)L(\lambda_i)d\lambda_i \right] \cos\theta, \tag{5}$$

in which E_r and E_f are independently observed at two distinct wavelengths λ_i and λ_o, respectively. The delta function $\delta(\lambda_i - \lambda_o)$ is associated with the reflective component because an ordinary reflective component only reflects light at the same wavelength as its incident light ($\lambda_i = \lambda_o$).

3.2   Bispectral Interreflection Model

We briefly review the interreflection model for the ordinary reflective component on a Lambertian surface [12] and extend the interreflection model for the fluorescent component.

Interreflection Model for Reflective Component. The interreflection geometry [12] between points $x \in \mathbb{R}^3$ and $x' \in \mathbb{R}^3$ is described by a kernel K as

$$K(x, x') = \frac{Pos[n(x)^T(x' - x)]Pos[n(x')^T(x - x')]}{\|x' - x\|^2}, \quad Pos[a] = \frac{a + |a|}{2}, \tag{6}$$

where $n(x) \in \mathbb{R}^3$ is the surface normal at point x. The outgoing radiance of the reflective component $I_r(x, \lambda)$ can be expressed as the sum of direct and indirect components as

$$I_r(x, \lambda) = \frac{\rho(x, \lambda)}{\pi}P(x, \lambda) + \frac{\rho(x, \lambda)}{\pi} \int K(x, x')I_r(x', \lambda)dx', \tag{7}$$

where $P(x, \lambda)$ is the irradiance from the light source towards the surface point x at wavelength λ. By defining iterated kernels K_m as

$$K_1(x, x') = \frac{K(x, x')}{\pi}, \quad K_m(x, x') = \int \frac{K(x, y)}{\pi}K_{m-1}(y, x')dy \ (m > 1), \tag{8}$$

Eq. (7) can be rewritten as the polynomial function of ρ as

$$I_r(x, \lambda) = \rho(x, \lambda)\frac{P(x, \lambda)}{\pi} + \sum_{m=2}^{\infty} \rho^m(x, \lambda) \int K_{m-1}(x, x')\frac{P(x', \lambda)}{\pi}dx'. \tag{9}$$

By defining

$$R_1(x, \lambda) = \frac{P(x, \lambda)}{\pi},$$

$$R_m(x, \lambda) = \int K_{m-1}(x, x') \frac{P(x', \lambda)}{\pi} dx' \quad (m > 1), \tag{10}$$

Eq. (9) becomes

$$I_r(x, \lambda) = \sum_{m=1}^{\infty} \rho^m(x, \lambda) R_m(x, \lambda). \tag{11}$$

as described in [15]. Interested readers can refer to [12], [19] and [15] for more details.

Interreflection Model for Fluorescent Component. Analogous to inter-reflections of the reflective component, the direct component of the fluorescent component is

$$\mu(x, \lambda_o) \frac{\int a(x, \lambda_i) P(x, \lambda_i) d\lambda_i}{\pi}. \tag{12}$$

From Eq. (6), we can see that the interreflection geometry $K(x, x')$ is independent of the albedo of the objects and the energy absorbed from the light source. Also, the fluorescence emissions are typically not re-absorbed by the same fluorescent material again[2]; therefore, the interreflection of fluorescence emissions behaves like that of the reflective components except for the initial emission. Therefore, the second-bounce component can be written as

$$\mu(x, \lambda_o) \rho(x, \lambda_o) \int K_1(x, x') \frac{\int a(x', \lambda_i) P(x, \lambda_i) d\lambda_i}{\pi} dx', \tag{13}$$

where $\rho(x, \lambda_o)$ is the reflective albedo at the outgoing wavelength λ_o. The radiance of the fluorescent component at surface point x is, therefore represented as the sum of the direct component and interreflections as

$$I_f(x, \lambda_o) = \mu(x, \lambda_o) \frac{\int a(x, \lambda_i) P(x, \lambda_i) d\lambda_i}{\pi} +$$
$$\sum_{m=1}^{\infty} \mu(x, \lambda_o) \rho^m(x, \lambda_o) \int K_m(x, x') \frac{\int a(x', \lambda_i) P(x, \lambda_i) d\lambda_i}{\pi} dx'. \tag{14}$$

By defining

$$F_1(x, \lambda_i) = \frac{\int a(x, \lambda_i) P(x, \lambda_i) d\lambda_i}{\pi},$$

$$F_m(x, \lambda_i) = \int K_{m-1}(x, x') \frac{\int a(x', \lambda_i) P(x, \lambda_i) d\lambda_i}{\pi} dx', \quad (m > 1), \tag{15}$$

---

[2] The overlap between absorption and emission spectra is small. As a result, only a negligible amount of emitted light is re-absorbed.

the interreflection model for the fluorescent component can be written as

$$I_f(x, \lambda_o) = \mu(x, \lambda_o)F_1(x, \lambda_o) + \sum_{m=1}^{\infty} \mu(x, \lambda_o)\rho^m(x, \lambda_o)F_{m+1}(x, \lambda_o). \qquad (16)$$

Unlike the conventional interreflection model for the reflective component (Eq. (11)), the derived model includes both fluorescent and reflective albedos at the outgoing wavelength λ_o.

3.3 Separation of Direct and Indirect Components

In theory, one would need an infinite-bounce model to fully describe interreflections. Fortunately, in practice, a 2-bounce model is sufficient for accurately modeling interreflections [6]. We thus restrict our attention to the 2-bounce case. If we observe the reflective component at the same wavelength ($\lambda_i = \lambda_o$) as the illumination, we obtain

$$I_r(x, \lambda_i) = \rho(x, \lambda_i)R_1(x, \lambda_i) + \rho^2(x, \lambda_i)R_2(x, \lambda_i). \qquad (17)$$

The fluorescent component can be observed at a longer wavelength as

$$I_f(x, \lambda_i, \lambda_o) = \mu(x, \lambda_o)F_1(x, \lambda_i) + \mu(x, \lambda_o)\rho(x, \lambda_o)F_2(x, \lambda_i). \qquad (18)$$

For convenience, we remove λ_i and λ_o in all functions in Eqs. (17) and (18) and use ρ_1 and ρ_2 to represent the reflective albedo at incident wavelength λ_i and outgoing wavelength λ_o, respectively. We also assume that the scene consists of a uniform material, so the albedos $\rho(x)$ and $\mu(x)$ will be the same for all points x and can be represented as ρ and μ. Therefore, Eqs. (17) and (18) can be rewritten as

$$I_r(x) = \rho_1 R_1(x) + \rho_1^2 R_2(x), \quad I_f(x) = \mu F_1(x) + \mu\rho_2 F_2(x). \qquad (19)$$

As will be detailed in Sec. 3.4, we condition $P(x, \lambda_i) = \int a(x, \lambda_i)P(x, \lambda_i)d\lambda_i$ so $R_m(x) = F_m(x)$(m=1,2). Thus Eq. (19) can then be written as

$$\begin{bmatrix} I_r(x) \\ I_f(x) \end{bmatrix} = \begin{bmatrix} \rho_1 & \rho_1^2 \\ \mu & \mu\rho_2 \end{bmatrix} \begin{bmatrix} R_1(x) \\ R_2(x) \end{bmatrix}. \qquad (20)$$

We later detail how ρ_1, ρ_2 and μ can be determined but provided they are known, we can solve for $R_1(x)$ and $R_2(x)$ in Eq. (20) by a matrix inverse. From this, $\rho_1 R_1(x)$ and $\mu R_1(x)$ would give us the direct component in the reflective and fluorescent parts respectively.

Compared with [15], our method requires one less image to capture. Since the 2-bounce model can accurately approximate interreflections in practice, our method can remove interreflections only with a single image. As demonstrated in later in experiments, this allows the interreflection removal of a dynamic scene by the straightforward recording of a video using a standard RGB camera.

(a) Blue light   (b) Red light

Fig. 3. Lighting and albedo calibration

3.4   Lighting and Albedo Calibration

The equality $R_m(x) = F_m(x)$ holds only if $P(x, \lambda_i) = \int a(x, \lambda_i)P(x, \lambda_i)d\lambda_i$, which is not the general case. Furthermore, in order to solve Eq. (20), the value of the albedos are required. We will address these two issues in the following.

Light Intensity Calibration. As in Eq. (19), $R_m(x) = F_m(x)$ only when irradiance $P(x, \lambda_i)$ is equal to $A(x) = \int a(x, \lambda_i)P(x, \lambda_i)d\lambda_i$. To make these two values equal, we would need to calibrate the fluorescent absorption spectrum and control the light source carefully. This would be technically very challenging so we instead use a simpler calibration procedure. Let us assume $P(x, \lambda_i)$ is α times $A(x)$, then for every surface point x, the radiance $L(\lambda_i)$ from the light source for the reflective component is also α times the absorbed energy $\int a(\lambda)L(\lambda_i)d\lambda_i$ for the fluorescent component with uniform albedo. That is,

$$\alpha = \frac{P(x, \lambda_i)}{\int a(x, \lambda_i)P(x, \lambda_i)d\lambda_i} = \frac{L(\lambda_i)}{\int a(\lambda_i)L(\lambda_i)d\lambda_i}. \tag{21}$$

Because of this relation, we can calculate a single α for all points x. As defined in Eqs. (10) and (15), $R_m(x)$ and $F_m(x)$ are linearly dependent on the irradiance $P(x, \lambda_i)$ and $\int a(x, \lambda_i)P(x, \lambda_i)d\lambda_i$, respectively:

$$R_1(x) = \alpha F_1(x), \text{ and } R_2(x) = \alpha F_2(x). \tag{22}$$

Therefore, Eq. (20) can be written as

$$\begin{cases} I_r(x) = \rho_1 R_1(x) + \rho_1^2 R_2(x) \\ I_f(x) = \frac{\mu}{\alpha}\left(R_1(x) + \rho_2 R_2(x)\right). \end{cases} \tag{23}$$

Albedo Ratio. We discussed earlier that with known reflective albedos ρ_1 and ρ_2 and fluorescent albedo μ, we can solve for the direct and indirect lighting components. However, directly measuring these values is actually quite difficult. From from Eq. (1) and Eq. (4), reflective albedo ρ and fluorescent albedo μ can be described as

$$\rho(x, \lambda) = \frac{E_r(x, \lambda)}{L(\lambda)\cos\theta}, \text{ and } \mu(x, \lambda_o) = \frac{E_f(x, \lambda_o)}{\left(\int a(x)L(\lambda_i)d\lambda_i\right)\cos\theta}. \tag{24}$$

Determining the albedos from Eq. (24) is difficult because we would need to know θ, the angle between the incident light and the surface normal.

Fortunately, a simple calibration procedure can be used to obtain albedo ratios which would also be sufficient for our purposes. If we take $\rho_1 R_1(x)$ and $\rho_1^2 R_2(x)$ as the unknown variables, Eq. (20) can be reformulated[3] as

$$\begin{bmatrix} I_r(x) \\ I_f(x) \end{bmatrix} = \begin{bmatrix} 1 & 1 \\ \frac{\mu}{\rho_1 \alpha} & \frac{\mu}{\rho_1 \alpha} \frac{\rho_2}{\rho_1} \end{bmatrix} \begin{bmatrix} \rho_1 R_1(x) \\ \rho_1^2 R_2(x) \end{bmatrix}. \tag{25}$$

Then measuring the relative surface albedo for a point x as opposed to the absolute value of the albedo can be simply done with the following ratios derived from Eq. (24)

$$\frac{\mu}{\rho_1 \alpha} = \frac{E_f(x, \lambda)}{E_{r1}(x, \lambda)}, \quad \text{and} \quad \frac{\rho_2}{\rho_1} = \frac{E_{r2}(x, \lambda)}{E_{r1}(x, \lambda)} \frac{L_1(\lambda)}{L_2(\lambda)}, \tag{26}$$

where L_1 and L_2 are blue and red lights respectively[4].

In the calibration process, the objects used to compute the albedo ratios should be made of the same material as the object under consideration, as well as being flat or convex to avoid any interreflections. As shown in Fig. 3, we use a flat fluorescent sheet and a spectrally flat white reflectance target to calibrate $\frac{\mu}{\rho_1 \alpha}$ and $\frac{\rho_2}{\rho_1}$. The scene is captured under blue and red light. $\frac{E_f}{E_{r1}}$ is the ratio of the intensity of the fluorescent sheet in the blue and red channels under the blue light. $\frac{E_{r2}}{E_{r1}}$ is the ratio of the intensity of the fluorescent sheet in the red channel under the red light and the blue channel under the blue light. $\frac{L_1}{L_2}$ is the ratio of the intensity of the white target in the blue channel under the blue light and the red channel under the red light.

So far, the possibility to make Eq. (25) work is based on the assumption that the surface reflective albedo cannot be constant across the entire spectrum ($\rho_1 \neq \rho_2$).

4   Experimental Results

We tested our method on real fluorescent objects. To obtain both reflective and fluorescent components effectively, we used pink fluorescent objects where the reflective component is strong in the blue channel and the fluorescent emission is strong in red channel. Such color characteristics make reflective-only and fluorescent-reflective capture ideal for use with a standard RGB camera. In practice, capture with other colors can also be done but different light sources or camera filters would be needed to remove some wavelengths so that reflective-only and fluorescent-reflective images can be captured. Our method requires all

---

[3] The reformulation solves for scaled versions of $R_1(x)$ and $R_2(x)$ but this is still sufficient for analyzing direct and indirect lighting.

[4] In our method, L_1 should be in the short wavelength range, and L_2 should be the same appearance with the fluorescent emission spectrum so that it shows the spectral reflectance in the fluorescent emission area.

surface points to exhibit the same color. In a real application, objects could be easily spray painted. We could then get the benefits of our method's ability to separate direct and indirect components for moving objects. For our experiments, we used objects that naturally exhibit fluorescence and a leaf dish that was painted. These objects were all illuminated by blue light and captured in the blue and red channels of a CCD camera (SONY DXC-9000).

4.1 Separation Results

In this section, we show the results for the separation of direct and indirect components. We first give an overview of the entire process. As shown in Fig. 1, an RGB image is first captured under blue light. Since we used our pink fluores-

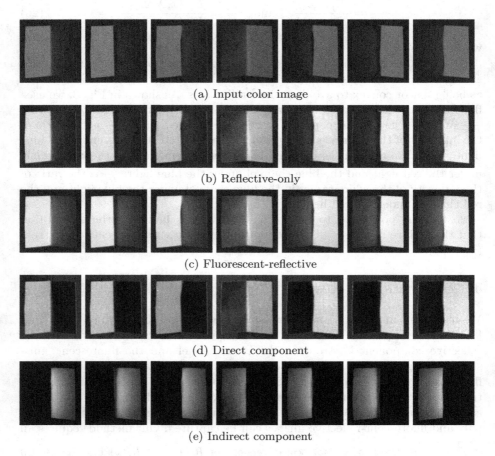

(a) Input color image

(b) Reflective-only

(c) Fluorescent-reflective

(d) Direct component

(e) Indirect component

Fig. 4. Separation results for the v-shape. (a) The input image captured under blue light. (b) The reflective-only image from (a)'s blue channel. (c) The fluorescent-reflective image from (a)'s red channel. (d) The separated direct component. (e) The separated indirect component.

cent color, the blue channel is a reflective-only image while the red channel is a fluorescent-reflective image. As described in Sec. 3.4, the lighting and albedo are then calibrated by images captured under blue and red light, where the calibration targets are both flat. After calibration, direct and indirect components are recovered by Eq. (25).

Our first scene is a pink fluorescent v-shape object. The scene was first taken under blue light (Fig. 4 (a)). Its blue channel is then a reflective-only image (Fig. 4 (b)) and the red channel is a fluorescent-reflective image (Fig. 4 (c)). We calibrated the lighting and albedo by using the method in the previous section and found $\frac{\mu}{\rho_1 \alpha}$ and $\frac{\mu}{\rho_1 \alpha} \frac{\rho_2}{\rho_1}$ to be 1.10 and 2.07 for the pink fluorescent sheet, respectively. After calibration, the direct and indirect components were separated by Eq. (25) as shown in Fig. 4(d) and (e). In the figures, we have scaled the indirect component to $0 \sim 255$, for visualization purposes. We can see that when we light one side of the v-shape, the direct component is strong on one side while the indirect component is strong in other side. This observation fits our

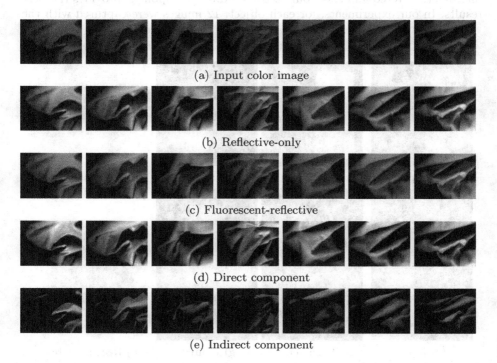

(a) Input color image

(b) Reflective-only

(c) Fluorescent-reflective

(d) Direct component

(e) Indirect component

Fig. 5. Separation results for the moving fluorescent cloth. (a) The input image captured under blue light. (b) The reflective-only image from (a)'s blue channel. (c) The fluorescent-reflective image from (a)'s red channel. (d) The separated direct component. (e) The separated indirect component.

expectations of how interreflections would physically behave and demonstrates that our method removes interreflection effectively.

As mentioned, our method only requires a one-shot measurement to separate the direct and indirect component and so is applicable to dynamic scenes. In Fig. 5, seven successive video frames for a dynamic pink fluorescent cloth are shown. We can see the changing of direct and indirect components in Fig. 5 (d) and (e) as a result of the object's motion. The direct component is strong in the flat area (Fig. 5 (d)) and the indirect component is strong in the wrinkled area. As with the v-shape, these observations fit our expectations of how interreflections would physically behave and demonstrates our method's effectiveness.

4.2 Photometric Stereo

To demonstrate a sample application and to further validate our separation results, we use the recovered direct component to perform photometric stereo [26]. We also tested using reflective-only and fluorescent-reflective images as inputs to photometric stereo and show our recovered direct component provides the best results. In our experiments, for each object, 12 images were captured with the

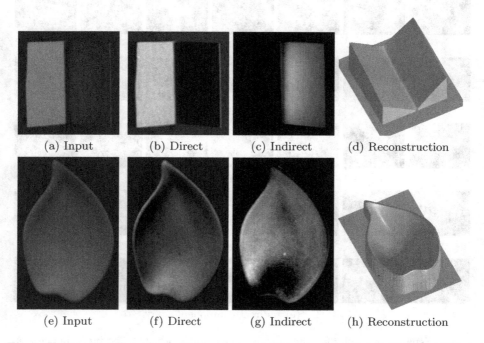

(a) Input   (b) Direct   (c) Indirect   (d) Reconstruction

(e) Input   (f) Direct   (g) Indirect   (h) Reconstruction

Fig. 6. Reconstructed results for the fluorescent v-shape and leaf dish. (a)(e) One of the input images captured under the directional blue light. The corresponding separated direct and indirect components are shown (b)(f) and (c)(g). (d)(h) The recovered shape form the direct components.

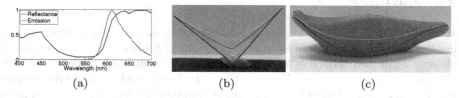

(a)   (b)   (c)

Fig. 7. (a) The reflectance and emission spectra for the fluorescent pink sheet. (b) and (c) The cross-sectional view of recovered shapes from fluorescent-reflective images (green line), reflective-only images (blue line) and direct components (dark line) superimposed into the side view of the v-shape and leaf dish, respectively.

object illuminated from different light source directions. The light source was about 1 m away from the object, which was 4 ∼ 10 cm in diameter.

We tested our method on the pink fluorescent v-shape sheet and a "leaf dish". Fig. 6 shows one of the input images and the corresponding separated direct and indirect components. The surface normals were recovered by photometric stereo and the shape was integrated from the normal map. Fig. 6(d)(h) show the recovered shapes by using our recovered direct components.

In [19], Nayar *et al.* showed that interreflections cause recovered shapes to be shallow. We quantitatively show the improvement in using our interreflection removal method by comparing against recovered shape depths from using the reflective-only images and fluorescent-reflective images as inputs to photometric stereo.

We can see that the shape recovered from the fluorescent-reflective images (Fig. 7(b) green line) is more shallow than that from the reflective-only images(Fig. 7(b) blue line). This is because the reflectance spectrum is stronger in the red channel than in the blue channel (Fig. 7(a)). Recall that the fluorescent indirect component shown in Eq. (25), $\frac{\mu}{\rho_1 \alpha} \frac{\rho_2}{\rho_1} = 2.07$ is greater than the reflective indirect component which is 1. Thus the indirect component $2.07\rho_1^2 R_2(x)$ in the fluorescent-reflective images is stronger than the $\rho_1^2 R_2(x)$ in the reflective-only images. From Fig. 7(a), we also see that the spectral reflectance has a strong overlap with the fluorescence emission spectrum. In the fluorescent photometric stereo work of [21] and [24], they both assume that spectral reflectance does not overlap with the fluorescent emission spectrum. This is not always the case and our method addresses situations where spectral reflectance does overlap with the fluorescent emission spectrum.

Finally, the recovered shape from the direct component (Fig. 7(b) dark line) is deepest one, which indicates that our method removes the indirect component effectively. The ground truth angle between the two sides for the v-shape is about 90 degrees. The recovered angles for the shape from the direct component, reflective-only and fluorescent-reflective cases are 91, 101 and 114 degrees, respectively. Thus our recovered direct component provided a result very close to the ground truth. Similar results can be seen for the leaf dish in Fig. 7(c).

5   Conclusion

We presented a novel method for separating direct and indirect components using the phenomenon of fluorescence. By exploiting Stokes shift, we were able to observe separated reflective and fluorescent components simultaneously in two channels of an RGB camera. While both channels still contained interreflections, we devised a simple but effective decomposition method for separating out interreflections. From this, we derived a general interreflection model for fluorescent materials and showed that a single shot measurement is sufficient for the decomposition. In contrast to existing methods, this single shot ability allowed for effective operation on complex dynamic scenes as demonstrated in the experiments. In addition, we showed that our method's effective recovery of the direct component greatly improved an existing photometric stereo method. Although we only demonstrated this on the photometric stereo method, our method can be easily applied to any methods that assume direct lighting and a uniform Lambertian surface. In the future, we would like to explore the benefits of separating for dynamic scenes through applications such as dynamic color relighting.

References

1. Achar, S., Nuske, S., Narasimhan, S.G.: Compensating for motion during direct-global separation. In: Proc. of International Conference on Computer Vision (ICCV), pp. 1481–1488 (December 2013)
2. Forsyth, D., Zisserman, A.: Mutual illumination. In: Proc. of IEEE Conference on Computer Vision and Pattern Recognition, CVPR, pp. 466–473 (June 1989)
3. Forsyth, D., Zisserman, A.: Shape from shading in the light of mutual illumination. Image Vision Computing 8(1), 42–49 (1990)
4. Y., Fu, L.A., Sato, I., Okabe, T., Sato, Y.: Separating reflective and fluorescent components using high frequency illumination in the spectral domain. In: Proc. of International Conference on Computer Vision, ICCV (2013)
5. Funt, B.V., Drew, M.S., Ho, J.: Color constancy from mutual reflection. International Journal of Computer Vision (IJCV) 6(1), 5–24 (1991)
6. Funt, B., Drew, M.: Color space analysis of mutual illumination. IEEE Trans. Pattern Analysis and Machine Intelligence (PAMI) 15(12), 1319–1326 (1993)
7. Glassner, A.S.: A model for fluorescence and phosphorescence. In: Photorealistic Rendering Techniques, pp. 60–70. Springer, Heidelberg (1995)
8. Han, S., Matsushita, Y., Sato, I., Okabe, T., Sato, Y.: Camera spectral sensitivity estimation from a single image under unknown illumination by using fluorescence. In: Proc. of IEEE Conference on Computer Vision and Pattern Recognition, CVPR (2012)
9. Hullin, M.B., Fuchs, M., Ihrke, I., Seidel, H.P., Lensch, H.P.A.: Fluorescent immersion range scanning. ACM Trans. on Graph (ToG) 27, 87:1–87:10 (2008)
10. Hullin, M.B., Hanika, J., Ajdin, B., Seidel, H.P., Kautz, J., Lensch, H.P.A.: Acquisition and analysis of bispectral bidirectional reflectance and reradiation distribution functions. ACM Trans. on Graph (ToG) 29, 97:1–97:7 (2010)
11. Johnson, G.M., Fairchild, M.D.: Full-spectral color calculations in realistic image synthesis. IEEE Computer Graphics and Applications 19, 47–53 (1999)

12. Koenderink, J.J., Van Doorn, A.J.: Geometrical modes as a general method to treat diffuse interreflections in radiometry. Journal of the Optical Soceity of America (JOSA) 73(6), 843–850 (1983)
13. Lakowicz, J.R.: Principles of Fluorescence Spectroscopy. Springer (2006)
14. Lam, A., Sato, I.: Spectral modeling and relighting of reflective-fluorescent scenes. In: Proc. of IEEE Conference on Computer Vision and Pattern Recognition, CVPR (2013)
15. Liao, M., Huang, X., Yang, R.: Interreflection removal for photometric stereo by using spectrum-dependent albedo. In: Proc. of IEEE Conference on Computer Vision and Pattern Recognition (CVPR), pp. 689–696 (2011)
16. McNamara, G., Gupta, A., Reynaert, J., Coates, T.D., Boswell, C.: Spectral imaging microscopy web sites and data. Cytometry. Part A: The Journal of the International Society for Analytical Cytology 69(8), 863–871 (2006)
17. Nayar, S.K., Gao, Y.: Colored interreflections and shape recovery. In: Proceedings of the Image Understanding Workshop (1992)
18. Nayar, S.K., Krishnan, G., Grossberg, M.D., Raskar, R.: Fast separation of direct and global components of a scene using high frequency illumination. In: ACM SIGGRAPH, pp. 935–944 (2006)
19. Nayar, S., Ikeuchi, K., Kanade, T.: Shape from interreflections. International Journal of Computer Vision (IJCV) 6(3), 173–195 (1991)
20. O'Toole, M., Mather, J., Kutulakos, K.N.: 3d shape and indirect appearance by structured light transport. In: Proc. of IEEE Conference on Computer Vision and Pattern Recognition (CVPR) (June 2014)
21. Sato, I., Okabe, T., Sato, Y.: Bispectral photometric stereo based on fluorescence. In: Proc. of IEEE Conference on Computer Vision and Pattern Recognition, CVPR (2012)
22. Sato, I., Zhang, C.: Image-based separation of reflective and fluorescent components using illumination variant and invariant color. IEEE Trans. Pattern Analysis and Machine Intelligence (PAMI) 35(12), 2866–2877 (2013)
23. Seitz, S.M., Matsushita, Y., Kutulakos, K.N.: A theory of inverse light transport. In: Proc. of International Conference on Computer Vision (ICCV), pp. 1440–1447 (2005)
24. Treibitz, T., Murez, Z., Mitchell, B.G., Kriegman, D.: Shape from fluorescence. In: Fitzgibbon, A., Lazebnik, S., Perona, P., Sato, Y., Schmid, C. (eds.) ECCV 2012, Part VII. LNCS, vol. 7578, pp. 292–306. Springer, Heidelberg (2012)
25. Wilkie, A., Weidlich, A., Larboulette, C., Purgathofer, W.: A reflectance model for diffuse fluorescent surfaces. In: International Conference on Computer Graphics and Interactive Techniques, pp. 321–331 (2006)
26. Woodham, R.J.: Photometric method for determining surface orientation from multiple images. Optical Engineering 19(1) (1980)

Intrinsic Face Image Decomposition
with Human Face Priors

Chen Li[1,*], Kun Zhou[1], and Stephen Lin[2]

[1] State Key Lab of CAD&CG, Zhejiang University, China
[2] Microsoft Research, Beijing, China

Abstract. We present a method for decomposing a single face photograph into
its intrinsic image components. Intrinsic image decomposition has commonly
been used to facilitate image editing operations such as relighting and re-texturing.
Although current single-image intrinsic image methods are able to obtain an approximate decomposition, image operations involving the human face require
greater accuracy since slight errors can lead to visually disturbing results. To
improve decomposition for faces, we propose to utilize human face priors as constraints for intrinsic image estimation. These priors include statistics on skin reflectance and facial geometry. We also make use of a physically-based model
of skin translucency to heighten accuracy, as well as to further decompose the
reflectance image into a diffuse and a specular component. With the use of priors and a skin reflectance model for human faces, our method is able to achieve
appreciable improvements in intrinsic image decomposition over more generic
techniques.

Keywords: intrinsic image decomposition, reflectance models, human face
priors.

1 Introduction

Algorithms for intrinsic image estimation aim to decompose an image into separate
components of shading and reflectance. Such a decomposition can facilitate computer
vision tasks that operate more effectively on images with just one of these components
and not the other. For example, shape-from-shading methods ideally should have shading images as input, while segmentation algorithms may perform better on reflectance
images. Intrinsic image decomposition can also be beneficial for image editing, where
changes in scene lighting can be produced by adjusting the shading component, and object colors and surface textures can be altered by modifying the reflectance component.

Intrinsic image decomposition, however, is a highly underconstrained problem, since
two unknowns (shading and reflectance) are to be solved for each observation (image
color) that is available. To obtain a realistic solution, previous work have applied various
constraints on the two intrinsic components, such as attributing large image gradients
to reflectance [19], or gradients with little chromatic change to shading [11]. More
recently, priors on the illumination environment and the underlying scene geometry

---

* This work was done while Chen Li was an intern at Microsoft Research.

D. Fleet et al. (Eds.): ECCV 2014, Part V, LNCS 8693, pp. 218–233, 2014.

have been incorporated to improve decompositions [2]. While gradual progress has been made on this problem, methods that operate with a single color image still have limited success, as observed in the comparative study of [13].

In this paper, we address the intrinsic image problem for human faces, which is especially challenging because slight errors in decomposition can lead to obviously unnatural results in downstream applications, since humans are highly sensitive to facial appearance. To heighten performance, we propose to take advantage of commonalities among human faces by incorporating priors on their reflectance properties and 3D shapes. Our work particularly makes use of statistics from the facial reflectance data captured in [30] with special measurement devices, and the 3D facial shape model in [31] developed from a face dataset. Moreover, our method accounts for the non-Lambertian reflectance properties of human skin by utilizing a bidirectional surface-scattering reflectance distribution function (BSSRDF) to model skin translucency, as well as an empirical model for specular reflections of light off the skin surface. With these human face priors and skin reflectance model, our method computes intrinsic images by jointly solving for face shape, illumination environment, and skin reflectance, in a manner inspired by the SIRFS technique [2].

Aside from the use of human face priors, our method contains other technical novelties of note in relation to previous works on intrinsic image estimation. One is its consideration of specular reflections and subsurface scattering of light radiance in modeling reflectance, in contrast to the Lambertian model that is typically assumed. We will later show experimentally the advantage of using this more advanced reflectance model for decomposition of human faces. Another is the use of priors in a generic-to-specific optimization scheme, in which reflectance priors are narrowed according to the population membership (e.g., race and age) inferred from the face at an earlier stage of the optimization. Our overall approach is shown to yield distinct improvements in decomposition of human face images over state-of-the-art intrinsic image methods which are designed for general objects and scenes.

2   Related Work

In this section, we briefly review previous work on intrinsic image estimation and related techniques on image-based face modeling.

Intrinsic image estimation. In decomposing an image into its reflectance and shading components, previous techniques have employed various constraints to make the problem more tractable. A common approach is to attribute image gradients to either reflectance or shading changes. This has been accomplished through thresholding image gradients [19,11,16] and by employing trained classifiers [28]. Recently, non-local constraints between non-adjacent pixels have been used to obtain greater global consistency in decomposition results [27,12,26,33]. In [2], generic priors were introduced on the illumination environment and the underlying 3D geometry, based on the notion that certain explanations of a scene are more likely than others. Our work also makes use of prior statistics, but in our case the priors are specific to our problem of decomposing a face image. We additionally utilize a reflectance model that better describes the physical interactions of light with human skin.

Several techniques use richer input data to better constrain the intrinsic image problem. These include methods that operate on RGB-D images [21,1,7], image sets taken under different lighting conditions [29,22,18], and images supplemented with user-supplied decomposition clues [5]. While the additional input data gives these methods a clear advantage over single-image techniques, the need for this extra data generally limits them to certain application settings.

Image-based face modeling. Often the most important element in a photograph, the human face has received much attention in computer vision. While most works focus on recognition, alignment and tracking, there are some that attempt to reconstruct a face model from an image, which can be useful for predicting its appearance under different viewing conditions. 3D facial geometry has been estimated with the help of 3D face datasets, whose elements are regarded as a basis set for shape reconstruction, with the reconstruction coefficients estimated via principal components analysis [3,31] or 3D regression [6] from the image positions of facial landmark points. In our work, we use the method in [31] to provide a constraint on 3D face shape.

In [20], the morphable face model of [3] is extended to additionally handle lighting variations, through a multilinear analysis on a dataset that contains each face under numerous lighting conditions. Though such basis representations are computationally convenient, their bounded dimensionality in practice limits their descriptive detail, and the datasets from which they are built do not encompass a full range of face variations (e.g., different expressions). These issues are overcome in [15] by utilizing shading information to recover detailed shape, as well as albedo and illumination, with the help of a single reference face image and its 3D shape. Estimation of these elements is formulated on the Lambertian reflectance model, which does not capture the translucency and specular surface reflections of human skin. In our experiments, we show that modeling these reflectance characteristics of skin, while using additional human face priors and intrinsic image constraints, leads to more accurate decomposition results.

3   Skin Reflectance Model

To model the translucency and specular surface reflections of human skin, we use the physically-based skin reflectance model of [30]. In this model, the outgoing radiance $L(x_o, \omega_o)$ at a surface point x_o in direction ω_o is computed by integrating the contributions of incoming radiance $L(x_i, \omega_i)$ from all incident light directions Ω over the surface C:

$$L(x_o, \omega_o) = \int_C \int_\Omega B(x_i, \omega_i, x_o, \omega_o) L(x_i, \omega_i)(N \cdot \omega_i) \, d\omega_i \, dC(x_i), \qquad (1)$$

where N is the surface normal vector at point x_i, and the function $B(x_i, \omega_i, x_o, \omega_o)$ is the BSSRDF, which relates light exiting from point x_o in direction ω_o to incoming light from direction ω_i at point x_i.

The integral can be separated into a specular reflectance component L_s and a diffuse subsurface scattering component L_d that models skin translucency:

$$L(x_o, \omega_o) = L_s(x_o, \omega_o) + L_d(x_o, \omega_o), \qquad (2)$$

with

$$L_s(x_o, \omega_o) = \int_\Omega f_s(x_o, \omega_o, \omega_i) L(x_o, \omega_i)(N \cdot \omega_i) \, d\omega_i, \tag{3}$$

$$L_d(x_o, \omega_o) = \int_C \int_\Omega B_d(x_i, \omega_i, x_o, \omega_o) L(x_i, \omega_i)(N \cdot \omega_i) \, d\omega_i \, dC(x_i) \tag{4}$$

where f_s is the bidirectional reflectance distribution function (BRDF) for specular reflection, and B_d is the diffuse BSSRDF which models only subsurface scattering.

The specular BRDF f_s is represented by the isotropic Blinn-Phong model as

$$f_s(x_o, \omega_o, \omega_i) = \rho_s \frac{n+2}{2\pi} \cos^n \delta, \tag{5}$$

where the scale factor ρ_s and specular exponent n are functions of x_o (dropped to simplify notation), and δ is the angle between the normal N and the half-angle vector $H = (\omega_i + \omega_o)/\|\omega_i + \omega_o\|$.

The diffuse BSSRDF B_d can be decomposed into a product of lower-dimensional functions:

$$B_d(x_i, \omega_i, x_o, \omega_o) \approx \frac{1}{\pi} F_t(x_i, \omega_i) P_d(\|x_i - x_o\|_2) F_t(x_o, \omega_o) \tag{6}$$

where F_t is the Fresnel transmittance at the entry and exit points x_i and x_o of light from the surface. The diffuse reflectance profile $P_d(x_i, x_o)$ describes the subsurface transport of light from x_i to x_o, and is modeled using a dipole diffusion approximation [14,8]:

$$P_d(r) = \frac{\alpha' z_r (1 + \sigma_{tr} d_r) e^{-\sigma_{tr} d_r}}{4\pi d_r^3} - \frac{\alpha' z_v (1 + \sigma_{tr} d_v) e^{-\sigma_{tr} d_v}}{4\pi d_v^3} \tag{7}$$

where $r = \|x_o - x_i\|_2$, $\sigma_{tr} = \sqrt{3\sigma_a \sigma_t'}$ is the effective transport coefficient, $\sigma_t' = \sigma_a + \sigma_s'$ is the reduced extinction coefficient, $\alpha' = \sigma_s'/\sigma_t'$ is the reduced albedo, and σ_a and σ_s' are the absorption and reduced scattering coefficients. $z_r = 1/\sigma_t'$ and $z_v = (1 + 4J/3)/\sigma_t'$ are the z-coordinates of the positive and negative dipole sources relative to the surface at $z = 0$, with $J = (1 + F_{dr})/(1 - F_{dr})$ where F_{dr} is the diffuse Fresnel reflectance computed from the refraction indices of air and skin [9]. The distances of these sources from a given surface point are $d_r = \sqrt{r^2 + z_r^2}$ and $d_v = \sqrt{r^2 + z_v^2}$, respectively.

Based on this skin reflectance model, a face image can be formulated as

$$I(x) = D(x) + S(x) \tag{8}$$

where x is a pixel location, and $D(x)$ and $S(x)$ are its diffuse and specular components expressed with the discrete forms of Eq. (3)-(4) as

$$D(p) = A(p) \sum_{q \in \mathcal{N}_p} \sum_{\omega_i \in \Omega} B_d(p, q, \omega_o, \omega_i) L(\omega_i)(N(p) \cdot \omega_i) \, d\omega_i \, d\mathcal{N}_q \tag{9}$$

$$S(p) = \rho_s \frac{n+2}{2\pi} \sum_{\omega_i \in \Omega} \cos^n \delta L(\omega_i)(N(p) \cdot \omega_i) \, d\omega_i. \tag{10}$$

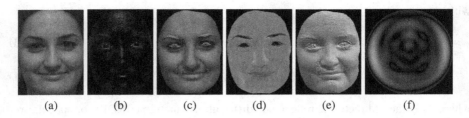

(a)	(b)	(c)	(d)	(e)	(f)

Fig. 1. Decomposed components with our approach. (a) Input image. (b) Specular shading. (c) Diffuse shading. (d) Reflectance (albedo). (e) 3D geometry (shown as surface normals for better visualization). (f) Illumination environment.

Here, $A(p)$ is the albedo of pixel p, which is used to account for the wavelength-dependency of P_d in Eq. (7). For computational efficiency we consider subsurface light transmission only within a local neighborhood $\mathcal{N}_p$ of each point.

In summary, the skin reflectance parameters for this model consist of spatially-varying albedo A, specular exponent n and specular scale ρ_s, and spatially-uniform reduced scattering coefficient σ'_s and absorption coefficient σ_a. We treat these all as scalar quantities except for albedo, which is an RGB vector.

4   Face Intrinsic Image Decomposition

Traditionally in intrinsic image decomposition, an image I is modeled as the product of a shading layer Sh and a reflectance layer R:

$$I = Sh \times R. \tag{11}$$

Our method further considers the specular shading component S_d which is unaffected by reflectance R, such that the equation above becomes the following:

$$I = S_d \times R + S_s, \tag{12}$$

where S_d is the diffuse reflection component. To separate a single face image into these elements, we first jointly estimate facial albedo A, skin reflectance parameters $\Theta = \{\rho_s, n, \sigma_a, \sigma'_s\}$, face geometry G, and illumination environment L through the following optimization problem:

$$\underset{A,\Theta,G,L}{\operatorname{argmin}} g(I(A,\Theta,G,L) - \hat{I}) + f(A) + h(\Theta) + z(G) + l(L) \tag{13}$$

where $\hat{I}$ is the input image, $I(A,\Theta,G,L)$ is the reflectance model in Eq. (8) with surface normals constructed from the depth map G, and g, f, h, z, l are cost functions for image formation, albedo, reflectance, geometry and illumination, respectively. The cost function g is defined simply as $g(x) = x^2$, and the remaining costs are presented in this section.

From the optimized values, the intrinsic components are solved as

$$R = A, \tag{14}$$
$$S_d = D/A, \tag{15}$$
$$S_s = S \tag{16}$$

for A, D and S from Eq. (9)–(10). An example result of this decomposition using our approach is shown in Fig. 1.

4.1 Face Reflectance

The cost functions related to face reflectance are formulated using human face reflectance priors from the the MERL/ETH Skin Reflectance Database [30]. This database contains reflectance parameter data for a set of 149 subjects. The subjects were imaged under a dome that consists of 16 cameras, 150 light sources, and a commercial 3D face scanning system. Additionally, translucency values were measured using a fiber-optic spectrometer. The reflectance data is classified according to age, gender, race and face region. We determine the region label for each pixel in a manner consistent to that in [30] for the database. We first apply the extended Active Shape Model of [24] to locate 76 facial landmark points as shown in Fig. 2(b). Cubic-splines are fit to these points to divide the face into 12 regions (Fig. 2(c)), from which region membership for a pixel can be determined.

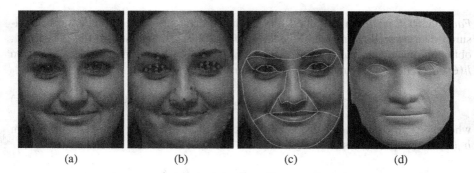

(a)   (b)   (c)   (d)

Fig. 2. Regions for face priors, and the geometry prior. (a) Input image. (b) Facial landmark points. (c) Face regions delineated by splines fit to landmark points. (d) Geometry prior for this face.

Face albedo prior. Among the reflectance parameters available for the measured data is albedo. To construct an albedo prior model, we fit a Gaussian mixture model (GMM) to the albedo data of each face region r, which yields the mean $\mu_A(r)$ and variance matrix $\Sigma_A(r)$ for the mixture components. The albedo cost function f is formed with this prior as

$$f(A) = \lambda_{fp} f_p(A) + \lambda_{fs} f_s(A) \tag{17}$$

where f_p is the prior term, f_s is a spatial smoothness regularization term, and λ_{fp} and λ_{fs} are balance weights. The prior term is derived from the GMM as

$$f_p(A) = \sum_{x \in \hat{I}} (A(x) - \mu_A(r_x))^T \Sigma_A(r_x)^{-1} (A(x) - \mu_A(r_x)) \qquad (18)$$

where r_x denotes the facial region of pixel x. The albedo smoothness term is defined as follows:

$$f_s(A) = \sum_{x \in \hat{I}} \sum_{y \in \aleph(x)} w_r w_c \|A(x) - A(y)\|^2 \qquad (19)$$

where $\aleph(x)$ denotes the four-connected neighbors of pixel x. This smoothness term is adaptively weighted by two factors. Since the face albedo prior is defined separately on different regions, smoothness in albedo across region boundaries is emphasized by the factor w_r. We additionally employ the common intrinsic image constraint that chromatic differences between adjacent pixels indicate a reflectance change. This is done through the factor w_c, which weakens the albedo smoothness term across such chromatic differences. These two factors are defined as follows:

$$w_r = \begin{cases} 1.5 & r_x! = r_y, \\ 1 & \text{otherwise} \end{cases}, \quad w_c = \begin{cases} 0.4 & \Upsilon_x{}^T \Upsilon_y < 0.9, \\ 1 & \text{otherwise} \end{cases} \qquad (20)$$

where Υ_x, Υ_y represent the normalized color vector of pixel x, y in input image $\hat{I}$, and r_x, r_y denote the region labels of x and y.

Face BSSRDF prior. In [30], the Blinn-Phong parameter n was computed for the measured data as well. Similar to albedo, we fit a Gaussian function to the data for n, obtaining mean value $\mu_n(r)$ and variance $\Sigma_n(r)$ for each region r. The cost function $h(\Theta)$ for reflectance parameters Θ is written as

$$h(\Theta) = \lambda_{hp} h_p(n) + \lambda_{hs} h_s(n, \rho_s) + \lambda_{hc} h_c(\sigma_a, \sigma_s') \qquad (21)$$

where λ_{hp}, λ_{hs}, and λ_{hc} balance the influence of each energy term. The prior term $h_p(n)$ is as expressed as

$$h_p(n) = \sum_{x \in \hat{I}} \frac{(n(x) - \mu_n(r))^2}{\sigma_n(r)}, \qquad (22)$$

and the smoothness term is

$$h_s(n, \rho_s) = \sum_{x \in \hat{I}} \sum_{y \in \aleph(x)} (n(x) - n(y))^2 + \sum_{x \in \hat{I}} \sum_{y \in \aleph(x)} (\rho_s(x) - \rho_s(y))^2. \qquad (23)$$

We note that the database also contains data on the specular scaling coefficient ρ_s, but we found that omitting or significantly downweighting a prior constraint on it leads to better specular decomposition results in our experiments.

No detailed quantitative data on the scattering parameters σ_a and σ_s' is provided in [30], but an approximately linear relationship between these parameters can be observed from plotted values. We fit a line of slope s_c and intercept i_c to the plot, and use it as a constraint between these parameters:

$$h_c(\sigma_a, \sigma_s') = \sum_{c \in \{R,G,B\}} \|\sigma_a(c) - s_c \sigma_s'(c) - i_c\|^2. \tag{24}$$

4.2   3D Geometry

Our work also takes advantage of a 3D face dataset as a geometric prior on face shape. Specifically, we use the single-image 3D face reconstruction algorithm in [31] to obtain approximate geometry $\hat{G}$ for the input face image. For the face shown in Fig. 2(a), the computed prior is shown in Fig. 2(d). We constrain the face shape to be similar to the prior through a cost function $Z(G)$ defined as follows:

$$z(G) = \lambda_{zp} Z_p(G) + \lambda_{zs} Z_s(G) \tag{25}$$

where the prior term $Z_p(G)$ and smoothness term $Z_s(G)$ are

$$Z_p(G) = \sum_{x \in \hat{I}} (G(x) - \hat{G}(x))^2, \tag{26}$$

$$Z_s(G) = \sum_{x \in \hat{I}} \sum_{y \in \aleph(x)} (G(x) - G(y))^2. \tag{27}$$

4.3   Illumination

Our illumination model consists of a scale factor P that represents overall lighting strength, an illumination chromaticity Γ, and spherical harmonics (SH) coefficients L_{sh} which describe the angular distribution of lighting over the range of incident directions Ω. Here we assume the lighting to be distant, and the primary light sources to have the same chromaticity, such that the illumination environment can be well-approximated with a single chromaticity. With this model, the illumination radiance $L(\omega_i)$ at incident direction ω_i is

$$L(\omega_i) = P \Gamma L_{sh}(\omega_i) \tag{28}$$

where $L_{sh}(\omega_i)$ is the value at ω_i of the spherical function modeled by SH coefficients L_{sh}.

Our method utilizes two priors to constrain estimates of the illumination environment. One is that the illumination chromaticity Γ lies on the Planckian locus that describes the chromaticity of black body radiators with respect to temperature [10]. To use this prior, we first express illumination chromaticity as (x_c', y_c') in CIE xy space, which can be converted from RGB as described in [4]. The Planckian locus in CIE xy space is defined as

$$y_c = \begin{cases} -1.1063814 x_c^3 - 1.34811020 x_c^2 + 2.18555832 x_c - 0.20219683 & 1667K \leqslant T < 2222K \\ -0.9549476 x_c^3 - 1.37418593 x_c^2 + 2.09137015 x_c - 0.16748867 & 2222K \leqslant T < 4000K \\ +3.0817580 x_c^3 - 5.87338670 x_c^2 + 3.75112997 x_c - 0.37001483 & 4000K \leqslant T < 25000K \end{cases} \tag{29}$$

where T is the temperature of the black body. Then our Planckian locus constraint on illumination chromaticity is expressed as

$$l_p(\Gamma) = (y_c(x'_c) - y'_c)^2. \tag{30}$$

For the second prior, we follow [2] by constraining the angular distribution of illumination to be consistent with a dataset of natural illumination environments. The illumination distribution prior is learned by fitting a Gaussian mixture model (mean μ_L and variance matrix Σ_L) to the SH coefficients L_{sh} of about 100 different environment maps from the *sIBL Archive*[1]. For each environment map, its intensity values are normalized, and its SH coefficients are computed in intensity space. Since the specular component requires a relatively accurate illumination model, we use a spherical harmonics representation of order 8, which provides a reasonably close approximation of environment lighting. The prior is enforced through the following cost functions, one for the SH distribution, l_{sh}, and one for normalization, l_n:

$$l_{sh}(L_{sh}) = (L_{sh} - \mu_L)^T \Sigma_L^{-1}(L_{sh} - \mu_L), \tag{31}$$

$$l_n(L_{sh}, \Gamma) = (\int_\Omega L_{sh}(\omega_i)\, d\omega_i - 4\pi)^2 + (\|\Gamma\|_1 - 1)^2. \tag{32}$$

Combining these illumination priors yields the overall cost function $l(L)$ for illumination:

$$l(\Gamma, L_{sh}) = \lambda_{lp} l_p(\Gamma) + \lambda_{lsh} l_{sh}(L_{sh}) + \lambda_{ln} l_n(L_{sh,\Gamma}), \tag{33}$$

where l_p is the Planckian locus cost, l_{sh} is the SH coefficient cost, and l_n is the intensity normalization term, with λ_{lb}, λ_{lsh}, λ_{ln} as balancing weights.

5   Optimization

Optimizing the proposed energy function in Eq. (13) is a challenge because of the large number of variables and some ambiguity in separating radiance between the spatially varying diffuse and specular components. To facilitate optimization, we use a three-step process that begins with computing an approximate separation of diffuse and specular components. The second stage obtains a solution using this diffuse-specular separation and the aforementioned human face priors. In the final step, we improve upon this initial solution by using priors specific to the population group that is inferred for the input face.

Separation stage. While existing methods could be used to separate the diffuse and specular components [32], we instead employ a simple technique based on color space analysis [17] in which the illumination chromaticity Γ is also estimated. We first plot the colors of face points in RGB space. Since most of the points have a similar skin chromaticity and the primary light sources are assumed to have the same chromaticity, a plane can be fit to these points according to the dichromatic reflectance model [25,23].

---

[1] http://www.hdrlabs.com/sibl/archive.html

We moreover assume that color samples whose intensity lies between 30% to 50% of the observed range are purely diffuse, with their mean chromaticity representing the channel-wise product of the illumination chromaticity and skin albedo in the following separation process. With this mean chromaticity and the Planckian locus model for lighting, the illumination chromaticity Γ is solved by minimizing the following function:

$$\operatorname*{argmin}_{\Gamma} l_p(\Gamma) + \sum_r l_{lp}(\Gamma) \qquad (34)$$

where the illumination chromaticity is constrained by the first term to lie on the Planckian locus, and by the second term to lie on the fitted color plane, where $l_{lp}(\Gamma) = (N^T \cdot \frac{\Gamma}{\|\Gamma\|})^2$, and N is the normal direction of the fitted color plane. After determining the two base colors (mean chromaticity and illumination chromaticity) for the color plane, we project each pixel color onto each base vector along the negative direction of the other base vector to obtain the diffuse and specular components, $\hat{D}$ and $\hat{S}$. With this separation, we revise the energy function to the following:

$$\operatorname*{argmin}_{A,\Theta,G,L} g(D(A,\Theta,G,L) - \hat{D}) + g(S(G,L) - \hat{S}) + f(A) + h(\Theta) + z(G) + l'(L) \quad (35)$$

where $D(A,\Theta,G,L)$ and $S(G,L)$ are the diffuse and specular components of $I(A,\Theta,G,L)$; l' is the same as l in Eq. (33) except that $l_p(\Gamma)$ is replaced with $g(\Gamma - \hat{\Gamma})$, where $\hat{\Gamma}$ denotes the illumination chromaticity estimated in this separation stage.

Generic priors stage. In the second stage, we solve Eq. (35) using priors for face reflectance parameters computed over all the data in the MERL/ETH database, including different genders, ages and races. Also, to save on computation we remove $z(G)$ from the energy function, use the prior $\hat{G}$ as the face geometry, and add $z(G)$ back in for the next stage. The modified energy function is optimized using L-BFGS to obtain initial estimates of albedo A', reflectance parameters Θ', and lighting environment L'.

We note that with the spherical harmonics model of lighting, the best fit to the illumination environment may generate negative lighting from certain directions, which can sometimes result in negative shading. To deal with this issue, we simply clamp $D(A,\Theta,G,L)$ and $S(G,L)$ so that they do not fall below a small predefined value.

Specific priors stage. From the initial estimates of albedo A' and reflectance parameters Θ' in the generic priors stage, we infer the population group of the face. Here, faces in the database are separated into 16 different groups according to 4 age categories (young: under 25, prime: 25-35, midlife: 35-50, and aged: over 50), and 4 skin color categories based on the Fitzpatrick skin type system (namely white, olive, brown and dark brown). The prior models for albedo and reflectance are learned for each of the 16 population groups, and then used to infer the population group for the input face by minimizing the following energy function:

$$\operatorname*{argmin}_{g} f_g(A') + h_g(\Theta') \qquad (36)$$

where g denotes a specific population group, and f_g and h_g correspond to versions of f and h with prior models learned for group g. To estimate g, Eq. (36) is solved for each group g and the one that yields the minimum energy is taken.

After determining the population group, we optimize Eq. (35) using priors specific to the group to refine the estimated parameters. Optimization is again computed using L-BFGS, and the parameters are initialized with the values obtained in the generic priors stage.

6   Results

To evaluate our method, we compared our decomposition results to the start-of-art single-image techniques for intrinsic image estimation [2] and face modeling [15]. We moreover compare the skin reflectance model and Lambertian model in decomposing faces, as well as compare the use of generic and specific population priors.

Our method was tested using both self-captured data and the *Bosphorus 3D Face Database*[2]. The Bosphorus images were assumed to be radiometrically linear, and our self-captured images were captured in RAW format. The parameters in our method were fixed to the following values: $\lambda_{fp} = \lambda_{hs} = \lambda_{zs} = \lambda_{ln} = 10.0$, $\lambda_{fs} = \lambda_{lp} = \lambda_{lsh} = 1.0$, $\lambda_{hp} = 0.5$, $\lambda_{hc} = 0.1$, and $\lambda_{zp} = 0.01$.

6.1   Comparisons with Related Techniques

Figure 3 displays intrinsic image and 3D shape results for our method, the SIRFS intrinsic image method [2], and the 3D face modeling technique in [15]. Shown in the figure are three different subjects with two facial expressions per subject. With its use of intrinsic image constraints, SIRFS tends to outperform the face modeling method on the decomposition problem, while the face modeling method generally obtains more detailed 3D geometry. For general images, SIRFS remains the state-of-the-art intrinsic decomposition method, but its general image priors are less suitable than ours for the case of human faces. In contrast to SIRFS which assumes a Lambertian reflectance model, our method utilizes a skin reflectance model that includes specular surface reflections, and thus can correctly associate specular highlights with the shading component. Also, the heavy reliance of SIRFS on smoothness priors leads it to produce overly smoothed geometry and shading results. Our method by contrast is able to recover the fine-scale effects of wrinkled skin on the shading component. Moreover, its use of reflectance priors helps to separate color more accurately between the reflectance and shading images. For additional comparison results, please view the supplemental material.

Our implementation currently does not account for self-occlusions of the lighting environment by other parts of the face (e.g., light blocked by the nose). Since 3D face geometry is estimated as part of the optimization, it could be used to determine such occlusions. More accurate modeling of incident illumination in this way could potentially elevate decomposition quality.

---

[2] http://bosphorus.ee.boun.edu.tr/default.aspx

Input	[15]	SIRFS [2]	Ours	Input	[15]	SIRFS [2]	Ours

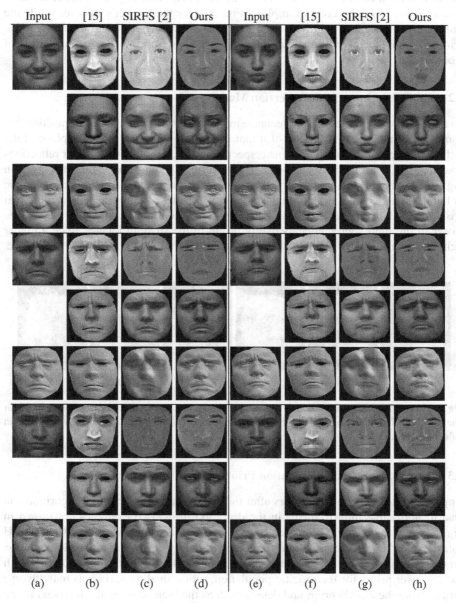

(a)	(b)	(c)	(d)	(e)	(f)	(g)	(h)

Fig. 3. Comparison of intrinsic images and 3D shapes. (a/e) Input images and ground-truth geometry. (b/f) Results of [15]. (c/g) Results of SIRFS [2]. (d/h) Our results. For each example, the first row is reflectance, the second row is shading, and the last row is a normal map.

We note that our human face priors account for the reflectance of human skin but not facial hair. As a result, facial hair color may not necessarily appear in the reflectance image, as seen in the second example of Fig. 3(h) for the subject's stubble. While the stubble affects the shading image as it likely should, an extension of the human face priors to model facial hair in certain face regions could improve the decomposition of those areas.

6.2   Skin Reflectance vs. Lambertian Model

To assess the effect of the skin reflectance model on intrinsic image decomposition, we compare our method to a version of it that uses the Lambertian model in place of the diffuse skin reflectance model and its respective priors. Handling of specular reflections was kept the same for both methods. The resulting shading images are displayed in Fig. 4. It can be seen that the Lambertian model yields a 'hard' shading uncharacteristic of human skin, whereas the skin reflectance model better captures the soft shading that arises from skin translucency. Also, for the Lambertian model, the side of the face closer to the light source appears overly bright in the shading images since a higher light intensity is needed to adequately boost the brightness of the other side of the face.

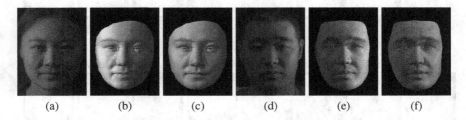

(a)   (b)   (c)   (d)   (e)   (f)

Fig. 4. Comparison between the skin reflectance model and the Lambertian model. (a/d) Input images. (b/e) Shading images using the Lambertian model. (c/f) Shading images using the skin reflectance model.

6.3   Generic vs. Specific Population Priors

Applying population-specific priors after the generic priors stage of our algorithm can lead to noticeable improvements in the decomposition. Two examples are shown in Fig. 5, where the generic priors are trained from all face samples in the MERL/ETH dataset, and the specific priors are trained from only faces in the inferred population group (young and white for the top face, and prime and olive for the bottom face). With the narrower priors for the specific population, subtle shading variations may diverge further from the albedo prior, and details such as the blemishes on the forehead in the top face become more visible in the reflectance image. For the bottom face, the check folds become less apparent in the reflectance image and appear more prominently and correctly in the shading image. We note that for these examples the geometry prior constraint was not omitted in computing the generic priors results.

Input   Generic prior   Specific prior

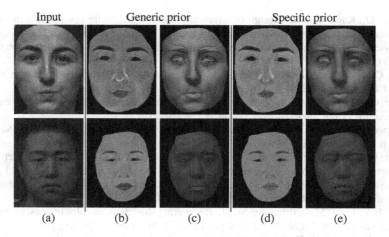

(a)   (b)   (c)   (d)   (e)

Fig. 5. Comparison between generic and specific priors. (a) Input image. (b/d) Estimated reflectance. (c/e) Estimated shading.

7   Conclusion

In this paper, we presented an intrinsic image decomposition method for human faces. Formulated in the optimization function are constraints derived from human face statistics and a reflectance model that well-represents properties of human skin. It is shown experimentally that this method generates decomposition results that compare favorably to state-of-the-art techniques for general intrinsic image estimation and 3D face modeling.

As mentioned previously, our reflectance priors presently account for human skin but not facial hair. A result of this is that facial hair might not correctly appear in reflectance images, because of inconsistency between its albedo and our facial skin priors. In future work, the prior model could potentially be expanded to account for facial hair in certain regions of the face.

Acknowledgements. The authors thank Muscle Wu of Microsoft Research for his implementation of the comparison technique from [15]. This work was partially supported by NSFC(No. 61272305) and the National Program for Special Support of Eminent Professionals.

References

1. Barron, J.T., Malik, J.: Intrinsic scene properties from a single rgb-d image. In: Proc. of IEEE Conf. on Computer Vision and Pattern Recognition, CVPR (2013)
2. Barron, J.T., Malik, J.: Shape, illumination, and reflectance from shading. Tech. Rep. UCB/EECS-2013-117, EECS, UC Berkeley (May 2013)
3. Blanz, V., Vetter, T.: A morphable model for the synthesis of 3d faces. In: Proc. of ACM SIGGRAPH, pp. 187–194 (1999)

4. Moon, O., Kang, C.H.B.: Design of advanced color - temperature control system for hdtv applications. Journal of the Korean Physical Society 41, 865–871 (2002)
5. Bousseau, A., Paris, S., Durand, F.: User-assisted intrinsic images. ACM Trans. on Graph. 28(5) (2009)
6. Cao, C., Weng, Y., Lin, S., Zhou, K.: 3d shape regression for real-time facial animation. ACM Trans. Graph. 32(4), 1–41 (2013)
7. Chen, Q., Koltun, V.: A simple model for intrinsic image decomposition with depth cues. In: Proc. of Int'l Conf. on Computer Vision, ICCV (2013)
8. Donner, C., Jensen, H.W.: Light diffusion in multi-layered translucent materials. ACM Trans. Graph. 24(3), 1032–1039 (2005)
9. Egan, W.G., Hilgeman, T.W., Reichman, J.: Determination of absorption and scattering co-efficients for nonhomogeneous media. 2: Experiment. Applied Optics 12, 1816–1823 (1973)
10. Finlayson, G.D., Schaefer, G.: Solving for colour constancy using a constrained dichromatic reflection model. Int. J. Comput. Vision 42(3), 127–144 (2001)
11. Funt, B.V., Drew, M.S., Brockington, M.: Recovering shading from color images. In: Sandini, G. (ed.) ECCV 1992. LNCS, vol. 588, pp. 124–132. Springer, Heidelberg (1992)
12. Gehler, P., Rother, C., Kiefel, M., Zhang, L., Schölkopf, B.: Recovering intrinsic images with a global sparsity prior on reflectance. In: Proc. of Neural Information Processing Systems, NIPS (2011)
13. Grosse, R., Johnson, M.K., Adelson, E.H., Freeman, W.T.: Ground truth dataset and baseline evaluations for intrinsic image algorithms. In: Proc. of Int'l Conf. on Computer Vision, ICCV (2009)
14. Jensen, H.W., Marschner, S.R., Levoy, M., Hanrahan, P.: A practical model for subsurface light transport. In: Proceedings of the 28th Annual Conference on Computer Graphics and Interactive Techniques, ACM SIGGRAPH 2001, pp. 511–518 (2001)
15. Kemelmacher-Shlizerman, I., Basri, R.: 3d face reconstruction from a single image using a single reference face shape. IEEE Transactions on Pattern Analysis and Machine Intelligence 33(2), 394–405 (2011)
16. Kimmel, R., Elad, M., Shaked, D., Keshet, R., Sobel, I.: A variational framework for retinex. Int'l Journal of Computer Vision 52, 7–23 (2003)
17. Klinker, G.J., Shafer, S.A., Kanade, T.: The measurement of highlights in color images. Int'l Journal of Computer Vision 2(1), 7–32 (1990)
18. Laffont, P.Y., Bousseau, A., Paris, S., Durand, F., Drettakis, G.: Coherent intrinsic images from photo collections. ACM Trans. on Graph. 31(6) (2012)
19. Land, E., McCann, J.: Lightness and retinex theory. Journal of the Optical Society of America A 3, 1684–1692 (1971)
20. Lee, J., Machiraju, R., Moghaddam, B., Pfister, H.: Estimation of 3d faces and illumination from single photographs using a bilinear illumination model. In: Proceedings of the Sixteenth Eurographics Conference on Rendering Techniques, EGSR 2005, pp. 73–82 (2005)
21. Lee, K.J., Zhao, Q., Tong, X., Gong, M., Izadi, S., Lee, S.U., Tan, P., Lin, S.: Estimation of intrinsic image sequences from image+Depth video. In: Fitzgibbon, A., Lazebnik, S., Perona, P., Sato, Y., Schmid, C. (eds.) ECCV 2012, Part VI. LNCS, vol. 7577, pp. 327–340. Springer, Heidelberg (2012)
22. Liu, X., Wan, L., Qu, Y., Wong, T.T., Lin, S., Leung, C.S., Heng, P.A.: Intrinsic colorization. ACM Trans. on Graph. 27(5) (2008)
23. Maxwell, B.A., Friedhoff, R.M., Smith, C.A.: A bi-illuminant dichromatic reflection model for understanding images. In: Proc. of IEEE Conf. on Computer Vision and Pattern Recognition, CVPR (2008)
24. Milborrow, S., Nicolls, F.: Locating facial features with an extended active shape model. In: Forsyth, D., Torr, P., Zisserman, A. (eds.) ECCV 2008, Part IV. LNCS, vol. 5305, pp. 504–513. Springer, Heidelberg (2008)

25. Shafer, S.A.: Using color to separate reflection components. Color Res. App. 10(4), 210–218 (1985)
26. Shen, J., Yang, X., Jia, Y., Li, X.: Intrinsic images using optimization. In: Proc. of IEEE Conf. on Computer Vision and Pattern Recognition, CVPR (2011)
27. Shen, L., Tan, P., Lin, S.: Intrinsic image decomposition with non-local texture cues. In: Proc. of IEEE Conf. on Computer Vision and Pattern Recognition, CVPR (2008)
28. Tappen, M.F., Adelson, E.H., Freeman, W.T.: Estimating intrinsic component images using non-linear regression. In: Proc. of IEEE Conf. on Computer Vision and Pattern Recognition (CVPR), pp. 1992–1999 (2006)
29. Weiss, Y.: Deriving intrinsic images from image sequences. In: Proc. of Int'l Conf. on Computer Vision (ICCV), pp. 68–75 (2001)
30. Weyrich, T., Matusik, W., Pfister, H., Bickel, B., Donner, C., Tu, C., McAndless, J., Lee, J., Ngan, A., Jensen, H.W., Gross, M.: Analysis of human faces using a measurement-based skin reflectance model. ACM Trans. Graph. 25(3), 1013–1024 (2006)
31. Yang, F., Wang, J., Shechtman, E., Bourdev, L., Metaxas, D.: Expression flow for 3d-aware face component transfer. ACM Trans. Graph. 30(4), 1–60 (2011)
32. Yang, Q., Wang, S., Ahuja, N.: Real-time specular highlight removal using bilateral filtering. In: Daniilidis, K., Maragos, P., Paragios, N. (eds.) ECCV 2010, Part IV. LNCS, vol. 6314, pp. 87–100. Springer, Heidelberg (2010)
33. Zhao, Q., Tan, P., Dai, Q., Shen, L., Wu, E., Lin, S.: A closed-form solution to retinex with nonlocal texture constraints. IEEE Trans. Pattern Anal. Mach. Intell. 34(7), 1437–1444 (2012)

Recovering Scene Geometry under Wavy Fluid via Distortion and Defocus Analysis*

Mingjie Zhang[1], Xing Lin[1], Mohit Gupta[2], Jinli Suo[1], and Qionghai Dai[1]

[1] Department of Automation, Tsinghua University
[2] Columbia University

Abstract. In this paper, we consider scenes that are immersed in transparent refractive media with a dynamic surface. We take the first steps to reconstruct both the 3D fluid surface shape and the 3D structure of immersed scene simultaneously by utilizing distortion and defocus clues. We demonstrate that the images captured through a refractive dynamic fluid surface are the distorted and blurred versions of all-in-focused (AIF) images captured through a flat fluid surface. The amounts of distortion and refractive blur are formulated by the shape of fluid surface, scene depth and camera parameters, based on our refractive geometry model of a finite aperture imaging system. An iterative optimization algorithm is proposed to reconstruct the distortion and immersed scene depth, which are then used to infer the 3D fluid surface. We validate and demonstrate the effectiveness of our approach on a variety of synthetic and real scenes under different fluid surfaces.

Keywords: underwater 3D reconstruction, dynamic fluid surface recovery, refractive blur, distortion, depth from defocus.

1 Introduction

In recent years, the problems of recovering scene structure immersed in refractive fluid and reconstructing the 3D shape of the dynamic fluid surface have drawn more attention in multiple research fields, including computer vision and oceanography. Although a lot of progress has been made [30,9,36,8,11,4], the solutions are not sufficiently general to be used in real-world scenarios. This is because most existing methods recovering scene geometry under fluid surface assume the fluid surface to be flat [8,34,3]. On the other hand, 3D fluid surface estimation approaches [22,9,24,30] assume a flat scene under the surface. These assumptions are rarely satisfied in real applications. The general scenario of recovering scene depths immersed in fluid with non-flat surfaces remains a challenging problem. In addition, most previous approaches are based on the pinhole imaging model. However, in practice, in order to achieve high signal-to-noise-ratio (SNR), cameras often use large apertures where pinhole model is not applicable, thus resulting in image blur.

---

* Electronic supplementary material - Supplementary material is available in the online version of this chapter at http://dx.doi.org/10.1007/978-3-319-10602-1_16. Videos can also be accessed at http://www.springerimages.com/videos/978-3-319-10601-4

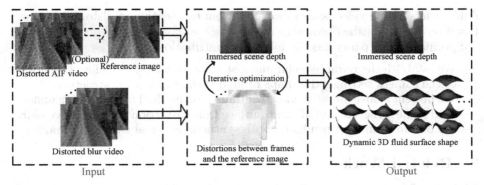

Fig. 1. Diagram of the proposed iterative optimization framework. The input of our approach are a captured refractive blur video and a reference image which could be estimated from another all-in-focused(AIF) video or captured under flat water. An iterative optimization is applied to recover the depth of immersed scene and the distortions, which are then used to estimate the dynamic 3D fluid surface shape.

Among the large numbers of depth estimation approaches (e.g. multi-view stereo, structure from motion, shape from shading), depth from defocus (DFD) is attractive due to its insensitivity to an occlusion and matching problem [29]. Different from performing DFD in clear air, the irregular refraction on the wavy interface causes distortion and blurring of the images of immersed scenes. The blur in images captured through a fluid surface is determined by not only camera parameters and scene depth but also the refraction on the fluid surface. Hence, we call it the **refractive blur.** Compared with stereo, DFD approach has a smaller baseline. Thus, all the rays emitted from a scene point reaching the sensor can be assumed to be sufficiently close so that the normals of the fluid surface where the rays cross the fluid interface can be assumed to be approximately constant. This reduces the number of unknowns as compared to stereo, where rays from a scene point cross the fluid interface at different points, and thus likely encounter different surface normals (details in the Sec. 6).

In this paper, we establish a geometric imaging model for refractive blur and distortion simultaneously, while most existing works do not account for refractive blur. Our imaging model represents the images captured through the fluid surface as the distorted and blurred version of the undistorted all-in-focus(AIF) image captured through a flat fluid surface.

The reconstruction steps of fluid surface and the underneath scene geometry are illustrated in Fig. 1. Our algorithm requires an out-of-focus video captured under large aperture setting and a reference image[1]. The reference image could be estimated from the pre-captured AIF video or captured under flat water with a small aperture. Then, based on the model established in Sec. 3, we construct an objective function and use an optimization procedure to compute the depth of the immersed scene and the distortions alternatively. Finally the dynamic 3D

---

[1] In this paper, the reference image refers to the undistorted all-in-focus(AIF) image captured under flat water with a small aperture.

fluid surface shape video is also recovered from the depth and distortions maps based on the established geometry model.

Specifically, the paper has the following contributions:

- We establish the refractive blur and distortion geometry model as a function of the camera settings, the shape of fluid surface and scene structure.
- We present a novel iterative global optimization method for recovering under-fluid scene structure and 3D fluid surface from distortion and refractive blur.
- We obtain promising results on both synthetic and real captured data.

2   Related Work

Fluid Surface Reconstruction. Several methods [22,9,24,30] recover the wavy fluid surface and undistorted image by analyzing the distortion in the video. These works require placing a flat plane with rich features under the fluid surface. In order to enhance the reconstruction performance, multi-camera methods [22,9,18] have also been proposed. Moreover, Tian and Narasimhan [30] model the distortion by the wave equation and present a tracking method without the need of undistorted image. There are also methods utilizing active illumination instead of a flat rich feature plane, such as [19,36]. Our paper estimates scene structure as well as fluid appearance, does not require active illumination, and owns wider applications.

Compensation of the Refractive Distortions. A variety of methods [11,10,33,31,26] have been proposed for removing the non-rigid distortions in the captured images without recovering the shape of the fluid surface. Most of these approaches adopt the lucky imaging strategy by seamlessly stitching the patches with least distortions, which can be searched or calculated via various techniques, such as clustering [11,10], iterative averaging [26], bispectral analysis [33] and progressive warping [31]. These works can be used for providing the reference image from a captured AIF sequence as an input for our algorithm.

Reconstruction of Geometry through Fluid. Reconstruction of 3D structure under or above the water surface is also an active area of research [8,4,3,14]. Chang and Chen [8] and Ferreira et al. [14] apply the structure from motion and stereo methods to reconstruct the 3D structure of scenes submerged in refractive fluid, respectively. A stochastic triangulation method is proposed by Alterman et al. [4] to recover the structure of scene above water from a video pair captured under water. These works provide some preliminary studies but are limited to static and flat fluid surface.

Depth from Defocus (DFD) in Clear Medium. DFD approaches capture two or multiple defocused images under different focal settings for recovering the scene structure [13,12,21]. These approaches assume that both the scene and the camera are in the same and clear medium. Applying DFD where the scene and the camera are immersed in different refractive media has received little attention. In this paper, we establish a refractive blur model to generalize the conventional defocus model and exploit it to estimate the scene depths under dynamic fluid surface using a reference image and a refractive blur video.

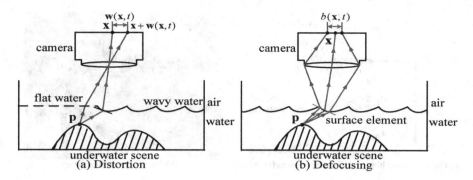

Fig. 2. Imaging through fluid surface with distortion (a) and defocusing (b). (a) The pixel $\mathbf{x} + \mathbf{w}(\mathbf{x}, t)$ in the reference image $I(\mathbf{x}, 0)$ is refracted to $\mathbf{x}$ at frame t. (b) The refracted light rays are further blurred into a refractive blur size $b(\mathbf{x}, t)$ due to the finite camera aperture size.

Other related works to ours include surface reconstruction of transparent refraction object [34,5,23,17], and camera calibration for imaging through the water-air interface [32,35].

3   The Refractive Blur and Distortion Geometry Model

3.1   Image Formulation Model

As shown in Fig. 2, this work supposes that a static non-plane scene is placed under a dynamic fluid surface, and a video camera is focused on a certain plane. For simplicity, we ignore scattering, light absorption and chromatic dispersion in the fluid. We assume that the exposure time is short enough to ignore the motion blur. Let $I(\mathbf{x}, t)$ denotes the tth AIF video frame taken through the fluid surface with $\mathbf{x} = \{x, y\}$ being the 2D spatial coordinates, and $I(\mathbf{x}, 0)$ denotes the reference image.

Without refractive blur, each AIF video frame $I(\mathbf{x}, t)$ is a distorted version of $I(\mathbf{x}, 0)$ as shown in Fig. 2 (a) and can be expressed as

$$I(\mathbf{x}, t) = I(x, y, t) = I(\mathbf{x} + \mathbf{w}(\mathbf{x}, t), 0) = I(x + u(\mathbf{x}, t), y + v(\mathbf{x}, t), 0), \quad (1)$$

where $\mathbf{w}(\mathbf{x}, t) = (u(\mathbf{x}, t), v(\mathbf{x}, t))$ denotes the distortion between the reference image and frame i correspondence to the point $\mathbf{x}$ at frame t, which will be formulated in Sec. 3.2 in detail.

Then considering both the refraction and the defocusing, as shown in Fig. 2 (b), rays emitted from an underwater scene point are deflected at the water surface and projected onto different positions of the sensor. Similar to the defocus blur occurring in the air, we call this deflection blur as "refractive blur". Detailed formulation of refractive blur will also be given in Sec. 3.2. Thus the refractive blur video acquired through a wavy water surface can be formulated as

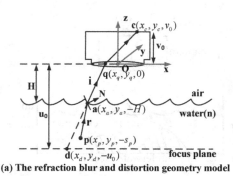
(a) The refraction blur and distortion geometry model

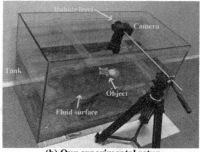
(b) Our experimental setup

Fig. 3. The refractive geometry of underwater imaging in 3D case (a), and our experiment setup (b). (a) One ray emitted from the scene point **p** is refracted at the fluid surface point **a** , passes through the aperture plane at **q** and is projected to point **c** on the sensor, which corresponds to point **d** on the focus plane. The coordinates axes are displayed with blue arrows and the origin is set at the camera optical center **O**. (b). Our camera's sensor is parallel with the flat water surface which is achieved by using bubble level.

$$B(\mathbf{x}, t) = \int_{\mathbf{y} \in N_{\mathbf{x}}} h_{\sigma^2(\mathbf{x},t)}(\mathbf{x}, \mathbf{y}) I(\mathbf{y}, t) d\mathbf{y} = \int_{\mathbf{y} \in N_{\mathbf{x}}} h_{\sigma^2(\mathbf{x},t)}(\mathbf{x}, \mathbf{y}) I(\mathbf{y} + \mathbf{w}(\mathbf{y}, t), 0) d\mathbf{y}, \quad (2)$$

where $B(\mathbf{x}, t)$ denotes the tth frame in the refractive blur video; $h_{\sigma^2(\mathbf{x},t)}(\mathbf{x}, \mathbf{y})$ denotes the refractive blur kernel of point $\mathbf{x}$ which can be approximately estimated by Gaussian kernel; $\sigma(\mathbf{x}, t)$ denotes the kernel size of point $\mathbf{x}$ at time t; and $\mathbf{y} \in N_{\mathbf{x}}$ denotes the pixels within $\mathbf{x}$'s neighborhood.

3.2   The Refractive Blur and Distortion Formulation

As shown in Fig. 3, suppose that the sensor is parallel with the flat water surface. H denotes the vertical distance from the camera to the flat water surface, n denotes the refractive index of water, u_0 denotes the distance between the lens and the focus plane, v_0 denotes the distance between the lens and the sensor plane, and the focal plane remains unchanged during the capture. Then based on the vector forms of Snell's law [20] in 3D space, we can obtain the relationship

$$\boldsymbol{i} \times \boldsymbol{N} = n\boldsymbol{r} \times \boldsymbol{N}, \quad (3)$$

where $\boldsymbol{i}$ denotes the unit vector along the light propagating in the air; $\boldsymbol{r}$ denotes the unit vector along the corresponding light propagating in the water; $\boldsymbol{N}$ denotes the unit normal vector of the refractive plane at the intersection point of $\boldsymbol{i}$ and $\boldsymbol{r}$; and $\times$ is the cross product.

In general 3D case, we use the thin lens model to analyze the light path and assume the x-axis and y-axis are parallel to the sensor plane, z-axis is aligned with the camera optical center **o**, represented by blue arrows in Fig. 3(a). Without the loss of generality, we also assume the amplitude of water wave is slight enough to ignore. Then Eq. 3 can be represented by the geometric locations of the underwater scene point $\mathbf{p} = (x_p, y_p, -s_p)$, the refractive point $\mathbf{a} = (x_a, y_a, -H)$ on the refractive plane and the intersection point $\mathbf{q} = (x_q, y_q, 0)$ on the aperture plane

$$i = \frac{\mathbf{q} - \mathbf{a}}{\|\mathbf{q} - \mathbf{a}\|}, \quad r = \frac{\mathbf{a} - \mathbf{p}}{\|\mathbf{a} - \mathbf{p}\|}. \tag{4}$$

As shown in Fig.3(a), this ray emitted from the immersed scene point $\mathbf{p}$ is projected to the sensor point $\mathbf{c}$, which corresponds to the point $\mathbf{d}$ on the focus plane. Based on the simple lens model, these two points have the relationship: $\mathbf{d} = (u_0/v_0)\mathbf{c}$. The three points $\mathbf{q}$, $\mathbf{a}$ and $\mathbf{d}$ are also collinear, thus point $\mathbf{a}$ can be represented by

$$\mathbf{a} = (1 - \frac{H}{u_0})\mathbf{q} - \frac{H}{u_0}\mathbf{d} = (1 - \frac{H}{u_0})\mathbf{q} - \frac{H}{v_0}\mathbf{c}. \tag{5}$$

Substitute Eq. 4 and Eq. 5 into Eq. 3, we can obtain the geometric function represented one ray emitted from the scene point $\mathbf{p}$ and projected to the sensor point $\mathbf{c}$, which also provides the relationship between these two points:

$$\begin{cases} \dfrac{(x_q + \frac{u_0}{v_0}x_c)n_z(\mathbf{a}) - u_0 n_x(\mathbf{a})}{\sqrt{\left(x_q + \frac{u_0}{v_0}x_c\right)^2 + \left(y_q + \frac{u_0}{v_0}y_c\right)^2 + u_0^2}} = n \dfrac{((1 - \frac{H}{u_0})x_q - \frac{H}{v_0}x_c - x_p)n_z(\mathbf{a}) - (s_p - H)n_x(\mathbf{a})}{\sqrt{\left((1 - \frac{H}{u_0})x_q - \frac{H}{v_0}x_c - x_p\right)^2 + \left((1 - \frac{H}{u_0})y_q - \frac{H}{v_0}y_c - y_p\right)^2 + (s_p - H)^2}} \\[4mm] \dfrac{(y_q + \frac{u_0}{v_0}y_c)n_z(\mathbf{a}) - u_0 n_y(\mathbf{a})}{\sqrt{\left(x_q + \frac{u_0}{v_0}x_c\right)^2 + \left(y_q + \frac{u_0}{v_0}y_c\right)^2 + u_0^2}} = n \dfrac{((1 - \frac{H}{u_0})y_q - \frac{H}{v_0}y_c - y_p)n_z(\mathbf{a}) - (s_p - H)n_y(\mathbf{a})}{\sqrt{\left((1 - \frac{H}{u_0})x_q - \frac{H}{v_0}x_c - x_p\right)^2 + \left((1 - \frac{H}{u_0})y_q - \frac{H}{v_0}y_c - y_p\right)^2 + (s_p - H)^2}}, \end{cases} \tag{6}$$

where $n_x(\mathbf{a})$, $n_y(\mathbf{a})$ and $n_z(\mathbf{a})$ are the 3D coordinates of the unit normal vector N at the refractive point $\mathbf{a}$, and s_p is the depth of the scene point $\mathbf{p}$.

With Eq. 6, we can project the underwater scene point to the sensor plane or conversely, thus the distortion between different frames can be calculated. By scanning the point $\mathbf{q}$ over the aperture plane while holding the scene point $\mathbf{p}$, we can also derive the blur kernel size of the scene point $\mathbf{p}$ on the sensor. Unfortunately, Eq. 6 is too complex to analyze. Therefore, we use the first order Taylor expansion for simplification (details in the Supplementary Material). We regard x_p and y_p as the independent variable and regard x_c and y_c as unknown variable. The first order Taylor expansion of Eq. 6 at point $x_p = x_{p0} = x_q - \frac{n_x(\mathbf{a})}{n_z(\mathbf{a})}s_p$ and $y_p = y_{p0} = y_q - \frac{n_y(\mathbf{a})}{n_z(\mathbf{a})}s_p$ is

$$\begin{cases} x_c \approx \dfrac{v_0}{u_0}(\dfrac{n_x(\mathbf{a})}{n_z(\mathbf{a})}u_0 - x_q) - (x_p - x_q + \dfrac{n_x(\mathbf{a})}{n_z(\mathbf{a})}s_p)\dfrac{nv_0}{s_p + (n-1)H} \\[4mm] y_c \approx \dfrac{v_0}{u_0}(\dfrac{n_y(\mathbf{a})}{n_z(\mathbf{a})}u_0 - y_q) - (y_p - y_q + \dfrac{n_y(\mathbf{a})}{n_z(\mathbf{a})}s_p)\dfrac{nv_0}{s_p + (n-1)H}. \end{cases} \tag{7}$$

Eq. 7 is the simple approximation function representing the light that is emitted from the scene point $\mathbf{p}$ and passes through the lens point $\mathbf{q}$ with the sensor projection $\mathbf{c}$. When we scan the aperture point $\mathbf{q}$ within the circle aperture to analyze the size of blur kernel, the refractive point $\mathbf{a}$ on the refractive plane is also changing, which makes the analysis difficult. However, as illustrated in Fig. 2 (b), when the varying area (i.e. the **surface element** shown in Fig. 2(b)) of the refractive point **a** is small enough (The detailed analysis will be presented in Sec. 3.3), we can ignore the changes of the normal vector $\boldsymbol{N}$. Then we can find that the area on the sensor corresponding to the scene point (i.e. the refractive blur kernel) is approximatively a circle, and **the refractive blur size** of pixel **x** at frame t is

$$\sigma(\mathbf{x}, t) = \kappa \frac{v_0 D}{2} \left| \frac{n}{s(\mathbf{x}) + (n-1)H} - \frac{1}{u_0} \right|, \tag{8}$$

where D is the aperture diameter of the lens, $s(\mathbf{x})$ is the depth map of reference image and κ is the calibration parameter converting world coordinate to image plane. Notice that if there is no fluid, i.e. $n = 1$, refractive blur size (Eq. 8) is degraded to the defocused blur size in the air [21]. In addition, Eq. 8 shows that the refractive blur size is independent of the water surface shape which means we can infer the immersed scene depth from refractive blur.

In order to derive the amount of distortion, we apply the perspective model by keeping an infinite small aperture size in our refractive geometry model. Then based on Eq. 7, we can also derive the 2D spatial coordinates **distortion** between reference image and other frames by back-projecting point to the scene through the wavy surface and forward-projecting it to the sensor through the flat surface

$$\begin{cases} u(\mathbf{x}, t) = -\kappa \left(\dfrac{n_x(\mathbf{x}, t)}{n_z(\mathbf{x}, t)} - \dfrac{n_x(\mathbf{x} + \mathbf{w}(\mathbf{x}, t), 0)}{n_z(\mathbf{x} + \mathbf{w}(\mathbf{x}, t), 0)} \right)(v_0 - \dfrac{n v_0 s(\mathbf{x} + \mathbf{w}(\mathbf{x}, t))}{s(\mathbf{x} + \mathbf{w}(\mathbf{x}, t)) + (n-1)H}) \\ v(\mathbf{x}, t) = -\kappa \left(\dfrac{n_y(\mathbf{x}, t)}{n_z(\mathbf{x}, t)} - \dfrac{n_y(\mathbf{x} + \mathbf{w}(\mathbf{x}, t), 0)}{n_z(\mathbf{x} + \mathbf{w}(\mathbf{x}, t), 0)} \right)(v_0 - \dfrac{n v_0 s(\mathbf{x} + \mathbf{w}(\mathbf{x}, t))}{s(\mathbf{x} + \mathbf{w}(\mathbf{x}, t)) + (n-1)H}), \end{cases} \tag{9}$$

where $n_x(\mathbf{x}, t)$, $n_y(\mathbf{x}, t)$ and $n_z(\mathbf{x}, t)$ are the 3D coordinates of the unit normal vector $\boldsymbol{N}$ corresponding to the point(x, y) at frame t.

3.3   The Condition of Model

As illustrated in Fig. 2(b) and the derivation in Sec. 3.2, due to the camera's finite aperture, a scene point **p** emits a cluster of rays projecting to the sensor. Each of these rays is deflected at different points on the water-air interface, and we call the area on the interface where these rays pass through the **surface element** corresponding to point **p**.

When we obtain Eq.8 from Eq.7, we assume that each scene point's surface element is small enough to be approximated by a plane. Thus **the size of surface element** is the minimum area of water surface that our model can distinguish, which is similar to the spatial resolution of traditional camera.

Based on Eq. 5 and Eq. 7, we can derive the coordinates of the refractive point **a**:

$$\mathbf{x}_a = \frac{s_p - H}{s_p + (n-1)H}(x_q + (n-1)H \frac{n_x(\mathbf{x}_a)}{n_z(\mathbf{x}_a)}) + \frac{n H x_p}{s_p + (n-1)H}. \tag{10}$$

Randomly select two points ($\mathbf{a_1}$ and $\mathbf{a_2}$) on the surface element corresponding to the same scene point $\mathbf{p}$, then the distance between them is

$$\mathbf{x}_{a_1} - \mathbf{x}_{a_2} = \frac{s_p - H}{s_p + (n-1)H}((x_{q_1} - x_{q_2}) + (n-1)H(\frac{n_{\mathbf{x}}(\mathbf{x}_{a_1})}{n_z(\mathbf{x}_{a_1})} - \frac{n_{\mathbf{x}}(\mathbf{x}_{a_2})}{n_z(\mathbf{x}_{a_2})})). \quad (11)$$

Assuming the model holds, we can derive the size of surface elements $\triangle_p$ corresponding to scene point $\mathbf{p}$:

$$\triangle_p = \max(\mathbf{x}_{a_1} - \mathbf{x}_{a_2}) = \frac{s_p - H}{s_p + (n-1)H}D \leq D \quad (12)$$

From Eq. 12, we know that the size of surface element is positively correlated with the aperture size, i.e. the size of baseline. Thus the smaller the baseline, the better performance and system's robustness. Obviously the DFD approaches usually have a smaller baseline than stereo method and are more suitable to this model in the paper.

4 Iterative Optimization Algorithm for Reconstructing Scene Depth and Water Surface Shape

In this section, we propose an iterative optimization method to reconstruct both the undistorted scene depth and the wavy water surface.

4.1 Optimization Model

Assume the depth of water, the refractive index of water, and the distance from the camera to the water surface are measured in advance, the camera's sensor is parallel with the water surface, and the focal plane remains unchanged during the capture. Then according to Eq. 2, the optimization problem for estimating the distortion $\mathbf{w}(\mathbf{x}, t)$ and the depth $s(\mathbf{x})$ can be formulated as

$$\min_{s,\mathbf{w}} J(s(\mathbf{x}), \mathbf{w}(\mathbf{x}, t)) = \min_{s,\mathbf{w}} E_d(s(\mathbf{x}), \mathbf{w}(\mathbf{x}, t)) + \alpha E_m(\mathbf{w}(\mathbf{x}, t)) + \beta E_m(s(\mathbf{x})), \quad (13)$$

where $J(s(\mathbf{x}), \mathbf{w}(\mathbf{x}, t))$, $E_d(s(\mathbf{x}), \mathbf{w}(\mathbf{x}, t))$, $E_m(s(\mathbf{x}))$ and $E_m(\mathbf{w}(\mathbf{x}, t))$ are objective function, data term, depth regularization term and distortion regularization term, respectively; $\alpha > 0$ and $\beta > 0$ are the regularization parameters that balance data term and two regularization terms, respectively; $s(\mathbf{x})$ denotes the depth corresponding to reference image $I(\mathbf{x}, 0)$.

Specifically, the data term can be written as

$$E_d(s(\mathbf{x}), \mathbf{w}(\mathbf{x}, t)) = \sum_{t=1}^{T} \int_{\Omega} \psi(\left\| B(\mathbf{x}, t) - \int_{\mathbf{y} \in N_{\mathbf{x}}} h_{\sigma^2(\mathbf{x}, t)}(\mathbf{x}, \mathbf{y}) I(\mathbf{y} + \mathbf{w}(\mathbf{y}, t), 0) d\mathbf{y} \right\|_2^2) d\mathbf{x}, \quad (14)$$

and depth and distortion regularization terms are

$$E_m(\mathbf{w}(\mathbf{x},t)) = \sum_{t=1}^{T} \int_{\Omega} \psi(\|\nabla u(\mathbf{x},t)\|_2^2 + \|\nabla v(\mathbf{x},t)\|_2^2) d\mathbf{x}, \tag{15}$$

$$E_m(s(\mathbf{x})) = \int_{\Omega} \|\nabla s(\mathbf{x})\|_2 d\mathbf{x}, \tag{16}$$

where $\Omega \subset \mathbb{R}^2$ is the range of $\mathbf{x}$; $\psi(\xi^2) = \sqrt{\xi^2 + \epsilon^2}$ is applied to reduce the outliers, similar to optical flow algorithms in [7,6]; and the distorted displacement $u(\mathbf{x},t)$, $v(\mathbf{x},t)$ and kernel size $\sigma(\mathbf{x},t)$ have been formulated in Eq. 8 and Eq. 9.

The optimization for Eq. 13 requires that the reference image $I(\mathbf{x},\mathbf{0})$ is known. According to Eq. 9, if we want to recover the normal vectors of dynamic fluid surface from distortions and scene depth, the reference image must be the AIF undistorted image taken through the flat water. In this paper, we capture the reference image directly by using the small aperture size under flat water. Besides, we also estimate the reference image from a captured AIF distorted video by an existing method [26], of which synthetic results are shown in the supplementary material and video.

To optimize Eq. 13, we apply an alternative minimization approach to iteratively estimate the distortion $\mathbf{w}(\mathbf{x},t)$ and blur size $s(\mathbf{x})$ which are detailed in Sec. 4.2 and Sec. 4.3, respectively. Next, surface shape could be reconstructed from $s(\mathbf{x})$ and $\mathbf{w}(\mathbf{x},t)$ as described in Sec. 4.4.

4.2   Distortion Refinement

For the minimization of distortion $\mathbf{w}(\mathbf{x},t)$, we keep the depth $s(\mathbf{x})$ fixed, then the optimization in Eq. 13 can be simplified as

$$\min_{\mathbf{w}} J_1(\mathbf{w}(\mathbf{x},t)) = \min_{\mathbf{w}} E_d(\mathbf{w}(\mathbf{x},t)) + \alpha E_m(\mathbf{w}(\mathbf{x},t)), \tag{17}$$

where $J_1(\mathbf{w}(\mathbf{x},t))$ is the objective function for distortion refinement; $E_d(\mathbf{w}(\mathbf{x},t))$ is the data-term defined in Eq. 14 with fixed $s(\mathbf{x})$; $E_m(\mathbf{w}(\mathbf{x},t))$ is the distortion regularization term defined in Eq. 15.

The distortion refinement objective function in Eq. 17 is similar to but different from the objective function of optical flow algorithm in [7,6] in two aspects: the distorted images $I(\mathbf{x},t)$ in [7] are replaced with the distorted and blur images $\int_{\mathbf{y} \in N_{\mathbf{x}}} h_{\sigma^2(\mathbf{x},t)}(\mathbf{x},\mathbf{y}) I(\mathbf{y} + \mathbf{w}(\mathbf{y},i), 0) d\mathbf{y}$; the weight γ of gradient image in [7] is set to zero. So we modify the numerical solution of existing optical flow algorithms in [7,6] for our problem:

$$\begin{cases} \psi'((I_z^k + I_x^k du^{k,l} + I_y^k dv^{k,l})^2) \cdot (I_x^k (I_z^k + I_x^k du^{k,l+1} + I_y^k dv^{k,l+1})) \\ \quad - \alpha \, div(\psi'(\left|\nabla(u + du^{k,l})\right|^2 + \left|\nabla(v + dv^{k,l})\right|^2) \nabla(u + du^{k,l+1})) = 0, \\ \psi'((I_z^k + I_x^k du^{k,l} + I_y^k dv^{k,l})^2) \cdot (I_y^k (I_z^k + I_x^k du^{k,l+1} + I_y^k dv^{k,l+1})) \\ \quad - \alpha \, div(\psi'(\left|\nabla(u + du^{k,l})\right|^2 + \left|\nabla(v + dv^{k,l})\right|^2) \nabla(v + dv^{k,l+1})) = 0, \end{cases} \tag{18}$$

where

$$I_z^k = \int_{\mathbf{y} \in N_{\mathbf{x}}} h_{\sigma^2(\mathbf{x},t)}(\mathbf{x},\mathbf{y}) I(\mathbf{y}+\mathbf{w}(\mathbf{y},i),0) d\mathbf{y} - B(\mathbf{x},i),$$

$$I_x^k = \int_{\mathbf{y} \in N_{\mathbf{x}}} h_{\sigma^2(\mathbf{x},t)}(\mathbf{x},\mathbf{y}) \partial_x I(\mathbf{y}+\mathbf{w}(\mathbf{y},i),0) + \frac{\partial h_{\sigma^2(\mathbf{x},t)}(\mathbf{x},\mathbf{y})}{\partial s(\mathbf{x}+\mathbf{w}(\mathbf{x},i))} \partial_x s(\mathbf{x}+\mathbf{w}(\mathbf{x},i)) I(\mathbf{x}+\mathbf{w}(\mathbf{y},i),0) d\mathbf{y}, \quad (19)$$

$$I_y^k = \int_{\mathbf{y} \in N_{\mathbf{x}}} h_{\sigma^2(\mathbf{x},t)}(\mathbf{x},\mathbf{y}) \partial_y I(\mathbf{y}+\mathbf{w}(\mathbf{y},i),0) + \frac{\partial h_{\sigma^2(\mathbf{x},t)}(\mathbf{x},\mathbf{y})}{\partial s(\mathbf{x}+\mathbf{w}(\mathbf{x},i))} \partial_y s(\mathbf{x}+\mathbf{w}(\mathbf{x},i)) I(\mathbf{y}+\mathbf{w}(\mathbf{y},i),0) d\mathbf{y},$$

which can be solved by Gauss-Seidel or SOR iterations.

4.3 Depth Refinement

For the minimization of scene depth $s(\mathbf{x})$, we keep the distorted displacement $\mathbf{w}(\mathbf{y},t)$ fixed, then Eq. 13 becomes

$$\min_s J_2(s(\mathbf{x})) = \min_s E_d(s(\mathbf{x})) + \beta E_m(s(\mathbf{x})), \quad (20)$$

where $J_2(s(\mathbf{x}))$ is the depth refinement objective function; $E_d(s(\mathbf{x}))$ is the data-term defined in Eq. 14 with fixed $\mathbf{w}(\mathbf{y},t)$; $E_m(s(\mathbf{x}))$ is the depth regularization term defined in Eq. 16.

The minimization in Eq. 20 resembles the DFD optimization problem in the air [12,21], except that defocused blur kernel size functions (Eq. 8) and the $\psi(\xi^2)$ function are different. Thus, we modify the numerical solution in [21] for our problem.

4.4 Recover Surface Shape

In Sec. 4.1 to 4.3, we have proposed the optimization method to estimate the distortion between the reference image and refractive blur video and the underneath scene depth in the reference image. Based on Eq. 8 and Eq. 9, the normal vectors map of the wavy water surface in each frame can be reconstructed by the following linear operator:

$$\begin{cases} f_x(\mathbf{x_a},t) = -\dfrac{n_x(\mathbf{x},t)}{n_z(\mathbf{x},t)} = -\dfrac{s(\mathbf{x}+\mathbf{w}(\mathbf{x},i))+(n-1)H}{\kappa v_0(n-1)(s(\mathbf{x}+\mathbf{w}(\mathbf{x},i)-H)} u(\mathbf{x},t) \\ f_y(\mathbf{x_a},t) = -\dfrac{n_y(\mathbf{x},t)}{n_z(\mathbf{x},t)} = -\dfrac{s(\mathbf{x}+\mathbf{w}(\mathbf{x},i))+(n-1)H}{\kappa v_0(n-1)(s(\mathbf{x}+\mathbf{w}(\mathbf{x},i)-H)} v(\mathbf{x},t), \end{cases} \quad (21)$$

where $f_x(\mathbf{x_a},t)$ and $f_y(\mathbf{x_a},t)$ are the x-axis and y-axis gradients of wavy water surface at the point $\mathbf{x_a}$ corresponding to the pixel $\mathbf{x}$ in frames t. Surface integration from a gradient field by solving the Poisson equation has been well studied. In this paper, we apply a similar approach in [2,1] to recover the wavy water surface from its gradients field obtained from Eq. 21.

5   Experimental Results

5.1   Synthetic Data

We evaluate the performance of our approach on synthetic image sequences generated by ray-tracing method. Firstly the ground truth AIF image is regarded as the reference image taken through flat water surface. Its pixels are projected into the scene immersed in water by tracking light through the flat interface. Then under wavy interface, we track each light ray emitted from the scene pixels back to search for each pixels' new locations and refractive blur size on the sensor. Finally we render the synthetic image sequences based on Eq. 2 in Sec. 3.1.

We use the "cloth", "barn" and "baby" data from the Middlebury Stereo Datasets [16,27] and downsample them to resolution 148×174 pixels as the ground truth AIF image and depth. We assume that the distance from the camera to the water surface is 1m, the water depth is 0.5m, the depth range of object under the water is 1.1∼1.5m (we linearly map the ground truth depth to this range under the water), the refractive index of water is 1.33, the virtual camera is focused on the bottom of the water, the camera's focal length $f = 35mm$, the $f/\# = 4$ and the calibration parameter $\kappa = 3e4$. In these experiments, we implement our method with Matlab on a PC with an Intel 2.50G Hz Xeon Quad-Core E5420 CPU.

We first conduct experiments assuming the water surface to be a sinusoidal wave $z(x, y, t) = -0.5 + 0.001\cos(\pi t \sqrt{x^2 + y^2}/300)$ meters (we call this wave wave 1 in this paper, the coordinate system is the same with Sec. 3.2, as shown in Fig. 3(a)). The computation time is about 120 minutes (17 frames,"cloth" data), 80 minutes (15 frames,"barn" data) and 110 minutes (15 frames,"baby" data), respectively. For each scene, we pick one frame from synthetic video and its reconstruction results (depth and fluid surface shape) as shown in Fig. 4 (the first row in each subgraph), and the fluid surface reconstruction error maps are visualized as well (sixth column in Fig. 4). We can see the accuracy of the recovered scene depth and dynamic surfaces results with comparison to the ground truth data. For quantitative evaluation, we also calculate the root mean square error (RMSE) of the immersed scene's depth and water surface's shape sequence. The RMSE of the reconstructed scene depths are respectively 0.0555m("cloth"), 0.0358m("barn") and 0.0839m("baby"), and the average RMSE of the recovered water surfaces are 0.0362mm("cloth"), 0.0317mm("barn") and 0.0618mm ("baby").

To verify our approach's robustness towards different water fluctuations, we apply a different synthetic sinusoidal wave $z(x, y, t) = -0.5 + 0.001\cos(\pi x/60 + 9\pi t/32)$m to three scenes repeatedly (we call this wave wave 2 in this paper), and display the results in second row of each Fig. 4's subgraph. The computation time is about 120 minutes ("cloth"), 90 minutes ("barn") and 130 minutes ("baby") on 17 frames, respectively. The RMSE of the reconstructed scene depth are 0.0441m("cloth"), 0.0433m("barn") and 0.0767m("baby"), and the average RMSE of the reconstructed surfaces are 0.0648mm("cloth"), 0.0677mm("barn") and 0.1426mm("baby"). The results show similar accuracy to that in the first

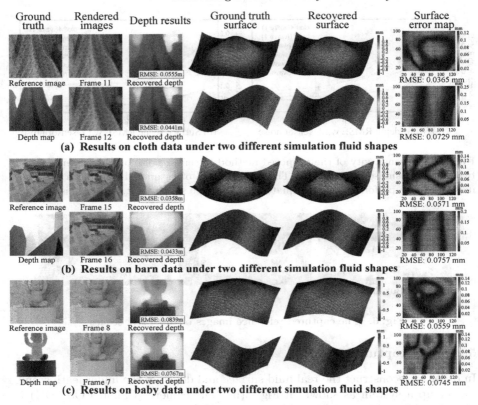

Fig. 4. Experimental results on three different synthetic data under two kinds of sinusoid waves. We synthesize the refractive blur images (second column) from reference image and its depth (first column) with known sinusoid waves (fourth column), then the depth and water surface are reconstructed (third and fifth column) with water surface error map (sixth column).

surface shape sequences. The complete recovered sequences can be found in the supplementary video. We also conduct similar experiments with the estimated reference reconstructed from the synthetic distorted AIF video by [26], of which results are shown in the supplementary material and video.

We also demonstrate the sensitivity of the proposed method by introducing different levels of additive white gaussian noises to the input video and the reference image. In implementation, Fig. 5 demonstrates the performance (RMSE of the reconstruction result) at varying noise levels. The curves show that the performance does not degenerate largely at increasing noise, especially on the rich-textured scene—'cloth', the RMSE on which is relatively lower than on the other scenes.

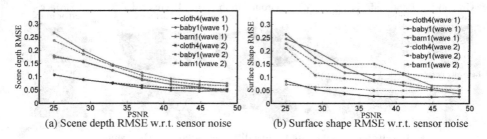

Fig. 5. The sensitivity of the proposed method to sensor noise on three scenes under two different sinusoid waves. (a) The performance of estimated depth w.r.t. sensor noise. (b) The performance of estimated fluid surface shape w.r.t. sensor noise.

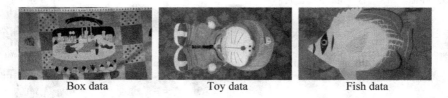

Box data   Toy data   Fish data

Fig. 6. The captured reference images of three real scenes

5.2 Real-captured Results

In order to reconstruct the real fluid surface and depth of the underneath scene, we set up a system as shown in Fig. 3(b). The camera (Canon EOS 5DII) is placed orthogonally to the flat water surface. The scene is uniformly lit from the side face of tank to avoid specular reflections. The distance from the camera to the bottom of the tank is about 72 cm and the depth of water is about 40 cm.

To test our approach's performance under a variety of conditions, we conduct a series of experiments on three immersed scenes with different texture richness of which reference images are shown in Fig. 6 and two different kinds of water fluctuation amplitudes. We firstly take an AIF image through the undisturbed water surface with a small aperture directly to avoid the inaccuracy of the reconstructed reference image by using [30,26], and regard it as the reference image in our approach. Then we capture a blurry video through wavy water with a large aperture, and apply our approach to above two inputs.

Firstly we test our approach under a slightly rippled water surface generated by dripping a drop of water into the tank. To eliminate influences on the video capturing, we drop the water at the corner and generate quarter-annular waves. The results in the first row of each Fig. 7's subgraph show that we achieve promising reconstruction in scenes with abundant texture (Fig. 7(a), with $f = 35mm$ and $f/\# = 4$), common texture scene (Fig. 7(b), with $f = 50mm$ and $f/\# = 4$) and textureless scene (Fig. 7(c), with $f = 50mm$ and $f/\# = 4$).

We also test our method under larger fluctuating water surface by blowing air onto it using a hair dryer. We repeat the same process to capture the reference image and refractive blurry video and reconstruct both the water surface shape

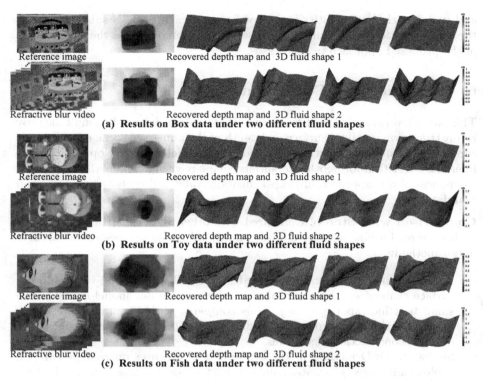

Fig. 7. Results on real-captured data. We reconstruct the depth (second column) and water surface (third to sixth columns) from a captured refractive blur video and a reference image (first column).

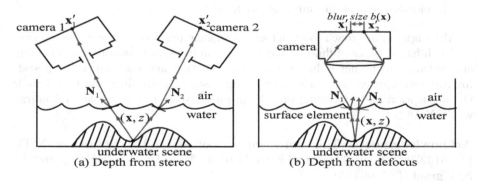

Fig. 8. Comparison of the stereo (a) and DFD approaches (b) applied for scenes under non-planar fluid surface. In stereo, rays leaving the same scene point crosses the fluid surface at different locations, which may have different normals. Compared to stereo, in DFD, two normal vectors of the refractive plane can be regarded as the same due to small baseline (aperture size).

and underneath scene depth. The second row in each Fig. 7's subgraph shows the reconstruction results on the three scenes and demonstrates the effectiveness of the proposed approach in such cases.

6   Discussion and Conclusions

This paper has presented the first method that exploits defocus to simultaneously reconstruct dynamic fluid surface and depth of the immersed scene using a single camera. We build a refractive blur geometry model and develop an iterative inference algorithm for depth and surface shape recovery. The performance and robustness of our approach are experimentally validated on both synthetic and real data.

Comparison with Stereo. Compared with other 3D reconstruction methods such as stereo for imaging through wavy fluid surface, there are some advantages of our method:

- As shown in Fig.8(b) and mentioned in Sec. 3.3, the normal vectors in the surface element can be assumed to be the same in our model owing to the small baseline (aperture size). Thus compared with Fig.8(a), there is less number of the unknowns in the geometry, which enhances the performance of our reconstruction algorithms.
- Similar to DFD method in the air, our approach uses only single camera, avoids multi-view registration and is robust to occlusion, as analyzed in [29]. Besides, the geometry registration in DFD method can be eliminated since we only change the aperture size during capturing and there is no scaling between images. The proposed model incorporates multiple controllable camera parameters (e.g., aperture diameter, focusing depth) and thus is flexible for developing high performance algorithms.

Although our approach could achieve promising performance on various scenes under different types of fluid surfaces, using multiple cameras or changing camera settings to further enhance the reconstruction accuracy are two interesting avenues of future research. Another interesting future direction is to handle the absorption and scattering of light in media such as fog, smoke and murky water[25,15,28].

Acknowledgments. This work was supported by the Project of NSFC (No.61327902, No.61035002 and No.61120106003), and Mohit was supported by NSF grant IIS 09-64429.

References

1. Agrawal, A., Chellappa, R., Raskar, R.: An algebraic approach to surface reconstruction from gradient fields. In: ICCV, vol. 1, pp. 174–181. IEEE (2005)
2. Agrawal, A., Raskar, R., Chellappa, R.: What is the range of surface reconstructions from a gradient field? In: Leonardis, A., Bischof, H., Pinz, A. (eds.) ECCV 2006, Part I. LNCS, vol. 3951, pp. 578–591. Springer, Heidelberg (2006)
3. Alterman, M., Schechner, Y., Perona, P., Shamir, J.: Detecting motion through dynamic refraction. PAMI 35(1), 245–251 (2013)
4. Alterman, M., Schechner, Y.Y., Swirski, Y.: Triangulation in random refractive distortions. In: ICCP, pp. 1–10. IEEE (2013)
5. Ben-Ezra, M., Nayar, S.K.: What does motion reveal about transparency? In: ICCV, pp. 1025–1032. IEEE (2003)
6. Brox, T., Bregler, C., Malik, J.: Large displacement optical flow. In: CVPR, pp. 41–48. IEEE (2009)
7. Brox, T., Bruhn, A., Papenberg, N., Weickert, J.: High accuracy optical flow estimation based on a theory for warping. In: Pajdla, T., Matas, J(G.) (eds.) ECCV 2004. LNCS, vol. 3024, pp. 25–36. Springer, Heidelberg (2004)
8. Chang, Y.-J., Chen, T.: Multi-view 3d reconstruction for scenes under the refractive plane with known vertical direction. In: ICCV, pp. 351–358. IEEE (2011)
9. Ding, Y., Li, F., Ji, Y., Yu, J.: Dynamic fluid surface acquisition using a camera array. In: ICCV, pp. 2478–2485. IEEE (2011)
10. Donate, A., Ribeiro, E.: Improved reconstruction of images distorted by water waves. In: Advances in Computer Graphics and Computer Vision, pp. 264–277. Springer, Heidelberg (2007)
11. Efros, A., Isler, V., Shi, J., Visontai, M.: Seeing through water. In: NIPS, vol. 17, pp. 393–400 (2005)
12. Favaro, P.: Recovering thin structures via nonlocal-means regularization with application to depth from defocus. In: CVPR, pp. 1133–1140. IEEE (2010)
13. Favaro, P., Soatto, S.: 3D shape reconstruction and image restoration: exploiting defocus and motion blur. Springer Verlag (2006)
14. Ferreira, R., Costeira, J.P., Santos, J.A.: Stereo reconstruction of a submerged scene. In: Marques, J.S., Pérez de la Blanca, N., Pina, P. (eds.) IbPRIA 2005. LNCS, vol. 3522, pp. 102–109. Springer, Heidelberg (2005)
15. Gupta, M., Narasimhan, S.G., Schechner, Y.Y.: On controlling light transport in poor visibility environments. In: CVPR, pp. 1–8. IEEE (2008)
16. Hirschmuller, H., Scharstein, D.: Evaluation of cost functions for stereo matching. In: CVPR, pp. 1–8. IEEE (2007)
17. Huynh, C.P., Robles-Kelly, A., Hancock, E.: Shape and refractive index recovery from single-view polarisation images. In: CVPR, pp. 1229–1236. IEEE (2010)
18. Ihrke, I., Goidluecke, B., Magnor, M.: Reconstructing the geometry of flowing water. In: ICCV, vol. 2, pp. 1055–1060. IEEE (2005)
19. Jähne, B., Klinke, J., Waas, S.: Imaging of short ocean wind waves: a critical theoretical review. JOSA A 11(8), 2197–2209 (1994)
20. Kidger, M.J.: Fundamental optical design, vol. 92. SPIE Press Bellingham, Washington, DC (2002)
21. Lin, X., Suo, J., Cao, X., Dai, Q.: Iterative feedback estimation of depth and radiance from defocused images. In: Lee, K.M., Matsushita, Y., Rehg, J.M., Hu, Z. (eds.) ACCV 2012, Part IV. LNCS, vol. 7727, pp. 95–109. Springer, Heidelberg (2013)

22. Morris, N.J., Kutulakos, K.N.: Dynamic refraction stereo. In: ICCV, vol. 2, pp. 1573–1580. IEEE (2005)
23. Morris, N.J., Kutulakos, K.N.: Reconstructing the surface of inhomogeneous transparent scenes by scatter-trace photography. In: ICCV, pp. 1–8. IEEE (2007)
24. Murase, H.: Surface shape reconstruction of an undulating transparent object. In: ICCV, pp. 313–317. IEEE (1990)
25. Narasimhan, S.G., Nayar, S.K., Sun, B., Koppal, S.J.: Structured light in scattering media. In: ICCV, vol. 1, pp. 420–427. IEEE ((2005)
26. Oreifej, O., Shu, G., Pace, T., Shah, M.: A two-stage reconstruction approach for seeing through water. In: CVPR, pp. 1153–1160. IEEE (2011)
27. Scharstein, D., Szeliski, R.: A taxonomy and evaluation of dense two-frame stereo correspondence algorithms. IJCV 47(1-3), 7–42 (2002)
28. Schechner, Y.Y., Karpel, N.: Recovery of underwater visibility and structure by polarization analysis. IEEE Journal of Oceanic Engineering 30(3), 570–587 (2005)
29. Schechner, Y.Y., Kiryati, N.: Depth from defocus vs. stereo: How different really are they? IJCV 39(2), 141–162 (2000)
30. Tian, Y., Narasimhan, S.G.: Seeing through water: Image restoration using model-based tracking. In: ICCV, pp. 2303–2310. IEEE (2009)
31. Tian, Y., Narasimhan, S.G.: A globally optimal data-driven approach for image distortion estimation. In: CVPR, pp. 1277–1284. IEEE (2010)
32. Treibitz, T., Schechner, Y., Kunz, C., Singh, H.: Flat refractive geometry. PAMI 34(1), 51–65 (2012)
33. Wen, Z., Lambert, A., Fraser, D., Li, H.: Bispectral analysis and recovery of images distorted by a moving water surface. Applied Optics 49(33), 6376–6384 (2010)
34. Wetzstein, G., Roodnick, D., Heidrich, W., Raskar, R.: Refractive shape from light field distortion. In: ICCV, pp. 1180–1186. IEEE (2011)
35. Yau, T., Gong, M., Yang, Y.-H.: Underwater camera calibration using wavelength triangulation. In: CVPR, pp. 2499–2506. IEEE (2013)
36. Ye, J., Ji, Y., Li, F., Yu, J.: Angular domain reconstruction of dynamic 3d fluid surfaces. In: CVPR, pp. 310–317. IEEE (2012)

Human Detection Using Learned Part Alphabet and Pose Dictionary

Cong Yao[1], Xiang Bai[1,*], Wenyu Liu[1], and Longin Jan Latecki[2]

[1] Department of Electronics and Information Engineering,
Huazhong University of Science and Technology
[2] Department of Computer and Information Sciences, Temple University
yaocong2010@gmail.com, {xbai,liuwy}@hust.edu.cn, latecki@temple.edu

Abstract. As structured data, human body and text are similar in many aspects. In this paper, we make use of the analogy between human body and text to build a compositional model for human detection in natural scenes. Basic concepts and mature techniques in text recognition are introduced into this model. A discriminative alphabet, each grapheme of which is a mid-level element representing a body part, is automatically learned from bounding box labels. Based on this alphabet, the flexible structure of human body is expressed by means of symbolic sequences, which correspond to various human poses and allow for robust, efficient matching. A pose dictionary is constructed from training examples, which is used to verify hypotheses at runtime. Experiments on standard benchmarks demonstrate that the proposed algorithm achieves state-of-the-art or competitive performance.

Keywords: Human detection, mid-level elements, part alphabet, pose dictionary, matching.

1 Introduction

Human detection in natural images has been an active research topic for decades and has attracted continuous attention from the computer vision community [21,32,1,5,34,41,10]. Though considerable progress has been made in recent years [8,13,20,23], detecting people in uncontrolled environments remains a challenging task. Human pose articulation, scale change, partial occlusion, low resolution, varied illumination, and complex background all constitute major challenges to human detection.

To tackle these challenges, a rich body of research has been devoted, among which part-based methods [1,11,22,20,4] have become increasingly popular in this field, due to their advantage in handling pose variation and partial occlusion. In this paper, we investigate the problem of human detection from a different perspective and propose a novel part-based human detection algorithm.

The algorithm is motivated by the key observation that human body and text are similar in many aspects. Notably: (1) They both consist of a set of basic

---

* Corresponding author.

D. Fleet et al. (Eds.): ECCV 2014, Part V, LNCS 8693, pp. 251–266, 2014.
© Springer International Publishing Switzerland 2014

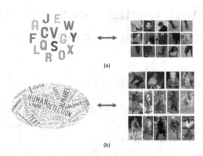

Fig. 1. Analogy between human body and text. (a) Letters *versus* parts. (b) Words *versus* poses.

primitives. For text, these basic primitives are letters in the alphabet, while for human body they are parts, such as head, shoulder, waist, and foot (Fig. 1 (a)). (2) They may exhibit significant variability. The type, number of primitives and their spatial relation are all very crucial as they jointly determine the expression of a particular object. The variation in the type and number of primitives and their spatial relation may lead to highly diverse expressions (different words in text and various poses in human body, as shown in Fig. 1 (b)). (3) They are both structured objects. The spatial relation of the primitives are not random, but instead with high degree of regularity. For example, in English text the letter 't' is very likely to be followed by 'h'. For human body, the position of head is tightly coupled with that of shoulders.

Since there are well established and widely used concepts and techniques in text recognition, we can make use of the analogy between human body and text and transfer some basic concepts and mature techniques in text recognition to the domain of human detection.

While an alphabet already exists for text, there is no visual alphabet for human in natural images. Therefore, an alphabet for human parts should be learned automatically from training data. In this paper, the discriminative clustering algorithm proposed by Singh et al. [36] is employed to learn the part alphabet.

Having learned the part alphabet, we are able to build a representation for human body. Similar to words in text, which are strings consisting of different types and numbers of letters, human poses can be represented in the form of sequences of parts. This representation converts the 3D structure of human body into 1D sequence. Though information loss is inevitable in this conversion, the ingredients of human body and their relationship are mostly preserved. Similar human poses have similar sequences while different human poses correspond to dissimilar sequences.

The benefit of representing human poses by sequences is that comparison and matching of human poses can be transformed into string matching [30], which has been proven to be both robust and efficient in text recognition. For human detection, hypothesis verification can be accomplished by matching the hypotheses with a set of reference poses. In this paper, the reference poses are given in the training data and are converted into a collection of symbolic sequences, which we call *pose dictionary*.

In summary, the contributions of this paper are three-fold: (1) We exploit automatically learned mid-level primitives to represent human parts; (2) We propose to express human poses using symbolic sequences; and (3) We employ string matching in text recognition to perform hypothesis verification for human detection.

To assess the performance of the proposed algorithm, we have conducted experiments on standard benchmarks. It is demonstrated that the proposed algorithm achieves state-of-the-art or competitive performance, compared to other competing methods.

The rest of the paper is organized as follows. Sec. 2 reviews related works in this field. We describe the details of the proposed method, including the procedure of learning part alphabet and pose dictionary as well as the pipeline of human detection, in Sec. 3. Sec. 4 summarizes the proposed algorithm and discusses its connections to existing methods. Sec. 5 presents experimental results. Conclusion remarks and future work are given in Sec. 6.

2   Related Work

As one of the most competitive domains in computer vision, human detection has attracted quite a lot of attention from the community [8,1,43,4,10,39]. Comprehensive surveys on this topic can be found in [17,15].

The analogy between text and visual data has inspired a number of researchers in the computer vision community. Basic ideas and models for processing text have been adapted to perform vision tasks. For example, Sivic et al. [37] proposed an approach to object matching in videos by recasting the problem as text retrieval; Fei-Fei et al. [19] adopted Bag-of-Words to represent images and perform scene categorization. In this paper, we learn an alphabet to represent human body parts and build a dictionary to characterize human poses. Furthermore, string matching [30], a technique widely used in text recognition and retrieval, is employed to verify hypotheses in human detection.

The work presented in this paper is also inspired by the discriminative clustering approaches proposed by Singh et al. [36] and Lee et al. [25]. In the algorithm of Singh et al., a set of representative patch clusters is automatically discovered from a large image set. The discovered patch clusters are mid-level representation for natural images, which can be used for a wide rang of tasks such as scene classification [36] and geographically-informed image retrieval [9]. We adopt this algorithm to learn part prototypes for human body.

In [31], Opelt et al. proposed to learn a visual alphabet of shape and appearance to represent and detect objects. Our approach is different from this algorithm in: (1) the type of local descriptors (HOG descriptors on patches *vs.* boundary fragments or SIFT descriptors on interest points); (2) the usage of alphabet graphemes (strong detectors *vs.* weak detectors); and (3) the manner of hypothesis verification (string matching *vs.* Adaboost classifier).

Fig. 2. Part alphabet generation. (a) Learned alphabet on the TUD-Pedestrians dataset [1]. Each row illustrates a cluster of part instances that constitute a grapheme in the alphabet. The images in the first column (orange rectangle) are the average of all the instances of that grapheme. The rest are top-ranked part instances. (b) Discovered part instances in original images. The learned part prototypes are tightly clustered in both appearance and configuration space. (c) Learned alphabet on the INRIA Person dataset [8].

Similar to our work, Andriluka et al. [1] and Bourdev et al. [5,4] learn part-based models to detect people in natural scenes. However, the part prototypes in their algorithms are obtained using detailed annotations of body parts, while in our model the part prototypes are inferred automatically without part annotations.

Wang et al. [42] presented a framework for discovering salient object parts, which was shown to be robust to object articulation. However, the framework used fixed number of parts and implicitly assumed common structure among different object instances, which can be violated in case of viewpoint change or occlusion. In contrast, in our model different object instances are represented in variable number of parts, and pose variation, viewpoint change and occlusion are treated as variants of symbolic sequences.

The proposed method shares the idea of predicting object centroid via Hough voting with [26] and [22], but the representation and detection pipeline are different from those of [26] and [22].

Most related to our work, the algorithm of Endres et al. [16] also learned mid-level elements to represent object parts. However, our work is different from [16] in that it learns the part detectors jointly while Endres et al. trained part detectors independently. Moreover, our part detectors are more efficient at runtime as the parts are described by HOGs with the same resolution and thus allow highly parallelized part detection.

3   Methodology

3.1   Part Alphabet Generation

Given a set of training images of humans $S = \{(I_i, B_i)\}_{i=1}^{n}$, where I_i is an image and B_i is a set of bounding boxes specifying the location and extent of the humans in the image I_i ($B_i = \emptyset$, if I_i is person-free), the goal of part alphabet generation is to learn a set of part prototypes Ω from S. The part prototypes should have two properties: (1) Representativeness. The prototypes should be able to capture the essential sub-structures of human body and be common across different human poses, at least for similar poses. (2) Discrimination. The prototypes should be distinctive from background and against each other, otherwise, there will be tremendous confusion and ambiguity when applying them to novel images, which will make the detection of human in natural images fail.

Since only bounding box annotations are available in S, these part prototypes should be automatically discovered. The discriminative clustering algorithm proposed by Singh et al. [36] meets the requirements well, as it can discover visual primitives that are both representative and discriminative from large image collections in an unsupervised manner. Inspired by [36] and [44], we adopt this algorithm to learn the part alphabet Ω from S.

Given a "discovery" image set $\mathcal{D}$ and a "natural world" image set $\mathcal{N}$, the algorithm of Singh et al. [36] is aimed to discover a set of representative patch clusters that are discriminative against other clusters in $\mathcal{D}$, as well as the rest visual world modelled by $\mathcal{N}$. The algorithm is an iterative procedure which alternates between two phases: clustering and training. Initially, examples (patches) are grouped into clusters in an unsupervised fashion and then a discriminative classifier is trained for each cluster using the patches in the cluster as positive examples and the rest as negative examples. In next iteration, these classifiers are used to find patches similar to those in the corresponding cluster in novel images, which is followed by a new round of training. The algorithm iterates until convergence.

The output of the algorithm is a set of top-ranked patch clusters K and a set of classifiers C. Each cluster K_j corresponds to a classifier C_j that can detect patches similar to those in K_j in novel images. These classifiers will serve as part detectors at runtime.

The algorithm of Singh et al. [36] was originally designed for discovering discriminative patches from generic natural images. To utilize it to discover part prototypes from training examples, we made the following customizations:

- The regions in the bounding boxes B constitute the discovery set $\mathcal{D}$ as we aim to discover discriminative parts for human and the rest regions of the training image set I are taken as the natural world set $\mathcal{N}$.
- At the initial clustering stage, each patch p_k from the discover set is represented by a location-augmented descriptor, which is the concatenation of the appearance descriptor and the normalized coordinates (x_{p_k}, y_{p_k}), following [29]. This makes the patches in each cluster more compact in configuration space.
- The scale of the patches (following [36], we also use square patches, i.e. the width w and height h are equal and $w = h = s$) sampled from the discovery set is adaptive to the scale of the bounding box bb. The scale of a specific patch is $s = r \cdot max(w(bb), h(bb))$, where $r \in (0, 1]$ is scale ratio which controls the relative scale of the patches.
- To make the learned parts distinctive from background cluster, we also randomly draw examples from the natural world set $\mathcal{N}$ at different scales.

- To make the trained classifiers more robust to scale change, the training set is enriched by rescaling the original images at multiple scales.
- The SVM classifier used in [36] was replaced by Random Forest [6] because Random Forest can achieve similarly high accuracy as SVM and directly gives probabilities, which are more intuitive and interpretable.
- The size of the patch descriptors (HOG [8]) is 3×3 (rather than 8×8) cells as they are sufficient for describing local body parts.

The learned part alphabet can be expressed as $\Omega = \{(K_j, C_j)\}_{j=1}^{\Gamma}$, where K and C are the discovered part prototypes and corresponding classifiers respectively, and Γ is the size of the alphabet. For each cluster K_j, the following information is stored: The set of all its members (patches) M_j, their offset vectors to object centroid V_j, and the average width $\bar{w}_j$ and height $\bar{h}_j$ of the parent rectangles, from which the members M_j originate. V_j, $\bar{w}_j$ and $\bar{h}_j{}^1$ will be used to estimate the location and extent of objects in the detection phase (see Sec. 3.3).

Fig. 2 depicts the alphabets (classifiers not shown) learned on the TUD-Pedestrians [1] and INRIA Person [8] dataset. The learned part prototypes are tightly clustered in both appearance and configuration space (Fig. 2 (b)), which are very much in common with poselets [5,4]. However, different from poselets, which are obtained using manually labeled part regions and keypoints, our part prototypes are automatically learned using human bounding boxes.

As shown in Fig. 2 (b), the learned part prototypes do not necessarily correspond to single semantic body part. For example, the part prototype in the bottom row fires on both left and right foot. However, this is reasonable as the patches are very similar in both appearance and configuration space. More importantly, the learned parts are sufficient for the task of human detection and work well in practice (see the experiments in Sec. 5).

3.2   Pose Dictionary Construction

Having learned an alphabet for representing human body parts, we are now able to construct a dictionary to describe human poses. The procedure of pose dictionary construction is illustrated in Fig. 3.

For each positive example in the training set, part detection is performed within the bounding box using the trained part detectors. In accordance with the alphabet generation stage, the scale of the detection windows is $s = r \cdot max(w(bb), h(bb))$. Non-maximum suppression is applied to the detection activations to eliminate redundancy. The scores of different part detectors are directly comparable as they are trained in a one-versus-all manner.

The detected parts are then sorted by the azimuth relative to the body center (yellow cross in Fig. 3). The azimuth angle of each part is measured clockwise from a north base line (red arrow in Fig. 3). A one-dimensional sequence is formed by successively recording the indices of the parts after sorting (orange

---

[1] We assume that V_j, $\bar{w}_j$ and $\bar{h}_j$ have been normalized with respect to the members M_j.

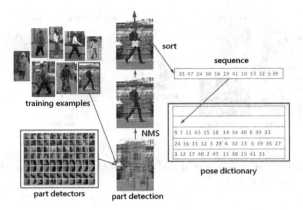

Fig. 3. Pose dictionary construction. Parts are detected by applying the trained part detectors to the positive training examples (different parts are marked in different colors). The detected parts are then sorted by the azimuth relative to the body center to convert a pose to a one-dimensional sequence. Due to variation or partial occlusion, different poses may correspond to sequences of variable lengths.

numbers in Fig. 3). The sequence is appended to the pose dictionary, which will be used in the detection phase to certificate human hypotheses. The production of the pose dictionary construction procedure is $\Phi = \{\phi_l\}_{l=1}^{\Pi}$, where each ϕ_l is a one-dimensional sequence that represents a pose in the training set and Π stands for the size of the dictionary.

To make the representation more robust, random jittering is applied to the starting point of the original sequence to generate multiple sequences for each training example.

The variability caused by pose variation and viewpoint change is implicitly encoded by the symbolic sequences. More importantly, in our model different poses are expressed in different number of parts (in contrast to fixed number of parts in [20]), which yields a more flexible representation for modelling articulated objects. More sophisticated approaches that are able to capture the 2D (or even 3D) nature of human body can be incorporated, however, the current strategy is already quite effective and efficient.

3.3 Detection Pipeline

Generally, the proposed detection pipeline works in a hypothesis generation and verification paradigm [40]. We follow up traditional object detection methods to search human instances in images in a multi-scale sliding-window manner and fuse activations of different locations and scales to form the final detections. In the detection phase, the images are fixed and windows of multiple scales are densely sampled and fed to the part detectors. In the following paragraphs, we present the processes of hypothesis generation and verification in an image at a single scale for simplicity.

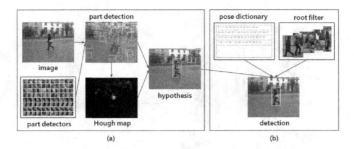

Fig. 4. Human detection at a single scale. (a) Hypothesis generation. (b) Hypothesis verification. See text for details.

Hypothesis Generation. Patches are densely sampled and described by HOG descriptors with 3×3 cells. Parts are detected using the learned detectors C. A Hough map is then generated by casting and accumulating the votes from the detected parts, similar to [26]. The vote of each part is the highest score the part receives from the detectors C. Centers of hypotheses are found by seeking maxima in the Hough map using Mean Shift [7].

For each hypothesis h, back-projection is performed to seek the parts (denoted as a set $Q(h)$) that have contributed to h. Non-maximum suppression is applied to $Q(h)$, to remove redundant parts, resulting in $Q'(h)$. A sequence $\psi(h)$ is formed using $Q'(h)$ in the same way as in the pose dictionary construction procedure.

The width and height of hypothesis h is estimated using the corresponding clusters the parts in $Q(h)$ belong to:

$$w(h) = \frac{\sum_l \rho(Q_l) \cdot w(Q_l) \cdot \bar{w}_{Q_l}}{\sum_l \rho(Q_l)}, \tag{1}$$

$$h(h) = \frac{\sum_l \rho(Q_l) \cdot h(Q_l) \cdot \bar{h}_{Q_l}}{\sum_l \rho(Q_l)}, \tag{2}$$

where $\rho(Q_l)$ is the detection score of Q_l, $w(Q_l)$ and $h(Q_l)$ stand for the width and height of Q_l, and $\bar{w}_{Q_l}$ and $\bar{h}_{Q_l}$ denote the average width and height of the cluster corresponding to Q_l, respectively.

The total vote of hypothesis h, $\alpha(h)$, is also calculated as follows: $\alpha(h) = \sum_l \rho(Q_l)$. We use total vote instead of mean vote as low level evidence, as hypotheses formed by spurious parts may have high mean vote, therefore using mean vote may lead to confusion.

Hypothesis Verification via Dictionary Search. Dictionary search [24,30] is a popular technique for error correction in text recognition. Basically, dictionary search tries to find the closest match(es) in the dictionary for a given string. The similarity between the input string and the matched entry (or entries) can be used to verify whether the input string is erroneous. We adopt this method to verify hypotheses, since they have been expressed in sequences.

The edit distance [27] is the most widely used technique in dictionary search, which can efficiently compute the distance (dissimilarity) of two strings (sequences). In the edit distance, three basic operations are allowable: insertion, deletion, and substitution. Interesting correspondence can be observed between these operations and part-based image matching: insertion corresponds to part missing, deletion corresponds to spurious part and substitution to incorrect part type. This correspondence makes the edit distance [27] particularly suitable for matching and verifying hypotheses for human detection, as it can tolerate errors in the bottom-up hypothesis generation stage.

Formally, given two sequences ψ and ϕ with edit distance $d(\psi, \phi)$, the normalized distance [28] is defined as:

$$\hat{d}(\psi, \phi) = \frac{2d(\psi, \phi)}{L(\psi) + L(\phi) + d(\psi, \phi)}, \tag{3}$$

where $L(\psi)$ and $L(\phi)$ denote the lengths of ψ and ϕ.

For a hypothesis h expressed in sequence $\psi(h)$, T closest entries $\{\phi_i\}_{i=1}^{T}$ in the dictionary Φ are searched. The score of hypothesis h via dictionary search, $\beta(h)$, is defined as the average similarity:

$$\beta(h) = \frac{1}{T} \sum_{i=1}^{T} (1 - \hat{d}(\psi(h), \phi_i)). \tag{4}$$

$\beta(h)$ measures the possibility of hypothesis h being a valid human pose.

Hypothesis Verification via Root Filter. Merely considering local parts may lose information from global structure of object, thus we also train a root filter [20] as compensation. The examples for training the root filter Υ are harvested by applying hypothesis generation to the training images and comparing the bounding boxes of the generated hypotheses and ground truth rectangles. A hypothesis is taken as positive example if it overlaps significantly with a ground truth rectangle (overlap ratio ≥ 0.5). The sub images within the bounding boxes are normalized and represented by HOG descriptors.

To deal with pose variation and viewpoint change, multiple components are introduced into the root filter, following [20]. The components are formed by clustering the training examples according to their aspect ratio. The optimal value of component number m depends on the variability of objects.

A Random Forest classifier [6] is trained for each component using the harvested examples. In the verification phase, for each hypothesis h the component with proximal aspect ratio is used to predict the probability of h being an object and this probability serves as the output of the root filter: $\gamma(h) = \Upsilon(h)$.

Metric Fusion. As described above, for each hypothesis h there are three metrics that measure the possibility of h representing a true object: $\alpha(h)$ stands for the local evidence from part detection; $\beta(h)$ characterizes the interactions among the parts of h; and $\gamma(h)$ induces global information. These metrics should be fused to give a unique score for h. However, since not all the three metrics are at the same scale ($\alpha(h)$ is the sum of multiple votes), simple linear combination will lead to poor result.

In this paper, we use the harmonic mean [33] for metric fusion, as it can handle metrics at different scales. The final score of hypothesis h is defined as:

$$\theta(h) = \frac{3}{\frac{1}{\alpha(h)} + \frac{1}{\beta(h)} + \frac{1}{\gamma(h)}} \tag{5}$$

4 Reflection

The proposed algorithm has many interesting connections to existing methods, which we briefly discuss below.

Deformable Part Model. In Deformable Part Model [20], a star-structured model with a root template and several part templates is designed to represent objects. In the detection procedure, the location of root template is first determined and the optimal placement of the part templates with respect to the root template are then searched. In our method, parts are detected and grouped together to form a global object hypothesis and deformation and articulation are verified by a set of reference poses. In this sense, our algorithm can be seen as a bottom-up deformable part model.

Grammar Model. The pioneer work of Zhu et al. [45] established a general grammar framework for images. Following this work, Girshick et al. proposed a Grammar Model [23], which defines formal grammar for people and utilizes a compositional hierarchy that provides choices between different part subtypes and allows for optional parts, to adapt to different poses and levels of visibility. In our model, variabilities caused by pose variation and occlusion, which the grammar in [23] aims to model, are implicitly reflected in the variance of the symbolic sequences.

Poselets. Poselets [5,4] are part primitives that are by construction tightly clustered in both appearance and configuration space, for representing and detecting people. At runtime, instances of poselets are found and combined to predict location and extent of humans. The proposed algorithm works in a similar way. But the key difference is that the primitives in the proposed algorithm are learned automatically without part annotations.

5 Experiments

We have evaluated the proposed algorithm on several standard benchmarks for human detection and compared it to other competing methods, including the leading algorithms in this field. We followed the evaluation criteria for each of the datasets used in previous works. All the experiments were conducted on a regular PC (2.8GHz 8-core CPU, 16G RAM and Windows 64-bit OS).

For all the Random Forest classifiers, 100 trees were used. $T = 5$ entries in the dictionary were sought in hypothesis verification. Detection windows were sampled at 10 scales to handle size variation of humans.

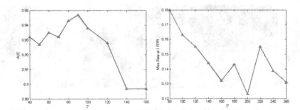

Fig. 5. Impact of alphabet size Γ on (*left*) TUD-Pedestrians and (*right*) INRIA Person

5.1   Datasets

TUD-Pedestrians. The TUD-Pedestrians dataset was proposed by Andriluka et al. in [1] and has become a widely used benchmark for assessing human detection algorithms. This database includes 250 test images of street scenes containing 311 side-view pedestrians with variability in pose, appearance and scale. As the backgrounds in the training set are with limited diversity, we also used the background images from the INRIA Person dataset [8], following [22].

INRIA Person. The INRIA Person dataset [8] is also a popular benchmark for pedestrian detection. This dataset is challenging because of pose articulation, scale change, partial occlusion, varying illumination and complex background clutter. There are 614 images with humans and 1218 person-free images for training. 741 images are used for testing. We evaluated the proposed algorithm on full images and reported per-image instead of per-window performance on this database, following [13,15].

As objects in different datasets exhibit different degrees of variability, the value of component number m varies for each dataset. In this paper, we set $m = 2, 3$ for TUD-Pedestrians and INRIA Person respectively.

5.2   Experimental Results

Scale ratio r is a crucial parameter as it determines the relative scale of the part prototypes in the alphabet. We investigated the impact of r on the TUD-Pedestrians dataset. As shown in Tab. 1, $r = 0.2$ leads to the best performance. Upon inspection, we found that too small parts only capture simple primitives like bars and corners and thus omit the characteristics of human body, while too large parts generalize poorly to novel images. Similar trend was also observed on the INRIA Person dataset, so r is fixed at 0.2 for all the following experiments.

We experimented with different alphabet sizes on the TUD-Pedestrians and INRIA Person dataset. As can be seen from Fig 5, the accuracy increases with

Table 1. Impact of scale ratio r (with $\Gamma = 80$)

r	0.1	0.2	0.3	0.4	0.5	0.6
AUC	0.608	0.943	0.596	0.133	0.043	0.009

Fig. 6. Detection examples on (*left*) TUD-Pedestrians and (*right*) INRIA Person. Note that the type and number of parts vary across different human instances, as we use more flexible representation and model to represent objects, which make our algorithm different from other part-based methods, such as [1,20].

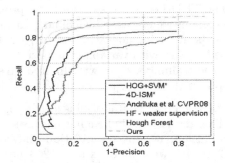

Fig. 7. Performance curves of different algorithms evaluated on the TUD-Pedestrians dataset [1]

alphabet size Γ upto a certain point and then falls. Excessive part prototypes may include redundancy and thus hurt the accuracy. The performance is not sensitive to alphabet size, as long as sufficient part prototypes are learned. Optimal result was obtained with $\Gamma = 90$ for TUD-Pedestrians and $\Gamma = 200$ for INRIA Person.

Fig. 6 depicts several detection examples of our method on the TUD-Pedestrians and INRIA Person dataset. The proposed algorithm is able to detect people of different poses and sizes under varying illumination and complex background.

Table 2. Performances of different methods evaluated on the TUD-Pedestrians dataset [1]

Algorithm	Recall at EER	Detection Rate
Ours	**0.920**	**0.965**
Hough Forest [22]	0.87	0.91
PartISM [1]	0.84	0.92
Feature Context [42]	0.73	0.84
4D-ISM [35]	0.69	0.81
HOG [8]	-	0.71

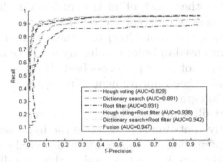

Fig. 8. Comparison of detection accuracy with different metrics and their combination

The quantitative results of different methods evaluated on the TUD-Pedestrians dataset are shown in Fig. 7 and Tab. 2. On this dataset, the proposed algorithm achieves AUC = 0.947 and recall-precision EER = 0.92, which outperforms all the competing algorithms by a large margin, including the state-of-the-art methods [1,22]. Note that in TUD-Pedestrians the test images are much more challenging than the images for training, as the variation in human pose and scale in the test images are more significant and the backgrounds are relatively more complex. This indicates that the proposed algorithm generalizes well to novel images, even though trained on simpler examples.

Without the extra negative images, our method still performs fairly well. The AUC is 0.84, on par with [1], which required detailed part annotations, and comparable to [22], which used those negative images.

Table 3. Performances of different methods evaluated on the INRIA Person dataset [1]

Algorithm	Miss Rate at 1 FPPI
Ours	0.12
Very Fast [3]	**0.07**
FPDW [12]	0.09
DPM-V2 [20]	0.09
Integral Channel Features [13]	0.14
HOG-LBP [43]	0.14
HOG [8]	0.23

The performances of the proposed algorithm and other competing methods on the INRIA Person dataset are depicted in Tab. 3. The proposed algorithm achieves miss rate of 0.12 at 1 false positive per image (FPPI), which is better than the traditional methods such as HOG [8], HOG-LBP [43] and Integral Channel Features [13], but still behind the best performers on this dataset [12,20,3]. The comparisons are fair, since those methods were also evaluated on full images.

We also investigated the effect of metric fusion on the TUD-Pedestrians dataset. The performances of different metrics (three types of cues from Hough voting, dictionary search and root filter) and their combinations are shown in Fig. 8. The three metrics used in isolation already lead to considerably good performance, among which root filter performs best. Hough voting and dictionary search indeed lead to further improvement. The optimal accuracy is achieved when all the cues are integrated.

On the surface, root filter provides bulk of the detection rate. However, part detection also implicitly contributes to it, since the hypotheses fed to root filter are a sparse set of bounding boxes estimated from detected parts; string matching further punishes invalid poses. Hence the considerable overall improvement is due to all 3 techniques.

On the TUD-Pedestrians dataset, the average processing time of the proposed algorithm is about 6 seconds[2], which is comparable to that of Hough Forest [22].

6   Conclusions and Future Work

We have presented a compositional model for human detection in natural scenes, which incorporates basic concepts (alphabet and dictionary) and mature techniques (edit distance and dictionary search) from text recognition. Specifically, a discriminative alphabet is learned to represent body parts. To characterize the flexible structure of human body, human poses are represented by one-dimensional sequences, which allow for robust and efficient matching. Experiments on standard benchmarks demonstrate that the proposed algorithm achieves state-of-the-art or competitive performance.

In this paper, we only demonstrated the strength of the proposed algorithm on the problem of human detection on moderate-sized datasets. Assessing the proposed algorithm on larger and more challenging datasets (such as the PASCAL VOC 2007 dataset [18] and Caltech Pedestrian Dataset [14]) is an ongoing work. The proposed model is actually quite general, thus it can be readily generalized to other object classes. We plan to build a universal model for multi-class object detection [31,20] in the future. Moreover, this work can be extended by learning part prototypes with different aspect ratios [38] and exploring the 2D/3D nature of object structure [2].

Acknowledgements. This work was primarily supported by National Natural Science Foundation of China (NSFC) (No. 61222308), and in part by NSFC (No. 61173120 and 60903096), Program for New Century Excellent Talents in University (No. NCET-12-0217) and Fundamental Research Funds for the Central Universities (No. HUST 2013TS115). This work was also supported by National Science Foundation under Grants OIA-1027897 and IIS-1302164. The authors would like to thank Xinggang Wang for the enlightening discussions and valuable suggestions.

---

[2] 6 threads are used to accelerate the process of part detection.

References

1. Andriluka, M., Roth, S., Schiele, B.: People-tracking-by-detection and people-detection-by-tracking. In: Proc. CVPR (2008)
2. Bai, X., Wang, X., Latecki, L.J., Liu, W.: Active skeleton for non-rigid object detection. In: Proc. ICCV (2009)
3. Benenson, R., Mathias, M., Timofte, R., Gool, L.V.: Pedestrian detection at 100 frames per second. In: Proc. CVPR (2012)
4. Bourdev, L., Maji, S., Brox, T., Malik, J.: Detecting people using mutually consistent poselet activations. In: Daniilidis, K., Maragos, P., Paragios, N. (eds.) ECCV 2010, Part VI. LNCS, vol. 6316, pp. 168–181. Springer, Heidelberg (2010)
5. Bourdev, L., Malik, J.: Poselets: Body part detectors trained using 3d human pose annotations. In: Proc. ICCV (2009)
6. Breiman, L.: Random forests. Machine Learning 45(1), 5–32 (2001)
7. Cheng, Y.: Mean shift, mode seeking, and clustering. IEEE Trans. PAMI 17(8), 790–799 (1995)
8. Dalal, N., Triggs, B.: Histograms of oriented gradients for human detection. In: Proc. CVPR (2005)
9. Doersch, C., Singh, S., Gupta, A., Sivic, J., Efros, A.A.: What makes paris look like paris? ACM Trans. Graphics 31(3), 101 (2012)
10. Dollár, P., Appel, R., Kienzle, W.: Crosstalk cascades for frame-rate pedestrian detection. In: Fitzgibbon, A., Lazebnik, S., Perona, P., Sato, Y., Schmid, C. (eds.) ECCV 2012, Part II. LNCS, vol. 7573, pp. 645–659. Springer, Heidelberg (2012)
11. Dollár, P., Babenko, B., Belongie, S., Perona, P., Tu, Z.: Multiple component learning for object detection. In: Forsyth, D., Torr, P., Zisserman, A. (eds.) ECCV 2008, Part II. LNCS, vol. 5303, pp. 211–224. Springer, Heidelberg (2008)
12. Dollar, P., Belongie, S., Perona, P.: The fastest pedestrian detector in the west. In: Proc. BMVC (2010)
13. Dollar, P., Tu, Z., Perona, P., Belongie, S.: Integral channel features. In: Proc. BMVC (2009)
14. Dollar, P., Wojek, C., Appel, R., Perona, P.: Pedestrian detection: A benchmark. In: Proc. CVPR (2009)
15. Dollar, P., Wojek, C., Schiele, B., Perona, P.: Pedestrian detection: An evaluation of the state of the art. IEEE Trans. PAMI 34(4), 743–761 (2012)
16. Endres, I., Shih, K.J., Jiaa, J., Hoiem, D.: Learning collections of part models for object recognition. In: Proc. CVPR (2013)
17. Enzweiler, M., Gavrila, D.M.: Monocular pedestrian detection: Survey and experiments. IEEE Trans. PAMI 31(12), 2179–2195 (2009)
18. Everingham, M., Gool, L.V., Williams, C.K.I., Winn, J., Zisserman, A.: The PASCAL Visual Object Classes (VOC) challenge. IJCV 88(2), 303–338 (2010)
19. Fei-Fei, L., Perona, P.: A bayesian heirarcical model for learning natural scene categories. In: Proc. CVPR (2005)
20. Felzenszwalb, P., Girshick, R., McAllester, D., Ramanan, D.: Object detection with discriminatively trained part-based models. IEEE Trans. PAMI 32(9), 1627–1645 (2010)
21. Forsyth, D., Fleck, M.: Body plans. In: Proc. CVPR (1997)
22. Gall, J., Lempitsky, V.: Class-specific hough forests for object detection. In: Proc. CVPR (2009)
23. Girshick, R., Felzenszwalb, P., McAllester, D.: Object detection with grammar models. In: Proc. NIPS (2011)

24. Kukich, K.: Techniques for automatically correcting words in text. ACM Computing Surveys 24(4), 377–439 (1992)
25. Lee, Y.J., Efros, A.A., Hebert, M.: Style-aware mid-level representation for discovering visual connections in space and time. In: Proc. ICCV (2013)
26. Leibe, B., Leonardis, A., Schiele, B.: Robust object detection with interleaved categorization and segmentation. IJCV 77(1-3), 259–289 (2008)
27. Levenshtein, V.I.: Binary codes capable of correcting deletions, insertions, and reversals. Soviet Physics Doklady 10(8), 707–710 (1996)
28. Li, Y., Liu, B.: A normalized levenshtein distance metric. IEEE Trans. PAMI 29(6), 1091–1095 (2007)
29. McCann, S., Lowe, D.G.: Spatially local coding for object recognition. In: Lee, K.M., Matsushita, Y., Rehg, J.M., Hu, Z. (eds.) ACCV 2012, Part I. LNCS, vol. 7724, pp. 204–217. Springer, Heidelberg (2013)
30. Navarro, G.: A guided tour to approximate string matching. ACM Computing Surveys 33(1), 31–88 (2001)
31. Opelt, A., Pinz, A., Zisserman, A.: Learning an alphabet of shape and appearance for multi-class object detection. IJCV 80(1), 16–44 (2008)
32. Papageorgiou, C., Poggio, T.: A trainable system for object detection. IJCV 38(1), 15–33 (2000)
33. Van Rijsbergen, C.: Information Retrieval, 2nd edn. Butterworths, London (1979)
34. Schwartz, W.R., Kembhavi, A., Harwood, D., Davis, L.S.: Human detection using partial least squares analysis. In: Proc. ICCV (2009)
35. Seemann, E., Schiele, B.: Cross-articulation learning for robust detection of pedestrians. In: Franke, K., Müller, K.-R., Nickolay, B., Schäfer, R. (eds.) DAGM 2006. LNCS, vol. 4174, pp. 242–252. Springer, Heidelberg (2006)
36. Singh, S., Gupta, A., Efros, A.A.: Unsupervised discovery of mid-level discriminative patches. In: Fitzgibbon, A., Lazebnik, S., Perona, P., Sato, Y., Schmid, C. (eds.) ECCV 2012, Part II. LNCS, vol. 7573, pp. 73–86. Springer, Heidelberg (2012)
37. Sivic, J., Zisserman, A.: Video google: A text retrieval approach to object matching in videos. In: Proc. ICCV (2003)
38. Song, X., Wu, T., Jia, Y., Zhu, S.C.: Discriminatively trained and-or tree models for object detection. In: Proc. CVPR (2013)
39. Tan, D., Li, Y., Kim, T.K.: Fast pedestrian detection by cascaded random forest with dominant orientation templates. In: Proc. BMVC (2012)
40. Tsai, S.S., Parameswarany, V., Berclazy, J., Vedanthamy, R., Grzeszczuky, R., Girod, B.: Design of a text detection system via hypothesis generation and verification. In: Proc. ACCV (2012)
41. Walk, S., Majer, N., Schindler, K., Schiele, B.: New features and insights for pedestrian detection. In: Proc. ICCV (2010)
42. Wang, X., Bai, X., Yang, X., Liu, W., Latecki, L.J.: Maximal cliques that satisfy hard constraints with application to deformable object model learning. In: Proc. NIPS (2011)
43. Wang, X., Han, T.X., Yan, S.: An HOG-LBP human detector with partial occlusion handling. In: Proc. ICCV (2009)
44. Yao, C., Bai, X., Shi, B., Liu, W.: Strokelets: A learned multi-scale representation for scene text recognition. In: Proc. CVPR (2014)
45. Zhu, S.C., Mumford, D.: A stochastic grammar of images. Foundations and Trends in Computer Graphics and Vision 2(4), 259–362 (1995)

SPADE: Scalar Product Accelerator by Integer Decomposition for Object Detection

Mitsuru Ambai and Ikuro Sato

Denso IT Laboratory, Inc.
{manbai,isato}@d-itlab.co.jp

Abstract. We propose a method for accelerating computation of an object detector based on a linear classifier when objects are expressed by binary feature vectors. Our key idea is to decompose a real-valued weight vector of the linear classifier into a weighted sum of a few ternary basis vectors so as to preserve the original classification scores. Our data-dependent decomposition algorithm can approximate the original classification scores by a small number of the ternary basis vectors with an allowable error. Instead of using the original real-valued weight vector, the approximated classification score can be obtained by evaluating the few inner products between the binary feature vector and the ternary basis vectors, which can be computed using extremely fast logical operations. We also show that each evaluation of the inner products can be cascaded for incorporating early termination. Our experiments revealed that the linear filtering used in a HOG-based object detector becomes 36.9× faster than the original implementation with 1.5% loss of accuracy for 0.1 false positives per image in pedestrian detection task.

Keywords: linear classifier, binary features, object detection.

1 Introduction

In spite of its simplicity, a linear classifier is widely acknowledged as a powerful tool for object detection. In many cases, both training and detection time of the linear classifier are greatly reduced compared to non-linear classifiers such as deep neural networks[11] and kernel methods[9,14]. Although the linear classifier simply defines a decision boundary by a hyper plane in a feature space, recent feature representations, e.g. Histograms of Oriented Gradients (HOG)[3], Fisher vector[16,15], explicit feature maps[21] and deformable part models[7], produce comparable classification performances to the non-linear object detectors.

However, even for the linear classifier, the detection time differs from real-time due to the fact that the detection task is done by sliding window approach, in which the linear classifier is exhaustively applied at all possible locations on an image. Coupled with the high-dimensionality of the recent feature representations, the computational cost of evaluating classification scores is enormous. This drawback becomes more serious when a part-based model is used[7] because such an object model must compute scores of multiple linear part filters. However,

D. Fleet et al. (Eds.): ECCV 2014, Part V, LNCS 8693, pp. 267–281, 2014.

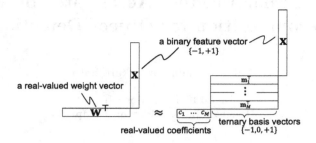

Fig. 1. A basic idea of our method. Classification score is approximated by weighted sum of inner products between binary feature vector and ternary basis vectors.

reducing the computational load is crucial issue for industrial applications, such as in-vehicle safety system.

Our aim with this study is to accelerate the score computation of the linear object detectors, such as HOG with SVM. Figure 1 illustrates the basic idea of our method. Our work was inspired by recent research on binary hashing[8,23] and binary descriptors[18,13,1], which represent a visual feature as a binary vector. In our framework, a feature vector is restricted to binary values -1 and +1. In this case, the classification score is formulated as an inner product between a real-valued weight vector (trained by a machine learning technique such as SVM) and the binary feature vector. Our key idea is to decompose the real-valued weight vector into a weighted sum of a few ternary basis vectors that only contain -1, 0, and +1. In this case, the classification score is approximated by the weighted sum of a few inner products between the ternary basis vectors and the binary feature vector. Instead of using time-consuming floating-point operations, each of the inner products can be computed extremely fast by simple logical operations such as XOR, AND, and bit counts. For this idea to work well, it is important to approximate the real-valued weight vector into a small number of ternary vectors with an allowable error. To address this issue, we introduce a data-dependent decomposition algorithm that minimizes the sum of squared errors between the original and approximated classification scores of training samples. In addition, cascading approach is introduced to reject a large number of object candidates without evaluating all the decomposed inner products.

1.1   Related Work

There have been extensive studies on accelerating linear object detectors. We review just a few representatives. Felzenszwalb et al.[6] introduced an idea of rejection cascade popularized by Viola and Johns[22] into deformable part models. Dubout et al.[5] processed the sliding-window filtering in a frequency domain. The filtering is accelerated by using a fast Fourier transform without any approximations. If a large number of multiple linear filters are needed, one solution is to approximate each of the given filters by a weighted sum of a smaller number of shared filters[20,19,17]. Song et al.[20,19] used this idea for multi-class object detection based on deformable part models. In their approach, a large number of part filters are decomposed into shared filters and are approximated by sparse linear combinations of them. Rigamonti *et al.*[17] proposed a method for finding shared filters under the condition in which each are separable. Since the responses of the separable filters can be computed by applying one-dimensional filters twice in the x- and y- directions, the total computation time can be drastically reduced. Lampert *et al.*[12] revealed that a branch-and-bound approach can directly find peaks of a filter response without exhaustive sliding-window search if a good quality bounding function is given. The closest idea to ours was proposed by Hare *et al.*[10] within the context of matching binary local descriptors. In their work, classifier weights are decomposed into a few binary basis vectors in a similar manner to ours. However, as shown later, our approach approximates the classifier weights with significantly smaller errors than the proposed by Hare *et al.*[10]. They also did not discuss the rejection cascade.

1.2 Contributions

We call our framework consisted of the following three components as Scalar Product Accelerator by integer DEcomposition (SPADE).

1. **Ternary representation:** The classification score is approximated using a small number of ternary basis vectors, as illustrated in Figure 1. We show that the inner product between the ternary basis vector and the binary feature vector can be computed extremely fast by a combination of three logical operations: XOR, AND, and bit counts.
2. **Data-dependent decomposition algorithm:** The ternary basis vectors and their coefficients are optimized to minimize the sum of squared errors between the original and approximated classifier scores of training samples. Although this minimization is a hard combinatorial optimization problem, we propose an efficient method for finding an approximated solution.
3. **Rejection cascade:** When M ternary basis vectors are given, we show that M-stage cascade can be built for early termination. With the introduction of the rejection cascade, we also propose a method for determining safe thresholds that do not decrease classification accuracy.

The rest of this paper is structured as follows. In Section 2, we introduce the three components of SPADE. In Section 3, we explain experimental results and give a discussion. We give concluding remarks in Section 4. Throughout this paper, AND, XOR, and bit count operations are denoted by $L_{and}(\mathbf{x}_1, \mathbf{x}_2)$, $L_{xor}(\mathbf{x}_1, \mathbf{x}_2)$ and $L_{pop}(\mathbf{x}_1)$, respectively, where $\mathbf{x}_1$ and $\mathbf{x}_2$ are binary vectors that contains only -1 or $+1$. The positive values are regarded as true bits, and the negative values are regarded as false bits.

2 Scalar Product Accelerator by Integer Decomposition

In this section, we introduce three key ideas of SPADE: ternary representation, data-dependent decomposition algorithm and rejection cascade. First we begin with formulating the linear classifier as follows.

$$f(\mathbf{x}) = \mathbf{w}^\top \mathbf{x} + b, \tag{1}$$

where $\mathbf{w} \in \mathbb{R}^D$ is a weight vector, $\mathbf{x} \in \{-1, +1\}^D$ is a binary feature vector extracted from an image, and $b \in \mathbb{R}$ is a bias term. Since the method for extracting a good binary feature is an application-specific issue, we skip this discussion until Section 3. In this section, we assume that the binary feature is properly designed for the object detection task.

Even though $\mathbf{x}$ is binary, Eq. (1) still requires $\mathcal{O}(D)$ floating-point operations. To reduce them, we introduce the following approximated classifier.

$$f_{\text{approx}}(\mathbf{x}) = \sum_{i=1}^{M} c_i \mathbf{m}_i^\top \mathbf{x} + b, \tag{2}$$

where $\mathbf{m}_i$ is an i-th integer basis vector, $c_i \in \mathbb{R}$ is its coefficient, and M is the number of the basis vectors used for this approximation. The difference between Eqs. (1) and (2) is that $\mathbf{w}$ is replaced with a linear combination of the integer vectors $\sum_{i=1}^{M} c_i \mathbf{m}_i$.

Hare $et\ al.$[10] investigated the case in which $\mathbf{m}_i \in \{-1, +1\}$. In this case, the inner product $\mathbf{m}_i^\top \mathbf{x}$ can be quickly computed using XOR followed by bit counts as follows[1]:

$$\mathbf{m}_i^\top \mathbf{x} = D - 2 \cdot L_{\text{pop}}(L_{\text{xor}}(\mathbf{m}_i, \mathbf{x})). \tag{3}$$

In this way, the order of floating-point operations to obtain $f_{\text{approx}}(\mathbf{x})$ is reduced from $\mathcal{O}(D)$ to $\mathcal{O}(M)$. For this method to work well, M must be small enough. Hare $et\ al.$[10] reported that only two binary basis vectors are sufficient for classifying binary local descriptors in the context of keypoint tracking. However, for accelerating a linear object detector, such as a HOG with an SVM, we found that much larger number of basis vectors is necessary to preserve the original classification accuracy. In the following three subsections, we introduce three key ideas of SPADE that greatly improve this drawback.

2.1 Ternary Representation

Even if M is set to a small value, good approximation can be obtained by permitting various values to be taken in $\mathbf{m}_i$. However, fast computation of $\mathbf{m}_i^\top \mathbf{x}$ may become more difficult. There is a trade-off between computation time and approximation quality depending on constraints on $\mathbf{m}_i$.

From the viewpoint of this trade-off, a good balanced approach is to use a ternary vector $\mathbf{m}_i = (m_{i1}, \cdots, m_{iD})^\top \in \{-1, 0, +1\}^D$. Even in this case, logical operations are available to compute $\mathbf{m}_i^\top \mathbf{x}$ similar to Eq. (3). By introducing $N_{\text{plus}}(\mathbf{m}_i, \mathbf{x})$ and $N_{\text{minus}}(\mathbf{m}_i, \mathbf{x})$, $\mathbf{m}_i^\top \mathbf{x}$ can be rewritten as follows.

$$\mathbf{m}_i^\top \mathbf{x} = N_{\text{plus}}(\mathbf{m}_i, \mathbf{x}) - N_{\text{minus}}(\mathbf{m}_i, \mathbf{x}), \tag{4}$$

---

[1] In the original work [10], this inner product is computed using AND operation instead of XOR. However, there are no essential difference between them.

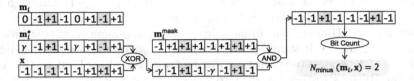

Fig. 2. N_{minus} is obtained by XOR, AND, and bit count operations by introducing two binary vectors $\mathbf{m}_i^*$ and $\mathbf{m}_i^{\mathrm{mask}}$ derived from $\mathbf{m}_i$. Locations that satisfy $m_{ij}x_j = -1$ are indicated by yellow boxes.

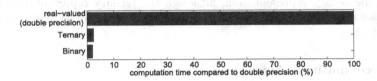

Fig. 3. Comparison of computation times of $\mathbf{m}_i^\top \mathbf{x}$. Three cases of $\mathbf{m}_i$: binary, ternary and real-valued, are shown in this figure. A dimension D is set to 4896 in this test.

where $N_{\mathrm{plus}}(\mathbf{m}_i, \mathbf{x})$ and $N_{\mathrm{minus}}(\mathbf{m}_i, \mathbf{x})$ are numbers of elements that satisfy $m_{ij}x_j = +1$ and $m_{ij}x_j = -1$, respectively. A formal definition of $N_{\mathrm{minus}}(\mathbf{m}_i, \mathbf{x})$ is

$$N_{\mathrm{minus}}(\mathbf{m}_i, \mathbf{x}) = \sum_{j=1}^{D} I(m_{ij}, x_j), \quad I(m_{ij}, x_j) = \begin{cases} 1 \text{ if } m_{ij}x_j = -1 \\ 0 \quad \text{otherwise} \end{cases}, \quad (5)$$

where $I(m_{ij}, x_j)$ is an indicator function. If $N_{\mathrm{minus}}(\mathbf{m}_i, \mathbf{x})$ are given, $N_{\mathrm{plus}}(\mathbf{m}_i, \mathbf{x})$ can be easily obtained as follows.

$$N_{\mathrm{plus}}(\mathbf{m}_i, \mathbf{x}) = D - z_i - N_{\mathrm{minus}}(\mathbf{m}_i, \mathbf{x}), \quad (6)$$

where z_i is a number of zero values in $\mathbf{m}_i$ and is pre-computable because $\mathbf{m}_i$ is determined at the training phase and is fixed when detecting objects. By substituting Eq. (6) into Eq. (4), we obtain

$$\mathbf{m}_i^\top \mathbf{x} = D - z_i - 2 \cdot N_{\mathrm{minus}}(\mathbf{m}_i, \mathbf{x}). \quad (7)$$

In practice, $N_{\mathrm{minus}}(\mathbf{m}_i, \mathbf{x})$ can be quickly computed by logical operations without the element-wise summation shown in Eq. (5). This is illustrated in Figure 2. Instead of directly using $\mathbf{m}_i$, we prepared two binary vectors $\mathbf{m}_i^{\mathrm{mask}} = (m_{i1}^{\mathrm{mask}}, \cdots, m_{iD}^{\mathrm{mask}})^\top$ and $\mathbf{m}_i^* = (m_{i1}^*, \cdots, m_{iD}^*)^\top$, which are defined as follows.

$$m_{ij}^{\mathrm{mask}} = \begin{cases} -1 \text{ if } m_{ij} = 0 \\ +1 \quad \text{otherwise} \end{cases}, \quad m_{ij}^* = \begin{cases} \gamma \quad \text{if } m_{ij} = 0 \\ m_{ij} \quad \text{otherwise} \end{cases}, \quad (8)$$

where γ is an arbitrary value that takes -1 or $+1$, $\mathbf{m}_i^{\mathrm{mask}}$ and $\mathbf{m}_i^*$ are binary vectors, and $N_{\mathrm{minus}}(\mathbf{m}_i, \mathbf{x})$ is given by the following equation.

$$N_{\mathrm{minus}}(\mathbf{m}_i, \mathbf{x}) = L_{\mathrm{pop}}(L_{\mathrm{and}}(L_{\mathrm{xor}}(\mathbf{m}_i^*, \mathbf{x}), \mathbf{m}_i^{\mathrm{mask}})). \quad (9)$$

The first XOR operation finds positions that satisfy $m_{ij}x_j = -1$. Although this operation may also find positions that satisfy $m_{ij}x_j = 0$, they are filtered out by the following AND operation. Finally, by counting the number of true bits, we obtain $N_{\mathrm{minus}}(\mathbf{m}_i, \mathbf{x})$. It should be noted that $N_{\mathrm{minus}}(\mathbf{m}_i, \mathbf{x})$ does not depend on the choice of γ because the corresponding locations are filtered out by the AND operation. By substituting Eq. (9) into Eq. (7), $\mathbf{m}_i^\top \mathbf{x}$ is obtained very fast.

Computation times of $\mathbf{m}_i^\top \mathbf{x}$ are compared in Figure 3. Three types of constraints: binary, ternary, and real-valued (no constraints), are imposed on $\mathbf{m}_i$. A *popcnt* instruction of Intel Core i7 processor was used for computing $L_{\mathrm{pop}}(\cdot)$. Interestingly, the computation time of the ternary representation was comparable to the binary representation, although the ternary representation potentially has a capability to reduce the approximation error better than the binary representation.

2.2   Decomposition Algorithms

In this subsection, we explain two different algorithms for decomposing $\mathbf{w}$ into $\mathbf{m}_i$ and c_i. One is a *data-dependent* algorithm and the other is a *data-independent* algorithm. These two algorithms minimize different cost function. The former uses training datasets, but the latter does not. First, we introduce each cost function and discuss their advantages and disadvantages. Next, two optimization algorithms that minimize them are proposed. Finally, a connection between our study and a related study[10] is discussed.

To preserve a decision boundary, it is natural to minimize the sum of the squared differences between the original and approximated classifier scores. This requires training datasets $\mathbf{X} = (\mathbf{x}_1, \cdots, \mathbf{x}_N) \in \{-1, +1\}^{D \times N}$, where $\mathbf{X}$ contains positive and negative samples used to train $\mathbf{w}$ and b. The cost function is defined as follows.

$$E_1 = \sum_{k=1}^{N}(f(\mathbf{x}_k) - f_{\mathrm{approx}}(\mathbf{x}_k))^2 = ||\mathbf{w}^\top \mathbf{X} - (\sum_{i=1}^{M} c_i \mathbf{m}_i)^\top \mathbf{X}||_2^2. \qquad (10)$$

We call this optimization *data-dependent* decomposition. While this decomposition well preserves the decision boundary, the above optimization is difficult to solve. An alternative solution is to minimize an L_2 norm of a residual vector between $\mathbf{w}$ and $\sum_{i=1}^{M} c_i \mathbf{m}_i$. The cost function is defined as follows.

$$E_2 = ||\mathbf{w} - \sum_{i=1}^{M} c_i \mathbf{m}_i||_2^2. \qquad (11)$$

We call this optimization *data-independent* decomposition because the training dataset $\mathbf{X}$ does not appear in this cost function. This optimization is relatively easier than the case of the data-dependent decomposition.

It should be noted that data-independent decomposition can be regarded as a special case of data-dependent decomposition. The two cost functions can be rewritten as follows.

Algorithm 1. *Data-independent decomposition* that minimizes E_2

---
function *data_independent_decomposition*$(\mathbf{w}, M)$
$\mathbf{r} = \mathbf{w}$
for $i = 1$ to M **do**
   initialize $\mathbf{m}_i$ by random three integer values $\{-1, 0, +1\}$
   repeat
      $c_i = \mathbf{m}_i^\top \mathbf{r} / \mathbf{m}_i^\top \mathbf{m}_i$
      $m_{ij} = \underset{\alpha \in \{-1,0,+1\}}{\arg\min} \ (r_j - c_i\alpha)^2 , \quad$ for $j = 1, \cdots, D$
   until c_i and $\mathbf{m}_i$ have not been updated.
   $\mathbf{r} \leftarrow \mathbf{r} - c_i\mathbf{m}_i$
end for
return $\{\mathbf{m}_i\}_{i=1}^M, \{c_i\}_{i=1}^M$

$$E_1 = (\mathbf{w} - \tilde{\mathbf{w}})^\top \mathbf{A}(\mathbf{w} - \tilde{\mathbf{w}}) \tag{12}$$

$$E_2 = (\mathbf{w} - \tilde{\mathbf{w}})^\top (\mathbf{w} - \tilde{\mathbf{w}}), \tag{13}$$

where $\tilde{\mathbf{w}} = \sum_{i=1}^M c_i\mathbf{m}_i$ and $\mathbf{A} = \mathbf{X}\mathbf{X}^\top$. If $\mathbf{A}$ is proportional to an identity matrix, E_1 becomes equivalent to E_2. Even when $\mathbf{A}$ does not satisfy this assumption, E_1 tends to decrease by minimizing E_2 in practice. Based on this observation, we propose a two-step algorithm, in which minimization of E_1 is started from a good initial solution obtained by minimizing E_2.

Data-independent decomposition is shown in Algorithm 1. Our strategy is to sequentially reduce the residual error in Eq. (11). At the i-th iteration, c_i and $\mathbf{m}_i$ are determined to minimize $||\mathbf{r} - c_i\mathbf{m}_i||_2^2$, where $\mathbf{r} = (r_1, \cdots, r_D)^\top$ is a residual vector initialized by $\mathbf{w}$ before the first iteration. This optimization is done using an alternative approach. When $\mathbf{m}_i$ is fixed, c_i is updated using a least square method. When c_i is fixed, the j-th element m_{ij} in $\mathbf{m}_i$ is separately updated by testing only three candidates $\{-1, 0, +1\}$. After the convergence, the residual vector $\mathbf{r}$ is updated by subtracting $c_i\mathbf{m}_i$ before going to the next $(i + 1)$-th iteration.

Data-dependent decomposition shown in Algorithm 2 uses Algorithm 1 to produce a good initial solution. At the i-th iteration, c_i and $\mathbf{m}_i$ are determined to minimize the following cost value.

$$\epsilon_i = ||(\mathbf{r} - c_i\mathbf{m}_i)^\top \mathbf{X}||_2^2 = (\mathbf{r} - c_i\mathbf{m}_i)^\top \mathbf{A}(\mathbf{r} - c_i\mathbf{m}_i). \tag{14}$$

If $\mathbf{m}_i$ is fixed, c_i is updated using a least square method as well as Algorithm 1.

$$c_i = \mathbf{m}_i^\top \mathbf{A}\mathbf{r} / \mathbf{m}_i^\top \mathbf{A}\mathbf{m}_i. \tag{15}$$

Even when c_i is fixed, optimizing $\mathbf{m}_i$ is still difficult due to the fact that the j-th element m_{ij} cannot be separately optimized to minimize ϵ_i unlike in the case of data-independent decomposition. To address this issue, our algorithm permits replacing only n_c randomly-chosen elements at the same time. In this

---

Algorithm 2. *Data-dependent decomposition* that minimizes E_1

---

  function *data_dependent_decomposition*$(\mathbf{w}, M, \mathcal{T}_{\min}, \rho)$
  $\mathbf{r} = \mathbf{w}$
  for $i = 1$ to M **do**
    initialize c_i and $\mathbf{m}_i$ by calling *data_independent_decomposition*$(\mathbf{r}, 1)$
    $N_{\text{iter}} = 0$; $N_{\text{update}} = 0$
    loop
      $N_{\text{iter}} \leftarrow N_{\text{iter}} + 1$
      if $(N_{\text{iter}} > \mathcal{T}_{\min})$ and $(N_{\text{update}}/N_{\text{iter}} < \rho)$ **then**
        break loop
      end if
      create Ω by randomly choosing n_c indices from $\{1, \cdots, D\}$
      $\mathbf{m}_{i,\Omega} = \underset{\boldsymbol{\alpha} \in \{-1,0,+1\}^{n_c}}{\arg \min} \epsilon_i(\boldsymbol{\alpha})$ $\{see\ Eq.(17)\}$
      if cost value ϵ_i is not improved, **then**
        continue loop
      end if
      $N_{\text{update}} \leftarrow N_{\text{update}} + 1$
      $c_i = \mathbf{m}_i^\top \mathbf{A} \mathbf{r} / \mathbf{m}_i^\top \mathbf{A} \mathbf{m}_i$
    end loop
    $\mathbf{r} \leftarrow \mathbf{r} - c_i \mathbf{m}_i$
  end for
  return $\{\mathbf{m}_i\}_{i=1}^M$, $\{c_i\}_{i=1}^M$

---

case, only 3^{n_c} candidates are necessary to be tested to update $\mathbf{m}_i$. Although such greedy-like optimization is seemingly difficult to sufficiently minimize the cost function, our algorithm gives good results because this optimization starts from the good initial solution produced by Algorithm 1.

When c_i is fixed, $\mathbf{m}_i$ is updated as follows. Let us define a set Ω containing indices of n_c randomly-chosen elements. Its complement is $\bar{\Omega} = \{1, \cdots, D\} \setminus \Omega$. The cost value ϵ_i can be rewritten as follows.

$$
\begin{aligned}
\epsilon_i = {}& (\mathbf{r}_\Omega - c_i \mathbf{m}_{i,\Omega})^\top \mathbf{A}_{\Omega\Omega} (\mathbf{r}_\Omega - c_i \mathbf{m}_{i,\Omega}) + \\
& (\mathbf{r}_{\bar{\Omega}} - c_i \mathbf{m}_{i,\bar{\Omega}})^\top \mathbf{A}_{\bar{\Omega}\bar{\Omega}} (\mathbf{r}_{\bar{\Omega}} - c_i \mathbf{m}_{i,\bar{\Omega}}) + \\
& 2(\mathbf{r}_\Omega - c_i \mathbf{m}_{i,\Omega})^\top \mathbf{A}_{\Omega\bar{\Omega}} (\mathbf{r}_{\bar{\Omega}} - c_i \mathbf{m}_{i,\bar{\Omega}}),
\end{aligned} \tag{16}
$$

where $\mathbf{m}_{i,\Omega}, \mathbf{m}_{i,\bar{\Omega}}, \mathbf{r}_\Omega$, and $\mathbf{r}_{\bar{\Omega}}$ are sub-vectors of $\mathbf{m}_i$ and $\mathbf{r}$ and $\mathbf{A}_{\Omega\Omega}$, $\mathbf{A}_{\bar{\Omega}\bar{\Omega}}$, and $\mathbf{A}_{\Omega\bar{\Omega}}$ are sub-matrices of $\mathbf{A}$. These sub-vectors and sub-matrices contain certain rows and columns indicated by their subscripts Ω and $\bar{\Omega}$. In the case of a matrix, the first subscript means row indices and the second subscript means column indices, e.g. $\mathbf{A}_{\Omega\bar{\Omega}}$ is an n_c-by-$(D - n_c)$ matrix. In Algorithm 2, not only c_i but also $\mathbf{m}_{i,\bar{\Omega}}$ are fixed. In this case, the cost value ϵ_i is simplified as follows.

$$
\begin{aligned}
\epsilon_i(\mathbf{m}_{i,\Omega}) = {}& c_i^2 \mathbf{m}_{i,\Omega}^\top \mathbf{A}_{\Omega\Omega} \mathbf{m}_{i,\Omega} \\
& + 2c_i \mathbf{m}_{i,\Omega}^\top (c_i \mathbf{A}_{\Omega\bar{\Omega}} \mathbf{m}_{i,\bar{\Omega}} - \mathbf{A}_{\Omega\Omega} \mathbf{r}_\Omega - \mathbf{A}_{\Omega\bar{\Omega}} \mathbf{r}_{\bar{\Omega}}) + \text{constant}. \tag{17}
\end{aligned}
$$

Algorithm 3. Fast classification by rejection cascade

---

    function *classify* $(\mathbf{x}, b, \mathbf{m}_1 \cdots, \mathbf{m}_M, R_1, \cdots, R_M, M)$

    $y = b;\ f = positive$

    for $i = 1$ to M **do**

        $y \leftarrow y + c_i \mathbf{m}_i^\top \mathbf{x}$

        if $y < R_i$ **then**

            $f = negative$; exit for loop

        end if

    end for

    return f

This sub-problem can be easily solved by testing only 3^{n_c} candidates $\{-1, 0, +1\}^{n_c}$ because $\mathbf{m}_{i,\Omega}$ is an n_c-dimensional ternary vector. Depending on the choice of Ω, the initial value of $\mathbf{m}_{i,\Omega}$ is already optimal for $\epsilon_i(\mathbf{m}_{i,\Omega})$. Therefore, we repeat the random choice and the sub-problem optimization until the cost value is improved. If the cost value is not improved for a long time, we go to the next $(i + 1)$-th iteration. This is controlled by two pre-defined thresholds $\mathcal{T}_{\min}$ and ρ. In practice, the parameters $\{n_c, \mathcal{T}_{\min}, \rho\}$ are set to $\{4, 100, 0.1\}$, respectively.

Obviously, with a slight modification, both Algorithms 1 and 2 are also available when $\mathbf{m}_i$ is constrained to binary values. In this case, Algorithm 1 produces the same results as a previous work[10]. From this perspective, the Algorithms 1 and 2 can be regarded as a generalization of their work.

2.3 Rejection Cascade

Since Algorithms 1 and 2 sequentially compute $\mathbf{m}_i$ by reducing the residual error one by one, $\mathbf{m}_i$ with the smaller index i more contributes to $\mathbf{w}$ in a similar way to a principal component analysis. In other words, the original decision boundary is almost reconstructed by the first basis vector $\mathbf{m}_1$ and its coefficient c_1. The rest of basis vectors $\mathbf{m}_2, \cdots, \mathbf{m}_M$ and coefficients $c_2, \cdots, c_M$ acts as correction terms for further fine reconstruction. This characteristic is very convenient to construct rejection cascade. In most cases, we can estimate the sign of the approximated classification score $f_{\text{approx}}(\mathbf{x})$ by using only the first several inner products $\mathbf{m}_i^\top \mathbf{x}$.

Algorithm 3 shows our strategy of the early termination. Our rejection cascade has M stages. A cumulative score y is initialized by the bias term b at the beginning. At i-th stage, $c_i \mathbf{m}_i^\top \mathbf{x}$ is added to y. The score y is thresholded by R_i to examine whether $\mathbf{x}$ belongs to a negative class or not.

The thresholds $R_1, \cdots, R_M$ must not cause a loss of accuracy. We discuss how the j-th threshold R_j should be determined. At the j-th stage, j weighted inner products $c_1 \mathbf{m}_1^\top \mathbf{x}, \cdots, c_j \mathbf{m}_j^\top \mathbf{x}$ have already been given. The rest of the weighted inner products are not given at this time. We split them as follows.

$$f_{\text{approx}}(\mathbf{x}) = \sum_{i=1}^{j} c_i \mathbf{m}_i^\top \mathbf{x} + b + \sum_{i=j+1}^{M} c_i \mathbf{m}_i^\top \mathbf{x}. \tag{18}$$

While the first and second terms of Eq. (18) are given at the j-th stage, the third term is not given yet. The problem is how we estimate whether $f(\mathbf{x})$ is negative without knowing the third term.

To address this issue, we consider replacing the unknown third term with a possible maximum value α_i defined as follows:

$$\alpha_i = \max_{\mathbf{x} \in \{\mathbf{x}_1, \cdots, \mathbf{x}_N\}} (c_i \mathbf{m}_i^\top \mathbf{x}), \tag{19}$$

where $\mathbf{x}_1, \cdots, \mathbf{x}_N$ are training samples. By replacing $c_i \mathbf{m}_i^\top \mathbf{x}$ in the third term of Eq. (18) with α_i, we obtain the upper bound of $f_{\mathrm{approx}}(\mathbf{x})$ as follows.

$$f_{\mathrm{approx}}(\mathbf{x}) \leq \sum_{i=1}^{j} c_i \mathbf{m}_i^\top \mathbf{x} + b + \sum_{i=j+1}^{M} \alpha_i. \tag{20}$$

If the upper bound is less than zero, $f_{\mathrm{approx}}(\mathbf{x})$ also takes a negative value. In this case, the feature vector $\mathbf{x}$ can be regarded as a negative sample. Therefore, the j-th threshold R_j can be determined as follows.

$$\sum_{i=1}^{j} c_i \mathbf{m}_i^\top \mathbf{x} + b + \sum_{i=j+1}^{M} \alpha_i < 0 \tag{21}$$

$$\sum_{i=1}^{j} c_i \mathbf{m}_i^\top \mathbf{x} + b < - \sum_{i=j+1}^{M} \alpha_i = R_j. \tag{22}$$

In addition, obviously $R_M = 0$.

3 Experiments and Discussion

We evaluated SPADE by taking pedestrian detection task as an example. We used INRIA pedestrian dataset[3] and a software supplied by [4] to evaluate miss rate against false positives per image (FPPI).

To avoid confusion, four different decompositions are abbreviated as follows.

- Data-Independent, binary basis vectors (DI2, DI2M1, $\cdots$,DI2M5)
- Data-Independent, ternary basis vectors (DI3, DI3M1, $\cdots$,DI3M5)
- Data-Dependent, binary basis vectors (DD2, DD2M1, $\cdots$,DD2M5)
- Data-Dependent, ternary basis vectors (DD3, DD3M1, $\cdots$,DD3M5)

The first 'DI' or 'DD' specifies the decomposition algorithm. The following digit, '2' or '3', defines the constraint on basis vectors. Optionally, the number of basis vectors M may be added to the end of the abbreviation. For example, 'DD3M5' uses data-dependent decomposition algorithm, ternary basis vectors and $M = 5$. It should be noted that DI2 is completely equivalent to the previous work[10], when the rejection cascade is not used.

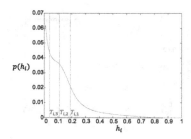

Fig. 4. probability distribution of h_i

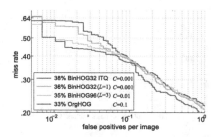

Fig. 5. Performance comparison

3.1 Implementation Details: Pedestrian Detector Using Binary HOG

While real-valued HOG feature is frequently used in object detection task[3,7,6], SPADE requires binary features. We show an interesting observation that the HOG can be converted to binary features by simple multi-level thresholding with little loss of detection accuracy. In our implementation[2], eight contrast-insensitive gradient orientations are used to form a 32-dimensional HOG feature $\mathbf{h} = (h_1, \cdots, h_{32})^\top$ per block. L-level thresholding is applied to h_i as follows.

$$h_{i,l} = \begin{cases} +1 & h_i \geq T_{i,l} \\ -1 & h_i < T_{i,l} \end{cases}. \tag{23}$$

The thresholds $T_{i,1}, \cdots, T_{i,L}$ for h_i are determined as follows. Each element h_i extracted from training samples are sorted in descending order, where $T_{i,l}$ is chosen to make the top $100l/(L+1)\%$ values take $+1$ and the rest take -1 in the sorted list. For example, when $L = 3$, three thresholds are chosen from values at the top 25, 50, and 75% positions in the sorted list. Figure 4 shows an example of a probability density distribution of h_i and the chosen three thresholds $T_{i,1}$, $T_{i,2}$, and $T_{i,3}$. In this way, a $32L$-dimensional binary feature per block is obtained.

Figure 5 compares the miss rates of the real-valued and the binarized HOG. Two parameters, $L = 1$ and 3, are tested. In addition, iterative quantization (ITQ) [8] is also tested to generate a 32-bit binary feature from $\mathbf{h}$. At the beginning of the captions, log-average miss rate[4] is denoted. The pedestrian models are trained using a linear SVM with appropriate soft margin parameters C, which are shown at the end of the captions. Interestingly, the binarized HOG produced comparable results to the real-valued HOG when L was set to 3. Even when $L = 1$, the log-average miss rate dropped only 3%. It should be also noted that our 32-bit HOG exhibited almost the same accuracy as that of ITQ. Since extracting binary features must also be fast, we used the simple multi-level thresholding instead of using the conventional binary hashing. In the following subsections, we use three abbreviations: 'BinHOG32', 'BinHOG96', and 'OrgHOG' that correspond to 32-bit($L = 1$), 96-bit($L = 3$) and 32-dimensional real-valued HOG, respectively. Unless otherwise specified, the BinHOG32 and rejection cascade were used in the following experiments.

---

[2] Unless otherwise stated, we followed the same parameters described in [3].

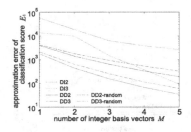
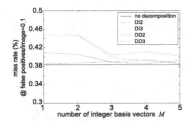

Fig. 6. Comparison of decompositions   **Fig. 7.** Miss rate v.s. M

3.2 Comparing Approximation Qualities of Classification Scores

Figure 6 shows total approximation errors of classification scores E_1 defined in Eq.(10) versus M. The y-axis is represented in a logarithmic scale. In addition to the above mentioned four methods: DI2, DI3, DD2, and DD3, the data-dependent decomposition algorithm initialized by random values (instead of using the optimized initial solution generated by the Algorithm 1) is also tested. This is denoted by 'DD2-random' and 'DD3-random'.

Although the approximation errors E_1 were decreased by increasing M in all cases, the approximation qualities were quite different for each case. The cases of the ternary representation: DI3, DD3, and DD3-random, produced better results than the cases of the binary representation: DI2, DD2, and DD2-random. The binary representation required the larger number of basis vectors M than the ternary representation. Interestingly, DI2 and DI3 decreased E_1 in spite of the fact that they do not directly minimize E_1 but E_2. This fact suggests that DI2 and DI3 can produce a good initial solution. In fact, DD2-random and DD3-random produced poor results compared to DD2 and DD3. The best approximation quality was obtained by using DD3.

3.3 Classification Accuracy and M

Figure 7 shows miss rates at 10^{-1} false positives per image versus M. We also tested a baseline method that does not decompose the weight vector $\mathbf{w}$ into integer basis vectors. This baseline detector runs very slow, but its classification scores do not include any errors. This is denoted by 'no decomposition' in this figure. In this experiment, consistent results with section 3.2 were observed. In all the four cases, the miss rates were approached to the same level of the baseline detector by increasing M. However convergence speed were obviously different among them. Even when M was set to a small value, DD3 achieved almost the same miss rate as the baseline detector.

Figure 8 shows performance curves obtained by testing different M, different binary features and different decomposition algorithms. The results of BinHOG32 and BinHOG96 are separately shown in (a) and (b). In addition to the four methods: DI2, DI3, DD2, and DD3, the baseline detector (without decomposing $\mathbf{w}$) is also tested as well as Figure 7. By increasing M, the results of all the

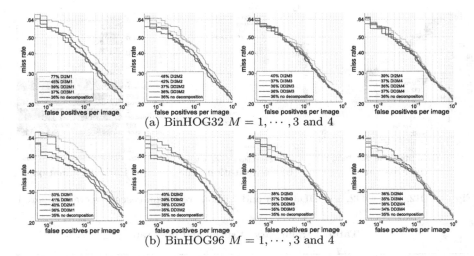

(a) BinHOG32 $M = 1, \cdots, 3$ and 4

(b) BinHOG96 $M = 1, \cdots, 3$ and 4

Fig. 8. In these figures, two kinds of binary features (BinHOG32 and BinHOG96), five approximation models(DI2, DI3, DD2, DD3, and no decomposition) and different $M = 1, \cdots, 4$ were tested to draw performance curves.

four methods (DI2, DI3, DD2, and DD3) approached to the performance curve of the baseline detector (without decomposition). The same trend was observed for BinHOG32 and BinHOG96. In both cases, DD3 reached at almost the same level of the baseline detector even when $M = 1$.

In summary, a conclusion resulting from Figure 6, 7, and 8 is that we should minimize the data-dependent cost function E_1 rather than the data-independent cost function E_2 addressed in the previous work[10]. Introducing the ternary decomposition helps to sufficiently minimize E_1, which brings significant performance gain over the (previously proposed) binary decomposition.

3.4   Effect of Rejection Cascade and Computation Time

Figure 9 summarizes the effect of our rejection cascade. The cases in which early termination is not used are indicated by 'w/o cascade'. Figure 9(a) compares miss rates. Figure 9(b) shows computation time ratios compared to the case in which **w** is not decomposed. Figure 9(c) shows frequency of early termination. x-axis means an average number of evaluated inner products in the rejection cascade. If the early termination works well, this value approaches to one. Throughout this experiment, a *popcnt* instruction of Intel Core i7 processor was used. It was observed from Figure 9(a) that the rejection cascade did not cause loss of classification accuracy. The detection results with and without the rejection cascade were completely consistent. Figure 9(b)(c) revealed that the rejection cascade obviously improved the runtime computation even when M was set to a large value. As shown in Figure 9(c), DD3 could reject the largest number of

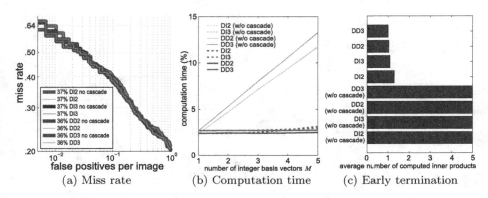

Fig. 9. DI2, DI3, DD2, and DD3 with and without rejection cascade were compared

Table 1. Summary of speed and miss rate

method	acceleration	miss rate@FPPI=0.025	miss rate@FPPI=0.1
OrgHOG (baseline)	1×	0.436	0.370
BinHOG32 DD3M5	36.9×	0.503	0.385
BinHOG96 DD3M5	12.9×	0.494	0.385
BinHOG32 DI2M5 w/o cascade (Hare et.al.[10])	8.6×	0.504	0.402

candidates than DI2, DI3 and DD2. These results suggest that the first ternary basis vector $\mathbf{m}_1$ obtained by DD3 sufficiently preserved the decision boundary.

Finally, we compared our method with the previous work proposed by Hare et.al.[10] as shown in Table 1. As pointed out in Section 2.2, Hare's study is regarded as 'DI2 w/o cascade'. Our method outperformed both computation time and accuracy compared to the previous work.

4   Conclusion

In this paper, we proposed SPADE that accelerated runtime computation of the linear classifier by introducing three ideas: ternary representation, data-dependent decomposition and rejection cascade. Since state-of-the-art object detection[2] is beginning to focus on the Hare's study[10] to boost the detection task, it is widely expected that SPADE is able to improve such detection methods based on binary features. Finally, we discuss possible extensions for future works. While we focused on a single class case throughout this paper, we believe that it is potentially feasible to extend our method to a multi-class recognition. In this case, ternary basis vectors should be shared within multiple real-valued weight vectors in a similar spirit of related works[20,19,17], because visual features are often shared among different classes. From the other perspective, it is also expected that SPADE is widely available not only for computer vision but also for the other field of researches based on linear classifiers and binary features.

References

1. Ambai, M., Yoshida, Y.: CARD: Compact and real-time descriptors. In: ICCV, pp. 97–104 (2011)
2. Cheng, M.-M., Zhang, Z., Lin, W.-Y., Torr, P.: BING: Binarized normed gradients for objectness estimation at 300fps. In: CVPR (2014)
3. Dalal, N., Triggs, B.: Histograms of oriented gradients for human detection. In: CVPR, pp. 886–893 (2005)
4. Dollár, P., Wojek, C., Schiele, B., Perona, P.: Pedestrian detection: An evaluation of the state of the art. In: PAMI, pp. 743–761 (2012)
5. Dubout, C., Fleuret, F.: Exact acceleration of linear object detectors. In: Fitzgibbon, A., Lazebnik, S., Perona, P., Sato, Y., Schmid, C. (eds.) ECCV 2012, Part III. LNCS, vol. 7574, pp. 301–311. Springer, Heidelberg (2012)
6. Felzenszwalb, P.F., Girshick, R.B., McAllester, D.: Cascade object detection with deformable part models. In: CVPR, pp. 2241–2248 (2010)
7. Felzenszwalb, P.F., Girshick, R.B., McAllester, D., Ramanan, D.: Object detection with discriminatively trained part based models. In: PAMI, pp. 1627–1645 (2010)
8. Gong, S.Y., Lazebnik: Iterative quantization: A procrustean approach to learning binary codes. In: CVPR, pp. 817–824 (2011)
9. Grauman, K., Darrell, T.: The pyramid match kernel: Discriminative classification with sets of image features. In: ICCV, pp. 1458–1465 (2005)
10. Hare, S., Saffari, A., Torr, P.H.S.: Efficient online structured output learning for keypoint-based object tracking. In: CVPR, pp. 1894–1901 (2012)
11. Krizhevsky, A., Sutskever, I., Hinton, G.E.: ImageNet classification with deep convolutional neural networks. In: NIPS, pp. 1106–1114 (2012)
12. Lampert, C.H., Blaschko, M.B., Hofmann, T.: Beyond sliding windows: Object localization by efficient subwindow search. In: CVPR, pp. 1–8 (2008)
13. Leutenegger, S., Chli, M., Siegwart, R.Y.: BRISK: Binary robust invariant scalable keypoints. In: ICCV, pp. 2548–2555 (2011)
14. Maji, S., Berg, A.C., Malik, J.: Classification using intersection kernel support vector machines is efficient. In: CVPR, pp. 1–8 (2008)
15. F., Perronnin, Y.L., Sanchez, J., Poirier, H.: Large-scale image retrieval with compressed fisher vectors. In: CVPR, pp. 3384–3391 (2010)
16. Perronnin, F., Sánchez, J., Mensink, T.: Improving the fisher kernel for large-scale image classification. In: Daniilidis, K., Maragos, P., Paragios, N. (eds.) ECCV 2010, Part IV. LNCS, vol. 6314, pp. 143–156. Springer, Heidelberg (2010)
17. Rigamonti, R., Sironi, A., Lepetit, V., Fua, P.: Learning separable filters. In: CVPR, pp. 2754–2761 (2013)
18. Rublee, E., Rabaud, V., Konolige, K., Bradski, G.: ORB: An efficient alternative to SIFT or SURF. In: ICCV, pp. 2564–2571 (2011)
19. Song, H.O., Girshick, R., Darrell, T.: Discriminatively activated sparselets. In: ECCV, pp. 196–204 (2013)
20. Song, H.O., Zickler, S., Althoff, T., Girshick, R., Fritz, M., Geyer, C., Felzenszwalb, P., Darrell, T.: Sparselet models for efficient multiclass object detection. In: Fitzgibbon, A., Lazebnik, S., Perona, P., Sato, Y., Schmid, C. (eds.) ECCV 2012, Part II. LNCS, vol. 7573, pp. 802–815. Springer, Heidelberg (2012)
21. Vedaldi, A., Zisserman, A.: Efficient additive kernels via explicit feature maps. In: PAMI, pp. 480–492 (2012)
22. Viola, P., Jones, M.: Rapid object detection using a boosted cascade of simple features. In: CVPR, pp. 511–518 (2001)
23. Weiss, Y., Torralba, A., Fergus, R.: Spectral hashing. In: NIPS, pp. 1753–1760 (2008)

Detecting Snap Points in Egocentric Video with a Web Photo Prior

Bo Xiong and Kristen Grauman

University of Texas at Austin, USA

Abstract. Wearable cameras capture a first-person view of the world, and offer a hands-free way to record daily experiences or special events. Yet, not every frame is worthy of being captured and stored. We propose to automatically predict *"snap points"* in unedited egocentric video— that is, those frames that look like they could have been intentionally taken photos. We develop a generative model for snap points that relies on a Web photo prior together with domain-adapted features. Critically, our approach avoids strong assumptions about the particular *content* of snap points, focusing instead on their *composition*. Using 17 hours of egocentric video from both human and mobile robot camera wearers, we show that the approach accurately isolates those frames that human judges would believe to be intentionally snapped photos. In addition, we demonstrate the utility of snap point detection for improving object detection and keyframe selection in egocentric video.

1 Introduction

Photo overload is already well-known to most computer users. With cameras on mobile devices, it is all too easy to snap images and videos spontaneously, yet it remains much less easy to organize or search through that content later. This is already the case when the user actively decides which images are worth taking. *What happens when that user's camera is always on, worn at eye-level, and has the potential to capture everything he sees throughout the day?* With increasingly portable wearable computing platforms (like Google Glass, Looxcie, etc.), the photo overload problem is only intensifying.

Of course, not everything observed in an egocentric video stream is worthy of being captured and stored. Even though the camera follows the wearer's activity and approximate gaze, relatively few moments actually result in snapshots the user would have intentionally decided to take, were he actively manipulating the camera. Many frames will be blurry, contain poorly composed shots, and/or simply have uninteresting content. This prompts the key question we study in this work: can a vision system predict **"snap points" in unedited egocentric video—that is, those frames that look like intentionally taken photos?**

To get some intuition for the task, consider the images in Figure 1. Can you guess which row of photos was sampled from a wearable camera, and which was sampled from photos posted on Flickr? Note that subject matter itself is not always the telling cue; in fact, there is some overlap in content between the

D. Fleet et al. (Eds.): ECCV 2014, Part V, LNCS 8693, pp. 282–298, 2014.

Fig. 1. Can you tell which row of photos came from an egocentric camera?

top and the bottom rows. Nonetheless, we suspect it is easy for the reader to detect that a head-mounted camera grabbed the shots in the first row, whereas a human photographer purposefully composed the shots in the second row. These distinctions suggest that it may be possible to learn the generic properties of an image that indicate it is well-composed, independent of the literal content.

While this anecdotal sample suggests detecting snap points may be feasible, there are several challenges. First, egocentric video contains a wide variety of scene types, activities, and actors. This is certainly true for human camera wearers going about daily life activities, and it will be increasingly true for mobile robots that freely explore novel environments. Accordingly, a snap point detector needs to be largely domain invariant and generalize across varied subject matter. Secondly, an optimal snap point is likely to differ in subtle ways from its less-good temporal neighbors, i.e., two frames may be similar in content but distinct in terms of snap point quality. That means that cues beyond the standard texture/color favorites may be necessary. Finally, and most importantly, while it would be convenient to think of the problem in discriminative terms (e.g., training a snap point vs. non-snap point classifier), it is burdensome to obtain adequate and unbiased labeled data. Namely, we'd need people to manually mark frames that appear intentional, and to do so at a scale to accommodate arbitrary environments.

We introduce an approach to detect snap points from egocentric video that requires no human annotations. The main idea is to construct a generative model of what human-taken photos look like by sampling images posted on the Web. Snapshots that people upload to share publicly online may vary vastly in their content, yet all share the key facet that they were intentional snap point moments. This makes them an ideal source of positive exemplars for our target learning problem. Furthermore, with such a Web photo prior, we sidestep the issue of gathering negatively-labeled instances to train a discriminative model, which could be susceptible to bias and difficult to scale. In addition to this prior, our approach incorporates domain adaptation to account for the distribution mismatch between Web photos and egocentric video frames. Finally, we designate features suited to capturing the framing effects in snap points.

We propose two applications of snap point prediction. For the first, we show how snap points can improve object detection reliability for egocentric cameras. It is striking how today's best object detectors fail when applied to arbitrary

Fig. 2. Understandably, while proficient for human-taken photos (left), today's best object detectors break down when applied to egocentric video data (right). Each image displays the person detections by the DPM [8] object detector.

egocentric data (see Figure 2). Unsurprisingly, their accuracy drops because detectors trained with human-taken photos (e.g., the Flickr images gathered for the PASCAL VOC benchmark) do not generalize well to the arbitrary views seen by an ego-camera. We show how snap point prediction can improve the precision of an off-the-shelf detector, essentially by predicting those frames where the detector is most trustworthy. For the second application, we use snap points to select keyframes for egocentric video summaries.

We apply our method to 17.5 hours of videos from both human-worn and robot-worn egocentric cameras. We demonstrate the absolute accuracy of snap point prediction compared to a number of viable baselines and existing metrics. Furthermore, we show its potential for object detection and keyframe selection applications. The results are a promising step towards filtering the imminent deluge of wearable camera video streams.

2   Related Work

We next summarize how our idea relates to existing work in analyzing egocentric video, predicting high-level image properties, and using Web image priors.

Egocentric Video Analysis: Egocentric video analysis, pioneered in the 90's [31,38], is experiencing a surge of research activity thanks to today's portable devices. The primary focus is on object [33,25] or activity recognition [37,5,21,32,7,34,25]. No prior work explores snap point detection.

We consider object detection and keyframe selection as applications of snap points for unconstrained wearable camera data. In contrast, prior work for detection in egocentric video focuses on controlled environments (e.g., a kitchen) and handheld objects (e.g., the mixing bowl) [33,25,37,5,7]. Nearly all prior keyframe selection work assumes third-person static cameras (e.g., [27,28]), where all frames are already intentionally composed, and the goal is to determine which are representative for the entire video. In contrast, snap points aim to discover intentional-looking frames, not maximize diversity or representativeness. Some video summarization work tackles dynamic egocentric video [23,30]. Such methods could exploit snap points as a filter to limit the frames they consider for summaries. Our main contribution is to detect human-taken photos, not a novel summarization algorithm.

We are not aware of any prior work using purely visual input to automatically trigger a wearable camera, as we propose. Methods in ubiquitous computing use manual intervention [31] or external non-visual sensors [13,14] (e.g., skin conductivity or audio) to trigger the camera. Our image-based approach is complementary; true snap points are likely a superset of those moments where abrupt physiological or audio changes occur.

Predicting High-Level Image Properties: A series of interesting work predicts properties from images like saliency [29], professional photo quality [18], memorability [16], aesthetics, interestingness [3,11], or suitability as a candid portrait [9]. These methods train a discriminative model using various image descriptors, then apply it to label human-taken photos. In contrast, we develop a generative approach with (unlabeled) Web photos, and apply it to *find* human-taken photos. Critically, a snap point need not be beautiful, memorable, etc., and it could even contain mundane content. Snap points are thus a broader class of photos. This is exactly what makes them relevant for the proposed object detection application; in contrast, an excellent aesthetics detector (for example) would fire on a narrower set of photos, eliminating non-aesthetic photos that could nonetheless be amenable to off-the-shelf object detectors.

Web Image Priors: The Web is a compelling resource for data-driven vision methods. Both the volume of images as well as the accompanying noisy metadata open up many possibilities. Most relevant to our work are methods that exploit the biases of human photographers. This includes work on discovering iconic images of landmarks [36,24,41] (e.g., the Statue of Liberty) or other tourist favorites [12,17,1,20] by exploiting the fact that people tend to take similar photos of popular sites. Similarly, the photos users upload when trying to sell a particular object (e.g., a used car) reveal that object's canonical viewpoints, which can help select keyframes to summarize short videos of the same object [19]. Our method also learns about human framing or composition biases, but, critically, in a manner that transcends the specific content of the scene. That is, rather than learn when a popular landmark or object is in view, we want to know when a well-composed photo of *any* scene is in view. Our Web photo prior represents the photos humans intentionally take, independent of subject matter.

Our approach uses a non-parametric representation of snap points, as captured by a large collection of Web photos. At a high level, this relates to work in vision exploiting big data and neighbor-based learning. This includes person detection [40], scene parsing with dense correspondences [26], geographic localization [12], action recognition [4] and pose estimation [35]. Beyond the fact our task is unique and novel, all these methods assume labels on the training data, whereas our method relies on the distribution of photos themselves.

3   Approach

Our goal is to detect snap points, which are those frames within a continuous egocentric video that appear as if they were composed with intention, as opposed

Fig. 3. Example images from the SUN dataset [42]

to merely observed by the person wearing the camera. In traditional camera-user relationships, this "trigger" is left entirely to the human user. In the wearable camera-user relationship, however, the beauty of being hands-free and always-on should be that the user no longer has to interrupt the flow of his activity to snap a photo. Notably, whether a moment in time is photoworthy is only partially driven by the subject matter in view. The way the photo is composed is similarly important, as is well-understood by professional photographers and intuitively known by everyday camera users.

We take a non-parametric, data-driven approach to learn what snap points look like. First, we gather unlabeled Web photos to build the prior (Sec. 3.1), and extract image descriptors that capture cues for composition and intention (Sec. 3.2). Then, we estimate a domain-invariant feature space connecting the Web and ego sources (Sec. 3.3). Finally, given a novel egocentric video frame, we predict how well it agrees with the prior in the adapted feature space (Sec. 3.4). To illustrate the utility of snap points, we also explore applications for object detection and keyframe selection (Sec. 3.5).

Section 4 will discuss how we systematically gather ground truth labels for snap points using human judgments, which is necessary to evaluate our method, but, critically, is *not* used to train it.

3.1   Building the Web Photo Prior

Faced with the task of predicting whether a video frame is a snap point or not, an appealing solution might be to train a discriminative classifier using manually labeled exemplars. Such an approach has proven successful for learning other high-level image properties, like aesthetics and interestingness [3,11], quality [18], canonical views [19], or memorability [16]. This is thanks in part to the availability of relevant meta-data for such problems: users on community photo albums manually score images for visual appeal [3,18], and users uploading ads online manually tag the object of interest [19].

However, this familiar paradigm is problematic for snap points. Photos that appear human-taken exhibit vast variations in appearance, since they may have almost arbitrary content. This suggests that large scale annotations would be necessary to cover the space. Furthermore, snap points must be isolated within

Fig. 4. Illustration of line alignment features on a short sequence of egocentric video frames. Each frame shows a bar in bottom right indicating how much its line alignment descriptor agrees with the Web prior. Here, the center frame in this mini-sequence would rate highest as a snap point (if using line alignment alone); note how it corresponds to the moment when the camera wearer looks straight at the scene.

ongoing egocentric video. This means that labeling *negatives* is tedious—each frame must be viewed and judged in order to obtain clean labels.

Instead, we devise an approach that leverages *unlabeled* images to learn snap points. The idea is to build a prior distribution using a large-scale repository of Web photos uploaded by human photographers. Such photos are by definition human-taken, span a variety of contexts, and (by virtue of being chosen for upload) have an enhanced element of *intention*. We use these photos as a generative model of snap points.

We select the SUN Database as our Web photo source [42], which originates from Internet search for hundreds of scene category names. Our choice is motivated by two main factors. First, the diversity of photos is high—899 categories in all drawn from 70K WordNet terms—and there are many of them ($130K$). Second, its scope is fairly well-matched with wearable camera data. Human- or robot-worn cameras observe a variety of daily life scenes and activities, as well as interactions with other people. SUN covers not just locations, but settings that satisfy "I am in a *place*, let's go to a *place*" [42], which includes many scene-specific interactions, such as shopping at a pawnshop, visiting an optician, driving in a car, etc. See Figure 3.

3.2 Image Descriptors for Intentional Cues

To represent each image, we designate descriptors to capture intentional composition effects.

Motion: Non-snap points will often occur when a camera wearer is moving quickly, or turning his head abruptly. We therefore extract a descriptor to summarize *motion blur*, using the blurriness estimate of [2].[1]

Composition: Snap points also reflect intentional framing effects by the human photographer. This leads to spatial regularity in the main line structures in the image—e.g., the horizon in an outdoor photo, buildings in a city scene, the table surface in a restaurant—which will tend to align with the image axes. Thus, we extract a *line alignment* feature: we detect line segments using the method

---

[1] We also explored flow-based motion features, but found their information to be subsumed by blur features computable from individual frames.

in [22], then record a histogram of their orientations with 32 uniformly spaced bins. To capture framing via the 3D structure layout, we employ the geometric class probability map [15]. We also extract GIST, HOG, self-similarity (SSIM), and dense SIFT, all of which capture alignment of interior textures, beyond the strong line segments. An accelerometer, when available, could also help gauge coarse alignment; however, these descriptors offer a fine-grained visual measure helpful for subtle snap point distinctions. See Figure 4.

Feature Combination: For all features but line alignment, we use code and default parameters provided by [42]. We reduce the dimensionality of each feature using PCA to compactly capture 90% of its total variance. We then standardize each dimension to ($\mu = 0, \sigma = 1$) and concatenate the reduced descriptors to form a single vector feature space X, which we use in what follows.

3.3   Adapting from the Web to the Egocentric Domain

While we expect egocentric video snap points to agree with the Web photo prior along many of these factors, there is also an inherent mismatch between the statistics of the two domains. Egocentric video is typically captured at low-resolution with modest quality lenses, while online photos (e.g., on Flickr) are often uploaded at high resolution from high quality cameras.

Therefore, we establish a domain-invariant feature space connecting the two sources. Given unlabeled Web photos and egocentric frames, we first compute a subspace for each using PCA. Then, we recover a series of intermediate subspaces that gradually transition from the "source" Web subspace to the "target" egocentric subspace. We use the algorithm of [10] since it requires no labeled target data and is kernel-based.

Let $\boldsymbol{x}_i$, $\boldsymbol{x}_j \in X$ denote image descriptors for a Web image i and egocentric frame j. The idea is to compute the projections of an input $\boldsymbol{x}_i$ on a subspace $\phi(t)$, for all $t \in [0, 1]$ along the geodesic path connecting the source and target subspaces in a Grassmann manifold. Values of t closer to 0 correspond to subspaces closer to the Web photo prior; values of t closer to 1 correspond to those more similar to egocentric video frames. The infinite set of projections is achieved implicitly via the geodesic flow kernel [10] (GFK):

$$K_{GFK}(\boldsymbol{x}_i, \boldsymbol{x}_j) = \langle \boldsymbol{z}_i^\infty, \boldsymbol{z}_j^\infty \rangle = \int_0^1 (\phi(t)^T \boldsymbol{x}_i)^T (\phi(t)^T \boldsymbol{x}_j) dt, \tag{1}$$

where $\boldsymbol{z}_i^\infty$ and $\boldsymbol{z}_j^\infty$ denote the infinite-dimensional features concatenating all projections of $\boldsymbol{x}_i$ and $\boldsymbol{x}_j$ along the geodesic path.

Intuitively, this representation lets the two slightly mismatched domains (Web and ego) "meet in the middle" in a common feature space, letting us measure similarity between both kinds of data without being overly influenced by their superficial resolution/sensor differences.

3.4   Predicting Snap Points

With the Web prior, image features, and similarity measure in hand, we can now estimate how well a novel egocentric video frame agrees with our prior. We take a simple data-driven approach. We treat the pool of Web photos as a non-parametric distribution, then estimate the likelihood of the novel ego frame under that distribution based on its nearest neighbors' distances.

Let $W = \{x_1^w, \ldots, x_N^w\}$ denote the N Web photo descriptors, and let x^e denote a novel egocentric video frame's descriptor. We retrieve the k nearest examples $\{x_{n_1}^w, \ldots, x_{n_k}^w\} \subset W$, i.e., those k photos that have the highest GFK kernel values when compared to x^e.[2] Then we predict the snap point confidence for x^e:

$$S(x^e) = \sum_{j=1}^{k} K_{GFK}(x^e, x_{n_j}^w), \tag{2}$$

where higher values of $S(x^e)$ indicate the test frame is more likely to be human-taken. For our dataset of $N = 130K$ images, similarity search is fairly speedy (0.01 seconds per test case in Matlab), and could easily be scaled for much larger N using hashing or kd-tree techniques.

This model follows in the spirit of prior data-driven methods for alternative tasks, e.g., [35,40,12,26], the premise being to keep the learning simple and let the data speak for itself. However, our approach is label-free, as all training examples are (implicitly) positives, whereas the past methods assume at least weak meta-data annotations.

While simple, our strategy is very effective in practice. In fact, we explored a number of more complex alternatives—one-class SVMs, Gaussian mixture models, non-linear manifold embeddings—but found them to be similar or inferior to the neighbor-based approach. The relatively lightweight computation is a virtue given our eventual goal to make snap point decisions onboard a wearable device.

3.5   Leveraging Snap Points for Egocentric Video Analysis

Filtering egocentric video down to a small number of probable snap points has many potential applications. We are especially interested in how they can bolster object detection and keyframe selection. We next devise strategies for each task that leverage the above predictions $S(x^e)$.

Object Detection: In the object recognition literature, it is already disheartening how poorly detectors trained on one dataset tend to generalize to another [39]. Unfortunately, things are only worse if one attempts to apply those same detectors on egocentric video (recall Figure 2). Why is there such a gap? Precisely because today's very best object detectors are learned from human-taken photos, whereas egocentric data on wearable cameras—or mobile robots—consist of very few frames that match those statistics. For example, a winning person detector on PASCAL VOC trained with Flickr photos, like the deformable

---

[2] We use $k = 60$ based on preliminary visual inspection, and found results were similar for other k values of similar order ($k \in [30, 120]$).

parts model (DPM) [8], expects to see people in similarly composed photos, but only a fraction of egocentric video frames will be consistent and thus detectable.

Our idea is to use snap points to predict those frames where a standard object detector (trained on human-taken images) will be most trustworthy. This way, we can improve precision; the detector will avoid being misled by incidental patterns in non-snap point frames. We implement the idea as follows, using the DPM as an off-the-shelf detector.[3] We score each test ego-frame by $S(\boldsymbol{x}^e)$, then keep all object detections in those frames scoring above a threshold τ. We set τ as 30% of the average distance between the Web prior images and egocentric snap points. For the remaining frames, we eliminate any detections (i.e., flatten the DPM confidence to 0) that fall below the confidence threshold in the standard DPM pipeline [8]. In effect, we turn the object detector "on" only when it has high chance of success.

Keyframe Selection: As a second application, we use snap points to create keyframe summaries of egocentric video. The goal is to take hours of wearable data and automatically generate a visual storyboard that captures key events. We implement a simple selection strategy. First, we identify temporal event segments using the color- and time-based grouping method described in [23], which finds chunks of frames likely to belong to the same physical location or scene. Then, for each such event, we select the frame most confidently scored as a snap point.

Our intent is to see if snap points, by identifying frames that look intentional, can help distill the main events in hours of uncontrolled wearable camera data. Our implementation is a proof of concept to demonstrate snap points' utility. We are not claiming a new keyframe selection strategy, a problem studied in depth in prior work [27,28,23,30].

4   Datasets and Collecting Ground Truth Snap Points

Datasets: We use two egocentric datasets. The first is the publicly available UT Egocentric Dataset (**Ego**)[4], which consists of four videos of 3-5 hours each, captured with a head-mounted camera by four people doing unscripted daily life activities (eating, working, shopping, driving, etc.). The second is a mobile robot dataset (**Robot**) newly collected for this project. We used a wheeled robot to take a 25 minute video both indoors and outdoors on campus (coffee shops, buildings, streets, pedestrians, etc.). Its camera moves constantly from left to right, pauses, then rotates back in order to cover a wide range of viewpoints.

Both the human and robot datasets represent incidentally captured video from always-on, dynamic cameras and unscripted activity. We found other existing ego collections less suited to our goals, either due to their focus on a controlled environment with limited activity (e.g., making food in a kitchen [7,25]) or their use of chest-mounted or fisheye lens cameras [32,6], which do not share the point of view of intentional hand-held photos.

---

[3] http://www.cs.berkeley.edu/~rbg/latent/
[4] http://vision.cs.utexas.edu/projects/egocentric_data

Ground Truth: Our method requires no labeled data for learning: it needs only to populate the Web prior with human-taken photos. However, to *evaluate* our method, it is necessary to have ground truth human judgments about which ego-frames are snap points. The following describes our crowdsourced annotation strategy to get reliable ground truth.

We created a "magic camera" scenario to help MTurk annotators understand the definition of snap points. Their instructions were as follows: *Suppose you are creating a visual diary out of photos. You have a portable camera that you carry all day long, in order to capture everyday moments of your daily life. ... Unfortunately, your magic camera can also trigger itself from time to time to take random pictures, even while you are holding the camera. At the end of the day, all pictures, both the ones you took intentionally and the ones accidentally taken by the camera, are mixed together.* **Your task is to distinguish the pictures that you took** *intentionally* **from the rest of pictures that were** *accidentally* **taken by your camera.**

Workers were required to rate each image into one of four categories: (a) very confidently intentional, (b) somewhat confident intentional, (c) somewhat confident accidental, and (d) very confident accidental. Since the task can be ambiguous and subjective, we issued each image to 5 distinct workers. We obtained labels for 10,000 frames in the Ego data and 2,000 frames in the Robot data, sampled at random.

We establish confidence-rated ground truth as follows. Every time a frame receives a rating of category (a), (b), (c), or (d) from any of the 5 workers, it receives 5, 2, -1, -2 points, respectively. This lets us rank all ground truth examples by their true snap point strength. To alternatively map them to binary ground truth, we threshold a frame's total score: more than 10 points is deemed intentional, otherwise it is accidental. See Supp. file for more details. Annotators found 14% of the Ego frames and 23% of the Robot frames to be snap points, respectively. The total MTurk cost was about $500.

5 Results

We experiment on the 2 datasets described above, Ego and Robot, which together comprise 17.5 hours of video. Since no existing methods perform snap point detection, we define several **baselines** for comparison:

- **Saliency [29]:** uses the CRF-based saliency method of [29] to score an image. This baseline reflects that people tend to compose images with a salient object in the center. We use the implementation of [3], and use the CRF's log probability output as the snap point confidence.
- **Blurriness [2]:** uses the blur estimates of [2] to score an image. It reflects that intentionally taken images tend to lack motion blur. Note, blur is also used as a feature by our method; here we isolate how much it would solve the task if used on its own, with no Web prior.
- **People likelihood:** uses a person detector to rank each frame by how likely it is to contain one or more people. We use the max output of the DPM [8] detector. The intuition is people tend to take images of their family and

friends to capture meaningful moments, and as a result, many human-taken images contain people. In fact, this baseline also implicitly captures how well-composed the image is, since the DPM is biased to trigger when people are clear and unoccluded in a frame (recall Figure 2).

– **Discriminative SVM**: uses a RBF kernel SVM trained with the ground truth snap points/non-snap points in the Ego data. We run it with a leave-one-camera-wearer-out protocol, training on 3 of the Ego videos and testing on the 4th. This baseline lets us analyze the power of the unlabeled Web prior compared to a standard discriminative method. Note, it requires substantially more training effort than our approach.

5.1   Snap Point Accuracy

First, we quantify how accurately our method predicts snap points. Figure 5 shows the precision-recall curves for our method and the three unsupervised baselines (saliency, blurriness, people likelihood). Table 1 shows the accuracy in terms of two standard rank quality metrics, Spearman's correlation ρ and Kendall's τ. While the precision-recall plots compare predictions against the binarized ground truth, these metrics compare the full orderings of the confidence-valued predictions against the raw MTurk annotators' ground truth scores (cf. Sec. 4). They capture that even for two positive intentional images, one might look better than the other to human judges. We show results for our method with and without the domain adaptation (DA) step.

Overall, our method outperforms the baselines. Notably, the same prior succeeds for both the human-worn and robot-worn cameras. Using both the Web prior and DA gives best results, indicating the value of establishing a domain-invariant feature space to connect the Web and ego data.

On Ego video 4 (v4), our method is especially strong, about a factor of 2 better than the nearest competing baseline (Blur). On v2, mAP is very low for all methods, since v2 has very few true positives (only 3% of its frames, compared to 14% on average for Ego). Still, we see stronger ranking accuracy with our Web prior and DA. On v3, People Likelihood fares much better than it does on all other videos, likely because v3 happens to contain many frames with nice portraits. On the Robot data, however, it breaks down, likely because of the increased viewpoint irregularity and infrequency of people.

While our method is nearly always better than the baselines, on v1 Blur is similar in ranking metrics and achieves higher precision for higher recall rates. This is likely due to v1's emphasis on scenes with one big object, like a bowl or tablet, as the camera wearer shops and cooks. The SUN Web prior has less close-up object-centric images; this suggests we could improve our prior by increasing the coverage of object-centric photos, e.g., with ImageNet-style photos.

Figure 6 shows examples of images among those our method ranks most confidently (top) and least confidently (bottom) as snap points, for both datasets. We see that its predictions capture the desired effects. Snap points, regardless of their content, do appear intentional, whereas non-snap points look accidental.

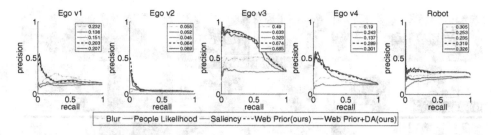

Fig. 5. Snap point detection precision/recall on the four Ego videos (left) and the Robot video (right). Numbers in legend denote mAP. Best viewed in color.

Table 1. Snap point ranking accuracy (higher rank correlations are better)

Methods	Ego v1		Ego v2		Ego v3		Ego v4		Robot	
rank coefficient	ρ	τ	ρ	τ	ρ	τ	ρ	τ	ρ	τ
Blurriness	**0.347**	**0.249**	0.136	0.094	0.479	0.334	0.2342	0.162	0.508	0.352
People Likelihood	0.002	0	-0.015	-0.011	0.409	0.289	0.190	0.131	0.198	0.134
Saliency	0.027	0.019	0.008	0.005	0.016	0.011	-0.021	-0.014	-0.086	-0.058
Web Prior (Ours)	0.321	0.223	0.144	0.100	**0.504**	**0.355**	**0.452**	0.317	0.530	0.373
Web Prior+DA (Ours)	0.343	0.239	**0.179**	**0.124**	0.501	0.353	**0.452**	**0.318**	**0.537**	**0.379**

Figure 8 (left) examines the effectiveness of each feature we employ, were we to take them individually. We see that each one has something to contribute, though they are best in combination (Fig. 5). HOG on Ego is exceptionally strong. This is in spite of the fact that the exact locations visited by the Ego camera wearers are almost certainly disjoint from those that happen to be in the Web prior. This indicates the prior is broad enough to capture the diversity in appearance of everyday environments.

All baselines so far required no labeled images, same as our approach. Next we compare to a discriminative approach that uses manually labeled frames to train a snap point classifier. Figure 7 shows the results, as a function of the amount of labeled data. We give the SVM labeled frames from the held-out Ego videos. (We do not run it for the Robot data, since the only available labels are scene-specific; it's not possible to run the leave-one-camera-wearer-out protocol.) *Despite learning without any explicit labels*, our method generally outperforms the discriminative SVM. The discriminative approach requires thousands of hand-labeled frames to come close to our method's accuracy in most cases. This is a good sign: while expanding the Web prior is nearly free, expanding the labeled data is expensive and tedious. In fact, if anything, Figure 7 is an optimistic portrayal of the SVM baseline. That's because both the training and testing data are captured on the very same camera; in general scenarios, one would not be able to count on this benefit.

The results above are essential to validate our main idea of snap point detection with a Web prior. Next we provide proof of concept results to illustrate the utility of snap points for practical applications.

Fig. 6. Frames our method rates as likely (top) or unlikely (bottom) snap points

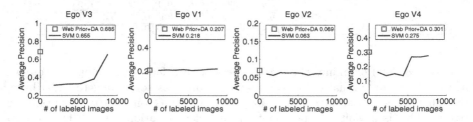

Fig. 7. Comparison to supervised baseline. SVM's mAP (legend) uses *all* labeled data.

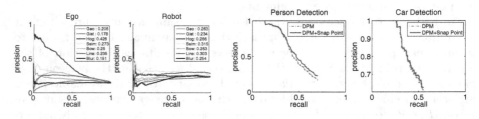

Fig. 8. Left: Accuracy per feature if used in isolation. Right: Snap points boost precision for an off-the-shelf object detector by focusing on frames that look human-taken.

5.2   Object Detection Application

Today's best object detection systems are trained thoroughly on human-taken images—for example, using labeled data from PASCAL VOC or ImageNet. This naturally makes them best suited to run on human-taken images at test time. Our data statistics suggest only 10% to 15% of egocentric frames may fit this bill. Thus, using the method defined in Sec. 3.5, we aim to use snap points to boost object detection precision.

We collected ground truth person and car bounding boxes for the Ego data via DrawMe [43]. Since we could not afford to have all 17.5 hours of video labeled, we sampled the labeled set to cover 50%-50% snap points and non-snap points. We obtained labels for 1000 and 200 frames for people and cars, respectively (cars are more rare in the videos).

Figure 8 (right) shows the results, using the PASCAL detection criterion. We see that snap points improve the precision of the standard DPM detector, since they let us ignore frames where the detector is not trustworthy. Of course, this comes at the cost of some recall at the tails. This seems like a good trade-off for detection in video, particularly, since one could anchor object tracks using these confident predictions to make up the recall.

5.3   Keyframe Selection Application

Keyframe or "storyboard" summaries are an appealing way to peruse long ego-centric video, to quickly get the gist of what was seen. Such summaries enable novel interfaces to let a user "zoom-in" on time intervals that appear most relevant. As a final proof-of-concept result, we apply snap points for keyframe selection, using the method defined in Sec. 3.5.

Figure 9 shows example results on Ego, where the average event length is 30 min. Keyframe selection requires subjective evaluation; we have no ground truth for quantitative evaluation. We present our results alongside a baseline that uses the exact same event segmentation as [23] (cf. Sec. 3.5), but selects each event's frame at random instead of prioritizing snap points. We see the snap point-based summaries contain well-composed images for each event. The baseline, while seeing the same events, uses haphazard shots that do not look intentionally taken. See Supp. file for more examples and comparisons to [28].

Fig. 9. Example keyframe selections for two 4-hour Ego videos. In each example, top row shows snap point result, bottom shows result using only event segmentation.

6 Conclusions and Future Work

An onslaught of lengthy egocentric videos is imminent, making automated methods for intelligently filtering the data of great interest. Whether for easing the transfer of existing visual recognition methods to the ego domain, or for helping users filter content to photoworthy moments, snap point detection is a promising direction. Our data-driven solution uses purely visual information and requires no manual labeling. Our results on over 17 hours of video show it outperforms a variety of alternative approaches.

Ultimately, we envision snap point detection being run online with streaming egocentric video, thereby saving power and storage for an always-on wearable device. Currently, a bottleneck is feature extraction. In future work we will consider ways to triage feature extraction for snap points, and augment the generative model with user-labeled frames to learn a personalized model of snap points. While we are especially interested in wearable data, our methods may also be applicable to related sources, such as bursts of consumer photos or videos captured on mobile phones.

Acknowledgements. This research is sponsored in part by ONR YIP and gifts from Intel and Google. We thank Piyush Khandelwal and Jacob Menashe for helping us collect the Robot video.

References

1. Chen, C.-Y., Grauman, K.: Clues from the Beaten Path: Location Estimation with Bursty Sequences of Tourist Photos. In: CVPR (2011)
2. Crete-Roffet, F., Dolmiere, T., Ladret, P., Nicolas, M.: The blur effect: Perception and estimation with a new no-reference perceptual blur metric. In: SPIE (2007)
3. Dhar, S., Ordonez, V., Berg, T.L.: High level describable attributes for predicting aesthetics and interestingness. In: CVPR (2011)
4. Efros, A., Berg, A., Mori, G., Malik, J.: Recognizing action at a distance. In: ICCV (2003)
5. Fathi, A., Farhadi, A., Rehg, J.: Understanding Egocentric Activities. In: ICCV (2011)
6. Fathi, A., Hodgins, J., Rehg, J.: Social interactions: a first-person perspective. In: CVPR (2012)
7. Fathi, A., Rehg, J.: Modeling actions through state changes. In: CVPR (2013)
8. Felzenszwalb, P., Girshick, R., McAllester, D., Ramanan, D.: Object detection with discriminatively trained part based models. PAMI 32(9) (2010)
9. Fiss, J., Agarwala, A., Curless, B.: Candid portrait selection from video. In: TOG (2011)
10. Gong, B., Shi, Y., Sha, F., Grauman, K.: Geodesic flow kernel for unsupervised domain adaptation. In: CVPR (2012)
11. Gygli, M., Grabner, H., Riemenschneider, H., Nater, F., Van Gool, L.: The interestingness of images. In: ICCV (2013)
12. Hays, J., Efros, A.: im2gps: estimating geographic information from a single image. In: CVPR (2008)

13. Healey, J., Picard, R.: Startlecam: a cybernetic wearable camera. In: Wearable Computers (1998)
14. Hodges, S., Williams, L., Berry, E., Izadi, S., Srinivasan, J., Butler, A., Smyth, G., Kapur, N., Wood, K.: SenseCam: A retrospective memory aid. In: Dourish, P., Friday, A. (eds.) UbiComp 2006. LNCS, vol. 4206, pp. 177–193. Springer, Heidelberg (2006)
15. Hoiem, D., Efros, A., Hebert, M.: Recovering surface layout from an image. IJCV (2007)
16. Isola, P., Xiao, J., Torralba, A., Oliva, A.: What makes an image memorable? In: CVPR (2011)
17. Kalogerakis, E., Vesselova, O., Hays, J., Efros, A., Hertzmann, A.: Image sequence geolocation with human travel priors. In: ICCV (2009)
18. Ke, Y., Tang, X., Jing, F.: The design of high-level features for photo quality assessment. In: CVPR (2006)
19. Khosla, A., Hamid, R., Lin, C.-J., Sundaresan, N.: Large-scale video summarization using web-image priors. In: CVPR (2013)
20. Kim, G., Xing, E.: Jointly aligning and segmenting multiple web photo streams for the inference of collective photo storylines. In: CVPR (2013)
21. Kitani, K., Okabe, T., Sato, Y., Sugimoto, A.: Fast unsupervised ego-action learning for first-person sports videos. In: CVPR (2011)
22. Kôsecká, J., Zhang, W.: Video compass. In: Heyden, A., Sparr, G., Nielsen, M., Johansen, P. (eds.) ECCV 2002, Part IV. LNCS, vol. 2353, pp. 476–490. Springer, Heidelberg (2002)
23. Lee, Y.J., Ghosh, J., Grauman, K.: Discovering important people and objects for egocentric video summarization. In: CVPR (2012)
24. Li, X., Wu, C., Zach, C., Lazebnik, S., Frahm, J.-M.: Modeling and recognition of landmark image collections using iconic scene graphs. In: Forsyth, D., Torr, P., Zisserman, A. (eds.) ECCV 2008, Part I. LNCS, vol. 5302, pp. 427–440. Springer, Heidelberg (2008)
25. Li, Y., Fathi, A., Rehg, J.M.: Learning to predict gaze in egocentric video. In: ICCV (2013)
26. Liu, C., Yuen, J., Torralba, A.: Nonparametric scene parsing: label transfer via dense scene alignment. In: CVPR (2009)
27. Liu, D., Hua, G., Chen, T.: A hierarchical visual model for video object summarization. PAMI 32(12), 2178–2190 (2010)
28. Liu, T., Kender, J.R.: Optimization algorithms for the selection of key frame sequences of variable length. In: Heyden, A., Sparr, G., Nielsen, M., Johansen, P. (eds.) ECCV 2002, Part IV. LNCS, vol. 2353, pp. 403–417. Springer, Heidelberg (2002)
29. Liu, T., Sun, J., Zheng, N., Tang, X., Shum, H.: Learning to detect a salient object. In: CVPR (2007)
30. Lu, Z., Grauman, K.: Story-driven summarization for egocentric video. In: CVPR (2013)
31. Mann, S.: Wearcam (the wearable camera): Personal imaging systems for long term use in wearable tetherless computer mediated reality and personal photo/videographic memory prosthesis. In: Wearable Computers (1998)
32. Pirsiavash, H., Ramanan, D.: Detecting activities of daily living in first-person camera views. In: CVPR (2012)
33. Ren, X., Gu, C.: Figure-ground segmentation improves handled object recognition in egocentric video. In: CVPR (2010)

34. Ryoo, M., Matthies, L.: First-person activity recognition: What are they doing to me? In: CVPR (2013)
35. Shakhnarovich, G., Viola, P., Darrell, T.: Fast Pose Estimation with Parameter-Sensitive Hashing. In: ICCV (2003)
36. Simon, I., Seitz, S.: Scene segmentation using the wisdom of crowds. In: ECCV (2008)
37. Spriggs, E., De la Torre, F., Hebert, M.: Temporal segmentation and activity classification from first-person sensing. In: Workshop on Egocentric Vision, CVPR (2009)
38. Starner, T., Schiele, B., Pentland, A.: Visual contextual awareness in wearable computing. In: Intl. Symp. on Wearable Comp. (1998)
39. Torralba, A., Efros, A.: Unbiased look at dataset bias. In: CVPR (2011)
40. Torralba, A., Fergus, R., Freeman, W.T.: 80 million Tiny Images: a Large Dataset for Non-Parametric Object and Scene Recognition. PAMI 30(11), 1958–1970 (2008)
41. Weyand, T., Leibe, B.: Discovering favorite views of popular places with iconoid shift. In: ICCV (2011)
42. Xiao, J., Hays, J., Ehinger, K., Oliva, A., Torralba, A.: SUN database: large-scale scene recognition from abbey to zoo. In: CVPR (2010)
43. Xiao, J.: Princeton vision toolkit (2013), http://vision.princeton.edu/code.html

Towards Unified Object Detection and Semantic Segmentation

Jian Dong[1], Qiang Chen[1], Shuicheng Yan[1], and Alan Yuille[2]

[1] Department of Electrical and Computer Engineering, NUS, Singapore
[2] Department of Statistics, UCLA, Los Angeles, CA, USA

Abstract. Object detection and semantic segmentation are two strongly correlated tasks, yet typically solved separately or sequentially with substantially different techniques. Motivated by the complementary effect observed from the typical failure cases of the two tasks, we propose a unified framework for joint object detection and semantic segmentation. By enforcing the consistency between final detection and segmentation results, our unified framework can effectively leverage the advantages of leading techniques for these two tasks. Furthermore, both local and global context information are integrated into the framework to better distinguish the ambiguous samples. By jointly optimizing the model parameters for all the components, the relative importance of different component is automatically learned for each category to guarantee the overall performance. Extensive experiments on the PASCAL VOC 2010 and 2012 datasets demonstrate encouraging performance of the proposed unified framework for both object detection and semantic segmentation tasks.

Keywords: Object Detection, Semantic Segmentation, Unified Approach.

1 Introduction

Object detection and semantic segmentation are two core tasks of visual recognition [13,19,36,3,42,6,35]. Object detection is often formulated as predicting a bounding box enclosing the object of interest [19] while semantic segmentation usually aims to assign a category label to each pixel from a pre-defined set [6]. Though strongly correlated, these two tasks have typically been approached as separate problems and handled using substantially different techniques.

Template based detection using sliding window scanning (*e.g.* HoG [13] and DPM [19]) has long been the dominant approach for object detection. Though good at finding the rough object positions, this approach usually fails to accurately localize the whole object via a tight bounding box. In fact, it has been found that the largest source of detection error is inaccurate bounding box localization ($0.1 \leq$ overlap < 0.5) [12,24]. This may arise from the limited representation ability of template-based detectors for non-rigid objects. For example, the deformable part-based model (DPM) [19] detector works much better for localizing rigid cat heads than for more amorphous cat bodies [32]. As shown in Figure 1 (a) and (b), the DPM detector often locates the head region only, which

D. Fleet et al. (Eds.): ECCV 2014, Part V, LNCS 8693, pp. 299–314, 2014.

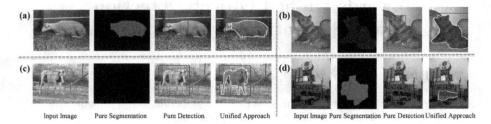

Fig. 1. The inconsistency of failure cases for object detection and semantic segmentation. The images in the top row show the scenario where detection is imperfect due to pose variance while the semantic segmentation works fine. The images in the bottom row show the scenario where semantic segmentation is not accurate while detectors can easily locate the objects. Thus, the two tasks are able to benefit each other, and more satisfactory results can be achieved for both tasks using our unified framework.

leads to the localization error. On the other hand, owing to their homogeneous appearances, the whole objects (cat and sheep) can be easily segmented out by the leading semantic segmentation techniques [6]. If poor localizations can be corrected with the help of semantic segmentation techniques [6], the overall detection performance would be improved considerably from additional true positives and fewer false positives.

Hypotheses based semantic segmentation has achieved great success during the past few years, which works by directly generating a pool of segment hypotheses for further ranking [2,6]. However, due to the lack of global shape models, these approaches may fail to recognize the hypotheses of objects with heterogeneous appearances in the cluttered background, especially when all the generated hypotheses have some artifacts. As shown in Figure 1 (c) and (d), the leading hypotheses based semantic segmentation approach [6] either fails to segment out the object of interest or selects a much larger segment hypothesis. In contrast, if the target object has strong shape cues, the template-based detector [19] can easily locate the object and thus provide valuable information for semantic segmentation. Recently, a line of works, called detection-based segmentation, explored directly utilizing the detection results as top-down guidance and then performing segmentation within the given bounding boxes [4,37]. However, such approaches usually have to make a hard decision about detection results at the early stage. Hence the error for detection, especially the localization error, will propagate to the segmentation results and could not be rectified. Intuitively it is beneficial to postpone making a hard decision till the last step of the pipeline [38].

Based on the above observations, we argue that object detection and semantic segmentation should be addressed jointly. Object detections should be consistent with some underlying segments to integrate local cues for better localization as shown in Figure 1 (a) and (b). Similarly, hypotheses based semantic segmentation should benefit from template-based object detectors to select better segment hypotheses as shown in Figure 1 (c) and (d). To this end, we propose a principled framework to unify current leading object detection and semantic segmentation techniques. By enforcing the consistency, our unified approach can benefit from the advantages of both techniques. In addition, some ambiguous object hypotheses may be difficult to classify from the information within the window/segment alone, but contextual information, such as local context around each object hypothesis and global image-level context, can help [28,34,11]. Hence, we further integrate contextual modeling into our framework. The major contributions of this work can be summarized as follows:

- We propose a principled framework for joint object detection and semantic segmentation. By enforcing the consistency between detection and segmentation results, our unified framework can effectively leverage the advantages of both techniques. Furthermore, both local and global context information are integrated into our unified framework to distinguish the ambiguous examples.
- With our unified framework, all information is accumulated at the final stage of the pipeline for decision making. Hence, it is avoided to make any hard decision at the early stage. The relative importance of different components is automatically learned for each category to guarantee the overall performance.
- Extensive experiments are conducted for both object detection and semantic segmentation tasks on the PASCAL VOC [17] datasets. The state-of-the-art performance of the proposed framework verifies its effectiveness, showing that performing object detection and semantic segmentation jointly is beneficial for both tasks.

2   Related Work

Recently, by noticing the limitation and complementarity of techniques for both tasks, some researchers have begun to investigate their correlations [25,2,40,5,39]. The early work [25] simply employs the masks from detectors to initialize graph-cuts based segmentations. In [27,37], more sophisticated models are proposed to refine the region within ground-truth bounding boxes. Rather than focusing on entire objects, Brox *et al.* employed Poselet detectors to predict masks for object parts [5]. Arbeláez *et al.* aggregated top-down information from detectors as activation features for bottom-up segments [2]. Conversely, segmentation techniques have also been explored to assist object detection. Dai *et al.* utilized segments extracted for each object detection hypothesis for better localization [12]. Some recent works [26,40] proposed to perform joint object detection and semantic segmentation. Unfortunately, nearly all the above approaches utilize a sequential manner to fuse detection and segmentation techniques. Hence, the overall performance heavily relies on the correctness of the initial results as the errors in the early stage are difficult to rectify. Our framework is different in the sense that we avoid making any hard decision at the early stage. All the information is aggregated at the final stage of the pipeline for decision making.

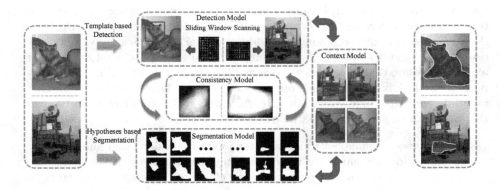

Fig. 2. Overview of the proposed unified object detection and semantic segmentation framework. Give a testing image, our UDS framework performs template based detection using sliding window scanning and hypotheses based semantic segmentation jointly. The agreement of the predictions from these two approaches is ensured by the consistency model. Both local context around the object hypothesis and global image context are also seamlessly integrated into our framework. The final output is the bounding box position and the index of the selected segment hypothesis.

Probably the most similar approach to ours is [20], which proposed to improve object detection based on semantic segmentation results. Similar to this work we utilize consistency between the detection windows and bottom-up segments. However, unlike [20] our features are computed on parts as well. Also, in [20] it is not described how to deal with a large number of segments, and their experiments are based on a few segments.

3   Unified Object Detection and Semantic Segmentation

In this section, we introduce the details of the proposed unified object detection and semantic segmentation (UDS) framework. We start with an overview of the system and then detail each key component.

Figure 2 illustrates the pipeline of the proposed UDS framework. For the segmentation component, we employ the hypotheses based approach. Thus, with a pool of generated segment hypotheses, the segmentation problem is converted into choosing the appropriate hypothesis. Given a testing image, we perform template based detection using sliding window scanning and hypotheses based semantic segmentation jointly. Successful detection and segmentation require the agreement of both detection and segmentation predictions, which is achieved by utilizing a consistency model. In addition, as context plays an important role in distinguishing ambiguous object hypotheses, we further design a context model to aggregate both local (around the target object) and global (image-level) context information. For different object categories, each of these four components may have a different level of importance, which is automatically decided during the learning process. The final output of our system is the bounding box position (p_0) and the selected segment index (id) for the target object.

Formally, the joint detection and segmentation is achieved via the maximization of the following score function:

$$S(I, z, id) = \lambda^{Dt} S^{Dt}(z|w^{Dt}, I) + \lambda^{Sg} S^{Sg}(id|w^{Sg}, I)$$
$$+\lambda^{Ct} S^{Ct}(z, id|w^{Ct}, I) + S^{Cs}(z, id|w^{Cs}), \tag{1}$$

where w^{Dt}, w^{Sg}, w^{Ct} and w^{Cs} are the parameters for detection, segmentation, context and consistency component, respectively. λ^{Dt}, λ^{Sg}, λ^{Ct} are scalar weights for the corresponding components. z captures the information for the template based detector and id denotes the index of the selected segment. The details of each component are introduced in the following subsections. Based on the proposed unified approach, we avoid making any hard decision at the early stage. The final decision is delayed to the last step of the pipeline with all the integrated information, which implicitly relies on the learning mechanism to assess the relative importance of different components for each object category to guarantee the overall performance.

Finally, we want to emphasize that the proposed UDS framework provides a principled way to unify detection and segmentation techniques. We can directly employ the existing techniques or design new approaches for each component. Hence, it is easy to tailor UDS for specific applications, such as simultaneous person detection and segmentation. In this work, we will focus on utilizing the UDS framework for general object detection and semantic segmentation to verify its effectiveness.

3.1   Template Based Detection Component

For the detection component, we aim to utilize the template based approach [19,14,20], as it is good at capturing the shape cue and thus complementary to the appearance based segmentation techniques [6,38]. In addition, through the mixture model strategy [19], these approaches can easily encode sub-category level top-down information (subcategory specific soft shape mask in this work). In this paper, we utilize the state-of-the-art deformable part-based model (DPM) [19]. Following [19,20], we define $z = \{c, p\}$, where $p = \{p_i\}_{i=0,\cdots,m}$. Here, c denotes the mixture component index. p_0 encodes the location and scale of the root bounding box in an image pyramid and $\{p_i\}_{i=1,\cdots,m}$ encodes the m part bounding boxes at the double resolution of the root. By concatenating the parameters for all mixtures as in [19,20], the score of a configuration can be written as

$$S^{Dt}(p, c|w^{Dt}, I) = \sum_{i=0}^{m} w_i^{Dt} \cdot \phi^{Dt}(I, p_i, c) + \sum_{i=1}^{m} w_{i,def}^{Dt} \cdot \phi^{Dt}(p_0, p_i, c), \tag{2}$$

where $\phi^{Dt}(I, p_i, c)$ and $\phi^{Dt}(p_0, p_i, c)$ are the HoG pyramid features and spring deformation features, respectively, as in [19,20]. As Eqn. (2) is linear in model parameters, it can be written compactly as:

$$S^{Dt}(p, c | w^{Dt}, I) = w^{Dt} \cdot \phi^{Dt}(I, p, c). \tag{3}$$

3.2   Hypotheses Based Segmentation Component

Hypotheses based semantic segmentation has achieved great success during the past few years [7,6,38]. This line of approaches mainly consist of two stages. The first stage generates a pool of segment hypotheses. The second stage ranks the generated hypotheses based on category-dependent information. The top ranked segments are returned as the final solution. Many efforts have been devoted to hypotheses generation through either a pure bottom-up approach [7,36,2] or a CRF based approach [38]. For the second stage, most approaches [7,36,38] simply employ the appearance based classification/regression for ranking. However, due to the limited discriminative ability of the appearance based ranking function, there exists a large gap between upper-bound accuracy of generated hypotheses (larger than 80%) and predicted accuracy of selected hypotheses (less than 50%) [7,38]. As shown in Figure 1, due to the lack of global shape models, semantic segmentation relying on pure appearance based ranking may fail to find the appropriate hypotheses.

Based on the above observation, it may be expected that considerable improvement over the current segmentation performance can be achieved by means of simply selecting better hypothesis without generating more hypotheses. Hence, in this work we use standard methods for hypotheses generation and similar to [20], focus on selecting better segment hypotheses. To allow direct comparison, we utilize the publicly available code of the second order pooling (O_2P) approach [6] for hypotheses generation. For the feature representation $\phi^{Sg}(I, id)$ of the selected hypothesis id, a naive strategy is directly employing the second order pooling features as in [6]. However, training a latent model with high dimension features may be intractable. Hence, rather than keeping $\phi^{Sg}(I, id)$ as a high dimensional vector of raw second order pooling features, we represent $\phi^{Sg}(I, id)$ as the scores of pre-trained support vector regressors (SVR) [6]. Then, the score function of the segmentation component can be written as:

$$S^{Sg}(id | w^{Sg}, I) = w^{Sg} \cdot \phi^{Sg}(I, id). \tag{4}$$

3.3   Consistency Component

The consistency component mainly aims to enforce the consistency between detection and segmentation prediction and thus leverage the advantages of both approaches. Soft shape mask has demonstrated to be effective for many detection guided techniques [39,2,8]. Hence, in this work, we measure the consistency between results of detection and segmentation approaches by calculating the correlations between their masks as shown below:

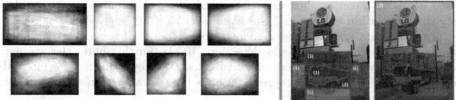

(a) Exemplar soft shape masks for bus and cat categories   (b) Regions for calculating context features

Fig. 3. (a) Examples of subcategory-specific soft shape masks for buses (top row) and cats (bottom row). (b) Illustration of regions defined for computing the context features. Based on the selected segment hypothesis and bounding box, we adaptively divide the image into 7 regions as described in Section 3.4.

$$S^{Cs}(z, id|w^{Cs}) = \sum_{i=0}^{m} w_i^{Cs} \cdot m(p_i, id, c) = w^{Cs} \cdot \phi^{Cs}(p, id, c), \qquad (5)$$

where $m(p_i, id, c)$ is the binary map $\{1, -1\}$ clipped from the segmentation hypothesis id by the localized bounding box p_i. Here, c in $m(p_i, id, c)$ is only used for padding 0 to make the equation with mixture models more compact, which is a common trick for the DPM approach [19].

Intuitively, the learned soft mask w^{Cs} from top-down detection techniques can be seen as a shape guidance for bottom-up segmentation techniques. Enforcing the correlation between masks from both approaches will guarantee the consistency of top-down and bottom-up information. In addition, the mixture model strategy is critical to cope with variance in the poses as well as the view points. To ensure obtaining a reliable shape mask for each mixture component, we employ a shape guided mixture initialization as introduced in Section 4.2. Some examples of such soft shape masks are visualized in Figure 3 (a).

3.4 Context Component

Both the local context around the target object [28,31] and the global image context [34,2,11,31] have shown to be effective for visual recognition. The local context directly models the interaction of the target object and the surrounding environment. For example, a horse is often occluded by a person riding on it. In contrast, the global context mainly captures the image level information and co-existence/exclusion relation between objects.

In order to leverage such informative context cues, we further enhance the framework with an adaptive context model. Specifically, given a bounding box p_0 and a segment id, similar to [31], we divide the image into 7 regions (segment region, surrounding region within p_0, 4 context boxes and the whole image) as shown in Figure 3 (b). The area of the context box is half of that of the bounding box p_0. Hence, the spatial extent of the local context will vary adaptively based on p_0. If a context box crosses the boundary of the image, we consider only the area within the image. Fisher Vector (FV) [21,9] is employed as region feature representation, as it has demonstrated the state-of-the-art performance for both object classification and detection [10,11]. Furthermore, the average pooling strategy for FV enables effective calculation by utilizing the integral graph. Thus, the raw context representation is the concatenation of FVs on the 7 regions mentioned above.

Similar to the segmentation component, the dimension of the raw context features is too high. Hence, we first train a separate classifier for each object category and then use the predicted scores as the final context features. Then, the context component can be written as:

$$S^{Ct}(z, id|w^{Ct}, I) = S^{Ct}(p_0, id|w^{Ct}, I) = w^{Ct} \cdot \phi^{Ct}(I, id, p_0), \qquad (6)$$

where $\phi^{Ctx}(I, id, p_0)$ is the concatenation of predicted scores for all classifiers. In fact, our context model can be seen as a variant of the appearance based detection approach to some extent. We still call it "context model" as it can provide valuable and complementary context information to the other three components.

4   Inference and Learning

This section introduces inference and learning of the proposed UDS framework. We begin with the general inference and learning procedure and then describe the implementation details in practice.

4.1   Inference

We employ the sliding windows strategy for inference. Similar to [19,20], the inference is performed by enumerating the segments. For a fixed root bounding box position p_0 and mixture index c, inference in our model can be done by solving the following optimization problem:

$$
\begin{aligned}
S(p_0, c) = \max_{p_1, \cdots, p_m, id} S(p, id, c) = \max_{id} [\lambda^{Dt} w_0^{Dt} \cdot \phi^{Dt}(I, p_0, c) \\
+ \lambda^{Sg} w^{Sg} \cdot \phi^{Sg}(I, id) + \lambda^{Ct} w^{Ct} \cdot \phi^{Ct}(I, id, p_0) + w_0^{Cs} \cdot m(p_0, id, c) \\
+ \max_{p_1, \cdots, p_m} \sum_{i=1}^{m} (\lambda^{Dt} w_i^{Dt} \cdot \phi^{Dt}(I, p_i, c) + \lambda^{Dt} w_{i,def}^{Dt} \cdot \phi^{Dt}(p_0, p_i, c) + w_i^{Cs} \cdot m(p_i, id, c))].
\end{aligned}
\tag{7}
$$

By defining

$$
\begin{aligned}
R_0(p_0, id, c) =& \lambda^{Dt} w_0^{Dt} \cdot \phi^{Dt}(I, p_0, c) + \lambda^{Sg} w^{Sg} \cdot \phi^{Sg}(I, id) \\
& + \lambda^{Ct} w^{Ct} \cdot \phi^{Ct}(I, id, p_0) + w_0^{Cs} \cdot m(p_0, id, c) \\
R_i(p_i, id, c) =& \lambda^{Dt} w_i^{Dt} \cdot \phi^{Dt}(I, p_i, c) + w_i^{Cs} \cdot m(p_i, id, c),
\end{aligned}
$$

the Eqn. (7) can be written compactly as:

$$S(p_0, c) = \max_{id}[R_0(p_0, id, c) + \max_{p_1, \cdots, p_m} \sum_{i=1}^{m} (R_i(p_i, id, c) + \lambda^{Dt} w_{i,def}^{Dt} \cdot \phi^{Dt}(p_0, p_i, c))].$$

$$(8)$$

With fixed segment index id, this scoring function is similar to that of DPM [19,20] and can thus be passed to an off-the-shelf DPM solver. Hence, the inference algorithm works as follows: First, we compute $R_0(p_0, id, c)$ for each root filter position p_0 and segment index id. Then, we prune the object hypotheses based on the score of R_0 without sacrificing the overall recall rate (validated on the validation set). For each retained segment hypothesis, we further run the full model (7) locally with the dynamic programming approach as in [19]. Finally, we compute the maximum over the mixture components to obtain the final score of the object hypothesis.

4.2   Learning

By defining the output variable $y = \{p_0, id\}$ and latent variable $h = \{p_1, \cdots, p_m, c\}$, the scoring function (1) can be rewritten as

$$S(I, y, h) = w \cdot \Phi(I, y, h),$$ $$(9)$$

where w is the concatenation of all model parameters (w^{Dt}, w^{Sg}, w^{Ct} and w^{Cs}). $\Phi(I, y, h)$ is the concatenation of all four components features weighted by their weights ($\lambda^{Dt}, \lambda^{Sg}$ and λ^{Ct}) with respect to the label y and latent variable h.

We note that Eqn. (9) is linear in the model parameter w, thus this model can be effectively learned based on the latent structure SVM framework [41,22]:

$$\min_{w} \frac{1}{2}||w||^2 + C[\sum_{j=1}^{n} \max_{\hat{y},\hat{h}}(w \cdot \Phi(x_j, \hat{y}, \hat{h}) + \Delta(y_i, \hat{y}, \hat{h})) - \sum_{j=1}^{n} \max_{h}(w \cdot \Phi(x_i, y_i, h))], (10)$$

where the loss function $\Delta(y_i, \hat{y}, \hat{h})$ is defined as the weighted sum of the Intersection over Union of the root filters and segment hypotheses (in current implementation, we simply use the average value of two IoUs).

The standard approach to solve the optimization problem (10) is the Concave-Convex Procedure (CCCP) [43,41]. However, as the CCCP algorithm only guarantees to converge to a local minimum, we learn the model progressively to ensure a reasonable initialization. More specifically, we first train each component separately and jointly learn the overall model with Eqn (10).

For the object detection component, we follow the original training approach of DPM [19] except for the mixture initialization and part discovery. Aspect ratio based clustering is used in [19] for mixture initialization. However, such an approach may ignore the potential pose/view variance. Hence, we employ the idea of "subcategory mining" [15,1,14] by utilizing the additional segmentation annotation to ensure a more reliable shape mask for each component. Specifically, we resize all the cropped segmentation masks to the same height and l_2 normalizes all the resized masks. Then, the similarity between two normalized masks a and b is defined as the maximal value of the convolution response map of a and b. Finally, the graph shift algorithm [29] is employed to discover the dense subgraphs, which correspond to the subcategories, as in [15]. The resulting subcategories are then used for mixture initialization. The original DPM approach [19] discovers the salient parts greedily by covering the high-energy region of the root HOG-template. Recently, [8] suggests that modifying this "saliency" measure by multiplying the HOG magnitude by the average segmentation mask for each component will lead to more semantic meaningful parts. Hence, we follow their approach by utilizing the modified 'saliency" measure for part discovery. For the consistency component, the pixel-wise mean of all segmentation masks for each component is utilized for initialization.

In the final joint learning stage, all model parameters (w^{Dt}, w^{Sg}, w^{Ct} and w^{Cs}) in Eqn. (10) are jointly optimized. Thus, the relative importance of each component will be automatically tuned for each category.

4.3   Implementation Details

As discussed in Section 3.3 and 3.4, we employ the predicted scores of the basic-level classifiers as features for both the segmentation ($\phi^{Sg}(I, id)$ in Eqn. (4)) and context ($\phi^{Ct}(I, id, p_0)$ in Eqn. (6)) components to improve the efficiency of the UDS framework. For the segmentation component, we follow the second-order pooling approach [33] by utilizing the public available implementation provided by the author. 150 top-ranked object hypotheses are generated with the CPMC method for each image [7]. The concatenation of scores from support vector regressors of all categories is employed as the segmentation component feature for each hypothesis. For the context component, the dense SIFT [30] and color moment are extracted as low-level features. Both features are projected to 64 dimensions using PCA and the size of Gaussian Mixture Model in FV [9] is set to 64. The concatenation of resulting FVs in all regions is then trained with the LibLinear library [18] in a similar manner with [13]. Finally, the confidence scores of classifiers for all categories are utilized as the context component features.

For the shape-guided DPM, the number of subcategories is automatically decided by the graph shift algorithm based on the expansion size, which is decided by cross-validation [29]. The resulting subcategory number for different object categories is generally from 4 to 8.

The weights $\lambda^{Dt}, \lambda^{Sg}$ and λ^{Ct} in Eqn. (1) are set as 0.1, 0.2 and 0.2, respectively, based on cross-validation. In fact, the final accuracy is not very sensitive to the variation of these parameters, as our UDS framework can automatically learn w to adjust the relative weights of different components.

5   Experiments

We extensively evaluate the proposed UDS framework on the challenging PASCAL Visual Object Challenge (VOC) datasets [17], which provide a common

Table 1. Proof-of-Concept experiments for object detection on VOC 2010 validation set

Method	plane	bike	bird	boat	bottle	bus	car	cat	chair	cow	table	dog	horse	motor	person	plant	sheep	sofa	train	tv	mAP
DPM	43.6	51.1	4.4	3.4	21.7	57.4	40.4	17.0	16.4	15.3	10.2	11.1	37.2	39.1	40.4	5.2	27.4	18.9	39.7	37.1	26.9
S-DPM	48.2	52.7	4.9	5.7	25.3	60.6	40.8	21.6	**16.6**	16.3	17.0	12.5	40.5	38.8	**41.3**	6.9	32.5	23.2	44.3	40.8	29.5
S-DPM+Sg	57.6	55.4	22.6	15.8	27.9	**64.3**	45.8	54.8	10.7	26.9	21.9	35.2	48.2	49.8	38.8	13.3	36.3	32.5	49.0	45.3	37.6
S-DPM+Sg+Ct	**59.2**	**56.7**	**22.8**	**16.4**	**28.9**	63.7	**46.6**	**56.2**	15.6	**29.1**	**25.1**	**36.9**	**49.5**	**50.7**	39.3	**14.4**	**38.2**	**36.1**	**49.2**	**46.2**	**39.0**

Table 2. Proof-of-Concept experiments for semantic segmentation on VOC 2010 validation set

Method	b/g	plane	bike	bird	boat	bottle	bus	car	cat	chair	cow	table	dog	horse	motor	person	plant	sheep	sofa	train	tv	avg
O₂P	83.2	70.0	22.0	43.8	39.6	40.3	60.3	64.9	55.7	13.2	37.1	20.2	42.5	**37.3**	47.1	50.5	31.9	51.5	27.2	58.6	50.6	45.1
S-DPM+ Sg	82.5	74.2	20.5	45.0	42.7	38.4	65.1	66.9	55.8	16.1	37.3	23.3	41.3	34.7	49.6	49.5	34.1	54.6	33.4	63.7	53.5	46.8
S-DPM+Sg+Ct	**83.2**	**74.9**	**22.9**	**45.7**	**43.4**	**40.6**	**66.2**	**68.1**	**56.4**	**16.8**	**39.8**	**24.0**	**44.2**	36.3	**49.9**	**50.9**	**34.4**	**56.7**	**34.1**	**64.8**	**54.4**	**48.0**

evaluation platform for both object detection and semantic segmentation. These datasets are extremely challenging since the images are crawled from the real-world photo sharing website and the objects contained vary significantly in size, pose, view point and appearance. The datasets contain 20 object classes and are divided into "train", "val" and "test" subsets. We follow the standard PASCAL protocol by employing Average Precision (AP) and Intersection over Union (IoU) as evaluation metric for object detection and semantic segmentation, respectively.

In the following section, we first conduct multiple Proof-of-Concept experiments on the validation set to assess the relative importance of each individual component. Then, we evaluate the optimal configuration of the proposed framework on the test set to compare with the state-of-the-art performance ever reported for both object detection and semantic segmentation tasks.

5.1 Proof-of-Concept Experiments

In this subsection, we evaluate the relative importance of individual components in our framework on VOC 2012 "train/val" datasets (i.e. "train" set for training and "val" set for test) with the extra segmentation annotation from [23] for proof of concept and ease of parameter tuning.

Table 1 and 2 show the detailed object detection and semantic segmentation results, respectively. It can be concluded from the tables that:

- Shape-guided subcategory mining does improve the detection performance. By better capturing the pose/viewpoint variance and adaptively deciding the number of subcategories, shape-guided DPM (S-DPM) can provide more reliable shape masks for our UDS framework.
- Object detection and semantic segmentation techniques are complementary. Performing two tasks jointly will boost the performance of each other. As shown in Table 1, the joint approach (S-DPM+Sg) significantly outperforms

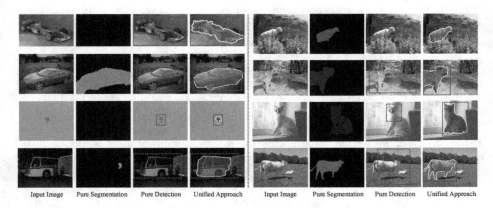

Input Image   Pure Segmentation   Pure Detection   Unified Approach   Input Image   Pure Segmentation   Pure Detection   Unified Approach

Fig. 4. More exemplar results on VOC 2012 from the proposed UDS framework and baseline methods (DPM [19] for detection and O$_2$P [6] for segmentation)

the detection baseline (S-DPM) by 8.1%. In fact, the DPM based detector mainly captures the shape cues. Hence, it may locate rigid parts only and thus leads to localization error. On the contrary, the underlying segmentation component mainly relies on the appearance cues and thus can help to rectify the bounding box position, especially for the objects with homogeneous appearances. Table 2 demonstrates that the joint approach (S-DPM+Sg) also outperforms the segmentation baseline (O$_2$P). For objects in the cluttered background, shape based detectors can provide valuable information to assist in selecting better segment hypotheses. More examples to illustrate the complementarity of the two tasks are shown in Figure 4.

- The context component can further improve the performance for both tasks. By employing both the local and global context cues, the full model (S-DPM+Sg+Ct) can better distinguish ambiguous objects and thus yields the best performance.

5.2   Comparison with State-of-the-arts

In this subsection, we evaluate our UDS framework on the Pasval VOC test set to have a direct comparison with the state-of-the-arts. Though our framework can perform joint detection and segmentation, these two tasks are usually evaluated using different image sets. Hence, we slightly tweak the training process to allow the direct comparison with previous methods. Specifically, for the detection task, we train the model on the VOC 2010 "main-trainval" set, as many leading methods [20,11] only reported their results on this dataset. For the segmentation task, we perform the experiments on the union of the VOC 2012 "main" and "seg" sets. The extra segmentation annotation from [23] are used for both tasks. We omit the results of VOC 2010 segmentation and VOC 2012 detection due to space limitation.

Table 3. Comparison of detection performance on VOC 2010 test set

Method	plane	bike	bird	boat	bottle	bus	car	cat	chair	cow	table	dog	horse	motor	person	plant	sheep	sofa	train	tv	mAP
DPM [19]	48.2	52.2	14.8	13.8	28.7	53.2	44.9	26.0	18.4	24.4	13.7	23.1	45.8	50.5	43.7	9.8	31.1	21.5	44.4	35.7	32.2
van de Sande *et al.* [36]	56.2	42.4	15.3	12.6	21.8	49.3	36.8	46.1	12.9	32.1	30.0	36.5	43.5	52.9	32.9	**15.3**	41.1	31.8	47.0	44.8	35.1
NLPR [17]	53.3	**55.3**	19.2	21.0	30.0	54.4	46.7	41.2	**20.0**	31.5	20.7	30.3	48.6	55.3	46.5	10.2	34.4	26.5	50.3	40.3	36.8
MITUCLA [44]	54.2	48.5	15.7	19.2	29.2	55.5	43.5	41.7	16.9	28.5	26.7	30.9	48.3	55.0	41.7	9.7	35.8	30.8	47.2	40.8	36.0
ContextSVM [34]	53.1	52.7	18.1	13.5	30.7	53.9	43.5	40.3	17.7	31.9	28.0	29.5	**52.9**	56.6	44.2	12.6	36.2	28.7	50.5	40.7	36.8
FV [11]	**65.9**	50.1	23.7	24.1	20.4	52.6	47.1	50.9	13.2	32.8	**31.8**	41.4	43.9	55.3	29.8	14.1	**41.7**	35.6	46.7	**46.9**	38.4
Using Extra Semantic Segmentation Annotation From [23]																					
segDPM [20]	58.7	51.4	25.3	24.1	33.8	52.5	49.2	48.8	11.7	30.4	21.6	37.7	46.0	53.1	46.0	13.1	35.7	29.4	52.5	41.8	38.1
segDPM+context [20]	61.4	53.4	**25.6**	**25.2**	**35.5**	51.7	50.6	50.8	19.3	33.8	26.8	40.4	48.3	54.4	**47.1**	14.8	38.7	35.0	52.8	43.1	40.4
Ours:UDS	60.1	54.3	23.9	22.9	31.8	**57.0**	**51.1**	**54.8**	17.6	**35.7**	26.7	**42.8**	51.2	**58.0**	41.7	**15.3**	37.8	**39.8**	**54.9**	45.6	**41.2**

Object Detection: The detailed comparison of the proposed framework with current leading approaches for object detection is presented in Table 3. The first two methods are the representative works for sliding windows strategy and selective search strategy, respectively. Despite their theoretical interest, these methods only focus on the information within the windows and thus ignore the informative context cues, which leads to inferior results compared with other competitors. All other methods are obtained through the combinations of multiple techniques in order to obtain better performance.

From Table 3, it can be observed that our proposed UDS outperforms all the competitors in terms of mAP. The proposed UDS framework achieves the best performance in 8 out of the 20 categories with an mAP of 41.2%, which is 3.1% higher than that of the state-of-the-arts (segDPM). (We think it is not fair to compare with segDPM+context, as this method uses the scores from the winner of VOC 2012 classification task, which utilizes many advanced tricks, such as multiple model fusion, and combine several learning detection techniques to achieve amazing classification performance [20].) With our unified approach, the advantages of both object detection and semantic segmentation techniques can be leveraged to improve the overall performance. In addition, it can be noted that our method can significantly improve the performance on the categories with homogeneous appearances, such as cats and dogs. For such categories, the underlying segmentation component can easily segment the objects out for rectifying the localization errors.

Semantic Segmentation: Table 4 shows the detailed comparison of the proposed framework with previous approaches on the VOC 2012 segmentation challenge. Based on the basic idea behind the methods, all the competing methods can be divided into two categories. The first category (O2P-CPMC-CSI, CMBR-O2P-CPMC-LIN, O2P-CPMC-FGT-SEGM and Yadollahpour) employs the hypotheses based segmentation. The difference among them mainly lies in the hypotheses generation procedure and ranking function design. Most of them provide the results with/without extra annotation from [23]. The other category (NUS-DET-SPR-GC-SP and Xia) estimates the semantic segmentation results based on the bounding boxes from object detection. Hence, these approaches heavily rely on the detector performance and need extra annotation for object detection.

Table 4. Comparison of segmentation performance on VOC 2012 test set

Method	b/g	plane	bike	bird	boat	bottle	bus	car	cat	chair	cow	table	dog	horse	motor	person	plant	sheep	sofa	train	tv	avg
O2P-CPMC-CSI [16]	85.0	59.3	27.9	43.9	39.8	41.4	52.2	**61.5**	56.4	13.6	44.5	26.1	42.8	51.7	57.9	51.3	29.8	45.7	28.8	49.9	43.3	45.4
CMBR-O2P-CPMC-LIN [16]	83.9	60.0	27.3	46.4	40.0	41.7	57.6	59.0	50.4	10.0	41.6	22.3	43.0	51.7	56.8	50.1	33.7	43.7	29.5	47.5	44.7	44.8
O2P-CPMC-FGT-SEGM [16]	85.1	65.4	29.3	51.3	33.4	44.2	59.8	60.3	52.5	13.6	**53.6**	32.6	40.3	57.6	57.3	49.0	33.5	53.5	29.2	47.6	37.6	47.0
Yadollahpour et al. [38]	**85.7**	62.7	25.6	46.9	43.0	54.8	58.4	58.6	55.6	14.6	47.5	31.2	44.7	51.0	60.9	**53.5**	36.6	50.9	30.1	50.2	46.8	48.1
Relying on Extra Object Detector																						
NUS-DET-SPR-GC-SP [16]	82.8	52.9	**31.0**	39.8	44.5	58.9	60.8	52.5	49.0	**22.6**	38.1	27.5	47.4	52.4	46.8	51.9	35.7	**55.3**	**40.8**	**54.2**	47.8	47.3
Xia et al. [37]	82.5	52.1	29.5	50.6	35.6	**59.8**	64.4	55.5	54.7	22.0	38.7	24.3	**48.3**	55.6	52.9	52.2	38.2	49.1	35.5	53.7	**53.5**	48.0
Using Extra Semantic Segmentation Annotation From [23]																						
O2P-CPMC-CSI [16]	85.0	63.6	26.8	45.6	41.7	47.1	54.3	58.6	55.1	14.5	49.0	30.9	46.1	52.6	58.2	53.4	32.0	44.5	34.6	45.3	43.1	46.8
CMBR-O2P-CPMC-LIN [16]	84.7	63.9	23.8	44.6	40.3	45.5	59.6	58.7	57.1	11.7	45.9	34.9	43.0	54.9	58.0	51.5	34.6	44.1	29.9	50.5	44.5	46.7
O2P-CPMC-FGT-SEGM [16]	85.2	63.4	27.3	**56.1**	37.7	47.2	57.9	59.3	55.0	11.5	50.8	30.5	45.0	58.4	57.4	48.6	34.6	53.3	32.4	47.6	39.2	47.5
Ours:UDS	85.2	**67.0**	24.5	47.2	**45.0**	47.9	**65.3**	60.6	**58.5**	15.5	50.8	**37.4**	45.8	**59.9**	**62.0**	52.7	**40.8**	48.2	36.8	53.1	45.6	**50.0**

The results in Table 4 demonstrate that the proposed UDS framework performs the best in 8 out of the 21 categories, achieving the best average performance of 50%. As discussed above, our unified approach can leverage the advantages of both object detection and semantic segmentation techniques. One main source of the improvement for semantic segmentation comes from the successful detection of objects in cluttered backgrounds. The bottom-up segmentation techniques may not be able to extract the accurate boundary of objects in cluttered backgrounds, which makes the following ranking problem very difficult. However, the template based detection mainly focuses on the object shape and thus is robust to the cluttered backgrounds to some extent. Hence, the proposed framework can significantly improve the semantic segmentation performance of rigid objects, such as aeroplane, bus and motorbike, as verified in Table 4.

6   Conclusions and Future Work

In this paper, we proposed a unified framework for joint object detection and semantic segmentation. Noticing the complementarity of current detection and segmentation approaches, we explicitly enforce the consistency between their outputs to leverage the advantages of both techniques. Both local and global context information are further integrated into the framework to better distinguish the ambiguous samples. All the information is aggregated at the end of the pipeline for decision making and thus hard decision is avoided to make at the early stage as in traditional pipelines. The relative importance of different components is automatically learned for each category to guarantee the overall performance. Extensive experimental results clearly demonstrated the proposed framework has achieved the state-of-the-art performance. In the future, we plan to integrate deep learning techniques into the current framework.

Acknowledgment. This research is supported by the Singapore National Research Foundation under its International Research Centre @Singapore Funding Initiative, Office of Naval Research ONR N00014-12-1-0883 and ONR MURI N000014-10-1-0933.

References

1. Aghazadeh, O., Azizpour, H., Sullivan, J., Carlsson, S.: Mixture component identification and learning for visual recognition. In: Fitzgibbon, A., Lazebnik, S., Perona, P., Sato, Y., Schmid, C. (eds.) ECCV 2012, Part VI. LNCS, vol. 7577, pp. 115–128. Springer, Heidelberg (2012)
2. Arbeláez, P., Hariharan, B., Gu, C., Gupta, S., Bourdev, L., Malik, J.: Semantic segmentation using regions and parts. In: CVPR (2012)
3. Boix, X., Gonfaus, J.M., van de Weijer, J., Bagdanov, A.D., Serrat, J., Gonzàlez, J.: Harmony potentials. IJCV (2012)
4. Brox, T., Bourdev, L., Maji, S., Malik, J.: Object segmentation by alignment of poselet activations to image contours. In: CVPR (2011)
5. Brox, T., Bourdev, L., Maji, S., Malik, J.: Object segmentation by alignment of poselet activations to image contours. In: CVPR (2011)
6. Carreira, J., Caseiro, R., Batista, J., Sminchisescu, C.: Semantic segmentation with second-order pooling. In: Fitzgibbon, A., Lazebnik, S., Perona, P., Sato, Y., Schmid, C. (eds.) ECCV 2012, Part VII. LNCS, vol. 7578, pp. 430–443. Springer, Heidelberg (2012)
7. Carreira, J., Sminchisescu, C.: Cpmc: Automatic object segmentation using constrained parametric min-cuts. TPAMI (2012)
8. Chai, Y., Lempitsky, V., Zisserman, A.: Symbiotic segmentation and part localization for fine-grained categorization. In: ICCV (2013)
9. Chatfield, K., Lempitsky, V., Vedaldi, A.: The devil is in the details: an evaluation of recent feature encoding methods. In: BMVC (2011)
10. Chen, Q., Song, Z., Hua, Y., Huang, Z., Yan, S.: Hierarchical matching with side information for image classification. In: CVPR (2012)
11. Cinbis, R.G., Verbeek, J., Schmid, C., et al.: Segmentation driven object detection with fisher vectors. In: ICCV (2013)
12. Dai, Q., Hoiem, D.: Learning to localize detected objects. In: CVPR (2012)
13. Dalal, N., Triggs, B.: Histograms of oriented gradients for human detection. In: CVPR (2005)
14. Divvala, S.K., Efros, A.A., Hebert, M.: How important are "deformable parts" in the deformable parts model? In: ECCV Workshops (2012)
15. Dong, J., Xia, W., Chen, Q., Feng, J., Huang, Z., Yan, S.: Subcategory-aware object classification. In: CVPR (2013)
16. Everingham, M., Van Gool, L., Williams, C.K.I., Winn, J., Zisserman, A.: The PASCAL Visual Object Classes Challenge (VOC2012) Results (2012)
17. Everingham, M., Van Gool, L., Williams, C.K.I., Winn, J., Zisserman, A.: The pascal visual object classes (voc) challenge. International Journal of Computer Vision 88(2), 303–338 (2010)
18. Fan, R.-E., Chang, K.-W., Hsieh, C.-J., Wang, X.-R., Lin, C.-J.: LIBLINEAR: A library for large linear classification. JMLR (2008)
19. Felzenszwalb, P., Girshick, R., McAllester, D., Ramanan, D.: Object Detection with Discriminatively Trained Part-Based Models. TPAMI (2010)
20. Fidler, S., Mottaghi, R., Yuille, A., Urtasun, R.: Bottom-up segmentation for top-down detection. In: CVPR (2013)
21. Perronnin, F., Sánchez, J., Mensink, T.: Improving the Fisher Kernel for Large-Scale Image Classification. In: Daniilidis, K., Maragos, P., Paragios, N. (eds.) ECCV 2010, Part IV. LNCS, vol. 6314, pp. 143–156. Springer, Heidelberg (2010)

22. Girshick, R.B., Felzenszwalb, P., Mcallester, D.: Object detection with grammar models. In: NIPS (2011)
23. Gu, C., Arbeláez, P., Lin, Y., Yu, K., Malik, J.: Multi-component models for object detection. In: Fitzgibbon, A., Lazebnik, S., Perona, P., Sato, Y., Schmid, C. (eds.) ECCV 2012, Part IV. LNCS, vol. 7575, pp. 445–458. Springer, Heidelberg (2012)
24. Hariharan, B., Arbeláez, P., Bourdev, L., Maji, S., Malik, J.: Semantic contours from inverse detectors. In: ICCV (2011)
25. Hoiem, D., Chodpathumwan, Y., Dai, Q.: Diagnosing error in object detectors. In: Fitzgibbon, A., Lazebnik, S., Perona, P., Sato, Y., Schmid, C. (eds.) ECCV 2012, Part III. LNCS, vol. 7574, pp. 340–353. Springer, Heidelberg (2012)
26. Kumar, M.P., Ton, P.H.S., Zisserman, A.: Obj cut. In: CVPR (2005)
27. Ladický, L., Sturgess, P., Alahari, K., Russell, C., Torr, P.H.S.: What, where and how many? Combining object detectors and cRFs. In: Daniilidis, K., Maragos, P., Paragios, N. (eds.) ECCV 2010, Part IV. LNCS, vol. 6314, pp. 424–437. Springer, Heidelberg (2010)
28. Lempitsky, V., Kohli, P., Rother, C., Sharp, T.: Image segmentation with a bounding box prior. In: 2009 IEEE 12th International Conference on Computer Vision (2009)
29. Li, C., Parikh, D., Chen, T.: Extracting adaptive contextual cues from unlabeled regions. In: ICCV (2011)
30. Liu, H., Yan, S.: Robust graph mode seeking by graph shift. In: ICML (2010)
31. Lowe, D.G.: Distinctive image features from scale-invariant keypoints. IJCV (2004)
32. Mottaghi, R., Chen, X., Liu, X., Cho, N.G., Lee, S.W., Fidler, S., Urtasun, R., Yuille, A.: The role of context for object detection and semantic segmentation in the wild. In: CVPR (2014)
33. Parkhi, O.M., Vedaldi, A., Jawahar, C.V., Zisserman, A.: The truth about cats and dogs. In: ICCV (2011)
34. Russakovsky, O., Lin, Y., Yu, K., Fei-Fei, L.: Object-centric spatial pooling for image classification. In: Fitzgibbon, A., Lazebnik, S., Perona, P., Sato, Y., Schmid, C. (eds.) ECCV 2012, Part II. LNCS, vol. 7573, pp. 1–15. Springer, Heidelberg (2012)
35. Song, Z., Chen, Q., Huang, Z., Hua, Y., Yan, S.: Contextualizing object detection and classification. In: CVPR (2011)
36. Tighe, J., Lazebnik, S.: Finding things: Image parsing with regions and per-exemplar detectors. In: CVPR (2013)
37. Uijlings, J.R.R., van de Sande, K., Gevers, T., Smeulders, A.W.M.: Selective search for object recognition. IJCV (2013)
38. Xia, W., Domokos, C., Dong, J., Cheong, L.F., Yan, S.: Semantic segmentation without annotating segments (2013)
39. Yadollahpour, P., Batra, D., Shakhnarovich, G.: Discriminative re-ranking of diverse segmentations. In: CVPR (2013)
40. Yang, Y., Hallman, S., Ramanan, D., Fowlkes, C.C.: Layered object models for image segmentation. PAMI (2012)
41. Yu, C.N.J., Joachims, T.: Learning structural svms with latent variables. In: ICML (2009)
42. Yuen, J., Zitnick, C.L., Liu, C., Torralba, A.: A framework for encoding object-level image priors. Tech. rep., Microsoft Research Technical Report
43. Yuille, A.L., Rangarajan, A.: The concave-convex procedure. Neural Computation (2003)
44. Zhu, L., Chen, Y., Yuille, A.L., Freeman, W.T.: Latent hierarchical structural learning for object detection. In: CVPR (2010)

Foreground Consistent Human Pose Estimation Using Branch and Bound*

Jens Puwein[1], Luca Ballan[1], Remo Ziegler[2], and Marc Pollefeys[1]

[1] Department of Computer Science, ETH Zurich, Switzerland
[2] Vizrt

Abstract. We propose a method for human pose estimation which extends common unary and pairwise terms of graphical models with a global foreground term. Given knowledge of per pixel foreground, a pose should not only be plausible according to the graphical model but also explain the foreground well.

However, while inference on a standard tree-structured graphical model for pose estimation can be computed easily and very efficiently using dynamic programming, this no longer holds when the global foreground term is added to the problem.

We therefore propose a branch and bound based algorithm to retrieve the globally optimal solution to our pose estimation problem. To keep inference tractable and avoid the obvious combinatorial explosion, we propose upper bounds allowing for an intelligent exploration of the solution space.

We evaluated our method on several publicly available datasets, showing the benefits of our method.

1 Introduction

Single image human pose estimation has received a lot of attention over the past few years. The goal is to localize each body part of a human body in a given image. This allows for a higher level of understanding of the image itself and, potentially, it can be used to facilitate other complementary computer vision tasks like image segmentation, 3D reconstruction, activity recognition, and image retrieval.

In this paper, we aim at estimating the 2D locations of all the joints of a human body under uncontrolled imaging conditions. A common approach to this problem is to use tree-structured graphical models to represent the human pose as a set of joints, or as a set of limbs, linked by edges representing bones or kinematic constraints between limbs, respectively [4,25].

While inference in these models can be carried out very efficiently using dynamic programming [25], they lack the possibility of considering global information depending on all the body parts at the same time. An example of such a scenario is when per pixel foreground probabilities of the given image are available. To account for this additional information, the pose should not only be

---

* Electronic supplementary material - Supplementary material is available in the online version of this chapter at http://dx.doi.org/10.1007/978-3-319-10602-1_21. Videos can also be accessed at http://www.springerimages.com/videos/978-3-319-10601-4

D. Fleet et al. (Eds.): ECCV 2014, Part V, LNCS 8693, pp. 315–330, 2014.
© Springer International Publishing Switzerland 2014

plausible with respect to the graphical model, but also explain the foreground. Therefore a more complex inference model needs to be used, which besides the common unary and pairwise terms also includes a global foreground term favoring solutions explaining the given foreground information.

In order to guarantee the global optimality of our solutions, we propose to optimize the model using a branch and bound based algorithm [10]. However, despite the fact that branch and bound intelligently explores only the promising regions of the solution space, it can be prohibitively slow since this space is actually the Cartesian product of all the domains of each individual unknown, and hence it grows exponentially with the number of unknowns. To keep our inference computationally tractable, we propose a set of upper bounds specifically designed for our pose estimation problem, and a way to decouple the estimation of rarely overlapping limbs while still maintaining the global optimality.

The performance of the proposed method was evaluated on four publicly available datasets (KTH, Parse, Leeds and Buffy [24,25,6,5]), showing the potential improvements achieved by our method.

2   Related Work

One of the most common and efficient ways of estimating a human pose from a single image is to formulate the problem as an inference on a tree-structured graphical model, where nodes express the position, the orientation, and the scale of each body limb [4] or the position of each body joint [25], and where edges between nodes correspond to kinematic constraints between limbs or to bones between joints. While inference on such models can be performed exactly and very efficiently using dynamic programming, it fails to capture some higher level dependencies that can occur between limbs, for instance when these are overlapping in the image space. This problem has been addressed by including occlusion terms [11,18] or repulsive edges [2]. A solution can be obtained through Gibbs sampling [11] or by using a loopy graphical model and loopy belief propagation [18,2]. Loopy models can also be expressed as an ensemble of tree-structured models by enforcing the equality of corresponding nodes in the different trees, as proposed by Sapp et al. [17]. In their work, different levels of agreement are proposed. For the full agreement between all submodels, convergence is not guaranteed. Another way of dealing with loopy models is branch and bound, which leads to a globally optimal solution and has been shown to be efficient [19,22,20]. Going beyond local reasoning, Kohli et al. [7] simultaneously solve for human pose and segmentation using dynamic graph cuts. Their algorithm, however, is susceptible to local minima and requires a good initialization of the pose. To solve for a model including global terms, sampling techniques are a popular choice. Zhang et al. [26] propose a data-driven Markov Chain Monte Carlo framework using a tree-based grammar to explore the space of human poses, trying to globally explain the foreground regions and the edges as well as possible while trying to fulfill body constraints. Similarly, Rauschert and Collins [15] use a data-driven, coarse-to-fine Metropolis Hastings sampling scheme also incorporating the likelihood of all image pixels and the domain knowledge in the proposal function.

Instead of relying on the maximum a posteriori (MAP) estimate of a tree structured model, Park and Ramanan [12] propose to infer the N-best solutions according to a tree structured model. Assuming that the correct pose is among the N best, further more expensive processing is applied to determine the correct solution. Starting from this idea, Vahid and Sullivan [24] extract the N-best poses and rerank them using an SVM-Rank formulation including a global segmentation term. Along the same paradigm, Ladicky et al. [8] introduce a joint pixel-wise and part-wise formulation. First, poses from the set of the N-best poses are added iteratively as long as it decreases the cost. Then, for all the added poses, each pixel is assigned to a person and to a body part. Their approach can deal with multiple people and missing/occluded body parts.

The approach presented in this paper builds on the model introduced by Yang and Ramanan [25]. However, please note that our method is not constrained to this model and any other efficient graphical model can be easily used in its place. A global segmentation term is added to this model, similarly to the work of Vahid and Sullivan [24]. However, differently from their approach, we propose to rely on a branch and bound optimization technique to avoid the premature selection of the N-best solutions, and hence to guarantee the optimal solution. The guarantee of global optimality differentiates our approach from sampling based techniques like [26,15].

3   Our Approach

3.1   Standard Model

We build upon the tree structured graphical model introduced by Yang and Ramanan [25], consisting of 14 joints as shown in Figure 1(a). Differently from them however, we consider an additional joint for the lower end of the spine between the left and the right hip joint, and define the torso as the body part identified by this new joint and the bottom of the head. Together with the edges of the human kinematic chain, these 15 joints, depicted in Figure 1(b), define a tree $G = (V, E)$ with nodes V and edges E. For each joint $i \in V$, let l_i identify its (x, y)-position in the image space, and let $t_i \in \{1, ..., T_i\}$ denote its type. The type essentially captures the relative orientation of a joint with respect to its parent in the tree model. Different orientations lead to different appearances. The appearance of each type t_i is modeled using a HOG descriptor [1], describing the distribution of image gradients in a local region. Let $\phi(I, l_i, t_i)$ denote the descriptor of joint i with type t_i extracted at location l_i in image I. Pairwise costs are given by a deformation model favoring frequently encountered relative positions of connected parts i and j. The corresponding feature vector $\psi(l_i, l_j)$ is given as $[(x_i - x_j), (x_i - x_j)^2, (y_i - y_j), (y_i - y_j)^2]^T$, encoding the differences in x- and y-coordinates, respectively. $\psi(l_i, l_j)$ is weighted differently for each type, providing a link between the appearance of a part and its relative location w.r.t. to its parent. Bias terms $b_i^{t_i}$ and $b_{i,j}^{t_i, t_j}$ capture the probabilities of encountering specific parts and types and pairs of parts and types. After adding the bias

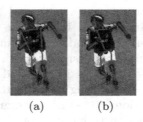

(a)   (b)

Fig. 1. (a) The standard model with 14 joints. (b) Our model with 15 joints.

terms and weighting the feature vectors from the appearance model ϕ and the deformation model ψ, we end up with the following scoring function S:

$$S(I,l,t) = \sum_{i \in V} \left(b_i^{t_i} + \phi(I,l_i,t_i)^T w_i^{t_i} \right) + \\ + \sum_{i,j \in E} \left(b_{i,j}^{t_i,t_j} + \psi(l_i,l_j)^T w_{i,j}^{t_i,t_j} \right) \tag{1}$$

Concatenating all the individual weight vectors and bias terms as w and subsuming all feature vectors within $\Phi(I,l,t)$, an equivalent linear model $S(I,l,t) = \Phi(I,l,t)^T w$ is obtained. Parameters w are learned using structured support vector machine [21,23]. For more details, please refer to [25].

3.2 Augmented Model

The scoring function $S(I,l,t)$ captures the local appearance and the deformations of a generic human body. However, in many scenarios, a good guess of the foreground shape of the body can be obtained from an image, for instance, through global color models, background subtraction or image/video matting. It is then desirable to find the pose which, globally, best accounts for the foreground shape, and is also plausible and faithful w.r.t. the scoring function $S(I,l,t)$.

Hence, given a per-pixel foreground estimate $FG(p)$, the pose should not only have a high score $S(I,l,t)$, but also explain foreground regions in $FG(p)$ as much as possible. To this end, we introduce a generative model Ω mapping joint positions l to sets of image points $\Omega(l)$ representing the human body silhouette in the image space in that specific pose. Each body part $(i,j) \in E$ is modeled as a rectangle $R(l_i,l_j)$ of predefined width, as illustrated in Figure 2(e). The silhouette $\Omega(l)$ is therefore defined as the union of all these rectangles, i.e. as $\Omega(l) = \bigcup_{i,j \in E} R(l_i,l_j)$. Using this generative model, the previously described scoring function $S(I,l,t)$ is augmented with a global foreground term $F(l)$ defined as

$$F(l) = \sum_{p \in \Omega(l)} FG(p), \tag{2}$$

where $FG(p) \in [0,1]$ is the per-pixel foreground estimate evaluated on a given pixel p, and it indicates the confidence value that that pixel belongs to the foreground.

Algorithm 1. Branch and bound inference

---

push pair $(\bar{E}(\mathcal{H}_0), \mathcal{H}_0)$ into queue and set $\hat{\mathcal{H}} = \mathcal{H}_0$
repeat
    split $\hat{\mathcal{H}} = \hat{\mathcal{H}}_1 \cup \hat{\mathcal{H}}_2$ with $\hat{\mathcal{H}}_1 \cap \hat{\mathcal{H}}_2 = \emptyset$
    push pair $(\bar{E}(\hat{\mathcal{H}}_1), \hat{\mathcal{H}}_1)$ into queue
    push pair $(\bar{E}(\hat{\mathcal{H}}_2), \hat{\mathcal{H}}_2)$ into queue
    pop $\hat{\mathcal{H}}$ with the highest score
until $|\hat{\mathcal{H}}| = 1$

The goal is now to maximize the following scoring function

$$\arg\max_{l,\, t} E(I, l, t) = S(I, l, t) + \lambda F(l), \tag{3}$$

where λ is a constant weighting the global foreground term w.r.t. $S(I, l, t)$.

Pose estimation aims at fitting a model, which typically has a predefined number of parts, into an image. Therefore, placing a part at a wrong location means that the foreground region which actually corresponds to that part is likely to not be explained (if that part does not overlap with another part), and hence lowering the overall score. In the absence of false foreground regions, regions wrongly labeled as background should not bias the model towards wrong solutions. However, false foreground regions might induce errors, since covering such a false region with a body part can increase the score E. This fact can be mitigated by using a conservative foreground mask.

3.3   Optimization

While inference on tree structured graphical models, like the one in Equation 1, can be performed very efficiently using dynamic programming, this no longer holds when a global term considering all the joints at the same time is added. This is the case with term $F(l)$ in Equation 3. Therefore, to optimize the new problem, a different optimization technique is required.

To this aim, we propose to use branch and bound on the set of possible joints configurations l, inspired by the work of Sun et al. [20], who applied branch and bound to loopy graphical models, and also inspired by Lampert et al. [9], who applied branch and bound to subwindow search. Apart from its generality, one of the advantages of branch and bound is that it guarantees to find the globally optimal solution.

We now describe how branch and bound is employed for our problem. The algorithm starts with the trivial set $\mathcal{H}_0$ defined as the set of all possible joint configurations hypotheses, $i.e. \mathcal{H}_0 = \prod_{i=1}^{15}\{1, ..., w_{image}\} \times \{1, ..., h_{image}\}$, the Cartesian product of the possible (x, y)-positions of all joints. Throughout the branch and bound iterations a priority queue is maintained where the considered sets of hypotheses are ordered in terms of a quality bound function $\bar{E}$ which upper bounds the maximum score E that any pose of a given set can possibly achieve. The best candidate $\hat{\mathcal{H}}$ of all the sets within the queue is considered for further processing. If $\hat{\mathcal{H}}$ consists of a single hypothesis, then the optimum is obtained. Otherwise, the set is split into two disjoint sets of hypotheses $\hat{\mathcal{H}}_1$ and $\hat{\mathcal{H}}_2$. Different branching strategies exist. We use a very simple strategy and split the hypotheses by splitting the largest remaining image coordinate interval of all joints in half. The new bounds $\bar{E}(\hat{\mathcal{H}}_1)$ and $\bar{E}(\hat{\mathcal{H}}_2)$ for those sets are computed, and both candidate sets are added to the priority queue. Since the bounds are tighter (smaller sets of hypotheses), it may be that none of these sets will be on top of the priority queue. The algorithm terminates when a single hypothesis is returned, and this hypothesis is guaranteed to be the global optimum. The advantage of using branch and bound is that it does not explore regions of the solution space which are not promising. The reader is referred to Algorithm 1 for a schematic illustration.

In order to guarantee the convergence of the branch and bound algorithm to the globally optimal solution, the quality bound function $\bar{E}$ needs to satisfy the following two conditions:

1. None of the hypotheses in $\mathcal{H}$ can achieve a higher score than $\bar{E}(\mathcal{H})$. More precisely, for each joint configuration $l \in \mathcal{H}$, and each type configuration t, $\bar{E}(\mathcal{H}) \geq E(I, l, t)$ has to hold.
2. If the set of hypotheses contains a single configuration, the bound has to be exact. More precisely, for each $l \in \mathcal{H}_0$, $\bar{E}(\{l\}) = \max_t E(I, l, t)$ has to hold.

3.4 Quality Bound Function $\bar{E}$

A valid quality bound function $\bar{E}$ can be defined in terms of multiple upper bounds $\bar{E}_i$ by always selecting the smallest value $\bar{E}_i$, i.e. $\bar{E} = \min_i \bar{E}_i$. It is easy to see that condition 1 is satisfied if every upper bound $\bar{E}_i$ satisfies condition 1, while condition 2 is satisfied if at least one of the bounds $\bar{E}_i$ satisfies condition 2. In the following sections, two different upper bounds $\bar{E}_1$ and $\bar{E}_2$ are introduced, each having its own advantages and disadvantages depending on the set of hypotheses being bounded. We combine these two upper bounds as $\bar{E} = \min(\bar{E}_1, \bar{E}_2)$.

Upper Bound $\bar{E}_1$. Let us first consider an alternative global foreground term $\tilde{F}$ defined as

$$\tilde{F} = \sum_{i,j \in E} Seg(l_i, l_j), \tag{4}$$

where each pairwise score $Seg(l_i, l_j)$ is defined as $\sum_{p \in R(l_i, l_j)} FG(p)$. Adding this new term $\tilde{F}$ to the scoring function $S(I, l, t)$ leads to the following scoring function

$$E_{pairwise}(I, l, t) = S(I, l, t) + \lambda \tilde{F}(l). \tag{5}$$

Differently from the original foreground term, the new $\tilde{F}$ maintains the tree structure of $S(I, l, t)$. Therefore inference on $E_{pairwise}(I, l, t)$ can be performed efficiently using dynamic programming.

However, $\tilde{F}$ counts foreground pixels multiple times if body parts overlap, and therefore we conclude that

$$E_{pairwise}(I, l, t) \geq E(I, l, t) \tag{6}$$

for every pose (l, t). In Equation 6, equality holds if and only if none of the rectangles defining the foreground silhouette overlap.

Hence, an upper bound for $E(I, l, t)$ can be defined as

$$\bar{E}_1(\mathcal{H}) = \max_{l \in \mathcal{H}, t} E_{pairwise}(I, l, t). \tag{7}$$

Due to the underlying tree structure, $\bar{E}_1(\mathcal{H})$ can be computed very efficiently by constraining the dynamic programming to the configurations in $\mathcal{H}$. In order to quickly evaluate $Seg(l_i, l_j)$ one can resort to integral images computed for rotated versions of the original foreground map $FG(p)$. In this way, each body part rectangle becomes an axis-aligned rectangle in the respective rotated foreground map. Integrals can then be evaluated using lookups in the corresponding integral images. In our implementation, integral image angles were quantized to steps of one degree.

Upper Bound $\bar{E}_2$. Since the new foreground term $\tilde{F}$ introduced in the previous section may count image foreground evidence multiple times, there is no guarantee that condition 2 holds in general for the upper bound $\bar{E}_1$. We therefore introduce a second upper bound $\bar{E}_2$ as follows.

Given the current set of hypotheses $\mathcal{H}$, a conservative estimate of the body silhouette is given by

$$\bar{\Omega}(\mathcal{H}) = \bigcup_{l \in \mathcal{H}} \Omega(l), \tag{8}$$

which equals to the union of all the silhouettes corresponding to each individual pose hypothesis. Hence, an upper bound for the original $F(l)$ is

$$\bar{F}(\mathcal{H}) = \sum_{p \in \bar{\Omega}(\mathcal{H})} FG(p). \tag{9}$$

Finally, we define the upper bound $\bar{E}_2$ as

$$\bar{E}_2(\mathcal{H}) = \bar{S}(I, \mathcal{H}) + \lambda \bar{F}(\mathcal{H}), \tag{10}$$

where $\bar{S}(I, \mathcal{H})$ is the maximum value achievable by $S(I, l, t)$ in $\mathcal{H}$, i.e., $\bar{S}(I, \mathcal{H}) = \max_{l \in \mathcal{H}, t} S(I, l, t)$. Due to the tree structured nature of $S(I, l, t)$, $\bar{S}(I, \mathcal{H})$ can be computed efficiently using dynamic programming on the set of hypotheses $\mathcal{H}$.

Note that the new upper bound $\bar{E}_2$ fulfills both condition 1 and 2 of the branch and bound algorithm.

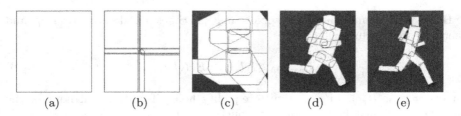

(a)   (b)   (c)   (d)   (e)

Fig. 2. Branch and bound: the algorithm iteratively narrows down the search space. White pixels indicate the set $\bar{\Omega}(\mathcal{H})$ of Equation 8. In the initial set of hypotheses, every joint can lie anywhere in the image (a). Once branch and bound terminates, the set of hypotheses corresponds to a single pose (e).

Combining $\bar{E}_1$ and $\bar{E}_2$. $\bar{E}_1$ and $\bar{E}_2$ are combined to form the upper bound $\bar{E} = \min(\bar{E}_1, \bar{E}_2)$. $\bar{E}$ fulfills conditions 1 and 2 of the branch and bound algorithm because both $\bar{E}_1$ and $\bar{E}_2$ fulfill condition 1 and $\bar{E}_2$ fulfills condition 2. While $\bar{E}_2$ alone would be sufficient in theory, $\bar{E}_1$ should be included in practice to decrease the computational complexity. Branch and bound terminates once the currently chosen set of hypotheses $\hat{\mathcal{H}}$ is of size one. Note that at this point, the upper bound equals the lower bound since they are both equal to the cost of the single remaining pose. The faster the upper bound decreases, the faster branch and bound terminates.

During the first branch and bound iterations, the chosen sets of hypotheses are large and lead to high values of $\bar{F}$. In these cases, $\bar{E}_1$ provides a much tighter bound than $\bar{E}_2$, and this holds until the double counting in $\bar{E}_1$ leads to $\bar{E}_1 > \bar{E}_2$. Therefore, at the beginning $\bar{E}_1$ quickly guides the branch and bound to a reasonable set of poses, and then $\bar{E}_2$ is active instead. An example of a branch and bound evolution is provided in Figure 2.

3.5   Efficient Inference

Sequential Branch and Bound. An alternative way to optimize $E(I, l, t)$ which does not guarantee global optimality is to apply the branch and bound algorithm sequentially on the tree structure. More precisely, the torso and the head are first inferred jointly (see Figure 3(c)). Subsequently, head and torso are kept fixed, and the legs are inferred (see Figure 3(d)). Finally, head, torso and legs are kept fixed and the configuration of the arms is inferred (see Figure 3(e)). The whole process is summarized in Figure 3. The results obtained in our experiments (and reported in Section 4) suggest that the detection of the torso is the most reliable by far, and correct with a high probability. This justifies estimating the torso and the head first, followed by legs and arms. Legs and arms only seldom interfere with each other, suggesting that, given the torso and the head, their configuration may be inferred correctly using sequential branch and bound.

Decoupling of States. The observations made in the previous section lead us to consider an additional expedient to speed up the branch and bound algorithm

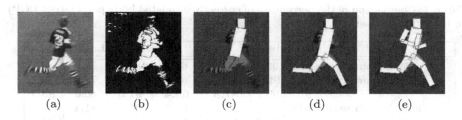

(a)   (b)   (c)   (d)   (e)

Fig. 3. Sequential branch and bound: (a) Input image. (b) Foreground probabilities $FG(p)$. In the sequential algorithm, torso and head are estimated first (c), followed by legs (d), and arms (e).

in a way that the global optimality property is preserved. As explained before, the complexity of our problem is caused by the global foreground term $F(l)$ which links all the body parts together, and makes them dependent on each other because of possible overlaps in the image space.

In a realistic scenario, however, not all the limbs overlap, and some of them do it very rarely. This is the case for head, arms and legs. Therefore, in most of the cases, it makes perfect sense to consider the head and the arms independently from the legs. We can exploit this natural characteristic of our solution space to speed up our global optimization. Basically, given a torso location, a very tight upper bound can be obtained by running branch and bound on the configurations of head and arms, and legs independently.

Therefore we first compute a lower bound for the scoring function $E(I, l, t)$ using the sequential approach described in the previous section. Then, for each torso location an upper bound is computed by maximizing $E_{pairwise}(I, l, t)$. Torso locations leading to upper bounds below the current lower bound can be safely discarded. For each remaining location of the torso a set of hypotheses is created and added to the priority queue. The already fixed torso in each set of hypotheses decouples upper and lower body to a large extent.

4 Results

The proposed method was tested on four publicly available datasets, namely: the KTH dataset [24], the Parse dataset [25], the Leeds dataset [6] and the Buffy dataset [5]. The KTH dataset consists of 771 images, where the first 180 images were used for training and the remaining 591 images were used for testing. The images show football players in different poses commonly observable in TV broadcasts. The Parse dataset instead consists of 305 images, where the first 100 images were used for training and the remaining 205 images were used for testing. The images show a wide variety of poses in unconstrained outdoor settings, similar to the Leeds dataset, which consists of 1000 training images and 1000 test images. The Buffy dataset is limited to the upper body and shows scenes from different episodes of the TV show 'Buffy'; 472 images were used for training and 276 for testing.

Table 1. Comparison of the percentage of correctly estimated body parts (strict PCP) on the **KTH** dataset

Method	Head	Torso	U. Arms	L. Arms	U. Legs	L. Legs	Total
[25], 26 parts	91.2	99.7	87.2	60.7	85.0	73.3	80.3
[25], 29 parts	91.7	**99.8**	85.2	62.8	85.8	73.9	80.7
[24]	91.7	99.7	**87.8**	**63.4**	**91.5**	80.0	**83.7**
Sequential BB (26 parts)	90.9	99.7	87.1	62.2	**91.5**	**81.1**	83.4
Sequential BB (29 parts)	91.5	**99.8**	84.8	59.7	90.1	79.3	81.9
Global BB (29 parts)	**92.2**	**99.8**	84.2	61.7	91.4	80.2	82.7

Table 2. Comparison of the percentage of correctly estimated body parts (strict PCP) on the **Parse** dataset

Method	Head	Torso	U. Arms	L. Arms	U. Legs	L. Legs	Total
[25], 26 parts	84.9	89.8	61.5	39.8	75.4	68.0	66.4
[25], 29 parts	84.9	87.8	59.0	36.8	77.6	70.5	66.0
[8]	75.1	83.9	56.8	33.9	71.0	63.9	61.0
[14]	**86.3**	**93.2**	**63.4**	**48.8**	77.1	68.0	**69.4**
Sequential BB	83.4	86.3	60.5	38.8	79.8	72.7	67.3
Global BB	**86.3**	92.7	59.8	40.0	**81.0**	**73.4**	68.7

Table 3. Comparison of the percentage of correctly estimated body parts (loose PCP) on the **Buffy** dataset

Method	Head	Torso	U. Arms	L. Arms	Total
[25], 21 parts	97.5	97.8	93.1	66.0	85.6
[8]	**100.0**	**100.0**	**97.5**	**75.4**	**90.9**
Global BB	**100.0**	**100.0**	95.6	71.5	89.0

Table 4. Comparison of the percentage of correctly estimated body parts (strict PCP) on the **Leeds** dataset

Method	Head	Torso	U. Arms	L. Arms	U. Legs	L. Legs	Total
[25], 29 parts, 12 types	80.1	84.8	54.0	38.0	71.5	66.5	62.5
[3]	80.1	86.5	56.5	37.4	74.9	69.4	64.3
[14]	**85.6**	**88.7**	**61.5**	**44.9**	**78.8**	**73.4**	**69.2**
Global BB, 29 parts, 12 types	80.0	86.6	53.8	38.8	75.4	70.0	64.3

Each test image is first pre-processed in order to estimate the per-pixel foreground confidence map $FG(p)$. To this aim, the standard tree-structured model of Yang and Ramanan [25] is used to retrieve an estimate of the pose. Subsequently, a mask around this estimate is created by dilating the convex hull of the estimated joints positions. In the end, grabcut [16] is initialized by this mask and used to obtain the foreground map $FG(p)$. Note that in many scenarios where information about foreground and/or background is given a priori, a better segmentation can be obtained. For the Buffy dataset, segmentations provided by [8] were used.

To increase the expressiveness of the original model $S(I, l, t)$ in Equation 1, 14 auxiliary joints are added to the graph G. This is coherent to what is also done in [25], and the main purpose is to provide appearance models also to the central part of each body limb. We do not branch on these additional unknowns. On the contrary, branch and bound is still run only on the (2x15)-dimensional solution space described before, and the positions of these auxiliary joints are estimated during the maximization procedures in $\bar{E}_1$ and $\bar{E}_2$.

To quantitatively evaluate the results obtained using our approach, the percentage of parts being correctly detected (PCP) was used [5]. Note that with the exception of the Buffy dataset, we use the strict PCP measure, not the loose PCP. In the strict version, if the maximum difference between the locations of two connected joints and the corresponding ground truth locations is less than 50% of the length of the corresponding body part, the location of that part is considered to be correctly estimated. In the loose version used for Buffy, not the maximum, but the average distance is considered. More details on this measure can be found in [13]. Notice that [24] used a different evaluation criterion for KTH.

Table 1, Table 2, Table 3 and Table 4 report the results obtained on all datasets by our branch and bound approach and the approaches proposed in [24], [8] and [25], where available. Note that these methods, including ours, use the model introduced by Yang and Ramanan as the underlying model. Additionally, we compare to state-of-the-arts results achieved by Eichner and Ferrari, and Pishchulin et al. [3,14]. In the KTH dataset, the tree structured model of [25] leads to a total score of 80.3% when 26 joints are used. The sequential branch and bound proposed in Section 3.5 outperforms this score by 3.1%, achieving 83.4%, similar to what is achieved using the re-ranking approach of [24]. Using the model consisting of 29 parts, our global branch and bound approach here scores 82.7%, outperforming the sequential version (81.9%). For this dataset, examples of successfully estimated poses are shown in Figure 4.

In the Parse dataset, the model of Yang and Ramanan achieves a score of 66.0% for the model with 29 joints. Our global branch and bound approach instead is able to achieve a score of 68.7%. Figure 5 shows some examples of correctly estimated poses compared with the ones obtained using [25] (29 parts). Figure 6, instead, shows failure cases on both methods. Although our approach is not able to detect the correct pose, its results are closer to the actual solution than the ones obtained using [25]. Figure 7 shows some more failure cases which might be caused by a wrong foreground map.

The loose PCP measure is commonly used for the Buffy dataset. We achieve 89.0% and perform 3.4% better than our baseline implementation of [25]. Note the significant increase in the detection of the lower arms, also shown qualitatively in Figure 8. The method of Ladicky et al. [8] performs very well on the Buffy dataset, but seems to have some shortcomings on the Parse dataset.

Fig. 4. KTH Dataset: The top row shows the results of the inference in the standard tree model [25]. The bottom row displays the results obtained using the proposed branch and bound algorithm.

Fig. 5. Parse Dataset: Comparison between the results obtained using the approach of Yang and Ramanan [25] (top row), and the results obtained using our approach (bottom row).

Fig. 6. Parse Dataset: Failure cases for both [25] and our global branch and bound approach

Fig. 7. Parse Dataset: Failure cases due to segmentation errors

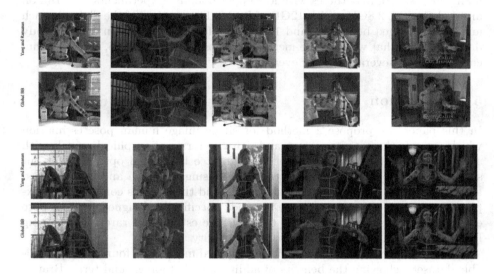

Fig. 8. Buffy Dataset: Comparison between the results obtained using the approach of Yang and Ramanan [25] (top row), and the results obtained using our approach (bottom row).

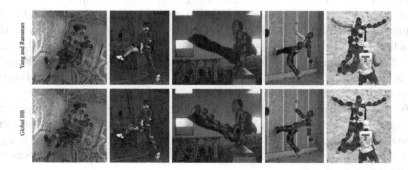

Fig. 9. Leeds Dataset: Comparison between the results obtained using the approach of Yang and Ramanan [25] (top row), and the results obtained using our approach (bottom row).

For all datasets observer centric labeling was used for training and testing. This means that the right arm and the right leg of a back facing person are labeled as left arm and left leg and vice versa.

The worst-case runtime complexity for our approach is exponential in the number of states. This happens when branch and bound degenerates to exhaustive search and the algorithm tries all the possible combinations of part positions. In practice, however, branch and bound terminates much earlier because only promising sets of hypotheses are divided further, ignoring and never exploring many large sets of hypotheses with low upper bounds. Experiments were run on an Intel Core i7, 2.8GHz, with 12GB of RAM. The runtime of the global branch and bound ranged between 2 and 10 minutes for most images in the full body datasets. Note that without the methods proposed in Section 3.5, the algorithm can take up to several hours or even days.

5   Conclusion

In this paper, we propose a method for single image human pose estimation which extends the common unary and pairwise terms of graphical models with a global foreground term. In order to guarantee the global optimality of our solutions, we propose to optimize the model using a branch and bound based algorithm. To keep inference tractable and avoid the obvious combinatorial explosion, we propose a set of upper bounds specifically designed for our pose estimation problem, and a way to decouple the estimate of rarely overlapping limbs while still maintaining the global optimality.

We evaluated the performance of the proposed method on four publicly available datasets, showing the benefits of adding a global foreground term. Branch and bound guarantees the best solution according to the specified model. Additionally, we show quantitative results of a sequential version of the proposed branch and bound algorithm.

In conclusion, the global foreground term improves the results when a reasonable segmentation or confidence map for the foreground $F(l)$ is available. Our automatic estimation of $F(l)$ works reasonably well in the tested datasets. However, when it fails, it influences the outcome of the pose estimation algorithm. Figure 7 shows some failure cases due to segmentation errors. Nevertheless, in many scenarios a good foreground model can be easily estimated and therefore we expect this algorithm to work well in such situations.

In future work, we plan to address pose estimation given multiple images of the same person either from multiple views or several neighboring frames of a video sequence. Encouraging consistency between several such input images suggests new challenges in terms of efficient inference and is an encouraging direction for more robustness.

Acknowledgments. This project is supported by a grant of CTI Switzerland, the 4DVideo ERC Starting Grant Nr. 210806 and the SNF Recording Studio Grant.

References

1. Dalal, N., Triggs, B.: Histograms of oriented gradients for human detection. In: Proc. CVPR (2005)
2. Eichner, M., Marin-Jimenez, M., Zisserman, A., Ferrari, V.: 2d articulated human pose estimation and retrieval in (almost) unconstrained still images. In: IJCV (2012)
3. Eichner, M., Ferrari, V.: Appearance sharing for collective human pose estimation. In: Lee, K.M., Matsushita, Y., Rehg, J.M., Hu, Z. (eds.) ACCV 2012, Part I. LNCS, vol. 7724, pp. 138–151. Springer, Heidelberg (2013)
4. Felzenszwalb, P.F., Huttenlocher, D.P.: Pictorial structures for object recognition. IJCV (2005)
5. Ferrari, V., Marin-Jiminez, M., Zisserman, A.: Progressive search space reduction for human pose estimation. In: Proc. CVPR (2008)
6. Johnson, S., Everingham, M.: Clustered pose and nonlinear appearance models for human pose estimation. In: Proc. BMVC (2010)
7. Kohli, P., Rihan, J., Bray, M., Torr, P.H.S.: Simultaneous segmentation and pose estimation of humans using dynamic graph cuts. IJCV (2008)
8. Ladicky, L., Torr, P.H.S., Zisserman, A.: Human pose estimation using a joint pixel-wise and part-wise formulation. In: Proc. CVPR (2013)
9. Lampert, C.H., Blaschko, M.B., Hofmann, T.: Efficient subwindow search: a branch and bound framework for object localization. TPAMI (2009)
10. Land, A.H., Doig, A.G.: An automatic method of solving discrete programming problems. Econometrica (1960)
11. Mori, G.: Guiding model search using segmentation. In: Proc. ICCV (2005)
12. Park, D., Ramanan, D.: N-best maximal decoders for part models. In: Proc. ICCV (2011)
13. Pishchulin, L., Jain, A., Andriluka, M., Thormaehlen, T., Schiele, B.: Articulated people detection and pose estimation: Reshaping the future. In: Proc. CVPR (2012)
14. Pishchulin, L., Andriluka, M., Gehler, P., Schiele, B.: Strong appearance and expressive spatial models for human pose estimation. In: Proc. ICCV (2013)
15. Rauschert, I., Collins, R.T.: A generative model for simultaneous estimation of human body shape and pixel-level segmentation. In: Fitzgibbon, A., Lazebnik, S., Perona, P., Sato, Y., Schmid, C. (eds.) ECCV 2012, Part V. LNCS, vol. 7576, pp. 704–717. Springer, Heidelberg (2012)
16. Rother, C., Kolmogorov, V., Blake, A.: 'grabcut' - interactive foreground extraction using iterated graph cuts. In: Proc. of ACM SIGGRAPH (2004)
17. Sapp, B., Weiss, D., Taskar, B.: Parsing human motion with stretchable models. In: CVPR (2011)
18. Sigal, L., Black, M.J.: Measure locally, reason globally: Occlusion-sensitive articulated pose estimation. In: Proc. CVPR (2006)
19. Singh, V.K., Nevatia, R., Huang, C.: Efficient inference with multiple heterogeneous part detectors for human pose estimation. In: Daniilidis, K., Maragos, P., Paragios, N. (eds.) ECCV 2010, Part III. LNCS, vol. 6313, pp. 314–327. Springer, Heidelberg (2010)
20. Sun, M., Telaprolu, M., Lee, H., Savarese, S.: An efficient branch-and-bound algorithm for optimal human pose estimation. In: Proc. CVPR (2012)
21. Taskar, B., Guestrin, C., Koller, D.: Max-margin markov networks. In: Proc. NIPS (2003)

22. Tian, T., Sclaroff, S.: Fast globally optimal 2d human detection with loopy graph models. In: Proc. CVPR (2010)
23. Tsochantaridis, I., Hofmann, T., Joachims, T., Altun, Y.: Support vector machine learning for interdependent and structured output spaces. In: Proc. ICML (2004)
24. Vahid, K., Sullivan, J.: Using richer models for articulated pose estimation of footballers. In: Proc. BMVC (2012)
25. Yang, Y., Ramanan, D.: Articulated human detection with flexible mixtures of parts. TPAMI (2013)
26. Zhang, X., Li, C., Tong, X., Hu, W., Maybank, S., Zhang, Y.: Efficient human pose estimation via parsing a tree structure based human model. In: Proc. ICCV (2009)

Human Pose Estimation
with Fields of Parts

Martin Kiefel and Peter Vincent Gehler

Max Planck Institute for Intelligent Systems, Tübingen Germany

Abstract. This paper proposes a new formulation of the human pose estimation problem. We present the *Fields of Parts* model, a binary Conditional Random Field model designed to detect human body parts of articulated people in single images.

The Fields of Parts model is inspired by the idea of Pictorial Structures, it models local appearance and joint spatial configuration of the human body. However the underlying graph structure is entirely different. The idea is simple: we model the presence and absence of a body part at every possible position, orientation, and scale in an image with a binary random variable. This results into a vast number of random variables, however, we show that approximate inference in this model is efficient. Moreover we can encode the very same appearance and spatial structure as in Pictorial Structures models.

This approach allows us to combine ideas from segmentation and pose estimation into a single model. The Fields of Parts model can use evidence from the background, include local color information, and it is connected more densely than a kinematic chain structure. On the challenging Leeds Sports Poses dataset we improve over the Pictorial Structures counterpart by 6.0% in terms of Average Precision of Keypoints.

Keywords: Human Pose Estimation, Efficient Inference.

1 Introduction

In this work we consider the challenging problem of human pose estimation from a single image. This task serves as a crucial pre-requisite step to many high level vision applications, for example human action recognition [16], and natural human computer interfaces [28]. Therefore, it is among the most studied problems in the field of computer vision.

The main difficulty of pose estimation is the weak local appearance evidence for every single body part. While heads nowadays can reliably be detected, localization of general body parts such as arms, legs, or hands remain challenging. Several factors complicate detection: fore-shortening and self-occlusion of parts; different clothing and light environments lead to variability in appearance; some parts might just be a few pixels in size which makes it hard to encode them robustly.

Consequently, the pre-dominant method for this problem are approaches that model both appearance and part configuration jointly. This idea of combining

D. Fleet et al. (Eds.): ECCV 2014, Part V, LNCS 8693, pp. 331–346, 2014.
© Springer International Publishing Switzerland 2014

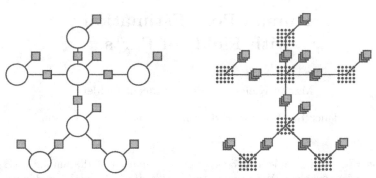

Fig. 1. From Pictorial Structure models (left) to the Fields of Parts model (right). For each body part in the PS model we introduce a field of binary random variables, one for each of its states. When two body parts are connected by a pairwise factor (left) we densely connect the corresponding fields (right), illustrated by the stacked factors. The binary variables 0/1 encode absence or presence of a body part at its location and type (rotation). This is a dense graph and thus contains multiple cycles. This is an illustration with six parts, resp. fields, only.

part appearance evidence with spatial configuration for part relations dates back to [13] and was popularized as a CRF model by [11]. The CRF approach of [11] elegantly expresses pose estimation in a statistical structured prediction problem and introduces with the distance transform an efficient exact inference technique. This model serves as a basis for many variants and thus resulted in significant empirical improvements on increasingly challenging datasets [24,12,17].

Most work focuses on the main dimensions of the pose estimation problem: use of discriminative appearance information ([25,22,23,33,34,10,9] and many more) and stronger models for the spatial body configuration [27,29,22]. Examples of better appearance models are the local image conditioned features used in [25], the use of mid-level representations via Poselets [14,3,22], or semantic segmentation information to include background evidence [10,31,20,4]. The spatial model of [11] is a tree, a limitation that obviously does not reflect dependencies in the human body, for example color relation between left and right limbs. This has been addressed by introducing loopy versions [29] or regression onto part positions directly [6,15]. Another dimension is inference efficiency, richer appearance features typically requires more computations, some approaches perform well but are slow. The same is true for changes in the graph, giving up the tree structure usually results in more involved inference techniques. To speed up inference in pose estimation models enabling the use of richer appearance or graph structure methods like cascading [26] or coarse-to-fine search [25] have been proposed.

In this work we propose the Fields of Parts (FoP) model; a re-formulation of the human pose estimation problem. The FoP model offers a different view on all three dimensions – appearance, structure, and inference. It is inspired by the Pictorial Structures (PS) model, but has different semantics which lead to interesting modeling possibilities. The main idea behind this model is simple: the presence or absence of a body part at every possible location, orientation, and scale of a body part is modelled using a binary random variable. This results in a huge number of variables, seemingly complicating the matter.

In this paper we show that this model is tractable and present a way to perform efficient marginal inference and more importantly, that this re-parametrization offers new and interesting modeling possibilities. In particular it allows to carry over many ideas from semantic segmentation. We achieve this without the need to explicitly include a segmentation layer or rely on a pose estimation pipeline as a pre-processing step in order to generate body part proposals. The FoP model provides a full interpretation of the image: the presence of a body is explained at every position simultaneously while including evidence from the background without the need for explicit segmentation variables. The graph topography is flexible, we are not bound to a tree structure with restricted potentials in order to use the distance transform. Nevertheless, it does not enforce the detection of a single person in the image anymore. Depending on the application domain this might be advantageous or unwanted.

The marginal inference technique that we propose, namely mean field, is approximate. However, we reason that this is not a severe limitation. We account for the approximation already during training time using Back-Mean-Field learning [7,8]. The inference complexity dependends only linearly on any important dimension of the model: number of part-connections, number of feature dimensions, and size of the image. Furthermore it is amendable to parallelization.

The FoP model is built upon advances from three separate domains: efficient inference for segmentation [18], parameter estimation with approximate inference [7,8], and expressive PS models [34]. We report on modeling, technical, and experimental contributions:

- A reformulation of the human pose estimation problem. This opens up new modelling flexibility and provides a new viewpoint on this well-studied problem (model in Sect. 3.1, discussion in Sect. 3.2).
- An generalization of the inference algorithm from [18]. This makes it possible to use efficient mean field inference in the FoP formulation (Sect. 4.1).
- A new estimator that is tailored to pose prediction using a binary CRF formulation. (Sect. 4.2).
- Experimentally, we demonstrate that the FoP model with the same set of parameters as [34] achieves a performance increase of 6.0% on the LSP dataset, novel variants improve this even further (Sect. 5).

2   Related Work

We adapt the part based formulation from [34] since it offers a good trade-off between flexibility and efficiency. The authors propose to model a body as a collection of body joints, with each body joint being represented as a point in the 2D plane for its position, and a multinomial type variable that accounts for appearance variations. For the FoP model we enumerate all those states and model each one with a binary random variable. A different way to model body part appearance is by a representation as boxes with a center, orientation and scale, e.g.[2]. The model in [23] combines both the body part and body joint representations into a single joint one. The authors report improved performance, however their proposed method has a runtime of several minutes per image. Other approaches introduce more connections in the factor graph to account for the dependencies of body parts not reflected in the tree structure. One such example is [29] that combines a densely connected model with efficient branch and bound inference.

PS models can be understood as body pose detectors that only model the foreground object while largely ignoring background information. Several authors used segmentation information within their pose estimation model [12,25], this typically complicates the inference process. Therefore, these methods either use sequential algorithms [12] or CRF inference methods with elaborate search based methods [26]. Another way to include background evidence is to explicitly include a separate segmentation layer [20,4,31,32]. Most of these works following this choice have in common that they rely on a separate pose estimation algorithm (e.g.,[2,33]) to retrieve a number of candidate poses. Based on these proposals a CRF structure is then instantiated with factors for segmentation and selector variables for the proposals. Additional CRF layers could be foreground/background segmentation [32], additionally body part segmentation [20], and combination with stereo estimation [31]. Finally, the authors of [10] exploit commonalities in the background appearance within a dataset by fitting a separate color likelihood term to an estimate of background on.

For inference and learning we build upon the advances from [18] that we generalize so it can be used for our purpose. The authors show that mean field inference in densely connected models with Gaussian pairwise potentials reduces to an application of bilateral filtering. The other connection that we draw is to marginal based learning techniques advocated in [7,8]. Domke argues that learning should both take the desired loss function as well as the approximate nature of the inference procedure into account. Our model implements this using Back-Mean-Field learning, also mentioned in [19].

3   Fields of Parts

The flexible body part model of [34] serves as the starting point for our derivation. The authors of [34] propose to model each body part p as a random variable $Y^p = (U, V, T)$ with three values: (U, V) for the position in the image I and $T \in \{1, \ldots, K\}$ a latent type variable. The idea of introducing T is to capture appearance differences of a part due to fore-shortening, rotation, etc, while at the same time increasing the flexibility of the body configuration. We gather all possible states of Y^p in the set $\mathcal{Y}^p$, the entire body is then represented as the concatenation $Y = (Y^1, \ldots, Y^P)$. This PS model defines a Gibbs distribution $p(Y|I, \theta)$, where θ denotes the collection of all model parameters.

In this work we propose a different kind of parametrization. In this section we will introduce the model (Section 3.1) and discuss the gained flexibility that it offers (Section 3.2). The technical contributions on inference (Section 4.1), and learning (Section 4.2) that enable the use of this parametrization are the topic of Section 4.

3.1   Model

We parametrize the problem in the following way: For every part p and every possible state in $\mathcal{Y}^p$ we introduce a binary random variable $X_i^p, i = 1, \ldots, |\mathcal{Y}^p|$. Each such variable represents the presence $X_i^p = 1$ and absence $X_i^p = 0$ of a part at its location, type, and scale in the image. We refer to the collection of variables for a part $X^p = \{X_i^p\}_{i=1,\ldots,|\mathcal{Y}^p|}$ as a *field of parts*. With X we denote the collection of all variables for all parts. The total number of variables per part p is $|\mathcal{Y}^p|$, the total number for all parts $S = \sum_p |\mathcal{Y}^p|$, and thus the state space of X is of size 2^S. We do introduce all variables on different image scales but do not use a super-/sub-script, so as not to clutter the notation. Next, we discuss how to connect the variables in a meaningful way.

Energy. Given an image I and model parameters θ, we write the energy of a Gibbs distribution as the sum of unary and pairwise terms

$$E(x|I, \theta) = \sum_{p=1}^{P} \sum_{i=1}^{|\mathcal{Y}^p|} \Psi_{\text{unary}}(x_i^p|I, \theta) + \sum_{p \sim p'} \sum_{i=1}^{|\mathcal{Y}^p|} \sum_{j=1}^{|\mathcal{Y}^{p'}|} \Psi_{\text{pairwise}}(x_i^p, x_j^{p'}|I, \theta). \quad (1)$$

Note, that the neighborhood relationship is defined between different fields $p \sim p'$, for example wrist and elbow. Between any two neighbouring fields, all pairs of random variables $(X_i^p, X_j^{p'})$ are connected by a factor node. We illustrate the resulting cyclic CRF graph in Figure 1 for the case of kinematic chain connections $p \sim p'$ and six body parts.

Unary Factors. Local appearance of body parts is captured through the unary factors Ψ_{unary}. In the simplest case this might be a log-linear model

$$\Psi_{\text{unary}}(x_i^p|I, \theta) = \langle \theta_{\text{unary}}^p, \psi_i(I) \rangle.$$

Concretely, we use exactly the same factors as in [34] in order to make the models comparable: HOG [5] responses $\psi(I)$ and a linear filter θ_{unary}^p of size 5×5 at different scales of the image.

Pairwise Factors. The important piece of the FoP model are the pairwise connections. Their form needs to fulfill two requirements: encode a meaningful spatial configuration between neighboring fields, and allow for efficient approximate inference. We are inspired by the observation of [18]. In their work they show that mean field inference in densely connected models with Gaussian pairwise potentials can be implemented as a bilateral filtering. Since for this operation exist highly optimized algorithms [1], the approximate inference is efficient. The pairwise terms in the FoP model have the following form

$$\Psi_{\text{pairwise}}(x_i^p, x_j^{p'} | I, \theta) = \sum_m L_m(x_i^p, x_j^{p'})\, k_m^{p,p'}\left(f_m(i, p; I, \theta), f_m(j, p'; I, \theta); \theta\right) \qquad (2)$$

$$k_m^{p,p'}(f, f'; \theta) = \exp\left(-\frac{1}{2}(f - f' - \mu_m^{p,p'})^T (\Sigma_m^{p,p'})^{-1}(f - f' - \mu_m^{p,p'})\right). \qquad (3)$$

The key observation is that this allows to encode the same spatial relation between body part variables X_i^p and $X_i^{p'}$, as the PS model does for Y^p and $Y^{p'}$. To see this, let us take a closer look at Eq. (2). This potential is a linear combination of Gaussian kernels k_m weighted by a compatibility matrix L. Remember that all random variables are binary, thus L is of size 2×2. The Gaussian kernel function k measures the influence of two variables i, j on each other; it has a high value if variables i and j should be in agreement.

To encode the same spatial relationship as PS models we use the 2D positions of the states i as features $f(i, p; I, \theta)$. Consider two variables $X_i^p, X_j^{p'}$, and their 2D image positions. The two states with maximal influence on each other are those whose 2D position are offset by exactly $\mu_m^{p,p'}$. This influence decreases exponentially depending on the distance of two states i, j and the variance $\Sigma_m^{p,p'}$.

Note that a state i also includes the type/mixture component T. For every part there are as many random variables at the same 2D location as we have mixture components K in the model. For every type/type pair we could use a different offset and variance. Again to enable comparison we implement the choice made in [34], namely that the offset only depends on one of the two types (in [34] the child type determines the offset and variance). In summary the same kind of flexible body part configuration is represented in the FoP model. A minor difference is that here, we use Gaussian potentials, whereas in the PS model the spatial term is log-linear (without the exp in Eq. (3)).

3.2   Discussion

The parametrization of the FoP model allows to carry over ideas from semantic segmentation into the pose estimation problem.

It is important to note, that the Gaussian pairwise terms are more general than using only positional information. In fact we can use any features $f(i, p; I, \theta) \in \mathbb{R}^D$ to modulate the influence of two states on each other. For example, we can encode color by appending RGB values to the image locations, resulting in a bilateral kernel. This is in contrast to PS models [11,34,2] where extra local image evidence can not easily be included. The reason is inference time, in order to use the distance transform, the features have to lie on a grid, and for example RGB values do not. Without this restricted form of the features, the general sum product algorithm scales quadratically in the number of states.

We exploit this new possibilities in three different ways: including color information, using foreground/background segmentation of a person, and connecting the CRF more densely.[1]

Additionally to the between-fields connections, we also connect the variables within a single field p using as a pairwise factor

$$\Psi_{\text{pairwise}}(x_i^p, x_j^p | I, \theta) = L(x_i^p, x_j^p) k^p \left(f(i, p; I, \theta), f(j, p; I, \theta); \theta \right). \tag{4}$$

We set $L(x, x') = \delta_{x=0 \text{ and } x'=0}$ and use as features $f(i, p; I, \theta)$ the 2D position and RGB color in a 3×3 neighborhood around the position of i. This potential affects variables X_i^p, X_j^p that are near each other in the image *and similar* in color. For example a variable may be certain that it does not represent a certain body part, a patch in the sky that is blue and is smooth. The term of (4) is "encouraging" all other blue patches in the image (it is densely connected) to also be in state 0. In effect this propagates color background information in the image over the random variables. This is the same type of a bilateral kernel as used in segmentation methods [18,31], in this case it aids prediction of body parts without explicitly reason over segmentation.

Fields of Parts - Segmentation. As a second example, we include a segmentation prediction as extra image evidence into the pairwise terms. The decision tree implementation of [21] and its features are used to train a person/background classifier on the training images. From ground truth bounding box annotations we construct 0/1 segmentation masks for training. The final decision tree yields a score in $d_{u,v} \in [0, 1]$ for every position (u, v) in the image, namely, the fraction of person-pixels in the corresponding leaf. We then append this score to the spatial features to all states i at the corresponding position. This again results in a bilateral kernel and allows for propagation of information to be different inside or outside of the predicted segmentation.

Fields of Parts - Loopy. The CRF of the FoP model is a loopy graph already. In the upcoming section we will show that the inference complexity depends only linear on the number of field-field $p \sim p'$ connections. This allows us to connect the fields more densely than rather along the kinematic chain with only a modest increase in computational complexity. In this variant (*Fields of Parts - Loopy*) we introduce 10 more connections between parts that contain spatial information about each other, like left and right hip, etc.

Future Work. We mention some additional possibilities that we plan to investigate in future work. Beyond standard RGB, different texture and color information can be encoded in f. An interesting example is the mid-level representation used in [22]. The authors condition the pairwise terms of a PS model *globally* on reponses of a poselet detector [3] and report impressive performance

---

[1] The precise details of the variants are included in the appendix.

gains. With the FoP model this type of evidence can be included *locally*. A connection strength between variables can be modulated given that they are in mutual agreement with a poselet response at a corresponding position.

Another route is to combine the FoP model with the different body parameterization as a collection of sticks/card-boards. For example a "field of sticks" can be fused into the model in the very same way the body part fields are connected.

3.3   Comparison to Pictorial Structures

There are two main differences between the FoP model and the PS model concerning the semantic of their outputs. PS models explain the foreground, they represent a conditional distribution $p(y|I, \theta)$ over all possible body configurations. In contrast the FoP model explains the entire image $p(X|I, \theta)$, i.e. foreground and background. Hence, the FoP model is not just a relaxation of the PS model in the sense that we allow multiple detections for one part. Consider for this again Eq. (2). If at least one of the arguments x_i^p, $x_j^{p'}$ is assigned the label 0 for background then a non-trivial term is added to the total energy. Contrast this to the energy for the PS model where no such term exists[2]. This is much more in spirit of works that try to combine segmentation information into the pose estimation problem [4,10,31,20] but with the crucial difference that the FoP model is designed for pose estimation. It does not require a separate algorithm to generate part proposals, nor is an explicit segmentation layer needed.

Second, consider the case of multiple, including no persons in an image. What would the optimal distribution be? With no person in the image the best a PS model can do is to achieve a uniform distribution over the body poses, it has no notion of absent body parts. In the case of multiple persons the distribution becomes multi-modal. Consequently, the probability mass has to be distributed over different persons and thus the scores will have to decrease. A similar effect will happen if the image size is increased. This can be undesirable depending on the application, the score/probability of a body pose should not depend on the number of people in the image or its size. Therefore a detection step is a crucial pre-requisite for the PS model.

4   Learning and Inference

In this section we present the technical extension of [18] that enables efficient inference (Sect. 4.1) in this model. We then present an estimator tailored to the pose prediction problem with this binary CRF (Sect. 4.2).

4.1   Inference

Exact inference in the FoP model is unfortunately prohibitive due to the loopy structure of the factor graph. We resort to approximate inference, and in particular to a mean field approximation. With mean field the intractable distribution is replaced by a factorizing approximation Q, usually by the product of

---

[2] The comparison of the LP-formulations of the two models in the appendix shows another perspective of this.

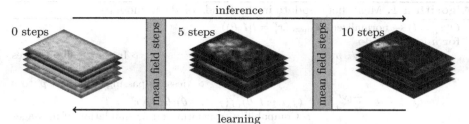

Fig. 2. Evolution of part fields over the filter steps of the mean field updates. For parameter estimation the FoP model builds the gradient w.r.t. the model parameters θ by backpropagating it through the filter steps of the mean field updates.

its marginals $Q(x|I,\theta) = \prod_i Q(x_i^p|I,\theta)$, that are then fit to yield a low KL divergence with the target distribution. Every binary state variable X_i^p gets its approximating probability distribution $Q(x_i^p)$. Note that by finding the factorizing distribution Q we gain all included state marginals of the X_i^p.

The authors of [18] have shown that the mean-field update equations in discrete CRF models with Gaussian pairwise potentials can be implemented by means of bilateral filtering. In the FoP model the mean field update equations can be derived to[3]

$$Q(x_i^p|I,\theta) \propto \exp(-\Psi_{\text{unary}}(x_i^p|I,\theta) - \sum_{p \sim p'} \sum_{l' \in \{0,1\}} \sum_m L_m(x_i^p,l')$$

$$\sum_{j=1}^{|\mathcal{Y}^{p'}|} k_m^{p,p'}(f(i,p;I,\theta),f(j,p';I,\theta);\theta)\, Q(x_j^{p'}=l'|I,\theta)). \tag{5}$$

This generalizes the results of [18] where there is no part connection relationship $p \sim p'$. In the update step Eq. (5) we can exploit the underlying structure of the factor graph to perform bilateral filtering of the two affected neighboring fields. There are two filtering operations – from p to p' and back – for every field connection $p \sim p'$. The full update algorithm is described in Algorithm 1.

As noted by the authors of [18] this block update scheme is not guaranteed to converge. In practice we have not seen any convergence problems for our model.

To come by the expensive operation of calculating the message from one part field p to another part field p', we also make use of an acceleration technique of the permutohedral lattice [1]. This reduces the computational cost to be linear in the number of states of the two involved fields in contrast to the quadratic cost in the number of states in a naive implementation. We loosen the probabilistic interpretation of the mean field update and allow the compability matrix $L^{p,p'}$ to differ for the messages passed from p to p' and vice-versa.

For images that contain a single person only we report, for each field separately, the state that is most probable to be of value 1,

$$\hat{i}^p = \underset{i \in \mathcal{Y}^p}{\text{argmax}}\, Q(x_i^p = 1|I,\theta). \tag{6}$$

---

[3] See appendix.

Algorithm 1. Mean field update in the Fields of Parts model

$Q(x_i^p = l) \leftarrow \text{normalize}(-\Psi_{\text{unary}}(x_i^p = l|I, \theta))$

for n iterations **do**

    $\tilde{Q}(x_i^p = l) \leftarrow 0, \forall i, p$ $\triangleright$ Initialize all messages

    for $p \sim p'$ **do**

                                    $\triangleright$ Message passing from part p' to p

        $\hat{Q}_{i,m}(l) \leftarrow \sum_{j=1}^{|\mathcal{Y}^{p'}|} k_m^{p,p'}(f(i,p;I,\theta), f(j,p';I,\theta); \theta)\, Q(x_j^{p'} = l)$

                        $\triangleright$ Compability transform and accumulation of messages

        $\tilde{Q}(x_i^p = l) \leftarrow \tilde{Q}(x_i^p = l) + \sum_{l' \in \{0,1\}} \sum_m L_m(l, l')\hat{Q}_{i,m}(l')$

    end for

    $Q(x_i^p = l) \leftarrow \text{normalize}(\exp(-\Psi_{\text{unary}}(x_i^p = l|I, \theta) - \tilde{Q}(x_i^p = l)))$

end for

Nevertheless, there is no reason not to use a different prediction rule, e.g. in the case of multiple persons in one image. The complexity of the inference algorithm scales very favorably, namely linear in every dimension: number of mean field iterations, number of Gaussian kernels m, linear in the number of pairwise features D, linear in the number of part-part connections $p \sim p'$. Furthermore the model is amendable to easy parallelizations, e.g. by calculating the messages sent by the part fields in parallel. In our current CPU implementation the model requires about $6s$ for inference on a single level in an image of size 100×200.

4.2 Parameter Estimation

Part annotations are available as 2D positions (u, v) of the separate body parts which needs to be translated into the binary CRF formulation. Using K types for part p, the FoP model contains K random variable that represent the position (u, v), one for each type. It is desirable to find parameters θ that yield a high probability for at least one of those variables being in state 1. Here we construct an max-margin objective that is tailored to pose estimation: the predicted state $\hat{i}^p$ (Eq. 6) should be at the correct image position. There is no loss for background states in pose estimation, and thus they are not included in the objective.

Prediction Loss. In practice the performance of body pose models is measured using loss functions that ideally represent the desired output of the systems. For the parametrization of body parts as 2D positions the Average Precision of Keypoints (APK) measure is natural, [34] refers to it as the "golden standard". A prediction is considered correct if it falls inside a small region of the annotated point. To be precise, for a given part at the annotated location i_*, the loss for a prediction $\hat{i}$ is defined to be

$$\Delta^p(i_*, \hat{i}) = I(\|i_* - \hat{i}\| > \alpha \max(h, w)), \tag{7}$$

where I stands for the indicator function. The loss depends on the size of the object to be found (namely height h and width w) and a threshold α to restrict the region where we count a part as detected. The authors of [34] choose α to be equal to 0.1 on full body pose estimation tasks.

Objective Function. We use a structured maximum-margin estimator [30] to encourage the model to fit parameters that lead to a low loss Δ^p. Similar to the loss we decompose the optimization problem along the parts

$$\text{minimize}_{\theta,\xi^p \geq 0} \sum_p \ell(\xi^p) + C(\theta) \tag{8}$$

$$\text{sb.t. } s_{i_*}^p - s_i^p \geq \Delta^p(i_*, i) - \xi^p \ \forall p, \forall i \in \mathcal{Y}^p \tag{9}$$

$$s_i^p := \sigma^{-1}(Q(x_i^p = 1)|\theta). \tag{10}$$

Equation (9) demands a margin of $\Delta^p(i_*, i)$ between the score of the annotated state i_* and every other state i. The score s_i^p is the result of an inverse sigmoid function[4] applied to the probability of the positive state of a state variable X_i^p. We allow the constraint to be violated by the slack variable ξ^p. The objective (8) consists of a Hingle-loss ℓ and a regularizer C to prevent over-fitting to training data. In our experiments we set C to be the squared norm of the parameter vector θ and weight the result with 0.001. We did not change this value over the course of the experiments.

Optimization. We can rewrite Eqns. (8)+(9) equivalently as an unconstrained optimization problem

$$\text{minimize}_\theta \sum_p \ell(\max(0, -s_{i_*}^p + \max_{i \in \mathcal{Y}^p}(s_i + \Delta^p(i_*, i)))) + C(\theta). \tag{11}$$

Every evaluation of the unconstrained objective contains solutions to a loss-augmented inference problem of the APK proxy loss. This problem decomposes over parts and the offending state is the maximum in each loss-augmented field. This objective is piecewise differentiable and we resort to stochastic sub-gradient methods. We apply ADADELTA [35], with decay parameter 0.95 and $\epsilon = 10^{-8}$.

In an implementation only a finite number of mean field iterations are executed, some termination criterion has to be applied. In our experiments we chose a fixed number of 10 iterations to calculate the marginals $Q(X_i^p)$ from Algorithm 1. Performance does not depend on any convergence that may occur when the inference is run longer. When optimizing (11) we take this into account by computing the gradient of the marginals w.r.t. parameters by back-propagating the objective Eq. (11) through the mean field updates as illustrated in Figure 2. This is an application of the Back-Mean-Field idea of [8], a procedure advocated for learning with approximate inference when predicting with marginal inference.

Fig. 3. Top row, from left to right: Result from [34], a visualization of the marginal inference result of the base model, inference result with added segmentation information. The part marginals are considerably sharpened by using the additional features in the pairwise connections. **Bottom row from left to right:** Result from [34], part marginals, stick predictions, for two positive results.

5   Experiments

We empirically test the proposed method with the standard benchmark dataset of "Leeds Sport Poses" (LSP) [17]. This dataset consists of 1000 training and 1000 test images of people performing various sports activities and is challenging due to strong body pose articulation.

5.1   Comparison to Pictorial Structures

The idea of reparametrization the body pose problem can in principle be applied to many PS variants. Here we chose the model [34], and thus it serves as the PS "counterpart" we compare against[5]. Note that the described FoP model uses *exactly the same* unary potentials and *exactly the same* features for the pairwise potentials. Also we use the same pre-processing steps: clustering and assignment of the types on the training dataset. Both models have almost identical number of parameters, a total of about $130k$ most of them unary parameters θ_{unary}. Any performance difference of the two methods thus can be attributed solely to the change in model structure, learning objective and inference.

The direct comparison using APK is reported in Table 1, some example detections are depicted in Figure 3. First we compare FoP to the PS counterpart and observe that we obtain an improvement for every body part, while being on par

---

[4] This maximizes the margin with respect to the ratio between the two 1 probabilities and the two 0 probabilities; see appendix.

[5] We thank the authors of [34] for making the code (version 1.3) publicly available.

Table 1. Comparison of pose estimation results on the LSP dataset. Shown are the APK results (observer-centric annotations [10]).

Model	Setting	Head	Shoulder	Elbow	Wrist	Hip	Knee	Ankle	avg
Fields of Parts	Unary only	44.7	28.7	2.1	3.3	5.6	5.8	25.8	16.6
Fields of Parts		83.1	76.5	55.2	29.0	74.8	70.3	63.7	64.7
Fields of Parts	Bilateral	83.3	77.0	56.2	30.9	76.1	71.2	64.5	65.6
Fields of Parts	Segmentation	84.9	77.7	56.9	29.7	78.1	71.9	65.2	66.4
Fields of Parts	Loopy	83.0	76.2	55.7	29.0	77.7	72.0	64.3	65.4
Yang&Ramanan [34]		80.0	75.2	48.2	28.9	70.4	60.5	53.2	59.5
Yang&Ramanan [34] (single det.)	79.5	74.9	47.6	28.4	69.9	59.0	51.6	58.7
Pishchulin et al., [23]		**88.0**	**80.6**	**60.4**	**38.2**	**81.8**	**74.9**	**65.4**	**69.9**

on "wrist". The improvement in average APK is 5.2%. For all FoP results we use the top prediction per image only, and have not implemented Non-Maximum-Supression to retrieve multiple detections. The results of [34] when reporting only the top scoring part are also included in the table, in this case we the performance gain is 6.0%. The results increase over all body parts, most prominently on the feet, for example more than 12% on ankles.

When comparing the extensions (Bilateral, Segmentation, Loopy) against the FoP model we observe a modest but consistent improvement. Again results increase across all parts. Since all models are trained in the very same way this effect can only be due to the image conditioning terms and extra connections that we introduced.

5.2   Comparison with State-of-the-Art

We also compare using the Percentage of Correct Parts (PCP) measure to [34] and recent results from the literature. The numbers are shown in Table 2. The FoP model performs better than the PS models [2,34].

Interestingly, when comparing the differences between [34] and the FoP models we observe that a higher APK number is not directly translating into higher PCP scores. Especially on the arms, the APK criterion with a threshold of $\alpha = 0.1$ that was used during training, appears not to be indicative of PCP performance. The FoP model makes more points correct in terms of APK and we conjecture that switching to a parametrization based on sticks, the model will improve results on the PCP loss.

Methods that make use of richer appearance information (Poselets [22], Poselets and extra DPM detectors for every body part [23], assumptions about the background color distribution [10]) achieve higher results in terms of PCP. We are encouraged by the result of [10] and believe that adapting their color background model should result in similar performance gains, especially, since they extend [34] by an additional unary factor. The methods of [22,23] make use of mid-level representations for bodies. We already discussed a possibility to adapt

Table 2. Pose estimation results using the PCP criterion on the LSP dataset. We compare our method against the current top performing methods in the literature.

Model	Setting	Torso	Upper leg	Lower leg	Upper arm	Fore-arm	Head	Total
Fields of Parts		82.2	71.8	66.5	52.0	27.7	76.8	59.5
Fields of Parts	Bilateral	83.4	72.8	67.0	52.2	28.0	77.0	60.0
Fields of Parts	Segmentation	84.4	74.4	67.1	53.3	27.4	78.4	60.7
Fields of Parts	Loopy	81.8	73.7	66.9	52.0	26.8	77.3	59.8
Yang&Ramanan [34]		81.0	67.4	63.9	51.0	31.8	77.3	58.6
Andriluka et al., [2]		80.9	67.1	60.7	46.5	26.4	74.9	55.7
Pishchulin et al., [22]		87.5	75.7	68.0	54.2	33.9	78.1	62.9
Pishchulin et al., [23]		**88.7**	**78.8**	**73.4**	**61.5**	**44.9**	**85.6**	**69.2**
Eichner&Ferrari [10]		86.2	74.3	69.3	56.5	37.4	80.1	64.3

and extend their approach to a locally conditioned term in Sect. 3.2. However their current implementation runs at several minutes per frame and thus would negatively affect inference time.

6   Conclusion

We have introduced the FoP model, a binary CRF formulation for human pose estimation. Despite being different in structure, it allows to encode a similar spatial dependency structure as done in PS. Further, it permits extensions with more general image conditioned part connections. We have shown two applications of this, by including color and segmentation information as extra features. We have demonstrated how to perform inference and learning in this model through a technical extension of [18], and a max-margin estimator for parameter learning. Because inference complexity depends linearly on almost all relevant model dimensions we also implemented a variant with denser connections than just along the kinematic chain. Experimentally, we validated that the FoP model outperforms [34] on equal ground.

The important new dimension of the proposed parametrization is that it opens up connections to image segmentation. We have discussed several interesting extensions of this model in Section 3.2: image conditioned part configurations, combination with cardboard models, changes in graph topology, etc. Extensions to an explicit person and/or body part segmentation can be easily included, especially, because the inference needs not to be changed.

An interesting aspect of the FoP model is that it explains the image locally at every position; it is not affected by image size, number of persons in the image, or their size. This output semantic differs drastically compared to the PS model. In the future we plan to investigate further along this direction, our goal is to remove the sequential process of current pose estimation pipelines into a single process that performs joint detection and pose estimation of multiple people.

Acknowledgment. The authors would like to thank Leonid Pishchulin for the helpful discussions. MK's work is supported by a grant from Microsoft Research Ltd.

References

1. Adams, A., Baek, J., Davis, M.A.: Fast high-dimensional filtering using the permutohedral lattice. Comput. Graph. Forum 29(2), 753–762 (2010)
2. Andriluka, M., Roth, S., Schiele, B.: Pictorial structures revisited: People detection and articulated pose estimation. In: CVPR (2009)
3. Bourdev, L., Malik, J.: Poselets: Body part detectors trained using 3D human pose annotations. In: ICCV (2009)
4. Bray, M., Kohli, P., Torr, P.: POSECUT: Simultaneous segmentation and 3D pose estimation of humans using dynamic graph-cuts. In: Leonardis, A., Bischof, H., Pinz, A. (eds.) ECCV 2006. LNCS, vol. 3952, pp. 642–655. Springer, Heidelberg (2006)
5. Dalal, N., Triggs, B.: Histograms of oriented gradients for human detection. In: CVPR (2005)
6. Dantone, M., Gall, J., Leistner, C., Gool., L.V.: Human pose estimation using body parts dependent joint regressors. In: CVPR (2013)
7. Domke, J.: Parameter learning with truncated message-passing. In: CVPR (2011)
8. Domke, J.: Learning graphical model parameters with approximate marginal inference. PAMI (2013)
9. Eichner, M., Ferrari, V.: Better appearance models for pictorial structures. In: BMVC (2009)
10. Eichner, M., Ferrari, V.: Appearance sharing for collective human pose estimation. In: Lee, K.M., Matsushita, Y., Rehg, J.M., Hu, Z. (eds.) ACCV 2012, Part I. LNCS, vol. 7724, pp. 138–151. Springer, Heidelberg (2013)
11. Felzenszwalb, P.F., Huttenlocher, D.P.: Pictorial structures for object recognition. IJCV (2005)
12. Ferrari, V., Marin, M., Zisserman, A.: Progressive search space reduction for human pose estimation. In: CVPR (2008)
13. Fischler, M.A., Elschlager, R.A.: The representation and matching of pictorial structures. IEEE Trans. Comput. (1973)
14. Gkioxari, G., Arbelaez, P., Bourdev, L., Malik, J.: Articulated pose estimation using discriminative armlet classifiers. In: CVPR (2013)
15. Jain, A., Tompson, J., Andriluka, M., Taylor, G.W., Bregler, C.: Learning human pose estimation features with convolutional networks. arXiv (2013)
16. Jhuang, H., Gall, J., Zuffi, S., Schmid, C., Black, M.J.: Towards understanding action recognition. In: ICCV (2013)
17. Johnson, S., Everingham, M.: Clustered pose and nonlinear appearance models for human pose estimation. In: BMVC (2010)
18. Krähenbühl, P., Koltun, V.: Efficient inference in fully connected CRFs with Gaussian edge potentials. In: NIPS (2011)
19. Krähenbühl, P., Koltun, V.: Parameter learning and convergent inference for dense random fields. In: ICML (2013)
20. Ladicky, L., Torr, P.H.S., Zisserman, A.: Human pose estimation using a joint pixel-wise and part-wise formulation. In: CVPR (2013)

21. Nowozin, S., Rother, C., Bagon, S., Sharp, T., Yao, B., Kohli, P.: Decision tree fields. In: ICCV (2011)
22. Pishchulin, L., Andriluka, M., Gehler, P., Schiele, B.: Poselet conditioned pictorial structures. In: CVPR (2013)
23. Pishchulin, L., Andriluka, M., Gehler, P., Schiele, B.: Strong appearance and expressive spatial models for human pose estimation. In: ICCV (2013)
24. Ramanan, D.: Learning to parse images of articulated objects. In: NIPS (2006)
25. Sapp, B., Jordan, C., Taskar, B.: Adaptive pose priors for pictorial structures. In: CVPR (2010)
26. Sapp, B., Toshev, A., Taskar, B.: Cascaded models for articulated pose estimation. In: Daniilidis, K., Maragos, P., Paragios, N. (eds.) ECCV 2010, Part II. LNCS, vol. 6312, pp. 406–420. Springer, Heidelberg (2010)
27. Sapp, B., Weiss, D., Taskar, B.: Parsing human motion with stretchable models. In: CVPR (2011)
28. Shotton, J., Fitzgibbon, A., Cook, M., Sharp, T., Finocchio, M., Moore, R., Kipman, A., Blake, A.: Real-time human pose recognition in parts from a single depth image. In: CVPR (2011)
29. Sun, M., Telaprolu, M., Lee, H., Savarese, S.: An efficient branch-and-bound algorithm for optimal human pose estimation. In: CVPR (2012)
30. Tsochantaridis, I., Joachims, T., Hofmann, T., Altun, Y.: Large margin methods for structured and interdependent output variables. JMLR 6, 1453–1484 (2005), http://dl.acm.org/citation.cfm?id=1046920.1088722
31. Vineet, V., Sheasby, G., Warrell, J., Torr, P.H.S.: PoseField: An efficient mean-field based method for joint estimation of human pose, segmentation, and depth. In: Heyden, A., Kahl, F., Olsson, C., Oskarsson, M., Tai, X.-C. (eds.) EMMCVPR 2013. LNCS, vol. 8081, pp. 180–194. Springer, Heidelberg (2013)
32. Wang, H., Koller, D.: Multi-level inference by relaxed dual decomposition for human pose segmentation. In: CVPR, pp. 2433–2440 (2011)
33. Yang, Y., Ramanan, D.: Articulated pose estimation with flexible mixtures-of-parts. In: CVPR (2011)
34. Yang, Y., Ramanan, D.: Articulated human detection with flexible mixtures of parts. PAMI 35 (2013)
35. Zeiler, M.: Adadelta: An adaptive learning rate method (December 2012)

Unsupervised Video Adaptation for Parsing Human Motion*

Haoquan Shen[1], Shoou-I Yu[2], Yi Yang[3], Deyu Meng[4], and Alexander Hauptmann[2]

[1] School of Computer Science, Zhejiang University, China
[2] School of Computer Science, Carnegie Mellon University, USA
[3] ITEE, The University of Queensland, Australia
[4] School of Mathematics and Statistics, Xi'an Jiaotong University, China
{shenhaoquan,yee.i.yang}@gmail.com, {iyu,alex}@cs.cmu.edu,
dymeng@mail.xjtu.edu.cn

Abstract. In this paper, we propose a method to parse human motion in unconstrained Internet videos without labeling any videos for training. We use the training samples from a public image pose dataset to avoid the tediousness of labeling
video streams. There are two main problems confronted. First, the distribution
of images and videos are different. Second, no temporal information is available
in the training images. To smooth the inconsistency between the labeled images
and unlabeled videos, our algorithm iteratively incorporates the pose knowledge
harvested from the testing videos into the image pose detector via an adjust-and-
refine method. During this process, continuity and tracking constraints are imposed to leverage the spatio-temporal information only available in videos. For
our experiments, we have collected two datasets from YouTube and experiments
show that our method achieves good performance for parsing human motions.
Furthermore, we found that our method achieves better performance by using
unlabeled video than adding more labeled pose images into the training set.

Keywords: Unsupervised Video Pose Estimation, Image to Video Adaptation,
Unconstrained Internet Videos.

1 Introduction

[1]In this paper, we focus on articulated pose estimation in unconstrained Internet videos.
While limited research efforts have been made to pose detection in videos [7,25,9,16],
they only consider clean video data (*e.g.*, TV shows) rather than Internet videos which
are much more noisy. Furthermore, the performance largely relies on the selection of
training data and the accuracy may drop dramatically if the distributions of training and
testing data are quite different. As such, the existing work have constrained the training and testing video to be similar. For example, in [7] and [25], researchers collected
both the training and testing data from the TV shows "Friends" and "Lost". In that way,
the scene, the person and apparel of both training and testing data are consistent. Pose
detection in those videos is simplified.

---

* Electronic supplementary material - Supplementary material is available in the online version of
this chapter at http://dx.doi.org/10.1007/978-3-319-10602-1_23. Videos
can also be accessed at http://www.springerimages.com/videos/978-3-
319-10601-4

[1] The code and datasets will be available upon request.

D. Fleet et al. (Eds.): ECCV 2014, Part V, LNCS 8693, pp. 347–360, 2014.
© Springer International Publishing Switzerland 2014

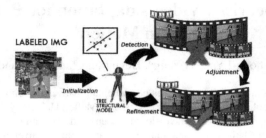

Fig. 1. The framework of our algorithm

The main unsolved challenge in current work is that Internet videos generally have huge apparel variations with different levels of occlusions and cluttered body parts. It is not reasonable to directly apply the model trained from clean TV shows to predict the poses in Internet videos, especially for articulated pose detection. To achieve reliable pose detection performance, it is necessary to have a large amount of training videos covering a variety of apparels, backgrounds (scenes) and poses. Yet it is very time consuming to label the poses and computationally intensive to train the models as a single video clip contains many frames in real cases. Compared to videos, it is much easier to label still images without the tediousness of reviewing the video streams. For example, the effort of labeling 100 images is much less than that of labeling 100 video clips. In addition, there are some image datasets, *e.g.*, PARSE [17], with labeled body parts that contain a variety of articulated poses. In this paper, we propose to leverage such free data to estimate poses in Internet quality videos. To the best of our knowledge, this is the first work on articulated pose detection without any labeled videos. The merit of our algorithms is that no human supervision is required.

As shown in Fig. 1, our algorithm starts with training an image pose estimator using an external pre-labeled image dataset. These pose estimators can be used as good initializations for Internet videos, since labeled images have relatively larger variations although less than Internet videos. We then propose a self-refining approach to adapt the pose knowledge from the testing videos, and incorporate the information into the next round of learning, during which both spatial and temporal constraints are utilized. More specifically, we first apply a self-adjustment approach to the results of image pose detection by tracking the trajectory of each body part across multiple frames with spatial smoothing constraints. Then, we use a scoring strategy to pick the frames with high confidence in the testing data, while preserving the diversity of selected key-frames and adding them as extra labeled poses to the training process.

Our contributions are summarized as follows:

1. We address the limitations of previous work, which are unable to deal with Internet videos with large variations and heavy clutters. We propose a self-refining approach to adapt the pose knowledge from static images to Internet videos.
2. We introduce a self-adjustment method to improve accuracy by tracking the trajectory of each body part across multiple frames with spatial smoothing constraints.
3. We collect a challenging pose detection dataset consisting of full-body and half-body dancing clips from Internet videos, which have large variations in terms of scene, person, apparel, *etc*.

2 Related Work

Pose detection is a very valuable but tough task in computer vision. Researchers have addressed the problem of pose detection in video dating back to the classic model-based approaches [15,8,21]. The difficulties are summarized as follows:

1. Huge variations of human poses on Internet videos, as depicted in Fig. 8 and Fig. 9: For example, human limbs are stretched and foreshortened. Left and right limbs reverse regularly due to rotation and self-occlusion. Appearances including skin color, clothing, body shape differ from one person to another. In some scenarios, multiple persons are seen simultaneously and occlude each other.
2. Poor quality of most Internet videos: Uploaded videos often have low resolution and serious motion blur.
3. Lack of generalizability. In fact, most of the existing methods are training-data-driven: When we detect poses in Internet videos which consist of more varied body shapes, apparel, backgrounds, *etc*, existing models generally cannot adapt well to the new domain.

Recent work has examined this problem for static images, assuming that techniques for static images will be needed in video-based articulated trackers. Other than the techniques exploring the tradeoff between generative and discriminative models from an overall perspective [11,28,23], multiple approaches advocate strong body models. The graph-based and tree-structured models are the two main approaches for this task. Loopy models [20,13,26,1,30] (graph-based models) have stricter constraints of different body parts and usually lead to good performance. But they are also harder to optimize and more time consuming. Other approaches are tree models, which allow for efficient inference, but are often plagued by the well-known phenomena of double counting [3,19,22]. In addition, researchers [24] also extend the single model to multiple model scenario and use model selection to improve performance. Recently, a novel tree structured framework [32,31] has received much attention. It extends the classic pictorial structure [3,6] and parameterizes body parts by both pixel locations and latent variable "orientations". This model realizes a good balance between performance and efficiency, which achieves state-of-the-art performance for static images and can be efficiently implemented when Structural SVM [5] and Dynamic Programming are applied.

There are also some research efforts to pose detection in video streams [7,25,9,16]. For example, a segmentation-based pose and flow framework is proposed in [7], which is similar to [9,10]. In [14], Ma et. al. proposed an algorithm to adapt the knowledge from clean lab-generated videos for action recognition in the real world videos, e.g., the YouTube videos. In [25], researchers approximate the full, intractable spatio-temporal loopy model of pose detection by decomposing it into an ensemble of tree models. Other pose detectors use labeled videos as training data and train pose detectors by applying both spatial and temporal constraints [2,16]. Several recent papers [27,12,18,4], enhance performance by using tracking methods. However, all of these use video data from TV shows or lab recorded videos which are cleaner than Internet video data. Furthermore, the performance largely relies on the selection of training data and the accuracy may drop dramatically if the distributions of training and testing data are quite different. To handle Internet videos well, in this paper, we propose a self-refining approach to uncover the pose knowledge of Internet videos.

3 Framework

The framework of our method is shown in Fig. 1. Specifically, we first initialize our model with a small number of labeled images. Then, we apply a self-refining approach to adapt the pose knowledge to the testing videos. This approach can be summarized as:

1. Detect human pose on every frame of the test videos using [32,31], which is a state-of-the-art image pose detector (Section 3.1).
2. Adjust pose detection results by using continuity and tracking constraints for the testing videos (Section 3.2).
3. Gradually add high confidence frames automatically found in the testing videos to the training set for the next round of learning (Section 3.3). Repeat step 1.

In the following sections, we introduce our three main implementation procedures in detail.

3.1 Pose Detection

For each iteration in the self-refining process, we first generate an image pose detector. In the initialization stage, only labeled images are used as training data. After that, additional high-confidence frames in the testing videos are automatically selected for use in training. Here we follow the tree-structured model [32,31] and write the score function of a candidate pose as follows:

$$\max_{p,t} \sum_{i \in vertex} b_i^{t_i} + \sum_{ij \in edge} b_{ij}^{t_i,t_j}$$
$$+ \sum_{i \in vertex} w_i^{t_i} \cdot \phi(f, p_i)$$
$$+ \sum_{ij \in edge} w_{ij}^{t_i,t_j} \cdot \psi(p_i - p_j) \tag{1}$$

In Eq. (1), *vertex* and *edge* are the nodes and edges of the pose tree. p_i, t_i stand for the pixel location and orientation of part i. The parameter $b_i^{t_i}$ favors a particular type of assignment for part i, while the pairwise parameter $b_{ij}^{t_i,t_j}$ favors particular co-occurrences of part types. $\phi(f, p_i)$ is the feature vector extracted from p_i. The third term can be viewed as the loss when part i is placed at location p_i with the orientation t_i. w^{t_i} is a template learned from Structural SVM by taking orientation t_i as a latent variable [32,31]. The last term stands for the loss of a "switching" spring which is the dot product of spring parameter $w_{ij}^{t_i,t_j}$ and pixel difference of parts. Following [32,31], we solve Eq. (1) by using Dynamic Programming (DP).

3.2 Pose Adjustment

Continuity Constraint. One important property of pose detection on videos is that the positions of human joints in consecutive frames will not change dramatically. We call this property Continuity Constraint. In this step, we adjust the pose detection results by using this continuity property. We denote V and f as video and frame. $next(f)$ is the frame after f. $vertex$ is the nodes of the tree models. p_i^f and $\widetilde{p}_i^f$ are the location for part i in frame f before and after the adjustment process. Our adjustment process can be converted into optimizing the following objective:

$$\min_{\widetilde{p}} \sum_{f \in V} \sum_{i \in vertex} \left(||\widetilde{p}_i^f - p_i^f||_2^2 + \alpha ||\widetilde{p}_i^{next(f)} - \widetilde{p}_i^f||_2^2 \right) \qquad (2)$$

In Eq. (2), the first term restricts the adjusted results to be similar to the original ones. The second term is the temporal constraint that joints in adjacent frames won't change much. α parameterizes the weight of the continuity constraint. By doing this, our insight is that wrong results will cause a big discontinuity to adjacent frames with high confidence score, resulting in a big loss to the second temporal term, which can be reduced in the optimization step. Fig. 2 shows two examples of pose adjustment using the continuity constraint, from which we can see a visible improvement after the adjustment.

Fig. 2. Pose detection results before (rows 1 & 3) and after (rows 2 & 4) adjustment with continuity constraint

Tracking Constraint. A tracking rectification algorithm, which tracks each body part across multiple frames, is used to rectify incorrect body parts. Given the pose detection results for a source frame f, one could track each body part forward or backward in time and produce hypotheses of part locations for neighboring frames. Inversely, neighboring frames of f will also produce body part location hypotheses for frame f. As shown in Fig. 4, to rectify the pose detection results for frame f, we perform a weighted fusion of all the hypotheses provided by the neighboring frames. The weight of each hypothesis is determined by the pose detection score in the source frame. Our insight is that high-scoring poses have more accurate predictions of body part locations, thus making the hypotheses generated by these detections also more reliable.

Specifically, as shown in Fig. 3, suppose that we want to use the results of the frame f to generate the tracking results after 25 frames (1 second). Taking the right wrist as

Fig. 3. Pose refinement using tracking cues. Frame f' is the frame 1 second after frame f. a) Pose detection results of frame f according to Eq. (1). b) Trajectory keypoints of the right arm in frame f. c) Wrong pose detection results of frame f' according to Eq. (1). d) Refined pose according to the arm trajectory key point of frame f'.

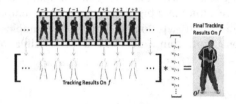

Fig. 4. Procedure to generate tracking results

an example, firstly, we can cover every joint with a box. Then, we detect all the dense trajectory keypoints in each box and track these trajectory keypoints by using [29]. Finally, the prediction results are generated by averaging the tracking points. Similarly, we can apply this method to other parts to generate the tracking results for the full human skeleton. In fact, the tracking results can be very good in practice as shown in Fig. 3.

We denote the fused tracking results of the i-th part in f as O_i^f and rewrite the Eq. (2) as the following:

$$\min_{\widetilde{p}} \sum_{f \in V} \sum_{i \in vertex} \left(||\widetilde{p}_i^f - p_i^f||_2^2 \right.$$
$$\left. + \alpha ||\widetilde{p}_i^{next(f)} - \widetilde{p}_i^f||_2^2 + \beta ||\widetilde{p}_i^f - O_i^f||_2^2 \right) \qquad (3)$$

In Eq. (3), other than what we have discussed before, the last term restricts the adjusted results to be similar with the tracking results. β parameterizes the degree that we trust the tracking results. As shown in Fig. 3, there often exists a situation where the pose detection results are wrong but the tracking results are correct. This will cause a big tracking error, which can be optimized by balancing the tracking error with other constraints.

Since (3) is a convex optimization problem, we can calculate the derivative for every variable $\widetilde{p}_i$ and solve it using an iterative method by setting the derivative to be zero.

3.3 Pose Detector Refinement

In the refinement process, we automatically select the frames with top scores in the testing videos and use them as extra training data in the next round of learning. Denote $\mathcal{R}$

as the pose detection results. S_S and S_T are the pose detection and the pose adjustment scores. We define the score of results $\mathcal{R}$ on frame f as follows:

$$S(f, \mathcal{R}) = S_S(f, \mathcal{R}) + S_T(f, \mathcal{R}) \tag{4}$$

Where, similar to Eq. (1) and (3), we write the spatial and temporal scores as follows:

$$
\begin{aligned}
S_S(f, \mathcal{R}) = &\sum_{i \in vertex} b_i^{t_i} + \sum_{ij \in edge} b_{ij}^{t_i, t_j} \\
&+ \sum_{i \in vertex} w_i^{t_i} \cdot \phi(f, \widetilde{p}_i) \\
&+ \sum_{ij \in edge} w_{ij}^{t_i, t_j} \cdot \psi(\widetilde{p}_i - \widetilde{p}_j)
\end{aligned} \tag{5}
$$

$$
\begin{aligned}
S_T(f, \mathcal{R}) = &-\gamma \sum_{i \in vertex} \left(\|\widetilde{p}_i^{next(f)} - \widetilde{p}_i^f\|_2^2 + \right. \\
&\left. \|\widetilde{p}_i^{prev(f)} - \widetilde{p}_i^f\|_2^2 \right) - \theta \sum_{i \in vertex} \|\widetilde{p}_i^f - O_i^f\|_2^2
\end{aligned} \tag{6}
$$

In Eq. (5), the spatial score S_S reflects both the confidence of every body part and the matching rate of every adjacent body part. In Eq. (6), the temporal score S_T is the negative loss in the adjustment procedure, in which the first and second terms stand for the location differences of every body part to adjacent two frames, and the third term stands for the error compared to the tracking results. Here, γ and θ parameterize the degree of punishment on frame discontinuity and tracking mismatch.

Note that even though Eq. (5) and (6) have the similar forms as Eq. (1) and (3), their purposes are different. For Eq. (1) and (3), they are used during optimization, whereas Eq. (5) and (6) are only used to compute scores. No optimization is done using Eq. (5) ans (6).

In our refinement process, to keep both the quality and diversity of added testing key-frames, we only select the frames which have scores above 0.4 in Eq. (4) and we select at most 4 frames from each video per iteration.

4 Experiments

Datasets: We have constructed one full-body and one upper-body dataset for testing purposes from the dancing videos of Youtube, which we call Full-body Youtube Dancing Pose (FYDP) dataset and Upper-body Youtube Dancing Pose (UYDP) dataset, respectively. Each of the FYDP and UYDP dataset contains 20 video clips. Each video clip lasts around 4 seconds and consists of around 100 consecutive annotated video frames. Specifically, our FYDP dataset contains dancing videos with fast and slow movements, rotating and split-leg positions, stretched and forshortened limbs. In the UYDP dataset, more intricate upper-body motions are included. Some typical frames in FYDP and UYDP are depicted in Fig. 8 and Fig.9, respectively. In addition to FYDP and UYDP, we also used the VideoPose2 dataset collected in [25] to evaluate the performance of the proposed algorithm.

In our experiments, the labeled images for initialization are selected from the PARSE dataset [17] and the BUFFY dataset [4], respectively. PARSE dataset contains 305 pose-annotated images of highly-articulated full body images of human poses, and the BUFFY dataset contains 748 upper-body-annotated images extracted from 5 episodes

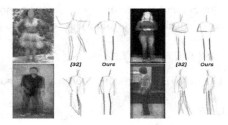

Fig. 5. A comparison between our model and that of [32]. This figure shows the aggregated frames sampled from dancing video clips of two seconds and the pose skeletons obtained by our model and [32], respectively.

of a TV show. Both datasets have specified the training and testing sets [32,31]. In each of our full-body and upper-body experiments, we respectively use three settings of PARSE and BUFFY images as initialization to test how sensitive our method is to the number of labeled data: half of the images from the training set, all the images from the training set, all images of the training and testing sets.

To train our image pose detector, we follow the experiment settings in [32,31] and use the negative training images from the INRIAPerson database [33]. These images tend to be outdoor scenes which do not contain people.

Evaluation Criteria. Following [32], in which researchers have discussed the limitations of PCP (Probability of a Correct Pose) [4], we use APK (Average Precision of Keypoints) and PCK (Percent of Correct Keypoints) [32] in our experiments with the threshold to be 0.1 for FYDP dataset and 0.2 for UYDP and VideoPose2 [25] datasets. When the bounding boxes of every person is given, PCK evaluates the percentage of correct keypoints. For comparison, APK is stricter, in that both missed-detections and false-positives are penalized.

Structure. We use 26 parts and 18 parts tree-structured models in our full-body and upper-body experiments, respectively, in which both joint positions and some midway points between limbs are included. For each part, we use 4(8) mixtures for full-body(upper-body) detector, which has shown to be a good tradeoff between performance and efficiency in [32].

Parameters. In our experiments, we iterate 3 times to adapt the domain knowledge of testing videos, which is demonstrated by our experiments to be a good balance between efficiency and performance. In our refining process, there are two parameters γ and θ. We empirically set $\gamma = 0.5, \theta = 1$, for which our method can consistently perform well. For α and β in Eq. (3), our experiments verify that the proposed framework is not sensitive to both parameters. We empirically set $\alpha = 5, \beta = 1$.

Table 1. Full-body pose detection results on FYDP dataset, when different number of training images from PARSE dataset are used

50% randomly sampled images from the training set of PARSE are used for training

Criteria	Method	Head	Shou	Elbo	Wris	Hip	Knee	Ankle	Total
APK	Yang et. al. [32]	92.9	85.7	57.0	27.1	73.2	70.2	71.3	68.2
	Our Model	**95.0**	**88.5**	**65.2**	**32.3**	**78.1**	**78.2**	**79.8**	**73.9**
PCK	Yang et. al. [32]	94.4	89.3	69.9	48.7	80.8	75.0	73.4	75.9
	Our Model	**95.5**	**91.2**	**74.6**	**50.8**	**82.4**	**81.6**	**77.2**	**79.0**

All images from the training set of PARSE are used for training

Criteria	Method	Head	Shou	Elbo	Wris	Hip	Knee	Ankle	Total
APK	Yang et. al. [32]	94.4	86.7	58.2	33.3	68.6	73.4	76.4	70.2
	Our Model	**95.9**	**88.8**	**67.3**	**35.4**	**79.7**	**79.3**	**79.3**	**75.1**
PCK	Yang et. al. [32]	95.2	89.9	69.0	53.1	78.1	78.2	77.7	77.3
	Our Model	**96.1**	**91.0**	**74.8**	**54.5**	**83.6**	**81.7**	**78.8**	**80.0**

All images of PARSE are used for training

Criteria	Method	Head	Shou	Elbo	Wris	Hip	Knee	Ankle	Total
APK	Yang et. al. [32]	95.3	86.9	66.2	41.1	73.8	75.2	76.8	73.6
	Our Model	**95.7**	**89.6**	**73.6**	**43.5**	**82.4**	**82.9**	**78.2**	**78.0**
PCK	Yang et. al. [32]	95.8	89.9	73.7	58.5	80.1	79.8	78.1	79.4
	Our Model	**96.2**	**91.7**	**78.4**	**60.3**	**85.4**	**83.8**	**79.2**	**82.1**

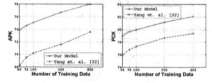 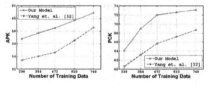

(a) Full-body pose detection results on FYDP dataset, when different number of training images from PARSE dataset are used

(b) Upper-body pose detection results on UYDP dataset, when different number of training images from BUFFY dataset are used

Fig. 6. Full-body and upper-body pose detection results

Compared Algorithms. In the experiments, we compare our method to [32,24], which are state-of-the-art pose detectors on static images. As the algorithm proposed in [24] is only able to detect three body parts, *i.e.* shoulder, elbow and wrist, we do not report the results of [24] on the full-body dataset FYDP. Note that we aim to parse human motion without labeling any videos for training. We are unable to compare our algorithm to [7,25] because both [7] and [25] require labeled *video clips* for training, which are unavailable in our experiments. Other than [32], which achieves both state-of-the-art results and high time efficiency, we could extend any image pose detector to the video scenario by simply replacing the pose detection process.

Table 2. Upper-body pose detection results on UYDP dataset, when different number of training images from BUFFY dataset are used

50% randomly sampled images from the training set of BUFFY are used for training

Criteria	Method	Head	Shou	Elbo	Wris	Hip	S. E. W. Avg	All Avg
APK	Sapp et. al. [24]	NA	67.1	**32.0**	35.3	NA	44.8	NA
	Yang et. al. [32]	84.2	74.2	22.5	44.3	41.9	47.0	53.4
	Our Model	**88.3**	**80.1**	22.6	**47.5**	**45.5**	**50.1**	**56.8**
PCK	Sapp et. al. [24]	NA	81.3	38.8	35.6	NA	51.9	NA
	Yang et. al. [32]	88.1	79.5	36.4	45.1	54.1	53.7	60.6
	Our Model	**89.8**	**87.4**	**38.9**	**48.8**	**55.7**	**58.4**	**64.1**

All images from the training set of BUFFY are used for training

Criteria	Method	Head	Shou	Elbo	Wris	Hip	S. E. W. Avg	All Avg
APK	Sapp et. al. [24]	NA	69.5	33.7	37.3	NA	46.8	NA
	Yang et. al. [32]	85.0	78.2	29.2	46.2	34.4	51.2	54.6
	Our Model	**90.9**	**83.5**	33.3	**47.7**	**36.9**	**54.8**	**58.5**
PCK	Sapp et. al. [24]	NA	82.2	39.6	38.1	NA	53.3	NA
	Yang et. al. [32]	90.9	84.9	43.6	51.4	57.7	59.9	65.7
	Our Model	**97.5**	**95.6**	**49.0**	**56.6**	**61.5**	**67.1**	**72.0**

All images of BUFFY are used for training

Criteria	Method	Head	Shou	Elbo	Wris	Hip	S. E. W. Avg	All Avg
APK	Sapp et. al. [24]	NA	72.0	**38.6**	39.6	NA	50.1	NA
	Yang et. al. [32]	88.0	81.3	33.9	50.7	39.1	55.3	58.6
	Our Model	**91.6**	**84.8**	37.2	**51.0**	**39.8**	**57.7**	**60.9**
PCK	Sapp et. al. [24]	NA	83.5	42.4	40.8	NA	55.6	NA
	Yang et. al. [32]	92.5	86.5	49.4	54.2	60.8	63.4	68.7
	Our Model	**97.7**	**94.8**	**53.8**	**55.6**	**63.4**	**68.1**	**73.1**

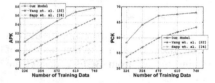

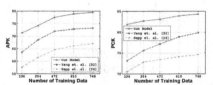

(a) Pose detection results on UYDP dataset, when different number of training images from BUFFY dataset are used.

(b) Pose detection results on VideoPose2 dataset, when different number of training images from BUFFY dataset are used.

Fig. 7. Three body parts (shoulder, elbow, wrist) pose detection results

Experimental Settings. In this paper, we have done three experiments separately to demonstrate the effectiveness of our proposed framework. In order to see whether our method is sensitive to the number of labeled training data, for each experiment, we show the results under three different settings based on the number of labeled training data to do initialization: half images of the training set (for either BUFFY or PARSE) are used for training, all images of the training set are used for training, all images of the training and testing set are used for training. The three experiments are as follows:

Table 3. Upper-body pose detection results on VideoPose2 dataset, when different number of training images from BUFFY dataset are used

50% randomly sampled images from the training set of BUFFY are used for training

Criteria	Method	Head	Shou	Elbo	Wris	Hip	S. E. W. Avg	All Avg
APK	Sapp et. al. [24]	NA	81.0	42.4	49.3	NA	57.6	NA
	Yang et. al. [32]	**92.3**	90.1	40.1	60.5	46.5	63.6	65.9
	Our Model	**92.3**	**92.5**	**58.3**	**63.5**	**49.6**	**71.4**	**71.2**
PCK	Sapp et. al. [24]	NA	90.8	61.3	59.3	NA	70.5	NA
	Yang et. al. [32]	96.1	94.7	56.6	67.9	71.3	73.1	77.3
	Our Model	**96.6**	**97.2**	**78.6**	**69.8**	**74.5**	**81.9**	**83.3**

All images from the training set of BUFFY are used for training

Criteria	Method	Head	Shou	Elbo	Wris	Hip	S. E. W. Avg	All Avg
APK	Sapp et. al. [24]	NA	84.6	57.1	52.0	NA	64.6	NA
	Yang et. al. [32]	**97.0**	94.4	56.4	65.2	51.3	72.0	72.9
	Our Model	96.7	**95.8**	**68.2**	**68.4**	**60.7**	**77.5**	**78.0**
PCK	Sapp et. al. [24]	NA	92.5	66.2	61.5	NA	73.4	NA
	Yang et. al. [32]	**97.2**	94.6	67.0	70.1	74.0	77.2	80.6
	Our Model	96.9	**97.5**	**78.4**	**73.3**	**77.8**	**83.1**	**84.8**

All images of BUFFY are used for training

Criteria	Method	Head	Shou	Elbo	Wris	Hip	S. E. W. Avg	All Avg
APK	Sapp et. al. [24]	NA	85.0	64.2	52.2	NA	67.1	NA
	Yang et. al. [32]	95.3	95.2	64.1	60.5	52.3	73.3	73.5
	Our Model	**96.6**	**95.9**	**74.5**	**68.2**	**61.7**	**79.5**	**79.4**
PCK	Sapp et. al. [24]	NA	93.3	69.3	61.3	NA	74.6	NA
	Yang et. al. [32]	97.0	96.1	73.4	70.2	71.0	79.9	81.5
	Our Model	**97.3**	**97.1**	**82.4**	**73.4**	**77.5**	**84.3**	**85.5**

1. We compare our full-body model to Yang et. al. [32] on FYDP by utilizing PARSE [17] to do initialization as shown in Table 1 and Fig. 6 (a).
2. We compare our upper-body model to Yang et. al. [32] on UYDP by utilizing BUFFY [4] to do initialization as shown in Table 2, Fig. 6 (b) and Fig. 7 (a).
3. We compare our upper-body model to Yang et. al. [32] and Sapp et. al. [24] on VideoPose2 dataset [25] by utilizing BUFFY [4] to do initialization as shown in Table 3 and Fig. 7 (b). We do not compare to video based method [7,25] since video data are not available in the training process.

Experiment Results. From Table 1, Table 2 and Table 3, we can see that our method achieves a significant improvement compared to the image pose detector. In addition, if we look at the results in detail, in Table 1, when we use half of the training set (50 images) to do training, we can obtain 73.9% APK and 79.0% PCK. If we instead trained a state-of-the-art image pose detector [32] with 305 images, it only achieves 73.6% APK and 79.4% PCK. This shows that our method, with only $\frac{1}{6}$ training data, can still generate comparable results to the state-of-the-art image pose detector [32].

Furthermore, from Fig. 6, we observe that: 1) when the number of labeled training images increases, both the performance of our method and [32] are improved. 2) our

Fig. 8. Key frame results on FYDP dataset. We show different parts of full-body skeleton using 6 different colors. Other than the last three images of the last row, all images show successful examples. By examining the failure cases, we find our model is still confused by foreshortened limbs, horizontal people and the left/right limb.

Fig. 9. Key frame results on UYDP dataset. We show different parts of half-body skeleton using 4 different colors. Other than the last three images of the last row, all the images show successful examples. We see our model still has difficulty to hidden parts, foreshortened limbs and self-occlusion.

model is always better than [32] when the number of training data varies. 3) our model is not very sensitive to the number of training data, and can generally get pretty good results when only 50 images are used for training.

To vividly compare our pose detection results to a state-of-the-art image-based pose detector [32], we visualize the human motion parsing results of a two-second video clip, which are shown in Fig. 5. The comparison shows that our model is more robust to noise and can clearly represent the movements. In addition, we also show some successful and failed examples of our full-body and upper-body results in Fig. 8 and Fig. 9.

5 Conclusion

We propose an unsupervised framework to adapt pose detector from images to uncon-strained Internet videos. A novel adjustment strategy is proposed to iteratively exploit the domain specific information in unconstrained videos, where no labeled videos are available. Temporal smoothness and body part consistency are simultaneously satis-fied to refine the pose detection model, which is initialized only by labeled images. The merit of our work is that the pre-trained model does not have to fit the testing data, which are unseen during initialization. Therefore, no human supervision is required when we adapt the image model to videos. Our framework is a general one, which can be read-ily extended to any other image pose detector for Internet videos. We demonstrate the effectiveness and robustness of our framework through the full-body and upper-body pose experiments based on a real world Internet video set. One limitation of the pro-posed algorithm is that if the video resolution is low, the tracking results may not be robust enough. In these cases, the improvement from tracking part will decrease. In the future, we will improve the tracking method.

Acknowledgments. This paper was partially supported by the US Department of De-fense the U. S. Army Research Office (W911NF-13-1-0277), partially supported by the National Science Foundation under Grant Number IIS-12511827, partially supported by the ARC DECRA project (DE130101311), the UQ ECR project (2013002401) and the NSFC projects with No.61373114. The U.S. Government is authorized to reproduce and distribute reprints for Governmental purposes notwithstanding any copyright annotation thereon. Disclaimer: The views and conclusions contained herein are those of the authors and should not be interpreted as necessarily representing the official policies or endorse-ments, either expressed or implied, of DoI/NBC, ARO, NSF, or the U.S. Government.

References

1. Bergtholdt, M., Kappes, J.: A study of parts-based object class detection using complete graphs. In: IJCV (2009)
2. Fablet, R., Black, M.J.: Automatic detection and tracking of human motion with a view-based representation. In: Heyden, A., Sparr, G., Nielsen, M., Johansen, P. (eds.) ECCV 2002, Part I. LNCS, vol. 2350, pp. 476–491. Springer, Heidelberg (2002)
3. Felzenszwalb, P., Huttenlocher, D.: Pictorial structures for object recognition. IJCV 61(1), 55–79 (2005)
4. Ferrari, V., Marin-Jimenez, M., Zisserman, A.: Progressive search space reduction for human pose estimation. In: CVPR (2008)
5. Finley, T., Joachims, T.: Training structural svms when exact inference is intractable. In: ICML (2008)
6. Fischler, M., Elschlager, R.: The representation and matching of pictorial structures, vol. 100, pp. 67–92 (1973)
7. Fragkiadaki, K., Hu, H., Shi, J.: Pose from flow and flow from pose. In: CVPR (2013)
8. Hogg, D.: Model-based vision: a program to see a walking person. Image and Vision com-puting 1(1), 5–20 (1983)
9. Jiang, H.: Human pose estimation using consistent maxcovering. In: ICCV (2009)
10. Ju, S.X., Black, M.J., Yacoob, Y.: Cardboard people: A parameterized model of articulated image motion. In: FG (1996)

11. Kumar, M., Zisserman, A., Torr, P.: Efficient discriminative learning of parts-based models. In: CVPR (2010)
12. Lan, X., Huttenlocher, D.: Beyond trees: Common-factor models for 2d human pose recovery. In: ICCV (2005)
13. Lee, M., Cohen, I.: Proposal maps driven mcmc for estimating human body pose in static images. In: CVPR (2004)
14. Ma, Z., Yang, Y., Nie, F., Sebe, N., Yan, S., Hauptmann, A.: Harnessing lab knowledge for real-world action recognition. International Journal of Computer Vision 109(1-2), 60–73 (2014)
15. O'Rourke, J., Badler, N.: Model-based image analysis of human motion using constraint propagation. PAMI 2(6), 522–536 (1980)
16. O'Rourke, J., Badler, N.: 2d human pose estimation in tv shows. Statistical and Geometrical Approaches to Visual Motion Analysis 1, 128–147 (2009)
17. Ramanan, D.: Learning to parse images of articulated bodies. In: NIPS (2007)
18. Ramanan, D., Forsyth, D., Zisserman, A.: Strike a pose: Tracking people by finding stylized poses. In: CVPR (2005)
19. Ramanan, D., Sminchisescu, C.: Training deformable models for localization. In: CVPR (2006)
20. Ren, X., Berg, A.C., Malik, J.: Recovering human body configurations using pairwise constraints between parts. In: ICCV (2005)
21. Rohr, K.: Towards model-based recognition of human movements in image sequences. CVGIP-Image Understanding 59(1), 94–115 (1994)
22. Ronfard, R., Schmid, C., Triggs, B.: Learning to parse pictures of people. In: Heyden, A., Sparr, G., Nielsen, M., Johansen, P. (eds.) ECCV 2002, Part IV. LNCS, vol. 2353, pp. 700–714. Springer, Heidelberg (2002)
23. Sapp, B., Jordan, C., Taskar, B.: Adaptive pose priors for pictorial structures. In: CVPR (2010)
24. Sapp, B., Taskar, B.: Modec: Multimodal decomposable models for human pose estimation. In: CVPR (2013)
25. Sapp, B., Weiss, D., Taskar, B.: Parsing human motion with stretchable models. In: CVPR (2011)
26. Sigal, L., Black, M.: Measure locally, reason globally: Occlusion-sensitive articulated pose estimation. In: CVPR (2006)
27. Sigal, L., Isard, M., Sigelman, B.H., Black, M.J.: Attractive people: Assembling loose-limbed models using non-parametric belief propagation. In: NIPS (2003)
28. Singh, V.K., Nevatia, R., Huang, C.: Efficient inference with multiple heterogeneous part detectors for human pose estimation. In: Daniilidis, K., Maragos, P., Paragios, N. (eds.) ECCV 2010, Part III. LNCS, vol. 6313, pp. 314–327. Springer, Heidelberg (2010)
29. Wang, H., Kläser, A., Schmid, C., Liu, C.: Action Recognition by Dense Trajectories. In: IEEE Conference on Computer Vision & Pattern Recognition, Colorado Springs, United States, pp. 3169–3176 (June 2011), http://hal.inria.fr/inria-00583818/en
30. Wang, Y., Mori, G.: Multiple tree models for occlusion and spatial constraints in human pose estimation. In: Forsyth, D., Torr, P., Zisserman, A. (eds.) ECCV 2008, Part III. LNCS, vol. 5304, pp. 710–724. Springer, Heidelberg (2008)
31. Yang, Y., Ramanan, D.: Articulated pose estimation using flexible mixtures of parts. In: CVPR (2011)
32. Yang, Y., Ramanan, D.: Articulated human detection with flexible mixtures of parts. PAMI 61(1), 55–79 (2013)
33. Yuille, A., Rangarajan, A.: The concave-convex procedure. Neural Computation 15(4), 915–936 (2003)

Training Object Class Detectors from Eye Tracking Data

Dim P. Papadopoulos, Alasdair D.F. Clarke, Frank Keller, and Vittorio Ferrari

School of Informatics, University of Edinburgh, UK

Abstract. Training an object class detector typically requires a large set of images annotated with bounding-boxes, which is expensive and time consuming to create. We propose novel approach to annotate object locations which can substantially reduce annotation time. We first track the eye movements of annotators instructed to find the object and then propose a technique for deriving object bounding-boxes from these fixations. To validate our idea, we collected eye tracking data for the trainval part of 10 object classes of Pascal VOC 2012 (6,270 images, 5 observers). Our technique correctly produces bounding-boxes in 50% of the images, while reducing the total annotation time by factor 6.8× compared to drawing bounding-boxes. Any standard object class detector can be trained on the bounding-boxes predicted by our model. Our large scale eye tracking dataset is available at groups.inf.ed.ac.uk/calvin/eyetrackdataset/.

1 Introduction

Object class detection is the task of predicting a bounding-box around each instance of an object class in a test image. Traditionally, training an object class detector requires a large set of images in which objects are manually annotated with bounding-boxes [8,14,15,47,50] (Fig. 1). Bounding-box annotation is time consuming and expensive. The authors of [20] report a 26s median time to draw a bounding-box during a large-scale annotation effort for ImageNet by crowd-sourcing on Mechanical Turk. Additionally, detailed annotation guidelines, annotator training based on these guidelines, and manual checking of the annotation are typically required [14,20]. Annotating large sets of images is therefore an enormous undertaking, which is typically supported by crowd sourcing [1,13].

In this paper, we propose a novel approach to training object detectors which can substantially reduce the time required to annotate images. Instead of carefully marking every training image with accurate bounding-boxes, our annotators only need to find the target object in the image, look at it, and press a button. By tracking the eye movements of the annotators while they perform this task, we obtain valuable information about the position and size of the target object (Fig. 1). Unlike bounding-box annotation, our eye tracking task requires no annotation guidelines and can be carried out by completely naive viewers. Furthermore, the task can be performed in a fraction of the time it takes to draw a bounding-box (about one second per image, Sec. 3).

Eye movement behavior in scene viewing has been the subject of a large body of research in cognitive science [22]. Experimental results indicate that human observers prefer to fixate objects, rather than the background of an image [12]. This tendency is particularly pronounced in visual search, as finding an object typically requires fixating it [51]. This strongly suggests that eye tracking data can be useful for training a

D. Fleet et al. (Eds.): ECCV 2014, Part V, LNCS 8693, pp. 361–376, 2014.

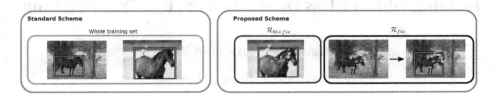

Fig. 1. (Left) The standard approach to training an object detector, where all images in the training set are manually annotated with bounding-boxes. (Right) In our approach most of the images are annotated only with human eye fixations ($\mathcal{R}_{fix}$ set). The key idea is to automatically predict bounding-boxes for the images in $\mathcal{R}_{fix}$ set given only their fixations. For this we first train a model to infer the spatial support of objects from the fixations, on a small subset of images annotated by both fixations and bounding-boxes ($\mathcal{R}_{bb+fix}$, only 7% of the images in our experiments).

system to automatically localize objects. However, fixation data only provides a rough indication of the spatial extent of an object: humans have a tendency to fixate the center of an object [33], and within animate objects (humans and animals), there is a strong preference for fixating faces [24]. Furthermore, the eye movement record will include fixations on salient non-target objects, and occasionally on the background.

Inspired by the above observations, we propose a technique for deriving a bounding-box covering the whole target object given the fixations on the image (Sec. 4). We cast bounding-box estimation as a figure-ground segmentation problem. We define a model that takes human eye movement data as input and infers the spatial support of the target object by labeling each pixel as either object or background. As the relation between fixations and bounding-boxes can be complex and vary between object classes, we train our model from a small subset of images annotated with bounding-boxes *and* fixations. The subset is only a small fraction of the dataset we want to annotate (7% of the images in our experiments). Once trained on this subset, we use our model to derive bounding-boxes from eye movement data for the whole dataset, which can then be used to train any standard object class detector, such as the Deformable Parts Model [15].

To test our hypothesis that eye tracking data can reduce the annotation effort required to train object class detectors, we collected eye tracking data for the complete training set of ten objects classes from Pascal VOC 2012 [13] (6,270 images in total). Each image is annotated with the eye movement record of five participants, whose task was to identify which object class was present in the image (Sec. 3). This dataset is publicly available at groups.inf.ed.ac.uk/calvin/eyetrackdataset/.

We demonstrate through extensive experiments on this dataset that our segmentation model can produce accurate bounding-boxes in about half the images, and that a modern object detector [15] can be trained from them (Sec. 5).

2 Related Work

Eye Movement Data in Computer Vision. Researchers in cognitive science have a long-standing interest in computational models that predict human eye movement behavior (e.g. [21,23,24]). Recently, however, a number of authors have started to use eye movement data for computer vision tasks. This includes work on image segmentation, which shows that using fixation data to help segmentation algorithms leads to improved performance [32,37,48]. Eye tracking data is also useful for face and text detection: [25] cluster fixations to find regions in which the targets are likely to be found, and then apply standard face and text detectors only there. Several authors have collected eye tracking data for video and shown that saliency maps computed from these data can improve action recognition [31,46].

Yun et al. [52] collect eye movement data for a 1,000 image subset of Pascal VOC 2008; three observers performed a three second free-viewing task. This data is then used to to re-rank the output of an object class detector [15] on test images. Our dataset is substantially larger (6,270 images, 5 observers), and our observers perform a visual search task, which is faster (one second per image) and more likely to result in fixations on the target objects (Sec. 3). Most importantly, we present a method for using eye tracking data to *train* an object class detector, replacing ground-truth bounding-boxes, rather than using them for post-processing at test time.

Weakly Supervised Learning. Our research is related to work trying to reduce the annotation effort required to train object class detectors. Weakly supervised methods train from a set of images labeled only as containing a certain object class, without location annotation [7,9,16,34,40,41,45]. These methods try to locate the object by searching for patterns of appearance recurring across the training images. However, learning a detector without location annotation is very difficult and performance is still below fully supervised methods [9,34,39]. Recently a few authors have tackled learning object class detectors from video, where the temporal continuity facilitates the task [28,36,42]. Another line of work leverages text naturally occurring near an image as a weak annotation for its contents [3,11,19,30], such as on web pages or newspapers. This form of supervision has been particularly successful for learning faces of specific people [3], in part because excellent generic face detectors are already available [47].

Our work provides a different way to reduce annotation effort which is complementary to those above. It could potentially be integrated with some of them for even greater savings.

3 Eye Tracking Dataset

3.1 Materials

The images in our dataset were taken from the 2012 edition of the Pascal VOC challenge [13]. We selected 10 of the 20 Pascal classes and included all trainval images for these classes in our dataset. We grouped our 10 classes into pairs as follows (see below for explanation): cat/dog, bicycle/motorbike, boat/aeroplane, horse/cow, sofa/diningtable. For each pair of classes, we removed all images that contained objects of both classes (e.g. images containing both horses and cows). This eliminated 91 images, or 1.4% of total, and resulted in a dataset containing 6,270 images.

(a) (b) (c)

Fig. 2. Examples of eye tracking data for three images of class motorbike. We show the sequence of fixations (circles) for five participants (color coded). Note how the first fixation falls outside the image (see main text for details).

3.2   Procedure

As explained in Sec. 2, results in the visual cognition literature indicate that free viewing may not be the optimal task for collecting eye tracking data for training automatic object detectors. A visual search task, in contrast, increases the likelihood that participants fixate the target object, as this facilitates finding the target and help complete the task correctly.

However, traditional visual search tasks require a large number of target-absent trials. For example, if the task is to search for horses (the participants presses a "yes" button if a horse is present in the image, and "no" otherwise), then the set of images shown to the participant needs to contain images without horses (typically 50%, to minimize guessing). Such a setup would mean that eye tracking data is collected for a large number of target-absent images, which then cannot be used to train a detector.

We therefore used the related task of *two-alternative forced choice object discrimination*, in which each image contains instances of one of two object classes (e.g. cow or horse), and participants have to press one of two buttons to indicate which class is present. This way, visual search data can be collected for two classes at a time, without the need for target-absent images. In adopting this approach, we paired object classes carefully, such that the two sets of images were similar in size (to minimize guessing), and such that the objects were easily confusable (similar size and background, etc.), as otherwise the task is too easy for human observers.

3.3   Apparatus

The experiment was conducted in a sound-attenuated room; participants were seated 60 cm from a 22" LCD screen (Samsung SyncMaster 2233, 100 Hz refresh rate, 5 ms response time) while their eye movements were recorded using an Eyelink 2000 eye tracker (SR Research Ltd., Ottawa), which sampled both eyes at a rate of 1,000 Hz, with a typical spatial resolution of $0.25°$ to $0.5°$. A head rest was used to minimize participants head movements and improve recording accuracy. Button presses were recorded using a Logitech gamepad that offers millisecond accuracy.

The experiment was controlled using Psychophysics Toolbox Version 3 [6]. Data collection started with a standard nine-point calibration and validation. As explained below, participants viewed images blocked by pairs of classes; the images within a block were presented in random order (a new sequence was generated for each participant). Each trial started with a central fixation cross, displayed for 500 ms, after which the image was displayed. The participant's task was to press one of the two response buttons to indicate the class to which the object(s) in the image belonged, after which the next trial was started automatically. Drift correction was performed after every 20 images; re-calibration was performed if the correction showed that this was necessary (after approximately every 200 images). Participants were offered a five minute break every 30 minutes.

The images in the Pascal dataset differ in size, and they are all smaller than the screen resolution used for the experiment (1,680 × 1,050 pixels). Instead of re-scaling the images to this resolution (which would result in visual artifacts and make the task unnatural), we presented the images in their original size, but at random offset from the center of the screen. This has the advantage that participants cannot easily develop a viewing strategy (e.g. always looking at the center of the screen, looking in the upper half), thus ensuring that we obtain maximally informative eye movement data.

3.4 Participants

A total of 28 participants (11 male) took part in the data collection, all students at the University of Edinburgh. They gave informed consent and were paid £10 per hour. The materials were divided into seven blocks of around 1,000 images each, where each block contained of all the images in one pair of classes, except for one large pairs of classes (cat/dog), which was split across three blocks. Each participant saw all the images in one block, except for five participants, who saw between two and four blocks in multiple sessions. Blocks were distributed across participants such that every image in every block was seen by five distinct participants.

3.5 Results

A total of around 178,000 fixations were collected, corresponding a mean of 5.7 fixations per participant per image. For example images with fixations superimposed, see Fig. 2. Note that we removed the first fixation of each trial, as it almost always falls on the location of the fixation cross, and thus is uninformative (as well as often being outside the image, due to the off-center presentation).

The mean response time per image (the time from the onset of the image to the button press) was 889 ms, ranging from 786 ms for cat 1090 ms for cow. This indicates that the task can be performed very efficiently by human observers, especially compared to the 26 seconds reported in [20] as the time required to draw a bounding-box. Participants were nevertheless highly accurate at the task, with a mean discrimination accuracy (percentage of correct button presses) of 95.2%, ranging from 92.9% for sofa/diningtable to 96.1% for boat/aeroplane.

We then compared the positions of the human fixations with the locations of the ground-truth bounding-boxes provided with the Pascal dataset. On average, 75.2% of all fixations on an image fell within one of the bounding-boxes for that image, ranging from 57.3% for boat to 89.6% for cat. This provides initial evidence of our claim that fixation

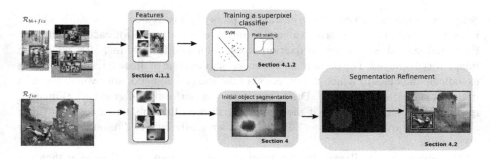

Fig. 3. Illustration of our method for predicting bounding-boxes from fixations. See sec. 4

data is useful for localizing objects, though it also indicates that there is considerable inter-class variability in fixation behavior.

4   From Fixations to Bounding-Boxes

We present here our method for localizing objects in an image given fixations (Fig. 1). We model this problem as figure-ground segmentation. Our model takes as input human fixations Φ for an image I in $\mathcal{R}_{fix}$ and infers the spatial support of the object by labeling each pixel as either object or background. The method has two stages (Fig. 3):

I) **Initial object segmentation** (Sec. 4.1) The first stage predicts an initial estimate of the object position by labeling each (super-)pixel individually. This predictor captures the relation between fixations and object positions. It is trained on the image set $\mathcal{R}_{bb+fix}$, which is annotated with both fixations and manual bounding-boxes. The output of this stage is a values for each pixel of I that corresponds to the probability to be on the object.

II) **Segmentation refinement** (Sec. 4.2). The second stage refines the segmentation with an energy model similar to GrabCut [38]. This includes pairwise dependencies between neighboring superpixels, acting as a prior preferring spatially smooth segmentations.

4.1   Initial Object Segmentation

We describe here the first stage of deriving object segmentations from fixations. We use an SVM to classify superpixels into object or background based on a diverse set of features computed from the fixations, such as the distance between a superpixel and the nearest available fixation. Before the classifier is ready to label superpixels in a new image, we train it on the set $\mathcal{R}_{bb+fix}$. In this fashion it can learn a relation between fixations and object positions specific for that object class (i.e. the relation between these features and the fact that a superpixel is on the object or not). After training, the classifier is applied to each image $I \in \mathcal{R}_{fix}$, resulting in a soft segmentation mask M (Fig. 3). Each pixel value in M corresponds to the estimated probability for it to be on the object.

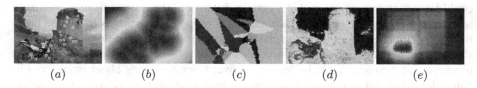

$$(a) \qquad (b) \qquad (c) \qquad (d) \qquad (e)$$

Fig. 4. (a) The positions of the fixations in an image. (b) The *near distance* feature. (c) The *rank* feature. (d) The *appearance* feature according to the distance of the nearest fixation. (e) The *objectness* feature.

Features. We start by over-segmenting each image I into superpixels S using the Turbopixels method [29]. Operating at the superpixel level greatly reduces the computational cost and memory requirements of our technique.

Let Φ be the set of fixations in the image. Each fixation is determined by four values: the (x, y) position, the duration and the rank of the fixation in chronological order.

Fixation Position Features. As mentioned in Sec. 3, we acquired fixations under a visual search task instead of the usual free-viewing task to increase the proportion of fixations on (or near) the target object. Therefore, the position of the fixations directly relates to the position of the object. This motivates us to construct good features indicating whether a superpixel s lies inside the object based on its position relative to the fixations (Fig. 5a):

- *mean distance:* the distance between the center of s and the mean position of all fixations in the image.
- *near distance:* the distance between the center of s and the position of the fixation nearest to s (Fig. 4b).
- *mean offsets:* the vertical and horizontal difference between the center of s and the mean position of all fixations in the image.
- *near offsets:* the vertical and horizontal difference between the center of s and the position of the fixation nearest to s.

Fixation Timing Features. In addition to the position of each fixation, the eye tracker also delivers timing information, such as the duration and rank of each fixation. These properties carry valuable information. Intuitively, the longer a fixation lasts, the more significant it is. Moreover, in most images the first few fixations will not fall on the target object yet, as the annotator is searching for it, while later fixations are likely to be on the target (Fig. 4c).

- *duration:* the duration of the fixation nearest to s.
- *rank:* the rank of the fixation nearest to s.

Fixation Appearance Features. The features considered so far support learning a *fixed* spatial relation between the fixations and the superpixels on the object. For example, we could learn that superpixels within a certain distance of the nearest fixation are likely to be on the object. Or we could learn that most of the object mass is below the mean fixation position (e.g. for the person class, as faces receive most fixations).

However, in images of natural objects this spatial relation might change from image to image and therefore might be hard to recover when reasoning about image coordinates alone. For instance, animals can appear in a wide range of viewpoint and deformations, but viewers tend to fixate mostly their heads. This makes it difficult to guess the full extent of their body based purely on the fixation positions.

Here we consider another family of features based on the *appearance* of superpixels (i.e. their color distribution). The key idea is that, while the fixations do not cover the whole object, many of them are on the object, and so provide examples of how it looks. Hence, we can learn about object appearance from a few superpixels hit by fixations. Analogously, we can learn about background appearance from superpixels far from fixations. We can then transfer this knowledge to all superpixels in the image. For example we might find out that a horse is brown and the background is green, even from just a few fixations, and use this knowledge to segment out the whole horse (Fig. 1). Note that this idea works regardless of the spatial relation between the shape and size of the horse in the image and the fixation positions. It effectively creates a mapping from fixation to segmentations that *adapts* to the contents of the target image.

More precisely, we estimate two Gaussian Mixture Models (GMM), one for the object and one for the background. Each GMM has 5 components, each of which is a full-covariance Gaussian over the RGB color space. We estimate the object GMM A_{obj} from all pixels inside all superpixels hit by any fixation, as these are likely on the object (Fig. 5b). Selecting background sample pixels is harder as the converse relation does not hold: the fact that a superpixel is not hit by any fixation does not reveal much about it being on the background or the object (in fact nearly all superpixels are not hit by a fixation, as fixations are extremely sparse). Therefore, we sample superpixels according to three criteria, leading to three different background GMM models A_{bg}, and we leave it to the learner to decide how to best weight them: (1) sample proportionally to the distance to the mean fixation, resulting in many samples far from the mean fixation and less and less samples as we get nearer; (2) sample proportionally to the distance to the nearest fixation. This is simply an alternative way to express 'far from the expected object location'; (3) sample inversely proportionally to the objectness probability (see next paragraph).

After estimating the appearance models A_{obj}, A_{bg}, we use them to evaluate every superpixel s in the image, resulting in per-pixel likelihoods of object/background $p(s|obj) = A_{obj}(s), p(s|bg) = A_{bg}(s)$. We combine these likelihoods in a per-pixel posterior probability of being on the object with Bayes' formula under a uniform prior: $p(obj|s) = p(s|obj)/(p(s|obj)+p(s|bg))$ (Fig. 4d). We compute three different posteriors, by using each of the three background models in turn, resulting in three appearance features for each super-pixel.

Objectness Feature. As an additional feature, we incorporate the *objectness* measure [2]. Objectness estimates the probability that an image window contains an object of *any* class. It is designed to distinguish windows containing an object with a well

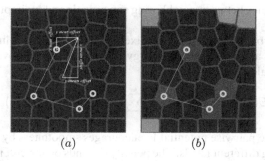

(a)   (b)

Fig. 5. Feature extraction. (a) Fixation position features. The yellow circles indicate the positions of the fixations in the image, while the red circle indicates the mean position of all fixations. The figure shows the distances from a superpixel center (red cross) that are required to compute all the feature position features. (b) Selecting foreground and background superpixels to estimate appearance models for the fixation appearance features. The selected foreground superpixels are indicated in red, while the sampled background superpixels according to the distance from the nearest fixation are in green.

defined boundary and center, such as cows and telephones, from amorphous background windows, such as grass and road. It measures distinctive characteristics of objects, such as appearing different from their surroundings, having a closed boundary, and sometimes being unique within the image.

We sample 1,000 windows using [2] according to their probability of containing an object. Then we convert this measure to per-superpixel probabilities by averaging the objectness value over all windows covering a super-pixel. This objectness feature helps by pushing the segmentation method towards objects and away from backgrounds (Fig. 4e).

Training a Superpixel Classifier. We train a separate classifier for each object class, as the relation between fixations and objects can be complex and vary between classes. As training samples we use the feature vectors of all superpixels from the $\mathcal{R}_{bb+fix}$ images of a class (Fig. 3). Each superpixel is labeled according to whether it is inside a ground-truth bounding-box or not. After whitening the features, we train a linear SVM with the very efficient implementation of [43] on a random 80% subset of the training data. We set the regularization parameter C by validation on a held-out 10% of the data, and then re-train the SVM on the total 90% of the data. In order to get a smooth, probabilistic output we apply Platt scaling [35] and fit a sigmoid to the output of the SVM on the remaining 10% of the training data.

Applying the classifier to a new image $I \in \mathcal{R}_{fix}$ yields a soft-segmentation mask M where each pixel value corresponds to the estimated probability of being on the target object. This is the output of the first stage of our method.

4.2   Segmentation Refinement

We describe here the second stage of deriving object segmentations from fixations. This refines the soft-segmentation M output by the first stage by taking into account pairwise dependencies between neighboring superpixels and by improving the appearance models.

Let $l_s \in \{0, 1\}$ be the label for superpixel s and L be the labeling of all l_s in the image. We employ a binary pairwise energy function E defined over the superpixels and their labels, analog to [26,38]

$$E(L) = \sum_s M_s(l_s) + \sum_s A_s(l_s) + \sum_{s,r} V(l_s, l_r) \tag{1}$$

As in [26,38], the pairwise potential V encourages smoothness by penalizing neighboring pixels taking different labels. The penalty depends on the color contrast between the pixels, being smaller in regions of high contrast (image edges). The summation over (s, r) is defined on an eight-connected pixel grid.

Because of the probabilistic nature of the soft segmentation mask M, we can use $M_s(l_s) = M(s)^{l_s}(1 - M(s))^{1-l_s}$ as a unary potential (with M_s the value of the mask at superpixel s). As M_s estimates the probability that superpixel s is on the object, this potential encourages the final segmentation to be close to M (see [26]). This anchors the segmentation to image regions likely to contain the target object, while letting this second stage refine its exact delineation.

The second unary potential A_s evaluates how likely a superpixel s is to take label l_s, according to object and background appearance models. As in the classic GrabCut [38], an appearance model consists of two GMMs, one for the object (used when $l_s = 1$) and one for the background (used when $l_s = 0$). Each GMM has five components, each a full-covariance Gaussian over the RGB color space.

In traditional work using similar energy models [4,38,49], estimating the appearance models requires user interaction to indicate the image region containing the object (typically a manually drawn bounding-box or scribbles). Recently, [26] proposed to automatically estimate the appearance models from a soft segmentation mask produced by transferring segmentations from manually annotated images in a training set. Inspired by that idea, we estimate our appearance models from the mask M obtained from fixations in Sec. 4.1 (so our method does not require training segmentations).

After this initial estimation, we follow [38] and alternate between finding the optimal segmentation L given the appearance models, and updating the appearance models given the segmentation. The first step is solved globally optimally by minimizing (1) using graph-cuts [5] as our pairwise potentials are submodular. The second step fits GMMs to labeled superpixels. Defining the energy over superpixels [18,27,44] instead of pixels brings great memory savings and reduces the cost to optimize over L. As demonstrated in [18], the accuracy of the superpixel model is essentially identical to the corresponding pixel model.

The final output of our method is a bounding-box enclosing the largest connected component in the segmentation (Fig. 3).

5   Experiments

We carry out experiments on the challenging Pascal VOC 2012 benchmark [13]. We first evaluate the ability of our method to derive object bounding-boxes from fixations

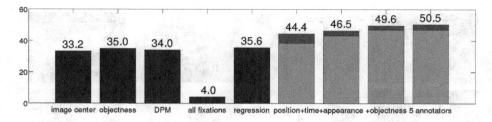

Fig. 6. CorLoc performance for the baselines (blue bars) and several stripped down versions of our model (green+red) bars. The height of the green bars indicate the performance of the initial segmentation method (i) using only position and timing features, (ii) adding appearance features, (iii) adding the objectness feature, and (iv) using all features and fixations from 5 annotators (the previous three bars use only 2 annotators). The height of the red bars show the improvement brought by the refinement stage.

on the trainval part of the dataset (Sec. 5.1). Next, we train the object class detector of [15] from these bounding-boxes and compare its performance on the test set to the original model trained from ground-truth bounding-boxes (Sec. 5.2).

5.1 From Fixations to Bounding-Boxes

Data. We consider 10 classes from Pascal VOC 2012, for a total of 6,270 images in the trainval part (see Sec. 3.1 for a list of classes). We split each class into two subsets $\mathcal{R}_{bb+fix}$ and $\mathcal{R}_{fix}$. We use both ground-truth bounding-boxes and human fixations from the set $\mathcal{R}_{bb+fix}$ to train our segmentation model. This subset contains only 7% of all trainval images. This fraction was chosen so that each class has $\geq$ 20 images. On average, each class has only 44 images. After training, we use our model to predict bounding-boxes for images in the $\mathcal{R}_{fix}$ set, which are annotated only by fixations.

Evaluation Measure. We report performance as CorLoc [9,34,36,40], i.e. the percentage of images in $\mathcal{R}_{fix}$ where a method correctly localizes an object of the target class according to the Pascal criterion [14] (intersection-over-union $\geq$ 0.5).

Baselines. In Fig. 6 we evaluate several informative baselines: **(1) image center:** a window in the image center with area set to the average over the object bounding-boxes in the $\mathcal{R}_{bb+fix}$ set. This baseline provides an indication of the difficulty of the dataset; **(2) all fixations:** a bounding-box around all fixations; **(3) objectness:** the window with the highest objectness probability, out of 1000 sampled using [2]; **(4) DPM:** the highest scored detection returned by a Deformable Parts Model detector [15] trained on the $\mathcal{R}_{bb+fix}$ set; **(5) regression:** linear regression from the mean and variance of the fixation positions to a bounding-box. This models the spatial relation between the cloud of fixations and the object with a single translation and anisotropic scaling transformation, constant across all images of a class.

As Fig. 6 shows, the *image center* baseline achieves 33.2% CorLoc, confirming the dataset contains mostly images with smaller, often off-center objects. Interestingly, *all*

Fig. 7. Qualitative results of our method for localizing objects given fixations. The fixations are indicated with yellow circles while the predicted bounding-boxes are in green. Successful examples are shown in the first four rows for various classes, while some failure cases are shown in the last row. Note how our method nicely outputs a bounding-box covering the whole object even when the fixations are concentrated on only part of it, often the center, or the head.

fixations fails entirely, demonstrating that the task of deriving bounding-boxes from fixations is far from trivial. *Regression* does much better, finding the object in 35.6% of the images. This highlights the need for learning the relation between fixations and bounding-boxes. Note how *Objectness* also performs quite well (35.0%). It can find some objects even when used on its own, confirming observations made by earlier research [17]. As *regression* and *objectness* incorporate elements of our full method, they set the standards to beat. Finally, the *DPM* baseline reaches only 34.0% CorLoc, showing that the problem cannot be solved simply by training an object detector on the small fully annotated set $\mathcal{R}_{bb+fix}$.

Results. Fig. 6 shows the CorLoc achieved by several stripped down version of our model. We study the impact of using increasingly more features (Sec. 4.1), and the difference between using only the initial segmentation stage (Sec. 4.1) or also the segmentation refinement stage (Sec. 4.2). To quantify the performance of the initial segmentation stage, we threshold the soft-segmentation mask M and fit a bounding-box around the largest segment. The threshold is optimized on the training set $\mathcal{R}_{bb+fix}$.

The results reveal several interesting observations: (1) all feature types we propose contribute to the overall performance of the full model, as adding each type in turn progressively leads to higher CorLoc; (2) with 49.6% CorLoc, our full model significantly outperforms all baselines, including *regression* and *objectness*. This shows that it can learn better, more complex relations between the fixations and the object's spatial extent than the regression baseline. It also shows that, while objectness is a valuable cue to the position of objects, our model goes well beyond it; (3) the segmentation refinement stage always helps, adding between 3% and 6% CorLoc depending on the features used in the initial segmentation stage.

As a reference, the recent weakly supervised method [39], which produces bounding-boxes on a set of images labelled only as containing a class, achieves 32% in a similar setting on Pascal VOC 2007 (which is a dataset of similar difficulty). This provides a ballpark for what can be expected when using such alternative methods.

Our results discussed above used fixations from just *two* annotators. This is an especially economical annotation scenario, as it takes only a total of about *two seconds* to annotate an image, substantially less than the 26 seconds it takes to draw a bounding-box [20]. However, as we collected fixations from five annotators per image (Sec. 3), for completeness we report also the performance of our model when using all annotators (rightmost bar in Fig. 6). As performance improves only marginally, we conclude that our model efficiently exploits the information provided by two annotators, and keep this as the default setting in the next experiment.

5.2   Training Object Class Detectors from Fixations

Settings. In the previous subsection we automatically derived bounding-boxes from fixations for the $\mathcal{R}_{fix}$ part of the Pascal VOC 2012 trainval set (i.e. 93% of the total). Here we use these predicted bounding-boxes, along with the 7% images in $\mathcal{R}_{bb+fix}$ with ground-truth bounding-boxes, to train a DPM detector per class [15]. Following the standard Pascal VOC protocol, the negative training set for a class contains all trainval images not containing that class. After training, the detectors are applied to the Pascal VOC 2012 test set (10,991 images). Performance is quantified by the mean average precision (mAP) over all 10 classes, as returned by the Pascal VOC evaluation server. We compare performance to DPM detectors trained from exactly the same images, but *all* annotated with ground-truth bounding-boxes.

Results. The mAP of detectors trained from bounding-boxes derived by our method is 12.5%, compared to 25.5% for the detectors trained from ground-truth bounding-boxes. We consider this an encouraging result, given that our scenario enables to train these detectors in 6.8× less total annotation time compared to drawing bounding-boxes on all images. This estimate takes into account all relevant factors, i.e. two annotators per image at one second per image, the time to set up and calibrate the eye tracker, breaks between blocks of images, and the time to draw bounding-boxes on the 7% images in $\mathcal{R}_{bb+fix}$. Interestingly, training DPMs from ground-truth bounding-boxes for a $6.8\times$ smaller training set leads to comparable performance as our method (13.7%).

6 Conclusions

We have presented a novel approach to train object detectors. Instead of the traditional, time consuming manual bounding-box annotation protocol, we proposed to learn the detector from eye movement data recorded while annotators simply look for the object in the training images. We proposed a technique to successfully derive object bounding-boxes from such eye movement data and demonstrated that they can be used to train a modern object detector [15].

In its current form, when given equal total annotation time, our scheme leads to detectors that are about as good as those trained from manual bounding-box annotations. In future work we plan to further improve the quality of our segmentation model, so as to localize more objects and more accurately, which should lead to training better detectors. Moreover, the bounding-boxes predicted by our method could be sent to Amazon Mechanical Turk for verification, leading to cleaner training sets at a small additional cost. As another direction, we plan to extend the work to connect it to weakly supervised models that look for repeated appearance patterns in multiple training images [10,40]. Finally, we would like to extend the work to video, ideally moving towards the dream paradigm of 'learning object detectors while watching TV'.

Acknowledgment. F. Keller was supported by the ERC under award "Synchronous Linguistic and Visual Processing". V. Ferrari was supported by ERC Starting Grant "Visual Culture for Image Understanding". We are grateful to Mukta Prasad for suggesting this research direction.

References

1. Imagenet large scale visual recognition challenge, ILSVRC (2011), http://www.image-net.org/challenges/LSVRC/2011/index
2. Alexe, B., Deselaers, T., Ferrari, V.: What is an object? In: CVPR (2010)
3. Berg, T., Berg, A., Edwards, J., Mair, M., White, R., Teh, Y., Learned-Miller, E., Forsyth, D.: Names and Faces in the News. In: CVPR (2004)
4. Blake, A., Rother, C., Brown, M., Perez, P., Torr, P.: Interactive image segmentation using an adaptive GMMRF model. In: Pajdla, T., Matas, J(G.) (eds.) ECCV 2004. LNCS, vol. 3021, pp. 428–441. Springer, Heidelberg (2004)
5. Boykov, Y., Kolmogorov, V.: An experimental comparison of min-cut/max-flow algorithms for energy minimization in vision. IEEE Trans. on PAMI 26(9), 1124–1137 (2004)
6. Brainard, D.H.: The Psychophysics Toolbox. Spatial Vision 10, 433–436 (1997)
7. Chum, O., Zisserman, A.: An exemplar model for learning object classes. In: CVPR (2007)
8. Dalal, N., Triggs, B.: Histogram of Oriented Gradients for human detection. In: CVPR (2005)

9. Deselaers, T., Alexe, B., Ferrari, V.: Weakly supervised localization and learning with generic knowledge. IJCV (2012)
10. Deselaers, T., Ferrari, V.: Global and efficient self-similarity for object classification and detection. In: CVPR (2010)
11. Duygulu, P., Barnard, K., de Freitas, J.F.G., Forsyth, D.: Object recognition as machine translation: Learning a lexicon for a fixed image vocabulary. In: Heyden, A., Sparr, G., Nielsen, M., Johansen, P. (eds.) ECCV 2002, Part IV. LNCS, vol. 2353, pp. 97–112. Springer, Heidelberg (2002)
12. Einhäuser, W., Spain, M., Perona, P.: Objects predict fixations better than early saliency. Journal of Vision 8, 1–26 (2008)
13. Everingham, M., Van Gool, L., Williams, C.K.I., Winn, J., Zisserman, A.: The PASCAL Visual Object Classes Challenge (VOC2012) Results (2012),
http://www.pascal-network.org/challenges/
VOC/voc2012/workshop/index.html
14. Everingham, M., Van Gool, L., Williams, C.K.I., Winn, J., Zisserman, A.: The pascal visual object classes (voc) challenge. IJCV (2010)
15. Felzenszwalb, P., Girshick, R., McAllester, D., Ramanan, D.: Object detection with discriminatively trained part based models. IEEE Trans. on PAMI 32(9) (2010)
16. Fergus, R., Perona, P., Zisserman, A.: Object class recognition by unsupervised scale-invariant learning. In: CVPR (2003)
17. Guillaumin, M., Ferrari, V.: Large-scale knowledge transfer for object localization in imagenet. In: CVPR (2012)
18. Guillaumin, M., Kuettel, D., Ferrari, V.: ImageNet Auto-annotation with Segmentation Propagation. Tech. rep., ETH Zurich (2013)
19. Gupta, A., Davis, L.S.: Beyond nouns: Exploiting prepositions and comparative adjectives for learning visual classifiers. In: Forsyth, D., Torr, P., Zisserman, A. (eds.) ECCV 2008, Part I. LNCS, vol. 5302, pp. 16–29. Springer, Heidelberg (2008)
20. Hao, S., Deng, J., Fei-Fei, L.: Crowdsourcing annotations for visual object detection. In: AAAI (2012)
21. Harel, J., Koch, C., Perona, P.: Graph-based visual saliency. In: NIPS (2007)
22. Henderson, J.: Human gaze control in real-world scene perception. Trends in Cognitive Sciences 7, 498–504 (2003)
23. Itti, L., Koch, C., Niebur, E.: A model of saliency-based visual attention for rapid scene analysis. IEEE Trans. on PAMI 20(11), 1254–1259 (1998)
24. Judd, T., Ehinger, K., Durand, F., Torralba, A.: Learning to predict where humans look. In: IEEE International Conference on Computer Vision, ICCV (2009)
25. Karthikeyan, S., Jagadeesh, V., Shenoy, R., Eckstein, M., Manjunath, B.: From where and how to whatwe see. In: ICCV (2013)
26. Kuettel, D., Ferrari, V.: Figure-ground segmentation by transferring window masks. In: CVPR (2012)
27. Ladicky, L., Russell, C., Kohli, P.: Associative hierarchical crfs for object class image segmentation. In: ICCV (2009)
28. Leistner, C., Godec, M., Schulter, S., Saffari, A., Bischof, H.: Improving classifiers with weakly-related videos. In: CVPR (2011)
29. Levinshtein, A., Stere, A., Kutulakos, K., Fleed, D., Dickinson, S.: Turbopixels: Fast super-pixels using geometric flows. IEEE Trans. on PAMI (2009)
30. Luo, J., Caputo, B., Ferrari, V.: Who's doing what: Joint modeling of names and verbs for simultaneous face and pose annotation. In: NIPS (2009)
31. Mathe, S., Sminchisescu, C.: Dynamic eye movement datasets and learnt saliency models for visual action recognition. In: Fitzgibbon, A., Lazebnik, S., Perona, P., Sato, Y., Schmid, C. (eds.) ECCV 2012, Part II. LNCS, vol. 7573, pp. 842–856. Springer, Heidelberg (2012)

32. Mishra, A., Aloimonos, Y., Fah, C.L.: Active segmentation with fixation. In: ICCV (2009)
33. Nuthmann, A., Henderson, J.M.: Object-based attentional selection in scene viewing. Journal of Vision 10(8), 1–19 (2010)
34. Pandey, M., Lazebnik, S.: Scene recognition and weakly supervised object localization with deformable part-based models. In: ICCV (2011)
35. Platt, J.: Probabilistic outputs for support vector machines and comparisons to regularized likelihood methods. Advances in large margin classifiers (1999)
36. Prest, A., Leistner, C., Civera, J., Schmid, C., Ferrari, V.: Learning object class detectors from weakly annotated video. In: CVPR (2012)
37. Ramanathan, S., Katti, H., Sebe, N., Kankanhalli, M., Chua, T.-S.: An eye fixation database for saliency detection in images. In: Daniilidis, K., Maragos, P., Paragios, N. (eds.) ECCV 2010, Part IV. LNCS, vol. 6314, pp. 30–43. Springer, Heidelberg (2010)
38. Rother, C., Kolmogorov, V., Blake, A.: Grabcut: interactive foreground extraction using iterated graph cuts. SIGGRAPH (2004)
39. Siva, P., Russell, C., Xiang, T., Agapito, L.: Looking beyond the image: Unsupervised learning for object saliency and detection. In: CVPR (2013)
40. Siva, P., Xiang, T.: Weakly supervised object detector learning with model drift detection. In: ICCV (2011)
41. Siva, P., Russell, C., Xiang, T.: In defence of negative mining for annotating weakly labelled data. In: Fitzgibbon, A., Lazebnik, S., Perona, P., Sato, Y., Schmid, C. (eds.) ECCV 2012, Part III. LNCS, vol. 7574, pp. 594–608. Springer, Heidelberg (2012)
42. Tang, K., Sukthankar, R., Yagnik, J., Fei-Fei, L.: Discriminative segment annotation in weakly labeled video. In: CVPR (2013)
43. Vedaldi, A., Fulkerson, B.: VLFeat: An open and portable library of computer vision algorithms (2008)
44. Veksler, O., Boykov, Y., Mehrani, P.: Superpixels and supervoxels in an energy optimization framework. In: Daniilidis, K., Maragos, P., Paragios, N. (eds.) ECCV 2010, Part V. LNCS, vol. 6315, pp. 211–224. Springer, Heidelberg (2010)
45. Vicente, S., Rother, C., Kolmogorov, V.: Object cosegmentation. In: CVPR, pp. 2217–2224 (2011)
46. Vig, E., Dorr, M., Cox, D.: Space-variant descriptor sampling for action recognition based on saliency and eye movements. In: Fitzgibbon, A., Lazebnik, S., Perona, P., Sato, Y., Schmid, C. (eds.) ECCV 2012, Part VII. LNCS, vol. 7578, pp. 84–97. Springer, Heidelberg (2012)
47. Viola, P.A., Platt, J., Zhang, C.: Multiple instance boosting for object detection. In: NIPS (2005)
48. Walber, T., Scherp, A., Staab, S.: Can you see it? Two novel eye-tracking-based measures for assigning tags to image regions. In: Li, S., El Saddik, A., Wang, M., Mei, T., Sebe, N., Yan, S., Hong, R., Gurrin, C. (eds.) MMM 2013, Part I. LNCS, vol. 7732, pp. 36–46. Springer, Heidelberg (2013)
49. Wang, J., Cohen, M.: An iterative optimization approach for unified image segmentation and matting. In: ICCV (2005)
50. Wang, X., Yang, M., Zhu, S., Lin, Y.: Regionlets for generic object detection. In: ICCV (2013)
51. Wolfe, J., Horowitz, T.S.: Visual search. Scholarpedia 3(7), 3325 (2008)
52. Yun, K., Peng, Y., Samaras, D., Zelinsky, G.J., Berg, T.L.: Studying relationships between human gaze, description, and computer vision. In: CVPR (2013)

Depth Based Object Detection from Partial Pose Estimation of Symmetric Objects

Ehud Barnea and Ohad Ben-Shahar

Dept. of Computer Science, Ben-Gurion University of the Negev, Beer Sheva, Israel
{barneaeh,ben-shahar}@cs.bgu.ac.il

Abstract. Category-level object detection, the task of locating object instances of a given category in images, has been tackled with many algorithms employing standard color images. Less attention has been given to solving it using range and depth data, which has lately become readily available using laser and RGB-D cameras. Exploiting the different nature of the depth modality, we propose a novel shape-based object detector with partial pose estimation for axial or reflection symmetric objects. We estimate this partial pose by detecting target's symmetry, which as a global mid-level feature provides us with a robust frame of reference with which shape features are represented for detection. Results are shown on a particularly challenging depth dataset and exhibit significant improvement compared to the prior art.

Keywords: Object detection, 3D computer vision, Range data, Partial pose estimation.

1 Introduction

The recent advances in the production of depth cameras have made it easy to acquire depth information of scenes in the form of RGB-D images or 3D point clouds. The depth modality, which is inherently different than color and intensity, is lately being employed to solve many kinds of computer vision problems, such as object recognition [12], object detection [7,26], pose estimation [24,1] and segmentation [25].

Owing to the growing research interest, several datasets that include depth information have also been publicly released [11,9,26], allowing to evaluate different algorithms requiring this kind of data. Like image databases for appearance-based detection (e.g., [5]), the Berkeley category-level 3D object dataset [9] contains a high variability of objects in different scenes and under many viewpoints. Together with available bounding box annotations this dataset is perfectly suitable for the task of object category detection.

Considering the available depth data, we propose to tackle the category-level object detection problem of *symmetric* objects. While this may seem limiting, a quick look around reveals the extent to which symmetry is present in our lives, and it may come as no surprise that most of the objects in the Berkeley category-level 3D object dataset [9] and in the Washington's RGB-D Object Dataset [11]

D. Fleet et al. (Eds.): ECCV 2014, Part V, LNCS 8693, pp. 377–390, 2014.

are symmetric as well. Our proposed detector therefore attempts to exploits symmetry to provide partial pose estimation and then constructs a representation that is based on this estimation. More specifically, once partial pose estimation is obtained from the symmetry, we construct a feature vector by processing surface normal angles and bins that are both calculated relative to the estimated partial pose. In what follows we discuss the relevant background (Section 2) followed by an elaborate description of our suggested algorithm (Section 3) and comparative results to previous methods (Section 4).

2   Background

2.1   Employing the Depth Modality

The depth modality has been applied to most kinds of computer vision problems, even more so following the release of the Kinect camera. This kind of data, in contrast to plain RGB, enables a much easier calculation of various things such as the separation of foreground from background (by thresholding distances), floor detection and removal (by finding the dominant plane in the scene [1]), segmentation of non-touching objects (by identifying and removing the floor [1]), or the estimation of surface normals and curvature (e.g., by fitting planes to 3D points in small neighborhoods [22]).

In previous studies, depth images were often treated as intensity images [26,9], allowing them to be used with previous algorithms requiring regular images. Exploiting surface *normals* as well, Hinterstoisser et al. [8] recently suggested a combined similarity measure by considering both image gradients and surface normals. This was done to combine the qualities of color with depth, as strong edges are prominent mostly *on* object silhouettes, whereas the normals make explicit the shape *between* silhouettes.

2.2   RGB-D Category-Level Object Detection

Object detection in color images has been a subject of research for many years. With the introduction of depth data to the field new challenges emerge such as how to properly use this kind of data, or how it may be used in conjunction with RGB data to combine the spatial characteristics of both channels.

A baseline study by Janoch et al. [9] employed the popular part-based detector by Felzenszwalb et al. [6]. Taking object's parts into account, this model is a variant of the HoG algorithm [4] that combines a sliding window approach together with a representation based on histograms of edge orientations. This detector was employed by running it on depth images while treating them as intensity images. The results indicated that applying this algorithm to color images always gives better results than applying it over depth images, though it is important to note that sometimes database objects have no depth information associated with them (see Figure 1), which gives a somewhat unfair advantage to color-based algorithms. Tang et al. [27] also uses the HoG formulation, but with histograms of surface normals that are characterized by two spherical angles.

Fig. 1. An example of a color and depth image pair from the Berkeley category-level 3D object dataset [9]. The cup, bottle and monitor at the border of the color image are almost completeley missing in the depth image due to a smaller field of view. Significant information is also missing from the monitor screen in the center (dark blue depicts missing depth information).

Since several previous algorithms require prior segmentation [2,21], Kim et al. [10] alleviate such requirement by detecting a small set of segmentation hypotheses. A part-based model generalized to 3D is used together with HoG features and other 3D features of the segmented objects. This scheme results in a feature vector containing both color features and 3D features, which gives better results in most categories. Depth information was also used for object size estimation [23,9] and to combine detector responses from different views [13].

Regardless of the color or depth features employed, an important issue of object detection is the treatment of object pose. A robust detector must be general enough to capture its sought-after object at different poses, and there are different ways of doing so. The naïve way, as shared by most detectors, is to rely on machine-learning classifiers to be able to generalize diverse training data. However, machine-learning methods have limitations (like any other method) and cannot always be expected to generalize well. In order to achieve better results some try and provide the learning algorithm with "easier" examples to learn from. This is done by estimating the object's pose prior to the classification phase [15], and using it to align the object to a canonical pose or to calculate features in relation to the estimation. For example, Tang et al.[27] sought detection by estimating the pose using the centroid of normal directions, but unfortunately with no improvement to detection results.

2.3 Symmetry Detection

Symmetry is a phenomenon occurring abundantly in nature. Extensive research has been done trying to detect all kinds of symmetry in both 2D [18] and 3D [17]. Complete symmetry detection (including the detection of multiple types of symmetry and across multiple objects in an image) is a hard problem due to the different types of symmetry found in nature. For this reason, research is usually focused on specific symmetries, ranging from rigid translation [29] and reflection [16,19], to non-rigid symmetry [20] and curved glide reflection [14] (which is a combination of reflection and translation relative to a curve).

Proposed symmetry detection methods may also be classified as solving for either partial or global symmetries. While an image containing various symmetric objects is likely to contain a great deal of local symmetries, the image itself may not necessarily be globally symmetric. Partial symmetry detection entails finding the symmetric parts of the image, in contrast to global symmetry detection in which all of the image pixels are expected to participate. More formally, global symmetry, being a special case of partial symmetry [17], is characterized by a transformation that maps the entire data to itself, while for partial symmetry a sought-after transformation maps only part of the data to itself.

Considered somewhere between global and local, images of *segmented* symmetric objects may contain only object points, but under various viewpoints some of the data will have no visible symmetric counterpart. Working with this kind of data, a shape reconstruction algorithm by Thrun et al. [28] detects symmetry by employing a probabilistic model to score hypothetical symmetries. This way, several types of symmetry are found, including point reflection, plane reflection, and axial symmetry. The several types are found efficiently by taking into account the relations between symmetry types, as the existence of some symmetries entails the existence of others as well.

3   Partial Pose Invariant Detector

Considering the abundance of symmetric objects, a robust detection of symmetry may prove a valuable mid-level feature for many computer vision tasks. Here, we propose to use it for object detection in depth data, and the overview below is followed by a detailed account of the calculations.

We first observe that when a complete estimation of an object's pose is given, one may improve detector performance. The target can be aligned to match a given model, or alternatively a richer representation may be obtained using the pose estimation as a reference. Indeed, a quick and accurate estimation prior to the detection process is not an easy task. Still, seeking to benefit from such information, we propose to estimate the object's pose at least partially, by exploiting its symmetry properties.

Even though complete pose invariance is highly desired, in practice many objects rarely appear in all possible poses. For example, looking from a human's point of view, surfaces of tables are usually visible but bottoms of cars are rarely so. In such cases (and many others), even partial knowledge regarding symmetry may supply most of the pose information of objects observed from likely viewpoints. Figure 2 presents such cases for one selected class of objects.

As it happens, many objects, including almost all of the objects in both Berkeley's category dataset [9] and Washington's RGB-D Object Dataset [11], are highly symmetric. Thus, we limit our scope to working with objects with reflection symmetry over a plane and note that axial symmetrical objects are also plane symmetric [28]. Using the detected reflection symmetry plane a reference

Fig. 2. Typical examples of chair poses. If the symmetry of these chairs (in this case, about a reflection plane) is known, most pose variability in these examples may be accounted for. Indeed, when viewed from a typical viewpoint, the pose of a chair varies by rotation about an axis normal to the floor. This uncertainty is removed once the chair symmetry plane is known.

frame is constructed, and estimated surface normals [22] are represented as 2 angles based on the known partial pose. The normals are grouped inside bins calculated relative to the complete reference frame and a feature vector is constructed using this resultant histograms.

To conveniently leverage the advantages of depth data mentioned in section 2 we scan the space with a fixed-size 3D box sliding over the cloud of points in space. This is done in an efficient manner, without considering empty parts of space, places that are too far away from the camera or those containing just a small batch of nearby points. For each box the best symmetry plane passing through the box's center is found, and features are calculated using the data points inside the box. This is followed by a classification of the resultant feature vector using SVM. Since several boxes are usually classified as containing the same object, nearby detections are removed using a non-maximum suppression process. In the next sections we describe the calculations performed for every 3D box, consisting of the symmetry detection process and the computation of the features and feature vector used for classification.

3.1   Symmetry Plane Detection and the Reference Frame

Taking into account every relevant box in space greatly simplifies the symmetry plane detection task. If it contains the target object, most points inside the box are likely to belong to that object, while the number of outliers is usually not too great, a property that distinguishes range data from intensity/color data. More importantly, scanning the entire space, we are assured that some box will have its center point coincide with the sought-after symmetry plane. Since a plane can be represented with a point and a normal, only the normal remains to solve for. Be that as it may, we assume that points are generated from

Fig. 3. Points with no visible symmetric partners are colored blue in the rightmost image of the two examples. The points are identified by the process described in the text, given the symmetry plane depicted in the 3rd image (in which points are colored according to their side of the plane). The RGB-D image for the right example is taken from the RGB-D People Dataset [26].

a perspective imaging device (from a single viewpoint), so the corresponding symmetric point of many inlier points (or even all of them) is simply not visible. These points are first identified following a scoring strategy that ranks every possible reflection plane normal. For that purpose, the 2 angles comprising the normal's spherical representation[1] are quantized and the best pair is chosen using a score penalizing symmetric point pairs (relative to the candidate plane) with non-symmetric surface normals (in contrast to Thrun et al. [28]). The formal details follow below.

Prior to calculating a score for a candidate symmetry plane, we first deal with the inlier points without symmetric partners. Self occlusion dictates that when observing an object from one side of the symmetry plane, most of the visible inlier points that are observed will be the ones that share the same side with the camera. For the same reason, inlier points that are observed on the other side should all have visible symmetric points in the camera's side (as portrayed by the "lady" object in Figure 3). Knowing this, we find these points on the closer side of the candidate plane with no partners on the farther side and disregard them from the score calculation. To do so we rely on surface normals, observing that a point $\mathbf{x}$ on a surface with an estimated surface normal [22] $\mathbf{n_x}$ is visible from viewpoint $\mathbf{p_v}$ if [22]:

$$\mathbf{n_x} \cdot (\mathbf{p_v} - \mathbf{x}) > 0. \tag{1}$$

Consequently, we look for points whose symmetric partner has a surface normal that points away from the camera. A point $\mathbf{x}$ with estimated normal $\mathbf{n_x}$ is reflected over a candidate symmetry plane with center point $\mathbf{p}$ and normal $\mathbf{n_p}$ by:

$$\tilde{\mathbf{x}} = \mathbf{x} - 2 \cdot \mathbf{n_p} \cdot d_x, \tag{2}$$

where d_x is the signed distance between the point $\mathbf{x}$ and the plane. Correspondingly, $\mathbf{x}$'s normal is reflected as well by:

$$\tilde{\mathbf{n}}_\mathbf{x} = \mathbf{n_x} - 2 \cdot \mathbf{n_p} \cdot d_n, \tag{3}$$

---

[1] A normal's magnitude is always 1 and thus only its direction should be represented.

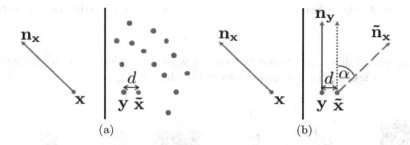

Fig. 4. Determining a reflection score for point **x** using its reflection $\tilde{\mathbf{x}}$, the closest point **y** is found (a), then the point is scored according to the distance d and normal difference α (b)

where $\mathbf{n_x}$ is the normal we wish to reflect and d_n is the signed distance between the normal's head and the candidate plane, centered at the camera's axes origin with normal $\mathbf{n_p}$. Thus **x** has no symmetric partner if:

$$\tilde{\mathbf{n}}_{\mathbf{x}} \cdot (\mathbf{p_v} - \tilde{\mathbf{x}}) \leq 0. \qquad (4)$$

Following that, each point is assigned a *point reflection score* that measures the "wellness" of its reflection. An observed point **y** with normal $\mathbf{n_y}$ closest to $\tilde{\mathbf{x}}$ (and in the same side) is found using a kd-tree data structure and the score of **x** is determined by:

$$x_{score} = d + w \cdot \alpha, \qquad (5)$$

where d is the distance between $\tilde{\mathbf{x}}$ and **y**, α is the angle between $\tilde{\mathbf{n}}_{\mathbf{x}}$ and $\mathbf{n_y}$ (see Figure 4), and w is a weighing factor. A lower value implies good symmetry and the best plane is chosen as the one that minimizes the mean score of all the contributing points [2].

In order to have a complete reference frame for the symmetry plane we endow $\mathbf{n_p}$ with another unit length reference vector **r** that lies *on* the plane. It is chosen to be on the verge of visibility according to equation 1, and to be directed upwards. Summarizing these constraints we get:

1. $\|\mathbf{r}\| = 1$ (**r** is of unit length)
2. $\mathbf{r} \cdot (\mathbf{p_v} - \mathbf{p}) = 0$ (**r** is on the verge of visibility)
3. $\mathbf{r} \cdot \mathbf{n_p} = 0$ (**r** is on the symmetry plane)
4. $\mathbf{r} \cdot [0, 1, 0] \leq 0$ (**r** points up[3])

Therefore, we calculate **r** with:

$$\mathbf{r} = \mathbf{n_p} \times \frac{(\mathbf{p_v} - \mathbf{p})}{\|\mathbf{p_v} - \mathbf{p}\|}, \qquad (6)$$

---

[2] Points from the farther side to the camera, and closer side points for which equation 4 does *not* hold.

[3] Working relative to the Kinect camera's coordinates (in which the y axis points down) the "up" direction is defined as the negative y direction.

and complete the reference frame by calculating the third orthonormal vector:

$$\mathbf{i} = \mathbf{n_p} \times \mathbf{r}. \tag{7}$$

Examples of detected symmetry together with a complete reference frame may be seen in Figure 5 for two objects from the chair category.

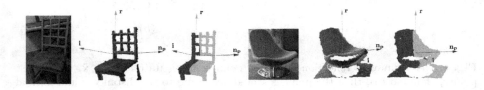

Fig. 5. The detected symmetry plane and reference frame of two chairs. The vector $\mathbf{n_p}$ is the normal of the detected plane (blue), $\mathbf{r}$ points up (green), and $\mathbf{i}$ is the cross product of the two vectors (red).

3.2   Feature Vector Construction

Our feature vector for the purpose of detecting objects with varying pose is based on histograms of normals that are accumulated into angular bins that are created relative to the reference frame. Our representation of normal directions is relative only to the estimated symmetry.

For every point in the box we use a representation of the surface normal based on two angles. However, instead of representing normals with regular spherical coordinates (that will depend on $\mathbf{r}$) we use two angles that are independent of our choice of reference frame. Let $\mathbf{x}$ be a cloud point with surface normal $\mathbf{n_x}$, and let $\bar{\mathbf{x}}$ and $\bar{\mathbf{n}}_\mathbf{x}$ be their projections on the symmetry plane $(\mathbf{p}, \mathbf{n_p})$. The first angle $\theta \in [0, \pi]$ we use is the one between the normal $\mathbf{n_x}$ and the plane normal $\mathbf{n_p}$:

$$\theta = cos^{-1}(\mathbf{n_x} \cdot \mathbf{n_p}). \tag{8}$$

The second angle $\phi \in [0, 2\pi)$ in our representation is the signed angle between the projected normal $\bar{\mathbf{n}}_\mathbf{x}$ and the vector connecting the box center $\mathbf{p}$ with the projected point $\bar{\mathbf{x}}$:

$$\phi = cos^{-1}\left(\frac{\bar{\mathbf{n}}_\mathbf{x}}{\|\bar{\mathbf{n}}_\mathbf{x}\|} \cdot \frac{\mathbf{p} - \bar{\mathbf{x}}}{\|\mathbf{p} - \bar{\mathbf{x}}\|}\right). \tag{9}$$

This is then followed by an addition of π depending on the direction of $\bar{\mathbf{n}}_\mathbf{x}$ relative to direction vector:

$$direction = \mathbf{n_p} \cdot \frac{\mathbf{p} - \bar{\mathbf{x}}}{\|\mathbf{p} - \bar{\mathbf{x}}\|}. \tag{10}$$

These two angles supply us with a representation that depends only on the estimated symmetry plane. We selected this particular representation of surface normals because it is fixed under different poses of an object.

The normals, represented using the above two angles, are accumulated in histograms based on the spatial location of their points. In order to be robust to variations of the arbitrarily chosen **r** vector a given box is divided into spatio-angular bins based on distance from the symmetry plane together with angular distance from **r**, as can be seen in Figure 6. Each bin is associated with two 1D histograms for the angles described above, which are then normalized and concatenated to form the feature vector that is then classified using RBF-kernel SVM [3].

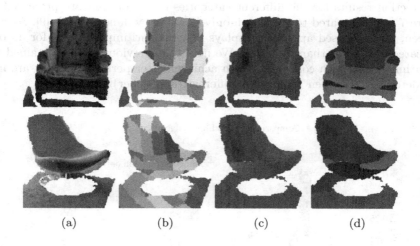

(a)   (b)   (c)   (d)

Fig. 6. Boxes are divided into spatio-angular bins (b). Each point is associated with two angles, depicted in (c) and (d).

4 Experimental Results

We evaluate our proposed approach over the Berkeley category-level 3D object dataset [9] that exhibits significant variations in terms of objects and poses. The dataset supplies basic object annotations in the form of 2D bounding boxes that we use for the evaluation of detector performance. However, our detector requires training examples in the form of fix-sized 3D bounding boxes in space. To this end we extended the provided annotations and added the 3D center point of every annotated object[4].

Object detection algorithms incorporating depth information may be grouped in two categories, either working with depth only, or combining depth and color. The former allows to understand the strength of the depth modality in itself (for object detection), while the latter better leads to an understanding of the

---

[4] Supplementary information, including our annotations, will be available at http://www.cs.bgu.ac.il/~icvl

role depth plays in relation to color (appearance) and the interaction between the two modalities. Seeking to properly compare the two groups of detectors, it is important to note that not only the latter contains more information, but also that depth-only detectors suffer an intrinsic disadvantage in this particular dataset, since objects' depth information is sometimes completely missing due to the smaller field of view of Kinect's depth camera compared to its color camera, or due to imaging artifacts resulting in pixels with no depth information (see Figure 1 again). For these reasons we compare our results to algorithms employing only depth information.

Detection results for the different categories in the dataset are presented in Figure 7 and compared to the depth-only baseline by Janoch et al. [9]. As can be seen, our proposed approach displays a significant improvement for all object categories other than monitors. We note that previous results obtained by algorithms using both color and depth achieve better performance but are not considered here for their reliance on different (and richer) sensory data.

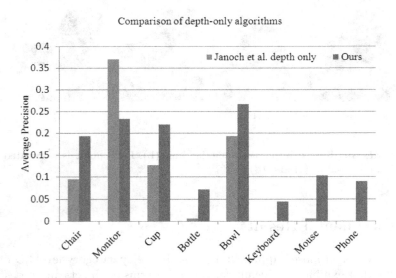

Fig. 7. Average precision of depth-only algorithms over the Berkeley category-level 3D object dataset [9]. Our method presents significant improvement for most categories except for the monitor class.

Finally, examples of true and false positives over selected categories are illustrated in Figure 8 (for chairs) and Figure 9 (for cups).

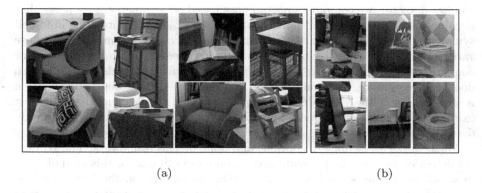

(a)   (b)

Fig. 8. Examples of true positives (a) and false positives (b) of chairs. As can be seen, chairs with different poses and different geometry are successfully detected, while scenes with chair-like geometry may lead to false detection. Such structures may be induced by couches, toilets, monitors placed on desks, or desks placed next to walls.

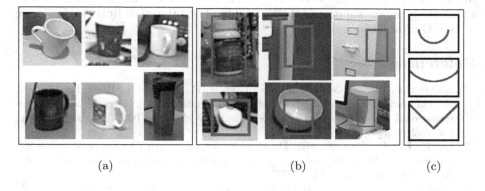

(a)   (b)   (c)

Fig. 9. Examples of true positives (a) and false positives (b) of cups. Cups with different shapes and poses are detected, and cup-like structures may lead to false detections. Red rectangles mark the precise locations of hallucinated cups, and as can be seen, may be induced by bottles, mice, bowl-parts, or corners of walls, drawers or speakers. The red curves in (c) illustrate a cross-sections of a cup, a bowl, and a corner (respectively, from top to bottom), portraying the large simmilarity between shapes.

5   Conclusions and Future Work

The current availability of depth cameras has made depth information easily accessible, with many possibilities for new and exciting directions of research. The unique properties of this kind of information raises the question of how to properly exploit it. Focusing on object detection from depth-only data, we addressed this question with an object detector involving pose estimation. Since a complete and accurate pose estimation would be too expensive for a sliding window detector, we compute a partial pose based on symmetry, a property that is robust as a mid-level and global feature over object's points. The obtained symmetry, detected using surface normals, may account for most of the pose variations of many objects, and is leveraged by a specially crafted feature vector consisting of angular binning and histograms of surface normals. Our approach does not require registration and can be used when only depth information is present (as is the case for most depth cameras). Under such conditions it exhibits significant improvement in performace compared to previous depth-only detection algorithms.

Much work can be done to continue and build on this framework. The symmetry detection process can be made better and more suitable for this kind of data, in which most points are inliers, and outliers usually lie on the box's borders. Incorporating the proposed approach together with color gradients is likely to present further improvement for cases where a registered pair of color and depth images are available.

Acknowledgements. This research was funded in part by the European Commission in the 7th Framework Programme (CROPS GA no. 246252). We also thank the generous support of the Frankel fund and the ABC Robotics Initiative at Ben-Gurion University.

References

1. Aldoma, A., Vincze, M., Blodow, N., Gossow, D., Gedikli, S., Rusu, R., Bradski, G.: Cad-model recognition and 6dof pose estimation using 3d cues. In: IEEE International Conference on Computer Vision Workshops (ICCV Workshops), pp. 585–592 (2011)
2. Bo, L., Lai, K., Ren, X., Fox, D.: Object recognition with hierarchical kernel descriptors. In: Proceedings of the IEEE Conference on Computer Vision and Pattern Recognition, pp. 1729–1736. IEEE (2011)
3. Chang, C.C., Lin, C.J.: LIBSVM: A library for support vector machines. ACM Transactions on Intelligent Systems and Technology 2(3), 27:1–27:27 (2011)
4. Dalal, N., Triggs, B.: Histograms of oriented gradients for human detection. In: Proceedings of the IEEE Conference on Computer Vision and Pattern Recognition, pp. 886–893 (2005)
5. Everingham, M., Van Gool, L., Williams, C., Winn, J., Zisserman, A.: The pascal visual object classes (voc) challenge. International Journal of Computer Vision 88(2), 303–338 (2010)
6. Felzenszwalb, P., McAllester, D., Ramanan, D.: A discriminatively trained, multi-scale, deformable part model. In: Proceedings of the IEEE Conference on Computer Vision and Pattern Recognition, pp. 1–8 (2008)
7. Hinterstoisser, S., Holzer, S., Cagniart, C., Ilic, S., Konolige, K., Navab, N., Lepetit, V.: Multimodal templates for real-time detection of texture-less objects in heavily cluttered scenes. In: Proceedings of the IEEE International Conference on Computer Vision, pp. 858–865 (2011)
8. Hinterstoisser, S., Cagniart, C., Ilic, S., Sturm, P., Navab, N., Fua, P., Lepetit, V.: Gradient response maps for real-time detection of textureless objects. IEEE Transactions on Pattern Analysis and Machine Intelligence 34(5), 876–888 (2012)

9. Janoch, A., Karayev, S., Jia, Y., Barron, J., Fritz, M., Saenko, K., Darrell, T.: A category-level 3-d object dataset: Putting the kinect to work. In: Consumer Depth Cameras for Computer Vision (2011)
10. Kim, B., Xu, S., Savarese, S.: Accurate localization of 3d objects from rgb-d data using segmentation hypotheses. In: Proceedings of the IEEE Conference on Computer Vision and Pattern Recognition, pp. 886–893 (2013)
11. Lai, K., Bo, L., Ren, X., Fox, D.: A large-scale hierarchical multi-view rgb-d object dataset. In: Proceedings of the IEEE International Conference on Robotics and Automation (2011)
12. Lai, K., Bo, L., Ren, X., Fox, D.: Sparse distance learning for object recognition combining rgb and depth information. In: Proceedings of the IEEE International Conference on Robotics and Automation, pp. 4007–4013 (2011)
13. Lai, K., Bo, L., Ren, X., Fox, D.: Detection-based object labeling in 3d scenes. In: Proceedings of the IEEE International Conference on Robotics and Automation, pp. 1330–1337 (2012)
14. Lee, S., Liu, Y.: Curved glide-reflection symmetry detection. IEEE Transactions on Pattern Analysis and Machine Intelligence 34(2), 266–278 (2012)
15. Lin, Z., Davis, L.S.: A pose-invariant descriptor for human detection and segmentation. In: Forsyth, D., Torr, P., Zisserman, A. (eds.) ECCV 2008, Part IV. LNCS, vol. 5305, pp. 423–436. Springer, Heidelberg (2008)
16. Loy, G., Eklundh, J.-O.: Detecting symmetry and symmetric constellations of features. In: Leonardis, A., Bischof, H., Pinz, A. (eds.) ECCV 2006. LNCS, vol. 3952, pp. 508–521. Springer, Heidelberg (2006)
17. Mitra, N., Pauly, M., Wand, M., Ceylan, D.: Symmetry in 3d geometry: Extraction and applications. In: EUROGRAPHICS State-of-the-art Report (2012)
18. Park, M., Lee, S., Chen, P., Kashyap, S., Butt, A., Liu, Y.: Performance evaluation of state-of-the-art discrete symmetry detection algorithms. In: Proceedings of the IEEE Conference on Computer Vision and Pattern Recognition, pp. 1–8 (2008)
19. Podolak, J., Shilane, P., Golovinskiy, A., Rusinkiewicz, S., Funkhouser, T.: A planar-reflective symmetry transform for 3d shapes. ACM Transactions on Graphics 25(3), 549–559 (2006)
20. Raviv, D., Bronstein, A., Bronstein, M., Kimmel, R.: Symmetries of non-rigid shapes. In: Non-rigid Registration and Tracking through Learning workshop (NRTL), IEEE International Conference on Computer Vision (ICCV), pp. 1–7 (2007)
21. Redondo-Cabrera, C., López-Sastre, R., Acevedo-Rodriguez, J., Maldonado-Bascón, S.: Surfing the point clouds: Selective 3d spatial pyramids for category-level object recognition. In: Proceedings of the IEEE Conference on Computer Vision and Pattern Recognition, pp. 3458–3465 (2012)
22. Rusu, R.: Semantic 3D Object Maps for Everyday Manipulation in Human Living Environments. Ph.D. thesis, Technische Universitaet Muenchen, Germany (2009)
23. Saenko, K., Karayev, S., Jia, Y., Shyr, A., Janoch, A., Long, J., Fritz, M., Darrell, T.: Practical 3-d object detection using category and instance-level appearance models. In: IEEE International Workshop on Intelligent Robots and Systems, pp. 1817–1824 (2011)
24. Shotton, J., Sharp, T., Kipman, A., Fitzgibbon, A., Finocchio, M., Blake, A., Cook, M., Moore, R.: Real-time human pose recognition in parts from single depth images. Communication of the ACM 56(1), 116–124 (2013)
25. Silberman, N., Fergus, R.: Indoor scene segmentation using a structured light sensor. In: IEEE International Conference on Computer Vision Workshops, ICCV Workshops (2011)

26. Spinello, L., Arras, K.: People detection in rgb-d data. In: IEEE International Workshop on Intelligent Robots and Systems, pp. 3838–3843 (2011)
27. Tang, S., Wang, X., Lv, X., Han, T.X., Keller, J., He, Z., Skubic, M., Lao, S.: Histogram of oriented normal vectors for object recognition with a depth sensor. In: Lee, K.M., Matsushita, Y., Rehg, J.M., Hu, Z. (eds.) ACCV 2012, Part II. LNCS, vol. 7725, pp. 525–538. Springer, Heidelberg (2013)
28. Thrun, S., Wegbreit, B.: Shape from symmetry. In: Proceedings of the IEEE International Conference on Computer Vision, pp. 1824–1831 (2005)
29. Zhao, P., Quan, L.: Translation symmetry detection in a fronto-parallel view. In: Proceedings of the IEEE Conference on Computer Vision and Pattern Recognition, pp. 1009–1016 (2011)

Edge Boxes: Locating Object Proposals from Edges

C. Lawrence Zitnick and Piotr Dollár

Microsoft Research

Abstract. The use of object proposals is an effective recent approach for increasing the computational efficiency of object detection. We propose a novel method for generating object bounding box proposals using edges. Edges provide a sparse yet informative representation of an image. Our main observation is that the number of contours that are wholly contained in a bounding box is indicative of the likelihood of the box containing an object. We propose a simple box objectness score that measures the number of edges that exist in the box minus those that are members of contours that overlap the box's boundary. Using efficient data structures, millions of candidate boxes can be evaluated in a fraction of a second, returning a ranked set of a few thousand top-scoring proposals. Using standard metrics, we show results that are significantly more accurate than the current state-of-the-art while being faster to compute. In particular, given just 1000 proposals we achieve over 96% object recall at overlap threshold of 0.5 and over 75% recall at the more challenging overlap of 0.7. Our approach runs in 0.25 seconds and we additionally demonstrate a near real-time variant with only minor loss in accuracy.

Keywords: object proposals, object detection, edge detection.

1   Introduction

The goal of object detection is to determine whether an object exists in an image, and if so where in the image it occurs. The dominant approach to this problem over the past decade has been the sliding windows paradigm in which object classification is performed at every location and scale in an image [1,2,3]. Recently, an alternative framework for object detection has been proposed. Instead of searching for an object at every image location and scale, a set of object bounding box proposals is first generated with the goal of reducing the set of positions that need to be further analyzed. The remarkable discovery made by these approaches [4,5,6,7,8,9,10,11] is that object proposals may be accurately generated in a manner that is agnostic to the type of object being detected. Object proposal generators are currently used by several state-of-the-art object detection algorithms [5,12,13], which include the winners of the 2013 ImageNet detection challenge [14] and top methods on the PASCAL VOC dataset [15].

High recall and *efficiency* are critical properties of an object proposal generator. If a proposal is not generated in the vicinity of an object that object

D. Fleet et al. (Eds.): ECCV 2014, Part V, LNCS 8693, pp. 391–405, 2014.

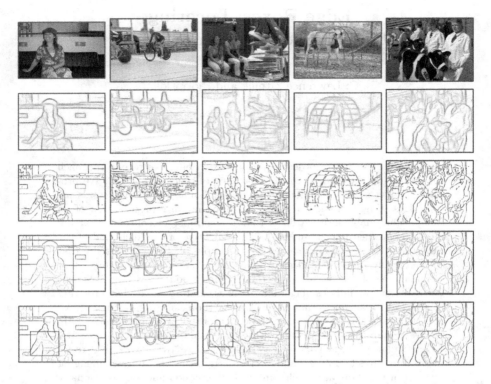

Fig. 1. Illustrative examples showing from top to bottom (first row) original image, (second row) Structured Edges [16], (third row) edge groups, (fourth row) example correct bounding box and edge labeling, and (fifth row) example incorrect boxes and edge labeling. Green edges are predicted to be part of the object in the box ($w_b(s_i) = 1$), while red edges are not ($w_b(s_i) = 0$). Scoring a candidate box based solely on the number of contours it *wholly encloses* creates a surprisingly effective object proposal measure. The edges in rows 3-5 are thresholded and widened to increase visibility.

cannot be detected. An effective generator is able to obtain high recall using a relatively modest number of candidate bounding boxes, typically ranging in the hundreds to low thousands per image. The precision of a proposal generator is less critical since the number of generated proposals is a small percentage of the total candidates typically considered by sliding window approaches (which may evaluate tens to hundreds of thousands of locations *per object category*). Since object proposal generators are primarily used to reduce the computational cost of the detector, they should be significantly faster than the detector itself. There is some speculation that the use of a small number of object proposals may even improve detection accuracy due to reduction of spurious false positives [4].

In this paper we propose *Edge Boxes*, a novel approach to generating object bounding box proposals directly from edges. Similar to segments, edges provide a simplified but informative representation of an image. In fact, line drawings of an image can accurately convey the high-level information contained in an image using only a small fraction of the information [17,18]. As we demonstrate, the use of edges offers many computational advantages since they may be efficiently computed [16] and the resulting edge maps are sparse. In this work we investigate how to directly detect object proposals from edge-maps.

Our main contribution is the following observation: the number of contours *wholly enclosed* by a bounding box is indicative of the likelihood of the box containing an object. We say a contour is wholly enclosed by a box if all edge pixels belonging to the contour lie within the interior of the box. Edges tend to correspond to object boundaries, and as such boxes that tightly enclose a set of edges are likely to contain an object. However, some edges that lie within an object's bounding box may not be part of the contained object. Specifically, edge pixels that belong to contours straddling the box's boundaries are likely to correspond to objects or structures that lie outside the box, see Figure 1. In this paper we demonstrate that scoring a box based on the number of contours it *wholly encloses* creates a surprisingly effective proposal measure. In contrast, simply counting the number of edge pixels within the box is not as informative. Our approach bears some resemblance to superpixels straddling measure introduced by [4]; however, rather than measuring the number of straddling contours we instead remove such contours from consideration.

As the number of possible bounding boxes in an image is large, we must be able to score candidates efficiently. We utilize the fast and publicly available Structured Edge detector recently proposed in [16,19] to obtain the initial edge map. To aid in later computations, neighboring edge pixels of similar orientation are clustered together to form groups. Affinities are computed between edge groups based on their relative positions and orientations such that groups forming long continuous contours have high affinity. The score for a box is computed by summing the edge strength of all edge groups within the box, minus the strength of edge groups that are part of a contour that straddles the box's boundary, see Figure 1.

We evaluate candidate boxes utilizing a sliding window approach, similar to traditional object detection. At every potential object position, scale and aspect ratio we generate a score indicating the likelihood of an object being present. Promising candidate boxes are further refined using a simple coarse-to-fine search. Utilizing efficient data structures, our approach is capable of rapidly finding the top object proposals from among millions of potential candidates.

We show improved recall rates over state-of-the-art methods for a wide range of intersection over union thresholds, while simultaneously improving efficiency. In particular, on the PASCAL VOC dataset [15], given just 1000 proposals we achieve over 96% object recall at overlap threshold of 0.5 and over 75% recall at an overlap of 0.7. At the latter and more challenging setting, previous state-of-the-art approaches required considerably more proposals to achieve similar recall. Our approach runs in quarter of a second, while a near real-time variant runs in a tenth of a second with only a minor loss in accuracy.

2   Related Work

The goal of generating object proposals is to create a relatively small set of candidate bounding boxes that cover the objects in the image. The most common use of the proposals is to allow for efficient object detection with complex and expensive classifiers [5,12,13]. Another popular use is for weakly supervised learning [20,21], where by limiting the number of candidate regions, learning with less supervision becomes feasible. For detection, recall is critical and thousands of candidates can be used, for weakly supervised learning typically a few hundred proposals per image are kept. Since it's inception a few years ago [4,9,6], object proposal generation has found wide applicability.

Generating object proposals aims to achieve many of the benefits of image segmentation without having to solve the harder problem of explicitly partitioning an image into non-overlapping regions. While segmentation has found limited success in object detection [22], in general it fails to provide accurate object regions. Hoiem et al. [23] proposed to use multiple overlapping segmentations to overcome errors of individual segmentations, this was explored further by [24] and [25] in the context of object detection. While use of multiple segmentations improves robustness, constructing coherent segmentations is an inherently difficult task. Object proposal generation seeks to sidestep the challenges of full segmentation by directly generating multiple overlapping object proposals.

Three distinct paradigms have emerged for object proposal generation. Candidate bounding boxes representing object proposals can be found by measuring their 'objectness' [4,11], producing multiple foreground-background segmentations of an image [6,9,10], or by merging superpixels [5,8]. Our approach provides an alternate framework based on *edges* that is both simpler and more efficient while sharing many advantages with previous work. Below we briefly outline representative work for each paradigm; we refer readers to Hosang et al. [26] for a thorough survey and evaluation of object proposal methods.

Objectness Scoring. Alexe et al. [4] proposed to rank candidates by combining a number of cues in a classification framework and assigning a resulting 'objectness' score to each proposal. [7] built on this idea by learning efficient cascades to more quickly and accurately rank candidates. Among multiple cues, both [4] and [7] define scores based on edge distributions near window boundaries. However, these edge scores do not remove edges belonging to contours intersecting the box boundary, which we found to be critical. [4] utilizes a superpixel straddling measure penalizing candidates containing segments overlapping the boundary. In contrast, we suppress straddling contours by propagating information across edge groups that may not directly lie on the boundary. Finally, recently [11] proposed a very fast objectness score based on image gradients.

Seed Segmentation. [6,9,10] all start with multiple seed regions and generate a separate foreground-background segmentation for each seed. The primary advantage of these approaches is generation of high quality segmentation masks, the disadvantage is their high computation cost (minutes per image).

Superpixel Merging. Selective Search [5] is based on computing multiple hierarchical segmentations based on superpixels from [27] and placing bounding boxes around them. Selective Search has been widely used by recent top detection methods [5,12,13] and the key to its success is relatively fast speed (seconds per image) and high recall. In a similar vein, [8] propose a randomized greedy algorithm for computing sets of superpixels that are likely to occur together. In our work, we operate on groups of edges as opposed to superpixels. Edges can be represented probabilistically, have associated orientation information, and can be linked allowing for propagation of information; properly exploited, this additional information can be used to achieve large gains in accuracy.

As far as we know, our approach is the first to generate object bounding box proposals directly from edges. Unlike all previous approaches we do not use segmentations or superpixels, nor do we require learning a scoring function from multiple cues. Instead we propose to score candidate boxes based on the number of contours *wholly enclosed* by a bounding box. Surprisingly, this conceptually simple approach out-competes previous methods by a significant margin.

3   Approach

In this section we describe our approach to finding object proposals. Object proposals are ranked based on a single score computed from the contours wholly enclosed in a candidate bounding box. We begin by describing a data structure based on edge groups that allows for efficient separation of contours that are fully enclosed by the box from those that are not. Next, we define our edge-based scoring function. Finally, we detail our approach for finding top-ranked object proposals that uses a sliding window framework evaluated across position, scale and aspect ratio, followed by refinement using a simple coarse-to-fine search.

Given an image, we initially compute an edge response for each pixel. The edge responses are found using the Structured Edge detector [16,19] that has shown good performance in predicting object boundaries, while simultaneously being very efficient. We utilize the single-scale variant with the sharpening enhancement introduced in [19] to reduce runtime. Given the dense edge responses, we perform Non-Maximal Suppression (NMS) orthogonal to the edge response to find edge peaks, Figure 1. The result is a sparse edge map, with each pixel p having an edge magnitude m_p and orientation θ_p. We define edges as pixels with $m_p > 0.1$ (we threshold the edges for computational efficiency). A contour is defined as a set of edges forming a coherent boundary, curve or line.

3.1   Edge Groups and Affinities

As illustrated in Figure 1, our goal is to identify contours that overlap the bounding box boundary and are therefore unlikely to belong to an object contained by the bounding box. Given a box b, we identify these edges by computing for each $p \in b$ with $m_p > 0.1$ its maximum affinity with an edge on the box boundary. Intuitively, edges connected by straight contours should have high affinity, where those not connected or connected by a contour with high curvature should have lower affinity. For computational efficiency we found it advantageous to group edges that have high affinity and only compute affinities between edge groups. We form the edge groups using a simple greedy approach that combines 8-connected edges until the sum of their orientation differences is above a threshold ($\pi/2$). Small groups are merged with neighboring groups. An illustration of the edge groups is shown in Figure 1, row 3.

Given a set of edge groups $s_i \in S$, we compute an affinity between each pair of neighboring groups. For a pair of groups s_i and s_j, the affinity is computed based on their mean positions x_i and x_j and mean orientations θ_i and θ_j. Intuitively, edge groups have high affinity if the angle between the groups' means in similar to the groups' orientations. Specifically, we compute the affinity $a(s_i, s_j)$ using:

$$a(s_i, s_j) = |\cos(\theta_i - \theta_{ij}) \cos(\theta_j - \theta_{ij})|^\gamma, \tag{1}$$

where θ_{ij} is the angle between x_i and x_j. The value of γ may be used to adjust the affinity's sensitivity to changes in orientation, with $\gamma = 2$ used in practice. If two edge groups are separated by more than 2 pixels their affinity is set to zero. For increased computational efficiency only affinities above a small threshold (0.05) are stored and the rest are assumed to be zero.

The edge grouping and affinity measure are computationally trivial. In practice results are robust to the details of the edge grouping.

3.2 Bounding Box Scoring

Given the set of edge groups S and their affinities, we can compute an object proposal score for any candidate bounding box b. To find our score, we first compute the sum m_i of the magnitudes m_p for all edges p in the group s_i. We also pick an arbitrary pixel position $\bar{x}_i$ of some pixel p in each group s_i. As we will show, the exact choice of $p \in s_i$ does not matter.

For each group s_i we compute a continuous value $w_b(s_i) \in [0, 1]$ that indicates whether s_i is wholly contained in b, $w_b(s_i) = 1$, or not, $w_b(s_i) = 0$. Let S_b be the set of edge groups that overlap the box b's boundary. We find S_b using an efficient data structure that is described in Section 3.3. For all $s_i \in S_b$, $w_b(s_i)$ is set to 0. Similarly $w_b(s_i) = 0$ for all s_i for which $\bar{x}_i \notin b$, since all of its pixels must either be outside of b or $s_i \in S_b$. For the remaining edge groups for which $\bar{x}_i \in b$ and $s_i \notin S_b$ we compute $w_b(s_i)$ as follows:

$$w_b(s_i) = 1 - \max_T \prod_j^{|T|-1} a(t_j, t_{j+1}), \tag{2}$$

where T is an ordered path of edge groups with a length of $|T|$ that begins with some $t_1 \in S_b$ and ends at $t_{|T|} = s_i$. If no such path exists we define $w_b(s_i) = 1$. Thus, Equation (2) finds the path with highest affinity between the edge group s_i and an edge group that overlaps the box's boundary. Since most pairwise affinities are zero, this can be done efficiently.

Using the computed values of w_b we define our score using:

$$h_b = \frac{\sum_i w_b(s_i) m_i}{2(b_w + b_h)^\kappa},$$ (3)

where b_w and b_w are the box's width and height. Note that we divide by the box's perimeter and not its area, since edges have a width of one pixel regardless of scale. Nevertheless, a value of $\kappa = 1.5$ is used to offset the bias of larger windows having more edges on average.

In practice we use an integral image to speed computation of the numerator in Equation (3). The integral image is used to compute the sum of all m_i for which $\bar{x}_i \in b$. Next, for all s_i with $\bar{x}_i \in b$ and $w_b(s_i) < 1$, $(1 - w_b(s_i))m_i$ is subtracted from this sum. This speeds up computation considerably as typically $w_b(s_i) = 1$ for most s_i and all such s_i do not need to be explicitly considered.

Finally, it has been observed that the edges in the center of the box are of less importance than those near the box's edges [4]. To account for this observation we can subtract the edge magnitudes from a box b^{in} centered in b:

$$h_b^{in} = h_b - \frac{\sum_{p \in b^{in}} m_p}{2(b_w + b_h)^\kappa},$$ (4)

where the width and height of b^{in} is $b_w/2$ and $b_h/2$ respectively. The sum of the edge magnitudes in b^{in} can be efficiently computed using an integral image. As shown in Section 4 we found h_b^{in} offers slightly better accuracy than h_b with minimal additional computational cost.

3.3   Finding Intersecting Edge Groups

In the previous section we assumed the set of edge groups S_b that overlap the box b's boundary is known. Since we evaluate a huge number of bounding boxes (Sec. 3.4), an efficient method for finding S_b is critical. Naive approaches such as exhaustively searching all of the pixels on the boundary of a box would be prohibitively expensive, especially for large boxes.

We propose an efficient method for finding intersecting edge groups for each side of a bounding box that relies on two additional data structures. Below, we describe the process for finding intersections along a horizontal boundary from pixel (c_0, r) to (c_1, r). The vertical boundaries may be handled in a similar manner. For horizontal boundaries we create two data structures for each row of the image. The first data structure stores an ordered list L_r of edge group indices for row r. The list is created by storing the order in which the edge groups occur along the row r. An index is only added to L_r if the edge group index changes from one pixel to the next. The result is the size of L_r is much smaller than the width of the image. If there are pixels between the edge groups that are not edges, a zero is added to the list. A second data structure K_r with the same size as the width of the image is created that stores the corresponding index into L_r for each column c in row r. Thus, if pixel p at location (c, r) is a member of edge group s_i, $L_r(K_r(c)) = i$. Since most pixels do not belong to

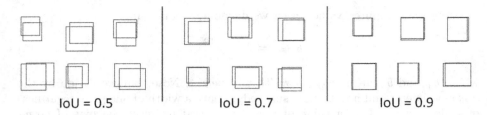

Fig. 2. An illustration of random bounding boxes with Intersection over Union (IoU) of 0.5, 0.7, and 0.9. An IoU of 0.7 provides a reasonable compromise between very loose (IoU of 0.5) and very strict (IoU of 0.9) overlap values.

an edge group, using these two data structures we can efficiently find the list of overlapping edge groups by searching L_r from index $K_r(c_0)$ to $K_r(c_1)$.

3.4 Search Strategy

When searching for object proposals, the object detection algorithm should be taken into consideration. Some detection algorithms may require object proposals with high accuracy, while others are more tolerant of errors in bounding box placement. The accuracy of a bounding box is typically measured using the Intersection over Union (IoU) metric. IoU computes the intersection of a candidate box and the ground truth box divided by the area of their union. When evaluating object detection algorithms, an IoU threshold of 0.5 is typically used to determine whether a detection was correct [15]. However as shown in Figure 2, an IoU score of 0.5 is quite loose. Even if an object proposal is generated with an IoU of 0.5 with the ground truth, the detection algorithm may provide a low score. As a result, IoU scores of greater than 0.5 are generally desired.

In this section we describe an object proposal search strategy based on the desired IoU, δ, for the detector. For high values of δ we generate a more concentrated set of bounding boxes with higher density near areas that are likely to contain an object. For lower values of δ the boxes can have higher diversity, since it is assumed the object detector can account for moderate errors in box location. Thus, we provide a tradeoff between finding a smaller number of objects with higher accuracy and a higher number of objects with less accuracy. Note that previous methods have an implicit bias for which δ they are designed for, e.g. Objectness [4] and Randomized Prim [8] are tuned for low and high δ, respectively, whereas we provide explicit control over diversity versus accuracy.

We begin our search for candidate bounding boxes using a sliding window search over position, scale and aspect ratio. The step size for each is determined using a single parameter α indicating the IoU for neighboring boxes. That is, the step sizes in translation, scale and aspect ratio are determined such that one step results in neighboring boxes having an IoU of α. The scale values range from a minimum box area of $\sigma = 1000$ pixels to the full image. The aspect ratio varies from $1/\tau$ to τ, where $\tau = 3$ is used in practice. As we discuss in Section

Original image   No contour removal   Contour removal

Fig. 3. Illustration of the computed score using (middle) and removing (right) contours that overlap the bounding box boundary. Notice the lack of clear peaks when the contours are not removed. The magnitudes of the scores are normalized for viewing. The box dimensions used for generating the heatmaps are shown by the blue rectangles.

4, a value of $\alpha = 0.65$ is ideal for most values of δ. However, if a highly accurate $\delta > 0.9$ is required, α may be increased to 0.85.

After a sliding window search is performed, all bounding box locations with a score h_b^{in} above a small threshold are refined. Refinement is performed using a greedy iterative search to maximize h_b^{in} over position, scale and aspect ratio. After each iteration, the search step is reduced in half. The search is halted once the translational step size is less than 2 pixels.

Once the candidate bounding boxes are refined, their maximum scores are recorded and sorted. Our final stage performs Non-Maximal Suppression (NMS) of the sorted boxes. A box is removed if its IoU is more than β for a box with greater score. We have found that in practice setting $\beta = \delta + 0.05$ achieves high accuracy across all values of δ, Section 4.

4 Results

In this section we explore the performance and accuracy of our Edge Boxes algorithm in comparison to other approaches. Following the experimental setup of previous approaches [7,5,8,4] we evaluate our algorithm on the PASCAL VOC 2007 dataset [15]. The dataset contains 9,963 images. All results on variants of our approach are reported on the validation set and our results compared to other approaches are reported on the test set.

4.1 Approach Variants

We begin by testing various variants of our approach on the validation set. Figure 4(a, b) illustrates the algorithm's behavior based on the parameters α and β that control the step size of the sliding window search and the NMS threshold, respectively, when generating 1000 object proposals.

As α is increased, the density of the sampling is increased, resulting in more candidate boxes being evaluated and slower runtimes, Table 1. Notice that the

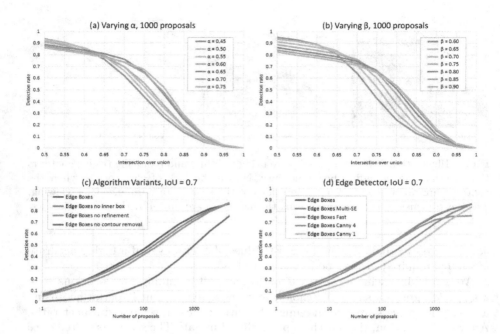

Fig. 4. A comparison of various variants of our approach. (a) The detection rate when varying the parameter α that varies the density of the sampling rate (default $\alpha = 0.65$). (b) Results while varying the parameter β controlling the NMS threshold (default $\beta = 0.75$). (c) The detection accuracy when various stages are removed from the algorithm, including the removal of edges in the inner box, the bounding box location refinement, and the removal of the contours that overlap the box's boundaries. (d) Detection accuracy when different edge detectors are used, including single-scale Structured Edges [16] (default), multi-scale Structure Edges, and a fast variant that runs at 10 fps without the edge sharpening enhancement introduced in [19]. Results using the Canny edge detector [28] with varying amounts of blur are also shown.

results for $\alpha = 0.65$ are better than or nearly identical to $\alpha = 0.70$ and $\alpha = 0.75$. Thus, if a lower IoU value δ is desired $\alpha = 0.65$ provides a nice accuracy vs. efficiency tradeoff. Depending on the desired IoU value of δ, the value of β may be adjusted accordingly. A value of $\beta = \delta + 0.05$ achieves high accuracy across all desired δ. As shown in Table 1, changes in β have minimal effect on runtime.

Three useful variants of our algorithm are shown in Table 1; Edge Boxes 50, Edge Boxes 70, and Edge Boxes 90 that have settings for α and β adjusted for IoU thresholds of $\delta = 0.5, 0.7$ and 0.9 respectively. For higher IoU thresholds that require extremely tight bounding boxes, α must be adjusted to search more densely resulting in longer runtimes. Otherwise, α may be kept fixed.

Our second set of experiments tests several variants of the algorithm, Figure 4(c, d). For these experiments we set δ to an intermediate value of 0.7 and show detection rates when varying the number of object proposals. The primary con-

Table 1. Accuracy measures and runtimes for three variants of our algorithm: Edge Boxes 50, Edge Boxes 70 and Edge Boxes 90. Accuracy measures include Area Under the Curve (AUC) and proposal recall at 1000 proposals. Parameter values for α and β are shown. All other parameters are held constant.

| | IoU = 0.5 | | IoU = 0.7 | | IoU = 0.9 | | | | |
	AUC	Recall	AUC	Recall	AUC	Recall	Runtime	α	β
Edge boxes 50	**.64**	**96%**	.36	55%	.04	5%	**.25s**	.65	.55
Edge boxes 70	.58	89%	**.45**	**76%**	.06	9%	**.25s**	.65	.75
Edge boxes 90	.38	59%	.28	46%	**.15**	**28%**	2.5s	.85	.95

tribution of our paper is that contours that overlap the bounding box's boundary should be removed when computing the box's score. Figure 4 shows that if these contours are not removed a significant drop in accuracy is observed. To gain intuition into the effect of the contour removal on the score, we illustrate the score computed with and without contour removal in Figure 3. With contour removal the scores have strong peaks around clusters of edges that are more likely to form objects given the current box's size. Notice the strong peak with contour removal in the bottom left-hand corner corresponding to the van. When contours are not removed strong responses are observed everywhere.

If the center edges are not removed, using h_b instead of h_b^{in}, a small drop in accuracy is found. Not performing box location refinement results in a more significant drop in accuracy. The quality of the initial edge detector is also important, Figure 4(d). If the initial edge map is generated using gradient-based Canny edges [28] with varying blur instead of Structured Edges [16] the results degrade. If multi-scale Structured Edges are computed instead of single-scale edges there is a minimal gain in accuracy. Since single-scale edges can be computed more efficiently we use single-scale edges for all remaining experiments. The runtime of our baseline approach which utilizes single-scale edges is 0.25s.

If near real-time performance is desired, the parameters of the algorithm may be adjusted to return up to 1000 boxes with only a minor loss in accuracy. Specifically, we can reduce α to 0.625, and increase the threshold used to determine which boxes to refine from 0.01 to 0.02. Finally, if we also disable the sharpening enhancement of the Structured Edge detector [19], the runtime of our algorithm is 0.09s. As shown in Figure 4(d), this variant, called Edge Boxes Fast, has nearly identical results when returning fewer than 1000 boxes.

4.2 Comparison with State-of-the-Art

We compare our Edge Boxes algorithm against numerous state-of-the-art algorithms summarized in Table 2. Results of all competing methods were provided by Hosang et al. [26] in a standardized format. Figure 5 (top) shows the detection rates when varying the number of object proposals for different IoU thresholds. For each plot, we update our parameters based on the desired value of δ using the parameters in Table 1. Edge Boxes performs well across all IoU

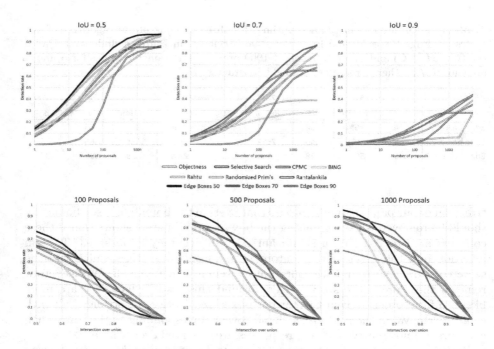

Fig. 5. Comparison of Edge Boxes to various state-of-the-algorithms, including Objectness [4], Selective Search [5], Randomized Prim's [8] and Rahtu [7]. The variations of our algorithm are tested using $\delta = 0.5, 0.7$ and 0.9 indicated by Edge Boxes 50, Edge Boxes 70 and Edge Boxes 90. (top) The detection rate vs. the number of bounding box proposals for various intersection over union thresholds. (bottom) The detection rate vs. intersection over union for various numbers of object proposals.

values and for both a small and large number of candidates. Selective Search [5] achieves competitive accuracy, especially at higher IoU values and larger number of boxes. CPMC [6] generates high quality proposals but produces relatively few candidates and is thus unable to achieve high recall. BING [11], which is very fast, generates only very loosely fitting proposals and hence is only competitive at low IoU. In contrast our approach achieves good results across a variety of IoU thresholds and quantity of object proposals. In fact, as shown in Table 2, to achieve a recall of 75% with an IoU of 0.7 requires 800 proposals using Edge Boxes, 1400 proposals using Selective Search, and 3000 using Randomized Prim's. No other methods achieve 75% recall using even 5000 proposals. Edge Boxes also achieves a significantly higher maximum recall (87%) and Area Under the Curve (AUC = 0.46) as compared to all approaches except Selective Search.

Figure 5 (bottom) shows the detection rate when varying the IoU threshold for different numbers of proposals. Similar to Figure 4(a,b), these plots demonstrate that setting parameters based on δ, the desired IoU threshold, leads to good performance. No single algorithm or set of parameters is capable of achieving superior performance across all IoU thresholds. However, Edge Boxes 70

Table 2. Results for our approach, Edge Boxes 70, compared to other methods for IoU threshold of 0.7. Methods are sorted by increasing Area Under the Curve (AUC). Additional metrics include the number of proposals needed to achieve 25%, 50% and 75% recall and the maximum recall using 5000 boxes. Edge Boxes is best or near best under every metric. All method runtimes were obtained from [26].

	AUC	N@25%	N@50%	N@75%	Recall	Time
BING [11]	.20	292	–	–	29%	**.2s**
Rantalankila [10]	.23	184	584	–	68%	10s
Objectness [4]	.27	27	–	–	39%	3s
Rand. Prim's [8]	.35	42	349	3023	80%	1s
Rahtu [7]	.37	29	307	–	70%	3s
Selective Search [5]	.40	28	199	1434	**87%**	10s
CPMC [6]	.41	15	111	–	65%	250s
Edge boxes 70	**.46**	**12**	**108**	**800**	**87%**	**.25s**

performs well over a wide range of IoU thresholds that are typically desired in practice (IoU between 0.5 and 0.8, Figure 2). Segmentation based methods along with Edge Boxes 90 perform best at very high IoU values.

We compare the runtime and summary statistics of our approach to other methods in Table 2. The runtimes for Edge Boxes includes the 0.1 seconds needed to compute the initial edges. Table 2 shows that our approach is significantly faster and more accurate than previous approaches. The only methods with comparable accuracy are Selective Search and CPMC, but these are considerably slower. The only method with comparable speed is BING, but BING has the worst accuracy of all evaluated methods at IoU of 0.7.

Finally, qualitative results are shown in Figure 6. Many of the errors occur with small or heavily occluded objects in the background of the images.

5   Discussion

In this paper we propose an effective method for finding object proposals in images that relies on one simple observation: the number of edges that are wholly enclosed by a bounding box is indicative of the likelihood of the box containing an object. We describe a straightforward scoring function that computes the weighted sum of the edge strengths within a box minus those that are part of a contour that straddles the box's boundary. Using efficient data structures and smart search strategies we can find object proposals rapidly. Results show both improved accuracy and increased efficiency over the state of the art.

One interesting direction for future work is using the edges to help generate segmentation proposals in addition to the bounding box proposals for objects. Many edges are removed when scoring a candidate bounding box; the location of these suppressed edges could provide useful information in generating seg-mentations. Finally we will work with Hosang at al. to add Edge Boxes to their

Fig. 6. Qualitative examples of our object proposals. Blue bounding boxes are the closest produced object proposals to each ground truth bounding box. Ground truth bounding boxes are shown in green and red, with green indicating an object was found and red indicating the object was not found. An IoU threshold of 0.7 was used to determine correctness for all examples. Results are shown for Edge Boxes 70 with 1,000 object proposals. At this setting our approach returns over 75% of object locations.

recent survey and evaluation of object proposal methods [26] and we also hope to evaluate our proposals coupled with state-of-the-art object detectors [13].

Source code for Edge Boxes will be made available online.

References

1. Viola, P.A., Jones, M.J.: Robust real-time face detection. IJCV 57(2), 137–154 (2004)
2. Dalal, N., Triggs, B.: Histograms of oriented gradients for human detection. In: CVPR (2005)
3. Felzenszwalb, P., Girshick, R., McAllester, D., Ramanan, D.: Object detection with discriminatively trained part based models. PAMI 32(9), 1627–1645 (2010)

4. Alexe, B., Deselaers, T., Ferrari, V.: Measuring the objectness of image windows. PAMI 34(11) (2012)
5. Uijlings, J.R.R., van de Sande, K.E.A., Gevers, T., Smeulders, A.W.M.: Selective search for object recognition. IJCV (2013)
6. Carreira, J., Sminchisescu, C.: Cpmc: Automatic object segmentation using constrained parametric min-cuts. PAMI 34(7) (2012)
7. Rahtu, E., Kannala, J., Blaschko, M.: Learning a category independent object detection cascade. In: ICCV (2011)
8. Manen, S., Guillaumin, M., Van Gool, L., Leuven, K.: Prime object proposals with randomized prims algorithm. In: ICCV (2013)
9. Endres, I., Hoiem, D.: Category-independent object proposals with diverse ranking. PAMI (2014)
10. Rantalankila, P., Kannala, J., Rahtu, E.: Generating object segmentation proposals using global and local search. In: CVPR (2014)
11. Cheng, M.M., Zhang, Z., Lin, W.Y., Torr, P.: BING: Binarized normed gradients for objectness estimation at 300fps. In: CVPR (2014)
12. Wang, X., Yang, M., Zhu, S., Lin, Y.: Regionlets for generic object detection. In: ICCV (2013)
13. Girshick, R.B., Donahue, J., Darrell, T., Malik, J.: Rich feature hierarchies for accurate object detection and semantic segmentation. In: CVPR (2014)
14. Deng, J., Dong, W., Socher, R., Li, L.J., Li, K., Fei-Fei, L.: Imagenet: A large-scale hierarchical image database. In: CVPR (2009)
15. Everingham, M., Van Gool, L., Williams, C.K.I., Winn, J., Zisserman, A.: The pascal visual object classes (voc) challenge. IJCV 88(2), 303–338 (2010)
16. Dollár, P., Zitnick, C.L.: Structured forests for fast edge detection. In: ICCV (2013)
17. Marr, D.: Vision: A computational investigation into the human representation and processing of visual information. Inc., New York, NY (1982)
18. Eitz, M., Hays, J., Alexa, M.: How do humans sketch objects? ACM Transactions Graphics 31(4) (2012)
19. Dollár, P., Zitnick, C.L.: Fast edge detection using structured forests. CoRR abs/1406.5549 (2014)
20. Deselaers, T., Alexe, B., Ferrari, V.: Localizing objects while learning their appearance. In: Daniilidis, K., Maragos, P., Paragios, N. (eds.) ECCV 2010, Part IV. LNCS, vol. 6314, pp. 452–466. Springer, Heidelberg (2010)
21. Siva, P., Xiang, T.: Weakly supervised object detector learning with model drift detection. In: ICCV (2011)
22. Gu, C., Lim, J.J., Arbeláez, P., Malik, J.: Recognition using regions. In: CVPR (2009)
23. Hoiem, D., Efros, A.A., Hebert, M.: Geometric context from a single image. In: ICCV (2005)
24. Russell, B.C., Freeman, W.T., Efros, A.A., Sivic, J., Zisserman, A.: Using multiple segmentations to discover objects and their extent in image collections. In: CVPR (2006)
25. Malisiewicz, T., Efros, A.A.: Improving spatial support for objects via multiple segmentations. In: BMVC (2007)
26. Hosang, J., Benenson, R., Schiele, B.: How good are detection proposals, really? In: BMVC (2014)
27. Felzenszwalb, P.F., Huttenlocher, D.P.: Efficient graph-based image segmentation. IJCV 59(2) (2004)
28. Canny, J.: A computational approach to edge detection. PAMI (6), 679–698 (1986)

Training Deformable Object Models for Human Detection Based on Alignment and Clustering

Benjamin Drayer and Thomas Brox

Department of Computer Science,
Centre of Biological Signalling Studies (BIOSS),
University of Freiburg, Germany
{drayer,brox}@cs.uni-freiburg.de

Abstract. We propose a clustering method that considers non-rigid alignment of samples. The motivation for such a clustering is training of object detectors that consist of multiple mixture components. In particular, we consider the deformable part model (DPM) of Felzenszwalb et al., where each mixture component includes a learned deformation model. We show that alignment based clustering distributes the data better to the mixture components of the DPM than previous methods. Moreover, the alignment helps the non-convex optimization of the DPM find a consistent placement of its parts and, thus, learn more accurate part filters.

1 Introduction

Much variability among images of persons is due to viewpoint and deformation/articulation. This variation makes it hard to pick discriminative features. Exemplar based classifiers are less affected by variation, as they learn the samples by heart, but they do not generalize well. The deformable part model (DPM) [9] has introduced two complementary concepts to deal with variation: mixture components address very different viewpoints and deformable parts can handle smaller viewpoint changes and articulation. Mixture components and a hierarchical part structure are also used in other recognition models, such as convolutional neural nets [16]. With their deep hierarchy of mixture components, they implement these concepts even more rigorously. However, the idea to also model typical deformations by including deformation costs is unique to the deformable part model.

As viewpoint labels and the part placement are not given in typical training sets, these need to be inferred in conjunction with the classifier training. This makes the training procedure a rather tough non-convex optimization problem, where a good initialization is crucial. Felzenszwalb et al. [9] address this by using the bounding box aspect ratio to initialize mixture components. Others, building on [9], suggested clustering the HOG descriptors [1,5,12]. In all these cases, parts are initialized at high energy positions of the root filters' positive weights. Initially, they do not account for deformation/movement within the

D. Fleet et al. (Eds.): ECCV 2014, Part V, LNCS 8693, pp. 406–420, 2014.

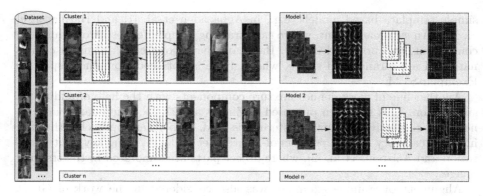

Fig. 1. On a training dataset (left), we compute alignment vector fields between all pairs of samples. This allows us to cluster the samples based on alignment-normalized similarities (middle). These clusters serve as mixture components for the deformable part model (right). The non-aligned samples in a cluster serve to train the root filter. Thanks to the alignment, we know a good initial placement of parts, which leads to more detailed part filters.

training samples, which leads to very blurred part filters in the first training iterations.

In this paper, we suggest running an alignment procedure on the training samples. This has two positive effects: (1) We enhance the clusters by enforcing that all samples in a cluster are similar up to a "regular" deformation, which directly results in stronger mixture components. (2) The initial part placement is improved.

In particular, we allow for deformations that can be well represented by the deformable model. We use distances for clustering that reflect this space of deformations better than typical distances defined on non-aligned samples. As a consequence, we obtain mixture components that generalize better over deformations while the classifier can learn more detailed structures that are specific to the respective component.

Additionally, the alignment allows us to initialize the part placement, since it tells us where the part should be placed in each training sample. Hence, the optimization of the DPM can train quite distinct part filters already in the first iteration. As a consequence, the final part filters can capture more detailed structures. An overview of our method is illustrated in Figure 1.

2   Related Work

Appearance based clustering of training data in the context of the deformable part model by Felzenszwalb et al. [9] was proposed by Gu et al. [12]. The bounding box aspect ratio is supplemented by a distance on the HOG descriptors as a criterion to define the mixture components. A pure appearance based clustering was proposed by Divalla et al. [5]. Clustering was also used in conjunction with simple template based models, e.g., in Aghazadeh et al. [1] and Hariharan el al. [13]. An extreme variant, where each training sample defines its own mixture component, was proposed in [18]. Based on that, Dong et al. [6] use a combination of appearance and shape, where shape is obtained from the respective Exemplar-SVM.

Another line of work defines mixture components with the help of additional supervision. This has been proposed in Zhu et al. [22,23], where landmark annotation, respectively human clustering, is used. Two other approaches that fall into this category are the poselets of Bourdev et al. [3,11] using keypoint annotation and Azizpour et al. [2], where object parts are annotated in the training images.

Alignment of training examples was also considered in the work of Gu et al. [11]. For each manually selected cluster representative, its 32 nearest neighbors are added to form a cluster. Both, their and our approach, align the examples with respect to the cluster representative. Different from their approach, we select the representatives automatically and apply an unsupervised, non-rigid alignment, whereas Gu et al. employ a transformation matrix optimizing the Procrustes distance between the keypoints.

In terms of the overall framework, the work of Ladicky et al. [17] is most related to ours, as it is the only one that combines the definition of mixture components with an unsupervised alignment procedure. Ladicky et al. rely on a locally affine model, which allows efficient optimization of the alignment variables in the structured SVM. In contrast, we have a more general non-rigid deformation model for clustering and provide a strong initialization for the star-model of Felzenszwalb et al. [9].

3   Alignment

Although HOG [4] is robust to some local deformation, clustering in HOG space generally cannot deal with larger image transformations and deformations. For example, already small rotation of the object in an image makes clustering fail. To address this problem, we use a distance we proposed in [7] that normalizes out all spatial transformations including non-rigid deformations and considers the similarity of the aligned HOG features as well as the deformation energy. In the scope of detection, we benefit from the alignment twice: The clusters improve and within a cluster we obtain correspondences for the various object parts.

For each pair of examples we aim for the optimum deformation field that aligns one example to the other. The cost function consists of the data term E_D, that aims for maximum feature overlap and a pairwise regularization term E_P, that penalizes strong deformations:

$$E(\mathbf{u}) = E_D(\mathbf{u}) + E_P(\mathbf{u}) \tag{1}$$

This cost function is minimized with respect to the deformation field $\mathbf{u}$. The globally normalized version of the HOG features $F/\|F\|_2$ allows us to compare the alignment energies of different image pairs.

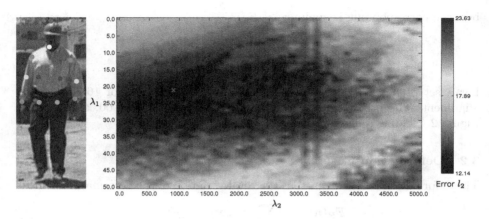

Fig. 2. Optimization of the weight parameters. **Left:** Exemplar of the given keypoint annotation. **Right:** l_2 distance between the corresponding keypoints after alignment with parameters λ_1 and λ_2, averaged over the image pairs. The optimum of 12.14 is achieved with $\lambda_1 = 21$ and $\lambda_2 = 900$ (marked in red). The l_2 distance before alignment is 16.29.

3.1   Data Term

We use a weighted combination of the l_1-norm and the dot product, as we introduced in [7]. The intuition behind this choice is to benefit from the robustness of the l_1-norm and the capability of the dot-product to match features of different magnitude. A grid search on the weighting parameters λ_1 and λ_2 shows that the best results are achieved by a combination of both distances; see Figure 2. One may expect this result, because the l_1-norm has problems matching features of different magnitude, whereas the dot product tends to many-to-one correspondences. The data term reads:

$$E_D\left(\mathbf{u}\right) = \sum_{\mathbf{x}} \lambda_1 \left|F_2(\mathbf{x} + \mathbf{u}(\mathbf{x})) - F_1(\mathbf{x})\right|_1 - \lambda_2 \langle F_2(\mathbf{x} + \mathbf{u}(\mathbf{x})), F_1(\mathbf{x})\rangle, \quad (2)$$

where $\mathbf{x}$ are the coordinates of the grid points and $F_1(\cdot)$, $F_2(\cdot)$ denote the feature representation of the images being aligned by $\mathbf{u}$. The influence of the deformation cost E_P is implicitly handled by the weighting parameters λ_1 and λ_2.

We select these parameters automatically using the keypoint annotation provided in the Buffy training set, which coincide with the human joints; see Figure 2. The usage of keypoints in our work is restricted to the optimization of the weighting parameters. For the non-rigid alignment, only HOG features are used.

In order to select the parameters, we take n pairs of images $(I_1, J_1), ..., (I_n, J_n)$ and the corresponding keypoint pairs $(p_1, q_1), ..., (p_n, q_n)$. With $u^{(i,j)}_{\lambda_1 \lambda_2}$ we denote the alignment between image pair (I_i, J_i) under the parameters λ_1, λ_2, where the optimal parameters correspond to the alignment that minimizes the l_2-distance between corresponding keypoints:

$$\operatorname*{argmin}_{\lambda_1,\lambda_2} \frac{1}{n} \sum_{i=1}^{n} \left\| q_i - u_{\lambda_1\lambda_2}^{(i,j)}(p_i) \right\|_2 . \tag{3}$$

For a set of $n = 20$ pairs, we have an average l_2-distance of 16.29 without alignment. The best result is achieved with $\lambda_1 = 21, \lambda_2 = 900$, as shown in Figure 2, yielding a distance of 12.14.

3.2   Deformation Cost

The deformation cost is defined as the total variation of the deformation field $\mathbf{u}$:

$$E_P(\mathbf{u}) = \sum_{\mathbf{x},\mathbf{y} \in \mathcal{N}(\mathbf{x})} |\mathbf{u}(\mathbf{x}) - \mathbf{u}(\mathbf{y})|_1 , \tag{4}$$

where $\mathcal{N}(\mathbf{x})$ denotes the neighborhood of $\mathbf{x}$. In our experiments, we use a 4-connected neighborhood. The total variation regularization prefers piecewise constant deformation fields and allows for discontinuities in the deformation field. This is necessary for handling the typical challenges of the dataset, e.g. raising arms, change in viewpoint and occlusion of body parts.

The resulting optimization problem can be solved efficiently with the Fast Primal-Dual solver of [14, 15]. On average, the alignment of a pair takes 0.11 seconds. The result is an approximation, but in practice it is very close to the global optimum [1].

4   Clustering

4.1   Pairwise Distances and Spectral Clustering

We directly use the energy E in (1) to define pairwise distances for clustering, which includes both the matching cost and the deformation cost. Figure 3 illustrates that the nearest neighbors more often contain the same instance or other similar instances if alignment is taken into account.

Based on the pairwise distances we apply spectral clustering [19, 21], by constructing the affinity matrix A in the following way:

$$A(i,j) = e^{-\frac{E(i,j)}{2\sigma^2}}, \tag{5}$$

with $\sigma = 0.7$. The alignment procedure and the derived distances are most informative for small distances. In case of large distances, a good alignment cannot be found, which indicates that the samples do not match. Therefore, we only keep the affinities of the 20 nearest neighbors of each sample and set all other affinities to zero. This ensures sufficient connectivity and keeps the graph of the dataset from splitting into tiny clusters, while at the same time a strong

---

[1] This can be read from the lower and upper bounds computed during optimization.

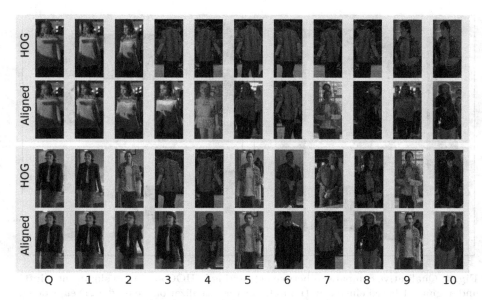

Fig. 3. Nearest neighbor queries showing query image **Q** and its 10 nearest neighbors. The 1st and 3rd row show the query result using HOG features without alignment. The 2nd and 4th row use alignment energy E as distance and show the nearest neighbors warped to the query image. The alignment based distance returns more similar instances, demonstrating that it is more invariant to deformations than simple HOG based distances.

preference is given to the most similar pairs. Since the 20 nearest neighbors are not the same for a pair of samples and the alignment is not enforced to be a diffeomorphism, the affinities are not symmetric. Thus, symmetry of the final affinity matrix is enforced by using $A + A^t$.

4.2   Clustering Performance

In order to evaluate the clustering performance and to justify some design choices quantitatively, we add some additional annotation to the training data of the Buffy dataset. Manually specifying unique ground truth clusters is impossible. There are many cases in which even humans do not agree on whether an object belongs to one or another cluster and setting the right number of clusters is even more difficult. Hence, rather than specifying clusters, we label pairs of examples by assigning them to one out of three categories. The first category comprises the pairs that are clearly similar and should end up in one cluster. The second category contains all pairs that are clearly different and should end up in different clusters. The last category is 'unknown' that takes all pairs, for which an assignment to one of the two other categories is difficult to make.

Based on this annotation, we can compute true and false positives, as well as true and false negatives. In clustering, the Jaccard index, the Rand index and

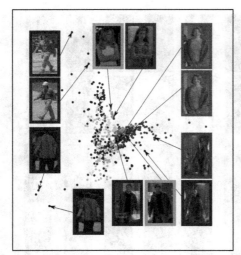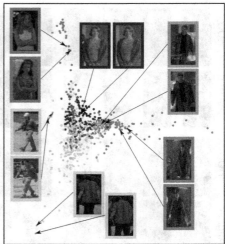

Fig. 4. Qualitative comparison between clustering in HOG space (no alignment) **(left)** and alignment based clustering **(right)**. For the visualization we used a 2D embedding (obtained with multidimensional scaling [20]) of the corresponding affinity matrices. Different colors indicate different clusters. Without alignment, some instances that should belong to the same cluster, e.g., the two cross-armed women, the men at the table, and the upper frontal bodies, end up in different clusters. With alignment similar examples are mapped closer together, e.g., the men walking to the left and the men from behind.

F-score are frequently used quality measures obtained from these values. However, one has to decide on the number of clusters using these measures, which is hard. In our scenario, it is more appropriate to compute precision and recall for the clustering. This way we do not need to fix the number of clusters and the average precision (AP) serves as measure for the overall quality.

As the number of pairs is quadratic in the number of examples, the effort to annotate all pairs is too high. However, we can resort to random sampling and the effect of large numbers. Labeling m pairs of images resembles the true distribution with a maximum deviation of

$$\varepsilon = z_{(1-\frac{\alpha}{2})} \frac{s}{\sqrt{m}}. \tag{6}$$

Here, $z_{(1-\frac{\alpha}{2})}$ is the z-quantile of the normal distribution and s denotes the standard deviation. Due to the underlying Bernoulli distribution with $s^2 = p(1-p)$, the upper bound of the standard deviation is 0.5. We manually labeled 4000 pairs of images and considering a confidence of 95% we obtain a maximum deviation of $\varepsilon \leq 1.6\%$. This means the computed AP for the clustering is the center of a confidence interval with length ≤ 3.2.

We evaluate the affinities of Equation 5 by varying the exponent corresponding to the distance. Namely, the weighted combination of l_1-norm and dot product,

Table 1. Average precision on the clustering task with and without alignment. Alignment improves the clustering AP by 4%. The deformation cost E_P alone is not sufficient for clustering.

E_D, $\mathbf{u} = 0$ (without alignment)	43.62
E_D	47.88
E_P (deformation cost only)	19.72
$E = E_D + E_P$	**48.04**

Table 2. Comparison of the DPM clustering and ours for a fixed number of clusters. The left column shows the F-measure of the initial clusters and the right column after reassignment by the mixture model. We evaluated the DPM with 3 and 5 aspect ratios, corresponding to 6 and 10 clusters. Our alignment based clustering yields stronger clusters than DPM.

	At initialization	After DPM training
DPM $K = 6$	0.3831	0.5012
DPM $K = 10$	0.4664	0.5013
$E = E_D + E_P$, $K = 10$	0.5251	**0.5308**

the energy of the data term E_D, the smoothness term E_P and the total energy of the alignment E. We achieve an improvement of more than 4% AP using the energy of the alignment instead of the unaligned features, see Table 1. Despite having an uncertainty of 1.6% this improvement is statistically significant.

We also evaluate how well the internal optimization of the mixture components of the DPM perform on the clustering task. The DPM first clusters the samples based on the bounding box aspect ratio and then splits each group into a so-called left- and right-facing cluster based on appearance. We evaluate 6 and 10 clusters (corresponding to 3 and 5 aspect ratios) and report the performance of the initial clusters and the final ones (after running the full DPM training). Since in this experiment the number of clusters is fixed and we only know a single precision-recall point, we compare performance based on the F-measure. As one may expect, Table 2 shows that optimization of the mixture components by the DPM improves the clustering performance compared to the initial cluster assignment. Therefore, the proposed clustering using non-rigid alignment E yields better clusters than the DPM.

A qualitative comparison of the alignment based clustering is given in Figure 4. The alignment based distance provides cleaner clusters than the purely appearance based distance. This is because the non-rigid alignment better deals with deformation in the data and hence provides more meaningful matches (see also Figure 3).

5   Training the Deformable Part Model

Given n training examples $(x_1, y_1), ..., (x_n, y_n)$ with $y_i \in \{-1, 1\}$, the DPM [9] tries to infer the assignment $z_i \in \{1, ..., K\}$ of a sample i to one of K mixture components, the hyperplane parameters w_{kj}, b_{kj} of a linear SVM for each mixture component k and part $j \in \{1, ...M\}$, and the deformation parameters θ_{kj} in a joint optimization process. The objective is highly non-convex. To initialize the model, [9] first train a model with just the root filters and no parts. The root filters then serve as an initialization for the parts.

5.1 Mixture Components

Without parts, the training objective becomes that of a mixture of linear SVMs:

$$\underset{w}{\operatorname{argmin}} \frac{1}{2} \sum_{k=1}^{K} \|w_{k0}\|_2^2 + C \sum_{i=1}^{n} \epsilon_i,$$
$$y_i \cdot s_i^{z_i} \geq 1 - \epsilon_i, \quad \epsilon_i \geq 0, \tag{7}$$
$$z_i = \underset{k}{\operatorname{argmin}} s_i^k,$$
$$s_i^k = w_{k0}^\top F(x_i) + b_{k0}$$

with regularization parameter C and slack variables ϵ_i. $F(x_i)$ denotes the feature representation (HOG) of sample i. The optimum parameters are estimated by alternating optimization of SVM parameters w_{k0}, b_{k0} and the latent assignment variables z_i. In fact, this strongly resembles clustering in an expectation-maximization style. So even without parts there is a strong dependency on the initialization.

In [9], the initial assignments z_i are based on the bounding box aspect ratio. Moreover, each cluster is split into left- and right-facing instances based on similarity of the HOG descriptors. We replace these initial mixture components simply by the clusters from the previous section.

5.2 Part Filters

[9] derives initial part filters from the root filters. The root filters are upsampled to the resolution of the part filters and parts are placed such that most of the positive weights of the root filters are covered. Clearly, no deformation is considered for the initial placement of the parts. This is left to the overall optimization over all model parameters.

We propose to use the non-rigid alignment from Section 3 to initialize the relative positions of the parts. It is easy to see that this can be reduced to the initialization procedure in [9] but using the clusters from Section 4 and warping all samples within a cluster k to one representative sample r_k of that cluster. This is possible, since for each pair of samples the respective deformation field **u** is available. The representatives r_k are selected as the samples with the lowest intra-cluster distance.

We train auxiliary root filters as in Section 5.1 but using the warped samples and high resolution HOG features (the same resolution as the part filters). We call these root filters *accurate*. Their only purpose is to obtain improved initial part filters, which again can be set by covering most of the positive weights.

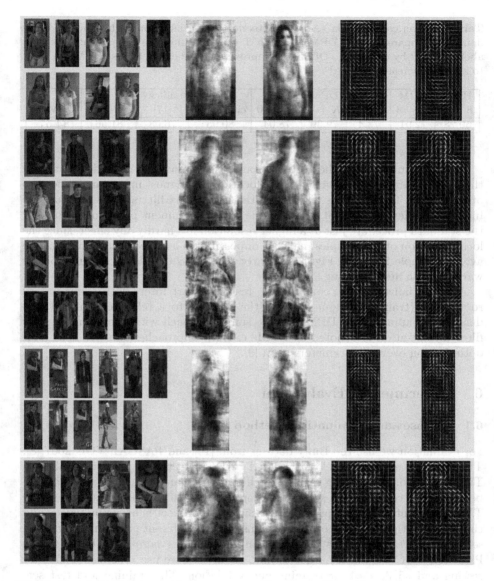

Fig. 5. Part initialization with accurate auxiliary root filters shown for 5 out of 10 mixture components. **Left:** Samples from the clusters, red marks the representative sample r_k. **Middle:** Overlay of all samples with (right) and without (left) alignment (images are histogram-normalized for better visualization). **Right:** Trained auxiliary root filter with (right) and without (left) alignment. Especially for the two top-most and the bottom cluster alignment leads to more detailed filters. In the head and shoulder region this is visible particularly well.

Table 3. Average precision (AP) on detection for various approaches on the Buffy dataset. Compared to the DPM [9] (with 3, 6 and 10 mixture components) we gain about 2% AP by clustering (DPM+c). Improving also the part filters (DPM+a) leads to another increase of 3% AP.

HOG $K = 3$	DPM $K = 3$	HOG $K = 6$	DPM $K = 6$	DPM $K = 10$	HOG clustering	Ladicky [17]	DPM+c	DPM+a
50.28	72.91	73.4	79.39	78.04	80.95	76.03	81.56	**84.57**

As shown in Figure 5, the accurate root filters are visibly more detailed since the warped samples agree on the same location of the most important structures of that filter. These details transfer to the initial part filters. We note that the higher accuracy of the root filters is due to the alignment procedure. Running the standard procedure just at a higher resolution has hardly any effect, since the local variation of the samples makes it impossible to learn consistent filters. The average sample image in Figure 5 clearly shows less detailed structures before warping than after warping.

After initialization, we combine the resulting part filters with the standard root filters (trained without aligning the samples to a reference sample). We denote this approach as DPM+a. The same approach with the standard part filter initialization is denoted as DPM+c. Both approaches run the final joint optimization over all parameters as in [9].

6   Experimental Evaluation

6.1   Dataset and Evaluation Method

For evaluation we use the Buffy dataset from [10] and PASCAL VOC 2007 [8]. The first was used in the closely related LADF detector by Ladicky et al. [17]. The dataset contains strong variation in illumination and truncated and occluded persons. It is composed of scenes from episodes $2 - 6$ of the fifth season of the TV-series "Buffy the Vampire Slayer". Since the dataset is based on videos and there are multiple samples of the same instance at different poses in the training set, it supports transitions between samples, whereas samples in datasets like PASCAL VOC are much harder to link. As in [17], we use $s5e2$, $s5e5$, $s5e6$ for testing and $s5e3$, $s5e4$ for training and validation. The training and test sets contain 276 and 472 images, respectively.

As usual, a detection is counted as positive if the intersection over union ratio with respect to ground truth bounding box is greater than 0.5. We report the average precision (AP) over the test set.

6.2   Results

Table 3 compares the AP of alignment based clustering (DPM+c) and initial part placement (DPM+a) against the classical DPM (with and without parts)

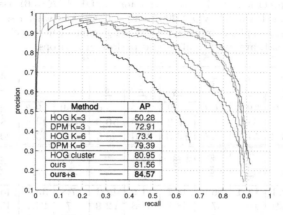

The table within the figure:

Method		AP
HOG K=3	———	50.28
DPM K=3	———	72.91
HOG K=6	———	73.4
DPM K=6	———	79.39
HOG cluster	———	80.95
ours	———	81.56
ours+a	———	**84.57**

Fig. 6. Precision-recall curves of our method (red) on the Buffy dataset. Baselines are DPM without (dark blue and dark green) and with left-right-splitting (violet and magenta). We clearly see that appearance based clustering improves the detection results and that the alignment improves the results twice: first by optimizing the clustering, which results in a better detection performance and second, by the better part placement, which gives the major improvement.

and the LADF detector by Ladicky et al. [17][2]. The DPM model uses 3 aspect ratios, with and without left-right-splitting, resulting in $K = 6$ and $K = 3$ mixture components. For our approach, we used $K = 10$ components, which corresponds to the K components of the LADF detector. Figure 6 shows the precision-recall curves of methods for which code was publicly available. Typical detection results of our method are shown in Figure 7.

In the previous sections, we discussed the importance of good clustering as initialization for the mixture model learning. The alignment based clustering as a starting point for the mixture components (DPM+c) has indeed a positive effect on detection with the DPM. It also slightly improves over clustering without alignment indicating that the improvement is not only due to the larger number of mixture components[3]. The main boost in performance is due to the better part initialization, included in DPM+a, which is due to the accurate root filters trained on warped samples. In total, we get an improvement of more than 5% AP compared to the DPM.

---

[2] The reviewing process revealed some inconsistencies between the dataset used in [17] and the one that is available for download. For the public dataset a few corrections in the annotation have been made, which is why the direct comparison to [17] should be taken with a grain of salt. The comparison to DPM is fair and the DPM results reported in [17] can be almost exactly reproduced when using DPM version 3 or the newer version with left-right-splitting turned off.

[3] More mixture components are not necessarily advantageous because a larger number of components leads to a smaller number of samples to train each component.

Table 4. Average precision (AP) on detection for the DPM ($K = 6$) baseline, DPM+c and DPM+a on the PASCAL VOC 2007 test set. Classes with less variation or a denser sampling e.g. aeroplane improve with the alignment, whereas classes with larger variability, such as cat, are hard to align and performance drops.

	aero	bike	bird	boat	bottle	bus	car	cat	chair	cow
DPM [9]	28.9	**59.5**	**10.0**	15.2	**25.5**	49.6	**57.9**	**19.3**	**22.4**	25.2
DPM+c	29.7	58.2	9.7	16.3	22.9	**50.3**	52	14.8	18.9	27.9
DPM+a	**33.2**	57.4	9.7	**16.9**	25.0	48.6	52.3	13.3	20.2	**30.3**

	table	dog	horse	mbike	person	plant	sheep	sofa	train	tv
DPM [9]	23.3	**11.1**	56.8	48.7	**41.9**	12.2	17.8	**33.6**	45.1	**41.6**
DPM+c	24.9	10.3	57.2	48.7	36.8	**12.9**	17	24.1	45.8	40.9
DPM+a	**26.6**	6.5	**60.1**	**49.1**	38.4	9.8	**18.7**	29.7	**47.3**	39.8

Fig. 7. Qualitative comparison between the detections of our model DPM+a(bottom rows) and the DPM (top rows). Green boxes indicate correct detections with an intersection over union ratio > 0.5; red boxes indicate false detections. With DPM+a, we capture a wider range of variation that does not only manifest in more detected people (ex 4, 7, 8, 12), but also in more precise bounding boxes (ex 6, 10, 11, 14). Both methods fail in case of highly occluded or truncated people, as in ex 5 and 10. Instances with few or no training data, as the sitting person in ex. 13, cannot be handled. These would require additional mixture components with corresponding additional training data.

The results of the object detection on PASCAL VOC 2007 are shown in Table 4. Both approaches DPM+c and DPM+a heavily depend on the alignment. If the specific class is too diverse in pose and appearance, such as for cat, dog, plant and person, alignment is too hard and even deteriorates the clustering and the DPM training. On the other hand, subcategories with a strong connectivity among the samples, such as for aeroplane, cow and horse, the DPM benefits from both clustering and alignment. We believe that the alignment is most beneficial when training samples from video showing the same instance in different poses are involved. Apart from the Buffy dataset, few data of that sort is yet available.

7   Conclusions

We have presented a new clustering method based on a pairwise non-rigid alignment. In the experiments, we have shown that such a strategy is most reasonable for datasets that allow for clear correspondences within subcategories such as in videos. Detailed analysis on the Buffy dataset has shown that the alignment improves the performance directly in terms of clustering AP

and indirectly by obtaining better detection results. Furthermore, we have demonstrated that alignment can help initialize the part placement in the deformable part model.

It is worth noting that we finally optimize the same energy model as the DPM. Apart from increasing the number of mixture components from $K = 6$ to $K = 10$ the model has not changed. The improvement is only due to a better initialization. This indicates that complex detection approaches which optimize many mutually dependent parameters can benefit from stronger optimization methods and sophisticated initialization strategies.

Acknowledgements. This study was supported by the Excellence Initiative of the German Federal and State Governments (EXC 294) and by the ERC Starting Grant VIDEOLEARN.

References

1. Aghazadeh, O., Azizpour, H., Sullivan, J., Carlsson, S.: Mixture component identification and learning for visual recognition. In: Fitzgibbon, A., Lazebnik, S., Perona, P., Sato, Y., Schmid, C. (eds.) ECCV 2012, Part VI. LNCS, vol. 7577, pp. 115–128. Springer, Heidelberg (2012)
2. Azizpour, H., Laptev, I.: Object detection using strongly-supervised deformable part models. In: Fitzgibbon, A., Lazebnik, S., Perona, P., Sato, Y., Schmid, C. (eds.) ECCV 2012, Part I. LNCS, vol. 7572, pp. 836–849. Springer, Heidelberg (2012)
3. Bourdev, L., Maji, S., Brox, T., Malik, J.: Detecting people using mutually consistent poselet activations. In: Daniilidis, K., Maragos, P., Paragios, N. (eds.) ECCV 2010, Part VI. LNCS, vol. 6316, pp. 168–181. Springer, Heidelberg (2010)
4. Dalal, N., Triggs, B.: Histograms of oriented gradients for human detection. In: CVPR, pp. 886–893. IEEE Computer Society (2005)

5. Divvala, S.K., Efros, A.A., Hebert, M.: How important are "Deformable parts" in the deformable parts model? In: Fusiello, A., Murino, V., Cucchiara, R. (eds.) ECCV 2012 Ws/Demos, Part III. LNCS, vol. 7585, pp. 31–40. Springer, Heidelberg (2012)

6. Dong, J., Xia, W., Chen, Q., Feng, J., Huang, Z., Yan, S.: Subcategory-aware object classification. In: CVPR, pp. 827–834. IEEE (2013)

7. Drayer, B., Brox, T.: Distances based on non-rigid alignment for comparison of different object instances. In: Weickert, J., Hein, M., Schiele, B. (eds.) GCPR 2013. LNCS, vol. 8142, pp. 215–224. Springer, Heidelberg (2013)

8. Everingham, M., Van Gool, L., Williams, C.K.I., Winn, J., Zisserman, A.: The PASCAL Visual Object Classes Challenge (VOC2007) Results (2007), http://www.pascal-network.org/challenges/VOC/voc2007/workshop/index.html

9. Felzenszwalb, P.F., Girshick, R.B., McAllester, D., Ramanan, D.: Object detection with discriminatively trained part-based models. IEEE Transactions on Pattern Analysis and Machine Intelligence 32(9), 1627–1645 (2010)

10. Ferrari, V., Marin-Jimenez, M., Zisserman, A.: Progressive search space reduction for human pose estimation. In: CVPR (2008)

11. Gu, C., Arbeláez, P., Lin, Y., Yu, K., Malik, J.: Multi-component models for object detection. In: Fitzgibbon, A., Lazebnik, S., Perona, P., Sato, Y., Schmid, C. (eds.) ECCV 2012, Part IV. LNCS, vol. 7575, pp. 445–458. Springer, Heidelberg (2012)

12. Gu, C., Ren, X.: Discriminative mixture-of-templates for viewpoint classification. In: Daniilidis, K., Maragos, P., Paragios, N. (eds.) ECCV 2010, Part V. LNCS, vol. 6315, pp. 408–421. Springer, Heidelberg (2010)

13. Hariharan, B., Malik, J., Ramanan, D.: Discriminative decorrelation for clustering and classification. In: Fitzgibbon, A., Lazebnik, S., Perona, P., Sato, Y., Schmid, C. (eds.) ECCV 2012, Part IV. LNCS, vol. 7575, pp. 459–472. Springer, Heidelberg (2012)

14. Komodakis, N., Tziritas, G.: Approximate labeling via graph cuts based on linear programming. IEEE Transactions on Pattern Analysis and Machine Intelligence 29(8), 1436–1453 (Aug 2007)

15. Komodakis, N., Tziritas, G., Paragios, N.: Performance vs computational efficiency for optimizing single and dynamic mrfs: Setting the state of the art with primal-dual strategies. Computer Vision and Image Understanding 112(1), 14–29 (2008)

16. Krizhevsky, A., Sutskever, I., Hinton, G.E.: Imagenet classification with deep convolutional neural networks. In: Advances in Neural Information Processing Systems. pp. 1106–1114 (2012)

17. Ladicky, L., Torr, P.H.S., Zisserman, A.: Latent svms for human detection with a locally affine deformation field. In: BMVC. BMVA Press (2012)

18. Malisiewicz, T., Gupta, A., Efros, A.A.: Ensemble of exemplar-svms for object detection and beyond. In: ICCV, pp. 89–96. IEEE Computer Society (2011)

19. Ng, A.Y., Jordan, M.I., Weiss, Y.: On spectral clustering: Analysis and an algorithm. In: Advances in Neural Information Processing Systems, pp. 849–856. MIT Press (2001)

20. Seber, G.: Multivariate observations. Wiley (1984)

21. Shi, J., Malik, J.: Normalized cuts and image segmentation. IEEE Transactions on Pattern Analysis and Machine Intelligence 22, 888–905 (1997)

22. Zhu, X., Ramanan, D.: Face detection, pose estimation, and landmark localization in the wild. In: CVPR, pp. 2879–2886. IEEE (2012)

23. Zhu, X., Vondrick, C., Ramanan, D., Fowlkes, C.C.: Do we need more training data or better models for object detection? In: BMVC. BMVA Press (2012)

Predicting Actions from Static Scenes

Tuan-Hung Vu[1], Catherine Olsson[2], Ivan Laptev[1],
Aude Oliva[2], and Josef Sivic[1]

[1] WILLOW, ENS/INRIA/CNRS UMR 8548, Paris, France
[2] CSAIL, MIT, Cambridge, Massachusetts, USA

Abstract. Human actions naturally co-occur with scenes. In this work
we aim to discover action-scene correlation for a large number of scene
categories and to use such correlation for action prediction. Towards this
goal, we collect a new SUN Action dataset with manual annotations
of typical human actions for 397 scenes. We next discover action-scene
associations and demonstrate that scene categories can be well identified
from their associated actions. Using discovered associations, we address
a new task of predicting human actions for images of static scenes. We
evaluate prediction of 23 and 38 action classes for images of indoor and
outdoor scenes respectively and show promising results. We also propose
a new application of geo-localized action prediction and demonstrate
ability of our method to automatically answer queries such as "Where is
a good place for a picnic?" or "Can I cycle along this path?".

Keywords: Action prediction, scene recognition, functional properties.

1 Introduction

Our environments, such as living rooms, cafes and offices, vary in objects and
geometry, but also in *actions* that we usually do in these places (e.g., we typically
work in offices and *cook* or *eat* in kitchens). As illustrated in Figure 1, scene types
are, indeed, often correlated with specific sets of typical actions. The goal of this
work is to explore such correlation and to develop algorithms able to answer
questions such as "What are typical actions for a given scene?", "Where is a good
place to have a picnic?" or "Can I cycle along this path?". Automatic answers
to such questions could be useful for several purposes. First, action prediction
could provide scene-specific priors when recognizing human actions. For example,
relaxing is common on beaches but not on streets; cooking is common in kitchens
but not in offices. Second, deviations from an expected set of actions could be
used to identify abnormal activities. Third, as we show in this paper, automatic
action prediction for geo-localized images could support the search of places
suited for particular purposes.

Computer vision has a rich body of work on recognizing human actions
[1,2,3,4,5] and scenes [6,7,8,9]. Most of this work addresses the problems of action and scene recognition separately. Recently, several methods have shown
advantages of recognizing actions or tracking people in the context of their environments [5,10]. Similarly, the interplay between human poses and objects has

D. Fleet et al. (Eds.): ECCV 2014, Part V, LNCS 8693, pp. 421–436, 2014.

Fig. 1. Images of scene classes `sandbar` and `temple_east_asia` from the SUN dataset [14] together with probabilities for the five most likely actions, predicted manually by people (red) and by our method (green).

been studied in [11,12,13]. While previous work has looked at functional properties for a few selected classes of scenes and objects, here we aim to exploit correlation between scenes and actions at a *large scale* of hundreds of scene categories. Using the discovered correlations, we demonstrate prediction of human actions for test images of outdoor scenes such as, for example, found on Google maps.

To reach our goal, we construct a new SUN Action dataset and collect manual annotations of human actions for 7940 images of 397 scene categories from the SUN dataset [14]. Analysis of this data reveals strong action-scene correlation for the majority of scene categories. Notably, we show that an image's scene category can be determined from corresponding textual descriptions of characteristic actions for that image.

Using the discovered relations between scenes and actions, we next address the task of automatic action prediction for images of static scenes. We consider 38 outdoor and 23 indoor action classes and associate typical action labels with 397 scene categories. Using such scene-based action annotation we learn visual classifiers for each action category and predict actions for images of static scenes as illustrated in Figure 1.

We finally demonstrate an application of our method to the new task of geo-localized action prediction. Our motivation comes from the large amount of publically-available geo-tagged images (e.g., on Flickr and Panoramio) which is expected to grow even faster with the introduction of new wearable devices such as Google Glass. Application of automatic action prediction to such images will enable the search for places based on their *function*, including specific actions such as swimming, having picnic, hiking and many others. In our experiments we use geo-localized images of outdoor scenes collected from `panoramio.com` and demonstrate examples of successful action prediction on the map of France.

In summary, we make the following three contributions. First, we present a new dataset with manual annotations of typical actions for 397 scene classes (see Section 3) and use it to analyze action-scene correlations (see Section 4). Second, based on the discovered correlations, we demonstrate successful action prediction for images of static scenes (see Section 5). Finally, we propose a new task of geo-localized action prediction. We apply our method to geo-tagged images on the web and show encouraging results of searching maps for locations suitable for particular activities (see Section 6).

2   Related Work

Relatively few papers explore relations between scenes and actions. Li *et al.* [15] propose a graphical model combining evidence from object and scene categories for action recognition in still images. Marszalek *et al.* [5] propose a joint framework for scene and action recognition in video. While most of the work in action recognition targets actions depicted in images or video, here we address a different task and predict actions in scene images with no action observations.

Action prediction has been recently addressed by Kitani *et al.* [10] and Walker *et al.* [16] aiming to model future motion of people and cars using priors derived from the scene. Yuen and Torralba [17] predict motion for images of static scenes by searching and transferring motion cues from video scenes with similar appearance. Our work complements these efforts and investigates action prediction for a large set of scenes and actions.

Recognition of functional properties of objects and scenes is an interesting but less explored area of computer vision. Relations between people and objects as well as between human poses and scene geometry have been investigated in [11,12,13]. Patterson and Hays [18] annotate scene images with a set of global attributes of various types (i.e: material, surface property, affordance and spatial envelope), and recognize attributes from scene images. Unlike any previous work, we here aim to model functional properties for a wide range of scene classes. Our work is similar in spirit to Arietta *et al.* [19] and Khosla *et al.* [20] who aim to predict non-observed scene properties such as crime rate in the area.

3   Dataset

Dataset annotation. To analyze correlations over a wide range of scene categories and a rich set of actions, we gather the novel *SUN Action* dataset (short for "Scene UNderstanding - Action") with manual annotations of typical human actions for images of static scenes. We use scene images from the SUN dataset [14]. For each of the 397 well-sampled scene categories we collect free-form annotations of typical actions for the twenty "most typical" images in that category [21], for a total of 7940 images. Annotations were crowdsourced using Amazon Mechanical Turk (AMT)[1]. AMT workers were shown images of scenes and were asked to list between one and three words or short phrases for each scene describing a typical action that one would usually do there. Scene category labels were not provided. All together we collected 137,558 responses: each image received 17.3 responses on average, and each category received an average of 346.4 responses.

Example images and corresponding responses from the SUN Action dataset are shown in Figure 2. We have observed a varying diversity of responses for different scene categories. The top row of Figure 2 shows a few examples of scene classes with low entropy of response histograms (high annotator agreement, low response diversity). Such scenes often correspond to places that have been

---

[1] AMT workers gave consent (set by the MIT IRB) for each HIT they chose to perform.

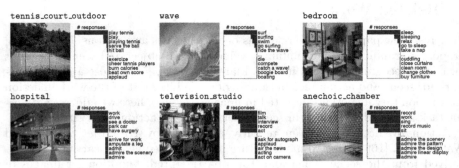

Fig. 2. SUN Action scene categories with corresponding histograms of action responses. Top row: Scene categories with low entropy of response histograms. Bottom row: scene categories with high entropy of response histograms. Low-entropy categories are often places designed for specific purposes (tennis court) or where the environment limits possible actions (wave). By comparison, high-entropy categories are places that afford many actions (television studio) or are unfamiliar (anechoic chamber)

Fig. 3. Histograms of words in action responses for two images of the scene class **crosswalk**. The presence of a cyclist in the image on the right biases responses to contain the action "bike", which is not present in other crosswalk images.

designed for specific purposes (tennis court) or where the natural environment limits the set of possible actions (wave). In contrast, scene classes with high entropy of responses (Figure 2, bottom) are places that afford many actions (e.g., a television studio, where many actions need to take place over the course of filming) or unfamiliar places (an anechoic chamber).

The majority of images in the SUN Action dataset contain no people. We found this property to be important for collecting unbiased annotations of typical actions. For a few images containing people we have observed a bias in action annotations towards actions depicted in the image. An example of such a bias is shown in Figure 3 illustrating two crosswalk scenes, one without people and one with a cycling person. In the scene containing the cyclist, the predominant response was "bike", unlike other images in the crosswalk category.

Processing of Action Responses. Action responses were gathered in free-form natural language and require preprocessing for our further analysis. Many of responses contain nearly identical information but differ in grammatical structure, such as "read the book while on the flight" and "read a book". Our first pass of preprocessing converts responses into simplified action annotations by extracting verbs or verb-noun patterns from each response. This strategy reduces the response space while preserving meaning. For example, responses like *"read the book while on the flight"* or *"avoid eye contact with neighbours"* are trimmed to *"read book"* and *"avoid eye contact"* respectively. We use the Stanford NLP toolbox [22] for part-of-speech tagging, stemming, and removal of stop words, and extract either verbs or verb-noun patterns from each response. Responses containing no verbs are removed. The words extracted in this stage of preprocessing are used as input to predict scene categories in Section 4.

For the action prediction task in Section 5 we manually group semantically similar action responses into action classes. To define action classes, we automatically extract 100 most frequent verb patterns, i.e. single verbs, verb+noun, etc., from action responses. Patterns with similar meaning are then manually merged yielding action labels, for example, "walk on grass" and "walk on sand" are merged into "walk". We note that the automatic parsing of natural language into action categories is an open problem beyond our work. In particular, we separate scenes into 197 outdoor and 203 indoor categories and define corresponding 38 outdoor and 23 indoor action classes as listed in Figure 7.

Given the average of 17.3 action responses per image in our database and a potentially large number of typical actions for a scene, our per-image annotation is not exhaustive. To address this problem, we assume that instances of the same scene category share the same functional properties. We found this assumption to be valid in most cases in our database. We therefore assign the same action labels to all instances of a given scene category using the following *label propagation* strategy. A scene category C is labeled by an action A if images of C are labeled with A at least 20 times. Following this procedure, for each action label A we obtain a set of *positive* scene categories. The *negative* scene categories for A are those containing no A labels for any of their images. Results of our preprocessing together with the original action responses are available from [23].

4   Analysis of Scene-Action Correlation

Are different scene categories correlated with distinctive sets of actions? Scene categories are often defined by what you would typically do there: for example, in an office one would typically *work*, whereas in a kitchen one would typically *cook*. Indeed, most man-made scenes around us have been created to facilitate certain actions.

This section verifies and quantifies relations between actions and scenes. We demonstrate successful recognition of a large number of scene categories from associated actions descriptions. We further investigate the structure of action-scene correlations with a hierarchical clustering analysis.

4.1   Predicting Scenes from Actions

To verify the hypothesized correlation between scene categories and actions, we conduct two classification experiments using action annotations in the SUN Action dataset. We take inspiration from the field of text classification. In the SUN

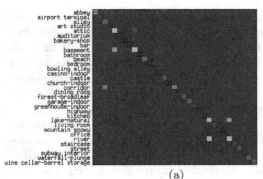

Method	33-cat	397-cat
Chance level	3.00	0.25
Nearest Centroid	85.80	40.31
ML Naive Bayes	**91.97**	**55.86**

(a)   (b)

Fig. 4. Results of action-based scene classification. (a): Confusion matrix for the 33-category subset using Maximum Likelihood Naive Bayes estimation. The strong red line along the diagonal indicates excellent classification performance. A few pairs of categories e.g., (basement,attic) and (river,lake) are confused due to similarity in their characteristic actions. (b): Average accuracy (%) of scene classification for the 33-category subset and for all 397 scene categories.

Action dataset, each image is associated with a collection of natural-language action descriptions. Classifying images based on a collection of associated responses is reminiscent of classifying documents based on their contents. However, there are two notable differences in our approach. First, the number of responses available per image (17.3 responses on average) is significantly lower compared to the number of words in a typical text document. Secondly, we wish to probe category membership using only a small collection of responses per image, to simulate asking a handful of people to provide a most typical action for the image and then performing classification based on the consensus of that set of responses. Therefore we use classification strategies that compare small queries to entire categories at a time.

Classification Methods. We classify images using two simple bag-of-words techniques – Nearest Centroid and Naive Bayes. First, we divide the images in each class into 10 folds for cross-validation. Within the training set, the responses for each image are split into individual words. These word counts are combined and normalized across all images within a given class, to generate a word distribution histogram for each scene category. Within the test set, responses for each image are randomly grouped into chunks of 7 responses for that image, to simulate asking a handful of people at a time to provide a most typical action for each image. Responses within each chunk are then split into individual words to form bag-of-words queries.

In nearest centroid classification, the bag-of-words queries are normalized to form histograms, which are compared with category histograms according to histogram intersection distance. The scene category centroid with the smallest distance from the query is selected as the class label.

In Maximum Likelihood Naive Bayes classification, the category histograms are interpreted as empirical likelihood estimates: the likelihood $\Pr(w|c)$ of

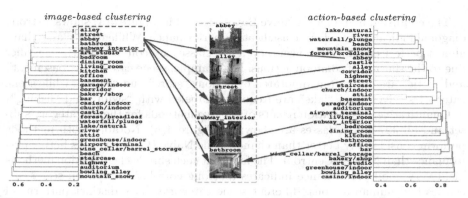

Fig. 5. Results of hierarchical clustering of 33 scene categories based on the similarity of image descriptors (left) and action similarity (right). Image-based similarity groups similar-*looking* scenes despite their large difference in semantics such as "alley" and "bathroom". In contrast, action-based similarity results in more semantically meaningful clusters. For example, "mountain, snowy" is placed in a category of its own according to the visual similarity, whereas it is grouped together with other outdoor places on the basis of action similarity.

observing word w in association with an image of class c is assumed to be the number or observations of w within the class c responses in the training set divided by the total number of words in all class c responses combined. The word observation likelihoods are assumed to be conditionally independent (the "naive Bayes assumption"), enabling us to compute the class-conditional likelihood of each bag-of-word query as the product of each constituent word's empirical class likelihood: $\Pr(w_1, w_2, \ldots w_n | c) = \Pr(w_1 | c) \times \Pr(w_2 | c) \times \ldots \times \Pr(w_n | c)$. The empirical likelihood estimate makes no explicit provision for estimating the likelihood of unobserved word-class pairs. To address this issue, we compute the minimum class-conditional likelihood over all words and classes in the dataset, $\min_{w,c}(\Pr(w | c))$, and use this probability to stand in as the class-conditional likelihood for unobserved words. We assume a uniform prior over scene categories, enabling maximum likelihood estimation: that is to say, bag-of-words queries are classified according to which class provides the largest class-conditional likelihood.

Results. Figure 4 illustrates results of scene classification. As visualizing results across 397 individual classes is difficult, we select a 33-category subset of well-recognized and semantically important scene categories. To select the 33-category subset, we have asked four of our collaborators to nominate 20-40 most important scene types. Out of the 80 scene types with most annotated images, 35 received at least two nominations and were slated for inclusion. "Cathedral" was removed for not being different enough from "church", and "abbey" and "coast" was removed for containing only aerial shots, leaving a final slate of 33 scene categories.

The confusion matrix for a Naive Bayes method in Figure 4(a) shows a strong diagonal indicating excellent classification performance. While most classes have almost perfect classification accuracy, a few classes are confused by the classifier due to the sharing of common actions. For example, scene categories "basement" and "attic" are both often annotated by actions "store" and "clean", while scene categories "river" and "lake" are frequently labeled with "swim" and "fishing".

Quantitative classification results of the two methods for the 33-category subset and all 397 scene classes are shown in Figure 4(b). Notably, both methods perform considerably better than chance while Naive Bayes provides better performance than Nearest Centroid. The fact that such simple classification methods yield very good performance indicates a strong correlation between scene categories and human actions: different scene categories have distinct patterns of associated actions. This confirms our initial hypothesis of a very strong relation between scene categories and their functional properties.

4.2 Action-Based Scene Clustering

We seek to further investigate the structure of correlations between scene categories and actions: Which scene categories are more similar in terms of their function? We use hierarchical clustering and group scene descriptors at multiple scales. At the finest scale, only the most similar scene types cluster together, whereas at coarse scales, clusters are larger and encompass more dissimilar scene types. Dendrogram visualizations in Figure 5 show the progression of clustering patterns from fine to coarse: categories are represented as "leaves"; branchings closer to the leaves of the tree connect classes that cluster together under fine-grained clusterings; and branchings closer to the trunk of the tree encompass broader clusterings. The height of each linkage in the dendrogram indicates the distance between the subclusters it connects.

The two dendrograms in Figure 5 illustrate image-based and action-based scene clustering. In the first case, distances between scenes were obtained as Eucledian distances of corresponding image descriptors (see Section 5). Clustering based on human action annotations was obtained using χ^2-distances between scene representations in terms of bag-of-words histograms (see Section 4.1). We observe that image-based similarity in Figure 5(left) captures substantially different information about scene classes as compared to action similarity Figure 5(right). For example, "alley", "bathroom" and "subway interior" are grouped together according to visual similarity due to their similar geometrty and texture, but are separated according to action similarity since alleys, bathrooms and subways have different function. Another example is that visual similarity places "mountain, snowy" is a category of its own because no other class commonly depicts open white peaks, whereas action similarity places mountains together with other outdoor places that are associated with hiking, taking photos, and related actions.

5 Visual Action Prediction

People can easily determine appropriate actions to perform in a given place. Are machines able to do the same thing? In Section 4 we have addressed the related problem of predicting scene categories from a set of associated actions. Here we turn to the problem of predicting typical actions for an image of a scene. We approach the problem of visual action prediction using standard image classification techniques in terms of local features and binary classifiers. To train image classifiers we use action labels derived from action annotations as described in Section 3. We predict actions separately for indoor and outdoor scenes.

We test two different schemes for action prediction. Under the first scheme (**S1**), we train action classifiers directly from images using action labels only. Under the second scheme (**S2**), we first classify images into scene categories as an intermediate step and then assign action scores based on the obtained scores of scene classifiers. We assume that any particular test image belongs to one scene category only, therefore a score for an action a in a given image is defined as a max scene score over scene categories S associated with a.

5.1 Implementation Details

Image representation. Our image classification pipeline follows standard approaches and consists of densely extracted local image features, a learned visual vocabulary and a feature encoding step. For local image features we use HOG2x2 [14], SIFT [24] and CSIFT [25,26] descriptors. Descriptor dimension is reduced by PCA. For the encoding phase we consider two popular encoding techniques: histogram encoding (BoW) and Fisher Vector encoding (FV). To exploit spatial information, we apply Spatial Pyramid framework [6], using grids of size 1x1, 2x2, 3x1. Each grid cell is represented either by BoW or FV vectors. The resulting vectors are normalized and concatenated to create the final representation. In the rest of this section we use the format $<descriptor>\_<encoding\ technique>$ to denote image representation techniques, e.g. CSIFT_FV as Fisher Vector encoding for CSIFT descriptors.

Classification. For the classification, we train SVM classifiers using LIBSVM toolbox [27]. Linear kernels are used for image representation by Fisher Vector. For the histogram representation (SIFT_BoW /CSIFT_BoW), we use χ^2 kernel [28]. With HOG_BoW, we exploit Histogram Intersection kernel. Training by SVM, we can boost up the performance by simply using a linear combination of kernels. In our experiments, we aggregate kernels with equal weights.

5.2 Experimental Results

For training and testing the classifiers, we randomly divide the dataset into two equal parts. Our training and testing splits are balanced in number of images per scene category. Our results for action prediction are summarized in Figures 6-8 and Table 1.

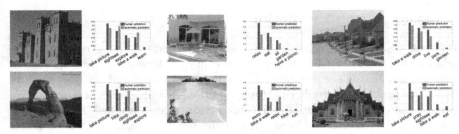

Fig. 6. Automatic visual action prediction for test images in SUN Action dataset.

We use mean Average Precision (mAP) as the performance measure. To get mAP, we first compute the area under precision-recall curve, or Average Precision (AP), for each class. Then mAP is determined as the mean of average precisions across all classes. We obtain best prediction mAP of 60.99% for outdoor actions and 52.09% for indoor actions using combination of HOG_BOW, HOG_FV and CSIFT_FV kernels. Our result is significantly higher than the mAP at chance level, i.e. 6.32% for outdoor action classes and 4.24% for indoor action classes. Figures 6-8 are produced with our best kernel combination.

In Figure 7, we show classification results with 38 outdoor and 23 indoor action classes sorted by AP. For better visualization of prediction results for some action classes, we show example images in Figure 8. The last two columns depict some hard positive and hard negative samples for each class. For outdoor scenes, action classes such as "hike", "pray", having rather typical color/structure, are easier to classify than other "can-do-almost-every-where" action classes like "learn". While people can often differentiate universities from other buildings based e.g., on the text and other cues, the task is still difficult for current vision systems, especially, for those exploiting global image representations. We notice that indoor actions are more structure-dependent than outdoor actions. In our experiment APs of indoor action classes are generally lower than APs of outdoor action classes. We also observe different levels of difficulty among indoor actions, e.g., detecting bowling lanes is easier than detecting sink-like structures. We found building action classifiers challenging, because positive samples are possibly images from very different scene categories, thus covering much larger range of visual texture and structure.

We also aggregate predicted action scores for test images and try to estimate the score contribution. Figure 6 shows some test images along with manual action annotations and automatic action predictions. For this visualization, we map SVM scores of test images to probabilities using Platt's sigmoid [29], with parameters estimated during the training phase. Even though the results are not perfect, we still observe a good match between distributions of annotated and predicted actions. Our predictors successfully give reasonable responses like "swim", "take a walk" and "relax" to a beach image, or "take picture", "pray" and "sightsee" to a temple image. Other qualitative results of action prediction by our method are available at [23].

For more quantitative analysis, we now consider Table 1. The table shows action prediction mAPs of two proposed training schemes combined with different image

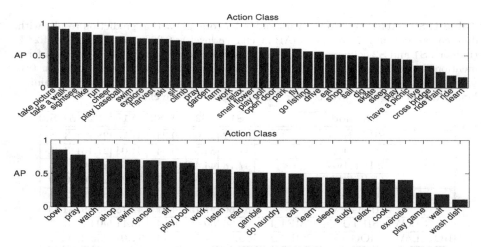

Fig. 7. Results of action prediction for all 38 outdoor actions (top) and 23 indoor actions (bottom) sorted in the decreasing order of Average Precision (AP)

Action	Precision Recall	Correct Predictions	Most Confident False Positives	Least Confident False Negatives
take picture	AP = 0.95			
hike	AP = 0.88			
pray	AP = 0.70			
learn	AP = 0.18			
bowl	AP = 0.85			
watch	AP = 0.70			
sleep	AP = 0.44			
wash dish	AP = 0.11			

Fig. 8. Selected SUN Action classification results - both outdoor (cyan) and indoor (orange) - with our best kernel combination

representation techniques. By comparing results of the two schemes, as shown in two columns **S1** and **S2**, we can conclude that learning action classifiers directly achieve better prediction performance than aggregating multiple scene classifiers. This improvement can be attributed to sharing similar functional properties across different scene classes. In terms of image representation techniques, Fisher Vector

Table 1. Scene-based outdoor (cyan) and indor (orange) action prediction results with different approaches. Note that mAP at chance level is 6.32% (outdoor) an d 4.24% (indoor). **S1** and **S2** columns respectively show classification mAP (%) of the two afore-mentioned training schemes. Column (**S1-S2**) shows the different mAP between two schemes. We observe consistently better performance of scheme **S1**: directly training binary action classifiers over scheme **S2**: aggregating scene classifiers.

Method	S1	S2	S1-S2	S1	S2	S1-S2
SIFT_BoW	40.92	40.68	0.24	31.75	28.71	3.04
SIFT_FV	41.15	34.51	6.64	31.04	27.13	3.91
CSIFT_BoW	47.78	44.43	3.35	32.53	27.90	4.63
CSIFT_FV	49.52	41.65	7.87	36.29	29.70	6.59
HOG_BoW	47.03	45.93	1.10	37.91	35.50	2.41
HOG_FV	52.66	47.75	4.91	42.78	43.89	-1.11
HOG_BoW+ SIFT_FV+ CSIFT_FV	56.60	50.06	6.54	46.11	40.04	6.07
HOG_BoW+ HOG_FV+ CSIFT_FV	**60.99**	54.25	6.74	**52.09**	45.98	6.11
SIFT_FV+ HOG_FV+ CSIFT_FV	56.48	49.61	6.87	45.76	41.41	4.35

encoding yields better performance compared to Histogram encoding. These results are consistent with recent works on scene classification [30]. Significant performance difference between SIFT and CSIFT proves that color information is useful for the task. Also, linear combination of multiple kernels does improve the performance. Among our three tested kernel combinations, using HOG_BoW, HOG_FV and CSIFT_FV yields the best result. In conclusion, we have shown high accuracy for a new task of action prediction evaluated on a large number of action and scene classes.

6   Image-Based Geo-Mapping of Actions

One possible application of scene-based action prediction is to search for places in which to do a specific action. For example, a user may ask "Where can I camp in the Mont Blanc valley?" or "Where can I sunbathe in Tuscany?". Such queries are currently not supported by map services such as Google Maps or Bing Maps. To address this problem, we introduce Image-based Geo-Mapping of Action (IGMA), an application for geo-localizing actions on a map and answering map queries of the type "Where can I do X?". Results are derived from geo-localized scene images publicly available on the Internet. IGMA is the first attempt to automatically answer geo-localized action queries. Our strategy of predicting actions at a broad spatial scale using geo-localized images enables us to go beyond manual location-action labels: for example, one can "have a picnic" not only at a designated picnic area, but also in a grassy countryside field.

Collecting the Panoramio Dataset. We use Panoramio image sharing service [31] to collect a dataset with geo-localized images. Like the SUN Action dataset, the images in Panoramio contain few to no people. The Panoramio service provides a REST API for selecting images: given a range of longitude and

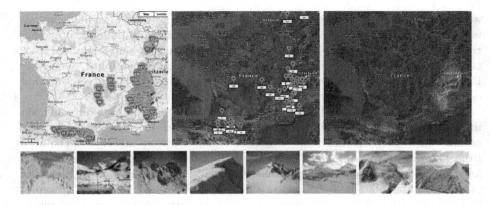

Fig. 9. "Where can I ski in France?" - (Top left) Official skiing stations in France [32]. (Top middle) Suggested places for skiing by IGMA. (Top right) Dense map of action "ski" generated by IGMA. (Bottom) Panoramio images of suggested places for skiing.

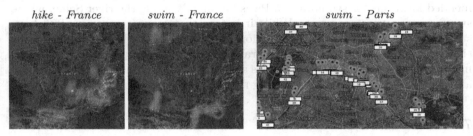

hike - France   *swim - France*   *swim - Paris*

Fig. 10. Geo-localized prediction of actions. (left): Predictions for actions "hike" and "swim" on the map of France. (right): Predictions for the action "swim" in Paris.

latitude values, Panoramio returns a JSON file of image properties including image URL and geographical position. For our experiment, we collected Panoramio images of France, with longitude from $-5°$ to $8°$ and latitude from $41°$ to $51°$. In total, our dataset contains over $38,000$ distinct geo-tagged images.

Dense Map of Actions. Our goal is to construct dense maps visualizing places where people would likely perform certain actions. We construct these maps by applying the scene-based action classifiers computed in Section 5.2 to the collected Panoramio dataset using the following procedure.

For a given action, we compute the top-scored Panoramio images. We generate a dense map from this list of scores and geo-locations by modeling the map using a Gaussian Mixture Model (GMM) with mixture components centered at the image locations and their weights set to corresponding action scores. The standard deviation σ for each component is set to a fixed value.

This initial dense map estimate is adjusted to compensate for non-uniform sampling of Panoramio images. Different population densities of the examined regions may introduce bias to the action density estimation. Therefore, we estimate the sampling density of Panoramio images. To estimate sampling density, we use the same GMM model above with the same σ for each Gaussian component as before, but with a uniform weight across all mixture model components rather than an action-score-based weight. The initial action map estimated from the highest scored images is normalized by the estimated sampling density of Panoramio images to correct the sampling density bias. We then get the final estimation of action density.

Figure 9 illustrates IGMA's suggestions for the question "Where can I ski in France?". We compare the estimated dense map produced by IGMA for the action "ski" with the the map of official skiing stations in France, acquired from [32]. Visually, our predictions have a high degree of correspondence with locations containing official skiing areas. Similarly, in Figure 10(left) we illustrate predictions for "hike" and "swim" in France. These results visually correspond to the sea-coast and mountain areas of France, confirming good geo-localization of actions.

Figure 10(right) illustrates an interesting result of predicting the "swim" action in Paris. This result suggests an area for further investigation: the recommended locations for swimming in Paris fall mainly along the river Seine, where swimming is very uncommon. While it is true that scene categories often have strong correlation with associated actions, not all scenes within a scene category share the same action affordances in practice. One possible approach to this issue might be to subdivide scene categories according to more fine-grained functional affordances, e.g. separately identifying rivers where people can and cannot swim.

7   Conclusion

In this work we have addressed a new problem of action prediction for a wide range of scene images. We have collected a new SUN Action dataset with manual annotations of typical actions for scene images, and discovered strong action-scene correlation for the majority of scene classes. Based on this correlation, we have learned to predict typical actions for a large set of scenes. Using standard state-of-the-art image classification techniques we have shown high accuracy of action prediction, which is an encouraging result for a new problem. To demonstrate potential advantages of our work, we have shown promising results on a new application Geo-Mapping of Actions (IGMA) enabling automatic answers to queries such as "Where can I do X?".

Acknowledgements. This work is partly funded by ERC Activia, US National Science Foundation grant 1016862, Google Research Awards, MSR-INRIA laboratory and EIT-ICT labs.

References

1. Laptev, I., Marszalek, M., Schmid, C., Rozenfeld, B.: Learning realistic human actions from movies. In: CVPR (2008)
2. Niebles, J.C., Chen, C.-W., Fei-Fei, L.: Modeling temporal structure of decomposable motion segments for activity classification. In: Daniilidis, K., Maragos, P., Paragios, N. (eds.) ECCV 2010, Part II. LNCS, vol. 6312, pp. 392–405. Springer, Heidelberg (2010)
3. Sadanand, S., Corso, J.: Action bank: A high-level representation of activity in video. In: CVPR (2012)
4. Wang, H., Kläser, A., Schmid, C., Cheng-Lin, L.: Action Recognition by Dense Trajectories. In: CVPR (2011)
5. Marszalek, M., Laptev, I., Schmid, C.: Actions in context. In: CVPR (2009)
6. Lazebnik, S., Schmid, C., Ponce, J.: Beyond bags of features: Spatial pyramid matching for recognizing natural scene categories. In: CVPR (2006)
7. Oliva, A., Torralba, A.: Modeling the shape of the scene: A holistic representation of the spatial envelope. IJCV 42, 145–175 (2001)
8. Quattoni, A., Torralba, A.: Recognizing indoor scenes. In: CVPR (2009)
9. Vogel, J., Schiele, B.: Natural scene retrieval based on a semantic modeling step. In: Enser, P.G.B., Kompatsiaris, Y., O'Connor, N.E., Smeaton, A.F., Smeulders, A.W.M. (eds.) CIVR 2004. LNCS, vol. 3115, pp. 207–215. Springer, Heidelberg (2004)
10. Kitani, K.M., Ziebart, B.D., Bagnell, J.A., Hebert, M.: Activity forecasting. In: Fitzgibbon, A., Lazebnik, S., Perona, P., Sato, Y., Schmid, C. (eds.) ECCV 2012, Part IV. LNCS, vol. 7575, pp. 201–214. Springer, Heidelberg (2012)
11. Grabner, H., Gall, J., Van Gool, L.: What makes a chair a chair? In: CVPR (2011)
12. Gupta, A., Satkin, S., Efros, A., Hebert, M.: From 3d scene geometry to human workspace. In: CVPR (2011)
13. Delaitre, V., Fouhey, D.F., Laptev, I., Sivic, J., Gupta, A., Efros, A.A.: Scene semantics from long-term observation of people. In: Fitzgibbon, A., Lazebnik, S., Perona, P., Sato, Y., Schmid, C. (eds.) ECCV 2012, Part VI. LNCS, vol. 7577, pp. 284–298. Springer, Heidelberg (2012)
14. Jianxiong, X., Hays, J., Ehinger, K., Oliva, A., Torralba, A.: Sun database: Large-scale scene recognition from abbey to zoo. In: CVPR, pp. 3485–3492 (2010)
15. Li, L.J., Fei-Fei, L.: What, where and who? classifying events by scene and object recognition. In: ICCV (2007)
16. Walker, J., Gupta, A., Hebert, M.: Patch to the future: Unsupervised visual prediction. In: CVPR (2014)
17. Yuen, J., Torralba, A.: A data-driven approach for event prediction. In: Daniilidis, K., Maragos, P., Paragios, N. (eds.) ECCV 2010, Part II. LNCS, vol. 6312, pp. 707–720. Springer, Heidelberg (2010)
18. Patterson, G., Hays, J.: Sun attribute database: Discovering, annotating, and recognizing scene attributes. In: CVPR (2012)
19. Arietta, S., Agrawala, M., Ramamoorthi, R.: On relating visual elements to city statistics. Technical Report UCB/EECS-2013-157, EECS Department, University of California, Berkeley (September 2013)
20. Khosla, A., An, B., Lim, J., Torralba, A.: Looking beyond the visible scene. In: CVPR (2014)
21. Ehinger, K.A., Xiao, J., Torralba, A., Oliva, A.: Estimating scene typicality from human ratings and image features (2011)

22. Toutanova, K., Klein, D., Manning, C., Singer, Y.: Feature-rich part-of-speech tagging with a cyclic dependency network. In: Conference of the North American Chapter of the Association for Computational Linguistics on Human Language Technology, pp. 173–180 (2003)
23. http://www.di.ens.fr/willow/research/actionsfromscenes
24. Lowe, D.G.: Distinctive image features from scale-invariant keypoints. IJCV 60(2), 91–110 (2004)
25. Abdel-Hakim, A.E., Farag, A.A.: Csift: A sift descriptor with color invariant characteristics. In: CVPR (2006)
26. van de Sande, K.E.A., Gevers, T., Snoek, C.G.M.: Empowering visual categorization with the gpu. IEEE Transactions on Multimedia 13(1), 60–70 (2011)
27. Chang, C.C., Lin, C.J.: Libsvm: A library for support vector machines. ACM Trans. Intell. Syst. Technol. 2(3), 27:1–27:27 (2011)
28. Zhang, J., Marszałek, M., Lazebnik, S., Schmid, C.: Local features and kernels for classification of texture and object categories: A comprehensive study. IJCV 73(2), 213–238 (2007)
29. Platt, J.C.: Probabilistic outputs for support vector machines and comparisons to regularized likelihood methods. In: Advances in Large Margin Classifiers, pp. 61–74. MIT Press (1999)
30. Perronnin, F., Dance, C.: Fisher kernels on visual vocabularies for image categorization. In: CVPR (2007)
31. Google: Panoramio service (2007), http://www.panoramio.com
32. Map of ski stations in france (2013), http://www.skiinfo.fr/france/carte.html

Exploiting Privileged Information from Web Data for Image Categorization

Wen Li*, Li Niu*, and Dong Xu

School of Computer Engineering, Nanyang Technological University, Singapore

Abstract. Relevant and irrelevant web images collected by tag-based image retrieval have been employed as loosely labeled training data for learning SVM classifiers for image categorization by only using the visual features. In this work, we propose a new image categorization method by incorporating the textual features extracted from the surrounding textual descriptions (tags, captions, categories, etc.) as privileged information and simultaneously coping with noise in the loose labels of training web images. When the training and test samples come from different datasets, our proposed method can be further extended to reduce the data distribution mismatch by adding a regularizer based on the Maximum Mean Discrepancy (MMD) criterion. Our comprehensive experiments on three benchmark datasets demonstrate the effectiveness of our proposed methods for image categorization and image retrieval by exploiting privileged information from web data.

Keywords: learning using privileged information, multi-instance learning, domain adaptation.

1 Introduction

Image categorization is a challenging problem in computer vision. A number of labeled training images are often required for learning a robust classifier for image categorization. However, collecting labeled training images based on human annotation is often time-consuming and expensive. Meanwhile, increasingly rich and massive social media data are being posted to the photo sharing websites like Flickr everyday, in which the web images are generally accompanied by valuable contextual information (*e.g.*, tags, captions, and surrounding text). Recently, relevant and irrelevant web images (*e.g.*, Flickr images) collected by tag-based image retrieval have been used as loosely labeled training data for learning SVM classifiers for various computer vision tasks (*e.g.*, image categorization and image retrieval)[43,33,31].

In this work, we extract the visual and textual features from the training web images and the associated textual descriptions (tags, captions, etc.), respectively. While we do not have the textual features in test images, the additional textual features extracted from the training images can still be used as privileged information, as shown in the work [42] from Vapnik and Vashist. Their work is

---

* Indicates equal contributions.

D. Fleet et al. (Eds.): ECCV 2014, Part V, LNCS 8693, pp. 437–452, 2014.

motivated by human learning, where a teacher provides the students with hidden information through explanations, comments, comparisons etc [42]. Similarly, we observe the surrounding textual descriptions more or less describe the content of training images. So the textual features can additionally provide hidden information for learning robust classifiers by bridging the semantic gap between the low-level visual features and the high-level semantic concepts.

For image categorization using massive web data, another challenging research issue is to cope with noisy labels of relevant training images. To solve this problem, the recent works [43,33,31] partitioned the training images into small subsets. By treating each subset as a "bag" and the images in each bag as "instances", the multi-instance learning (MIL) methods like Sparse MIL (sMIL) [5], mi-SVM [1] and MIL-CPB [33] were used for image categorization and image retrieval.

Based on the above observations, in Section 3, we first propose a new method called *sMIL using privileged information* (sMIL-PI) for image categorization by learning from loosely labeled web data, which not only takes advantage of the additional textual features but also effectively copes with noisy labels of relevant training images. When the training and testing samples are from different datasets, we also observe the data distributions between the training and testing samples may be very different. Our proposed sMIL-PI method can further be extended to reduce the data distribution mismatch. We name the extended method as sMIL-PI-DA, in which we additionally add a regularizer based on the Maximum Mean Discrepancy (MMD) criterion.

In Section 4, we conduct comprehensive experiments for two tasks, image categorization and image retrieval. Our results demonstrate our newly proposed method sMIL-PI outperforms its corresponding existing MIL method (*i.e.*, sMIL), and sMIL-PI is also better than the learning methods using privileged information as well as other related baselines. Moreover, our newly proposed domain adaptation method sMIL-PI-DA achieves the best results when the training and testing samples are from different datasets.

2   Related Work

Researchers have proposed effective methods to employ massive web data for various computer vision applications [37,40,17,27]. Torralba *et al.* [40] used a nearest neighbor (NN) based approach for object and scene recognition by leveraging a large dataset with 80 million tiny images. Fergus *et al.* [17] proposed a topic model based approach for object categorization by exploiting the images retrieved from Google image search, while Hwang and Grauman [27] employed kernel canonical correlation analysis (KCCA) for image retrieval using different features. Recently, Chen *et al.* [6] proposed the NEIL system for automatically labeling instances and extracting the visual relationships.

Our work is more related to [43,11,31,32,33], which explicitly coped with noise in the loose labels of relevant training web images. Those works first partitioned the training images into small subsets. By treating each subset as a "bag" and the images in each bag as "instances", they formulated this task as a multi-instance learning problem. The bag-based MIL method Sparse MIL as well as its variant were used in [43], while an instance-based approach called MIL-CPB was developed in [33]. The works in [43,33] did not consider the additional features in training data, and thus they can only employ the visual features for learning MIL classifiers for image categorization[1]. In contrast, we propose a new image categorization method by incorporating the additional textual features of training images as privileged information.

Our approach is motivated by the work on learning using privileged information (LUPI) [42], in which training data contains additional features (*i.e.*, privileged information) which are not available at the testing stage. Privileged information was also used for distance metric learning [20], multiple task learning [35] and learning to rank [38]. However, all those works only considered the supervised learning scenario using training data with accurate supervision. In contrast, we formulate a new MIL-PI method in order to cope with noise in the loose labels of relevant training web images.

Our work is also related to attributes based approaches [19,15], in which the attribute classifiers are learnt to extract the mid-level features. However, the mid-level features can be extracted from both training and testing images. Similarly, the classeme based approaches [41,30] proposed to use the training images from additionally annotated concepts to obtain the mid-level features. Those methods can be readily applied to our application by using the mid-level features as the main features to replace our current visual features (*i.e.*, the DeCAF features [10] in our experiments). However, the additional textual features, which are not available in the testing images, can still be used as privileged information in our sMIL-PI method. Moreover, those works did not explicitly reduce the distribution mismatch between the training and testing images as in our sMIL-PI-DA method.

Finally, our work is also related to the domain adaptation methods [2,3,18,26,22,21,29,13,4,14,12,34]. Huang *et al.* [26] proposed a two-step approach by re-weighting the source domain samples. For domain adaptation, Kulis *et al.* [29] proposed a metric learning method by learning an asymmetric nonlinear transformation, while Gopalan *et al.* [22] and Gong *et al.* [21] interpolated intermediate domains. SVM based approaches [13,4,14,12] were also developed to reduce the distribution mismatch. Some recent approaches aim to learn a domain invariant subspace [2] or align two subspaces from both domains [18]. Bergamo and Torresani [3] proposed a domain adaptation method which can cope with the loosely labeled training data. However, their method requires the labeled training samples from the target domain which are not required in our domain adaptation method sMIL-PI-DA. Moreover, our sMIL-PI-DA method achieves the best results when the training and testing samples are from different datasets.

---

[1] The work in [33] used both visual and textual features in the training process. However, it also requires the textual features in the testing process.

3 Multi-Instance Learning Using Privileged Information

Our goal is to learn robust classifiers for image categorization by using automatically collected web images. Given any category name, relevant and irrelevant web images can be collected as training data by using tag-based image retrieval. However, those collected relevant and irrelevant web images may be associated with noisy and inaccurate labels. Moreover, we also observe that web images are usually associated with rich textual descriptions (*e.g.*, tags, captions, and surrounding texts), which provide semantic descriptions to the content of the image to some extent.

To this end, we propose a new learning paradigm called multi-instance learning using privileged information (MIL-PI) for image categorization, in which we not only take advantage of the additional textual descriptions (*i.e.*, privileged information) in training data but also effectively cope with noise in the loose labels of relevant training images. Based on the Sparse MIL (sMIL) method [5], we develop a new method called sMIL-PI in Section 3.2.

When the training and testing samples are from different datasets, the distributions of training and testing samples may be very different. To reduce the data distribution mismatch, we further extend our sMIL-PI method as sMIL-PI-DA for domain adaptation by adding a regularizer based on the Maximum Mean Discrepancy (MMD) criterion into the dual formulation of our sMIL-PI in Section 3.3.

In the remainder of this paper, we use a lowercase/uppercase letter in boldface to denote a vector/matrix (*e.g.*, $\mathbf{a}$ denotes a vector and $\mathbf{A}$ denotes a matrix). The superscript $'$ denotes the transpose of a vector or a matrix. We denote $\mathbf{0}_n, \mathbf{1}_n \in \mathbb{R}^n$ as the n-dim column vectors of all zeros and all ones, respectively. For simplicity, we also use $\mathbf{0}$ and $\mathbf{1}$ instead of $\mathbf{0}_n$ and $\mathbf{1}_n$ when the dimension is obvious. Moreover, we use $\mathbf{A} \circ \mathbf{B}$ to denote the element-wise product between two matrices $\mathbf{A}$ and $\mathbf{B}$. The inequality $\mathbf{a} \leq \mathbf{b}$ means that $a_i \leq b_i$ for $i = 1, \ldots, n$.

3.1 Problem Statement

To cope with label noise in the training data, we partition the relevant and irrelevant web images into bags as in the recent works [43,33]. The training bags constructed from relevant images are labeled as positive and those from irrelevant images are labeled as negative.

Formally, let us represent the training data as $\{(\mathcal{B}_l, Y_l) \,|_{l=1}^{L}\}$, where $\mathcal{B}_l$ is a training bag, $Y_l \in \{+1, -1\}$ is the corresponding bag label, and L is the total number of training bags. Each training bag $\mathcal{B}_l$ consists of a number of training instances, *i.e.*, $\mathcal{B}_l = \{(\mathbf{x}_i, \tilde{\mathbf{x}}_i, y_i)|_{i \in \mathcal{I}_l}\}$, where $\mathcal{I}_l$ is the set of indices for the instances inside $\mathcal{B}_l$, $\mathbf{x}_i$ is the visual feature of the i-th sample, $\tilde{\mathbf{x}}_i$ is the corresponding textual feature (*i.e.*, privileged information), and $y_i \in \{+1, -1\}$ is the ground truth label of the instance which is unknown. Without loss of generality, we assume the positive bags are the first L^+ training bags.

In our method, we use the generalized constraints for the MIL problem [33]. As shown in [33], the relevant images usually contain a portion of positive images, while it is more likely that the irrelevant images are all negative images. Namely, we have

$$
\begin{cases}
\sum_{i \in \mathcal{I}_l} \frac{y_i+1}{2} \geq \sigma |\mathcal{B}_l|, & \forall Y_l = 1, \\
y_i = -1, & \forall i \in \mathcal{I}_l \text{ and } Y_l = -1,
\end{cases}
\tag{1}
$$

where $|\mathcal{B}_l|$ is the cardinality of the bag $\mathcal{B}_l$, and $\sigma > 0$ is a predefined ratio based on prior information. In other words, each positive bag is assumed to contain at least a portion of true positive instances, and all instances in a negative bag are assumed to be negative samples.

Recall the textual descriptions associated with the training images are also noisy, so privileged information may not be always reliable as in [42,38]. Considering the labels of instances in the negative bags are known to be negative [43,33], and the results after employing noisy privileged information for the instances in the negative bags are generally worse (see our experiments in Section 4.3), we only utilize privileged information for positive bags in our method. However, it is worth mentioning that our method can be readily used to employ privileged information for the instances in all training bags.

3.2 MIL Using Privileged Information

MIL methods can be generally classified into bag-level methods [7,5] and instance-level methods [1,33]. Since bag-level methods are generally fast and effective, we focus on bag-level methods in this paper. Specifically, we take the bag-level MIL method sMIL [5] as a showcase to explain how to exploit privileged information from loosely labeled training data. We refer to our new method as *sMIL-PI*. By transforming each training bag to one training sample, the MIL problem becomes a supervised learning problem [5], because the labels of training bags are known. Such a strategy can also be applied in our sMIL-PI method.

SVM+: Before describing our sMIL-PI method, we briefly introduce the existing work SVM+. Let us denote the training data as $\{(\mathbf{x}_i, \tilde{\mathbf{x}}_i, y_i)|_{i=1}^n\}$, where $\mathbf{x}_i$ is main feature for the i-th training sample, $\tilde{\mathbf{x}}_i$ is the corresponding feature representation of privileged information which is not available for testing data, $y_i \in \{+1, -1\}$ is the class label, and n is the total number of training samples. The goal of SVM+ [42] is to learn the classifier $f(\mathbf{x}) = \mathbf{w}'\phi(\mathbf{x}) + b$, where $\phi(\cdot)$ is a nonlinear feature mapping function. Let us define another nonlinear feature mapping function $\tilde{\phi}(\cdot)$ for privileged information, and the objective of SVM+ is as follows,

$$
\min_{\tilde{\mathbf{w}}, \tilde{b}, \mathbf{w}, b} \frac{1}{2} \left(\|\mathbf{w}\|^2 + \gamma \|\tilde{\mathbf{w}}\|^2 \right) + C \sum_{i=1}^n \xi(\tilde{\mathbf{x}}_i),
\tag{2}
$$
$$
\text{s.t. } y_i(\mathbf{w}'\phi(\mathbf{x}_i) + b) \geq 1 - \xi(\tilde{\mathbf{x}}_i), \quad \xi(\tilde{\mathbf{x}}_i) \geq 0, \quad \forall i,
$$

where γ and C are the tradeoff parameters, $\xi(\tilde{\mathbf{x}}_i) = \tilde{\mathbf{w}}'\tilde{\phi}(\tilde{\mathbf{x}}_i) + \tilde{b}$ is the *slack function*, which replaces the slack variable $\xi_i \geq 0$ in the hinge loss in SVM. Such a slack function plays a role of the teacher in the training process [42]. Recall the slack variable ξ_i in SVM tells about how difficult to classify the training sample $\mathbf{x}_i$. The slack function $\xi(\mathbf{x}_i)$ is expected to model the optimal slack variable ξ_i by using privileged information analogous to the comments and explanations from the teacher in human learning [42]. Similar to SVM, SVM+ can be solved in the dual form by optimizing a quadratic programming problem.

sMIL-PI: Let us denote $\psi(\mathcal{B}_l)$ as the feature mapping function which converts a training bag into a single feature vector. The feature mapping function in sMIL is defined as the mean of instances inside the bag, *i.e.*, $\psi(\mathcal{B}_l) = \frac{1}{|\mathcal{B}_l|} \sum_{i \in \mathcal{I}_l} \phi(\mathbf{x}_i)$, where $|\mathcal{B}_l|$ is the cardinality of the bag $\mathcal{B}_l$. Recall the labels for negative instances are assumed to be negative, so we only apply the feature mapping function on the positive training bags. For ease of presentation, we denote a set of virtual training samples $\{\mathbf{z}_j|_{j=1}^m\}$, in which $\mathbf{z}_1, \ldots, \mathbf{z}_{L^+}$ are the samples mapped from the positive bags $\{\psi(\mathcal{B}_j)|_{j=1}^{L^+}\}$, the remaining samples $\mathbf{z}_{L^++1}, \ldots, \mathbf{z}_m$ are the instances $\{\phi(\mathbf{x}_i)|i \in \mathcal{I}_l, Y_l = -1\}$ in the negative bags.

When there are additional privileged information for training data, we additionally define a feature mapping function $\tilde{\psi}(\mathcal{B}_l)$ on each training bag as the mean of the instances inside the bag by using privileged information, *i.e.*, $\tilde{\mathbf{z}}_j = \tilde{\psi}(\mathcal{B}_j) = \frac{1}{|\mathcal{B}_j|} \sum_{i \in \mathcal{I}_j} \tilde{\phi}(\tilde{\mathbf{x}}_i)$ for $j = 1, \ldots, L^+$. Based on the SVM+ formulation, the objective of our sMIL-PI can be formulated as,

$$\min_{\mathbf{w},b,\tilde{\mathbf{w}},\tilde{b},\eta} \frac{1}{2} \left(\|\mathbf{w}\|^2 + \gamma \|\tilde{\mathbf{w}}\|^2 \right) + C_1 \sum_{j=1}^{L^+} \xi(\tilde{\mathbf{z}}_j) + C_2 \sum_{j=L^++1}^{m} \eta_j, \tag{3}$$

$$\text{s.t.} \quad \mathbf{w}'\mathbf{z}_j + b \geq p_j - \xi(\tilde{\mathbf{z}}_j), \quad \forall j = 1, \ldots, L^+, \tag{4}$$

$$\mathbf{w}'\mathbf{z}_j + b \leq -1 + \eta_j, \qquad \forall j = L^+ + 1, \ldots, m, \tag{5}$$

$$\xi(\tilde{\mathbf{z}}_j) \geq 0, \quad \forall j = 1, \ldots, L^+, \tag{6}$$

$$\eta_j \geq 0, \qquad \forall j = L^+ + 1, \ldots, m \tag{7}$$

where $\mathbf{w}$ and b are the variables of the classifier $f(\mathbf{z}) = \mathbf{w}'\mathbf{z} + b$, γ, C_1 and C_2 are the tradeoff parameters, $\boldsymbol{\eta} = [\eta_{L^++1}, \ldots, \eta_m]'$, the slack function is defined as $\xi(\tilde{\mathbf{z}}_j) = \tilde{\mathbf{w}}'\tilde{\mathbf{z}}_j + \tilde{b}$, and p_j is the virtual label for the virtual sample $\mathbf{z}_j$. In sMIL [5], the virtual label is calculated by leveraging the instance labels of each positive bag. As sMIL assumes that there is at least one true positive sample in each positive bag, the virtual label of positive virtual sample $\mathbf{z}_j$ is $p_j = \frac{1-(|\mathcal{B}_j|-1)}{|\mathcal{B}_j|} = \frac{2-|\mathcal{B}_j|}{|\mathcal{B}_j|}$. Similarly, for our sMIL-PI using the generalized MIL constraints in (1), we can derive it as $p_j = \frac{\sigma|\mathcal{B}_j|-(1-\sigma)|\mathcal{B}_j|}{|\mathcal{B}_j|} = 2\sigma - 1$.

By introducing dual variable $\boldsymbol{\alpha} = [\alpha_1, \ldots, \alpha_m]'$ for the constraints in (4) and (5), and also introducing dual variable $\boldsymbol{\beta} = [\beta_1, \ldots, \beta_{L^+}]'$ for the constraints in (6), respectively, we arrive at the dual from of (3) as follows,

$$\min_{\boldsymbol{\alpha},\boldsymbol{\beta}} -\mathbf{p}'\boldsymbol{\alpha} + \frac{1}{2}\boldsymbol{\alpha}'(\mathbf{K} \circ \mathbf{yy}')\boldsymbol{\alpha} + \frac{1}{2\gamma}(\hat{\boldsymbol{\alpha}} + \boldsymbol{\beta} - C_1\mathbf{1})'\tilde{\mathbf{K}}(\hat{\boldsymbol{\alpha}} + \boldsymbol{\beta} - C_1\mathbf{1}), \tag{8}$$

$$\text{s.t.} \quad \boldsymbol{\alpha}'\mathbf{y} = 0, \quad \mathbf{1}'(\hat{\boldsymbol{\alpha}} + \boldsymbol{\beta} - C_1\mathbf{1}) = 0, \quad \bar{\boldsymbol{\alpha}} \leq C_2\mathbf{1}, \quad \boldsymbol{\alpha} \geq \mathbf{0}, \quad \boldsymbol{\beta} \geq \mathbf{0},$$

where $\hat{\alpha} \in \mathbb{R}^{L^+}$ and $\bar{\alpha} \in \mathbb{R}^{m-L^+}$ are from $\alpha = [\hat{\alpha}', \bar{\alpha}']'$, $\mathbf{y} = [\mathbf{1}'_{L^+}, -\mathbf{1}'_{m-L^+}]'$ is the label vector, $\mathbf{p} = [p_1, \ldots, p_{L^+}, \mathbf{1}'_{m-L^+}]' \in \mathbb{R}^m$, $\mathbf{K} \in \mathbb{R}^{m \times m}$ is the kernel matrix constructed by using the visual features, $\tilde{\mathbf{K}} \in \mathbb{R}^{L^+ \times L^+}$ is the kernel matrix constructed by using privileged information (*i.e.*, the textual features). The above problem is jointly convex in α and β, which can be efficiently solved by optimizing a quadratic programming problem.

3.3 Domain Adaptive MIL-PI

The collected web images may have very different statistical properties with the test images (*e.g.*, the images in the Caltech-256 dataset), which is also known as the dataset bias problem [39]. To reduce domain distribution mismatch, we proposed an effective method by re-weighting the source domain samples when learning the sMIL-PI classifier. In the following, we develop our domain adaptation method, which is referred as sMIL-PI-DA.

Inspired by Kernel Mean Matching (KMM) [26], we also propose to learn the weights for the source domain samples by minimizing Maximum Mean Discrepancy (MMD) between two domains. However, KMM is a two-stage method, in which they first learn the weights for the source domain samples and then utilize the weights to train a weighted SVM. Though the recent work [8] proposed to combine the primal formulation of weighted-SVM and a regularizer based on the MMD criterion, their objective function is non-convex. Thus the global optimal solution cannot be guaranteed. To this end, we propose a convex formulation by adding the regularizer based on the MMD criterion to the dual formulation of our sMIL-PI in (8). Formally, let us denote the target domain samples as $\{\mathbf{x}_i^t|_{i=1}^{n_t}\}$, and also denote $\mathbf{z}_i^t = \phi(\mathbf{x}_i^t)$ as the corresponding nonlinear feature. To distinguish the two domains, we append a superscript s to the source domain samples, *i.e.*, $\{\mathbf{z}_i^s|_{i=1}^m\}$ is the set of source domain virtual samples used in our sMIL-PI-DA. We denote the objective in (8) as $H(\alpha, \beta) = -\mathbf{p}'\alpha + \frac{1}{2}\alpha'(\mathbf{K} \circ \mathbf{yy}')\alpha + \frac{1}{2\gamma}(\hat{\alpha} + \beta - C_1\mathbf{1})'\tilde{\mathbf{K}}(\hat{\alpha} + \beta - C_1\mathbf{1})$ and also denote the weights for source domain samples as $\theta = [\theta_1, \ldots, \theta_m]'$. Then, we formulate our sMIL-PI-DA as follows,

$$\min_{\alpha, \beta, \theta} \quad H(\alpha, \beta) + \frac{\mu}{2}\|\frac{1}{m}\sum_{i=1}^m \theta_i \mathbf{z}_i^s - \frac{1}{n_t}\sum_{i=1}^{n_t} \mathbf{z}_i^t\|^2 \tag{9}$$

$$\text{s.t.} \quad \alpha'\mathbf{y} = 0, \quad \mathbf{1}'(\hat{\alpha} + \beta - C_1\mathbf{1}) = 0, \quad \bar{\alpha} \le C_2\mathbf{1}, \quad \beta \ge \mathbf{0} \tag{10}$$

$$0 \le \alpha \le C_3\theta, \quad \mathbf{1}'\theta = m, \tag{11}$$

where C_3 is a parameter and θ_i is the weight for $\mathbf{z}_i^s$. The last term in (9) is a regularizer based on the MMD criterion which aims to reduce the domain distribution mismatch between two domains by reweighting the source domain samples as in KMM, and the constraints in (10) are from sMIL-PI. Note in (11), we use the box constraint $0 \le \alpha \le C_3\theta$ to regularize the dual variable α, which is similarly used in weighted SVM [26]. The second constraint $\mathbf{1}'\theta = m$ is used to enforce the expectation of sample weights to be 1. The problem in (9) is jointly convex with respect to $\boldsymbol{\alpha}$, $\boldsymbol{\beta}$ and $\boldsymbol{\theta}$, and thus we can obtain the global optimum by optimizing a quadratic programming problem.

Interestingly, the primal form of (9) is closely related to the formulation of SVM+, as described below,

Proposition 1. *The primal form of (9) is equivalent to the following problem,*

$$\min_{\mathbf{w},b,\tilde{\mathbf{w}},\tilde{b},\hat{\mathbf{w}},\hat{b},\boldsymbol{\eta}} \quad J(\mathbf{w},b,\tilde{\mathbf{w}},\tilde{b},\boldsymbol{\eta}) + \frac{\lambda}{2}\|\hat{\mathbf{w}} - \rho\mathbf{v}\|^2 + C_3 \sum_{i=1}^{m} \zeta(\mathbf{z}_i^s), \tag{12}$$

$$s.t. \quad \mathbf{w}'\mathbf{z}_i^s + b \geq p_i - \xi(\tilde{\mathbf{z}}_i^s) - \zeta(\mathbf{z}_i^s), \quad \forall i = 1,\ldots,L^+, \tag{13}$$

$$\mathbf{w}'\mathbf{z}_i^s + b \leq -1 + \eta_i + \zeta(\mathbf{z}_i^s), \quad \forall i = L^+ + 1,\ldots,m, \tag{14}$$

$$\xi(\tilde{\mathbf{z}}_i^s) \geq 0, \quad \forall i = 1,\ldots,L^+, \tag{15}$$

$$\eta_i \geq 0, \quad \forall i = L^+ + 1,\ldots,m, \tag{16}$$

$$\zeta(\mathbf{z}_i^s) \geq 0, \quad \forall i = 1,\ldots,m, \tag{17}$$

where $J(\mathbf{w},b,\tilde{\mathbf{w}},\tilde{b},\boldsymbol{\eta}) = \frac{1}{2}\left(\|\mathbf{w}\|^2 + \gamma\|\tilde{\mathbf{w}}\|^2\right) + C_1 \sum_{j=1}^{L^+} \xi(\tilde{\mathbf{z}}_j^s) + C_2 \sum_{j=L^++1}^{m} \eta_j$ *is the objective function in (3),* $\zeta(\mathbf{z}_i^s) = \hat{\mathbf{w}}'\mathbf{z}_i^s + \hat{b}$, $\mathbf{v} = \frac{1}{m}\sum_{i=1}^{m}\mathbf{z}_i^s - \frac{1}{n_t}\sum_{i=1}^{n_t}\mathbf{z}_i^t$, $\lambda = \frac{(mC_3)^2}{\mu}$ *and* $\rho = \frac{mC_3}{\lambda}$.

Proof. We prove the dual form of (12) can be equivalently rewritten as (9). Let us introduce the dual variables $\hat{\boldsymbol{\alpha}} = [\alpha_1,\ldots,\alpha_{L^+}]' \in \mathbb{R}^{L^+}$ for the constraints in (13), $\bar{\boldsymbol{\alpha}} = [\alpha_{L^++1},\ldots,\alpha_m]' \in \mathbb{R}^{m-L^+}$ for the constraints (14), $\boldsymbol{\beta} = [\beta_1,\ldots,\beta_{L^+}]' \in \mathbb{R}^{L^+}$ for the constraints in (15), $\boldsymbol{\tau} = [\tau_1,\ldots,\tau_{m-L^+}]' \in \mathbb{R}^{m-L^+}$ for the constraints in (16), and $\boldsymbol{\nu} = [\nu_1,\ldots,\nu_m]'$ for the constraints in (17). We also define $\boldsymbol{\alpha} = [\hat{\boldsymbol{\alpha}}',\bar{\boldsymbol{\alpha}}']'$, $\mathbf{Z} = [\mathbf{z}_1^s,\ldots,\mathbf{z}_m^s]$, $\tilde{\mathbf{Z}} = [\tilde{\mathbf{z}}_1^s,\ldots,\tilde{\mathbf{z}}_{L^+}^s]$, and $\mathbf{y} = [\mathbf{1}_{L^+}', -\mathbf{1}_{m-L^+}']'$. By setting the derivatives of the Lagrangian of (12) w.r.t. $\mathbf{w},b,\tilde{\mathbf{w}},\tilde{b},\hat{\mathbf{w}},\hat{b},\boldsymbol{\eta}$ to zeros and substituting the derived equations back into the Lagrangian of (12), we obtain the following dual form,

$$\min_{\boldsymbol{\alpha},\boldsymbol{\beta},\boldsymbol{\nu}} \quad -\mathbf{p}'\boldsymbol{\alpha} + \frac{1}{2}\boldsymbol{\alpha}'(\mathbf{K} \circ \mathbf{y}\mathbf{y}')\boldsymbol{\alpha} + \frac{1}{2\gamma}(\hat{\boldsymbol{\alpha}} + \boldsymbol{\beta} - C_1\mathbf{1})'\tilde{\mathbf{K}}(\hat{\boldsymbol{\alpha}} + \boldsymbol{\beta} - C_1\mathbf{1}) \tag{18}$$

$$+ \frac{1}{2\lambda}(\boldsymbol{\alpha} + \boldsymbol{\nu} - C_3\mathbf{1}_m)'\mathbf{K}(\boldsymbol{\alpha} + \boldsymbol{\nu} - C_3\mathbf{1}_m) + \rho\mathbf{v}'\mathbf{Z}(\boldsymbol{\alpha} + \boldsymbol{\nu} - C_3\mathbf{1}_m)$$

$$s.t. \quad \boldsymbol{\alpha}'\mathbf{y} = 0, \quad \mathbf{1}_{L^+}'(\hat{\boldsymbol{\alpha}} + \boldsymbol{\beta} - C_1\mathbf{1}_{L^+}) = 0, \quad \bar{\boldsymbol{\alpha}} \leq C_2\mathbf{1}_{m-L^+},$$

$$\mathbf{1}_m'(\boldsymbol{\alpha} + \boldsymbol{\nu} - C_3\mathbf{1}_m) = 0, \quad \boldsymbol{\alpha},\boldsymbol{\beta},\boldsymbol{\nu} \geq \mathbf{0}.$$

Let us define $\boldsymbol{\theta} = \frac{1}{C_3}(\boldsymbol{\alpha} + \boldsymbol{\nu})$, and the feasible set for $(\boldsymbol{\alpha},\boldsymbol{\beta},\boldsymbol{\nu})$ becomes $\mathcal{A} = \{\boldsymbol{\alpha}'\mathbf{y} = 0, \mathbf{1}_{L^+}'(\hat{\boldsymbol{\alpha}} + \boldsymbol{\beta} - C_1\mathbf{1}_{L^+}) = 0, \bar{\boldsymbol{\alpha}} \leq C_2\mathbf{1}_{m-L^+}, \mathbf{1}_m'\boldsymbol{\theta} = m, \boldsymbol{\alpha} \leq C_3\boldsymbol{\theta}, \boldsymbol{\alpha},\boldsymbol{\beta} \geq \mathbf{0}\}$, then we arrive at,

$$\min_{(\boldsymbol{\alpha},\boldsymbol{\beta},\boldsymbol{\theta})\in\mathcal{A}} \quad -\mathbf{p}'\boldsymbol{\alpha} + \frac{1}{2}\boldsymbol{\alpha}'(\mathbf{K} \circ \mathbf{y}\mathbf{y}')\boldsymbol{\alpha} + \frac{1}{2\gamma}(\hat{\boldsymbol{\alpha}} + \boldsymbol{\beta} - C_1\mathbf{1})'\tilde{\mathbf{K}}(\hat{\boldsymbol{\alpha}} + \boldsymbol{\beta} - C_1\mathbf{1}) \tag{19}$$

$$+ \frac{(C_3)^2}{2\lambda}(\boldsymbol{\theta} - \mathbf{1}_m)'\mathbf{K}(\boldsymbol{\theta} - \mathbf{1}_m) + \rho C_3\mathbf{v}'\mathbf{Z}(\boldsymbol{\theta} - \mathbf{1}_m).$$

Recall that we have defined $\lambda = \frac{(C_3 m)^2}{\mu}$ and $\rho = \frac{C_3 m}{\lambda} = \frac{\mu}{C_3 m}$. By substituting the equation $\mathbf{v}'\mathbf{Z} = \frac{1}{m}\mathbf{1}'_m\mathbf{K} - \frac{1}{n_t}\mathbf{1}'_{n_t}\mathbf{K}_{ts}$ into the objective and replacing the constant terms with $\frac{\mu}{2n_t^2}\mathbf{1}'_{n_t}\mathbf{K}_t\mathbf{1}_{n_t}$, where $\mathbf{K}_{ts} \in \mathbb{R}^{n_t \times m}$ is the kernel matrix between the target domain samples and the source domain samples, and $\mathbf{K}_t \in \mathbb{R}^{n_t \times n_t}$ is the kernel matrix on the target domain samples, then the optimization problem in (19) finally becomes,

$$\min_{(\boldsymbol{\alpha},\boldsymbol{\beta},\boldsymbol{\theta})\in\mathcal{A}} H(\boldsymbol{\alpha},\boldsymbol{\beta}) + \frac{\mu}{2}\|\frac{1}{m}\sum_{i=1}^{m}\theta_i\mathbf{z}_i^s - \frac{1}{n_t}\sum_{i=1}^{n_t}\mathbf{z}_i^t\|^2, \tag{20}$$

where $H(\boldsymbol{\alpha},\boldsymbol{\beta})$ is defined as in (9). We complete the proof here. $\square$

Compared with the objective function in (3), we introduce one more slack function $\zeta(\mathbf{z}_i^s) = \hat{\mathbf{w}}'\mathbf{z}_i^s + \hat{b}$, and also regularize the weight vector of this slack function by using the regularizer $\|\hat{\mathbf{w}} - \rho\mathbf{v}\|^2$. Recall that the witness function in MMD is defined as $g(\mathbf{z}) = \frac{1}{\|\mathbf{v}\|}\mathbf{v}'\mathbf{z}$ [23], which can be deemed as the mean similarity between $\mathbf{z}$ and the source domain samples (*i.e.*, $\frac{1}{m}\sum_{i=1}^{m}\mathbf{z}_i^{s'}\mathbf{z}$) minus the mean similarity between $\mathbf{z}$ and the target domain samples (*i.e.*, $\frac{1}{n_t}\sum_{i=1}^{n_t}\mathbf{z}_i^{t'}\mathbf{z}$). In other words, we conjecture that the witness function outputs a lower value when the sample $\mathbf{z}$ is closer to the target domain samples and vice versa. By using the regularizer $\|\hat{\mathbf{w}} - \rho\mathbf{v}\|^2$, we expect the new slack function $\zeta(\mathbf{z}_i^s) = \hat{\mathbf{w}}'\mathbf{z}_i^s + \hat{b}$ shares the similar trend[2] with the witness function $g(\mathbf{z}_i^s) = \frac{1}{\|\mathbf{v}\|}\mathbf{v}'\mathbf{z}_i^s$. As a result, the training error of the training sample $\mathbf{z}_i^s$ (*i.e.*, $\xi(\tilde{\mathbf{z}}_i^s) + \zeta(\mathbf{z}_i^s)$ for the samples in positive bags or $\eta_i + \zeta(\mathbf{z}_i^s)$ for negative samples) will tend to be lower if it is closer to the target domain, which is helpful for learning a more robust classifier to better predict the target domain samples.

4 Experiments

In this section, we evaluate our method sMIL-PI for image retrieval and image categorization, respectively. Then we demonstrate the effectiveness of our domain adaptation method sMIL-PI-DA for image categorization.

We extract both textual features and visual features from the training web images. The textual features are used as privileged information.

- **Textual feature:** A 200-dim term-frequency (TF) feature is extracted for each image by using the top-200 words with the highest frequency as the vocabulary. Stop-word removal is performed to remove the meaningless words.
- **Visual feature:** We extract DeCAF features [10], which has shown promising performance in various tasks. Following [10], we use the outputs from the 6th layer as visual features, which leads to 4,096-dim DeCAF_6 features.

In all our experiments for image retrieval and image categorization, the test data does not contain textual information. So we can only extract the same type of visual features (*i.e.*, DeCAF_6 features) for the images in the test set.

---

[2] The bias term $\hat{b}$ and the scalar terms ρ and $\frac{1}{\|\mathbf{v}\|}$ will not change the trend of functions.

4.1   Image Retrieval

Baselines: For image retrieval, we firstly compare our proposed method with two sets of baselines: the recent LUPI methods including pSVM+ [42] and Rank Transfer (RT) [38], as well as the conventional MIL method sMIL [5]. We also include SVM as a baseline, which is trained by only using the visual features. Moreover, we also compare our method with Classeme [41] and multi-view learning methods KCCA and SVM-2K, because they can also be used for our application.

- *Kernel Canonical Correlation Analysis (KCCA)* [25]: We apply KCCA on the training set by using the textual features and visual features, and then train the SVM classifier by using the common representations of visual features. In the testing process, the visual features of test samples are transformed into their common representations for the prediction.
- *SVM-2K* [16]: We train the SVM-2K classifiers by using the visual features and text features from the training samples, and apply the visual feature based classifier on the test samples for the prediction.
- *Classeme* [41]: For each word in the 200-dim textual features, we retrieve relevant and irrelevant images to construct positive bags and negative bags, respectively. Then we follow [30] to use mi-SVM to train the classeme classifier for each word. For each training image and test image, 200 decision values are obtained by using 200 learnt classeme classifiers and the decision values are augmented with the visual features. Finally, we train the SVM classifiers for classifying the test images based on the augmented features.

We also compare our method with MIML [44]. While we treat the top 200 words in the textual descriptions as noisy class labels, MIML cannot be directly applied to our task because the 200 words are not as the same as the concepts names. Thus, we use the decision values from the MIML classifiers as the features, similarly as in Classeme.

Experimental Settings. We use two web image datasets NUS-WIDE [9] and WebQuery [28] to evaluate our sMIL-PI method for image retrieval [43,33].

The NUS-WIDE dataset contains $269,648$ images, which is officially split into a training set (60%) and a test set (40%). All images in NUS-WIDE are associated with noisy tags, which are also manually annotated as 81 concepts. The WebQuery dataset contains $71,478$ web images retrieved from 353 textual queries. Each image in WebQuery is associated with textual descriptions in English or other languages (*e.g.*, French). In this work, we only use the images associated with English descriptions, and divide those images into a training set (60%) and a test set (40%). The textual queries with less than 100 training images are discarded. Finally, we obtain $19,665$ training images and $13,114$ test images from 163 remaining textual queries on the WebQuery dataset.

For both datasets, we train the classifiers using the training set and evaluate the performances of different methods on the test set. For the NUS-WIDE dataset, we follow [33] to construct 25 positive bags and 25 negative bags by respectively using relevant and irrelevant images, in which each training bag

Table 1. MAPs (%) of different methods for image retrieval. The results in boldface are from our method.

Method	Dataset	
	NUS-WIDE	WebQuery
SVM	54.41	48.51
pSVM+	57.92	50.35
RT	42.63	31.92
Classeme	54.14	48.48
MIML	54.23	48.56
KCCA	54.62	47.86
SVM-2K	54.43	49.04
sMIL	56.72	51.42
sMIL-PI	**60.88**	**52.63**

contains 15 instances. We strictly follow [33] to uniformly partition the ranked relevant images into bags. For the WebQuery dataset, we use the retrieved images from each textual query to construct the positive bags, and randomly sample the same number of images from other queries to construct the negative bags. Considering only about $100 \sim 150$ training images are retrieved from each textual query, we set the bag size as 5 to construct more training bags. Note the ground truth labels of training images are not used in the training process for both datasets. The positive ratio is set as $\sigma = 0.6$, as suggested in [33]. In our experiments, we use Gaussian kernel for visual features and linear kernel for textual features for our method and the baseline methods except RankTransfer (RT). The objective function of RT is solved in the primal form, so we can only use linear kernel instead of Gaussian kernel for visual features.

Considering the users are generally more interested in the top-ranked images, we use Average Precision (AP) based on the 100 top-ranked images for performance evaluation as suggested in [33]. The mean of APs (MAP) over all classes is used to compare different methods. We empirically fix $C_1 = C_2 = 1$ and $\gamma = 10$ for our method. For baseline methods, we choose the optimal parameters according to their MAPs on the test dataset.

Experimental Results. The MAPs of all methods are shown in Table 1. By exploiting the additional textual features, pSVM+ outperforms SVM. The multi-view learning methods KCCA and SVM-2K are also comparable or better than SVM. RankTransfer (RT) is much worse than SVM, possibly because it can only use the linear kernel. We also observe that Classeme and MIML only achieve comparable results with SVM. The sMIL method outperforms SVM, which demonstrates it is beneficial to cope with label noise by using sMIL.

Our method is better than SVM, the existing LUPI methods pSVM+ and RT, Classeme, MIML, and multi-view learning methods KCCA and SVM2K, which demonstrates the effectiveness of our sMIL-PI method for image retrieval by coping with loosely labeled web data and simultaneously taking advantage of the additional textual features as privileged information. Our sMIL-PI method also

Table 2. The left subtable lists the MAPs (%) of different methods without using domain adaptation. The right subtable reports the MAPs (%) of SVM, sMIL-PI and different domain adaptation methods. For SA, TCA, DIP, KMM, GFK and SGF, the first number is obtained by using the SVM classifiers and the second number in the parenthesis is obtained by using our sMIL-PI. The results in boldface are from our methods.

Method	Training Set	
	NUS-WIDE	Flickr
SVM	65.33	31.41
pSVM+	66.61	35.84
RT	55.53	19.09
Classeme	66.58	34.57
MIML	66.66	34.60
KCCA	65.94	35.69
SVM-2K	66.61	35.09
sMIL	67.73	35.26
sMIL-PI	**68.55**	**39.49**

Method	Training Set	
	NUS-WIDE	Flickr
SVM	65.33	31.41
sMIL-PI	68.55	39.49
sMIL-PI-DA	**70.56**	**41.35**
DASVM	67.96	33.52
STM	65.73	28.52
SA	56.13(68.73)	30.15(39.61)
TCA	61.28(66.64)	27.91(37.57)
DIP	61.08(65.32)	26.49(35.16)
KMM	60.32(68.78)	32.08(37.85)
GFK	62.98(64.60)	23.90(29.24)
SGF	66.29(68.57)	30.08(37.46)

outperforms its corresponding conventional MIL method sMIL. It again demonstrates it is beneficial to exploit the textual features as privileged information for training a more robust visual feature based classifier.

4.2 Image Categorization without Domain Adaptation

For image categorization without considering domain distribution mismatch, we use the same baselines as in image retrieval.

Experimental Settings. We evaluate our sMIL-PI method for image categorization on the benchmark dataset Caltech-256 [24]. We use the training set of NUS-WIDE as the training data. Considering different datasets contain different class names, we use their common class names for performance evaluation. Specifically, there are 17 common class names between NUS-WIDE and Caltech-256. We use the images from these 17 common classes as the test images. In total, we have 2,620 test images for performance evaluation.

Since most of the class names in the WebQuery dataset consist of multiple words, it is ambiguous to define common classes between WebQuery and Caltech-256. So we do not use WebQuery as the training set here. Instead, we construct a new training dataset called "Flickr", in which we crawl 142,081 Flickr images using the class names in Caltech-256 as the queries. The whole Caltech-256 dataset which contains 29,780 images is used as the test set for performance evaluation. This setting is more challenging because we have a large number of classes and test images.

We use Average Precision (AP) based on all test images for performance evaluation. The mean of APs (MAP) over all classes is used to compare different methods. For our method, we use the same parameters as in image retrieval. For the baseline methods, we choose the optimal parameters based on their MAPs on the test dataset.

Experimental Results. The MAPs of all methods are reported in the left subtable of Table 2. As in the image retrieval application, pSVM+ is better than SVM and RT is worse than SVM. Moreover, sMIL outperforms SVM. Classeme, MIML, and Multi-view learning methods KCCA and SVM-2K are also better than SVM.

We observe that our method sMIL-PI is better than SVM, pSVM+, RT, Classeme, MIML and multi-view learning methods, which clearly demonstrates the effectiveness of our method sMIL-PI for image categorization. Moreover, our method sMIL-PI is better than its corresponding conventional MIL method sMIL, which again demonstrates it is beneficial to exploit the additional textual features as privileged information.

4.3   How to Utilize Privileged Information

As discussed in Section 3, in our sMIL-PI method, we use privileged information for relevant images (*i.e.*, positive bags) only, because privileged information (*i.e.*, textual features) may not be always reliable. To verify it, we evaluate SVM+ by utilizing privileged information for all training samples.

We report the results for image retrieval and image categorization by using NUS-WIDE as the training set. The MAPs of SVM+ and pSVM+ are 54.95% and 57.92% (*resp.*, 64.29% and 66.61%) for image retrieval (*resp.*, image categorization), which demonstrates the advantage of only utilizing privileged information for positive training bags.

4.4   Image Categorization with Domain Adaptation

Baselines. We compare our domain adaptation method sMIL-PI-DA with the existing domain adaptation methods GFK [21], SGF [22], SA [18], TCA [36], KMM [26], DIP [2], DASVM [4] and STM [8]. We notice that the feature-based domain adaptation methods such as GFK, SGF, SA, TCA, DIP can be combined with the SVM classifier or our sMIL-PI method, so we report two results by using the SVM classifier and our sMIL-PI classifier for these methods.

Experiment Settings. We use the same setting as in Section 4.2. sMIL-PI-DA has two more parameters (i.e., C_3 and λ) when compared with sMIL-PI. We empirically fix C_3 as 10 and λ as 10^4. For the baseline methods, we choose the optimal parameters based on their MAPs on the test dataset.

Experimental Results. The MAPs of all methods by using NUS-WIDE and Flickr as the training datasets are reported in the right subtable of Table 2.

The existing feature-based domain adaptation methods GFK, SGF, SA, TCA, DIP by using the SVM (*resp.*, sMIL-PI) classifier are generally comparable or even worse when compared with SVM (*resp.*, sMIL-PI). One possible explanation is the feature distributions of web images and the images from Caltech-256 are quite different. For these feature-based baselines, their results after using sMIL-PI classifier are better when compared with those using SVM classifier, which again shows the effectiveness of our sMIL-PI for image categorization by coping with label noise and simultaneously taking advantage of the additional textual features as privileged information. Moreover, DASVM is better than SVM, possibly because it can better utilize noisy training samples by progressively removing some source domain samples during the training process.

Our method is more related to KMM and STM. We also report two results for KMM because KMM can be combined with SVM or our sMIL-PI, in which the instance weights are learnt in the first step and we use the learnt instance weights to reweight the loss function of SVM or sMIL-PI in the second step. We observe that our method is better than STM and KMM with SVM or sMIL-PI, because our method can solve for the global solution while KMM is a two-step approach and STM can only achieve a local optimum.

We also observe that our method sMIL-PI-DA outperforms sMIL-PI and all the existing domain adaptation baselines, which demonstrates the advantage of our domain adaptation method sMIL-PI-DA.

5   Conclusion

In this paper, we have proposed a new method sMIL-PI for image categorization by learning from web data. Our method not only takes advantage of the additional textual features in training web data but also effectively copes with noise in the loose labels of relevant training images. We also extend sMIL-PI to handle the distribution mismatch between the training and test data, which leads to our new domain adaptation method sMIL-PI-DA. Extensive experiments for image retrieval and image categorization clearly demonstrate the effectiveness of our newly proposed methods by exploiting privileged information from web data.

Acknowledgement. This work was carried out at the Rapid-Rich Object Search (ROSE) Lab at the Nanyang Technological University, Singapore. The ROSE Lab is supported by a grant from the Singapore National Research Foundation and administered by the Interactive & Digital Media Programme Office at the Media Development Authority. This work is also supported by the Singapore MoE Tier 2 Grant (ARC42/13).

References

1. Andrews, S., Tsochantaridis, I., Hofmann, T.: Support vector machines for multiple-instance learning. In: NIPS (2003)
2. Baktashmotlagh, M., Harandi, M., Brian Lovell, M.S.: Unsupervised domain adaptation by domain invariant projection. In: ICCV (2013)
3. Bergamo, A., Torresani, L.: Exploiting weakly-labeled web images to improve object classification: a domain adaptation approach. In: NIPS (2010)

4. Bruzzone, L., Marconcini, M.: Domain adaptation problems: A DASVM classification technique and a circular validation strategy. T-PAMI 32(5), 770–787 (2010)
5. Bunescu, R.C., Mooney, R.J.: Multiple instance learning for sparse positive bags. In: ICML (2007)
6. Chen, X., Shrivastava, A., Gupta, A.: NEIL: Extracting visual knowledge from web data. In: ICCV (2013)
7. Chen, Y., Bi, J., Wang, J.Z.: MILES: Multiple-instance learning via embedded instance selection. T-PAMI 28(12), 1931–1947 (2006)
8. Chu, W.S., DelaTorre, F., Cohn, J.: Selective transfer machine for personalized facial action unit detection. In: CVPR (2013)
9. Chua, T.S., Tang, J., Hong, R., Li, H., Luo, Z., Zheng, Y.: NUS-WIDE: a real-world web image database from National University of Singapore. In: CIVR (2009)
10. Donahue, J., Jia, Y., Vinyals, O., Hoffman, J., Zhang, N., Tzeng, E., Darrell, T.: DeCAF: A deep convolutional activation feature for generic visual recognition. In: ICML (2014)
11. Duan, L., Li, W., Tsang, I.W., Xu, D.: Improving web image search by bag-based re-ranking. T-IP 20(11), 3280–3290 (2011)
12. Duan, L., Xu, D., Tsang, I.W.: Domain adaptation from multiple sources: A domain-dependent regularization approach. T-NNLS 23(3), 504–518 (2012)
13. Duan, L., Tsang, I.W., Xu, D.: Domain transfer multiple kernel learning. T-PAMI 34(3), 465–479 (2012)
14. Duan, L., Xu, D., Tsang, I.W., Luo, J.: Visual event recognition in videos by learning from web data. T-PAMI 34(9), 1667–1680 (2012)
15. Farhadi, A., Endres, I., Hoiem, D., Forsyth, D.: Describing objects by their attributes. In: CVPR (2009)
16. Farquhar, J.D.R., Hardoon, D.R., Meng, H., Shawe-Taylor, J., Szedmak, S.: Two view learning: SVM-2K, theory and practice. In: NIPS (2005)
17. Fergus, R., Fei-Fei, L., Perona, P., Zisserman, A.: Learning object categories from Google's image search. In: ICCV (2005)
18. Fernando, B., Habrard, A., Sebban, M., Tuytelaars, T.: Unsupervised visual domain adaptation using subspace alignment. In: ICCV (2013)
19. Ferrari, V., Zisserman, A.: Learning visual attributes. In: NIPS (2007)
20. Fouad, S., Tino, P., Raychaudhury, S., Schneider, P.: Incorporating privileged information through metric learning. T-NNLS 24(7), 1086–1098 (2013)
21. Gong, B., Shi, Y., Sha, F., Grauman, K.: Geodesic flow kernel for unsupervised domain adaptation. In: CVPR (2012)
22. Gopalan, R., Li, R., Chellappa, R.: Domain adaptation for object recognition: An unsupervised approach. In: ICCV (2011)
23. Gretton, A., KBorgwardt, K.M., Rasch, M.J., Schölkopf, B., Smola, A.: A kernel two-sample test. JMLR 13, 723–773 (2012)
24. Griffin, G., Holub, A., Perona, P.: Caltech-256 object category dataset. Tech. rep., California Institute of Technology (2007)
25. Hardoon, D.R., Szedmak, S., Shawe-taylor, J.: Canonical correlation analysis: An overview with application to learning methods. Neural Computation 16(12), 2639–2664 (2004)
26. Huang, J., Smola, A., Gretton, A., Borgwardt, K., Scholkopf, B.: Correcting sample selection bias by unlabeled data. In: NIPS (2007)
27. Hwang, S.J., Grauman, K.: Learning the relative importance of objects from tagged images for retrieval and cross-modal search. IJCV 100(2), 134–153 (2012)
28. Krapac, J., Allan, M., Verbeek, J., Jurie, F.: Improving web image search results using query-relative classifier. In: CVPR (2010)

29. Kulis, B., Saenko, K., Darrell, T.: What you saw is not what you get: Domain adaptation using asymmetric kernel transforms. In: CVPR (2011)
30. Li, Q., Wu, J., Tu, Z.: Harvesting mid-level visual concepts from large-scale internet images. In: CVPR (2013)
31. Li, W., Duan, L., Tsang, I.W., Xu, D.: Batch mode adaptive multiple instance learning for computer vision tasks. In: CVPR, pp. 2368–2375 (2012)
32. Li, W., Duan, L., Tsang, I.W., Xu, D.: Co-labeling: A new multi-view learning approach for ambiguous problems. In: ICDM, pp. 419–428 (2012)
33. Li, W., Duan, L., Xu, D., Tsang, I.W.: Text-based image retrieval using progressive multi-instance learning. In: ICCV, pp. 2049–2055 (2011)
34. Li, W., Duan, L., Xu, D., Tsang, I.W.: Learning with augmented features for supervised and semi-supervised heterogeneous domain adaptation. T-PAMI 36(6), 1134–1148 (2014)
35. Liang, L., Cai, F., Cherkassky, V.: Predictive learning with structured (grouped) data. Neural Networks 22, 766–773 (2009)
36. Pan, S.J., Tsang, I.W., Kwok, J.T., Yang, Q.: Domain adaptation via transfer component analysis. T-NN 22(2), 199–210 (2011)
37. Schroff, F., Criminisi, A., Zisserman, A.: Harvesting image databases from the web. T-PAMI 33(4), 754–766 (2011)
38. Sharmanska, V., Quadrianto, N., Lampert, C.H.: Learning to rank using privileged information. In: ICCV (2013)
39. Torralba, A., Efros, A.A.: Unbiased look at dataset bias. In: CVPR (2011)
40. Torralba, A., Fergus, R., Freeman, W.T.: 80 million tiny images: A large data set for nonparametric object and scene recognition. T-PAMI 30(11), 1958–1970 (2008)
41. Torresani, L., Szummer, M., Fitzgibbon, A.: Efficient object category recognition using classemes. In: Daniilidis, K., Maragos, P., Paragios, N. (eds.) ECCV 2010, Part I. LNCS, vol. 6311, pp. 776–789. Springer, Heidelberg (2010)
42. Vapnik, V., Vashist, A.: A new learning paradigm: Learning using privileged infromatin. Neural Networks 22, 544–557 (2009)
43. Vijayanarasimhan, S., Grauman, K.: Keywords to visual categories: Multiple-instance learning for weakly supervised object categorization. In: CVPR (2008)
44. Zhou, Z., Zhang, M.: Multi-instance multi-label learning with application to scene classification. In: NIPS (2006)

Multi-modal Unsupervised Feature Learning for RGB-D Scene Labeling

Anran Wang[1], Jiwen Lu[2], Gang Wang[1,2], Jianfei Cai[1], and Tat-Jen Cham[1]

[1] Nanyang Technological University, Singapore
[2] Advanced Digital Sciences Center, Singapore

Abstract. Most of the existing approaches for RGB-D indoor scene labeling employ hand-crafted features for each modality independently and combine them in a heuristic manner. There has been some attempt on directly learning features from raw RGB-D data, but the performance is not satisfactory. In this paper, we adapt the unsupervised feature learning technique for RGB-D labeling as a multi-modality learning problem. Our learning framework performs feature learning and feature encoding simultaneously which significantly boosts the performance. By stacking basic learning structure, higher-level features are derived and combined with lower-level features for better representing RGB-D data. Experimental results on the benchmark NYU depth dataset show that our method achieves competitive performance, compared with state-of-the-art.

Keywords: RGB-D scene labeling, unsupervised feature learning, joint feature learning and encoding, multi-modality.

1 Introduction

Scene labeling is an integral part of scene understanding and involves densely assigning a category label to each pixel in an image. Most previous scene labeling work dealt with outdoor scenarios [1,2,3,4,5,6]. Comparatively, indoor scenes are more challenging due to a number of factors: relative poor light condition, messy object distribution, and large variance of features for objects in different scene types. However, low-cost RGB-D cameras such as the Kinect can be used on indoor scenes to provide both color and depth measurements, leading to improvements in accuracy and robustness of labeling.

Hand-crafted features were used in several previous works on RGB-D scene labeling. These include the use of SIFT [7], KDES (kernel descriptors) [8] and other sophisticated features [9]. However, the accuracy of such feature extractors is highly dependent on variations in hand-crafting and combinations, and thus hard to systematically extend to different modalities. In addition, features are often designed for RGB and depth independently, with the shared information between RGB and depth left unexploited. Inspired by the recent success of unsupervised feature learning technique in many applications including object recognition [10] and action recognition [11], we propose to adapt the existing unsupervised feature learning technique to directly learn features from multi-modal

D. Fleet et al. (Eds.): ECCV 2014, Part V, LNCS 8693, pp. 453–467, 2014.

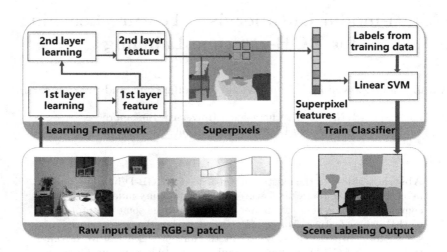

Fig. 1. Our framework for RGB-D indoor scene labeling. Our method learns features from raw RGB-D input with two-layer stacking structure. Features of the two layers are concatenated to train linear SVMs over superpixels for labeling task.

raw data in RGB-D indoor scene labeling so as to avoid the problem of hand-crafting features. To the best of our knowledge, very few works have applied feature learning for RGB-D indoor scene labeling. Recently, supervised feature learning method [12], convolutional neural networks (CNN), is used for RGB-D feature learning. In another work [13], pixels of patches are encoded with selected example patches. Both of these two methods obtain limited performance.

The approach proposed in this paper attempts to learn visual patterns from RGB and depth in a joint manner via an unsupervised learning framework. This is illustrated in Figure 1. At the heart of our unsupervised learning algorithm, we perform feature learning and feature encoding jointly in a two-layer stacked structure. A dense sampling of patches is initially obtained from RGB-D images, forming the input into the learning structure. The output of the learning is a collection of superpixels, in which each superpixel represents a combination of features obtained from all patches whose centers fall into the catchment region of the superpixel. Subsequently, linear SVMs are trained to map superpixel features to scene labels.

2   Related Work

2.1   Scene Labeling

Early work on scene labeling focused on outdoor color imagery, and typically used CRF or MRF. The nodes of the graphical models were pixels [14,15], super-pixels [1,4] or a hierarchy of regions [2]. Local interactions between nodes were captured by pairwise potentials, while unary potentials were used to represnt image observations, via features such as SIFT [16] and HOG [17]. An alternative inference framework was presented in [3], in which a very efficient recursive neural network (RNN) was used to greedily merge neighboring superpixels according to a learned scoring function. In a departure from the earlier approaches involving hand-crafted feature extraction, Grangier et al. [5] used convolutional networks for scene labeling. Farabet et al. [6] later adopted multiscale convolutional networks to automatically learn low and high-level textures as well as shape features from raw pixels, and further proposed the "purity" of class distributions as an optimization goal, in order to maximize the likelihood that each segment contained only one object. They achieved state-of-the-art performance on the commonly used Stanford Background [18] and SIFT Flow datasets [19].

Indoor scene labeling is a harder problem, but is recent more accessible with the advent of affordable RGB-D cameras such as Kinect. Silberman and Fergus [7] released a large-scale RGB-D dataset containing 7 scene types and 13 semantic labels. They employed RGB-D SIFT and 3D location priors as features and used MRFs to ensure contextual consistency. Koppula et al. [20] achieved high accuracy on semantic labeling of point clouds through a mixed integer optimization method. They however require the extraction of richer geometry features from 3D+RGB point clouds rather than the more limited height field from a single RGB-D image, and also depend on a computationally intensive optimization process with long running time. In an extension to Silberman and Fergus's work, Ren et al. [8] evaluated six kernel descriptors and chose four. Additionally, more comprehensive geometry features of superpixels were added to further boost performance. With these features, they achieved state-of-the-art performance on the NYU depth dataset V1. Recently, Cadena and Kosecka [9] proposed various new features including entropy for associating superpixel boundaries to vanishing points, and neighborhood planarity. A CRF is applied to the superpixels to obtain final scene labels. These methods mentioned require manual fine-tuning in feature design and also in the way that different features are combined. To reduce the dependency on hand-crafted features, Couprie et al. [12] applied the convolutional neural network method of Farabet et al. [6] to indoor RGB-D scene labeling. The depth data was treated as an additional channel besides RGB, and a multiscale convolutional network was used to ensure the features captured a larger spatial context. Although this method was demonstrated to be effective for outdoor scenes, the performance on RGB-D indoor scenes is much less satisfactory. Pei et al. [13] learned features by projecting raw pixels of patches onto selected example patches. Such an encoding method may not be powerful enough since the input raw pixel values are usually redundant and noisy.

2.2 Feature Learning

Feature learning has been applied to action recognition [11], handwritten digits recognition [21] and image classification [10,22,23]. It is also a central aspect of the RGB-D labeling framework in this paper, in which we jointly consider the two modalities of color and depth.

A number of previous work also applied feature learning to data with multiple modalities. Potamianos et al. [24] applied it to audio-visual speech recognition. Ngiam et al. [25] proposed a framework to train deep networks over multiple modalities (video and audio) using RBM (Restricted Boltzmann Machines) as basic learning units. Their method focused on learning better features for one modality when multiple modalities were present. Socher et al. [26] treated color and depth information as two modalities in object classification problem. Each modality was processed separately, wherein low-level features were extracted using a single-layer CNN and combined using RNN. Finally features from two modalities were concatenated together. However as their framework was designed only for determining a single label for each image, and did not involve classifying different regions in an image, it was not suitable for the scene labeling task in this paper.

3   Approach

3.1   Single-Layer Feature Learning Structure

Our approach is based on the unsupervised feature learning algorithm [10], which is to minimize the following objective function

$$\underset{W}{\text{minimize}} \left\| W^T W Z - Z \right\|_2^2 + \lambda_1 g(WZ) \tag{1}$$

where Z is a set of d-dimensional raw input data vectors, i.e. $Z = [z_1, \cdots z_m] \in \mathbb{R}^{d \times m}$, $W \in \mathbb{R}^{d' \times d}$ is the transform matrix which projects Z into a d'-dimensional feature space, g is the smooth L_1 penalty function [10], and λ_1 is a tradeoff factor. Eq. (1) essentially is to seek the transformation matrix W that can minimize the reconstruction error (first term) and the penalty of the approximated orthonormal constraint (second term). The transform matrix $W \in \mathbb{R}^{d' \times d}$ is often chosen to be overcomplete, i.e. $d' > d$, for better performance, as demonstrated in the study [27]. Note that Z has gone through the whitening preprocess, i.e. the input data vectors are linearly transformed to have zero mean and identity covariance [10]. Such unsupervised feature learning method has been proven to be successful in the application of object recognition [10].

Here, we adopt Eq. (1) to learn multi-modality features for RGB-D scene labeling. Instead of learning W for color and depth information separately, we consider different modalities jointly and their relationship is implicitly reasoned. In particular, let $X = [x_1, \cdots x_m] \in \mathbb{R}^{d_1 \times m}$ denote the input RGB vectors, and $Y = [y_1, \cdots y_m] \in \mathbb{R}^{d_2 \times m}$ denote the input depth vectors. Then, Z in Eq. (1) is simply formed by cascading color and depth information as $Z = [X; Y] \in \mathbb{R}^{d \times m}$ $(d = d_1 + d_2)$.

Moreover, the previous methods [11,28] show that better performance can be achieved by further applying feature encoding over the learned features to build "bag of words" type features. However, they perform feature learning and feature encoding separately. It is clear that there is inconsistency between these two components, i.e. feature learning is not optimized for feature encoding and vice versa. Thus, in this paper, we propose to perform feature learning and feature encoding in a joint framework with the following objective function:

$$\underset{W,V,U}{\text{minimize}} \quad \left\| W^T W Z - Z \right\|_2^2 + \lambda_1 g(WZ) + \lambda_2 \left\| WZ - UV \right\|_2^2 + \lambda_3 |V|_1$$

$$\text{subject to} \quad \|u_k\|_2 \leq 1, \ k = 1, 2, \ldots, K. \tag{2}$$

where $U = [u_1, \cdots u_K] \in \mathbb{R}^{d' \times K}$ represents the dictionary which has K bases, and V denotes the feature encoding coefficients. Compared with Eq. (1), the newly added two terms in Eq. (2) aim to find sparse feature representation for the learned feature WZ. At the same time, there is a L2-norm constraint for u_k to avoid trivial solutions which just scale down V and scale up U. By jointly learning W, V and U in Eq. (2), we integrate feature learning and feature encoding into a coherent framework. With the optimized W, transformed data WZ could be encoded by more descriptive dictionary U and the final features V become more efficient.

Optimization Process. In the proposed unsupervised feature learning Eq. (2), we need to optimize W, U and V together. We solve this problem by updating three variables iteratively. W, U and V are initialized randomly. Given a training data matrix Z, we first fix U and V, the cost function can then be minimized by using the unconstrained optimizer (e.g. L-BFGS [29], CG [29]) to update W. When fixing W and U, similar to the sparse coding work [22], Eq. (2) becomes a linear regression problem with regularization on the coefficients, which can be solved efficiently by optimization over each coefficient v_m with the feature-sign search algorithm [30]. At last, when W and V are fixed, it becomes a least square problem with quadratic constraints, which can be easily solved. The optimization process is shown in Algorithm 1.

3.2   Hierarchical Structure

What we present in section 3.1 is just one-layer feature learning structure. Considering that there exists multi-level information in visual data such as intensity, edge, object, etc [31], it is often preferred to learn hierarchical features so as to describe low-level and high-level properties simultaneously. In our case, we can stack the single-layer feature learning structure to capture the higher-level features. Particularly, we first learn the low-level features using the single-layer structure. Then, the output of low-level structure is treated as raw data input for the higher level. Considering the output of the first-layer learning structure is of high dimension, PCA is used to reduce its dimension so that the same structure can be reused for the high-layer feature learning. In the stacked structure, the input Z of higher level would contain lower-level features from the two modalities produced by the lower-level feature learning.

Input: Raw data from multiple modalities: Z

Output: Transformation matrix W, Dictionary U, Sparse encoding V

Step 1: Initialization.

W, U and V are randomly initialized;

Step 2: Iteratively optimize over W, U and V.

while $iter \leq max\_iter$ **do**

Fix U and V:
Solved by unconstrained optimizer L-BFGS and update W

Fix W and U:
A linear regression problem over V with L1 norm regularization on the coefficients.

Optimized by feature-sign search algorithm and update V

Fix W and V:
A least square problem with quadratic constraints over U

Optimized by Lagrange dual and update U
end

Algorithm 1: Optimization process

3.3   Application in RGB-D Scene Labeling

In the RGB-D scene labeling application, when the input data has large size, the learning process becomes less efficient. To address this, we make use of small patch features to represent big patches. Our main framework for RGB-D labeling is as follows. We first run our unsupervised learning on randomly sampled small patches ($s \times s$) to learn the optimal transform matrix W and the dictionary U. Then, for each densely sampled big patch ($S \times S$, $S > s$), with the obtained W and U we derive the feature vector V for its overlapped $s \times s$ small patches. Features of $S \times S$ patches are then obtained by concatenating all its overlapped $s \times s$ patches' features together. Finally, superpixel technique is incorporated to ensure that pixels in the same superpixel take the same label.

Fig. 2 shows the detailed first-layer feature extraction process. In particular, we extract input raw data from two different modalities (color and depth). We convert the color image to grayscale. At the beginning, m $s \times s$ RGB-D small image patches are randomly sampled. For each $s \times s$ small patch, X is s^2-d raw color data by flatting the patch into a vector. The same goes for raw depth data Y. Concatenating them together, we have Z, $2s^2$-d data. For each $S \times S$ big patch, there are $(S - s + 1)^2$ $s \times s$ small patches. After the unsupervised feature learning process, a small patch is then represented by a sparse vector V (K-dimensional) computed from W and U. Concatenating the features of $(S - s + 1)^2$ small patches together, we obtain the features of a big patch. To avoid over-fitting caused by the high dimensionality of the big patch features, we use max-pooling to reduce the dimensionality.

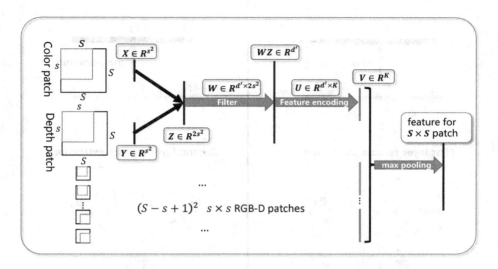

Fig. 2. Detailed illustration of feature extraction of the first layer: $s \times s$ color and depth patches are flatted to vectors X and Y. Z is the feature vector obtained by concatenating X and Y. With learned filter matrix W and dictionary U, the sparse encoding coefficients V can be derived, which represents the feature of a $s \times s$ patch. By concatenating the features of $(S - s + 1)^2$ $s \times s$ small patches, we get the feature of a $S \times S$ big patch.

To capture higher-level features, we stack two above single-layer structure together. Fig. 3 shows the two-layer feature learning structure, where the output features of the first layer are used as the input for the second layer. Specifically, the first-layer output feature vectors are further processed through dimension reduction by PCA so that the vectors could be resized to $S \times S$ data patches. Same as the first layer, $s \times s$ small patches in these $S \times S$ big patches are sampled as training data of the second layer. After the learning process of the second layer, these $S \times S$ patches are represented by the concatenated features of their $s \times s$ patches. At last, the features from the two different layers are concatenated together as the final representation of the raw patches.

In our patch size setting, we set S as 10 and s as 7 for both layers. The input data is normalized between the two modalities. We choose the dictionary size K as 1024. With learned W and U, the output of the first layer is 1024-d V. After PCA transformation, it is rescaled as 100-d data. The 100-d data is then resized to 10×10 patches, where the overlapping 7×7 patches are the training input for the second layer. By concatenating 16 1024-d features, we get a 16384-d feature vector for a 10×10 patch. Then, max-pooling is used to reduce the dimension to 1024-d for one layer. Concatenating the features of the two layers, we finally obtain a 2048-d feature for each 10×10 patch.

After feature learning process, scene labeling is done using the learned patch features. Considering that predicting the pixel-wise labeling independently could

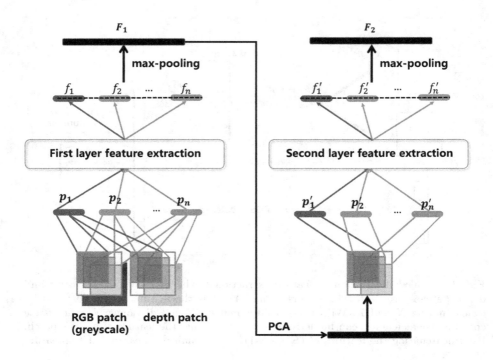

Fig. 3. Left: the unsupervised learning structure of the first layer. Right: the second layer structure. F_1 is the first-layer feature. F_2 is the second-layer feature.

be noisy and pixels with same color in local regions should take the same label, we oversegment RGB-D images using the gPb hierarchical segmentation method [32], where we follow the adaption to RGB-D images proposed by Ren et al. [8] to linearly combine the Ultrametric Contour Maps (UCM) results. The 10×10 patches are obtained by densely sampling over a grid with a unit distance of eight pixels. Finally, each superpixel is represented by averaging the features of all the patches whose centers are located in the region.

4   Experiment

Dataset. The benchmark dataset, the NYU depth dataset [7,33] including version 1 and version 2, are used for evaluation. The V1 dataset contains 2347 RGB-D images captured in 64 different indoor scenes labeled with 12 categories plus an unknown class. The V2 dataset consists of 1449 images captured in 464 different scenes.

Training Details. The parameters λ_1, λ_2 and λ_3 in Eq. (2) are empirically set to 0.1, 0.5 and 0.15. For each layer, we randomly sample 20000 7×7 patches as training data. We run 50 iterations to learn W, U in our unsupervised learning framework. Each iteration takes about 17 minutes on average on a PC with Intel i5 3.10GHz CPU and 8G memory. For a superpixel, we calculate the mean values of all its 10×10 patches' features. With the labelled superpixels in the training list, we train a 1-vs-all linear SVM for each category. For NYU depth dataset V1 [7], we use 60% data for training and 40% data for testing which is the same as that of [8]. For NYU depth dataset V2 [33], we use the training/testing splits provided by the dataset: 795 images for training and 654 images for testing.

We produce a confusion matrix whose diagonal represents the pixel-level labeling accuracy of each category. The average value of the diagonal of the confusion matrix is used as the performance metric. Note that different oversegmentation levels lead to different scene labeling results. We report the best performance of different oversegmentation levels. We would also like to point out that in this research we focus on feature learning and thus we did not further apply contextual models such as MRFs to smooth the class labels. For fair comparison, we only report the results of other methods without further smoothing.

Table 1. Class-average accuracy comparison of different methods on the NYU depth dataset V1

Results on V1		
Single feature	Ours	61.71%
	gradient KDES [8]	51.84%
	color KDES [8]	53.27%
	spin/surface normal KDES [8]	40.28%
	depth gradient KDES [8]	53.56%
Combined feature	Silberman and Fergus [7]	53.00%
	Pei et al. [13]	50.50%
	Ren et al. [8]	71.40%
	Combining our features with Ren's	72.94%

Result Comparisons on Dataset V1. Table 1 shows the average labeling results of different methods on the NYU detph dataset V1. We compare the result of our two-layer feature learning method with: 1) the result of Silberman and Fergus [7]; 2) the result of Pei et al. [13]; 3) the result of single kernel descriptor(KDES) [8]; 4) the result of Ren et al. [8] (combining four KDESs and geometry features); 5) the result of combining the features of our method and Ren's.

It can be seen from Table 1 that our method significantly outperforms the method of Silberman and Fergus, as they mainly use SIFT features on color and depth images. Our method also outperforms the method of Pei et al. [13], as they use selected patches which are usually redundant and noisy in encoding. However, our result does not outperform that of Ren et al. [8]. We argue that Ren et al. [8] evaluated six kernel based features, integrated four of them: gradient, color, depth gradient, spin/surface normal, and developed a sophisticated

Table 2. Class-average accuracy results of our method with different settings on the NYU depth dataset V1

Result on V1	
Our method (first layer)	54.76%
Sparse coding after feature learning	45.67%
k-means feature encoding after feature learning	22.32%
Separate learning from two modalities with our cost function	50.74%
Our method (second layer)	52.90%

Table 3. Individual class label accuracy on the NYU depth dataset V1 with only one-layer features. Second column: learning from color modality alone. Third column: learning from two modalities separately. Forth column: joint learning from two modalities. The bold numbers are to indicate the cases that extra depth features hurt the performance. In contrast, the performance is boosted when jointly learning from two modalities for all the categories.

	Learning only from color modality	Separate learning from two modalities	Joint learning from two modalities
bed	58.08%	**57.11% ↓**	62.55%
blind	56.63%	**55.19% ↓**	60.40%
book	54.88%	**47.97% ↓**	60.99%
cabinet	34.66%	38.40%	44.77%
ceiling	61.77%	79.52%	75.36%
floor	67.70%	83.20%	81.37%
picture	35.56%	47.35%	51.71%
sofa	43.99%	57.37%	54.48%
table	19.27%	23.68%	30.40%
tv	47.56%	59.83%	73.15%
wall	70.75%	**69.73% ↓**	71.62%
window	33.69%	36.50%	38.73%
other	3.70%	3.87%	6.28%

method to carefully select the best combination of the four features. In contrast, we just learn a single type of features directly from raw pixel values. If we compare our result with that of each single descriptor of [8], our method achieves superior performance. Compared to [8], our method does not need any detailed hand-crafting of features. Moreover, by combining our and Ren's features together, the classification accuracy can be further improved, suggesting that our features capture visual patterns which cannot be captured by those of [8].

Detailed Evaluations on Different Settings. Here we give detailed evaluations on our method with only one-layer features under different settings. In particular, we compare the following five setups: 1) our method with the features learned from the first layer; 2) separate learning: conducting feature

Table 4. Class labeling accuracy on the NYU depth dataset V2.

	Ground	Structure	Furniture	Props	class average
Ours	90.1%	81.4%	46.3%	43.3%	65.3%
Couprie et al. [12]	87.3%	45.3%	35.5%	86.1%	63.5%
Cadena and Kosecka [9]	87.3%	60.6%	33.7%	74.8 %	64.1%

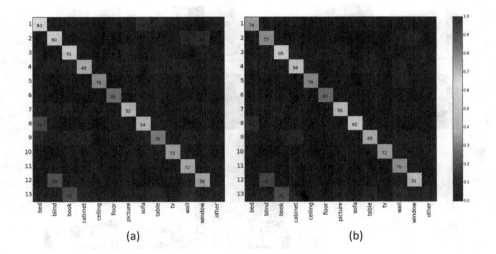

(a)   (b)

Fig. 4. The confusion matrices of: (a) our results with one-layer structure; (b) our results with two-layer structure.

learning with Eq. (1) to get filter matrix W and then performing sparse coding to encode filtered data WZ; 3) conducting feature learning with Eq. (1) and then use k-means clustering result as hard quantization to encode filtered data WZ; 4) learning features from two modalities separately with our cost function; 5) our method with the features learned from the second layer alone. Table 2 shows the results of the five different setups.

Comparing the results of methods 1, 2 and 3 in Table 2, we can see that joint feature learning and encoding performs much better than the methods using separate processing. Particularly, for method 2, we run 50 iterations to update W and then conduct sparse coding for 50 iterations to encode WZ. Compared with the way of iteratively updating W and U for 50 iterations in method 1, method 2 cannot guide W to help find descriptive U. For method 3, important feature information is lost when quantized by k-means.

Comparing the results of methods 1 and 4 in Table 2, we can see that joint learning from two modalities outperforms separate learning. This is because separate learning ignores the correlation information between the two modalities, for which the extra features learned from depth alone might hurt the perfor-

Fig. 5. 15 example results. Rows 1st, 4th and 7th: color images. Rows 2nd, 5th and 8th: the results of combining our features and Ren's features. Rows 3rd, 6th and 9th: ground truth. Note that since we focus on feature learning, we did not use CRFs or MRFs to smooth the labels. So the results might look a bit noisy.

Table 5. Labeling accuracy on the NYU depth dataset V2. Second column: the results of Couprie et al. [12]. Third column: the results of our method with two-layer structure.

	Couprie et al. [12]	Ours
bed	38.1%	47.6%
objects	8.7%	12.4%
chair	34.1%	23.5%
furnit.	42.4 %	16.7%
ceiling	62.6%	68.1%
floor	87.3%	84.1%
deco.	40.4%	26.4%
sofa	24.6%	39.1%
table	10.2%	35.4%
wall	86.1%	65.9%
window	15.9%	52.2%
books	13.7%	45.0%
TV	6.0%	32.4%
class average	36.2%	42.2%

mance, as shown in Table 3. On the contrary, our algorithm implicitly infers the correlation between the two modalities and could find better combination of them, which leads to better performance for all the classes (see Table 3).

Comparing the results of methods 1 and 5 in Table 2, we can see that the high-level features captured by the second layer alone are not sufficient. Only when combining with low-level features together, we can achieve a performance improvement of 7% (see Table 1), compared with using the first-layer features alone. The detailed comparison of confusion matrixes between one-layer learning and two-layer learning is shown in Fig. 4.

Result Comparisons on Dataset V2. We also compare our results on NYU depth dataset V2 with the following two existing works that have reported results on the dataset V2: 1) Couprie et al. [12]; 2) Cadena and Kosecka [9]. [9] includes a lot of hand-crafted appearance and geometry features. Couprie et al. [12] automatically learns features from raw data input which is similar to our method. Table 4 shows the labeling accuracy results on the NYU depth dataset V2, where the four structural classes, structure, floor, furniture and prop, are often used for comparison. It can be seen that our method achieves the best average accuracy, although our method performs poorly on the prop class, which contains many small table items.

Considering that both [12] and our method are feature-learning based approaches, we give a further comparison between them using the 13 fine categories defined in [12]. Table 5 shows the comparison results. It can be seen that the performance of [12] is not satisfactory, although their hierarchical convolutional neural network system succeeds in scene labeling on outdoor color image dataset. Our average accuracy outperforms theirs by 6%.

Fig. 5 shows some examples of pixel labeling results. The visualization results demonstrate that the learned local features can well represent objects in the scene. Note that since our work focuses on feature learning, we did not use CRFs or MRFs to smooth class labels.

5 Conclusion

In this paper, we presented an unsupervised feature learning method that learns features from RGB-D data for scene labeling task. We pose it as a multi-modality learning problem containing color and depth. Our method considers unsupervised feature learning and feature encoding problem together and implicitly infers the relationship between two modalities. By stacking the learning framework, our method could learn hierarchical features. Linear SVMs are trained on superpixels to produce the final labeling. We carried experiments on NYU depth dataset V1 and V2 and get comparable results with state-of-the-art methods including those use hand-crafted features and those learns features from raw data.

Acknowledgment. This research, which is carried out at BeingThere Centre, is supported by Singapore MoE AcRF Tier-1 Grant RG30/11 and the Singapore National Research Foundation under its International Research Centre @ Singapore Funding Initiative and administered by the IDM Programme Office. The research is also in part supported by MOE Tier 1 RG84/12 and SERC 1321202099.

References

1. Micusik, B., Kosecka, J.: Semantic segmentation of street scenes by superpixel co-occurrence and 3d geometry. In: ICCV Workshops, pp. 625–632 (2009)
2. Lempitsky, V.S., Vedaldi, A., Zisserman, A.: Pylon model for semantic segmentation. In: NIPS, pp. 1485–1493 (2011)
3. Socher, R., Lin, C.C., Manning, C., Ng, A.Y.: Parsing natural scenes and natural language with recursive neural networks. In: ICML, pp. 129–136 (2011)
4. Galleguillos, C., Rabinovich, A., Belongie, S.: Object categorization using co-occurrence, location and appearance. In: CVPR, pp. 1–8 (2008)
5. Grangier, D., Bottou, L., Collobert, R.: Deep convolutional networks for scene parsing. In: ICML Deep Learning Workshop (2009)
6. Farabet, C., Couprie, C., Najman, L., LeCun, Y.: Learning hierarchical features for scene labeling. IEEE Trans. Pattern Anal. Mach. Intell. 35(8), 1915–1929 (2013)
7. Silberman, N., Fergus, R.: Indoor scene segmentation using a structured light sensor. In: ICCV Workshops, pp. 601–608 (2011)
8. Ren, X., Bo, L., Fox, D.: Rgb-(d) scene labeling: Features and algorithms. In: CVPR, pp. 2759–2766 (2012)
9. Cadena, C., Košecka, J.: Semantic parsing for priming object detection in rgb-d scenes. In: Workshop on Semantic Perception, Mapping and Exploration (2013)
10. Le, Q.V., Karpenko, A., Ngiam, J., Ng, A.Y.: Ica with reconstruction cost for efficient overcomplete feature learning. In: NIPS, pp. 1017–1025 (2011)
11. Le, Q.V., Zou, W.Y., Yeung, S.Y., Ng, A.Y.: Learning hierarchical invariant spatio-temporal features for action recognition with independent subspace analysis. In: CVPR, pp. 3361–3368 (2011)

12. Couprie, C., Farabet, C., Najman, L., LeCun, Y.: Indoor semantic segmentation using depth information. arXiv preprint arXiv:1301.3572 (2013)
13. Pei, D., Liu, H., Liu, Y., Sun, F.: Unsupervised multimodal feature learning for semantic image segmentation. In: IJCNN (2013)
14. He, X., Zemel, R., Carreira-Perpindn, M.: Multiscale conditional random fields for image labeling. In: CVPR (2004)
15. Shotton, J., Winn, J.M., Rother, C., Criminisi, A.: *textonBoost*: Joint appearance, shape and context modeling for multi-class object recognition and segmentation. In: Leonardis, A., Bischof, H., Pinz, A. (eds.) ECCV 2006, Part I. LNCS, vol. 3951, pp. 1–15. Springer, Heidelberg (2006)
16. Lowe, D.G.: Object recognition from local scale-invariant features. In: ICCV, pp. 1150–1157 (1999)
17. Dalal, N., Triggs, B.: Histograms of oriented gradients for human detection. In: CVPR, pp. 886–893 (2005)
18. Gould, S., Fulton, R., Koller, D.: Decomposing a scene into geometric and semantically consistent regions. In: ICCV (2009)
19. Liu, C., Yuen, J., Torralba, A.: Sift flow: Dense correspondence across scenes and its applications. PAMI (2011)
20. Koppula, H.S., Anand, A., Joachims, T., Saxena, A.: Semantic labeling of 3d point clouds for indoor scenes. In: NIPS, pp. 244–252 (2011)
21. Hinton, G.E., Osindero, S., Teh, Y.W.: A fast learning algorithm for deep belief nets. Neural Computation 18(7), 1527–1554 (2006)
22. Yang, J., Yu, K., Gong, Y., Huang, T.: Linear spatial pyramid matching using sparse coding for image classification. In: CVPR, pp. 1794–1801 (2009)
23. Kumar, A., Rai, P., Daumé III, H.: Co-regularized multi-view spectral clustering. In: NIPS, pp. 1413–1421 (2011)
24. Potamianos, G., Neti, C., Luettin, J., Matthews, I.: Audio-visual automatic speech recognition: An overview. Issues in Visual and Audio-Visual Speech Processing 22, 23 (2004)
25. Ngiam, J., Khosla, A., Kim, M., Nam, J., Lee, H., Ng, A.Y.: Multimodal deep learning. In: ICML, pp. 689–696 (2011)
26. Socher, R., Huval, B., Bhat, B., Manning, D.: C., Ng, A.Y.: Convolutional-Recursive Deep Learning for 3D Object Classification. In: NIPS, pp. 665–673 (2012)
27. Coates, A., Ng, A.Y., Lee, H.: An analysis of single-layer networks in unsupervised feature learning. In: International Conference on Artificial Intelligence and Statistics, pp. 215–223 (2011)
28. Wang, H., Ullah, M.M., Klaser, A., Laptev, I., Schmid, C., et al.: Evaluation of local spatio-temporal features for action recognition. In: BMVC, pp. 124.1–124.11 (2009)
29. Schimidt, M.: minfunc. (2005)
30. Lee, H., Battle, A., Raina, R., Ng, A.Y.: Efficient sparse coding algorithms. In: NIPS, pp. 801–808 (2006)
31. Lee, H., Grosse, R., Ranganath, R., Ng, A.Y.: Convolutional deep belief networks for scalable unsupervised learning of hierarchical representations. In: ICML, pp. 609–616 (2009)
32. Arbelaez, P., Maire, M., Fowlkes, C., Malik, J.: Contour detection and hierarchical image segmentation. PAMI, 898–916 (2011)
33. Silberman, N., Hoiem, D., Kohli, P., Fergus, R.: Indoor segmentation and support inference from RGBD images. In: Fitzgibbon, A., Lazebnik, S., Perona, P., Sato, Y., Schmid, C. (eds.) ECCV 2012, Part V. LNCS, vol. 7576, pp. 746–760. Springer, Heidelberg (2012)

Discriminatively Trained Dense Surface Normal Estimation

L'ubor Ladický, Bernhard Zeisl, and Marc Pollefeys

ETH Zürich, Switzerland
{lubor.ladicky,bernhard.zeisl,marc.pollefeys}@inf.ethz.ch

Abstract. In this work we propose the method for a rather unexplored problem of computer vision - discriminatively trained dense surface normal estimation from a single image. Our method combines contextual and segment-based cues and builds a regressor in a boosting framework by transforming the problem into the regression of coefficients of a local coding. We apply our method to two challenging data sets containing images of man-made environments, the indoor NYU2 data set and the outdoor KITTI data set. Our surface normal predictor achieves results better than initially expected, significantly outperforming state-of-the-art.

1 Introduction

Recently, single-view reconstruction methods, estimating scene geometry directly by learning from data, have gained quite some popularity. While resulting 3D reconstructions of such methods are of debatable quality, coarse information about the 3D layout of a scene has shown to help boost the performance of applications such as object detection [1], semantic reasoning [2] or general scene understanding [3].

The principal underlying idea behind these methods [4,5,6] is, that particular structures have a certain real world size, and thus their size in an image gives rise to the scene depth. We argue that this is a rather weak hypothesis, since structures are likely to exist at different size in reality and perspective projection distorts them. As a consequence it renders the problem of single image depth estimation ill-posed in general. However, perspective cues are not harmful, but actually helpful, because they carry information about the local surface orientation and allow to reason about the scene, for example about the viewpoint of the camera. We argue that it is beneficial to directly estimate first order derivatives of depth, i.e. surface normals, as it can provide more accurate results than estimation of absolute depth. In addition we do not need to worry about depth discontinuities, e.g. due to occlusions, which are difficult to detect and harm single image reconstruction [5,6].

While data-driven normal estimation seems to be a more promising approach, it has not been exploited much so far. We believe this is due to the lack of available ground truth data, which is hard to obtain, as recording requires accurate capturing devices. With the recent advances in low cost commodity depth sensors such as Kinect, ToF cameras or laser scanners, acquisition was made easier

D. Fleet et al. (Eds.): ECCV 2014, Part V, LNCS 8693, pp. 468–484, 2014.
© Springer International Publishing Switzerland 2014

and there are multiple data sets [7,8] available nowadays, which should foster research in this direction.

The importance of surface normal estimation has been already recognized long before such data was available. Due to the lack of data, proposed approaches [9,10,11] had to rely purely on the knowledge of underlying physics of light and shading. Thus, resulting methods work only under strong assumptions about the knowledge of locations of light sources and properties of the material, such as the assumption of Lambertian surfaces. However, these approaches do not work in more complex scenarios such as indoor or outdoor scenes, and thus are not applicable for general problems. The first approach, that directly tries to estimate surface normals from the data was proposed in [12]. The method aims to extract a set of both visually-discriminative and geometrically-informative primitives from training data. For test images the learned detector fires at sparse positions with similar appearance and hypothesizes about the underlying surface orientations by means of the learned primitives. Hoiem et al. [13] do not directly estimate normal directions, but formulate the task as a labeling problem with more abstract surface orientations, such as left- or right-facing, vertical, etc. in order to estimate the 3D contextual frame of an image. In [14] Gupta et al. extracted a qualitative physical representation of an outdoor scene by reasoning about the pairwise depth relations (and thus also not via absolute depth); though their model is approximated to consist of blocks only. Other authors have simplified the task to be more robust and incorporated strong orientation priors such as vanishing points and lines [15,16] or Manhattan world constrains [17,18,19].

In this work we aim to extract surface normals for each pixel in a single image without any measured knowledge about the underlying 3D scene geometry. We present a discriminative learning approach to estimate pixel-wise surface orientation solely from the image appearance. We do not incorporate any kind of geometric priors; rather we utilize recent work in image labelling as often used for semantic image segmentation, where context enhanced pixel-based and segment-based feature representations proved best performances. For the semantic segmentation problem it is reasonable to assume that all pixels within a detected segment share the same label, i.e. segments correspond to objects. However, for normal estimation this assumption of label-consistency holds only for planar regions, such as segments on a wall; for segments related to non-planar objects, e.g. a cylindrical shaped pot, it is violated.

We account for this property and propose a feature representation, that combines the cues of pixel-wise and segment-based methods. The strength of our approach stems from the fact that we join both representations and intrinsically learn, when to use which. It has the desired effect that results tend to follow segment (and by this object) boundaries, but do not necessarily have to. Then we formulate the surface normal estimation as a regression of coefficients of the local coding, to make the learning problem more discriminative. Finally, we adapt the standard boosting framework to deal with this specific learning problem. The whole pipeline is illustrated in Figure 1. We apply our method to two data sets from two different man-made environments - indoors [7] and outdoors [8].

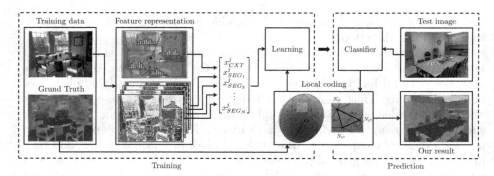

Fig. 1. Workflow of the algorithm. In the training stage images are segmented using multiple unsupervised segmentations, dense features are extracted and discriminative feature representations combining contextual and segment-based features are built. Ground truth normals are approximated using the local coding by a weighted sum of representative normals and the discriminative regressor for these coefficients is trained. In the test stage the likelihood of each representative normal is predicted by the classifier and the output normal is recovered as a weighted sum of representative normals. The colours of the half-sphere represent corresponding normal directions.

Our classifier obtains surprisingly good results, successfully recognizing surface normals for a wide range of different scenes.

Our paper is structured as follows: In Section 2 we explain the details of our feature representation and draw connections to related work. Our learning procedure is illustrated in Section 3. In Section 4 we describe more implementation details, in Section 5 the acquisition of the ground truth data, and finally Section 6 reports our experimental results.

2   Feature Representation for Surface Normal Estimation

The standard label prediction pipeline for recognition tasks in computer vision consists of dense or sparse feature extraction, the composition of suitable compact discriminative feature representations, and the application of an appropriate machine learning algorithm, capable of discriminating between different labels corresponding to the different possible outcomes for the given task. For pixel-wise tasks, such as semantic segmentation, the feature representations are typically built either over pixels, or alternatively over segments (a.k.a. superpixels), obtained using any unsupervised segmentation technique [20,21,22,23]. Next we elaborate more on both approaches.

2.1   Context-Based Pixel-Wise Methods

For pixel-based approaches only a local feature vector of a pixel itself is insufficient to predict the label. Thus, a certain form of context [24,25,26,27], combining information from neighbouring pixels capturing a spatial configuration of features, has to be used. The context is captured either using a pixel-based or rectangle-based context representation. In a pixel-based context approach [25,26], the contextual information for a given pixel is obtained by concatenating individual feature vectors of neighbouring pixels, placed at a fixed set of displacements from the reference pixel. In a rectangle-based context approach [24,27], the feature representation for a pixel j is obtained by concatenating bag-of-words representations $bow(r_i + j)$ for a fixed set of rectangles $r_i \in R$, placed relative to the pixel j; i.e. $\mathbf{x}_{CXT}^j = [bow(r_1 + j), bow(r_2 + j), .., bow(r_{|R|} + j)]$. For both forms of context, multiple local features can be used jointly [27].

In practice, even for a small data set it is impossible to store these huge feature representations for all training samples in memory. Typically, the feature representation values are evaluated on the fly during the learning process. For a pixel-based context, the context is quickly evaluated from individual feature vector maps stored in memory. For a rectangle-based approach, the contextual information is obtained efficiently using integral images, calculated individually for each visual word. The response for one individual dimension, corresponding to the number of certain visual words in a rectangle, placed relative to the given pixel, is often referred to as a shape-filter response [24].

The predictions using context based approaches are typically very noisy, do not follow object boundaries, and thus require some form of regularization [28,27]. The rectangle-based context representation is typically more robust and leads to better performance quantitatively [24,25,27]. On the other hand the pixel-based approach is much faster and with a suitable learning method it can be evaluated in real-time [25,26] during testing. In this work we are more interested in high performance of our method, and thus we build on the superior rectangle-based rather than the faster pixel-based context.

2.2   Segment-Based Methods

Segment-based methods [29,30,31,32] are built upon the assumption, that predicted labels are consistent over segments obtained by unsupervised segmentation. This assumption plays two significant roles. First, the learning and evaluation over pixels can be reduced to a much smaller problem over segments, which allows for more complex and slower learning methods to be used, such as kernel SVMs [33]. Second, it allows us to build robust feature representations by combining features of all pixels in each segment. The most common segment-based representation is a L^1-normalized bag-of-words [29,30,31,27,32], modelling the distribution of visual words within a segment. Recently, several other alternatives beyond bag-of-words have been proposed [34,35,36], suitable for labelling of segments.

All standard segmentation methods [20,21,22,23] have free colour and spatial range parameters, that can be tuned specially for each individual task or data set, and are either hand-tuned or chosen based on an appropriate quality measure [37] to satisfy the label consistency in segments. However, even choosing the best

Input Image   Mean-shift [20]   Normalized cut [21]   SLIC [23]   Graph-cut [22]

Fig. 2. The example segmentations obtained by 4 different unsupervised methods [20,21,22,23]. The segments largely differ in terms of smoothness, shape consistency or variances of size. The notion of their quality largely depends on the task they are applied to. For semantic segmentation similar sized segments have typically more discriminant feature representations, but methods producing segments of different scales are more suitable for enforcing label consistency in segments [28]. For normal estimation a single unsupervised segmentation method can not produce label-consistent segments in general, e.g. the lamp in an image is not planar at any scale. Optimally, the learning method should decide by itself, which method – if any – and which features are more suitable for each specific task.

unsupervised segmentation method is harder than it seems. Human perception of the segment quality is very misleading, see Figure 2. Methods producing segments of large variation in size [20], capturing information over the right scale, may look visually more appealing, but the feature representations obtained using methods producing similar sized segments [22,23] may be more stable, and thus more discriminative. Choosing the right parameters is even harder; to obtain segments that will not contain multiple labels, the parameters of the unsupervised segmentation method must be chosen to produce a large number of very small segments. However, at that point the information in each segment is often not sufficient to correctly predict the label. Two kinds of approaches have been proposed to deal with this problem. In [32], the feature representation of segments also includes a feature representation of the union of neighbours to encode contextual information. Alternatively in [27] multiple segmentations are combined in the CRF framework by finding the smooth labelling that agrees with most of the predictions of individual pixel-wise and segment-wise classifiers and enforces label-consistency of segments as a soft constraint (see also [28]).

For normal estimation, the assumption of label-consistency is even more damming. It would imply, that all segments must be planar. It is a very good assumption for floor or walls, however, some objects are intrinsically not planar, such as cylindrical thrash bins or spherical lamp shades.

2.3   Joint Context-Based Pixel-Wise and Segment-Method

In our approach we propose a joint feature representation, that can deal with the weaknesses of individual context-based and segment-based methods. In particular, we overcome the inability of context-based approaches to produce smooth labellings tightly following boundaries and to capture the information on the correct object-based level, and the inability of segment-based methods to learn from a suitable-sized context. Unlike in [27], the contextual and segment cues are combined directly during in the learning stage.

This can be achieved by a very simple trick. Any learning method defined over segments, with a loss function weighted by the size of the segment, is equivalent to a learning method defined over pixels, with the feature vector $\mathbf{x}_{SEG}^{j} = \mathbf{x'}_{SEG}^{s(j)}$, where $s(j)$ is the segment the pixel j belongs to, and $\mathbf{x'}_{SEG}^{k}$ is any segment-based feature representation of the segment k. This transformation allows us to trivially combine feature representations over multiple segmentations as $\mathbf{x}_{MSEG}^{j} = (\mathbf{x}_{SEG_1}^{j}, \mathbf{x}_{SEG_2}^{j}, .., \mathbf{x}_{SEG_N}^{j})$, where $\mathbf{x}_{SEG_i}^{j}$ is the representation for an i-th segmentation. Learning over such pixel representations becomes equivalent to learning over intersections of multiple segmentations [38]. And finally, we concatenate this representation with contextual information $\mathbf{x}^{j} = (\mathbf{x}_{CXT}^{j}, \mathbf{x}_{MSEG}^{j})$. For normal estimation, this representation is powerful enough to learn the properties, such as *wall*-like features are more discriminative for segments from a particular segmentation or context-driven features can determine correct normals for spherical objects. Unlike in [27], the framework is able to potentially enforce label inconsistency in segments, which are identified to be non-planar.

3   Learning Normals

Due to a large dimensionality of the problem, we preferred learning algorithms, that use only a small randomly sampled subset of dimensions in each iteration, such as random forests [39] or Ada-boost [40]. Direct application of a even a simple linear regression would not be feasible. In practice Ada-boost typically performs better in terms of performance [24,25], random forests in terms of speed. Similarly to the choice of contextual representation, we chose better over faster. Intuitively the most discriminative contextual features will correspond to the local configuration of corner-like dense features, each one discriminant for a narrow range of normals. Thus, we make the learning problem simpler by lifting it to the problem of regressing coefficients of local coding [41,42,43], typically used in the feature space to increase the discriminative power of linear SVM classifiers. Standard multi-class Ada-boost [44] is designed for classification over a discrete set of labels, not for continuous regression. We adapt the learning algorithm to deal with a set of continuous ground truth labels, both during training and evaluation.

3.1   Local Coding in the Label Space

We start by performing standard k-means clustering on the set of ground truth normals n^j in the training set. In each iteration we back-project each cluster mean to the unit (half-)sphere. We refer to the cluster mean as the reference normal N_k. The Delaunay triangulation is evaluated on the set of reference normals to obtain the set of triangles T, where each triangle $t_i \in T$ is an unordered triplet of cluster indexes $\{t_i^1, t_i^2, t_i^3\}$. For each ground truth normal n^j we find the closest triangle $t(j)$ by solving the non-negative least squares problem [41]:

$$t(j) = \arg\min_{t_i \in T} \min_{\alpha_{t_i}^j} |n^j - \sum_{p=1}^{3} \alpha_{t_i^p}^j N_{t_i^p}|^2, \tag{1}$$

such that $\sum_{p=1}^{3} \alpha_{t_i^p}^j = 1$ and $\alpha_{t_i^p}^j \geq 0, \forall p \in \{1, 2, 3\}$. Each ground truth normal is approximated by $n^j \approx \sum_k \alpha_k^j N_k$, where 3 potentially non-zero coefficients α_k^j come from the corresponding problem (1) for the triplet in $t(j)$ and for all other coefficients $\alpha_k^j = 0$. In general, any reconstruction based local coding can be used.

3.2 Multi-class Boosting with Continuous Ground Truth Labels

A standard boosting algorithm builds a strong classifier $H(\mathbf{x}, l)$ for a feature vector $\mathbf{x}$ and a class label $l \in \mathcal{L}$ as a sum of weak classifiers $h(\mathbf{x}, l)$ as:

$$H(\mathbf{x}, l) = \sum_{m=1}^{M} h^{(m)}(\mathbf{x}, l), \tag{2}$$

where M is the number of iterations (boosts). The weak classifiers $h(\mathbf{x}, l)$ are typically found iteratively as: $H^{(m)}(\mathbf{x}, l) = H^{(m-1)}(\mathbf{x}, l) + h^{(m)}(\mathbf{x}, l)$.

Standard multi-class Ada-boost [44] with discrete labels minimizes the expected exponential loss:

$$J = \sum_{l \in \mathcal{L}} E\left[e^{-z^l H(\mathbf{x}, l)}\right], \tag{3}$$

where the $z_l \in \{-1, 1\}$ is the membership label for a class l. A natural extension to continuous ground truth labels is to minimize the weighted exponential loss defined as:

$$J = \sum_{l \in \mathcal{L}} E\left[\alpha_l e^{-H(\mathbf{x}, l)} + (1 - \alpha_l) e^{H(\mathbf{x}, l)}\right], \tag{4}$$

where α_l is the coefficient of a cluster mean l of the local coding, in our case corresponding to a reference normal. This cost function can be optimized using adaptive Newton steps by following the procedure in [40]. Each weak classifier $h^{(m)}(\mathbf{x}, l)$ is chosen to minimize the second order Taylor expansion approximation of the cost function (4). Replacing expectation by an empirical risk leads to a minimization of the error [40,44]:

$$J_{wse} = \sum_{l \in \mathcal{L}} \sum_j (\alpha_l^j e^{-H^{(m-1)}(\mathbf{x}^j, l)} (1 - h^{(m)}(\mathbf{x}^j, l))^2$$

$$+ (1 - \alpha_l^j) e^{H^{(m-1)}(\mathbf{x}^j, l)} (1 + h^{(m)}(\mathbf{x}^j, l))^2). \tag{5}$$

Defining two sets of weights:

$$w_l^{j,(m-1)} = \alpha_l^j e^{-H^{(m-1)}(\mathbf{x}^j,l)}, \tag{6}$$

$$v_l^{j,(m-1)} = (1 - \alpha_l^j) e^{H^{(m-1)}(\mathbf{x}^j,l)}, \tag{7}$$

the minimization problem transforms into:

$$J_{wse} = \sum_{l \in \mathcal{L}} \sum_j (w_l^{j,(m-1)}(1 - h^{(m)}(\mathbf{x}^j,l))^2 + v_l^{j,(m-1)}(1 + h^{(m)}(\mathbf{x}^j,l))^2). \tag{8}$$

The weights are initialized to $w_l^{j,(0)} = \alpha_l^j$ and $v_l^{j,(0)} = 1 - \alpha_l^j$ and updated iteratively as:

$$w_l^{j,(m)} = w_l^{j,(m-1)} e^{-h^{(m)}(\mathbf{x}^j,l)}, \tag{9}$$

$$v_l^{j,(m)} = v_l^{j,(m-1)} e^{h^{(m)}(\mathbf{x}^j,l)}. \tag{10}$$

The most common weak classifier for multi-class boosting are generalized decision stumps, defined as [44]:

$$h^{(m)}(\mathbf{x}, l) = \begin{cases} a^{(m)}\delta(x_{i^{(m)}} > \theta^{(m)}) + b^{(m)} & \text{if } l \in \mathcal{L}^{(m)} \\ k_l^{(m)} & \text{otherwise,} \end{cases} \tag{11}$$

where $x_{i^{(m)}}$ is one particular dimension of $\mathbf{x}$, $\mathcal{L}^{(m)} \subseteq \mathcal{L}$ is the subset of labels the decision stump is applied to; and $i^{(m)}$, $a^{(m)}$, $b^{(m)}$, $k_l^{(m)}$ and $\theta^{(m)}$ parameters of the weak classifier.

In each iteration the most discriminant weak classifier is found by randomly sampling dimensions $i^{(m)}$ and thresholds $\theta^{(m)}$ and calculating the set of remaining parameters $a^{(m)}$, $b^{(m)}$, $k_l^{(m)}$ and $\mathcal{L}^{(m)}$ by minimising the cost function (8). The parameters $a^{(m)}$, $b^{(m)}$ and $k_l^{(m)}$ are derived by setting the derivative of (8) to 0, leading to a close form solution:

$$b^{(m)} = \frac{\sum_{l \in \mathcal{L}^{(m)}} \sum_j (w_l^{j,(m-1)} - v_l^{j,(m-1)})\delta(x_{i^{(m)}} \le \theta^{(m)})}{\sum_{l \in \mathcal{L}^{(m)}} \sum_j (w_l^{j,(m-1)} + v_l^{j,(m-1)})\delta(x_{i^{(m)}} \le \theta^{(m)})}, \tag{12}$$

$$a^{(m)} = \frac{\sum_{l \in \mathcal{L}^{(m)}} \sum_j (w_l^{j,(m-1)} - v_l^{j,(m-1)})\delta(x_{i^{(m)}} > \theta^{(m)})}{\sum_{l \in \mathcal{L}^{(m)}} \sum_j (w_l^{j,(m-1)} + v_l^{j,(m-1)})\delta(x_{i^{(m)}} > \theta^{(m)})} - b^{(m)}, \tag{13}$$

$$k_l^{(m)} = \frac{\sum_j (w_l^{j,(m-1)} - v_l^{j,(m-1)})}{\sum_j (w_l^{j,(m-1)} + v_l^{j,(m-1)})}, \forall l \notin \mathcal{L}^{(m)}. \tag{14}$$

The subset of labels $\mathcal{L}^{(m)}$ is found greedily by iterative inclusion of additional labels, if they decrease the cost function (8).

3.3   Prediction of the Surface Normal

During test time the responses $H(\mathbf{x}, l)$ for each reference normal are evaluated and the most probable triangle is selected by maximizing:

$$t(\mathbf{x}) = \arg\max_{t_i \in T} \sum_{p=1}^{3} e^{H(\mathbf{x}, t_i^p)}. \tag{15}$$

The non-zero local coding coefficients for each index k of a triangle $t(\mathbf{x})$ are obtained as:

$$\alpha^j_{t(\mathbf{x})^k} = \frac{e^{H(\mathbf{x}, t(\mathbf{x})^k)}}{\sum_{p=1}^{3} e^{H(\mathbf{x}, t(\mathbf{x})^p)}}, \tag{16}$$

and the resulting normal $n^j(\mathbf{x})$ for a pixel j is recovered by computing the linear combination projected to the unit sphere:

$$n^j(\mathbf{x}) = \frac{\sum_{p=1}^{3} \alpha^j_{t(\mathbf{x})^p} N_{t(\mathbf{x})^p}}{|\sum_{p=1}^{3} \alpha^j_{t(\mathbf{x})^p} N_{t(\mathbf{x})^p}|}, \tag{17}$$

corresponding to the expected value under standard probabilistic interpretation of boosted classifier [40]. Weighted prediction leads to better performance both qualitatively and quantitatively (see Figure 6).

4   Implementation Details

The complete work flow of our method is shown in the Figure 1. In our implementation four dense features were extracted for each pixel in each image - texton [45], SIFT [46], local quantized ternary patters [47] and self-similarity features [48]. Each feature was clustered into 512 visual words using k-means clustering, and for each pixel a soft assignment for 8 nearest cluster centres is calculated using distance-based exponential kernel weighting [49]. The rectangle-based contextual part of the feature representation consists of a concatenation of soft-weighted bag-of-words representations over 200 rectangles, resulting in $200 \times 4 \times 512$ dimensional feature vector $\mathbf{x}^j_{CXT}$. The Segment-based part $\mathbf{x}^j_{SEG}$ consists of soft-weighted bag-of-words representations over 16 unsupervised segmentations obtained by varying kernel parameters of 4 different methods, 4 segmentations each - Mean-shift [20], SLIC [23], normalized cut [21] and graph-cut based segmentation [22]. In the boosting process, the same number of dimensions from the contextual and segment part of the feature representation were sampled in each iteration, to balance different dimensionality of these representations. This was achieved by increasing the sampling probability of each dimension of the segment-part $\frac{200}{16}$ times. The strong classifier consisted of 5000 weak classifiers. The whole learning procedure has been applied independently for 5 different colour models - RGB, Lab, Luv, Opponent and GreyScale. Each individual classifier was expected to perform approximately the same, and thus the final classifier response was simply averaged over these 5 classifiers without any additional training of weights for each individual colour space. In practice this averaging procedure has similar effects to the use of multiple decision trees in the random forest; it leads to smoother results and avoids over-fitting to noise.

5   Ground Truth Acquisition

Required ground truth measurements about the underlying 3D scene geometry can be captured with active devices, such as laser scanners, commodity depth sensors, stereo cameras or from dense 3D reconstructions of image collections. In all cases the depth measurements are likely to contain noise, which will get amplified in their first derivatives. Since our aim is to obtain piecewise constant normal directions – as reflected typically in man-made environments – we leverage (second order) Total Generalized Variation (TGV) [50] for denoising. The optimization is formulated as a primal-dual saddle point problem and solved via iterative optimization; for more detail we refer the interested reader to [51]. Normals are then computed on the 3D point cloud for each point in a local 3D spatial neighborhood. Compared to computations on the depth map itself, this guarantees that measurements of distant structures in 3D which project to neighboring pixels do not get intermixed. Finally, for point-wise normal estimation we utilize a least squares regression kernel in a RANSAC scheme in order to preserve surface edges. Given the quality of the depth data, obtained ground truth normals look visually significantly better than the direct first derivatives of the original raw depth data. However, the quality of normals often degrades in the presence of reflective surfaces, near image edges or in regions without sufficient amount of direct depth measurements.

6   Experiments

We trained our classifier on the indoor NYU2 [7] and on the outdoor KITTI [8] data set to demonstrate the ability of our method to predict normals in various man-made environments.

6.1   NYU2 Data Set

The NYU2 data set [7] consists of 795 training and 654 test images of resolution 640×480, containing pixel-wise depth obtained by a Kinect sensor. The data set covers a wide range of types of indoor scenes, such as offices, bedrooms, living rooms, kitchens or bathrooms. To train the classifier, the ground truth normals were clustered into 40 reference normals. The mean angle between neighbouring reference normals was 18 degrees. The training of the classifier took three weeks on five 8-core machines. Thus, the parameters of our method (such as number of normal clusters, segmentations or boosts) have been chosen based on our expert knowledge and not tweaked at all. The evaluation took 40 minutes per image on

Input Image   Our result   Ground Truth | Input Image   Our result   Ground Truth

Fig. 3. Qualitative results on NYU2 data set. The colours, corresponding to different normals, are shown in Figure 1. Our algorithm consistently predicted high quality surface normals for a single image. Note, the imperfect quality of the ground truth labelling (see for example the image in bottom-right).

Input Image   Our result   3DP [12] result   Input Image   Our result   3DP [12] result

Fig. 4. Qualitative comparison of our method with 3DP [12] on the RMRC data set. Both methods were trained on the NYU2 training data. Several images of RMRC data set were taken from unusual viewpoints, not present in the NYU2 data set, causing troubles to both methods.

Input Image   Our result   Input Image   Our result   Input Image   Our result

Fig. 5. Additional results of our method using the classifier trained on NYU2 data set

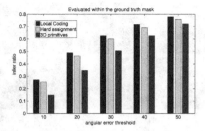 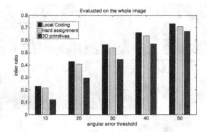

Fig. 6. Quantitative comparison of locally coded and hard assigned version of our method with 3DP [12] method on the NYU2 data set. The performance is evaluated in term of ratio of pixels within different angular error (10, 20, 30, 40 and 50) and calculated either over the masks, corresponding to the regions with direct depth measurements; or over the whole image. Our method estimated approximately half of normals in the masked region within 20 degree error. The numbers do not fully reflect the quality of our results due to the imperfection of the ground truth (see Figure 3).

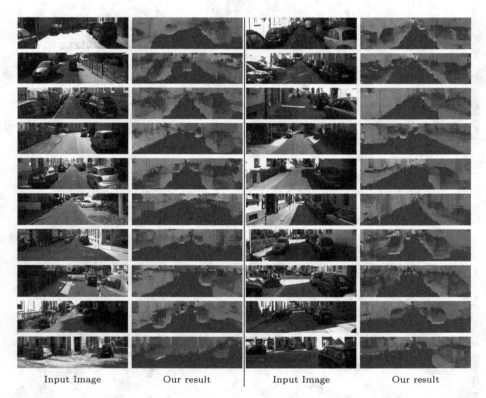

Input Image   Our result   Input Image   Our result

Fig. 7. Qualitative results of our method on the KITTI data set. The ground truth colours are the same as for the NYU2 data set. Our classifier essentially learnt the typical geometrical layout of the scene and the spatial configuration of surface normals of cars seen from various viewpoints.

a single core; however, it can be easily parallelized. The results are significantly better than initially expected. Our classifier consistently managed to successfully predict normals for various complicated indoor environments. The qualitative results are shown in Figure 3. Quantitative comparisons of our classifier (weighted by local coding coefficients and hard-assigned to the normal cluster with the highest response) to the state-of-the-art [12] are shown in Figure 6. The results are reported for full images (561×427 sub-window) and on the masks (as in [12]), that define the regions containing direct depth measurements. Approximately for one half of the pixels in the masks the predicted normals were within 20 degrees angle. The numbers do not reflect the quality of our results, because even in a flat surfaces the normals of the ground truth often vary by 10 or 20 degrees (see for example the ground truth of the bottom-right image in Figure 3). To get an idea of the interpretation of the error, the average angular error of the visually very appealing result on the test image in Figure 1 is 28 degrees.

The success of our method on this data set lead us to further experiments using the already trained classifier. We applied it to the Reconstruction-Meets-Recognition depth challenge (RMRC) data set [52], consisting of 558 images. Qualitative comparisons with the method [12] are shown in Figure 4. Ground truth depth images are not publicly available. Our method was able to successfully predict normals for images that looked visually similar to the NYU2 data. However, for images, that were not taken upright (as in NYU2), our classifier predicted normals as if they were. We evaluated our classifier also on images captured by ourselves, see Figure 5.

6.2   KITTI Data Set

The KITTI depth data set [8] consists of 194 training images and 195 test outdoor images, containing sparse disparity maps obtained by a Velodyne laser scanner. The distribution of normals within an image seemed much more predictable than for indoor scenes, due to a very typical image layout and lower variety of normals. Thus, to train a classifier we clustered normals only into 20 clusters. The training took five days on five 8-core machines. The evaluation took 20 minutes per image on a single core. Qualitative results are shown in Figure 7. The ground truth depths are not publicly available, thus we do not provide any quantitative results.

7   Conclusions and Future Work

In this paper we proposed a method for dense normal estimation from RGB images by combining state-of-the-art context-based and segment-based cues in a continuous Ada-Boost framework. The results have the potential to be applied to several other reconstruction problems in computer vision, such as stereo, single-view or 3D volumetric reconstruction, as a geometric prior for their regularization. In the future we would like to do further research along these lines.

References

1. Hoiem, D., Efros, A.A., Hebert, M.: Putting objects in perspective. In: Conference on Computer Vision and Pattern Recognition (2006)
2. Ladicky, L., Shi, J., Pollefeys, M.: Pulling things out of perspective. In: Conference on Computer Vision and Pattern Recognition (2014)
3. Hoiem, D., Efros, A.A., Hebert, M.: Closing the loop on scene interpretation. In: Conference on Computer Vision and Pattern Recognition (2008)
4. Saxena, A., Chung, S.H., Ng, A.Y.: 3-D Depth Reconstruction from a Single Still Image. International Journal of Computer Vision (2007)
5. Saxena, A., Sun, M., Ng, A.Y.: Make3D: learning 3D scene structure from a single still image. Transactions on Pattern Analysis and Machine Intelligence (2009)
6. Liu, B., Gould, S., Koller, D.: Single image depth estimation from predicted semantic labels. In: Conference on Computer Vision and Pattern Recognition (2010)
7. Silberman, N., Hoiem, D., Kohli, P., Fergus, R.: Indoor segmentation and support inference from RGBD images. In: Fitzgibbon, A., Lazebnik, S., Perona, P., Sato, Y., Schmid, C. (eds.) ECCV 2012, Part V. LNCS, vol. 7576, pp. 746–760. Springer, Heidelberg (2012)
8. Geiger, A., Lenz, P., Urtasun, R.: Are we ready for autonomous driving? the kitti vision benchmark suite. In: Conference on Computer Vision and Pattern Recognition (2012)
9. Horn, B.K.P., Brooks, M.J. (eds.): Shape from Shading. MIT Press (1989)
10. Mallick, S.P., Zickler, T.E., Kriegman, D.J., Belhumeur, P.N.: Beyond lambert: reconstructing specular surfaces using color. In: Conference on Computer Vision and Pattern Recognition (2005)
11. Ikehata, S., Aizawa, K.: Photometric stereo using constrained bivariate regression for general isotropic surfaces. In: Conference on Computer Vision and Pattern Recognition (2014)
12. Fouhey, D., Gupta, A., Hebert, M.: Data-driven 3d primitives for single image understanding. In: International Conference on Computer Vision (2013)
13. Hoiem, D., Efros, A.A., Hebert, M.: Recovering Surface Layout from an Image. International Journal of Computer Vision (2007)
14. Gupta, A., Efros, A.A., Hebert, M.: Blocks world revisited: Image understanding using qualitative geometry and mechanics. In: Daniilidis, K., Maragos, P., Paragios, N. (eds.) ECCV 2010, Part IV. LNCS, vol. 6314, pp. 482–496. Springer, Heidelberg (2010)
15. Delage, E., Lee, H., Ng, A.: A Dynamic Bayesian Network Model for Autonomous 3D Reconstruction from a Single Indoor Image. In: Conference on Computer Vision and Pattern Recognition (2006)
16. Barinova, O., Konushin, V., Yakubenko, A., Lee, K., Lim, H., Konushin, A.: Fast Automatic Single-View 3-d Reconstruction of Urban Scenes. In: Forsyth, D., Torr, P., Zisserman, A. (eds.) ECCV 2008, Part II. LNCS, vol. 5303, pp. 100–113. Springer, Heidelberg (2008)
17. Lee, D.C., Hebert, M., Kanade, T.: Geometric reasoning for single image structure recovery. In: Conference on Computer Vision and Pattern Recognition (2009)
18. Flint, A., Mei, C., Reid, I., Murray, D.: Growing semantically meaningful models for visual SLAM. In: Conference on Computer Vision and Pattern Recognition (2010)

19. Flint, A., Mei, C., Murray, D., Reid, I.: A dynamic programming approach to reconstructing building interiors. In: Daniilidis, K., Maragos, P., Paragios, N. (eds.) ECCV 2010, Part V. LNCS, vol. 6315, pp. 394–407. Springer, Heidelberg (2010)
20. Comaniciu, D., Meer, P.: Mean shift: A robust approach toward feature space analysis. Transactions on Pattern Analysis and Machine Intelligence (2002)
21. Shi, J., Malik, J.: Normalized cuts and image segmentation. Transactions on Pattern Analysis and Machine Intelligence (2000)
22. Zhang, Y., Hartley, R.I., Mashford, J., Burn, S.: Superpixels via pseudo-boolean optimization. In: International Conference on Computer Vision (2011)
23. Achanta, R., Shaji, A., Smith, K., Lucchi, A., Fua, P., Susstrunk, S.: SLIC superpixels compared to state-of-the-art superpixel methods. Transactions on Pattern Analysis and Machine Intelligence (2012)
24. Shotton, J., Winn, J.M., Rother, C., Criminisi, A.: textonBoost: Joint appearance, shape and context modeling for multi-class object recognition and segmentation. In: Leonardis, A., Bischof, H., Pinz, A. (eds.) ECCV 2006, Part I. LNCS, vol. 3951, pp. 1–15. Springer, Heidelberg (2006)
25. Shotton, J., Johnson, M., Cipolla, R.: Semantic texton forests for image categorization and segmentation. In: Conference on Computer Vision and Pattern Recognition (2008)
26. Shotton, J., Fitzgibbon, A., Cook, M., Blake, A.: Real-time human pose recognition in parts from single depth images. In: Conference on Computer Vision and Pattern Recognition (2011)
27. Ladicky, L., Russell, C., Kohli, P., Torr, P.H.S.: Associative hierarchical CRFs for object class image segmentation. In: International Conference on Computer Vision (2009)
28. Kohli, P., Ladicky, L., Torr, P.H.S.: Robust higher order potentials for enforcing label consistency. In: Conference on Computer Vision and Pattern Recognition (2008)
29. Yang, L., Meer, P., Foran, D.J.: Multiple class segmentation using a unified framework over mean-shift patches. In: Conference on Computer Vision and Pattern Recognition (2007)
30. Batra, D., Sukthankar, R., Tsuhan, C.: Learning class-specific affinities for image labelling. In: Conference on Computer Vision and Pattern Recognition (2008)
31. Galleguillos, C., Rabinovich, A., Belongie, S.: Object categorization using co-occurrence, location and appearance. In: Conference on Computer Vision and Pattern Recognition (2008)
32. Boix, X., Cardinal, G., van de Weijer, J., Bagdanov, A.D., Serrat, J., Gonzalez, J.: Harmony potentials: Fusing global and local scale for semantic image segmentation. International Journal on Computer Vision (2011)
33. Guyon, I., Boser, B., Vapnik, V.: Automatic capacity tuning of very large vc-dimension classifiers. In: Advances in Neural Information Processing Systems (1993)
34. Perronnin, F., Sánchez, J., Mensink, T.: Improving the fisher kernel for large-scale image classification. In: Daniilidis, K., Maragos, P., Paragios, N. (eds.) ECCV 2010, Part IV. LNCS, vol. 6314, pp. 143–156. Springer, Heidelberg (2010)
35. Zhou, X., Yu, K., Zhang, T., Huang, T.S.: Image classification using super-vector coding of local image descriptors. In: Daniilidis, K., Maragos, P., Paragios, N. (eds.) ECCV 2010, Part V. LNCS, vol. 6315, pp. 141–154. Springer, Heidelberg (2010)

36. Carreira, J., Caseiro, R., Batista, J., Sminchisescu, C.: Semantic Segmentation with Second-Order Pooling. In: Fitzgibbon, A., Lazebnik, S., Perona, P., Sato, Y., Schmid, C. (eds.) ECCV 2012, Part VII. LNCS, vol. 7578, pp. 430–443. Springer, Heidelberg (2012)

37. Rabinovich, A., Vedaldi, A., Galleguillos, C., Wiewiora, E., Belongie, S.: Objects in context. In: International Conference on Computer Vision (2007)

38. Pantofaru, C., Schmid, C., Hebert, M.: Object recognition by integrating multiple image segmentations. In: Forsyth, D., Torr, P., Zisserman, A. (eds.) ECCV 2008, Part III. LNCS, vol. 5304, pp. 481–494. Springer, Heidelberg (2008)

39. Breiman, L.: Random forests. In: Machine Learning (2001)

40. Friedman, J., Hastie, T., Tibshirani, R.: Additive Logistic Regression: a Statistical View of Boosting. The Annals of Statistics (2000)

41. Roweis, S.T., Saul, L.K.: Nonlinear dimensionality reduction by locally linear embedding. Science (2000)

42. Yu, K., Zhang, T., Gong, Y.: Nonlinear learning using local coordinate coding. In: Advances in Neural Information Processing Systems (2009)

43. Wang, J., Yang, J., Yu, K., Lv, F., Huang, T.S., Gong, Y.: Locality-constrained linear coding for image classification. In: Conference on Computer Vision and Pattern Recognition (2010)

44. Torralba, A., Murphy, K., Freeman, W.: Sharing features: efficient boosting procedures for multiclass object detection. In: Conference on Computer Vision and Pattern Recognition (2004)

45. Malik, J., Belongie, S., Leung, T., Shi, J.: Contour and texture analysis for image segmentation. International Journal of Computer Vision (2001)

46. Lowe, D.G.: Distinctive image features from scale-invariant keypoints. International Journal of Computer Vision (2004)

47. Hussain, S.u., Triggs, B.: Visual Recognition Using Local Quantized Patterns. In: Fitzgibbon, A., Lazebnik, S., Perona, P., Sato, Y., Schmid, C. (eds.) ECCV 2012, Part II. LNCS, vol. 7573, pp. 716–729. Springer, Heidelberg (2012)

48. Shechtman, E., Irani, M.: Matching local self-similarities across images and videos. In: Conference on Computer Vision and Pattern Recognition (2007)

49. van Gemert, J.C., Geusebroek, J.-M., Veenman, C.J., Smeulders, A.W.M.: Kernel codebooks for scene categorization. In: Forsyth, D., Torr, P., Zisserman, A. (eds.) ECCV 2008, Part III. LNCS, vol. 5304, pp. 696–709. Springer, Heidelberg (2008)

50. Bredies, K., Kunisch, K., Pock, T.: Total Generalized Variation. SIAM Journal on Imaging Sciences 3, 492–526 (2010)

51. Chambolle, A., Pock, T.: A First-Order Primal-Dual Algorithm for Convex Problems with Applications to Imaging. Journal of Mathematical Imaging and Vision (2010)

52. Urtasun, R., Fergus, R., Hoiem, D., Torralba, A., Geiger, A., Lenz, P., Silberman, N., Xiao, J., Fidler, S.: Reconstruction Meets Recognition Challenge (2013), http://ttic.uchicago.edu/~rurtasun/rmrc/

Numerical Inversion of SRNFs for Efficient Elastic Shape Analysis of Star-Shaped Objects

Qian Xie[1], Ian Jermyn[2], Sebastian Kurtek[3], and Anuj Srivastava[1]

[1] Florida State University, Tallahassee, Florida, United States
qxie@stat.fsu.edu, anuj@fsu.edu
[2] Durham University, Durham, County Durham DH1, United Kingdom
ian.jermyn@inria.fr
[3] Ohio State University, Columbus, Ohio, United States
kurtek.1@stat.osu.edu

Abstract. The elastic shape analysis of surfaces has proven useful in several application areas, including medical image analysis, vision, and graphics. This approach is based on defining new mathematical representations of parameterized surfaces, including the square root normal field (SRNF), and then using the $\mathbb{L}^2$ norm to compare their shapes. Past work is based on using the pullback of the $\mathbb{L}^2$ metric to the space of surfaces, performing statistical analysis under this induced Riemannian metric. However, if one can estimate the inverse of the SRNF mapping, even approximately, a very efficient framework results: the surfaces, represented by their SRNFs, can be efficiently analyzed using standard Euclidean tools, and only the final results need be mapped back to the surface space. Here we describe a procedure for inverting SRNF maps of star-shaped surfaces, a special case for which analytic results can be obtained. We test our method via the classification of 34 cases of ADHD (Attention Deficit Hyperactivity Disorder), plus controls, in the Detroit Fetal Alcohol and Drug Exposure Cohort study. We obtain state-of-the-art results.

Keywords: Statistical shape analysis, elastic shape analysis, parameterized surface, geodesic computation, deformation analysis.

1 Introduction

The analysis of the shapes of 3D objects is an important area of research with a wide variety of applications. The need for shape analysis arises in many branches of science, for example, medical image analysis, protein structure analysis, computer graphics, and 3D printing and prototyping. Many of these are especially concerned with capturing variability within and across shape classes, and so the main focus of research has been on statistical shape analysis and on comparing shapes [2,22,28]. The main differences among the different approaches proposed so far lie in the mathematical representations and metrics used in the analysis. One may use chosen landmarks to represent shapes, and perform Kendall-type shape analysis [8], or use point clouds and apply thin plate splines or ICP [3]. One may represent shapes using medial surfaces [4], level sets [21], or deformable templates [11]. However, the most natural representation for studying

D. Fleet et al. (Eds.): ECCV 2014, Part V, LNCS 8693, pp. 485–499, 2014.

the shapes of 3D objects would seem to be their continuous boundaries. Windheuser et al. [26] solve a dense registration problem, but use linear interpolation between registered pairs of points in $\mathbb{R}^3$ to compute geodesic paths. Kilian et al. [17] represent parameterized surfaces by discrete triangulated meshes, assume a Riemannian metric on the space of such meshes, and compute geodesic paths between given meshes. The method has the limitation that it assumes the correspondence between points on the two meshes to be known. Heeren et al. [12] propose a method to compute geodesic-based deformations of thin shell shapes. Some papers use SPHARM or SPHARM-PDM [5,24] to tackle this problem by choosing a fixed arc-length type parameterization. This is a major restriction, and does not allow elastic shape analysis of surfaces. They also assume that the surfaces are already in full correspondence. A large set of papers in the literature treat the parameterization (or registration) and comparison steps in a disjoint manner [4,29,10,7,25]. In other words, they take a set of surfaces and use some energy function, such as the entropy or the minimum description length, to register points across surfaces. Once the surfaces are registered, they are compared using standard procedures. Because these two steps are often performed under different metrics, the resulting registrations and shape comparisons tend to be suboptimal.

Recently there has been increasing interest in frameworks for studying the shapes of parameterized surfaces, and in particular in methods that provide invariance to shape-preserving transformations such as rigid motions, global scaling, and reparameterizations. These frameworks are predominantly Riemannian: one identifies an appropriate representation space for the relevant surfaces, endows it with a Riemannian metric, and develops an algorithm for computing geodesic paths under that metric. Invariance to shape-preserving transformations is obtained by forming quotient spaces under these groups, and geodesic calculations are then transferred to this quotient space using an *alignment* step. The key idea is to choose a mathematical representation and an associated Riemannian metric so that the desired invariances are obtained, and geodesic computations are rendered simple. This has been achieved in the shape analysis of **curves** by using as representation and metric, the *square-root velocity function (SRVF)* and a particular member of the family of *elastic metrics*: the resulting metric in the SRVF space is then the $\mathbb{L}^2$ metric [23]. The $\mathbb{L}^2$ metric greatly simplifies computations, and enables sophisticated statistical analyses that require fast geodesic calculations. Critical to its utility is the fact that the mapping from the space of curves to the SRVF space is a bijection (up to a translation). Solutions found in SRVF space using the $\mathbb{L}^2$ metric can thus be uniquely mapped back to the original curve space, which is significantly more efficient than calculating in the curve space itself. This paper contributes to the search for a similarly efficient framework for the shape analysis of **surfaces**.

Kurtek et al. [18,20] took the first steps in this direction. Let $f : \mathbf{S}^2 \to \mathbb{R}^3$ be a parameterized surface and let $\mathcal{F}$ be the space of all such smooth mappings. Suppose $\mathbf{S}^2$ is parameterized by the pair $s \equiv (u, v)$ for all $s \in \mathbf{S}^2$. Kurtek et al. introduced a surface representation defined by $q(s) = \sqrt{|n(s)|} f(s)$, where $n(s) = f_u(s) \times f_v(s)$ is the unnormalized normal to the surface at $f(s)$; this was termed the *square-root map* (SRM). Equipping the space of SRMs with the $\mathbb{L}^2$ metric greatly simplifies geodesic calculations, and also has the crucial property that Γ, the group of all orientation-preserving diffeomorphisms of $\mathbf{S}^2$, acts by isometries. Unfortunately, the representation has several limitations, including that the metric distance between two shapes changes if they are both translated by the same amount; that it is difficult to invert (indeed may not have an inverse); and that the metric has no clear physical interpretation in terms of surfaces.

Jermyn et al. [16] introduced a new representation that avoids some of the limitations of the SRM, while preserving its advantages: the *square-root normal field* (SRNF) sends $f \mapsto Q(f)$, where $Q(f)(s) \equiv n(s)/|n(s)|^{1/2}$. Equipping the space of SRNFs, $\mathcal{Q}$, with the $\mathbb{L}^2$ metric again trivializes geodesic calculations, and Γ again acts by isometries. Now, however, the representation is translation invariant by definition, while the $\mathbb{L}^2$ metric on $\mathcal{Q}$ corresponds to a partial elastic Riemannian metric on $\mathcal{F}$ strictly analogous to the elastic metric used in the case of curves.

The SRNF shares one difficulty with the SRM, however, and that is the problem of inversion. Knowing $Q(f)$ is equivalent to knowing the Gauss map $\tilde{n} = n/|n|$ and the induced measure $|n|^{1/2}$. While the Gauss map together with the induced *metric* is sufficient to reconstruct the surface up to translations and rotations [1,9] (or in combination with only the conformal class of the metric, up to translations, rotations and scale [13]), it is not clear that Q is injective up to simple transformations.[1] (In addition, Q is almost certainly not surjective, a point to which we will return.) If one cannot invert the representation, geodesics and statistical analyses conducted in $\mathcal{Q}$ cannot be moved back to $\mathcal{F}$. One can always pull the $\mathbb{L}^2$ metric back to $\mathcal{F}$ and perform computations there [27], but this defeats the purpose of introducing the representation and the $\mathbb{L}^2$ metric on it.

An alternative is to proceed pragmatically, supposing invertibility until it creates problems. (It is worth noting that even if f is not unique given $Q(f)$, the distance between any two such surfaces is zero, and thus any two geodesics in $\mathcal{F}$ mapping to a geodesic in $\mathcal{Q}$ will have the same length.) We take this pragmatic approach in this paper. The problem we wish to solve is this: Given $q \in \mathcal{Q}$, find $f \in \mathcal{F}$ such that $Q(f) = q$. Were it solved, geodesics, mean shapes, PCA, etc. could be computed in $\mathcal{Q}$ under the $\mathbb{L}^2$ metric and then mapped back to $\mathcal{F}$, just as is possible in the case of curves using the SRVF, with resulting large gains in computational efficiency with respect to *e.g.* [16,27]. For general surfaces, this can only be done numerically. We develop a numerical method to find such an f if it exists, and to find the closest (in the elastic metric) f to the set $Q^{-1}(q)$ if it does not. This numerical procedure is expensive, however, and in this paper we do not use it directly to invert Q for general surfaces. Rather, we show that for an important subset of surfaces, an *analytic* solution exists to the inversion problem. These are the 'star-shaped' surfaces, *i.e.* those whose enclosed volumes are star domains, a large family of surfaces with great relevance for many real problems. Combining the analytic result with the numerical procedure, we are able to compute geodesics and perform statistical analyses in the space of star-shaped surfaces in a very efficient manner: in fact the computational cost is reduced by an order of magnitude.

The paper is organized as follows. Section 2 gives an overview of the statistical tasks we use as points of comparison, and describes algorithms for these tasks under previous and proposed methods. Section 3 describes the analytic solution to the inversion

---

[1] It is not simply a case of applying Bonnet's theorem, because in addition to dn, the second fundamental form involves the derivative df, which is the quantity we are trying to find.

problem, while Section 4 describes the algorithms in detail. Section 5 describes the use of the methods for the classification of subjects with Attention Deficit Hyperactivity Disorder (ADHD) using the shapes of brain subcortical structures, and demonstrates state-of-the-art classification results at greatly reduced computational cost.

2   Model Problems

In order to illustrate the advantages of the new methods, we have selected as points of comparison, several algorithmic and computational tasks that are fundamental to statistical shape analysis:

1. **Geodesic Path Construction**: Given two surfaces f_1 and f_2, one wants to construct a geodesic path $\alpha(t)$ s.t. $\alpha(0) = f_1$ and $\alpha(1) = f_2$.
2. **Shooting Geodesics**: Given a surface f and a tangent vector v_0 at f, one wants to construct a geodesic path $\alpha(t)$ s.t. $\alpha(0) = f$ and $\dot{\alpha}(0) = v$.
3. **Statistical Summaries of Shapes**: Given a sample of observed surfaces $f_1, \ldots, f_n$, one wants to estimate the mean shape and principal directions of variation.
4. **Random Sampling from Shape Models**: Given a sample of observed surfaces $f_1, \ldots, f_n$, one wants to fit a probability model to the data and sample random shapes from it.
5. **Transferring Deformations between Shapes**: Given surfaces f_1, h_1 and f_2, one wants to find h_2 such that f_2 deforms to it in a similar way f_1 deforms to h_1.

Table 1 outlines the algorithms for performing these tasks using both previous and the proposed methods. Computationally intensive steps are underlined, and the computational complexity is indicated in boxes.

3   The Inversion Problem

In order to exploit the SRNF to full advantage, we need to be able to find a surface f such that $Q(f) = q$. In this section, we describe solutions to this problem, first for arbitrary surfaces, and then for star-shaped surfaces.

3.1   General Surfaces

We formulate the inversion problem as an optimization problem by defining an energy function $E_0 : \mathcal{F} \to \mathbb{R}_+$ such that

$$E_0(f; q) = \|Q(f) - q\|_2^2 . \tag{1}$$

Finding an $f \in \mathcal{F}$ such that $Q(f) = q$ is then equivalent to seeking zeros of E_0. If no such f exists, then a minimizer of E will be a nearest such f under the elastic metric. We define $f^* = \arg\min_{f \in \mathcal{F}} E_0(f; q)$.

Minimization is performed using a gradient descent approach. Since $\mathcal{F}$ is an infinite-dimensional vector space, we will approximate the gradient using a finite basis for $\mathcal{F}$. From a computational point of view, it may be easier to express the deformation of

Table 1. Comparison of Algorithms

	Previous	Proposed
Karcher Mean	**Algorithm 1** *Let μ_f^0 be an initial estimate. Set $j = 0$.* 1. *Register $f_1, \ldots, f_n$ to μ_f^j.* 2. *For each $i = 1, \ldots, n$, construct a <u>geodesic</u> to connect f_i to μ_f^j and evaluate $v_i = \exp_{\mu_f^j}^{-1}(q_i)$.* 3. *Compute the average direction $\bar{v} = \frac{1}{n}\sum_{i=1}^{n} v_i$.* 4. *If $\|\bar{v}\|$ is small, stop. Else, update $\mu_f^{j+1} = \exp_{\mu_f^j}(\epsilon\bar{v})$ by shooting a <u>geodesic</u>, $\epsilon \dot{\iota} 0$, small.* 5. *Set $j = j + 1$ and return to Step 1.* $\boxed{n \text{ geodesics per iteration}}$	**Algorithm 2** *Let $\bar{q} = Q(\mu_f^0)$ with μ_f^0 as an initial estimate. Set $j = 0$.* 1. *Register $Q(f_1), \ldots, Q(f_n)$ to $\bar{q}$.* 2. *Update the average $\bar{q} = \frac{1}{n}\sum_{i=1}^{n} q_i$.* 3. *If change in $\|\bar{q}\|$ is small, stop. Else, set $j = j + 1$ and return to Step 1.* *Find μ_f by <u>inversion</u> s.t. $Q(\mu_f) = \bar{q}$.* $\boxed{1 \text{ inversion}}$
Parallel Transport	**Algorithm 3** *Find a <u>geodesic</u> $\alpha(t)$ connecting f_1 to f_2. For $\tau = 1, \ldots, m$, do the following.* 1. *<u>Parallel transport</u> $V(\frac{\tau-1}{m})$ from $\alpha(\frac{\tau-1}{m})$ to $\alpha(\frac{\tau}{m})$ and name it $V(\frac{\tau}{m})$.* *Set $v^{\|} = V(1)$.* $\boxed{1 \text{ geodesic} + m \text{ parallel transports}}$	**Algorithm 4** *Parallel transport on $\mathbb{L}^2$ remains constant.* 1. *Compute $w = Q_{*,f_1}(v)$ (differential of the mapping Q).* 2. *Find f by <u>inversion</u> s.t. $Q(f) = Q(f_2) + \epsilon w$, ϵ is small.* 3. *Evaluate $\frac{f-f_2}{\epsilon}$ and set it to be $v^{\|}$.* $\boxed{1 \text{ inversion}}$
Transfer Deformation	**Algorithm 5** 1. *Find a <u>geodesic</u> $\beta(t)$ connecting f_1 to h_1 and evaluate $v = \exp_{f_1}^{-1}(h_1)$.* 2. *Find a <u>geodesic</u> $\alpha(t)$ connecting f_1 to f_2. Set $V(0) = v$. For $\tau = 1, \ldots, m$, do the following.* (a) *<u>Parallel transport</u> $V(\frac{\tau-1}{m})$ from $\alpha(\frac{\tau-1}{m})$ to $\alpha(\frac{\tau}{m})$ and name it $V(\frac{\tau}{m})$.* 3. *Shoot a <u>geodesic</u> $\beta'(t)$ from f_2 with velocity $v^{\|} = V(1)$ and set $h_2 = \beta'(1)$.* $\boxed{3 \text{ geodesics} + m \text{ parallel transports}}$	**Algorithm 6** *Parallel transport on $\mathbb{L}^2$ remains constant.* 1. *Compute $v = Q(h_1) - Q(f_1)$.* 2. *Find h_2 by <u>inversion</u> s.t. $Q(h_2) = Q(f_2) + v$.* $\boxed{1 \text{ inversion}}$

a surface, rather than the surface itself, using a basis. We therefore set $f = f_0 + w$, where $w = \sum_{b \in \mathcal{B}} \alpha_b b$, with $\alpha_b \in \mathbb{R}$, and where $\mathcal{B}$ forms an orthonormal basis of $\mathcal{F}$. (In practice, we use spherical harmonics.) Here f_0 denotes the current estimate of f^*, and w is a deformation of f_0. Then, we minimize the new energy

$$E(w; q) = \|Q(f_0 + w) - q\|_2^2 , \tag{2}$$

with respect to w. One can view f_0 as an initial guess of the solution or a known surface with shape similar to the one being estimated. If no initial guess is possible, one can initialize f_0 as a unit sphere or even set $f_0 = 0$.

We need to evaluate the directional derivatives of E. The directional derivative of E at $f_0 + w$ in the direction of b, $\nabla_b E(w; q)$, is given by:

$$\nabla_b E(w; q, f_0) = \frac{d}{d\epsilon}|_{\epsilon=0} \|Q(f_0 + w + \epsilon b) - q\|_2^2 = 2\langle Q(f_0 + w) - q, Q_{*, f_0+w}(b)\rangle . \tag{3}$$

Here $Q_{*, f}$ denotes the differential of Q at f. This can be evaluated using the following expression: for all $s \in \mathbf{S}^2$,

$$Q_{*, f}(b)(s) = \frac{n_b(s)}{\sqrt{|n(s)|}} - \frac{n(s) \cdot n_b(s)}{2|n(s)|^{5/2}} n(s) \tag{4}$$

where $n_b(s) = f_u(s) \times b_v(s) + b_u(s) \times f_v(s)$. From the perspective of numerical accuracy, the second term can be replaced by a more stable form, $\frac{\tilde{n}(s) \cdot n_b(s)}{2\sqrt{|n(s)|}} \tilde{n}(s)$, resulting in

$$Q_{*, f}(b)(s) = \frac{1}{\sqrt{|n(s)|}} \left(n_b(s) - \frac{\tilde{n}(s) \cdot n_b(s)}{2} \tilde{n}(s) \right) . \tag{5}$$

Finally, the update is determined by the gradient $\nabla E(f_0; q) = \sum_{b \in \mathcal{B}} (\nabla_b E(b; q, f_0)) b$ obtained using Eqn. 3, 4 and 5.

3.2   Star-Shaped Surfaces

The numerical solution is for general surfaces. However, solving the optimization problem in this general case is difficult due to the high dimensionality of the search space. We now restrict attention to a special subspace of 'star-shaped' surfaces. Remarkably, in this case an analytic solution to the inversion problem exists. At the same time, such surfaces are of great relevance for many applications.

By a 'star-shaped' surface, we mean a parameterized surface $f \in \mathcal{F}$ that, up to translation, can be written in the form $f(u, v) = r(u, v)e(u, v)$, where $r(u, v) \in \mathbb{R}$, and $e(u, v) \in \mathbf{S}^2$ is the unit vector in $\mathbb{R}^3$ given in Euclidean coordinates by $e(u, v) = (\cos(u)\sin(v), \sin(u)\sin(v), \cos(v))$. It can be seen by inspection that the form of e means that the angular spherical coordinates (θ, ϕ) of points on the surface are simply given by $(\theta(u, v), \phi(u, v)) = (u, v)$. Note that the volume enclosed by a star-shaped surface is a star domain, that is, there exists a point in the enclosed volume such that the straight line segments from that point to every point on the surface all lie entirely in the enclosed volume, but that in addition to this purely geometric property, we demand that the surface have a particular parameterization.

In the case of star-shaped surfaces, the map Q can be *analytically* inverted, as follows. The radial component of the normal vector n of an star-shaped surface is, by definition, given by

$$n^r(u,v) = \langle n(u,v), e(\theta(u,v), \phi(u,v)) \rangle \tag{6}$$

since $e(\theta, \phi)$ is the radial unit vector in the direction in $\mathbb{R}^3$ defined by (θ, ϕ). If the star-shaped surface were in general parametrization, we could not compute n^r because we would not know θ and ϕ, the angular coordinates of the surface we are trying to recover. In the special parameterization, however, the expression just becomes

$$n^r(u,v) = \langle n(u,v), e(u,v) \rangle \tag{7}$$

and this can be calculated. The result is very simple:

$$n^r(u,v) = r^2(u,v). \tag{8}$$

As a result, given an SRNF q and a parameterization e, the star-shaped surface $\tilde{f}$ corresponding to this q, i.e. such that $Q(\tilde{f}) = q$, takes the form:

$$\tilde{f}(u,v) = \left(\sqrt{|q(u,v)| \, q^r(u,v)} \right) e(u,v), \tag{9}$$

where $q^r = \langle q, e \rangle$ is the radial component of q.

Note that $\tilde{f}$ depends on both q and a fixed parameterization $e(u,v)$. If both are known, then Q can be analytically inverted, as above. If a surface encloses a star domain, but is in a general parameterization (and hence not star-shaped by definition), one can still choose to apply Eqn. 9. In this case, the resulting $\tilde{f}$ will not in general be the original surface f, but it may provide a good initialization for solving the reconstruction-by-optimization problem. The numerical inversion method also provides a way to check whether a given SRNF q corresponds to a star-shaped surface: simply construct $\tilde{f}$ and then compute $Q(\tilde{f})$; if one finds $Q(\tilde{f}) = q$, then q corresponds to a star-shaped surface.

One can thus use the analytic result together with numerical inversion to construct geodesics in $\mathcal{F}$ between two star-shaped surfaces. First, find the geodesic in $\mathcal{Q}$ between the corresponding SRNFs, which is trivially a straight line. It is not guaranteed, however, that all intermediate SRNFs correspond to star-shaped surfaces; thus the analytic form $\tilde{f}$ may not be the right inversion. One can use $\tilde{f}$, however, as an initial guess for the original surface, thereby better initializing the reconstruction-by-optimization problem.

Reconstruction Examples. To explain the inversion problem further, we present results on reconstructing a synthetic surface in Fig. 1. In this experiment, the target surface is f_o which serves as the ground truth. We compute $q_o = Q(f_o)$ and the goal is to recover the target surface f_o with only q_o known. A surface computed using the analytic inversion in Eqn. 9 is shown as $\tilde{f}$. Using the unit sphere as initialization, the numerical solution to the optimization problem is shown as f^*. In order to check the convergence of the optimization problem, the energy plotted against iterations is shown in the bottom left panel. The energies, $E(\tilde{f}; q_o)$ and $E(f^*; q_o)$ are shown below the respective surfaces and compared to $E(f_o; q_o) = 0$ if we get a perfect reconstruction. The pixelwise errors, $|\tilde{f}(s) - f_o(s)|$ and $|f^*(s) - f_o(s)|$ are also shown for the analytic and the numerical solutions in that order. The surface from analytic inversion is very close to the targeted ground truth surface with an energy on the order of 10^{-4}; the numerical method then brings the energy down further towards zero. The two reconstructed surfaces have very small pointwise errors with respect to the ground truth surface.

We also show results on inverting anatomical surfaces in Fig. 2. For these the experiments, all the energies converge to a small value and the constructed surfaces resemble the ground truth surfaces very well.

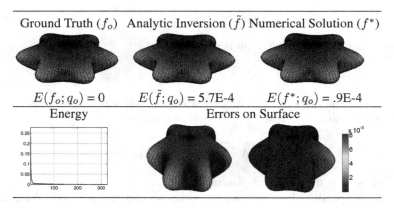

Fig. 1. Reconstructing a surface from its SRNF. A target surface (f_o) is numerically reconstructed as f^* with initialization as the unit sphere. The energy plot shows the evolution of energies against iterations with initialization as a unit sphere. The analytically inverted surface $\tilde{f}$ is shown for comparison. The energies $E(\tilde{f}; q_o)$ and $E(f^*; q_o)$ are shown correpondingly. The errors between the reconstructed surfaces and the ground truth are shown on the ground truth surface with colors representing the magnitudes, i.e. $|f^*(s) - f_o(s)|$ for all $s \in \mathbf{S}^2$.

4   Statistical Analysis of Surfaces under Inversion

The ability to invert Q enormously simplifies the algorithms used for various analyses. Compared to the previous framework [27], where analysis is performed on a Riemannian manifold, the new framework performs analysis in the $\mathbb{L}^2$ space of SRNFs, and only brings the results to the shape space at the very end (Fig. 3).

The basic algorithms for computing the Karcher mean shape, for parallel transport, and for transferring deformations from one shape to another are described in Table 1. Here, we elaborate on the list of target analyses and the mechanisms under inversion.

1. **Geodesic Path Reconstruction**: Given two surfaces f_1 and f_2, one wants to construct a geodesic path $\alpha(t)$ s.t. $\alpha(0) = f_1$ and $\alpha(1) = f_2$. Let $q_i = Q(f_i), i = 1, 2$ be the SRNFs of the given surfaces f_1 and f_2. Let $\beta : [0, 1] \rightarrow \mathbb{L}^2(\mathbf{S}^2, \mathbb{R}^3)$ denote the geodesic path, obtained via a straight line connecting q_1 and q_2. Then, for any arbitrary point $\beta(\tau) \in \mathbb{L}^2(\mathbf{S}^2, \mathbb{R}^3)$, we want to find a surface $\alpha(\tau)$ such that

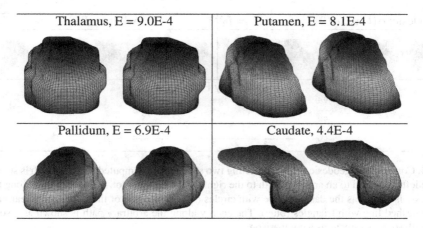

Fig. 2. Four examples of reconstructing anatomical surfaces. In each cell, the surface on the left is the ground truth (f_o) while the reconstruction (f^*) is on the right. The corresponding energies $\|Q(f^*) - Q(f_o)\|^2$ are shown at the top.

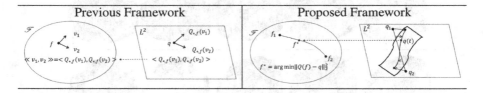

Fig. 3. Inversion from SRNF space to shape space gives an alternative way to analyze shapes. Previous methods require pulling back the metric and working with the Riemannian metric on $\mathcal{F}$ (left). The proposed method performs analysis in $\mathbb{L}^2$ space (right) and pulls back the results onto the shape space (left) by inversion.

$Q(\alpha(\tau)) = \beta(\tau)$. In practice, we will accomplish this sequentially. For any $\epsilon > 0$, we start by solving for $f(\epsilon)$. Since our search is gradient-based, we need a good initial condition for starting the search. In this case $\alpha(0) = f_1$ provides such an initial condition. For the next shape, $f(2\epsilon)$, we can use the previous step $f(\epsilon)$ to initialize the search, and so on.

Figure 4 shows results of computing a geodesic connecting two known endpoints given by synthetic surfaces. The path of shapes is initialized by linear interpolation of SRNFs and then optimized numerically to form a geodesic path. An arbitrary path is shown to the right for comparison. Paths of energies are shown in the bottom panel. The energy paths of the arbitrary path, the linear path and the numerically computed geodesic path are shown in green, blue and red, respectively. We observe that the analytically inverted path has low energy and is close to the solution. The computed geodesic is shown in the left panel: it smoothly deforms one shape into the other. Similar experiments are performed with anatomical surfaces; the geodesics are shown in Fig. 5.

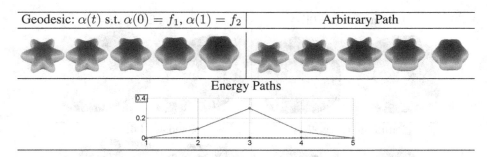

Fig. 4. Constructing geodesic paths connecting two shapes. The computed geodesic path is shown to the left compared to an arbitrary path to the right. In the bottom plot, the energy path along the geodesic is shown as the dash-dot line with circles (red), while that of the initialized linear path is the dashed line with triangles (blue). The energy along the arbitrary path is shown as a solid line with squares (green) as a comparison.

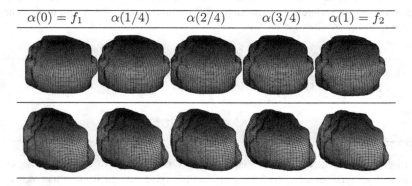

Fig. 5. Two geodesics computed for anatomical surfaces. Geodesics connecting the given two endpoint surfaces, f_1 and f_2, are shown as $\alpha(t)$ at discrete time stamps for the thalamus and the pallidum.

2. **Shooting Geodesics**: Given a surface f and a tangent vector v_0 at f, one wants to construct a geodesic path $\alpha(t)$ s.t. $\alpha(0) = f$ and $\dot{\alpha}(0) = v$. Here $\dot{\alpha} = d\alpha/dt$. Note that shooting a geodesic is essentially evaluating the exponential map $\exp_f(tv_0) = \alpha(t), t = [0, 1]$ numerically. Let $\beta : [0, 1] \to \mathbb{L}^2(\mathbf{S}^2, \mathbb{R}^3)$ denote a straight line, i.e. $\beta(t) = Q(f) + tQ_{*,f}(v_0)$, where $Q_{*,f}$ is the differential of Q at f as previously mentioned. Then the desired geodesic path $\alpha(t)$ is of the form $Q(\alpha(t)) = \beta(t)$. This path $\alpha(t)$ is computed sequentially similarly to the first case. Some statistical analyses computed using shooting geodesics are shown in Fig. 6 and 7.

3. **Statistical Summaries of Shapes**: When given a sample of observed surfaces $f_1, \ldots, f_n$, one wants to estimate the mean shape and principal directions of variation.

   The mean shape μ_f is computed as shown in Table 1. Let $q_i, i = 1, \ldots, n$, be the SRNFs of the registered surfaces in the sample and u_q^k be the k-th principal component of $q_1, \ldots, q_n$. The k-th principal mode of variation for the SRNFs is given by $\mu_q \pm \lambda u_q^k$, $\lambda \in \mathbb{R}^+$. In order to visualize the principal directions in the shape space, we need to find f^k such that $Q(f^k) = \mu_q \pm \lambda u_q^k$. This is essentially a shooting geodesic type of problem.

We generated two groups of synthetic surfaces, each with 8 observations, as shown in Fig. 6. Within each group, we computed the mean shape and performed principal component analysis. The first three principal directions (PD) are shown on the mean shapes of each group as their local magnitudes. Computed mean shapes and modes of variation on anatomical surfaces are presented in Fig. 7. Under the proposed framework, to compute the Karcher mean, computational cost per iteration (Algorithm 2 in Table 1) is 174 seconds comparing to 397 seconds in the previous method (Algorifhm 1 in Table 1) using the PCA basis (8 of them, see [27]) and more than 4 hours using 200 spherical harmonic basis. Inverting the μ_q takes 6 seconds.

4. **Random Sampling from Shape Models**: When given a sample of observed surfaces $f_1, \ldots, f_n$, one wants to fit a probability model to the data and generate random samples from it. Let $q_1, \ldots, q_n$ be the SRNFs of the registered surfaces

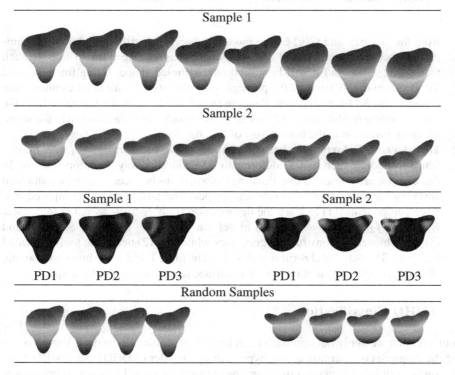

Fig. 6. Statistical analysis of synthetic data sets. Each sample has eight observations. The first three principal directions (PD) are shown plotted on the corresponding mean shapes for both samples (middle). Deformation magnitude is shown by color (blue small, red large). Random samples from Gaussian models are shown at the bottom.

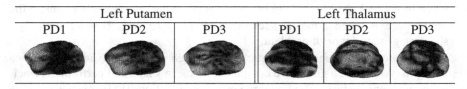

Left Putamen			Left Thalamus		
PD1	PD2	PD3	PD1	PD2	PD3

Fig. 7. Plots of mean shape and principal directions (PD) for medical surfaces. Deformation magnitude is shown by color (blue small, red large) and plotted on mean shapes.

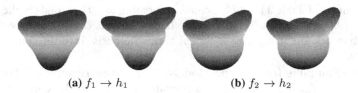

(a) $f_1 \to h_1$ **(b)** $f_2 \to h_2$

Fig. 8. Transfer of a deformation across shapes. Surfaces f_1, h_1 and f_2 are given. Deformation from f_1 to h_1 is learnt and used to deform f_2 to get the new surface h_2.

from the last step and $G(q)$ be the model probability distribution. A random sample can be generated from G and we denote it as q_s. We want to find f_s such that $Q(f_s) = q_s$ and it will be a randomly sampled shape. Using the registered SRNFs from Fig. 6, we used the principal components and estimated a multivariate Gaussian model for each group. Random samples of SRNFs are generated from the corresponding models and random shapes from both models are shown in the shape space by inversion in the bottom row of Fig. 6.

5. **Transferring Deformation between Shapes**: Given surfaces f_1, h_1 and f_2, one wants to find h_2 such that f_2 deforms to it in a similar way f_1 deforms to h_1. In this case we are interested in estimating deformations between two shapes and then applying the deformations to new test shapes. The task can be decomposed into three components: (1) to learn the deformation from f_1 to h_1 as v, (2) to transfer v at f_1 to f_2 resulting $v^\parallel$ and (3) to deform f_2 into h_2 using $v^\parallel$. Steps (1) and (3) are achieved by constructing geodesics while step (2) needs the tool of parallel transport. The detailed algorithm is described in Table 1. Figure 8 shows an example of transferring a deformation from one surface to another in the shape space.

5   ADHD Classification

In this section we apply our approach to an important problem in medical image analysis: the diagnosis of attention deficit hyperactivity disorder (ADHD) using MRI scans. The surfaces of brain structures used here were extracted from T1 weighted brain magnetic resonance images of young adults aged between 18 and 21. These subjects were recruited from the Detroit Fetal Alcohol and Drug Exposure Cohort [15,14,6]. Among the 34 subjects studied, 19 were diagnosed with ADHD and the remaining 15 were controls (non-ADHD). Some examples of left structures are displayed in Fig. 9. First

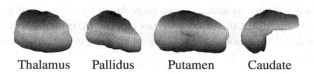

| Thalamus | Pallidus | Putamen | Caudate |

Fig. 9. Left anatomical structures in the brain

Table 2. Classification Performance for Five Different Techniques

Method Structure (%)	SRNF Gauss **Proposed**	SRM Gauss [19]	SRM NN [18]	Harmonic	ICP [3]	SPHARM PDM [24]
L. Caudate	67.7	-	41.2	64.7	32.4	61.8
L. Pallidus	85.3	88.2	76.5	79.4	67.7	44.1
L. Putamen	94.1	82.4	82.4	70.6	61.8	50.0
L. Thalamus	67.7	-	58.8	67.7	35.5	52.9
R. Caudate	55.9	-	50.0	44.1	50.0	70.6
R. Pallidus	76.5	67.6	61.8	67.7	55.9	52.9
R. Putamen	67.7	82.4	67.7	55.9	47.2	55.9
R. Thalamus	67.7	-	58.8	52.9	64.7	64.7

we register the extracted surfaces as described in [16] and map them into the $\mathbb{L}^2$ space of SRNFs using Q. In order to distinguish ADHD and control samples, we use the Gaussian classifier on principal components as defined in Section 4.

Table 2 shows the single structure, LOO nearest neighbor classification rate in %. The best performance is attained using the proposed SRNF Gaussian classifier between left putamen surfaces. We compare our results to those obtained using: the SRM Gaussian classifier; the SRM NN classifier; the iterative closest point (ICP) algorithm; an approach using fixed surface parametrization and $\mathbb{L}^2$ distance between the surfaces; and the SPHARM-PDM approach. The performance measures for these approaches were taken from Kurtek et al. [19] and other previously published papers. The results suggest that the parametrization-invariant metric and the probability models in our approach provides improved matching and modeling of the surfaces, resulting in a superior ADHD classification. In summary, our method is not only more efficient: the computational cost is an order of magnitude less than SRM and related ideas; but also provides significantly improved classification.

6   Conclusions

The SRNF representation is potentially an important tool in statistical shape analysis of parameterized surfaces. Previous methods built tools for analysis directly in the surface space, which is computationally inefficient. We have introduced methods for approximating the inverse mapping Q^{-1}. This map can be used to convert results computed in SRNF space back to the shape space. Since the SRNF space is a vector space with $\mathbb{L}^2$-metric, the cost of statistical analysis in this space is very low, thus simplifying typical shape analysis tasks. In general, by adopting the proposed framework, computational cost of algorithms for various analyses can be reduced by an order of magnitude. Experimental results show that the same analyses can be performed under the simplified framework, and that the method achieves state-of-the-art performance on the classification of ADHD data.

Acknowledgement. This research was supported in part by the NSF grants DMS 1208959, IIS 1217515, and CCF 1319658. We also thank the producers of datasets used here for making them available to public.

References

1. Abe, K., Erbacher, J.: Isometric immersions with the same Gauss map. Mathematische Annalen 215(3), 197–201 (1975)
2. Allen, B., Curless, B., Popović, Z.: The space of human body shapes: Reconstruction and parameterization from range scans. ACM Transactions on Graphics 22(3), 587–594 (2003)
3. Besl, P.J., McKay, N.D.: A method for registration of 3-D shapes. IEEE Transactions on Pattern Analysis and Machine Intelligence 14(2), 239–256 (1992)
4. Bouix, S., Pruessner, J.C., Collins, D.L., Siddiqi, K.: Hippocampal shape analysis using medial surfaces. In: Niessen, W.J., Viergever, M.A. (eds.) MICCAI 2001. LNCS, vol. 2208, pp. 33–40. Springer, Heidelberg (2001)
5. Brechbühler, C., Gerig, G., Kübler, O.: Parameterization of closed surfaces for 3D shape description. Computer Vision and Image Understanding 61(2), 154–170 (1995)
6. Burden, M.J., Jacobson, J.L., Westerlund, A., Lundahl, L.H., Morrison, A., Dodge, N.C., Klorman, R., Nelson, C.A., Avison, M.J., Jacobson, S.W.: An event-related potential study of response inhibition in ADHD with and without prenatal alcohol exposure. Alcoholism: Clinical and Experimental Research 34(4), 617–627 (2010)
7. Davies, R.H., Twining, C.J., Cootes, T.F., Taylor, C.J.: Building 3-D statistical shape models by direct optimization. IEEE Transactions on Medical Imaging 29(4), 961–981 (2010)
8. Dryden, I., Mardia, K.: Statistical Shape Analysis. John Wiley & Sons (1998)
9. Eschenburg, J.-H., Kruglikov, B.S., Matveev, V.S., Tribuzy, R.: Compatibility of Gauss maps with metrics. Differential Geometry and its Applications 28(2), 228–235 (2010)
10. Gorczowski, K., Styner, M., Jeong, J.Y., Marron, J.S., Piven, J., Hazlett, H.C., Pizer, S.M., Gerig, G.: Multi-object analysis of volume, pose, and shape using statistical discrimination. IEEE Transactions on Pattern Analysis and Machine Intelligence 32(4), 652–661 (2010)
11. Grenander, U., Miller, M.I.: Computational anatomy: An emerging discipline. Quarterly of Applied Mathematics LVI(4), 617–694 (1998)
12. Heeren, B., Rumpf, M., Wardetzky, M., Wirth, B.: Time-discrete geodesics in the space of shells. Computer Graphics Forum 31(5), 1755–1764 (2012)
13. Hoffman, D.A., Osserman, R.: The Gauss map of surfaces in R3 and R4. Proceedings of the London Mathematical Society 3(1), 27–56 (1985)
14. Jacobson, S.W., Jacobson, J.L., Sokol, R.J., Chiodo, L.M., Corobana, R.: Maternal age, alcohol abuse history, and quality of parenting as moderators of the effects of prenatal alcohol exposure on 7.5-year intellectual function. Alcoholism: Clinical and Experimental Research 28(11), 1732–1745 (2004)
15. Jacobson, S.W., Jacobson, J.L., Sokol, R.J., Martier, S.S., Chiodo, L.M.: New evidence for neurobehavioral effects of in utero cocaine exposure. The Journal of Pediatrics 129(4), 581–590 (1996)

16. Jermyn, I., Kurtek, S., Klassen, E., Srivastava, A.: Elastic shape matching of parameterized surfaces using square root normal fields. In: IEEE European Conference on Computer Vision, vol. 5(14), pp. 805–817 (2012)
17. Kilian, M., Mitra, N.J., Pottmann, H.: Geometric modeling in shape space. In: ACM SIG-GRAPH (2007)
18. Kurtek, S., Klassen, E., Ding, Z., Jacobson, S., Jacobson, J., Avison, M., Srivastava, A.: Parameterization-invariant shape comparisons of anatomical surfaces. IEEE Transactions on Medical Imaging 30(3), 849–858 (2011)
19. Kurtek, S., Klassen, E., Ding, Z., Avison, M.J., Srivastava, A.: Parameterization-invariant shape statistics and probabilistic classification of anatomical surfaces. In: Székely, G., Hahn, H.K. (eds.) IPMI 2011. LNCS, vol. 6801, pp. 147–158. Springer, Heidelberg (2011)
20. Kurtek, S., Klassen, E., Gore, J.C., Ding, Z., Srivastava, A.: Elastic geodesic paths in shape space of parameterized surfaces. IEEE Transactions on Pattern Analysis and Machine Intelligence 34(9), 1717–1730 (2012)
21. Osher, S., Fedkiw, R.: Level Set Methods and Dynamic Implicit Surfaces (Applied Mathematical Sciences). 2003 edn. Springer(November 2002)
22. Ovsjanikov, M., Li, W., Guibas, L., Mitra, N.J.: Exploration of continuous variability in collections of 3D shapes. ACM Transactions on Graphics 30(4), 33:1–33:10 (2011)
23. Srivastava, A., Klassen, E., Joshi, S.H., Jermyn, I.H.: Shape analysis of elastic curves in Euclidean spaces. IEEE Transactions on Pattern Analysis and Machine Intelligence 33(7), 1415–1428 (2011)
24. Styner, M., Oguz, I., Xu, S., Brechbuehler, C., Pantazis, D., Levitt, J., Shenton, M., Gerig, G.: Framework for the statistical shape analysis of brain structures using SPHARM-PDM. Insight Journal (July 2006)
25. Van Kaick, O., Zhang, H., Hamarneh, G., Cohen-Or, D.: A Survey on Shape Correspondence. Computer Graphics Forum 30(6), 1681–1707 (2011)
26. Windheuser, T., Schlickewei, U., Schmidt, F.R., Cremers, D.: Geometrically consistent elastic matching of 3D shapes: A linear programming solution. In: IEEE International Conference on Computer Vision, pp. 2134–2141 (November 2011)
27. Xie, Q., Kurtek, S., Le, H., Srivastava, A.: Parallel transport of deformations in shape space of elastic surfaces. In: IEEE International Conference on Computer Vision (December 2013)
28. Yang, Y.L., Yang, Y.J., Pottmann, H., Mitra, N.J.: Shape space exploration of constrained meshes. ACM Transactions on Graphics 30(6), 124:1–124:12 (2011)
29. Zhang, H., Sheffer, A., Cohen-Or, D., Zhou, Q., Van Kaick, O., Tagliasacchi, A.: Deformation-driven shape correspondence. Computer Graphics Forum 27(5), 1431–1439 (2008)

Non-associative Higher-Order Markov Networks for Point Cloud Classification

Mohammad Najafi, Sarah Taghavi Namin,
Mathieu Salzmann, and Lars Petersson

Australian National University (ANU)
NICTA*, Canberra, Australia
{mohammad.najafi,sarah.namin,mathieu.salzmann,lars.petersson}@nicta.com.au

Abstract. In this paper, we introduce a non-associative higher-order graphical model to tackle the problem of semantic labeling of 3D point clouds. For this task, existing higher-order models overlook the relationships between the different classes and simply encourage the nodes in the cliques to have consistent labelings. We address this issue by devising a set of non-associative context patterns that describe higher-order geometric relationships between different class labels within the cliques. To this end, we propose a method to extract informative cliques in 3D point clouds that provide more knowledge about the context of the scene. We evaluate our approach on three challenging outdoor point cloud datasets. Our experiments evidence the benefits of our non-associative higher-order Markov networks over state-of-the-art point cloud labeling techniques.

Keywords: Non-associative Markov networks, Higher-order graphical models, 3D point clouds, Semantic labeling.

1 Introduction

Semantic labeling of 3D point clouds for terrain classification remains a very challenging task, despite recent advances in the field. Outdoor environments are to a large extent irregular in nature and often present complex relationships between the different objects in the scene. Furthermore, the substantial presence of noise in data captured outdoors makes labeling even more difficult. In this paper, we introduce a non-associative higher-order Markov network to address the problem of outdoor terrain classification from 3D point cloud data.

In the past few years, pairwise graphical models have been frequently used for indoor and outdoor point cloud labeling [2,32,28,21,1,19,29]. However, pairwise networks can generally not adequately describe the complex contextual information that exists in natural scenes. In contrast, higher-order networks enable us to better model this information and take into account the structural relationships present between groups of objects in the data. In the context of 3D

---

* NICTA is funded by the Australian Government as represented by the Department of Broadband, Communications and the Digital Economy and the ARC through the ICT Centre of Excellence program.

D. Fleet et al. (Eds.): ECCV 2014, Part V, LNCS 8693, pp. 500–515, 2014.

point cloud classification, a handful of approaches have exploited higher-order models in the form of Associative Markov Networks (AMN) [22,6]. While AMNs consider groups of multiple neighboring nodes jointly, they only encourage these nodes to have an identical label. Therefore, AMNs cannot describe complex relationships between the different classes in the scene and, as a result, have only limited ability to model contextual information. To the best of our knowledge, no model has yet managed to exploit the full representative power of higher-order graphical models for 3D point cloud labeling.

In this paper, we introduce a new higher-order model for 3D point cloud classification that takes into account the non-associative geometric context between different classes. This lets us exploit more information than common pairwise models or associative higher-order models to describe the semantic structure of the scene. As a consequence, our model typically yields more accurate labelings.

More specifically, we build a graph in which each node represents a segment (i.e., group) of 3D points. We then build higher-order cliques by projecting the 3D segments to the ground plane and grouping the segments with substantial overlap. Intuitively, in outdoor scenes, grouping segments along the vertical direction will carry more information than along horizontal ones (e.g., leaves are above tree trunks, which are above the ground). To model this information, we devise four geometric context patterns that describe non-associative relationships between the segments in the cliques. Importantly, these context patterns are independent of the number and size of the segments inside the cliques.

We evaluate our model on three benchmark point cloud datasets (VMR-Oakland-V2, RSE-RSS and GML-PCV). Our approach outperforms state-of-the-art point cloud labeling techniques, which evidences the importance of modeling the complex higher-order relations of the classes in the scene.

2   Related Work

There is a considerable amount of literature on point cloud classification in both indoor and outdoor environments. In particular, over the years, there has been a strong focus on designing new feature types, such as FPFH (Fast Point Feature Histogram) [26], histogram descriptors [3], hierarchical kernel descriptors [4], and on adapting geometric and shape-based features [7,16] to improve the performance of point cloud classification systems. As with RGB images, the performance of local features can typically be improved by exploiting the context of the scene via a graphical model.

Graphical models enable us to encode the spatial and semantic relationships between objects via a set of edges between the nodes in a graph. A number of works [21,2,18,25] have studied the impact of pairwise graphical models on point cloud classification and have demonstrated that adding a label consistency constraint between neighboring nodes improves the classification accuracy significantly. However, these simple label consistency constraints, which define an AMN, often suffer from the drawback of over-smoothing the labeling.

To address this problem, the authors of [28,1,19] investigated the use of pairwise non-AMNs for point cloud labeling. Non-AMNs can exploit the complex contextual information existing between the objects in the scene by exploring various combinations of classes rather than just enforcing homogeneous labelings of the graph nodes. For instance, the observation that A is "above" B cannot be modeled with an AMN, whereas non-AMNs can encode this information. While existing non-AMNs have proven useful for both indoor [1] and outdoor [28] point cloud classification, the current models remain limited to modeling pairwise interactions.

In contrast, higher-order models can be used to capture the complex relationships in the scene that cannot be described using pairwise models [10,11,31,12,30,14]. In our context, in [22,6], Munoz et al. exploited $\mathcal{P}^n$ Potts potentials [10] on groups of multiple 3D points. In [9], a *Voxel-CRF* framework was introduced to tackle the occlusion and 2D-3D mismatch problems by utilizing a higher-order model based on Hough voting and categorical object detection. In both cases, however, the resulting higher-order graphical model is an AMN, and is thus limited to encoding simple label consistency potentials.

The main contribution of our work lies in proposing a non-AMN higher-order graphical model that better describes the scene context and thus yields improved 3D point cloud classification. Our higher-order potentials belong to the category of *pattern-based* potentials [12]. However, in contrast to most instances in this category (e.g., $\mathcal{P}^n$ Potts model, co-occurrence potentials), our potentials account for the geometric context that exists in the scene, and thus form a non-AMN.

Some recent works on point cloud labeling have proposed to incorporate contextual information without using a graphical model [33,8,23]. In particular, in [33], which is the most relevant work here, the authors used a sequence of hierarchical classifiers at different scales (i.e., at point level and at segment level). Due to the non-standard form of their model, they had to design a special inference method. Here, in contrast, we can leverage the vast research on inference in higher-order graphical models to propose a principled approach to point cloud classification.

3 Method

In this section, we introduce our approach to point cloud labeling. To this end, we first present our higher-order CRF. For a comprehensive discussion of CRFs, we refer the reader to [15].

Given N 3D point segments $\mathbf{x} = [x_1, \ldots, x_2, x_N]$ obtained from a point cloud, our goal is to assign a label $y_i \in [1, \cdots, L]$ to each segment x_i. To this end, we construct a Condition Random Field (CRF) over the labels, where each node corresponds to a segment. In this CRF, the joint distribution of the labels of all nodes given the segments can be expressed as

$$\mathbf{P}(\mathbf{y}|\mathbf{x}) = \frac{1}{Z}\exp\left(-\sum_{i=1}^{N}\boldsymbol{\Phi}(y_i, x_i) - \sum_{(ij)\in\mathcal{E}}\boldsymbol{\Psi}_{\mathbf{p}}(y_i, y_j, x_i, x_j) - \sum_{c\in C}\boldsymbol{\Psi}_{\mathbf{h}}(y_c, x_c)\right)$$

$$(1)$$

where Z is the partition function, $\mathcal{E}$ is the set of second-order (pairwise) edges and C is the set of higher-order cliques in the graph. The unary potential function $\mathbf{\Phi}$ expresses the likelihood of an individual segment to be assigned to each class. The pairwise potential $\mathbf{\Psi_p}$ imposes consistent labeling to the neighboring nodes. In contrast, the clique potential $\mathbf{\Psi_h}$ encodes the compatibility of the different possible class assignments of multiple segments. As will be shown later, we make use of this clique potential to encode the geometric relationships between groups of segments.

To obtain the best labeling for the problem at hand, we seek to compute a MAP estimate of the labels given by $arg\,max\,\mathbf{P}(\mathbf{y}|\mathbf{x})$. This can be achieved by minimizing the energy corresponding to the CRF, given by

$$\mathbf{E}(\mathbf{y}|\mathbf{x}) = \sum_{i=1}^{N} \mathbf{\Phi}(x_i, y_i) + \sum_{(ij)\in\mathcal{E}} \mathbf{\Psi_p}(y_i, y_j, x_i, x_j) + \sum_{c\in C} \mathbf{\Psi_h}(y_c, x_c) \qquad (2)$$

Minimizing this energy is achieved by performing inference in the CRF. To this end, here, we employ Loopy Belief Propagation [24] .

In the remainder of this section, we present the potentials that we use in the energy of Eq. 2. In particular, we introduce new pattern-based potentials that, as opposed to most existing pattern-based potentials, let us model complex geometric relationships across groups of segments.

3.1 Higher-Order Context-Based Potentials

Clique Structure. To be able to capture informative semantic context patterns, we construct cliques from segments that are located in the same vertical structures in the point cloud. The intuition behind this is that the horizontal placement of objects in outdoor scenes is often arbitrary (e.g., a car can be located anywhere near a building) and thus conveys less geometric information. In contrast, the relative vertical positioning of objects is often well-constrained (e.g., leaves are above tree-trunks which are above the ground). To build our cliques, we therefore project the segments to the ground plane (which is achieved by removing the z-coordinate of all the points) and find the overlapping segments on this ground plane. More specifically, we create a clique for each segment i and add any segment with a significant overlap with i (i.e., more than 50% overlap) to this clique. Cliques containing a single segment are then discarded. This strategy to create cliques is illustrated in Fig.1-a. While one could think of using a simple grid-based technique to determine the base of the vertical structure of the cliques, in the presence of thin segments such as *tree trunks* and *utility poles*, this approach would be very sensitive to the exact placement of the grid. In contrast, in our scheme all the segments are completely surrounded by at least one clique structure.

Pattern-Based Potentials. As mentioned earlier, in this work we design new pattern-based potentials to encode the geometric relationships within the cliques

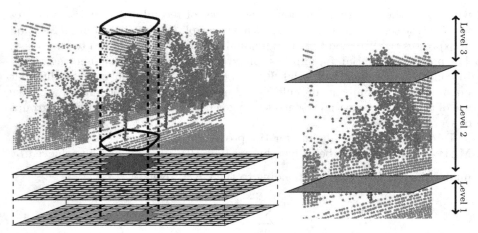

a) The vertical structure of a clique in our model. The cliques are created by analyzing every individual segment and checking whether its projection on the ground plane overlaps with the projection of other segments in the point cloud. Here for instance, the projection of the *leaves* covers the *tree trunk* and has a substantial overlap with the *ground*. Hence, a clique from these three segments is formed and our context patterns are extracted from this vertical structure.

c) Height signature pattern. The vertical structure of the clique (shown in Fig.1-a) is cut horizontally into K levels (here $K = 3$). Then each level is explored to check if any of the L class labels is present. The resulting pattern vector for this example is given in Fig.1-d.

Simple Co-occurrence

W	P	G	L	T	B	V
0	0	**1**	**1**	**1**	0	0

b) The simple co-occurrence pattern records the class labels that are found within the vertical structure.

Height Signature (3 levels)

W	P	G	L	T	B	V	W	P	G	L	T	B	V	W	P	G	L	T	B	V
0	0	**1**	0	**1**	0	0	0	0	0	0	**1**	**1**	0	0	0	0	0	**1**	0	0	0

⟵——— Level 1 ———⟶ ⟵——— Level 2 ———⟶ ⟵——— Level 3 ———⟶

d) The height signature pattern shows how the class labels inside the clique are spread vertically. The pattern vector is computed according to Fig. 1-c.

Geometric Co-occurrence

	W	P	G	L	T	B	V
W	0	0	0	0	0	0	0
P	0	0	0	0	0	0	0
G	0	0	0	0	0	0	0
L	0	0	**1**	0	**1**	0	0
T	0	0	**1**	0	0	0	0
B	0	0	0	0	0	0	0
V	0	0	0	0	0	0	0

e) The geometric co-occurrence pattern indicates how the class labels are vertically located inside the clique. Element (i,j) of this matrix is **1** if there is at least one segment with label i, above another segment with label j.

Within Clique Adjacency

	W	P	G	L	T	B	V
W	-	0	0	0	0	0	0
P	-	-	0	0	0	0	0
G	-	-	-	0	**1**	0	0
L	-	-	-	-	**1**	0	0
T	-	-	-	-	-	0	0
B	-	-	-	-	-	-	0
V	-	-	-	-	-	-	-

f) The within clique adjacency indicates which class labels are connected to each other inside the clique.

Fig. 1. Extracting the cliques and the higher-order context patterns from the point cloud. Here, the classes are {W:*wire*, P:*pole*, G:*ground*, L:*leaves*, T:*tree trunk*, B:*building*, V:*vehicle*}.

of our graph. In their general form, pattern-based potentials were introduced by Komodakis and Paragios [12] as potential functions defined as

$$\Psi_h(\mathbf{P}) = \begin{cases} H(\mathbf{P}) & \mathbf{P} \in \mathcal{P} \\ H_{max} & \text{otherwise} \end{cases} \tag{3}$$

where $\mathbf{P}$ is a context pattern vector which describes the clique, $\mathcal{P}$ is the set of all pattern vectors that are considered valid and H_{max} is the cost assigned to the patterns that are not listed in $\mathcal{P}$ (i.e., invalid patterns). This formulation is very general and only imposes that $H_{max} \geq H(\mathbf{P})$. However, most existing methods employ such potentials to define simple label consistency constraints, such as $\mathcal{P}^n$ Potts and co-occurrence potentials.

Here, we make use of these potentials to define much more complex relationships between the segments in a clique. In particular, we compute four higher-order patterns defined as $\mathbf{P}_1$: *Simple Co-occurrence*, $\mathbf{P}_2$: *Geometric Co-occurrence*, $\mathbf{P}_3$: *Within Clique Adjacency* and $\mathbf{P}_4$: *Height Signature*. Our complete context pattern is then obtained by concatenating these patterns as

$$\mathbf{P} = [\mathbf{P}_1{}^\mathsf{T}, \mathbf{P}_2{}^\mathsf{T}, \mathbf{P}_3{}^\mathsf{T}, \mathbf{P}_4{}^\mathsf{T}]^\mathsf{T}. \tag{4}$$

As will be shown below, the primary advantage of our context patterns is that they are defined based on the class labels of the segments. In other words, we analyze the relationships of the abstract class labels rather than of the specific segments inside the cliques. This property makes our patterns invariant to the size and number of the segments from each class [14]. In our work, to create the set of valid patterns, we make use of the training data and record all the observed context patterns. The collection of observed patterns along with their number of occurrences forms the codebook $\mathcal{P}$. In practice, we ignore cliques of order 6 or higher to keep inference computationally tractable. Furthermore, we take into account all the patterns regardless of their number of occurrences. The intuition is that even patterns that have been observed a small number of times, can be important. We set $H(\mathbf{P}) = 0$ in Eq. 3, which means that we assign no higher-order cost to the valid patterns. The optimization algorithm then tries to find a labeling of the cliques such that they form valid patterns, while also having low unary and pairwise costs.

In the following, we describe the four different patterns that we employ in more detail.

Simple Co-occurrence. Label co-occurrence is a pattern vector that indicates which classes are present inside a higher-order clique. We represent the co-occurrence pattern by $\mathbf{P}_1 : \{p_1^i\}_{i=1:L}$ which is a binary vector with L elements, where L is the number of class labels. If a segment with class label i is present inside the clique, p_1^i is set to 1 (see Fig. 1-b).

Geometric Co-occurrence. The main drawback of simple co-occurrence is that it just provides us with a symmetric description of the clique and can not capture the geometric relationships between the nodes. For instance, the label configuration of *tree trunk* above *leaves* is undesirable, but the simple co-occurrence pattern vector for this clique will make it a valid configuration. To address this problem, we utilize non-associative features to build a geometric co-occurrence pattern. To this end, we project all the 3D segments onto the ground. Then, for each clique, all segment pairs with a significant projection overlap (larger than 50%) are recorded, and the segment with a higher centroid is considered to be *above* the other one. We encode the *above* relationships between any pair of class labels within the clique as an $L \times L$ binary matrix (Fig. 1-e), which can then form the pattern $\mathbf{P}_2 : \{p_2^i\}_{i=1:L^2}$. Note that, while we compare pairs of segments inside the cliques, the final pattern vector considers all the pairs jointly. Therefore, our geometric co-occurrence potential cannot be expressed as a pairwise potential.

Within Clique Adjacency. To make the context pattern more informative, we check whether there is a spatial connection between any pair of class labels within the clique. Here, we consider that two 3D segments are spatially connected if the shortest Euclidean distance between any two of their points is lower than a pre-defined threshold (in practice 0.6m). This pattern can be stored in the $L(L-1)/2$ dimensional vector $\mathbf{P}_3 : \{p_3^i\}_{i=1:L(L-1)/2}$ (see Fig. 1-f).

Height Signature. This context pattern acts as a vertical location prior in our classification framework. It indicates whether a specific class label is observed in a certain range of height above the ground. To compute this pattern, we partition the point cloud inside each clique into K horizontal levels. At each level, we then record the presence of any of the L classes. This results in the pattern of height signature $\mathbf{P}_4 : \{p_4^i\}_{i=1:LK}$ (see Fig. 1-(c,d)). In practice, we divide the vertical space into $K = 3$ partitions whose boundaries are determined during training.

3.2 Pairwise Potential

In addition to the higher-order terms, we also encode pairwise potentials in our graphical model. In particular, we specify a pairwise link for each pair of 3D segments that are neighbors. Two segments are treated as neighbors if the shortest distance between any two of their points is less than a pre-defined threshold (in practice 0.6 m). We then define a pairwise potential that depends on the class labels of the segments, as well as on their local shape features. This potential can be expressed as

$$\mathbf{\Psi}_\mathbf{P}(y_i, y_j, \theta_i, \theta_j) = \begin{cases} \frac{1}{1+|\theta_i - \theta_j|/T} & (y_i \neq y_j) \\ 0 & \text{otherwise} \end{cases} \tag{5}$$

where T is a normalization factor set to $90°$ in practice, and θ is the angle between the direction of the normal vector of the segment and the direction of the vertical axis. Here, the normal vector of a segment is computed by taking the average of the normal vectors of all its points. Intuitively, this potential favors assigning identical labels to two segments if their normal vectors have a similar deviation from the vertical axis.

3.3   Unary Potential

Feature Set. Our unary potential relies on a classifier applied to features extracted at each point of the cloud. In particular, we use the following features: (i) FPFH descriptors that describe the geometric relationships between a point and its neighbors in terms of distance and normal vector orientations [26]; (ii) Eigenvalue features that provide us with measures of scatter, linearity and planarity of a point distribution. (iii) Deviation of the normal vector direction of each point from the z-axis, which helps distinguishing between the horizontal and vertical planar surfaces; (iv) Height of the point.

The FPFH and Eigenvalue features are computed over two local neighborhoods around the point of interest. To obtain the height of each point, a proper estimation of the ground level is essential. As the ground points are not evenly distributed on a horizontal surface, particularly in complex outdoor environments, we perform local approximations of the ground by considering horizontal patches in the point cloud and taking the lowest point as a part of the ground.

Point-Wise Classification. Given the aforementioned features, we employ a probabilistic SVM classifier [20,5] to compute the class probabilities for each 3D point. We then compute the class probability vector of each segment by averaging over the class probabilities of all its constituent 3D points. The unary potential in our graphical model is obtained by taking the negative logarithm of this probability vector. In practice, we used an RBF kernel in our SVM classifier, and set the hyper-parameters of the SVM to $C = 5$ and $\gamma = 0.1$.

3.4   Segmentation

As mentioned throughout this section, we use point segments as nodes in our graphical model. This lets us effectively handle very large point clouds. To obtain these segments, we first apply the efficient fully connected CRF (Dense-CRF) [13] to the results of the point-wise classifier using Gaussian kernels on 3D positions and surface normals (implemented in PCL [27]). This allows us to reduce the noise and produce point classification results that are better suited to segmentation. The final segments are computed by dividing the entire set into L distinct groups, corresponding to the labeling of the Dense-CRF, and clustering each group into smaller segments via k-means clustering. We found that this two-step segmentation scheme yields a cleaner set of segments than directly applying k-means clustering to the point cloud. The number of segments, k, is determined by the k-means algorithm of PCL (about 300 segments in practice).

4   Experiments

We evaluated the performance of our method using the same three datasets as in [33]. The first dataset, VMR-Oakland-V2[1], represents street scenes collected using a terrestrial laser scanner. It is composed of approximately 3 million 3D points separated into 36 point cloud blocks (pcd-files). The points are labeled according to seven categories of outdoor objects, i.e., *wire, pole, ground, leaves, tree trunk, building* and *vehicle*. The number of points belonging to each class is strongly unbalanced, which makes training very challenging. To facilitate the comparison with previously-reported results on this dataset, we follow the evaluation procedure of [33], which sets aside 6 pcd-files to tune the parameters of the classifier and defines 30 pcd-files to train and test the model. These 30 files are further split into 5 sets, which let us perform 5-fold cross-validation.

Table 1 reports the performance of our approach and of state-of-the-art point cloud labeling baselines in terms of the precision, recall and F1-score ($F1 = \frac{precision \times recall \times 2}{precision + recall}$) for each class. Our approach yields an average F1-score of 0.79, which is higher than the state-of-the-art on this dataset [8]. Note that the performance of the unary potentials is 0.63, which was impressively improved by our non-associative higher-order model. This confirms the importance of our context-aware higher-order potentials. Note that we also computed the F1-scores of the non-associative pairwise model (NA-pairwise) incorporating all our pattern potentials, but computed only on pairwise cliques (formed using our region overlap criterion). This model achieved an average F1-score of 0.73, which shows that, while it yields a better performance than the simple associative pairwise model (0.65), it is outperformed by our higher-order model. In addition, we performed an ablation study in which the results of our model using a single type of higher-order potential at a time were computed. This led to the average F1-scores of 0.74, 0.75, 0.75 and 0.72 for $\mathbf{P}_1$, $\mathbf{P}_2$, $\mathbf{P}_3$ and $\mathbf{P}_4$, respectively.

Fig. 2 illustrates how our method can improve the results of the unary potential. For a more detailed analysis, we magnified one of the regions of Fig. 2-a in Fig. 3-a. Note that the segment located underneath the tree leaves was originally incorrectly classified as *vehicle* by the unary potentials. Since the pattern {*leaves*-above & adjacent-*vehicle*-above & adj.-*ground*} does not occur in the codebook $\mathcal{P}$ generated from the training data, it is penalized in our non-associative graphical model. As depicted in Fig. 3, our labeling yields the valid (and correct) pattern {*leaves*-above & adj.-*trunk*-above & adj.-*ground*}. Fig. 3 illustrates other cases where our non-associative higher-order model has leveraged the geometrical relationships between several clusters in a clique to find the correct labels of the nodes.

Fig. 4 illustrates a failure case of our approach. In this image, the unary potential has classified the top of the building as vegetation. This resulted in the pattern $\mathbf{p}^0$: {*leaves*-above & adj.-*building*} which does not exist in the training pattern codebook $\mathcal{P}$. Since the building pillars look very similar to the *tree trunk* class and are beneath and connected to the top segment labeled as leaves,

---

[1] http://www.cs.cmu.edu/~vmr/datasets/oakland_3d/

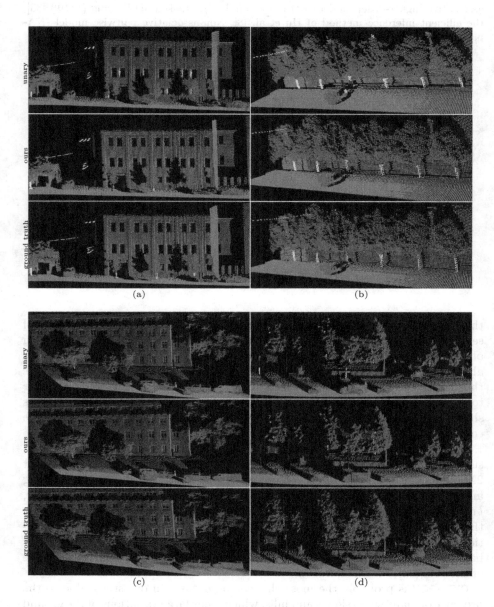

Fig. 2. Qualitative results of four different scenes in VMR-Oakland-V2. For each scene, we show the results of (top) our unary potentials, (middle) our full model. Ground-truth labels are shown in the bottom image. The classes are colored as {*wire*: white, *pole*: blue, *ground*: gray, *leaves*: green, *tree trunk*: yellow, *building*: brown, *vehicle*: pink}.

Table 1. Classification results for VMR-Oakland-V2. We report the results of: Non-associative higher-order model (*NAHO*, our method), Stacked 3D Parsing (*S3DP*) [33], the efficient inference method of Hu et al. [8], Non-associative pairwise model (NA-pairwise), simple associative pairwise model and our unary potentials.

		Wire	Pole	Ground	Leaves	Tree Trunk	Building	Vehicle	avg
Recall	NAHO (ours)	**.89**	.56	**.99**	.94	**.49**	.94	**.87**	
	Hu et al. [8]	.61	.62	.98	.95	.30	**.97**	.72	
	S3DP [33]	.75	**.67**	.98	.93	.41	.93	.74	
	NA-Pairwise	.85	.48	**.99**	**.97**	.25	.93	.78	
	Pairwise	.78	.54	.98	.92	.32	.90	.52	
	Unary Potential	.73	.60	**.99**	.91	.38	.89	.49	
Precision	NAHO (ours)	.66	.70	**.99**	.95	.52	.91	.75	
	Hu et al. [8]	**.86**	**.72**	.97	**.96**	**.72**	.92	**.85**	
	S3DP [33]	.73	.51	**.99**	**.96**	.65	.83	.79	
	NA-Pairwise	.40	.70	**.99**	.93	.61	**.94**	.76	
	Pairwise	.30	.37	**.99**	.95	.41	.83	.52	
	Unary Potential	.34	.25	**.99**	**.96**	.37	.81	.47	
F1-score	NAHO (ours)	**.76**	.62	**.99**	.94	**.50**	.92	**.81**	**.79**
	Hu et al. [8]	.72	**.67**	.98	**.96**	.43	**.94**	.78	.78
	S3DP [33]	.74	.58	.98	.94	**.50**	.88	.76	.76
	NA-Pairwise	.54	.57	**.99**	.95	.35	.93	.77	.73
	Pairwise	.43	.44	.98	.93	.36	.87	.53	.65
	Unary Potential	.46	.35	**.99**	.93	.37	.85	.48	.63

the model matches the pattern $\mathbf{p}^1$: {*leaves*-above & adj.-*trunk*} to this pair of segments. In addition, trees with the same height as this building have been observed in the training data, which means that the height signature context is also supporting the undesirable pattern $\mathbf{p}^1$ for this clique. The final decision is thus left to the unary classifier, which due to the similarity of the building pillar to a tree trunk assigns the wrong labels to these segments. A similar situation is shown in Fig. 3-d, where, in contrast, the problem was resolved, thanks to the considerable height of the building pillars.

As a second experiment, we used the GML-PCV[2] dataset. This dataset consists of two separate aerial point clouds A and B, each of which contains about 2M points and is divided into two approximately equally-sized splits for training and test. The object classes present in this dataset are *ground, building, vehicle, bushes/low vegetation* and *trees/high vegetation*. Due to the lack of samples from the vehicles class in dataset B, this class is commonly dropped from the evaluation procedure. Table 2 provides the results of our approach and state-of-the-art baselines on this dataset. Note that, as before, our system outperforms the state of the art ([33]) on this dataset.

GML-PCV is probably the most challenging dataset in our study, due to the presence of many steep slopes and hills, which incur large variations of the ground height. This issue adversely affects our context patterns that are extracted from the clique structures. To address this problem, we performed ground estimation in small patches of $5\,\mathrm{m} \times 5\,\mathrm{m}$. Furthermore, note that this aerial data provides us with a bird's eye view of the scenes which yields much fewer informative vertical

---

[2] http://graphics.cs.msu.ru/en/node/922

(a)   (b)

(c)   (d)

Fig. 3. Examples of misclassifications of the unary potentials (left image) which are fixed using our higher-order model (right image). Context pattern vectors that are not found in the pattern codebook are penalized and thus corrected by our approach. The classes are color-coded as in Fig. 2.

unary   ours

Fig. 4. Example where context was not sufficient to correct the unary results. The presence of leaves on top of the building in conjunction with the similarity of the building pillars to the class of *tree trunk* has caused the higher-order model to consider this scene as *leaves*-above-*trunk*. Note that some other regions of this point cloud were corrected by our model. Class labels are color-coded as in Fig. 2.

patterns. Therefore, most of the extracted cliques contain only two segments. Nonetheless, our approach managed to extract the relevant information from the data (e.g., *height signature*) to overcome these problems. Qualitative results on this dataset are depicted in Fig. 5-a, where the non-associative higher-order model was able to recover some of the buildings and disambiguate low-vegetation from high-vegetation in some regions.

Finally, we evaluated our model on the RSE–RSS[3] dataset [17], which contains 10 blocks of point clouds from urban scenes, captured using a terrestrial LIDAR

---

[3] http://www.cs.washington.edu/homes/kevinlai/datasets.html

Table 2. Classification results for the dataset GML-PCV using different approaches: Non-associative higher-order model (*NAHO*, our method), Stacked 3D Parsing (*S3DP*) [33], non-associative pairwise model (NA-pairwise) and Unary Potentials.

Dataset A		Ground	Building	Vehicle	High Veg	Low Veg	avg
Recall	NAHO (ours)	.94	.72	.38	.97	.72	
	S3DP [33]	**.98**	**.77**	.10	**.98**	.36	
	NA-pairwise	.93	.70	.37	.97	**.74**	
	Unary Potential	.90	.73	**.40**	.96	.73	
Precision	NAHO (ours)	.97	.81	.42	.98	.17	
	S3DP [33]	.95	**.91**	**.54**	**.99**	**.31**	
	NA-pairwise	.96	.76	.41	.98	.17	
	Unary Potential	**.98**	.49	.40	**.99**	.13	
F1-score	NAHO (ours)	.95	.76	**.40**	.98	.28	**.67**
	S3DP [33]	**.96**	**.83**	.17	.98	**.33**	.66
	NA-pairwise	.94	.73	.39	.97	.28	.66
	Unary Potential	.94	.59	**.40**	.97	.22	.62

Dataset B		Ground	Building	High Veg	Low Veg	avg
Recall	NAHO (ours)	**.99**	**.93**	**.97**	**.55**	
	S3DP [33]	**.99**	.92	**.97**	.52	
	NA-pairwise	.99	.83	.93	.54	
	Unary Potential	**.99**	.77	.96	.37	
Precision	NAHO (ours)	**.99**	**.91**	**.97**	**.57**	
	S3DP [33]	**.99**	.83	**.97**	.53	
	NA-pairwise	.99	.86	.97	.51	
	Unary Potential	.98	.90	.94	.40	
F1-score	NAHO (ours)	**.99**	**.92**	**.97**	**.56**	**.86**
	S3DP [33]	**.99**	.87	**.97**	.52	.84
	NA-pairwise	.99	.84	.95	.52	.83
	Unary Potential	.98	.83	.95	.38	.79

Table 3. Classification results for the dataset RSE-RSS using different approaches: Non-associative higher-order model (*NAHO*, our method), Stacked 3D Parsing (*S3DP*) [33], non-associative pairwise model (NA-pairwise) and Unary Potentials.

		Background	Street Sign	Ground	Tree	House	Fence	Person	Vehicle	avg
Recall	NAHO (ours)	.81	**.51**	**.93**	**.75**	.81	**.61**	.39	**.49**	
	NA-pairwise	**.83**	.25	**.93**	.74	.81	.27	.44	.43	
	Unary Potential	.78	.41	.92	.69	**.82**	.51	**.57**	.43	
Precision	NAHO (ours)	.96	**.12**	.91	**.68**	**.88**	.27	.18	**.44**	
	NA-pairwise	.92	.04	.92	.66	.86	**.40**	**.25**	.41	
	Unary Potential	**.97**	.07	**.93**	.67	.82	.32	.10	.40	
F1-score	NAHO (ours)	**.88**	.19	.92	**.71**	**.84**	.37	.25	.46	**.58**
	S3DP [33]	.79	**.28**	**.94**	.66	.83	.31	.20	**.49**	.56
	NA-pairwise	.87	.07	.92	.70	.83	.32	**.32**	.42	.56
	Unary Potential	.86	.12	.92	.68	.82	**.39**	.17	.41	.54

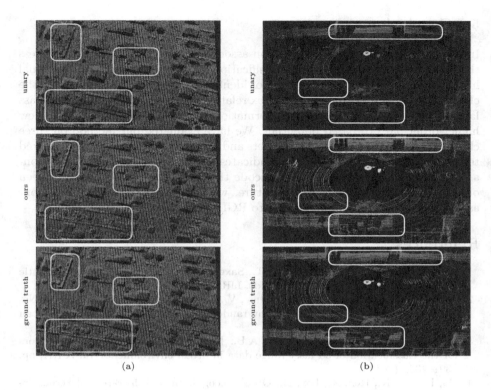

(a)   (b)

Fig. 5. Qualitative results of two scenes from GML-PCV (a) and RSE-RSS (b). For each scene, we show the results of (top) our unary potentials, and (middle) our full model. Ground-truth is shown in the bottom image. The highlighted frames indicate the regions whose labels were corrected using our model. Color codes for (a): {*ground*: gray, *building*: brown, *high-vegetation*: dark green, *low-vegetation*: bright green}, and for (b): {*background*: yellow, *street signs*: blue, *ground*: gray, *tree*: green, *building*: brown, *person*: red, *vehicle*: pink}.

scanner. The dataset is composed of 3D points from eight object categories: *street sign, ground, tree, building, fence, person, vehicle* and *background*, which includes every object not belonging to the previous classes. Table 3 reports the performance of our method obtained using the evaluation procedure of [33].

As discussed in [33], it is very difficult to record descriptive context patterns from this dataset. Nevertheless, as depicted in Table 3, our higher-order model has improved the F1-scores of the unary classifier significantly. This improvement is mostly noticeable in the classes *street sign, tree, person* and *vehicle*. One reason behind this improvement could be the size of these objects and the fact that they are more likely to be included in clique structures (Fig. 1) with descriptive context information. Fig. 5-b provides qualitative results of our method on one scene of this dataset.

5 Conclusion

In this paper, we have introduced a non-associative higher-order CRF to address the problem of semantic 3D point classification. In contrast to many conventional higher-order models, which simply favor identical labeling of the nodes inside the cliques, our model accounts for complex relationships between the different class labels. To model such contextual information we have introduced a set of new higher-order pattern-based potentials. We have evaluated our method on three challenging outdoor point cloud datasets and achieved superior results compared to state-of-the-art techniques. This indicates the importance of exploiting non-associative higher-order models to encode the geometric relationships between objects in outdoor scenes. In the future, we intend to study how such non-associative potentials can be applied to RGB image semantic labeling.

References

1. Anand, A., Koppula, H., Joachims, T., Saxena, A.: Contextually guided semantic labeling and search for 3d point clouds. IJRR (2012)
2. Anguelov, D., Taskar, B., Chatalbashev, V., Koller, D., Gupta, D., Heitz, G., Ng, A.: Discriminative learning of markov random fields for segmentation of 3d scan data. In: CVPR, pp. 169–176 (2005)
3. Behley, J., Steinhage, V., Cremers, A.B.: Performance of histogram descriptors for the classification of 3d laser range data in urban environments. In: ICRA, pp. 4391–4398 (2012)
4. Bo, L., Lai, K., Ren, X., Fox, D.: Object recognition with hierarchical kernel descriptors. In: CVPR, pp. 1729–1736 (2011)
5. Chang, C.C., Lin, C.J.: LIBSVM: A library for support vector machines. ACM TIST 2, 27:1–27:27 (2011)
6. Daniel Munoz, N.V., Hebert, M.: Onboard contextual classification of 3-d point clouds with learned high-order markov random fields. In: ICRA (2009)
7. Gould, S., Baumstarck, P., Quigley, M., Ng, A., Koller, D.: Integrating visual and range data for robotic object detection. In: ECCV Workshop (2008)
8. Hu, H., Munoz, D., Bagnell, J.A., Hebert, M.: Efficient 3-d scene analysis from streaming data. In: ICRA, pp. 2297–2304 (2013)
9. Kim, B.S., Kohli, P., Savarese, S.: 3d scene understanding by voxel-crf. In: ICCV (2013)
10. Kohli, P., Kumar, M., Torr, P.: P3 and beyond: Move making algorithms for solving higher order functions. PAMI 31(9), 1645–1656 (2009)
11. Kohli, P., Ladicky, L., Torr, P.: Robust higher order potentials for enforcing label consistency. IJCV 82(3) (2009)
12. Komodakis, N., Paragios, N.: Beyond pairwise energies: Efficient optimization for higher-order mrfs. In: CVPR, pp. 2985–2992 (2009)
13. Krähenbühl, P., Koltun, V.: Efficient inference in fully connected crfs with gaussian edge potentials. In: NIPS, pp. 109–117 (2011)
14. Ladicky, L., Russell, C., Kohli, P., Torr, P.H.S.: Inference methods for crfs with co-occurrence statistics. IJCV 103(2), 213–225 (2013)
15. Lafferty, J.D., McCallum, A., Pereira, F.C.N.: Conditional random fields: Probabilistic models for segmenting and labeling sequence data. In: ICML, pp. 282–289 (2001)

16. Lai, K., Bo, L., Ren, X., Fox, D.: Sparse distance learning for object recognition combining rgb and depth information. In: ICRA, pp. 4007–4013 (2011)
17. Lai, K., Fox, D.: Object recognition in 3d point clouds using web data and domain adaptation. IJRR 29(8), 1019–1037 (2010)
18. Lim, E.H., Suter, D.: 3d terrestrial lidar classifications with super-voxels and multi-scale conditional random fields. CAD 41(10), 701–710 (2009)
19. Lin, D., Fidler, S., Urtasun, R.: Holistic scene understanding for 3d object detection with rgbd cameras. In: ICCV (2013)
20. Lin, H.T., Lin, C.J., Weng, R.C.: A note on platt's probabilistic outputs for support vector machines. ML 68(3), 267–276 (2007)
21. Lu, Y., Rasmussen, C.: Simplified markov random fields for efficient semantic labeling of 3d point clouds. In: IROS, pp. 2690–2697 (2012)
22. Munoz, D., Bagnell, J.A., Vandapel, N., Hebert, M.: Contextual classification with functional max-margin markov networks. In: CVPR, pp. 975–982 (2009)
23. Munoz, D., Bagnell, J.A., Hebert, M.: Co-inference for multi-modal scene analysis. In: Fitzgibbon, A., Lazebnik, S., Perona, P., Sato, Y., Schmid, C. (eds.) ECCV 2012, Part VI. LNCS, vol. 7577, pp. 668–681. Springer, Heidelberg (2012)
24. Murphy, K.P., Weiss, Y., Jordan, M.I.: Loopy belief propagation for approximate inference: An empirical study. In: UAI, pp. 467–475 (1999)
25. Niemeyer, J., Rottensteiner, F., Soergel, U.: Contextual classification of lidar data and building object detection in urban areas. ISPRS JPRS 87, 152–165 (2014)
26. Rusu, R.B., Blodow, N., Beetz, M.: Fast point feature histograms (fpfh) for 3d registration. In: ICRA, pp. 1848–1853 (2009)
27. Rusu, R.B., Cousins, S.: 3D is here: Point Cloud Library (PCL). In: ICRA (2011)
28. Shapovalov, R., Velizhev, A., Barinova, O.: Non-associative markov networks for 3d point cloud classification. In: PCV, vol. 38, pp. 103–108 (2010)
29. Shapovalov, R., Vetrov, D., Kohli, P.: Spatial inference machines. In: CVPR, pp. 2985–2992 (2013)
30. Vineet, V., Warrell, J., Torr, P.H.S.: Filter-based mean-field inference for random fields with higher-order terms and product label-spaces. In: Fitzgibbon, A., Lazebnik, S., Perona, P., Sato, Y., Schmid, C. (eds.) ECCV 2012, Part V. LNCS, vol. 7576, pp. 31–44. Springer, Heidelberg (2012)
31. Wegner, J.D., Montoya-Zegarra, J.A., Schindler, K.: A higher-order crf model for road network extraction. In: CVPR, pp. 1698–1705 (2013)
32. Xiong, X., Huber, D.: Using context to create semantic 3d models of indoor environments. In: BMVC. pp. 45.1–45.11 (2010)
33. Xiong, X., Munoz, D., Bagnell, J.A.D., Hebert, M.: 3-d scene analysis via sequenced predictions over points and regions. In: ICRA (2011)

Learning Where to Classify
in Multi-view Semantic Segmentation

Hayko Riemenschneider[1], András Bódis-Szomorú[1],
Julien Weissenberg[1], and Luc Van Gool[1,2]

[1] Computer Vision Laboratory, ETH Zurich, Switzerland
[2] K.U. Leuven, Belgium
{hayko,bodis,julienw,vangool}@vision.ee.ethz.ch

Abstract. There is an increasing interest in semantically annotated 3D models, e.g. of cities. The typical approaches start with the semantic labelling of all the images used for the 3D model. Such labelling tends to be very time consuming though. The inherent redundancy among the overlapping images calls for more efficient solutions. This paper proposes an alternative approach that exploits the geometry of a 3D mesh model obtained from multi-view reconstruction. Instead of clustering similar views, we predict the best view before the actual labelling. For this we find the single image part that bests supports the correct semantic labelling of each face of the underlying 3D mesh. Moreover, our single-image approach may surprise because it tends to increase the accuracy of the model labelling when compared to approaches that fuse the labels from multiple images. As a matter of fact, we even go a step further, and only explicitly label a subset of faces (e.g. 10%), to subsequently fill in the labels of the remaining faces. This leads to a further reduction of computation time, again combined with a gain in accuracy. Compared to a process that starts from the semantic labelling of the images, our method to semantically label 3D models yields accelerations of about 2 orders of magnitude. We tested our multi-view semantic labelling on a variety of street scenes.

Keywords: semantic segmentation, multi-view, efficiency, view selection, redundancy, ranking, importance, labeling.

1 Introduction

Multi-view 3D reconstructions are common these days. Not only have tourist data become ubiquitous [1, 2] but the images also often result from deliberate mobile mapping campaigns [3–6]. The images have to exhibit sufficient redundancy – overlap – in order to be suited for Structure-from-Motion (SfM) and Multi-View Stereo (MVS) reconstruction. In the meantime, solutions have been worked out to keep the number of images within bounds, primarily for making the reconstruction pipelines applicable to larger scenes. For instance, the redundancy can be captured by measuring visual similarity between images, and the scene can be summarized, e.g. by constructing a graph of iconic views [2].

D. Fleet et al. (Eds.): ECCV 2014, Part V, LNCS 8693, pp. 516–532, 2014.

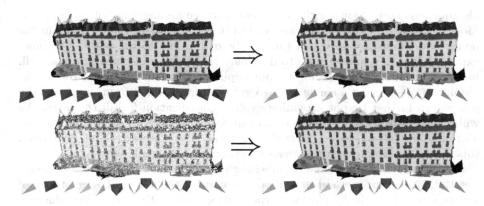

Fig. 1. View overlap is ignored by existing work in semantic scene labelling, and features in all views for all surface parts are extracted redundantly and expensively (top left). In turn, we propose a fine-grained view selection (top right), as well as to reduce scene coverage (bottom left) by only classifying regions essential in terms of classification accuracy. The labels of the classified regions are then spread into all regions (bottom right). This sparsity increases efficiency by orders of magnitude, while also increasing the accuracy of the final result (bottom right vs. top left).

In the aftermath of SfM/MVS reconstruction processes arise recent efforts to make these 3D models widely applicable. An important step in that direction is to augment the models with semantic labels, i.e. to identify parts of the 3D data to belong to certain object classes (e.g. building, tree, car, etc), or object part classes (e.g. door, window, wheel, etc). Typically, the semantic labelling is carried out in all the overlapping images used for 3D reconstruction [7, 8]. This implies that many parts of the scene get labeled multiple times, resulting in a large computational overhead in the order of the redundancy of the image set. The runtime of semantic classification pipelines still lies between 10 s and 300 s per image [8]. Worse, these speeds are reported for moderately sized images of 320×240 pixels, and not for the high-resolution megapixel-sized images common for SfM. The bottleneck of redundant labelling is not in the classification step [9–11], but rather in feature extraction and description. Also, an extra step is needed after labelling the images, namely, to fuse the different labels of the same 3D patch in order to obtain a consistently labelled model.

We propose an alternative strategy to semantically label the 3D model. We start by producing the mesh model and then determine for each of its faces which *single* image is best suited to well capture the true semantic assignment of the face. Not only do we avoid to needlessly process a multitude of images for the same mesh face, but we also have the advantage that we can exploit both geometry (3D model) and appearance (image). Moreover, the accuracy of the semantic labelling will be shown to improve over that of multi-view labelling.

A somewhat similar problem is known from texture mapping or image-based rendering. There decisions have to be made about which image to use to render the local appearance of the model. As to avoid the texture getting blurred, it is also quite usual to look for the best source image among a set of possibilities. Most methods use criteria that are related to the size of the model patch in the image and the degree to which the view is orthogonal to the patch. One may expect to find the same criteria to dominate the choice in segmentation as well, but that intuition is misleading for our application, as we will also show.

On top of selecting a single view to get each face's label from, we speed the process up further by not providing explicit classification for all the faces. We will demonstrate that it suffices to do this for about 30% of the faces, whereas all remaining labels can be inferred from those that were extracted. Moreover, this second parsimony again increases the accuracy of labelling.

We demonstrate our semantic labelling approach for different street scenes. Yet the core of our method is general and can be applied to different types of scenes and objects. In keeping with the central goals of the paper, we achieve a speedup with about two orders of magnitude while improving the label accuracy. In summary our contributions are the following.

1. An alternative approach is proposed for multi-view semantic labelling, efficiently combining the geometry of the 3D model and the appearance of a single, appropriately chosen view - denoted as reducing view redundancy.
2. We show the beneficial effect of reducing the initial labelling to a well-chosen subset of discriminative surface parts, and then using these labels to infer the labels of the remaining surface. This is denoted as scene coverage.
3. As a result, we accelerate the labelling by two orders of magnitude and make a finer-grained labelling of large models (e.g. of cities) practically feasible.
4. Finally, we provide a new 3D dataset of densely labelled images.

2   Related Work

The research in the field of semantic segmentation has enjoyed much attention and success in the last years (+17% in 5 years on PASCAL [12]). Yet most semantic segmentation approaches still rely on redundant independent 2D analysis. Only recently some dived into the 3D realm and exploit joining the domains.

In the 2D domain, the initial works dealt mostly with feature description and learning. [13] introduced TextonBoost which exploits multiple texture filters with an effective boost learning algorithm. [14] uses the output of the trained classifier as new feature input for training several cascades. Additional works included higher-order terms [15, 16] and simplification by superpixels [17, 18]. Others focused on better graphical models [19, 20] or including detectors [7, 21].

None of the above focus on the scalability issue of large scenes and only operate on individual images. Pure 2D scalable semantic classification was addressed in [8], which reduces by nearest neighbor searching for images and superpixels.

For the 2D domain in streetside, where surfaces are more structured than in arbitrary scenes, fewer works have been carried out. [22] pioneered the feel for architectural scene segmentation. [23] carried out 2D classification with a generic image height prior. [24, 25] both used streetside object detectors on top of local features to improve the classification performance. Yet classification is performed on 2D images. 3D is introduced only at a procedural level [26–28].

[29] exploit temporal smoothness on highway scenes. The idea is that redundant time-adjacent frames should be consistently labeled, where assumption is that between frames the motion is not too strong (always forward looking and high-frame rate) and scene content is redundantly present.

For the 3D domain in streetside, [5] were the first to combine sparse SfM and semantic classification. [3] interleaved 2.5D depth estimation and semantic labelling. In these lines [30] used dense 2.5D depth images for classification and [31] used semantic segmentation for deciding where to use 2.5D depth for plane fitting. [32] again worked only on sparse 3D data and yet provides a method for linking these different densities of the full 2D image and sparse 3D domain. [4] classified 2D images and then aggregated their labels to provide an overhead map of the scene. This uses a homography assumption to aggregate the birdseye map of the scenes. Most accuracy problems arise because of occlusions and averaging of multiple views. Recently, [33, 34] combined the creation of geometry with the semantic labelling implicitly evaluating all data redundantly.

Most related to our baseline are the works [9, 10] who used 3D meshes to directly label 3D scenes. This has the benefit of using 3D features and operating in one place to fuse the classification yet still requires description and classification. [10] showed how a common 3D classification can speed up the labelling over redundant 2D classification. [9] introduced decision tree fields for 3D labelling to learn which pairwise connections are important for efficient inference.

Yet in summary, all of the 3D semantic research uses all data redundantly. All images are fully analyzed, described and all its features classified.

Related work for the view selection has only been carried out on an image level. Before SfM, the visual graphs are analyzed and clustered for iconic scenes [1, 2] to split the data into coherent scene parts. After SfM, camera and geometry information are used to select clusters and non-redundant views - again only at the image level [35, 36].

Our work is inspired by the related world of 3D model texturing, where the goal is to find an optimal single texture file for a 3D model [37–39]. Usually, for finding the single best texture, the largest projection in terms of area size or most fronto-parallel view is used in addition to lighting constancy constraints.

We propose to change this paradigm and only analyze the most discriminative views of the data. To the best of our knowledge, we are the first to actively exploit this redundancy in a multi-view semantic labeling. Further, we propose a novel view to select the best such view by selecting the best view according to its ability to classify the scene correctly.

A further note on 3D datasets, most related work only shows examples on small outdoor scenes of single coarse buildings or small indoor scenes like the NYU 3D scenes [40]. The datasets for semantic streetside labeling consist of very few coarse labels (building, vegetation, road) and do not focus on the details of the scenes. For example, datasets like Leuven [3], Yotta [4], CamVid [5] and the KITTI [6] labelled for semantics by [10] only contain these coarse scenes

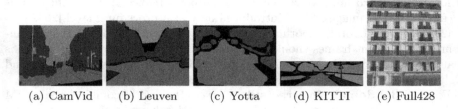

(a) CamVid   (b) Leuven   (c) Yotta   (d) KITTI   (e) Full428

Fig. 2. Dataset overview - most are coarsely labelled at low resolution. We use a pixel accurate labelling with fine details at 1-3 megapixel resolution. (rightmost).

labels, see Figure 2. Except for CamVid where there exist 700 accurately labelled ground truth images, the other datasets only contain coarsely labelled images (in order of user strokes) from 70 to 89 images for training and testing.

In this work, we move to finely detailed ground truth labels including building detail such as windows, doors, balconies, etc. Further, the dataset is used for SfM with high resolution images of 1-3 megapixels and pixel-accurate dense labels.

3 3D Surface and Semantic Classification

Our final goal is to label each part of the scene – a 3D mesh surface – by detailed semantic labels (wall, window, door, sky, road, etc). We briefly describe the multi-view reconstruction methods to obtain the surface, the cues for semantic scene labelling, and then dive into the multi-view scene labelling problem.

3.1 Multi-view Surface Reconstruction

Our input is a set of images which are initially fed to standard SfM/MVS algorithms to produce a mesh. SIFT features [41] are extracted and matched across the images, and reconstructed along with the cameras by using incremental bundle adjustment [42]. The estimated views are clustered and used to compute depth maps via dense MVS. Volumetric fusion is performed by tetrahedral partitioning of space over the obtained dense 3D point cloud, and by exploiting point-wise visibility information in a voting scheme [43, 44]. The final surface is recovered using a robust volumetric graph cuts optimization [45].

The output of the reconstruction procedure is the set of cameras $\mathcal{C} = \{c_j\}$ and a surface mesh $\mathcal{M}$, which consists of a set of 3D vertices, a set of face edges and a set of triangular faces $\mathcal{F} = \{f_i\}$. Since we are about to assign semantic labels to faces f_i, we will represent this mesh as a graph, where nodes correspond to mesh faces and edges correspond to face adjacencies.

3.2 Heavy vs. Light Features for Semantic Labelling

For semantic labelling, we extract simple 2D image and geometric features. The typical approach is to extract features for every location of every single image

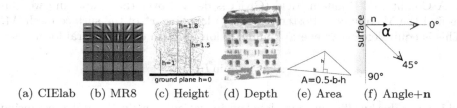

Fig. 3. Features like color and gradient filters are expensive since they are densely calculated in the entire image. Geometry-based are more light-weight. Extra features like denseSIFT should improve the baseline, yet are even heavier to calculate.

in the dataset. We deviate from this dense computational scheme to a sparse computation, which is a main contribution of this paper.

In contrast to related work [9, 10], we split the features into two sets. The first set consists of features that will take longer time to compute:

$$\mathcal{X}^{heavy} = (L^*, a^*, b^*, \mathbf{t}, h, d, \mathbf{n}), \tag{1}$$

This is a 16-dimensional feature vector containing the CIELAB Lab^* color components, 8 responses of the MR8 filter bank [46, 47] in vector $\mathbf{t}$, the height h defined as the distance from the ground plane, the depth d w.r.t. the dominant plane (e.g. facade plane), and the surface normal $\mathbf{n}$, shown in Figure 3. One could use additional features here, e.g. dense SIFT, etc. See [8, 10, 16] for inspiration.

To aggregate features over the projection of a face $f \in \mathcal{F}$ in any observing camera c, we use Sigma Points [48], which efficiently capture the first two statistical moments of the feature vectors.

The second set contains only lightweight features:

$$\mathcal{X}^{light} = (A_{2D}, A_{3D}, A_{2D}/A_{3D}, \alpha), \tag{2}$$

where A_{3D} is the area of a mesh face $f \in \mathcal{F}$, A_{2D} is the area of its 2D projection in a specific camera $c \in \mathcal{C}$, and α is the angle of observation of the face from c.

It should be emphasized that $\mathcal{X}^{heavy}$ relies on image content, whereas $\mathcal{X}^{light}$ relies on geometric information only. In practice, calculation of $\mathcal{X}^{light}$ takes only a fraction of the time (120 seconds for all 1.8 million faces and 428 camera views vs. 21+ hours needed to calculate $\mathcal{X}^{heavy}$ for the Full428 dataset).

3.3   Multi-view Optimization for 3D Surface Labelling

We define a mesh graph $\mathcal{G}_{\mathcal{M}} = (\mathcal{F}, \mathcal{E})$, where the nodes represent the triangular faces $\mathcal{F} = \{f_i\}$ of the surface mesh $\mathcal{M}$, and $\mathcal{E}$ is the set of graph edges, which encode 3D adjacencies between the faces. We aim to assign a label x_i from the set of possible semantic labels $\mathcal{L} = \{l_1, l_2, \ldots, l_L\}$ to each of the n faces f_i. A possible complete labelling of the mesh is denoted by $x = (x_1, x_2, \ldots, x_n)$.

A Conditional Random Field (CRF) is defined over this graph and we aim to find the Maximum-A-Posteriori (MAP) labelling x^* of the surface mesh $\mathcal{M}$. This is equivalent to an energy minimization problem of the general form

$$x^* = \operatorname*{argmin}_{x \in \mathcal{L}^n} E(x),$$

which we solve by efficient multi-label optimization, namely, the alpha-expansion graphcuts [49–51]. Our energy consists of unary data terms for every face f_i, and pairwise regularity terms for every pair of adjacent faces (f_i, f_j).

$$E(x) = \sum_{f_i \in \mathcal{F}} \sum_{c_j \in \mathcal{C}} \Theta(f_i, c_j, x_i) + \lambda \cdot \sum_{(f_i, f_j) \in \mathcal{E}} \Psi(f_i, f_j, x_i, x_j) \tag{3}$$

where $\sum_{c_j} \Theta(f_i, c_j, x_i)$ is the potential (penalty) for face f_i obtaining label x_i. $\Theta(f_i, c_j, x_i)$ is a per-view subterm, which relies on the single specific projection (an observation) of face f_i into view c_j. It can be written as the log-likelihood

$$\Theta(f_i, c_j, l) = -\log p(l \mid \mathcal{X}_{ij}), \tag{4}$$

where $\mathcal{X}_{ij} = \mathcal{X}(f_i, c_j)$ denotes the feature vector associated to the projection of face f_i into camera c_j, and $p(l \mid \mathcal{X}_{ij})$ is the likelihood of label $l \in \mathcal{L}$ for this particular projection of the face. In our scenario, the likelihoods $p(l \mid \mathcal{X})$ are provided by a random forest classifier trained on ground truth labels using the features described in Section 3.2.

The pairwise potential $\Psi(f_i, f_j, x_i, x_j)$ in Eq. 3 enforces spatially smooth labelling solutions over the mesh faces by penalizing occurrences of adjacent faces f_i and f_j obtaining different labels ($x_i \neq x_j$). We use a Potts model

$$\Psi(x_i, x_j) = \begin{cases} 0 & \text{if} \quad x_i = x_j \\ \nabla & \text{if} \quad x_i \neq x_j \end{cases}, \tag{5}$$

where $\nabla = 1$ is a constant penalty. In the future, we plan to weight ∇ in function of the dihedral angles or plane distances between neighboring faces.

The coefficient λ in Eq. 3 controls the balance between unary and pairwise, data and smoothness terms. A grid search showed that $\lambda = 0.5$ works best.

Now for the fun part, it should be emphasized that each triangle f_i is typically observed from multiple cameras c_j. This redundant set of observations poses a computational challenge when extracting the feature vectors $\mathcal{X}(f_i, c_j)$ over all views c_j and for each face f_i. In the classical formulation, every view is considered and the final unary potential is aggregated over all views (see the second sum over the camera set $\mathcal{C}$ in the unary term of Eq. 3). In our findings, this is unnecessary. In the following section we describe our model of view importance and how it can be used to reduce the redundant set of views to the single most discriminative view for a more efficient semantic scene classification.

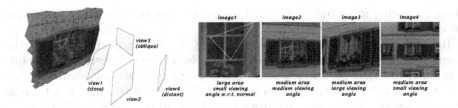

Fig. 4. Geometric link between 3D model and 2D image space. Contrary to related work in view clustering, we look for the best view $c^*(f_i)$ per mesh triangle f_i. For small viewing angles the texture is visually pleasing but not best for semantic classification.

4   Multi-view Observation Importance

In a multi-view scenario redundancy is inherent due to the view overlaps needed for SfM/MVS. Prior work ignored the relationship between these views. In turn, we start by defining two characteristics of the computational burden.

First, **view redundancy** R_i is the number of redundant camera views a mesh face f_i is observed in. See the top of Figure 7 and Table 1 for some typical average view redundancy values. Each triangle of the scene is visible in up to 50 cameras ($\bar{R} = 49$) on average! We aim for zero view redundancy ($R_i \equiv 0, \forall f_i$).

Second, we define (**prior**) **scene coverage** S as the percentage of mesh faces used for feature extraction and semantic classification. Traditionally, the entire scene is classified ($S = 100\%$). However, small areas or parts of homogeneous areas may not need to be classified individually, as the graphcut optimization in Section 3 is capable of spreading the correct labelling into these regions from "covered" regions, i.e. regions where the unaries in Eq. 3 are actually evaluated.

Our method aims at reducing both the view redundancy and the scene coverage for an efficient classification, while also improving accuracy. An initial idea could be to use a single global texture by fusing all images, and to only use this texture for extracting and classifying the heavy features. However, as we will show, the visually best texture is not always the best for semantic classification. Hence, we avoid using a fused texture, and rather keep the rich multi-view environment to decide which views are discriminative, yet before classification.

4.1   Ranking Observations by Importance

In this section, we are looking for the most discriminative view per mesh face in terms of semantic classification. Since SfM also delivers the exact camera models $\mathcal{C} = \{c_j\}$, we can accurately relate each 3D surface element f_i (triangular mesh face) to each of the views c_j, as shown in Figure 4. For efficiency, we aim to eliminate observations which are redundant or less important.

For this, we introduce the term **observation importance** $\mathcal{I}$, which deviates from the existing paradigms of pairwise view clustering and ranking. In our work, we require a relationship to the 3D scene, and define $\mathcal{I}_{ij}$ per observation of a mesh face f_i in any camera c_j. Furthermore, our observation importance

ranks according to usefulness for final semantic scene classification rather than
for camera clustering or texturing.

Inspired by its success in texture mapping, we will rank the views by the
simple texture features such as area and angle. However generally, we define
a ranking function that weights the cheap geometric cues for predicting the
likelihood of the final classifier performance. The goal is to rank each triangle
projection without the heavy feature set. Our importance rank is defined as

$$\mathcal{I}_{ij} = p(f_i \text{ is classified correctly in } c_j | \mathcal{X}_{ij}^{light}). \tag{6}$$

We learn to regress these probabilities, by requiring that $\mathcal{I}_{ij}$ correlates with
view and face-wise classification accuracies resulted from the classical scenario,
i.e. when all views and all faces are used to extract all features. A view c_j is
reliable for classifying face f_i if the semantic label $x_i^* = \text{argmin}_{l \in \mathcal{L}} \Theta(f_i, c_j, l)$
equals the ground truth label. Hence, for the training set, we extract all features
and classify all observations of every mesh face. This provides binary labels for
reliability (correct/incorrect). We use these and the features $\mathcal{X}^{light}$ (including,
e.g. area A_{ij}^{2D}, observation angle α_{ij}) to train a meta-classifier. For this, we use
random forests again and, according to Eq. 6, we use the final leaf probability,
i.e. classifier confidence, as a measure of the importance $\mathcal{I}_{ij}$. Intuitively, views
c_j with small apparent area A_{ij}^{2D} of face f_i, or views observing the face from a
sharper angle α_{ij} should be less reliable. For completeness, we also experimented
using individual features, such as area A_{ij}^{2D}, angle α_{ij}, class likelihood Θ defined
in Eq. 4, or its entropy $H[\Theta]$, to replace the importance $\mathcal{I}_{ij}$.

4.2   Reducing View Redundancy and Scene Coverage

For both characteristics – view redundancy and scene coverage – we use the
observation ranking in Eq. 6 to remove redundant views.

For **view redundancy**, we optimize for the best observation $c^*(f_i)$ of each
face f_i over all views $c_j \in \mathcal{C}$. This simplifies the energy function in Eq. 3 to

$$E_R(x) = \sum_{f_i \in \mathcal{F}} \Theta(f_i, c^*(f_i), x_i) + \dots, \quad \text{with} \quad c^*(f_i) = \underset{\forall c_j \in \mathcal{C}}{\text{argmax}}(\mathcal{I}_{ij}), \tag{7}$$

where we select only the maximally informative view per triangle instead of
merging unary potentials from all observations. Thus, X^{heavy} only needs to be
extracted, described and classified in these most informative views.

For **scene coverage**, we only classify a subset of all triangles that are present
in the surface mesh. We choose for each face f_i the most informative view $c^*(f_i)$
having importance I_{i*}. We then rank faces according to their values I_{i*} and only
use the set of top k faces $\mathcal{F}^k \subset \mathcal{F}$ for further heavy feature extraction, rather
than the full set $\mathcal{F}$. This further simplifies the energy to

$$E_S(x) = \sum_{f_i \in \mathcal{F}^k} \Theta(f_i, c^*(f_i), x_i) + \lambda \cdot \sum_{(f_i, f_j) \in \mathcal{E}} \Psi(f_i, f_j, x_i, x_j) \tag{8}$$

Table 1. Summary of all results (details in supplemental). Semantic Segmentation accuracy (PASCAL IOU in %) for Full428, Sub28 and CamVid102 datasets. By reducing redundancy to zero and also scene coverage to 1/6th, we speedup by 2 orders of magnitude. Ranking by area is better than angle yet the 1st ranks are not best (bold).

	Full428	Sub28	CamVid102	Description
Stats	1794k	185k	46k	# Triangles
	428 (8)	28 (8)	102 (11)	# Images (# Categories)
	9 ± 3	8 ± 2	50 ± 27	Redundancy
Baseline Eq. (3)	35.77	26.05	42.61	MAP SUMALL ($\lambda = 0$)
	35.25	25.13	29.25	MAP MINENTROPY ($\lambda = 0$)
	35.57	25.19	33.21	MAP BESTPROB ($\lambda = 0$)
	37.33	26.63	**50.80**	GC SUMALL (baseline)
	37.82	**26.93**	36.73	GC MINENTROPY $\forall C_j$
	38.27	25.42	37.31	GC MAXPROB $\forall C_j$
SingleView Eq. (7)	37.38 (8px)	26.09 (18px)	52.19 (135px)	Ranked 1st GC AREA (avg)
	37.38 (8px)	26.60 (15px)	54.60 (62px)	Ranked 4th GC AREA (avg)
	35.73 (9°)	25.64 (8°)	47.84 (37°)	Ranked 1st GC ANGLE (avg)
	36.06 (15°)	26.34 (24°)	50.04 (41°)	Ranked 4th GC ANGLE (avg)
	37.04 (0.19)	26.19 (0.49)	52.62 (0.70)	Ranked 1st GC LEARN (avg)
	37.64 (0.18)	**26.86** (0.47)	**56.01** (0.63)	Ranked 4th GC LEARN (avg)
Coverage Eq. (8)	**38.37** (15%)	**28.28** (27%)	**61.07** (35%)	Best Accuracy (AREA)
	37.68 (14%)	26.39 (12%)	57.08 (20%)	1st as Baseline (AREA)
	35.73 (35%)	26.83 (74%)	54.37 (16%)	Best Accuracy (ANGLE)
	35.67 (35%)	25.76 (22%)	52.20 (13%)	1st as Baseline (ANGLE)
	37.08 (35%)	27.97 (40%)	60.57 (31%)	Best Accuracy (LEARN)
	36.15 (33%)	25.96 (34%)	52.98 (13%)	1st as Baseline (LEARN)
Timing	1280min	88min	184min	TIME Full View Redundancy
	11.9x	8.6x	52.6x	SPEEDUP Zero Redundancy
	108min	10.2min	3.5min	TIME Zero Redundancy
	7.1x	8.3x	5.0x	SPEEDUP 1st Coverage as Eq. (3)
	15min	1.2min	0.7min	TIME 1st Coverage as Eq. (3)
	85x	72x	262x	SPEEDUP Overall
	+1.04%	+1.65%	+11.81%	GAIN Overall (absolute)
	103%	106%	124%	GAIN Overall (relative)

which contains unary potentials for only the top k mesh faces, i.e. we set the unaries of all remaining faces to zero. The smoothness term will take care of propagating labels into these areas. An optimal labelling over the complete face set $\mathcal{F}$ defines our final labelling solution (see bottom right of Figure 1).

This is where we again deviate from existing approaches, which evaluate all potentials as they have no means to rank them. Only a recent work [11] introduced the so-called Expected Label Change (ELC) ranking after sampling where to evaluate Θ and running full optimization multiple times. In a multi-view scenario, our methods avoids such a redundant graphcut optimization to estimate the ranking, as we propose the light geometric features to directly estimate the ranking.

5   Experimental Evaluation

In this section we analyze the effect of eliminating view redundancy and reducing scene coverage at the classification stage. As shown below our method considerably reduces computational burden, while showing that we not only maintain but can also improve the final classification accuracy.

We divide our experiments into two investigations summarized in Figure 2 and Table 1. First, we evaluate various importance measures as detailed in Section 4.1 to find the most discriminative view per mesh face. Second, we evaluate the effect of reducing the scene coverage at the classification stage.

Our datasets consist of three outdoor urban scenes annotated with ground truth labels, such as road, wall, window, door, street sign, balcony, door, sky, sidewalk, etc. CamVid [5] is a public dataset. We use its sequence 0016E5, which contains the most buildings and frames. Note that SfM/MVS was only stable for a subset sequence of 102 of its 300 frames. We introduce the larger ETHZ RueMonge 2014 dataset (short: Full428) showing 60 buildings in 428 images covering 700 meters along Rue Monge street in Paris. It has dense and accurate ground-truth labels (Figure 2). Sub28 is a smaller set of 28 images showing four buildings. The CamVid dataset is taken from a car driving forward on a road (with an average viewing angle of 40°) while in the other two datasets the human camera man points more or less towards the buildings (avg. angle $\approx 10°$).

We split each dataset into independent training and testing buildings of roughly 50% of the images and train using all observations of all triangles of the training set. We train both classifiers using a random forest [52, 53] because of its inherent abilities to handle multiple classes, label noise and non-linearity of the features. The number of trees is optimized to 10 and depth to 20 levels.

Please note that our method to reduce view redundancy and scene coverage is general and the speedup generalizes to other semantic classification pipelines. Hence, to study the exact differences, we use the graphcut optimization explained in Eq. (3) over all views as our main baseline (see Table 1).

5.1   Single Discriminative Views – Zero Redundancy

In this first experiment, we determine the most discriminative measure for observation importance. We evaluate the measures in terms of semantic scene classification using PASCAL IOU accuracy averaged over all classes. Table 1 is a summary of our findings. Please look in the supplemental material and website for more detailed results.

As one would expect, exploiting all of the view redundancy and averaging the classifier confidence from each observation (SUMALL) provides stable results. However, these approaches do not provide any speedup and require all the heavy features to be extracted over all observations.

Yet calculating all potentials is the time consuming task, hence we focus on how to find the best observation from cheap geometric features only. The measures to rank are apparent face area A^{2D} (AREA), viewing angle α (ANGLE), and our importance in Eq. 6 (LEARN).

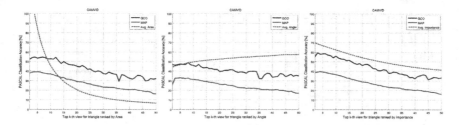

Fig. 5. Removing View Redundancy: showing accuracy for the single k-th ranked feature on x-axis (e.g. 1st largest area, 10th smallest angle, 4th learned importance) and average feature value (red dash). The smaller the area or the larger the angle, the worse performance gets. Our learned performance captures the combination of area and angle better. This is CamVid, other datasets are in supplemental material.

From the evaluations, we have three conclusions. First, on average using the 2D projection area works better than the viewing angle. This is likely due to more robust statistics of larger areas and implicit preference for closer views, as the viewing angle is scale-invariant. Despite the challenging datasets of hugely varying appearance (training to testing performance drops roughly by 30%), other experiments show that the view invariance of the classifier is inherently quite high, which could further explain why the minimum angle is not as useful.

Second and surprisingly, our findings show that neither the largest 2D area nor the most fronto-parallel view deliver the best performance. Rows 10-14 in Table 1 show the average area/angle to change several units for slightly better results. This gain is higher for CamVid because of the steep forward-looking camera and also because of the different semantic classes. For more detail over the class-averaged measures in Figure 5, we also looked at classwise results for area. For all datasets, the classes captured by changing thin 3D surfaces (pole, fence, door, window, sign/pole, etc) experience a gain in accuracy with less frontal projections. These findings suggest that for these classes slanted views better capture the 3D structure.

Overall, our learned combination of the light features works best, since it can balance the distortion of the area and the extreme viewing angles.

5.2 Reduction of Scene Coverage

In the second experiment, we investigate how many total mesh faces are really essential for good performance semantic classification in multi-view scenarios. Going one step further, we reduce the scene coverage and only select the top k triangles after selecting the most discriminative view per triangle.

Here our baselines are a) using all redundancies and the zero redundancy of b) area and c) angle - all at full coverage. The results are shown as average over all classes (top) and as classwise results (bottom) in Figure 6. First conclusion is that the area is usually better at selecting the important triangles for coverage. Its curve climbs faster and overall its accuracy is higher, except for steep-angled

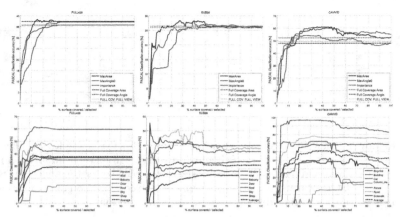

Fig. 6. Reducing Scene Coverage: showing accuracy over percentage of selected triangles within graph optimization. Dashed lines are accuracy at full coverage (allviews, maxarea, minangle, importance). On average 30% are sufficient to label the entire scene as correctly as 100% coverage! Last rows show classwise results (see text for details).

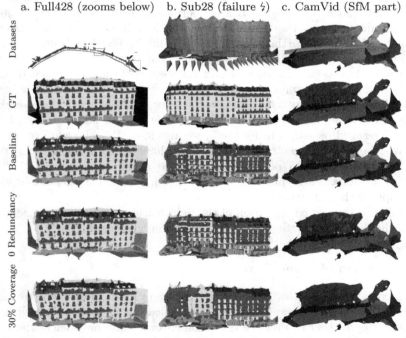

Fig. 7. Overview of results - top left is full street, view redundancy as heatmap (more redundancy, the greener), ground truth (zoomed for two parts of street), and results for full redundancy, single best view and best score for coverage (at stable 30%). Overall, the accuracy are the same after all our speedups. Middle column shows failure cases (↯), where the initial classifier already fails and gracefully further smoothes the results.

CamVid dataset. Here the angle measure works better, and overall our learned importance combining the two is best.

Second conclusion may surprise again, we can even get better than the baselines at full coverage (dashed lines)! This is explained by the smaller classes (which occur less frequently and cover less space). Not sampling these early, removes competition for the large classes, which perform much better here. Hence, it is the size of the area that matters. As the importance measure is less good at the early coverage (below 10% coverage), we visualized the three measures and learned that the area is spread across the scene where our learned ranking focuses more on high confidence classes like building and road.

Third and most important conclusion, for large classes it is enough to use 10% of the scene coverage to reach the baselines. Overall, around 30% scene coverage stable results are obtained for all classes. This means that 70% of the potentials usually calculated for semantic scene segmentation are not necessary. The same accuracy can be achieved by using our proposed observation importance and optimization over the graph neighborhood.

6   Conclusions

In this work we investigated methods for reducing the inherent data overlap of multi-view semantic segmentation. As the speeds for other parts have been improved, the bottleneck is the redundant feature extraction and classification.

By exploiting the geometry and introducing single discriminative views per detailed scene part (a triangle), we avoid the redundancy and only classify a single time. This provides a speedup in the order of the data redundancy.

Further, we showed that simple features used for texture mapping are not best when the goal is semantic scene classification. Our learned importance better combines the features like area and viewing angle and improves the ranking.

Lastly, we proposed further efficiency by reducing the scene coverage and classifying only 30% of the scene and still obtain accurate labels for the entire scene. All in all, after reducing the redundancy and coverage we even increase the overall accuracy.

For future work we noticed that the overall accuracy of the scene classification depends on the resolution of this mesh as too large triangles cover semantic units and small triangles are not reliable for classification. Hence we plan to find the best resolution and rank even features in terms of the their computational effort.

Acknowledgements. This work was supported by the European Research Council (ERC) under the project VarCity (#273940) at www.varcity.eu.

References

1. Gammeter, S., Quack, T., Tingdahl, D., van Gool, L.: Size does matter: Improving object recognition and 3D reconstruction with cross-media analysis of image clusters. In: Daniilidis, K., Maragos, P., Paragios, N. (eds.) ECCV 2010, Part I. LNCS, vol. 6311, pp. 734–747. Springer, Heidelberg (2010)

2. Li, X., Wu, C., Zach, C., Lazebnik, S., Frahm, J.-M.: Modeling and Recognition of Landmark Image Collections Using Iconic Scene Graphs. In: Forsyth, D., Torr, P., Zisserman, A. (eds.) ECCV 2008, Part I. LNCS, vol. 5302, pp. 427–440. Springer, Heidelberg (2008)

3. Ladicky, L., Sturgess, P., Russell, C., Sengupta, S., Bastanlar, Y., Clocksin, W., Torr, P.: Joint Optimization for Object Class Segmentation and Dense Stereo Reconstruction. Intern. Journal of Computer Vision (IJCV) 100(2), 122–133 (2012)

4. Sengupta, S., Sturgees, P., Ladicky, L., Torr, P.: Automatic dense visual semantic mapping from street-level imagery. In: Proc. Intern. Conf. on Intelligent Robots Systems, IROS (2012)

5. Brostow, G.J., Shotton, J., Fauqueur, J., Cipolla, R.: Segmentation and recognition using structure from motion point clouds. In: Forsyth, D., Torr, P., Zisserman, A. (eds.) ECCV 2008, Part I. LNCS, vol. 5302, pp. 44–57. Springer, Heidelberg (2008)

6. Geiger, A., Lenz, P., Urtasun, R.: Are we ready for Autonomous Driving? The KITTI Vision Benchmark Suite. In: Proc. IEEE Conf. on Computer Vision and Pattern Recognition, CVPR (2012)

7. Ladický, Ľ., Sturgess, P., Alahari, K., Russell, C., Torr, P.H.S.: What, Where and How Many? Combining Object Detectors and CRFs. In: Daniilidis, K., Maragos, P., Paragios, N. (eds.) ECCV 2010, Part IV. LNCS, vol. 6314, pp. 424–437. Springer, Heidelberg (2010)

8. Tighe, J., Lazebnik, S.: SuperParsing: Scalable Nonparametric Image Parsing with Superpixels. Intern. Journal of Computer Vision (IJCV) 101(2), 329–349 (2012)

9. Koehler, O., Reid, I.: Efficient 3D Scene Labeling Using Fields of Trees. In: Proc. IEEE Intern. Conf. on Computer Vision, ICCV (2013)

10. Sengupta, S., Valentin, J., Warrell, J., Shahrokni, A., Torr, P.: Mesh Based Semantic Modelling for Indoor and Outdoor Scenes. In: Proc. IEEE Conf. on Computer Vision and Pattern Recognition, CVPR (2013)

11. Roig, G., Boix, X., Ramos, S., de Nijs, R., Van Gool, L.: Active MAP Inference in CRFs for Efficient Semantic Segmentation. In: Proc. IEEE Intern. Conf. on Computer Vision, ICCV (2013)

12. Everingham, M., Van Gool, L., Williams, C.K.I., Winn, J., Zisserman, A.: The PASCAL Visual Object Classes Challenge (VOC 2012) Results (2012), http://www.pascal-network.org/challenges/VOC/voc2012/workshop/index.html

13. Shotton, J., Winn, J.M., Rother, C., Criminisi, A.: *textonBoost*: Joint appearance, shape and context modeling for multi-class object recognition and segmentation. In: Leonardis, A., Bischof, H., Pinz, A. (eds.) ECCV 2006, Part I. LNCS, vol. 3951, pp. 1–15. Springer, Heidelberg (2006)

14. Tu, Z.: Auto-context and its application to high-level vision tasks. In: Proc. IEEE Conf. on Computer Vision and Pattern Recognition, CVPR (2008)

15. Kohli, P., Ladicky, L., Torr, P.: Robust higher order potentials for enforcing label consistency. Intern. Journal of Computer Vision (IJCV) 82(3), 302–324 (2009)

16. Ladicky, L., Russell, C., Kohli, P., Torr, P.: Associative Hierarchical CRFs for Object Class Image Segmentation. In: Proc. IEEE Intern. Conf. on Computer Vision, ICCV (2009)

17. Kluckner, S., Mauthner, T., Roth, P., Bischof, H.: Semantic image classification using consistent regions and individual context. In: Proc. British Machine Vision Conference, BMVC (2009)

18. Gould, S., Rodgers, J., Cohen, D., Koller, D., Elidan, G.: Multi-class segmentation with relative location prior. Intern. Journal of Computer Vision (IJCV) 80(3), 300–316 (2008)

19. Munoz, D., Bagnell, J.A., Hebert, M.: Stacked Hierarchical Labeling. In: Daniilidis, K., Maragos, P., Paragios, N. (eds.) ECCV 2010, Part VI. LNCS, vol. 6316, pp. 57–70. Springer, Heidelberg (2010)
20. Kraehenbuehl, P., Koltun, V.: Efficient Inference in Fully Connected CRFs with Gaussian Edge Potentials. In: Advances in Neural Information Processing Systems, NIPS (2011)
21. Wojek, C., Schiele, B.: A dynamic conditional random field model for joint labeling of object and scene classes. In: Forsyth, D., Torr, P., Zisserman, A. (eds.) ECCV 2008, Part IV. LNCS, vol. 5305, pp. 733–747. Springer, Heidelberg (2008)
22. Berg, A., Grabler, F., Malik, J.: Parsing images of architectural scenes. In: Proc. IEEE Intern. Conf. on Computer Vision, ICCV (2007)
23. Xiao, J., Quan, L.: Multiple view semantic segmentation for street view images. In: Proc. IEEE Intern. Conf. on Computer Vision, ICCV (2009)
24. Riemenschneider, H., Krispel, U., Thaller, W., Donoser, M., Havemann, S., Fellner, D., Bischof, H.: Irregular lattices for complex shape grammar facade parsing. In: Proc. IEEE Conf. on Computer Vision and Pattern Recognition, CVPR (2012)
25. Martinović, A., Mathias, M., Weissenberg, J., Van Gool, L.: A Three-Layered Approach to Facade Parsing. In: Fitzgibbon, A., Lazebnik, S., Perona, P., Sato, Y., Schmid, C. (eds.) ECCV 2012, Part VII. LNCS, vol. 7578, pp. 416–429. Springer, Heidelberg (2012)
26. Teboul, O., Simon, L., Koutsourakis, P., Paragios, N.: Segmentation of building facades using procedural shape prior. In: Proc. IEEE Conf. on Computer Vision and Pattern Recognition, CVPR (2010)
27. Simon, L., Teboul, O., Koutsourakis, P., Van Gool, L., Paragiosn, N.: Parameter-free/pareto-driven procedural 3d reconstruction of buildings from ground-level sequences. In: Proc. IEEE Conf. on Computer Vision and Pattern Recognition, CVPR (2012)
28. Müller, P., Wonka, P., Haegler, S., Ulmer, A., Van Gool, L.: Procedural modeling of buildings. In: Proc. of the Intern. Conf. on Computer graphics and interactive techniques, SIGGRAPH (2006)
29. Floros, G., Leibe, B.: Joint 2D-3D Temporally Consistent Semantic Segmentation of Street Scenes. In: Proc. IEEE Conf. on Computer Vision and Pattern Recognition, CVPR (2012)
30. Zhang, C., Wang, L., Yang, R.: Semantic segmentation of urban scenes using dense depth maps. In: Daniilidis, K., Maragos, P., Paragios, N. (eds.) ECCV 2010, Part IV. LNCS, vol. 6314, pp. 708–721. Springer, Heidelberg (2010)
31. Gallup, D., Frahm, J., Pollefeys, M.: Piecewise planar and non-planar stereo for urban scene reconstruction. In: Proc. IEEE Conf. on Computer Vision and Pattern Recognition, CVPR (2010)
32. Munoz, D., Bagnell, J.A., Hebert, M.: Co-inference for Multi-modal Scene Analysis. In: Fitzgibbon, A., Lazebnik, S., Perona, P., Sato, Y., Schmid, C. (eds.) ECCV 2012, Part VI. LNCS, vol. 7577, pp. 668–681. Springer, Heidelberg (2012)
33. Haene, C., Zach, C., Cohen, A., Angst, R., Pollefeys, M.: Joint 3D Scene Reconstruction and Class Segmentation. In: Proc. IEEE Conf. on Computer Vision and Pattern Recognition, CVPR (2013)
34. Kim, B., Kohli, P., Savarese, S.: 3D Scene Understanding by Voxel-CRF. In: Proc. IEEE Intern. Conf. on Computer Vision, ICCV (2013)
35. Furukawa, Y., Curless, B., Seitz, S., Szeliski, R.: Towards Internet-scale Multi-view Stereos. In: Proc. IEEE Conf. on Computer Vision and Pattern Recognition, CVPR (2010)

36. Mauro, M., Riemenschneider, H., Van Gool, L., Leonardi, R.: Overlapping camera clustering through dominant sets for scalable 3D reconstruction. In: Proc. British Machine Vision Conference, BMVC (2013)

37. Debevec, P., Borshukov, G., Yu, Y.: Efficient View-Dependent Image-Based Rendering with Projective Texture-Mapping. In: Eurographics Rendering Workshop (1998)

38. Laveau, S., Faugeras, O.: 3-D scene representation as a collection of images. In: Proc. IEEE Intern. Conf. on Computer Vision, ICCV (1994)

39. Williams, L., Chen, E.: View interpolation for image synthesis. In: Proc. of the Intern. Conf. on Computer graphics and interactive techniques, SIGGRAPH (1993)

40. Silberman, N., Hoiem, D., Kohli, P., Fergus, R.: Indoor Segmentation and Support Inference from RGBD Images. In: Fitzgibbon, A., Lazebnik, S., Perona, P., Sato, Y., Schmid, C. (eds.) ECCV 2012, Part V. LNCS, vol. 7576, pp. 746–760. Springer, Heidelberg (2012)

41. Lowe, D.: Distinctive image features from scale-invariant keypoints. Intern. Journal of Computer Vision (IJCV) 60(2), 91–110 (2004)

42. Wu, C.: Towards linear-time incremental structure from motion. In: Proc. of Intern. Symp. on 3D Data, Processing, Visualiz. and Transmission (3DPVT) (2013)

43. Labatut, P., Pons, J., Keriven, R.: Efficient Multi-View Reconstruction of Large-Scale Scenes using Interest Points, Delaunay Triangulation and Graph Cuts. In: Proc. IEEE Intern. Conf. on Computer Vision, ICCV (2007)

44. Hiep, V., Labatut, P., Pons, J., Keriven, R.: High Accuracy and Visibility-Consistent Dense Multi-view Stereo. IEEE Trans. on Pattern Analysis and Machine Intelligence (PAMI) 34(5), 889–901 (2012)

45. Jancosek, M., Pajdla, T.: Multi-View Reconstruction Preserving Weakly-Supported Surfaces. In: Proc. IEEE Conf. on Computer Vision and Pattern Recognition, CVPR (2011)

46. Varma, M., Zisserman, A.: A statistical approach to texture classification from single images. Intern. Journal of Computer Vision (IJCV) 62(1-2), 61–81 (2005)

47. Geusebroek, J., Smeulders, A., van de Weijer, J.: Fast Anisotropic Gauss Filtering. IEEE Trans. on Image Processing (TIP) 12(8), 938–943 (2003)

48. Kluckner, S., Mauthner, T., Roth, P.M., Bischof, H.: Semantic classification in aerial imagery by integrating appearance and height information. In: Zha, H., Taniguchi, R.-i., Maybank, S. (eds.) ACCV 2009, Part II. LNCS, vol. 5995, pp. 477–488. Springer, Heidelberg (2010)

49. Boykov, Y., Veksler, O., Zabih, R.: Fast approximate energy minimization via graph cuts. IEEE Trans. on Pattern Analysis and Machine Intelligence (PAMI) 23(11), 1222–1239 (2001)

50. Boykov, Y., Kolmogorov, V.: An experimental comparison of min-cut/max-flow algorithms for energy minimization in vision. IEEE Trans. on Pattern Analysis and Machine Intelligence (PAMI) 26(9), 124–1137 (2004)

51. Kolmogorov, V., Zabih, R.: What energy functions can be minimized via graph cuts? IEEE Trans. on Pattern Analysis and Machine Intelligence (PAMI) 26(2), 147–159 (2004)

52. Amit, Y., August, G., Geman, D.: Shape quantization and recognition with randomized trees. Neural Computation 9, 1545–1588 (1996)

53. Breiman, L.: Random forests. Machine Learning 45(1), 5–32 (2001)

Stixmantics: A Medium-Level Model
for Real-Time Semantic Scene Understanding

Timo Scharwächter[1,2], Markus Enzweiler[1], Uwe Franke[1], and Stefan Roth[2]

[1] Environment Perception, Daimler R&D, Sindelfingen, Germany
[2] Department of Computer Science, TU Darmstadt, Germany

Abstract. In this paper we present *Stixmantics*, a novel medium-level scene representation for real-time visual semantic scene understanding. Relevant scene structure, motion and object class information is encoded using so-called *Stixels* as primitive elements. Sparse feature-point trajectories are used to estimate the 3D motion field and to enforce temporal consistency of semantic labels. Spatial label coherency is obtained by using a CRF framework.

The proposed model abstracts and aggregates low-level pixel information to gain robustness and efficiency. Yet, enough flexibility is retained to adequately model complex scenes, such as urban traffic. Our experimental evaluation focuses on semantic scene segmentation using a recently introduced dataset for urban traffic scenes. In comparison to our best baseline approach, we demonstrate state-of-the-art performance but reduce inference time by a factor of more than 2,000, requiring only 50 ms per image.

Keywords: semantic scene understanding, bag-of-features, region classification, real-time, stereo vision, stixels.

1 Introduction

Robust visual scene understanding is one of the fundamental requirements for artificial systems to interpret and act within a dynamic environment. Essentially, two main levels of scene and object representation have been proposed, with contradicting benefits and drawbacks.

Object-centric approaches, *i.e.* sliding window detectors [9,15], have shown remarkable recognition performance due to strong scene and geometric model constraints (holistic or deformable bounding-boxes), easy cue integration and strong temporal tracking-by-detection models. The scene content is represented very concisely as a set of individual detected objects. However, the generalization to partial occlusion cases, object groups or geometrically not well-defined classes, such as road surface or building, is difficult.

Region-centric models, *i.e.* (semantic) segmentation approaches, such as [6,20,28,37,44] among many others, operate in a bottom-up fashion and usually do not recover an object-level scene description. They are rather generic in terms of the geometry and the number of object classes involved. However, grouping

D. Fleet et al. (Eds.): ECCV 2014, Part V, LNCS 8693, pp. 533–548, 2014.

Fig. 1. Different scene representation levels trading-off specificity (object-centric) and generality (region-centric). We advocate the use of a medium-level *scene-centric* model to balance this trade-off and gain efficiency.

is based on pixel-level intensity, depth or motion discontinuities with only few geometry or scene constraints leading to noise in the recovered scene models. Furthermore, segmentation approaches are often computationally expensive and the final representation, a pixel-wise image labeling, is overly redundant for many real-world applications, *e.g.* mobile robotics or intelligent vehicles.

To balance this trade-off between specificity (objects) and generality (regions), as shown in Fig. 1, we consider the ideal model for visual semantic scene understanding to be a medium-level *scene-centric* representation that builds upon the strengths of both object-centric and region-centric models. The framework we propose in this paper, called Stixmantics, is based on the *Stixel World* [35], a compact environment representation computed from dense disparity maps. The key aspect that qualifies Stixels as a good medium-level representation is simply the fact that it is based on depth information and that it maps the observed scene to a well-defined model of ground surface and upright standing objects. This makes it adhere more to boundaries of actual objects in the scene than standard superpixels. Yet, in contrast to object-centric approaches, the separation into thin stick-like elements (the Stixels) retains enough flexibility to handle complex geometry and partial occlusions. More precisely, a Stixel models a part of an elevated (upright standing) object in the scene and is defined by its 3D foot point, height, width and distance to the camera.

Fig. 2. System overview. A spatio-temporally regularized medium-level scene model (bottom center) is estimated in real-time. This model represents the scene in terms of 3D scene structure, 3D velocity and semantic class labels at each Stixel. Dense stereo and Stixel visualization (top center) is color-encoded depending on distance. Stixel-based proposal regions for classification are shown in false-color (top right). In all other images, colors represent semantic object classes.

In this work, we augment this Stixel representation with spatio-temporally regularized semantic object category and motion information, so that our recovered scene model gives easy access to all relevant information about objects in the scene. To this end, we aggregate intensity and depth information through a semantic bag-of-features classification model that takes Stixel-based proposal regions as input. Reliable sparse point trajectories are used to estimate ego-motion corrected 3D velocity and to enforce temporal coherence of semantic labels in a recursive fashion. Finally, spatial consistency is imposed by a conditional random field using individual Stixels as nodes. See Fig. 2 for an overview.

For unparalleled real-time inference in semantic scene understanding, our framework operates on a few hundred Stixels as opposed to millions of pixels without loss of scene representation quality. Although specialized real-time implementations of pixel dense semantic segmentation exist [7,37], we believe only a medium-level aggregation will enable unrivaled computational efficiency.

2   Related Work

Among the wealth of existing literature about semantic segmentation [6,20,28,37] and scene understanding [13,22,45], we focus on models imposing temporal coherency upon the segmentation result. On a broad level, existing work can be distinguished into *offline* and *online* methods. Offline or batch methods, *e.g.* [24], have the potential to yield best possible segmentation performance, as they can access all available information from all time steps during inference. However, being not causal, they cannot be applied to streaming video analysis, which is a requirement for many applications, such as mobile robotics.

In contrast, online methods only require observations from previous time steps. A closer look reveals fundamental differences, mainly separating *recursive* models [12,44,45] from models considering longer time history [10,16,33]. The latter also include models performing inference in a 3D graphical model (space and time) over a stack of several frames.

Furthermore, the position in the processing pipeline and the level of abstraction on which temporal consistency is enforced has several important implications. For example, low-level motion segmentation (detection-by-tracking) methods, such as [10] or [34], can provide temporally stable proposal regions as input for semantic labeling but require prominent motion of an object in the image for proper detection. In [31], a post-processing algorithm for causal temporal smoothing of frame-by-frame segmentation results is proposed. Requiring dense optical flow, temporal contributions are weighted according to a pixel-wise similarity measure.

Over the last years, prevalent consensus has emerged that increasing the level of abstraction from pixels to superpixels or larger image regions allows for richer models and more efficient inference. In fact, most state-of-the-art methods rely on superpixels, *e.g.* [3,6]. However, as superpixels are typically built in a bottom-up fashion, their boundaries often fluctuate when applied to consecutive frames in a video sequence. The difficulty of registering and aligning superpixels over time has recently been addressed by [8] and [43]. Alternatively, using the warped previous segmentation as initialization for superpixels in the current frame is exploited in [1] and [30]. In [40], spatio-temporal segments are extracted from video data and are subsequently ranked according to weakly labeled categories provided with the video. However, even with perfect temporal registration of superpixels and object shapes, the semantic label decision can still be incorrect, mainly due to temporal noise in the classification results [36,41]. We provide a method to encourage temporal label coherence which is independent of the used superpixel approach.

Further related work addresses the recovery of a rough 3D scene layout from single images [26] or from video data using structure-from-motion point clouds [5]. None of these methods exploits dense stereo as well as motion information at the same time.

We consider the main contribution of this paper to be the spatio-temporally regularized Stixmantics scene model, where structure, motion and semantics are aggregated on local scene elements, the so-called Stixels. Most closely related to this work is [36], which also combines Stixels and a bag-of-features classification scheme for semantic segmentation. However, their model does not use motion information at all and includes neither spatial nor temporal regularization. Another related Stixel-based approach is [12], where Stixels are grouped into objects, based on discrete motion directions only. This method does not involve any semantic information. Furthermore, we rely on long-term point trajectories for temporal label coherence by applying a recursive Bayesian filtering scheme on trajectory-level. This effectively combines the efficiency of recursive methods [12,13,44,45] with the robustness of considering a longer temporal window [16,33].

Our Stixmantics approach delivers state-of-the-art performance on the public Daimler Urban Segmentation Dataset but at a fraction of the computational cost of previously reported methods. In the same way as Stixels have dramatically improved processing speeds for object detection [4,11] and motion segmentation [12], we demonstrate a real-time method for semantic 3D scene understanding.

3   Generation and Classification of Proposal Regions

One of the foundations of our framework is a bag-of-features model to classify free-form proposal regions. In this context, meaningful initial regions are crucial for semantic segmentation performance [3,6,36]. To rapidly obtain good regions, we follow the method of [36], who first showed how to leverage medium-level depth information of the Stixel World for semantic scene understanding. In this section, we briefly summarize their work, which is the foundation for our Stixmantics model.

Semi-global matching (SGM) [25] is used to obtain dense disparity maps and from that the Stixel representation is computed as described in [35]. To efficiently obtain larger proposal regions R_k, the authors group Stixels according to their 3D spatial proximity, leveraging the fact that Stixels model upright standing objects on the ground surface at different distances. This approach comes with a bias towards objects on the ground, which however holds true for outdoor traffic scenes and in fact strongly helps to regularize the resulting scene representation. For more details, the reader is referred to [36].

To describe the appearance information within the resulting free-form proposal regions, dense multi-scale SIFT descriptors [29] are encoded with extremely randomized clustering forests and finally pooled over each region R_k. Height information, another medium-level cue, is incorporated in terms of *height pooling*, where visual words are pooled into different locations in the histogram according to their height above the ground plane to introduce a vertical geometric ordering into the descriptor [36]. The resulting bag-of-features region histogram $\mathbf{h}(R_k)$ is subsequently classified by means of a multi-class SVM with histogram-intersection kernel. We refer to the per-label classification confidence for region R_k as $\Gamma_i(\mathbf{h}(R_k)) \in (0, 1)$, with $i = 1 \ldots L$ and L denoting the number of labels.

This model, as introduced in [36], does not contain any spatial or temporal integration of semantic class labels. Our proposed Stixmantics model fills this gap. Note that the ideas presented in the next sections are conceptually independent from the particular proposal generation, feature descriptor, codebook method or classifier.

4   Temporal Filtering on Trajectory-Level

In order to obtain a temporally consistent representation, we propose a method to efficiently incorporate knowledge from previous time steps into our medium-level scene model. In contrast to existing methods, which aim to filter the semantic label information either densely on pixel-level or focus explicitly on registering superpixels over time, we aggregate information over time locally on sparse long-term point trajectories, where correspondence is very reliable and can be computed efficiently. For this we rely on the well-established KLT feature tracker [42]. We deliberately do not use pixel-level dense optical flow, as it can be spatially redundant, is often overly smooth at object boundaries due to the required regularization term and is, despite modern parallel GPU implementations, computationally expensive. This choice is supported by [10], where the combination of sparse point tracks with superpixels results in more efficient models with adequate performance.

In the following, we describe our methods to filter the discrete semantic label decision (Sec. 4.1), as well as continuous velocity information (Sec. 4.2) for each KLT trajectory over time.

4.1   Label Integration

To integrate the semantic region classification output $\Gamma_i(\mathbf{h}(R_k))$ from Sec. 3 over time, we opt for a Hidden Markov Model (HMM) approach. We model label transitions as a Markov chain for each trajectory and perform label filtering in

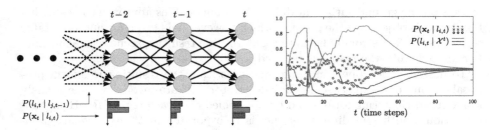

Fig. 3. Illustration of the recursive label filtering scheme, which is applied to each point trajectory. Unfolded directed Markov model with three labels (left). Arrows indicate possible causal transitions. Simulated result for a trajectory of length 100 (time steps), where dots represent noisy observations and solid lines show the resulting filtered posterior for the labels in each time step, given all previously observed data (right). In time step 10, we place a strong outlier in the observation and starting from time step 40, we quickly shift all observations towards a uniform value of $P(\mathbf{x}_t \mid l_{i,t}) = \frac{1}{3} \forall i$ to demonstrate the filtering effect of the model. Note that in practice we never observed such strong outliers as simulated in time step 10. The weight α is set to $\alpha = 0.95$, as in all our experiments.

the Bayesian sense, as shown in Fig. 3. For a trajectory with an age of t time steps, we estimate the posterior $P(l_{i,t} \mid \mathcal{X}^t)$ of label $l_{i,t}$, given the set of all previous and current observations $\mathcal{X}^t = \{\mathbf{x}_0, \mathbf{x}_1, \ldots, \mathbf{x}_t\}$ up to time t. Prediction is performed using forward inference, which involves recursive application of predict (1) and update (2) steps [32]:

$$P\big(l_{i,t} \mid \mathcal{X}^{t-1}\big) = \sum_j P\big(l_{i,t} \mid l_{j,t-1}\big) P\big(l_{j,t-1} \mid \mathcal{X}^{t-1}\big) \tag{1}$$

$$P\big(l_{i,t} \mid \mathcal{X}^t\big) = \frac{P(\mathbf{x}_t \mid l_{i,t}) P\big(l_{i,t} \mid \mathcal{X}^{t-1}\big)}{\sum_j P(\mathbf{x}_t \mid l_{j,t}) P\big(l_{j,t} \mid \mathcal{X}^{t-1}\big)} . \tag{2}$$

The term $P(l_{i,t} \mid l_{j,t-1})$ in (1) corresponds to the transition model of labels between two subsequent time steps and acts as the temporal regularizer in our setup. Note that ideally objects do not change their label over time, especially not on trajectory-level. The only two causes for a label change are errors in the observation model $P(\mathbf{x}_t \mid l_{i,t})$ or measurement errors in the trajectory, $i.e.$ the tracked point is accidentally assigned to another object. Thus, we assign a relatively large weight $\alpha \in (0, 1)$ to the diagonal entries of the transition matrix (self loops) and a small value to the remaining entries, such that we obtain a proper probability distribution:

$$P(l_{i,t} \mid l_{j,t-1}) = \begin{cases} \alpha & i = j \\ \dfrac{1 - \alpha}{L - 1} & i \neq j . \end{cases} \tag{3}$$

Fig. 4. Scene labeling result with averaged velocity information, indicated by the arrow at the bottom of each Stixel (left). 3D scene reconstruction showing the corresponding Kalman filtered velocity information for each tracked feature point (right). The arrows indicate the predicted position in 500 ms and the color encodes velocity from slow (green) to fast moving (red).

We empirically choose $\alpha = 0.95$ in our experiments. Alternatively, the transition probabilities could be learned from training data. However, we point out again that the resulting transitions would only reflect erroneous correspondences in the trajectory and do not correspond to actual semantic object relations.

Following Sec. 3, we model the observation $\mathbf{x}_t$ as the bag-of-features histogram $\mathbf{h}(R_k)$ of the region R_k covering the tracked feature point in time step t. We relate the per-label classification output $\Gamma_i(\mathbf{h}(R_k))$ to the observation model given uniform label priors as $P(\mathbf{x}_t \mid l_{i,t}) \propto \Gamma_i(\mathbf{h}(R_k))$.

To maintain a constant number of tracks, new trajectories are instantiated in every time step to account for lost tracks. The label prior of a new trajectory is chosen uniformly as $P(l_{i,t=0} \mid \emptyset) = \frac{1}{L}$. In Fig. 3, we illustrate the recursive label filtering process and provide a simulation for better insight into the model behavior. To assign the track-wise filtered label posteriors back to proposal regions, we compute the average posterior over all trajectories a within region R_k, where $A(R_k)$ is the total number of trajectories in the region, *i.e.*

$$\overline{P}(l_i) = \frac{1}{A(R_k)} \sum_{a=1}^{A(R_k)} P_a\left(l_{i,t} \mid \mathcal{X}^t\right) . \tag{4}$$

4.2   Kalman Filter Tracking

In addition to the recursive label filtering scheme, we apply a Kalman filter to each trajectory in order to estimate the 3D world position and velocity of the feature point using stereo information. To compensate for apparent motion induced by the moving observer, we obtain odometry information from the vehicle and incorporate ego velocity $v_{\text{ego},t}$ and yaw-rate $\dot{\psi}_t$ into the estimation process.

As with the filtered label decision, we assign the averaged Kalman filtered 3D velocity information to each Stixel using the corresponding proposal region R_k for averaging. Fig. 4 shows a 3D point cloud of the reconstructed scene and each tracked feature point is depicted with an arrow, indicating the predicted position in 500 ms. We adopt the system model and estimation process from [18]. For more details, please consult this paper.

5   Spatial Regularization

One side effect of most data-driven grouping schemes, *e.g.* superpixels or Stixels, is local spatial over-segmentation. To incorporate global smoothness properties, we formulate a conditional random field (CRF) in each time step, where Stixels are connected within a graphical model. More formally, a graph $\mathcal{G} = \{\mathcal{V}, \mathcal{E}\}$ consisting of vertices $\mathcal{V}$ and edges $\mathcal{E}$ is built, where $|\mathcal{V}| = N$ is the number of nodes (Stixels). We assign a set of discrete random variables $\mathcal{Y} = \{y_n \mid n = 1 \ldots N\}$, where each y_n can take a value of the label set $\mathcal{L} = \{l_i \mid i = 1 \ldots L\}$. A labeling $\mathbf{y} \in \mathcal{L}^N$ defines a joint configuration of all random variables assigned to a specific label. In a CRF, the labeling $\mathbf{y}$ is globally conditioned on all observed data $\mathbf{X}$ and follows a Gibbs distribution: $p(\mathbf{y} \mid \mathbf{X}) = \frac{1}{Z} \exp\left(-\sum_{c \in \mathcal{C}} \psi_c(\mathbf{y}_c)\right)$, where Z is a normalizing constant, $\mathcal{C}$ is the set of maximal cliques, $\mathbf{y}_c$ denotes all random variables in clique c and $\psi_c(\mathbf{y}_c)$ are potential functions for each clique [27], having the data $\mathbf{X}$ as implicit dependency.

Finding the maximum a posteriori (MAP) labeling $\hat{\mathbf{y}}$ is equivalent to finding the corresponding minimum Gibbs energy, *i.e.* $\hat{\mathbf{y}} = \arg\max_{\mathbf{y}} p(\mathbf{y} \mid \mathbf{X}) = \arg\min_{\mathbf{y}} E(\mathbf{y})$. For semantic labeling problems, the energy function $E(\mathbf{y})$ typically consists of unary (ψ_n) and pairwise (ψ_{nm}) potentials and is defined as

$$E(\mathbf{y}) = \sum_{n \in \mathcal{V}} \psi_n(y_n) + \sum_{(n,m) \in \mathcal{E}} \psi_{nm}(y_n, y_m) \ . \tag{5}$$

Note that we do not model spatial and temporal consistency jointly to allow better pipelining of the process. Instead, we use the temporally smoothed results from Sec. 4.1 during inference to additionally facilitate spatial smoothness. Inference is performed using five sweeps of α-expansion. In the following, we discuss the potential functions in more detail.

5.1   Unary Potentials

For the unary potential of a vertex, we employ the filtered label posterior from Sec. 4.1, averaged over the corresponding proposal region as

$$\psi_n(y_n = l_i) = -\log\left(\overline{P}(l_i)\right) \ . \tag{6}$$

Note that this unary potential not only incorporates data from a single Stixel locally but from the larger proposal region. In CRFs (compared to MRFs) the labeling $\mathbf{y}$ is globally conditioned on the data $\mathbf{X}$, so this is a valid choice to increase the robustness of the unary term.

5.2   Pairwise Potentials

To encourage neighboring Stixels to adopt the same label, the pairwise potentials take the form of a modified Potts model. In pixel-level CRFs, the Potts model is often extended to be contrast-sensitive to disable smoothing when strong changes

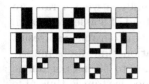
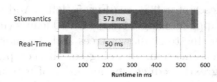

Fig. 5. 8×8 pixel Haar wavelet basis feature set (left). White, black and gray areas denote weights of +1, -1 and 0, respectively. Adapted from [38]. Average runtime in milliseconds of the proposed Stixmantics approach and the real-time variant (right).

in image intensities occur, *e.g.* [39]. In contrast, our Stixel-level model allows us to make smoothing sensitive to more concise and less noisy measures such as spatial proximity or different motion direction. Here, we propose a measure of common boundary length between Stixels as a proxy for spatial proximity. Hence, we define the pairwise potentials as

$$\psi_{nm}(y_n, y_m) = \begin{cases} 0 & y_n = y_m \\ \gamma\,\Omega(n,m) & y_n \neq y_m, \end{cases} \tag{7}$$

where γ is a smoothness factor. The term $\Omega(n, m)$ measures the affinity of adjacent Stixels. For two adjacent Stixels n and m, let b_n be the number of pixels on the boundary of Stixel n. Further let c_{nm} be the number of pixels on the boundary of Stixel n, which are direct neighbors of Stixel m. The terms b_m and c_{mn} are defined accordingly. The common boundary length is then defined as

$$\Omega(n, m) = \frac{c_{nm} + c_{mn}}{b_n - c_{nm} + b_m - c_{mn}}. \tag{8}$$

By definition, the measure is symmetric and limited to the range $[0, 1)$ for non-overlapping Stixels and the cost of a label change is reduced if two adjacent Stixels only have a small common boundary.

6   Going Real-Time

Our approach is implemented single-threaded in C++ using an Intel i7-3.33 GHz CPU and an NVIDIA GeForce GTX 770 GPU (for KLT feature tracking). We use a pipelining strategy where SGM stereo and Stixel computation are performed on dedicated FPGA hardware [17,21], which effectively increases the system latency by two frames (100 ms at a framerate of 20 Hz). For clarity of presentation, we set aside this additional delay in our reported timings as it is equally present in all systems except for the first baseline from [28].

Fig. 5 (right) shows, that SIFT feature extraction (red) and random forest encoding coupled with SVM classification (green) are the computational bottlenecks of the system. To address those bottlenecks, we replace the multi-scale SIFT features by simpler and faster descriptors. In particular, we use single-scale 8×8 pixel features derived from a 2D Haar wavelet basis resulting in a

15-dimensional descriptor [38], see Fig. 5 (left). Additionally, a weaker random forest encoder is applied using 5 trees with 50 leaves (instead of 500 leaves) each. Encoding is faster due to shallower trees and the shorter histograms also result in faster SVM classification. In doing so, the computation time for semantic class labeling is greatly reduced by an order of magnitude to 50 ms per image on average, see Fig. 5 (right). In total, our whole pipelined system is thus able to operate at a real-time framerate of 20 Hz. This includes the full estimation of 3D scene structure and motion (SGM, Stixels and KLT tracking) in additional to semantic class labeling.

7   Experiments

7.1   Dataset

For experimental evaluation we use the public Daimler Urban Segmentation Dataset[1] and the corresponding evaluation methodology as introduced in [36]. This dataset contains 5,000 stereo images captured in urban traffic with vehicle ego-motion data, where every 10-th image has exact pixel-wise semantic annotation, see Fig. 7. Note that other public datasets such as PASCAL VOC [14], MSRC [37] or KITTI [23] do not have all necessary data, *i.e.* stereo images, odometry and semantic labeling, available at the same time.

7.2   Discussion of Baselines

To provide adequate baselines, we use the publicly available ALE software with the framework proposed in [28] to exploit depth information. This method uses a bank of several local feature descriptors and performs joint optimization of class labels and dense disparity maps and arguably provides state-of-the-art performance in this domain (Joint-Optim. ALE in Table 1). For an additional external baseline, we apply Iterative Context Forests [19], adapted by adding the disparity image as additional feature channel and Stixel segments to regularize the per-pixel classification result (Depth-enabled ICF in Table 1). Note, that this baseline compared favorably to many other approaches on different datasets and in related applications [19]. As a final reference, we re-implemented the method of [36]. Here, Stixels are also used to create proposal regions but the whole system does neither incorporate any temporal analysis nor spatio-temporal regularization. We also provide numbers for the variant, where intensity-based SLIC superpixels [2] are used instead of Stixel-based proposal regions. The variants are called Stixbaseline and SLICbaseline in Table 1 respectively, where both correspond to the ERC_G^{HP} version in [36]. Note that with our re-implementation, we slightly improve over their originally reported results. In contrast to [36], we improve the segmentation of sky regions by including a prior based on location and intensity.

---

[1] The dataset is available at http://www.6d-vision.com/scene-labeling/

Table 1. Semantic segmentation results (PASCAL VOC IU measure) for all considered approaches. The best result per class is marked in **boldface**, the second best in *italics*. Besides the average performance over all classes, we additionally give the average for the most application-relevant dynamic object classes only, *i.e.* vehicle and pedestrian. We additionally report the computation time per frame for each method, where SLIC related timings assume a real-time implementation of SLIC superpixels.

	Baselines			
Class \ Method	Joint-Optim. ALE [28]	Depth-enabled ICF [19]	SLICbaseline [36]	Stixbaseline [36]
Ground	**89.9**	86.2	81.4	87.5
Vehicle	63.8	53.5	49.8	66.2
Pedestrian	**63.6**	34.9	40.4	53.4
Sky	**86.7**	35.1	27.1	51.4
Building	59.1	53.9	52.6	**61.1**
Average (all)	**72.6**	52.8	50.2	63.9
Average (dyn)	*63.7*	44.2	45.1	59.8
Runtime/frame	111 s	3.2 s	544 ms	544 ms

	This paper			
Class \ Method	Stixmantics (real-time)	Stixmantics (real-time/NR)	SLICmantics	Stixmantics
Ground	*87.6*	*87.6*	87.4	*87.6*
Vehicle	*67.4*	61.8	60.9	**68.9**
Pedestrian	57.8	51.5	47.4	*59.0*
Sky	*61.4*	55.2	48.0	57.6
Building	60.1	60.9	54.2	*60.2*
Average (all)	*66.9*	63.4	59.6	66.7
Average (dyn)	62.6	56.7	54.2	**64.0**
Runtime/frame	*50 ms*	**23 ms**	571 ms	571 ms

7.3   Results

We compare four of our own system variants against the four baselines discussed above using identical data and evaluation criteria. Although we estimate a full medium-level scene model including 3D structure, 3D motion and semantic labeling, we focus on evaluating the semantic segmentation performance at this point. Segmentation accuracy is evaluated using the standard PASCAL VOC intersection-over-union (IU) measure [14]. Temporal regularization is evaluated using an additional object-centric score. In Table 1 (bottom) we show our four system variants. In the first and second column, we provide results for the Stixmantics real-time version, and the real-time version without spatio-temporal

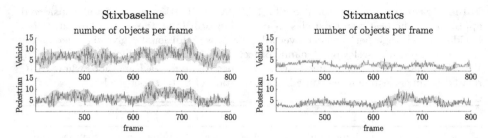

Fig. 6. Number of detected objects per frame, for the Stixbaseline (left) and our Stix-mantics approach (right). We show an excerpt from frame $400 - 800$ of the `test_2` sequence for the dynamic object classes, *i.e.* vehicle and pedestrian. The TF_i score is shown as solid band in the background, illustrating the strength of local temporal fluctuations in the labeling decision. Our Stixmantics model clearly provides stronger temporal consistency.

regularization (NR). Furthermore, we show results when Stixel-based proposal regions are replaced with SLIC superpixels computed on the intensity images (SLICmantics). Finally, we show results for our full Stixmantics model.

One problem with the IU measure is its pixel-wise nature. It is strongly biased towards close objects that take up large portions of the image and small objects of the same class barely contribute to the final score. The same holds true for small temporal fluctuations in the result. To account for this fact, we provide an additional object centric evaluation to support the spatio-temporal regularization proposed in this paper. Fig. 6 shows the number of detected objects o_i over the frames i, for the Stixbaseline approach (left) and our Stixmantics approach (right). To approximate the number of objects, we count each closed image region with identical class label as one instance. Although the absolute number of objects is non-informative without ground-truth data, a lower temporal fluctuation in the number of objects indicates stronger temporal consistency. We define a temporal fluctuation measure TF_i at frame i as sliding mean squared deviation to the sliding average $\bar{o}_j$:

$$\text{TF}_i = \frac{1}{2w+1} \sum_{j=i-w}^{i+w} (o_j - \bar{o}_j)^2 \quad \text{with } \bar{o}_j = \frac{1}{2w+1} \sum_{k=j-w}^{j+w} o_k, \qquad (9)$$

where w is the temporal window size and is set to 10 frames in our evaluation. We show the TF_i score as $\bar{o}_i \pm \text{TF}_i$ for each frame i as solid band in the background of Fig. 6. In Table 2, we show the averaged TF score over all 2,000 frames of the test sequences. Qualitative results of our Stixmantics framework are shown in Fig. 7.

From the reported results, we draw several conclusions. First, our proposed Stixmantics approach delivers state-of-the-art performance but requires only a fraction of the computational costs compared to all baseline methods, with the real-time variant being several orders of magnitude faster than Joint-Optim. ALE [28]. For the vehicle class, it even outperforms the method of [28] on this

Fig. 7. Comparison of results obtained with our Stixmantics model against ground-truth labels. Colors denote the recovered semantic object classes. Arrows at the bottom of each underlying Stixel depict the ego-motion corrected 3D velocities of other traffic participants. Images are taken from the real-time version of our approach.

dataset. As apparent from Fig. 6 and Table 2, our regularized Stixmantics model consistently outperforms Stixbaseline throughout all object classes except for the Sky class w.r.t. the TF measure. The average numbers in Table 1 also support this.

We also observe that for dynamic objects the benefit of regularization is more pronounced when using simpler features, *cf*. Stixmantics (real-time) *vs*. Stixmantics (real-time/NR) with Stixmantics *vs*. Stixbaseline. We take this as evidence for the strength of our integrated medium-level model, where weaker classification performance can be compensated for by stronger constraints on the model. Non-surprisingly, the gain of temporal integration is also stronger when SLIC superpixels are utilized instead of Stixel-based proposal regions, given that they are inherently less temporally consistent than Stixels, *cf*. SLICmantics *vs*. SLICbaseline with Stixmantics *vs*. Stixbaseline. In general, results improve significantly when Stixel-based proposal regions are used.

Table 2. Average TF measure per class for the Stixbaseline and our Stixmantics approach. Lower scores indicate less temporal fluctuation. The best result per class is marked in **boldface**.

Method \ Class	Ground	Vehicle	Pedestrian	Sky	Building
Stixbaseline [36]	0.25	1.92	1.98	**2.43**	0.67
Stixmantics	**0.18**	**0.67**	**0.53**	3.10	**0.25**

8   Conclusion

In this paper, we presented a novel comprehensive scene understanding model that can be computed in 50 ms from stereo image pairs. At the same time, we achieve close to state-of-the-art performance in semantic segmentation of urban traffic scenes. Our spatio-temporally coherent model extracts application-relevant scene content and encodes it in terms of the medium-level Stixel representation with 3D position, height, 3D velocity and semantic object class information available at each Stixel. From a mobile vision and robotics application point-of-view, the richness, flexibility, compactness and efficiency of the proposed scene description make it an ideal candidate to serve as a generic interface layer between raw pixel values and higher level reasoning algorithms, such as for path planning and localization.

References

1. Abramov, A., Pauwels, K., Papon, J., Worgotter, F., Dellen, B.: Real-Time Segmentation of Stereo Videos on a Portable System With a Mobile GPU. IEEE Transactions on Circuits and Systems for Video Technology 22(9) (2012)
2. Achanta, R., Shaji, A., Smith, K., Lucchi, A., Fua, P., Süsstrunk, S.: SLIC Superpixels Compared to State-of-the-art Superpixel Methods. Trans. PAMI 34(11) (2012)
3. Arbeláez, P., Hariharan, B., Gu, C., Gupta, S., Bourdev, L., Malik, J.: Semantic Segmentation using Regions and Parts. In: CVPR (2012)
4. Benenson, R., Mathias, M., Timofte, R., Gool, L.V.: Fast Stixel Computation for Fast Pedestrian Detection. In: CVVT Workshop, ECCV (2012)
5. Brostow, G.J., Shotton, J., Fauqueur, J., Cipolla, R.: Segmentation and Recognition Using Structure from Motion Point Clouds. In: Forsyth, D., Torr, P., Zisserman, A. (eds.) ECCV 2008, Part I. LNCS, vol. 5302, pp. 44–57. Springer, Heidelberg (2008)
6. Carreira, J., Caseiro, R., Batista, J., Sminchisescu, C.: Semantic Segmentation with Second-Order Pooling. In: Fitzgibbon, A., Lazebnik, S., Perona, P., Sato, Y., Schmid, C. (eds.) ECCV 2012, Part VII. LNCS, vol. 7578, pp. 430–443. Springer, Heidelberg (2012)
7. Costea, A., Nedevschi, S.: Multi-Class Segmentation for Traffic Scenarios at Over 50 FPS. In: IV Symposium. pp. 1–6 (2014)
8. Couprie, C., Farabet, C., LeCun, Y.: Causal Graph-based Video Segmentation. In: ICIP (2013)
9. Dollár, P., Wojek, C., Schiele, B., Perona, P.: Pedestrian Detection: An Evaluation of the State of the Art. Trans. PAMI 34(4) (2012)
10. Ellis, L., Zografos, V.: Online Learning for Fast Segmentation of Moving Objects. In: Lee, K.M., Matsushita, Y., Rehg, J.M., Hu, Z. (eds.) ACCV 2012, Part II. LNCS, vol. 7725, pp. 52–65. Springer, Heidelberg (2013)
11. Enzweiler, M., Hummel, M., Pfeiffer, D., Franke, U.: Efficient Stixel-Based Object Recognition. In: IV Symposium (2012)
12. Erbs, F., Schwarz, B., Franke, U.: Stixmentation - Probabilistic Stixel based Traffic Scene Labeling. In: BMVC (2012)

13. Ess, A., Mueller, T., Grabner, H., Gool, L.V.: Segmentation-Based Urban Traffic Scene Understanding. In: BMVC (2009)
14. Everingham, M., Gool, L.V., Williams, C.K.I., Winn, J., Zisserman, A.: The Pascal Visual Object Classes (VOC) Challenge. IJCV 88(2) (2010)
15. Felzenszwalb, P.F., Girshick, R.B., McAllester, D., Ramanan, D.: Object Detection with Discriminatively Trained Part Based Models. Trans. PAMI 32(9) (2010)
16. Floros, G., Leibe, B.: Joint 2D-3D Temporally Consistent Semantic Segmentation of Street Scenes. In: CVPR (2012)
17. Franke, U., Pfeiffer, D., Rabe, C., Knoeppel, C., Enzweiler, M., Stein, F., Herrtwich, R.G.: Making Bertha See. In: CVAD Workshop, ICCV (2013)
18. Franke, U., Rabe, C., Badino, H., Gehrig, S.K.: 6D-Vision: Fusion of Stereo and Motion for Robust Environment Perception. In: Kropatsch, W.G., Sablatnig, R., Hanbury, A. (eds.) DAGM 2005. LNCS, vol. 3663, pp. 216–223. Springer, Heidelberg (2005)
19. Fröhlich, B., Rodner, E., Denzler, J.: Semantic Segmentation with Millions of Features: Integrating Multiple Cues in a Combined Random Forest Approach. In: Lee, K.M., Matsushita, Y., Rehg, J.M., Hu, Z. (eds.) ACCV 2012, Part I. LNCS, vol. 7724, pp. 218–231. Springer, Heidelberg (2013)
20. Fulkerson, B., Vedaldi, A., Soatto, S.: Class segmentation and object localization with superpixel neighborhoods. In: ICCV (2009)
21. Gehrig, S.K., Eberli, F., Meyer, T.: A Real-Time Low-Power Stereo Vision Engine Using Semi-Global Matching. In: Fritz, M., Schiele, B., Piater, J.H. (eds.) ICVS 2009. LNCS, vol. 5815, pp. 134–143. Springer, Heidelberg (2009)
22. Geiger, A., Lauer, M., Wojek, C., Stiller, C., Urtasun, R.: 3D Traffic Scene Understanding from Movable Platforms. Trans. PAMI (2013)
23. Geiger, A., Lenz, P., Urtasun, R.: Are we ready for Autonomous Driving? The KITTI Vision Benchmark Suite. In: CVPR (2012)
24. Grundmann, M., Kwatra, V., Han, M., Essa, I.: Efficient Hierarchical Graph-based Video Segmentation. In: CVPR (2010)
25. Hirschmüller, H.: Stereo Processing by Semiglobal Matching and Mutual Information. Trans. PAMI 30(2) (2008)
26. Hoiem, D., Efros, A.A., Hebert, M.: Closing the Loop in Scene Interpretation. In: CVPR (2008)
27. Koller, D., Friedman, N.: Probabilistic Graphical Models: Principles and Techniques. The MIT Press (2009)
28. Ladický, L., Sturgess, P., Russell, C., Sengupta, S., Bastanlar, Y., Clocksin, W., Torr, P.H.S.: Joint Optimisation for Object Class Segmentation and Dense Stereo Reconstruction. In: BMVC (2010)
29. Lowe, D.G.: Distinctive Image Features from Scale-Invariant Keypoints. IJCV 60(2) (2004)
30. Mester, R., Conrad, C., Guevara, A.: Multichannel Segmentation Using Contour Relaxation: Fast Super-Pixels and Temporal Propagation. In: Heyden, A., Kahl, F. (eds.) SCIA 2011. LNCS, vol. 6688, pp. 250–261. Springer, Heidelberg (2011)
31. Miksik, O., Munoz, D., Bagnell, J.A., Hebert, M.: Efficient Temporal Consistency for Streaming Video Scene Analysis. In: ICRA (2013)
32. Murphy, K.P.: Machine Learning: A Probabilistic Perspective. The MIT Press (2012)
33. de Nijs, R., Ramos, S., Roig, G., Boix, X., Gool, L.V., Kühnlenz, K.: On-line Semantic Perception using Uncertainty. In: IROS (2012)
34. Ochs, P., Brox, T.: Object Segmentation in Video: A Hierarchical Variational Approach for Turning Point Trajectories into Dense Regions. In: ICCV (2011)

35. Pfeiffer, D., Franke, U.: Towards a Global Optimal Multi-Layer Stixel Representation of Dense 3D Data. In: BMVC (2011)
36. Scharwächter, T., Enzweiler, M., Franke, U., Roth, S.: Efficient Multi-cue Scene Segmentation. In: Weickert, J., Hein, M., Schiele, B. (eds.) GCPR 2013. LNCS, vol. 8142, pp. 435–445. Springer, Heidelberg (2013)
37. Shotton, J., Winn, J., Rother, C., Criminisi, A.: TextonBoost for Image Understanding: Multi-Class Object Recognition and Segmentation by Jointly Modeling Texture, Layout, and Context. IJCV (2009)
38. Stollnitz, E.J., DeRose, T.D., Salesin, D.H.: Wavelets for Computer Graphics: A Primer. IEEE Computer Graphics and Applications 15 (1995)
39. Sturgess, P., Alahari, K., Ladický, L., Torr, P.H.S.: Combining Appearance and Structure from Motion Features for Road Scene Understanding. In: BMVC (2009)
40. Tang, K., Sukthankar, R., Yagnik, J., Fei-Fei, L.: Discriminative Segment Annotation in Weakly Labeled Video. In: CVPR. IEEE (2013)
41. Tighe, J., Lazebnik, S.: SuperParsing: Scalable Nonparametric Image Parsing with Superpixels. In: Daniilidis, K., Maragos, P., Paragios, N. (eds.) ECCV 2010, Part V. LNCS, vol. 6315, pp. 352–365. Springer, Heidelberg (2010)
42. Tomasi, C., Kanade, T.: Detection and Tracking of Point Features. Tech. Rep. CMU-CS-91-132, Carnegie Mellon University (1991)
43. Vazquez-Reina, A., Avidan, S., Pfister, H., Miller, E.: Multiple Hypothesis Video Segmentation from Superpixel Flows. In: Daniilidis, K., Maragos, P., Paragios, N. (eds.) ECCV 2010, Part V. LNCS, vol. 6315, pp. 268–281. Springer, Heidelberg (2010)
44. Wojek, C., Schiele, B.: A Dynamic Conditional Random Field Model for Joint Labeling of Object and Scene Classes. In: Forsyth, D., Torr, P., Zisserman, A. (eds.) ECCV 2008, Part IV. LNCS, vol. 5305, pp. 733–747. Springer, Heidelberg (2008)
45. Wojek, C., Walk, S., Roth, S., Schindler, K., Schiele, B.: Monocular Visual Scene Understanding: Understanding Multi-Object Traffic Scenes. Trans. PAMI 35(4) (2013)

Sparse Dictionaries for Semantic Segmentation

Lingling Tao[1], Fatih Porikli[2], and René Vidal[1]

[1] Center for Imaging Science, Johns Hopkins University, USA
[2] Australian National University & NICTA ICT, Australia

Abstract. A popular trend in semantic segmentation is to use top-down object information to improve bottom-up segmentation. For instance, the classification scores of the Bag of Features (BoF) model for image classification have been used to build a top-down categorization cost in a Conditional Random Field (CRF) model for semantic segmentation. Recent work shows that discriminative sparse dictionary learning (DSDL) can improve upon the unsupervised K-means dictionary learning method used in the BoF model due to the ability of DSDL to capture discriminative features from different classes. However, to the best of our knowledge, DSDL has not been used for building a top-down categorization cost for semantic segmentation. In this paper, we propose a CRF model that incorporates a DSDL based top-down cost for semantic segmentation. We show that the new CRF energy can be minimized using existing efficient discrete optimization techniques. Moreover, we propose a new method for jointly learning the CRF parameters, object classifiers and the visual dictionary. Our experiments demonstrate that by jointly learning these parameters, the feature representation becomes more discriminative and the segmentation performance improves with respect to that of state-of-the-art methods that use unsupervised K-means dictionary learning.

Keywords: discriminative sparse dictionary learning, conditional random fields, semantic segmentation.

1 Introduction

Semantic image segmentation is the problem of inferring an object class label for each pixel [17,12,16,33,27]. This is a fundamental problem in computer vision with many applications in scene understanding, automatic driving, surveillance, etc. However, this problem is significantly more complex than image classification, where one needs to find a single label for the image. This is because the joint labeling of all pixels involves reasoning about the image neighborhood structure, as well as capturing long-range interactions and high-level object class priors.

Prior Work. The most common approach to semantic segmentation is to model the image with a Conditional Random Field (CRF) model [17]. A CRF captures the fact that image regions corresponding to the same object class should have similar features, and regions that are similar to each other (in location or feature space) should be more likely to share the same label. In a second-order CRF model, the features coming from each region are usually modeled by the CRF

D. Fleet et al. (Eds.): ECCV 2014, Part V, LNCS 8693, pp. 549–564, 2014.
© Springer International Publishing Switzerland 2014

unary potentials, which are based on appearance, context and semantic relations, while pairwise relationships are modeled by the CRF pairwise potentials, which are based on neighborhood similarity and co-occurrence information. For example, early works use patch/super-pixel/region based features such as a Bag of Features (BoF) representation of color, SIFT features [7,8], textonboost [24], co-occurrence statistics [8], relative location features [9], etc. Once the CRF model has been constructed, multi-label graph cuts [13] or other approximate graph inference algorithms can be used to efficiently find an optimal segmentation.

In spite of their success, a major disadvantage of second-order CRF models is that the features they use are too local to capture long-range interactions and object-level information. To address this issue, various methods have been proposed. One family of methods [3,15,33,22,27] uses other cues such as object detection scores, shape priors, motion information and scene information, to improve object segmentation. For instance, [15,22] combine object detection results with pixel-based CRF models; [33] further improves the algorithm by combining object detection results with shape priors and scene classification information for holistic scene understanding; and [27] uses exemplar-SVMs to get the detection results together with shape priors, and combines them with appearance models. Another family of methods uses more complex higher-order or hierarchical CRF models. For instance, [12] shows that the integration of higher-order robust P^N potentials improves over the second-order CRF formulation. Also [16] proposes a hierarchical CRF combining both segment-based and pixel-based CRF models using robust P^N potentials. However, a major drawback of these methods is that the CRF cliques need to be predefined. Hence they cannot capture global information about the entire object because the segmentation is unknown.

To address this issue, [26] proposes to augment the second-order CRF energy with a global, top-down categorization potential based on the BoF representation for image classification [6,18]. This potential is obtained as the sum of the scores of a multi-class SVM classifier applied to multiple BoF histograms per image, one per object class. Since each histogram depends on the unknown segmentation, during inference one effectively searches for a segmentation of the image that gives a good classification score for each histogram. While in this approach of [26] the visual words are learned independently from the classifiers, [10] shows how to extend this method by using a discriminative dictionary of visual words, which is learned jointly with the CRF parameters. Both approaches are, however, limited by the simplicity of the BoF framework. Recent work shows that discriminative sparse representations can improve over the basic BoF model for classification due to their ability to capture discriminative features from different classes. For instance, [20] proposes to learn a discriminative dictionary such that the classification scores based on the sparse representation are well separated; [32] shows that extracting sparse codes with a max-pooling scheme outperforms BoF for object and scene classification; [2] further improves classification performance by jointly learning the dictionary and the classifier parameters; and [1] presents a general formulation for supervised dictionary learning adapted to various tasks. However, these approaches have not been applied to semantic segmentation.

Paper Contributions. In this paper, we propose a novel framework for semantic segmentation based on a new CRF model with a top-down discriminative sparse dictionary learning cost. Our main contributions are the following:

1. A new categorization cost for semantic segmentation based on discriminative sparse dictionary learning. Although similar approaches have been explored in image classification tasks [20,32,2,1] and shown good performance, they have not been used to model top-down information in semantic labeling.
2. A new algorithm for jointly learning a sparse dictionary and the CRF parameters, which makes the learned dictionary more discriminative and specifically trained for the segmentation task. Prior work in this area either learned the dictionary beforehand or used energies that are linear on the dictionary and classifier parameters, which makes the learning problem amenable to structural SVMs [11] or latent structural SVMs [34]. In sharp contrast, we use a sparse dictionary learning cost, which makes the energy depend nonlinearly on the dictionary atoms. The learning problem we confront is, thus, significantly more difficult and requires the development of an ad-hoc learning method. Here, we propose a method based on stochastic gradient descent.
3. From a computational perspective, our approach is more scalable than that of [26]. This is because the approach in [26] is based on minimizing an energy involving the histogram intersection kernel, which requires the construction of graphs with many auxiliary variables. On the other hand, our learning scheme utilizes a stochastic gradient descent method, which requires fewer graph-cut inference computations for each training loop.

To the best of our knowledge, there is little work on using discriminative sparse dictionaries for semantic segmentation. This is arguably due to the complexity of jointly learning the dictionary and the CRF parameters. The only related works we are aware of are [35,31]. In [35], a sparse dictionary is used to build a sparse reconstruction weight matrix for all the super-pixels. Then a set of representative super-pixels for each class is learned based on the weight matrix, and classification is done by comparing reconstruction errors from each class. However, the atoms of the dictionary used in this model are all the data samples from one object class, thus there is no learning involved. On the other hand, in [31], a grid-based CRF is defined to model the top-down saliency of the image. The unary cost for each point on the grid is associated with the sparse representation of the SIFT descriptor at that point. A max-margin formulation and gradient descent optimization is then used to jointly learn the dictionary and the classifier. But this model gives only a binary segmentation on the grid, and requires fitting one dictionary per class, which could be computationally expensive for semantic segmentation tasks with a large number of classes.

Paper Outline. The rest of the paper is organized as follows. In §2 we review the basic CRF model and the CRF model with higher-order BoF potentials. In §3 we introduce higher-order potentials based on discriminative sparse dictionary learning. We describe how inference is done and propose a gradient descent method for jointly learning the dictionary and CRF parameters. In §4 we present some experimental results as well as a discussion of possible improvements.

2   Review of CRF Models for Semantic Segmentation

In this section, we describe how the semantic segmentation problem is formulated using a CRF model. In principle, the goal is to compute an object category label for each pixel in the image. In practice, however, the image is often over-segmented into super-pixels and the goal becomes to label each super-pixel. To that end, the image I is associated with a graph $G = (V, E)$, where V is the set of nodes and $E \subset V \times V$ is the set of edges. Each node $i \in V$ is a super-pixel and is associated with a label $x_i \in \{1, \ldots, L\}$, where L is the number of object classes. Two nodes are connected by an edge if their super-pixels share a boundary.

To find a labeling $X = \{x_i\}_{i=1}^{|V|}$ for image I, rather than modeling the joint distribution of all labels $P(X)$, a CRF models the conditional distribution of the labels given the observations $P(X \mid I)$ with a Gibbs distribution of the form

$$P(X \mid I) \propto \exp\left(-E(X, I)\right), \tag{1}$$

where the energy function $E(X, I)$ is the sum of potentials from all cliques of G.

Second-Order CRF Model. In the basic second-Order CRF model, the energy function is given as

$$E(X, I) = \lambda_1 \sum_{i \in V} \phi_i^U(x_i, I) + \lambda_2 \sum_{(i,j) \in E} \phi_{ij}^P(x_i, x_j, I). \tag{2}$$

The unary potential $\phi^U(x_i, I)$ models the cost of assigning class label x_i to super-pixel i, while the pairwise potential $\phi_{ij}^P(x_i, x_j, I)$ models the cost of assigning a pair of labels (x_i, x_j) to a pair of neighboring super-pixels $(i, j) \in E$. Then, the best labeling is the one that maximizes the conditional probability, and thus minimizes the energy function. In this work, we will use different state-of-art choices for the unary and pairwise potentials, as described in the experiments.

Top-Down BoF Categorization Cost. As discussed before, the basic CRF model does not capture high-level information about an object class. To address this issue, [26] proposes a higher-order potential based on the BoF approach. The key idea is to represent an image I with L class-specific histograms $\{h_l(X)\}_{l=1}^L$, each one capturing the distribution of image features for one of the object classes. Let D be a dictionary of K visual words learned from all training images using K-means. Let $b_j \in \mathbb{R}^K$ be the encoding of feature descriptor f_j at the j-th interest point, i.e., $b_{jk} = 1$ if the j-th descriptor is associated with the k-th visual word, and $b_{jk} = 0$ otherwise. A BoF histogram for class l is constructed by accumulating b_j over interest points that belong to super-pixels with label l, that is

$$h_l(X) = \sum_{j \in S} b_j \delta(x_{s_j} = l), \tag{3}$$

where S is the set of all interest points in image I and $s_j \in V$ is the super-pixel containing interest point j. A top-down categorization cost is then defined by applying a classifier $\phi_l^O(\cdot)$ to this BoF histogram. To encourage the optimal segmentation to be such that the distribution of features within each segment resemble that of one of the object categories, the L categorization costs are integrated with the basic CRF model by defining the following energy

$$E(X, I) = \lambda_1 \sum_{i \in V} \phi_i^U(x_i, I) + \lambda_2 \sum_{(i,j) \in E} \phi_{ij}^P(x_i, x_j, I) + \sum_{l=1}^{L} \phi_l^O(h_l(X)). \quad (4)$$

It is shown in [26] that if the classifiers ϕ_l^O are linear or intersection-kernel SVMs, the minimization of the energy can be done using extensions of graph cuts and that the CRF parameters can be learned by structural SVMs.

One drawback of the approach in [26] is that the dictionary is fixed and learned independently from the CRF parameters via K-means. To address this issue, [10] proposes to learn the dictionary of visual words jointly with the CRF parameters by defining a classifier for each visual word and augmenting the energy with a dictionary learning cost. Since the assignments of visual descriptors to visual words are unknown, these assignments become latent variables for the energy. The optimal segmentation and visual words assignments can be found via a combination of graph cuts and loopy belief propagation [21], and the dictionary and CRF parameters are then jointly learned by latent structural SVMs [34].

3   Proposed Discriminative Dictionary Learning CRF Cost

In this section, we present a discriminative sparse dictionary learning cost for semantic segmentation. As in [26,10], this cost is based on the construction of a classifier applied to a class-specific histogram. However, the key difference is that our histogram is a sum pooling over the sparse coefficients of all feature descriptors associated with a class. While histograms of this kind have been used for classification (see, e.g., [32]), the fundamental challenge when using them for segmentation is that the histograms depend on both the segmentation and the dictionary. In particular, the histograms depend nonlinearly on the dictionary, which makes learning methods based on latent structural SVMs no longer applicable. In what follows, we describe the details of the new categorization cost as well as how we solve the inference and learning problems.

Top-Down Sparse Dictionary Learning Cost. Let $D \in \mathbb{R}^{F \times K}$ be an unknown dictionary of K visual words, with each visual word normalized to unit norm. Each feature descriptor f_j is encoded with respect to D via sparse coding, which involves solving the following problem:

$$\alpha_j(D) = \underset{\alpha}{\operatorname{argmin}} \{ \frac{1}{2} \| f_j - D\alpha \|^2 + \lambda \|\alpha\|_1 \}. \quad (5)$$

Note the implicit nonlinear dependency of α on D. The sparse codes of all feature descriptors associated with class l are then used to construct a histogram

$$h_l(X, D) = \sum_{j \in S} \alpha_j(D) \delta(x_{s_j} = l) = \sum_{i \in V} \sum_{j \in S_i} \alpha_j(D) \delta(x_i = l), \quad (6)$$

where S_i is the set of feature points that belong to super-pixel i. Note the dependency of h_l on both the segmentation X and the dictionary D. Finally, let $w_l \in \mathbb{R}^F$ be the parameters of a linear classifier for class l, where we remove the bias term to simplify the computation. Then the energy function in (4) becomes

$$E(X, I) = \lambda_1 \sum_{i \in V} \phi_i^U(x_i, I) + \lambda_2 \sum_{(i,j) \in E} \phi_{ij}^P(x_i, x_j, I) + \sum_{l=1}^{L} w_l^\top h_l(X, D). \quad (7)$$

Inference. Given an image I, the CRF parameters λ_1, λ_2, the classifier parameters $\{w_l\}_{l=1}^{L}$, and the dictionary D, our goal is to compute the labeling X^* that maximizes the conditional probability, i.e.,

$$X^* = \operatorname*{argmax}_X P(X \mid I) = \operatorname*{argmin}_X E(X, I). \quad (8)$$

To that end, notice that the top-down categorization term can be decomposed as a summation of unary potentials

$$\sum_{l=1}^{L} w_l^\top h_l(X, D) = \sum_{l=1}^{L} w_l^\top \sum_{i \in V} \sum_{j \in S_i} \alpha_j(D) \delta(x_i = l) = \sum_{i \in V} \overbrace{w_{x_i}^\top \sum_{j \in S_i} \alpha_j(D)}^{\psi_i^O(x_i, I)}. \quad (9)$$

Therefore, we can represent the cost function as

$$E(X, I) = \sum_{i \in V} \{\lambda_1 \phi_i^U(x_i, I) + \psi_i^O(x_i, I)\} + \lambda_2 \sum_{(i,j) \in E} \phi_{ij}^P(x_i, x_j, I). \quad (10)$$

Since this energy is the sum of unary and pairwise potentials, it can be minimized using approximate inference algorithms, such as α expansion, $\alpha - \beta$ swap, etc.

Parameter and Dictionary Learning. Given a training set of images $\{I^n\}_{n=1}^{N}$ and their corresponding segmentations $\{X^n\}_{n=1}^{N}$, we now show how to learn the CRF parameters λ_1, λ_2, the classifier parameters $\{w_l\}_{l=1}^{L}$, and the dictionary D.

When D is known, we can approach the learning problem using the structural SVM framework [11]. To that end, we first rewrite the energy function as

$$E(X, I) = W^\top \Phi(X, I, D), \quad (11)$$

where

$$W = \begin{bmatrix} \lambda_1 \\ \lambda_2 \\ w_1 \\ \vdots \\ w_L \end{bmatrix} \quad \text{and} \quad \Phi(X, I, D) = \begin{bmatrix} \sum_{i \in V} \phi^U(x_i, I) \\ \sum_{(i,j) \in E} \phi_{ij}^P(x_i, x_j, I) \\ \sum_{i \in V} \sum_{j \in S_i} \alpha_j \delta(x_i = 1) \\ \vdots \\ \sum_{i \in V} \sum_{j \in S_i} \alpha_j \delta(x_i = L) \end{bmatrix}. \quad (12)$$

We then seek a vector of parameters W of small norm such that the energy at the ground truth segmentation $E(X^n, I^n)$ is smaller than the energy at any other segmentation $E(\hat{X}^n, I^n)$ by a loss $\Delta(\hat{X}^n, X^n)$.[1] That is, we solve the problem

---

[1] We use a scaled Hamming loss $\Delta(\hat{X}^n, X^n) = \gamma \sum_{l=1}^{L} \frac{1}{N_l} \sum_{i \in V} \delta(\hat{x}_i^n = x_i^n) \delta(x_i^n = l)$.

$$\min_{W,\{\xi_n\}} \quad \frac{1}{2}\|W\|^2 + \frac{C}{N}\sum_{n=1}^{N}\xi_n$$

$$\text{s.t.} \quad \forall n \in \{1,\ldots,N\}, \forall \hat{X}^n$$

$$W^\top \Phi(\hat{X}^n, I^n, D) - W^\top \Phi(X^n, I^n, D) \geq \Delta(\hat{X}^n, X^n) - \xi_n, \tag{13}$$

where $\{\xi_n\}$ are slack variables that account for the violation of the constraints.

The problem in (13) is a quadratic optimization problem subject to a combinatorial number of linear constraints in W, one for each labeling $\hat{X}^n$. As shown in [11], this problem can be solved using a cutting plane method that alternates between two steps: given W one finds the most violated constraint by solving for $\bar{X}^n = \operatorname{argmin}_{\hat{X}}\{W^\top \Phi(\hat{X}, I^n, D) - \Delta(\hat{X}, X^n)\}$, and given a set of constraints $\bar{X}^n$ one solves for W with this constraint added.

Unfortunately, in our case both W and D are unknown. Moreover, the energy is not linear in D and its dependency on D is not explicit. As a result, the cutting plane method does not apply to our problem. Therefore, we propose an alternative approach inspired by recent work on image classification [1,2,31].

Let us first rewrite the optimization problem in (13) over both W and D as:

$$J(W, D) = \tag{14}$$

$$\frac{1}{2}\|W\|^2 + \frac{C}{N}\sum_{n=1}^{N}\left[W^\top \Phi(X^n, I^n, D) - \min_{\hat{X}^n}\{W^\top \Phi(\hat{X}^n, I^n, D) - \Delta(\hat{X}^n, X^n)\}\right].$$

The basic idea is to solve this problem by stochastic gradient descent and the key challenge is the computation of the gradient with respect to D. Let us denote the variables after the t-th iteration as D_t and W_t, and the most violated constraint as $\{\bar{X}_t^n\}$. We can easily compute the derivative of J with respect to W as:

$$\frac{\partial J}{\partial W}\bigg|_{W_t,D_t} = W_t + \frac{C}{N}\sum_{n=1}^{N}(\Phi(X^n, I^n, D_t) - \Phi(\bar{X}_t^n, I^n, D_t)). \tag{15}$$

To compute the derivative of J with respect to D, notice that J depends implicitly on D through the sparse codes $\{\alpha_j\}$. Thus, we can compute $\partial J/\partial D$ using the chain rule, which requires computing $\partial J/\partial \alpha$ and $\partial \alpha/\partial D$.

Under certain assumptions, $\partial \alpha/\partial D$ can be computed as shown in [1,2,31]. Specifically, since $\mathbf{0}$ has to be a subgradient of the objective function in (5), the sparse representation α of feature descriptor f must satisfy

$$D^\top(D\alpha - f) = -\lambda\operatorname{sign}(\alpha). \tag{16}$$

Now, suppose that the support of α (denoted as Λ) does not change when there is a small perturbation of D and let $A = (D_\Lambda^\top D_\Lambda)^{-1}$, where D_Λ is a submatrix of D whose columns are indexed by Λ. After taking the derivative of (16) with respect to D we get:

$$\frac{\partial \alpha_{(k)}}{\partial D} = (f - D\alpha)A_{[k]} - (DA^\top)_{\langle k\rangle}\alpha^\top \quad \forall k \in \Lambda, \tag{17}$$

Algorithm 1. Parameter Learning for Semantic Labeling with Sparse Dictionaries

---

1: Initialize the parameter with W_0 and D_0
2: **while** iter $t \leq$ maxiter **do**
3:     Randomly select Q images
4:     **for** $q = 1, \ldots, Q$ **do**
5:         Compute sparse code α for q-th image using Eqn. (5)
6:         Find the most violated constraint $\bar{X}^q$ for this sample
7:     **end for**
8:     Compute the partial gradient of W and D corresponding to these Q samples using Eqn. (15) and Eqn. (19). Denote them as g_{Wt} and g_{Dt} respectively.
9:     Gradient Descent: $W_{t+1} = W_t - \tau_t g_{Wt}$, $D_{t+1} = D_t - \tau_t g_{Dt}$
10:     $D_{t+1}=\text{normalize}(D_t)$
11:     $t++$
12: **end while**

---

where (k), $[k]$, and $\langle k \rangle$ denote the k-th entry, row, and column, respectively.

Given the set of images $\{I^n\}_{n=1}^N$ with the corresponding set of feature points $\{S^n\}_{n=1}^N$, one can apply the chain rule to compute $\frac{\partial J}{\partial D}$. Denote $z_j^n = \frac{\partial J}{\partial \alpha_j^n}$ as the partial derivative of J with respect to the sparse codes α_j^n of feature point j in image I^n, then

$$z_j^n = \frac{\partial J}{\partial \alpha_j^n}\bigg|_{W_t, D_t} = w_{x_{s_j}^n, t} - w_{\hat{x}_{s_j}^n, t, t}, \tag{18}$$

where $x_{s_j}^n, \hat{x}_{s_j, t}^n$ denote the ground-truth label and the computed label of feature point f_j^n at iteration t respectively. According to the chain rule, we have

$$\frac{\partial J}{\partial D} = \sum_{n=1}^N \sum_{j \in S^n} \frac{\partial J}{\partial \alpha_j^n}^\top \frac{\partial \alpha_j^n}{\partial D} = \sum_{n=1}^N \sum_{j \in S^n} \sum_{k \in \Lambda_j^n} \frac{\partial J}{\partial \alpha_j^n(k)}^\top \frac{\partial \alpha_j^n(k)}{\partial D}$$

$$= \sum_{n=1}^N \sum_{j \in S^n} \sum_{k \in \Lambda_j^n} z_j^n(k)\{(f_j^n - D\alpha_j^n)A_{j[k]}^n - (DA_j^{n\top})_{\langle k \rangle}\alpha_j^{n\top}\}$$

$$= \sum_{n=1}^N \sum_{j \in S^n} (f_j^n - D\alpha_j^n)(A_j^n z_j^n)^\top - DA_j^{n\top} z_j^n \alpha_j^{n\top}, \tag{19}$$

where $A_j^n = (D_{\Lambda_j^n}^\top D_{\Lambda_j^n})^{-1}$. For simplicity, we removed the sub-script t from all the variables that change through iterations.

Instead of summing over all the image samples, in our algorithm, we use stochastic gradient descent, i.e., at each iteration we select a small subset of sample images and compute the gradient based on this subset only. The detailed algorithm is described in Algorithm 1.

Since the problem of jointly learning D and W is non-convex, it is very important to have a good initialization for Algorithm 1. We compute D_0 by applying the sparse dictionary learning algorithm of [19] to all feature descriptors $\{f_j\}$.

We then compute W_0 as $[\lambda_1, \lambda_2, \lambda_3 w_1, \ldots, \lambda_3 w_L]$, where $\{w_l\}_{l=1}^L$ are the parameters of a multi-class linear SVM classifier (without bias term) trained on the histograms $\{h_l(X^n, D_0)\}$, and $\lambda_1, \lambda_2, \lambda_3$ are the parameters of the model

$$E(X, I) = \lambda_1 \sum_{i \in V} \phi^U(x_i, I) + \lambda_2 \sum_{(i,j) \in E} \phi_{ij}^P(x_i, x_j, I) + \lambda_3 \sum_{l=1}^L w_l^\top h_l(X, D_0) \quad (20)$$

trained on the segmentations $\{X^n\}$ using standard structural SVM learning.

4 Experimental Results

Datasets. We evaluate our algorithm on three datasets: the Graz-02 dataset, the PASCAL VOC 2010 dataset and the MSRC21 dataset. The Graz-02 Dataset [23] contains 900 images of size 480×640. Each image is labeled with 4 categories: bike, pedestrian, car and background. In our experiments, we use 450 images for training and the other 450 for testing. The PASCAL VOC 2010 dataset [5] contains 1928 images labeled with 20 object classes and a background class. Following [14], since there is no publicly available groundtruth for the test data, we split the training/validation dataset and use 600 images among them for training, 364 for validation and 964 for testing. The MSRC21 dataset [25] consists of 591 color images of size 320×213 and corresponding ground-truth labeling for 21 classes. The standard train-validation-test split is used as described in [25].

Metric. We evaluate our algorithm using two performance metrics: accuracy and intersection-union metric (VOC measure). We compute the per-class accuracy as the percentage of pixels that are classified correctly for each object class, and report the 'average' accuracy (the mean of the per-class percentages) and the 'global' accuracy (the percentage of pixels from all classes that are classified correctly). We compute the VOC measure for each object class as $\frac{\#TP}{\#TP + \#FP + \#FN}$, where $\#TP$, $\#FP$ and $\#FN$ are the number of true positives, false positives and false negatives, respectively, and report the mean VOC measure over all classes.

Top-Down Term. Since this framework is general, it can be applied with different unary, pairwise and top-down terms with different features. In our experiments, we used three different methods to extract feature points and compute object-level histograms. In the first method (TP1), we extract sparse SIFT features for each image at detected interest points, similar to [26,10]. In this case, each super-pixel region can contain 0, 1 or more feature points, and we use the absolute value of the sparse code for our top-down term. In the second method (TP2), we extract one SIFT feature at the center of each super-pixel region, to capture the texture of the whole region. In the third method (TP3), we compute the vectorized average TextonBoost scores of all pixels in each super-pixel as feature points. In the last two methods, each super-pixel is associated with only one feature point. The first two methods are used for the Graz02 dataset, while the third method is used for both the PASCAL VOC and MSRC21 datasets.

Unary Potentials. We use different unary potentials for different datasets. For the Graz-02 dataset, we use the same unary potentials as in [26,10] in order to make our results comparable. Specifically, we first create super-pixels by over-segmenting each image using the Quick Shift algorithm [30]. Then we extract dense SIFT features on each image, and compute the BoF representation for each super-pixel region. We then train an SVM with a χ^2-RBF kernel using LibSVM [4]. For each super-pixel, we apply the SVM classifier to the associated histogram and compute the logarithm of the output probability as the unary potential. For the PASCAL VOC and MSRC21 datasets, we use the pixel-wise unaries based on TextonBoost classifier provided by [14]. The super-pixel unary potentials are then computed by first taking the logarithm of the probabilities and then averaging over all pixels inside each super-pixel.

Pairwise Potentials. For all datasets, we use a contrast sensitive cost $\frac{B_{ij}}{1+\|C_i-C_j\|}$ [10] as pairwise potentials, where B_{ij} is the length of shared boundary between super-pixel i and j, and C_i is the mean color of super-pixel i.

Implementation Details. We use the VL_feat toolbox [29] for preprocessing. We use vl_quickshift to generate super-pixels and set the parameter that controls super-pixel size to $\tau = 8$. When extracting dense SIFT features to construct the unaries, we use the vl_dsift function with spatial bin size set to 12. To define the top-down cost, when computing sparse SIFT features (TP1), we apply the vl_sift function with default settings, while for TP2, we set the position for SIFT features to be the center position of each super-pixel, and the spatial bin size to 8. For initializing the linear classifiers $w_1, \ldots, w_L$, we use the Matlab Structural SVM toolbox [28]. For initializing the dictionary and computing sparse representations, we use the sparse coding toolbox provided by [19], where λ is set to 0.1, and the dictionary is of size 400 for SIFT feature points, and 50 for TextonBoost based feature points. The parameter C in our Max-Margin formulation is set to 1000. The scale γ of the hamming loss is set to 1000. For gradient descent, we use an initial step size $\tau_0 =$1e-6. We run 100 iterations for Graz02, and 600 iterations for PASCAL VOC and MSRC21. For PASCAL VOC and MSRC21, we use the validation data to train our parameters, while the unary potentials from [14] are computed based on training data. For Graz02, both unary potentials and model parameters are computed based on training data.

4.1   Graz-02 Dataset

Results. Tables 1 and 2 show the VOC measure and per-class accuracy, respectively, on the Graz-02 dataset. Since we randomly sampled super-pixels to compute the unary potentials for this dataset, we run the experiment 5 times and calculate the mean and variance of the result (reported in parenthesis). In the tables, U+P refers to the basic CRF model described by Eqn. (2), and TP1 and TP2 refer to the first two methods for extracting top-down feature points. Notice that the U+P result is computed by our implementation, while results from [26,10] are taken from the original paper. To show that these results are comparable, we observe that in [10], their U+P implementation gives an average of 50.82% in VOC measure metric, and 80.36% in average per-class accuracy, which means our method and [10] are built based on comparable baselines.

Table 1. VOC measure on Graz-02 Dataset

	U+P	[26]	[10]	Ours-TP1	Ours-TP2
BG	79.4 (0.8)	82.3	78.0	86.4 (0.1)	87.2 (0.1)
Bike	44.3 (0.3)	46.2	55.6	52.8 (0.1)	52.5 (0.1)
Car	40.6 (1.5)	36.5	41.5	44.1 (0.3)	48.4 (0.6)
Human	37.9 (1.2)	39.0	37.3	41.2 (0.8)	44.1 (0.6)
Mean	50.6 (0.3)	51.0	53.1	56.1 (0.1)	58.0 (0.1)

Table 2. Accuracy on Graz-02 Dataset

	U+P	[26]	[10]	Ours-TP1	Ours-TP2
BG	81.6 (0.3)	86.4	75.9	90.6 (0.1)	91.2 (0.1)
Bike	85.9 (0.1)	73.0	84.9	77.8 (1.7)	76.3 (0.5)
Car	78.9 (0.8)	68.7	76.7	66.3 (6.6)	68.2 (1.6)
Human	80.0 (1.4)	71.3	79.8	66.7 (5.5)	70.0 (1.2)
Mean	81.6 (0.1)	74.9	79.3	75.4 (0.6)	76.4 (0.1)
Global	81.72 (0.2)	N/A	N/A	87.6 (0.1)	88.1 (0.1)

| Image | Ground Truth | U+P | [26] | Ours-TP1 | Ours-TP2 |

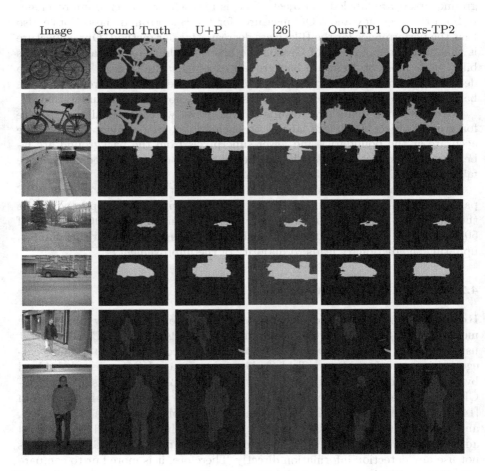

Fig. 1. Example segmentation results for the Graz02 dataset using different methods. The background, bikes, cars and humans are color coded as blue, cyan, yellow and red respectively.

Discussion. From Table 1 we can see that our method outperforms both our baseline U+P and other state-of-art methods (except for the bike category). However, the per-class accuracy in Table 2 is not improved except for the Background category. This is understandable since our goal is to reduce the false negative rate as well as the false positive rate, while the accuracy metric focuses on the true positive rate exclusively. Note that for the Car and Human category, the VOC measure is improved by around 7% while the accuracy decreases by around 10%. This implies that a lot of false positives are removed, i.e. less background pixels are labeled as object. That is also why we observe improvement in both the accuracy and VOC measures for the Background class. Notice also that the performance for the Bike class decreases for our method. Our conjecture is that in the annotations of Graz02 the pixels inside the wheel are labeled as bike, while most of them are background except for the spokes. This leads to decreased performance, since some of the pixels inside the wheel are classified as background. We would expect better results with more detailed annotations.

We show some qualitative results in Fig. 1. As we can see, although more foreground object pixels are labeled as background, the segmentation is more accurate at the boundaries and fewer superpixels from the background are labeled as other class. For example, for the Bike category, our method can remove false positives in the triangle area (row 2 in Fig. 1).

To further understand the effect of jointly learning the dictionary and the CRF parameters, we run experiments where only the weights W is updated, while the dictionary D is fixed. In this case, we achieve an average VOC measure of 50.1% for TP1 and 51.0% for TP2, which seems to suggest that for this dataset, updating the dictionary leads to majority of the improvement.

4.2 PASCAL VOC2010

Results. Fig. 2 shows the per-class VOC measure obtained by the baseline method (U+P) and our proposed method on the PASCAL VOC2010 dataset using the third feature extraction method (TP3) to construct the top-down categorization cost. In addition, Table 3 shows the average VOC measure obtained by both methods together with the results of [25,14,33] for comparison. The grid-CRF method refers to the one used by [25], while its performance is reported in [14]. Notice that the dense-CRF in [14] models each pixel as a node of the graph, and the work in [33] uses also detection scores. On the other hand, our method adopts a super-pixel based CRF instead of a dense pixel based CRF and does not use any detection information directly. Therefore, it is more fair to compare our results with those of the grid-CRF method in [25].

Discussion. As expected, our U+P baseline performs as good as the grid-CRF model, since they have similar graph size. Our method with jointly updating dictionary and CRF leads to a 1.4% improvement in VOC measure and the performance is comparable with more complex methods [14,33]. As we can see in Fig. 2, for most of the object classes, we obtain an improvement of up to 5%.

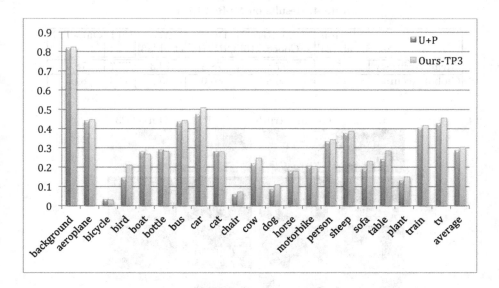

Fig. 2. VOC measure on VOC 2010 dataset using baseline U+P and our method

Table 3. Results on VOC2010 Dataset

	grid-CRF [25]	dense-CRF [14]	[33]	U+P	Ours-TP3
VOC measure	28.3	30.2	31.2	28.9	30.3

4.3 MSRC21

Results. Table 4 gives the mean and global accuracy obtained by the baseline method (U+P) and our proposed method on the MSRC21 dataset using the TextonBoost based unary potential and top-down terms, as for the PASCAL VOC2010 dataset. The results of [24,15,14,33] are also reported for comparison, while the performance of [15] on MSRC21 dataset is reported in [33]. We also show some qualitative results in Fig. 3.

Discussion. The global accuracy given by our algorithm is slightly worse than that of other methods. However, the mean accuracy is on par with the performance of the dense-CRF model [14], and is only 1% less than the performance of [33]. As explained before, [33] combines both scene information and object information, while our method only uses TextonBoost feature. This suggests that our algorithm gives comparable result while using simpler models. Finally, while our results are just marginally better than those of the U+P baseline, when looking at the example segmentations in in Fig. 3 we observe that our methods gives qualitatively better segmentations.

Table 4. Results on MSRC21 Dataset

	Shotton et al. [24]	HCRF + Coocc. [15]	Dense CRF [14]	Yao et al.[33]	U+P	Ours-TP3
Mean Accuracy	67	77.8	78.3	79.3	77.7	78.4
Global Accuracy	72	86.5	86.0	86.2	84.3	84.5

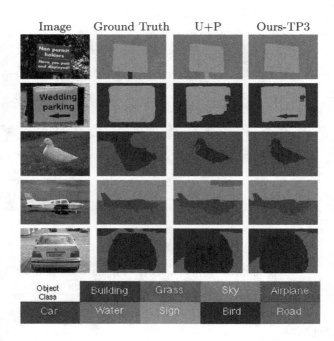

Fig. 3. Example segmentation results for the MSRC21 dataset using the U+P baseline and our proposed method

5 Conclusion

In this paper, we presented a new semantic segmentation framework that incorporates a top-down object categorization cost based on a discriminative sparse representation of each object. We proposed an optimization framework to jointly learn the sparse dictionary and the CRF parameters, so that the dictionary is specifically trained for the segmentation task. Experimental results showed that our algorithm outperforms the basic CRF model and the top-down model with BoF representation, suggesting that a jointly learned dictionary can help to improve segmentation performance compared with a pre-learned BoF dictionary.

Acknowledgements. We thank Florent Couzinié-Devy for interesting discussions about the gradient computation. The first and last author were supported in part by grants NSF 1218709, ONR N000141310116 and ERC VideoWorld. Part of the work was conducted when the first two authors were at Mitsubishi Electric Research Laboratories (MERL). This part was funded by MERL only.

References

1. Bach, F., Mairal, J., Ponce, J.: Task-driven dictionary learning. IEEE Transactions on Pattern Analysis and Machine Intelligence 34(4), 791–804 (2012)
2. Boureau, Y.L., Bach, F., LeCun, Y., Ponce, J.: Learning mid-level features for recognition. In: IEEE Conference on Computer Vision and Pattern Recognition (2010)
3. Brostow, G.J., Shotton, J., Fauqueur, J., Cipolla, R.: Segmentation and recognition using structure from motion point clouds. In: Forsyth, D., Torr, P., Zisserman, A. (eds.) ECCV 2008, Part I. LNCS, vol. 5302, pp. 44–57. Springer, Heidelberg (2008)
4. Chang, C.C., Lin, C.J.: LIBSVM: a library for support vector machines (2001), software available at http://www.csie.ntu.edu.tw/~cjlin/libsvm
5. Everingham, M., Van Gool, L., Williams, C.K.I., Winn, J., Zisserman, A.: The pascal visual object classes (voc) challenge. Int. Journal of Computer Vision 88(2), 303–338 (2010)
6. Fei-Fei, L., Perona, P.: A bayesian hierarchical model for learning natural scene categories. In: IEEE Computer Society Conference on Computer Vision and Pattern Recognition, CVPR 2005 (2005)
7. Fulkerson, B., Vedaldi, A., Soatto, S.: Class segmentation and object localization with superpixel neighborhoods. In: IEEE Int. Conf. on Computer Vision (2009)
8. Galleguillos, C., Rabinovich, A., Belongie, S.: Object categorization using co-occurrence, location and appearance. In: IEEE Conf. on Computer Vision and Pattern Recognition (2008)
9. Gould, S., Rodgers, J., Cohen, D., Elidan, G., Koller, D.: Multi-class segmentation with relative location prior. International Journal of Computer Vision 80(3), 300–316 (2008)
10. Jain, A., Zappella, L., McClure, P., Vidal, R.: Visual dictionary learning for joint object categorization and segmentation. In: Fitzgibbon, A., Lazebnik, S., Perona, P., Sato, Y., Schmid, C. (eds.) ECCV 2012, Part V. LNCS, vol. 7576, pp. 718–731. Springer, Heidelberg (2012)
11. Joachims, T., Finley, T., Yu, C.N.J.: Cutting-plane training of structural SVMs. Machine Learning 77(1), 27–59 (2009)
12. Kohli, P., Ladicky, L., Torr, P.H.S.: Robust higher order potentials for enforcing label consistency. In: IEEE Conf. on Computer Vision and Pattern Recognition (2008)
13. Kolmogorov, V., Zabih, R.: What energy functions can be minimized via graph cuts? IEEE Trans. on Pattern Analysis and Machine Intelligence 26(2), 147–159 (2004)
14. Krähenbühl, P., Koltun, V.: Efficient inference in fully connected crfs with gaussian edge potentials. In: Neural Information Processing Systems, pp. 109–117 (2011)
15. Ladický, Ľ., Sturgess, P., Alahari, K., Russell, C., Torr, P.H.S.: What, where and how many? Combining object detectors and cRFs. In: Daniilidis, K., Maragos, P., Paragios, N. (eds.) ECCV 2010, Part IV. LNCS, vol. 6314, pp. 424–437. Springer, Heidelberg (2010)
16. Ladicky, L., Russell, C., Kohli, P., Torr, P.: Associative hierarchical CRFs for object class image segmentation. In: IEEE Int. Conf. on Computer Vision (2009)
17. Lafferty, J.D., McCallum, A., Pereira, F.C.N.: Conditional random fields: Probabilistic models for segmenting and labeling sequence data. In: ICML (2001)
18. Laptev, I.: On space-time interest points. International Journal of Computer Vision 64(2-3), 107–123 (2005)

19. Lee, H., Battle, A., Raina, R., Ng, A.Y.: Efficient sparse coding algorithms. In: Neural Information Processing Systems, pp. 801–808 (2007)
20. Mairal, J., Bach, F., Ponce, J., Sapiro, G., Zisserman, A.: Discriminative learned dictionaries for local image analysis. IEEE Conference on Computer Vision and Pattern Recognition (2008)
21. Murphy, K.P., Weiss, Y., Jordan, M.I.: Loopy belief propagation for approximate inference: An empirical study. In: Proceedings of Uncertainty in AI, pp. 467–475 (1999)
22. Naikal, N., Singaraju, D., Sastry, S.S.: Using models of objects with deformable parts for joint categorization and segmentation of objects. In: Lee, K.M., Matsushita, Y., Rehg, J.M., Hu, Z. (eds.) ACCV 2012, Part II. LNCS, vol. 7725, pp. 79–93. Springer, Heidelberg (2013)
23. Opelt, A., Pinz, A.: The TU Graz-02 database (2002), http://www.emt.tugraz.at/~pinz/data/GRAZ02/
24. Shotton, J., Johnson, M., Cipolla, R.: Semantic texton forests for image categorization and segmentation. In: IEEE Conf. on Computer Vision and Pattern Recognition (2008)
25. Shotton, J., Winn, J.M., Rother, C., Criminisi, A.: Textonboost for image understanding: Multi-class object recognition and segmentation by jointly modeling texture, layout, and context. Int. Journal of Computer Vision 81(1), 2–23 (2009)
26. Singaraju, D., Vidal, R.: Using global bag of features models in random fields for joint categorization and segmentation of objects. In: IEEE Conference on Computer Vision and Pattern Recognition (2011)
27. Tighe, J., Lazebnik, S.: Finding things: Image parsing with regions and per-exemplar detectors. In: IEEE Conf. on Computer Vision and Pattern Recognition (2013)
28. Vedaldi, A.: A MATLAB wrapper of SVM^{s}truct (2011), http://www.vlfeat.org/~vedaldi/code/svm-struct-matlab.html
29. Vedaldi, A., Fulkerson, B.: VLFeat: An open and portable library of computer vision algorithms (2008), http://www.vlfeat.org/
30. Vedaldi, A., Soatto, S.: Quick shift and kernel methods for mode seeking. In: Forsyth, D., Torr, P., Zisserman, A. (eds.) ECCV 2008, Part IV. LNCS, vol. 5305, pp. 705–718. Springer, Heidelberg (2008)
31. Yang, J., Yang, M.: Top-down visual saliency via joint crf and dictionary learning. In: IEEE Conference on Computer Vision and Pattern Recognition (2012)
32. Yang, J., Yu, K., Gong, Y., Huang, T.: Linear spatial pyramid matching using sparse coding for image classification. In: IEEE Conference on Computer Vision and Pattern Recognition (2009)
33. Yao, J., Fidler, S., Urtasun, R.: Describing the scene as a whole: Joint object detection, scene classification and semantic segmentation. In: IEEE Conf. on Computer Vision and Pattern Recognition (2012)
34. Yu, C.N.J., Joachims, T.: Learning structural svms with latent variables. In: Proceedings of the 26th Annual International Conference on Machine Learning, ICML 2009, pp. 1169–1176. ACM, New York (2009)
35. Zhang, K., Zhang, W., Zheng, Y., Xue, X.: Sparse reconstruction for weakly supervised semantic segmentation. In: Proceedings of the Twenty-Third International Joint Conference on Artificial Intelligence, pp. 1889–1895 (2013)

Video Action Detection with Relational Dynamic-Poselets

Limin Wang[1,2], Yu Qiao[2,*], and Xiaoou Tang[1,2]

[1] Department of Information Engineering,
The Chinese University of Hong Kong, Hong Kong
[2] Shenzhen Key Lab of CVPR, Shenzhen Institutes of Advanced Technology
Chinese Academy of Sciences, Shenzhen, China
07wanglimin@gmail.com, yu.qiao@siat.ac.cn, xtang@ie.cuhk.edu.hk

Abstract. Action detection is of great importance in understanding human motion from video. Compared with action recognition, it not only recognizes action type, but also localizes its spatiotemporal extent. This paper presents a relational model for action detection, which first decomposes human action into temporal "key poses" and then further into spatial "action parts". Specifically, we start by clustering cuboids around each human joint into dynamic-poselets using a new descriptor. The cuboids from the same cluster share consistent geometric and dynamic structure, and each cluster acts as a mixture of body parts. We then propose a sequential skeleton model to capture the relations among dynamic-poselets. This model unifies the tasks of learning the composites of mixture dynamic-poselets, the spatiotemporal structures of action parts, and the local model for each action part in a single framework. Our model not only allows to localize the action in a video stream, but also enables a detailed pose estimation of an actor. We formulate the model learning problem in a structured SVM framework and speed up model inference by dynamic programming. We conduct experiments on three challenging action detection datasets: the MSR-II dataset, the UCF Sports dataset, and the JHMDB dataset. The results show that our method achieves superior performance to the state-of-the-art methods on these datasets.

Keywords: Action detection, dynamic-poselet, sequential skeleton model.

1 Introduction

Action understanding in video [1] has attracted a great deal of attention in the computer vision community due to its wide applications in surveillance, human computer interaction, and content-based retrieval. Most of the research efforts have been devoted to the problem of action recognition using the Bag of Visual Words (BoVW) framework or variants thereof [29,24,11]. These particular designed methods for action recognition usually require a short video clip to be

---

* Corresponding author.

D. Fleet et al. (Eds.): ECCV 2014, Part V, LNCS 8693, pp. 565–580, 2014.
© Springer International Publishing Switzerland 2014

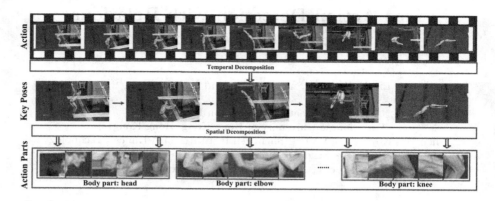

Fig. 1. Illustration of action decomposition. A video sequence first can be temporally decomposed into several short snippets, each of which corresponds to a key pose. For each key pose, the action can then be further decomposed spatially into several action parts (red boxes), each of which describes the appearance and motion of body part in a specific configuration. A body part is described by multiple action parts. Best view in color.

cropped from a continuous video stream. Apart from the class label, however, they cannot provide further information about the action, such as the location and pose of the actor. To overcome these limitations, we focus on the problem of action detection. Given a long video stream, we aim not only to recognize on-going action class, but also to localize its spatiotemporal extent (that is, the bounding box of the actor and the temporal duration of action), and estimate the pose of the actor.

Previous studies have shown that *pose* [23,13,10,17,7] and *motion* [27,30,15,5] are key elements in understanding human actions from videos. Pose captures the static configurations and geometric constraints of human body parts, while motion refers to the local articulated movements of body parts and global rigid kinematics. As Figure 1 shows, an action sequence can be decomposed temporally into several snippets. In these snippets, the actors exhibit discriminative configurations of body parts for action understanding. We call these discriminative configurations of body parts as the *key poses* of an action. There is a temporal structure and global rigid motion (for example, translation) among these key poses. Each key pose can be further broken down spatially to *action parts*, each of which describes the appearance and motion of body part in a specific configuration. As in Figure 1, each red box corresponds to an action part and a body part is described by multiple action parts. However, modeling the action class still presents the following challenges:

- How to discover a collection of tightly-clustered action parts from videos. As the same body part exhibits large variations in the action (see Figure 1), it is not feasible to describe the body part using a single template. Mixture model will be a more suitable choice to handle large intra-variations of body parts. The cuboids belonging to the same mixture (action part) should not

only share similar visual appearance and pose configuration, but also exhibit consistent motion patterns. It is necessary to design effective descriptors to help tightly cluster body parts and satisfy these requirements.
- How to model the spatiotemporal relations of action parts. To handle large intra-class variation, each body part is represented by a mixture of action part. Each mixture component (action part) represents the feature template of the body part in a specific pose and motion configuration. A key pose can be viewed as a spatial arrangement of action parts, and an action contains a sequence of moving key poses. Thus, the action model must take into account the spatiotemporal relations among body part, co-occurrences of different mixture types, and local part templates jointly.

In order to address these issues, this paper proposes a unified approach to discover effective action parts and model their relations. Specifically, we first annotate articulated human poses in training video sequences to leverage the human-supervised information. Based on these annotations, we design an effective descriptor to encode both the geometric and motion properties of each cuboid. Using this descriptor, we are able to cluster cuboids that share similar pose configuration and motion patterns into consistent action parts, which we call *dynamic-poselets*. These dynamic-poselets then act as mixture components of body parts, and we propose a relational model, called *sequential skeleton model* (SSM), that is able to jointly learn the composites of mixture dynamic-poselets, spatiotemporal structures of action parts, and the local model for each part. Using a mixture of dynamic-poselet enables SSM to be robust for large intra-class variation, such as viewpoint changes and motion speed variations. We formulate the model learning problem in a structured SVM framework [21] and use the dual coordinate-descent solver [31] for parameter optimization. Due to the fact that the sequential skeleton model is tree-structured, we can efficiently detect the action instance by dynamic programming algorithm. We conduct experiments on three public datasets: the MSR-II dataset [4], the UCF Sports dataset [14], and the JHMDB dataset [7]. We show that our framework achieves state-of-the-art performance for action detection in these challenging datasets.

2   Related Works

Action recognition has been extensively studied in recent years [1]. This section only covers the works related to our method.

Action Detection. Action detection has been comprehensively studied [8,14,34,4,5,32,9,33,20,19]. Methods in [4,34,9] used Bag of Visual Words (BoVW) representation to describe action and conduct a sliding window scheme for detection. Yuan *et al.* [34] focused on improving search efficiency, while Cao *et al.* [4] mainly evaluated cross-dataset performance. Methods in [8,14,5] untilized global template matching with different features. Yao *et al.* [32] and Yu *et al.* [33] resorted to the Hough voting method of local cuboids for action detection, while Lan *et al.* [9] resorted to latent learning to locate action automatically.

Tran *et al.* [20] casted action detection task as a spatiotemporal structure regression problem and leveraged efficient Max-Path search method for detection. Tian *et al.* [19] extended the 2D part deformable model to 3D cases. Our method is different from these other methods in that we consider motion and pose in a unified framework for video-based action detection.

Parts in Action. The concept of "action part" appeared in several previous works, either implicitly or explicitly [12,13,27,22,26]. Raptis *et al.* [12] clustered trajectories of similar motion speed in a local region, with each cluster center corresponding to an action part. They modeled action in a graphical model framework to constrain the spatiotemporal relations among parts. Ullah *et al* [22] presented a supervised approach to learn the motion descriptor of actlets from synthetic videos. Wang *et al.* [27] proposed to cluster cuboids with high-motion salience into 3D parts, called *motionlets*, based on low-level features such as HOG and HOE. Raptis *et al.* [13] resorted to the poselet part proposed for static image, and used a sequence model to model the temporal structure. Wang *et al.* [26] designed a discriminative clustering method to discover the "temporal parts" of action, called *motion atoms*. Inspired by the success of poselets [2] and phraselets [6] in image-based tasks, we have designed spatiotemporal action part, called dynamic-poselets. Dynamic-poselets capture both the pose configuration and motion pattern of local cuboids, which are suitable for action detection in video.

Relational Model in Action. Several previous works [9,3,19,28,18] have considered the relations among parts for action recognition and detection. Lan *et al.* [9] detected 2D parts frame-by-frame with tracking constraints using CRF. Brendel *et al.* [3] proposed a spatiotemporal graph to model the relations over tubes and to represent the structure of action. Tian *et al.* [19] proposed a spatiotemporal deformable part models for action and obtained state-of-the-art performance. Wang *et al.* [28] designed a Latent Hierarchical Model (LHM) to capture the temporal structure among segments in a coarse-to-fine manner. Sun *et al.* [18] considered the temporal relations of segments by exploiting activity concept transitions in video events. Our relational model differs from these models in two main aspects. Firstly, our model is constructed by explicitly modeling the human pose, which has been proved to be an important cue for action understanding [7]. Secondly, our model is composed of mixtures of parts, similar to that of [31] for static pose estimation, and this mixture representation is effective at handling large intra-class variations in action.

3   Dynamic-Poselets

This section describes the method for learning action parts or dynamic-poselets, specific to a given action class. Dynamic-poselets are cuboids that are tightly clustered in both pose and motion configuration space. Due to the large intra-class variation and low resolution quality of action video, it is difficult to directly group cuboids based on low-level appearance and motion features such as HOG

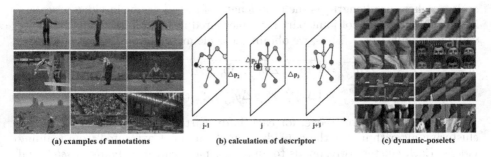

(a) examples of annotations   (b) calculation of descriptor   (c) dynamic-poselets

Fig. 2. Illustration of dynamic-poselet construction. (a) Some examples of human pose annotations in the training videos. (b) The descriptor extraction for dynamic-poselet clustering. For each joint, we calculate its spatial offset ΔP_1 with respect to its parent, and its temporal offsets ΔP_2 and ΔP_3 with respect to itself in previous and subsequent frames. (c) Some examples of clusters (dynamic-poselets) in training videos.

and HOF [24]. Similar to the methods of constructing image representation such as poselet [2] and phraselet [6], we leverage the human annotations of human joints, and propose a new descriptor based on the geometric configuration and the moving direction of a cuboid.

For a specific action class, we assume that we have been given training videos with human joint annotations. Typical human joints (body parts) include head, shoulder, elbow and so on. Some annotation examples are shown in Figure 2. Let K be the number of body parts in our annotations, and $i \in \{1, \cdots, K\}$ denote the ith human body part. Let $p_{i,j}^v = (x_{i,j}^v, y_{i,j}^v)$ denote the position of body part i in the jth frame of video v. Let M_i be the number of mixture for body part i and $t_{i,j}^v \in \{1, \cdots, M_i\}$ denote the mixture type of body part i in the jth frame of video v. In the remaining part of this section, we will show how to obtain the mixture types of body parts for training videos.

Intuitively, the spatial geometric configuration of a human body part with respect to others in the same frames will determine its pose and appearance, and the temporal displacement with respect to the same joints from adjacent frames will represent the articulated motion. Based on this assumption, we have designed the following new descriptor for a cuboid around each human joint:

$$f(p_{i,j}^v) = [\Delta p_{i,j}^{v,1}, \Delta p_{i,j}^{v,2}, \Delta p_{i,j}^{v,3}], \tag{1}$$

where $\Delta p_{i,j}^{v,1} = p_{i,j}^v - p_{par(i),j}^v$ is the offset of joint i with respect to its parent $par(i)$ in current frame j of video v, $\Delta p_{i,j}^{v,2} = p_{i,j}^v - p_{i,j-1}^v$ and $\Delta p_{i,j}^{v,3} = p_{i,j}^v - p_{i,j+1}^v$ denote the temporal displacements of joint i with respect to the same joints in previous and subsequent frames of video v, respectively (see Figure 2). Essentially, $\Delta p_{i,j}^{v,1}$ encodes the pose and appearance information, and $\Delta p_{i,j}^{v,2}$ and $\Delta p_{i,j}^{v,3}$ capture the motion information.

To make the descriptor invariant to scale, we estimate the scale for each body part in a video v. The scale of body part is estimated by $s_{i,j}^v = \text{headlength}_j^v \times$

scale$_{i,j}$, where headlength$_j^v$ is the head length of the jth frame in video v, scale$_{i,j}$ is the canonical scale of joint part (i, j) measured in human head length, whose value is usually 1 or 2. Thus, we obtain the scale invariant descriptor as follows:

$$\overline{f(p_{i,j}^v)} = [\overline{\Delta p_{i,j}^{v,1}}, \overline{\Delta p_{i,j}^{v,2}}, \overline{\Delta p_{i,j}^{v,3}}],$$
$$\overline{\Delta p_{i,j}^{v,k}} = [\Delta x_{i,j}^{v,k}/s_{i,j}^v, \Delta y_{i,j}^{v,k}/s_{i,j}^v](k = 1, 2, 3). \tag{2}$$

Using the descriptor above, for each body part, we separately run k-means clustering algorithm over the cuboids around this joint extracted from training videos. Each cluster corresponds to an action part, called *dynamic poselet*, and the body part is represented as a mixture of action part (dynamic poselet). The cluster label is the mixture type t of body parts in training videos. Some examples of clusters (dynamic-poselets) are shown in Figure 2. These results indicate that the proposed descriptor is effective at obtaining tightly-clustered cuboids with similar pose, appearance, and movement. Meanwhile, we find it is important to leverage the motion term (i.e., $\Delta p_{i,j}^{v,2}$, $\Delta p_{i,j}^{v,3}$) in the descriptor to cluster dynamic-poselets. See the examples of the top row in Figure 2, where the two kinds of dynamic-poselets are from hand-waving action. If we ignore the motion term in our descriptor, the two kinds of dynamic-poselets will be merged in the same cluster because they share similar appearance and pose configuration. However, the two kinds of dynamic-poselets are different in motion, with one corresponds to moving down and the other to moving up.

4   Sequential Skeleton Model

Figure 3 provides an overview of our approach. During the training phase, we first cluster the cuboids into consistent dynamic-poselets using the descriptor (Equation (2)) in the previous section. Then, based on the clustering the results, we develop a *Sequential Skeleton Model* (SSM) to describe each action class. The SSM is described in the remainder of this section, and the learning and inference algorithms are proposed in the next section.

We now propose the SSM of a specific action class to describe the spatiotemporal configuration of a collection of action parts (dynamic-poselets). Our model not only imposes the spatiotemporal structure and geometric arrangement of dynamic-poselets, but also learns the co-occurrence of mixture types for action parts. The two goals interact with each other, and the geometric arrangement of action parts affects the mixture types, and vice versa. To encode such relationships jointly, we extend the framework of mixture-of-parts [31] to spatiotemporal domain and design a relational model (that is, SSM).

Let $G = (V, E)$ be a spatiotemporal graph with node $V = \{(i, j)\}_{i,j=1}^{K,N}$ denoting the body part in human action where K is the number of body parts, N is the number of key poses, and edge $E = \{(i, j) \sim (m, n)\}$ denote the relations among adjacent body parts (see Figure 3). How to determine the location of key pose of training videos will be specified in next section. Let v be a video clip, p be the pixel positions of body parts in key poses, and t be the mixture types of

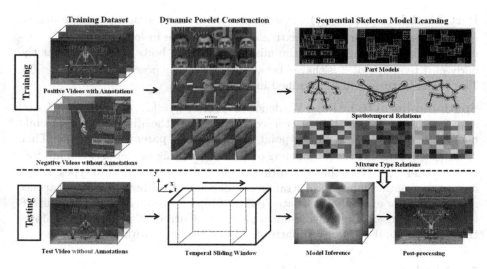

Fig. 3. Overview of our approach. For training, we annotate human joints for several key poses in the positive samples. We first cluster the cuboids around each human joint into dynamic-poselets. Then, each dynamic-poselet acts as a mixture of body parts and is fed into the SSM training. Our SSM is composed of three components: part models, spatiotemporal relations, and mixture type relations. For testing, we first use a temporal sliding window and then conduct inference of SSM. Finally, we resort to post-processing techniques such as no-maximum suppression to obtain the detection results. It is worth **noting that** there is no annotation for testing samples.

body parts in key poses. The discriminative score with the current configuration of dynamic poselets is then defined as follows:

$$S(v, p, t) = b(t) + \sum_{j=1}^{N} \sum_{i=1}^{K} \alpha_i^{t_{i,j}} \phi(v, p_{i,j}) + \sum_{(i,j) \sim (m,n)} \beta_{(i,j),(m,n)}^{t_{i,j} t_{m,n}} \psi(p_{i,j}, p_{m,n}), \quad (3)$$

where $(\{b\}, \{\alpha\}, \{\beta\})$ are model parameters, ϕ and ψ are visual features.

Mixture Type Relations. $b(t)$ is used to define a "prior" with preference to some mixture combinations, which factors into a summation of the following terms :

$$b(t) = \sum_{j=1}^{N} \sum_{i=1}^{K} b_{i,j}^{t_{i,j}} + \sum_{(i,j) \sim (m,n)} b_{(i,j),(m,n)}^{t_{i,j} t_{m,n}}, \quad (4)$$

where term $b_{(i,j),(m,n)}^{t_{i,j} t_{m,n}}$ encodes the compatibility of mixture types. Intuitively, some configurations of mixture types are more compatible with current action class than others. In the case of hand-waving action, moving-up arms tends to co-occur with moving-up hands, while moving-down arms tends to co-occur with moving-down hands. With this term in the relational model, we are able to discover these kinds of co-occurrence patterns.

Part Models. $\alpha_i^{t_{i,j}} \phi(v, p_{i,j})$ is the model for a single action part. We denote $\phi(v, p_{i,j})$ as the feature vector extracted from video v in location $p_{i,j}$. $\alpha_i^{t_{i,j}}$ denotes the feature template for the mixture $t_{i,j}$ of ith body part. Note that the body part template $\alpha_i^{t_{i,j}}$ is shared between different key poses of the same action. The visual features will be specified in Section 6.

Spatiotemporal Relations. We denote $\psi(p_{i,j}, p_{m,n}) = [dx, dy, dz, dx^2, dy^2, dz^2]$ as a quadratic deformation vector computed from the displacement of child node (i, j) relative to its anchor point determined by parent node (m, n). Then $\beta_{(i,j),(m,n)}^{t_{i,j} t_{m,n}}$ represents the parameters of quadratic spring model between mixture type $t_{i,j}$ and $t_{m,n}$. Note that the spring model is related to mixture types, which means the spatiotemporal constraints are dependent on both local appearance and motion. For example, the spatial relationship between hands and arms is different in moving-up and moving-down processes. Currently, we explicitly enforce that the temporal locations of parts should be the same within a key pose.

5 Model Learning and Inference

The *learning task* aims to determine the structure of Graph $G = (V, E)$ and estimate the model parameters $\theta = (\{b\}, \{\alpha\}, \{\beta\})$ in Equation (3) for each action class. For graph structure, we currently resort to a simple initialization method. For each key pose, we determine its structure as a skeleton tree model independently. For each action, in the temporal domain, we add an edge between the heads of adjacent key poses. This method is simple but effective for determining the graph structure.

Given the action-specific graph G and a training set $\{v_i, y_i, p^{v_i}, t^{v_i}\}_{i=1}^{M}$, the score function of Equation (3) is linear with model parameters θ, and we can rewrite the score function in the form $\theta \cdot \Phi(v_i, p^{v_i}, t^{v_i})$. Thus, we formulate the parameter learning problem in the following structured SVM framework [21]:

$$\arg \min_{\theta, \{\xi_i \geq 0\}} \frac{1}{2} \|\theta\|_2^2 + C \sum_{i=1}^{M} \xi_i$$

$$\text{s.t. } \theta \cdot \Phi(v_i, p^{v_i}, t^{v_i}) \geq 1 - \xi_i, \text{ if } y_i = 1$$

$$\theta \cdot \Phi(v_i, p, t) \leq -1 + \xi_i, \quad \forall(p, t), \text{ if } y_i = -1. \tag{5}$$

The negative examples are collected from the action videos with different labels. This is a standard convex optimization problem, and many well-tuned solvers are public available. Here we use the dual coordinate-decent solver [31]. Together with the process of dynamic-poselets clustering, the whole learning process is shown in Algorithm 1.

Firstly, for each positive example, we extract the descriptors for the annotated human parts and conduct k-means to cluster these cuboids into dynamic-poselets. From the clustering results, we obtain the mixture labels for the parts of positive examples. We then train each dynamic-poselet independently using classical SVM. This training process provides an initialization for the template

---

Algorithm 1. Dynamic-poselets clustering and model learning.

Data: Positive samples: $\mathcal{P} = \{v_i, p^{v_i}, y_i\}_{i=1}^{T_1}$, negative samples: $\mathcal{N} = \{v_j, y_j\}_{j=1}^{T_2}$.
Result: Graph: G and parameters: θ.
// Dynamic-poselets clustering
- Extract the descriptors of each body part (i, j).
- Using the descriptors, run k-means on the local cuboids, and obtain the
mixture type $t_{i,j}$ for each body part.
// Model parameter learning
- Initialize the graph structure G.
foreach *part i and mixture type t_i* **do**
$\quad | \quad \alpha_i^{t_i} \longleftarrow$ SVMTrain $(\{v_i, p^{v_i}, t^{v_i}\}, i, t_i)$.
end
- Use the part template above to initialize the model parameters θ.
for $i \leftarrow 1$ **to** C **do**
$\quad | \quad$ - Mining Hard negative examples: $N \leftarrow$ NegativeMining$(\theta, G, \mathcal{N})$.
$\quad | \quad$ - Retrain model jointly: $\theta \leftarrow$ JointSVMTrain$(\theta, G, N, \{v_i, p^{v_i}, y^{v_i}\})$.
end
- **return** *graph G and parameters θ*.

---

parameters in the relational model. Based on this initialization, we iterate between mining hard negative examples and retraining model parameters jointly as in the Structured SVM. The iteration is run for a fixed number of times.

Implementation Details. In the current implementation, the number of key poses is set as 3. Due to the subjectivity of key pose, we design a simple yet effective method to determine the locations of key pose given a specific video. We start by dividing the video into three segments of equal duration. Then, in each segment, we uniformly sample a frame as the key pose. To handle the temporal miss-alignment of training videos, we conduct uniform sampling four times and obtain four instances for each positive video. This method also increases the number of training samples for structured SVM learning and makes the learning procedure more stable. The iteration times C of Algorithm 1 is set as 5.

The *inference task* is to determine the locations and mixture types (p, t) of a given video v by maximizing the discriminative score $S(v, p, t)$ defined in Equation (3). Since our relational graph $G = (V, E)$ is a tree, this can be done efficiently with dynamic programming. For a node (i, j) at location $p_{i,j}$ with mixture type $t_{i,j}$, we can compute its score according to the message passed from its children $kids((i, j))$:

$$S_{i,j}(p_{i,j}, t_{i,j}) = b_{i,j}^{t_{i,j}} + \alpha_i^{t_{i,j}} \phi(v, p_{i,j}) + \sum_{(m,n) \in kids((i,j))} C_{m,n}(p_{i,j}, t_{i,j}), \quad (6)$$

$$C_{m,n}(p_{i,j}, t_{i,j}) = \max_{t_{m,n}} \left\{ b_{(m,n),(i,j)}^{t_{m,n} t_{i,j}} + \right.$$
$$\left. \max_{p_{m,n}} \left[S_{m,n}(p_{m,n}, t_{m,n}) + \beta_{(m,n),(i,j)}^{t_{m,n} t_{i,j}} \psi(p_{m,n}, p_{i,j}) \right] \right\}. \quad (7)$$

Equation (6) computes the local score of part (i, j) located at $p_{i,j}$ with mixture type $t_{i,j}$, and Equation (7) collects message from the child nodes and computes scores for every mixture type $t_{m,n}$ and possible location $p_{m,n}$ to obtain the best score given the parent's location $p_{i,j}$ and type $t_{i,j}$. Based on these recursive functions, we can evaluate the score in a depth-first-search (DFS) order and pass the message from leaf nodes to the root node. Once the message has been passed to the root node, $S_{1,1}(p_{1,1}, t_{1,1})$ represents the best score for each root position and mixture type.

Implementation Details. During detection, we will use the temporal sliding window of 40 frames with a step size of 20, if the testing sample is a video stream instead of a video clip. For final detection, we choose a threshold of -2 for detection score to generate multiple detections, and use the post-processing technique of non-maximum suppression to avoid repeated detections [31].

6   Experiments

In this section, we present the experimental results on three public datasets: the MSR-II dataset [4], the UCF Sports dataset [14], and the JHMDB dataset [7].

Experiment Details. For all these datasets, we extract Histogram of Oriented Gradients (HOG) and Histogram of Optical Flow (HOF) as low-level features [24]. HOG features capture the static appearance and HOF features describe the motion information. The feature cell size is up to the resolution of the video, and we select a cell size of $4 \times 4 \times 2$ for the MSR-II dataset, and $8 \times 8 \times 2$ for the UCF Sports and the JHMDB dataset. The cuboid size of each part is determined automatically according to the size of the person in the video. For the mixture number of each part, the default setting is 8.

Results on the MSR-II Dataset. The MSR-II dataset includes three action classes: boxing, hand-waving, and hand-clapping. The dataset is composed of 54 video sequences that are captured in realistic scenarios such as parties, schools, and outer traffics, with cluttered background and moving people. Following the scheme in [4], we use a subset of the KTH [16] for training and test our model on the MSR-II dataset. Specifically, we train our model on the KTH dataset with 20 positive examples for each class and the number of joints is 10 (see Figure 2). For action detection evaluation, we use the same scheme in [4] and report the average precision (AP) for each class. Although the action class is relatively simple, the MSR-II dataset is a challenging benchmark for action detection due to its realistic scene and the cross-dataset testing scheme. The experimental results can demonstrate the effectiveness of our approach for detecting simple action in realistic scenarios.

We plot the precision-recall (PR) curves in Figure 4 and report the average precision (AP) for each class in Table 1. Our method performs quite well on the action of hand waving but relatively poorly on the action of boxing. This result could be due to the fact that the action of boxing involves heavy occlusion with two arms and pose estimation in the action of boxing is more difficult than

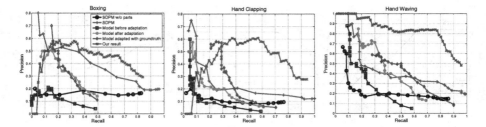

Fig. 4. Results on the MSR-II dataset. We plot the PR curves for the three action classes: boxing, hand-clapping, and hand-waving. We compare our results with GMM methods with or without adaption [4] and SDPM [19] (state-of-the-art). Best viewed in color.

in hand waving. We compare our results with two other methods: GMM adaption method [4] (baseline) and spatiotemporal deformation part model (SDPM) (state-of-the-art method) [19]. We observe that our method outperforms these methods in all action classes. Especially for the actions of hand-waving and hand-clapping, our APs are almost twice those of state-of-the-art results. In these two action classes, key poses are well detected and yield important cues for discriminating action from other classes. For the action of boxing, the improvement of our method is not so significant. The superior performance demonstrates the effectiveness of our key pose based approach for detecting simple actions in realistic scenarios.

Table 1. Results on the the MSR-II dataset. We report the APs for the three action class and mean AP (mAP) over all classes. We compare our results with GMM methods with or without adaption [4] and SDPM [19] (state-of-the-art).

Method	Boxing	Hand-clapping	Hand-waving	mAP
Baseline [4]	17.48%	13.16%	26.71%	19.12%
SDPM [19]	38.86%	23.91%	44.70%	35.82%
Our result	41.70%	50.15%	80.85%	**57.57%**

Results on the UCF Sports Dataset. The UCF Sports dataset [14] is composed of 150 realistic videos from sports broadcasts. The dataset has 10 action classes including diving, lifting, skating and so on (see Figure 5). Following the experimental setting [9], we split the dataset into 103 samples for training and 47 samples for testing. We evaluate the action localization using the "intersection-over-union" criterion and a detection is regarded as correct if the measure is larger than 0.2 and the predicted label matches. We plot the ROC curves and report the AUC for each action class. The UCF Sports dataset is more challenging than the MSR-II dataset due to the fact that the videos are cropped from sports broadcasts with large intra-class variations caused by camera motion, scale changes, viewpoint changes, and background clutter. The experiments on the UCF sports dataset can verify the effectiveness of our approach for more complex actions with articulated poses.

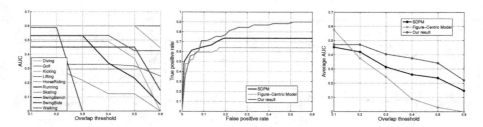

Fig. 5. Results on the UCF Sports dataset. **Left**: We plot the AUC per class of our detection result with a varying overlap thresholds. **Center**: We compare our results with the Figure-Centric Model [9] and the SDPM (state of the art) [19], when the overlap threshold is set as 0.2. **Right**: We compare the detection performances of these methods with varying thresholds (from 0.1 to 0.6). Best viewed in color.

Figure 5 shows the results of our method. We first plot the AUC of the ROC curve for each action class with respect to the varying overlap threshold in the left of Figure 5. These curves show that our method achieves a high detection rate for many action classes, such as lifting, horse-riding, and walking. We compare our approach with two recently published methods: figure-centric model (FCM) [9] and spatiotemporal deformable part model (SDPM) [19]. The FCM resorts to latent learning and detects 2D parts frame-by-frame with smooth constraints. The SDPM obtains the state-of-the-art detection performance on the UCF Sports dataset. From the comparison of the ROC curve and the AUC curve with respect to varying overlap thresholds in Figure 5, we conclude that our method outperforms the others and obtains the state-of-the-art performance on this challenging dataset. These results demonstrate that our method is not only suitable for simple action class such as MSR-II dataset, but also effective for more realistic action classes recorded in unconstrained environment.

Results on the JHMDB Dataset. The JHMDB dataset is a recently proposed dataset with full human annotation of body joints [7]. It is proposed for a systematic action recognition performance evaluation using thoroughly human annotated data. It also selects a subset of videos, called **sub-JHMDB**, each of which has all the joints inside the frames. The sub-JHMDB contains 316 clips distributed over 12 categories, including catch, pick, and swing (see Figure 6). The results in [7] show that this subset is much more challenging for action recognition than the whole dataset. No action detection results are reported in this subset and we have made the first attempt with our method. Using the same evaluation in the UCF Sports dataset, we plot the ROC curves and report the AUC for each action class.

We plot the AUC of ROC curve for each action class with respect to the varying overlap thresholds in the left of Figure 6. From the results, we observe that our method still performs quite well for some action classes on this more challenging dataset, such as golf, swing, and push. However, due to the challenges caused by low resolution, strong camera shaking, illumination changes, some action classes obtain relatively low detection rates such as jump and climbstairs. In order to compare our method with others, we adapt the state-of-the-art

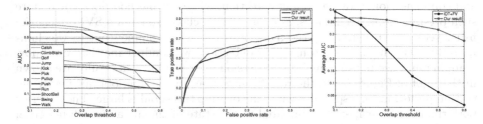

Fig. 6. Results of the sub-JHMDB dataset. **Left**: We plot the AUC per class of our detection result with varying overlap thresholds. **Center**: We compare our results with the state-of-the-art approach in action recognition [25], when the overlap threshold is set as 0.2. **Right**: We compare the detection performance with varying thresholds (from 0.1 to 0.6). Best viewed in color.

Fig. 7. Examples of action detection in three datasets. Our model is able to detect human actions and also estimate human poses accurately in most cases. Best viewed in color.

approach [25] in action recognition to action detection, and design a very competitive baseline method. Specifically, we use the improved dense trajectories (iDTs) as low-level features and choose Fisher Vector as encoding method. It should be noted that the iDTs are improved version of dense trajectories (DTs) [24] with several pre-processing techniques such as camera motion estimation and compensation, moving human detection, while our method does not require such pre-processing techniques. For each action class, we train a SVM using the fisher vector that aggregates the iDTs from the actor volume; that is, we eliminate the iDTs in the background. For detection, we conduct multiscale window scanning and use non-maximum suppression. Our comparison results are shown in the right of Figure 6 and the results show that our method obtains better detection performance, especially when the overlap threshold is large. The superior performance of our method compared to the state-of-the-art approach in action recognition indicates the importance of human pose in action understanding, especially for accurate action localization.

Examples of Detection Results. Some action detection examples on the three datasets are shown in Figure 7. We show the key poses automatically detected by our method. From these examples, we observe that our model is able to not only detect human actions, but also estimate human pose accurately in most cases.

7 Conclusion

This paper has proposed an approach for action detection in video by taking account of both cues of motion and pose. To handle the large variations of body part in action videos, a *action part* is designed as a mixture component. Guided by *key pose* decomposition, a relational model is then developed for joint modeling of spatiotemporal relations among body part, co-occurrences of mixture type, and local part templates. Our method achieves superior performance, as evidenced by comparing them to the state-of-the-art methods. In addition to action detection, our model is able to estimate human pose accurately in many cases, which also provides insights for the research of human pose estimation in videos.

Acknowledgement. We would like to thank the anonymous reviewers for their valuable suggestions in improving this paper. We also like to thank Xiaojiang Peng and Zhuowei Cai for their help in the annotatios of the UCF Sports dataset. Yu Qiao is supported by National Natural Science Foundation of China (91320101), Shenzhen Basic Research Program (JCYJ20120903092050890, JCYJ20120617114614438, JCYJ20130402113127496), 100 Talents Programme of Chinese Academy of Sciences, and Guangdong Innovative Research Team Program (No.201001D0104648 280).

References

1. Aggarwal, J.K., Ryoo, M.S.: Human activity analysis: A review. ACM Comput. Surv. 43(3), 16 (2011)
2. Bourdev, L.D., Maji, S., Malik, J.: Describing people: A poselet-based approach to attribute classification. In: ICCV (2011)

3. Brendel, W., Todorovic, S.: Learning spatiotemporal graphs of human activities. In: ICCV (2011)
4. Cao, L., Liu, Z., Huang, T.S.: Cross-dataset action detection. In: CVPR (2010)
5. Derpanis, K.G., Sizintsev, M., Cannons, K.J., Wildes, R.P.: Efficient action spotting based on a spacetime oriented structure representation. In: CVPR (2010)
6. Desai, C., Ramanan, D.: Detecting actions, poses, and objects with relational phraselets. In: Fitzgibbon, A., Lazebnik, S., Perona, P., Sato, Y., Schmid, C. (eds.) ECCV 2012, Part IV. LNCS, vol. 7575, pp. 158–172. Springer, Heidelberg (2012)
7. Jhuang, H., Gall, J., Zuffi, S., Schmid, C., Black, M.J.: Towards understanding action recognition. In: ICCV (2013)
8. Ke, Y., Sukthankar, R., Hebert, M.: Event detection in crowded videos. In: ICCV (2007)
9. Lan, T., Wang, Y., Mori, G.: Discriminative figure-centric models for joint action localization and recognition. In: ICCV (2011)
10. Packer, B., Saenko, K., Koller, D.: A combined pose, object, and feature model for action understanding. In: CVPR (2012)
11. Peng, X., Wang, L., Wang, X., Qiao, Y.: Bag of visual words and fusion methods for action recognition: Comprehensive study and good practice. CoRR abs/1405.4506 (2014)
12. Raptis, M., Kokkinos, I., Soatto, S.: Discovering discriminative action parts from mid-level video representations. In: CVPR (2012)
13. Raptis, M., Sigal, L.: Poselet key-framing: A model for human activity recognition. In: CVPR (2013)
14. Rodriguez, M.D., Ahmed, J., Shah, M.: Action mach a spatio-temporal maximum average correlation height filter for action recognition. In: CVPR (2008)
15. Sadanand, S., Corso, J.J.: Action bank: A high-level representation of activity in video. In: CVPR (2012)
16. Schüldt, C., Laptev, I., Caputo, B.: Recognizing human actions: A local svm approach. In: ICPR (2004)
17. Singh, V.K., Nevatia, R.: Action recognition in cluttered dynamic scenes using pose-specific part models. In: ICCV (2011)
18. Sun, C., Nevatia, R.: Active: Activity concept transitions in video event classification. In: ICCV (2013)
19. Tian, Y., Sukthankar, R., Shah, M.: Spatiotemporal deformable part models for action detection. In: CVPR (2013)
20. Tran, D., Yuan, J.: Max-margin structured output regression for spatio-temporal action localization. In: NIPS (2012)
21. Tsochantaridis, I., Hofmann, T., Joachims, T., Altun, Y.: Support vector machine learning for interdependent and structured output spaces. In: ICML (2004)
22. Ullah, M.M., Laptev, I.: Actlets: A novel local representation for human action recognition in video. In: ICIP (2012)
23. Wang, C., Wang, Y., Yuille, A.L.: An approach to pose-based action recognition. In: CVPR (2013)
24. Wang, H., Kläser, A., Schmid, C., Liu, C.L.: Dense trajectories and motion boundary descriptors for action recognition. IJCV 103(1) (2013)
25. Wang, H., Schmid, C.: Action recognition with improved trajectories. In: ICCV (2013)
26. Wang, L., Qiao, Y., Tang, X.: Mining motion atoms and phrases for complex action recognition. In: ICCV (2013)
27. Wang, L., Qiao, Y., Tang, X.: Motionlets: Mid-level 3D parts for human motion recognition. In: CVPR (2013)

28. Wang, L., Qiao, Y., Tang, X.: Latent hierarchical model of temporal structure for complex activity classification. TIP 23(2) (2014)
29. Wang, X., Wang, L., Qiao, Y.: A comparative study of encoding, pooling and normalization methods for action recognition. In: Lee, K.M., Matsushita, Y., Rehg, J.M., Hu, Z. (eds.) ACCV 2012, Part III. LNCS, vol. 7726, pp. 572–585. Springer, Heidelberg (2013)
30. Yang, Y., Saleemi, I., Shah, M.: Discovering motion primitives for unsupervised grouping and one-shot learning of human actions, gestures, and expressions. TPAMI 35(7) (2013)
31. Yang, Y., Ramanan, D.: Articulated pose estimation with flexible mixtures-of-parts. In: CVPR (2011)
32. Yao, A., Gall, J., Gool, L.J.V.: A Hough transform-based voting framework for action recognition. In: CVPR (2010)
33. Yu, G., Yuan, J., Liu, Z.: Propagative hough voting for human activity recognition. In: Fitzgibbon, A., Lazebnik, S., Perona, P., Sato, Y., Schmid, C. (eds.) ECCV 2012, Part III. LNCS, vol. 7574, pp. 693–706. Springer, Heidelberg (2012)
34. Yuan, J., Liu, Z., Wu, Y.: Discriminative subvolume search for efficient action detection. In: CVPR (2009)

Action Recognition with Stacked Fisher Vectors

Xiaojiang Peng[1,3,2], Changqing Zou[3,2], Yu Qiao[2,4,*], and Qiang Peng[1]

[1] Southwest Jiaotong University, Chengdu, China
[2] Shenzhen Key Lab of CVPR,
Shenzhen Institutes of Advanced Technology, CAS, China
[3] Department of Computer Science, Hengyang Normal University, Hengyang, China
[4] The Chinese University of Hong Kong, China

Abstract. Representation of video is a vital problem in action recognition. This paper proposes Stacked Fisher Vectors (SFV), a new representation with multi-layer nested Fisher vector encoding, for action recognition. In the first layer, we densely sample large subvolumes from input videos, extract local features, and encode them using Fisher vectors (FVs). The second layer compresses the FVs of subvolumes obtained in previous layer, and then encodes them again with Fisher vectors. Compared with standard FV, SFV allows refining the representation and abstracting semantic information in a hierarchical way. Compared with recent mid-level based action representations, SFV need not to mine discriminative action parts but can preserve mid-level information through Fisher vector encoding in higher layer. We evaluate the proposed methods on three challenging datasets, namely Youtube, J-HMDB, and HMDB51. Experimental results demonstrate the effectiveness of SFV, and the combination of the traditional FV and SFV outperforms state-of-the-art methods on these datasets with a large margin.

Keywords: Action recognition, Fisher vectors, stacked Fisher vectors, max-margin dimensionality reduction.

1 Introduction

Action recognition in realistic videos has been an active research area in recent years due to its wide range of potential applications, such as smart video surveillance, video indexing, human-computer interface, etc. Though significant progresses have been made [31,32,26,16], action recognition still remains a challenging task due to high-dimensional video data, large intra-class variations, camera motions and view point changes, and other fundamental difficulties [1].

By far, the most popular video representation for action recognition has been the Bag-of-Visual-Words (BoVW) model [29,23] or its variants [21,24] based on spatial-temporal local features. This representation mainly contains four steps: feature extraction, codebook generation, feature encoding and pooling, and normalization. As for traditional BoVW, we usually extract local features from videos, learn a visual dictionary in training set by k-means or Gaussian Mixture Model (GMM), encode features and pool them for each video, and finally

---

* Corresponding author.

D. Fleet et al. (Eds.): ECCV 2014, Part V, LNCS 8693, pp. 581–595, 2014.

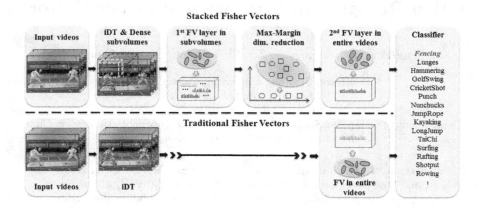

Fig. 1. Comparison between our approach and traditional Fisher vectors. Top: The pipeline of proposed Stacked Fisher vectors with two layers. Bottom: traditional pipeline of single layer Fisher vectors. The video representations of SFV are constructed based on large subvolumes which contain richer semantic information than those local cuboids.

normalize the pooled vectors as video representations. These representations are subsequently fed into a pre-trained SVM classifier. The good performance of BoVW model should be partly ascribed to the development of more elaborately designed low-level features (e.g., dense trajectory features [31,32] and spatial-temporal co-occurrence descriptors [22]) and more sophisticated encoding methods (e.g., Fisher vector encoding [24]). Currently, the pipeline of Fisher vector encoding based on improved Dense Trajectory (iDT) features provides state-of-the-art results on most action datsets [32].

More recently, many efforts have focused on developing mid-level representations [19,35,34,7,37,27] for action recognition. These methods usually mine discriminative action parts, such as attributes [19], motionlets [35], actons [37], and train a classifier for each type of parts, and then summarize the outputs of these classifiers as video representations by max-pooling. Therefore, the contribution of each subvolume for the final representation is summarized as a single value (if this subvolume obtains the highest response) or null (otherwise). This limits the capacity of the mid-level representations. From another aspect, hierarchical feature learning with deep network has attracted much attention for action recognition [18,11,12], which can partly alleviate the above dilemma. These works are partly inspired by the success of Deep Neural Network (DNN) for image representation and classification [14]. Though these methods can describe videos from low level features to more abstract and semantic representation using deep structures, they are very computationally expensive to directly learn effective deep neural network for video-based action recognition. Recently, improvement has also been observed in shallow but still hierarchically layered models based on traditional encoding methods for object classification [28,25].

Inspired by these previous works, we propose Stacked Fisher Vectors (SFV), a new representation based on Fisher Vector (FV) encoding [24], for action recognition. Figure 1 compares the traditional single layer Fisher vector encoding method with our SFV. Unlike traditional single layer FV pipeline that directly encodes and summarizes all local descriptors of input video with Fisher vectors , our SFV pipeline first performs Fisher vector encoding in densely sampled subvolumes based on low-level features, and then discriminatively compresses these subvolume-level FVs, and finally employs another FV encoding layer based on compressed subvolume-level representations. Specially, subvolumes are extracted in multiple scales. As it is known, the raw FVs are too high-dimensional to serve as inputs for the next FV layer. To compress these high-dimensional vectors significantly, we learn a projection matrix via a max-margin learning framework (Section 4), which is very important for the performance of SFV. The compressed FVs delivered to the 2nd layer contain rich semantic information and are powerful to describe those large volumes as they come from high-dimensional space. Our experimental results on three popular datasets demonstrate that our SFV representation can provide significant complementary information w.r.t the traditional FV representation, and the SFV performs comparably with traditional FV. Specially, when combining SFV with traditional FV, we obtain significantly superior recognition performance than the current state-of-the-art results on Youtube (93.77%), J-HMDB (69.03%), and HMDB51 (66.79%).

1.1 Related Work

Early researches in action recognition widely made use of low-level features with BoVW model. Typical low-level features in action videos include histogram of oriented gradients (HOG) [16], 3D-HOG [13], histogram of optical flow (HOF) [16] and motion boundary histogram (MBH) [30], which are computed in local cuboids obtained by spatial-temporal interesting points (STIP) detectors [17] or dense sampling schemes [33,30]. These local features especially the dense trajectory features demonstrate excellent performance on many challenging datasets [33,30,32].

As discussed in [4,36], selection of encoding methods is important to recognition performance in the BoVW framework. Recently, advanced feature encoding methods have been introduced for action recognition, such as soft-assignment [21,36], vector of locally aggregated descriptors [9,8], and Fisher coding [24,36,32]. In [36], Wang *et al.* evaluated most of these encoding methods for action recognition and observed that Fisher coding method performs the best among them. Wang *et al.* [32] also adopted this coding method with improved dense trajectory features, and obtained state-of-the-art results on many action datasets.

Besides those low-level features and encoding methods, recent efforts for action recognition have been devoted to mining discriminative mid-level action representations [19,35,7,37,27]. Wang *et al.* [35] developed motionlets which are defined as representative and discriminative 3D parts obtained by clustering and ranking algorithms. Jain *et al.* [7] learned discriminative cuboids by exemplar-SVM. Both Sapienza *et al.* [7] and Zhu *et al.* [37] adopted multiple instance learning framework to mine discriminative action parts or actons. Specially, all these methods made use of the part responses, and then pooled them as video representations. The mined 3D parts in this type methods are large subvolumes and expected to contain rich semantic information which is related to action categories. Along the line of this idea, but unlike these previous works, we do not mine discriminative action parts, and instead we encode densely sampled subvolumes via FV encoding, and project them to a low-dimensional subspace, and use another FV layer with those compressed FVs to construct video-level representations. Perhaps the most similar work to ours is Deep Fisher Networks proposed by Simonyan et al. [27]. Deep Fisher Networks used multiple layer of Fisher Vector encoding for image representation and classification. However, video based action recognition is different from image classification. A large portion of video is irrelevant to action, and the extracted features (such as iDT) mainly concentrate on foreground. The irregular distribution and spasticity of action related features makes it difficult to directly apply Deep Fisher Networks for action recognition. In our SFV, the sampling strategy and dimensionality reduction method are different from those of Deep Fisher Networks.

2   Fisher Vectors for Action Recognition

Fisher Vector (FV) coding method, derived from Fisher kernel, was originally proposed for large scale image categorization [24]. FV encoding assumes the generation process of local descriptors $\mathbf{X}$ can be modeled by a probability density function $p(\cdot; \theta)$ with parameters θ. The gradient of the log-likelihood w.r.t a parameter can describe how that parameter contributes to the generation process of $\mathbf{X}$ [6]. Then the video can be described by [6]:

$$G_\theta^{\mathbf{X}} = \frac{1}{N} \nabla_\theta \log p(\mathbf{X}; \theta). \tag{1}$$

The probability density function is usually modeled by Gaussian Mixture Model (GMM), and $\theta = \{\pi_1, \mu_1, \sigma_1, \cdots, \pi_K, \mu_K, \sigma_K\}$ are the model parameters denoting the mixture weights, means, and diagonal covariances of GMM. K and N are the mixture number and the number of local features, respectively. X denotes spatial-temporal local features (e.g., HOG and HOF) in action videos. Perronnin et al. [24] proposed an improved fisher vector as follows,

$$\mathcal{G}_{\mu,k}^{\mathbf{X}} = \frac{1}{N\sqrt{\pi_k}} \sum_{n=1}^{N} \gamma_n(k) \left(\frac{\mathbf{x}_n - \mu_k}{\sigma_k} \right), \tag{2}$$

$$\mathcal{G}_{\sigma,k}^{\mathbf{X}} = \frac{1}{N\sqrt{2\pi_k}} \sum_{n=1}^{N} \gamma_n(k) \left[\frac{(\mathbf{x}_n - \mu_k)^2}{\sigma_k^2} - 1 \right], \tag{3}$$

where $\gamma_n(k)$ is the weight of local feature $\mathbf{x}_n$ for the i-th Gaussian:

$$\gamma_n(k) = \frac{\pi_k \mathcal{N}(\mathbf{x}_n; \mu_k, \sigma_k)}{\sum_{i=1}^{K} \pi_i \mathcal{N}(\mathbf{x}_n; \mu_i, \sigma_i)}, \tag{4}$$

where $\mathcal{N}(\mathbf{x}; \mu_k, \Sigma_k)$ is d-dimensional Gaussian distribution. The final fisher vector is the concatenation of all $\mathcal{G}^{\mathbf{X}}_{\mu,k}$ and $\mathcal{G}^{\mathbf{X}}_{\sigma,k}$ which is a $2Kd$-dimensional super vector.

Fisher vector encoding with dense features yields the best performance on both image classification [4] and video-based action recognition [32]. Compared with other coding methods such as vector quantization and sparse coding, FV encoding can easily obtain high-dimensional feature codes with small codebook size, which is very important for performance improvement when using linear classifiers. We apply power normalization followed by ℓ_2 normalization to each FV block $\mathcal{G}^{\mathbf{X}}_{\mu,k}$ and $\mathcal{G}^{\mathbf{X}}_{\sigma,k}$ before normalizing them jointly, which demonstrates good performance in previous works [27].

3   Stacked Fisher Vectors

The traditional FV effectively encodes the local features of action video in a high-dimensional space, and aggregates the codes into a super vector by sum pooling over the entire video. This representation describes the video from the local feature space (approximated by GMM), which can not directly depict more global and complex structures. Deep structures (e.g., DNN [14]) are able to capture complex structures by local spatial pooling and refining the representation from one layer to the next. In this section, we present a "deep" structure by stacking two FV encoding layers, which we call *Stacked Fisher Vectors*.

The motivation of SFV is to describe the entire video with higher level representation extracted from large cuboids, which contains rich semantic information. One may argue that increasing the size of spatial-temporal patches for feature extraction may address this motivation. But, unfortunately, extracting low-level features like HOG and HOF to depict large subvolumes is not robust due to huge pose and temporal variations in action videos [27], and it has been demonstrated that very large patches is inferior to small ones (e.g., 32×32) [31]. The pipeline of SFV is shown in Figure 1. In this paper, we consider SFV with two layers. One can generalize it to more layers without difficulty. The detailed description of each layer is as follows.

3.1   The First-Layer FV

Given an video $\mathbf{V}$ with size $W \times H \times L$, we first extract improved dense trajectories [32] described by concatenated HOG, HOF, and MBH descriptors. Let $\mathbf{X} = [\mathbf{x}_1, \mathbf{x}_2, \cdots, \mathbf{x}_N] \in \mathbb{R}^{d \times N}$ be the trajectory features in the video. To meet the assumption of diagonal covariances for GMM, all the features are decorrelated using PCA+Whitening before feeding into the Fisher encoder, which shows good performance in previous works [32]. Then we perform FV on each trajectory feature ($N = 1$ in Equation (1)) using a pre-learned GMM with size of K_1 in training set. We call these sparse high-dimensional vectors $\mathbf{X}' = [\mathbf{x}'_1, \mathbf{x}'_2, \cdots, \mathbf{x}'_N] \in \mathbb{R}^{2K_1 d \times N}$ as *tiny FVs*.

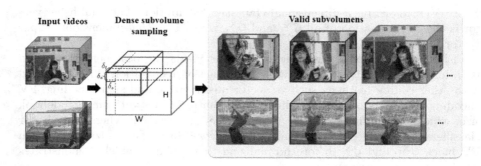

Fig. 2. Dense sampling strategy for subvolumes and some representative subvolumes from "brush hair" and "golf" action videos

Once these tiny FVs are obtained, we aggregate them within multi-scale subvolumes scanned densely over spatial-temporal domain with strides of δ_s and δ_t. The subvolumes range from small cuboids to larger ones, allowing for two scales in width (i.e. $W/2$ and W), two scales in height (i.e. $H/2$ and H), and three scales in time (i.e. $L/3$, $2L/3$, and L), where the largest scale stretches over the entire video. To avoid meaningless statistics in near motion empty subvolumes, we check the number of trajectories within subvolumes and only perform aggregating over those subvolumes where the number of trajectories is more than a given threshold T. Figure 2 summarizes the sampling process and shows some examples of valid subvolumes. We observe that most of the valid subvolumes can deliver sufficient characteristics to discriminate action categories. We call these locally aggregated FVs $\mathbf{A} = [\mathbf{a}_1, \mathbf{a}_2, \cdots, \mathbf{a}_M] \in \mathbb{R}^{2K_1 d \times M}$ as *local FVs*, where M is the number of valid subvolumes in the video. It is worth noting that M can be varied in different videos. The local FVs are sequently normalized by power+ℓ_2 normalization per component before performing ℓ_2-normalization jointly.

3.2   The Second-Layer FV

The FVs from the 1st FV layer are too high-dimensional to be directly used as the inputs of next FV layer. Here we adopt a max-margin dimensionality reduction algorithm to compress the local FVs, which make the dimensions of compressed local FVs comparable to those local features at the first layer. The details of max-margin dimensionality reduction algorithm will be described in Section 4.

The compressed local FVs are sequently decorrelated by PCA+Whitening, and then serve as the inputs of the 2nd FV layer. After learning a GMM with size of K_2, we perform another FV layer with these pre-processed local FVs and aggregate them over the entire video. The output vector is sequently normalized using the same scheme as that in the 1st layer, and serves as the final video representation of SFV.

4   Max-margin Dimensionality Reduction

This section presents the max-margin dimensionality reduction algorithm used to compress the local FVs of subvolumes.

As explained in Section 3.2, we need to learn a projection matrix $\mathbf{U} \in \mathbb{R}^{p \times 2Kd}, p \ll 2Kd$ to significantly reduce the dimension of local FV. Note that only the whole video is assigned action label. Taking into account the fact that there are too many local FVs to us in the leaning process, we learn U from a subset of local FVs. Specially, to make all the labels of local FVs in this subset available, we sample those local FVs from entire videos and large subvolumes with size of $W \times H \times 2L/3$ which inherit the labels of their corresponding videos.

Suppose the selected local FVs and their labels are $\{\phi_i, y_i\}_{i=1,\cdots,N_l}$, where N_l denotes the number of local FVs. We aim to find the projection $\mathbf{U}$ where $\{U\phi_i\}_{i=1,\cdots,N_l}$ are as linearly separable as possible. In this paper, we perform multi-class classification with a *one-vs-all* approach, and impose there is a margin of at least one between positive and negative local FVs. This results in the following constraints,

$$y_i(\mathbf{w}U\phi_i + b) > 1, \quad i = 1, \cdots, N_l, \tag{5}$$

where $\mathbf{w} \in \mathbb{R}^{p \times 1}$ is the linear model of a certain category, and $y_i \in \{+1, -1\}$. Incorporating regularization to all the model parameters of C categories and the projection U with hinge-loss, we obtain the following objective function,

$$\arg\min_{U,W,b} \frac{\lambda}{2}\|U\|_F^2 + \frac{\beta}{2}\sum_{j=1}^{C}\|\mathbf{w}_j\|^2 + \sum_{i=1}^{N_l}\sum_{j=1}^{C}\max\{0, 1 - y_i(\mathbf{w}_jU\phi_i + b)\}, \tag{6}$$

where λ and β are the regularization constants. Though the learning objective is non-convex w.r.t $\mathbf{w}$ and U, it is convex w.r.t one of them when fixing the other. The optimum can be obtained by alternately solve the convex optimization problems of $\mathbf{w}$ and U. Both of the problems can be solved by sub-gradient method. Specially, we leverage standard SVM [3] to optimize linear model $\mathbf{w}$ and use sub-gradient algorithm to optimize U. We initialize U by PCA-Whitening matrix U_0 obtained from the local FVs, and perform the following update for U in the j-th model at each iteration,

$$\mathbf{U}_{t+1}^j = \begin{cases} -\gamma\lambda\mathbf{U}_t^j, \text{ if } y_i(\mathbf{w}_jU_t\phi_i + b) > 1, \forall\, i \in \{1, \cdots, N_l\} \\ -\gamma(\lambda\mathbf{U}_t^j + \sum_i -y_i\mathbf{w}_j\phi_i), \text{ otherwise,} \end{cases} \tag{7}$$

where $\gamma > 0$ is a given learning rate, and the final updated projection matrix is $\mathbf{U}_{t+1} = \mathbf{U}_t + \sum_{j=1}^{C}\mathbf{U}_{t+1}^j$ at the t-th iteration. Once both optimization objectives have converged, the model $\mathbf{w}$ is discarded, and only $\mathbf{U}$ is saved.

5   Experiments

In this section, we evaluate the performance of the proposed SFV and traditional FV for action recognition on three popular datasets, and compare it with several

Fig. 3. From left to right, example frames from (a)YouTube, (b)HMDB51, and (c) J-HMDB

state-of-the-art methods. Moreover, we also provide evaluations on the mixture number of GMM used in the 2nd FV layer, and on the parameters of dense sampling (i.e. δ_s, δ_t, etc.).

5.1   Datasets

We conduct experiments on three action datasets, namely Youtube [20], HMDB51 [15], and J-HMDB [10]. Some example frames are illustrated in Figure 3. We summarize them and the experimental protocols as follows.

The **Youtube** dataset [20] is collected from YouTube videos. It contains 11 action categories: basketball *shooting*, volleyball *spiking*, trampoline *jumping*, soccer *juggling*, horse back *riding*, *cycling*, *diving*, *swinging*, *golf-swinging*, *tennis-swinging*, and *walking* (with a dog). A total of 1,168 video clips are available. Following [20], we use Leave-One-Group-Out cross-validation and report the average accuracy over all classes.

The **HMDB51** dataset [15] is a large action video database with 51 categories. Totally, there are 6,766 manually annotated clips which are extracted from a variety of sources ranging from digitized movies to YouTube. It contains facial actions, general body movements and human interactions. It is a very challenging benchmark due to its high intra-class variation and low video quality. We follow the experimental settings in [15] where three train/test splits are available, and report the mean average accuracy over three splits.

The **J-HMDB** dataset [10] is a subset of HMDB51 with 21 action categories, which is annotated in details. This dataset excludes categories from HMDB51 that contain facial expressions like smiling, interactions with others such as shaking hands, and focuses on single body action. From Figure 3(c), we observe that most of the videos contain the actor in a relative small region. This ensures that sampled subvolumes can cover most of action region. The person in each frame is annotated with his/her 2D joint positions, scale, viewpoint, segmentation, puppet mask and puppet flow, which are used to evaluate the mid-level

Table 1. Performance of traditional FV, the proposed SFV, and their combination

Method (Dim.)	Youtube (%)	HMDB51 (%)	J-HMDB (%)
Traditional FV (102,400)	90.69	57.29	62.83
Stacked FV (102,400)	88.68	56.21	59.27
Combination (204,800)	93.38	66.79	67.77

(e.g., bounding box) and high-level features (e.g., pose feature and joints). We follow the experimental settings in [10], and report the mean average accuracy.

5.2 Experimental Setup

In all the following experiments, we densely extract improved trajectories using the code from Wang [32]. Each trajectory is described by concatenating HOG, HOF, and MBH descriptors, which is a 396-dimensional vector. We reduce the dimensionality of these descriptors to 200 by performing PCA and Whitening. For traditional FV pipeline and the first layer of SFV, we randomly sample 1,000,000 features and learn the GMM with 256 components via the EM algorithm [2], which has been shown to empirically give good results for a wide range of datasets [32]. The default values of δ_s, δ_t, and T are 10, 5, and 100, respectively. These parameters are closely related to the number of valid subvolumes, which are evaluated in Section 5.4.

We reduce the dimensionality of local FV to 400 by default. The discriminative projection matrix is initialized by PCA-Whitening matrix and learned in the training set for each dataset. λ and γ are fixed as 0.1 and 0.01, respectively. We stop the iteration once the training accuracy keeps unchanged. For the second layer of SFV, we decorrelate those compressed local FV by PCA and Whitening and further reduce the dimensionality from 400 to 200. And then we learn GMM with 256 components from a randomly sampled subset of 100,000 decorrelated local FVs. In our experiments, we choose linear SVM as our classifier with the implementation of LIBSVM [3]. For multi-class classification, we use the *one-vs-rest* approach and select the class with the highest score.

5.3 Experimental Results

We evaluate the recognition performance by default parameters in this experiment. Table 1 shows the results of traditional FV, SFV, and their combination. The FV and SFV are combined in representation level since this strategy exhibits high performance [23]. Combining the FV and SFV can double the dimension of video representation. As for higher dimension of traditional FV, please refer to our recent study in [23].

On all the datasets we used, the proposed SFV achieves comparable performance w.r.t traditional FV. This may be explained by the fact that the number of local FVs for the 2nd layer of SFV is about one-tenth of that of traditional FV.

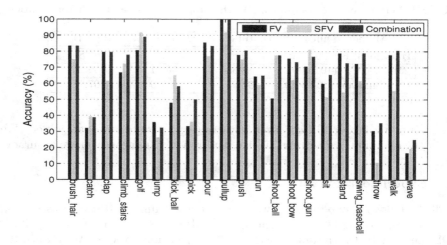

Fig. 4. The results of all the action categories from the J-HMDB dataset

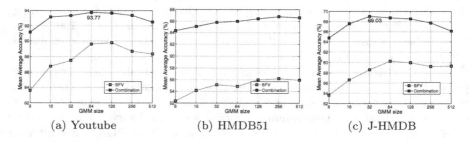

(a) Youtube   (b) HMDB51   (c) J-HMDB

Fig. 5. Performance of SFV and FV+SFV with varying GMM size on the Youtube, HMDB51, and J-HMDB datasets

However, somewhat surprisingly, the proposed SFV provides significant complementary information to traditional FV. When combining SFV to FV, we improve the results by 2.69% on Youtube, 9.5% on HMDB51, and 4.94% on J-HMDB. To further investigate the effects of SFV on traditional FV, we illustrate the individual recognition results of all the action classes of J-HMDB dataset in Figure 4. From Figure 4, we observe that the proposed SFV is effective for the actions with less variations like golf, kick ball, shoot_ball, and shoot_gun. This can be interpreted by the properties of large volumes (described by local FVs): *global* and *discriminative* [35]. However, the global nature makes them sensitive to intra-class variation and deformation. Therefore, the performance of our SFV representation is not high for those actions with large variations.

Considering that there are less local FVs or subvolumes than local features, we also evaluate the GMM size for the 2nd layer of SFV. Figure 5 shows the results of SFV and FV+SFV with different GMM sizes. It is worth noting that the GMM sizes of both the traditional FV and the 1st layer of SFV are fixed

Table 2. Evaluation of multi-scale sampling strategy for dense subvolumes on Youtube, and J-HMDB

	Youtube		J-HMDB	
sizes	volumes/video	accuracy	volumes/video	accuracy
$0.5W \times 0.5H \times \frac{L}{3}$	~1,500	83.60	~600	53.82
$0.5W \times \{0.5H, H\} \times \frac{L}{3}$	~3,200	86.35	~1,100	56.22
$\{0.5W, W\} \times 0.5H \times \frac{L}{3}$	~3,200	86.52	~1,000	56.29
$\{0.5W, W\} \times \{0.5H, H\} \times \frac{L}{3}$	~4,600	86.78	~1,600	57.96
Default	~6,000	88.68	~2,500	60.27

as 256, and only that of the 2nd layer of SFV is changed. For all the datasets, increasing the GMM size K improves the performance in the beginning. However, the recognition performance decreases when GMM sizes are larger than 128 and 64 on Youtube and J-HMDB, respectively. For the combination performance, the best results are observed with GMM sizes 64, 256, and 32 on Youtube, HMDB51, and J-HMDB datasets, respectively.

5.4 Evaluation of Sampling Parameters

In this section, we evaluate the impact of the sampling parameters for subvolumes on the performance. We report results for Youtube and J-HMDB datasets. Specially, we study the impact of multi-scale, spatial and temporal sampling steps, spatial and temporal sizes of subvolumes. In these experiments, unless otherwise stated, we carry out the evaluation for one parameter at a time, and fix the other ones to the default values, i.e., 12 scales for subvolumes, spatial sampling step $\delta_s = 10$, temporal sampling step $\delta_t = 5$.

Multi-scale vs. Single Scale. Results for multi-scale sampling are shown in Table 2. Considering various multi-scale schemes can can lead to different numbers of subvolumes, we also show the approximate number of valid subvolumes per video. From Table 2, it is clear that using multi-scale subvolumes is beneficial compared to a single scale on both datasets. The results from single scale $0.5W \times 0.5H \times \frac{L}{3}$ are inferior to the default settings by 5.08% and 6.45% on Youtube and J-HMDB, respectively. The main reason is that there is not enough subvolumes to cover the entire video.

Sampling Step. We evaluate the spatial and temporal sampling steps on J-HMDB dataset with single scale $0.5W \times 0.5H \times \frac{L}{3}$. With respect to the spatial sampling step δ_s, Figure 6(a) presents the results for $\delta_s = 2$ pixels to $\delta_s = 40$ pixels. The performance increases with a higher sampling density. Figure 6(b) shows the results of different temporal sampling steps. For both spatial and temporal sampling steps, lower sampling density obtains less number of valid subvolumes, which is harmful to the recognition performance.

Volume Size. We also evaluate the spatial and temporal sizes of subvolumes with single scale on J-HMDB dataset. Figure 6(c) and Figure 6(d) show the results of various spatial and temporal sizes, respectively. The worst results are

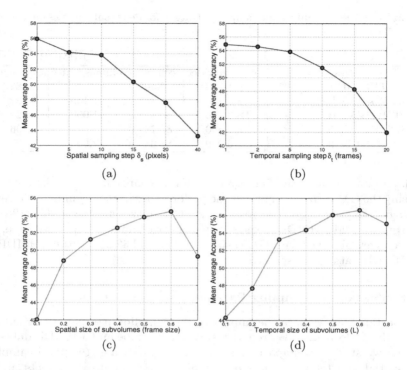

Fig. 6. Evaluation of the sampling parameters and subvolume sizes on the J-HMDB dataset with single scale. (a) spatial sampling step, (b) temporal sampling step, (c) the spatial size of subvolumes related to frame size, (d) the temporal length of subvolumes related to video length L.

those from the smallest spatial and temporal sizes. Small sizes of subvolumes suffer from two issues. On one hand, there are a small number of local features within subvolumes which results in very few valid local FVs. On the other hand, pooling tiny FVs (from local features) in a small 3D patch may lead to less meaningful statistics [27]. Enlarging the size of subvolumes boosts the performance up to 60 percent of frame size and video length L. However, subvolume sizes larger than 60 percent of frame size and L decrease the performance, as there is a limited sampling space for subvolumes.

5.5   Comparison with State of the Art

In this section, we compare our results to the state of the art on each dataset. Table 3 displays our best results and several recently published results in the literature.

These methods (e.g., motionlets [35], mid-level parts [27], and actons [37]) that utilize the responses of discriminative action parts combined with low-level features perform inferior to our method (FV+SFV) with a certain margin on

Table 3. Comparison of our approach (FV+SFV) with the state-of-the-art results on Youtube, HMDB51, and J-HMDB. *Our own implementation. [+] It leverages human annotation on actors with person mask or pose, but ours don't require.

Youtube		HMDB51		J-HMDB	
Liu et al. [20]	71.2	Actons [37]	54.0		
Ikizler et al. [5]	75.21	Motionlets [35]	42.1	DT+BoVW [10]	56.6
Mid-level parts [27]	84.5	Mid-level parts [27]	37.2	iDT+FV*	62.8
DT+BoVW [31]	85.4	DT+BoVW [31]	46.6	Masked DT+BoVW [10][+]	69.0
iDT+FV *	90.69	iDT+FV [32]	57.2	Pose+BoVW [10] [+]	76.0
Our method	**93.77**	Our method	**66.79**	Our method	69.03

all three datasets. This demonstrates the effectiveness of the proposed stacked Fisher vectors. For a fair comparison, we use the results of "iDT+FV" as baselines. From Table 3, our approach outperforms the best previous results by 3.08% on Youtube, and 9.59% on HMDB51. As for J-HMDB, the method [10] using annotated pose features with BoVW model provides the highest performance. Without the high-level human annotated pose information, our method significantly improves the baseline by 6.2%.

6 Conclusions

Mid-level action parts prove to be effective for action recognition [35,7,37,27]. However, previous methods only leveraged the responses of discriminative parts for subvolumes which have limited representative ability. In this paper, we propose stacked Fisher vectors, which is a hierarchical structure based on the off-the-shelf Fisher coding. It describes the densely sampled subvolumes by high-dimensional super vectors. The high-dimensional nature allows it to preserve richer information for each subvolume. After discriminative dimensionality reduction by a max-margin approach, we utilize another Fisher coding layer to construct a global representation for videos. Extensive experiments on three widely-used datasets indicate the effectiveness of our SFV representation. Combining our SFV and standard Fisher vectors, we achieve superior performance on the Youtube and HMDB51 datasets than state-of-the-art methods.

Acknowledgements. This work is partly supported by Natural Science Foundation of China (91320101, 61036008, 60972111), Shenzhen Basic Research Program (JC201005270350A, JCYJ20120903092050890, JCYJ20120617114614438), 100 Talents Program of CAS, Guangdong Innovative Research Team Program (201001D0104648280), and the construct program of the key discipline in Hunan province.

References

1. Aggarwal, J.K., Ryoo, M.S.: Human activity analysis: A review. ACM Computing Surveys 43(3), 16 (2011)
2. Bishop, C.M., Nasrabadi, N.M.: Pattern recognition and machine learning, vol. 1 (2006)
3. Chang, C.-C., Lin, C.-J.: Libsvm: a library for support vector machines. ACM Transactions on Intelligent Systems and Technology (TIST) 2(3), 27 (2011)
4. Chatfield, K., Lempitsky, V., Vedaldi, A., Zisserman, A.: The devil is in the details: an evaluation of recent feature encoding methods. In: BMVC (2011)
5. Ikizler-Cinbis, N., Sclaroff, S.: Object, scene and actions: Combining multiple features for human action recognition. In: Daniilidis, K., Maragos, P., Paragios, N. (eds.) ECCV 2010, Part I. LNCS, vol. 6311, pp. 494–507. Springer, Heidelberg (2010)
6. Jaakkola, T., Haussler, D., et al.: Exploiting generative models in discriminative classifiers. In: NIPS pp. 487–493 (1999)
7. Jain, A., Gupta, A., Rodriguez, M., Davis, L.S.: Representing videos using mid-level discriminative patches. In: CVPR, pp. 2571–2578 (2013)
8. Jain, M., Jégou, H., Bouthemy, P.: Better exploiting motion for better action recognition. In: CVPR, pp. 2555–2562 (2013)
9. Jégou, H., Douze, M., Schmid, C., Pérez, P.: Aggregating local descriptors into a compact image representation. In: CVPR, pp. 3304–3311 (2010)
10. Jhuang, H., Gall, J., Zuffi, S., Schmid, C., Black, M.J., et al.: Towards understanding action recognition. In: ICCV (2013)
11. Ji, S., Xu, W., Yang, M., Yu, K.: 3d convolutional neural networks for human action recognition. TPAMI, 221–231 (2013)
12. Karpathy, A., Toderici, G., Shetty, S., Leung, T., Sukthankar, R., Fei-Fei, L.: Large-scale video classification with convolutional neural networks. In: CVPR (2014)
13. Klaser, A., Marszałek, M., Schmid, C.: et al.: A spatio-temporal descriptor based on 3d-gradients. In: BMVC (2008)
14. Krizhevsky, A., Sutskever, I., Hinton, G.E.: Imagenet classification with deep convolutional neural networks. In: NIPS, vol. 1, p. 4 (2012)
15. Kuehne, H., Jhuang, H., Garrote, E., Poggio, T., Serre, T.: Hmdb: a large video database for human motion recognition. In: ICCV, pp. 2556–2563 (2011)
16. Laptev, I., Marszalek, M., Schmid, C., Rozenfeld, B.: Learning realistic human actions from movies. In: CVPR, pp. 1–8 (2008)
17. Laptev, I.: On space-time interest points. IJCV 64(2), 107–123 (2005)
18. Le, Q.V., et al.: Learning hierarchical invariant spatio-temporal features for action recognition with independent subspace analysis. In: CVPR, pp. 3361–3368 (2011)
19. Liu, J., Kuipers, B., Savarese, S.: Recognizing human actions by attributes. In: CVPR, pp. 3337–3344 (2011)
20. Liu, J., Luo, J., Shah, M.: Recognizing realistic actions from videos in the wild. In: CVPR. pp. 1996–2003 (2009)
21. Liu, L., Wang, L., Liu, X.: In defense of soft-assignment coding. In: ICCV, pp. 2486–2493 (2011)
22. Peng, X., Qiao, Y., Peng, Q., Qi, X.: Exploring motion boundary based sampling and spatial-temporal context descriptors for action recognition. In: BMVC, pp. 1–11 (2013)
23. Peng, X., Wang, L., Wang, X., Qiao, Y.: Bag of visual words and fusion methods for action recognition: Comprehensive study and good practice. CoRR abs/1405.4506 (2014)

24. Perronnin, F., Sánchez, J., Mensink, T.: Improving the fisher kernel for large-scale image classification. In: Daniilidis, K., Maragos, P., Paragios, N. (eds.) ECCV 2010, Part IV. LNCS, vol. 6314, pp. 143–156. Springer, Heidelberg (2010)
25. Ren, X., Ramanan, D.: Histograms of sparse codes for object detection. In: CVPR, pp. 3246–3253 (2013)
26. Sadanand, S., Corso, J.J.: Action bank: A high-level representation of activity in video. In: CVPR, pp. 1234–1241 (2012)
27. Sapienza, M., Cuzzolin, F., Torr, P.H.: Learning discriminative space–time action parts from weakly labelled videos. IJCV, 1–18 (2014)
28. Simonyan, K., Vedaldi, A., Zisserman, A.: Deep fisher networks for large-scale image classification. In: NIPS, pp. 163–171 (2013)
29. Sivic, J., Zisserman, A.: Video google: A text retrieval approach to object matching in videos. In: ICCV, pp. 1470–1477 (2003)
30. Wang, H., Klaser, A., Schmid, C., Liu, C.-L.: Action recognition by dense trajectories. In: CVPR, pp. 3169–3176 (2011)
31. Wang, H., Kläser, A., Schmid, C., Liu, C.-L.: Dense trajectories and motion boundary descriptors for action recognition. IJCV, 1–20 (2013)
32. Wang, H., Schmid, C., et al.: Action recognition with improved trajectories. In: ICCV (2013)
33. Wang, H., Ullah, M.M., Klaser, A., Laptev, I., Cordelia, Schmid, o.: Evaluation of local spatio-temporal features for action recognition. In: BMVC (2009)
34. Wang, L., Qiao, Y., Tang, X.: Mining motion atoms and phrases for complex action recognition. In: ICCV, pp. 2680–2687 (2013)
35. Wang, L., Qiao, Y., Tang, X.: Motionlets: Mid-level 3d parts for human motion recognition. In: CVPR, pp. 2674–2681 (2013)
36. Wang, X., Wang, L., Qiao, Y.: A comparative study of encoding, pooling and normalization methods for action recognition. In: Lee, K.M., Matsushita, Y., Rehg, J.M., Hu, Z. (eds.) ACCV 2012, Part III. LNCS, vol. 7726, pp. 572–585. Springer, Heidelberg (2013)
37. Zhu, J., Wang, B., Yang, X., Zhang, W., Tu, Z.: Action recognition with actons. In: ICCV (2013)

A Discriminative Model with Multiple Temporal Scales for Action Prediction

Yu Kong[1], Dmitry Kit[1], and Yun Fu[1,2]

[1] Department of Electrical and Computer Engineering,
Northeastern University, Boston, MA, USA
[2] College of Computer and Information Science,
Northeastern University, Boston, MA, USA
{yukong,dkit,yunfu}@ece.neu.edu

Abstract. The speed with which intelligent systems can react to an action depends on how soon it can be recognized. The ability to recognize ongoing actions is critical in many applications, for example, spotting criminal activity. It is challenging, since decisions have to be made based on partial videos of temporally incomplete action executions. In this paper, we propose a novel discriminative multi-scale model for predicting the action class from a partially observed video. The proposed model captures temporal dynamics of human actions by explicitly considering all the history of observed features as well as features in smaller temporal segments. We develop a new learning formulation, which elegantly captures the temporal evolution over time, and enforces the label consistency between segments and corresponding partial videos. Experimental results on two public datasets show that the proposed approach outperforms state-of-the-art action prediction methods.

Keywords: Action Prediction, Structured SVM, Sequential Data.

1 Introduction

Human action recognition [17,10,8,18] has been of great interest for the computer vision community for many decades due to its practical importance, such as video analysis and visual surveillance. A majority of action recognition approaches focus on classifying the action after fully observing the entire video. However, in many real-world scenarios (e.g. vehicle accident and criminal activity), intelligent systems do not have the luxury of waiting for the entire video before having to react to the action contained in it. For example, being able to predict a dangerous driving situation before it occurs; opposed to recognizing it thereafter. Unfortunately, most of the existing action recognition approaches are unsuitable for such early classification tasks as they expect to see the entire set of action dynamics extracted from a full video.

Different from action recognition, visual data arrives sequentially in action prediction. Therefore, to achieve accurate prediction as early as possible, it is essential to maximize the discriminative power of the beginning temporal segments in an action video. In addition, accurate action prediction relies on effectively

D. Fleet et al. (Eds.): ECCV 2014, Part V, LNCS 8693, pp. 596–611, 2014.

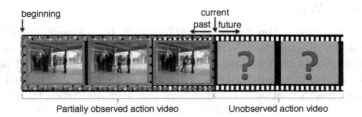

Fig. 1. Our method predicts action label given a partially observed video. Action dynamics are captured by both local templates (solid rectangles) and global templates (dashed rectangles).

utilizing useful history action information. As the action data are progressively observed, the confidence of the partial history observations should also increase.

In this paper, we propose a novel multiple temporal scale support vector machine (MTSSVM) for the early recognition of unfinished actions. Our model characterizes human actions at two different temporal granularities (Fig. 1) to learn the evolution and dynamics of actions, and predicts action labels from partially observed videos containing temporally incomplete action executions. Local templates in the MTSSVM consider the sequential nature of human actions at the fine granularity. The discriminative power of the beginning temporal segments are maximized by enforcing their label consistency. The temporal arrangements of these local templates also implicitly capture temporal orderings of inhomogeneous action segments.

We also build coarse global templates to capture the history action information. The global templates summarize action evolutions at different temporal lengths, from the start of the video to the current point in time. Our model uses this information to learn how to differentiate between classes using all available information. For example, for the action class "Push" the important feature is that the "arm is up", which can be used to distinguish it from the class "Kick". By learning a model for increasing amount of information, our model captures the evolution of actions in each class.

We develop a new convex learning formulation based on the structured SVM to consider the nature of the sequentially arriving action videos. This is achieved by introducing new constraints into the learning formulation. We enforce the label consistency between segments and their corresponding full video to maximize the discriminative power of the beginning temporal segments. In addition, we introduce a principled monotonic score function for the global template. This allows us to use the prior knowledge that informative action information is increasing as the data arrive sequentially. We show in Section 3.3 that the objective of the new learning formulation minimizes an upper bound of the empirical risk of the training data.

2   Related Work

Action Recognition: Human actions [17,26,15,3] have been popularly represented by a set of quantized local spatiotemporal features, known as bag-of-words. Bag-of-words models have shown to be robust to background noise but may not be expressive enough to describe actions in the presence of large appearance and pose variations. This problem has been addressed by introducing human knowledge into models and using semantic descriptions or attributes to characterize complex human actions [7,8,10]. In addition, recognizing human actions from a set of keyframes [12,22] and static images [25,24] have also been investigated in previous studies. However, most of existing action recognition methods were designed for recognizing complete actions, assuming the action in each testing video has been fully executed. This makes these approaches unsuitable for predicting action labels in partial videos.

Another line of work captures temporal evolutions of appearance or pose using sequential state models [11,23,20,19]. These approaches treat a video as a composition of temporal segments. However, they do not model temporal action evolution with respect to observation ratios. Therefore, they cannot characterize partially observed actions and are unsuitable for prediction. In contrast, we simulate the sequential data arrival in prediction and use large temporal scale templates to capture action evolutions from the beginning of the video to the current observed frame. Therefore, our model can recognize incomplete actions at different observation ratios.

Action Prediction: Most of the existing work in action prediction aims at recognizing unfinished action videos. Ryoo [14] proposed the integral bag-of-words (IBoW) and dynamic bag-of-words (DBoW) approaches for action prediction. The action model of each progress level is computed by averaging features of a particular progress level in the same category. However, the learned model may not be representative if the action videos of the same class have large appearance variations, and it is sensitive to outliers. To overcome these two problems, Cao et al.[1] built action models by learning feature bases using sparse coding and used the reconstruction error in the likelihood computation. Li et al.[9] explored long-duration action prediction problem. However, their work detects segments by motion velocity peaks, which may not be applicable on complex outdoor datasets. Compared with [1,9,14], our model incorporates an important prior knowledge that informative action information is increasing when new observations are available. However, their methods have not taken advantage of this prior. In addition, our method models label consistency of segments, which is not presented in their methods. The label consistency provides discriminative local information and implicitly captures context information, which is beneficial for the prediction task. Moreover, we capture action dynamics in both global and local temporal scales while [1,14] capture dynamics in one single scale.

Additionally, an early event detector [4] was proposed to localize the starting and ending frames of an incomplete event, which is different from our goal. Activity forecasting, which aims at reasoning about the preferred path for people given a destination in a scene, has been investigated in [6].

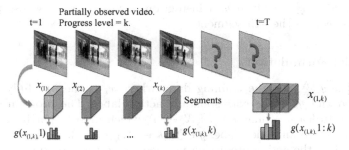

Fig. 2. Example of video segments $x_{(k)}$, partial video $x_{(1,k)}$, feature representations $g(x_{(1,k)}, l)$ of segments ($l = 1, \cdots, k$), and the representation of the partial video $g(x_{(1,k)}, 1 : k)$

3 Our Method

The aim of this work is to predict the action class y of a partially observed action video $x[1, t]$ before the action ends. Here 1 and t in $x[1, t]$ indicate the indices of the starting frame and the last observed frame of the partial video $x[1, t]$, respectively. Index t ranges from 1 to length T of a full video $x[1, T]$: $t \in \{1, \cdots, T\}$, to generate different partial videos. An action video is usually composed of a set of inhomogeneous temporal units, which are called segments. In this work, we uniformly divide a full video $x[1, T]$ into K segments $x[\frac{T}{K} \cdot (l-1) + 1, \frac{T}{K} \cdot l]$, where $l = 1, \cdots, K$ is the index of segment. The length of each segment is $\frac{T}{K}$. Note that for different videos, their lengths T may be different. Therefore, the length of segments of various videos may be different. For simplicity, let $x_{(k)}$ be the k-th segment $x[\frac{T}{K} \cdot (k - 1) + 1, \frac{T}{K} \cdot k]$ and $x_{(1,k)}$ be the partially observed sequence $x[1, \frac{T}{K} \cdot k]$ (see Fig. 2). The progress level k of a partially observed video is defined as the number of observed segments that the video has. The observation ratio is the ratio of the number of frames in a partially observed video $x[1, t]$ to the number of frames in the full video $x[1, T]$, which is $\frac{t}{T}$. For example, if $T = 100$, $t = 30$ and $K = 10$, then the progress level of the partially observed video $x[1, t]$ is 3 and its observation ratio is 0.3.

3.1 Action Representations

We use the bag-of-words models to represent segments and partial videos. The procedure of learning the visual word dictionary for action videos is as follows. Spatiotemporal interest points detector [3] and tracklet [13] are employed to extract interest points and trajectories from a video, respectively. The dictionaries of visual words are learned by clustering algorithms.

We denote the feature of the partial video $x_{(1,k)}$ at progress level k by $g(x_{(1,k)}, 1 : k)$, which is the histogram of visual words contained in the entire partial video, starting from the first segment to the k-th segment (Fig. 2). The representation of the l-th ($l \in \{1, \cdots, k\}$) segment $x_{(l)}$ in the partial video is denoted by $g(x_{(1,k)}, l)$, which is a histogram of visual words whose temporal locations are within the l-th segment.

3.2   Model Formulation

Let $\mathcal{D} = \{x_i, y_i\}_{i=1}^N$ be the training data, where x_i is the i-th fully observed action video and y_i is the corresponding action label. The problem of action prediction is to learn a function $f : \mathcal{X} \to \mathcal{Y}$, which maps a partially observed video $x_{(1,k)} \in \mathcal{X}$ to an action label $y \in \mathcal{Y}$ ($k \in \{1, \cdots, K\}$).

We formulate the action prediction problem using the structured learning as presented in [21]. Instead of searching for f, we aim at learning a discriminant function $F : \mathcal{X} \times \mathcal{Y} \to \mathcal{R}$ to score each training sample (x, y). The score measures the compatibility between a video x and an action label y. Note that, in action prediction, videos of different observation ratios from the same class should be classified as the same action category. Therefore, we use the function F to score the compatibility between the videos of different observation ratios $x_{(1,k)}$ and the action label y, where $k \in \{1, \cdots, K\}$ is the progress level.

We are interested in a linear function $F(x_{(1,k)}, y; \mathbf{w}) = \langle \mathbf{w}, \Phi(x_{(1,k)}, y) \rangle$, which is a family of functions parameterized by $\mathbf{w}$, and $\Phi(x_{(1,k)}, y)$ is a joint feature map that represents the spatio-temporal features of action label y given a partial video $x_{(1,k)}$. Once the optimal model parameter $\mathbf{w}^*$ is learned, the prediction of the action label y^* is computed by

$$y^* = \arg\max_{y \in \mathcal{Y}} F(x_{(1,k)}, y; \mathbf{w}^*) = \arg\max_{y \in \mathcal{Y}} \langle \mathbf{w}^*, \Phi(x_{(1,k)}, y) \rangle. \tag{1}$$

We define $\mathbf{w}^T \Phi(x_{(1,k)}, y)$ as a summation of the following two components:

$$\mathbf{w}^T \Phi(x_{(1,k)}, y) = \alpha_k^T \psi_1(x_{(1,k)}, y) + \sum_{l=1}^K \left[\mathbf{1}(l \leqslant k) \cdot \beta_l^T \psi_2(x_{(1,k)}, y) \right], \tag{2}$$

where $\mathbf{w} = \{\alpha_1, \cdots \alpha_K, \beta_1, \cdots, \beta_K\}$ is model parameter, k is the progress level of the partial video $x_{(1,k)}$, l is the index of progress levels, and $\mathbf{1}(\cdot)$ is the indicator function. The two components in Eq.(2) are summarized as follows.

Global Progress Model (GPM). $\alpha_k^T \psi_1(x_{(1,k)}, y)$ indicates how likely the action class of an unfinished action video $x_{(1,k)}$ (at progress level k) is y. We define GPM as

$$\alpha_k^T \psi_1(x_{(1,k)}, y) = \sum_{a \in \mathcal{Y}} \alpha_k^T \mathbf{1}(y = a) g(x_{(1,k)}, 1 : k). \tag{3}$$

Here, feature vector $g(x_{(1,k)}, 1{:}k)$ of dimensionality D is an action representation for the partial video $x_{(1,k)}$, where features are extracted from the entire partial video, from its beginning (i.e., progress level 1) to its current progress level k. Parameter α_k of size $D \times |\mathcal{Y}|$ can be regarded as a progress level-specific template. Since the partial video is at progress level k, we select the template α_k at the same progress level, from K parameter matrices $\{\alpha_1, \cdots, \alpha_K\}$. The selected template α_k is used to score the unfinished video $x_{(1,k)}$. Define $A = [\alpha_1, \cdots, \alpha_K]$ as a vector of all the parameter matrices in the GPM. Then A is a vector of size $D \times K \times |\mathcal{Y}|$ encoding the weights for the configurations between progress levels and action labels, with their corresponding video evidence.

The GPM simulates the sequential segment-by-segment data arrival for training action videos. Essentially, the GPM captures the action appearance changes as the progress level increases, and characterizes the entire action evolution over time. In contrast to the IBoW model [14], our GPM does not assume any distributions on the data likelihood; while the IBoW model uses the Gaussian distribution. In addition, the compatibility between observation and action label in our model is given by the linear model of parameter and feature function, rather than using a Gaussian kernel function [14].

Local Progress Model (LPM). $\mathbf{1}(l \leqslant k) \cdot \beta_l^{\mathrm{T}} \psi_2(x_{(1,k)}, y)$ indicates how likely the action classes of all the temporal segments $x_{(l)}$ ($l = 1, \cdots, k$) in an unfinished video $x_{(1,k)}$ are all y. Here, the progress level of the partial video is k and we consider all the segments of the video whose temporal locations l are smaller than k. We define LPM as

$$\beta_l^{\mathrm{T}} \psi_2(x_{(1,k)}, y) = \sum_{a \in \mathcal{Y}} \beta_l^{\mathrm{T}} \mathbf{1}(y = a) g(x_{(1,k)}, l), \tag{4}$$

where feature vector $g(x_{(1,k)}, l)$ of dimensionality D extracts features from the l-th segment of the unfinished video $x_{(1,k)}$. β_l of size $D \times |\mathcal{Y}|$ is the weight matrix for the l-th segment. We use the indicator function $\mathbf{1}(l \leqslant k)$ to select all the segment weight matrices, $\beta_1, \cdots, \beta_k$, whose temporal locations are smaller than or equal to the progress level k of the video. Then the selected weight matrices are used to score the corresponding segments. Let $B = [\beta_1, \cdots, \beta_K]$ be a vector of all the parameters in the LPM. Then B is a vector of size $D \times K \times |\mathcal{Y}|$ encoding the weights for the configurations between segments and action labels, with their corresponding segment evidence.

The LPM considers the sequential nature of a video. The model decomposes a video of progress level k into segments and describes the temporal dynamics of segments. Note that the action data preserve the temporal relationship between the segments. Therefore, the discriminative power of segment $x_{(k)}$ is critical to the prediction of $x_{(1,k)}$ given the prediction results of $x_{(1,k-1)}$. In this work, the segment score $\beta_k^{\mathrm{T}} g(x_{(1,k)}, k)$ measures the compatibility between the segment $x_{(k)}$ and all the classes. To maximize the discriminability of the segment, the score difference between the ground-truth class and all the other classes is maximized in our learning formulation. Thus, accurate prediction can be achieved using the newly-introduced discriminative information in the segment $x_{(k)}$.

3.3   Structured Learning Formulation

The MTSSVM is formulated based on the structured SVM [21,5]. The optimal model parameter $\mathbf{w}^*$ of MTSSVM in Eq.(1) is learned by solving the following convex problem given training data $\{x_i, y_i\}_{i=1}^{N}$:

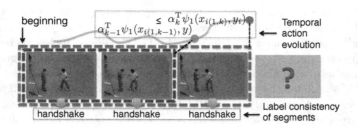

Fig. 3. Graphical illustration of the temporal action evolution over time and the label consistency of segments. Blue solid rectangles are LPMs, and purple and red dashed rectangles are GPMs.

$$\min \frac{1}{2}\|\mathbf{w}\|^2 + \frac{C}{N}\sum_{i=1}^{N}(\xi_{1i} + \xi_{2i} + \xi_{3i}) \tag{5}$$

$$\text{s.t. } \mathbf{w}^{\mathrm{T}}\Phi(x_{i(1,k)}, y_i) \geqslant \mathbf{w}^{\mathrm{T}}\Phi(x_{i(1,k)}, y) + K\delta(y, y_i) - \frac{\xi_{1i}}{u(k/K)}, \quad \forall i, \forall k, \forall y, \tag{6}$$

$$\alpha_k^{\mathrm{T}}\psi_1(x_{i(1,k)}, y_i) \geqslant \alpha_{k-1}^{\mathrm{T}}\psi_1(x_{i(1,k-1)}, y) + K\delta(y, y_i) - \frac{\xi_{2i}}{u(k/K)},$$
$$\forall i, k = 2, \cdots, K, \forall y, \tag{7}$$

$$\beta_k^{\mathrm{T}}\psi_2(x_{i(k)}, y_i) \geqslant \beta_k^{\mathrm{T}}\psi_2(x_{i(k)}, y) + kK\delta(y, y_i) - \frac{\xi_{3i}}{u(1/K)}, \quad \forall i, \forall k, \forall y, \tag{8}$$

where C is the slack trade-off parameter similar to that in SVM. ξ_{1i}, ξ_{2i} and ξ_{3i} are slack variables. $u(\cdot)$ is a scaling factor function: $u(p) = p$. $\delta(y, y_i)$ is the 0-1 loss function.

The slack variables ξ_{1i} and the Constraint (6) are usually used in SVM constraints on the class labels. We enforce this constraint for all the progress levels k since we are interested in learning a classifier that can correctly recognize partially observed videos with different progress levels k. Therefore, we simulate the segment-by-segment data arrival for training and augment the training data with partial videos of different progress levels. The loss function $\delta(y, y_i)$ measures the recognition error of a partial video and the scaling factor $u(\frac{k}{K})$ scales the loss based on the length of the partial video.

Constraint (7) considers **temporal action evolution** over time (Fig. 3). We assume that the score $\alpha^{\mathrm{T}}\psi_1(x_{i(1,k)}, y_i)$ of the partial observation $x_{i(1,k)}$ at progress level k and ground truth label y_i must be greater than the score $\alpha^{\mathrm{T}}\psi_1(x_{i(1,k-1)}, y)$ of a previous observation $x_{i(1,k-1)}$ at progress level $k-1$ and all incorrect labels y. This provides a monotonically increasing score function for partial observations and elaborately characterizes the nature of sequentially arriving action data in action prediction. The slack variable ξ_{2i} allows us to model outliers.

The slack variables ξ_{3i} and the Constraint (8) are used to maximize the discriminability of segments $x_{(k)}$. We encourage the **label consistency** between segments and the corresponding full video due to the nature of sequential data in action prediction (Fig. 3). Assume a partial video $x_{(1,k-1)}$ has been correctly recognized, then the segment $x_{(k)}$ is the only newly-introduced information and its discriminative power is the key to recognizing the video $x_{(1,k)}$. Moreover, context information of segments is implicitly captured by enforcing the label consistency. It is possible that some segments from different classes are visually similar and may not be linearly separable. We use the slack variable ξ_{3i} for each video to allow some segments of a video to be treated as outliers.

Empirical Risk Minimization: We define $\Delta(y_i, y)$ as the function that quantifies the loss for a prediction y, if the ground-truth is y_i. Therefore, the loss of a classifier $f(\cdot)$ for action prediction on a video-label pair (x_i, y_i) can be quantified as $\Delta(y_i, f(x_i))$. Usually, the performance of $f(\cdot)$ is given by the empirical risk $R_{\mathrm{emp}}(f) = \frac{1}{N} \sum_{i=1}^{N} \Delta(y_i, f(x_i))$ on the training data (x_i, y_i), assuming data samples are generated i.i.d.

The nature of continual evaluation in action prediction requires aggregating the values of loss quantities computed during the action sequence process. Define the loss associated with a prediction $y = f(x_{i(1,k)})$ for an action x_i at progress level k as $\Delta(y_i, y)u(\frac{k}{K})$. Here $\Delta(y_i, y)$ denotes the misclassification error, and $u(\frac{k}{K})$ is the scaling factor that depends on how many segments have been observed. In this work, we use summation to aggregate the loss quantities. This leads to an empirical risk for N training samples: $R_{\mathrm{emp}}(f) = \frac{1}{N} \sum_{i=1}^{N} \sum_{k=1}^{K} \left\{ \Delta(y_i, y)u(\frac{k}{K}) \right\}$.

Denote by ξ_1^*, ξ_2^* and ξ_3^* the optimal solutions of the slack variables in Eq. (5-8) for a given classifier f, we can prove that $\frac{1}{N} \sum_{i=1}^{N} (\xi_{1i}^* + \xi_{2i}^* + \xi_{3i}^*)$ is an upper bound on the empirical risk $R_{\mathrm{emp}}(f)$ and the learning formulation given in Eq. (5-8) minimizes the upper bound of the empirical risk $R_{\mathrm{emp}}(f)$[1].

3.4 Discussion

We highlight here some important properties of our model, and show some differences from existing methods.

Multiple Temporal Scales. Our method captures action dynamics in both local and global temporal scales, while [1,4,14] only use a single temporal scale.

Temporal Evolution over Time. Our work uses the prior knowledge of temporal action evolution over time. Inspired by [4], we introduce a principled monotonic score function for the GPM to capture this prior knowledge. However, [4] aims at finding the starting frame of an event while our goal is to predict action class of an unfinished video. The methods in [1,14,9] do not use this prior.

Segment Label Consistency. We effectively utilize the discriminative power of local temporal segments by enforcing label consistency of segments. However, [1,14,9,4] do not consider the label consistency. The consistency also implicitly

---

[1] Please refer to the supplemental material for details.

models temporal segment context by enforcing the same label for segments while [1,14,4] explicitly treat successive temporal segments independently.

Principled Empirical Risk Minimization. We propose a principled empirical risk minimization formulation for action prediction, which is not discussed in [1,14,9].

3.5   Model Learning and Testing

Learning. We solve the optimization problem (5-8) using the regularized bundle algorithm [2]. The basic idea of the algorithm is to iteratively approximate the objective function by adding a new cutting plane to the piecewise quadratic approximation.

The equivalent unconstrained problem of the optimization problem (5-8) is $\min_{\mathbf{w}} \frac{1}{2}\|\mathbf{w}\|^2 + \frac{C}{N} \cdot L(\mathbf{w})$, where $L(\mathbf{w}) = \sum_{i=1}^{N}(U_i + Z_i + V_i)$ is the empirical loss. Here, U_i, Z_i and V_i are given by

$$U_i = \sum_{k=1}^{K} u(\frac{k}{K}) \max_y \left[K\delta(y, y_i) + \mathbf{w}^T \Phi(x_{i(1,k)}, y) - \mathbf{w}^T \Phi(x_{i(1,k)}, y_i) \right], \qquad (9)$$

$$Z_i = \sum_{k=2}^{K} u(\frac{k}{K}) \max_y \left[K\delta(y, y_i) + \alpha_{k-1}^T \psi_1(x_{i(1,k-1)}, y) - \alpha_k^T \psi_1(x_{i(1,k)}, y_i) \right],$$

$$\tag{10}$$

$$V_i = \sum_{k=1}^{K} u(\frac{1}{K}) \max_y \left[kK\delta(y, y_i) + \beta_k^T \psi_2(x_{i(k)}, y) - \beta_k^T \psi_2(x_{i(k)}, y_i) \right]. \qquad (11)$$

The regularized bundle algorithm requires the subgradient of the training loss with respect to the parameter, $\frac{\partial L}{\partial \mathbf{w}} = \sum_{i=1}^{N}(\frac{\partial U_i}{\partial \mathbf{w}} + \frac{\partial Z_i}{\partial \mathbf{w}} + \frac{\partial V_i}{\partial \mathbf{w}})$, in order to find a new cutting plane to be added to the approximation[2].

Testing. Given an unfinished action video with progress level k (k is known in testing), our goal is to infer the class label y^* using the learned model parameter $\mathbf{w}^*$: $y^* = \arg\max_{y \in \mathcal{Y}} \langle \mathbf{w}^*, \Phi(x_{(1,k)}, y) \rangle$. Note that testing phase does not require sophisticated inference algorithms such as belief propagation or graph cut since we do not explicitly capture segment interactions. However, the context information between segments is implicitly captured in our model by the label consistency in Constraint (8).

4   Experiments

We test the proposed MTSSVM approach on three datasets: the UT-Interaction dataset (UTI) Set 1 (UTI #1) and Set 2 (UTI #2) [16], and the BIT-Interaction dataset (BIT) [7]. UTI #1 were taken on a parking lot with mostly static background and little camera jitters. UTI #2 were captured on a lawn with slight

---

[2] Please refer to the supplemental material for details.

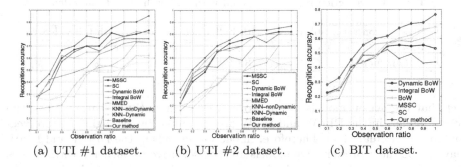

(a) UTI #1 dataset. (b) UTI #2 dataset. (c) BIT dataset.

Fig. 4. Prediction results on the UTI #1, UTI #2 and BIT dataset

background movements (e.g. tree moves) and camera jitters. Both of the two sets consist of six types of human actions, with ten videos per class. We adopt the leave-one-out training scheme on the two datasets. The BIT dataset consists of eight types of human actions between two people, with fifty videos per class. For this dataset, a random sample of 272 videos is chosen as training samples, and the remaining 128 videos are used for testing. The dictionary size for interest point descriptors is set to 500, and the size for tracklet descriptors is automatically determined by the clustering method in all the experiments.

MTSSVM is evaluated for classifying videos of incomplete action executions using 10 observation ratios, from 0.1 to 1, representing the increasing amount of sequential data with time. For example, if a full video containing T frames is used for testing at the observation ratio of 0.3, the accuracy of MTSSVM is evaluated by presenting it with the first $0.3 \times T$ frames. At observation ratio of 1, the entire video is used, at which point MTSSVM acts as a conventional action recognition model. The progress level k of testing videos is known to all the methods in our experiments.

4.1 Results

UTI #1 and UTI #2 Datasets. The MTSSVM is compared with DBoW and IBoW in [14], the MMED [4], the MSSC and the SC in [1], and the method in [12]. The KNN-nonDynamic, the KNN-Dynamic, and the baseline method implemented in [1] are also used in comparison. The same experiment settings in [1] are followed in our experiments.

Fig. 4(a) shows the prediction results on the UTI #1 dataset. Our MTSSVM achieves better performance over all the other comparison approaches. Our method outperforms the MSSC method because we not only model segment dynamics but also characterize temporal evolutions of actions. Our method can achieve an impressive 78.33% recognition accuracy when only the first 50% frames of testing videos are observed. This result is even higher than the SC method with full observations. Results of our method are significantly higher than the DBoW and IBoW for all observation ratios. This is mainly due to the

Table 1. Prediction results compared with [12] on half and full videos

Observation ratio	Accuracy with half videos	Accuracy with full videos
Raptis and Sigal [12]	73.3%	93.3%
Our model	**78.33%**	**95%**

fact that the action models in our work are discriminatively learned while the action models in the DBoW and IBoW are computed by averaging feature vectors in a particular class. Therefore, the action models in the DBoW and IBoW may not be the representative models and are sensitive to outliers. MMED does not perform well as other prediction approaches since it is optimized for early detection of the starting and ending frame of an action. This is a different goal from this paper, which is to classify unfinished actions. We also compare with [12] on half and full video observations. Results in Table 1 show that our method achieves better performance over [12].

Comparison results on the UTI #2 datasets are shown in Fig. 4(b). The MTSSVM achieves better performance over all the other comparison approaches in all the cases. At 0.3, 0.5 and 1 observation ratios, MSSC achieves 48.33%, 71.67%, and 81.67% prediction accuracy, respectively, and SC achieves 50%, 66.67%, and 80% accuracy, respectively. By contrast, our MTSSVM achieves 60%, 75% and 83.33% prediction results, respectively, which is consistently higher than MSSC and SC. Our MTSSVM achieves 75% accuracy when only the first 50% frames of testing videos are observed. This accuracy is even higher than the DBoW and IBoW with full observations.

To demonstrate that both the global progress model (GPM) and the local progress model (LPM) are important for action prediction, we compare the performance of MTSSVM with the model that only uses one of the two sources of information on the UTI #1 dataset. Fig. 5 shows the scores of the GPM and LPM ($\alpha_k^T \psi_1(x_{(1,k)}, y)$ of the GPM and $\sum_{l=1}^{K} \mathbf{1}(l \leqslant k) \cdot \beta_l^T \psi_2(x_{(1,k)}, y)$ of the LPM), and compare them to the scores of the full MTSSVM model with respect to the observation ratio. Results show that the LPM captures discriminative temporal segments for prediction. LPM characterizes temporal dynamics of segments and discriminatively learns to differentiate segments from different classes. In most cases, the score of LPM is monotonically increasing, which indicates a discriminative temporal segment is used for prediction. However, in some cases, segments from different classes are visually similar and thus are difficult to discriminate. Therefore, in the middle of the "handshake" class and the "hug" class in Fig. 5 (observation ratio from 0.3 to 0.7), adding more segment observations does not increase LPM's contribution to MTSSVM. Fig. 6 shows examples of visually similar segments of the two classes at $k = 6$. However, when such situations arise, GPM can provide necessary appearance history information and therefore increases the prediction performance of MTSSVM.

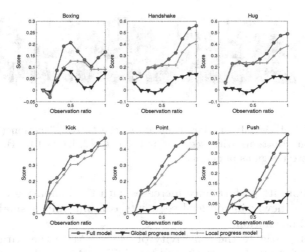

Fig. 5. Contributions of the global progress model and the local progress model to the prediction task

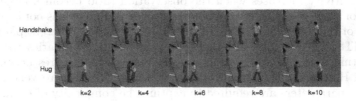

Fig. 6. Examples of segments in "handshake" and "hug". Segments $k = 6, 8, 10$ in the two classes are visually similar.

BIT-Interaction Dataset. We also compare MTSSVM with the MSSC, SC, DBoW and IBoW on the BIT-Interaction dataset. A BoW+SVM method is used as a baseline. The parameter σ in DBoW and IBoW is set to 36 and 2, respectively, which are the optimal parameters on the BIT-Interaction dataset. Results shown in Fig. 4(c) demonstrate that MTSSVM outperforms MSSC and SC in all cases due to the effect of the global progress model, which effectively captures temporal action evolution information. MTSSVM also outperforms the DBoW and IBoW. Our method achieves 60.16% recognition accuracy with only the first 50% frames of testing videos are observed, which is better than the DBoW and IBoW at all observation ratios. Note that the performance of DBoW and IBoW do not increase much when the observation ratios are increased from 0.6 to 0.9. The IBoW performs even worse. This is due to the fact that some video segments from different classes are visually similar; especially the segments in the second half of the videos, where people return to their starting positions (see Fig. 7). However, because MTSSVM models both the segments and the

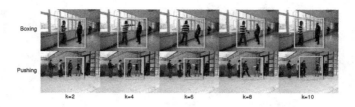

Fig. 7. Examples of visually similar segments in the "boxing" action (Top) and the "pushing" action (Bottom) with segment index $k \in \{2, 4, 6, 8, 10\}$. Bounding boxes indicate the interest regions of actions

entire observation, its performance increases with the increasing of observation ratio even if the newly introduced segments contain only a small amount of discriminative information.

We further investigate the sensitivity of MTSSVM to the parameters C in Eq. (5). We set C to 0.5, 5, and 10, and test MTSSVM on all parameter combinations with observation ratios 0.3, 0.5, and 0.8. Results in Table 2 indicate that MTSSVM is not sensitive to the parameters when the observation ratio is low but the sensitivity increases when the observation ratio becomes large. In the beginning of a video, the small number of features available does not capture the variability of their class. Therefore, it does not help to use different parameters, because MTSSVM cannot learn the appropriate class boundaries to separate all the testing data. As observation ratio increases, the features become more expressive. However, since structural features in MTSSVM are very complex, appropriate parameters are required to capture the complexity of data.

Table 2. Recognition accuracy of our model on videos of observation ratio 0.3, 0.5, and 0.8 with different C parameters

Observation ratio	C=0.5	C=5	C=10
0.3	42.97%	39.84%	38.28%
0.5	54.69%	57.03%	51.56%
0.8	66.41%	61.72%	55.47%

Finally, we also evaluate the importance of each component in the MTSSVM, including the Constraint (7), the Constraint (8), the local progress model (LPM in Eq. (4)) and the global progress model (GPM in Eq. (3)). We remove each of these components from the MTSSVM, and obtain four variant models, the no-cons2 model (remove the Constraint (7) from MTSSVM), the no-cons3 model (remove the Constraint (8)), the no-LPM model (remove the LPM and Constraint (8)), and the no-GPM model (remove the GPM and Constraint (7)). We compare MTSSVM with these variants with parameter C of 1 and 100. Results in Fig. 8 show that the GPM is the key component in the MTSSVM.

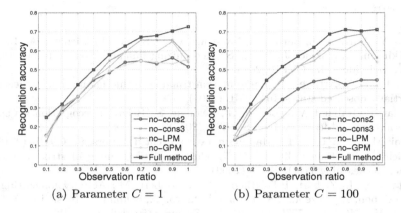

(a) Parameter $C = 1$ (b) Parameter $C = 100$

Fig. 8. Prediction results of each component in the full MTSSVM with C parameter 1 and 100

Without the GPM, the performance of the no-GPM model degrades significantly compared with the full MTSSVM model, especially with parameter C of 100. The performances of the no-cons3 model and the no-LPM model are worse compared with the full method in all cases. This is due to the lack of the segment label consistency in the two models. The label consistency can help use the discriminative information in segments and also implicitly model context information. In the ending part of videos in BIT dataset, since most of observations are visually similar (people return back to their normal position), label consistency is of great importance for discriminating classes. However, due to the lack of label consistency in the the no-cons3 model and the no-LPM model, they cannot capture useful information for differentiating action classes.

5   Conclusion

We have proposed the multiple temporal scale support vector machine (MTSSVM) for recognizing actions in incomplete videos. MTSSVM captures the entire action evolution over time and also considers the temporal nature of a video. We formulate the action prediction task as a structured SVM learning problem. The discriminability of segments is enforced in the learning formulation. Experiments on two datasets show that MTSSVM outperforms state-of-the-art approaches.

Acknowledgements. This research is supported in part by the NSF CNS award 1314484, ONR award N00014-12-1-1028, ONR Young Investigator Award N00014-14-1-0484, U.S. Army Research Office Young Investigator Award W911NF-14-1-0218, and IC Postdoc Program Grant 2011-11071400006.

References

1. Cao, Y., Barrett, D., Barbu, A., Narayanaswamy, S., Yu, H., Michaux, A., Lin, Y., Dickinson, S., Siskind, J., Wang, S.: Recognizing human activities from partially observed videos. In: CVPR (2013)
2. Do, T.-M.-T., Artieres, T.: Large margin training for hidden markov models with partially observed states. In: ICML (2009)
3. Dollar, P., Rabaud, V., Cottrell, G., Belongie, S.: Behavior recognition via sparse spatio-temporal features. In: VS-PETS (2005)
4. Hoai, M., De la Torre, F.: Max-margin early event detectors. In: CVPR (2012)
5. Joachims, T., Finley, T., Yu, C.-N.: Cutting-plane training of structural svms. Machine Learning 77(1), 27–59 (2009)
6. Kitani, K.M., Ziebart, B.D., Bagnell, J.A., Hebert, M.: Activity forecasting. In: Fitzgibbon, A., Lazebnik, S., Perona, P., Sato, Y., Schmid, C. (eds.) ECCV 2012, Part IV. LNCS, vol. 7575, pp. 201–214. Springer, Heidelberg (2012)
7. Kong, Y., Jia, Y., Fu, Y.: Learning human interaction by interactive phrases. In: Fitzgibbon, A., Lazebnik, S., Perona, P., Sato, Y., Schmid, C. (eds.) ECCV 2012, Part I. LNCS, vol. 7572, pp. 300–313. Springer, Heidelberg (2012)
8. Kong, Y., Jia, Y., Fu, Y.: Interactive phrases: Semantic descriptions for human interaction recognition. TPAMI (2014)
9. Li, K., Hu, J., Fu, Y.: Modeling complex temporal composition of actionlets for activity prediction. In: Fitzgibbon, A., Lazebnik, S., Perona, P., Sato, Y., Schmid, C. (eds.) ECCV 2012, Part I. LNCS, vol. 7572, pp. 286–299. Springer, Heidelberg (2012)
10. Liu, J., Kuipers, B., Savarese, S.: Recognizing human actions by attributes. In: CVPR (2011)
11. Niebles, J.C., Chen, C.-W., Fei-Fei, L.: Modeling temporal structure of decomposable motion segments for activity classification. In: Daniilidis, K., Maragos, P., Paragios, N. (eds.) ECCV 2010, Part II. LNCS, vol. 6312, pp. 392–405. Springer, Heidelberg (2010)
12. Raptis, M., Sigal, L.: Poselet key-framing: A model for human activity recognition. In: CVPR (2013)
13. Raptis, M., Soatto, S.: Tracklet descriptors for action modeling and video analysis. In: Daniilidis, K., Maragos, P., Paragios, N. (eds.) ECCV 2010, Part I. LNCS, vol. 6311, pp. 577–590. Springer, Heidelberg (2010)
14. Ryoo, M.S.: Human activity prediction: Early recognition of ongoing activities from streaming videos. In: ICCV (2011)
15. Ryoo, M.S., Aggarwal, J.K.: Spatio-temporal relationship match: Video structure comparison for recognition of complex human activities. In: ICCV, pp. 1593–1600 (2009)
16. Ryoo, M., Aggarwal, J.: UT-Interaction Dataset, ICPR contest on Semantic Description of Human Activities, SDHA (2010)
17. Schuldt, C., Laptev, I., Caputo, B.: Recognizing human actions: A local svm approach. In: ICPR, vol. 3, pp. 32–36. IEEE (2004)
18. Shapovalova, N., Vahdat, A., Cannons, K., Lan, T., Mori, G.: Similarity constrained latent support vector machine: An application to weakly supervised action classification. In: Fitzgibbon, A., Lazebnik, S., Perona, P., Sato, Y., Schmid, C. (eds.) ECCV 2012, Part VII. LNCS, vol. 7578, pp. 55–68. Springer, Heidelberg (2012)

19. Shi, Q., Cheng, L., Wang, L., Smola, A.: Human action segmentation and recognition using discriminative semi-markov models. IJCV 93, 22–32 (2011)
20. Tang, K., Fei-Fei, L., Koller, D.: Learning latent temporal structure for complex event detection. In: CVPR (2012)
21. Tsochantaridis, I., Joachims, T., Hofmann, T., Altun, Y.: Large margin methods for structured and interdependent output variables. JMLR 6, 1453–1484 (2005)
22. Vahdat, A., Gao, B., Ranjbar, M., Mori, G.: A discriminative key pose sequence model for recognizing human interactions. In: ICCV Workshops. pp. 1729–1736 (2011)
23. Wang, Z., Wang, J., Xiao, J., Lin, K.-H., Huang, T.S.: Substructural and boundary modeling for continuous action recognition. In: CVPR (2012)
24. Yao, B., Fei-Fei, L.: Action recognition with exemplar based 2.5D graph matching. In: Fitzgibbon, A., Lazebnik, S., Perona, P., Sato, Y., Schmid, C. (eds.) ECCV 2012, Part IV. LNCS, vol. 7575, pp. 173–186. Springer, Heidelberg (2012)
25. Yao, B., Fei-Fei, L.: Recognizing human-object interactions in still images by modeling the mutual context of objects and human poses. TPAMI 34(9), 1691–1703 (2012)
26. Yu, T.-H., Kim, T.-K., Cipolla, R.: Real-time action recognition by spatiotemporal semantic and structural forests. In: BMVC (2010)

Seeing is *Worse* than Believing: Reading People's Minds Better than Computer-Vision Methods Recognize Actions

Andrei Barbu[1], Daniel P. Barrett[2], Wei Chen[3], Narayanaswamy Siddharth[4],
Caiming Xiong[5], Jason J. Corso[6], Christiane D. Fellbaum[7], Catherine Hanson[8],
Stephen José Hanson[8], Sébastien Hélie[2], Evguenia Malaia[9],
Barak A. Pearlmutter[10], Jeffrey Mark Siskind[2],
Thomas Michael Talavage[2], and Ronnie B. Wilbur[2]

[1] MIT, Cambridge, MA, USA
andrei@0xab.com
[2] Purdue University, West Lafayette, IN, USA
{dpbarret,shelie,qobi,tmt,wilbur}@purdue.edu
[3] SUNY Buffalo, Buffalo, NY, USA
wchen23@buffalo.edu
[4] Stanford University, Stanford, CA, USA
nsid@stanford.edu
[5] University of California at Los Angeles, Los Angeles, CA, USA
caimingxiong@ucla.edu
[6] University of Michigan, Ann Arbor, MI, USA
jjcorso@eecs.umich.edu
[7] Princeton University, Princeton, NJ, USA
fellbaum@princeton.edu
[8] Rutgers University, Newark, NJ, USA
{cat,jose}@psychology.rutgers.edu
[9] University of Texas at Arlington, Arlington, TX, USA
malaia@uta.edu
[10] National University of Ireland Maynooth, Co. Kildare, Ireland
barak@cs.nuim.ie

Abstract. We had human subjects perform a one-out-of-six class action recognition task from video stimuli while undergoing functional magnetic resonance imaging (fMRI). Support-vector machines (SVMs) were trained on the recovered brain scans to classify actions observed during imaging, yielding average classification accuracy of 69.73% when tested on scans from the same subject and of 34.80% when tested on scans from different subjects. An apples-to-apples comparison was performed with all publicly available software that implements state-of-the-art action recognition on the same video corpus with the same cross-validation regimen and same partitioning into training and test sets, yielding classification accuracies between 31.25% and 52.34%. This indicates that one can read people's minds better than state-of-the-art computer-vision methods can perform action recognition.

Keywords: action recognition, fMRI.

D. Fleet et al. (Eds.): ECCV 2014, Part V, LNCS 8693, pp. 612–627, 2014.

1   Introduction

There has been considerable recent interest in action recognition in the computer vision community. By our count, there were 236 papers related to action recognition published in major computer-vision conferences over the past three years.[1] A recent survey paper [17] reports the performance of a variety of different systems on a variety of different datasets. On some datasets with small numbers of classes (e.g. KTH [25], 6 classes; Weizmann [1], 9 classes) the best performance is perfect or near perfect. This has prompted many to conclude that action recognition with small numbers of classes is a solved problem, motivating many to work on datasets with larger numbers of classes (e.g. UCF50 [22], HMDB51 [14], and even UCF101 [26]).

Here we show that this conclusion might be premature. We present a new dataset with only six classes: *carry, dig, hold, pick up, put down,* and *walk*. Our dataset is innocuous; there is no attempt to subvert the recognition process. The actions are, arguably, easily interpretable by humans and, similar to KTH [25] and Weizmann [1], occur largely unoccluded in an outdoor setting with an uncluttered background. We applied *every* state-of-the-art, recently published action-recognition system for which code is publicly available (as well as several for which code is not publicly available) to this dataset and obtained classification accuracies between 31.25% and 52.34%. (Chance performance is 16.67%.) As a point of comparison, we showed these same videos to human subjects undergoing *functional magnetic resonance imaging* (fMRI). We trained classifiers on the brain-scan data and obtained an average within-subject classification accuracy of 69.73%. Note that as discussed in the next section, our dataset is *difficult*. While we do not have a precise human-performance baseline against which to compare the above classification accuracies, the next section does discuss human annotation that we have gathered and used to measure the level of difficulty of the corpus.

Figure 1 summarizes our experiment. We train and test state-of-the-art computer vision action-recognition software (C2 [12], Action Bank [24], Stacked ISA [16], VHTK [18], Cao's implementation [2] of Ryoo's method [23], Cao's method [2], and our own implementation of the classifier described in [28] on top of the Dense Trajectories [27,28,29] feature extractor) to classify video clips depicting one of six action classes and achieve accuracy of about 50%. We show the same video clips as stimuli to human subjects undergoing fMRI and train and test state-of-the-art brain-scan classifiers to classify the same six action classes and achieve accuracy of about 70%. This was an apples-to-apples comparison. Both conditions involved the same eight-fold cross-validation procedure with the same splits of data into training and test sets.

---

[1] 49 (5 oral and 44 poster) in CVPR 2011, 24 (4 oral and 20 poster) in ICCV 2011, 20 (2 oral and 18 poster) in CVPR 2012, 7 (3 oral and 4 poster) in BMVC 2012, 51 (5 oral and 46 poster) in ECCV 2012, 23 (3 oral and 20 poster) in ACCV 2012, 20 (2 oral and 18 poster) in CVPR 2013, and 42 (all poster) in ICCV 2013.

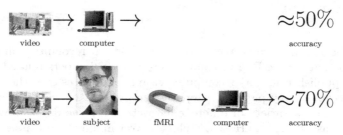

Fig. 1. A summary of our experiment. We train and test state-of-the-art computer-vision action-recognition software to classify video clips depicting one of six action classes and achieve accuracy of about 50%. We show the same video clips as stimuli to human subjects undergoing fMRI, train and test state-of-the-art brain-scan classifiers to classify the same six action classes, and achieve accuracy of about 70%.

2   Dataset

We employed a small portion of the video dataset gathered as part of the Year 2 evaluation for the DARPA Mind's Eye program.[2] (Note that we did not design the corpus or film the video ourselves; it was designed and filmed by DARPA and provided to all teams funded by the Mind's Eye program.) In particular, we used data from two components of that dataset: the portion known as C-D2b, which was intended to be used as training data, and the portion known as y2-evaluation, what was used as test data for the actual evaluation. Of C-D2b, we used solely the Country_Road portion (both Country_Road_1 and Country_Road_2), videos filmed on a rural country road depicting the specified action classes. This portion contains 22 video clips ranging in length from about 13.5 minutes to about 41 minutes totaling about 8.5 hours of video. Of y2-evaluation, we used all of the videos employed for evaluating the 'Recognition' and 'Description' tasks that were part of the Year 2 evaluation. This portion contains 11 video clips ranging in length from about 6 minutes to about 13 minutes totaling about 2 hours of video. Two of these video clips were filmed in a country-road setting while the remainder were filmed in a 'Safe House' setting, a simulated middle-eastern urban environment. Nominally, this dataset depicts 24 distinct action classes: *approach, arrive, bury, carry, chase, dig, drop, enter, exchange, exit, flee, follow, give, hold, leave, pass, pick up, put down, replace, run, stop, take, turn,* and *walk.* However, the video is streaming; action occurrences start and stop at arbitrary points in the time course of the video, and often overlap.

There is no official ground-truth action labeling associated with this dataset. To remedy this, we had five humans annotate the entire Country_Road portion of C-D2b (both Country_Road_1 and Country_Road_2) and had a different set of five annotators (with one annotator in common) annotate the entire set of videos for the Recognition and Description portions of y2-evaluation. Each

---

[2] http://www.visint.org/datasets#Year_2_Videos

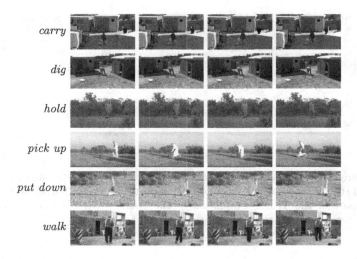

Fig. 2. Key frames from sample stimuli for each of the six action classes

annotator annotated the entire corpus portion independently, labeling each occurrence of the 24 specified action classes along with the start and end times for each occurrence. Thus we have five complete redundant annotations of the entire corpus. Having multiple annotators allows us to measure intercoder agreement, which we did for all pairs of annotators. We considered two annotated action occurrences to match when they were labeled with the same action class and temporally overlapped by a minimum specified amount. The temporal overlap was measured using a 1-dimensional variant of the 2-dimension spatial-overlap metric used in PASCAL VOC [6], namely the ratio of the length of the intersection of the two intervals to the length of their union. We then computed the F1 score for each pair of annotators as a function of overlap. The result is shown in Fig. 3. The F1 score naturally decreases monotonically with increasing minimum overlap and goes to zero when the required overlap is 100%, indicating that human annotators never agree on the precise temporal extent of the actions in question. But the F1 score ranged between 0.27 and 0.8 at 50% overlap and between 0.39 and 0.81 at 0% overlap (which still requires temporal adjacency).

This surprisingly low level of human-human intercoder agreement indicates that even in this setting where the actions are easily interpretable by humans and occur largely unoccluded in an outdoor setting with an uncluttered background, the task of delineating temporal extent of action occurrences is ambiguous. Thus we selected a subset of 6 out of the 24 action classes with the highest level of intercoder agreement: *carry*, *dig*, *hold*, *pick up*, *put down*, and *walk*. For each of these classes, we selected intervals of at least 2.5 seconds where at least two human annotators agreed on the label with at least 50% overlap. From these, we attempted to select 30 random 2.5-second clips for each of the six classes. The 2.5-second clips were chosen to maximally coincide with the intersection of

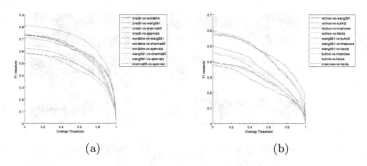

(a)   (b)

Fig. 3. Intercoder agreement for each annotator pair on (a) the `C-D2b/Country_Road` dataset and (b) the Recognition and Description portions of the `y2-evaluation` dataset that were part of the Year 2 evaluation of the DARPA Mind's Eye program, as a function of requisite temporal overlap.

the human-annotated intervals. However, two classes did not have sufficient clips with the requisite level of intercoder agreement: *dig* with 23 and *hold* with 26. Thus we selected a total of 169 distinct clips across all six action classes with the highest possible level of intercoder agreement.[3] Key frames from sample stimuli are shown in Fig. 2.

We employed a technique to further reduce the potential ambiguity in determining the intended action-class label for each stimulus. This technique was borrowed and adapted from the Natural Language Processing community. Natural language exhibits lexical polysemy: words can have multiple senses, which leads to ambiguity in contexts. WordNet [7,19] represents word meanings with synsets, unordered sets of words that share a same meaning. A polysemous word with n different meanings occurs in n different synsets, along with its synonyms. For example, the verb *break* is found in the synsets {*break, interrupt*} and {*break, bust*}. To further reduce the potential ambiguity in the intended class label depicted by each video, we constructed pairs of video clips with the same label, in the spirit of WordNet's synsets. In other words, we constructed longer stimuli as pairs of different video clips with the same intended action-class label, where each might otherwise be mildly ambiguous as to which action class was intended, but where together, the ambiguity is resolved. Sequences of such video-clip pairs constituted both the stimuli presented to human subjects during fMRI as well as training and test sets for computer-vision action recognition.

3   Action Recognition Software

We sought to try our corpus with as many published action-recognition methods as possible. We searched all papers on action recognition published in all conferences listed under *Computer Vision Paper Indexes*[4] since 2011, namely ICCV

---

[3] Code and data at `http://upplysingaoflun.ecn.purdue.edu/~qobi/eccv2014/`.

[4] `http://www.cvpapers.com/index.html`

2011 and 2013, CVPR 2011, 2012, and 2013, ECCV 2012, ACCV 2012, BMVC 2012, SIGGRAPH 2011, EUROGRAPHICS 2011, and IJCAI 2011, for indication that their code was publicly available. We sought **end-to-end** implementations that included both feature extraction and classification. (Some authors release only the code for feature extraction, for example binaries for STIP [15][5] and source for Dense Trajectories [27,28,29][6]. The lack of a compatible released classifier makes it difficult to run and further difficult to compare with the precise published method.) The only papers that we found that indicated such were for C2 [12,14][7] and Action Bank [24].[8] C2 is particularly relevant to our comparison with fMRI as [14] claims that it

> uses a hierarchical architecture modeled after the ventral and dorsal streams of the primate visual cortex for the task of object and action recognition, respectively.

Additionally, we posted a query for available action-recognition software to CVNet which yielded a single response pointing us to the code for Stacked ISA [16].[9] Furthermore, we contacted Rogerio Feris to see if any code was collected for the study in [17]. He pointed us to a website[10] that yielded only one available system that we hadn't already been aware of, namely Velocity Histories of Tracked Keypoints (VHTK) [18].[11] As far as we can tell, these are the only published action-recognition methods for which there are corresponding publicly available **end-to-end** implementations.

Note that the released code for Stacked ISA is only able to perform binary classification and so must differ from that used to generate the published results which include evaluation of KTH that requires multi-label classification. Also note that for VHTK, the documentation for the released code states that the released code differs from that used to produce the results in the corresponding publication; the actual code used to produce the results in the corresponding publication has not been publicly released. Thus the only publicly available systems that we are aware of that can replicate the associated published results are C2 and Action Bank.

We also have access to two action-recognition software packages that are not publicly available. Cao [2] reports that they reimplemented Ryoo's method [23] as it is not publicly available. We tested against both Cao's implementation [2] of Ryoo's method [23] as well as Cao's method [2]. Further, we implemented our own classifier using the methods described in [28] on top of the publicly available source code for the Dense Trajectories [27,28,29] feature extraction and tested against this as well (with 4000 GMM components).

---

[5] http://www.di.ens.fr/~laptev/download.html
[6] https://lear.inrialpes.fr/people/wang/download/
    dense_trajectory_release_v1.2.tar.gz
[7] https://github.com/hueihan/Action_Recognition
[8] http://www.cse.buffalo.edu/~jcorso/r/actionbank/
[9] http://ai.stanford.edu/~quocle/video_release.tar.gz
[10] http://rogerioferis.com/VisualRecognitionAndSearch2014/Resources.html
[11] http://www.cs.rochester.edu/~rmessing/uradl/

4   Overview of FMRI

For a general overview of fMRI see [11]. Modern 3T clinical MRI scanners can perform a high-resolution anatomical scan in about 8 minutes. This yields a spatial resolution of approximately 1mm and produces a 3D image of the brain with about 11 million voxels, with about 13 bits of information per voxel. Functional MRI trades off spatial resolution for scan time, yielding a 3D image containing about 150,000 voxels with a spatial resolution of about 3mm every two seconds. While some state-of-the-art scanners support higher-frequency functional scans about every 250ms, we do not have access to such. Thus, in our experiments, the scan time approximately coincides with the length of the video stimulus.

Most verbs describe state changes that happen over time. For example, *pick up* involves a state change of an object being at rest somewhere to being held by someone. Computer-vision methods can process frame sequences that reflect such changes. Presumably, there are also changes in brain activity to reflect such state changes in the perceived world. But they happen at a time scale that is too short to measure given the temporal resolution of fMRI. A single TR is 2s. The whole video stimulus takes 2.5s. So we get a single brain volume (after the HRF delay) that presumably reflects some smearing of the brain activity during the entire video clip but does not contain explicit information of the time course of processing. This means that while computer-vision action recognition can potentially avail itself of the temporally variant pixel values over the course of a video clip, the fMRI analysis methods we employ cannot, and process a single static brain volume for each video clip.

FMRI does not directly measure neural activity. It measures the *blood oxygenation level dependent* (BOLD) signal. Greater neural activity requires greater energy which in turn requires greater blood flow. Blood flow is shunted to different brain regions according to temporally variant neural activity. However, such shunting is delayed. It takes roughly 8–10 seconds for the BOLD response to peak after a stimulus onset that induces brain activity. Moreover, the deviation in BOLD response can persist for roughly 30 seconds after such. This is called the *hemodynamic response function* (HRF). It induces a smearing in the temporal signature of the brain activity indicated by the BOLD response; adjacent stimuli can induce overlapping BOLD response. To compensate for the HRF, we separate presentation of stimuli to the subject with blanking periods where there is no stimulus except for a fixation crosshair. Moreover, we analyze the brain-scan sample from the third TR after each stimulus, which roughly corresponds to the HRF delay.

Since the spatial resolution of a functional scan is only about 3mm, the scanning process can tolerate a small amount of subject head movement. Subject's heads are confined to a headrest in the head coil and subjects are instructed to attempt to minimize head movement. Preprocessing of BOLD involved correcting for drift, standard motion correction, and between session normalization.

State-of-the-art brain-activity classification involves a small number of concept classes, where the stimuli are still images of objects or orthographic presentation of nouns. Just et al. [13] perform classification on orthographic nouns, 5 exemplars from each of 12 classes, achieving a mean rank accuracy of 72.4% on a one-out-of-60 classification task, both within and across subjects. (Note that rank accuracy differs from classification accuracy and denotes "the normalized rank of the correct label in the classifier's posterior-probability-ordered list of classes" [13, p. 5].) Pereira et al. [20] reanalyze the preceding data in the context of a prior from Wikipedia and achieve a mean accuracy of 13.2% on a one-out-of-12 classification task and 1.94% on a one-out-of-60 classification task. Hanson & Halchenko [9] perform classification on still images of two object classes: faces and houses, and achieve an accuracy above 93% on a one-out-of-two classification task. Connolly et al. [3] perform classification on still images of objects, two instances of each of three classes: bugs, birds, and primates, and achieve an accuracy between 60% and 98% on a one-out-of-two within-class classification task and an accuracy between 90% and 98% on a one-out-of-three between-class classification task. Haxby et al. [10] perform cross-subject classification of image and video stimuli achieving between 60% and 70% between-subject accuracy on image data with 6 to 7 classes and video data with all 18-second clips from *Raiders of the Lost Ark*. To our knowledge, this is the first study that classifies brain scans of subjects observing actions in video, and moreover compares the performance of such to computer-vision action-recognition methods.

5   FMRI Experiment

Video clips were shown to subjects who were asked to think about the action class depicted in the video during imaging. No behavioral or motor response of any kind was elicited. Specifically, subjects were not asked to push buttons or produce words, either oral or visual (written, signed). Subjects were shown sample video prior to imaging and informed of the intended set of action classes.

Because fMRI acquisition times are slow, roughly coinciding with the stimulus length, a single brain volume that corresponds to the brain activation induced by each stimulus was classified to recover the actions that the subjects were asked to think about. Multiple runs were performed for each subject, separated by several minutes, during which no stimuli were presented, no data was gathered, and subjects engaged in unrelated conversation with the experimenters. This separation between runs allowed runs to constitute folds for cross validation without introducing spurious correlation in brain activity between runs.

Imaging used a 3T GE Signa HDx scanner (Waukesha, Wisconsin) with a Nova Medical (Wilmington, Massachusetts) 16 channel brain array to collect whole-brain volumes via a gradient-echo EPI sequence with 2000ms TR, 22ms TE, 200mm×200mm FOV, and 77° flip angle. We acquired 35 axial slices with a 3.000mm slice thickness using a 64×64 acquisition matrix resulting in 3.125mm×3.125mm×3.000mm voxels.

Eight runs were acquired per subject, using a rapid event-related design [13], with stimuli counterbalanced across all six action classes within each run. We presented pairs of 2.5s video clips at 10fps, depicting the same action class. Each such presentation consisted of a 2.5s video clip, 0.5s blanking without a fixation crosshair, a 2.5s video clip, and 0.5s of fixation, totaling 6s that was aligned to three consecutive TR boundaries. Each such was followed by a minimum of one fixation TR. Each run started with a minimum of four fixation TRs and ended with a minimum of 10 fixation TRs. An additional 48 fixation TRs were randomly placed before, between, and after video-clip-pair presentations. All such fixation TRs were aligned to TR boundaries. Each run comprised 48 presentations spanning 254 captured brain volumes. The 48 stimulus presentations constituted eight instances of each of the six action classes. The eight instances for each action class were selected randomly from a uniform distribution over the set of 23 to 30 video clips for each class. A given clip could appear more than once both within and across runs, but never within a pair. The same stimulus order, both within and across runs, was used for all subjects (and also for the computer-vision action-recognition experiments).

Scan data was gathered for eight subjects and was processed using AFNI [5] to skull-strip each volume, motion correct and detrend each run, and align each subject's runs to each other. Voxels within a run were z-scored, subtracting the mean value of that voxel for the run and dividing by its variance. Since each brain volume has very high dimension, 143,360 voxels, voxels were eliminated by computing a per-voxel Fisher score on the training set and keeping the 4,000 highest-scoring voxels (12,000 for the cross-subject analyses). The Fisher score of a voxel v for a classification task with C classes where each class c has n_c examples was computed as $\frac{\sum_{c=1}^{C} n_c (\mu_{c,v} - \mu)^2}{\sum_{c=1}^{C} n_c \sigma_{c,v}^2}$ where $\mu_{c,v}$ and $\sigma_{c,v}$ are the per-class per-voxel means and variances and μ was the mean for the entire brain volume. The resulting voxels were then analyzed with Linear Discriminant Dimensionality Reduction [8] to select a smaller number of potentially-relevant voxels, selecting on average 1,084 voxels per-subject per-fold (12,000 for the cross-subject analyses). Both stages of voxel selection were performed independently for the training set for each fold of the analysis. The set of voxels to consider was determined solely from the training set. That same subset of voxels was used in the test set for classification.

A linear support vector machine (SVM) [4] was employed to classify the selected voxels. One run was taken as the test set and the remaining runs were taken as the training set. To account for the HRF, the third brain volume after the onset of each stimulus was used for training and classification.

Two kinds of analyses were performed: within subject and cross subject. The within-subject analyses trained and tested each classifier on the same subject. In other words, classifiers were trained on the data for subject s and also tested on the data for subject s. This was repeated for all eight subjects. While we trained and tested on data from the same subject, this does *not* constitute training on the test data since *different* brain scans for *different* video clips were used for training and test. For these, leave-one-out cross validation was performed by run: when testing on run r, the classifiers were trained on all runs *except* run r. Such cross validation precludes training on the test data. Partitioning by run ensures that information could not flow from the training set to the test set through the

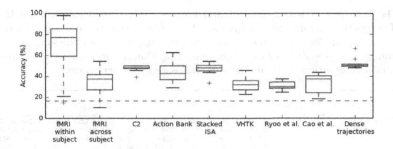

Fig. 4. Box plot corresponding to the results in Table 1, aggregated across subject and run for fMRI and aggregated across run for the computer-vision methods. Red lines indicate medians, box extents indicate upper and lower quartiles, error bars indicate maximal extents, and crosses indicate outliers. The dashed green lines indicates chance performance.

hemodynamic response function (HRF). This was repeated for all eight runs, thus performing eight-fold cross validation.

The cross-subject analyses trained and tested each classifier on different subjects. In particular, a classifier was trained on the data for all subjects except subject s and then tested on the data for subject s. This was repeated for all eight subjects. For these, leave-one-out cross validation was performed by both subject and run: when testing on run r for subject s, the classifiers were trained on all runs *except* run r for all subjects *except* subject s. While there is no potential for training on the test data, even without cross validation by run, there is potential for a different HRF-based confound. Due to the HRF, each scan potentially contains information from prior stimuli in the same run. Since the presentation order did not vary by subject, it is conceivable that classifier performance is due, in part, to the current stimulus in the context of previous stimuli in the same run, not just the current stimulus. One could control for this confound by randomizing presentation order across subject, but this was not part of the experiment design. Cross validation by run is an alternative control for this confound.

The results are presented in Table 1 and Figs. 4 and 5. All results are statistically significant with $p \leq .005$, when aggregated across subject, across run, or both, taking a binomial distribution (repeated independent Bernoulli trials with a uniform distribution over possible outcomes) as the null hypothesis. Assuming independence between trials, with each trial uniformly distributed, is warranted because all runs were counterbalanced. This demonstrates the ability to recover the action class that the subjects were thinking about when watching the video. Note that the confusion matrices are mostly diagonal, with the highest numbers of errors being made distinguishing *carry* and *hold*, *carry* and *walk* (which are both pairs of mutually ambiguous stimuli), and *pick up* and *put down*.[12]

---

[12] The instructions given to subjects delineated *carry*, which required horizontal agent motion, from *hold*, which required the agent to be stationary.

Table 1. Accuracy of within-subject and cross-subject classification of fMRI brain scans of subjects watching video clips on a 1-out-of-6 action-recognition task (chance performance is 0.1666), by subject and run, aggregated across subject, aggregated across run, and aggregated across subject and run. Comparison with seven computer-vision action-recognition methods, by run and aggregated across run.

analysis	subject	mean	stddev	run 1	2	3	4	5	6	7	8
fMRI within subject	1	0.7943	0.0783	0.8333	0.8125	0.8958	0.8542	0.7292	0.8125	0.7708	0.6458
	2	0.8880	0.0589	0.8750	0.9375	0.9792	0.9167	0.8958	0.7917	0.8333	0.8750
	3	0.7500	0.0568	0.7917	0.7083	0.7292	0.7500	0.7500	0.6458	0.8125	0.8125
	4	0.3828	0.0945	0.4583	0.5417	0.3750	0.3542	0.3750	0.2083	0.3750	0.3750
	5	0.9063	0.0686	0.8750	0.8542	0.9583	0.9583	0.9583	0.9583	0.9167	0.7708
	6	0.8385	0.0348	0.8750	0.8750	0.8542	0.8333	0.8125	0.8542	0.7708	0.8333
	7	0.5104	0.2260	0.1667	0.1458	0.6875	0.5417	0.6875	0.6875	0.6042	0.5625
	8	0.5078	0.1531	0.2083	0.6458	0.5208	0.6458	0.3958	0.4375	0.6042	0.6042
	mean	0.6973		0.6354	0.6901	0.7500	0.7318	0.7005	0.6745	0.7109	0.6849
	stddev		0.2171	0.3092	0.2557	0.2156	0.2061	0.2136	0.2450	0.1734	0.1694
fMRI across subject	1	0.2917	0.1045	0.2708	0.1458	0.2917	0.3750	0.3542	0.2708	0.1667	0.4583
	2	0.4141	0.0901	0.5417	0.5208	0.3750	0.3958	0.2500	0.3958	0.4167	0.4167
	3	0.3698	0.0761	0.4167	0.4375	0.2917	0.3750	0.3333	0.3125	0.2917	0.5000
	4	0.2917	0.1210	0.4167	0.2292	0.4792	0.2500	0.3958	0.1667	0.2292	0.1667
	5	0.3568	0.0550	0.3958	0.4167	0.3125	0.3333	0.3958	0.3750	0.3750	0.2500
	6	0.4036	0.0695	0.4375	0.3750	0.3333	0.3542	0.3333	0.5208	0.4792	0.3958
	7	0.3698	0.1677	0.1042	0.1042	0.4375	0.4792	0.3958	0.4375	0.5000	0.5000
	8	0.2865	0.0770	0.1458	0.2917	0.2917	0.3958	0.2708	0.2500	0.3750	0.2708
	mean	0.3480		0.3411	0.3151	0.3516	0.3698	0.3411	0.3411	0.3542	0.3698
	stddev		0.1068	0.1527	0.1475	0.0725	0.0647	0.0567	0.1135	0.1173	0.1254
C2 [12]		0.4740	0.0348	0.5000	0.4792	0.3958	0.4792	0.4583	0.5000	0.5000	0.4792
Action Bank [24]		0.4427	0.1112	0.5625	0.4583	0.2917	0.6250	0.3958	0.4792	0.3542	0.3750
Stacked ISA [16]		0.4688	0.0649	0.5208	0.5000	0.5417	0.4583	0.3333	0.5000	0.4375	0.4583
VHTK [18]		0.3255	0.0721	0.3750	0.2708	0.2708	0.3333	0.2292	0.3542	0.4583	0.3125
Ryoo's method*[23]		0.3125	0.0459	0.2500	0.2708	0.3750	0.3750	0.3333	0.2917	0.3750	0.3125
Cao's method [2]		0.3333	0.0964	0.3958	0.2292	0.2500	0.4375	0.1875	0.4167	0.3958	0.3542
Dense Trajectories [27,28,29]		0.5234	0.0634	0.6667	0.5625	0.5000	0.5000	0.4792	0.4792	0.5000	0.5000

*as implemented in Cao et al. [2]

As expected, the cross-subject average classification accuracy is lower than the within-subject average classification accuracy. This is because there is significant cross-subject anatomical variation. This is ameliorated to an extent, but not completely by warping the scan data to align the subjects to each other. But this process is imperfect. Few fMRI researchers perform cross-subject classification, testing classifiers trained on different subjects [10,13,21]. None that we are aware of do so for short video stimuli intended to be classified into object or event classes that correspond to nouns or verbs. Nonetheless, the average cross-subject classification accuracy is *far* above chance and is statistically significant.

6   Computer-Vision Action-Recognition Experiments

We applied C2 [12], Action Bank [24], Stacked ISA [16], VHTK [18], Cao's implementation [2] of Ryoo's method [23], Cao's method [2], and our own implementation of the classifier described in [28] on top of the Dense Trajectories [27,28,29] feature extractor to the same dataset.[13] When running Action Bank,

---

[13] These experiments were analogous to the within-subject fMRI experiment. It would be meaningless to perform a computational analog of the cross-subject fMRI experiments because there would be no variation between different runs of the same program.

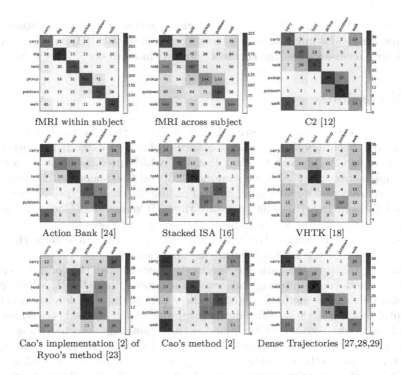

Fig. 5. Confusion matrices corresponding to the results in Table 1, aggregated across subject and run for fMRI and aggregated across run for the computer-vision methods.

we used the precomputed 205-template bank that was provided with the release. These experiments employed the same eight-fold leave-one-run-out cross validation. One complication arises, however. Since the stimuli were selected randomly from a uniform distribution over the set of available video clips, the same video clip could appear both within a given run and across runs. In the case of computer-vision systems, which directly process the stimuli, this would constitute training on the test data. In particular, several of the computer-vision systems that we evaluated are memory-based and would gain an unfair advantage by recalling from memory the class labels of test videos that occur in the training set. This is not a problem for the fMRI experiments because we did not directly process the stimuli; we process the brain-scan data that was evoked by the stimuli and there is significant natural variation in such.

To ameliorate this problem when performing the computer-vision experiments, we removed from each training set any pair that contained a video clip shared with a pair in the test set. This kept each test set unmodified but resulted in slightly smaller training sets. After removing such pairs, the two video clips from each pair were temporally concatenated in the same order as presented to human subjects to yield the training and test samples for the computer-vision action-recognition experiments. The results are presented in Table 1 and

Figs. 4 and 5. Note that all the computer-vision action-recognition systems that we tested on yield similar accuracy to the cross-subject fMRI experiments and *much* lower accuracy than the corresponding within-subject fMRI experiments.

7   Discussion

Figure 4 illustrates some interesting issues. It shows that Action Bank [24] has lower median accuracy and a higher variance profile that extends to much lower accuracy than C2 [12] and Stacked ISA [16] which predate it. It shows that Cao's implementation [2] of Ryoo's method [23] and Cao's method [2] have lower median accuracy and a much lower span of accuracies than C2 [12], Action Bank [24], and Stacked ISA [16] which predate them. It shows that Cao's method [2] has higher variance than Cao's implementation [2] of Ryoo's method [23] which predates it. Thus generally, the newer methods perform worse than the older ones; it shows that the field is basically not progressing.

Figure 5 gives some indication as to why. It shows that all the computer-vision methods tested confuse *carry* and *walk* much more than fMRI, which could be explained if these methods detected these action classes solely by detecting horizontal motion. It shows that all the computer-vision methods tested confuse *dig* and *hold*, which could be explained if these methods detected these action classes solely by detecting the lack of horizontal motion. It shows that all the computer-vision methods tested confuse *pick up* and *put down*, which could be explained if these methods detected these action classes solely by detecting vertical motion, without detecting the object being picked up or put down and without accounting for the temporal ordering of the motion. It also suggests that the semantics of human perception may play a role in action recognition, which the statistical classifiers cannot pick up. This is all to be expected when one considers that, generally, most current computer-vision methods employ techniques that look solely at local image features at very short spatial and/or temporal scales. Even Action Bank ultimately relies on local image gradients to define its templates. And none of the methods, even Dense Trajectories which can incorporate a person detector, detect the objects being interacted with as part of the action class. In other words, they don't detect the object being *carried*, the shovel used to *dig*, the hole in the ground that is *dug*, or the objects being *held*, *picked up*, or *put down*. Moreover, they don't model the time course of the changing human pose and relative position and orientation of the person and the object interacted with. These are the semantic characteristics of the action class. Thus it shows that none of these methods are, in fact, doing action recognition.

While cross-subject fMRI yields lower accuracy than within-subject fMRI, accuracy that is on par with the computer-vision methods, the confusion matrices indicate that the source of the error in the cross-subject fMRI is different than that in the computer-vision methods. There is less *pick up:put down* confusion, far less *dig:hold* confusion, and somewhat more *carry:walk* confusion. This indicates that even cross subject, the fMRI results appear to be using a degree of semantic inference that is absent in the computer-vision methods and the reduced accuracy of cross-subject fMRI is due more to issues of registration than to anything fundamental about the classification process.

8 Conclusion

Despite the explosive growth of interest in action recognition over the past three years and the perfect or near-perfect classification accuracies reported on datasets with small numbers of action classes, we show that the problem remains difficult. Uniformly, the newer methods we tried performed *no better* than or even *worse* than the older methods on this new dataset. One potential explanation is that the field as a whole is collectively overfitting to the datasets, i.e. having individual researchers repeatedly hone their methods to a small number of datasets and having the community collectively perform hill climbing on these datasets is tantamount to training on the test data. We advocate ameliorating this problem by testing methods on *read-once data*, data that has never been processed by the method. We practice what we preach by demonstrating our methods with data gathered *live* on stage during our presentations. Our ability to perform action recognition by reading minds is sufficiently robust to allow us to do something that computer-vision researchers rarely, if ever, do and neuroscientists never do, namely live demos as part of conference presentations. In the past, we have filmed live video during a talk, sent it via wireless internet to a remote imaging center, presented such video as stimuli to a subject waiting in a scanner, scanned them while watching said video, classified the brain scans, and sent the classification results back via wireless internet for live presentation. Moreover, all of the computer-vision methods we tested performed *far* worse than basic machine-learning methods applied to brain-scan data, which is surprising. We classify brain-scan data using SVMs; most computer-vision methods for action recognition do so as well. In essence, what we have done is replace the feature-extraction component with a brain-fMRI combination. This suggests that the computer-vision community may benefit by looking at neuroscience to motivate the development of better feature extraction.

Acknowledgments AB, DPB, NS, and JMS were supported, in part, by Army Research Laboratory (ARL) Cooperative Agreement W911NF-10-2-0060, AB, in part, by the Center for Brains, Minds and Machines (CBMM), funded by NSF STC award CCF-1231216, WC, CX, and JJC, in part, by ARL Cooperative Agreement W911NF-10-2-0062 and NSF CAREER grant IIS-0845282, CDF, in part, by NSF grant CNS-0855157, CH and SJH, in part, by the McDonnell Foundation, and BAP, in part, by Science Foundation Ireland grant 09/IN.1/I2637. The views and conclusions contained in this document are those of the authors and should not be interpreted as representing the official policies, either express or implied, of the supporting institutions. The U.S. Government is authorized to reproduce and distribute reprints for Government purposes, notwithstanding any copyright notation herein. Dr. Gregory G. Tamer, Jr. provided assistance with imaging and analysis.

References

1. Blank, M., Gorelick, L., Shechtman, E., Irani, M., Basri, R.: Actions as space-time shapes. In: International Conference on Computer Vision, vol. 2, pp. 1395–1402 (2005)
2. Cao, Y., Barrett, D., Barbu, A., Narayanaswamy, S., Yu, H., Michaux, A., Lin, Y., Dickinson, S., Siskind, J.M., Wang, S.: Recognizing human activities from partially observed videos. In: Computer Vision and Pattern Recognition, pp. 2658–2665 (2013)
3. Connolly, A.C., Guntupalli, J.S., Gors, J., Hanke, M., Halchenko, Y.O., Wu, Y.C., Abdi, H., Haxby, J.V.: The representation of biological classes in the human brain. The Journal of Neuroscience 32(8), 2608–2618 (2012)
4. Cortes, C., Vapnik, V.: Support-vector networks. Machine Learning 20(3), 273–297 (1995)
5. Cox, R.W.: AFNI: software for analysis and visualization of functional magnetic resonance neuroimages. Computers and Biomedical Research 29(3), 162–173 (1996)
6. Everingham, M., Van Gool, L., Williams, C.K.I., Winn, J., Zisserman, A.: The PASCAL visual object classes (VOC) challenge. International Journal of Computer Vision 88(2), 303–338 (2010)
7. Fellbaum, C.: WordNet: an electronic lexical database. MIT Press, Cambridge (1998)
8. Gu, Q., Li, Z., Han, J.: Linear discriminant dimensionality reduction. In: Gunopulos, D., Hofmann, T., Malerba, D., Vazirgiannis, M. (eds.) ECML PKDD 2011, Part I. LNCS, vol. 6911, pp. 549–564. Springer, Heidelberg (2011)
9. Hanson, S.J., Halchenko, Y.O.: Brain reading using full brain support vector machines for object recognition: there is no "face" identification area. Neural Computation 20(2), 486–503 (2009)
10. Haxby, J.V., Guntupalli, J.S., Connolly, A.C., Halchenko, Y.O., Conroy, B.R., Gobbini, M.I., Hanke, M., Ramadge, P.J.: A common, high-dimensional model of the representational space in human ventral temporal cortex. Neuron 72(2), 404–416 (2011)
11. Huettel, S.A., Song, A.W., McCarthy, G.: Functional magnetic resonance imaging. Sinauer Associates, Sunderland (2004)
12. Jhuang, H., Serre, T., Wolf, L., Poggio, T.: A biologically inspired system for action recognition. In: International Conference on Computer Vision, pp. 1–8 (2007)
13. Just, M.A., Cherkassky, V.L., Aryal, S., Mitchell, T.M.: A neurosemantic theory of concrete noun representation based on the underlying brain codes. PloS One 5(1), e8622 (2010)
14. Kuehne, H., Jhuang, H., Garrote, E., Poggio, T., Serre, T.: HMDB: a large video database for human motion recognition. In: International Conference on Computer Vision, pp. 2556–2563 (2011)
15. Laptev, I.: On space-time interest points. International Journal of Computer Vision 64(2-3), 107–123 (2005)
16. Le, Q.V., Zou, W.Y., Yeung, S.Y., Ng, A.Y.: Learning hierarchical invariant spatiotemporal features for action recognition with independent subspace analysis. In: Computer Vision and Pattern Recognition, pp. 3361–3368 (2011)
17. Liu, H., Feris, R., Sun, M.T.: Benchmarking datasets for human activity recognition, ch. 20, pp. 411–427. Springer (2011)
18. Messing, R., Pal, C., Kautz, H.: Activity recognition using the velocity histories of tracked keypoints. In: International Conference on Computer Vision, pp. 104–111 (2009)

19. Miller, G.A.: WordNet: a lexical database for English. Communications of the ACM 38(11), 39–41 (1995)
20. Pereira, F., Botvinick, M., Detre, G.: Using Wikipedia to learn semantic feature representations of concrete concepts in neuroimaging experiments. Artificial Intelligence 194, 240–252 (2012)
21. Poldrack, R.A., Halchenko, Y.O., Hanson, S.J.: Decoding the large-scale structure of brain function by classifying mental states across individuals. Psychological Science 20(11), 1364–1372 (2009)
22. Reddy, K.K., Shah, M.: Recognizing 50 human action categories of web videos. Machine Vision and Applications 24(5), 971–981 (2013)
23. Ryoo, M.S.: Human activity prediction: early recognition of ongoing activities from streaming videos. In: International Conference on Computer Vision, pp. 1036–1043 (2011)
24. Sadanand, S., Corso, J.J.: Action Bank: A high-level representation of activity in video. In: Computer Vision and Pattern Recognition, pp. 1234–1241 (2012)
25. Schuldt, C., Laptev, I., Caputo, B.: Recognizing human actions: a local SVM approach. In: International Conference on Pattern Recognition, vol. 3, pp. 32–36 (2004)
26. Soomro, K., Zamir, A.R., Shah, M.: UCF101: a dataset of 101 human actions classes from videos in the wild. Computing Research Repository abs/1212.0402 (2012)
27. Wang, H., Kläser, A., Schmid, C., Liu, C.L.: Action recognition by dense trajectories. In: Computer Vision and Pattern Recognition, pp. 3169–3176 (2011)
28. Wang, H., Kläser, A., Schmid, C., Liu, C.L.: Dense trajectories and motion boundary descriptors for action recognition. International Journal of Computer Vision 103(1), 60–79 (2013)
29. Wang, H., Schmid, C.: Action recognition with improved trajectories. In: International Conference on Computer Vision, pp. 3551–3558 (2013)

Weakly Supervised Action Labeling in Videos under Ordering Constraints

Piotr Bojanowski[1,*], Rémi Lajugie[1,**], Francis Bach[1,**], Ivan Laptev[1,*],
Jean Ponce[2,*], Cordelia Schmid[1,***], and Josef Sivic[1,*]

[1] INRIA, France
[2] École Normale Supérieure, France

Abstract. We are given a set of video clips, each one annotated with
an *ordered* list of actions, such as "walk" then "sit" then "answer phone"
extracted from, for example, the associated text script. We seek to temporally localize the individual actions in each clip as well as to learn a
discriminative classifier for each action. We formulate the problem as a
weakly supervised temporal assignment with ordering constraints. Each
video clip is divided into small time intervals and each time interval of
each video clip is assigned one action label, while respecting the order in
which the action labels appear in the given annotations. We show that
the action label assignment can be determined together with learning
a classifier for each action in a discriminative manner. We evaluate the
proposed model on a new and challenging dataset of 937 video clips with
a total of 787720 frames containing sequences of 16 different actions from
69 Hollywood movies.

1 Introduction

Significant progress towards action recognition in realistic video settings has
been achieved in the past few years [22,24,26,30,35]. However action recognition
is often cast as a classification or detection problem using fully annotated data,
where the temporal boundaries of individual actions, e.g. in the form of pre-
segmented video clips, are given during training. The goal of this paper is to
exploit the supervisory power of the temporal ordering of actions in a video
stream, as illustrated in figure 1.

Gathering fully annotated videos with accurately time-stamped action labels
is quite time consuming in practice. This limits the utility of fully supervised
machine learning techniques on large-scale data. Using data redundancy, weakly
and semi-supervised methods are a promising alternative in this case. On the
other hand, it is easy to gather videos with some level of textual annotation but
poor temporal localization, from movie scripts for example. This type of weak
supervisory signal has been used before in classification [22] and temporal localization [7] tasks. However, the crucial information on the ordering of actions

* WILLOW project-team, DI/ENS, ENS/INRIA/CNRS UMR 8548, Paris, France.
** SIERRA project-team, DI/ENS, ENS/INRIA/CNRS UMR 8548, Paris, France.
*** LEAR team, INRIA Grenoble Rhône-Alpes, France.

D. Fleet et al. (Eds.): ECCV 2014, Part V, LNCS 8693, pp. 628–643, 2014.
© Springer International Publishing Switzerland 2014

open door ⟶ stand up ⟶ shake hand

stand up ⟶ shake hand ⟶ open door

Fig. 1. Examples of video clips with associated actions sequence annotations such as provided in our dataset. Both examples contain the same set of actions but occurring in a different order. In this work we use the type and order of events as a supervisory signal to learn a classifier of each action and temporally localize each action in the video.

has, to the best of our knowledge, been ignored so far in the weakly supervised setting. Following recent work on discriminative clustering [3,37], image [18] and video [5] cosegmentation, we propose to exploit this information in a discriminative framework where both the action model and the optimal assignments under temporal constraints are learned together.

1.1 Related Work

The temporal ordering of actions, e.g. in the form of Markov models or action grammars, have been used to constrain action prediction in videos [13,15,21,23,29,34]. These kinds of spatial and temporal constraints have been also used in the context of group activity recognition [2,20]. Similar to us, these papers exploit the temporal structure of videos, but focus on inferring action sequences from noisy but pre-defined action detectors, often in constrained surveillance and laboratory settings with a limited number of actions and static cameras. In contrast, in this work we explore the temporal structure of actions for learning action classifiers in a weakly supervised set-up and show results on challenging videos from feature length movies.

Related is also work on recognition of **composite activities** [28], where atomic action models ("cut", "open") are learned given full supervision on a cooking video dataset. Composite activity models ("prepare pizza") are learned on top of the atomic actions, using the prediction scores for the atomic actions as features. Annotations are, however, used without taking into account the ordering of actions.

Temporal models for recognition **of individual actions** have been explored in e.g. [22,26,33]. Implicit models in the form of temporal pyramids have been used with bag-of-features representations [22]. Others have used more explicit temporal models in the form of, e.g. latent action parts [26] or hidden Markov models [33]. Contrary to these methods, we do not use an a priori model of the temporal structure of individual actions, but instead exploit the given ordering constraints between actions to learn better individual actions models.

Weak supervision for learning actions has been explored in [5,7,22]. These methods use uncertain temporal annotations of actions provided by movie scripts. Contrary to these works our method learns multiple actions simultaneously and incorporates temporal ordering constraints on action labels obtained, e.g. from the movie scripts.

Dynamic time warping algorithms (DTW) can be used to match temporal sequences, and are extensively used in speech recognition, e.g. [9,27]. In computer vision, the temporal order of events has been exploited in [25], where a DTW-like algorithm is used at test time to improve the performance of non-maximum suppression on the output of pre-trained action detectors.

Discriminative clustering is an unsupervised method that partitions data by minimizing a discriminative objective, optimizing over both classifiers and labels [3,37]. Convex formulations of discriminative clustering have been explored in [3,10]. In computer vision these methods have been successfully applied to co-segmentation [19]. The approach presented in this paper is inspired by this framework, but adds to it the use of ordering constraints.

In this work, we make use of the **Frank-Wolfe algorithm** (a.k.a conditional gradient) to minimize our cost function. The Frank-Wolfe algorithm [8,17] is a classical convex optimization procedure that permits optimizing a continuously differentiable convex function over a convex compact domain only by optimizing linear functions over the domain. In particular, it does not require any projection steps. It has recently received increased attention in the context of large-scale optimization [11,17].

1.2   Problem Statement and Contributions

The temporal assignment problem addressed in the rest of this paper and illustrated by Fig. 1 can be stated as follows: We are given a set of N video clips (or clips for short in what follows). A clip is defined as a contiguous video segment consisting of F frames, and may correspond, for example, to a scene (as defined in a movie script) or a collection of subsequent shots. Each clip is divided into T small *time intervals* (chunks of videos consisting of $F/T = 10$ frames in our case), and annotated by an ordered list of K elements taken from some action set $\mathcal{A}$ of size $A = |\mathcal{A}|$ (that may consist of labels such as "open door", "stand up", "answer phone", etc., as in Fig. 1 for example). Note that clips are not of the same length but for the sake of simplicity, we assume they are. We address the problem of assigning to each time interval of each clip one action in $\mathcal{A}$, respecting the order in which the actions appear in the original annotation list (Fig. 2).

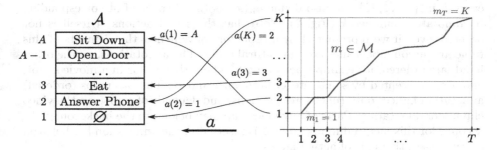

Fig. 2. Right: The goal is to find assignment of video intervals 1 to T (x-axis) to the ordered list of action annotations $a(1)$ to $a(K)$ indexed by integer k from 1 to K (y-axis). Left: The ordered annotation index k is mapped, through mapping a to action labels from the set $\mathcal{A}$, in that example $a(3) =$"Eat". To preserve the given ordering of annotations we only consider assignments $\mathcal{M}$ that are non-decreasing. One such assignment m is shown in red.

Contributions. We make the following contributions: **(i)** we propose a discriminative clustering model (section 2) that handles weak supervision in the form of temporal ordering constraints and recovers a classifier for each action together with the temporal localization of each action in each video clip; **(ii)** we design a convex relaxation of the proposed model and show it can be efficiently solved using the conditional gradient (Frank-Wolfe) algorithm (section 3); and finally **(iii)** we demonstrate improved performance of our model on a new action dataset for the tasks of temporal localization (section 6) and action classification (section 7). All the data and code are publicly available at http://www.di.ens.fr/willow/research/ordering.

2   Discriminative Clustering with Ordering Constraints

In this section we describe the proposed discriminative clustering model that incorporates label ordering constraints. The input is a set of video clips, each annotated with an ordered list of action labels specifying the sequence of actions present in the clip. The output is the temporal assignment of actions to individual time intervals in each clip respecting the ordering constraint provided by the annotations together with a learnt classifier for each action, common for all clips. In the following, we first formulate the temporal assignment of actions to individual frames as discriminative clustering (section 2.1), then introduce a parametrization of temporal assignments using indicator variables (section 2.2), and finally we describe the choice of a loss function for the discriminative clustering that leads to a convex cost (section 2.3).

2.1   Problem Formulation

Let us now formalize the temporal assignment problem. We denote by $x_n(t)$ in $\mathbb{R}^d$ some local descriptor of video clip number n during time interval number t. For every k in $\{1, \ldots, K\}$, we also define $a_n(k)$ as the element of $\mathcal{A}$ corresponding to annotation number k (Fig. 2). Note that the set of actions $\mathcal{A}$ itself is not ordered: even if we represent $\mathcal{A}$ by a table for convenience, the elements of this table are action labels and have no natural order. The annotations, on the other hand, are ordered, for example according to where they occur in a movie script, and are represented by some integer between 1 and K. Thus a_n maps (ordered) annotation indices onto (unordered) actions, and depends of course on the video clip under annotation. Parts of any video clip may belong to the background. To account for this fact, a dummy label $\varnothing$ is inserted in the annotation list between every consecutive pair of actual labels.

Let us denote by $\mathcal{M}$ the set of *admissible assignments* on $\{1, \ldots, T\}$, that is, the set of sequences $m = (m_1, \ldots, m_T)$ with elements in $\{1, \ldots, K\}$ such that $m_1 = 1$, $m_T = K$, and $m_{t+1} = m_t$ or $m_{t+1} = m_t + 1$ for all t in $\{1, \ldots, T-1\}$ Such an assignment is illustrated in Fig. 2.

Let us also denote by $\mathcal{F}$ the space of classifiers of interest, by $\Omega : \mathcal{F} \to \mathbb{R}$ some regularizer on this space and by $\ell : \mathcal{A} \times \mathbb{R}^A \to \mathbb{R}_+$ an appropriate loss function. For a given clip n and a fixed classifier f, the problem of assigning the clip intervals to the annotation sequence can be written as the minimization of the cost function:

$$E(m, f, n) = \frac{1}{T} \sum_{t=1}^{T} \ell\left(a_n(m_t), f(x_n(t))\right) \tag{1}$$

with respect to assignment m in $\mathcal{M}$. The regularizer Ω prevents overfitting and we therefore define a scalar parameter λ to control this effect. Jointly learning the classifiers and solving the assignment problem corresponds to the following optimization problem:

$$\min_{f \in \mathcal{F}} \left[\sum_{n=1}^{N} \min_{m \in \mathcal{M}} E(m, f, n) \right] + \lambda \Omega(f). \tag{2}$$

2.2   Parameterization Using an Assignment Matrix

As will be shown in the following sections, it is convenient to reformulate our problem in terms of indicator variables. The corresponding multi-class loss is $\ell : \{0, 1\}^A \times \mathbb{R}^A \to \mathbb{R}_+$, and the classifiers are functions $f : \mathbb{R}^d \to \mathbb{R}^A$. For a clip n, let us define the *assignment matrix* $Z^n \in \mathbb{R}^{T \times A}$ which is composed of entries z_{ta}^n such that $z_{ta}^n = 1$ if the interval t of clip n is assigned to class a.

Let Z_t^n denote the row vector of dimension A corresponding to the t-th row of Z^n. The cost function $E(m, f, n)$, defined in Eq. (1) can be rewritten as $\frac{1}{T} \sum_{t=1}^{T} \ell(Z_t^n, f(x_n(t)))$.

Note: To avoid cumbersome double summations, we suppose from now that we work with a single clip. This allows us to drop the superscript notation, we replace Z^n by Z and skip the sum over clips. We also replace the descriptor notation $x_n(t)$ by x_t and the row extraction notation Z_t^n by Z_t. This is without

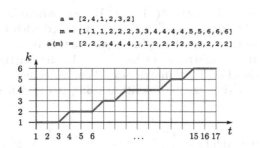
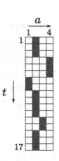

Fig. 3. Illustration of the correspondence between temporal assignments (left) and associated valid assignment matrices that map action labels a to time intervals t (right). **Left**: a valid assignment non-decreasing $m_t = k$. **Right**: the corresponding assignment matrix Z. One can build the assignment matrix Z given the assignment m and the annotation sequence a by putting a 1 at index $(t, a(m_t))$ in Z for every t. One obtains m given Z by iteratively constructing a sequence of integers of length T such that $m_{t+1} = m_t$ if the t-th and $(t+1)$-th row of Z are identical, and $m_{t+1} = m_t + 1$ otherwise.

loss of generality, and our method as described in the sequel handles multiple clips with some simple bookkeeping.

Because of temporal constraints, we want the assignment matrices Z to correspond to valid assignments m. This amounts to imposing some constraints on Z. Let us therefore define $\mathcal{Z}$, the set of all valid assignment matrices as:

$$\mathcal{Z} = \left\{ Z \in \{0,1\}^{T \times A} \mid \exists\, m \in \mathcal{M}, \text{ s.t., } \forall\, t,\ Z_{ta} = 1 \iff a(m_t) = a \right\}. \quad (3)$$

There is a bijection between the sets $\mathcal{Z}$ and $\mathcal{M}$. For each m in $\mathcal{M}$ there exists a unique corresponding Z in $\mathcal{Z}$ and *vice versa*. Figure 3 gives an intuitive illustration of this bijection.

The set $\mathcal{Z}$ is a subset of the set of stochastic matrices (positive matrices whose rows sum up to 1), formed by the matrices whose columns consist of exactly K blocks of contiguous ones occurring in a predefined order ($K = 6$ in Fig. 3). There are as many elements in $\mathcal{Z}$ as ways of choosing $(K - 1)$ transitions among $(T - 1)$ possibilities, thus $|\mathcal{Z}| = \binom{T-1}{K-1}$, which can be extremely large in our setting (in our setting $T \approx 100$ and $K \approx 10$). Furthermore, it is very difficult to describe explicitly the algebraic constraints on stochastic matrices that define $\mathcal{Z}$. This point will prove important in Sec. 3 when we propose an optimization algorithm for learning our model. Using these notations, Eq. (2) is equivalent to:

$$\min_{f \in \mathcal{F}, Z \in \mathcal{Z}} \frac{1}{T} \sum_{t=1}^{T} \ell\left(Z_t, f(x_t)\right) + \lambda \Omega(f). \quad (4)$$

2.3 Quadratic Cost Functions

We now choose specific functions ℓ and f that will lead to a quadratic cost function. This choice leads, to a convex relaxation of our problem. We use multi-class linear classifiers of the form $f(x) = x^T W + b$, where $W \in \mathbb{R}^{d \times A}$ and $b \in \mathbb{R}^{1 \times A}$. We choose the square loss function, regularized with the Frobenius norm of W, because in that case the optimal parameters W and b can be computed in closed form through matrix inversion. Let X be the matrix in $\mathbb{R}^{T \times d}$ formed by the concatenation of all $1 \times d$ matrices x_t. For this choice of loss and regularizer, our objective function can be rewritten using the matrices defined above as:

$$\frac{1}{T} \sum_{t=1}^{T} \ell(Z_t, f(x_t)) + \lambda \Omega(f) = \frac{1}{T} \|Z - XW - b\|_F^2 + \frac{\lambda}{2} \|W\|_F^2. \tag{5}$$

This is exactly a ridge regression cost. Minimizing this cost with respect to W and b for fixed Z can be done in closed form [3,12]. Setting the partial derivatives with respect to W and b to zero and plugging the solution back yields the following equivalent problem:

$$\min_{Z \in \mathcal{Z}} \operatorname{Tr}\left(ZZ^T B\right), \text{ where } B = \frac{1}{T} \Pi_T (I_T - X \left(X^T \Pi_T X + T\lambda I_d\right)^{-1} X^T)\Pi_T, \tag{6}$$

and the matrix Π_p is the $p \times p$ centering matrix $I_p - \frac{1}{p}\mathbf{1}_p\mathbf{1}_p^T$. This corresponds to implicitly learning the classifier while finding the optimal Z by solving a quadratic optimisation problem in Z. The implicit classifier parameters W and b are shared among all video clips and can be recovered in closed-form as:

$$W = (X^T \Pi_d X + \lambda I)^{-1} X^T \Pi_T Z D^{1/2}, \qquad b = \frac{1}{T}\mathbf{1}^T(Z - Xw)D^{1/2}. \tag{7}$$

3   Convex Relaxation and the Frank-Wolfe Algorithm

In Sec. 2, we have seen that our model can be interpreted as the minimization of a convex quadratic function (B is positive semidefinite) over a very large but discrete domain. As is usual for this type of hard combinatorial optimization problem, we replace the discrete set $\mathcal{Z}$ by its convex hull $\overline{\mathcal{Z}}$. This allows us to find a continuous solution of the relaxed problem using an appropriate and efficient algorithm for convex optimization.

3.1   The Frank-Wolfe Algorithm

We want to carry out the minimization of a convex function over a complex polytope $\overline{\mathcal{Z}}$, defined as the convex hull of a large but finite set of integer points defined by the constraints associated with admissible assignments. When it is possible to optimize a linear function over a constraint set of this kind, but other usual operations (like projections) are not tractable, a good way to optimize a convex objective function is to use the iterative Frank-Wolfe algorithm (a.k.a. conditional gradient method) [4,8]. We show in Sec. 3.2 that we can minimize linear functions over $\overline{\mathcal{Z}}$, so this is an appropriate choice in our case.

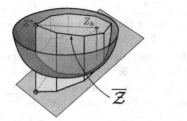 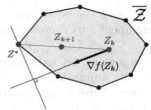

Fig. 4. Illustration of a Frank-Wolfe step (see [17] for more details). **Left**: the domain $\overline{\mathcal{Z}}$ interest, objective function (red), and its linearization at current point (blue). **Right**: top view of $\overline{\mathcal{Z}}$. Note that, in the algorithm, we actually minimize a linear function at each step. Adding a constant to it does not affect the solution of the minimization problem. That is why, we depicted an hyperplane that seems shifted from the origin.

The idea behind the Frank-Wolfe algorithm is rather simple. An affine approximation of the objective function is minimized yielding a point Z^* on the edge of $\overline{\mathcal{Z}}$. Then a convex combination of Z^* and the current point Z_t is computed. This is repeated until convergence (see Alg. 1). The interpolation parameter γ can be chosen either by using the universal step size $\frac{2}{p+1}$, where p is the iteration counter (see [17] and references therein) or, in the case of quadratic functions, by solving a univariate quadratic equation. In our implementation, we use the latter. A good feature of the Frank-Wolfe algorithm is that it provides a duality gap (referred to as the linearization duality gap [17]) that can be used as a certificate of sub-optimality and stopping criterion. The procedure is described in the special case of our relaxed problem in Algorithm 1. Figure 4 illustrates one step of the optimization.

3.2   Minimizing Linear Functions over $\overline{\mathcal{Z}}$ by Dynamic Programming

It is possible to minimize linear functions over the binary set $\mathcal{Z}$. Simple arguments (see for instance Prop B.21 of [4]) show that the solution over $\mathcal{Z}$ is also a solution over $\overline{\mathcal{Z}}$. We will therefore focus on the minimization problem on $\mathcal{Z}$ and keep in mind that it also gives a solution over $\overline{\mathcal{Z}}$ as required by the Frank-Wolfe algorithm. Minimizing a linear function on $\mathcal{Z}$ amounts to solving

---

$k \leftarrow 0$
while $\mathrm{Tr}(\nabla_f(Z_k)(Z_k - Z^*)) \geq \epsilon$ **do**
    Compute the current gradient in Z, $\nabla_f(Z_k) = Z_k^T B$.
    Choose Z^* in $\arg\min_{Z \in \overline{\mathcal{Z}}} \mathrm{Tr}(Z\nabla_f(Z_k))$ using dynamic programming.
    Compute the optimal Frank-Wolfe step size γ.
    $Z_{k+1} = Z_k + \gamma(Z^* - Z_k)$
    $k \leftarrow k + 1$.
end

Algorithm 1: The Frank-Wolfe optimization procedure

the problem: $\min_{Z \in \mathcal{Z}} \mathrm{Tr}\left(C^T Z\right) = \sum_{t=1}^{T} \sum_{a=1}^{A} Z_{ta} C_{ta}$, where C is a cost matrix in $\mathbb{R}^{T \times A}$. Using the equivalence between the assignment matrix (Z) and the plain assignment (m) representations (Fig. 3), this is equivalent to solving $\min_{m \in \mathcal{M}} \sum_{t=1}^{T} \sum_{a=1}^{A} \mathbb{1}_{a(m_t)=a} C_{ta}$. To better deal with the temporal structure of the assignment, let us denote by $D \in \mathbb{R}^{T \times K}$ the matrix with entries $D_{tk} = C_{ta(k)}$. The minimization problem then becomes $\min_{m \in \mathcal{M}} \sum_{t=1}^{T} D_{tm_t}$, which can be solved using dynamic time warping. Indeed, let us define for all $t \in \{1, \ldots, T\}$ and $k \in \{1, \ldots, K\}$: $P_t^*(k) = \min_{m \in \mathcal{M}} \sum_{s=1}^{t} D_{sm_s}$. We can think of $P_t^*(k)$ as the cost of the optimal path from $(1,1)$ to (t,k) in the graph defined by admissible assignments, and we have the following dynamic programming recursion: $P_t^*(k) = D_{tk} + \min(P_{t-1}^*(k-1), P_{t-1}^*(k))$.

The optimal value $P_T^*(K)$ can be computed in $O(TK)$ using dynamic programming, by precomputing the matrix D, incrementally computing the corresponding $P_t^*(k)$ values, and maintaining at each node (t,k) back pointers to the appropriate neighbors.

3.3 Rounding

At convergence, the Frank-Wolfe algorithm finds the (non-integer) global optimum $\hat{Z}$ of Eq. (6) over $\overline{\mathcal{Z}}$. Given $\hat{Z}$, we want to find an appropriate nearby point Z in $\mathcal{Z}$. The simplest geometric rounding scheme consists in finding the closest point of $\mathcal{Z}$ according to the Frobenius distance : $\min_{Z \in \mathcal{Z}} \|\hat{Z} - Z\|_F^2$. Expanding the norm yields: $\|\hat{Z} - Z\|_F^2 = \mathrm{Tr}(\hat{Z}^T \hat{Z}) + \mathrm{Tr}(Z^T Z) - 2\mathrm{Tr}(\hat{Z}^T Z)$.

Since $\hat{Z}$ is fixed, its norm is a constant. Moreover, since Z is an element of $\mathcal{Z}$, its squared norm is constant and equal to T. The rounding problem is therefore equivalent to: $\min_{Z \in \mathcal{Z}} -2\mathrm{Tr}(\hat{Z}^T Z)$, that is to the minimization of a linear function over $\overline{\mathcal{Z}}$. This can be done, as in Sec. 3.2, using dynamic programming.

4   Practical Concerns

In this section, we detail some refinements of our model. First, we show how to tackle a semi-supervised setting where some time-stamped annotations are available. Second, we discuss how to avoid the trivial solutions, a common issue in discriminative clustering methods [3,10,18].

4.1   Semi-supervised Setting

Let us suppose that we are given some fully annotated clips (in the sense that they are labeled with time-stamped annotations), corresponding to a total of L time intervals. For every interval l we have a descriptor X_l in $\mathbb{R}^d$ and a class label a_l in $\mathcal{A}$. We can incorporate this data by modifying the optimization problem as follows:

$$\min_{f \in \mathcal{F}} \left[\min_{m \in \mathcal{M}} E(m, f, n) \right] + \frac{1}{L} \sum_{l=1}^{L} \ell(a_l, f(X_l)) + \lambda \Omega(f). \tag{8}$$

The first term is the weakly supervised assignment cost and the second one is the loss on annotated data. This supervised model does not change the optimization procedure, which remains valid.

4.2   Minimum Size Constraints

There are two inherent problems with discriminative clustering. First, the constant assignment matrix is typically a trivial optimum because, as explained in [10], the optimization domain is symmetruc over the permutations of labels. Thanks to our temporal constraints, the set $\mathcal{Z}$ is not symmetric and thus we are not subject to this effect. The second difficulty is linked to the use of the centering matrix Π_T in Eq. (6). Indeed, we notice that the constant vector of length T is an eigen vector of Π_T and thus the column-wise constant matrices are trivial solutions to our problem. Due to the temporal ordering constraints these solutions are not admissible, but in practice we have noticed that the algorithm returned an assignment with the label $\varnothing$ being dominant. We cope with these issues by adding a class penalizing linear term and by weighting the different classes. We refer the reader to [6] for more details.

5   Dataset and Features

Dataset. Our input data consists of challenging video clips annotated with sequences of actions. One possible source for such data is movies with their associated scripts [5,7,22,32]. The annotations provided by this kind of data are noisy and do not provide ground-truth time-stamps for evaluation. To address this issue, we have constructed a new action dataset, containing clips annotated by sequences of actions. We have taken the 69 movies from which the clips of the Hollywood2 dataset were extracted [22], and manually added full time-stamped annotation for 16 classes (12 of these classes are already present in Hollywood2). To build clips that form our input data, we search in the annotations for action chains containing at least two actions. To do so, we pad the temporal action annotations by 250 frames and search for overlapping intervals. A chain of such overlapping annotations forms one video clip with associated action sequence in our dataset. In the end we obtain 937 clips, with the number of actions ranging from 2 to 11. We subdivide each clip into temporal intervals of length 10 frames. Clips contain on average 84 intervals, the shortest containing 11, the longest 289.

Feature Representation. We have to define a feature vector for every interval of a clip. We build a bag-of-words vector x_t per interval t. Recall that intervals are of length 10 frames. To aggregate enough features, we decided to pool features from the 30-frame-long window centered on the interval. We compute video descriptors following [36]. We generate a vocabulary of size 2000 for HOF features. We restricted ourselves to one channel to improve the running time, while being aware that by doing so we sacrifice some performance. In our informal experiments, we also tried the MBH channels yielding very close performance. We use the Hellinger kernel to obtain the explicit feature map by square-rooting the l_1 normalized histograms. Every data point is associated with a vector x_t in $\mathbb{R}^{2000}$.

Fig. 5. Splitting of the data described in Sec. 6

6   Action Labeling Experiments

Experimental Setup. To carry out the action labeling experiments, we split 90% of the dataset into three parts (Fig. 5) that we denote *Sup* (for supervised), *Eval* (for evaluation) and *Val* (for validation). *Sup* is the part of data that has time-stamped annotations, and it is used only in the semi-supervised setting described in Sec. 4.1. *Val* is the set of examples on which we automatically adjust the hyper-parameters for our method (λ, κ, D). In practice we fix the *Val* set to contain 5% of the dataset. This set is provided with fully time-stamped annotations, but these are not used during the cost optimization. None of the reported results are computed on this set. We evaluate the quality of the assignment on the *Eval* set. Note that we carry out the Frank-Wolfe optimization on the union of all three sets. The annotations from the *Sup* set are used to constrain Z in the semi-supervised setup while those from the *Val* set are only used for choosing our hyper parameters. The supervisory information used over the rest of the data are the ordered annotations without time stamps. Please also keep in mind that there are no "training" and "testing" phases *per se* in this primary assignment task. All our experiments are conducted over five random splits of the data. This allows us to present results with error bars.

Performance Measure. Several measures may be used to evaluate the performance of discriminative clustering algorithms. Some authors propose to use the output classifier to perform a classification task [7,37] or use the output partition of the data as a solution of the segmentation task [18]. Yet another way to evaluate is to use a loss between partitions [14] as in [3]. Note that because of temporal constraints, for every clip we have a set of corresponding (prediction, ground-truth) pairs. We have thus chosen to measure the assignment quality for every ground-truth action interval I^* and prediction I as $|I \cap I^*|/|I|$. This measure is similar to the standard Jaccard measure used for comparing ensembles [16]. Therefore, with a slight abuse of notation, we refer to this measure as the Jaccard measure. This performance measure is well suited for our problem since it respects the following properties: **(1)** it is high if the action predicted is included in the ground-truth annotation, **(2)** it is low if the prediction is bigger than the annotation, **(3)** it is lowest if the prediction is out of the annotation, **(4)** it does not take into account the prediction of the background class. The score is averaged across all ground-truth intervals. The perfect score of 1 is achieved when all actions are aligned to the correct annotations, but accurate temporal segmentation is not required as long as the predicted labels are within the ground truth interval.

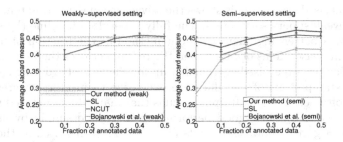

Fig. 6. Alignment evaluation for all considered models. **Left**: weakly-supervised methods. This graph is shown for various fractions of fully supervised data only to compare to the SL baseline. "Weak" methods do not make use of this supervision. **Right**: semi-supervised methods. See project webpage [1] for qualitative results.

Baselines. We compare our method to the three following baselines. All these are trained using the same features as the ones used for our method. For all baselines, we round the obtained solution Z using the scheme described in Sec. 3.3.
Normalized Cuts (NCUT). We compare our method to normalized cuts (or spectral clustering) [31]. Let us define B as the symmetric Laplacian of the matrix E: $B = I - D^{-\frac{1}{2}} E D^{-\frac{1}{2}}$, where $D = \text{Diag}(E1)$. E measures both the proximity and appearance similarity of intervals. For all (i, j) in $\{1, \ldots, T\}^2$, we compute: $E_{ij} = e^{-\alpha|i-j|-\beta d_{\chi^2}(X_i, X_j)} \mathbb{1}_{|i-j|<d_{\min}}$, where d_{χ^2} is the Chi-squared distance. More precisely, we minimize over all cuts Z the cost $g(Z) = \text{Tr}(ZZ^T B)$. g is convex (B is positive semidefinite) and we can use the Frank-Wolfe optimization scheme developed for our model. Intuitively, this baseline is searching for a partition of the video such that time intervals falling into the same segments have close-by features according to the Chi-squared distance.
Bojanowski et al. [5]. We also consider our own implementation of the weakly-supervised approach proposed in [5]. We replace our ordering constraints by the corresponding "at least one" constraints. When an action is mentioned in the sequence, we require it appears at least once in the clip. This corresponds to a set of linear constraints on Z. We adapt this technique in order to work on our dataset. Indeed, the available implementation requires storing a square matrix of the size of the problem. Instead, we choose to minimize the convex objective of [5] using the Frank-Wolfe algorithm which is more scalable.
Supervised Square Loss (SL). For completeness, we also compare our method to a fully supervised approach. We train a classifier using the square loss over the annotated *Sup* set and score all time intervals in *Eval*. We use the square loss since it is used in our method and all other baselines.

Weakly Supervised Setup. In this setup, all baselines except (SL) have only access to weak supervision in the form of ordering constraints. Figure 6 (left) illustrates the quality of the predicted asignmentss and compares our method to baselines. Our method performs better than all other weakly-supervised methods. Both the Bojanowski et al. and NCUT baselines have low scores in the weakly-supervised setting. This shows the advantage of exploiting temporal constraints as weak supervisory signal. The fully supervised baseline (blue) eventually recovers a better alignment than our method as the fraction of fully annotated data increases. This occurs (when the red line crosses the blue line) at the 25% mark, as the supervised data makes up for the lack of ordering constraints. Fully time-stamped annotated data are expensive to produce whereas movies scripts are often easy to get. It appears thus that manually annotated videos are not always necessary since good performance is reached simply by using weak supervision. Figure 7 shows the results for all weakly-supervised methods for all classes. We notice that we outperform the baselines on the most frequent classes (such as "Open Door", "Sit Down" and "Stand Up").

Semi-supervised Setup. Figure 6 (right) illustrates the performance of our model when some supervised data is available. The fraction of the supervised data is given on the x-axis. First, note that our semi-supervised method (red) is always and consistently (Cf error bars) above the square loss baseline (blue). Of course, during the optimization, our method has access to weak annotations over the whole dataset, and to full annotations on the *Sup* set whereas the SL baseline has access only to the latter. This demonstrates the benefits of exploiting temporal constraints during learning. The semi-supervised Bojanowski et al. baseline (orange) has low performance, but it improves with the amount of full supervision provided.

7   Classification Experiments

The experiments in the previous section evaluate the quality of the recovered assignment matrix Z. Here we evaluate instead the quality of the recovered classifiers on a held-out test set of data for an action classification task. We recover these classifiers as explained later in this section. We can treat them as K independent, one-versus-rest classifiers and use them to score the samples from the test set. We evaluate this performance by computing per-class precision and recall and report the corresponding average precision for each class.

Experimental Setup. The models are trained following the procedure described in the previous section. To test the performance of our classifiers, we

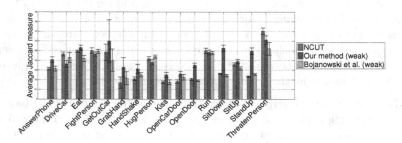

Fig. 7. Alignment performance for various weakly-supervised methods for all classes

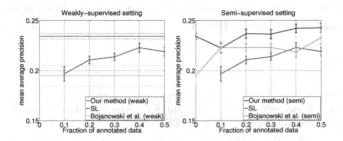

Fig. 8. Classification performance for various models. **Left**: weakly-supervised methods. **Right**: semi-supervised methods. See project webpage [1] for qualitative results.

use the held out set of clips. This set is made of 10% of the clips from the original data. The clips from this set are identical in nature to the ones used to train the models. We also perform multiple random splits to report results with error bars.

Recovering the Classifiers. One of the nice features of our method is that we can estimate the implicit classifiers corresponding to our solution Z^*. We do so using the expression from Eq. 7.

Baselines. We compare the classifiers obtained by our method to those obtained by the Bojanowski et al. baseline [5]. We also compare them to the classifiers learned using the (SL) baseline.

Weakly Supervised Setup. Classification results are presented in Fig. 8 (left). We observe a behavior similar to the action labeling experiment. But the supervised classifier (SL) trained on the *Sup* set using the square loss (blue) always performs worse than our model (red). This can be explained by the fact that the proposed model makes use of mode data. Even though our model has only access to weak annotation, it can prove sufficient to train good classifiers. The weakly-supervised method from Bojanowski et al. (orange) is performing worst, exactly as in the previous task. This can be explained by the fact that this method does not have access to full supervision or ordering constraints.

Semi-supervised Setup. In the semi-supervised setting (Fig. 8 (left)), our method (red) performs better than the supervised SL baseline (blue). The action model we recover is consistently better than the one obtained using only fully supervised data. Thus, our method is able to perform well semi-supervised learning. The Bojanowski et al. baseline (orange) improves when the fraction of annotated examples increases. Nonetheless, we see that making use of ordering constraints as used by our method signigicantly improves over simple linear inequalities ("at least one" constraints as formulated in [5]).

Acknowledgements. This work was supported by the European integrated project AXES, the MSR-INRIA laboratory, EIT-ICT labs, a Google Research

Award, a PhD fellowship from the EADS Foundation, the Institut Universitaire de France and ERC grants ALLEGRO, VideoWorld, Activia and Sierra.

References

1. http://www.di.ens.fr/willow/research/actionordering/
2. Amer, M.R., Todorovic, S., Fern, A., Zhu, S.C.: Monte carlo tree search for scheduling activity recognition. In: ICCV (2013)
3. Bach, F., Harchaoui, Z.: DIFFRAC: a discriminative and flexible framework for clustering. In: NIPS (2007)
4. Bertsekas, D.: Nonlinear Programming. Athena Scientific (1999)
5. Bojanowski, P., Bach, F., Laptev, I., Ponce, J., Schmid, C., Sivic, J.: Finding Actors and Actions in Movies. In: ICCV (2013)
6. Bojanowski, P., Lajugie, R., Bach, F., Laptev, I., Ponce, J., Schmid, C., Sivic, J.: Weakly Supervised Action Labeling in Videos Under Ordering Constraints. In: arXiv (2014)
7. Duchenne, O., Laptev, I., Sivic, J., Bach, F., Ponce, J.: Automatic annotation of human actions in video. In: ICCV (2009)
8. Frank, M., Wolfe, P.: An algorithm for quadratic programming. Naval Research Logistics Quarterly (1956)
9. Gold, B., Morgan, N., Ellis, D.: Speech and Audio Signal Processing - Processing and Perception of Speech and Music, Second Edition. Wiley (2011)
10. Guo, Y., Schuurmans, D.: Convex Relaxations of Latent Variable Training. In: NIPS (2007)
11. Harchaoui, Z.: Conditional gradient algorithms for machine learning. In: NIPS Workshop (2012)
12. Hastie, T., Tibshirani, R., Friedman, J.: The elements of statistical learning: data mining, inference and prediction. Springer (2009)
13. Hongeng, S., Nevatia, R.: Large-scale event detection using semi-hidden markov models. In: ICCV (2003)
14. Hubert, L., Arabie, P.: Comparing partitions. Journal of classification (1985)
15. Ivanov, Y.A., Bobick, A.F.: Recognition of visual activities and interactions by stochastic parsing. PAMI (2000)
16. Jaccard, P.: The distribution of the flora in the alpine zone. New Phytologist (1912)
17. Jaggi, M.: Revisiting Frank-Wolfe: Projection-free sparse convex optimization. In: ICML (2013)
18. Joulin, A., Bach, F., Ponce, J.: Discriminative Clustering for Image Co-segmentation. In: CVPR (2010)
19. Joulin, A., Bach, F., Ponce, J.: Multi-class cosegmentation. In: CVPR (2012)
20. Khamis, S., Morariu, V.I., Davis, L.S.: Combining per-frame and per-track cues for multi-person action recognition. In: Fitzgibbon, A., Lazebnik, S., Perona, P., Sato, Y., Schmid, C. (eds.) ECCV 2012, Part I. LNCS, vol. 7572, pp. 116–129. Springer, Heidelberg (2012)
21. Kwak, S., Han, B., Han, J.H.: Scenario-based video event recognition by constraint flow. In: CVPR (2011)
22. Laptev, I., Marszalek, M., Schmid, C., Rozenfeld, B.: Learning realistic human actions from movies. In: CVPR (2008)
23. Laxton, B., Lim, J., Kriegman, D.J.: Leveraging temporal, contextual and ordering constraints for recognizing complex activities in video. In: CVPR (2007)

24. Liu, J., Kuipers, B., Savarese, S.: Recognizing human actions by attributes. In: CVPR (2011)
25. Nguyen, M.H., Lan, Z.Z., la Torre, F.D.: Joint segmentation and classification of human actions in video. In: CVPR (2011)
26. Niebles, J.C., Chen, C.-W., Fei-Fei, L.: Modeling Temporal Structure of Decomposable Motion Segments for Activity Classification. In: Daniilidis, K., Maragos, P., Paragios, N. (eds.) ECCV 2010, Part II. LNCS, vol. 6312, pp. 392–405. Springer, Heidelberg (2010)
27. Rabiner, L.R., Juang, B.H.: Fundamentals of speech recognition. Prentice Hall (1993)
28. Rohrbach, M., Regneri, M., Andriluka, M., Amin, S., Pinkal, M., Schiele, B.: Script Data for Attribute-Based Recognition of Composite Activities. In: Fitzgibbon, A., Lazebnik, S., Perona, P., Sato, Y., Schmid, C. (eds.) ECCV 2012, Part I. LNCS, vol. 7572, pp. 144–157. Springer, Heidelberg (2012)
29. Ryoo, M.S., Aggarwal, J.K.: Recognition of composite human activities through context-free grammar based representation. In: CVPR (2006)
30. Sadanand, S., Corso, J.J.: Action bank: A high-level representation of activity in video. In: CVPR (2012)
31. Shi, J., Malik, J.: Normalized Cuts and Image Segmentation. In: CVPR (1997)
32. Sivic, J., Everingham, M., Zisserman, A.: "Who are you?" - Learning person specific classifiers from video. In: CVPR (2009)
33. Tang, K., Fei-Fei, L., Koller, D.: Learning latent temporal structure for complex event detection. In: CVPR (2012)
34. Vu, V.T., Bremond, F., Thonnat, M.: Automatic video interpretation: A novel algorithm for temporal scenario recognition. In: IJCAI (2003)
35. Wang, H., Kläser, A., Schmid, C., Liu, C.L.: Action recognition by dense trajectories. In: CVPR (2011)
36. Wang, H., Schmid, C.: Action Recognition with Improved Trajectories. In: ICCV (2013)
37. Xu, L., Neufeld, J., Larson, B., Schuurmans, D.: Maximum Margin Clustering. In: NIPS (2004)

Active Random Forests: An Application to Autonomous Unfolding of Clothes*

Andreas Doumanoglou[1,2], Tae-Kyun Kim[1],
Xiaowei Zhao[1], and Sotiris Malassiotis[2]

[1] Imperial College London, London, UK
[2] Center for Research and Technology Hellas (CERTH), Thessaloniki, Greece

Abstract. We present *Active Random Forests*, a novel framework to address active vision problems. State of the art focuses on best viewing parameters selection based on single view classifiers. We propose a multi-view classifier where the decision mechanism of optimally changing viewing parameters is inherent to the classification process. This has many advantages: a) the classifier exploits the entire set of captured images and does not simply aggregate probabilistically per view hypotheses; b) actions are based on learnt disambiguating features from all views and are optimally selected using the powerful voting scheme of Random Forests and c) the classifier can take into account the costs of actions. The proposed framework is applied to the task of autonomously unfolding clothes by a robot, addressing the problem of best viewpoint selection in classification, grasp point and pose estimation of garments. We show great performance improvement compared to state of the art methods.

Keywords: Active Vision, Active Random Forests, Deformable Object Recognition, Robotic Vision.

1 Introduction

Object recognition and pose estimation has been studied extensively in the literature achieving in many cases good results [15,24]. However, single-view recognition systems are often unable to distinguish objects which depict similar appearance when observed from certain viewpoints. An autonomous system can overcome this limitation by actively collecting relevant information about the object, that is, changing viewpoint, zooming to a particular area or even interacting with the object itself. This procedure is called *active vision* and the key problem is how to optimally plan the next actions of the system (usually a robot) in order to disambiguate any conflicting evidence about the object of interest.

The majority of state of the art techniques [7,13,12] in active vision share the following idea: one single-view classifier is trained to recognize the type and pose of target objects, whereas a subsequent step uses the inference probabilities to plan the next actions so that conflicting hypotheses are disambiguated. Although

---

* Electronic supplementary material - Supplementary material is available in the online version of this chapter at `http://dx.doi.org/10.1007/978-3-319-10602-1_42`. Videos can also be accessed at `http://www.springerimages.com/videos/978-3-319-10601-4`

D. Fleet et al. (Eds.): ECCV 2014, Part V, LNCS 8693, pp. 644–658, 2014.

| (a) | (b) | (c) | (d) |

Fig. 1. Robot autonomously unfolding a shirt. a) Grasping lowest point. b) grasping 1st grasp point. c) grasping 2nd grasp point. d) final unfolded configuration

intuitive, this approach makes the combination of features from multiple views difficult whereas hypotheses from different views can only be exploited a posteriori (i.e. Bayesian formulations). In addition, their performance heavily relies on the performance of the single-view classifier. However, designing a classifier that can generalize across views is particularly challenging especially when illumination variations or deformations are considered. Another problem in active vision which hasn't been addressed by many state of the art techniques [13,12], is defining the cost associated with each action.

To cope with the above challenges, we propose *Active Random Forests* which can be considered as an *"active classifier"*. The framework is based on classical Random Forests [3] having also the ability to control viewing parameters during on-line classification and regression. The key difference is that the classifier itself decides which actions are required in order to collect information which will disambiguate current hypotheses in an optimal way. As we will demonstrate, this combination of classification and viewpoint selection outperforms solutions which employ these two components in isolation [7,13,12]. Furthermore, inference is made using the entire set of captured images, taking advantage of the various feature associations between different viewpoints. The on-line inference and action planning become extremely fast by the use of Random Forests, making the framework very suitable for real-time applications such as robotics. In summary, the main contributions of our framework are:

- **A multi-view active classifier** which combines features from multiple views and is able to make decisions about further actions in order to accomplish classification and regression tasks in an optimal way.
- **Novel decision making criteria** based on distribution divergence of training and validation sets while growing the decision trees.
- **A decision selection method** during classification and regression using the powerful voting scheme inherent to Random Forests.
- A method for taking into account the possible **costs of actions**.

Letting the classifier decide the next disambiguating actions introduces much discriminative power to the framework, as will be shown in Section 5. We demonstrate the proposed framework in the challenging problem of recognizing and unfolding clothes autonomously using a bimanual robot, focusing on the problem of best viewpoint selection for classification, grasp point and pose estimation of garments.

2　Related Work

Active vision literature focuses mainly on finding efficient methods for selecting observations optimally while little attention is paid to the classifier which is kept simple. The majority of works adopted an off-line approach which consists of precomputing disambiguating features from training data. Schiele et al. [18] introduced "transinformation", the transmission of information based on statistical representations, which can be used in order to assess the ambiguity of their classifier and consequently find the next best views. Arbel et al. [1] developed a navigation system based on entropy maps, a representation of prior knowledge about the discriminative power of each viewpoint of the objects. In a subsequent study, they presented a sequential recognition strategy using Bayesian chaining [2]. Furthermore, Callari *et al.* [4] proposed a model-based active recognition system, using Bayesian probabilities learned by a neural network and Shannon entropy to drive the system to the next best viewpoints. Also, Sipe and Casasent [19] introduced the probabilistic feature space trajectory (FST) which can make estimation about the class and pose of objects along with the confidence of the measurements and the location of the most discriminative view. Such methods are computationally efficient both in training and testing. On the other hand, they rely mainly on their best hypotheses based on prior knowledge which can in fact have low probabilities on a test object while features from the visited viewpoints are assumed independent in order to make the final inference.

One of the most representative works in the same direction was made by Denzler *et al.* [7] who tried to optimally plan the next viewpoints by using mutual information as the criterion of the sequential decision process. They also presented a Monte-Carlo approach for efficiently calculating this metric. Later, Sommerlade and Reid [20] extended this idea in tracking of multiple targets on a surveillance system. One drawback of this approach was that the accumulated evidence about the visited viewpoints did not affect the viewpoint selection strategy which was based on precomputed leant actions. An improvement over this idea was made by Laporte and Arbel [13] who introduced an on-line and more efficient way of computing dissimilarity of viewpoints by using the Jeffrey Divergence weighted by the probabilistic belief of the state of the system at each time step. This work however, combines viewpoint evidence probabilistically using Bayesian update which relies on the consistent performance of the features or the single-view classifier used (in at least some viewpoints), which is generally challenging in high dimensional feature spaces like the problem of pose estimation of deformable objects. A recent work on active vision was made by Jia et al. [12] who used a similarity measure based on the Implicit Shape Model and other prior knowledge combined in a boosting algorithm in order to plan the next actions. However the employed similarity measure is not suitable for highly deformable objects such as garments, whereas the boosting strategy based on certain priors makes a minor improvement over [7] and [13]. Finally, there are some active vision applications to robotic systems in real scenarios [22,14,23,17] mainly based on the previously described works, showing promising results.

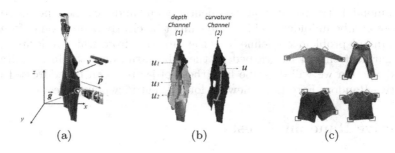

Fig. 2. Clothes Analysis. a) Grasp point g and pose vector p. b) The depth and curvature channels and the random positions used in binary pixel tests. c) Possible lowest points of clothes. Gray boxes are the symmetric points of the blue ones. Green diamonds show the desired grasping points for unfolding

Our work is based on the method proposed in [8]. In that work the authors have used Random Forests for identifying garments and grasping points, while they also propose an active scheme based on POMDPs for dealing with uncertainty. In that work, viewpoint selection was made sequentially by taking nearby viewpoints, which is a sub-optimal solution whilst in some cases slows down the entire process. Our work is built on the same principles, making active vision faster and more efficient by the use of Active Random Forests. In addition, we estimate the pose of the garment in order to guide the robot's gripper to grasp a desired point, which reduced grasping errors compared to the local plane fitting techniques employed in [8]. Most importantly, our framework can be easily extended to other active vision problems.

3   Problem Overview

We will describe our framework of Active Random Forests in the context of our target application: autonomously unfolding clothes using a dual-arm robot. This problem consists of picking a garment from a table in a random configuration, recognizing it and bringing it into a predefined unfolded configuration. In order to unfold a garment, the robot has to grasp the article from two certain grasp points sequentially (e.g. the shoulders of a shirt) and hang it freely to naturally unfold by gravity, imitating the actions of a human (Fig. 1). There are three underlying objectives in such procedure: Garment type classification, grasp points detection and pose estimation as shown in Fig. 2(a). We will describe in short these objectives, based on [8]:

For classification, 4 basic garment types are considered: shirts, trousers, shorts and T-shirts. In order to reduce the configuration space of a garment picked up randomly, the robot first grasps its lowest point[8]. Fig 2(c) shows the possible lowest points which are 2 for shorts and T-shirts, and one for shirts and trousers. Therefore, the classes considered are 6, corresponding to the possible lowest points. The grasp points used for unfolding are manually defined, shown in Fig.

2(c) (diamonds). The robot should sequentially find and pick these points so that a garment can be unfolded. While pose cannot be clearly defined on deformable objects, in our problem we define it as the direction from which a desired point on the garment should be grasped by the robot arm, depicted in Fig. 2(a). In the next Section we will describe how these objectives can be addressed using our Active Random Forests framework for efficient viewpoint selection.

4   Active Random Forests

4.1   Training

One training sample of Active Random Forests should consist of all the images that can be obtained from a certain training object using the possible actions and controllable viewing parameters available in the system. In our problem, only viewpoint selection is considered and therefore training samples can be represented as a tuple $(\mathbf{I}(v), c, \mathbf{g}(v), \mathbf{p}(v)), v \in \mathbf{V}$ where $\mathbf{I}$ is a vector containing the depth image of the garment, c is the class, $\mathbf{g}$ is a 2D vector containing the position of the desired grasp point in the depth image (thus depicting a 3D point), $\mathbf{p}$ is a 2D vector containing the pose of the cloth defined in the XY plane as shown in Fig. 2(a) and $\mathbf{V}$ is the set of all possible viewpoints v of the garment. Viewpoints are considered around the Z axis which coincides with the holding gripper, covering the whole $360°$ degrees. We discretized the infinite viewpoint space into V equal angle bins. Vector $\mathbf{g}(v)$ is not defined if the point is not visible from viewpoint v.

Each split node of Random Decision Trees stores an array of the already seen viewpoints $\mathbf{V}'$ which also passes to its children. Starting at the root node, the only seen viewpoint is the current one ($\mathbf{V}' = \{V_0\}$). Following [8], at each node a random set of splitting tests is generated with each test containing a random seen viewpoint $v \in \mathbf{V}'$ taken from uniform distribution over $\mathbf{V}'$, a feature channel $C_i = \{C_1, C_2\}$, a tuple of random positions $\mathbf{M}(\mathbf{u_1}, \mathbf{u_2}, \mathbf{u_3})$ on the image (Fig. 2(b)) and a binary test $f(v, C_i, \mathbf{M}) > t$ using threshold t, selected from a pool of possible binary tests. Channel C_1 is the raw depth data of the garment as captured from a depth sensor and channel C_2 is the mean curvature of the surface[8]. Also we used the binary tests proposed in [8] containing simple pixel tests in the depth or curvature channel, which showed good results and low execution time.

While in [8] two separate forests and a POMDP were applied sequentially for classification, grasp point detection and rotation actions respectively, our new forest is able to make classification, grasp point detection and pose estimation using the same tree structure. To achieve this, we apply a hierarchical coarse to fine quality function for node splitting as in [21], so that the upper part of the trees perform classification of garments hanging from their lowest point and the lower part perform regression of grasp point or pose vectors. The overall quality function has the following form:

$$Q = \alpha Q_c + (1 - \alpha)Q_r \tag{1}$$

where Q_c is a quality function for classification, Q_r a quality function for regression and α an adapting parameter. We adopt the traditional information gain using Shannon Entropy for Q_c and the corresponding information gain for continuous Gaussian distributions as defined in [5] for Q_r. Specifically, letting S be the set of training samples reaching a split node, and f be a random binary function applied to S, the latter will be split into two subsets, S_l and S_r, according to a random threshold t. Then, Q_c is the sum of the entropies of the 2 children nodes while the quality function for regression Q_r is defined as:

$$Q_r = -\sum_i^{\{l,r\}} \frac{|S_i|}{|S|} \sum_{v=1}^{V} \ln |\Lambda_{\mathbf{q}(v)}(S_i)| \tag{2}$$

where $\Lambda_{\mathbf{q}(v)}$ is the covariance matrix of the vectors $\mathbf{q}(v)$, with $\mathbf{q}(v) = \mathbf{g}(v)$ or $\mathbf{p}(v)$ chosen randomly. For switching between classification and regression (of $\mathbf{p}$ or $\mathbf{q}$), the maximum posterior probability of the samples in a node is used, with the parameter α is set to:

$$\alpha = \begin{cases} 1, & \text{if } \max P(c) \leq t_c \\ 0, & \text{if } \max P(c) > t_c \end{cases} \tag{3}$$

where t_c is a predefined threshold, typically set to 0.9. At a split node, the quality function in Eq. (1) is evaluated against a random set of split tests, and the one that maximizes Q is finally selected. When the maximum posterior probability $\max P(c)$ of a class in a node is below t_c, the tree performs classification, otherwise performs regression of grasp point location or pose, selected randomly, in a course to fine manner.

4.2   Incorporating Actions

When object recognition is not feasible by single view observations, some actions should be taken to change the current viewing conditions. Furthermore, such actions are also needed when searching for a particular region of the object which is not visible in the current view. In contrary, actions may have an execution cost which should be taken into account in the selection process. Therefore, the criteria for making a decision about an action should be the informativeness of the current observations, the belief about the visibility of the region of interest in the current observations and the execution cost of a potential action.

The analysis in section 4.1 was made taking into account the set of already seen viewpoints of the object $\mathbf{V}'$, which at the root node contains only the current view V_0. The split nodes keep splitting the training set for a few times using this view, until, in some cases in certain depth of the trees, the current view stops being informative and the tree starts overfitting on the training samples reached the nodes. The point at which such behaviour appears is crucial and requires a further action to be taken (or another viewpoint to be seen in our problem) so that more disambiguating information can be collected. We achieve this by using a validation set in parallel with the training set and measure the divergence of the posterior distributions among these two sets in a node. Specifically, we split the initial training set S into 2 equal-sized random subsets, with S_T being the actual training set and S_D the validation set. For finding the best split candidates at a node only the training set is considered. However, the validation set is also split using the best binary test found and is passed to the left or right child accordingly. Thus, at node j, the sample sets that arrive are the training set S_T^j and the validation set S_D^j.

In order to determine the presence of overfitting, the training set is compared against the validation set at each split node. For measuring the divergence of two sets, we have experimented with two alternative metrics which were tested and compared in the experimental results (Section 5). The first is the *Hellinger distance*[16], a statistical measure defined over validation set S_T^j and S_D^j as:

$$HL(S_T^j \| S_D^j) = \frac{1}{\sqrt{2}} \sqrt{\sum_{c=1}^{C} \left(\sqrt{P_{S_T^j}(c)} - \sqrt{P_{S_D^j}(c)} \right)^2} \tag{4}$$

when comparing the class distributions of the training set S_T^j and validation set S_D^j having C classes. $P_S(c)$ is the class probability distribution of the set S. The Hellinger distance satisfies the property $0 \le HL \le 1$ and it takes its lowest value 0 when training and validation set distributions are identical and its maximum value 1 when one distribution is 0 when the other is positive. Similarly, assuming that grasp point and vectors at node j are normally distributed variables, the averaged squared Hellinger distance over the possible viewpoints is:

$$HL^2(S_T^j \| S_D^j; \mathbf{q}) = \frac{1}{V} \sum_{v \in \mathbf{V}} 1 - \frac{\left(|A_{\mathbf{q}(v)}(S_T^j) \| A_{\mathbf{q}(v)}(S_D^j)| \right)^{\frac{1}{4}}}{|A|^{\frac{1}{2}}} \exp\{-\frac{1}{8} \mathbf{u}^T A^{-1} \mathbf{u}\} \tag{5}$$

where

$$\mathbf{u} = \boldsymbol{\mu}_{\mathbf{q}(v)}(S_T^j) - \boldsymbol{\mu}_{\mathbf{q}(v)}(S_D^j) \tag{6}$$

$\boldsymbol{\mu}_{\mathbf{q}(v)}()$ is the mean value of vectors $\mathbf{q}$ ($= \mathbf{g}(v)$ or $\mathbf{p}(v)$) in viewpoint v and A the average covariance matrix of S_T^j and S_D^j.

The other metric is the so called *Jensen–Shannon divergence* which measures the information divergence of two probability distributions and is actually a symmetric version of the *Kullback–Leibler* divergence. Measuring the class distribution divergence of training and validation sets, Jensen–Shannon divergence is defined as:

$$JS(S_T^j \| S_D^j) = \frac{1}{C} \sum_{c=1}^{C} P_{S_T^j}(c) \log \frac{P_{S_T^j}(c)}{P_m(c)} + P_{S_D^j}(c) \log \frac{P_{S_D^j}(c)}{P_m(c)} \tag{7}$$

where P_m is the average class distribution of S_T and S_D. Again, JS satisfies the property $0 \le JS \le 1$, where 0 indicates identical distributions while 1 indicates maximum divergence. For measuring the information divergence of our continuous variables over two sets, we substitute (7) with multi-variate Gaussian distributions and compute the average over viewpoints $\mathbf{V}$, which results in:

$$
JS(S_T^j \| S_D^j; \mathbf{q}) = \frac{1}{2V} \sum_{v \in \mathbf{V}} \left(\mathbf{u}^T \left(\Lambda_{\mathbf{q}(v)}(S_T^j)^{-1} + \Lambda_{\mathbf{q}(v)}(S_D^j)^{-1} \right) \mathbf{u} \right.
$$
$$
\left. + tr \left(\Lambda_{\mathbf{q}(v)}(S_T^j)^{-1} \Lambda_{\mathbf{q}(v)}(S_D^j) + \Lambda_{\mathbf{q}(v)}(S_D^j)^{-1} \Lambda_{\mathbf{q}(v)}(S_T^j) - 2\mathbf{I} \right) \right)
\tag{8}
$$

where $\mathbf{u}$ is defined in Eq. (6). More details about (8) can be found in [16].

When the divergence of the training and validation set Δ (= JS or HL) is above a threshold t_Δ, the node becomes an *action-selection node* and an action should be taken in order to change the viewing parameters, which in our problem is a rotation of the robot gripper in order to change the viewpoint v. Therefore, in an action-selection node the whole set of possible viewpoints $\mathbf{V}$ is considered in the selection of the best random test.

There are two main directions regarding the selection criteria of a new viewpoint, from which only the first has been studied in the literature [12,19,7,13,4]:

- Viewpoints can be reached at the same cost, while when moving from viewpoint i to viewpoint j, no further information can be captured from the viewpoints in between.
- Moving from viewpoint i to viewpoint j has a cost relative to the distance of i and j, while when moving from i to j, images from the intermediate viewpoints can be also captured without additional cost.

Our problem belongs to the second category, however we consider also the first case for comparison with previous works. Assuming no cost for the transition between viewpoints, the distribution of $\mathbf{V}$ used for randomly selecting a new viewpoint in an action-selection node is uniform (Fig. 3(a)). For our problem however, it is more realistic to assume a cost relevant to the degrees of rotation of the gripper needed to see a viewpoint, while during rotation, all intermediate images can be captured. The distribution of $\mathbf{V}$ in an action-selection node in this case is depicted in Fig. 3(b). If the furthest viewpoint seen so far is v_{max}, then all viewpoints $v = 1...v_{max}$ are also seen and have equal distribution ρ to be selected, as no action is required. The next viewpoints have an exponential distribution $\rho e^{-(v-v_{max})/V}$ for $v = (v_{max}+1)...V$. Parameter ρ can be easily found by solving $\sum_{v=1}^{V} P(v) = 1$. Using such distribution, further viewpoints are less likely to be selected by a split test. Modifying the distribution from which the viewpoints v are randomly selected and tested, is equivalent to weighting them.

One other issue when searching for a particular region of an object like a grasp point on a garment, is that it may be invisible in the acquired images. In this case, a viewpoint is needed so that not only it disambiguates the current belief about the category or the pose of the object, but it also makes the particular region visible. The visibility of samples reaching a node can be measured by the vectors in $\mathbf{g}(v)$ where viewpoints with non-visible grasp points are not defined.

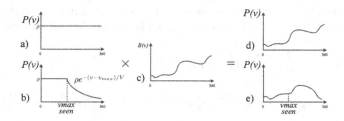

Fig. 3. Viewpoint distribution for random test selection. a) Uniform distribution, b) weighted distribution, c) Visibility map, d) Final distribution using (a), e) final distribution using (b).

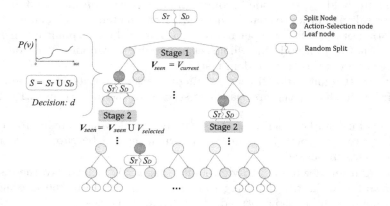

Fig. 4. Active Random Forests Training procedure

To achieve this, a visibility map B is constructed as:

$$B(v) = \frac{\sum_{s \in S^j} b(s,v)}{\sum_{v' \in \mathbf{V}} \sum_{s \in S^j} b(s,v')}, \quad b(s,v) = \begin{cases} 1, & \text{if } \mathbf{g}_s(v) \text{ exists} \\ 0, & \text{if } \mathbf{g}_s(v) \text{ is not defined} \end{cases} \quad (9)$$

An example is shown in Fig. 3(c). When visibility is low in the collected views, $B(v)$ is multiplied with the current distribution of the set $\mathbf{V}$ calculated previously, so that preference is given to the viewpoints where the grasp point is more probable to be visible, as shown in Fig. 3(d)–(e).

An action-selection node can now select the next best viewpoint v_{best} randomly evaluating binary tests from viewpoints taken from the calculated distribution $P(v)$. The random tests are evaluated on the whole set $S = S_T^j \cup S_D^j$. This results in finding the best viewpoint v_{best} which optimally separates the diverging samples and helps the tree disambiguate its hypotheses. The samples that arrive at each child of the action-selection node are again split randomly into training and validation sets and the tree enters the next stage where again only the seen viewpoints are considered, which are now increased by 1 (Fig. 4). That is: $\mathbf{V}' = \mathbf{V}'_{parent} \cup v_{best}$. This stage follows the same hierarchical quality

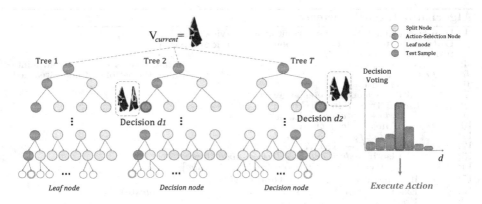

Fig. 5. Active Random Forests Inference procedure

function in Eq. (1) and the tree continues growing until another action-selection node is encountered or a leaf node is created. The criteria of making a leaf node is setting a minimum number of samples allowed in a node. Finally, in the leaf nodes, along with the class distribution $P(c)$ we store only the first 2 modes of $\mathbf{g}(v)$ and $\mathbf{p}(v)$ per class as in [9], weighted by the class probability, for memory efficiency during inference.

4.3 Inference

In order to make an inference using an Active Random Forest, the current arbitrary view of a garment, which is grasped and hanging from its lowest point, is captured and starts traversing the trees. Although in some trees the current view can reach a leaf node, in other trees it reaches an action-selection node where other viewing parameters are needed or another viewpoint is required (Fig. 5). Then, the action-selection nodes vote for the next best action that should be taken for collecting more information, in a similar way that leaf nodes vote for the best class of an object. Next, the most voted action is executed and another image is captured. The trees that voted for the selected action can be now traversed further by using the newly acquired image, and some of them may reach a leaf node. However, if there are not enough leaf nodes, being below a threshold N_L, this process continues iteratively until N_L leafs are reached. In each iteration, the most voted action is executed. The system updates the set of images captured at the end of each iteration with the last observation so that the whole set can be used by the trees in order to be traversed as deep as possible. The final inference about the class is made by averaging the class distribution of the leaf nodes. Grasp point detection and pose estimation are made using Hough voting from the vectors $\mathbf{g}$ and $\mathbf{p}$ of the leafs in the 3D space, combining all the viewpoints seen. Algorithm 1 summarizes the inference procedure and Fig. 5 illustrates the framework. We should mention that it is not required that all the trees should reach a leaf node, as some may have ended in an action-selection node. Parameter N_L is discussed in the experimental results, in Section 5.

Algorithm 1. ARF Inference

1: **Input:** A trained ARF, the current arbitrary viewpoint $V_{current}$
2: **Output:** garment class c, grasp point location **g** and pose **p**
3: **function** INFERENCE(ARF)
4:     $V_{seen} = \{V_{current}\}$ ▷ Initialize the set of seen viewpoints
5:     $Leafs = \emptyset$ ▷ Initialize the set of leaf nodes reached
6:     **while** $true$ **do**
7:         Initialize $decisionVotes$ array to 0
8:         **for all** Trees T in ARF **do**
9:             $node \leftarrow traverse(T, V_{seen})$
10:             **if** $node = leaf$ **then**
11:                 $Leafs \leftarrow Leafs \cup node$
12:                 $ARF \leftarrow ARF \backslash T$
13:             **else if** $node = action\_selection$ node **then**
14:                 Increase $decisionVotes[node \rightarrow decision]$
15:         **if** Number of $Leafs > N_L$ **then** $break$
16:         Execute Action for Decision: $d = \text{argmax}_d(decisionVotes(d))$
17:         Update current view $V_{current}$
18:         $V_{seen} \leftarrow V_{seen} \cup V_{current}$
19:         **return** Average class c and Hough Votes $H_{\mathbf{g}(v)}$, $H_{\mathbf{p}(v)}$ from $Leafs$

We should also note that in the experiments, this voting scheme produces a response similar to a delta function, significantly concentrated to one action. Such response is the result of the combination of many weak classifiers which vote for the most discriminating view at a time. We finally note that the more discriminative a view is, the more leaf nodes are reached, while if the first view is discriminative enough, no further actions may be required.

5   Experimental Results

Experimental Setup. To evaluate the ARF framework, we used our database which consists of 24 clothes, 6 of each type. Each garment was grasped by the robot gripper from each lowest point(s) 20 times to capture the random cloth configurations, collecting 40 depth images while it was rotating 360 degrees around its vertical axis. The total number of images collected is 57,600 taking into account the symmetric images as well. Another 480 unseen images for each category were used as our test samples. The training samples consist of sets of images $\mathbf{I}(v)$ containing images of a certain garment from every viewpoint v and having every arbitrary view as the first view. The steps involved in the unfolding process using the robot are: grasp the lowest point, recognize the garment and detect the 1st desired grasp point and pose, grasp desired point, search for the 2nd desired grasp point and pose (no classification needed), grasp final point and unfold. In the experiments bellow, classes $c_1 - c_6$ correspond to: *shirts, trousers, shorts grasped from 1st lowest point (leg), shorts grasped from the 2nd lowest point (waist), T-shirts grasped from the 1st lowest point (waist), T-shirts grasped from the 2nd lowest point (sleeve)*. We train an ARF using these classes so that the robot can recognize the cloth and grasp the first desired point, based on its pose. Furthermore, we train another ARF which is used to detect the 2nd desired point and pose. The second ARF does not perform classification as it is already addressed. The second ARF is trained using images from clothes hanging from their first grasp point. Thus, we define as c_i-2 the class c_i when hanging from the 1st grasp point and no classification is calculated for it. Last, We have discretized the possible viewpoints into 40 equal bins of 9 degrees each, which provides enough accuracy keeping training time reasonable(few hours). We assume a correct grasp point estimation if it is at most 10cm close to ground truth, whereas 18 degrees divergence is allowed for a correct pose estimation.

Parameter Analysis. An important issue in the experiments was setting up the parameters correctly. The first parameter which needs to be defined is t_Δ, the threshold of the divergence of the training and validation sets of a node, above which a new decision should be made. Fig. 6(a) shows the average performance of classification, grasp point and pose estimation of an ARF containing a large number of trees (discussed below) with t_Δ varying from 0 to 1 for both metrics HL and JS. When t_Δ is 0, every node in the forest becomes an action-selection node and the forest tends to overuse the possible viewpoints available for inference increasing the total number of actions required. On the other hand, when t_Δ is 1, there is no action-selection node and the forest behaves as a single-view classifier. Fig. 6(a) shows that when HL is used, performance starts decreasing for $t_\Delta > 0.2$ while the same happens when JS is used for $t_\Delta > 0.1$. These are the limit values for t_Δ, above which the classifier tends to behave as a single-view classifier and below which it starts using redundant actions. Having t_Δ defined for both of our metrics, the next parameters that should be defined are the total number of trees and the minimum number of leaf nodes N_L needed by an ARF in order to make an inference. Because ARFs have a decision voting scheme along with the leaf-node aggregation, we make the following observation: Assuming that N_x leaf nodes are sufficient to make an inference and an ARF has reached $N_x - 1$ leafs, it would be desired to have another N_x trees to vote for the next decision. Therefore, N_L is set to $N_T/2$, which is half the number of trees in the forest. Fig. 6(b) shows the average accuracy of our ARF, making use of the previous observation. Both metrics reach the same level of accuracy with JS requiring more trees. However, Fig. 6(c) shows that by using JS the forest requires significantly less movements than HL to achieve the same results. Therefore, JS was used for all the subsequent experiments.

Performance and Comparisons. Fig. 6(d) shows the performance of ARF in all possible situations, with pose estimation being the most challenging objective. This figure was created without considering the weights of the actions. In the opposite case however results were very similar, thus Fig. 6(d) represents both scenarios. These two cases are compared in Fig. 6(e) which shows that weighting actions slightly increases the required viewpoints needed for inference. On the other hand, in Fig. 6(f), the required actions in the case of considering their weights have significantly lower cost than the actions in the first case, without sacrificing accuracy. The cost of an action was considered to be the degrees of rotation the gripper required in order to reach the desired viewpoint. Fig. 6(f)

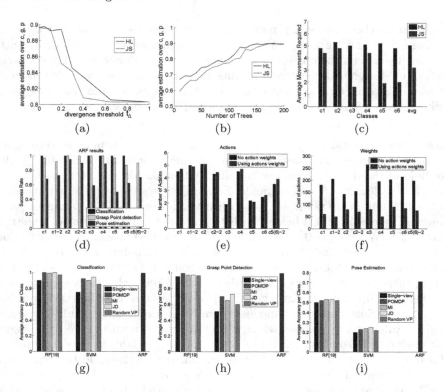

Fig. 6. Plots from experimental results showing: a) the divergence threshold t_Δ, b) Number of trees, c) average number of movements, d) ARF success rates, e) Number of movements for weighted and non-weighted actions policy f) average cost of actions of the two policies, g-h-i) Classification-Grasp Point-Pose estimation

shows the sum of the costs of all the actions needed for inference. In order to compare the ARF results, we have used two kinds of baseline methods: 1)single-view classification methods without incorporating actions; 2) active viewpoint selection methods based on a single-view method and utilizing information from entire history of selected viewpoints by updating the probability of the current state after each action. The first single-view classifier is based on Random Forests[8], modified to perform pose estimation. The second such classifier is based on multi-class and regression SVM[11,10]. The features used were the raw depth image of a garment and the HOG features[6] applied on the depth image. The first active vision technique used is based on POMDP[8], the second uses the viewpoint selection criterion proposed in [7] based on mutual information (displayed as *MI*) and the third uses Jeffrey Divergence metric as proposed in [13](displayed as *JD*). In all cases, we executed a random viewpoint selection for comparison. Finally, for a fair comparison we did not take into account the costs of actions and the visibility map (Eq. 9). Fig. 6(g) - 6(i) show the results for classification, grasp point detection and pose estimation respectively. In all cases, methods based on the SVM classifier had the worst performance. In classification

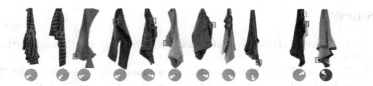

Fig. 7. Success and failure cases (the last two) of some clothes. The arrow under each cloth indicates its pose. The first error is in grasp point detection, the second in pose estimation.

and point detection, the single-view classifiers have consistent good performance and therefore the active vision approaches had a positive impact on the inference. In both cases, ARF achieves equal accuracy with the best active vision technique in each case. The power of ARFs however, is shown in Fig. 6(i), where they outperform previous works for pose estimation by almost 20%. The reason is that when dealing with such a challenging problem, the single-view inference has low accuracy producing many equally probable hypotheses. This makes classical active vision approaches perform similar to a random viewpoint selection strategy. In contrast, ARF combines features from the most discriminant views learned in training, and thus is not so affected from single-view uncertainty. Last, for achieving all the three objectives all active vision techniques were allowed to execute at most 20 actions, above which no further improvement was noticed, even when all viewpoints were seen. In contrast, as shown in Fig. 6(c), ARF shows high accuracy with an average of 3.5 moves, which is significantly lower. Fig. 7 shows some success and failure cases using some test clothes. The failures on the right are due to wrong grasp point detection and wrong pose estimation respectively. Also our supplementary video[1] shows the whole unfolding procedure using a dual arm robot, along with comparisons of ARF with the state of the art in real scenarios.

6   Conclusion

We presented Active Random Forests, a framework for addressing active vision problems, and applied it to the task of autonomously unfolding clothes. We have focused on best viewpoint selection in classification, key point detection and pose estimation of 4 types of garments. The idea of incorporating the decision process of executing disambiguating actions inside Random Forests and combining features from multiple views outperformed classical active vision techniques, especially in the challenging problem of pose estimation of clothes. Furthermore, the required number actions is significantly reduced. This framework is also open to other actions which can be integrated like zooming to a particular region or any kind of interaction with the object. This direction is left as future work.

Acknowledgment. This work was supported by the EC under the project FP7-288553 CloPeMa. A. Doumanoglou is also supported by the scholarship, and X. Zhao and T-K Kim are in part supported by EPSRC grant (EP/J012106/1).

---

[1] Supplementary material can be found at: `http://clopema.iti.gr/ECCV-2014/`

References

1. Arble, T., Ferrie, F.P.: Viewpoint selection by navigation through entropy maps. In: ICCV (1999)
2. Arble, T., Ferrie, F.P.: On the sequential accumulation of evidence. IJCV (2001)
3. Breiman, L.: Random forests. Machine Learning 45(1), 5–32 (2001)
4. Callari, F.G., Ferrie, F.P.: Recognizing large 3-d objects through next view planning using an uncalibrated camera. In: ICCV (2001)
5. Criminisi, A.: Decision forests: A unified framework for classification, regression, density estimation, manifold learning and semi-supervised learning. Foundations and Trends in Computer Graphics and Vision 7(2-3), 81–227 (2011)
6. Dalal, N., Triggs, B.: Histograms of oriented gradients for human detection. In: CVPR, vol. 1, pp. 886–893 (2005)
7. Denzler, J., Brown, C.M.: Information theoretic sensor data selection for active object recognition and state estimation. PAMI (2002)
8. Doumanoglou, A., Kargakos, A., Kim, T.K., Malassiotis, S.: Autonomous active recognition and unfolding of clothes using random decision forests and probabilistic planning. In: ICRA (2014)
9. Girshick, R., Shotton, J., Kohli, P., Criminisi, A., Fitzgibbon, A.: Efficient regression of general-activity human poses from depth images. In: ICCV (2011)
10. Guo, G., Fu, Y., Dyer, C.R., Huang, T.S.: Head pose estimation: Classification or regression? In: ICPR (2008)
11. Hastie, T., Tibshirani, R., Friedman, J., Hastie, T., Friedman, J., Tibshirani, R.: The elements of statistical learning, vol. 2. Springer, Heidelberg (2009)
12. Jia, Z., Chang, Y.-J., Chen, T.: A general boosting-based framework for active object recognition. In: BMVC (2010)
13. Laporte, C., Arbel, T.: Efficient discriminant viewpoint selection for active bayesian recognition. IJCV (2006)
14. Meger, D., Gupta, A., Little, J.J.: Viewpoint detection models for sequential embodied object category recognition. In: ICRA (2010)
15. Ozuysa, M., Lepetit, V., Fua, P.: Pose estimation for category specific multiview object localization. In: CVPR (2009)
16. Pardo, L.: Statistical inference based on divergence measures. CRC Press (2005)
17. Rasolzadeh, B., Bjorkman, M., Huebner, K., Kragic, D.: An active vision system for detecting, fixating and manipulating objects in the real world. IJRR (2010)
18. Schiele, B., Crowley, J.L.: Transinformation for active object recognition. In: ICCV, pp. 249–254 (1998)
19. Sipe, M.A., Casasent, D.: Feature space trajectory methods for active computer vision. PAMI (2002)
20. Sommerlade, E., Reid, I.: Information-theoretic active scene exploration. In: CVPR (2008)
21. Tang, D., Yu, T., Kim, T.K.: Real-time articulated hand pose estimation using semi-supervised transductive regression forests. In: ICCV (2013)
22. Vogel, J., de Freitas, N.: Target-directed attention: Sequential decision-making for gaze planning. In: ICRA (2008)
23. Welke, K., Issac, J., Schiebener, D., Asfour, T., Dillmann, R.: Autonomous acquisition of visual multi-view object representations for object recognition on a humanoid robot. In: ICRA (2010)
24. Zhao, X., Kim, T.K., Luo, W.: Unified face analysis by iterative multi-output random forests. In: CVPR (2014)

Model-Free Segmentation and Grasp Selection of Unknown Stacked Objects*

Umar Asif, Mohammed Bennamoun, and Ferdous Sohel

School of Computer Science & Software Engineering,
The University of Western Australia, Crawley, Perth, WA, Australia
umar.asif@research.uwa.edu.au,
{mohammed.bennamoun,ferdous.sohel}@uwa.edu.au

Abstract. We present a novel grasping approach for unknown stacked objects using RGB-D images of highly complex real-world scenes. Specifically, we propose a novel 3D segmentation algorithm to generate an efficient representation of the scene into segmented surfaces (known as surfels) and objects. Based on this representation, we next propose a novel grasp selection algorithm which generates potential grasp hypotheses and automatically selects the most appropriate grasp without requiring any prior information of the objects or the scene. We tested our algorithms in real-world scenarios using live video streams from Kinect and publicly available RGB-D object datasets. Our experimental results show that both our proposed segmentation and grasp selection algorithms consistently perform superior compared to the state-of-the-art methods.

Keywords: 3D segmentation, grasp selection.

1 Introduction

Grasping unknown objects in real-world environments is still a challenging task for visual perception and autonomous robot manipulation [3]. There are two main problems in a general grasping pipeline. **First**, an accurate segmentation of an object of interest is required to separate it from the environment. This is an intrinsically challenging problem, especially when the scene contains a large variety (textured, non-textured, planar and non-planar) of stacked objects with no information about their sizes, shapes or, visual appearance (e.g., color, or texture). The difficulty is compounded with the additional challenges of real-world environments (e.g., variable lighting conditions, shadows, clutter, and inherent sensor noise). Many state-of-the-art approaches handle this task either through recognition-based methods (e.g., [11,6,18,34,30,2]) or learning-based methods (e.g., [27,20]). While the former methods restrict the system to a fixed number of objects (whose models were previously stored or learned), the latter are also not suitable due to their high computational runtime when dealing with unknown objects in unknown environments (e.g., home or workplace).

---

* Electronic supplementary material - Supplementary material is available in the online version of this chapter at http://dx.doi.org/10.1007/978-3-319-10602-1_43. Videos can also be accessed at http://www.springerimages.com/videos/978-3-319-10601-4

D. Fleet et al. (Eds.): ECCV 2014, Part V, LNCS 8693, pp. 659–674, 2014.
© Springer International Publishing Switzerland 2014

Second, the selection of the most appropriate grasp from nearly an infinite number of possible grasps is a great challenge in the case of unknown stacked objects. Many approaches (e.g., [8,29]) use 2D or 3D object models to determine feasible grasps. Other approaches (e.g., [12,19,5]) assume that the objects to be grasped belong to a particular set of shape compositions and therefore reduce the number of possible grasps by fitting shape primitives (e.g., boxes, cylinders, or superquadrics). However, these shape abstractions are not accurate in the case of stacked and occluded objects. Learning-based approaches (e.g., [17,32,24,3]) handle the case of unknown objects using 2D and 3D features. However, all these approaches consider simple situations where the objects are isolated on a table. In the case of stacked and occluded objects, it is a very challenging task to generate the most appropriate grasp from a noisy partial view of the object (particularly from a single camera viewpoint).

We present a purely vision-based approach which addresses both the aforementioned problems in a model-free manner. **To handle the first problem**, we present a novel 3D segmentation algorithm (Sec. 3.1-3.2) which segments the scene into surfels and object hypotheses. **For the second problem**, we present a novel algorithm (Sec. 3.3) which generates potential grasps (specifically two-finger pinch-grasps) using surfels and automatically selects the most appropriate grasp for the objects in the scene. We tested our algorithms using live video streams from Microsoft Kinect and challenging object datasets, where we demonstrate that our algorithms improve both the segmentation and grasp selection performance for unknown stacked and occluded objects (Sec. 4). In summary, the contributions of this paper are:

1. Our proposed 3D segmentation algorithm segments unknown stacked and occluded objects compared to the methods in [24,28], which only segment objects isolated from each other. Our algorithm is completely **model-free** compared to the methods in [27,20] which require learning and parameter tuning on specific datasets. Hence, our algorithm is capable of separating a large variety of objects without any prior information about the objects or the scene (e.g., prior information about the table plane, or background). Our segmentation results are superior compared to the state-of-the-art methods (Sec. 4.2)
2. Our proposed grasp selection algorithm generates potential grasps and automatically selects the most appropriate grasp for unknown stacked and occluded objects. To the best of our knowledge, this is the first work to deal with unknown stacked objects in a complete **model-free** way. Our grasp selection results outperform the state-of-the-art grasp-selection methods (Sec. 4.3).
3. We evaluate the performance of our algorithms in real-world environments using our in-house mobile robot with a 7-DOF arm to grasp unknown stacked objects (see video in the supplementary material).

2   Related Work

Vision-based object grasping approaches can be divided into three main categories [3], grasping of known, familiar, and unknown objects. **For grasping**

known objects, active-exploration-based methods (e.g., [25]), or learning-based techniques (e.g., [31,22]) assume that a detailed 2D or 3D model of the object is available which is matched to the current scene for segmentation and pose estimation. Based on the model and the estimated pose, a large number of grasp hypotheses are generated and their quality is evaluated to compute the most appropriate grasp. Methods (e.g., [4]) use analytical approaches (by modeling the interaction between a gripper and an object using tactile sensing [23]) to generate force-closure grasps and rank them by optimizing the parameters of a dexterous hand [35]. Others use learning through demonstration approaches (e.g., [9]) to efficiently associate grasps to known objects. Recently, methods (e.g., [12,19]) evaluate the shape of the object by fitting shape primitives (e.g., boxes, cylinders, cones, and superquadrics) thereby reducing the number of potential grasps. However, all these methods require a prior knowledge about the objects, which restricts their application in real-world environments containing unknown objects.

For grasping familiar objects, methods (e.g.,[32,22,7]) learn relationships between visual features and grasp quality on a set of training objects. This knowledge is then used to grasp resembling objects. For instance, in [32], grasp hypotheses were learned based on a set of local 2D image features (edges, textures and color) using synthetic data to grasp novel objects. The method of [22] used a support vector machine (SVM) to predict the grasp quality based on the hand configuration and the parameters of the superquadric representation of the objects. In the work of [7], grasp selection was learned on a set of simple geometrical shapes and applied to grasp novel objects. However, most of these methods were trained using synthetic models and implemented in simulation. **Grasping unknown objects** is acknowledged to be a difficult problem particularly in the presence of a large variety of objects (i.e., with different sizes, shapes, textures, and layouts) and scenes (i.e., with clutter, indistinguishable background, and different lighting conditions). In this context, [21] used 2D contours of objects to approximate their centers of mass for grasp selection. The method in [28] used a selection algorithm to determine grasping points on the top-surface of an object. The method in [24] used a bottom-up segmentation algorithm and an SVM to learn the grasp selection of unknown objects. Recently, an early cognitive system presented in [14] was applied to the problem of grasping unknown objects based on edge and texture features. However, all of these methods consider the simple scenario of objects isolated from each other, which undermines the segmentation problem. This is not true when dealing with unknown real-world situations (e.g., Fig. 1B). Considering the important requirements for the next generation of service robots [14]), the grasping capabilities need to be implemented and evaluated in complex situations (i.e., scenes with unknown stacked and occluded objects).

In this paper, we present a purely vision-based grasping approach which has the following advantages, compared to the other methods: **First**, it is a fully model-free approach (i.e., no prior information about the objects or the scene is required), in contrast to the methods (e.g., [3,17,16,24,14]) which learn grasp

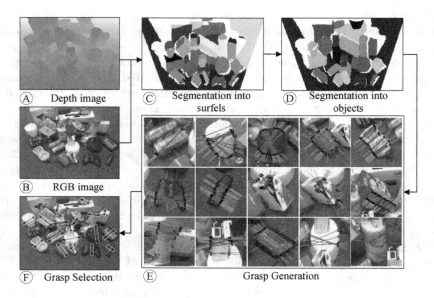

Fig. 1. Overview of our proposed grasping approach. First, we take a depth image (A) and a color image (B) as input and generate two segmentations: mid-level surfels (C), and high-level object hypotheses (D). Next, we use surfels to generate grasp hypotheses (E) and subsequently select the most appropriate grasp (F).

selection on training data using specific datasets. This allows our approach to generalize to different real-world environments (e.g., kitchen, or a workplace). **Second**, our approach successfully handles a large variety of unknown objects in unknown layouts compared to the methods (e.g., [17,16,24,28,14]) which considered only simple situations.

3 Proposed Grasping Approach

As illustrated in Fig. 1, **first**, we produce a 3D segmentation of the scene into mid-level surfaces (known as surfels), and high-level object hypotheses. **Second**, we use these segmentations to generate potential grasp hypotheses. Our overall approach addresses two key problems: **i)** accurate segmentation of unknown stacked and occluded objects and **ii)** selection of the most appropriate grasp in a model-free manner. **For the first problem**, we propose a new 3D segmentation algorithm which produces a layered representation of the scene in terms of mid-level and high-level information (i.e., surfels, and objects respectively). On the mid-level, our algorithm (see Sec. 3.1) follows an optimization procedure using simulated annealing to partition a given point cloud into surfels. On the high-level, our algorithm (see Sec. 3.2) combines perceptually similar surfels into object hypotheses using graph-cuts. **For the second problem**, we propose a novel algorithm (see Sec. 3.3) which generates potential grasp hypotheses and

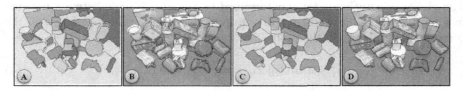

Fig. 2. Segmentation into surfels and their refinement. A-B: initial partitioning used for initialization, C-D: partitioning after 5 iterations of simulated annealing.

subsequently evaluates them to select the most appropriate grasp in a model-free manner.

3.1 Segmentation into Surfels

As illustrated in Fig. 2, our segmentation proceeds in two stages: **i)** initial segmentation (see Fig. 2A) and **ii)** its iterative refinement (see Fig. 2C). **In the first stage**, our algorithm produces an initial partitioning of the point cloud in terms of surfels. **In the second stage**, the algorithm iteratively refines these surfels (by exchanging boundary points between neighbors) so that their boundaries accurately conform to the physical object boundaries in the scene.

Initial Segmentation. The algorithm starts with a clustering technique in which structurally homogeneous points (i.e., those which have close 3D proximities, and similar local- and global-orientations of their surface normals) are grouped into distinct clusters. Our clustering algorithm is similar to the two-pass binary image labeling technique described in [33]. It has been, however, modified to label point cloud using our distance metric D_c. We define a comparator function $\mathbb{C}$, which compares a point i with its neighboring point j as given below:

$$\mathbb{C}(i,j) = \begin{cases} true & if(D_c < \delta_{D_c}). \\ false & otherwise \end{cases} \tag{1}$$

If $\mathbb{C}(i,j) = true$, then a common label is assigned to both the points i and j, otherwise a new label is created by incrementing the largest assigned label by one. Our distance metric D_c is a linear combination of three terms: 3D proximity, co-planarity, and global-orientation disparity. D_c can be written as:

$$D_c = \sqrt{||\mathbf{p}(i) - \mathbf{p}(j)||^2 + ||\beta_n(i) - \beta_n(j)||^2 + ||\gamma_n(i) - \gamma_n(j)||^2}, \tag{2}$$

where, $||.||$ represents the normalization within the local neighborhood. The terms $\mathbf{p}$, β_n, and γ_n represent the 3D coordinates, surface normal local orientation, and surface normal global-orientation of a query point respectively. For a point i, the orientation $\beta_n(i)$ is determined by the average dot product between its surface normal $\boldsymbol{n}_i$ and the normals of all the points in a local neighborhood $\boldsymbol{\Omega}$ of radius σ as:

$$\beta_n(i) = \frac{\sum_{j=1}^{size(\boldsymbol{\Omega})} acos(dot(\boldsymbol{n}_i, \boldsymbol{n}_j))}{size(\boldsymbol{\Omega})}. \tag{3}$$

The global-orientation $\gamma_n(i)$ is determined by the $atan2$ angle between the surface normal $\boldsymbol{n}_i$ and a vector $\boldsymbol{v}_c$ (drawn from the camera reference frame to the corresponding point i in the point cloud) as:

$$\gamma_n(i) = atan2(||cross(\boldsymbol{n}_i, \boldsymbol{v}_c)||, dot(\boldsymbol{n}_i, \boldsymbol{v}_c)). \tag{4}$$

Our algorithm proceeds as follows: the first point of the point cloud is assigned a unique label. For the remaining points, each unlabeled point i is compared to its left, left-top, and top neighbors using Eq. 1. If multiple neighbors with different labels satisfy the criterion in Eq. 1, the label of one of the neighbors is assigned to the current point i and equivalences are set for all of these neighbors. Otherwise, a new label is assigned to the point i by incrementing the largest assigned label by one. This procedure is iteratively repeated until all points are labelled. In the second pass, the labelled image is scanned again, and all equivalent regions are assigned the same region label using the union-find algorithm as in [33]. This produces a partitioning into regions whose boundaries are subsequently refined using an optimization technique as described in the following.

Refinement. We introduce an objective function, which when optimized, enforces structural homogeneity (i.e., similar normal orientations) of the points within each surfel. The optimization is based on a simulated annealing algorithm which proceeds as follows: The algorithm uses the initial segmentation as an initial solution and iteratively updates the solution by exchanging boundary points between neighboring surfels to generate a new partitioning. The algorithm terminates if the objective function does not increase or when the maximum number of iterations is reached (if the algorithm is allowed to run for a fixed number of iterations). In order to converge to a solution close to the global optimum, it is important to start with a good partition. We use our initial segmentation as a first rough partitioning for the simulated annealing algorithm. In our experiments, we found that there are several advantages of this initialization which include: **i)** the initial segmentation is automatic (i.e., our clustering algorithm automatically segments the point cloud into structurally distinct clusters). **ii)** Our initial segmentation is perceptually accurate because structurally homogeneous points are grouped into distinct clusters. Since the initialization is close to the optimal solution, this speeds up the convergence of the simulated annealing algorithm. Let K be the number of surfels we obtain from the initial segmentation. We define $S = \{s_1, s_2, \ldots, s_K\}$ to describe the initial partitioning where, each surfel s_k is represented by a cluster of 3D points in the point cloud as shown in Fig. 1C.

Objective Function Our objective function is defined to evaluate the homogeneity as a distribution of local orientations (ϕ, ψ, and α) of the surface normals of the points within each surfel s_k. The orientations are measured in the same manner as in [30]. Mathematically, the ϕ, ψ, and α values of a point $i \in s_k$ are computed with respect to its surfel's centroid s_{k_c} as:

$$\phi(i) = acos(dot(\mathbf{n}_i, \boldsymbol{v}_n)), \psi(i) = acos(dot(\mathbf{n}_{s_k}, \boldsymbol{v}_n)), \alpha(i) = atan2(\rho, \tau),$$
$$\rho = dot(cross(\mathbf{n}_{s_k}, cross(\boldsymbol{v}_n, \mathbf{n}_i)), \tau = dot(\mathbf{n}_{s_k}, \mathbf{n}_i) \tag{5}$$

where $\boldsymbol{v}_n$ is a normalized vector between $\mathbf{p}(i)$ and surfel centroid s_{k_c}. In order to define our objective function, we first define three feature histograms Φ, Ψ, and Ω based on the distribution of ϕ, ψ, and α values of the points in s_k respectively. Mathematically, Φ, Ψ, and Ω are written as:

$$\Phi_{s_k} = ||hist(\{\phi_i\})||, \Psi_{s_k} = ||hist(\{\psi_i\})||, \Omega_{s_k} = ||hist(\{\alpha_i\})||, \forall i \in s_k, \tag{6}$$

where, the term $||hist||$ represents the normalized histogram. For a given initial solution S, our objective function $C(S)$ is given by:

$$C(S) = \sum_{k=1}^{K} \left(\sqrt{\frac{1}{n_b} \sum_{j=1}^{n_b} (\Phi_{s_k}^j)^2} + \sqrt{\frac{1}{n_b} \sum_{j=1}^{n_b} (\Psi_{s_k}^j)^2} + \sqrt{\frac{1}{n_b} \sum_{j=1}^{n_b} (\Omega_{s_k}^j)^2} \right), \tag{7}$$

where $\Phi_{s_k}^j$, $\Psi_{s_k}^j$, and $\Omega_{s_k}^j$ represent the number of entries in the jth bin of the corresponding histograms. The term n_b represents the total number of bins of the corresponding histogram. In our experiments, we divide the ϕ and ψ values in 50 bins ranging from 0 to 180 deg, and the α values in 50 bins ranging from $-\pi$ to π. The simulated annealing algorithm updates S iteratively as follows: at each iteration, the algorithm generates a new partitioning S_{new} based on the previous one (i.e., S_{old}) by moving the boundary points between the neighboring regions. A boundary movement proceeds as follows: first, the algorithm places a rectangular patch of $\sigma \times \sigma$ pixels around a query boundary point p and computes its distance with respect to each surfel center s_k which lies within the patch and is adjacent in the point cloud (i.e., the minimum pairwise distance between p and the points of s_k is less than a distance threshold $\delta_{adj} = 5mm$), as:

$$\zeta(p, s_k) = \sqrt{||c_p - \bar{c}_{s_k}||^2 + ||\beta_p - \bar{\beta}_{s_k}||^2}, \tag{8}$$

where, $\bar{c}_{s_k}$, and $\bar{\beta}_{s_k}$ represent the mean of the CIELab color, and β values of all points within the surfel s_k respectively. Next, the algorithm assigns the label of the surfel with the minimum ζ value to the query boundary point p. This procedure is repeated for all boundary points of each surfel in S to generate S_{new}. The new partitioning (S_{new}) is evaluated using the objective function in Eq. 7 and is accepted as valid if it increases $C(S)$. This iterative refinement is repeated until either of the two following termination conditions is met: i) the change in the cost between two successive iterations is less than a threshold ε, or ii) the total number of iterations exceeds a predefined number N_{max}. The final partitioning, S^*, is subsequently used to produce high-level object hypotheses (Sec. 3.2). Our proposed initial segmentation algorithm has several advantages including: i) simulated annealing refines the surfels iteratively and produces a valid segmentation at the end of each iteration. This is advantageous because

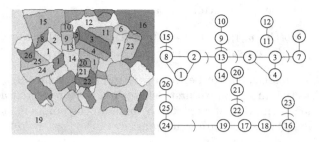

Fig. 3. The merging process of surfels based on graph-cut. Left: the segmentation into surfels. Right: our undirected graph structure. Cuts (arcs) are placed between the nodes which do not satisfy convex shape relationship.

we can stop the algorithm at any iteration and still achieve a valid segmentation, compared to the graph-based or region-growing methods, where one has to wait until all the cuts have been added to the graph, or until the growing is completely performed. **ii)** Our algorithm successfully recovers boundary errors (caused by missing depth information or smooth variations in the normal directions of touching surfaces) from a single RGB-D image of the scene. This is advantageous in situations where only a single partial view of the environment is available.

3.2   Perceptual Grouping into High-Level Object Hypotheses

The next key contribution is the merging of the surfels (i.e., whether two surfels correspond to the same object instance) to generate high-level object hypotheses in a model-free manner (i.e, without any prior knowledge of the objects in the scene). Our perceptual grouping algorithm follows a graph-based merging approach in which an undirected adjacency graph (built on surfels using adjacency relations such as 3D proximity) is reduced in a greedy manner. As illustrated in Fig. 3, the nodes of the graph represent the surfels and an edge between any pair represents the adjacency between the corresponding surfels. The cuts are placed on the edges which do not satisfy the merging criterion. Our merging criterion is based on the shape relationship (i.e., convex or concave) between two adjacent surfels. To estimate the shape relationship between two adjacent surfels s_k, and s_j, we construct a straight line between a point from s_k (i.e., the point which is maximally distant above/below the s_j plane) and a point from s_j (i.e., the point which is maximally distant above/below the s_k plane). As illustrated in Fig. 4, this line lies below both the surfels when they belong to the same object instance (e.g., two sides of a box shown in Fig. 4A). When the surfels belong to different object instances (e.g., box placed on a cylindrical container as shown in Fig. 4C), this line lies above either of the two surfels. Mathematically, we compute the projected distance d_p of the midpoint of the line from each surfel plane (see Fig. 4). If $d_p < 0$ for both the surfels, we report that the two surfels have a

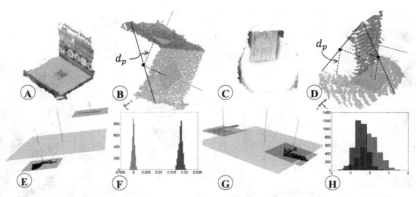

Fig. 4. Top row: Shape relationship analysis between two adjacent surfels. (A-B): when surfaces belong to the same object instance, the line lies below both surfels. (C-D): when one surface protrudes from its supporting surface, the respective line lies above either of the two surfaces. Bottom row: Co-planarity between two surfaces. (E-F): when surfaces are not aligned, their distance histograms do not intersect. (G-H): the distance histograms of co-planar surfaces intersect.

convex-shape, otherwise a concave-shape relationship. We iteratively check this condition for a set of 5 lines (in our experiments) and merge the two surfels if all lines satisfy the convex-shape relationship criterion. This procedure efficiently combines surfels which belong to distinct object instances however, ignores those which are not adjacent in the 3D Cartesian space (e.g., in Fig. 3, surfels 16, 17, 18, and 19 belong to the floor surface but are not connected in the 3D Cartesian space). To efficiently handle this problem, we detect surfels which are co-planar and do not have a convex relationship with any surfel (e.g., see edges represented by the dotted lines in Fig. 3-Right), and merge them subsequently. To measure co-planarity between two surfels, we check if they have similar mean normal directions and are aligned. The alignment is checked by building a histogram of the projected distances of each surfel points from the combined plane (i.e., the plane which best fits the 3D points of the union of the two surfels) and computing their intersection. As shown in Fig. 4F, the histograms of two non-aligned surfels do not intersect. On the other hand, the histograms of a co-planar pair intersect (as shown in Fig. 4H).

3.3 Grasp Synthesis

We apply our layered representation of the scene (i.e., surfels and object hypotheses) to perform grasp synthesis of unknown objects in a model-free manner. Our proposed algorithm proceeds in two steps. **i)** grasp generation, and **ii)** grasp selection. **For grasp generation**, the algorithm generates pairs of grasping points using reflection symmetry (i.e, co-linearity of the 3D points and similar orientations of their surface normals in the 2D image plane and the 3D Cartesian space) between points along the boundaries of the surfel. **For grasp selection**,

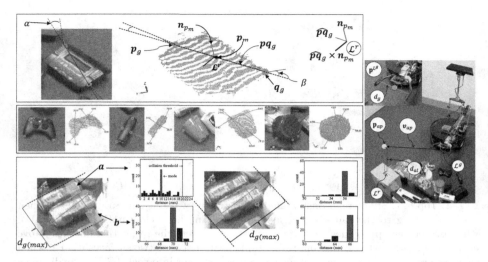

Fig. 5. Grasp synthesis using surfels. Left (top row): shows the angles α and β in the 2D image plane and the 3D Cartesian space respectively. Left (middle row): shows grasping points which satisfy our reflection symmetry criterion. Left (bottom row): shows the patches a and b used to extract shape descriptors. Their corresponding distance histograms show mode values (highlighted in red) smaller and larger than a threshold ($20mm$) for the cases when majority points are collision (e.g., a) and void (e.g., b) respectively. Right: illustration reference frames L^g and L^r, the approach point $\boldsymbol{p}_{ap}$, and the approach vector $\boldsymbol{v}_{ap}$.

the algorithm evaluates the grasp hypotheses based on the shape descriptors (a distance histogram representing the distances between a grasping point and all points in a rectangular region) of their corresponding grasping points to select the most appropriate grasp.

Grasp Generation. Our general grasp notation G for a surfel s is defined as:

$$G_s = \{\boldsymbol{p}_g, \boldsymbol{q}_g, L^r, \boldsymbol{p}_{ap}\} \tag{9}$$

As illustrated in Fig. 5, $\boldsymbol{p}_g$ and $\boldsymbol{q}_g$ are two grasping points located on the boundary of the surfel s. L^r is a local reference frame whose origin is the midpoint $\boldsymbol{p}_m$ of the vector $\boldsymbol{p}_g\boldsymbol{q}_g$ (i.e., straight line connecting the two grasping points). The x, z and y axes of L^r correspond to the direction vector $\boldsymbol{p}_g\hat{}\boldsymbol{q}_g$, surface normal $\boldsymbol{n}_{p_m}$ and $\boldsymbol{p}_g\hat{}\boldsymbol{q}_g \times \boldsymbol{n}_{p_m}$ respectively. $\boldsymbol{p}_{ap}$ is a point located at a distance d_{al} from L^r along $+n_{p_m}$ (positive direction of the normal) and is used as the approach point to align the gripper for the corresponding grasp (see Fig. 5-right). The grasping points are determined by finding two points from the surfel boundaries, which satisfy the reflection symmetry criteria in both the 2D image plane and the 3D Cartesian space (i.e., their surface normals minimize the angles α, and β as shown in Fig. 5-left-top). The algorithm stores all pairs of $(\boldsymbol{p}_g, \boldsymbol{q}_g)$ whose corresponding angles α, and β, are within ± 2 (as shown in Fig. 5-left-middle). This procedure is repeated for each surfel and the generated grasp hypotheses are subsequently ranked as explained in the following.

Grasp Selection. For each object of the segmented scene, its generated grasp hypotheses are first ranked in the order of increasing distance to the mean position of their corresponding surfel. This encourages the grasping of the object from a point that is close to its center of gravity. Next, the ranked grasp hypotheses are evaluated in terms of the shape descriptors of their corresponding grasping points. The extraction of our shape descriptor proceeds in two steps: i) a rectangular patch is constructed in the 2D image plane such that its major and minor axes are co-linear and perpendicular to the the line $p_g q_g$ respectively (see Fig. 5-left-bottom). ii) Next, each neighboring point (i.e, the point which lies in the rectangular patch and does not belong to the corresponding surfel) is iteratively classified as void or collision (i.e., if its distance to the corresponding grasping point is greater or less than a distance threshold respectively). If several points in the patch are classified as collision (i.e., the mode of patch's distance histogram is less than a fixed threshold), the corresponding grasp hypothesis is discarded. This facilitates the selection of grasp hypotheses, whose corresponding grasping points have sufficient void space for the gripper to fit its fingers without collision with the neighboring surfaces. After the evaluation of the grasp hypotheses based on their shape descriptors, the highest ranked grasp is selected as the most appropriate for grasp execution.

Grasp Execution. This section describes our grasp execution procedures. Once the most appropriate grasp is selected by the grasp selection algorithm, inverse kinematics is used to drive the gripper to the grasp location. Inverse kinematics represent the following mapping:

$$G_s = (p_g, q_g, L^r, p_{ap}) \rightarrow (L^g, d_g). \tag{10}$$

As illustrated in Fig. 5-right, L^g denotes the gripper reference frame calibrated with respect to the camera. The orientation of L^g is such that z^{L^g} (z-axis of L^g frame) is parallel to the grippers fingers, x^{L^g} connects the fingers and $y^{L^g} = z^{L^g} \times x^{L^g}$, and the origin p^{L^g} is placed between the two fingers. The term d_g corresponds to the distance between the fingers. The grasp execution algorithm proceeds as follows: the gripper is set to a pre-grasp configuration (i.e., $d_g = d_{g(max)}$), and is moved to the approach point, p_{ap} (i.e., $p^{L^g} = p_{ap}$), along the shortest directed path v_{ap}. Next, the gripper orientation is set to align with the object surface (i.e., $z^{L^g} = n_{p_m}$), and $x^{L^g} = p_g\hat{q}_g$, and the gripper is translated along the direction n_{p_m} until it reaches the grasp-position (i.e., $p^{L^g} > p_m$). Finally, the fingers move from the pre-grasp configuration to the grasp-configuration (i.e., $d_g \leq |p_g q_g|$) and the grasp-execution concludes when the joints settle in a static configuration. There are several advantages of our grasp selection algorithm which include: i) Using surfels to generate pairs of grasping points facilitates the determination of appropriate pairs and reduces outliers (i.e., grasping points which belong to other object instances). This also reduces the computational complexity by analyzing a fixed number of object surfaces compared to the methods (e.g., [14,17]), which search for grasping points in the entire image space or the entire point cloud. ii) The reflection symmetry criterion reduces the number of grasp hypotheses to a small number of appropriate grasps from which the best grasp is automatically selected using our ranking procedure (based on the shape descriptors of the corresponding grasping points). This is computationally more efficient compared to the methods which use shape abstractions to evaluate a nearly infinite number of possible grasp hypotheses [12].

4   Experiments

We evaluated the performance of our algorithms in terms of segmentation accuracy (Sec. 4.2) and grasp selection accuracy (Sec. 4.3). To quantify the performance and to comprehensively compare with the state-of-the-art methods, we used three popular object datasets which are publicly available. We also tested the performance on live video streams from Microsoft Kinect to validate the suitability of our algorithms for robotic applications (see video in the supplementary material). All experiments were done on a multi-core i7 machine without any GPU support.

4.1   Datasets

We used two datasets for the evaluation of our segmentation performance. The first dataset is the Washington RGB-D object dataset (WRGBD) [15], which provides 8 different video sequences of office and kitchen environments. Each video sequence in the dataset is a series of RGB-D images captured using a Kinect sensor from different viewpoints. The variable characteristics of the scenes such as different illumination settings, variable viewpoints, and a large variety of objects, make WRGBD a very challenging dataset for object segmentation purposes. The ground truth of the WRGBD dataset is available in two forms: 2D bounding boxes around salient objects in each scene and, labeled point clouds for each video sequence. The second dataset is the Object Segmentation Database (OSD) [26]. OSD contains RGB-D images of table-top scenes in which a large variety of objects are stacked over each other in several layouts. This is a great challenge for the segmentation algorithms to separate distinct objects particularly when they occlude each other. The ground truth for this dataset is available in the form of manually annotated segmentation masks for each object in the scene. For the evaluation of our grasp selection algorithm, we used the Cornell grasping dataset [13]. This dataset contains 1035 images of 280 different objects in different layouts, each annotated with several ground-truth positive and negative grasping rectangles. A grasping rectangle is an oriented rectangle in the image plane, which defines the orientation of a parallel gripper with respect to the image plane [13].

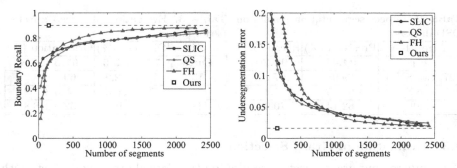

Fig. 6. 3D Boundary recall (left) and 3D under-segmentation errors (right) of our algorithm compared to the other methods on the OSD dataset.

Table 1. Object segmentation results on WRGBD dataset

Object category	percentage of objects detected						
	Soda Can	Coffee Mug	Cap	Bowl	Flashlight	Cereal Box	Average
Method in [20]	90.3%	84.2%	88.0%	85.5%	98.3%	95.4%	90.3%
Ours	**93.5%**	**87.3%**	**91.7%**	**90.5%**	**98.5%**	**98.2%**	**93.3%**

4.2   Evaluation of Object Segmentation

To quantitatively measure segmentation quality (i.e., how accurately the boundaries of its segments conform to the physical object boundaries), we used two standard metrics namely: 3D boundary recall, and 3D under-segmentation error as suggested in [37]. We compared our results with three state-of-the-art segmentation methods namely: hierarchical graph-based (GBH) [10], SLIC [1] and Quickshift (QS) [36]. The boundary recall and under-segmentation results are shown in Fig. 6-left and Fig. 6-right respectively. The results show that the performance of our algorithm is not dependent on the number of segments. On the contrary, other methods (i.e., [10,1,36]) improve as the number of segments (specified by the user) increase. Furthermore, our algorithm achieved the best boundary recall and under-segmentation results compared to the other methods. These improvements are credited to our proposed optimization-based segmentation refinement procedure (see Sec. 3.1 for details), which results in superior conformity of the surfel boundaries to the physical boundaries compared to state-of-the-art methods. Table. 1 shows our object segmentation results on the WRGBD. As shown in the table, our approach achieved the best performance in the four selected object categories and, on average, attained at least a 3.0% higher average precision compared to the method in [20]. On the OSD dataset, our algorithm achieved the best performance in the precision scores compared to the methods in [27] and [20] as shown in Table 2. These improvements are credited to our proposed merging criteria (see Sec. 3.2 for details), which efficiently combines perceptually similar surfels into distinct object hypotheses.

Table 2. Object segmentation results on OSD dataset

Algorithm	Precision (%)	Recall (%)
Ours	**94.41**	**96.20**
[27] two SVMs	89.98	97.05
[27] one SVM	93.75	95.48
[20]	62.14	70.93

Table 3. Evaluation of Grasp selection performance

Algorithm	Distance (%)	Orientation (%)
Ours	**77.6 ± 2.5**	**61.5 ± 1.8**
[13]	75.3 ± 2.9	60.1 ± 3.2
[24]	70.3 ± 6.3	58.5 ± 7.2
[28]	68.6 ± 10.5	52.9 ± 8.8

4.3 Evaluation of Grasp Selection

We compared our grasp selection results (on the Cornell grasping dataset) with the methods in [28,24]. For our evaluation, we compared the top-ranked rectangle for each method with the set of ground-truth rectangles for each image. We present our results using distance and orientation metrics as suggested in [13]. Table. 3 shows the results of our proposed grasp selection algorithm compared with the other methods. Our proposed algorithm outperforms the other segmentation-based grasp selection methods [24,28] by up to 7.3% for the distance metric and 3% for the orientation metric. Our results also show a superior performance (i.e., an improvement of 2.3% for the distance and 1.4% for the orientation metrics respectively) compared to the learning-based method in [13]. These improvements are credited to the use of our proposed reflection symmetry criteria to generate appropriate grasp hypotheses on surfel boundaries which are subsequently evaluated using our proposed shape descriptor to automatically select the most appropriate grasp for an unknown object in a model-free manner (see Sec. 3.3 for detail).

5   Conclusion

We successfully addressed the challenging problems of the segmentation and grasp selection of unknown stacked and occluded objects without the use of any prior information (model-free) of the objects or the environment. This was accomplished by the introduction of a novel 3D segmentation algorithm, which efficiently handles the case of stacked and occluded objects. We subsequently presented a novel grasp selection algorithm, which generates appropriates grasps hypotheses using surfel boundaries and automatically selects the most appropriate grasp in a model-free manner. Our segmentation and grasp-selection results show superior performance compared to the state-of-the-art methods.

Acknowledgment. This work was supported by Australian Research Council grants (DP110102166, DE120102960).

References

1. Achanta, R., Shaji, A., Smith, K., Lucchi, A., Fua, P., Susstrunk, S.: Slic superpixels compared to state-of-the-art superpixel methods. PAMI 34(11), 2274–2282 (2012)

2. Asif, U., Bennamoun, M., Sohel, F.: Real-time pose estimation of rigid objects using rgb-d imagery. In: ICIEA, pp. 1692–1699 (2013)
3. Bohg, J., Kragic, D.: Learning grasping points with shape context. Robotics and Autonomous Systems 58(4), 362–377 (2010)
4. Borst, C., Fischer, M., Hirzinger, G.: Grasp planning: How to choose a suitable task wrench space. In: ICRA, vol. 1, pp. 319–325 (2004)
5. Bowers, D.L., Lumia, R.: Manipulation of unmodeled objects using intelligent grasping schemes. IEEE Transactions on Fuzzy Systems 11(3), 320–330 (2003)
6. Collet, A., Martinez, M., Srinivasa, S.S.: The moped framework: Object recognition and pose estimation for manipulation. IJRR 30(10), 1284–1306 (2011)
7. Curtis, N., Xiao, J.: Efficient and effective grasping of novel objects through learning and adapting a knowledge base. In: IROS, pp. 2252–2257 (2008)
8. Dogar, M.R., Hsaio, K., Ciocarlie, M., Srinivasa, S.: Physics-based grasp planning through clutter (2012)
9. Ekvall, S., Kragic, D.: Integrating object and grasp recognition for dynamic scene interpretation. In: ICAR, pp. 331–336 (2005)
10. Felzenszwalb, P.F., Huttenlocher, D.P.: Efficient graph-based image segmentation. IJCV 59(2), 167–181 (2004)
11. Fenzi, M., Dragon, R., Leal-Taixé, L., Rosenhahn, B., Ostermann, J.: 3d object recognition and pose estimation for multiple objects using multi-prioritized ransac and model updating. In: Pattern Recognition, pp. 123–133 (2012)
12. Huebner, K., Ruthotto, S., Kragic, D.: Minimum volume bounding box decomposition for shape approximation in robot grasping. In: ICRA, pp. 1628–1633 (2008)
13. Jiang, Y., Moseson, S., Saxena, A.: Efficient grasping from rgbd images: Learning using a new rectangle representation. In: ICRA, pp. 3304–3311 (2011)
14. Kootstra, G., Popović, M., Jørgensen, J.A., Kuklinski, K., Miatliuk, K., Kragic, D., Krüger, N.: Enabling grasping of unknown objects through a synergistic use of edge and surface information. IJRR 31(10), 1190–1213 (2012)
15. Lai, K., Bo, L., Ren, X., Fox, D.: A large-scale hierarchical multi-view rgb-d object dataset. In: ICRA, pp. 1817–1824 (2011)
16. Le, Q.V., Kamm, D., Kara, A.F., Ng, A.Y.: Learning to grasp objects with multiple contact points. In: ICRA, pp. 5062–5069 (2010)
17. Lenz, I., Lee, H., Saxena, A.: Deep learning for detecting robotic grasps. arXiv preprint arXiv:1301.3592 (2013)
18. Li, X., Guskov, I.: 3d object recognition from range images using pyramid matching. In: ICCV. pp. 1–6 (2007)
19. Miller, A.T., Allen, P.K.: Graspit! a versatile simulator for robotic grasping. IEEE Robotics & Automation Magazine 11(4), 110–122 (2004)
20. Mishra, A.K., Shrivastava, A., Aloimonos, Y.: Segmenting "simple" objects using rgb-d. In: ICRA. pp. 4406–4413 (2012)
21. Morales, A., Sanz, P.J., Del Pobil, A.P., Fagg, A.H.: Vision-based three-finger grasp synthesis constrained by hand geometry. Robotics and Autonomous Systems 54(6), 496–512 (2006)
22. Pelossof, R., Miller, A., Allen, P., Jebara, T.: An svm learning approach to robotic grasping. In: ICRA, vol. 4, pp. 3512–3518 (2004)
23. Platt, R.: Learning grasp strategies composed of contact relative motions. In: 7th IEEE-RAS International Conference on Humanoid Robots, pp. 49–56 (2007)
24. Rao, D., Le, Q.V., Phoka, T., Quigley, M., Sudsang, A., Ng, A.Y.: Grasping novel objects with depth segmentation. In: IROS, pp. 2578–2585 (2010)

25. Recatalá, G., Chinellato, E., Del Pobil, Á.P., Mezouar, Y., Martinet, P.: Biologically-inspired 3d grasp synthesis based on visual exploration. Autonomous Robots 25(1-2), 59–70 (2008)
26. Richtsfeld, A., Morwald, T., Prankl, J., Zillich, M., Vincze, M.: Segmentation of unknown objects in indoor environments. In: IROS, pp. 4791–4796 (2012)
27. Richtsfeld, A., Mörwald, T., Prankl, J., Zillich, M., Vincze, M.: Learning of perceptual grouping for object segmentation on rgb-d data. Journal of Visual Communication and Image Representation 25(1), 64–73 (2014)
28. Richtsfeld, M., Vincze, M., et al.: Grasping of unknown objects from a table top. In: Workshop on Vision in Action: Efficient Strategies for Cognitive Agents in Complex Environments (2008)
29. Rosales, C., Porta, J.M., Ros, L.: Global optimization of robotic grasps. In: Proceedings of Robotics: Science and Systems VII (2011)
30. Rusu, R.B., Bradski, G., Thibaux, R., Hsu, J.: Fast 3d recognition and pose using the viewpoint feature histogram. In: IROS, pp. 2155–2162 (2010)
31. Saxena, A., Driemeyer, J., Kearns, J., Osondu, C., Ng, A.Y.: Learning to grasp novel objects using vision. In: ISER (2006)
32. Saxena, A., Driemeyer, J., Ng, A.Y.: Robotic grasping of novel objects using vision. IJRR 27(2), 157–173 (2008)
33. Shapiro, L., Stockman, G.C.: Computer vision. In: Computer Vision 2001, pp. 69–75. Prentice Hall (2001)
34. Sun, M., Bradski, G., Xu, B.-X., Savarese, S.: Depth-encoded hough voting for joint object detection and shape recovery. In: Daniilidis, K., Maragos, P., Paragios, N. (eds.) ECCV 2010, Part V. LNCS, vol. 6315, pp. 658–671. Springer, Heidelberg (2010)
35. Tegin, J., Ekvall, S., Kragic, D., Wikander, J., Iliev, B.: Demonstration-based learning and control for automatic grasping. Intelligent Service Robotics 2(1), 23–30 (2009)
36. Vedaldi, A., Soatto, S.: Quick shift and kernel methods for mode seeking. In: Forsyth, D., Torr, P., Zisserman, A. (eds.) ECCV 2008, Part IV. LNCS, vol. 5305, pp. 705–718. Springer, Heidelberg (2008)
37. Veksler, O., Boykov, Y., Mehrani, P.: Superpixels and supervoxels in an energy optimization framework. In: Daniilidis, K., Maragos, P., Paragios, N. (eds.) ECCV 2010, Part V. LNCS, vol. 6315, pp. 211–224. Springer, Heidelberg (2010)

Convexity Shape Prior for Segmentation

Lena Gorelick[1], Olga Veksler[1], Yuri Boykov[1], and Claudia Nieuwenhuis[2]

[1] University of Western Ontario, Canada
[2] UC Berkeley, USA

Abstract. Convexity is known as an important cue in human vision. We propose shape convexity as a new high-order regularization constraint for binary image segmentation. In the context of discrete optimization, object convexity is represented as a sum of 3-clique potentials penalizing any 1-0-1 configuration on all straight lines. We show that these non-submodular interactions can be efficiently optimized using a trust region approach. While the quadratic number of all 3-cliques is prohibitively high, we designed a dynamic programming technique for evaluating and approximating these cliques in linear time. Our experiments demonstrate general usefulness of the proposed convexity constraint on synthetic and real image segmentation examples. Unlike standard second-order length regularization, our convexity prior is scale invariant, does not have shrinking bias, and is virtually parameter-free.

Keywords: segmentation, convexity shape prior, high-order functionals, trust region, graph cuts.

1 Introduction

Length-based regularization is commonly used for ill-posed segmentation problems, in part because efficient global optimization algorithms are well-known for both discrete and continuous formulations, e.g. [1,2]. Nevertheless, the shrinking bias and the sensitivity to the weight of the length term in the energy are widely recognized as limitations of this form of regularization. These problems motivate active research on optimization of higher-order regularization energies, e.g. curvature [3,4,5,6], which can alleviate the shrinking bias and other issues.

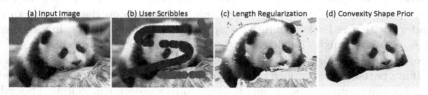

Fig. 1. Segmentation with convexity shape prior: (a) input image, (b) user scribbles, (c) segmentation with contrast sensitive length regularization. We optimized the weight of length with respect to ground truth. (d) segmentation with convexity shape prior.

D. Fleet et al. (Eds.): ECCV 2014, Part V, LNCS 8693, pp. 675–690, 2014.
© Springer International Publishing Switzerland 2014

We propose a new higher-order regularization model: convexity shape constraint, see Fig.1. Convexity was identified as an important cue in human vision [7,8]. Many natural images have convex or nearly convex objects. Convex objects are also common in medical images. Yet, to the best of our knowledge, we are the first to introduce a convexity shape prior into discrete segmentation energy.

We develop an energy-based formulation for convexity prior in discrete optimization framework and propose an efficient optimization algorithm for the corresponding non-submodular high-order term $E_{convexity}(S)$. The overall segmentation energy $E(S)$ can combine our convexity prior with user-defined hard-constraints and linear intensity appearance [9], boundary length [1], color separation [10], or any others standard submodular terms $E_{sub}(S)$

$$E(S) = E_{convexity}(S) + E_{sub}(S). \tag{1}$$

Convexity of segment S is expressed as a penalty for all ordered triplet configurations 1-0-1 along any straight line, see Fig.2(c). Similar straight 3-cliques also appear in curvature modeling [6], but they also need 0-1-0 configurations to penalize negative curvature. Moreover, they use only local triplets to evaluate curvature. In contrast, convexity **is not** a local property of the segment boundary. Therefore, we have to penalize 1-0-1 configurations on straight intervals of any length. Consequently, our convexity energy model has a much larger number of cliques. We propose an efficient dynamic programming technique to evaluate and approximate these cliques in the context of trust region optimization [11].

Related Work. Many related shape priors were introduced in the past. Common length-based regularizer [1] penalizes segment perimeter favoring smooth solutions that are closer to circles and, therefore, more convex. However, as shown in our experiments, this prior needs to be carefully balanced with the appearance term as it has a strong shrinking bias. Connectivity regularizer [12,13] does not have shrinking bias but might suffer from connecting thin structure artifacts.

Another related regularizer is the *star shape prior* [14,15], which imposes convexity constraints only along the lines passing through a reference point given by the user: these lines are allowed to enter and exit the object only once. In contrast to our convexity prior, the star shape allows for non-convex objects.

There are also part-based shape priors [16,17,18]. A shape is partitioned into several parts and each part imposes certain constraints on the direction of the boundary with the background. This approach can model some simple convex shapes, e.g. a rectangle, but it can not represent a general convexity prior.

Most related work is in [19], which models the object as an n-sided convex polygon. It is a part-based approach that uses one foreground and n background labels. For an accurate segmentation of an arbitrary convex object, e.g. a circle, a finer discretization (i.e. more background parts) is required, significantly increasing runtime. The larger the object, the worse is the problem. In contrast, we can obtain an arbitrary convex object for any choice of orientation discretization. Moreover,

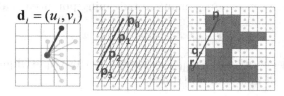

Fig. 2. Left: Example of discretized orientations given by a 5×5 stencil. One orientation d_i is highlighted. Middle: Set L_i of all discrete lines on image grid that are parallel to d_i. Right: Example of a triple clique (p, q, r) that violates convexity constraint.

[19] relies on continuous optimization and is not efficient without GPU. Additional related work on optimization is discussed in Sec. 4.3.

Contributions. We introduce a new discrete convexity shape regularizer. It is virtually parameter free: there is almost no variation in segmentation results for different values of the convexity weight, once the value is high enough, see Sec. 4. This leads to scale invariance, another desirable property. We develop an optimization algorithm based on trust region and show how to use dynamic programming to significantly improve efficiency. Finally, we experimentally validate the advantage of our covexity vs. the length regularizer for segmentation.

The paper is organized as follows. Sec. 2 formulates convexity energy and explains efficient evaluation. Sec. 3 explains trust-region optimization and its efficient implementation. Sec. 4 demonstrates the usefulness of convexity shape prior, and discusses alternative models, optimization schemes, and limitations.

2   Energy

Denote by Ω the set of all image pixels and let $S \subset \Omega$ be a segment. Let $\mathbf{x}$ be a vector of binary indicator variables $x_p \in \{0, 1\}, p \in \Omega$ such that $S = \{p \mid x_p = 1\}$. Due to one-to-one correspondence, we will use either $\mathbf{x}$ or S interchangeably.

In this paper we focus on convexity shape prior and propose a novel formulation to incorporate this prior into segmentation energy. In continuous case, segment S is convex if and only if for any $p, r \in S$ there is no q on a line between them s.t. $q \notin S$. In discrete case, we approximate convexity constrains as follows.

Let $i \in \{1, \ldots, m\}$ enumerate discrete line orientations, see Fig. 2a, and let L_i be the set of all *discrete lines* $l \subset \Omega$ of given orientation d_i such that

$$l = \{p_0, p_1, ..., p_n \mid p_t = p_0 + t \cdot d_i, \ t \in \mathcal{Z}^+, \ p_t \in \Omega\}. \tag{2}$$

Fig. 2b illustrates set L_i for one particular orientation d_i. One way to represent discrete convexity constraint can be based on potential $\phi : \{0, 1\}^3 \to \mathcal{R}$ defined for all triplets of ordered pixels (p, q, r) along any discrete line $l \in \bigcup L_i$

$$\phi(x_p, x_q, x_r) = \begin{cases} \infty & \text{if } (x_p, x_q, x_r) = (1, 0, 1) \\ 0 & \text{otherwise.} \end{cases}$$

In practice we use some finite penalty ω redefining potential ϕ algebraically as

$$\phi(x_p, x_q, x_r) = \omega \cdot x_p(1 - x_q)x_r. \tag{3}$$

The convexity energy $E_{\text{convexity}}(\mathbf{x})$ integrates this triple clique potential over all orientations, all lines and all triplets:

$$E_{\text{convexity}}(\mathbf{x}) = \sum_{l \in \bigcup L_i} \sum_{(p,q,r) \in l} \phi(x_p, x_q, x_r). \tag{4}$$

As discussed below, 3rd-order energy (4) is hard to optimize for two reasons: it is non-submodular and it has a prohibitively large number of cliques.

It is easy to verify that this energy is non-submodular [20]. It is enough to show that there exist segments $S, T \subset \Omega$ such that $E(S) + E(T) < E(S \cap T) + E(S \cup T)$. Consider the example on the right. Since both S and T are convex, the left hand side is zero, while the right hand side is infinite since the union of S and T is not convex. Therefore, our energy cannot be optimized with standard methods for submodular functions.

At the first glance, is seems prohibitively expensive to even evaluate our energy on reasonably sized images. For example, for an image of size 200×300, with just 8 orientations, there are roughly 32 billion triple cliques. In Sec. 2.1, 3.2 we show how to evaluate and approximate the $E_{\text{convexity}}$ in time linear wrt image size using dynamic programming. Then, in Sec. 3 we show how to optimize our energy using trust region techniques [21,11]. Other sparser convexity models and alternative optimization schemes are discussed in Sec. 4.3.

2.1   Energy Evaluation via Dynamic Programming

This section explains how to evaluate our convexity term $E_{convexity}(\mathbf{x})$ efficiently. We show how to compute the inner summation in (4) for one given line l. The idea is to use dynamic programming to efficiently count the number of triplets $(1, 0, 1)$ on a line violating convexity constraints.

Let $\mathbf{x}_l$ denote a vector of binary indicator variables on line l. Let $s, t, v \in \mathcal{Z}^+$, $s < t < v$ be non-negative integers enumerating the set of pixels on l as in definition (2). With some abuse of notation we denote by x_s, x_t, x_v the corresponding binary variables for pixels $p_s, p_t, p_v \in l$ and rewrite

$$E_{convexity}(\mathbf{x}_l) = \sum_{(p,q,r) \in l} \phi(x_p, x_q, x_r) = \omega \cdot \sum_t \sum_{s<t} \sum_{v>t} x_s \cdot (1 - x_t) \cdot x_v.$$

Consider pixels $p_s, p_t, p_v \in l$. We say pixel p_s *precedes* pixel p_t on line l if $s < t$. Similarly, pixel p_v *succeeds* pixel p_t if $v > t$. Let $C^-(t)$ be the number of pixels p_s preceding pixel p_t such that $x_s = 1$, and $C^+(t)$ be the number of pixels p_v succeeding pixel p_t such that $x_v = 1$:

$$C^-(t) = \sum_{s<t} x_s, \quad C^+(t) = \sum_{v>t} x_v. \tag{5}$$

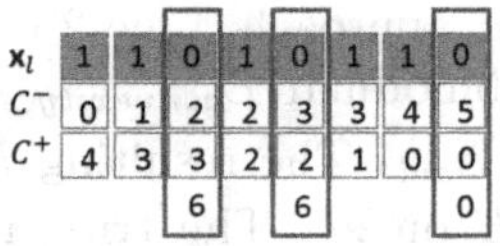

Fig. 3. Evaluation of $E_{convexity}$. The top row shows current configuration $\mathbf{x}_l$ of pixels on line l. The second and the third rows show the number of pixels p_s with $x_s = 1$ before and after each pixel p_t, that is, functions $C^-(t)$ and $C^+(t)$. The last row shows the number of violated constraints for each p_t with $x_t = 0$.

To count the number of all violating configuration $(1, 0, 1)$ for ordered triplets on line l we first consider one fixed pixel $p_t \in l$ with zero label $x_t = 0$. Each preceding pixel with label one and each succeeding pixel with label one form configuration $(1, 0, 1)$. Thus, the total combinatorial number of ordered triplets (p_s, p_t, p_v), $s < t < v$, with configuration $(1, 0, 1)$ is given by $C^+(t) \cdot C^-(t)$, see Fig. 3. Summing over all zero label pixels on line l gives

$$E_{convexity}(\mathbf{x}_l) = \omega \cdot \sum_t C^+(t) \cdot C^-(t) \cdot (1 - x_t).$$

Note that $C^-(t) = C^-(t-1) + x_{t-1}$. Hence both $C^+(t)$ and $C^-(t)$ can be computed for all pixels on a line in one pass using running sums. For a particular orientation d_i, each pixel appears in one line only. Therefore, the total number of operations needed to compute $E_{convexity}(\mathbf{x})$ is $O(mN)$, where $N = |\Omega|$ is the number of pixels in the image and m is the number of distinct orientations.

3   Optimization

This section describes our optimization algorithm for segmentation energy (1) with the convexity shape prior. In terms of indicator variables $\mathbf{x}$ this energy is

$$E(\mathbf{x}) = E_{convexity}(\mathbf{x}) + E_{sub}(\mathbf{x}) \tag{6}$$

where E_{sub} is any submodular term[1] that can be optimized with graph cuts, e.g. boundary length [1], color separation [10], etc. As mentioned earlier, our energy term $E_{convexity}$ is non-submodular. Therefore, (6) is hard to optimize. An additional difficulty is the large number of triple cliques in $E_{convexity}(\mathbf{x})$.

For optimization, we use iterative trust region framework [21], which has been shown promising for various non-submodular energies [11,6,22]. In each iteration, we construct an approximate tractable model $\tilde{E}^k$ of the energy E in (6) near current solution $\mathbf{x}^k$. The model is only accurate within a small region around $\mathbf{x}^k$ called "trust region". The approximate $\tilde{E}^k$ is then optimized within the trust region to obtain a candidate solution. This step is called *trust region sub-problem*. The size of the trust region is adjusted in each iteration based on the quality of the current approximation. See [21] for a review of trust region.

---

[1] The submodularity of the last term in (6) is assumed for clarity. The proposed trust region approach can approximate non-submodular terms jointly with $E_{convexity}$.

Algorithm 1 summarizes our approach. Line 2 computes unary approximate energy E_{approx}^k for the non-submodular $E_{convexity}$ around $\mathbf{x}^k$. Line 3 combines E_{approx}^k with the submodular E_{sub}. The resulting $\tilde{E}^k$ is submodular and coincides with the exact energy E on $\mathbf{x}^k$. The trust region sub-problem requires minimization of $\tilde{E}^k$ within a small region $||\mathbf{x} - \mathbf{x}^k|| \leq d_k$ around $\mathbf{x}^k$. Unfortunately, minimizing $\tilde{E}^k$ under distance constraints is NP-hard [22]. Instead, we use a simpler formulation of the trust region sub-problem proposed in [22,11] based on unconstrained optimization of submodular Lagrangian

$$L^k(\mathbf{x}) = \tilde{E}^k(\mathbf{x}) + \lambda_k ||\mathbf{x} - \mathbf{x}^k||. \tag{7}$$

Here parameter λ_k controls the trust region size indirectly instead of distance d_k. The distance term in (7) can be expressed using unary terms [11,22]. Therefore $L_k(\mathbf{x})$ is a submodular function. Line 5 solves (7) for some fixed λ_k using one graph-cut. The candidate solution $\mathbf{x}^*$ is accepted whenever the original energy decreases (line 11). The Lagrange multiplier λ_k is adaptively changed (line 13), based on the quality of the current approximation and as motivated by empirical inverse proportionality relation between λ_k and d_k (see discussion in [11]).

Algorithm 1. TRUST REGION CONVEXITY

---

1 **Repeat Until Convergence**
2   Compute approximation $E_{approx}^k(\mathbf{x})$ for $E_{convexity}(\mathbf{x})$ around $\mathbf{x}^k$ (see Sec. 3.1)
3      $\tilde{E}_k(\mathbf{x}) = E_{approx}^k(\mathbf{x}) + E_{sub}(\mathbf{x})$ // keep the submodular part unchanged
4   //**Trust region sub-problem: optimize approximate energy**
5      $\mathbf{x}^* \longleftarrow \operatorname{argmin}_{\mathbf{x}} L^k(\mathbf{x})$ (7)
6   //**Update current solution**
7   Evaluate $E_{convexity}(\mathbf{x}^k), E_{convexity}(\mathbf{x}^*)$ (see Sec. 2.1)
8   Evaluate $E_{approx}^k(\mathbf{x}), E_{approx}^k(\mathbf{x}^*)$ (see Sec. 3.2)
9      $R = E(\mathbf{x}^k) - E(\mathbf{x}^*)$ //actual reduction in energy
10     $P = \tilde{E}_k(\mathbf{x}^k) - \tilde{E}^k(\mathbf{x}^*)$ //predicted reduction in energy
11     $\mathbf{x}^{k+1} \longleftarrow \begin{cases} \mathbf{x}^* \text{ if } R/P > \tau_1 \\ \mathbf{x}^k \text{ otherwise} \end{cases}$
12   //**Adjust the trust region**
13     $d_{k+1} \longleftarrow \begin{cases} \lambda_k/\alpha \text{ if } R/P > \tau_2 \\ \lambda_k \cdot \alpha \text{ otherwise} \end{cases}$

3.1   Linear Approximation of $E_{convexity}$

In this section we derive linear approximation $E_{approx}^k(\mathbf{x})$ for the energy term $E_{convexity}(\mathbf{x})$ in (4) around current solution $\mathbf{x}^k$

$$E_{approx}^k(\mathbf{x}) = \sum_{l \in \bigcup L_i} \sum_{(p,q,r) \in l} \phi^k(x_p, x_q, x_r)$$

where $\phi^k(x_p, x_q, x_r)$ is a linear approximation of the corresponding triple clique potential $\phi(x_p, x_q, x_r)$ in (3) around $\mathbf{x}^k$, as explained below.

Property 1. For any potential $\phi(\mathbf{x}) : \{0,1\}^n \to \mathcal{R}$ of n binary variables $\mathbf{x} = (x_1, \ldots, x_n)$ and any subset $A \subset \{0,1\}^n$ of $n+1$ distinct binary configurations of $\mathbf{x}$, there is a linear function $L_A(\mathbf{x}) = a_0 + a_1 x_1 + a_2 x_2 + \ldots + a_n x_n$ such that $\phi(\mathbf{x}) = L(\mathbf{x})$ for any $\mathbf{x} \in A$.

For example, Fig.2 in [22] shows linear approximations of any pairwise potential ($n = 2$) that are exact for $n + 1 = 3$ out of $2^n = 4$ binary configurations.

Based on Prop. 1, one way to approximate potential $\phi(\mathbf{x})$ in (3) is to compute $n + 1$ unknown coefficients of $L_A(\mathbf{x})$ by solving a system of $n + 1$ equations $\phi(\mathbf{x}) = L_A(\mathbf{x})$ for $n + 1$ binary configurations in some chosen A. We take an alternative practical approach that avoids solving systems of equations and implicitly selects a specific set A. Note, any discrete potential ϕ can be written as a combination of *multilinear* functions of variables $(x_1, \ldots, x_n)$, see (3). In this case, it is easy to verify that Taylor expansion ϕ^k of the potential ϕ around configuration $\mathbf{x}^k$ is a linear function satisfying Prop. 1. That is, $\phi^k(\mathbf{x})$ agrees with $\phi(\mathbf{x})$ on configuration $\mathbf{x}^k$ and n other "neighboring" configurations obtained by flipping one of the variables in $\mathbf{x}^k = (x_1^k, \ldots, x_n^k)$. Omitting the constant terms, Taylor expansion of (3) around $\mathbf{x}^k$ yields[2]:

$$\phi^k(x_p, x_q, x_r) = (1 - x_q^k) \cdot x_r^k \cdot x_p - x_r^k \cdot x_p^k \cdot x_q + (1 - x_q^k) \cdot x_p^k \cdot x_r. \qquad (8)$$

The components in (8) have an intuitive interpretation. Consider the first component $(1 - x_q^k) \cdot x_r^k \cdot x_p$. Recall that pixels p, q, r are on a line and q is between p and r. If the current configuration $\mathbf{x}^k$ is such that $x_q^k = 0$, and $x_r^k = 1$, then assigning label 1 to pixel p violates convexity, assuming q and r keep their labels unchanged from $\mathbf{x}^k$. The unary term $(1 - x_q^k) \cdot x_r^k \cdot x_p$ penalizes this violation: assignment $x_p = 1$ carries a penalty, whereas $x_p = 0$ is not penalized. The other two components in (8) have similar intuitive interpretations.

Approximation in (8) gives three unary terms for each triple clique. Consider line l. Pixel p can be either the leftmost, middle, or rightmost member of a clique on that line. Sum the terms from all triple cliques on line l involving pixel p. First with p being on the left, then in the middle and finally on the right of the clique. All these terms contribute to the unary potential for a single pixel p:

$$u_p^l(x_p) = \sum_{(p,q,r)\in l}(1 - x_q^k) \cdot x_r^k \cdot x_p - \sum_{(q,p,r)\in l} x_q^k \cdot x_r^k \cdot x_p + \sum_{(q,r,p)\in l} (1 - x_r^k) \cdot x_q^k \cdot x_p. \qquad (9)$$

The full Taylor based unary term for pixel p sums $u_p^l(x_p)$ over all lines,

$$u_p(x_p) = \sum_{l \in \bigcup L_i} u_p^l(x_p) \qquad (10)$$

Fig. 5 illustrates the resulting unary terms arising from such approximation. They encourage any holes in the foreground segment to be filled in, and any protrusions to be erased. Efficient computation of (10) is discussed in Section 3.2.

There is a relation between the Taylor unary terms in (10) and parallel ICM algorithm, noted in [23]. However, our trust region framework has many differences from parallel ICM [23]. See [22] for a detailed comparison.

---

[2] Here we assume $\omega = 1$. If $\omega \neq 1$, all the derived formulas should be multiplied by ω.

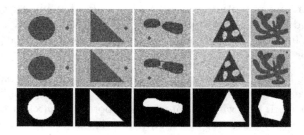

Fig. 4. First row shows synthetic images with added noise $\sigma_{noise} = 0.2$; Second and third rows show contours and masks of segmentation, $\omega = 0.1$. We used log-likelihood appearance terms, $(\mu_{fg} = 0, \sigma_{fg} = 0.1)$ and $(\mu_{bg} = 1, \sigma_{bg} = 0.1)$. The convexity prior removes noise, connects components and fills holes while preserving sharp corners.

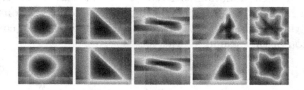

Fig. 5. First and second rows show unary approximation terms of $E_{convexity}$ as in (10) during the first and second iterations of trust region for the examples in Fig. 4. Red-yellow colors denote preference to background, and blue-cyan colors - preference to foreground. Unary terms encourage filling of holes and removal of protrusions.

3.2   Energy Approximation via Dynamic Programming

Naive computation of the summations in (10) is too costly. We now explain how to compute the unary terms in (10) efficiently. Similarly to Sec. 2.1, the speedup is achieved with running sums on each line. In (10), each u_p sums over all lines $l \in \bigcup L_i$. As in Sec. 2.1 we first show how to efficiently compute $u_p^l(x_p)$ in (9).

Let $s, t, v \in \mathcal{Z}^+$ enumerate pixels on l and rewrite (9)

$$u_t(x_t) = x_t \left(\sum_{s>t}\sum_{v>s}(1 - x_s^k) \cdot x_v^k - \sum_{s<t}\sum_{v>t} x_s^k \cdot x_v^k + \sum_{v<t}\sum_{s<v} x_s^k \cdot (1 - x_v^k) \right). \quad (11)$$

In (11), the first sum counts the number of pixel pairs (p_s, p_v) such that $t < s < v$ and $x_s^k = 0, x_v^k = 1$. The second sum counts the number of pixels pairs (p_s, p_v) such that $s < t < v$ and $x_s^k = x_v^k = 1$. The last sum counts the number of pixels pairs (p_s, p_v) such that $s < v < t$ and $x_s^k = 1, x_v^k = 0$.

Let C^- and C^+ be as in (5). Recall that each of them can be computed in one pass over the line. Then the second sum in (11) is simply $C^-(t) \cdot C^+(t)$. For the other two sums, we need additional running sums.

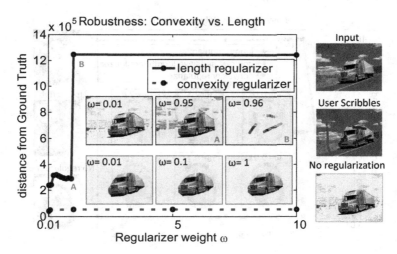

Fig. 6. Illustration of robustness to parameter ω: results for length regularization are shown with blue color and for convexity shape prior - with green. See text for details.

Denote by $A^-(t)$ the number of pixel pairs (p_s, p_v) preceding pixel p_t such that $x_s^k = 1$, $x_v^k = 0$ and pixel p_s precedes pixel p_v,

$$A^-(t) = \sum_{v<t}\sum_{s<v} x_s^k \cdot (1 - x_v^k).$$

Given C^-, we compute A^- in one pass over line l using $A^-(0) = A^-(1) = 0$ and recurrence $A^-(t) = A^-(t-1) + (1 - x_{t-1}^k) \cdot C^-(t-1)$.

Similarly, we define $A^+(t)$ as the number of pixel pairs (p_s, p_v) succeeding pixel p_t such that $x_s^k = 0$, $x_v^k = 1$ and pixel p_v succeeds pixel p_s,

$$A^+(t) = \sum_{s>t}\sum_{v>s} (1 - x_s^k) \cdot x_v^k.$$

A^+ is computed analogously to A^-, given C^+. Then the first sum in (11) is $A^+(t)$ and the third sum is $A^-(t)$, and $u_t(x_t) = A^+(t) - C^-(t) \cdot C^+(t) + A^-(t)$.

Computing A^- and A^+ is linear in the number of pixels on a line. For orientation d_i, each pixel appears on one line only. Therefore we can compute A^- and A^+ for all lines in $O(mN)$ time, where m is the number of orientations and $N = |\Omega|$. Then the unary term for each pixel is computed in $O(m)$ time. Thus the total time to compute Taylor based unary terms for all pixels is $O(mN)$.

4   Experiments

Below we apply convexity shape prior to image segmentation. We discretized orientations using 11×11 stencil yielding 40 orientations for all synthetic images. For natural images we found a 5×5 stencil yielding 8 orientations sufficient. The code is available from http://vision.csd.uwo.ca/code/.

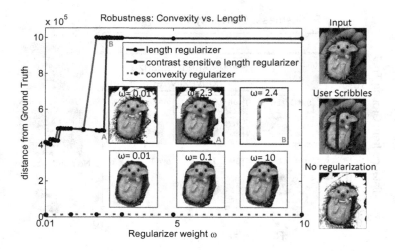

Fig. 7. Illustration of robustness to parameter ω: results for length regularization are shown with blue color and for convexity shape prior - with green. See text for details.

4.1 Synthetic Images

First we validate our method on synthetic images with noise $\mathcal{N}(0, 0.2)$, see Fig. 4. We assume given target appearance distributions for foreground and background, and combine standard log-likelihood data terms with the convexity shape prior

$$E(\mathbf{x}) = E_{app}(\mathbf{x}) + E_{convexity}(\mathbf{x}).$$

Here $E_{app}(\mathbf{x}) = \sum_{p \in \Omega} D_p(x_p)$ is the appearance term, $D_p(x_p) = -\log Pr(I_p|x_p)$ and $E_{convexity}(\mathbf{x})$ is as in (4). Fig. 4 demonstrates that our convexity prior removes noise, insures connectivity and fills in holes while preserving sharp corners.

4.2 Real Images

Next, we use convexity prior in interactive segmentation of natural images with user scribbles. The convexity prior is especially useful for images where there is an overlap between the foreground and background appearance, see Figures 6-9. Such overlap often leads to holes in the foreground or larger parts of the background erroneously segmented as the foreground, see Figures 6-8(bottom-right). The convexity prior prevents such results. Length regularization is either too weak to remove the noise or too strong causing shrinking.

We now specify the details of our interactive segmentation. For appearance we use the recent submodular L_1 *color separation* term proposed in [10]. This term is based on L_1 distance between unnormalized histograms of foreground and background colors. Unlike standard appearance models, the color separation does not require re-estimation of the parameters and can be efficiently and globally optimized. We use 16 bins per color channel and combine the color separation

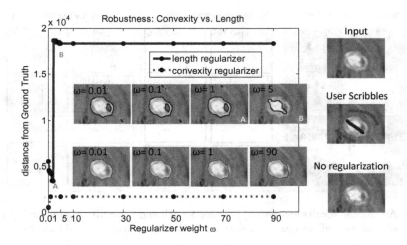

Fig. 8. Illustration of robustness to parameter ω: results for length regularization are shown with blue color and for convexity shape prior - with green. See text for details.

term with the convexity prior, subject to hard constraints on the user scribbles

$$E(\mathbf{x}) = E_{L1}(\mathbf{x}) + E_{convexity}(\mathbf{x}).$$

We then compare with the standard length regularization

$$E(\mathbf{x}) = E_{L1}(\mathbf{x}) + \sum_{(pq)\in\mathcal{N}} \omega[x_p \neq x_q].$$

Figures 6-8 show segmentation results on two natural and one medical image. We vary the weight ω for our convexity prior in (3) and optimize as discussed in Sec. 3. Similarly, we vary the weight ω for the length regularizer above and optimize with one graph-cut [10]. We then plot the distance between the resulting segment and the ground truth as a function of ω (green line - for convexity prior, blue - for length). We also show segmentations for several key points on the plot (green frames - for convexity, blue - for length) and compare them with the results obtained without regularization. The length regularization is either too weak to remove the noise or too strong and has a shrinking bias.

We experiment both with contrast sensitive length (ω depends on pixel pair (p, q) as in [9]) and pure length, see Fig. 7. There is no significant difference in their performance. The same sensitivity to the parameter values is observed; compare the red (contrast sensitive) curve with the blue one (pure length).

Our model is scale invariant due to infinity cost constraints. In practice, we have to choose finite ω. There is almost no variation in segmentation results for different values of ω, once the value is high enough, making it a virtually parameter-free regularizer. In fact, for each image we can compute finite ω such that violating a single constraint is more expensive than the initial solution. In

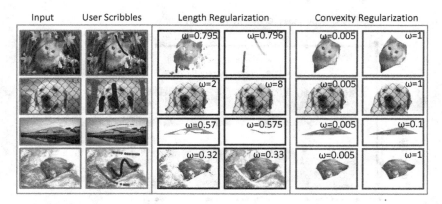

Fig. 9. Additional results comparing between length and convexity regularizers. Except for the second row, all images demonstrate sensitivity to length weight ω.

cases where using such large ω leads to poor local minimum, gradually increasing the weight ω (annealing) can potentially escape to a better solution.

4.3 Alternative Convexity Models and Optimization

Below we discuss some variations of our convexity model and optimization.

Central Cliques Model. One natural question regarding our model is whether we need *all* the triple cliques on a line to enforce convexity. Indeed, it is sufficient to use a smaller subset consisting only of *central* triple cliques (p, q, r), i.e. $|p - q| = |q - r|$, see example on the right. This reduces the number of triple cliques from $O(n^3)$ to $O(n^2)$ for a line with n pixels. However, our dynamic programming procedures for evaluation (Sec. 2.1) and for approximation (Sec. 3.2) are no longer applicable. Brute force computation takes $O(n^2)$ operations per line with n pixels, as opposed to linear time with our dynamic programming for the full model. Nonetheless, we compare between our full model and the central cliques model, see Fig.10. Since the resulting segmentations have no convexity violations their energies can be directly compared. The energy is slightly better with the central cliques, but its running time is 25-30 times longer. The difference in time will be even more significant for larger images.

Alternative Optimization Methods. The most related optimization method is LSA [22], which is also based on trust region framework. However, it was designed for non-submodular energies with only *pairwise* cliques. For this class of energies, LSA reports state-of-the-art results [22]. LSA approximates the energy by replacing non-submodular pairwise cliques with their Taylor expansions while preserving all submodular pairwise cliques. Even though our convexity prior is not pairwise, it is possible to reduce each triple clique to several pairwise po-

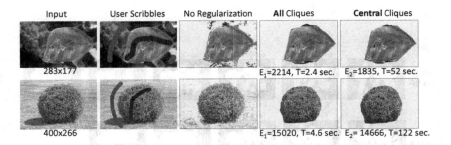

Fig. 10. Comparison between the full convexity model with all triple cliques vs. central cliques convexity model. The later does not allow efficient evaluation and approximation of $E_{convexity}$ using dynamic programming and therefore is much slower.

tentials using an additional auxiliary node [24] and optimize them with LSA. We call this reduced version r-LSA. Reducing all triple cliques would result in a prohibitively large number of auxiliary nodes and pairwise cliques for our full convexity model. Even for the central clique model the number of resulting pairwise cliques is quite large. An $n \times n$ image with m orientations for central cliques produces $O(mn^3)$ pairwise potentials, which is very costly both to optimize and to evaluate. Nonetheless, we tried this approach on a small 91×122 image. The first two rows in Figure 11 compare r-LSA approach to our method. We apply both methods to the central clique model[3] and vary ω. Note that r-LSA is an order of magnitude slower than the slow version of our method. As the value of ω increases, r-LSA fails to obtain satisfactory solutions. We believe that there could be serious drawbacks in splitting clique $\phi(x_p, x_q, x_r)$ into individual submodular and supermodular parts and then approximating the supermodular part. One sign of a problem is that there are infinitely many such decompositions and it is not clear which one would give a better approximation.

Our full model with all triple cliques is also prohibitively expensive for standard optimization methods designed for non-submodular energies, such as QPBO [25] and TRWS [26]. However, we can use these methods to optimize the more compact central clique model as well. The last two rows in Figure 11 show segmentation results of QPBO and TRWS for several values of ω. For values of ω that are not sufficiently large to enforce convexity, all four methods, QPBO, TRWS, r-LSA and Trust Region, return globally optimum, but useless solutions. However, when ω is large enough, QPBO, TRWS and r-LSA fail to obtain a satisfactory result. Our trust region approach obtains good results in all cases.

4.4   Optimization Limitations

Trust region framework is a local iterative optimization and therefore we can only guarantee a local minimum [11]. Figure 12 demonstrates some sensitivity with

---

[3] Even though the full model is more efficient for our method, for this experiment we use central cliques to have identical energies for direct comparison.

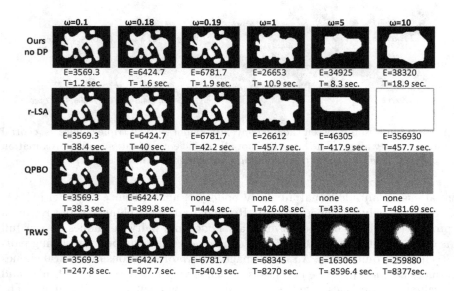

Fig. 11. Comparison between our method without dynamic programming (no DP), r-LSA, QPBO and TRWS on the central clique model with 8 orientations. We use thresholded appearance terms for initialization when needed. As ω increases, making the energy more difficult, QPBO was not able to label any pixel (shown in gray) and TRWS did not converge after 5000 iterations, which took several hours. For ω large enough to enforce convexity, all methods except ours fail.

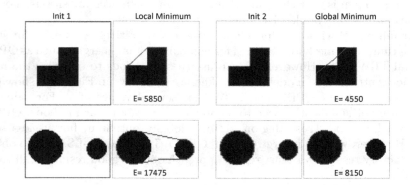

Fig. 12. Local optimization of convexity shape prior might yeild different segmentation results for different initializations. We used 40 orientations, $\omega = 10$ and given target appearance models $(\mu_{fg} = 0, \sigma_{fg} = 0.1)$, $(\mu_{bg} = 1, \sigma_{bg} = 0.1)$.

respect to initialization. A trivial initialization with all pixels in the foreground, denoted by "init 1" and delineated by the red contour, leads to a local minimum. Initializing with the maximum likelihood label per pixel, denoted by "init 2" results in a global optimum, verified by geometrical arguments. Empirically, we obtain better results starting with maximum likelihood labels. This is consistent for all the experiments, both on synthetic and real images.

5   Conclusion and Future Work

We propose convexity prior as a new regularizer and develop efficient discrete optimization based on trust region and dynamic programming. Our regularizer is scale invariant, does not have shrinking bias, and is virtually parameter-free.

In the future, we plan to explore meaningful relaxations of strict convexity. For example, we can explore contrast sensitive convexity, which is similar to contrast sensitive length. The penalty for convexity violation by triplet (p, q, r) can carry a smaller weight if there is a high contrast on a line connecting pixels p and r. This formulation is straightforward, but the main difficulty will be extending our dynamic programming algorithms to handle this case. Another direction is to extend our model to handle objects with multiple convex parts.

References

1. Boykov, Y., Kolmogorov, V.: Computing geodesics and minimal surfaces via graph cuts. In: International Conference on Computer Vision, pp. 26–33 (2003)
2. Pock, T., Cremers, D., Bischof, H., Chambolle, A.: Global solutions of variational models with convex regularization. SIAM Journal on Imaging Sciences 3, 1122–1145 (2010)
3. Schoenemann, T., Kahl, F., Masnou, S., Cremers, D.: A linear framework for region-based image segmentation and inpainting involving curvature penalization. Int. Journal of Computer Vision (2012)
4. Bredies, K., Pock, T., Wirth, B.: Convex relaxation of a class of vertex penalizing functionals. J. Math. Imaging and Vision 47(3), 278–302 (2013)
5. Olsson, C., Ulen, J., Boykov, Y., Kolmogorov, V.: Partial enumeration and curvature regularization. In: International Conference on Computer Vision (ICCV), Sydney, Australia (December 2013)
6. Nieuwenhuis, C., Töppe, E., Gorelick, L., Veksler, O., Boykov, Y.: Efficient regularization of squared curvature. In: IEEE conference on Computer Vision and Pattern Recognition (CVPR), pp. 4098–4105 (June 2014)
7. Liu, Z., Jacobs, D., Basri, R.: The role of convexity in perceptual completion: beyond good continuation. Vision Research 39, 4244–4257 (1999)
8. Mamassian, P., Landy, M.: Observer biases in the 3d interpretation of line drawings. Vision Research 38, 2817–2832 (1998)
9. Boykov, Y., Jolly, M.P.: Interactive graph cuts for optimal boundary and region segmentation of objects in N-D images. In: IEEE International Conference on Computer Vision, ICCV (2001)
10. Tang, M., Gorelick, L., Veksler, O., Boykov, Y.: Grabcut in one cut. In: International Conference on Computer Vision (2013)

11. Gorelick, L., Schmidt, F.R., Boykov, Y.: Fast trust region for segmentation. In: IEEE conference on Computer Vision and Pattern Recognition (CVPR), Portland, Oregon, pp. 1714–1721 (June 2013)
12. Vicente, S., Kolmogorov, V., Rother, C.: Graph cut based image segmentation with connectivity priors. In: IEEE Conference on Computer Vision and Pattern Recognition, CVPR (2008)
13. Nowozin, S., Lampert, C.H.: Global interactions in random field models: A potential function ensuring connectedness. SIAM J. Imaging Sciences 3(4), 1048–1074 (2010)
14. Veksler, O.: Star shape prior for graph-cut image segmentation. In: Forsyth, D., Torr, P., Zisserman, A. (eds.) ECCV 2008, Part III. LNCS, vol. 5304, pp. 454–467. Springer, Heidelberg (2008)
15. Gulshan, V., Rother, C., Criminisi, A., Blake, A., Zisserman, A.: Geodesic star convexity for interactive image segmentation. In: IEEE Conference on Computer Vision and Pattern Recognition (CVPR (June 2010)
16. Winn, J., Shotton, J.: The layout consistent random field for recognizing and segmenting partially occluded objects. In: IEEE Conference on Computer Vision and Pattern Recognition (CVPR), pp. 37–44 (2006)
17. Liu, X., Veksler, O., Samarabandu, J.: Order-preserving moves for graph-cut based optimization. Transactions on Pattern Analysis and Machine Intelligence (tPAMI) 32, 1182–1196 (2010)
18. Felzenszwalb, P., Veksler, O.: Tiered scene labeling with dynamic programming. In: IEEE Conference on Computer Vision and Pattern Recognition, CVPR (2010)
19. Strekalovskiy, E., Cremers, D.: Generalized ordering constraints for multilabel optimization. In: International Conference on Computer Vision, ICCV (2011)
20. Fujishige, S.: Submodular functions and optimization. Annals of Discrete Mathematics (1991)
21. Yuan, Y.: A review of trust region algorithms for optimization. In: The Fourth International Congress on Industrial & Applied Mathematics, ICIAM (1999)
22. Gorelick, L., Boykov, Y., Veksler, O., Ben Ayed, I., Delong, A.: IEEE Conference on Computer Vision and Pattern Recognition (CVPR), pp. 1154–1161 (June 2014)
23. Leordeanu, M., Hebert, M., Sukthankar, R.: An integer projected fixed point method for graph matching and map inference. In: Neural Information Processing Systems (NIPS), pp. 1114–1122 (2009)
24. Kolmogorov, V., Zabih, R.: What energy functions can be minimized via graph cuts? IEEE Trans. Pattern Anal. Mach. Intell. 26(2), 147–159 (2004)
25. Boros, E., Hammer, P.L.: Pseudo-boolean optimization. Discrete Applied Mathematics 123, 2002 (2001)
26. Kolmogorov, V., Schoenemann, T.: Generalized sequential tree-reweighted message passing. arXiv:1205.6352 (2012)

Pseudo-bound Optimization for Binary Energies

Meng Tang[1], Ismail Ben Ayed[1,2], and Yuri Boykov[1]

[1] University of Western Ontario, Canada
[2] GE Healthcare, Canada

Abstract. High-order and non-submodular pairwise energies are important for image segmentation, surface matching, deconvolution, tracking and other computer vision problems. Minimization of such energies is generally *NP-hard*. One standard approximation approach is to optimize an *auxiliary function* - an upper bound of the original energy across the entire solution space. This bound must be amenable to fast global solvers. Ideally, it should also closely approximate the original functional, but it is very difficult to find such upper bounds in practice.

Our main idea is to relax the upper-bound condition for an auxiliary function and to replace it with a family of pseudo-bounds, which can better approximate the original energy. We use fast polynomial parametric maxflow approach to explore all global minima for our family of submodular pseudo-bounds. The best solution is guaranteed to decrease the original energy because the family includes at least one auxiliary function. Our Pseudo-Bound Cuts algorithm improves the state-of-the-art in many applications: appearance entropy minimization, target distribution matching, curvature regularization, image deconvolution and interactive segmentation.

Keywords: Binary energy minimization, high-order and non-submodular functions, auxiliary functions, parametric maxflow, pseudo-bounds.

1 Introduction

Recently high-order [2,3,12,13,15,26,29,37] and non-submodular pairwise [11,16,21,19] energy minimization have drawn tremendous research interests. Those energy functions arise naturally in many computer vision and image processing applications. Examples of high-order functions include but are not limited to constraints on segment volume [12,37], clique labeling consistency [13,18,35] and matching target distributions [2,3,12,29]. Pairwise non-submodular energies occur in deconvolution [11], curvature regularization [8,11,28], inpainting [16] and surface registration [16].

In general, optimization of high-order or non-submodular pairwise energy is *NP-hard*. Existing approximation methods make optimization tractable either by *global* or *local* linearization. Well established LP relaxation methods such as QPBO [4,30] and TRWS [19] are examples of global linearization techniques for solving non-submodular energies in vision [16]. By relaxing the integrality constraints, they globally transform the original function into a linear function

D. Fleet et al. (Eds.): ECCV 2014, Part V, LNCS 8693, pp. 691–707, 2014.
© Springer International Publishing Switzerland 2014

with extra variables and linear constraints. Unlike global linearization, local techniques iteratively approximate the original energy around current solution, for instance, using Taylor approximations [11,12,17,24] or auxiliary functions [2,3,11,27,29,31]. The recent Fast Trust Region (FTR) method [12] finds the optimal solution of a local approximation within a trust region, *i.e.* a region near current solution where the approximation can be trusted. The trust region size is adaptively adjusted depending on the quality of current approximation using well-known trust region paradigms [38]. The recent studies [11,12] have shown that FTR achieved the state of the art performance in many applications. Our work is more closely related to bound optimizers, which take auxiliary functions [2,3,11,22,27,29,31] as local approximations and were recently shown to yield competitive performances in several vision problems [3,11,29].

1.1   Bound Optimization

We tackle binary energy functions $E(S)$ where $S = \{s_p \,|\, p \in \Omega\}$ is a vector of binary variables for pixels $p \in \Omega$. *Bound optimizers* iteratively minimize an *auxiliary function* bounding the original energy across the entire solution space.

Definition 1 (Auxiliary function). $A_t(S)$ *is an auxiliary function of $E(S)$ at current solution S_t if it satisfies the following conditions:*

$$E(S) \leq A_t(S), \forall S \tag{1a}$$
$$E(S_t) = A_t(S_t). \tag{1b}$$

Then, the current solution S_t is updated to the global optimum of the auxiliary function:

$$S_{t+1} = \arg\min_{S} A_t(S), \quad t = 1, 2, \ldots \tag{2}$$

Ideally optimization of the auxiliary function is easier than that of the original energy. Bound optimizers guarantee not to increase the original energy at each iteration since we have

$$E(S_{t+1}) \leq A_t(S_{t+1}) \leq A_t(S_t) = E(S_t). \tag{3}$$

Examples of well-known bound optimizers include mean-shift [9], difference of convex functions (DC) programming techniques [1], expectation maximization (EM) and submodular-supermodular procedures [27]. Besides, bound optimizers successfully tackled various problems in machine learning [39], computational statistics [22] and nonnegative matrix factorization [23].

In vision, bound optimizers were recently used for high-order or non-submodular pairwise energies [3,29,11,31]. The recent Auxiliary Cuts [3] work derived bounds for certain class of high-order functions. A variant of Auxiliary Cuts (LSA-AUX) is proposed in [11] for quadratic pseudo-boolean optimization.

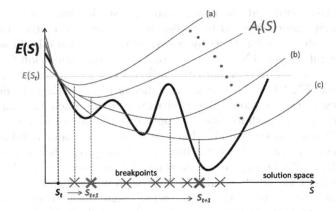

Fig. 1. Illustration of how pseudo-bound optimization framework updates current solution from S_t to S_{t+1}. Instead of optimizing only one auxiliary function $A_t(S)$, we explore a parametric family of pseudo-bounds. The best solution with the minimum original energy is chosen among the set of all global minima for the family. They correspond to breakpoints of parametric maxflow method [20] that can be efficiently explored in polynomial time. By optimizing the family of pseudo-bounds, larger decrease in energy is achieved ($S_t \rightarrow S_{t+1}$). [Best viewed in color]

1.2   Motivation and Contributions

Typically, for bound optimizers, one auxiliary function is chosen and optimized at each iteration. Furthermore, such an auxiliary function has to be an upper bound for the original energy $E(S)$ across the entire solution space, see $A_t(S)$ in Fig.1. However, in practice, it is difficult to find bounds that approximate well the original energy while being amenable to fast global solvers. Although working well for some applications, *auxiliary cuts* [3,11] may converge to undesirable solutions for several types of functions, see a representative example in Fig. 2.

Our main idea is to relax the bound condition for an auxiliary function replacing it with pseudo-bounds, which may better approximate the original energy. Consider the example in Fig.1. Auxiliary function $A_t(S)$ does guarantee that its global minimum decreases the original energy $E(S)$, see Sec.1.1. However, there are many other approximation functions whose global minimum also decrease the original energy. For example, optimal solutions for (a) and (c) decrease $E(S)$ because these functions are local upper bounds for $E(S)$ around their global minima. Function (b) does not have this local bound property, but its global minimum still decreases the original energy. Moreover, solutions obtained by minimizing other approximation functions, e.g. (c), could be better than the one from the upper bound, *i.e.* auxiliary function $A_t(S)$. In that sense, relaxing the upper bound constraint allows better approximations of $E(S)$.

We want to design an optimization algorithm using a larger class of relaxed bounds, which could give better solutions than proper auxiliary functions. The key challenge is choosing such *pseudo-bounds* so as to guarantee the original energy decrease; note that the upper bound constraint was used when proving (3). One way to proceed could be to design some specific relaxed bounds that guarantee the decrease for $E(S)$ by construction. For example, in some applications it might be possible to design a particular approximation function that is guaranteed to locally dominate the original energy only around its global optimum, as in Fig.1 (a) or (c), which is sufficient to prove the decrease of $E(S)$.

This paper follows an alternative approximation approach. Instead of a single auxiliary function, at each iteration we optimize a family of *pseudo-bounds* that includes only one proper bound, while the bound constraint is relaxed for the other functions. As shown in Sec.2.1, inclusion of one proper bound is sufficient to guarantee the original energy decrease when the best solution is selected among global minima for the whole family. As illustrated in Fig.1 and confirmed by our practical experiments, relaxation of the bound constraint allows to significantly improve the quality of optimization compared to auxiliary functions, even when pseudo-bounds come from the same class of globally optimizable functionals.

A parametric family of pseudo-bounds is built as follows. We start from a known optimizable, *i.e.* submodular, auxiliary function and add a unary *bound relaxation* term weighted by a parameter. In order to explore all global minima for the whole parametric family efficiently, we propose parametric maxflow [20,14,10], reviewed in Sec. 2.2. To find all global minima for the whole family in polynomial time, the unary bound relaxation term must be monotone w.r.t. parameter. This practical consideration is important when selecting parametric pseudo-bound families for specific applications, e.g (12), (16), or (19). Note that parametric maxflow can be easily parallelized to further accelerate our algorithm.

Our contributions can be summarized as follows.

- This paper proposes a new general *pseudo-bound optimization* paradigm for approximate iterative minimization of high-order and non-submodular binary energies. It is a generalization of the standard *majorize-minimize* principle relaxing the bound constraint for an auxiliary function.
- We optimize a parametric family of pseudo-bounds at each iteration. To guarantee the energy decreases we include one proper bound in the family.
- In the context of discrete optimization, we propose parametric maxflow technique [20,14,10] to explore all global minima for the whole family in low-order polynomial time. To guarantee this complexity, we can choose families of pseudo-bounds with *monotone* dependence on parameter.
- We propose and discuss several examples of pseudo-bound families for different high-order and non-submodular pairwise energies.
- Our *parametric Pseudo-Bound Cuts* algorithm (pPBC) improves the-state-of-the-art in many energy minimization problems, e.g. entropy based image segmentation, target distributions matching, curvature regularization and image deconvolution. In particular, we outperform the standard GrabCut algorithm [32] both in terms of energy and segmentation error statistics. Our pseudo-bound approach is more robust to initialization and binning. Our pPBC algorithm also gives lower energy than *Auxiliary Cuts* [3] and *Fast Trust Region* [12] for distribution matching, see Fig. 2, and other challenging optimization problems in computer vision, see Section 4.

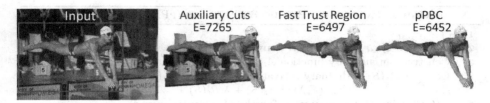

Fig. 2. Matching target foreground color distribution using auxiliary cuts [3], fast trust region [12] and pPBC. pPBC achieves the lowest energy.

2   Parametric Pseudo-bound Cuts (pPBC)

2.1   Our Pseudo-bound Framework

First, we define a family of *pseudo-bounds* for a scalar parameter λ with values in some set $\Lambda \subseteq \mathbb{R}$, for example $\Lambda = [\lambda^{min}, \lambda^{max}]$.

Definition 2 (Pseudo-Bound). *Assume energy $E(S)$, some current solution $S_t \in \{0,1\}^{\Omega}$ and parameter $\lambda \in \Lambda$. Then, function $\mathcal{F}_t(S, \lambda) : \{0,1\}^{\Omega} \times \Lambda \to \mathbb{R}$ is called a* pseudo bound *for energy $E(S)$ if there exists $\lambda' \in \Lambda$ such that $\mathcal{F}_t(S, \lambda')$ is an auxiliary function for $E(S)$ at current solution S_t.*

We may informally refer to pseudo-bound function $\mathcal{F}_t(S, \lambda)$ as a family of pseudo-bounds or a parametric family.

Our goal is to iteratively update current solution S_t for energy $E(S)$. Instead of bound optimization discussed in Sec.1.1, we propose Algorithm 1 that computes new better solution S_{t+1} by optimizing pseudo-bound $\mathcal{F}_t(S, \lambda)$ as follows.

Proposition 1. *Assume energy $E(S)$, current solution S_t and a pseudo-bound family $\mathcal{F}_t(S, \lambda)$ over parameter $\lambda \in \Lambda$. Let S^{λ} denote an optimal solution for $\mathcal{F}_t(S, \lambda)$ at any particular λ:*

$$S^{\lambda} = \arg\min_{S} \mathcal{F}_t(S, \lambda). \tag{4}$$

Then, $\lambda^* = \arg\min_{\lambda} E(S^{\lambda})$ gives solution $S_{t+1} := S^{\lambda^*}$ reducing original energy

$$E(S_{t+1}) = E(S^{\lambda^*}) \leq E(S_t).$$

Proof. Pseudo-bound family $\mathcal{F}_t(S, \lambda)$ contains an auxiliary function $\mathcal{F}_t(S, \lambda')$ for some λ'. Optimization over the whole family should give better solution than one particular function $E(S^{\lambda^*}) \leq E(S^{\lambda'})$. Then, the proposition follows from the property of auxiliary functions $E(S^{\lambda'}) \leq E(S_t)$, see (3). □

We construct a pseudo-bound family at current solution S_t by augmenting some auxiliary function $A_t(S)$ with a weighted *bound relaxation* term $R_t(S)$:

$$\mathcal{F}_t(S, \lambda) = A_t(S) + \lambda\, R_t(S). \tag{5}$$

Algorithm 1. PARAMETRIC PSEUDO-BOUND CUTS (pPBC)

---

1 $S_0 \longleftarrow S_{init}$
2 **For** $t = 0, 1, 2, ...,$ **repeat until convergence**
3   Construct an auxiliary function $A_t(S)$ at current solution S_t;
4   Combine $A_t(S)$ with unary relaxation term $R_t(S)$ to form pseudo-bound
$$\mathcal{F}_t(S, \lambda) = A_t(S) + \lambda \, R_t(S)$$
5   //**Optimize the parametric family of pseudo-bounds**
$$S^\lambda = \arg\min_S \mathcal{F}_t(S, \lambda), \text{ for } \lambda \in \Lambda$$
6   //**Score candidate solutions and update**
$$\lambda^* = \arg\min_\lambda E(S^\lambda), \qquad S_{t+1} \longleftarrow S^{\lambda^*}$$

Note that for $\lambda = 0$ our pseudo-bound $\mathcal{F}_t(S, \lambda)$ in (5) reduces to auxiliary function $A_t(S)$. Starting from the same current solution S_t, our pseudo-bound optimization is guaranteed to find at least as good or better solution than optimization of bound $A_t(S)$. While pseudo-bound may not be a proper bound for $\lambda \neq 0$, it may better approximate the original energy $E(S)$, see Fig.1.

In the context of binary energies $E(S)$ we typically choose some submodular $A_t(S)$ and modular (unary) $R_t(S)$. The resulting pseudo-bound family (5) is of the form (6) that allows to efficiently explore the whole set of solutions S^λ with standard *parametric maxflow* techniques reviewed in Sec. 2.2. The next solution $S_{t+1} = S^{\lambda^*}$ can be computed by selecting S^λ with the lowest value of original energy $E(S)$, as summarized in Alg.1.

2.2   Overview of *Parametric maxflow*

Parametric maxflow technique [20,14,10] is a building block in our proposed algorithm. For all λ in some interval $\Lambda = [\lambda^{min}, \lambda^{max}]$, parametric maxflow can efficiently generate a (finite) set of all distinct solutions $S^\lambda \in \{0, 1\}^\Omega$ minimizing energy $E(S, \lambda)$ of form

$$S^\lambda = \arg\min_S \overbrace{\sum_{p \in \Omega} (a_p + \lambda b_p) s_p + \sum_{(p,q) \in \mathcal{N}} \phi_{pq}(s_p, s_q)}^{E(S,\lambda)} \qquad (6)$$

where ϕ_{pq} are submodular pairwise terms for a set of pairwise factors $\mathcal{N}$. Note that the unary terms in (6) *linearly* depend on parameter λ.

As discussed in [7,20], interval Λ can be broken into a finite set of subintervals between *breakpoints* $\lambda_1 < \lambda_2 < ... < \lambda_k \in \Lambda$ such that any λ inside each given interval $[\lambda_i, \lambda_{i+1}]$ gives the same solution $S^\lambda = S^i$. Parametric maxflow identifies all breakpoints and solutions S^i by making a finite number of calls to the maxflow procedure, see [20,7] for details. Importantly, in *monotonic* case when coefficients b_p in (6) are either all non-negative or all non-positive, optimal solutions S^i have a *nestedness* property leading to guaranteed *polynomial* complexity. This necessitates our choice of relaxation term $R_t(S)$ to have unary coefficients of the same sign.

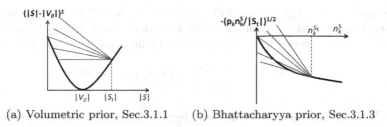

(a) Volumetric prior, Sec.3.1.1   (b) Bhattacharyya prior, Sec.3.1.3

Fig. 3. Pseudo-bound families for two cardinality functions. Auxiliary functions are red.

3   Examples of Pseudo-bounds

Algorithm 1 for minimizing energy $E(S)$ depends on pseudo-bound (5) and requires specific choices of a submodular auxiliary function $A_t(S)$ and a unary relaxation term $R_t(S)$. This section provides practical pseudo-bound examples for a wide range of high-order and non-submodular pairwise energies $E(S)$.

3.1   High-Order Energies

3.1.1   Volumetric Potential [12,37] like $\psi(|S| - V_0)$ for convex symmetric function $\psi(\cdot)$ penalize deviation of segment size $|S|$ from target volume V_0. For example, if $\psi(x) = x^2$ and $S \subset S_t$ we can use the following pseudo bound family[1] illustrated in Fig.3(a)

$$\mathcal{F}_t(S, \lambda) = \underbrace{(|S_t| - 2V_0)|S| + V_0^2}_{A_t(S)} + \lambda \underbrace{(|S| - |S_t|)}_{R_t(S)}. \tag{7}$$

3.1.2   Appearance Entropy was proposed for image segmentation in [35] as a general color consistency criterion that can be combined with other standard terms, e.g. boundary smoothness, as in the following binary segmentation energy

$$E(S) \;=\; |S| \cdot H(S) + |\bar{S}| \cdot H(\bar{S}) \;+\; |\partial S| \tag{8}$$

where $H(S)$ and $H(\bar{S})$ are entropies of color histograms inside foreground S and background $\bar{S}$ and $|\partial S| = \sum_{\{p,q\} \in \mathcal{N}} \omega_{pq}|s_p - s_q|$ is segmentation boundary length. Indirectly, color entropy was also used for segmentation in [40,32,6]. Entropy can also be used as a clustering criterion for any image features that can be binned. In fact, entropy and related *information gain* criterion are widely used in learning, e.g. for contextual clustering [25] or decision trees [34].

---

[1] For $\psi(x) = x^2$ our volumetric potential is non-submodular pairwise, see also Sec.3.2.

Entropy-based energy (8) from [35] is related to a well-known *minimum description length* (MDL) functional [40,6] for color model fitting. In particular, for two segments it reduces to a color model fitting energy in GrabCut [32]

$$E(S, \theta^1, \theta^0) = - \sum_{p \in \Omega} \log Pr(I_p|\theta^{s_p}) + |\partial S| \qquad (9)$$

where θ^1 and θ^0 are variables corresponding to unknown color models for foreground S and background $\bar{S}$. As shown in [35], globally optimal S for high-order energy (8) and mixed optimization functional (9) coincide if color models θ are represented by histograms. Since (9) is known to be *NP-hard* [36], it follows that high-order entropy energy in (8) is also *NP-hard*.

Equivalence of global solutions for entropy (8) and color-model fitting (9) suggests that (8) is minimized indirectly when applying standard *block-coordinate descent* (BCD) techniques [40,32,6] to energy (9) separately optimizing variables S and θ at each iteration. Below, we show that BCD in [32] can be seen as a bound optimization method for entropy (8). Then, we use the corresponding auxiliary function to build a family of pseudo-bounds that generate significantly better results, as shown by our experiments in Sec.4.1.

Proposition 2. *Assume fixed histograms θ_t^1 and θ_t^0 computed from the colors of current solution S_t (foreground) and its complement $\bar{S}_t$ (background). Then,*

$$A_t(S) := E(S, \theta_t^1, \theta_t^0), \qquad (10)$$

with E as in (9), is an auxiliary function *for entropy-based energy (8) at S_t.*

Proof. It follows from a cross entropy discussion in [35]. Indeed, as easy to check

$$E(S, \theta_t^1, \theta_t^0) = |S| \cdot H(S|S_t) + |\bar{S}| \cdot H(\bar{S}|\bar{S}_t) + |\partial S| \qquad (11)$$

where $H(\cdot|\cdot)$ is a cross-entropy of color distributions in two sets of pixels. Inequality $H(A|B) \geq H(A|A) = H(A)$ for $\forall A, B \subset \Omega$ implies

$$E(S, \theta_t^1, \theta_t^0) \geq E(S)$$

where $E(S)$ is from (8). It is also easy to check that $E(S_t, \theta_t^1, \theta_t^0) = E(S_t)$. $\quad\square$

Corollary 1. *Block-coordinate descent (BCD) for mixed functional (9), as in GrabCut [32], is a bound optimization for entropy-based energy (8), see Sec.1.1.*

Proof. Two steps during each iteration of BCD in GrabCut are (I) optimization of segment S by applying graph cuts to energy (9) with fixed color models, as in Boykov-Jolly [5], and (II) optimization of color models θ^1, θ^2 in energy (9) with fixed segmentation. Prop. 2 implies that the segmentation step optimizes auxiliary function $A_t(S)$ for energy (8) at S_t and gives

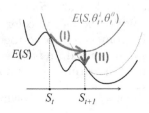

next solution S_{t+1}, as illustrated on the right. Color model re-estimation step gives new auxiliary function $A_{t+1}(S)$ at S_{t+1}. $\qquad\square$

Our proposed pPBC method for entropy-based segmentation energy (8) augments the auxiliary function $A_t(S)$ in (10) with weighted bound relaxation term $\lambda(|S| - |S_t|)$ giving the following family of pseudo-bounds:

$$\mathcal{F}_t(S, \lambda) = E(S, \theta_t^1, \theta_t^0) + \lambda \left(|S| - |S_t|\right). \tag{12}$$

3.1.3 Matching Color Distributions [3,12,29,2] One way of matching target color distributions is to minimize Bhattacharyya measure:

$$Bha(S) = -\sum_k \sqrt{p_k n_k^S / |S|}, \tag{13}$$

where n_k^S is the number of foreground pixels in color bin k and $\sum_k p_k = 1$ is the target distribution. For $S \subset S_t$, a family of pseudo-bounds (Fig. 3) is given as:

$$\mathcal{F}_t(S, \lambda) = \underbrace{-\sum_k \sqrt{\frac{p_k}{n_k^{S_t}|S_t|}} n_k^S}_{A_t(S)} + \lambda \underbrace{(|S| - |S_t|)}_{R_t(S)} \tag{14}$$

Another option for matching distributions is to use the KL divergence [3]:

$$KL(S) = \sum_k p_k \log \frac{p_k}{n_k^S / |S| + \epsilon} = \sum_k p_k \log p_k - \sum_k p_k \log \left(\frac{n_k^S}{|S|} + \epsilon\right), \tag{15}$$

where ϵ is a small constant used to avoid numerical issue. In this case, for $S \subset S_t$, we have the following family of pseudo-bounds (omitting constant $\sum_k p_k \log p_k$):

$$\mathcal{F}_t(S, \lambda) = \underbrace{\sum_k \frac{p_k}{n_k^{S_t}} \left(\log \frac{\epsilon}{\frac{n_k^{S_t}}{|S_t|} + \epsilon}\right) n_k^S - \log \epsilon}_{A_t(S)} + \lambda \underbrace{(|S| - |S_t|)}_{R_t(S)}, \tag{16}$$

where $A_t(S)$ is the auxiliary function derived recently in [3].

3.2 Non-submodular Pairwise Energies

We consider a general class of binary pairwise non-submodular energies, which are useful in various vision applications [16,11], e.g., segmentation, stereo, inpainting, deconvolution, and many others. Such energies can be expressed as:

$$E(S) = \sum_{(p,q) \in \mathcal{N}} m_{pq} s_p s_q = S^T M S, \qquad S \in \{0, 1\}^\Omega \tag{17}$$

where $M = \{m_{pq} \in \mathbb{R} \mid p, q \in \Omega\}$ is a symmetric matrix containing pairwise potentials. if $m_{pq} \leq 0 \ \forall (p, q)$, energy (17) is *submodular* and, therefore, global

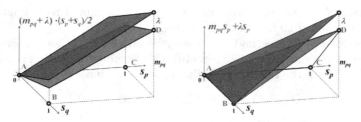

Fig. 4. pPBC-T: Pseudo-bounds (purple) and auxiliary functions (red) of non-submodular potential $m_{pq}s_p s_q$ for current configuration $s_{p,t} = 0, s_{q,t} = 0$ (left) and $s_{p,t} = 0, s_{q,t} = 1$ (right).

Table 1. Auxiliary functions [11] and weighted bound relaxation term for pPBC-T

$(s_{p,t}, s_{q,t})$	Auxiliary function	relaxation term (pPBC-T)
$(0,0)$	$m_{pq}(s_p + s_q)/2$	$\lambda(s_p - s_{p,t} + s_q - s_{q,t})$
$(0,1)$	$m_{pq}s_p$	$\lambda(s_p - s_{p,t})$
$(1,0)$	$m_{pq}s_q$	$\lambda(s_q - s_{q,t})$
$(1,1)$	$m_{pq}(s_p + s_q)/2$	$\lambda(s_p - s_{p,t} + s_q - s_{q,t})$

optima can be reached in a low-order polynomial time using graph cuts [4]. The general non-submodular case is *NP-hard*. In the following, we propose three different pseudo-bounds families for (17) for non-submodular pairs ($m_{pq} > 0$).

   pPBC-T(touch) gives pseudo-bounds for each non-submodular potential $m_{pq}s_p s_q, m_{pq} > 0$. Depending on the current configuration $s_{p,t}$ and $s_{q,t}$ for s_p and s_q, we augment the bound recently proposed in [11] with the relaxation terms specified as in Table 1. Fig. 4 shows the auxiliary functions in red and pseudo-bounds in purple for current configuration $(0,0)$ and $(0,1)$. Note that the bound relaxation term for current configuration $(0,1)$ and $(1,0)$ is different from that of $(0,0)$ and $(1,1)$. This relaxation allows the pseudo-bounds to *touch* the original energy at as many points as possible, yielding better approximation.

   pPBC-B(ballooning) This option uses the auxiliary function in Table 1 augmented with a linear ballooning term $\lambda(|S| - |S_t|)$.

   pPBC-L(Laplacian) We derive the third pseudo-bounds family based on the *Laplacian* matrix. Let $d(p) = \sum_q m_{pq}$ and D be the diagonal matrix having d on its diagonal. Notice that, in the case of supermodular terms ($m_{pq} \geq 0$), D is diagonally positive and, therefore, positive semidefinite. With symmetric matrix M, it is well known that the corresponding *Laplacian* matrix $L = D - M$ is positive semidefinite [33]. Now we write (17) as follows for $\lambda \in \Lambda$:

$$E(S) = \underbrace{S^T(M - \lambda D)S}_{G(S)} + \lambda \underbrace{S^T DS}_{H(S)}. \qquad (18)$$

H is a unary potential for binary variables: $H(S) = \sum_p d(p)s_p^2 = \sum_p d(p)s_p$. Also, notice that $\forall \lambda \geq 1$, G is concave w.r.t S because $M - \lambda D$ is negative semidefinite (as it is the sum of two negative semidefinite matrices:

Fig. 5. Left: interactive segmentations with BCD (GrabCut) or pPBC from different initialization (ellipses). Proposed pPBC method is more robust to inferior initialization. Right: unsupervised figure-ground segmentation with pPBC. Average color is shown.

$M - \lambda D = -L + (1 - \lambda)D$). Therefore, let ∇ denotes the gradient, we have the following pseudo-bounds at current solution S_t which includes bounds of (17) for $\lambda \geq 1$.

$$\mathcal{F}_t(S, \lambda) = G(S_t) + \nabla G(S_t)^T (S - S_t) + \lambda H(S)$$
$$= \underbrace{G(S_t) - \nabla G(S_t)^T S_t}_{\text{Constant}} + \underbrace{2[(M - \lambda D)S_t]^T S + \lambda H(S)}_{\text{Unary potential}} \quad (19)$$

4 Experiments

4.1 Appearance Entropy Based Segmentation

Robustness w.r.t Initialization and Binning. We use GrabCut and BCD interchangeably for the rest of the paper. Left part of Fig. 5 depicts an example of interactive segmentation with BCD or our proposed pPBC, and shows that BCD is sensitive to initializations, unlike pPBC. pPBC can even tolerate trivial initialization, see an un-supervised segmentation example in the right of Fig. 5.

Furthermore, we observed that with more appearance model variables, namely the number of color bins, BCD is more likely to get stuck in weak local minima. We randomly generated 500 box-like initializations for an input image, and run BCD and pPBC for different numbers of color bins, ranging from 16^3 to 128^3. From the solutions we obtained with BCD or pPBC, we computed the corresponding error rates and energies. Fig. 6 depicts the scatter plots of error rates

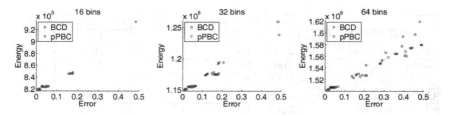

Fig. 6. Scatter plots; error rates versus energies for 500 solutions of BCD and pPBC

	Error rate	Time
GrabCut (16^3 bins)	$7.1\%^2$	1.78 s
GrabCut (32^3 bins)	8.78%	1.63 s
GrabCut (64^3 bins)	9.31%	1.64 s
GrabCut (128^3 bins)	11.34%	1.45 s
DD (16^3 bins)	10.5%	576 s
One-Cut (16^3 bins)	8.1%	5.8 s
One-Cut (32^3 bins)	6.99%	2.4 s
One-Cut (64^3 bins)	6.67%	1.3 s
One-Cut (128^3 bins)	6.71%	0.8 s
pPBC (16^3 bins)	5.80%	11.7 s
pPBC (32^3 bins)	5.60%	11.9 s
pPBC (64^3 bins)	5.56%	12.3 s
pPBC (128^3 bins)	7.51%	15.9 s

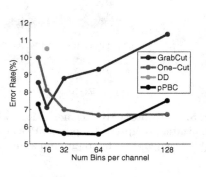

Fig. 7. Error rates and speed on GrabCut dataset for GrabCut [32], Dual Decomposition (DD) [36], One-Cut [35] and our pPBC method.

versus energies for the 500 solutions. Points on bottom-left give low energy and small error rate. The wider these dots spread across the plane, the more local minima the algorithm converged to. pPBC works much better than BCD for finer binning and is more robust to initializations.

Comparisons with the State of the Art [35,36] We compare with Grab-Cut, which as demonstrated in Sec.3.1.2, can be viewed as a bound optimizer. We run both algorithms on the GrabCut dataset [32] (The cross image excluded for comparison with [36]). We set the weight of the 8-connected contrast-sensitive smoothness term to 15 and vary number of color bins. As shown in Tab.3, pPBC consistently gives lower energies and misclassification errors. Our current implementation does not use a straightforward multi-core CPU parallelization of parametric maxflow by breaking the range of λ into intervals. Thus, significant speed up of our pPBC algorithm is possible. In the next experiment we tuned the smoothness term weight for pPBC and other methods [32,35] to obtain the best error statistics for each. Fig. 7 shows a competitive performance of pPBC.

Table 3. Statistics of pPBC and GrabCut [32] over the GrabCut database

	Mean Energy	# of lower energy	Mean time(s)
GrabCut [32] - 16^3 bins	1.2349×10^6	1	**1.0s**
pPBC - 16^3 bins	$\mathbf{1.2335 \times 10^6}$	**38**	11.2s
GrabCut [32] - 32^3 bins	1.7064×10^6	2	**0.9s**
pPBC - 32^3 bins	$\mathbf{1.7029 \times 10^6}$	**37**	11.7s
GrabCut [32] - 64^3 bins	2.2408×10^6	1	**0.9s**
pPBC - 64^3 bins	$\mathbf{2.2361 \times 10^6}$	**47**	14.1s

Table 4. Matching color distribution (KL or Bhattacharyya distance) with Auxiliary Cuts [3], FTR [12], pPBC and its limited version with $\lambda \leq 0$ for the pseudo-bounds.

Method	KL divergence (15)			Bhattacharyya distance (13)		
	Mean energy	Mean error	Time	Mean energy	Mean error	Time
Auxiliary Cuts [3]	6189	16.54%	**1.8s**	-12402	24.1%	**1.7s**
pPBC($\lambda \leq 0$)	6150	14.88%	N/A	-12451	23.7%	N/A
FTR [12]	5868	7.70%	4.40s	-14499	3.2%	2.71s
pPBC($\lambda \in [-\infty, +\infty]$)	**5849**	**3.63%**	2.98s	**-14504**	**2.9%**	1.99s

4.2 Matching Color Distributions

We experiment on the database [32], and used the bounding boxes as initializations. Similar to [3,12], the target distribution is learned from the ground truth. We compared pPBC with auxiliary cuts [3] and FTR [12]. We also tested a limited version of pPBC where only non-positive λ's were explored within the family of pseud-bounds. Note that, when λ is non-positive, the parametric family includes only auxiliary functions. The mean error rate, energy and running time are reported in Table 4. Exploring only a family of auxiliary functions ($\lambda \leq 0$) did not improve the results. pPBC with parameter $\lambda \in \mathbb{R}$ yielded the best performance, while being slightly slower than auxiliary cuts (even though pPBC explores a family of functions instead of only one). FTR yielded comparable mean energy to pPBC, but is slower. Fig. 2 depicts typical examples.

4.3 Curvature Regularization

We applied our framework to the curvature model proposed in [8], which penalizes 90 degree angles in a 4-connect neighborhood system. We also compare pPBC to the recent algorithms (LSA-AUX and LSA-TR) in [11], which were shown to outperform standard state-of-the-art methods such as QPBO [30] and TRWS [19]. Fig. 8 plots the energies of the solutions with different weights of the curvature term. pPBC-T gives the lowest energy among all methods. We also observed that the best λ for pPBC-T often does not make the pseudo-bound an auxiliary function, which means the bounding constraint is violated.

Table 5. Average energy with 10 random noisy images

Noise σ	LSA-AUX [11]	LSA-TR [11]	pPBC-L	pPBC-B	pPBC-T
0.05	40.34	30.83	39.49	39.65	**30.81**
0.10	130.24	**119.84**	128.68	128.06	121.20
0.15	277.27	**263.06**	275.89	276.62	266.35
0.20	482.54	**451.78**	480.80	482.09	471.11

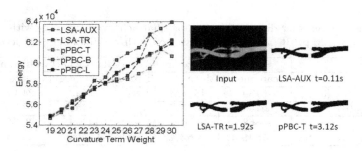

Fig. 8. Segmentation with the curvature regularization model in [8]

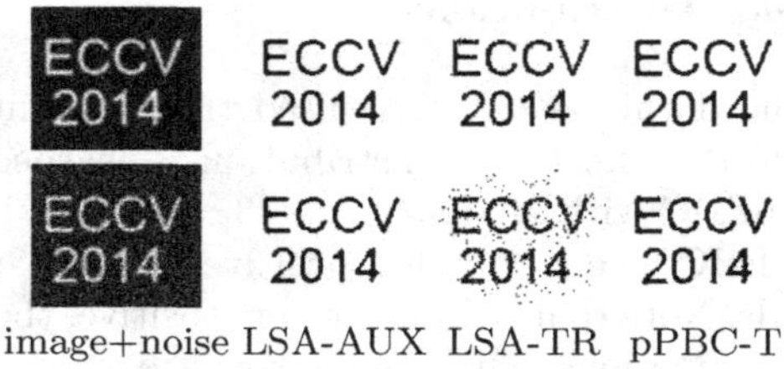

image+noise LSA-AUX LSA-TR pPBC-T

Fig. 9. Deconvolution results. Top row: noise $\sigma = 0.10$, bottom row: $\sigma = 0.2$.

4.4 Deconvolution

Fig. 9 depicts a binary image convolved with a mean 3×3 filter, with a Gaussian noise added. The purpose is to recover the original image via optimizing the energy: $E(S) = \sum_{p \in \Omega} (I_p - \frac{1}{9} \sum_{q \in \mathcal{N}_p} s_q)^2$, where $\mathcal{N}_p$ is a 3×3 neighborhood window centered at pixel p. In this energy, all pairwise interactions are supermodular. We compared our pPBC-B, L or T to the recent algorithms in [11] (LSA-AUX and LSA-TR). Table 5 shows average energy of those methods. Note that LSA-TR achieves lower energy but visually worse deconvolution. For $\sigma = 0.05$ noise, LSA-AUX takes 0.12s, LSA-TR 0.73s and pPBC-T 1.46s.

5   Conclusion

This paper proposes a new general *pseudo-bound optimization* paradigm for approximate iterative minimization of high-order and non-submodular binary energies. It generalizes the standard *majorize-minimize* principle relaxing the bound constraint for an auxiliary function. We propose to optimize a family of pseudo-bounds at each iteration. To guarantee the energy decreases we include at least one bound in the family. We propose parametric maxflow [20,14,10] to explore all global minima for the whole family in low-order polynomial time.

To guarantee polynomial time complexity, pseudo-bounds families with *monotone* dependence on parameter are chosen. We propose and discuss several options of pseudo-bound families for various high-order and non-submodular pairwise energies. Our *parametric Pseudo-Bound Cuts* algorithm (pPBC) improves the-state-of-the-art in many energy minimization problems, e.g. entropy based segmentation, target distributions matching, curvature regularization and deconvolution. In particular, we show that the well-known GrabCut algorithm [32] is a bound optimizer. Our pseudo-bound approach is more robust to inferior initialization and finer binning for image segmentation. Our pPBC algorithm also gives lower energy than *Auxiliary Cuts* [3] and *Fast Trust Region* [12] for distribution matching and other challenging optimization problems in vision.

References

1. An, L.T.H., Tao, P.D., Canh, N.N., Thoai, N.V.: Dc programming techniques for solving a class of nonlinear bilevel programs. J. Global Optimization 44(3), 313–337 (2009)
2. Ben Ayed, I., Chen, H.M., Punithakumar, K., Ross, I., Li, S.: Graph cut segmentation with a global constraint: Recovering region distribution via a bound of the bhattacharyya measure. In: CVPR, pp. 3288–3295 (2010)
3. Ben Ayed, I., Gorelick, L., Boykov, Y.: Auxiliary cuts for general classes of higher order functionals. In: IEEE Conference on Computer Vision and Pattern Recognition (2013)
4. Boros, E., Hammer, P.L.: Pseudo-boolean optimization. Discrete Applied Mathematics 123, 2002 (2001)
5. Boykov, Y., Jolly, M.-P.: *Interactive graph cuts* for optimal boundary & region segmentation of objects in N-D images. In: ICCV, vol. I, pp. 105–112 (July 2001)
6. Delong, A., Osokin, A., Isack, H., Boykov, Y.: Fast approximate energy minimization with label costs. International Journal of Computer Vision 96, 1–27 (2012)
7. Eisner, M.J., Severance, D.G.: Mathematical techniques for efficient record segmentation in large shared databases. J. ACM 23(4), 619–635 (1976)
8. El-Zehiry, N., Grady, L.: Fast global optimization of curvature. In: Proc. of CVPR 2010. IEEE Computer Society. IEEE (June 2010)
9. Fashing, M., Tomasi, C.: Mean shift is a bound optimization. IEEE Transactions on Pattern Analysis and Machine Intelligence 27, 471–474 (2005)
10. Gallo, G., Grigoriadis, M.D., Tarjan, R.E.: A fast parametric maximum flow algorithm and applications. SIAM J. Comput. 18(1), 30–55 (1989)
11. Gorelick, L., Boykov, Y., Veksler, O., Ayed, I.B., Delong, A.: Submodularization for binary pairwise energies. In: IEEE conference on Computer Vision and Pattern Recognition (CVPR), Columbus, Ohio (June 2014)
12. Gorelick, L., Schmidt, F.R., Boykov, Y.: Fast trust region for segmentation. In: IEEE Conference on Computer Vision and Pattern Recognition (CVPR), Portland, Oregon, pp. 1714–1721(June 2013)
13. Gould, S.: Max-margin learning for lower linear envelope potentials in binary markov random fields. In: ICML (2011)
14. Hochbaum, D.S.: Polynomial time algorithms for ratio regions and a variant of normalized cut. IEEE Trans. Pattern Anal. Mach. Intell. 32(5), 889–898 (2010)
15. Jiang, H.: Linear solution to scale invariant global figure ground separation. In: CVPR. pp. 678–685 (2012)
16. Kappes, J.H., Andres, B., Hamprecht, F.A., Schnorr, C., Nowozin, S., Batra, D., Kim, S., Kausler, B.X., Lellmann, J., Komodakis, N., Rother, C.: A comparative

study of modern inference techniques for discrete energy minimization problem. In: IEEE Conference on Computer Vision and Pattern Recognition (CVPR). pp. 1328–1335 (2013)

17. Kim, J., Kolmogorov, V., Zabih, R.: Visual correspondence using energy minimization and mutual information. In: Int. Conf. on Comp. Vision (ICCV), vol. 2, pp. 1033–1040 (October 2003)

18. Kohli, P., Ladický, L., Torr, P.H.: Robust higher order potentials for enforcing label consistency. Int. J. Comput. Vision 82(3), 302–324 (2009)

19. Kolmogorov, V., Schoenemann, T.: Generalized sequential tree-reweighted message pass. In: arXiv:1205.6352 (2012)

20. Kolmogorov, V., Boykov, Y., Rother, C.: Applications of parametric maxflow in computer vision. In: IEEE International Conference on Computer Vision (2007)

21. Kolmogorov, V., Rother, C.: Minimizing non-submodular functions with graph cuts - a review. IEEE transactions on Pattern Analysis and Machine Intelligence 29(7), 1274–1279 (July 2007)

22. Lange, K., Hunter, D.R., Yang, I.: Optimization transfer using surrogate objective functions. Journal of Computational and Graphical Statistics 9(1), 1–20 (2000)

23. Lee, D.D., Seung, H.S.: Algorithms for non-negative matrix factorization. In: NIPS, pp. 556–562 (2000)

24. Leordeanu, M., Hebert, M., Sukthankar, R.: An integer projected fixed point method for graph matching and map inference. In: NIPS, pp. 1114–1122 (2009)

25. Li, T., Ma, S., Ogihara, M.: Entropy-based criterion in categorical clustering. In: Proc. of Intl. Conf. on Machine Learning (ICML), pp. 536–543 (2004)

26. Mukherjee, L., Singh, V., Dyer, C.R.: Half-integrality based algorithms for cosegmentation of images. In: CVPR. pp. 2028–2035 (2009)

27. Narasimhan, M., Bilmes, J.A.: A submodular-supermodular procedure with applications to discriminative structure learning. In: UAI, pp. 404–412 (2005)

28. Nieuwenhuis, C., Toeppe, E., Gorelick, L., Veksler, O., Boykov, Y.: Efficient squared curvature. In: IEEE Conference on Computer Vision and Pattern Recognition (CVPR), Columbus, Ohio (June 2014)

29. Pham, V.Q., Takahashi, K., Naemura, T.: Foreground-background segmentation using iterated distribution matching. In: CVPR. pp. 2113–2120 (2011)

30. Rother, C., Kolmogorov, V., Lempitsky, V., Szummer, M.: Optimizing binary mrfs via extended roof duality. In: IEEE CVPR (2007)

31. Rother, C., Minka, T.P., Blake, A., Kolmogorov, V.: Cosegmentation of image pairs by histogram matching - incorporating a global constraint into mrfs. In: CVPR. pp. 993–1000 (2006)

32. Rother, C., Kolmogorov, V., Blake, A.: Grabcut - interactive foreground extraction using iterated graph cuts. In: ACM Tran. on Graphics, SIGGRAPH (2004)

33. Shi, J., Malik, J.: Normalized cuts and image segmentation. IEEE Trans. Pattern Anal. Mach. Intell. 22(8), 888–905 (2000)

34. Shotton, J., Sharp, T., Kohli, P., Nowozin, S., Winn, J., Criminisi, A.: Decision jungles: Compact and rich models for classification. In: Advances in Neural Information Processing Systems (NIPS), pp. 234–242 (2013)

35. Tang, M., Gorelick, L., Veksler, O., Boykov, Y.: Grabcut in one cut. In: International Conference on Computer Vision (ICCV), Sydney, Australia (2013)

36. Vicente, S., Kolmogorov, V., Rother, C.: Joint optimization of segmentation and appearance models. In: IEEE ICCV (2009)

37. Woodford, O.J., Rother, C., Kolmogorov, V.: A global perspective on map inference for low-level vision. In: ICCV, pp. 2319–2326 (2009)
38. Yuan, Y.: A review of trust region algorithms for optimization. In: Proceedings of the Fourth International Congress on Industrial and Applied Mathematics, ICIAM (1999)
39. Zhang, Z., Kwok, J.T., Yeung, D.Y.: Surrogate maximization/minimization algorithms and extensions. Machine Learning 69, 1–33 (2007)
40. Zhu, S.C., Yuille, A.: Region competition: Unifying snakes, region growing, and Bayes/MDL for multiband image segmentation. IEEE Transactions on PAMI 18(9), 884–900 (1996)

A Closer Look at Context:
From Coxels to the Contextual Emergence
of Object Saliency

Rotem Mairon and Ohad Ben-Shahar

Dept. of Computer Science, Ben-Gurion University of the Negev, Beer Sheva, Israel
{rotemra,ben-shahar}@cs.bgu.ac.il

Abstract. Visual context is used in different forms for saliency computation. While its use in saliency models for fixations prediction is often reasoned, this is less so the case for approaches that aim to compute saliency at the *object* level. We argue that the types of context employed by these methods lack clear justification and may in fact interfere with the purpose of capturing the saliency of whole visual objects. In this paper we discuss the constraints that different types of context impose and suggest a new interpretation of visual context that allows the emergence of saliency for more complex, abstract, or multiple visual objects. Despite shying away from an explicit attempt to capture "objectness" (e.g., via segmentation), our results are qualitatively superior and quantitatively better than the state-of-the-art.

1 Introduction

The remarkable ability of the visual system to rapidly attend towards salient stimuli enables humans to effortlessly filter visual input and allocate attentional resources differentially to salient regions. The computational prediction of this outcome can facilitate numerous applications in both the analysis of images (i.e., in computer vision) and their synthesis (i.e., in graphics). For example, the need to adjust visual context to a range of display devices has motivated image/video retargeting and content-aware resizing techniques that rely on saliency prediction [12,49,4,34,19]. A capacity to predict what is salient or not has also spared much computational resources in image classification [39], retrieval [13], object recognition [43] image and video compression [15,50], and served various other applications such as image thumbnailing [34,45], visualization and symmetrization [47,18,42] and object segmentation [21,30].

Judging by this variety of applications, the abundance of existing work on saliency computation and the need for perceptually-consistent and accurate saliency predictions are not surprising. We begin this work by taking a closer look at the mechanisms used to compute saliency and to examine the constraints and limitations they may pose on the computational process. Central to our exploration is the concept of "context" and part of our goal is to argue that it (i.e., context) alone is a sufficient substrate from which saliency can fully emerge. As we show later, despite using this single building block, our saliency results exceed state-of-the-art performance from methods that employ diverse set of additional tools and mechanisms.

D. Fleet et al. (Eds.): ECCV 2014, Part V, LNCS 8693, pp. 708–724, 2014.

1.1 Saliency and Context

From an ecological perspective, the saliency of a constituent in a visual scene is the degree to which it demands the allocation of computational (attentional) resources in order to better inquire its role in the visual stimulus. In practice, as is also acknowledged in both perceptual [46,38,16] and computational [29,14] accounts, saliency is strongly influenced (and often fully determined) by the degree to which the constituent stands out from its context. Combining the two, the saliency of a visual constituent cannot be determined without knowledge or understanding of the context in which it is embedded. Interestingly, this constituent-context duality has taken different forms in previous research of saliency computation.

Saliency is primarily driven in a bottom-up manner, depending on low level visual cues in the visual scene. In one of the first biologically plausible computational models for controlling visual attention, Koch and Ullman [31] followed Treisman and Gelade [46] and introduced the idea of a saliency map. Visual input is first decomposed into several maps encoding early visual features. Spatial competition in terms of hierarchical center-surround differences then determines their convergence to a unique map encoding saliency at each location. Most subsequent bottom-up saliency algorithms followed this model and compute the saliency of pixel constituents based on their local context (i.e., neighborhood) at multiple scales [27,22,10,25]. Alternatively, context was also considered globally, e.g., as a smoothed version of the amplitude [23] or the phase [20] spectrum of the image. Deviations from the original non-smoothed spectrum with respect to this global context are then considered as salient locations when transformed back to the spatial domain.

In addition to its categorization as local or global, bottom-up saliency may also be viewed at the level at which it operates. Unlike the models mentioned above, that mainly act spatially in order to reproduce human visual search strategies or predict visual fixations, other methods aim at detecting saliency at the higher level of *objects*. While the (local) visual context used by the first class of methods is reasonably intuitive, the forms of visual context employed by the latter (object-level) approaches typically remain unexplained. We argue below that this somewhat obscure relationship often constrains the nature of visual objects they may capture in order to measure their saliency.

Considering the scope of saliency as discussed above, we define visual context of a constituent as follows:

Definition 1. *The visual context of a constituent is the set of visual units in the image that are used in the computational process that measures its saliency.*

This somewhat general definition intentionally lacks a particular spatial relationship between the constituent and it context. It is used in Sec. 2 to discuss the contribution of different types of visual context to detecting saliency at the object level and to point at the constraints that these types of context may impose. Then, in Sec. 3, we suggest a novel approach to visual context, which is intuitively justified and can capture object saliency for both simple, complex, and abstract objects (Fig. 1) all without explicit reference to "objectness" or the use of segmentation.

Before beginning our closer look at visual context, one disclaimer is advised. Like many others, in this work we too discuss the notion of visual context that is associated

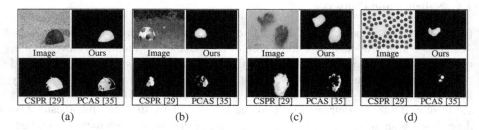

Fig. 1. Salient objects in visual stimuli can have different flavors. As is typical in virtually all benchmark databases, salient objects can be uniform singletons (panel a). However, salient objects can be multi-part and heterogeneous (panel b), they can have some multiplicity (panel c), or they can even be completely abstract (like the "hole" in panel d). By their implied notion of visual context, most computational saliency models impose certain constraints on the types of objects they can handle, with practical success limited to the simpler cases. Here we show computed saliency map (thresholded at 80%) from two state-of-the-art algorithms (CSPR [29] and PCAS [35]) and our own method. By modeling context instead of the objects we significantly reduce the constraints on the nature of objects that may be detected as salient, as is illustrated by the better assignment of saliency in all these cases.

with bottom-up saliency. But the latter may be strongly modulated or even overridden by top-down factors as well, including the experience (or expertise) of an observer or his biases due to task definition [26]. Such factors give rise to other forms of visual context and modulation of bottom-up saliency by semantic interrelations between visual objects [7,5] or the global structuring of a scene [6,41,37,40]. These types of context remain outside the scope of our present work.

2   Background and Related Work

Approaches to salient object detection embrace the same notion of a saliency map discussed above (sometimes with additional steps like segmentation) but employ different types of visual context (in the sense of the Def. 1) to compute such maps (see Fig. 2). To address the specific contribution of the types of context used we roughly categorize the different approaches into the following two groups:

Contrast-Based Saliency: In the first group are approaches that associate saliency with high contrast between local or regional structures. To measure this contrast, the computational mechanisms employ various center-surround structures. The visual constituent for which a measure of saliency is computed is regarded as the center and is spatially surrounded by its context. Some approaches define the surround component independent of visual content, e.g., as the local neighborhood of a pixel [24,48,1,32] or larger regular blocks [33]. In other approaches, the surrounding context depends on a grouping process which typically results in a superpixel representation of the image [29,11]. Apart from reducing computational costs, superpixels are preferable due to their capacity to preserve locally coherent structures

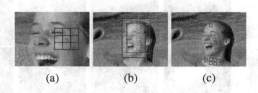

(a)   (b)   (c)

Fig. 2. Different types of visual context (marked in red) of a visual constituent (marked in blue).
(a) The local neighborhood of a pixel. **(b)** Pixels at the surround of a larger scale region. **(c)**
k-nearest neighbors of a patch.

(unlike pixels or predefined blocks). To a certain extent, these structures facilitate
meaningful central constituents when measuring contrast and therefore are more
suitable for saliency assignment.

Rarity-Based Saliency: The second group of approaches consider saliency as distinct-
ness or rarity. Intuitively, these may signal the importance of a visual constituent
compared with the redundancy of recurring visual information. Often in this approach the context is a global representation of the entire visual input. A constituent
is then considered salient if its representation does not conform with the context.
For example, such a representation may be the image mean color vector that is
used as reference to measure the saliency at all other pixels [2,4]. Alternative representation has considered a smoothed version of the phase spectrum [28] in order to suppress non-salient components in the original spectrum and thus highlight
salient locations after transforming back to the spatial domain. In a somewhat related way, image patches that are highly dissimilar to their k-nearest neighbors were
considered salient as this indicates their dissimilarity to all other patches [19,11].
Recently, this measure of dissimilarity has been shown oblivious to patch statistics,
leading to a new measure based on the distance of each patch to the average patch
along the principal components of the patch distribution [35].

An important factor in approaches from both of the groups above is the scale at
which saliency is computed. When the context is predefined as the surround in a certain center-surround structure or as a global description of the visual input, its scale
may be selected arbitrarily. In case it is determined by a grouping process, the scale
may be influenced by different input parameters. However, in both cases there is no
single appropriate scale. Tightly localized context would essentially capture edge information while context of excessive spatial scale may falsely signal non-salient areas and
incorporate visual information whose relevance to the saliency of a visual constituent
is unclear. Thus, the saliency map is often a combined result of computations across
multiple scales.

Other complexities that visual objects may exhibit pose additional constraints to the
nature of visual objects that may be captured during saliency computation. Indeed, the
implicit motivation underlying contrast-based saliency is the possibility that at a certain
scale the center part of the center-surround structure will capture the object to allow

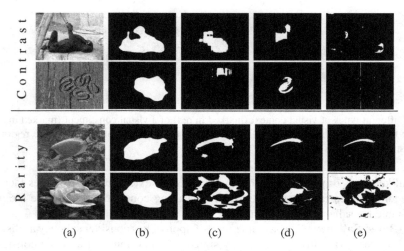

Contrast

Rarity

(a)   (b)   (c)   (d)   (e)

Fig. 3. Binarized saliency maps demonstrate the challenges in capturing whole salient objects by contrast (top) and rarity (bottom) based approaches. The two leftmost columns in each category show example images and our maps. **Constrast:** Saliency maps in columns c and d are generated as part of saliency computation algorithms, but are not their final output (which includes additional steps). They are shown here to demonstrate how capturing large or discontiguous objects is constrained when relying on regional center-surround. In column c computation is based on rectangular structures of varying size and aspect ratio [32] whereas in column d neighboring superpixels were used to estimate contrast [29]. The constraints are even more restrictive when only local considerations are involved [1] as shown in column e. **Rarity:** The challenge remains when relying on rarity aspects of saliency, as demonstrated by the maps in columns c-e [19,35,14]. When the object consists of multiple parts, only those with rare appearance are detected. The bottom map in panel e demonstrates how a large object may render the appearance of its surrounding more rare and therefore more computationally salient.

the comparison of its appearance against its surroundings. This implies that the object is expected to be compact and spatially continuous. Compactness and spatial continuity may not be required for rarity-based saliency, which assumes that the target object constitutes few units with rare visual properties with respect to the entire visual input. However, this approach ignores spatial relations between elements forming the context and may not account for figure-ground relations. In fact, when relying on rarity, the surrounding of a visual object may be considered more salient when the object is larger. The rarity aspect of saliency is also challenged when it comes to considering composite/heterogeneous objects. In these cases, different parts of a salient object may be assigned very different saliency values (see Fig. 3).

The limitations just discussed have led many scientists to use additional information and computational processes to possibly capture the nature of visual objects. Often, saliency maps are used as input to subsequent segmentation processes such as adaptive thresholding [2] fuzzy-growing [33], compactness and density analysis [24], and iterative region expansion [52]. Additional considerations are configural cues such as convexity [48] or closure [29], or higher-level factors such as objectness [11] and visual organization priors [35,19]. In other cases, the additional information used is more explicit and extracted directly from a collection of images (e.g., [32]).

While many of the approaches above indeed improve the original saliency mapping, The difficulty of modeling the nature of visual objects often leads to ad hoc methods that blur the distinction between bottom-up saliency and its applications in subsequent computations. In this work we propose a completely different approach. Instead of trying to capture the object, we put the emphasis on modeling the context that leads to visual saliency. As we show later, this paradigm shift leads to superior saliency results even if no additional object-specific information or computational processes (like segmentation) are employed.

3   Modeling Visual Context to Compute Saliency

Essentially, the same fundamental question is at the basis of most approaches to saliency computation: "To what extent does a visual constituent stand out from its context". This question implies that a certain constituent is at hand when its saliency is measured or estimated. When the desired constituent is an object, this idea raises the issues described above that limit the performance. Instead of trying to capture the object, we wish to consider a somewhat dual question: "What are the characteristics of visual context which allow to consider the visual information it embeds (be it an object or not) as salient".

To answer this question, we suggest to model visual context based on the several characteristics of visual information. Given a particular representation of the units that compose it (pixels, superpixels, patches, etc...), we consider a single *context element*, or *coxel*, to be a region or a subset of the image with the following properties (see Fig. 4):

Smoothness: Nearby units that compose the coxel are expected to have similar visual appearance. The more distant the units, more leeway is allowed in their similarity.

Apathy to contiguity: A coxel may be either contiguous or not, i.e., it may constitute several distinct connected components in the image plane.

Enclosure: To qualify as a saliency coxel, the spatial layout of the context element should "enclose" (strictly or approximately) some visual information.

While many ways can be used to define elementary image units from which coxels are composed, we elect to do so via the approximately regular, boundary adhesive patches such as those obtained from the SLIC superpixels algorithm [3]. Let $V = \{v_1, \ldots, v_n\}$ be the set of all these patches. Each patch is associated with a single coxel, the latter being a subset of V with the properties outlined above. Let C be the mapping from each patch to its coxel, such that $C(v_i)$ is the coxel of patch v_i. We denote the set of all coxels by $\mathbb{C}$. Initially, $\forall i, C(v_i) = \{v_i\}$ and $|\mathbb{C}| = N$.

Let $G = (V, E)$ be the weighted *complete* graph on V, where the weight $w(E_{ij})$ of each E_{ij} reflects the *contextual gap* between its corresponding patches v_i and v_j. Two general factors affect the contextual gap – similarity in appearance and image distance. The contextual gap as a whole, and the similarity distance in particular, can be evaluated in various ways. Here we choose to use a particularly simple form that takes only the raw color as a measure of appearance and the following blend of color and distance to express contextual gap

$$w(E_{ij}) = 1 - \left(\frac{1 - \alpha * s_{ij}}{1 + \beta * c_{ij}} \right) \tag{1}$$

where c_{ij} and s_{ij} are the appearance (color) distance and the spatial distance between the pair of patches, respectively, and α and β control their significance ($\alpha = 0.5$ and $\beta = 7$ were used). This results with contextual gaps in the range [0, 1] that are lower for edges linking similar and nearby patches and higher otherwise. The choice to express appearance similarity very simply via color only is intentional since it implies that the strength of our approach must emerge from the proposed concept of context and the derived estimation of saliency. Indeed, as we'll show, while our algorithm can accept arbitrarily sophisticated appearance measures, even the naïve one employed here already results in better than state-of-the-art saliency performance (even without endowing it with segmentation or other additional computational processes).

With the initial coxels set and pairwise contextual gaps between patches determined, our algorithm proceeds by repeatedly altering between two computational phases. The first phase enables coxels to extend by gradually merging together coxels of increasing contextual gap. The second phase accumulates saliency votes for visual information that is embedded in (i.e., enclosed by) coxels. Upon convergence, the entire image becomes a single coxel and the saliency map is finalized.

More formally, given the graph G and a predefined desired quantization level of contextual gaps $0 = w_1 < w_2 < \ldots < w_m = 1$, the steps described in Algorithm 1 (and illustrated in Fig. 5) are repeated until a single coxel is reached. In the first phase, coxels are extended by merging existing coxels by progressively relaxing the contextual gap allowed. Leveraging the smoothness property, initially only nearby and highly similar components are considered for merging. Apathy to contiguity is supported by the fact

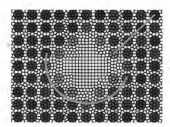

Fig. 4. The complexity and diversity of visual context that our model allows is demonstrated by this synthetic image. White, colored, and grayscale patches (superpixels) compose a scene of circles surrounding an "empty" salient region (cf. Fig. 1d). Context elements can be regarded at the level of these patches or at a higher level depicting circles and white background. Although the appearance of context units varies around the empty salient region (e.g., along the curved green path) and away from it (straight green line), at some level they should be considered as part of the *same* context element. In our approach to context this is possible due to the smoothness property and the lack of contiguity which allow context elements from different sides of the salient region to merge.

that the increased contextual gaps w_l gradually permit the merging of more distant and less similar coxels even if they are disconnected. Thus, a pair of patches v_i and v_j may (and at some point, will surely) belong to the same coxel, such that $C(v_i) = C(v_j)$.

Algorithm 1 Contextual Emergence of Saliency

1: $S(E_{ij}) := 0 \ \forall i, j = 1..n$ {Initial votes for saliency bridges}
2: $l := 0$
3: **while** $|\mathbb{C}| > 1$ **do**
        {Phase I: Extend coxels}
4:      **for all** E_{ij}, s.t $w(E_{ij}) \leq w_l$ and $C(v_i) \neq C(v_j)$ **do**
5:          $\mathbb{C} = \mathbb{C} - C(v_j)$
6:          $C(v_i) = C(v_i) \cup C(v_j)$
7:      **end for**
        {Phase II: Accumulate saliency votes}
8:      **for all** E_{ij} s.t $C(v_i) = C(v_j)$ **do**
9:          $T := \{v_k : E_{ij} \text{ traverses } v_k\} - \{v_i, v_j\}$
10:         **if** $|T| = |T - C(v_i)|$ **then**
11:             $S(E_{i,j}) = S(E_{i,j}) + 1$
12:         **end if**
13:     **end for**
14:     $l := l + 1.$
15: **end while**

During the second phase of each iteration, coxels that emerged up to this point are used to add saliency for the visual information they enclose. This is done by considering "visibility edges" or "saliency bridges", i.e., edges between patches of the *same* coxel that do *not* traverse another patch from that coxel. More abstractly, saliency bridges reflect interference in their associated context element and therefore suggest that visual information they traverse deserve a quota of saliency (all in the spirit of seeking the "extent to which a visual constituent stands out from its context"). The longer (i.e., more iterations) the relationship between a coxel and its enclosed region endures, the more "votes" saliency bridges will accumulate to indicate so.

It is easy to see that the algorithm always terminates. Since merging coxels reduces their total number, and since for every edge E_{ij} there exist some threshold w_l that exceeds its contextual gap $w(E_{ij})$, the iteration must end. Indeed, when $w_l = 1$ all remaining coxels merge into one final element, no saliency bridges are possible any longer, and the iteration terminates. In practice we represent saliency bridges by the image pixels they traverse and votes are accumulated in those pixels. Although one could employ different ways to obtain a dense map from the spatially distributed votes assigned to pixels, we apply a kernel density estimation [9,44] to produce the final saliency map.

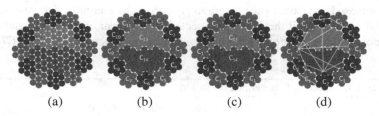

(a)   (b)   (c)   (d)

Fig. 5. Schematic depiction of the two phases of Algorithm 1. **(a)** Initial coxels (SLIC superpixels [3]) with their color-coded appearance content. **(b)** Coxels with small contextual gaps (initially, those which are very proximate and similar) are merged to larger, uniquely labeled components. Note that at this time no saliency bridges occur as any edge between two patches from the same component traverses another patch from that component. **(c)** At a future merging step, the threshold on contextual gaps is large enough to allow distant coxels to merge (implied by similar labels). **(d)** At this point, saliency bridges cross image patches from other coxels, leading to accumulation of their saliency measure. To avoid clutter, only selected number of saliency bridges are shown.

To conclude, we consider context as relevant to the saliency of a visual constituent when it exhibits certain properties that allow it to form coherently while spatially enclosing the constituent. By considering any visual information that is not part of a context element as salient, we successfully disregard issues of shape, size, contiguity, or topology, thus significantly reducing the constraints on the nature of objects that may be detected as salient (see Figs. 1 and 3). We note that the saliency bridges mechanism implicitly encourages enclosure, the third property we defined as desired. Indeed, saliency is voted for along saliency bridges, and the latter are more frequent for coxels that better enclose an image region. In addition, since saliency bridges are more likely to occur closer to the image center, an implicit central bias is predicted. This may in fact support the biological plausibility of the model and perhaps partially explain why humans have central bias. Finally, since coxels are apathetic to contiguity, the entire approach can capture abstract salient objects in the form of "holes" or "gaps" in a group of scattered similar elements (cf. Fig. 1).

4   Evaluation

To evaluate our model [1], we use the five datasets employed in the proposed benchmark by Borji et al. [8] and an additional dataset that was published recently by Yan et al. [51], all of which are described below.

MSRA: 5000 images of resolution 400×300. For each image, nine users annotated what they considered the most salient object by a single bounding-box.

ASD: 1000 images (taken from the MSRA daset). For each image, a single annotator manually labeled the boundaries of a single salient object (or several of them in a few cases).

---

[1] Implementation will be made publicly available at http://www.cs.bgu.ac.il/~icvl

SED1,SED2: Each contains 100 images, of resolution $\sim 300 \times 225$. The datasets were designed to avoid ambiguities by only including images that clearly depict a single (SED1) and exactly two salient objects (SED2). Each of three annotators manually labeled the boundaries of a single or two salient objects, respectively.

SOD: 300 images of resolution 481×321, selected from the Berkeley Segmentation Dataset (BSD) [36] and labeled by seven annotators. Each annotator was shown a random subset of possible segmentations depicted as boundaries overlapped on the image and chose the segments composing salient objects by clicking on them.

ECSSD: 1000 images of resolution $\sim 400 \times 300$, taken from BSD, the VOC dataset [17] and the internet. Salient objects were manualy segmented by five annotators. However, the produced ground truth maps are binary.

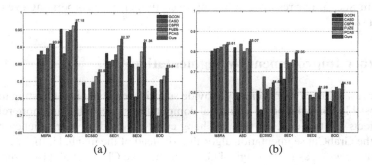

(a)   (b)

Fig. 6. Detection accuracy: (a) AUC scores of the "Top-4" algorithms, GCON, CASD, CSPR and FUZE, are compared with the rarity based approach recently suggested by Margolin et al. (PCAS) and our approach. On the MSRA dataset, our approach is comparable to PCAS which outperforms the "Top-4" algorithms. More significant improvements are obtained for the other four datasets. The most significant improvement is for the SED2 dataset, specifically designed to include two salient objects in every image. (b) F-Measure scores of the "Top-4" algorithms, PCAS and our approach, based on the precision-recall curve. Excluding the ECSSD dataset on which the CSPR algorithm that employs shape prior shows better scores, our approach is better than or comparable to other algorithms on all other datasets despite using nothing else but raw contextual consideration.

According to the recent benchmark by Borji et al. [8], the 4 highest scoring algorithms (henceforth, the "Top-4") to-date are FUZE [11], CSPR [29], CASD [19] and GCON [14]. Recently, Margolin et al. [35] have shown their approach (henceforth PCAS) outperforms these methods on all datasets used for the benchmark in terms of area under the ROC curve (AUC) scores. We compare our results to these five state-of-the-art algorithms, based on the same ranking used in the Borji et al. benchmark [8], both in terms of AUC scores and in terms of F-measure. Figure 6a shows AUC scores for each dataset, based on true positive rate and false positive rate, by varying a threshold from 0 to 1 on the normalized saliency maps. Our approach is comparable to PCAS on the MSRA dataset and outperforms all five algorithms on all other datasets. Interestingly, the most significant improvement is achieved on the SED2 dataset, which

includes two salient objects in every image and departs the most from the typical scenarios of single salient object around the center of the image.

Figure 6b shows the evaluation results according to the *precision-recall* curve (PR),
obtained during the calculation of the ROC curve. The reported scores are based on
the F-Measure defined as $F_\alpha = \frac{(1+\alpha)Precision \times Recall}{\alpha \times Precision + Recall}$. As in previous evaluations
[8,14,2], we set $\alpha = 0.3$ to weigh precision more than recall.

While the quantitative evaluation reveals superior results, it is important to note that
this happens despite being done on unequal grounds. As discussed in Sec. 2, almost all
previous approaches to which we compare use additional processes and biases to improve the raw saliency maps by incorporating object properties [11], shape priors [29],
face detection [19], or center bias [35]. Our results so far are intentionally stripped of
any such additional computations and yet the proposed contextual computation outperforms the state-of-the-art (despite also using the most naïve similarity measure). As
we show in Sec. 5, our results can be improved further by incorporating even simple
additional steps.

5   Further Improvement by Segmentation

While our raw saliency maps already provide superior results, it is interesting to examine the possible contribution of additional computational steps that are more related to
visual objects. To this end, we follow Cheng et al. [14] and use our saliency maps to
initialize the GrabCut segmentation algorithm (instead of the manual initialization with
a rectangular region, as in the original GrabCut). Unlike Cheng et al. [14], who initialized GrabCut with binary saliency maps based on a fixed threshold, we sought a way to
compare results across thresholds so they can be evaluated against the results presented
in Sec. 4. Hence, the task becomes one of combining GrabCut with information from
our raw (and graded) saliency maps in order to improve overall saliency results.

A possible approach to pursue the above would initialize GrabCut with binarized
saliency maps based on all threshold values $0 \leq \tau_i \leq 1$. New foreground regions suggested by GrabCut at each threshold (if they indeed emerge) would then be assigned
saliency values in a revised map. This still leaves open the particular strategy of assigning saliency values to aggregated foreground regions. As the segmentation may not
capture the entire object or it might include non object regions, careless assignment of
saliency values may significantly reduce true-positives (TP) or increase false-positives
(FP) and thus reduce performance rather than improving it.

If new foreground regions were assigned their raw saliency values, then FP rate in
the revised map could not exceed that in the raw map. Indeed, empirical results based
on this approach reduced preformance, implying that the GrabCut segmentation misses
parts of the objects that contributed to the results (hence decreasing TP rate). In order
to enhance the saliency of foreground regions while preserving the saliency of missed
objects parts, we use the following strategy (demonstrated in Fig.7). At each threshold,
any suggested foreground region in the revised map is assigned its raw saliency, normalized to the range between the average and maximum values of that region. Only after
all threshold values are considered, the remaining regions in the revised map (possibly
including missed object parts) are assigned their raw saliency values.

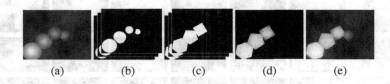

(a)	(b)	(c)	(d)	(e)

Fig. 7. A schematic demonstration of the GrabCut based improvement. The original saliency map (a) is thresholded at different levels (b) to initialize GrabCut, which may suggest new foreground regions at each level (c). New regions are accumulated in the revised map (d). Whenever a region is added to that map, its saliency values are normalized to the range between the average and the maximum values of that region in the original map. The remaining regions are assigned their original saliency values (e).

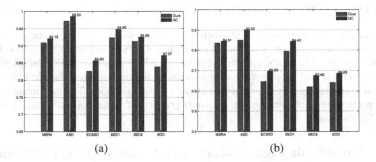

(a)   (b)

Fig. 8. Improvement of our original results using the GrabCut segmentation algorithm. Scores are presented in terms of AUC (panel a) and in terms of F-Measure (panel b).

Using the procedure above, Fig. 8 shows the improvement with respect to our previous results (based on the same evaluation metrics). More specifically, using this segmentation step, original AUC scores improve by $\sim 1\% - 3\%$ and F-measures increase by $\sim 1\% - 5\%$. Since many of the previous algorithms also use additional computations beyond raw saliency, an equal ground comparison to the prior art should consider *these* numbers (rather than those from Sec. 4, which already outperform existing approaches), that indicate that our algorithm exhibits performance which is better than the state-of-the-art by a large margin.

Finally, although it is important to consider objective quantitative measures and results as above, we believe that much of the strength of our approach is revealed at the qualitative level. Indeed, most benchmark databases for saliency detection include relatively simple saliency scenarios, with one (usually visually coherent) salient object typically at a central position. As we argue, the principles underlying previous saliency algorithms (i.e., contrast-based or rarity-based) permit to handle these cases to some extent, but constrain the complexity, frequency, and level of abstraction of the detectable salient objects. In focusing on modeling the context only, our approach is more flexible as indeed was demonstrated already in Fig. 1. Another qualitative comparison for novel images that depict more general saliency scenarios is shown in Fig. 9.

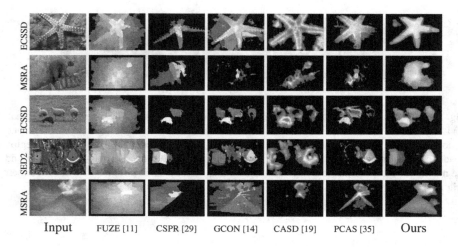

Input   FUZE [11]   CSPR [29]   GCON [14]   CASD [19]   PCAS [35]   Ours

Fig. 9. Example images and normalized saliency maps (thresholded at 30%). The datasets from which the input images are taken are noted on the left. Our saliency maps seem to coherently indicate the saliency of large and complex objects as a whole (first two rows) and allow the detection of multiple salient objects (following two rows). In contrast, no certain level of saliency seems to allow similar detection accuracy by state-of-the-art methods. The last image of a pyramid demonstrates the significance of the enclosure property of visual context for the detection of abstract salient regions.

6   An Unavoidable Commentary about Salient Object Databases

The evaluation of any apcroach inherently depends on two aspects of the dataset to which it is applied. One aspect is ground truth representation. With respect to the datasets above, an apparent problem in this regard is the bounding-box approach used for labeling the MSRA dataset which, as already criticized by Achanta et al. [2], provides limited accuracy. A simple case where this approach may clearly distort evaluation results is when the area ratio between the object and its bounding box is small (e.g., a boomerang). In such a case, false positives within the bounding-box would wrongfully enhance performance while a perfect detection would result in a lower score. To provide a more accurate representation of ground truth, Achanta et al. [2] proposed the ASD dataset in which objects are manually segmented. However, since the data were labeled by a single annotator, the ground truth saliency maps are binary (as is also the case for the ECSSD dataset) whereas the evaluated algorithms may produce graded saliency maps. This discrepancy alone already questions the evaluation reliability.

A second aspect concerns the visual content of the datasets. Although widely used and having size and stimulus variety, the existing datasets are rather restricted in many other ways. For example, as analyzed by Borji et al. [8], these datasets have a strong location-bias and most scenes have low-clutter. An undesired implication is the overfitting of models to existing datasets. Moreover, the suggested ground truth does not allow to evaluate other levels of saliency. This is demonstrated in Borji's benchmark, where methods aiming at fixation prediction show significantly lower performance than methods that seek saliency at the object level.

7 Discussion and Future Directions

We argue that the implicit assumption of having a certain visual constituent at hand when its saliency is measured is at the basis of using different types of context to detect salient objects. The intent for this constituent to be an object motivates its modelling in terms of contrast and rarity. Thus, the nature of visual objects that may be captured is constrained, which necessitates object-specific information and additional computational processes to facilitate better predictions. By modelling visual context instead, we disregard object appearance and reduce these constraints. This allows the saliency of more complex, abstract, or multiple visual objects to emerge. In contrast with previous methods, our approach cannot be categorized as based on contrast or rarity. Our new interpretation of context relies on more basic, general principles.

The ability of our model to outperform the state-of-the-art with no explicit use of object-specific information indicates the dependency of object-based saliency computation on the way context is interpreted in the first place. This is further emphasized by the fact that this superior performance is obtained from low level patches and a single, simple visual feature (i.e., color). Indeed, further development of the suggested theory for contextual emergence of saliency could incorporate additional and more sophisticated features and consider pixels as basic context units. We believe that this would allow to explore the nature of our context based saliency approach for a variety of more complex scenes and perhaps its feasibility for predicting human fixations. However, according to the critisism in section 6, this would require to extend the datasets with more general scenes in terms of complexity, multiplicity, and spatial location. In addition, it would require a new type and more general ground truth that allows to evaluate saliency detection across different levels (fixations and objects). We hope that our novel definition of low-level, non-semantic visual context and the contextual emergence of saliency that follows it would motivate further work in these directions.

Acknowledgements. This work was supported in part by the National Institute for Psychobiology in Israel (grant no. 9-2012/2013) founded by the Charles E. Smith Family, by the Israel Science Foundation (ISF grants no. 259/12 and 1274/11), and by the European Commission in the 7th Framework Programme (CROPS GA no. 246252). We also thank the Frankel Fund, the ABC Robotics initiative, and the Zlotowski Center for Neuroscience at Ben-Gurion University for their generous support.

References

1. Achanta, R., Estrada, F.J., Wils, P., Süsstrunk, S.: Salient region detection and segmentation. In: Gasteratos, A., Vincze, M., Tsotsos, J.K. (eds.) ICVS 2008. LNCS, vol. 5008, pp. 66–75. Springer, Heidelberg (2008)
2. Achanta, R., Hemami, S., Estrada, F., Susstrunk, S.: Frequency-tuned salient region detection. In: Proceedings of the IEEE Conference on Computer Vision and Pattern Recognition, pp. 1597–1604 (2009)
3. Achanta, R., Shaji, A., Smith, K., Lucchi, A., Fua, P., Süsstrunk, S.: Slic superpixels. École Polytechnique Fédéral de Lausssanne (EPFL), Tech. Rep. (2010)

4. Achanta, R., Susstrunk, S.: Saliency detection for content-aware image rresizing. In: Proceedings of the IEEE International Conference on Image Processing, pp. 1005–1008 (2009)
5. Bar, M., Ullman, S.: Spatial context in recognition. Perception 25, 343–352 (1996)
6. Biederman, I.: Perceiving real-world scenes. Science 177, 77–80 (1972)
7. Biedermanl, I., Mezzanote, R., Rabinowitx, J.: Scene perception: Detecting and judging objects undergoing relational violations. Cognitive Psychology 14(2), 143–177 (1982)
8. Borji, A., Sihite, D.N., Itti, L.: Salient object detection: A benchmark. In: Fitzgibbon, A., Lazebnik, S., Perona, P., Sato, Y., Schmid, C. (eds.) ECCV 2012, Part II. LNCS, vol. 7573, pp. 414–429. Springer, Heidelberg (2012)
9. Botev, Z., Grotowski, J., Kroese, D.: Kernel density estimation via diffusion. The Annals of Statistics 38(5), 2916–2957 (2010)
10. Bruce, N., Tsotsos, J.: Saliency based on information maximization. In: Neural Information Processing Systems, pp. 155–162 (2005)
11. Chang, K., Liu, T., Chen, H., Lai, S.: Fusing generic objectness and visual saliency for salient object detection. In: Proceedings of the IEEE International Conference on Computer Vision, pp. 914–921 (2011)
12. Chen, L.Q., Xie, X., Fan, X., Ma, W.Y., Zhang, H.J., Zhou, H.Q.: A visual attention model for adapting images on small displays. Multimedia Systems 9(4), 353–364 (2003)
13. Chen, T., Cheng, M.M., Tan, P., Shamir, A., Hu, S.M.: Sketch2photo: internet image montage. ACM Transactions on Graphics (TOG) 28, 124 (2009)
14. Cheng, M., Zhang, G., Mitra, N., Huang, X., Hu, S.: Global contrast based salient region detection. In: Proceedings of the IEEE Conference on Computer Vision and Pattern Recognition, pp. 409–416 (2011)
15. Christopoulos, C., Skodras, A., Ebrahimi, T.: The jpeg2000 still image coding system: an overview. IEEE Transactions on Consumer Electronics 46(4), 1103–1127 (2000)
16. Duncan, J., Humphreys, G.: Visual search and stimulus similarity. American Psychological Association 96(3), 433–458 (1989)
17. Everingham, M., Van Gool, L., Williams, C.K.I., Winn, J., Zisserman, A.: The PASCAL Visual Object Classes Challenge (VOC2012) Results (2012),
http://www.pascal-network.org/challenges/
VOC/voc2012/workshop/index.html
18. Goferman, S., Tal, A., Zelnik-Manor, L.: Puzzle-like collage. Computer Graphics Forum 29, 459–468 (2010)
19. Goferman, S., Zelnik-Manor, L., Tal, A.: Context-aware saliency detection. IEEE Transactions on Pattern Analysis and Machine Intelligence 34(10), 1915–1926 (2012)
20. Guo, C., Zhang, L.: A novel multiresolution spatiotemporal saliency detection model and its applications in image and video compression. IEEE Transactions on Image Processing 19(1), 185–198 (2010)
21. Han, J., Ngan, K., Li, M., Zhang, H.J.: Unsupervised extraction of visual attention objects in color images. IEEE Transactions on Circuits and Systems for Video Technology 16(1), 141–145 (2006)
22. Harel, J., Koch, C., Perona, P.: Graph-based visual saliency. In: Neural Information Processing Systems, pp. 545–552 (2006)
23. Hou, X., Zhang, L.: Saliency detection: A spectral residual approach. In: Proceedings of the IEEE Conference on Computer Vision and Pattern Recognition, pp. 1–8 (2007)
24. Hu, Y., Xie, X., Ma, W.-Y., Chia, L.-T., Rajan, D.: Salient region detection using weighted feature maps based on the human visual attention model. In: Aizawa, K., Nakamura, Y., Satoh, S. (eds.) PCM 2004. LNCS, vol. 3332, pp. 993–1000. Springer, Heidelberg (2004)
25. Itti, L., Baldi, P.: Bayesian surprise attracts human attention. In: Neural Information Processing Systems, pp. 547–554 (2005)

26. Itti, L., Koch, C.: Computational modelling of visual attention 2(3), 194–203 (2001)
27. Itti, L., Koch, C., Niebur, E.: A model of saliency-based visual attention for rapid scene analysis. IEEE Transactions on Pattern Analysis and Machine Intelligence 20(11), 1254–1259 (1998)
28. Jian, L., Saliency, L.M.A.X.H.H.: detection based on frequency and spatial domain analyses. In: British Machine Vision Conference, pp. 86.1–86.11 (2011)
29. Jiang, H., Wang, J., Yuan, Z., Liu, T., Zheng, N., Li, S.: Automatic salient object segmentation based on context and shape prior. In: British Machine Vision Conference (2011)
30. Ko, B.C., Nam, J.Y.: Object-of-interest image segmentation based on human attention and semantic region clustering. J. Opt. Soc. Am. A 23(10), 2462–2470 (2006)
31. Koch, C., Ullman, S.: Shifts in selective visual attention: towards the underlying neural circuitry 4(4), 219–227 (1985)
32. Liu, T., Yuan, Z., Sun, J., Wang, J., Zheng, N., Tang, X., Shum, H.: Learning to detect a salient object. IEEE Transactions on Pattern Analysis and Machine Intelligence 33(2), 353–367 (2011)
33. Ma, Y., Zhang, H.: Contrast-based image attention analysis by using fuzzy growing. In: Proceedings of the Eleventh ACM international conference on Multimedia, pp. 374–381 (2003)
34. Marchesotti, L., Cifarelli, C., Csurka, G.: A framework for visual saliency detection with applications to image thumbnailing. In: Proceedings of the IEEE International Conference on Computer Vision, pp. 2232–2239 (2009)
35. Margolin, R., Tal, A., Zelnik-Manor, L.: What makes a patch distinct? In: Proceedings of the IEEE Conference on Computer Vision and Pattern Recognition (2013)
36. Martin, D., Fowlkes, C., Tal, D., Malik, J.: A database of human segmented natural images and its application to evaluating segmentation algorithms and measuring ecological statistics. In: Proceedings of the IEEE International Conference on Computer Vision, pp. 416–423 (2001)
37. Navon, D.: Forest before the trees: the precedence of global features in visual perception. Cognitive Psychology 9, 353–383 (1977)
38. Nothdurft, H.: Salience from feature contrast: additivity across dimensions. Vision Research 40(10), 1073–1078 (2000)
39. Nowak, E., Jurie, F., Triggs, B.: Sampling strategies for bag-of-features image classification. In: Leonardis, A., Bischof, H., Pinz, A. (eds.) ECCV 2006. LNCS, vol. 3954, pp. 490–503. Springer, Heidelberg (2006)
40. Oliva, A., Torralba, A., Castelhano, M.S., Henderson, J.: Top-down control of visual attention in object detection. In: Proceedings of the IEEE International Conference on Image Processing (2003)
41. Palmer, S.: The effects of contextual scenes on the identification of objects. Memory & Cognition 3, 519–526 (1975)
42. Rother, C., Bordeaux, L., Hamadi, Y., Blake, A.: Autocollage. In: ACM SIGGRAPH 2006 Papers. pp. 847–852. ACM Press (2006)
43. Rutishauser, U., Walther, D., Koch, C., Perona, P.: Is bottom-up attention useful for object recognition. In: Proceedings of the IEEE Conference on Computer Vision and Pattern Recognition, vol. 2, pp. 37–44 (2004)
44. Silverman, B.: Density estimation for statistics and data analysis, vol. 26. CRC press (1986)
45. Suh, B., Ling, H., Bederson, B.B., Jacobs, D.W.: Automatic thumbnail cropping and its effectiveness. In: Proceedings of the 16th Annual ACM Symposium on User Interface Software and Technology, pp. 95–104 (2003)
46. Treisman, A.M., Gelade, G.: A feature-integration theory of attention. Cognitive Psychology 12(1), 97–136 (1980)
47. Wang, J., Quan, L., Sun, J., Tang, X., Shum, H.Y.: Picture collage. In: 2006 IEEE Computer Society Conference on Computer Vision and Pattern Recognition, vol. 1, pp. 347–354 (2006)

48. Wang, L., Xue, J., Zheng, N., Hua, G.: Automatic salient object extraction with contextual cue. In: Proceedings of the IEEE International Conference on Computer Vision, pp. 105–112 (2011)
49. Wang, Y.S., Tai, C.L., Sorkine, O., Lee, T.Y.: Optimized scale-and-stretch for image resizing. ACM Transactions on Graphics (TOG) 27, 118 (2008)
50. Xue, J., Li, C., Zheng, N.: Proto-object based rate control for jpeg2000: an approach to content-based scalability 20(4), 1177–1184 (2011)
51. Yan, Q., Xu, L., Shi, J., Jia, J.: Hierarchical saliency detection. In: Proceedings of the IEEE Conference on Computer Vision and Pattern Recognition, pp. 1155–1162. IEEE (2013)
52. Zhai, Y., Shah, M.: Visual attention detection in video sequences using spatiotemporal cues. In: Proceedings of the 14th Annual ACM International Conference on Multimedia, pp. 815–824

Geodesic Object Proposals

Philipp Krähenbühl[1] and Vladlen Koltun[2]

[1] Stanford University, USA
[2] Adobe Research

Abstract. We present an approach for identifying a set of candidate objects in a given image. This set of candidates can be used for object recognition, segmentation, and other object-based image parsing tasks. To generate the proposals, we identify critical level sets in geodesic distance transforms computed for seeds placed in the image. The seeds are placed by specially trained classifiers that are optimized to discover objects. Experiments demonstrate that the presented approach achieves significantly higher accuracy than alternative approaches, at a fraction of the computational cost.

Keywords: perceptual organization, grouping.

1 Introduction

Many image parsing pipelines use sliding windows to extract densely overlapping bounding boxes that are then analyzed [7,11,22]. This approach has well-known disadvantages: the number of bounding boxes per image must be very large to achieve good recognition accuracy, most of the computational effort is wasted on futile bounding boxes, and the rectangular boxes aggregate visual information from multiple objects and background clutter. Both recognition accuracy and computational performance suffer as a result.

An alternative approach is to use segmentation to extract a set of proposed objects to be analyzed [5,9,12,15,21]. Ideal object proposals of this kind should encapsulate the visual signal from one object and have informative boundary shape cues that can assist subsequent tasks. Image analysis pipelines based on such segmentation-driven object proposals have recently achieved state-of-the-art performance on challenging benchmarks [3,4].

In this paper, we present an approach that produces highly accurate object proposals with minimal computational overhead per image. Our key idea is to identify critical level sets in geodesic distance transforms computed for judiciously placed seeds in the image. The seeds are placed by classifiers that are trained to discover objects. Since the geodesic distance transform can be computed in near-linear time and since each computed transform is used to generate proposals at different scales, the pipeline is extremely efficient.

Our experiments demonstrate that the presented approach achieves significantly higher accuracy than alternative approaches as measured by both bounding box overlap and detailed shape overlap with ground-truth objects. It is also substantially faster, producing a high-performing set of object proposals for a raw input image in less than a second using a single CPU thread.

D. Fleet et al. (Eds.): ECCV 2014, Part V, LNCS 8693, pp. 725–739, 2014.

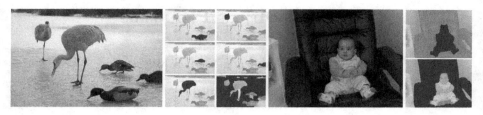

Fig. 1. Object proposals (in red) produced by the presented approach for two images from the PASCAL VOC2012 dataset

2 Overview

Our overall proposal generation pipeline is illustrated in Figure 2. Given an image, we compute an oversegmentation into superpixels and a boundary probability map that associates a boundary probability with each superpixel edge. This step uses existing techniques. Next we identify a set of seed superpixels. The goal is to hit all objects in the image with a small set of automatically placed seeds. In Section 3 we describe a reasonable seed placement heuristic that outperforms other heuristic approaches, such as regular seed placement, random seed placement, or saliency-based placement. In Section 4 we develop a learning-based approach that uses trained classifiers to adaptively place seeds. As shown in Section 6, this approach outperforms all other approaches. For example, it hits 50% of objects in the VOC2012 dataset with just 4 seeds per image. With 20 seeds per image the approach discovers 80% of all objects, many of which are not much larger than a single superpixel. Figure 2b shows the output of the approach with a budget of 8 seeds.

For each seed we generate foreground and background masks that will be used to compute the geodesic distance transform. As described in Section 3, a simple and effective approach is to use the seed itself as the foreground mask and the image boundary or the empty set as background. We can improve upon this by using a learning-based approach for computing the masks. This approach is developed in Section 4. Examples of such masks are shown in Figure 2c.

For each foreground-background mask we compute a signed geodesic distance transform (SGDT) over the image [2,6]. Each level set of the SGDT specifies an image region, but not all such regions form good proposals. As described in Section 3, we can extract a small set of high-quality object proposals by identifying certain critical level sets of the SGDT. Proposals formed by these critical level sets are shown in Figure 2e.

In the final step we sort all proposals produced for all seeds and masks to filter out near-duplicates. The overall pipeline yields state-of-the-art accuracy on standard datasets, as demonstrated in Section 6.

3 Proposal Generation

Preliminaries. Given an input image $\mathcal{I}$, we compute an oversegmentation into superpixels and a boundary probability map represented as a weighted graph

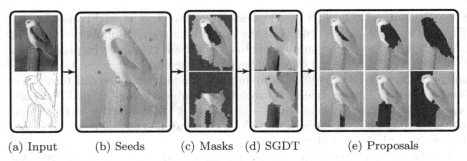

(a) Input   (b) Seeds   (c) Masks   (d) SGDT   (e) Proposals

Fig. 2. Overall proposal generation pipeline. (a) Input image with a computed super-pixel segmentation and a boundary probability map. (b) Seeds placed by the presented approach. (c) Foreground and background masks generated by the presented approach for two of these seeds. (d) Signed geodesic distance transforms for these masks. (e) Object proposals, computed by identifying critical level sets in each SGDT.

$G_\mathcal{I} = (V_\mathcal{I}, E_\mathcal{I})$. This is done using existing techniques, as described in Section 5. Each node $x \in V_\mathcal{I}$ corresponds to a superpixel, each edge $(x, y) \in E_\mathcal{I}$ connects adjacent superpixels, and the edge weight $w(x, y)$ represents the likelihood of object boundary at the corresponding image edge.

The geodesic distance $d_{x,y}$ between two nodes $x, y \in V_\mathcal{I}$ is the length of the shortest path between the nodes in $G_\mathcal{I}$. The geodesic distance transform (GDT) measures the geodesic distance from a set of nodes $Y \subset V_\mathcal{I}$ to each node $x \in V_\mathcal{I}$:

$$D(x; Y) = \min_{y \in Y} d_{x,y}. \qquad (1)$$

The GDT for all nodes in $V_\mathcal{I}$ can be computed exactly using Dijkstra's algorithm in total time $O(n \log n)$, where n is the number of superpixels. Linear-time approximations exist for regular grids [20,23], but our domain is not regular and we use the exact solution.

The geodesic distance transform can be generalized to consider a foreground set $F \subset V_\mathcal{I}$ and a background set $B \subset V_\mathcal{I}$ [2,6]. In this case, the signed geodesic distance transform (SGDT) is defined as

$$D(x; F, B) = D(x; F) - D(x; B). \qquad (2)$$

Each level set λ of the SGDT encloses a unique image segment, which can be used as an object proposal:

$$\mathcal{P}_\lambda = \{x : D(x; F, B) < \lambda\}. \qquad (3)$$

Our approach consists of computing promising foreground and background sets and identifying a small set of appropriate level sets λ for each foreground-background pair. The rest of this section describes the different stages of the approach. We begin by computing a set of foreground seeds: individual super-pixels that are likely to be located inside objects. For each such seed, we construct foreground and background masks. For each pair of masks, we identify a small set of level sets. Each level set specifies an object proposal.

Seed Placement. Our first task is to identify a small set of seed nodes $S \subset V_{\mathcal{I}}$. The goal is to hit all the objects in the image with a small number of seeds, so as to minimize the overall number of object proposals that must be processed by the recognition pipeline. As shown in Section 6, naive seed selection strategies do not perform well. Both regular sampling and random sampling fail to discover small objects in images unless an exorbitant number of seeds is used. Saliency-based seed placement also performs poorly since it is not effective at identifying less prominent objects. We now describe a better seed selection heuristic, based on greedy minimization of geodesic distances.

The heuristic proceeds iteratively. The first seed is placed in the geodesic center of the image:

$$S \leftarrow \{\arg\min_{s} \max_{y \in V_{\mathcal{I}}} d_{s,y}\}. \tag{4}$$

The geodesic center is the superpixel for which the maximal geodesic distance to all other superpixels is minimized. It lies halfway on the longest geodesic path in the superpixel graph and can be found using three consecutive shortest path computations.

Each of the following seeds is placed so as to maximize its geodesic distance to previous seeds:

$$S \leftarrow S \cup \{\arg\max_{s} D(s; S)\}. \tag{5}$$

This is repeated until the desired number of seeds is reached. The $\arg\max$ in Equation 5 can be evaluated with one execution of Dijkstra's algorithm on $G_{\mathcal{I}}$, thus the total runtime of the algorithm is $O(N_S n \log n)$, where N_S is the number of seeds. The algorithm can be interpreted as greedy minimization of the maximal geodesic distance of all superpixels to the seed set.

This algorithm considerably outperforms the naive approaches. It will in turn be superseded in Section 4 by a learning-based approach, but it is a simple heuristic that performs well and may be sufficient for some applications.

Foreground and Background Masks. For each seed $s \in S$, we generate foreground and background masks $F_s, B_s \subset V_{\mathcal{I}}$ that are used as input to the SGDT. The goal here is to focus the SGDT on object boundaries by possibly expanding the foreground mask to include more of the interior of the object that contains it, as well as masking out parts of the image that are likely to be outside the object. This is a challenging task because at this stage we don't know what the object is: it may be as small as a single superpixel or so large as to span most of the image. We will tackle this problem systematically in Section 4, where a learning-based approach to generate foreground and background masks will be developed. As a baseline we will use the seed itself as the foreground mask. For the background we will use two masks: an empty one and the image boundary.

Critical Level Sets. Given a foreground-background mask, our goal is to compute a small set of intermediate level sets that delineate the boundaries of objects that include the foreground. Prior work on interactive geodesic segmentation considered a single segmentation specified by the zero level set of the SGDT [2,6,19].

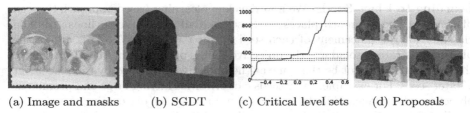

(a) Image and masks   (b) SGDT   (c) Critical level sets   (d) Proposals

Fig. 3. (a) An image with a foreground mask (red) and a background mask (blue). (b) The corresponding signed geodesic distance transform. (c) Critical level sets identified by our algorithm. (d) Corresponding object proposals.

However, the zero level set is sensitive to the detailed form of the masks and may not adhere to object boundaries [18]. We perform a more detailed analysis that yields a small number of level sets that capture object boundaries much better in the absence of interactive refinement by a human user.

Our analysis is based on the growth of the region $\mathcal{P}_\lambda$ as a function of λ. Specifically, let $A(\lambda) = |\mathcal{P}_\lambda|$ be the area enclosed by $\mathcal{P}_\lambda$. This function is illustrated in Figure 3c. Observe that when the λ level set reaches an object boundary, the evolution of the level set slows down. On the other hand, when the level set propagates through an object interior, it evolves rapidly. We can thus identify level sets that follow object boundaries by analyzing their evolution rate, given by the derivative $\frac{dA}{d\lambda}$. Specifically, to extract object proposals that adhere to object boundaries, we identify strong local minima of $\frac{dA}{d\lambda}$.

Selecting level sets purely by their evolution rate can lead to a lopsided selection, in which most proposals specify almost identical regions. To ensure diversity in the level set selection, we enforce the additional constraint that no two selected proposals can overlap by a factor of more than α. Overlap is defined as the Jaccard coefficient of two regions: $\mathcal{J}(\mathcal{P}_{\lambda_i}, \mathcal{P}_{\lambda_j}) = \frac{|\mathcal{P}_{\lambda_i}|}{|\mathcal{P}_{\lambda_j}|}$ for $\lambda_i < \lambda_j$. (Note that $\lambda_i < \lambda_j$ implies $\mathcal{P}_{\lambda_i} \subseteq \mathcal{P}_{\lambda_j}$.) We greedily select the critical level sets by iteratively choosing non-overlapping proposals with the lowest evolution rate. We stop when the desired number of proposals is reached or when no more non-overlapping level sets remain.

Once all proposals from all seeds are generated, we sort them by their evolution rate, which serves as a proxy for their quality. We then greedily select proposals that overlap with prior selections by at most α. To efficiently check the overlap between two proposals we use a hierarchical spatial data structure.

4   Learning Seed Placement and Mask Construction

The proposal generation pipeline described in Section 3 performs very well, as shown in Section 6. However, we can enhance its performance further by replacing two heuristic steps in the pipeline with learning-based approaches. These two steps are the seed placement algorithm and the construction of foreground and background masks.

Learning to Place Seeds. We now develop a learning-based approach for seed placement. The approach places seeds sequentially. We train a linear ranking classifier for the placement of each seed s_i, for $i = 1, \ldots, N_S$. This allows the placement strategy to adapt: the objective that is optimized by the placement of the first seeds need not be the same as the objective optimized by the placement of later seeds. For example, early seeds can prioritize hitting large and prominent objects in the image, while later seeds can optimize for discovering a variety of smaller objects that may require specialized objectives.

At each iteration i, we compute features $\mathbf{f}_x^{(i)}$ for each possible seed location $x \in V_\mathcal{I}$. These features include static features such as location within the image and adaptive features such as distance to previously placed seeds. In general, the feature values are a function of previously placed seeds: $\mathbf{f}_x^{(i)} \neq \mathbf{f}_x^{(j)}$ for $i \neq j$. The specific features we use are listed in Section 5.

The classifier for iteration i is trained after classifiers for iterations $j < i$. For iteration i, we train a linear ranking classifier that associates a score $\mathbf{w}_i^\top \mathbf{f}$ with any feature vector $\mathbf{f}$. During inference we place seed s_i in the top ranking location as determined by the trained classifier: $s_i = \arg\max_x \mathbf{w}_i^\top \mathbf{f}_x^{(i)}$. The training optimizes the weight vector $\mathbf{w}_i$. For the training, we partition each training image $\mathcal{I}$ into a positive region $P_\mathcal{I}$ and a negative region $N_\mathcal{I}$. The positive region consists of all superpixels contained in ground truth objects in the image that have not been hit by previously placed seeds. (The seeds are placed by classifiers previously trained for iterations $j < i$.) The negative region is simply the complement of the positive region: $N_\mathcal{I} = V_\mathcal{I} \setminus P_\mathcal{I}$. We will now formulate a learning objective that encourages the placement of seed s_i inside the positive region $P_\mathcal{I}$ in as many images $\mathcal{I}$ as possible.

Our learning objective differs substantially from standard ranking methods [13]. Standard algorithms aim to learn a ranking that fits a given complete or partial ordering on the data. In our setting, such a partial ordering can be obtained by ranking feature vectors associated with each positive region ($\mathbf{f}_x^{(i)}$ for $x \in P_\mathcal{I}$) above feature vectors associated with the corresponding negative region $N_\mathcal{I}$. While this standard objective works well for early seeds, it ceases to be effective in later iterations when no parameter setting $\mathbf{w}_i$ can reasonably separate the positive region from the negative.

Our key insight is that we do not need to rank all positive seed locations above all negative ones. Our setting only demands that the highest-ranking location be in the positive set, since we only place one seed s_i at iteration i. This objective can be formalized as finding a weight vector $\mathbf{w}_i$ that ranks the highest-ranking positive seed $\hat{x} \in P_\mathcal{I}$ above the highest-ranking negative seed $\hat{y} \in N_\mathcal{I}$. We use logistic regression on the difference between the two scores: $\mathbf{w}_i^\top \mathbf{f}_{\hat{x}}^{(i)} - \mathbf{w}_i^\top \mathbf{f}_{\hat{y}}^{(i)}$. The log-likelihood of the logistic regression is given by

$$\ell_\mathcal{I}(\mathbf{w}_i) = \log\left(1 + \exp\left(\max_{x \in N_\mathcal{I}} \mathbf{w}_i^\top \mathbf{f}_x^{(i)} - \max_{x \in P_\mathcal{I}} \mathbf{w}_i^\top \mathbf{f}_x^{(i)}\right)\right). \tag{6}$$

This objective is both non-convex and non-smooth, which makes it impossible to compute gradients or subgradients. However, we can replace each maximum

$\max_x \mathbf{w}_i^\top \mathbf{f}_x^{(i)}$ in Equation 6 with the softmax $\log \sum_x \exp(\mathbf{w}_i^\top \mathbf{f}_x^{(i)})$, which can be used to simplify the objective to

$$\ell_{\mathcal{I}}(\mathbf{w}_i) = \log \sum_{x \in V_{\mathcal{I}}} \exp\left(\mathbf{w}_i^\top \mathbf{f}_x^{(i)}\right) - \log \sum_{x \in P_{\mathcal{I}}} \exp\left(\mathbf{w}_i^\top \mathbf{f}_x^{(i)}\right). \tag{7}$$

This objective is smooth and any gradient-based optimization algorithm such as L-BFGS can be used to minimize it. While the second term in the objective is still non-convex, the optimization is very robust in practice. In our experiments, a wide variety of different initializations yield the same local minimum.

Learning to Construct Masks. Given a seed $s \in S$, we generate foreground and background masks $F_s, B_s \subset V_{\mathcal{I}}$. These masks give us a chance to further direct the geodesic segmentation to object boundaries by labeling some image regions as foreground or background. Given the formulation of the SGDT, these masks must be conservative: the foreground mask must be contained inside the sought object and the background mask must be outside.

To construct masks, we train one linear classifier for the foreground mask and one linear classifier for the background mask. Both classifiers operate on features $\mathbf{f}_x^{(s)}$, where s is the given seed and $x \in V_{\mathcal{I}}$ is a superpixel in the image. The training optimizes a weight vector $\mathbf{w}_F$ for the foreground classifier and a weight vector $\mathbf{w}_B$ for the background classifier.

We begin by considering the learning objective for the foreground classifier. This objective should reward the generation of the largest foreground mask $F_s \subseteq O_s$, where O_s is the ground-truth object that encloses seed s. The containment in O_s is a hard constraint: the foreground mask should not leak outside the object boundary. This can be formalized as follows:

$$\begin{aligned} \underset{\mathbf{w}_F}{\text{minimize}} \quad & \sum_s \sum_{x \in O_s} \rho\left(\mathbf{w}_F^\top \mathbf{f}_x^{(s)}\right) \\ \text{subject to} \quad & \forall s \in S \ \forall y \notin O_s \ \mathbf{w}_F^\top \mathbf{f}_y^{(s)} < 0. \end{aligned} \tag{8}$$

Here ρ is a penalty function that maximizes the number of true positives. We use the hinge loss, which allows us to minimize Equation 8 as a standard linear SVM with a high negative class weight.

The hard constraints in Equation 8 need to be satisfied for a large number of training objects O_s with hugely varying appearance and size. In our initial experiments, simply optimizing this objective led to trivial classifiers that simply produce the initial seed as the foreground mask and the empty set for the background mask. (The learning objective for the background mask is analogous to Equation 8.) To overcome this difficulty, we modify the formulation to train several classifiers. At inference time, we simply use each of the trained classifiers to generate object proposals. The basic idea is that one of the learned classifiers absorbs the challenging training examples that demand a highly conservative response (trivial foreground and background masks), while others can handle examples that allow larger masks.

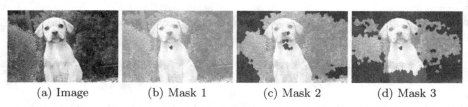

| (a) Image | (b) Mask 1 | (c) Mask 2 | (d) Mask 3 |

Fig. 4. The output of learned mask classifiers. (a) Input image. (b-d) Foreground and background masks generated for a given seed by the learned classifiers. The first classifier is maximally conservative, the others are more risk-taking.

Specifically, we train K foreground classifiers, with weight vectors $\mathbf{w}_F^{(k)}$ for $k = 1, \ldots, K$. (We use $K = 3$.) In addition to the weight vectors, we also optimize a label k_s for each seed s. This is a latent variable $k_s \in \{1, \ldots, K\}$ that associates each training seed s with one of the classifiers. The classifiers and the associations are optimized in concert using the following objective:

$$\operatorname*{minimize}_{\mathbf{w}_F^{(k)}, k_s} \quad \sum_s \sum_{x \in O_s} \rho\left(\mathbf{w}_F^{(k_s)} \cdot \mathbf{f}_x^{(s)}\right) \tag{9}$$
$$\text{subject to} \quad \forall s \in S \;\; \forall y \notin O_s \;\; \mathbf{w}_F^{(k_s)} \cdot \mathbf{f}_y^{(s)} < 0.$$

We use alternating optimization. The different classifiers $\mathbf{w}_F^{(k)}$ are initialized by picking K random seeds and optimizing the objective in Equation 8 for each of these seeds separately. We next optimize the associations k_s by evaluating each classifier on each seed s and associating each seed with the classifier that yields the lowest objective value on that seed. We then alternate between optimizing the classifier parameters given fixed associations and optimizing the associations given fixed classifiers. Note that each step decreases the compound objective in Equation 9.

The extension of the objective and the algorithm to incorporate background mask classifiers is straightforward. In the complete formulation, we train K pairs $(\mathbf{w}_F^{(k)}, \mathbf{w}_B^{(k)})$ of foreground and background classifiers. For each seed, the label k_s associates it with both the foreground classifier $\mathbf{w}_F^{(k_s)}$ and the background classifier $\mathbf{w}_B^{(k_s)}$.

Figure 4 demonstrates the output of the learned mask classifiers on an example test seed. As expected, one of the classifiers is conservative, using the input seed as the foreground and the empty set as the background. The other classifiers are more risk-taking. At test time we use all K masks for each seed to generate object proposals.

5   Implementation

We compute a boundary probability image using structured forests [8]. This boundary probability image is used to produce a superpixel segmentation. We use the geodesic k-means algorithm, which produces a regular oversegmentation that adheres to strong boundaries [17]. Both algorithms are extremely efficient, with a combined runtime of 0.5 seconds for images of size 350×500.

Seed features used by the classifiers described in Section 4 include image coordinates x and y, normalized to the interval $[-1, 1]$, as well as absolute and squared normalized coordinates. We further use the minimal color and spatial distance to previously placed seeds, as well as the color covariance between the given superpixel pixels and all seed pixels. We also add geodesic distances to previously placed seeds, as well as to the image boundary. For computing these distances, we use both graphs with constant edge weights and with boundary probability weights.

Mask features used by the classifiers described in Section 4 include location relative to the seed, distance to each of the image boundary edges, and color similarity to the seed in both RGB and Lab color space. We also compute color histograms for each superpixel and use the χ^2 distance between the color histogram of the given superpixel and the seed superpixel. Finally we add an indicator feature for the seed itself, which ensures that there always exists a parameter setting satisfying Equation 9.

6   Evaluation

We evaluate the presented approach on the PASCAL VOC2012 dataset [10]. All segmentation experiments are performed on the 1449 validation images of the VOC2012 segmentation dataset. Bounding box experiments are performed on the larger detection dataset with 5823 annotated validation images. We train all classifiers on the 1464 segmentation training images. Training all seed and mask classifiers takes roughly 10 minutes in total. All experiments were performed on a 3.4 GHz Core i7 processor. Runtimes for all methods are reported for single-threaded execution and cover all operations, including boundary detection and oversegmentation.

To evaluate the quality of our object proposals we use the Average Best Overlap (ABO), covering, and recall measures [5]. The ABO between a ground truth object set S and a set of proposals $\mathcal{P}$ is computed using the overlap between each ground truth region $R \in S$ and the closest object proposal $R' \in \mathcal{P}$:

$$\text{ABO} = \frac{1}{|S|} \sum_{R \in S} \max_{R' \in \mathcal{P}} \mathcal{J}(R, R').$$

Here the overlap of two image regions R and R' is defined as their Jaccard coefficient $\mathcal{J}(R, R') = \frac{|R \cap R'|}{|R \cup R'|}$. Figure 5 illustrates the relationship between the precision of fit of the two image regions and the corresponding Jaccard coefficient values.

Covering is an area-weighted measure:

$$\text{Covering} = \frac{1}{\sum_{R \in S} |R|} \sum_{R \in S} |R| \max_{R' \in \mathcal{P}} \mathcal{J}(R, R').$$

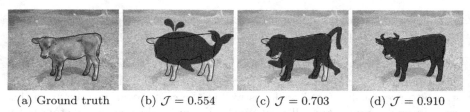

(a) Ground truth   (b) $\mathcal{J} = 0.554$ (c) $\mathcal{J} = 0.703$ (d) $\mathcal{J} = 0.910$

Fig. 5. The relationship between region similarity and the Jaccard coefficient $\mathcal{J}$. A Jaccard coefficient of 0.5 admits rather significant departures from the ground truth shape. A Jaccard coefficient of 0.7 is more discriminative and a coefficient of 0.9 demands a very tight fit.

It discounts small and thin objects and assigns higher importance to larger objects.

The recall measure is defined as the fraction of ground truth segments with a maximum overlap larger than α [5,21]. It is also referred to as the detection rate [16]. A fairly lenient $\alpha = 50\%$ recall threshold has sometimes been used [21]. However, this threshold allows poorly fitting proposals to qualify, as shown in Figure 5b. A high recall at 50% can be achieved by covering the image evenly with generic proposals, rather than producing detailed object shapes. Our work focuses on generating object proposals with informative spatial support. In the best case, our pipeline can precisely delineate objects in the image, as shown in Figure 1. To evaluate the precision of object proposals produced by different approaches more stringently, we also report results for the tighter $\alpha = 70\%$ recall threshold.

Seed Placement. We first compare the geodesic seed placement heuristic described in Section 3, the learning-based seed placement approach described in Section 4, and four alternative seed placement strategies: regular sampling, random sampling, saliency-weighted random sampling, and sampling based on an oversegmentation of the image. The oversegmentation-based seed placement is modeled on the approach of Carreira et al. [5] and uses a hierarchical segmentation algorithm. For saliency-based seed placement we randomly sample superpixels weighted by their saliency as given by the algorithm of Perazzi et al. [17]. For each seed placement strategy we generate a single-seed foreground mask and use the image boundary as background.

Both saliency-based and regular seeds are able to discover a reasonable number of objects with up to 3 seeds, as shown in Figure 6a. However, both methods make less progress after the first few seeds. The saliency-based method biases the placement to prominent objects, missing less salient ones. Regular and random sampling both miss many smaller objects. Oversegmentation-based seeds generally perform better, but not as well as our geodesic or learned seeds.

Figures 6b shows the ABO of our pipeline for a fixed parameter setting and an increasing number of seeds. Random, saliency-weighted, and regular sampling perform equally well and about 5% and 7% worse than geodesic seed placement in ABO and recall respectively. Segmentation-based seeds perform better, but

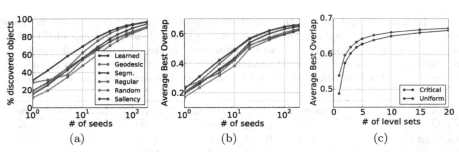

(a)   (b)   (c)

Fig. 6. (a,b) Comparison of our seed placement algorithms (heuristic and learned) to other seed placement algorithms: (a) percentage of objects discovered by placed seeds, (b) accuracy achieved by the proposal pipeline given seeds placed by different algorithms. (c) Comparison of our level set selection algorithm to uniform selection: the figure shows the accuracy achieved by the pipeline using each of these level set selection algorithms.

still 1-2% worse than geodesic seeds in both metrics. With a high seed budget, the geodesic and learned strategies perform similarly, however the learned strategy usually produces 5% fewer proposals, as seeds sometimes collide and produce duplicate proposals that are then filtered out.

Level Set Selection. Next, we compare the critical level set selection algorithm developed in Section 3 to simple uniform selection. For this experiment we use 100 geodesic seeds, with single-seed foreground masks and the image boundary as background. As shown in Figure 6c, our level set selection algorithm outperforms uniform selection, especially with a low budget of proposals per seed. For a single level set, our algorithm achieves a 5% higher ABO and 4% higher recall than the zero level set. Our algorithm consistently outperforms uniform selection. For 20 level sets our algorithm is within 0.5% of the maximal achievable ABO obtained with an oracle level set selector that uses the ground truth, while uniform selection requires twice as many level sets to achieve this level of accuracy.

Boundary Detection. In Figure 7, we evaluate the effect of the boundary detection procedure on the final proposal quality. We compare Sobel filtering, sketch tokens [14], and structured forests (single-scale and multi-scale) [8]. Sobel filtering yields poor accuracy since it produces a fairly inaccurate boundary map. Our pipeline performs well with all other boundary detectors. Multi-scale structured forests yield the best results and we use this procedure for all other experiments.

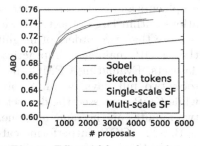

Fig. 7. Effect of boundary detection procedure

Object Proposals. We now use the VOC2012 segmentation dataset to evaluate the accuracy of object proposals produced by the baseline pipeline described in Section 3 and the enhanced pipeline that uses the seed placement and mask

Table 1. Accuracy and running time for three state-of-the-art object proposal methods compared to accuracy and running time for our approach. Results are provided for our baseline pipeline (Baseline GOP) and the enhanced pipeline that uses seed placement and mask construction classifiers (Learned GOP). Different budgets (N_S,N_A) for seed placement and level set selection control the number of generated proposals (# prop).

Method	# prop.	ABO	Covering	50%-recall	70%-recall	Time
CPMC [5]	646	0.703	0.850	0.784	0.609	252s
Cat-Ind OP [9]	1536	0.718	0.840	0.820	0.624	119s
Selective Search [21]	4374	0.735	0.786	0.891	0.597	2.6s
Baseline GOP (130,5)	653	0.712	0.812	0.833	0.622	0.6s
Baseline GOP (150,7)	1090	0.727	0.828	0.847	0.644	0.65s
Baseline GOP (200,10)	2089	0.744	0.843	0.867	0.673	0.9s
Baseline GOP (300,15)	3958	0.756	0.849	0.881	0.699	1.2s
Learned GOP (140,4)	652	0.720	0.815	0.844	0.632	1.0s
Learned GOP (160,6)	1199	0.741	0.835	0.865	0.673	1.1s
Learned GOP (180,9)	2286	0.756	0.852	0.877	0.699	1.4s
Learned GOP (200,15)	4186	0.766	0.858	0.889	0.715	1.7s

construction classifiers described in Section 4. Table 1 compares the accuracy of our pipeline (GOP) to three state-of-the-art object proposal methods, each of which produces a different number of segments. We set the number of seeds N_S and number of level sets N_A in our pipeline to different values to roughly match the number of proposals produced by the other approaches. Accuracy is evaluated using ABO, covering, and recall at $\mathcal{J} \geq 50\%$ and $\mathcal{J} \geq 70\%$.

Our baseline performs slightly better than CPMC [5] in ABO and 70%-recall and greatly outperforms it at 50%-recall. CPMC is better at proposing larger objects, which leads to higher covering results. Figure 8 provides a more detailed comparison. CPMC is based on graph cuts and is less sensitive to texture variations within large objects. However, CPMC is more than two orders of magnitude slower than GOP, making it impractical for larger datasets. Evaluating CPMC on 1464 images took two full days on an 8-core processor, while GOP processed the dataset in less than two minutes on the same machine. (0.6 seconds per image on a single core.)

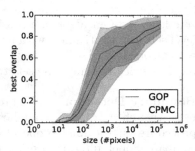

Fig. 8. Accuracy of CMPC and GOP as a function of segment size

Baseline GOP outperforms category-independent object proposals [9] using just two-thirds of the number of proposals. Again our approach is two orders of magnitude faster.

Selective search [21] performs extremely well at 50%-recall. However, when the recall threshold is increased to 70% our approach significantly outperforms selective search. At this threshold, Baseline GOP with 660 proposals outperforms the recall achieved by selective search with more than 4000 proposals. When the

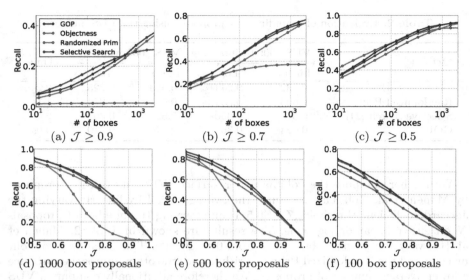

(a) $\mathcal{J} \geq 0.9$ (b) $\mathcal{J} \geq 0.7$ (c) $\mathcal{J} \geq 0.5$

(d) 1000 box proposals   (e) 500 box proposals   (f) 100 box proposals

Fig. 9. Recall for bounding box proposals. (a-c) Recall at above a fixed threshold rate $\mathcal{J}$ for a varying number of generated proposals. (d-f) Recall at different thresholds for fixed proposal budgets.

proposal budget for GOP is increased to match the number of proposals produced by selective search, our 70%-recall is 10% higher.

The seed placement and mask construction classifiers yield a noticeable increase in proposal accuracy, as reflected in the ABO and 70%-recall measures. The classifiers increase the ABO by about 1% and the 70%-recall by up to 3%. The additional computational cost of evaluating the classifiers increases the running time by about half a second and is primarily due to the feature computation.

Bounding Box Proposals. We also evaluate the utility of the presented approach for generating bounding box proposals. We produce bounding box proposals simply by taking the bounding boxes of object proposals produced by GOP. In this mode, using mask construction classifiers does not confer an advantage over simple foreground-background masks since segmentation accuracy is less important. We thus use baseline foreground-background masks for this experiment. The seed placement classifiers still reduce the number of generated proposals by 5% and yield higher accuracy, especially for a small number of seeds.

To evaluate the accuracy of bounding box proposals we use the VOC2012 detection dataset and follow the evaluation methodology of Manén et al. [16]. The results are shown in Figure 9. Our approach is compared to three state-of-the-art methods: objectness [1], selective search [21], and the Randomized Prim algorithm [16]. We measure recall for different Jaccard coefficient thresholds and for different proposal budgets N. For objectness and selective search we select the N highest ranking proposals produced by these methods. For Randomized Prim and GOP we generate N proposals by varying the algorithms' parameters.

Table 2. Evaluation of bounding box proposals using the VUS measure

Method	VUS 10000 windows		VUS 2000 windows		Time
	Linear	Log	Linear	Log	
Objectness [1]	0.332	0.244	0.323	0.225	2.2s
Randomized Prim [16]	0.603	0.334	0.511	0.274	1.1s
Selective search [21]	0.573	0.350[1]	0.528	0.301	2.6s
GOP	0.624	0.363	0.546	0.310	0.9s

We further compute the volume under surface (VUS) measure as proposed by Manén et al. [16]. This measures the average recall by linearly varying the Jaccard coefficient threshold $\mathcal{J} \in [0.5, 1]$ and varying the number of proposals N on either linear or log scale. The results are shown in Table 2. Manén et al. [16] vary the proposal budget N from 0 to 10,000. This unfairly favors our method and the Randomized Prim algorithm since the other approaches produce a lower average number of proposals. We therefore additionally compute a VUS for 2,000 windows, for which each algorithm produces approximately the same number of proposals.

Objectness performs best at 50%-recall and a low proposal budget, since it is able to rank proposals very well. However, its performance degrades quickly when the recall threshold is increased.

Both selective search and GOP consistently outperform Randomized Prim. Selective search has the edge at high recall with a low proposal budget, while our approach performs better in all other regimes. This is also reflected in the results for the VUS measure (Table 2). GOP outperforms all other approaches in both linear and logarithmic VUS measure, for both 2000 and 10000 windows. The running time of our approach is again the lowest.

7   Discussion

We presented a computationally efficient approach for identifying candidate objects in an image. The presented approach outperforms the state of the art in both object shape accuracy and bounding box accuracy, while having the lowest running time. In the future it would be interesting to also learn the metric on which the geodesic distance transform is computed. In addition, joint learning of all parameters for all steps in the pipeline could exploit correlations between the different learned concepts and further increase the accuracy of the approach.

Acknowledgements. Philipp Krähenbühl was supported by the Stanford Graduate Fellowship.

---

[1] Note that our results for selective search differ significantly from the results reported by Manén et al. [16]. We use the highest-ranking bounding boxes in the evaluation instead of randomly subsampling them.

References

1. Alexe, B., Deselaers, T., Ferrari, V.: Measuring the objectness of image windows. PAMI 34(11) (2012)
2. Bai, X., Sapiro, G.: Geodesic matting: A framework for fast interactive image and video segmentation and matting. IJCV 82(2) (2009)
3. Carreira, J., Caseiro, R., Batista, J., Sminchisescu, C.: Semantic segmentation with second-order pooling. In: Fitzgibbon, A., Lazebnik, S., Perona, P., Sato, Y., Schmid, C. (eds.) ECCV 2012, Part VII. LNCS, vol. 7578, pp. 430–443. Springer, Heidelberg (2012)
4. Carreira, J., Li, F., Sminchisescu, C.: Object recognition by sequential figure-ground ranking. IJCV 98(3) (2012)
5. Carreira, J., Sminchisescu, C.: CPMC: Automatic object segmentation using constrained parametric min-cuts. PAMI 34(7) (2012)
6. Criminisi, A., Sharp, T., Rother, C., Pérez, P.: Geodesic image and video editing. ACM Trans. Graph. 29(5) (2010)
7. Dalal, N., Triggs, B.: Histograms of oriented gradients for human detection. In: CVPR (2005)
8. Dollár, P., Zitnick, C.L.: Structured forests for fast edge detection. In: ICCV (2013)
9. Endres, I., Hoiem, D.: Category-independent object proposals with diverse ranking. PAMI 36(2) (2014)
10. Everingham, M., Van Gool, L.J., Williams, C.K.I., Winn, J.M., Zisserman, A.: The Pascal Visual Object Classes (VOC) challenge. IJCV 88(2) (2010)
11. Felzenszwalb, P.F., Girshick, R.B., McAllester, D.A., Ramanan, D.: Object detection with discriminatively trained part-based models. PAMI 32(9) (2010)
12. Gu, C., Lim, J.J., Arbelaez, P., Malik, J.: Recognition using regions. In: CVPR (2009)
13. Joachims, T.: Optimizing search engines using clickthrough data. In: KDD (2002)
14. Lim, J.J., Zitnick, C.L., Dollár, P.: Sketch tokens: A learned mid-level representation for contour and object detection. In: CVPR (2013)
15. Malisiewicz, T., Efros, A.A.: Improving spatial support for objects via multiple segmentations. In: BMVC (2007)
16. Manén, S., Guillaumin, M., Gool, L.V.: Prime object proposals with randomized Prim's algorithm. In: ICCV (2013)
17. Perazzi, F., Krähenbühl, P., Pritch, Y., Hornung, A.: Saliency filters: Contrast based filtering for salient region detection. In: CVPR (2012)
18. Price, B.L., Morse, B.S., Cohen, S.: Geodesic graph cut for interactive image segmentation. In: CVPR (2010)
19. Sinop, A.K., Grady, L.: A seeded image segmentation framework unifying graph cuts and random walker which yields a new algorithm. In: ICCV (2007)
20. Toivanen, P.J.: New geodesic distance transforms for gray-scale images. Pattern Recognition Letters 17(5) (1996)
21. Uijlings, J.R.R., van de Sande, K.E.A., Gevers, T., Smeulders, A.W.M.: Selective search for object recognition. IJCV 104(2) (2013)
22. Viola, P.A., Jones, M.J.: Rapid object detection using a boosted cascade of simple features. In: CVPR (2001)
23. Yatziv, L., Bartesaghi, A., Sapiro, G.: O(n) implementation of the fast marching algorithm. J. Comput. Physics 212(2) (2006)

Microsoft COCO: Common Objects in Context

Tsung-Yi Lin[1], Michael Maire[2], Serge Belongie[1], James Hays[3], Pietro Perona[2], Deva Ramanan[4], Piotr Dollár[5], and C. Lawrence Zitnick[5]

[1] Cornell
[2] Caltech
[3] Brown
[4] UC Irvine
[5] Microsoft Research

Abstract. We present a new dataset with the goal of advancing the state-of-the-art in object recognition by placing the question of object recognition in the context of the broader question of scene understanding. This is achieved by gathering images of complex everyday scenes containing common objects in their natural context. Objects are labeled using per-instance segmentations to aid in precise object localization. Our dataset contains photos of 91 objects types that would be easily recognizable by a 4 year old. With a total of 2.5 million labeled instances in 328k images, the creation of our dataset drew upon extensive crowd worker involvement via novel user interfaces for category detection, instance spotting and instance segmentation. We present a detailed statistical analysis of the dataset in comparison to PASCAL, ImageNet, and SUN. Finally, we provide baseline performance analysis for bounding box and segmentation detection results using a Deformable Parts Model.

1 Introduction

One of the primary goals of computer vision is the understanding of visual scenes. Scene understanding involves numerous tasks including recognizing what objects are present, localizing the objects in 2D and 3D, determining the objects' and scene's attributes, characterizing relationships between objects and providing a semantic description of the scene. The current object classification and detection datasets [1,2,3,4] help us explore the first challenges related to scene understanding. For instance the ImageNet dataset [1], which contains an unprecedented number of images, has recently enabled breakthroughs in both object classification and detection research [5,6,7]. The community has also created datasets containing object attributes [8], scene attributes [9], keypoints [10], and 3D scene information [11]. This leads us to the obvious question: what datasets will best continue our advance towards our ultimate goal of scene understanding?

We introduce a new large-scale dataset that addresses three core research problems in scene understanding: detecting non-iconic views (or non-canonical perspectives [12]) of objects, contextual reasoning between objects and the precise 2D localization of objects. For many categories of objects, there exists an iconic view. For example, when performing a web-based image search for the

D. Fleet et al. (Eds.): ECCV 2014, Part V, LNCS 8693, pp. 740–755, 2014.

(a) Image classification   (b) Object localization   (c) Semantic segmentation   (d) This work

Fig. 1. While previous object recognition datasets have focused on (a) image classification, (b) object bounding box localization or (c) semantic pixel-level segmentation, we focus on (d) segmenting individual object instances. We introduce a large, richly-annotated dataset comprised of images depicting complex everyday scenes of common objects in their natural context

object category "bike," the top-ranked retrieved examples appear in profile, unobstructed near the center of a neatly composed photo. We posit that current recognition systems perform fairly well on iconic views, but struggle to recognize objects otherwise – in the background, partially occluded, amid clutter [13] – reflecting the composition of actual everyday scenes. We verify this experimentally; when evaluated on everyday scenes, models trained on our data perform better than those trained with prior datasets. A challenge is finding natural images that contain multiple objects. The identity of many objects can only be resolved using context, due to small size or ambiguous appearance in the image. To push research in contextual reasoning, images depicting scenes [3] rather than objects in isolation are necessary. Finally, we argue that detailed spatial understanding of object layout will be a core component of scene analysis. An object's spatial location can be defined coarsely using a bounding box [2] or with a precise pixel-level segmentation [14,15,16]. As we demonstrate, to measure either kind of localization performance it is essential for the dataset to have every instance of every object category labeled and fully segmented. Our dataset is unique in its annotation of instance-level segmentation masks, Fig. 1.

To create a large-scale dataset that accomplishes these three goals we employed a novel pipeline for gathering data with extensive use of Amazon Mechanical Turk. First and most importantly, we harvested a large set of images containing contextual relationships and non-iconic object views. We accomplished this using a surprisingly simple yet effective technique that queries for pairs of objects in conjunction with images retrieved via scene-based queries [17,3]. Next, each image was labeled as containing particular object categories using a hierarchical labeling approach [18]. For each category found, the individual instances were labeled, verified, and finally segmented. Given the inherent ambiguity of labeling, each of these stages has numerous tradeoffs that we explored in detail.

The Microsoft Common Objects in COntext (MS COCO) dataset contains 91 common object categories with 82 of them having more than 5,000 labeled instances, Fig. 6. In total the dataset has 2,500,000 labeled instances in 328,000 images. In contrast to the popular ImageNet dataset [1], COCO has fewer categories but more instances per category. This can aid in learning detailed object models capable of precise 2D localization. The dataset is also significantly larger in number of instances per category than the PASCAL VOC [2] and SUN [3] datasets. Additionally, a critical distinction between our dataset and others is

(a) Iconic object images (b) Iconic scene images (c) Non-iconic images

Fig. 2. Example of (a) iconic object images, (b) iconic scene images, and (c) non-iconic images. In this work we focus on challenging non-iconic images.

the number of labeled instances per image which may aid in learning contextual information, Fig. 5. MS COCO contains considerably more object instances per image (7.7) as compared to ImageNet (3.0) and PASCAL (2.3). In contrast, the SUN dataset, which contains significant contextual information, has over 17 objects and "stuff" per image but considerably fewer object instances overall.

An extended version of this work with additional details is available [19].

2   Related Work

Throughout the history of computer vision research datasets have played a critical role. They not only provide a means to train and evaluate algorithms, they drive research in new and more challenging directions. The creation of ground truth stereo and optical flow datasets [20,21] helped stimulate a flood of interest in these areas. The early evolution of object recognition datasets [22,23,24] facilitated the direct comparison of hundreds of image recognition algorithms while simultaneously pushing the field towards more complex problems. Recently, the ImageNet dataset [1] containing millions of images has enabled breakthroughs in both object classification and detection research using a new class of deep learning algorithms [5,6,7].

Datasets related to object recognition can be roughly split into three groups: those that primarily address object classification, object detection and semantic scene labeling. We address each in turn.

Image Classification. The task of object classification requires binary labels indicating whether objects are present in an image; see Fig. 1(a). Early datasets of this type comprised images containing a single object with blank backgrounds, such as the MNIST handwritten digits [25] or COIL household objects [26]. Caltech 101 [22] and Caltech 256 [23] marked the transition to more realistic object images retrieved from the internet while also increasing the number of object categories to 101 and 256, respectively. Popular datasets in the machine learning community due to the larger number of training examples, CIFAR-10 and CIFAR-100 [27] offered 10 and 100 categories from a dataset of tiny 32×32 images [28]. While these datasets contained up to 60,000 images and hundreds of categories, they still only captured a small fraction of our visual world.

Recently, ImageNet [1] made a striking departure from the incremental increase in dataset sizes. They proposed the creation of a dataset containing 22k categories with 500-1000 images each. Unlike previous datasets containing entry-level categories [29], such as "dog" or "chair," like [28], ImageNet used the Word-Net Hierarchy [30] to obtain both entry-level and fine-grained [31] categories. Currently, the ImageNet dataset contains over 14 million labeled images and has enabled significant advances in image classification [5,6,7].

Object Detection. Detecting an object entails both stating that an object belonging to a specified class is present, and localizing it in the image. The location of an object is typically represented by a bounding box, Fig. 1(b). Early algorithms focused on face detection [32] using various ad hoc datasets. Later, more realistic and challenging face detection datasets were created [33]. Another popular challenge is the detection of pedestrians for which several datasets have been created [24,4]. The Caltech Pedestrian Dataset [4] contains 350,000 labeled instances with bounding boxes.

For the detection of basic object categories, a multi-year effort from 2005 to 2012 was devoted to the creation and maintenance of a series of benchmark datasets that were widely adopted. The PASCAL VOC [2] datasets contained 20 object categories spread over 11,000 images. Over 27,000 object instance bounding boxes were labeled, of which almost 7,000 had detailed segmentations. Recently, a detection challenge has been created from 200 object categories using a subset of 400,000 images from ImageNet [34]. An impressive 350,000 objects have been labeled using bounding boxes.

Since the detection of many objects such as sunglasses, cellphones or chairs is highly dependent on contextual information, it is important that detection datasets contain objects in their natural environments. In our dataset we strive to collect images rich in contextual information. The use of bounding boxes also limits the accuracy for which detection algorithms may be evaluated. We propose the use of fully segmented instances to enable more accurate detector evaluation.

Semantic Scene Labeling. The task of labeling semantic objects in a scene requires that each pixel of an image be labeled as belonging to a category, such as sky, chair, floor, street, etc. In contrast to the detection task, individual instances of objects do not need to be segmented, Fig. 1(c). This enables the labeling of objects for which individual instances are hard to define, such as grass, streets, or walls. Datasets exist for both indoor [11] and outdoor [35,14] scenes. Some datasets also include depth information [11]. Similar to semantic scene labeling, our goal is to measure the pixel-wise accuracy of object labels. However, we also aim to distinguish between individual instances of an object, which requires a solid understanding of each object's extent.

A novel dataset that combines many of the properties of both object detection and semantic scene labeling datasets is the SUN dataset [3] for scene understanding. SUN contains 908 scene categories from the WordNet dictionary [30] with segmented objects. The 3,819 object categories span those common to object detection datasets (person, chair, car) and to semantic scene labeling (wall, sky, floor). Since the dataset was collected by finding images depicting various scene types, the number of instances per object category exhibits the long tail phenomenon. That is, a few categories have a large number of instances (wall: 20,213, window: 16,080, chair: 7,971) while most have a relatively modest number of instances (boat: 349, airplane: 179, floor lamp: 276). In our dataset, we ensure that each object category has a significant number of instances, Fig. 5.

Other Vision Datasets. Datasets have spurred the advancement of numerous fields in computer vision. Some notable datasets include the Middlebury datasets for stereo vision [20], multi-view stereo [36] and optical flow [21]. The Berkeley Segmentation Data Set (BSDS500) [37] has been used extensively to evaluate both segmentation and edge detection algorithms. Datasets have also been created to recognize both scene [9] and object attributes [8,38]. Indeed, numerous areas of vision have benefited from challenging datasets that helped catalyze progress.

3   Image Collection

We next describe how the object categories and candidate images are selected.

Common Object Categories. The selection of object categories is a nontrivial exercise. The categories must form a representative set of all categories, be relevant to practical applications and occur with high enough frequency to enable the collection of a large dataset. Other important decisions are whether to include both "thing" and "stuff" categories [39] and whether fine-grained [31,1] and object-part categories should be included. "Thing" categories include objects for which individual instances may be easily labeled (person, chair, car) where "stuff" categories include materials and objects with no clear boundaries (sky, street, grass). Since we are primarily interested in precise localization of object instances, we decided to only include "thing" categories and not "stuff." However, since "stuff" categories can provide significant contextual information, we believe the future labeling of "stuff" categories would be beneficial.

The specificity of object categories can vary significantly. For instance, a dog could be a member of the "mammal", "dog", or "German shepherd" categories. To enable the practical collection of a significant number of instances per category, we chose to limit our dataset to entry-level categories, i.e. category labels that are commonly used by humans when describing objects (dog, chair, person). It is also possible that some object categories may be parts of other object categories. For instance, a face may be part of a person. We anticipate the inclusion of object-part categories (face, hands, wheels) would be beneficial for many real-world applications.

We used several sources to collect entry-level object categories of "things." We first compiled a list of categories by combining categories from PASCAL VOC [2] and a subset of the 1200 most frequently used words that denote visually identifiable objects [40]. To further augment our set of candidate categories, several children ranging in ages from 4 to 8 were asked to name every object they see in indoor and outdoor environments. The final 271 candidates may be found in [19]. Finally, the co-authors voted on a 1 to 5 scale for each category taking into account how commonly they occur, their usefulness for practical applications, and their diversity relative to other categories. The final selection of categories attempts to pick categories with high votes, while keeping the number of categories per super-category (animals, vehicles, furniture, etc.) balanced. Categories for which obtaining a large number of instances (greater than 5,000) was difficult were also removed. To ensure backwards compatibility all categories from PASCAL VOC [2] are also included. Our final list of 91 proposed categories is in Fig. 5(a).

Non-iconic Image Collection. Given the list of object categories, our next goal was to collect a set of candidate images. We may roughly group images into three types, Fig. 2: iconic-object images [41], iconic-scene images [3] and non-iconic images. Typical iconic-object images have a single large object in a canonical perspective centered in the image, Fig. 2(a). Iconic-scene images are shot from canonical viewpoints and commonly lack people, Fig. 2(b). Iconic images have the benefit that they may be easily found by directly searching for specific categories using Google or Bing image search. While iconic images generally provide high quality object instances, they can lack important contextual information and non-canonical viewpoints.

Our goal was to collect a dataset such that a majority of images are non-iconic, Fig. 2(c). It has been shown that datasets containing more non-iconic images are better at generalizing [42]. We collected non-iconic images using two strategies. First as popularized by PASCAL VOC [2], we collected images from Flickr which tends to have fewer iconic images. Flickr contains photos uploaded by amateur photographers with searchable metadata and keywords. Second, we did not search for object categories in isolation. A search for "dog" will tend to return iconic images of large, centered dogs. However, if we searched for pairwise combinations of object categories, such as "dog + car" we found many more non-iconic images. Surprisingly, these images typically do not just contain the two categories specified in the search, but numerous other categories as well. To further supplement our dataset we also searched for scene/object category pairs, see [19]. We downloaded at most 5 photos taken by a single photographer within a short time window. In the rare cases in which enough images could not be found, we searched for single categories and performed an explicit filtering stage to remove iconic images. The result is a collection of 328,000 images with rich contextual relationships between objects as shown in Figs. 2(c) and 6.

4   Image Annotation

We next describe how we annotated our image collection. Due to our desire to label over 2.5 million category instances, the design of a cost efficient yet high quality annotation pipeline was critical. The annotation pipeline is outlined in Fig. 3. For all crowdsourcing tasks we used workers on Amazon's Mechanical Turk (AMT). Examples of our user interfaces can be found in [19].

Annotation Pipeline

dog, bottle

(a) Category labeling   (b) Instance spotting   (c) Instance segmentation

Fig. 3. Our image annotation pipeline is split into 3 primary worker tasks: (a) Labeling the categories present in the image, (b) locating and marking all instances of the labeled categories, and (c) segmenting each object instance.

Category Labeling. The first task in annotating our dataset is determining which object categories are present in each image, Fig. 3(a). Since we have 91 potential categories and a large number of images, asking workers to answer 91 binary classification questions per image would be prohibitively expensive. Instead, we used a hierarchical approach [18]. Individual object categories are grouped into 11 super-categories (see [19]). For a given image, a worker was presented with each group of categories in turn and asked to indicate whether any instances exist for that super-category. This greatly reduces the time needed to classify the various categories. For instance, a worker may easily determine whether any animals are present in the image without having to specifically look for cats, dogs, etc. If a worker determines an instance in the super-category is present (animal), they indicate the instance's specific category (dog, cat, etc.) by dragging the category's icon onto the image over one instance of the category. The placement of these icons is critical for the following stage. To ensure high recall, five workers were asked to label each image; a detailed analysis of performance is presented shortly. This stage took 17,751 worker hours to complete.

Instance Spotting. In the next stage all instances of the object categories in an image were labeled, Fig. 3(b). In the previous stage each worker labeled one instance of a category, but multiple category instances may exist. For each image, a worker was asked to place crosses on top of each instance of a specific category found in the previous stage. To boost recall, the location of the instance found by the worker in the previous stage was shown to the current worker to help them in finding an initial instance. Without this priming, it can be difficult for a worker to quickly find an instance of a category upon first seeing the image. The workers could also use a magnifying glass to find small instances. Each worker was asked to label at most 10 instances of a specific category per image. Each image was completed by 5 workers for a total of 8,417 worker hours.

Instance Segmentation. Our final stage is the laborious task of segmenting each category instance, Fig. 3(c). For this stage we modified the excellent user interface developed by Bell et al. [16] for image segmentation. Our interface asks

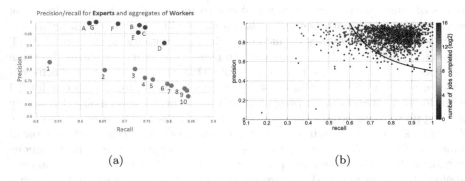

Fig. 4. (a) Precision and recall of experts (red) and the majority vote of AMT workers (blue). Note that the aggregate of 3 workers has better or similar recall to most experts. (b) illustrates the precision and recall of workers, with color indicating how many jobs they completed. For details and definition of ground truth for each plot see text.

the worker to segment a category instance specified by a worker in the previous stage. If other instances have already been segmented in the image, those segmentations are shown to the worker. If the worker does not see an instance of the category in the image (false positive from the previous stage) the worker may click "No <object name> in the image." Similarly if a worker does not find an unsegmented instance in the image they may specify "No unsegmented <object name> in the image."

Segmenting 2,500,000 object instances is an extremely time consuming task requiring over 22 worker hours per 1,000 segmentations. To minimize cost we only had a single worker segment each image. However, we initially found that most workers only produce a coarse outline of the instance resulting in poor segmentations. As a consequence, we required all workers to complete a training task for each object category. After reading the instructions, the training task asked workers to segment an object instance. If the worker's segmentation did not adequately match the ground truth segmentation the worker is repeatedly asked to improve their segmentation until it passes. The use of a training task vastly improves the quality of the workers (only about 1 in 3 workers passed the training stage) and resulting segmentations. Finally, the work of approved workers was periodically verified to ensure segmentation quality remains high. Example segmentations may be viewed in Fig. 6.

In some images many instances of the same category are tightly grouped together and it is hard to distinguish individual instances. For example, it might be difficult to segment an individual person from a crowd. In these cases, the group of instances is marked as one segment and labeled "do not care" for evaluation, e.g., finding people in a crowd will not affect a detector's score.

Annotation Performance Analysis. To ensure the quality of our annotations we analyze the quality of our workers by comparing them to expert workers. In Fig. 4 we show results for the task of category labeling. We compare the precision and recall of seven expert workers (co-authors of the paper) with the results obtained by taking the union of one to ten AMT workers. For this task precision is of less importance since false positives will be removed at later stages, where adding false negatives is much more difficult. Fig. 4(a) shows that 5 AMT workers, the same number as was used to collect our labels, achieves the same recall as most of the expert workers. Note that the expert labelers achieved between 65% and 80% recall. These low values of recall are due to our liberal definition of a category being present. If only one expert labels an object category as being present, we assume the category is indeed present. However, the presence of many categories is often ambiguous. Upon closer inspection, we find recall values of 70% to 75% are generally sufficient to capture the non-ambiguous categories. Fig. 4(b) shows the precision and recall of our workers on category labeling. Unlike in Fig. 4(a), the ground truth labels were now estimated using a majority vote. The color indicates the number of jobs completed by each worker. Notice that workers who complete more hits have generally higher precision and recall. All jobs from workers below the black line were rejected.

5   Dataset Statistics

Next, we analyze the properties of the Microsoft Common Objects in COntext (MS COCO) dataset in comparison to several other popular datasets. These include the ImageNet [1], PASCAL VOC 2012 [2], and SUN [3] datasets. Each of these datasets varies significantly in size, list of labeled categories and types of images. ImageNet was created to capture a large number of object categories, many of which are fine-grained. SUN focuses on labeling scene types and the objects that commonly occur in them. Finally, PASCAL VOC's primary application is object detection in natural images. MS COCO is designed for the detection and segmentation of objects occurring in their natural context. The number of instances per category for all 91 categories collected so far are shown in Fig. 5(a). The completion of our final segmentation stage is still ongoing. Please see [19] for a complete list of collected segmentations, including over 580,000 people.

A summary of the datasets showing the number of object categories and the number of instances per category is shown in Fig. 5(d). While MS COCO has fewer categories than ImageNet and SUN, it has more instances per category which we hypothesize will be useful for learning complex models capable of precise localization. In comparison to PASCAL VOC, MS COCO has both more categories and instances.

An important property of our dataset is we strive to find non-iconic images containing objects in their natural context. The amount of contextual information present in an image can be estimated by examining the number of object categories and instances per image, Fig. 5(b, c). For ImageNet we plot the object detection validation set, since the training data only has a single object labeled. On average our dataset contains 3.5 categories and 7.7 instances per image. In comparison ImageNet and PASCAL VOC both have less than 2 categories and 3 instances per image on average. Another interesting comparison is only 10% of the images in MS COCO have only one category per image, in comparison to

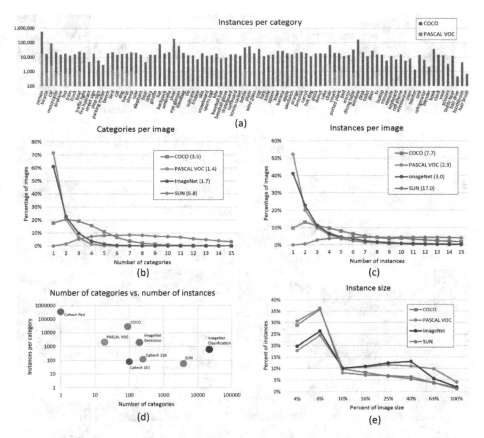

Fig. 5. (a) Number of annotated instances per category for MS COCO and PASCAL VOC. (b,c) Number of annotated categories and annotated instances, respectively, per image for MS COCO, ImageNet Detection, PASCAL VOC and SUN (average number of categories and instances are shown in parentheses). (d) Number of categories vs. the number of instances per category for a number of popular object recognition datasets. (e) The distribution of instance sizes for the MS COCO, ImageNet Detection, PASCAL VOC and SUN datasets.

over 60% of images containing a single object category in ImageNet and PASCAL VOC. As expected, the SUN dataset has the most contextual information since it is scene-based.

Finally, we analyze the average size of objects in the datasets. Generally smaller objects are harder to recognize and require more contextual reasoning to recognize. As shown in Fig. 5(e), the average sizes of objects is smaller for both MS COCO and SUN.

Fig. 6. Samples of annotated images in the MS COCO dataset

6   Algorithmic Analysis

To establish a concrete benchmark, we split our dataset into training, validation, and test data. We have a training set of 164,000 images and a validation and test set of 82,000 images each. We took care to minimize the chance of near-duplicate images existing across splits by explicitly removing duplicates (detected with [43]) and splitting images by date and user. Following now-established protocol, we will release annotations for train and validation images, but not test.

Bounding-box Detection. We begin by examining the performance of the well-studied 20 PASCAL object categories on our dataset. We take a subset of 55,000 images from train/val data for the following experiment and obtain tight-fitting bounding boxes from the annotated segmentation masks. We evaluate

Table 1. Top: Detection performance evaluated on **PASCAL VOC 2012**. DPMv5-P is the performance reported by Girshick et al. in VOC release 5. DPMv5-C uses the same implementation, but is trained with MS COCO. **Bottom**: Performance evaluated on **MS COCO** for DPM models trained with PASCAL VOC 2012 (DPMv5-P) and MS COCO (DPMv5-C). For DPMv5-C we used 5000 positive and 10000 negative training examples. While MS COCO is considerably more challenging than PASCAL, use of more training data coupled with more sophisticated approaches [5,6,7] should improve performance substantially.

	plane	bike	bird	boat	bottle	bus	car	cat	chair	cow	table	dog	horse	moto	person	plant	sheep	sofa	train	tv	Avg.
DPMv5-P	**45.6**	49.0	11.0	11.6	**27.2**	50.5	**43.1**	**23.6**	**17.2**	23.2	**10.7**	**20.5**	42.5	**44.5**	41.3	**8.7**	**29.0**	**18.7**	**40.0**	34.5	**29.6**
DPMv5-C	43.7	**50.1**	**11.8**	2.4	21.4	**60.1**	35.6	16.0	11.4	**24.8**	5.3	9.4	**44.5**	41.0	35.8	6.3	28.3	13.3	38.8	**36.2**	26.8
DPMv5-P	35.1	17.9	3.7	2.3	**7**	45.4	**18.3**	8.6	**6.3**	17	4.8	**5.8**	35.3	25.4	**17.5**	4.1	**14.5**	9.6	31.7	27.9	16.9
DPMv5-C	**36.9**	20.2	**5.7**	**3.5**	6.6	**50.3**	16.1	**12.8**	4.5	**19.0**	9.6	4.0	**38.2**	29.9	15.9	**6.7**	13.8	**10.4**	39.2	37.9	19.1

models tested on both the MS COCO and PASCAL datasets, see Table 1. We evaluate two different models. **DPMv5-P**: the latest implementation of [44] (release 5 [45]) trained on PASCAL VOC 2012. **DPMv5-C**: the same implementation trained on COCO (5000 positive and 10000 negative images). We use the default parameter settings for training COCO models.

If we compare the average performance of DPMv5-P on PASCAL VOC and MS COCO, we find that average performance on MS COCO drops by nearly a *factor of 2*, suggesting that MS COCO does include more difficult (non-iconic) images of objects that are partially occluded, amid clutter, etc. We notice a similar drop in performance for the model trained on MS COCO (DPMv5-C).

The effect on detection performance of training on PASCAL VOC or MS COCO may be analyzed by comparing DPMv5-P and DPMv5-C. They use the same implementation with different sources of training data. Table 1 shows DPMv5-C still outperforms DPMv5-P in 6 out of 20 categories when testing on PASCAL VOC. In some categories (e.g., dog, cat, people), models trained on MS COCO perform worse, while on others (e.g., bus, tv, horse), models trained on our data are better.

Consistent with past observations [46], we find that including difficult (non-iconic) images during training may not always help. Such examples may act as noise and pollute the learned model if the model is not rich enough to capture such appearance variability. Our dataset allows for the exploration of such issues.

Torralba and Efros [42] proposed a metric to measure cross-dataset generalization which computes the 'performance drop' for models that train on one dataset and test on another. The performance difference of the DPMv5-P models across the two datasets is 12.7 AP while the DPMv5-C models only have 7.7 AP difference. Moreover, overall performance is much lower on MS COCO. These observations support two hypotheses: 1) MS COCO is significantly more difficult than PASCAL VOC and 2) models trained on MS COCO can generalize better to easier datasets such as PASCAL VOC given more training data. To gain insight into the differences between the datasets, see [19] for visualizations of person and chair examples from the two datasets.

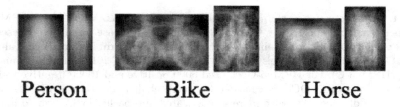

Person   Bike   Horse

Fig. 7. We visualize our mixture-specific shape masks. We paste thresholded shape masks on each candidate detection to generate candidate segments.

Fig. 8. Evaluating instance detections with segmentation masks versus bounding boxes. Bounding boxes are a particularly crude approximation for articulated objects; in this case, the majority of the pixels in the (**blue**) tight-fitting bounding-box do not lie on the object. Our (**green**) instance-level segmentation masks allows for a more accurate measure of object detection and localization.

Generating Segmentations from Detections. We now describe a simple method for generating object bounding boxes and segmentation masks, following prior work that produces segmentations from object detections [47,48,49,50]. We learn aspect-specific pixel-level segmentation masks for different categories. These are readily learned by averaging together segmentation masks from aligned training instances. We learn different masks corresponding to the different mixtures in our DPM detector. Sample masks are visualized in Fig. 7.

Detection Evaluated by Segmentation. Segmentation is a challenging task even assuming an object detector reports correct results as it requires fine localization of object part boundaries. To decouple segmentation evaluation from detection correctness, we benchmark segmentation quality using only correct detections. Specifically, given that the object detector reports a correct bounding box, how well does the predicted segmentation of that object match the groundtruth segmentation? As criterion for correct detection, we impose the standard requirement that intersection over union between predicted and groundtruth boxes is at least 0.5. We then measure the intersection over union of the predicted and groundtruth segmentation masks, see Fig. 8. To establish a baseline for our dataset, we project learned DPM part masks onto the image to create segmentation masks. Fig. 9 shows results of this segmentation baseline for the DPM learned on the 20 PASCAL categories and tested on our dataset.

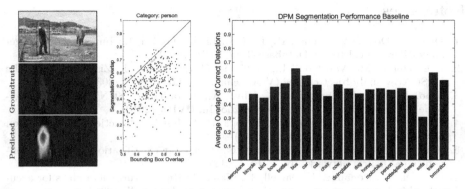

Fig. 9. A predicted segmentation might not recover object detail even though detection and groundtruth bounding boxes overlap well (left). Sampling from the person category illustrates that on a per-instance basis, predicting segmentation from top-down projection of DPM part masks is difficult even for correct detections (center). Averaging over instances for each of the PASCAL VOC categories on our dataset demonstrates that it presents a challenge for object segmentation algorithms (right).

7 Discussion

We described a new dataset for detecting and segmenting objects found in everyday life in their natural environments. Utilizing around 60,000 worker hours, a vast collection of category instances was gathered, annotated and organized to drive the advancement of object detection and segmentation algorithms. Emphasis was placed on finding non-iconic images of objects in natural environments and varied viewpoints. Dataset statistics indicate the images contain rich contextual information with many objects present per image.

There are several promising directions for future annotations on our dataset. We currently only label "things", but labeling "stuff" may also provide significant contextual information that may be useful for detection. Many object detection algorithms benefit from additional annotations, such as the amount an instance is occluded [4] or the location of keypoints on the object [10]. Finally, our dataset could provide a good benchmark for other types of labels, including scene types [3], attributes [9,8] and full sentence written descriptions [51].

To download and learn more about MS COCO please see the project website[1]. Additional details are presented in an extended version of this work [19]. MS COCO will evolve and grow over time; up to date information is available online.

Acknowledgments. Funding for all crowd worker tasks was provided by Microsoft. P.P. and D.R. were supported by ONR MURI Grant N00014-10-1-0933. We would like to thank all members of the community who provided valuable feedback throughout the process of defining and collecting the dataset.

---

[1] http://mscoco.org/

References

1. Deng, J., Dong, W., Socher, R., Li, L.J., Li, K., Fei-Fei, L.: ImageNet: A Large-Scale Hierarchical Image Database. In: CVPR (2009)
2. Everingham, M., Van Gool, L., Williams, C.K.I., Winn, J., Zisserman, A.: The PASCAL visual object classes (VOC) challenge. IJCV 88(2), 303–338 (2010)
3. Xiao, J., Hays, J., Ehinger, K.A., Oliva, A., Torralba, A.: SUN database: Large-scale scene recognition from abbey to zoo. In: CVPR (2010)
4. Dollár, P., Wojek, C., Schiele, B., Perona, P.: Pedestrian detection: An evaluation of the state of the art. PAMI 34 (2012)
5. Krizhevsky, A., Sutskever, I., Hinton, G.: ImageNet classification with deep convolutional neural networks. In: NIPS (2012)
6. Girshick, R., Donahue, J., Darrell, T., Malik, J.: Rich feature hierarchies for accurate object detection and semantic segmentation. In: CVPR (2014)
7. Sermanet, P., Eigen, D., Zhang, S., Mathieu, M., Fergus, R., LeCun, Y.: OverFeat: Integrated recognition, localization and detection using convolutional networks. In: ICLR (April 2014)
8. Farhadi, A., Endres, I., Hoiem, D., Forsyth, D.: Describing objects by their attributes. In: CVPR (2009)
9. Patterson, G., Hays, J.: SUN attribute database: Discovering, annotating, and recognizing scene attributes. In: CVPR (2012)
10. Bourdev, L., Malik, J.: Poselets: Body part detectors trained using 3D human pose annotations. In: ICCV (2009)
11. Silberman, N., Hoiem, D., Kohli, P., Fergus, R.: Indoor segmentation and support inference from RGBD images. In: Fitzgibbon, A., Lazebnik, S., Perona, P., Sato, Y., Schmid, C. (eds.) ECCV 2012, Part V. LNCS, vol. 7576, pp. 746–760. Springer, Heidelberg (2012)
12. Palmer, S., Rosch, E., Chase, P.: Canonical perspective and the perception of objects. Attention and Performance IX 1, 4 (1981)
13. Hoiem, D., Chodpathumwan, Y., Dai, Q.: Diagnosing error in object detectors. In: Fitzgibbon, A., Lazebnik, S., Perona, P., Sato, Y., Schmid, C. (eds.) ECCV 2012, Part III. LNCS, vol. 7574, pp. 340–353. Springer, Heidelberg (2012)
14. Brostow, G., Fauqueur, J., Cipolla, R.: Semantic object classes in video: A high-definition ground truth database. PRL 30(2), 88–97 (2009)
15. Russell, B., Torralba, A., Murphy, K., Freeman, W.: LabelMe: a database and web-based tool for image annotation. IJCV 77(1-3), 157–173 (2008)
16. Bell, S., Upchurch, P., Snavely, N., Bala, K.: OpenSurfaces: A richly annotated catalog of surface appearance. SIGGRAPH 32(4) (2013)
17. Ordonez, V., Kulkarni, G., Berg, T.: Im2text: Describing images using 1 million captioned photographs. In: NIPS (2011)
18. Deng, J., Russakovsky, O., Krause, J., Bernstein, M., Berg, A., Fei-Fei, L.: Scalable multi-label annotation. In: CHI (2014)
19. Lin, T., Maire, M., Belongie, S., Hays, J., Perona, P., Ramanan, D., Dollár, P., Zitnick, C.L.: Microsoft COCO: Common objects in context. CoRR abs/1405.0312 (2014)
20. Scharstein, D., Szeliski, R.: A taxonomy and evaluation of dense two-frame stereo correspondence algorithms. IJCV 47(1-3), 7–42 (2002)
21. Baker, S., Scharstein, D., Lewis, J., Roth, S., Black, M., Szeliski, R.: A database and evaluation methodology for optical flow. IJCV 92(1), 1–31 (2011)
22. Fei-Fei, L., Fergus, R., Perona, P.: Learning generative visual models from few training examples: An incremental bayesian approach tested on 101 object categories. In: CVPR Workshop of Generative Model Based Vision, WGMBV (2004)

23. Griffin, G., Holub, A., Perona, P.: Caltech-256 object category dataset. Technical Report 7694, California Institute of Technology (2007)
24. Dalal, N., Triggs, B.: Histograms of oriented gradients for human detection. In: CVPR (2005)
25. Lecun, Y., Cortes, C.: The MNIST database of handwritten digits (1998)
26. Nene, S.A., Nayar, S.K., Murase, H.: Columbia object image library (coil-20). Technical report, Columbia Universty (1996)
27. Krizhevsky, A., Hinton, G.: Learning multiple layers of features from tiny images. Computer Science Department, University of Toronto, Tech. Rep. (2009)
28. Torralba, A., Fergus, R., Freeman, W.T.: 80 million tiny images: A large data set for nonparametric object and scene recognition. PAMI 30(11), 1958–1970 (2008)
29. Ordonez, V., Deng, J., Choi, Y., Berg, A., Berg, T.: From large scale image categorization to entry-level categories. In: ICCV (2013)
30. Fellbaum, C.: WordNet: An electronic lexical database. Blackwell Books (1998)
31. Welinder, P., Branson, S., Mita, T., Wah, C., Schroff, F., Belongie, S., Perona, P.: Caltech-UCSD Birds 200. Technical Report CNS-TR-201, Caltech. (2010)
32. Hjelmås, E., Low, B.: Face detection: A survey. CVIU 83(3), 236–274 (2001)
33. Huang, G.B., Ramesh, M., Berg, T., Learned-Miller, E.: Labeled faces in the wild. Technical Report 07-49, University of Massachusetts, Amherst (October 2007)
34. Russakovsky, O., Deng, J., Huang, Z., Berg, A., Fei-Fei, L.: Detecting avocados to zucchinis: what have we done, and where are we going? In: ICCV (2013)
35. Shotton, J., Winn, J., Rother, C., Criminisi, A.: TextonBoost for image understanding: Multi-class object recognition and segmentation by jointly modeling texture, layout, and context. IJCV 81(1), 2–23 (2009)
36. Seitz, S.M., Curless, B., Diebel, J., Scharstein, D., Szeliski, R.: A comparison and evaluation of multi-view stereo reconstruction algorithms. In: CVPR (2006)
37. Arbelaez, P., Maire, M., Fowlkes, C., Malik, J.: Contour detection and hierarchical image segmentation. PAMI 33(5), 898–916 (2011)
38. Lampert, C., Nickisch, H., Harmeling, S.: Learning to detect unseen object classes by between-class attribute transfer. In: CVPR (2009)
39. Heitz, G., Koller, D.: Learning spatial context: Using stuff to find things. In: Forsyth, D., Torr, P., Zisserman, A. (eds.) ECCV 2008, Part I. LNCS, vol. 5302, pp. 30–43. Springer, Heidelberg (2008)
40. Sitton, R.: Spelling Sourcebook. Egger Publishing (1996)
41. Berg, T., Berg, A.: Finding iconic images. In: CVPR (2009)
42. Torralba, A., Efros, A.: Unbiased look at dataset bias. In: CVPR (2011)
43. Douze, M., Jégou, H., Sandhawalia, H., Amsaleg, L., Schmid, C.: Evaluation of gist descriptors for web-scale image search. In: CIVR (2009)
44. Felzenszwalb, P., Girshick, R., McAllester, D., Ramanan, D.: Object detection with discriminatively trained part-based models. PAMI 32(9), 1627–1645 (2010)
45. Girshick, R., Felzenszwalb, P., McAllester, D.: Discriminatively trained deformable part models, release 5. PAMI (2012)
46. Zhu, X., Vondrick, C., Ramanan, D., Fowlkes, C.: Do we need more training data or better models for object detection? In: BMVC (2012)
47. Brox, T., Bourdev, L., Maji, S., Malik, J.: Object segmentation by alignment of poselet activations to image contours. In: CVPR (2011)
48. Yang, Y., Hallman, S., Ramanan, D., Fowlkes, C.: Layered object models for image segmentation. PAMI 34(9), 1731–1743 (2012)
49. Ramanan, D.: Using segmentation to verify object hypotheses. In: CVPR (2007)
50. Dai, Q., Hoiem, D.: Learning to localize detected objects. In: CVPR (2012)
51. Rashtchian, C., Young, P., Hodosh, M., Hockenmaier, J.: Collecting image annotations using Amazon's Mechanical Turk. In: NAACL Workshop (2010)

Efficient Joint Segmentation, Occlusion Labeling, Stereo and Flow Estimation

Koichiro Yamaguchi[1], David McAllester[2], and Raquel Urtasun[3]

[1] Toyota Central R&D Labs., Inc., Aichi, 480-1192, Japan
[2] Toyota Technological Institute at Chicago, USA
[3] University of Toronto, Canada

Abstract. In this paper we propose a slanted plane model for jointly recovering an image segmentation, a dense depth estimate as well as boundary labels (such as occlusion boundaries) from a static scene given two frames of a stereo pair captured from a moving vehicle. Towards this goal we propose a new optimization algorithm for our SLIC-like objective which preserves connecteness of image segments and exploits shape regularization in the form of boundary length. We demonstrate the performance of our approach in the challenging stereo and flow KITTI benchmarks and show superior results to the state-of-the-art. Importantly, these results can be achieved an order of magnitude faster than competing approaches.

1   Introduction

Most autonomous vehicles rely on active sensing (e.g., lidar) to construct point cloud representations of the environment. However, passive computer vision holds out the potential to provide richer geometric representations at lower cost. In this paper we are interested in the problem of recovering image segmentations, dense depth, and segment boundary labels from stereo video — a sequence of stereo image pairs taken over time from a moving vehicle. This is an important estimation problem as it is a fundamental step to perform navigation and recognition tasks such as path planning, obstacle avoidance, semantic segmentation and object detection.

Current leading techniques are slanted plane methods, which assume that the 3D scene is piece-wise planar and the motion is rigid or piece-wise rigid [30,31,26]. Unfortunately, these slanted plane methods have involved time-consuming optimization algorithms (several minutes per frame) such as particle belief propagation [30,31] or algorithms based on plane proposals with fusion moves and iterated cut-based segmentations [26]. This makes to date slanted plane methods non-practical for robotics applications such as autonomous driving.

To address this issue, in this paper we propose a fast and accurate slanted plane algorithm that operates on three images — a stereo pair and an image from the left stereo camera at a later point in time. Our approach exploit the fact that in autonomous driving scenarios most of the scene is static and utilizes the stereo and video pairs to produce a joint estimate of depth, an image segmentation as

D. Fleet et al. (Eds.): ECCV 2014, Part V, LNCS 8693, pp. 756–771, 2014.

well as boundary labels in the reference image. Importantly, it does so at least an order of magnitude faster than existing slanted plane methods [30,31,26], while outperforming the state-of-the-art on the challenging KITTI benchmark [9].

Following [30,31], our algorithm first uses semi global block matching (SGM) [13] to construct a semi-dense depth map on the reference image. A contribution here is the development of an SGM algorithm based on the joint evidence of the stereo and video pairs. The semi-dense SGM depth map is then used as input to our slanted plane method for inferring the segmentation, planes and boundary labels.

Our new inference algorithm is a form of block-coordinate descent on a total energy involving the segmentation, the planes assigned to the segments, an "outlier-flag" at each pixel, and a line label assigned to each pair of neighboring segments giving the occlusion-status of the boundary between those segments. In particular, each slanted plane can be optimized by a closed-form least-squares fit holding the segmentation, outlier-flags, and line-labels fixed. The line labels can be optimized holding the segments, planes and outlier flags fixed. The segmentation and the outlier flags are optimized jointly. The segmentation objective is an extension of the SLIC energy to handle both color and depth as well as a shape prior regularizing the length of the boundary. Importantly, our segmentation optimization subroutine uses unit-time single pixel moves restricted to the boundaries of segments, preserving the invariant that each segment is simply connected (connected and without holes).

Our block-coordinate descent algorithm is guaranteed to converge as the optimization over each set of variables (including the segmentation) is guaranteed to reduce the total energy. Importantly, this objective can be optimized over all unknowns on a single core in as little as 3s, while achieving state-of-the-art results. As a byproduct, when ignoring the depth energy term, our topology preserving segmentation subroutine can be used to create superpixels from single images.

2   Related Work

Recovering depth from a stereo and a video pair with a common reference image is a special case of the more general structure from motion problem, where scene geometry is recovered from multiple images taken from different camera angles. There is a very large literature on structure from motion, for example see [23,7,10,21]. Here, we are interested in a particular three-image setting. The three image case has been studied from the perspective of the tri-focal tensor — a generalization of the fundamental matrix to three images [11]. In our setting we are given the calibration between the two images of the stereo pair and for this reason we chose to work with the single fundamental matrix defined by the ego-motion underlying the video pair.

Although we assume a static scene, it is useful to review work on scenes with moving objects such as pedestrians and cars. The widely cited Tomasi-Kanade matrix factorization method for structure from motion [23] has been generalized to the case of scenes containing moving objects [6]. This algorithm groups points (correspondences) into rigid objects and assigns both a position in space and a six dimensional motion to each rigid object. However, it assumes that correspondences are given and the cameras are projective.

The term "scene flow" was introduced in [24] for the problem of assigning both positions and motions to a dense set of points on the surface of objects in the scene. While an object has a six dimentional motion, a point does not rotate and thus only three degrees of freedom are necessary (a flow). Several papers have tackled the problem of estimating the 3D flow-field [28,17,14,2]. To date, good performance has not yet been shown in challenging real-world scenarios.

Vogel et. al. [26] handles scenes with moving objects using a segmentation of a reference image with both a planar surface and a six dimensional rigid motion associated with each image segment. They incorporate the rigid-scene assumption using a soft bias, while it is a hard constraint in our approach. Both systems do inference by minimizing an energy defined on planes associated with segments, however, our method is an order of magnitude faster and achieves greater accuracy on the KITTI benchmark for both stereo and flow.

Our approach is also related to the stereo and motion-stereo algorithms of Yamaguchi et. al. [30,31]. As in [31], our approach first computes a semi-dense SGM depth map which then undergoes slanted-plane smoothing. The difference is that our SGM depth map is derived by joint inference from a stereo and a video pair and that our slanted-plane algorithm is roughly three orders of magnitude faster. Our system spends 25 seconds computing SGM fields and as little as 10 seconds on the slanted plane smoothing. Furthermore, the smoothing time can be reduced to 3 seconds with very little loss of accuracy. Slanted plane models for stereo have a long history going back at least to [3]. They have proved quite successful on the Middlebury [20,15,4,27] and KITTI [30] stereo benchmarks.

The topology-preserving segmentation algorithm proposed here is related to SLIC superpixels [1]. However, our segmentation algorithm preserves the invariant that segments remain simply connected. This eliminates the need for the post-processing step in the SLIC algorithm to simplify segments. This is important as this post-processing step can result in large increases of the total energy. Furthermore, this speeds-up inference, as only boundary pixels are considered at each iteration. Our segmentation method also incorporates a length of boundary energy for shape regularization, as well as the evidence from the stereo and video pairs, which SLIC does not.

3   SGM for Joint Stereo and Flow

Our approach first estimates a semi-dense depth map on the reference image $\mathcal{I}_{L,t}$ using a variant of SGM [13] which integrates evidence from both a stereo pair $\{\mathcal{I}_{L,t}, \mathcal{I}_{R,t}\}$ and a video pair $\{\mathcal{I}_{L,t}, \mathcal{I}_{L,t+1}\}$. We then smooth these results to create a dense field using a slanted plane method, which we explain in the next section. An overview of our approach is shown in Fig. 1.

Following [31], we first use semi-global matching (SGM) [13] to independently compute a semi-dense disparity field from the stereo pair — SGM-stereo —

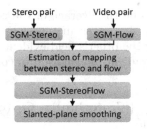

Stereo pair   Video pair

SGM-Stereo   SGM-Flow

Estimation of mapping
between stereo and flow

SGM-StereoFlow

Slanted-plane smoothing

Fig. 1. Processing flow of our approach

and a semi-dense epipolar flow field from the motion pair — SGM-flow. These two fields are then used to estimate a scaling relationship between stereo and flow. More specifically, let b be the distance between the stereo cameras (the stereo baseline), let f be the focal length of the cameras, and let $Z_\mathbf{p}$ be the Z coordinate of the point in the scene imaged at pixel p in the coordinate system defined by the reference image $\mathcal{I}_{L,t}$. The stereo disparity field, which is estimated by SGM-stereo, is defined by the following equation

$$d_\mathbf{p} = \frac{b}{Z_\mathbf{p}} f \tag{1}$$

Let v_z be the distance that the left camera moved in the Z direction (as defined by the reference image) from time t to $t + 1$. The SGM-flow field [31] is an estimate of the following "V over Z" field, also called VZ-ratio

$$\omega_\mathbf{p} = \frac{v_z}{Z_\mathbf{p}} \tag{2}$$

When the scene is static, we get a constant (across pixels) relationship between these two fields $\alpha = \omega_p/d_p = v_z/(bf)$. However, due to errors in calibration and registration, we formulate α as a linear function of the image coordinates

$$\omega_\mathbf{p} = \alpha(\mathbf{p})d_\mathbf{p} = (\alpha_x p_x + \alpha_y p_y + \alpha_c)d_\mathbf{p} \tag{3}$$

In practice, we robustly estimate $\alpha = (\alpha_x, \alpha_y, \alpha_c)$ using RANSAC from the set of pixels from which we have both an estimate of flow and stereo.

Given an estimate of $(\alpha_x, \alpha_y, \alpha_c)$, we formulate an SGM algorithm to jointly estimate stereo and flow by making use of Eq. (3). For the SGM algorithm we define the energy of the system to be the sum of a data energy $C_\mathbf{sf}$ and a smoothness energy $S_\mathbf{sf}$

$$E_\mathrm{sf}(\mathbf{d}) = \sum_\mathbf{p} C_\mathrm{sf}(\mathbf{p}, d_\mathbf{p}) + \sum_{\{\mathbf{p},\mathbf{q}\}\in\mathcal{N}} S_\mathrm{sf}(d_\mathbf{p}, d_\mathbf{q}) \tag{4}$$

where $\mathbf{d}$ is a field assigning a disparity to each reference pixel.

We say that a pixel is occluded in the flow (stereo) field, if the SGM-flow (SGM-stereo) does not return an estimate for that pixel. We define the unary cost of a depth at a pixel to be the average of the costs of the flow and stereo matchings. When the pixel is flagged as an outlier by a field, the cost function is simply computed using only the other's field evidence. In particular, we employ the Census transform and gradient information to compute the cost function of the stereo pair as follows

$$C_{\text{st}}(\mathbf{p}, d_{\mathbf{p}}) = \sum_{\mathbf{q} \in \mathcal{W}(\mathbf{p})} \{|\mathcal{G}_{L,t}(\mathbf{q}, \mathbf{h}(\mathbf{q})) - \mathcal{G}_{R,t}(\mathbf{q}'_{\text{st}}(\mathbf{q}, d_{\mathbf{q}}), \mathbf{h}(\mathbf{q}))|$$
$$+ \lambda_{\text{cen}} H(\mathcal{T}_{L,t}(\mathbf{q}), \mathcal{T}_{R,t}(\mathbf{q}'_{\text{st}}(\mathbf{q}, d_{\mathbf{q}}))) \} \tag{5}$$

where $\mathcal{G}(\cdot, \cdot)$ is the directional derivative in the image and $\mathbf{h}(\mathbf{p})$ is the epipolar line passing through pixel $\mathbf{p}$. $\mathcal{T}(\cdot)$ is the Census transform and $H(\cdot, \cdot)$ is the Hamming distance between two binary descriptors, with λ_{cen} a constant parameter, and $\mathbf{q}'_{\text{st}}(\mathbf{q}, d_{\mathbf{q}})$ the corresponding pixel in the right image whose disparity is $d_{\mathbf{q}}$, that is $\mathbf{q}'_{\text{st}}(\mathbf{q}, d_{\mathbf{q}}) = (q_x - d_{\mathbf{q}}, q_y)$. In a similar manner, we define the cost function of the motion pair

$$C_{\text{fl}}(\mathbf{p}, d_{\mathbf{p}}) = \sum_{\mathbf{q} \in \mathcal{W}(\mathbf{p})} \{|\mathcal{G}_{L,t}(\mathbf{q}, \mathbf{e}'(\mathbf{q})) - \mathcal{G}_{L,t+1}(\mathbf{q}'_{\text{fl}}(\mathbf{q}, d_{\mathbf{q}}), \mathbf{e}'(\mathbf{q}))|$$
$$+ \lambda_{\text{cen}} H(\mathcal{T}_{L,t}(\mathbf{q}), \mathcal{T}_{L,t+1}(\mathbf{q}'_{\text{fl}}(\mathbf{q}, d_{\mathbf{q}}))) \} \tag{6}$$

where $\mathbf{e}'(\mathbf{q})$ is the epipolar line of pixel $\mathbf{q}$ and $\mathbf{q}'_{\text{fl}}(\mathbf{q}, d_{\mathbf{q}})$ is the corresponding pixel in the left image at time $t + 1$ whose VZ-ratio is $\omega_{\mathbf{q}} = \alpha(\mathbf{q}) d_{\mathbf{q}}$.

The smoothness term $S(d_{\mathbf{p}}, d_{\mathbf{q}})$ is defined to be 0, if $d_{\mathbf{p}} = d_{\mathbf{q}}$, and two different penalties ($0 \geq \lambda_{s1} \geq \lambda_{s2}$) depending whether they are 1 or more integers apart. This scheme permits adapting to slanted or curved surfaces.

The motion and stereo fields can then be estimated jointly by solving for the disparities $\{d_{\mathbf{p}}\}$ by minimizing the energy in Eq. (4). While this global minimization is NP hard, we adopt the strategy of [13] and aggregate the matching cost in 1D from all directions equally

$$L(\mathbf{p}, d_{\mathbf{p}}) = \sum_j L_j(\mathbf{p}, d_{\mathbf{p}})$$

with L_j the cost of direction j. This can be done efficiently by employing dynamic programming and recursively computing

$$L_j(\mathbf{p}, d_{\mathbf{p}}) = C(\mathbf{p}, d_{\mathbf{p}}) + \min_i \{L_j(\mathbf{p} - \mathbf{j}, i) + S_{sf}(d_{\mathbf{p}}, i)\}$$

After minimizing Eq.(4) with respect to $\mathbf{d}$, we refine the disparity map by subpixel estimation and removing spurious regions. We called this algorithm *SGM-StereoFlow*. While effective, SGM-StereoFlow provides only semi-dense estimations of both fields. Furthermore, it employs very local regularization, which exploits only the relationships between neighboring pixels. In the next section we derive an efficient and effective slanted plane method which estimates dense flow and stereo fields while reasoning about segmentation, occlusion and outliers.

4 Slanted Plane Smoothing

The slanted-plane smoothing constructs an image segmentation, a slanted plane foreach segment, an outlier flag for each pixel, and a line label for each pair of neighboring segments. This is done by performing a form of block-coordinate descent on a joint energy involving all these latent structures. In particular, our algorithm is very efficient and it only updates the necessary components in an online fashion when possible.

4.1 Energy Definition

We denote our overall energy as $E(s, \theta, f, o, \mathcal{I}, d)$ where s is a segmentation, θ assigns a plane to each segment, f assigns an "outlier flag" to each pixel, o assigns a line label to each pair of neighboring segments, $\mathcal{I}$ is the reference image (for defining mean segment colors), and d is the semi-dense depth field being smoothed. Let s_p be the index of the segment that segmentation s assigns to pixel p, and let μ_i and c_i be the mean position and color respectively of segment i. In our implementation to be computationally efficient, the mean positions and colors are maintained incrementally as pixels shift between segments. Let $\theta_i = (A_i, B_i, C_i)$ be the disparity plane that θ assigns to segment i. At each pixel the disparity can be computed as

$$\hat{d}(\mathbf{p}, \theta_i) = A_i p_x + B_i p_y + C_i, \tag{7}$$

where (p_x, p_y) are the coordinates of pixel $\mathbf{p}$. We use the disparity estimate $\hat{d}(p, \theta_{s_p})$ at pixel p, where the plane is indexed by the variable s_p. In the following we will use the terms superpixel and segment interchangeably. Further, let $f_p \in \{0, 1\}$ be the outlier flag of pixel $\mathbf{p}$.

We define the energy of the system to be the sum of energies encoding appearance, location, disparity, smoothness and boundary energies as follows

$$E(s, \theta, f, o, \mathcal{I}, d) = \underbrace{\sum_{\mathbf{p}} E_{\text{col}}(\mathbf{p}, c_{s_p})}_{color-data} + \lambda_{\text{pos}} \underbrace{\sum_{\mathbf{p}} E_{\text{pos}}(\mathbf{p}, \mu_{s_p})}_{location} + \lambda_{\text{depth}} \underbrace{\sum_{\mathbf{p}} E_{\text{depth}}(\mathbf{p}, \theta_{s_p}, f_p)}_{depth-data}$$

$$+ \lambda_{\text{smo}} \underbrace{\sum_{\{i,j\} \in \mathcal{N}_{\text{seg}}} E_{\text{smo}}(\theta_i, \theta_j, o_{i,j})}_{plane-smoothness} + \lambda_{\text{com}} \underbrace{\sum_{\{i,j\} \in \mathcal{N}_{\text{seg}}} E_{\text{prior}}(o_{i,j})}_{label-prior}$$

$$+ \lambda_{\text{bou}} \underbrace{\sum_{\{\mathbf{p},\mathbf{q}\} \in \mathcal{N}_8} E_{\text{bou}}(s_p, s_q)}_{boundary-length} \tag{8}$$

where we have left the dependence on $\mathcal{I}$ and d implicit and where $\mathcal{N}_8$ is the set of pairs of 8-neighbor pixels. We now define the energy components in more detail.

Location: We define an energy term that prefers well-shaped segments

$$E_{\text{pos}}(\mathbf{p}, \mu_{s_p}) = ||\mathbf{p} - \mu_{s_p}||_2^2, \tag{9}$$

Appearance. This term simply encourages pixels to be in a superpixel if they agree on their color

$$E_{col}(\mathbf{p}, c_{s_p}) = ||\mathcal{I}_{L,t}(\mathbf{p}) - c_{s_p}||_2^2 \tag{10}$$

Disparity. This term encourages the plane estimates to agree with the image evidence (i.e., SGM-StereoFlow estimate). When the pixel is an outlier, we simply pay a constant factor λ_d. This prevents the trivial solution where all pixels are outliers. Thus

$$E_{depth}(\mathbf{p}, \theta_{s_p}, f_p) = \begin{cases} (d(\mathbf{p}) - \hat{d}(\mathbf{p}, \theta_{s_p}))^2 & \text{if } f_p = 0 \\ \lambda_d & \text{otherwise} \end{cases} \tag{11}$$

where λ_d is a constant parameter.

Complexity. We encourage simple explanations (i.e., co-planarity) by defining

$$E_{prior}(o_{i,j}) = \begin{cases} \lambda_{occ} & \text{if } o_{i,j} = lo \ \vee \ o_{i,j} = ro \\ \lambda_{hinge} & \text{if } o_{i,j} = hi \\ 0 & \text{if } o_{i,j} = co \end{cases} \tag{12}$$

where $\lambda_{occ}, \lambda_{hinge}$ are constants with $\lambda_{occ} > \lambda_{hinge} > 0$. In the absence of this term discontinuous solutions are preferred.

Boundary-Plane Agreement. The plane smoothness energy encourages the planes of adjacent segments to be similar if they belong to the same object. Therefore the smoothness energy between adjacent planes depends on the line label between them: If two neighboring segments are co-planar then the two planes should agree in the full segment, if they form a hinge, they should agree in the boundary, and if they form an occlusion boundary, the occluder should be closer in depth to the camera (i.e., higher disparity). We thus write

$$E_{smo}(\theta_i, \theta_j, o_{i,j}) = \begin{cases} \phi_{occ}(\theta_i, \theta_j) & \text{if } o_{i,j} = lo \\ \phi_{occ}(\theta_j, \theta_i) & \text{if } o_{i,j} = ro \\ \frac{1}{|\mathcal{B}_{i,j}|} \sum_{\mathbf{p} \in \mathcal{B}_{i,j}} \left(\hat{d}(\mathbf{p}, \theta_i) - \hat{d}(\mathbf{p}, \theta_j) \right)^2 & \text{if } o_{i,j} = hi \\ \frac{1}{|\mathcal{S}_i \cup \mathcal{S}_j|} \sum_{\mathbf{p} \in \mathcal{S}_i \cup \mathcal{S}_j} \left(\hat{d}(\mathbf{p}, \theta_i) - \hat{d}(\mathbf{p}, \theta_j) \right)^2 & \text{if } o_{i,j} = co \end{cases} \tag{13}$$

where $\mathcal{B}_{i,j}$ is the set of pixels on the boundary between segments i, j, $\mathcal{S}_i$ is the set of pixels in segment i, and $\phi_{occ}(\theta_{front}, \theta_{back})$ is a function which penalizes occlusion boundaries that are not supported by the plane parameters

$$\phi_{occ}(\theta_{front}, \theta_{back}) = \begin{cases} \lambda_{pen} & \text{if } \sum_{\mathbf{p} \in \mathcal{B}_{front,back}} (\hat{d}(\mathbf{p}, \theta_{front}) - \hat{d}(\mathbf{p}, \theta_{back})) < 0 \\ 0 & \text{otherwise} \end{cases} \tag{14}$$

Boundary Length. This term encourages super pixels to be regular, preferring straight boundaries

$$E_{bou}(s_p, s_q) = \begin{cases} 0 & \text{if } s_p = s_q \\ 1 & \text{otherwise} \end{cases} \tag{15}$$

Algorithm 1. Our Block Coordinate Descent algorithm

Init segmentation to a regular grid.

Compute μ_i and c_i for each segment i.

Init assigments by running TPS (Algorithm 3)

forall the *segments* i **do**

    | Initialize θ_i using RANSAC to approximately minimize

    | $\sum_{\{p|s_p=i\}} E_{\text{depth}}(\mathbf{p}, \theta_i)$

end

for $k = 1$ *to out* $-$ *iters* **do**

    | Obtain $\mathbf{s}, \mathbf{f}$ by running ETPS (i.e., Algorithm 2)

    | **for** $j = 1$ *to in* $-$ *iters* **do**

    | | **forall the** *boundaries* (i, j) **do**

    | | | $o_{i,j} = \text{argmin}_{o_{i,j}} E(s, \mu, c, \theta, o, f)$

    | | **end**

    | | **forall the** *segments* i **do**

    | | | $\theta_i = \text{argmin}_{\theta_i} E(s, \mu, c, \theta, o, f)$

    | | **end**

    | **endfor**

endfor

4.2   Efficient Block Coordinate Descent Inference

The minimization of Eq. (8) is NP-hard. Furthermore, it is particularly challenging as it involves inference in a Markov random field (MRF) containing a large number of both discrete (i.e., $\{s, f, o\}$) and continuous variables (i.e., $\{\theta, \mu, c\}$). Previous work employed particle methods to solve continuous-discrete problems by forming a sequence of discrete MRFs, which can be minimized using message passing algorithms [30,31] or fusion moves with QPBO [26]. This however is computationally very expensive.

In contrast, in this paper we derive a simple yet effective block coordinate descent algorithm which is several orders of magnitude faster than particle methods. Our approach alternates three steps: (i) jointly solving for the pixel-wise outlier flags f, the pixel-to-segment assignments s, as well as the location μ and appearance descriptions c of the segments, (ii) estimating the segment boundary labels o, and (iii) estimating the plane parameters θ. Algorithm 1 summarizes our block coordinate descent algorithm including the initialization of the latent information. We now describe these three steps and initialization in more detail.

Extended Topology-Preserving Segmentation. Our first step optimizes jointly over the segmentation, pixel-wise outlier flags as well as the appearance and location of the segments, while enforcing that each segment is composed of a single connected component with no holes. Note that this is in contrast with segmentation algorithms such as SLIC [1], which require a post processing step to guarantee connectivity and hole-free solutions. Towards this goal, we derive a novel algorithm, called Extended Topology Preserving Segmentation (ETPS), which works as follows. We initialize the stack to contain all boundary

---

Algorithm 2. ETPS: Extended Topology Preserving Segmentation

Initialize the stack to contain all boundary pixels.
while *not empty stack* **do**
   Take pixel **p** off the stack.
   if valid_connectivity(p) $= 0$ **then**
    | continue
   end
   $\{f_p, s_p\} = \operatorname{argmin}_{\{f_p, s_p \in \cup \{s_{\mathcal{N}_4(\mathbf{p})}\}\}} E(s, \mu, c, \theta, o, f)$
   if s_p *updated* **then**
    | incrementally update μ and c for the two altered segments.
    | Push the boundary pixels in $\mathcal{N}_4(\mathbf{p})$ onto the stack.
   end
end

Algorithm 3. TPS: Topology Preserving Segmentation

Initialize the stack to contain all boundary pixels.
while *not empty stack* **do**
   Take pixel **p** off the stack.
   if valid_connectivity(p) $= 0$ **then**
    | continue
   end
   $s_p = \operatorname{argmin}_{\{s_p \in \cup \{s_{\mathcal{N}_4(\mathbf{p})}\}\}} E_{\mathrm{col}}(\mathbf{p}, c_{s_p}) + \lambda_{\mathrm{pos}} E_{\mathrm{pos}}(\mathbf{p}, \mu_{s_p}) +$
   $\lambda_{bou} \sum_{p,q \in N8} E_{bou}(s_p, s_q)$
   if s_p *updated* **then**
    | incrementally update μ and c for the two altered segments.
    | Push the boundary pixels in $\mathcal{N}_4(\mathbf{p})$ onto the stack.
   end
end

---

pixels. While the stack is not empty, we take a pixel from the stack and check whether changing its segment assignment will break connectivity. If not, we update the assignment and the outlier flag for that pixel, as well as the location and appearance of the two segments with membership changes (i.e., the segment that pixel **p** was assigned in the previous iteration as well as the new assigned segment). This can be done very efficiently using the incremental mean equation, i.e., given the previous estimate m_{n-1} and a new element a_n the mean can computed as

$$m_n = m_{n-1} + \frac{a_n - m_{n-1}}{n}$$

We then push onto the stack the new boundary pixels using a 4-neighborhood around **p**, as the boundary has changed due to the change of assignment of pixel **p**. We refer the reader to Algorithm 2 for a summary of ETPS.

Boundary and Slanted Planes. We solve for the superpixel boundaries (second step) by iteratively computing the maximal argument for each boundary.

Table 1. Stereo: Comparison with the state-of-the-art on the test set of KITTI. We highlight in bold when our approach outperforms the state-of-the-art. Ours (stereo only) stands for our slanted plane algorithm when using only the stereo pair, Ours (joint) utilizes both stereo and video pairs.

	> 2 pixels		> 3 pixels		> 4 pixels		> 5 pixels		End-Point	
	Non-Occ	All	Non-Occ	All	Non-Occ	All	Non-Occ	All	Non-Occ	All
ALTGV [16]	7.88 %	9.30 %	5.36 %	6.49 %	4.17 %	5.07 %	3.42 %	4.17 %	1.1 px	1.2 px
iSGM [12]	7.94 %	10.00 %	5.11 %	7.15 %	3.84 %	5.82 %	3.13 %	5.02 %	1.2 px	2.1 px
ATGV [18]	7.08 %	9.05 %	5.02 %	6.88 %	3.99 %	5.76 %	3.33 %	5.01 %	1.0 px	1.6 px
wSGM [22]	7.27 %	8.72 %	4.97 %	6.18 %	3.88 %	4.89 %	3.25 %	4.11 %	1.3 px	1.6 px
PR-Sceneflow [26]	6.26 %	7.36 %	4.36 %	5.22 %	3.43 %	4.10 %	2.85 %	3.40 %	0.9 px	1.1 px
PCBP [30]	6.08 %	7.62 %	4.04 %	5.37 %	3.14 %	4.29 %	2.64 %	3.64 %	0.9 px	1.1 px
PR-Sf+E [26]	5.79 %	6.88 %	4.02 %	4.87 %	3.15 %	3.82 %	2.62 %	3.17 %	0.9 px	1.0 px
StereoSLIC [31]	5.76 %	7.20 %	3.92 %	5.11 %	3.04 %	4.04 %	2.49 %	3.33 %	0.9 px	1.0 px
PCBP-SS [31]	5.19 %	6.75 %	3.40 %	4.72 %	2.62 %	3.75 %	2.18 %	3.15 %	0.8 px	1.0 px
Ours (Stereo only)	**4.98 %**	**6.28 %**	**3.39 %**	**4.41 %**	**2.72 %**	**3.52 %**	**2.33 %**	**3.00 %**	0.9 px	1.0 px
Ours (Joint)	**4.30 %**	**5.39 %**	**2.83 %**	**3.64 %**	**2.24 %**	**2.89 %**	**1.90 %**	**2.46 %**	**0.8 px**	**0.9 px**

Solving for the plane parameters (third step) can be done in closed form as the energy is the sum of quadratic functions, including the disparity energy in Eq. (11) and the boundary-plane agreement energy in Eq. (13).

Initialization. As our approach is guaranteed to converge to a local optima, initialization is important. We first initialize the segmentation to form a regular grid, and compute in closed form the mean appearance and location of the superpixels. We then derive a version of ETPS which takes into account the image appearance and not the disparity, and returns superpixels forming a single hole-free connected component. We call this algorithm Boundary-Aware segmentation (TPS). We refer the reader to Algorithm 3. The disparity planes are initialized by minimizing the scene flow energy in Eq. (11) using RANSAC. For each pixel $\mathbf{p}$, f_p is set to 0 when the distance between the initial plane and SGM-StereoFlow estimate is less than a threshold. We then run the iterative algorithm given this initialization as summarized in Algorithm 1.

5   Experimental Evaluation

We performed our experimentation on the challenging KITTI dataset [9], which consists of 194 training and 195 test high-resolution real-world images. The ground truth is semi-dense covering approximately 30 % of the pixels. We employ two different metrics to evaluate our approach: the average number of pixels whose error is bigger than a fixed threshold, as well as the end-point error. We report this for two settings, when only non-occluded pixels are considered as well as predicting all pixels. Unless otherwise stated, we employ the same parameters for all experiments. We set the number of superpixels $n = 1000$, $\lambda_{pos} = 500$, $\lambda_{dis} = 2000$, $\lambda_{smo} = \lambda_{com} = 400$, $\lambda_{bou} = 1000$, $\lambda_d = 9$, $\lambda_{occ} = 15$, $\lambda_{hinge} = 5$, $\lambda_{pen} = 30$ and use 10 inner and outer loop iterations.

Comparison to State-of-the-Art. We begin our experimentation by comparing our approach to the state-of-the-art. As show in Fig. 1 and Fig. 2 our approach significantly outperforms all stereo, flow and scene flow approaches in the test set of KITTI. The improvements are particularly significant in terms of

Table 2. Flow: Comparison with the state-of-the-art on the test set of KITTI. We highlight in bold when our approach outperforms the state-of-the-art. Ours (flow only) stands for our slanted plane algorithm when using only the video pair, Ours (joint) utilizes both stereo and video pairs.

	> 2 pixels		> 3 pixels		> 4 pixels		> 5 pixels		End-Point	
	Non-Occ	All	Non-Occ	All	Non-Occ	All	Non-Occ	All	Non-Occ	All
CRTflow [8]	13.11 %	22.83 %	9.43 %	18.72 %	7.79 %	16.51 %	6.86 %	15.06 %	2.7 px	6.5 px
TVL1-HOG [19]	12.06 %	23.06 %	7.91 %	18.90 %	6.20 %	16.83 %	5.26 %	15.45 %	2.0 px	6.1 px
DeepFlow [29]	9.31 %	20.44 %	7.22 %	17.79 %	6.08 %	16.02 %	5.31 %	14.69 %	1.5 px	5.8 px
Data-Flow [25]	9.16 %	17.41 %	7.11 %	14.57 %	6.05 %	12.91 %	5.34 %	11.72 %	1.9 px	5.5 px
TGV2ADCSIFT [5]	8.04 %	17.87 %	6.20 %	15.15 %	5.24 %	13.43 %	4.60 %	12.27 %	1.5 px	4.5 px
MotionSLIC [31]	5.68 %	13.20 %	3.91 %	10.56 %	3.10 %	9.08 %	2.60 %	8.04 %	0.9 px	2.7 px
PR-Sceneflow [26]	5.67 %	10.32 %	3.76 %	7.39 %	2.96 %	5.98 %	2.52 %	5.14 %	1.2 px	2.8 px
PCBP-Flow [31]	5.28 %	10.62 %	3.64 %	8.28 %	2.90 %	7.01 %	2.46 %	6.16 %	0.9 px	2.2 px
PR-Sf+E [26]	5.58 %	10.13 %	3.57 %	7.07 %	2.69 %	5.48 %	2.17 %	4.49 %	0.9 px	1.6 px
Ours (Flow only)	5.01 %	12.41 %	3.38 %	10.06 %	2.69 %	8.79 %	2.28 %	7.90 %	0.9 px	2.9 px
Ours (Joint)	4.75 %	8.69 %	2.82 %	5.61 %	2.03 %	4.10 %	1.61 %	3.26 %	0.8 px	1.3 px

Table 3. Performance of each step on the training set of KITTI. Jointly estimating stereo and motion fields improves significantly performance over the independent baselines. By incorporating segmentation and explicit occlusion reasoning our slanted plane method improves even further.

Stereo										
	> 2 pixels		> 3 pixels		> 4 pixels		> 5 pixels		End-Point	
	Non-Occ	All	Non-Occ	All	Non-Occ	All	Non-Occ	All	Non-Occ	All
SGM-Stereo	7.42 %	8.62 %	4.93 %	5.89 %	3.73 %	4.50 %	3.01 %	3.65 %	0.9 px	1.1 px
SGM-StereoFlow	6.21 %	7.42 %	4.06 %	5.03 %	3.04 %	3.85 %	2.46 %	3.13 %	0.8 px	1.0 px
Slanted Plane	4.83 %	5.87 %	3.18 %	3.99 %	2.50 %	3.19 %	2.12 %	2.71 %	0.8 px	0.9 px

Flow										
	> 2 pixels		> 3 pixels		> 4 pixels		> 5 pixels		End-Point	
	Non-Occ	All	Non-Occ	All	Non-Occ	All	Non-Occ	All	Non-Occ	All
SGM-Flow	5.55 %	15.31 %	3.67 %	12.62 %	2.83 %	10.97 %	2.35 %	9.74 %	0.9 px	2.9 px
SGM-StereoFlow	5.03 %	8.81 %	3.14 %	5.90 %	2.29 %	4.41 %	1.82 %	3.51 %	0.7 px	1.2 px
Slanted Plane	4.40 %	7.69 %	2.67 %	4.93 %	1.96 %	3.61 %	1.58 %	2.87 %	0.7 px	1.1 px

the occluded pixels, demonstrating the benefit of having a joint energy which reasons about outliers at the level of the pixels and occlusions boundaries between superpixels. Note that our slanted plane method can also be used with only the stereo or the video pair. This is shown in Fig. 1 and Fig. 2 under Ours (Stereo only) and Ours (Flow only). Note that utilizing both pairs results in much better estimation particularly for occluded pixels in flow.

Importance of Every Step. In the next experiment we look at the importance of every step. As shown in Table 3, reasoning jointly about stereo and flow (last two entries) brings large performance improvements with respect to independently estimating each field (i.e., SGM-Stereo and SGM-Flow). This is particularly significant for occluded pixels in flow. Furthermore, our slanted plane algorithm significantly improves over our intermediate steps.

Number of Iterations. In the next experiment we look at performance of our slanted plane method as a function of the number of outer loop iterations for different number of inner loop iterations. As shown in Fig. 2, very good performance can be achieved with a small number of both inner and outer loop iterations. Fig. 3 (right) depicts convergence of the energy in Eq. 8 as a function

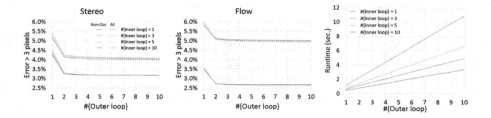

Fig. 2. Performance as a function of the number of iterations

	Joint	Stereo only	Flow only
SGM-Stereo	1.5	1.5	-
Camera motion est.	3.7	-	3.7
SGM-Flow	4.0	-	4.0
Alpha estimation	1.0	-	-
SGM-StereoFlow	12.8	-	-
Slanted plane	3.3	3.3	3.3
Total	26.3 s	4.8 s	11.0 s

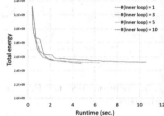

Fig. 3. Runtime (in seconds) of each step of our approach as well total energy for different number of inner loop iterations as a function of time.

of the number of inner and outer loop iterations. Note that we can converge extremely quickly with 1 inner loop iteration.

Running Time. We next evaluate the running time of our approach in a single core machine. Fig. 3 (left) illustrates the average running time for each step of the algorithm. Note that results superior to the state of the art can be achieved in as little as 3 seconds for our slanted plane algorithm. In comparison, slanted plane methods such as [26,30,31] take more than 10 minutes in a single core. Thus, our approach is between 2 to 3 orders of magnitude faster.

Number of superpixels: Fig. 4 shows results as a function of the number of superpixels. Note that performance saturates around 1000 superpixels. This is the number we used for all other experiments.

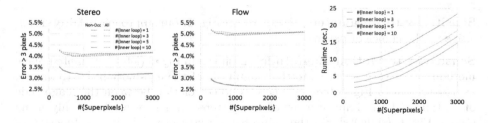

Fig. 4. Performance as a function of the number of superpixels: The performance saturates after 1000 superpixels.

Fig. 5. Sensitivity to Parameters: Our slanted plane model is not sensitive to parameters

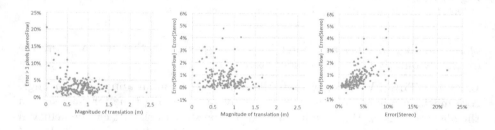

Fig. 6. Sensitivity to Motion Magnitude: (left) Error of our slanted plane method as a function of magnitude of motion. (center) Improvement of using stereo and flow w.r.t. only using stereo as a function of motion magnitude. As observed in the figure there is no correlation between the magnitude of motion and the improvement of using stereo + flow w.r.t. only using stereo. (right) Gain of using stereo + flow as a function of the errors of using stereo alone. The gain of using both flow and stereo is large when the error of using only stereo is also large.

Sensitivity to Parameters. As shown in Fig. 5, our approach is fairly insensitive to the choice of parameters.

Sensitivity to Motion Magnitude. As shown in Fig. 6 (left) our slanted plane method is not very sensitive to the magnitude of the ego-motion. Furthermore, as observed in in Fig. 6 (center) there is no correlation between the magnitude of motion and the improvement of using stereo and flow w.r.t. to only using stereo. Fig. 6 (right) shows the gain of using stereo and flow as a function of the errors of using only stereo information. Joint inference using flow and stereo helps particularly to correct large errors.

Left image at time t		
Superpixel segments		
Boundary labels		
Disparity image		
Disparity error		
Flow image		
Flow error		

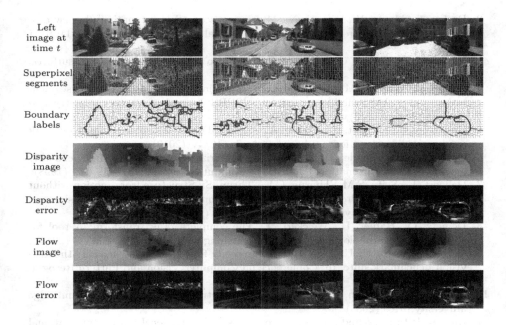

Fig. 7. Qualitative results for our slanted plane model: From top to bottom we show the original left image, our segmentation, boundary labels and the corresponding disparity and flow estimates with their errors. Note that our approach can accurately estimate occlusion boundaries (red/blue) as well as hinge (green) and coplanar (gray) relations

Qualitative Results: Fig. 7 illustrates qualitative results on KITTI. Note that our approach is able to estimate occlusion boundaries as well as hinge labels very accurately.

6   Conclusion

We have proposed a fast and accurate algorithm to recover dense depth and motion from stereo video under the assumption that the scene is static. We have demonstrated the effectiveness of our approach in the challenging KITTI dataset, showing state-of-the-art result. Importantly, our approach achieves one order of magnitude speed-ups over current slanted plane methods. We are currently investigating parallel implementations of our approach that can run in real-time in the autonomous driving platform. Furthermore, we believe that the extension to moving objects by employing motion segmentation is also a very interesting venue of future work.

References

1. Achanta, R., Shaji, A., Smith, K., Lucchi, A., Fua, P., Susstrunk, S.: Slic superpixels compared to state-of-the-art superpixel methods. IEEE Transactions on Pattern Analysis and Machine Intelligence 34(11), 2274–2282 (2012)

2. Basha, T., Moses, Y., Kiryati, N.: Multi-view scene flow estimation: A view centered variational approach. International journal of computer vision 101(1), 6–21 (2013)
3. Birchfield, S., Tomasi, C.: Multiway cut for stereo and motion with slanted surfaces. In: CVPR, vol. 1, pp. 489–495. IEEE (1999)
4. Bleyer, M., Gelautz, M.: A layered stereo matching algorithm using image segmentation and global visibility constraints. ISPRS Journal of Photogrammetry and Remote Sensing 59(3), 128–150 (2005)
5. Braux-Zin, J., Dupont, R., Bartoli, A.: A general dense image matching framework combining direct and feature-based costs. In: ICCV (2013)
6. Costeira, J.P., Kanade, T.: A multibody factorization method for independently moving objects. International Journal of Computer Vision 29(3), 159–179 (1998)
7. Dellaert, F., Seitz, S.M., Thorpe, C.E., Thrun, S.: Structure from motion without correspondence. In: Proceedings of the IEEE Conference on Computer Vision and Pattern Recognition, vol. 2, pp. 557–564. IEEE (2000)
8. Demetz, O., Hafner, D., Weickert, J.: The complete rank transform: A tool for accurate and morphologically invariant matching of structure. In: BMVC (2013)
9. Geiger, A., Lenz, P., Urtasun, R.: Are we ready for autonomous driving? the kitti vision benchmark suite. In: Conference on Computer Vision and Pattern Recognition, CVPR (2012)
10. Hartley, R., Zisserman, A.: Multiple view geometry in computer vision. Cambridge university press (2003)
11. Hartley, R.I.: Lines and points in three views and the trifocal tensor. International Journal of Computer Vision 22(2), 125–140 (1997)
12. Hermann, S., Klette, R.: Iterative semi-global matching for robust driver assistance systems. In: Lee, K.M., Matsushita, Y., Rehg, J.M., Hu, Z. (eds.) ACCV 2012, Part III. LNCS, vol. 7726, pp. 465–478. Springer, Heidelberg (2013)
13. Hirschmuller, H.: Accurate and efficient stereo processing by semi-global matching and mutual information. In: IEEE Computer Society Conference on Computer Vision and Pattern Recognition, CVPR 2005, vol. 2, pp. 807–814. IEEE (2005)
14. Huguet, F., Devernay, F.: A variational method for scene flow estimation from stereo sequences. In: IEEE 11th International Conference on Computer Vision, ICCV 2007, pp. 1–7. IEEE (2007)
15. Klaus, A., Sormann, M., Karner, K.: Segment-based stereo matching using belief propagation and a self-adapting dissimilarity measure. In: 18th International Conference on Pattern Recognition, ICPR 2006, vol. 3, pp. 15–18. IEEE (2006)
16. Kuschk, G., Cremers, D.: Fast and accurate large-scale stereo reconstruction using variational methods. In: ICCV Workshop on Big Data in 3D Computer Vision (2013)
17. Rabe, C., Müller, T., Wedel, A., Franke, U.: Dense, robust, and accurate motion field estimation from stereo image sequences in real-time. In: Daniilidis, K., Maragos, P., Paragios, N. (eds.) ECCV 2010, Part IV. LNCS, vol. 6314, pp. 582–595. Springer, Heidelberg (2010)
18. Ranftl, R., Pock, T., Bischof, H.: Minimizing TGV-based Variational Models with Non-Convex Data terms. In: ICSSVM (2013)
19. Rashwan, H.A., Mohamed, M.A., García, M.A., Mertsching, B., Puig, D.: Illumination robust optical flow model based on histogram of oriented gradients. In: Weickert, J., Hein, M., Schiele, B. (eds.) GCPR 2013. LNCS, vol. 8142, pp. 354–363. Springer, Heidelberg (2013)
20. Scharstein, D., Szeliski, R.: Middlebury stereo vision page (2002), http://www.middlebury.edu/stereo

21. Snavely, N., Seitz, S.M., Szeliski, R.: Photo tourism: exploring photo collections in 3d. ACM Transactions on Graphics (TOG) 25(3), 835–846 (2006)
22. Spangenberg, R., Langner, T., Rojas, R.: Weighted semi-global matching and center-symmetric census transform for robust driver assistance. In: Wilson, R., Hancock, E., Bors, A., Smith, W. (eds.) CAIP 2013, Part II. LNCS, vol. 8048, pp. 34–41. Springer, Heidelberg (2013)
23. Tomasi, C., Kanade, T.: Shape and motion from image streams under orthography: a factorization method. International Journal of Computer Vision 9(2), 137–154 (1992)
24. Vedula, S., Baker, S., Rander, P., Collins, R., Kanade, T.: Three-dimensional scene flow. In: The Proceedings of the Seventh IEEE International Conference on Computer Vision 1999, vol. 2, pp. 722–729. IEEE (1999)
25. Vogel, C., Roth, S., Schindler, K.: An evaluation of data costs for optical flow. In: Weickert, J., Hein, M., Schiele, B. (eds.) GCPR 2013. LNCS, vol. 8142, pp. 343–353. Springer, Heidelberg (2013)
26. Vogel, C., Roth, S., Schindler, K.: Piecewise rigid scene flow. In: ICCV (2013)
27. Wang, Z.-F., Zheng, Z.-G.: A region based stereo matching algorithm using co-operative optimization. In: IEEE Conference on Computer Vision and Pattern Recognition, CVPR 2008, pp. 1–8. IEEE (2008)
28. Wedel, A., Rabe, C., Vaudrey, T., Brox, T., Franke, U., Cremers, D.: Efficient dense scene flow from sparse or dense stereo data. Springer (2008)
29. Weinzaepfel, P., Revaud, J., Harchaoui, Z., Schmid, C.: DeepFlow: Large displacement optical flow with deep matching. In: ICCV (2013)
30. Yamaguchi, K., Hazan, T., McAllester, D., Urtasun, R.: Continuous markov random fields for robust stereo estimation. In: Fitzgibbon, A., Lazebnik, S., Perona, P., Sato, Y., Schmid, C. (eds.) ECCV 2012, Part V. LNCS, vol. 7576, pp. 45–58. Springer, Heidelberg (2012)
31. Yamaguchi, K., McAllester, D., Urtasun, R.: Robust monocular epipolar flow estimation. In: CVPR (2013)

Robust Bundle Adjustment Revisited

Christopher Zach

Toshiba Research Europe, Cambridge, UK*

Abstract. In this work we address robust estimation in the bundle adjustment procedure. Typically, bundle adjustment is not solved via a generic optimization algorithm, but usually cast as a nonlinear least-squares problem instance. In order to handle gross outliers in bundle adjustment the least-squares formulation must be robustified. We investigate several approaches to make least-squares objectives robust while retaining the least-squares nature to use existing efficient solvers. In particular, we highlight a method based on *lifting* a robust cost function into a higher dimensional representation, and show how the lifted formulation is efficiently implemented in a Gauss-Newton framework. In our experiments the proposed lifting-based approach almost always yields the best (i.e. lowest) objectives.

Keywords: Bundle adjustment, nonlinear least-squares optimization, robust cost function.

1 Introduction

Large scale nonlinear least-squares optimization occurs frequently in geometric computer vision and robotics to refine a set of continuous unknowns given all the observations extracted from acquired (image) data. Least-squares estimation in general has an underlying Gaussian noise (or residual) assumption if viewed as inference in a probabilistic model. This Gaussian assumption is typically violated whenever large residuals are observed, and consequently least-squares formulations are robustified to cope with such large residuals. Nevertheless, least-squares methods are popular even in the robustified setting because of their simplicity, efficiency, and the general availability of respective implementations. Thus, a robustified problem has to be cast as a nonlinear least-squares instance in order to make use of existing software and algorithms. Recent improvements for large-scale nonlinear estimation in geometric computer vision focus on the aspect of efficiently solving least-squares optimization, but usually do not explicitly address robustness of the formulation. In this work we focus on different options to cast a robustified objective into a nonlinear least-squares one. Thus, our contributions include:

- we review a number of approaches to make nonlinear least squares robust (Section 3)

---

* Much of this work was done while the author was with MSR Cambridge.

D. Fleet et al. (Eds.): ECCV 2014, Part V, LNCS 8693, pp. 772–787, 2014.

- we provide an in-depth discussion of lifting schemes (Section 3.4),
- we show how to make the lifting approach computationally attractive (Section 4),
- and experimentally compare the discussed approaches on large scale bundle adjustment instances (Section 5).

In our experiments the lifting method shows generally a very promising performance by reaching a much better local minimum in most test cases.

The main application of nonlinear least-squares in 3D computer vision is in the bundle adjustment routine, which refines the camera parameters (such as their pose, focal lengths and distortion coefficients) and the 3D point positions. We refer to [11] for a general treatment of geometric computer vision and to [22] for an in-depth discussion of bundle adjustment. Since the number of cameras of a typical dataset is in the hundreds or thousands (with about 10 scalar unknowns each) and the number of 3D points is in the millions, a modern bundle adjustment implementation must be able to cope with such large-scale problem instances.

The current work horse for bundle adjustment is the Levenberg-Marquardt algorithm [16,19], which at its core solves a sequence of linear systems of *normal* equations with a (strictly) positive definite and generally very sparse system matrix. The standard tool to solve such linear systems are sparse Cholesky factorization [8] in combination with a column reordering scheme to reduce the fill-in. More recently, iterative conjugate-gradient based solvers to address the normal equations have been explored to speed up bundle adjustment (e.g. [4,6,15,14]). To our knowledge none of these recent works on bundle adjustment provide guidelines on how to incorporate a robust cost function into a least-squares objective such that existing solvers can be reused. The standard method to utilize robust costs into a nonlinear least-squares framework is iteratively reweighted least squares (IRLS), i.e. by reweighting the terms in the objective according to the current residual values. Two notable exceptions are [22] and [9], which are discussed in more detail in Section 3. Although the Levenberg-Marquardt method is by far the most popular to address nonlinear least-squares problems, related trust-region methods may be more efficient for bundle adjustment tasks [18]. It is also possible to reduce the problem size in bundle adjustment significantly by algebraically eliminating some unknowns (often the 3D points) and optimizing essentially over multi-view relations directly [23,20,12]. We stay with the classical projection-based formulation (optimizing over camera parameters and 3D points) for bundle adjustment, since we feel that a robustified noise model is most appropriate in that setting.

2   Background

In this section we introduce some notation and terminology, and provide a brief description of nonlinear least-squares objectives playing a central role in this work.

2.1 Notations

We address minimization problems of the form

$$\Theta^* = \arg \min_{\Theta \in \mathbb{R}^n} \sum_{k=1}^{M} \psi\big(r_k(\Theta)\big), \tag{1}$$

where $r_k(\Theta) : \mathbb{R}^n \to \mathbb{R}^d$ is the k-th residual function dependent on the unknown vector Θ. Therefore d is the dimension of the residuals, which is usually 2 in a standard bundle adjustment instance. All of the residual functions are assumed to be differentiable.

Without loss of generality all the (differentiable) penalizing functions ψ are the same for the residual terms. Typical choices for ψ have the properties that $\psi(r) \geq 0$, $\psi(0) = 0$, and ψ is monotonically increasing with respect to the norm of its argument (the residual vector). Sensible choices for ψ feature a sub-linear growth of its function value in order to make the objective robust to outlier residuals. Therefore we call ψ a robust kernel in this work. Nevertheless, we assume that small residuals are penalized in the least-squares sense, i.e. the Hessian of ψ is the identity matrix, which corresponds to a Gaussian noise assumption in the underlying probabilistic model. This explains in particular the $1/2$ scaling factor in many of the objectives stated below, and also the choice of scaling for robust kernels ψ in Section 3.4.

While $\psi : \mathbb{R}^d \to \mathbb{R}_0^+$ maps residual vectors to non-negative costs, in Section 3.2 we will use functions $\rho : \mathbb{R}_0^+ \to \mathbb{R}_0^+$ mapping squared norms of residual vectors to costs. A choice of ρ induces ψ via $\psi(r) = \rho(\|r\|_2^2)$. Note that ρ penalizes residuals isotropically ignoring the direction of r_k. In the following we drop the explicit subscript to denote the Euclidean norm, and every occurrence of a norm $\|\cdot\|$ should be always read as $\|\cdot\|_2$.

Further, we stack the residual vector r_k and the respective Jacobians $J_k \overset{\text{def}}{=} \nabla_\Theta r_k$ into a large vector and matrix, respectively,

$$\mathbf{r}(\Theta) \overset{\text{def}}{=} \begin{pmatrix} r_1(\Theta) \\ \vdots \\ r_M(\Theta) \end{pmatrix} \qquad \mathbf{J}(\Theta) \overset{\text{def}}{=} \begin{pmatrix} J_1(\Theta) \\ \vdots \\ J_M(\Theta) \end{pmatrix}. \tag{2}$$

In general, bold-face letters indicate quantities spanning the whole objective not only individual residual terms.

Finally, for a positive semi-definite (p.s.d.) matrix A we denote the respective square root matrix either by $\sqrt{A}$ or $A^{1/2}$, $A = (\sqrt{A})^2 = (A^{1/2})^2$.

2.2 Nonlinear Least Squares Optimization

Nonlinear least squares optimization aims to find a minimizer Θ^* of a least-squares objective,

$$\Theta^* = \arg \min_\Theta \frac{1}{2} \sum_k \|r_k(\Theta)\|^2 = \arg \min_\Theta \frac{1}{2} \|\mathbf{r}(\Theta)\|^2. \tag{3}$$

It is beneficial to exploit the outer least-squares structure instead of solely relying on general minimization methods such as gradient descent, conjugate gradients, or quasi-Newton methods. Most popular methods to solve Eq. 3 are based on first order expansion of the residual r_k,

$$r_k(\Theta + \Delta\Theta) \approx r_k(\Theta) + J_k(\Theta)\Delta\Theta, \tag{4}$$

where $J_k(\Theta)$ is the Jacobian of r_k with respect to the parameters Θ (and evaluated at the current linearization point Θ). In the following we implicitly assume the dependence of r_k and J_k on Θ and consequently drop the respective argument Θ. Plugging the first order expansion into Eq. 3 and rearranging terms yields the normal equations of the Gauss-Newton method,

$$\mathbf{J}^T\mathbf{J}\Delta\Theta = -\mathbf{J}^T\mathbf{r}. \tag{5}$$

While it may be numerically advisable to solve the overconstraint linear equation $\mathbf{J}\Delta\Theta = -\mathbf{r}$ directly e.g. via a QR-decomposition [22], to our knowledge all methods to solve large scale instances of Eq. 3 are based on the Gauss-Newton method and the normal equations. In particular, the Levenberg-Marquardt method using augmented normal equations,

$$\left(\mathbf{J}^T\mathbf{J} + \mu\mathbf{I}\right)\Delta\Theta = -\mathbf{J}^T\mathbf{r}, \tag{6}$$

with $\mu > 0$, became very popular over the last years. The key requirement for Gauss-Newton-type methods to be competitive solvers is that $\mathbf{J}^T\mathbf{J}$ is a sparse matrix, which can be exploited to solve the (augmented) normal equations efficiently. In terms of the original problem formulation (Eq. 3) the sparsity of $\mathbf{J}^T\mathbf{J}$ means, that each residual r_k depends only on a small subset of parameters in Θ.

Most available implementations for large scale nonlinear least squares problems have an interface, that allows the user to specify the residual vector $\mathbf{r}$ and the Jacobian $\mathbf{J}$ (as sparse matrix). In some implementations a weight or even a covariance matrix may be provided with each residual. Two of the methods described in Section 3 require a minimal extension to such an interface: in the computation of $\mathbf{J}^T\mathbf{J}$ and $\mathbf{J}^T\mathbf{r}$ we allow block diagonal matrices to be inserted, i.e. we facilitate the efficient computation of

$$\mathbf{J}^T\mathbf{D}\mathbf{J} \qquad \text{and} \qquad \mathbf{J}^T\bar{\mathbf{D}}\mathbf{r} \tag{7}$$

for block diagonal matrices $\mathbf{D}$ and $\bar{\mathbf{D}}$ with $d \times d$ non-zeros blocks along the diagonal. Note that $\mathbf{J}^T\mathbf{J}$ and $\mathbf{J}^T\mathbf{D}\mathbf{J}$ will have the same sparsity pattern.

3   Robustified Nonlinear Least-Squares

The objective given in Eq. 1 has, at a first glance, little in common with nonlinear least-squares instances in Eq. 3 (other than that the objective is composed of individual terms). Often $\psi(\cdot)$ in Eq. 1 behaves like a quadratic function for small arguments, i.e. for residual vectors r close to 0 we have that $\psi(r) \approx \|r\|^2/2$. This usually corresponds to a Gaussian assumption on the noise model for inliers, which are characterized by having non-heavy tail residuals. In most estimation tasks the majority of observations are inliers, hence the majority of terms in Eq. 1 are (close to) quadratic functions near the minimizer Θ^*. Consequently, it appears beneficial to cast the problem Eq. 1 as nonlinear least-squares instance (Eq. 3) in order to leverage available efficient solvers for the latter problem class. Below we discuss several options to introduce robustness into least-squares estimation.

3.1   Iteratively Reweighted Least Squares

We assume that ψ is isotropic, i.e. $\psi(r) = \phi(\|r\|)$ for a function $\phi : \mathbb{R}_0^+ \to \mathbb{R}_0^+$. Then the first-optimality condition for Θ^* in Eq. 1 are

$$
0 = \sum_k \phi'(\|r_k(\Theta^*)\|) \frac{r_k^T(\Theta^*)}{\|r_k(\Theta^*)\|} \frac{\partial r_k}{\partial \Theta}(\Theta^*) = \sum_k \underbrace{\frac{\phi'(\|r_k(\Theta^*)\|)}{\|r_k^T(\Theta^*)\|}}_{\stackrel{\text{def}}{=} \omega(r_k(\Theta^*))} r_k^T(\Theta^*) J_k(\Theta^*)
$$

$$
= \sum_k \omega(r_k(\Theta^*)) r_k^T(\Theta^*) J_k(\Theta^*).
$$

If the (scalar) values $\omega_k^* \stackrel{\text{def}}{=} \omega(r_k(\Theta^*))$ are known for a minimizer Θ^* (and therefore constant), the optimality conditions above are the ones for a standard nonlinear least-squares problem,

$$
\Theta^* = \arg\min_\Theta \frac{1}{2} \sum_k \omega_k^* \|r_k(\Theta)\|^2. \tag{8}
$$

Since the weights ω_k^* are usually not known, one can employ an estimate based on the current solution maintained by the optimization algorithm. This also implies that the objective to minimize varies with each update of the current solution. Further, algorithms such as the Levenberg-Marquardt method have a built-in "back-tracking" step, which discards updates leading to an inferior objective value. Depending on the programming interface this back-tracking stage may only see the surrogate objective in Eq. 8 or the true cost in Eq. 1.

3.2   Triggs Correction

For completeness we review the approach outlined in [22] (and termed "Triggs correction" in [3]) to introduce robustness into a (nonlinear) least-squares method. Let $\rho : \mathbb{R}_0^+ \to \mathbb{R}_0^+$ be a robust kernel mapping the squared residual norm to a real number i.e. the objective is

$$
\min_\theta \frac{1}{2} \sum_k \rho\left(\|r_k(\theta)\|^2\right). \tag{9}
$$

A first-order expansion of $r_k(\Theta + \Delta\Theta) \approx r_k + J_k\Delta\Theta$ (dropping the explicit dependence of r_k and J_k on the current linearization point Θ) together with a second-order expansion of

$$h_k(\Delta\Theta) \stackrel{\text{def}}{=} \frac{1}{2}\rho\left(\|r_k + J_k\Delta\Theta\|^2\right) \tag{10}$$

yields

$$h_k(\Delta\Theta) \approx \rho' r_k^T J_k \Delta\Theta + \frac{1}{2}(\Delta\Theta)^T J_k^T \underbrace{\left(\rho' I + 2\rho'' r_k r_k^T\right)}_{\stackrel{\text{def}}{=} H_k} J\Delta\Theta + const, \tag{11}$$

where ρ' and ρ'' are evaluated at r_k. This expression is rewritten in [22] as a nonlinear least-squares instance by replacing J with $\tilde{J} = \sqrt{H_k}J$ (given that H_k is strictly p.d.[1]). In theory, any existing algorithm for nonlinear least squares minimization can be used, provided that the implementation allows sufficient powerful reweighting of the residuals and the Jacobian.[2]

Observe that one eigenvector of H_k is r_k with corresponding eigenvalue $\rho' + 2\rho''\|r_k\|^2$, and all other eigenvalues are ρ' (which is non-negative since a sensible function ρ is monotonically increasing) with eigenvectors $v \perp r_k$. Consequently, H_k is p.s.d. iff $\rho' + 2\rho''\|r_k\|^2$ is non-negative. If H_k is indefinite, one approach is to drop the ρ'' term entirely (i.e. set ρ'' to 0, as e.g. done in the Ceres Solver [3]). This amounts to representing the mapping $\Delta\Theta \mapsto \frac{1}{2}\rho(\|r(\Theta + \Delta\Theta)\|^2)$ locally at Θ via the (strictly) convex surrogate function

$$\Delta\Theta \mapsto \rho' r_k J_k \Delta\Theta + \frac{\rho'}{2}(\Delta\Theta)^T J_k^T J_k \Delta\Theta + const. \tag{12}$$

One could replace an indefinite H_k by its closest p.s.d. approximation $\tilde{H}_k$, which (using the Frobenius norm as distance between matrices) is determined by

$$\tilde{H}_k = \begin{cases} H_k & \text{if } H_k \succeq 0 \\ \rho'\left(I - \frac{r_k r_k^T}{\|r_k\|^2}\right) & \text{otherwise.} \end{cases} \tag{13}$$

Consequently, the respective normal equations to solve in each iteration read as

$$\sum_k J_k^T \tilde{H}_k J_k \Delta\Theta = -\sum_k \rho' J_k^T r_k. \tag{14}$$

In practice this approach converged to higher objectives, and therefore we use the same strategy as Ceres for indefinite H_k.

---

[1] One way to model $\sqrt{H_k}$ is using the ansatz $\sqrt{H_k} = \sqrt{\rho'}(I + \alpha r_k^0 (r_k^0)^T)$ for an α [22].
[2] The Jacobian and the residuals need to be reweighted differently.

3.3 Square-Rooting the Kernel

Another option proposed in [9] is to rewrite $\psi(r)$ as $\left(\sqrt{\psi(r)}\right)^2$, which implies that $\sqrt{\psi(r)}$ is now employed as the residual in the outer least-squares formulation. In some way this is a complete opposite approach to the "Triggs correction" above, since the robust kernel is pulled into the inner scope of the minimization problem. Note that by naive "square rooting" the robust kernel one effectively replaces a d-dimensional residual r with a one-dimensional one, $\sqrt{\psi(r)}$, which loses structural information. By noting that for any d-dimensional vector u with unit norm we have

$$\psi(r) = \left\langle \sqrt{\psi(r)}u, \sqrt{\psi(r)}u \right\rangle = \left\| \sqrt{\psi(r)}u \right\|^2, \tag{15}$$

we can use the specific choice of $u = r/\|r\|$ to obtain $\psi(r) = \left\| \sqrt{\psi(r)}/\|r\| \cdot r \right\|^2$, which means that the original residual r is weighted by a factor of $\sqrt{\psi(r)}/\|r\|$, which is a different one than used in IRLS (Section 3.1), since—first of all—this weight is explicitly dependent on Θ. Further, for convenience we state the derivative of this modified residual with respect to the unknowns Θ,

$$\frac{d}{d\Theta} \left(\frac{\sqrt{\psi(r)}}{\|r\|} r \right) = \left(\frac{1}{2\|r\|\sqrt{\psi(r)}} r \frac{d\psi(r)}{dr} + \frac{\sqrt{\psi(r)}}{\|r\|^3} \left(\|r\|^2 I - rr^T \right) \right) \frac{dr}{d\Theta}. \tag{16}$$

3.4 Lifting the Kernel

Another way to represent a robust cost function within a (nonlinear) least-squares framework is by introducing extra variables playing the role of "confidence weights" for each residual. Converting a minimization problem to a higher-dimensional one by augmenting the set of unknowns is often termed "lifting" in the optimization literature. Sometimes lifting allows a global optimal solution for an otherwise difficult minimization problem (e.g. [13,7]). Our motivation for enriching the set of unknowns is different: we hope to circumnavigate the flat regions in robust kernels by indirectly representing the robustness and therefore have better chances to reach a good local minimum. Initial evidence for such an improved behavior of lifted costs in a synthetic line-fitting experiment is given in [24]. Rewriting non-convex robust costs via lifting has a long history: "half-quadratic" optimization introduces additional variables to allow efficient minimization by using a block-coordinate method in the context of low-level vision tasks [10,5]). More recently, "switching constraints" (analogous to confidence weights) are employed to make pose graph optimization robust [21,1] (where the robust kernel is identified as the Geman-McClure one). These methods use an IRLS approach to incorporate robustness into a non-linear least-squares solver.

In our setting, one instance of a lifted kernel for robust objectives is

$$\min_{\Theta} \sum_k \frac{1}{2}\psi\big(\|r_k(\Theta)\| \big) = \min_{\Theta,\mathbf{w}} \sum_k \underbrace{\frac{1}{2}\left(w_k^2 \|r_k(\Theta)\|^2 + \kappa^2(w_k^2) \right)}_{\overset{\text{def}}{=}\hat{\psi}(r_k(\Theta),w_k)}, \tag{17}$$

where w_k is the confidence weight for the k-th residual. We denote the lifted kernel of $\psi(\cdot)$ as $\hat{\psi}(\cdot, \cdot)$. Depending on the choice of κ one arrives at different kernels ψ, and in the following we briefly discuss a few sensible choices for κ.

L^1-*cost:* The choice of $\hat{\psi}(r, w) = \frac{1}{2}\left(w^2 r^2 + \frac{1}{w^2}\right)$, i.e. $\kappa^2(w^2) = 1/w^2$, results in $\psi(r) = \min_w \hat{\psi}(r, w) = \|r\|/2$.

Tukey's biweight: One can lift the robust biweight kernel

$$\psi(r) = \begin{cases} \frac{\tau^2}{6}\left(1 - \left(1 - \frac{\|r\|^2}{\tau^2}\right)^3\right) \\ \frac{\tau^2}{6} \end{cases} = \begin{cases} \frac{\|r\|^2}{2}\left(1 - \frac{\|r\|^2}{\tau^2} + \frac{\|r\|^4}{3\tau^4}\right) & \text{if } \|r\|^2 \leq \tau^2 \\ \frac{\tau^2}{6} & \text{otherwise} \end{cases} \tag{18}$$

by setting

$$\hat{\psi}(r, w) = \frac{1}{2}w^2\|r\|^2 + \frac{1}{6}(|w| - 1)^2(2|w| + 1). \tag{19}$$

Note that the regularizer of w, $(|w| - 1)^2(2|w| + 1)/6$, is a double-well potential with minima at $w = \pm 1$ (inlier case), finite cost at $w = 0$ (outlier), and unbounded cost as $|w| \to \infty$ (see also Fig. 2). Formally we have in this setting

$$\kappa^2(w^2) = \frac{1}{6}\left(\sqrt{w^2} - 1\right)^2\left(2\sqrt{w^2} + 1\right).$$

Smooth truncated quadratic: The kernel of our main interest was proposed in [17] (but without establishing the strong connection between the introduced weights and robust estimation) and is given by

$$\kappa^2(w^2) = \frac{\tau^2}{2}\left(w^2 - 1\right)^2 \qquad \text{or} \qquad \kappa(w^2) = \frac{\tau}{\sqrt{2}}\left(w^2 - 1\right). \tag{20}$$

Again the regularizer $\kappa^2(w^2)$ is a double-well potential with zero cost at $w = \pm 1$, finite cost at $w = 0$ (outlier case), and unbounded cost for $|w| \to \infty$ (see Fig. 2). It can be easily shown that

$$\psi(r) = \frac{1}{2}\min_w\left\{w^2\|r\|^2 + \frac{\tau^2}{2}\left(w^2 - 1\right)^2\right\} = \begin{cases} \frac{1}{2}\|r\|^2\left(1 - \frac{\|r\|^2}{2\tau^2}\right) & \text{if } \|r\|^2 \leq \tau^2 \\ \tau^2/4 & \text{otherwise,} \end{cases} \tag{21}$$

which is a particular smooth approximation to a truncated quadratic kernel. We can create a family of such smooth approximations by making κ dependent on a parameter $p > 1$, e.g.

$$\kappa^2(w^2) = \frac{\tau^2}{p}\left(w^2 - 1\right)^p, \tag{22}$$

which corresponds to the robust kernel

$$\psi(r) = \begin{cases} \frac{1}{2}\|r\|^2 \left(1 - \frac{p-1}{p}\left(\frac{\|r\|^2}{\tau^2}\right)^{\frac{1}{p-1}}\right) & \text{if } \|r\|^2 \leq \tau^2 \\ \frac{\tau^2}{2p} & \text{otherwise,} \end{cases} \tag{23}$$

In the limit $p \to 1$ this kernel ψ approaches the truncated quadratic cost (see also Fig. 1(a)). Fig. 1(b) illustrates the lifted kernel $\hat{\psi}$, which has almost nowhere a zero gradient (in contrast to the one-dimensional function ψ, which has a zero gradient whenever the argument is larger than τ). Our hypothesis therefore is, that it is exactly this feature that enables lifted representations to have a better chance of escaping poor local minima than direct robust kernels.

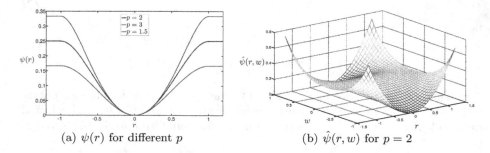

(a) $\psi(r)$ for different p (b) $\hat{\psi}(r, w)$ for $p = 2$

Fig. 1. Different robust kernels ψ for different values of p in Eq. 23 (left), and the visualization of the lifted kernel $\hat{\psi}$ for $p = 2$. Note that the lifted kernel appears "relatively convex" for large residuals.

From weight functions to lifted representations: As in Section 3.1 we now assume $\psi(r) = \phi(\|r\|)$ for a function $\phi : \mathbb{R}_0^+ \to \mathbb{R}_0^+$. We will use $e = \|r\|$ in the following. The *weight function* ω for the kernel ϕ is given by $\omega(e) \overset{\text{def}}{=} \phi'(e)/e$. This weight function plays a crucial role in iteratively reweighted least-squares. In order to lift ϕ (and consequently ψ), we have to find a function κ^2, such that

$$\phi(e) = \min_w \hat{\phi}(e, w) = \min_w \frac{1}{2}\left(w^2 e^2 + \kappa^2(w^2)\right).$$

First order optimality conditions imply $w = 0$ or $e^2 + (\kappa^2)'(w^2) = 0$. Since in a reweighted approach, $\omega(e)$ plays the role of w^2 in the lifted formulation, we use the ansatz $w^2 = \omega(e)$, leading to $e = \omega^{-1}(w^2)$ or $e^2 - \left(\omega^{-1}(w^2)\right)^2 = 0$. Comparing this with the first-order optimality condition we read that

$$(\kappa^2)'(w^2) = -\left(\omega^{-1}(w^2)\right)^2,$$

where ω^{-1} is the inverse function of ω (if it exists). For instance, the Cauchy kernel, $\phi(e) = \frac{\tau^2}{2}\log\left(1 + e^2/\tau^2\right)$, has a weight function $\omega(e) = 1/(1 + e^2/\tau^2)$ and a lifted representation

$$\hat{\phi}(e,w) = \frac{1}{2}w^2e^2 + \frac{\tau^2}{4}\left(w^4 - 2\log(w^2) - 1\right). \tag{24}$$

Similarly, lifted formulations for all robust kernels with strictly monotonically decreasing weight function ω can be derived. This construction is related but not equivalent to the one in [5].

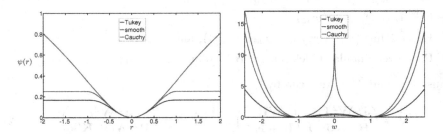

Fig. 2. Tukey's biweight, the smooth truncated quadratic (Eq. 21), and the Cauchy kernels (left). The associated regularization $w \mapsto \kappa^2(w^2)$ in the lifted representation (right).

Note that for all the choices of $\hat{\psi}$ above we can rewrite $\hat{\psi}(r,w)$ as

$$\hat{\psi}(r,w) = \frac{1}{2}\left(w^2\|r\|^2 + \kappa^2(w^2)\right) = \frac{1}{2}\left\|\begin{matrix} wr \\ \kappa(w^2) \end{matrix}\right\|^2, \tag{25}$$

i.e. $\hat{\psi}$ can be written as a nonlinear least-squares term over a lifted residual $\hat{r} \stackrel{\text{def}}{=} \begin{pmatrix} wr \\ \kappa(w^2) \end{pmatrix}$, and therefore lifted kernels can be immediately incorporated into a standard nonlinear least squares solver. This is probably not advisable, since having a potentially huge number of extra unknowns puts extra burden on the column reordering step and on the employed matrix factorization method. Consequently, we describe a more efficient implementation of lifted approaches in the next section.

4   Efficient Implementation of Lifted Kernels

Lifting the robust kernel requires maintaining one extra variable per residual. While we believe that the cost of storing an extra confidence weight is negligible, the computational burden in particular in Gauss-Newton-type solvers seems to increase significantly using a lifted representation. In this section we demonstrate that the computational complexity is essentially the same for lifted and non-lifted representations. Since a confidence weight w_k is linked to exactly one residual

r_k, the sparsity structure of the lifted Jacobian stays the same. If we consider the lifted residual as in Eq. 25, then we have for the lifted full Jacobian $\hat{\mathbf{J}}$,

$$\hat{\mathbf{J}} = \begin{pmatrix} \mathbf{WJ} & \mathbf{R} \\ \mathbf{0} & \mathbf{K}' \end{pmatrix} \qquad\qquad \hat{\mathbf{r}} = \begin{pmatrix} \mathbf{Wr} \\ \mathbf{k} \end{pmatrix} \qquad (26)$$

where

- $\mathbf{W} \stackrel{\text{def}}{=} \operatorname{diag}(w_1, \ldots, w_M) \otimes I_{d \times d}$,
- $\mathbf{k} \stackrel{\text{def}}{=} \left(\kappa(w_1), \ldots, \kappa(w_M)\right)^T$,
- $\mathbf{K}' \stackrel{\text{def}}{=} 2\operatorname{diag}\left(w_1 \kappa'(w_1^2), \ldots, w_M \kappa'(w_M^2)\right)$, and
- $\mathbf{R}$ is a rectangular block matrix $\mathbf{R} \stackrel{\text{def}}{=} \operatorname{diag}(r_1, \ldots, r_M)$.

Thus, $\hat{\mathbf{J}}^T \hat{\mathbf{J}}$ and $\hat{\mathbf{J}}^T \mathbf{r}$ are given by

$$\hat{\mathbf{J}}^T \hat{\mathbf{J}} = \begin{pmatrix} \mathbf{J}^T \mathbf{W}^2 \mathbf{J} & \mathbf{J}^T \mathbf{WR} \\ \mathbf{R}^T \mathbf{WJ} & \mathbf{R}^T \mathbf{R} + \mathbf{K}'^2 \end{pmatrix} \qquad \hat{\mathbf{J}}^T \hat{\mathbf{r}} = \begin{pmatrix} \mathbf{J}^T \mathbf{W}^2 \mathbf{r} \\ \mathbf{R}^T \mathbf{Wr} + \mathbf{K}' \mathbf{k} \end{pmatrix}. \qquad (27)$$

Note that $\mathbf{R}^T \mathbf{R} = \operatorname{diag}\left(\|r_1\|^2, \ldots, \|r_M\|^2\right)$, and we have the vector

$$\mathbf{R}^T \mathbf{Wr} + \mathbf{K}' \mathbf{k} = \left(w_k \left(\|r_k\|^2 + 2\kappa'(w_k^2)\kappa(w_k^2)\right)\right)_{k=1,\ldots,M}.$$

Since the confidence weights are only appearing in exactly one residual term, one can eliminate all w_k in parallel from the (augmented) normal equations

$$\left(\hat{\mathbf{J}}^T \hat{\mathbf{J}} + \mu \mathbf{I}\right) \begin{pmatrix} \Delta\Theta \\ \Delta\mathbf{w} \end{pmatrix} = -\hat{\mathbf{J}}^T \hat{\mathbf{r}}, \qquad (28)$$

via the Schur complement, which leads to the reduced system

$$\left(\mathbf{J}^T \mathbf{W}(\mathbf{I} - \mathbf{DRR}^T)\mathbf{WJ} + \mu \mathbf{I}\right) \Delta\Theta = \text{r.h.s.} \qquad (29)$$

where $\mathbf{D} = (\mathbf{R}^T \mathbf{R} + \mathbf{K}'^2 + \mu \mathbf{I})^{-1}$ is a diagonal matrix with

$$\mathbf{D}_{kk} = \frac{1}{\|r_k\|^2 + (2w_k \kappa'(w_k^2))^2 + \mu}, \qquad (30)$$

and $\mathbf{RR}^T$ is a block diagonal matrix with $d \times d$ blocks $(\mathbf{RR}^T)_{kk} = r_k r_k^T$. Note that $\mathbf{I} - \mathbf{DRR}^T \succ 0$ for $\mu > 0$. Further, the (block) non-zero structure of $\mathbf{J}^T \mathbf{W}(\mathbf{I} - \mathbf{DRR}^T)\mathbf{WJ}$ is the same as for $\mathbf{J}^T \mathbf{J}$, since $\mathbf{W}(\mathbf{I} - \mathbf{DRR}^T)\mathbf{W}$ is a block diagonal matrix with $d \times d$ blocks along the diagonal. One can easily calculate a square root of $\mathbf{I} - \mathbf{DRR}^T$ via the ansatz $(\mathbf{I} - \mathbf{DRR}^T)^{1/2} = \mathbf{I} - \tilde{\mathbf{D}}\mathbf{RR}^T$ with $\tilde{\mathbf{D}}$ being a diagonal matrix,

$$\tilde{\mathbf{D}}_{kk} = \frac{1}{\|r_k\|^2} \left(1 - \sqrt{\frac{(2w_k \kappa'(w_k^2))^2 + \mu}{\|r_k\|^2 + (2w_k \kappa'(w_k^2))^2 + \mu}}\right). \qquad (31)$$

Consequently, the modified Jacobian can be easily computed by left-multiplication with a block-diagonal matrix, i.e.

$$\mathbf{J} \rightsquigarrow \left(\mathbf{I} - \tilde{\mathbf{D}} \mathbf{R} \mathbf{R}^T\right) \mathbf{W} \mathbf{J}, \tag{32}$$

which is provided to the solver. The right hand side in Eq. 29 is given by

$$\text{r.h.s.} = \mathbf{J}^T \mathbf{W} \left(\mathbf{R} \mathbf{D} \left(\mathbf{R}^T \mathbf{W} \mathbf{r} + \mathbf{K}' \mathbf{k}\right) - \mathbf{W} \mathbf{r}\right) = -\mathbf{J}^T \mathbf{W} \tilde{\mathbf{r}}, \tag{33}$$

which corresponds to using a reweighted and adjusted residual vector,

$$\tilde{r}_k \stackrel{\text{def}}{=} w_k \left(1 - \frac{\|r_k\|^2 + 2\kappa'(w_k^2)\kappa(w_k^2)}{\|r_k\|^2 + (2w_k\kappa'(w_k^2))^2 + \mu}\right) r_k \tag{34}$$

together with a reweighted Jacobian $\mathbf{W}\mathbf{J}$. Backsubstitution to determine Δw_k leads to

$$\Delta w_k = -w_k \frac{r_k^T \left(r_k + J_k \Delta\Theta\right) + 2\kappa'(w_k^2)\kappa(w_k^2)}{\|r_k\|^2 + (2w_k\kappa'(w_k))^2 + \mu}. \tag{35}$$

With the minimal extension to a standard Levenberg-Marquardt code as outlined in Section 2.2, it is straightforward to implement this Schur-complement approach by solving

$$\left(\mathbf{J}^T \mathbf{B} \mathbf{J} + \mu \mathbf{I}\right) \Delta\Theta = -\mathbf{J}^T \bar{\mathbf{B}} \mathbf{r}$$

in each iteration, where $\mathbf{B}$ and $\bar{\mathbf{B}}$ are appropriate block diagonal matrices.

5   Numerical Results

We use a freely available sparse Levenberg-Marquardt C++ implementation[3] and extended its interface to allow insertion of block-diagonal matrices as indicated in Section 2.2. The test problems are the ones used in [4] based on structure-from-motion datasets generated from community photo collections [2]. We had to leave out the larger problem instances due to their memory consumption. The utilized objective in our bundle adjustment is

$$\sum \psi\big(f_i\eta_i\left(\pi(R_i X_j + t_i)\right) - \hat{p}_{ij}\big), \tag{36}$$

where $\hat{p}_{ij} \in \mathbb{R}^2$ is the observed image observation of the j-th 3D point in the i-image, $X_j \in \mathbb{R}^3$ is the j-th 3D point, $R_i \in SO(3)$ and $t_i \in \mathbb{R}^3$ are the orientation parameters of the i-th camera, $\pi : \mathbb{R}^3 \to \mathbb{R}^2$, $\pi(X) = X/X_3$ is the projection, and f_i is the respective focal length. η_i is the lens distortion function with $\eta_i(p) = (1 + k_{i,1}\|p\|^2 + k_{i,2}\|p\|^4)p$, and ψ is the robust kernel from Eq. 21 with $\tau = 1$ (i.e.

---

[3] We selected the "simple sparse bundle adjustment" software, http://www.inf.ethz.ch/personal/chzach/oss/SSBA-3.0.zip, mostly because of the simplicity of the underlying API.

Table 1. The main characteristics of the used datasets

Number	Dataset	# cameras	# 3D points	# observations
1	Trafalgar	257	65132	225911
2	Dubrovnik	356	226730	1255268
3	Ladybug	598	69218	304170
4	Venice	427	310384	1699145
5	Final-93	93	61203	287451
6	Final-394	394	100368	534408

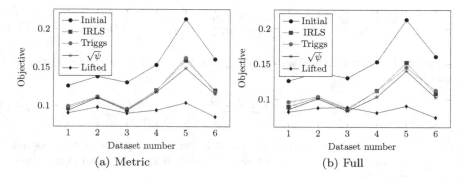

Fig. 3. Initial and final objectives (normalized with the observation count) reached by the different methods

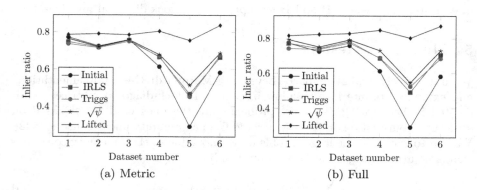

Fig. 4. Initial and reached final ratios obtained by the different methods. The inlier ratio is an indicator of how many terms in the objective are in the flat outlier region.

inliers may have up to 1 pixel reprojection error). We run bundle adjustment in two modes: the "metric" mode optimizes only over X_j, R_i and t_i and keeps the focal lengths and lens distortion parameters fixed, and the "full" mode optimizes over all unknowns. We report both settings in order to determine whether the additional nonlinearity induced by the internal camera parameters has an impact on the results.

The runtime varies between the datasets and ranges from about 1 minute (Final-93 using metric refinement only) and 30 minutes (Final-394 with full adjustment) on a standard laptop computer. The computational complexity of all approaches is similar. The median slowdown (with respect to IRLS) of one LM iteration is 1.0 (IRLS), 1.0337 (Triggs), 1.6643 ($\sqrt{\psi}$), and 1.5814 (lifted). Please refer to the supplementary material for detailed runtimes.

The maximum number of iterations in the Levenberg-Marquardt algorithm is 100, and the iterations stop when the relative updates are less than 10^{-12} in magnitude. Table 1 summarizes the relevant figures for the tested datasets. The initial and obtained final objective values for the different approach to robustification (called "IRLS", "Triggs", $\sqrt{\psi}$, and "lifted" with the weights w_k initialized to one) are illustrated in Fig. 3. With the exception of the "Ladybug" dataset in full refinement mode, the lifted representation achieves the lowest objectives. The other methods cluster around similar (usually higher) final objective values with the square-root approach slightly ahead of the others.

Another interesting statistics is the inlier ratio (i.e. the fraction of residuals with at most $\tau = 1$ pixels reprojection error), which is depicted in Fig. 4. This number indicates how many residuals are "active", i.e. contribute to the overall gradient for our choice of robust kernel. Interestingly, the inlier ratio is always the highest for the lifted approach, which may be an advantage in bundle adjustment instances with large initial drift (such as often induced by loop closure). More experimental results can be found in the supplementary material.

6   Conclusions

In this work we addressed how robust cost functions can be incorporated into a nonlinear least-squares framework. We discussed several options how to combine robust costs with a Gauss-Newton-type solver, including iteratively reweighted least-squares, the Triggs correction, square rooting the robust kernel, and finally lifting the kernel. In terms of achieved objective the lifted approach outperforms the other ones by far in most tested problem instances. Consequently, we believe that lifting a kernel function is a promising method to incorporate robustness into an otherwise non-robust objective, especially since lifting comes with negligible extra computational cost,

One direction of future work is to make the square-root and the lifted approach accessible in the recently very popular Ceres solver (which currently implements robust cost functions via the Triggs correction). Source code based on a direct sparse Levenberg-Marquardt implementation for non-linear least squares is available at http://github.com/chzach/SSBA.

Ackowledgements. I am very grateful to Andrew Fitzgibbon for extensive discussions and to Andrea Cohen for contributing Figures 1 and 2. Further, I would like to thank Sameer Agarwal and the area chairs for pointing out additional literature.

References

1. Agarwal, P., Tipaldi, G.D., Spinello, L., Stachniss, C., Burgard, W.: Robust map optimization using dynamic covariance scaling. In: 2013 IEEE International Conference on Robotics and Automation (ICRA), pp. 62–69. IEEE (2013)
2. Agarwal, S., Furukawa, Y., Snavely, N., Simon, I., Curless, B., Seitz, S.M., Szeliski, R.: Building rome in a day. Communications of the ACM 54(10), 105–112 (2011)
3. Agarwal, S., Mierle, K.: Others: Ceres solver, https://code.google.com/p/ceres-solver/
4. Agarwal, S., Snavely, N., Seitz, S.M., Szeliski, R.: Bundle adjustment in the large. In: Daniilidis, K., Maragos, P., Paragios, N. (eds.) ECCV 2010, Part II. LNCS, vol. 6312, pp. 29–42. Springer, Heidelberg (2010)
5. Black, M.J., Rangarajan, A.: On the unification of line processes, outlier rejection, and robust statistics with applications in early vision. IJCV 19(1), 57–91 (1996)
6. Byröd, M., Åström, K.: Conjugate gradient bundle adjustment. In: Daniilidis, K., Maragos, P., Paragios, N. (eds.) ECCV 2010, Part II. LNCS, vol. 6312, pp. 114–127. Springer, Heidelberg (2010)
7. Chan, T.F., Esedoglu, S., Nikolova, M.: Algorithms for finding global minimizers of image segmentation and denoising models. SIAM Journal on Applied Mathematics 66(5), 1632–1648 (2006)
8. Chen, Y., Davis, T., Hager, W., Rajamanickam, S.: Algorithm 887: CHOLMOD, supernodal sparse Cholesky factorization and update/downdate. ACM Transactions on Mathematical Software 35(3), 1–14 (2008)
9. Engels, C., Stewénius, H., Nistér, D.: Bundle adjustment rules. In: Photogrammetric Computer Vision, PCV (2006)
10. Geman, D., Reynolds, G.: Constrained restoration and the recovery of discontinuities. IEEE Transactions on Pattern Analysis and Machine Intelligence 14(3), 367–383 (1992)
11. Hartley, R., Zisserman, A.: Multiple View Geometry in Computer Vision. Cambridge University Press (2000)
12. Indelman, V., Roberts, R., Beall, C., Dellaert, F.: Incremental light bundle adjustment. In: Proc. BMVC (2012)
13. Ishikawa, H.: Exact optimization for Markov random fields with convex priors. IEEE Trans. Pattern Anal. Mach. Intell. 25(10), 1333–1336 (2003)
14. Jeong, Y., Nister, D., Steedly, D., Szeliski, R., Kweon, I.S.: Pushing the envelope of modern methods for bundle adjustment. IEEE Trans. Pattern Anal. Mach. Intell. 34(8), 1605–1617 (2012)
15. Jian, Y.D., Balcan, D.C., Dellaert, F.: Generalized subgraph preconditioners for large-scale bundle adjustment. In: Proc. ICCV (2011)
16. Levenberg, K.: A method for the solution of certain non-linear problems in least squares. Quarterly of Applied Mathematics 2(2), 164–168 (1944)
17. Li, H., Sumner, R.W., Pauly, M.: Global correspondence optimization for non-rigid registration of depth scans. In: Proc. SGP, pp. 1421–1430. Eurographics Association (2008)
18. Lourakis, M.I., Argyros, A.A.: Is levenberg-marquardt the most efficient optimization algorithm for implementing bundle adjustment? In: ICCV, vol. 2, pp. 1526–1531. IEEE (2005)
19. Marquardt, D.: An algorithm for the least-squares estimation of nonlinear parameters. SIAM Journal of Applied Mathematics 11(2), 431–441 (1963)

20. Steffen, R., Frahm, J.-M., Förstner, W.: Relative bundle adjustment based on trifocal constraints. In: Kutulakos, K.N. (ed.) ECCV 2010 Workshops, Part II. LNCS, vol. 6554, pp. 282–295. Springer, Heidelberg (2012)

21. Sunderhauf, N., Protzel, P.: Switchable constraints for robust pose graph slam. In: 2012 IEEE/RSJ International Conference on Intelligent Robots and Systems (IROS), pp. 1879–1884. IEEE (2012)

22. Triggs, B., McLauchlan, P.F., Hartley, R.I., Fitzgibbon, A.W.: Bundle adjustment – A modern synthesis. In: Triggs, B., Zisserman, A., Szeliski, R. (eds.) ICCV-WS 1999. LNCS, vol. 1883, pp. 298–372. Springer, Heidelberg (2000)

23. Zhang, J., Boutin, M., Aliaga, D.: Robust bundle adjustment for structure from motion. In: Proc. ICIP (2006)

24. Zollhöfer, M., Nießner, M., Izadi, S., Rehmann, C., Zach, C., Fisher, M., Wu, C., Fitzgibbon, A., Loop, C., Theobalt, C., Stamminger, M.: Real-time non-rigid reconstruction using an rgb-d camera. ACM Transactions on Graphics, TOG (2014)

Accurate Intrinsic Calibration of Depth Camera with Cuboids

Bingwen Jin, Hao Lei, and Weidong Geng

State Key Lab. of CAD&CG,
College of Computer Science and Technology, Zhejiang University,
Hangzhou, 310027, China

Abstract. Due to the low precision, the consumer-grade depth sensor is often calibrated jointly with a color camera, and the joint calibration sometimes presents undesired interactions. In this paper, we propose a novel method to carry out the high-accuracy intrinsic calibration of depth sensors merely by the depth camera, in which the traditional calibration rig, checker-board pattern, is replaced with a set of cuboids with known sizes, and the objective function for calibration is based on the length, width, and height of cuboids and its angle between the neighboring surfaces, which can be directly and robustly calculated from the depth-map. We experimentally evaluate of the accuracy of the calibrated depth camera by measuring the angles and sizes of cubic object, and it is empirically shown that the resulting calibration accuracy is higher than that in the state-of-the-art calibration procedures, making the commodity depth sensors applicable to more interesting application scenarios such as 3D measurement and shape modeling etc.

Keywords: intrinsic calibration, depth camera, 3D measurement, depth map, cuboids.

1 Introduction

Nowadays there has been an increasing number of depth cameras available at commodity prices, such as Microsoft Kinect. Although it was primarily designed for natural interaction for video game, the low cost, reliability and speed of the measurement promises of Kinect-type cameras have created a lot of interesting new research applications [26,16], such as 3D scanning and modeling [10,22,30,13,9]. Unfortunately Kinect-type 3D sensors are usually low accuracy, low precision devices. Diverse studies [14,16] show that their accuracy decreases with myopic intrinsic parameters [27] when the distance from sensor increases. This level of accuracy is quite satisfactory in human interaction applications. However, it is definitely insufficient in many exciting applications (e.g., indoor navigation, 3D measurement or fine manipulation) that require a relatively high accuracy of depth sensors.

Depth cameras (Kinect etc.) are usually pre-calibrated with a proprietary algorithm. The calibrated parameters are stored in the device during manufacturing and are used by the official drivers to calculate the 3D point clouds. The

D. Fleet et al. (Eds.): ECCV 2014, Part V, LNCS 8693, pp. 788–803, 2014.

manufacturer's calibration does not correct the depth distortion, and accuracy can be improved by software correction of sensor outputs later on. The correction is based on a specific calibration model whose intrinsic parameters are identified during the calibration process. In general, the calibration of a sensor measuring a quantity is the estimation of the relationship between the measured quantity and the actual quantity (also called the ground truth) [3].

The depth data from depth cameras are usually in low precision, and therefore it is often calibrated jointly with a color camera, which has a potential of improving the accuracy of optimal solution. However the joint calibration sometimes presents undesired interactions [14], e.g. in [11], it shows that a refinement of depth model can paradoxically lead to enlargement of reprojection errors of RGB camera.

In this paper, we aim at providing an intrinsic calibration algorithm with higher accuracy for the Kinect community merely by depth camera. Cuboids with known size, instead of traditional checker-board, are chosen as the reference calibration rig, since the depth camera itself can robustly measure the length, width, and height of cuboids and its angle between the neighboring surfaces. Therefore the known sizes and angles in reference cuboids could be registered as the ground truth for the calibration of depth sensor, and the resulting sizes and angles in 3D shape modeling could also have a higher accuracy potentially. The work here focused on a calibration and analysis of accuracy of Kinect sensor, but the results and the approach are applicable to other similar sensors.

The paper proceeds with a short review of representative works on calibration of Kinect-type sensors in section 2. In section 3 the calibration model and its algorithmic steps are presented. Section 4 analyzed the accuracy of the resulting intrinsic calibration. Section 5 summarizes conclusions on the novel approach.

2   Related Work

Kinect-type 3D sensors considered in this work operate as structured light sensors. Accuracy of them can be improved by intrinsic calibration, which can be classified into two categories: supervised calibration and unsupervised calibration, by the principle of whether the dimensions of the calibration rig are known in advance or not.

2.1   Supervised Calibration

Calibration of Kinect-type 3D sensors is naturally split into two parts: identification of parameters of sensor cameras and identification of parameters of depth measurement model. The early works from Burrus [2] and Zhang and Zhang [29] identified intrinsic parameters of sensor cameras using checker-board pattern. Later, researchers propose methods to achieve calibration of sensor depth measurement model, e.g. Khoshelham and Elberink [16], Smisek et al. [26], Kim et al [17], Herrera. et al. [11] and its enhanced method in [24]. In these work, approaches are proposed for depth map conversion from disparity maps provided by the sensor. As a nominal factory model in OpenNI and Microsoft Kinect SDK already can convert disparity data into depth, a reformulation of depth calibration model was proposed in [14,15], utilizing a linear relationship between actual and sensor-provided depth data.

An important issue in depth model calibration is how to get the accurate depth data as it normally requires either a special 3D calibration rig or an external measuring tool. In [16], depth was measured using a simple measuring tape. In [11], correspondence between depth map and RGB camera image was established using external corners of calibration table. A similar approach was proposed by Draelos et al. [4]. Geiger et al. [6] employed multiple checker-boards as reference objects. Shibo and Qing [25] designed a specific planar board with regularly-spaced drilled holes allowing their easy identification in both RGB images and depth maps.

In our work, cuboids with known sizes are employed as a depth calibration rig for subsequent calibration of the depth model based on ground-truth angles and dimensions externally measured in advance.

2.2   Unsupervised Calibration

The accuracy problem will arise occasionally in depth measurement, due to the myopic property of Kinect-type depth camera. In order to facilitate this problem, the calibration without the pre-measured ground-truth, called unsupervised calibration, is preferred. One of the popular approaches to carry out unsupervised calibration is to couple the calibration procedure with specific application scenarios such as 3D mapping or registration of depth map [21]. Yamazoe et al. [28] estimate the intrinsic parameters by showing a planar board with unknown size to the depth camera with different poses and distances with the objective function of minimizing the plane-fitting errors. Kummerle et al. [19] embed the calibration procedure into the application scenarios and solve the objective function with simultaneous localization and mapping (SLAM). Using SLAM, one can capture relatively accurate close range data and build a map. Then inaccurate long range data could be compared with the expected measurements from the map. Based on this idea, Teichman et al. [27] further presented a generic approach to make RGBD intrinsic calibration with CLAMS: (Calibrating, Localizing, and Mapping, Simultaneously) by recording a few minutes of data from natural environments, and neither special calibration targets nor measurements of the environment is required.

From the point of view of manipulation, the unsupervised calibration will be much easy and convenient for the end user or a dedicated application scenario, however the estimated parameters will usually be less accuracy than that in supervised calibration [5].

3   Calibration Method

In Kinect-type 3D sensors, depth is calculated by sensor software on the basis of disparity of reflected patterns with respect to the reference patterns obtained for a plane placed at a known distance from the sensor. Its intrinsic calibration is in essence to collect sensor outputs and compare them to reference data, using a special calibration rig. In our approach, it is a cubic object of precisely known dimensions from a high-precision external measurement.

Our intrinsic calibration of depth sensor can be viewed as fine-tuning the intrinsic parameters by minimizing the errors of angles and sizes of reference cuboids in depth images. The proposed calibration procedure consists of an iterative optimization loop of calibration of sensor's IR cameras, calibration of depth measurement model and disparity distortion correction.

3.1 IR Camera Calibration

To calibrate IR camera in depth sensor, we use the pinhole model [7,8]. Given a point P whose coordinates in the camera coordinate system are $(x, y, z)^T$, it is firstly normalized as $\mathbf{x}_n$:

$$\mathbf{x}_n = \begin{bmatrix} x_n \\ y_n \end{bmatrix} = \begin{bmatrix} x/z \\ y/z \end{bmatrix}. \tag{1}$$

We have the image coordinates:

$$\begin{bmatrix} u \\ v \end{bmatrix} = \begin{bmatrix} f_x & 0 \\ 0 & f_y \end{bmatrix} \begin{bmatrix} x_n \\ y_n \end{bmatrix} + \begin{bmatrix} c_x \\ c_y \end{bmatrix}, \tag{2}$$

where $[f_x, f_y]$ is the focal length in the x and y axis respectively, and $[c_x, c_y]$ is the principal point. Given these notations, the camera model can be described by $[f_x, f_y, c_x, c_y]$.

3.2 Depth Measurement Calibration

Several models have been proposed for depth calibration [12,2,4], transforming disparity d_k into depth value z. We use the calibration function proposed in [12,2] since it strongly resembles the functional form of the relationship between depth and pixel offset given on the ROS.org wiki page [18]. The function is defined as:

$$z(u, v) = \frac{1}{\gamma_1 d_k(u, v) + \gamma_0} \tag{3}$$

where $d_k(u, v)$ is the disparity value at image coordinate $[u, v]$, γ_0 and γ_1 are part of the intrinsic parameters in depth sensor to be estimated.

3.3 Disparity Distortion Correction

We take the same distortion model in as [11] that has per-pixel coefficients and decays exponentially with increasing disparity:

$$d_k(u, v) = d(u, v) + D(u, v) \cdot \exp(\alpha_0 - \alpha_1 d(u, v)) \tag{4}$$

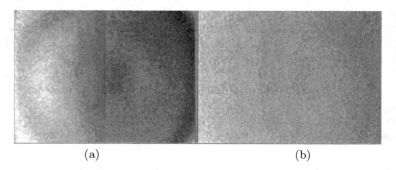

(a)   (b)

Fig. 1. Depth images before (a) and after (b) disparity distortion correction

where $d(u, v)$ is the disparity returned by the device, D is a matrix containing the per-pixel coefficients, $[\alpha_0, \alpha_1]$ models the decay of the error pattern, and $d_k(u, v)$ is calculated by Equation 3 with measured distance. An example of disparity distortion correction is given in Fig. 1.

It raises the problem of how to get the ground truth of depth value, as it is difficult for us to accurately measure the absolute distance between the depth camera and a fronto-parallel surface. However we observe that it is much easier for us to precisely measure the relative distance between two camera positions, with the assistance of software toolkit that can approximately determine whether the current sensor is vertical to the planar surface or not. Therefore we developed a toolkit to help acquire the desired depth data, and compute the ground truth of distance in an optimal sense by taking $d_k(u, v)$ as the internal variable in the iterative optimization. Its initial value is the approximate distance measured between the camera and the planar surface in the first reference camera position. The ground truth distance of the other camera positions are accordingly calculated by the precisely measured relative distances to the same reference camera position.

3.4   Iterative Optimization

The overall objective function for intrinsic parameter estimation has two components - the distance error and the angle error computed from the reference cuboids. The calculation of the distances between parallel surfaces and the angles of neighboring surface of cuboids is easy. It firstly builds up the plane equations of the relevant surfaces by fitting the converted 3D point clouds from the visible disparity image after the correction of IR camera and disparity distortion. Then the length, width and height of the cuboids are computed from the plane equations of the corresponding parallel surfaces, and the angles between the neighboring surfaces are calculated from the plane normals of neighboring surfaces in cuboids.

Formally, the overall objective function for intrinsic calibration is defined as the linear combination of angle and distance errors:

$$E = S \sum_{\text{view}} (\lambda E_a + (1 - \lambda) E_d), \tag{5}$$

where $S = 1/(\sum_{\text{view}} \sum_{i,j} 1)$, E_a is the angle errors, E_d is the distance errors, and λ is the weight of E_a. An instance of E_a and E_d is defined as

$$E_a = \sum_{i,j} \left(\frac{\theta_{i,j} - \bar{\theta}_{i,j}}{\bar{\theta}_{i,j}} \right)^2, \tag{6}$$

$$E_d = \sum_{i,j} \left(\frac{\delta_{i,j} - \bar{\delta}_{i,j}}{\bar{\delta}_{i,j}} \right)^2, \tag{7}$$

where $\theta_{i,j}$ and $\delta_{i,j}$ are computed angle and distance respectively, whose externally measured ground truth values are $\bar{\delta}_{i,j}$ and $\bar{\theta}_{i,j}$ respectively. More definitions for E_a and E_d are discussed and evaluated in Sec 4.3.

$\delta_{i,j}$ and $\theta_{i,j}$ are calculated by following equations:

$$\delta_{i,j} = \left(\frac{1}{|Q_i|} \sum_{\mathbf{q}_k \in Q_i} \frac{|\mathbf{P}_j \cdot \hat{\mathbf{q}}_k|}{|\mathbf{n}_j|} + \frac{1}{|Q_j|} \sum_{\mathbf{q}_k \in Q_j} \frac{|\mathbf{P}_i \cdot \hat{\mathbf{q}}_k|}{|\mathbf{n}_i|} \right)/2, \tag{8}$$

$$\theta_{i,j} = \arccos \left(\frac{\mathbf{n}_i \cdot \mathbf{n}_j}{|\mathbf{n}_i||\mathbf{n}_j|} \right), \tag{9}$$

where $\mathbf{P}_i = (a_i, b_i, c_i, d_i)$ and $\mathbf{P}_j = (a_j, b_j, c_j, d_j)$ represent two planes equations fitted from two 3D point sets Q_i and Q_j respectively, $\hat{\mathbf{q}}_k = (x_k, y_k, z_k, 1)$, $\mathbf{n}_i$ and $\mathbf{n}_j$ are the normals of $\mathbf{P}_i$ and $\mathbf{P}_j$ respectively. Q_i and Q_j are converted from two depth pixel sets $\tilde{Q}_i$ and $\tilde{Q}_j$ respectively. Each depth pixel set corresponds to a manually marked region. For a depth pixel $(u, v, d(u, v))$, we convert it into a 3D point using

$$x = \frac{z(u - c_x)}{f_x}, \tag{10}$$

$$y = \frac{z(v - c_y)}{f_y}, \tag{11}$$

$$z = \frac{1}{r_1(d(u, v) + D(u, v) \cdot \exp(\alpha_0 - \alpha_1 d(u, v))) + r_0}. \tag{12}$$

Equations (10), (11), and (12) are derived from Equation (1), (2), (3), and (4). Accordingly, Q can be defined as

$$Q = g_{\text{cvt}}(\tilde{Q}, \mathbf{M}), \tag{13}$$

where $\mathbf{M} = (f_x, f_y, c_x, c_y, \gamma_0, \gamma_1, \alpha_0, \alpha_1, D)$ represents a vector composed of depth camera intrinsic parameters.

Given a 3D point set Q, the plane $\mathbf{P} = (a, b, c, d)$ are fitted through

$$\mathbf{P} = g_{\text{fit}}(Q) \tag{14}$$

$$= \arg \min_{a,b,c,d} \sum_{\mathbf{q}_i \in Q} (ax_i + by_i + cz_i + d)^2. \tag{15}$$

In our implementation, we employ VCG library [23] to solve it.

Given Equations (8), (9), (13), and (14), we can see $\delta_{i,j}$ and $\theta_{i,j}$ are functions of intrinsic parameters $\mathbf{M}$ and two depth pixel sets $\tilde{Q}_i$ and $\tilde{Q}_j$:

$$\delta_{i,j} = g_{\text{dis}}(\tilde{Q}_i, \tilde{Q}_j, \mathbf{M}), \tag{16}$$

$$\theta_{i,j} = g_{\text{ang}}(\tilde{Q}_i, \tilde{Q}_j, \mathbf{M}). \tag{17}$$

According to Equation (5), (6), (7), (16), and (17), we rewrite the overall objective function explicitly depending on the intrinsic parameters as

$$E = S \sum_{\text{view}} \left(\lambda \sum_{i,j} \left(\frac{g_{\text{ang}}(\tilde{Q}_i, \tilde{Q}_j, \mathbf{M}) - \bar{\theta}_{i,j}}{\bar{\theta}_{i,j}} \right)^2 + \right.$$
$$\left. (1 - \lambda) \sum_{i,j} \left(\frac{g_{\text{dis}}(\tilde{Q}_i, \tilde{Q}_j, \mathbf{M}) - \bar{\delta}_{i,j}}{\bar{\delta}_{i,j}} \right)^2 \right). \tag{18}$$

The iterative optimization for minimizing E follows a two step procedure as that in [11]. During the first step we optimize parameters $(f_x, f_y, c_x, c_y, \gamma_0, \gamma_1)$ over the cost E using the Levenberg Marquardt algorithm [20]. The initial value of these parameters are from the standard calibration of IR camera as that in [26], where the IR images for calibration are captured with libfreenect [1] (all raw data from the camera is captured with libfreenect in out implementation). The disparity correction parameters, i.e. D, α_0 and α_1 are initially set to 0. In the second step the optimized parameter values from the first step are fixed, and α_0 and α_1 are further optimized using the Levenberg Marquardt algorithm with a set of fronto-parallel surfaces spanning the entire view. Optimized α_0 and α_1 are then used to linearly solve each coefficient in D. The two steps iterate till the residual error is stable.

4   Evaluation of Sensor Accuracy

We have implemented the calibration algorithm, and in this section we will validate our approach by similar principles in [16].

4.1   Calibration Setting-Up

In our work, at least 3 well-manufactured cuboids are required for calibration, as 2 distances and 3 angles are minimally needed for an acceptable calibration. Sizes of cuboids are externally measured, $399.574 \times 249.596 \times 299.436mm$,

Fig. 2. Cuboids setting-up to calibrate the depth camera. Plane annotations are given in the right image

Table 1. Ground truth for calibration. Cuboids and plane annotations are shown in Fig. 2

Angle Between Planes	Degree	Distance Between Planes	Millimeter
$\bar{\theta}_{1,2}$	89.97	$\bar{\delta}_{1,10}$	399.57
$\bar{\theta}_{1,3}$	89.97	$\bar{\delta}_{4,10}$	180.25
$\bar{\theta}_{2,3}$	89.89	$\bar{\delta}_{5,2}$	199.19
$\bar{\theta}_{4,5}$	89.96	$\bar{\delta}_{7,10}$	219.43
$\bar{\theta}_{4,6}$	89.67	$\bar{\delta}_{9,3}$	198.95
$\bar{\theta}_{5,6}$	89.91		
$\bar{\theta}_{7,8}$	89.99		
$\bar{\theta}_{7,9}$	90.00		
$\bar{\theta}_{8,9}$	89.99		

Fig. 3. 10 views of captured calibration data in 3 different distances. The 1st, 2nd, and 3rd rows are captured with the distances from camera to cuboids as $75 - 115cm$, $90 - 135cm$, and $115 - 155cm$ respectively.

$349.326 \times 180.252 \times 199.192mm$, and $198.948 \times 249.378 \times 219.434mm$ respectively. The combination and its 10 numbered planar regions are illustrated in Fig. 2. Table 1 gives the ground truth measurements among these planar regions used for calibration. We capture data roughly at three different distances: 75-115cm, 90-135cm, and 115-155cm. In each distance, 10 frames of depth images are captured from 10 different views (see Fig. 3). For each frame, we first convert the raw depth image into a normal map by calculating the normal of each point.

Secondly we manually marked the visible surface on cuboid based on the normal map, as shown in Fig. 4. Each marked region has a corresponding plane annotated in Fig. 2. It is worth noting that there are invalid depth pixels in the object boundaries. These invalid pixels should be avoided in the estimation of normals. In Fig. 4, we can clearly see that boundaries are not included while manually marking regions of interest. In case a marked region still includes invalid pixels, we can remove them easily since their disparity values all equal to a constant value far from valid ones'.

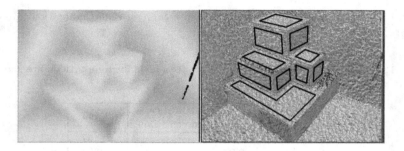

Fig. 4. The disparity map (left), the normal map, and manual segmentation (right)

In order to correct the disparity distortion, the depth data of fronto-parallel surface spanning the entire view are captured from 1m to 1.9m. However, it is difficult to manually align camera direction with the normals of fronto-parallel surfaces. Therefore, we develop a tool to semi-automatically help user make the decision. When camera is online, this tool lays a uniform grid over the depth image of each frame, and computes an averaged depth value in every rectangle. Since all depth pixels are valid except the ones near the right edge of the depth image, the grid is generated to be smaller than the depth image to exclude invalid depth pixels. As distortion pattern in depth image is centrosymmetric (see Fig. 1 (a)), the tool will alert user and automatically save current frame as a depth image for the fronto-parallel surface, when each averaged depth value is almost the same as the one computed in the symmetric box with respect to image center. With this tool, we can easily capture depth data for disparity distortion correction.

4.2   Calibration Accuracy

To evaluate the calibration accuracy, we firstly use a "hollow cube" as that in [11]. Three neighboring planes are fitted to the 3D point cloud from disparity image. The computed angles errors between neighboring planes are $0.4°$, $0.05°$, and $0.4°$. It achieves a comparable accuracy in their evaluation experiment [11].

Combo 1   Combo 2

Fig. 5. Cuboids setup for the validation experiment. Plane annotations are also shown in this Fig.

However, with a "hollow cube", only angles can be estimated. For a more general evaluation which includes both angles and distances, we employ a set of combos of solid cubes.

Depth images are captured from two combos of cuboids (see Fig. 5) different from those in calibration. Table 2 summarizes the ground truth measurements among planar regions used for evaluation. The height of the cuboid refers to the distance between plane 1 and 4 (see Fig. 5) of a cuboid. We compare the accuracy of our calibration method and the-state-of-the-art method proposed by Herrera et al. [11]. The depth data for evaluation are also captured in three different distances: 75-115cm, 90-135cm, and 115-155cm. We assign indexes 1, 2, and 3 to the three distances for convenience. At each distance, 20 frames of depth images are captured from 20 different views respectively. Given a depth image, the evaluation error for angles is defined as $\hat{\theta} = (|\theta_{1,2} - \bar{\theta}_{1,2}| + |\theta_{1,3} - \bar{\theta}_{1,3}| + |\theta_{2,3} - \bar{\theta}_{2,3}|)/3$. The evaluation error for height is defined as $\hat{\delta} = |\delta_{1,4} - \bar{\delta}_{1,4}|$.

Firstly, we empirically set calibration parameter λ to 0.75, and the calibration result is $[f_x, f_y, c_x, c_y, \gamma_0, \gamma_1, \alpha_0, \alpha_1] = [580.083, 585.555, 311.101, 238.108, 3.0582, -0.00280854, -19.0559, 0.0023218]$ (matrix D is too large to be shown here). The resulting evaluation is presented in Fig. 6. To evaluate Herrera et al.'s method [11], we use their matlab toolbox for calibration. In Herrera et al.'s matlab toolbox (see doc\doc_2_1.pdf in their latest toolbox), they recommend capturing 30 images for calibration. Therefore, 30 images are captured for both methods while calibrating them (in fact 10 images are sufficient for our calibration). The resultant precision of our method at all distances are higher than that in the peer method [11]. When sufficient images are given, Raposo et al. [24] achieves similar results to that in Herrera et al [11]. Hence, in this situation, our method can deliver better results than Raposo et al. [24]. In current implementation, we use the method of Smisek et al. [26] for initialization, while some other methods [29][2] can also be used for initialization. In principle, calibration accuracy of Zhang and Zhang's method [29] will not be higher than that of Smisek et al. [26], who also stated that their method is better than Burrus' one [2]. Fig. 6 also shows resultant evaluation of Smisek's method [26], which are obviously worse than ours. Therefore, our calibration accuracy is also higher than that in methods [2][29].

Table 2. Cube measurements for evaluation. Cuboids and plane annotations are shown in Fig. 5.

Angle Between Planes	Degree	Distance Between Planes	Millimeter
Combo 1			
$\theta_{1,2}$	89.99	$\delta_{1,4}$	349.25
$\theta_{1,3}$	90.02		
$\theta_{2,3}$	90.02		
Combo 2			
$\theta_{1,2}$	90.02	$\delta_{1,4}$	300.08
$\theta_{1,3}$	89.99		
$\theta_{2,3}$	90.02		

To evaluate the role of weight λ in the objective function, we experiment five different values from 0 to 1 (see Fig. 7). To clearly demonstrate the effect of λ, for each test value of λ, we average the angle and height errors as

$$\varepsilon_a = \frac{1}{60} \sum_{j=1}^{3} \sum_{i=1}^{20} \hat{\theta}_{i,j}, \tag{19}$$

$$\varepsilon_d = \frac{1}{60} \sum_{j=1}^{3} \sum_{i=1}^{20} \hat{\delta}_{i,j}, \tag{20}$$

where i is the index of frame and j is the index of distance from camera to cuboids. We clearly see that minimum errors of angle and height are both achieved when λ is roughly from 0.5 to 0.75. Hence, both the angle and distance constraints in cuboids should be taken into consideration when building up the objective functions for intrinsic calibration.

The distance from depth camera to the cuboids is also an important factor of evaluation error. Hence, we average the angle and height errors as $\frac{1}{20} \sum_{i=1}^{20} \hat{\theta}_{i,j}$ and $\frac{1}{20} \sum_{i=1}^{20} \hat{\delta}_{i,j}$ respectively, where i is also the index of frame. Fig. 8 shows the errors computed with 3 different capturing distances, when $\lambda = 0.75$. We observe from the averaged errors that 90-135cm is the best working distance.

4.3   Discussion of Objective Function

There are alternative approaches to calculate the errors of angle and distance in a combo of solid cubes. With relative and absolute metrics, more definitions on

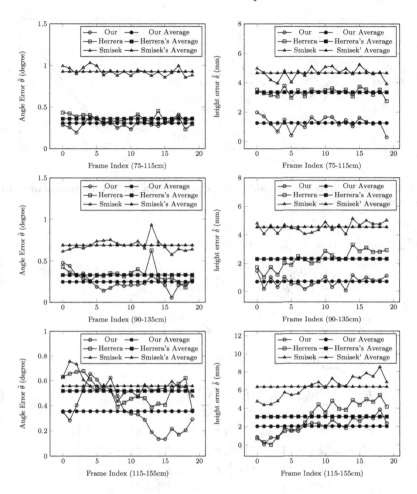

Fig. 6. Errors of evaluation across frames.

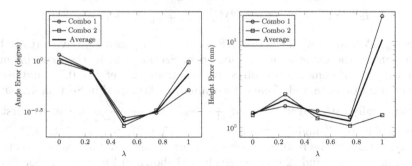

Fig. 7. Comparing errors of the calibrated depth camera with different λ values.

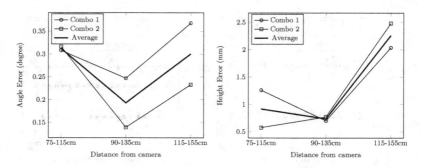

Fig. 8. Comparing errors of the calibrated depth camera with evaluation data captured in three different distances.

the objective function are given below:

$$E_a^1 = \sum_{i,j} \left(\frac{\theta_{i,j} - \bar{\theta}_{i,j}}{\bar{\theta}_{i,j}} \right)^2, E_d^1 = \sum_{i,j} \left(\frac{\delta_{i,j} - \bar{\delta}_{i,j}}{\bar{\delta}_{i,j}} \right)^2, \tag{21}$$

$$E_a^2 = \sum_{i,j} \left| \frac{\theta_{i,j} - \bar{\theta}_{i,j}}{\bar{\theta}_{i,j}} \right|, E_d^2 = \sum_{i,j} \left| \frac{\delta_{i,j} - \bar{\delta}_{i,j}}{\bar{\delta}_{i,j}} \right|, \tag{22}$$

$$E_a^3 = \sum_{i,j} (\theta_{i,j} - \bar{\theta}_{i,j})^2, E_d^3 = \sum_{i,j} (\delta_{i,j} - \bar{\delta}_{i,j})^2, \tag{23}$$

$$E_a^4 = \sum_{i,j} |\theta_{i,j} - \bar{\theta}_{i,j}|, E_d^4 = \sum_{i,j} |\delta_{i,j} - \bar{\delta}_{i,j}|, \tag{24}$$

$$E_a^5 = \omega_a^5 E_a^1 + (1 - \omega_a^5) E_a^2, E_d^5 = \omega_d^5 E_d^1 + (1 - \omega_d^5) E_d^2, \tag{25}$$

$$E_a^6 = \omega_a^6 E_a^1 + (1 - \omega_a^6) E_a^3, E_d^6 = \omega_d^6 E_d^1 + (1 - \omega_d^6) E_d^3, \tag{26}$$

$$E_a^7 = \omega_a^7 E_a^1 + (1 - \omega_a^7) E_a^4, E_d^7 = \omega_d^7 E_d^1 + (1 - \omega_d^7) E_d^4, \tag{27}$$

$$E_a^8 = \omega_a^8 E_a^2 + (1 - \omega_a^8) E_a^3, E_d^8 = \omega_d^8 E_d^2 + (1 - \omega_d^8) E_d^3, \tag{28}$$

$$E_a^9 = \omega_a^9 E_a^2 + (1 - \omega_a^9) E_a^4, E_d^9 = \omega_d^9 E_d^2 + (1 - \omega_d^9) E_d^4, \tag{29}$$

$$E_a^{10} = \omega_a^{10} E_a^3 + (1 - \omega_a^{10}) E_a^4, E_d^{10} = \omega_d^{10} E_d^3 + (1 - \omega_d^{10}) E_d^4, \tag{30}$$

where $\omega_a^i, \omega_d^i \in (0, 1)$ with $i = 5, 6, 7, 8, 9, 10$. Note E_a^1 and E_d^1 have already been utilized in all the experiments presented in Section 4.2. In the experiment for evaluating the aforementioned objective functions, we set $\lambda = 0.75$, and use the same calibration data and Combo 1's evaluation data used in Section 4.2. ω_a^i, ω_d^i are empirically assigned in terms of $\frac{\omega_a^i E_a^j}{(1-\omega_a^i) E_a^k} \approx 1$, $\frac{\omega_d^i E_d^j}{(1-\omega_d^i) E_d^k} \approx 1$ in the first 100 computations of E_a^i and E_d^i, where $(i, j, k) = (5, 1, 2), (6, 1, 3), (7, 1, 4), (8, 2, 3),$ $(9, 2, 4), (10, 3, 4)$. The resulting average errors of angle and height are calculated with Equation (19) and (20) respectively and shown in Fig. 9 (Equation (21-30) are numbered as $1, 2, \cdots, 10$ respectively in Fig. 9). Due to the difficult tradeoff between the errors of angle and distance, we will not recommend which one is the best objective function. However, we can clearly see that all the average

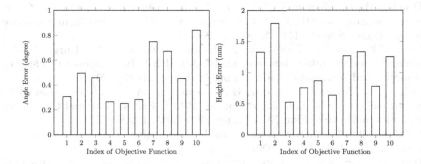

Fig. 9. The resulting errors evaluated with the candidate objective functions

angle errors are less than 1 degree, and all the average height errors are around 1mm. Such a calibrated precision is applicable to most 3D measurement and shape modeling.

5 Conclusion

The major contributions in our depth camera calibration system are 1) providing an alternative approach to estimate the intrinsic parameters of depth sensors merely by the depth data itself; 2) a relatively high-accuracy calibration of the low-precision depth sensors, better-fitted to the application of 3D measurements and shape modeling where high geometrical accuracy is usually required. What's more, our method is also useful in popularizing high-precise 3D modelling for CAD and 3D printing, since Kinect is much cheaper than other accurate 3D scanners.

The limitation of our approach is also obvious. Tens of thousands of 3D points are involved in the iterative plane fitting and non-linear optimization, and the calibration process is time-consuming. It takes around 5 minutes to accomplish the iterative optimization on a PC equipped with 4GB memory and an AMD Phenom^{TM}II X4 955 CPU 3.20GHz. In the future, we plan to develop a GPU-based parallel algorithmic pipeline for iterative plane fitting and non-linear optimization. Also we plan to extend our calibration system with an automatic or semi-automatic segmentation process, and develop a flexible extension to other types of depth cameras.

References

1. Blake, J., et al.: Openkinect, http://openkinect.org
2. Burrus, N.: Kinect calibration, http://nicolas.burrus.name/index.php/Research/Kinect
3. Dal Mutto, C., Zanuttigh, P., Cortelazzo, G.M.: Time-of-Flight Cameras and Microsoft Kinect^{TM}. Springer (2012)

4. Draelos, M., Deshpande, N., Grant, E.: The kinect up close: Adaptations for short-range imaging. In: 2012 IEEE Conference on Multisensor Fusion and Integration for Intelligent Systems (MFI), pp. 251–256. IEEE (2012)
5. Endres, F., Hess, J., Engelhard, N., Sturm, J., Cremers, D., Burgard, W.: An evaluation of the rgb-d slam system. In: 2012 IEEE International Conference on Robotics and Automation (ICRA), pp. 1691–1696. IEEE (2012)
6. Geiger, A., Moosmann, F., Car, O., Schuster, B.: Automatic camera and range sensor calibration using a single shot. In: 2012 IEEE International Conference on Robotics and Automation (ICRA), pp. 3936–3943. IEEE (2012)
7. Heikkila, J.: Geometric camera calibration using circular control points. PAMI 22(10), 1066–1077 (2000)
8. Heikkila, J., Silven, O.: A four-step camera calibration procedure with implicit image correction. PAMI, 1106–1112 (1997)
9. Henry, P., Krainin, M., Herbst, E., Ren, X., Fox, D.: RGB-D mapping: Using depth cameras for dense 3D modeling of indoor environments. In: Khatib, O., Kumar, V., Sukhatme, G. (eds.) Experimental Robotics. Springer Tracts in Advanced Robotics, vol. 79, pp. 477–491. Springer, Heidelberg (2012)
10. Herbst, E., Henry, P., Ren, X., Fox, D.: Toward object discovery and modeling via 3-d scene comparison. In: 2011 IEEE International Conference on Robotics and Automation (ICRA), pp. 2623–2629. IEEE (2011)
11. Herrera, C., Kannala, J., et al.: Joint depth and color camera calibration with distortion correction. PAMI 34(10), 2058–2064 (2012)
12. Herrera, D., Kannala, J., Heikkilä, J.: Accurate and practical calibration of a depth and color camera pair. In: Real, P., Diaz-Pernil, D., Molina-Abril, H., Berciano, A., Kropatsch, W. (eds.) CAIP 2011, Part II. LNCS, vol. 6855, pp. 437–445. Springer, Heidelberg (2011)
13. Izadi, S., Kim, D., Hilliges, O., Molyneaux, D., Newcombe, R., Kohli, P., Shotton, J., Hodges, S., Freeman, D., Andrew, Davison, o.: Kinectfusion: real-time 3d reconstruction and interaction using a moving depth camera. In: UIST, pp. 559–568. ACM (2011)
14. Karan, B.: Accuracy improvements of consumer-grade 3d sensors for robotic applications. In: 2013 IEEE 11th International Symposium on Intelligent Systems and Informatics (SISY), pp. 141–146. IEEE (2013)
15. Karan, B.: Calibration of depth measurement model for kinect-type 3d vision sensors (2013)
16. Khoshelham, K., Elberink, S.O.: Accuracy and resolution of kinect depth data for indoor mapping applications. Sensors 12(2), 1437–1454 (2012)
17. Kim, J.-H., Choi, J.S., Koo, B.-K.: Calibration of multi-kinect and multi-camera setup for full 3d reconstruction. In: 2013 44th International Symposium on Robotics (ISR), pp. 1–5. IEEE (2013)
18. Konolige, K., Mihelich, P.: kinect calibration/technical.ros.org, http://www.ros.org/wiki/kinectcalibration/technical
19. Kummerle, R., Grisetti, G., Burgard, W.: Simultaneous calibration, localization, and mapping. In: 2011 IEEE/RSJ International Conference on Intelligent Robots and Systems (IROS), pp. 3716–3721. IEEE (2011)
20. Lourakis, M.: levmar: Levenberg-marquardt nonlinear least squares algorithms in C/C++, http://users.ics.forth.gr/%7elourakis/levmar/
21. Macknojia, R., Chávez-Aragón, A., Payeur, P., Laganière, R.: Calibration of a network of kinect sensors for robotic inspection over a large workspace. In: 2013 IEEE Workshop on Robot Vision (WORV), pp. 184–190. IEEE (2013)

22. Menna, F., Remondino, F., Battisti, R., Nocerino, E.: Geometric investigation of a gaming active device. In: SPIE Optical Metrology. pp. 80850G–80850G. International Society for Optics and Photonics (2011)
23. Paolo Cignoni, F.G.: The visualization and computer graphics library, http://vcg.isti.cnr.it/~cignoni/newvcglib/html/index.html
24. Raposo, C., Barreto, J.P., Nunes, U.: Fast and accurate calibration of a kinect sensor. In: 2013 International Conference on 3DTV-Conference, pp. 342–349. IEEE (2013)
25. Shibo, L., Qing, Z.: A new approach to calibrate range image and color image from kinect. In: 2012 4th International Conference on Intelligent Human-Machine Systems and Cybernetics (IHMSC), vol. 2, pp. 252–255. IEEE (2012)
26. Smisek, J., Jancosek, M., Pajdla, T.: 3d with kinect. In: 2011 IEEE International Conference on Computer Vision Workshops (ICCV Workshops), pp. 1154–1160. IEEE (2011)
27. Teichman, A., Miller, S., Thrun, S.: Unsupervised intrinsic calibration of depth sensors via slam. In: Robotics: Science and Systems, RSS (2013)
28. Yamazoe, H., Habe, H., Mitsugami, I., Yagi, Y.: Easy depth sensor calibration. In: 2012 21st International Conference on Pattern Recognition (ICPR), pp. 465–468. IEEE (2012)
29. Zhang, C., Zhang, Z.: Calibration between depth and color sensors for commodity depth cameras. In: 2011 IEEE International Conference on Multimedia and Expo (ICME), pp. 1–6. IEEE (2011)
30. Zollhöfer, M., Martinek, M., Greiner, G., Stamminger, M., Süßmuth, J.: Automatic reconstruction of personalized avatars from 3d face scans. Computer Animation and Virtual Worlds 22(2-3), 195–202 (2011)

Statistical Pose Averaging with Non-isotropic and Incomplete Relative Measurements

Roberto Tron and Kostas Daniilidis

GRASP Lab, University of Pennsylvania, Philadelphia, PA, USA
{tron,kostas}@cis.upenn.edu

Abstract. In the last few years there has been a growing interest in optimization methods for averaging pose measurements between a set of cameras or objects (obtained, for instance, using epipolar geometry or pose estimation). Alas, existing approaches do not take into consideration that measurements might have different uncertainties (i.e., the noise might not be isotropically distributed), or that they might be incomplete (e.g., they might be known only up to a rotation around a fixed axis). We propose a Riemannian optimization framework which addresses these cases by using covariance matrices, and test it on synthetic and real data.

Keywords: Pose averaging, Riemannian geometry, Error propagation, Anisotropic filtering, Incomplete measurements.

1 Introduction

Consider N reference frames, each representing, e.g., the pose of a camera or of an object. Assume that we can completely or partially measure the relative rigid body transformations for a subset of all possible pairs of frames (see Figure 1). Our goal is to combine all these measurements and obtain an estimate of the position of each frame with respect to some global reference. In order to do so, if there are enough measurements available, we can exploit the geometric constraints induced by combining the poses in cycles. This usually takes the form of an optimization problem that "averages" the poses. However, we need to take into account that the estimates might be partially erroneous or unknown. For instance, the noise in the estimated translations could be higher in some direction, or two rotations could be constrained to be coplanar and have the same z-axis, but differ otherwise. If these errors and ambiguities are not correctly handled, they could propagate and bias the entire result. However, if correctly combined, the different measurements can complement each other into a complete and accurate solution. In this paper we propose to explicitly model non-isotropic noise and incomplete poses through the use of covariance matrices. This is similar to the idea of *gradient-weighted least-squares fitting* in the statistics literature [22]. More in detail, we propose to proceed as follows:

1. Estimate the relative rigid body transformations between pairs of references and their uncertainties or ambiguities.

D. Fleet et al. (Eds.): ECCV 2014, Part V, LNCS 8693, pp. 804–819, 2014.

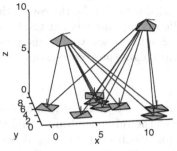

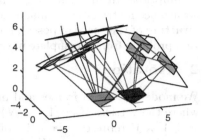

(a) Camera-Targets (CT) dataset.

(b) Camera-Depth sensor-Target (CDT) dataset.

Fig. 1. Example of different graphs of relative poses. Green pyramids: cameras. Green squares: targets with known structure. Blue pyramids: depth sensors. White squares: planes. Blue lines: complete pose estimates. Red lines: incomplete pose estimates. More details on this examples are given in §7.1.

2. Setup a graphical model for the joint probability of the poses.
3. Optimize the cost function associated with this model.

Note that our unknowns are poses, which lie on a Riemannian manifold. We will show in this work how this affects the steps above.

Prior Work. The idea of estimating covariance matrices to obtain better estimation accuracies has been a long-standing idea, even in the context of computer vision [23], [7]. In this work we use similar ideas, although from the more formal setting of Riemannian geometry.

Regarding pose averaging, this problem has been considered in numerous existing papers. The first contributions tried to solve the problem linearly using quaternions [11] or rotation matrices [15]. Following works are based on local optimization approaches: [12] uses Lie groups approximations, [19] applies gradient descent on the sum of squared Riemannian distances (i.e., an ℓ_2 norm), while [13, 20] use absolute distances (i.e., an ℓ_1 norm). In practice, the latter approaches are sensitive to local minimizers. Therefore, more recent work tackles the problem of obtaining good initializations: [4] solves a discretization of the problem using Belief Propagation, while [8] uses a formulation based on Lagrangian duality and [2] proposes a spectral method and an SDP relaxation. Closer to our approach is [5], where Belief Propagation is used for inference on the graphical models of the poses. However, no conditions for a consistent solution were imposed and the non-Euclidean structure of the rotations was not rigorously considered. Finally, Cramer-Rao bounds for this type of problems are considered in [3].

Paper Contributions. In almost all the previous work, the authors make the implicit or explicit assumptions that either the noise in the measurements is isotropically distributed or that the measurements themselves are complete. The major contribution of the present paper is to propose a feasible way to remove these assumptions. In addition, we give in §5 detailed formulae for the estimation of the covariance matrices from image data (while taking into account the Riemannian structure of the space of poses), and, in §6.2, a linear solution to the pose estimation problem from incomplete measurements (plane/pose correspondences).

2   Notation

We model the set of frames and measurements as a directed graph $G = \{V, E\}$, where the vertices $V = \{1, \ldots, N\}$ represent the reference frames and the edges $E \subseteq V \times V$ represent the pairs of nodes for which we have a rigid body transformation measurement. We denote the pose of each reference frame as a pair $g_i = (R_i, T_i) \in SE(3)$, where $SE(3) = SO(3) \times \mathbb{R}^3$ is the space of 3-D poses and $SO(3) = \{R \in \mathbb{R}^{3 \times 3} : R^T R = I, \det(R) = 1\}$ is the space of 3-D rotations. We also denote as $\tilde{g}_{ij} = (\tilde{R}_{ij}, \tilde{T}_{ij}) \in SE(3)$, $(i, j) \in E$, the measured relative rigid body transformations. We use the convention that (R_i, T_i) represents the transformation from local to global reference frames. Then, ideal, complete and noiseless measurements are given as $g_{ij} = (R_{ij}, T_{ij}) = g_i^{-1} g_j = (R_i^T R_j, R_i^T (T_j - T_i))$. The *tangent space* at $g \in SE(3)$ is given by $T_g SE(3) = T_R SO(3) \times \mathbb{R}^3$, where $T_R SO(3) = \{RV : V \in \mathfrak{so}(3)\}$ is the tangent space at $R \in SO(3)$ and where $\mathfrak{so}(3)$ is the space of 3×3, skew symmetric matrices. We can identify a tangent vector $V_R \in T_R SO(3)$ with a vector $v_R \in \mathbb{R}^3$ using the *hat* $(\cdot)^\wedge$ and *vee* $(\cdot)^\vee$ operators, given by the relations

$$v_R = \begin{bmatrix} v_{R1} \\ v_{R2} \\ v_{R3} \end{bmatrix} \overset{(\cdot)^\wedge}{\underset{(\cdot)^\vee}{\rightleftarrows}} V_R = R \begin{bmatrix} 0 & -v_{R3} & v_{R2} \\ v_{R3} & 0 & -v_{R1} \\ -v_{R2} & v_{R1} & 0 \end{bmatrix}. \tag{1}$$

Similarly, we can identify a vector $V = (\hat{v}_R, v_T) \in T_g SE(3)$ with a vector $v = \text{stack}(v_R, v_T) \in \mathbb{R}^6$. Given two tangent vectors $V_1, V_2 \in T_g SE(3)$ and the corresponding vector representations $v_1, v_2 \in \mathbb{R}^6$, we use the following Riemannian metric for $SE(3)$:

$$\langle V_1, V_2 \rangle = v_1^T v_2. \tag{2}$$

This metric is equivalent to consider $SE(3)$ as the cartesian (instead of semi-direct) product of $SO(3)$ and $\mathbb{R}^3$, and then summing the standard metrics of the two.

For a given $R \in SO(3)$, the *exponential* and *logarithm* map are denoted, respectively, as $\exp_R : T_R SO(3) \to SO(3)$ and $\log_R : U_R \to T_R SO(3)$, where $U_R \subset SO(3)$ is the maximal set containing R for which $\exp_R$ is diffeomorphic. For convenience, we also define $\text{Log} : U_I \to \mathbb{R}^3$, the vectorized version of the logarithm map at the identity, i.e., $\text{Log}(R) = (\log_I(R))^\vee \in \mathbb{R}^3$, where $R \in SO(3)$. For any given rotation $R \in SO(3)$, we denote as $\text{DLog}(R)$ the matrix representation of the differential of the logarithm. More precisely, let $R(t)$ be a smooth curve such that $R(0) = R_0$ and $\dot{R}(0) = \hat{v}_R$, then

$$\frac{\mathrm{d}}{\mathrm{d}t} \text{Log}(R)|_{t=0} = \text{DLog}(R_0) v_R. \tag{3}$$

The operators Log and DLog can be computed in closed-form [18].

For a given $g \in SE(3)$, the exponential and logarithm map are defined by the same maps applied independently on the rotation and translation components:

$$\exp_{(R,T)}(\hat{v}_R, v_T) = (\exp_R \hat{v}_R, T + v_T), \tag{4}$$

$$\log_{(R_1,T_1)}(R_2, T_2) = (\log_{R_1} R_2, T_2 - T_1). \tag{5}$$

Note that these definition are consistent with the choice of Riemannian metric in (2), and are different than the so-called *screw-motions* (see, e.g., [14]). If $\tilde{g} = (\tilde{R}, \tilde{T}) \in SE(3)$ is a random variable with distribution $p(\tilde{g})$, the covariance matrix with respect to $g = (R, T)$ (which is conventionally taken to be the mean) is defined as

$$\Sigma = \int_{SE(3)} v_{\tilde{g}g} v_{\tilde{g}g}^T p(\tilde{g}) \mathrm{d}SE(3), \tag{6}$$

where $v = \mathrm{stack}(\mathrm{Log}(\bar{R}^T \tilde{R}), \tilde{T} - \bar{T})$ and $\mathrm{d}SE(3)$ denotes the measure induced by the Riemannian metric [17]. Note that v is not defined on the so-called *cut locus* of g (i.e., outside of the set U_R mentioned above). However, it can be shown [9] that the cut locus has measure zero. Hence, for well-behaved distributions (such as those considered here), the integral in (6) is well defined.

Given a function $f : SE(3) \to \mathbb{R}^D$, we denote as $\mathrm{grad}_g f$ a unique set of tangent vectors $\{\mathrm{grad}_g^d f\}_{d=1}^D$ such that, for any tangent vector $v \in T_g SE(3)$, we have

$$\langle \mathrm{grad}_g^d f, v \rangle = \frac{\mathrm{d}}{\mathrm{d}t} f_d(\tilde{g}(t)) \Big|_{t=0}, \tag{7}$$

where f_d is the d-th component of f and $\tilde{g}(t)$ is a curve in $SE(3)$ such that $\tilde{g}(0) = g$ and $\dot{\tilde{g}}^\vee = v$. In practice, using the identification given by the hat operator, $\mathrm{grad} f$ can be expressed as a $6 \times d$ matrix. This is equivalent to the definition of gradient and Jacobian for the case where f is defined on the usual Euclidean space.

Lastly, we use I_d and 0_d to denote the identity and square zero matrix in $\mathbb{R}^{d \times d}$, respectively. Also, we denote with $\{e_d\}_{d=1}^3$ and $\{e_d'\}_{d=1}^2$ the standard bases in $\mathbb{R}^3$ and $\mathbb{R}^2$.

3   Problem Setting

For complete measurements $\tilde{g}_{ij}$, we assume a clipped Gaussian distribution with mean at the true values g_{ij}. This distribution has the form

$$p(\tilde{g}_{ij}; g_i, g_j) = k_{ij} \exp\left(-\frac{v_{ij}^T \Gamma_{ij} v_{ij}}{2}\right) \tag{8}$$

where

$$v_{ij} = \begin{bmatrix} v_{Rij} \\ v_{Tij} \end{bmatrix}, \quad v_{Rij} = \mathrm{Log}(\tilde{R}_{ij}^T R_i^T R_j), \quad v_{Tij} = \tilde{T}_{ij} - R_i^T(T_j - T_i), \tag{9}$$

Notation-wise, we will use the following partition of Γ_{ij}:

$$\Gamma_{ij} = \begin{bmatrix} \Gamma_{RRij} & \Gamma_{RTij} \\ \Gamma_{RTij}^T & \Gamma_{TTij} \end{bmatrix}, \tag{10}$$

where $\Gamma_{RRij}, \Gamma_{RTij}, \Gamma_{TTij} \in \mathbb{R}^{3\times3}$. The clipped Gaussian has been shown [17] to be a generalization of the usual Gaussian distribution in $\mathbb{R}^D$ to the manifold case, in the sense that it is the distribution that maximizes the entropy for a given covariance matrix Σ_{ij}. The constant k_{ij} is chosen such that $p(g_{ij})$ integrates to one over $SE(3)$ [17]. If the distribution is relatively concentrated (intuitively, far from a uniform distribution), the *dispersion* or *information matrix* Γ_{ij} is related, as a first order approximation [17], to the covariance matrix by the formula

$$\Gamma_{ij} \simeq \Sigma_{ij}^{-1} - \frac{1}{3}\text{Ric}, \tag{11}$$

where Ric is the matrix form in normal coordinates of the *Ricci* (or *scalar*) *curvature tensor*. In our case, we have the following:

Proposition 1. *With the choice of metric for $SE(3)$ made in §2, we have*

$$\text{Ric} = \begin{bmatrix} \frac{1}{2}I_3 & 0_3 \\ 0_3 & 0_3 \end{bmatrix}. \tag{12}$$

See the additional material for a proof. Intuitively, the correction in (11) takes into account the effect of clipping the tails of the Gaussian distribution.

For incomplete measurements, we model the unknown degrees of freedom as directions along which the covariance Σ_{ij} is infinite. In practice, this leads to dispersion matrices Γ_{ij} which are singular along the same directions.

Under the additional assumption that the noise terms affecting different edges $(i,j) \in E$ are independent, the joint distribution of the measurements is given by

$$p(\{\tilde{g}_{ij}\}_{(i,j)\in E}; \{g_i\}_{i\in V}) = \prod_{(i,j)\in E} p(\tilde{g}_{ij}; g_i, g_j). \tag{13}$$

We then formulate the problem of estimating the poses $\{g_i\}_{i\in V}$ as a maximum likelihood problem, i.e., as minimizing the following log-likelihood.

$$l(\{g_i\}_{i\in V}) = -\frac{1}{2} \sum_{(i,j)\in E} v_{ij}^T \Gamma_{ij} v_{ij}. \tag{14}$$

Note that in (14) we have excluded the constant terms containing the normalization constants k_{ij}, because they are not relevant for the optimization problem.

4   Minimization Algorithm

For the minimization of the cost (14), we will employ Riemmannian gradient descent with exact line search. The general form of this algorithm is given in

Algorithm 1. Riemannian gradient descent with exact line search

Input: Initial elements $\{g_{0i}\}_{i \in V} \in SE(3)^N$, a maximum step size $\bar{t}$.

1. **Initialize** $g_i(0) = g_{0i}$
2. **For** $l \in \mathbb{N}$, **repeat**
   (a) Compute the gradient $\{h_i\}_{i \in V}$ defined by (15)
   (b) Solve the line search problem

$$t^* = \operatorname*{argmin}_{t \in [0, \bar{t}]} l(\{\exp_{g_i(l)}(th_i)\}_{i \in V} \tag{19}$$

   (c) Compute the update

$$g_i(l + 1) = \exp_{g_i(l)}(t^* h_i), \quad i \in V \tag{20}$$

Algorithm 1. Other variations are also possible (e.g., using an inexact line search or a fixed step size). See [1] for details on such variations and for convergence proofs. The only part of the algorithm that is specific to our problem is in the computation of the gradient, which is given by the following.

Proposition 2. *The gradient of the negative log-likelihood function* (14) *is given by*

$$\operatorname{grad}_{g_i} l(\{g_i\}_{i \in V}) =$$

$$\left(\sum_{(i,j) \in E} (R_i^T R_j h'_{Rij} + h''_{Rij}) - \sum_{(j,i) \in E} h'_{Rji}, \ \sum_{(j,i) \in E} h_{Tji} - \sum_{(i,j) \in E} h_{Tij} \right) \tag{15}$$

where

$$h'_{Rij} = \mathrm{DLog}(R_{ij}^T R_i^T R_j)^T (\Gamma_{RRij} v_{Rij} + \Gamma_{RTij} v_{Tij}) \tag{16}$$

$$h''_{Rij} = \left(R_i^T (T_j - T_i) \right)^{\wedge} (\Gamma_{RTij}^T v_{Rij} + \Gamma_{TTij} v_{Tij}) \tag{17}$$

$$h_{Tij} = R_i (\Gamma_{RTij}^T v_{Rij} + \Gamma_{TTij} v_{Tij}); \tag{18}$$

See the Appendix for a proof.

4.1   Numerical Normalization

Notice that terms in (15) depend directly on the entries of $\{\Gamma_{ij}\}_{(i,j) \in E}$, which can be relatively large or small when the measurements are either really precise (small variances) or not precise at all (large variances). In practice, this has the effect that the step size t found by Algorithm 1 could become very small or very large. In order to avoid potential numerical problems that could arise, we rescale the cost (14) by performing the substitution

$$\Gamma_{ij} \leftarrow \frac{\Gamma_{ij}}{\mu_\Gamma} \tag{21}$$

where

$$\mu_\Gamma = \frac{1}{6|E|} \sum_{(i,j)\in E} \text{tr}(\Gamma_{ij}). \tag{22}$$

With this normalization the average of the eigenvalues of Γ_{ij} will be equal to one. Note that this rescaling does not affect where the minimizers of (14) are located.

5   Computing the Dispersion Matrices

In this section, we give details on how to compute the dispersion matrices Γ_{ij}. We consider the cases where we estimate complete poses from image data and where we have incomplete pose constraints.

5.1   Complete Poses from Image Data

In most applications, each relative transformation $\tilde{g}_{ij}$ is estimated as the solution to some minimization problem of the form

$$\tilde{g}_{ij} = \underset{g_{ij}}{\text{argmin}} \sum_{k=1}^{K} f(g_{ij}, x_{ij}^{(k)}), \tag{23}$$

where $\{x_{ij}^{(k)}\}_{k=1}^{K}$ represents a set of K measurements in $\mathbb{R}^D$ (e.g., matched image point coordinates). Then, one can think of the noise in $\tilde{g}_{ij}$ as being a consequence of the noise present in the data $x_{ij}^{(k)}$. We can extend well-known error propagation techniques (see, e.g., [7, 22, 23]) to the case of manifolds. Define $\nabla f(g_{ij}, x_{ij}^{(k)}) = \text{grad}_{g_{ij}} f(g_{ij}, x_{ij}^{(k)})$. The solution $\tilde{g}_{ij}$ of (23) implies the condition

$$\sum_{k} \nabla f(g_{ij}, x_{ij}^{(k)}) = 0 \tag{24}$$

Writing the first order Taylor expansion of (24) with respect to both g_{ij} and $x_{ij}^{(k)}$, we have

$$\sum_{k=1}^{K} H_{ijk} v_{ij} + \sum_{k=1}^{K} J_{ijk} v_{xij}^k \simeq 0, \tag{25}$$

where

$$H_{ijk} = \text{grad}_{g_{ij}} \nabla f(g_{ij}, x_{ij}^{(k)}) \tag{26}$$

$$J_{ijk} = \text{grad}_{x_{ij}^{(k)}} \nabla f(g_{ij}, x_{ij}^{(k)}) \tag{27}$$

and $v_{ij} \in T_{g_{ij}} SE(3)$, $v_{xij}^k \in \mathbb{R}^D$ represent the errors in the estimate g_{ij} and the measurements $x_{ij}^{(k)}$, respectively. Under the assumption that errors in the image point are corrupted by an isotropic Gaussian noise with zero mean and covariance $E[v_{xij}^k v_{xij}^k{}^T] = \sigma I_4$ for some $\sigma \in \mathbb{R}$, we can compute the covariance matrix of v_{ij} as

$$\Sigma_{ij} = E[v_{ij} v_{ij}^T] = (\sum_{k=1}^{K} H_{ijk})^{-1} (\sum_{k=1}^{K} J_{ijk} J_{ijk}^T)(\sum_{k=1}^{K} H_{ijk})^{-T}. \tag{28}$$

This result can then be plugged into (11) to obtain the dispersion matrices for the optimization problem.

As a concrete example, consider the estimation of the pose of a camera i from an object j with known geometry by minimizing the sum of reprojection errors

$$f(R_{ij}, T_{ij}, x_{ij}^{(k)}) = \|\pi(R_{ij}^T(X_{ij}^{(k)} - T_{ij})) - x_{ij}^{(k)}\|^2, \tag{29}$$

where X is the 3-D coordinate vector of a known point in the object's reference frame, x is its (measured) projection in the camera's image and π represents the perspective projection operator with unit focal length. The camera is assumed to be calibrated. Then, we have the following.

Proposition 3. *The matrices J_{ijk} and H_{ijk} in (28) for the cost (29) are*

$$H_{ijk} = J_x^T J_x + \sum_{d=1}^{2}(x_p - x_{ij}^{(k)})^T e_d H_{xd}, \qquad J_{ijk} = -J_x, \tag{30}$$

where

$$J_x = \frac{1}{\lambda_c^2} P M J_X w, \qquad \lambda_c = e_3^T X_c \tag{31}$$

$$H_{xd} = \frac{1}{\lambda_c^2}\left(\frac{1}{\lambda_c} J_X^T e_3 e_d^T M J_X + J_X^T(e_3 e_d^T - e_d e_3^T)J_X + \sum_{d'=1}^{3}(e_d^T M e_{d'} H_{Xd'})\right), \tag{32}$$

$$M = (\lambda_c I_3 - X_c e_3^T), \qquad P = \begin{bmatrix} I_2 & 0_2 \end{bmatrix}, \qquad x_p = \frac{1}{\lambda_c} P X_c \tag{33}$$

$$J_X = \begin{bmatrix} \hat{X}_c & R_{ij}^T \end{bmatrix}, \qquad H_{Xd} = \begin{bmatrix} \hat{X}_c \hat{e}_d & \hat{e}_d^T R_{ij}^T \\ R_{ij}\hat{e}_d & 0_3 \end{bmatrix}, \qquad X_c = R_{ij}^T(X_{ij}^{(k)} - T_{ij}). \tag{34}$$

See the additional material for a proof. Note that this result could also be used in PnP problems or in a bundle-adjustment iteration when the 3-D structure is fixed.

5.2 Partial Pose Constraints

In different applications, especially those combining sensors of different modalities, we can only obtain partial constraints between pairs of poses. For instance, consider the problem of calibrating the extrinsic transformation between a depth sensor and a camera using measurements from a plane in different positions (see Figure 1b, for instance). Using a known pattern on the plane, one can compute the relative transformation between the camera frame and a frame attached to the pattern. From the depth sensor, however, we can only estimate the equation of the plane. The relative transformation between the depth sensor and the plane frames can therefore be obtained only up to an in-plane rotation and translation. Similarly, consider the case where multiple known patterns are attached to the plane. We can then add the constraint that the reference frames should differ only by an in-plane rotation and translation.

Mathematically, these cases can be considered as follows. Assume that the measurement $\tilde{g}_{ij}$ is without noise, but with an ambiguity given by a rotation and translation in a plane with normal n, $\|n\| = 1$. We then have $\tilde{g}_{ij} = g_{ij}g_n$, where $g_n = (R_n(\theta), v_n)$, $R_n(\theta)$ is a rotation around of θ radiants around n and v_n is a vector orthogonal to n, i.e., $v^T n = 0$. Note that $\text{Log}(R_n(\theta)) = \theta n$. It then follows that the tangent vector v_{ij} is given by

$$v_{ij} = \begin{bmatrix} \theta n \\ v_n \end{bmatrix}. \tag{35}$$

We then propose to use the following dispersion matrix

$$\Gamma_{ij} = \begin{bmatrix} I_3 - nn^T & 0_3 \\ 0_3 & nn^T \end{bmatrix}. \tag{36}$$

It is then easy to check that the term $v_{ij}^T \Gamma_{ij} v_{ij}$ in (14) is zero if and only if v_{ij} is of the form (35), i.e., this quantity can be used to measure the similarity between the poses $g_i^{-1} g_j$ and $\tilde{g}_{ij}$.

6   Initialization

Since Algorithm 1 represents a local optimization, using good initial values for $\{g_i\}_{(i,j)\in E}$ is important. These can be found by using linear algorithms. We consider in this section the two cases of complete or incomplete pose estimates.

6.1   Complete Poses

For this case, we can use the spectral method of [2] to estimate the rotations. For the translations, we solve the least squares problem

$$\min_{\{T_i\}} \sum_{(i,j)\in E} \|\tilde{T}_{ij} - R_i^T(T_j - T_i)\|^2, \tag{37}$$

which can be rewritten in the form

$$\min_T \frac{1}{2} T^T A T + b^T T, \tag{38}$$

where $T = \text{stack}(\{T\}_{i \in V}) \in \mathbb{R}^{3N}$, and where the matrix $A \in \mathbb{R}^{3N \times 3N}$ and the vector $b \in \mathbb{R}^{3N}$ can be computed from $\{R_i\}_{i \in V}$ and $\{T_{ij}\}_{(i,j) \in E}$. Note that A is singular, due to the fact that if $\{T_i\}_{i \in V}$ is a minimizer of (37), then also $\{T_i + \tilde{T}\}_{i \in V}$ will be a minimizer for any $\tilde{T} \in \mathbb{R}^3$. In practice, one needs only to compute $T = A^\dagger b$, where $A^\dagger$ is the Moore-Penrose pseudoinverse of A.

6.2   Incomplete Poses

Assume that we have a node i for which all the measurements $\{g_{ij}\}_{j:(i,j) \in E}$ contain the ambiguity described in §5.2 and all the poses $\{g_i\}_{j:(i,j) \in E}$ are known (e.g., they can be directly measured). Assume that the equation of the plane for the ambiguity in g_{ij} is described as $n_{ij}^T X_i + d_{ij} = 0$ in the frame g_i, and $n_{ji}^T X_j + d_{ji} = 0$ in the frame g_j. Then, we have

$$n_{ij}^T R_{ij} X_j + n_{ij}^T T_{ij} + d_{ij} = 0, \tag{39}$$

from which we can obtain the following constraints:

$$R_i n_{ij} = R_j n_{ji}, \tag{40}$$

$$n_{ij}^T R_i^T (T_j - T_i) + d_{ij} = d_{ji}. \tag{41}$$

It follows that we can first estimate R_i through (40) and an orthogonal Procrustes analysis [10]. In practice, defining $C = \sum_{j:(i,j) \in E} R_i n_{ij} n_{ji}^T$, we can set $R_i = U \, \text{diag}(1, 1, \det(UV^T)) V^T$, where U, V are given by the SVD decomposition $C = U \Sigma V^T$. Once R_i is determined, we can use (41) to estimate T_i linearly in a least-squares sense.

7   Experiments

7.1   Synthetic Datasets

We first test the minimization algorithm described in §4 on two synthetic datasets.

Cameras-Targets (CT) Dataset. In the first dataset, we generate $N = 10$ reference frames where two frames (which represent "cameras") lie on the $z = 10$ plane and point downward while the remaining eight frames (which represent "targets" with known structure) lie on the plane $z = 0$ and point upward. The x and y coordinates of each frame are taken uniformly at random in a square with side length $L = 15$. The graph is formed by connecting each camera with the other and with each target. An example of this setup is depicted in Figure 1a. This scenario is meant to represent two poses of a camera moving above targets with known 3-D structure but unknown location. We generate each dispersion matrix (for the rotation part) as $\Gamma_{RRij} = U \Lambda^{-1} U^T$, where $U \in \mathbb{R}^{3 \times 3}$ is drawn uniformly at random from the space of orthonormal matrices and $\Lambda \in \mathbb{R}^{3 \times 3}$ is a diagonal matrix whose elements are variances drawn uniformly at random between 0.01 and 0.5 radiants (which are roughly equivalent to 0.5 and 30 degrees, respectively). A similar approach is taken for the translation part Γ_{TTij}, but with variances drawn uniformly between 0.1 and 2. For the cross-covariance matrices Γ_{RTij}, each entry is taken from a Gaussian distribution with standard deviation 0.01. The measurement $(\tilde{R}_{ij}, \tilde{T}_{ij})$ for each edge is generated by corrupting the true transformation according to the model in (8) and the generated covariances $\{\Gamma_{ij}\}_{(i,j)\in E}$. We then run the minimization algorithm of §4 on the generated dataset, first using the true covariance matrices $\{\Gamma_{ij}\}_{(i,j)\in E}$ ("Covariances"), and then again with $\Gamma_{ij} \leftarrow \frac{\mathrm{tr}(\Gamma_{ij})}{6} I_6$ ("Weighted") and $\Gamma_{ij} \leftarrow I_6$ ("Isotropic") for all $(i, j) \in E$. The last two configurations correspond, respectively, to just using the variance information without considering any coupling between rotation and translation, and to assuming that the errors are all isotropic and identically distributed. We repeated this experiment 50 times and, for each edge, we computed the angles between the relative rotations and between the relative translations from the poses obtained with the minimization algorithms (including the spectral initialization of §6.1) and those obtained from the ground truth. Figure 2 shows the empirical distributions of these errors, while Table 1 contains the corresponding mean and standard deviations. As a reference, we also include the same statistics for the initialization described in §6.1 ("Spectral").

From Figures 2a, 2b and Table 1a we can see that by averaging the measurements across the graph the errors (especially for the translations) are greatly reduced, both in mean and standard deviation. Also, by taking into account the correct covariance matrices, we obtain around 40% reduction in the mean error for the rotations and around 20% reduction for the translations. Intuitively, this is because our algorithm uses the fact that different measurements have different uncertainties in different directions.

Camera-Depth sensor-Targets (CDT) dataset. In the second dataset, we simulate a camera-depth sensor extrinsic calibration task. We pose the problem by using a plane with three targets on it and assume that each the camera can independently measure the pose of each target, while the depth sensor can only measure the normal and distance of the plane on which the targets reside. The

Table 1. Mean and standard deviation for the errors after localization and for the initial measurements. The errors are in degrees between ground truth and estimated rotation axes. The same applies to the translation directions.

(a) CT dataset

	Rotations Mean	Std	Translations Mean	Std
Covariances	4.130	2.041	1.856	1.063
Weighted	6.259	4.061	2.315	1.429
Isotropic	6.369	4.079	2.306	1.421
Spectral	9.208	4.381	3.971	2.267

(b) CDT dataset

	Rotations Mean	Std	Translations Mean	Std
Covariances	1.019	0.538	1.114	0.686
Linear	1.070	0.491	1.544	1.055

in-plane transformation between the targets is assumed unknown. We generate 20 random plane positions, and corrupt the corresponding measurements with an isotropic noise with variance 0.05 for both rotation and translation in the pose estimates, and both normal and distance in the plane estimates. We build the graph for our algorithm with edges between the camera and each target (complete poses), between each target and the depth sensor (incomplete poses) and between targets belonging to the same plane (incomplete poses). An illustration of this setup (with only three planes visualized) can be found in Figure 1b. We initialize our algorithm by fixing the camera frame at the origin, the targets' frames at their measured poses and the depth sensor frame at the solution given by the linear algorithm of §6.2. We repeat the localization for 50 different plane configurations, and measure the error on the rotation and translation direction for the pose of the depth sensor with respect to the camera. Similarly to before, Figures 2c, 2d and Table 1b show the cumulative distributions and the mean and standard deviation of the errors. Again, our algorithm improves the localization results with respect to the linear initialization, especially for the translation part.

7.2   Real Dataset

The dataset for this section has been obtained by collecting a sequence of 65 images of 6 AprilTags [16] (our targets) from a moving camera strapped onboard a quadcopter. The ground truth pose of each tag has been collected using a commercial VICON system, while the measurements of the relative pose between each visible tag and the camera are obtained using the software of [16] followed by a routine to minimize the reprojection error of the four corners of each tag. This dataset is particularly challenging because we have only four points available for pose estimation for each target and the dataset also contains a few mis-detections, which introduce outliers.

For both datasets, we use the method described in §5 to compute the covariance matrices for each estimate and run the same algorithms as in §7.1. For the evaluation, we consider only the nodes of the graph corresponding to the targets. Since we are interested in the error on the absolute pose, we align the result of each optimization to the ground truth using a Procrustes analysis. We record the root mean square error of the translations and the angle between the rotations. The results are reported in Table 2. the result using full covariance matrices ("Covariances") is strictly better than the result using equally weighted isotropic

Table 2. Errors on the pose of the tags (average angle for rotations, and root mean squared error for translations) with respect to ground truth for the Tag dataset.

	Rotations [deg]	Translations [cm]
Covariances	2.066	2.378
Weighted	3.293	1.853
Isotropic	2.331	2.670
Spectral	1.559	2.563

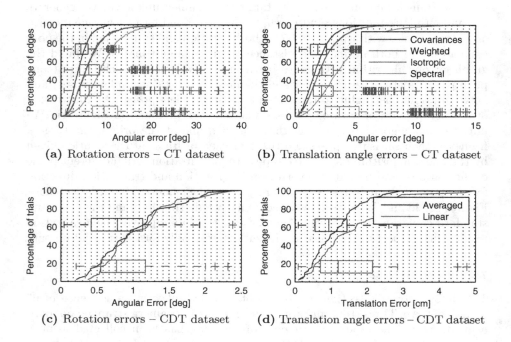

Fig. 2. Empirical cumulative distributions and box plots of the errors after localization. The various lines correspond to the estimation with exact, weighted and isotropic covariances and to the spectral initialization.

Fig. 3. Some of the images in the Tag dataset.

covariances ("Isotropic"). Using only the trace of the covariances ("Weighted") gives mixed results, with better translations but significantly worse rotations. We believe this might be due to the fact that, from only four points, the estimate of the covariance matrices is less indicative of the true covariance, and using only the trace might give better results. Finally, in both cases the initialization with the algorithm of [2] gives better rotation estimates but worse translation estimates. This might due to the fact that the datasets contain outliers due to wildly incorrect pose estimations, and the Frobenious-norm distance used for the rotations in [2] is slightly more robust to outliers than the Riemannian distance used here.

8   Conclusions and Future Work

In this paper we proposed an optimization method for averaging poses along a graph with non-istropic and incomplete measurements. Our technique can be seen as the extension of weighted least squares to this problem. We have also examined a method for analytically estimating the necessary covariance matrices in the case of pose estimation from objects with known geometry or with partial plane-pose constraints. We plan to expand this work by considering noise models with outliers and other kinds of ambiguities in the measurements, possibly combining it with other recent approaches such as [7, 23].

Acknowledgements. We gratefully acknowledge the support of grants ARL MAST CTA W911NF-08-2-0004, ARL Robotics CTA W911NF-10-2-0016, NSF-DGE-0966142, and NSF-IIS-1317788.

References

1. Absil, P.A., Mahony, R., Sepulchre, R.: Optimization Algorithms on Matrix Manifolds. Princeton University Press, Princeton(2008)
2. Arie-Nachimson, M., Kovalsky, S., Kemelmacher-Shlizerman, I., Singer, A., Basri, R.: Global motion estimation from point matches. In: International Conference on 3D Imaging, Modeling, Processing, Visualization and Transmission, pp. 81–88 (2012)
3. Boumal, N.: On intrinsic Cramer-Rao bounds for Riemannian submanifolds and quotient manifolds. IEEE Transactions on Signal Processing 61(7), 1809–1821 (2013)
4. Crandall, D., Owens, A., Snavely, N., Huttenlocher, D.P.: Discrete-continuous optimization for large-scale structure from motion. In: IEEE Conference on Computer Vision and Pattern Recognition. pp. 3001–3008 (2011)
5. Devarajan, D., Cheng, Z., Radke, R.: Calibrating distributed camera networks. Proceedings of the IEEE 96(10), 1625–1639 (2008)
6. Enqvist, O., Kahl, F., Olsson, C.: Non-sequential structure from motion. In: Workshop on Omnidirectional Vision, Camera Networks and Non-Classical Cameras, pp. 264–271 (2011)
7. Faugeras, O.: Three dimensional computer vision: A geometric viewpoint. The MIT Press (1993)
8. Fredriksson, J., Olsson, C.: Simultaneous multiple rotation averaging using lagrangian duality. In: Lee, K.M., Matsushita, Y., Rehg, J.M., Hu, Z. (eds.) ACCV 2012, Part III. LNCS, vol. 7726, pp. 245–258. Springer, Heidelberg (2013)
9. Gallier, J.: Notes on Differential Geometry and Lie Groups (in preparation, 2014), http://www.cis.upenn.edu/%7Ejean/gbooks/manif.html
10. Golub, G.H., Loan, C.F.V.: Matrix computations, vol. 3. Johns Hopkins University Press (1996)
11. Govindu, V.M.: Combining two-view constraints for motion estimation. In: IEEE Conference on Computer Vision and Pattern Recognition, vol. 2, pp. 218–225 (2001)
12. Govindu, V.M.: Lie-algebraic averaging for globally consistent motion estimation. In: IEEE Conference on Computer Vision and Pattern Recognition, vol. 1, pp. 684–691 (2004)

13. Hartley, R., Aftab, K., Trumpf, J.: L1 rotation averaging using the Weiszfeld algorithm. In: IEEE Conference on Computer Vision and Pattern Recognition (2011)
14. Ma, Y.: An invitation to 3-D vision: from images to geometric models. Springer (2004)
15. Martinec, D., Pajdla, T.: Robust rotation and translation estimation in multiview reconstruction. In: IEEE Conference on Computer Vision and Pattern Recognition, pp. 1–8 (2007)
16. Olson, E.: AprilTag: A robust and flexible visual fiducial system. In: IEEE International Conference on Robotics and Automation, pp. 3400–3407. IEEE (May 2011)
17. Pennec, X.: Intrinsic statistics on Riemannian manifolds: Basic tools for geometric measurements. Journal of Mathematical Imaging and Vision 25, 127–154 (2006)
18. Tron, R.: Distributed optimization on manifolds for consensus algorithms and camera network localization. Ph.D. thesis, The Johns Hopkins University (2012)
19. Tron, R., Vidal, R.: Distributed image-based 3-D localization in camera sensor networks. In: IEEE International Conference on Decision and Control (2009)
20. Dai, Y., Trumpf, J., Li, H., Barnes, N., Hartley, R.: Rotation averaging with application to camera-rig calibration. In: Zha, H., Taniguchi, R.-i., Maybank, S. (eds.) ACCV 2009, Part II. LNCS, vol. 5995, pp. 335–346. Springer, Heidelberg (2010)
21. Zach, C., Klopschitz, M., Pollefeys, M.: Disambiguating visual relations using loop constraints. In: IEEE Conference on Computer Vision and Pattern Recognition, pp. 1426–1433 (2010)
22. Zhang, Z.: Parameter estimation techniques: A tutorial with application to conic fitting. Image and Vision Computing 15, 59–76 (1997)
23. Zhang, Z., Faugeras, O.: 3D dynamic scene analysis: a stereo based approach. Springer (1992)

Appendix

This appendix contains the proof of Proposition 2. The proofs for the other results can be found in the additional material. In general, we will need to compute the gradient of some function f defined on $SE(3)$. The approach we use is as follows. First, we define the curves $(R_i(t), T_i(t))$ such that $\frac{\mathrm{d}}{\mathrm{d}t}(R_i(t), T_i(t))\big|_{t=0} = (\dot{R}_i(0), \dot{T}_i(0)) = (v\hat{}_{Ri}, v_{Ti}) = v$. Then, we compute the directional derivative at $t = 0$ of the function along such curves, which we will denote as $\dot{f}(v)$ (where v indicates the direction of the derivative). The result for the gradient will then follow from the definition in (7). Note that, in order to avoid clutter, we will omit, in the following, the explicit dependency of R_i, T_i, etc., on the variable t.

Proof of Proposition 2

We will need the following derivatives. We will use the fact that $R\hat{v}R^T = (Rv)^\wedge$ for $R \in SO(3)$.

$$\frac{\mathrm{d}}{\mathrm{d}t}\tilde{R}_{ij}R_i^T R_j = R_{ij}\dot{R}_i^T R_j + \tilde{R}_{ij}R_i^T \dot{R}_j = \tilde{R}_{ij}\hat{v}_{Ri}^T R_i^T R_j + R_{ij}R_i^T R_j \hat{v}_{Rj}$$
$$= \tilde{R}_{ij}R_i^T R_j(-R_j^T R_i \hat{v}_{Ri} R_i^T R_j + \hat{v}_{Rj}) = \tilde{R}_{ij}R_i^T R_j(-R_j^T R_i v_{Ri} + v_{Rj})^\wedge \quad (42)$$

$$\frac{d}{dt} v_{Tij} = -\hat{v}_{Ri}^T R_i^T (T_j - T_i) - R_i^T (v_{Tj} - v_{Ti}) = \left(R_i^T (T_i - T_j) \right)^\wedge v_{Ri} + R_i^T (v_{Ti} - v_{Tj}) \tag{43}$$

$$\frac{d}{dt} v_{Rij} = \text{DLog}(\tilde{R}_{ij} R_i^T R_j)(-R_j^T R_i v_i + v_j) \tag{44}$$

We can now take the derivative of the negative log-likelihood.

$$\frac{d}{dt} l(\{g_i\}_{i \in V}) = \frac{d}{dt} \frac{1}{2} \sum_{(i,j) \in E} (v_{Rij}^T \Gamma_{RRij} v_{Rij} + 2 v_{Rij}^T \Gamma_{RTij} v_{Tij} + v_{Tij}^T \Gamma_{TTij} v_{Tij})$$

$$= \sum_{(i,j) \in E} \Big((v_{Rij}^T \Gamma_{RRij} + v_{Tij}^T \Gamma_{RTij}^T) D_{ij} (-R_j^T R_i v_{Ri} + v_{Rj})$$

$$- (v_{Rij}^T \Gamma_{RTij} + v_{Tij}^T \Gamma_{TTij}) \big(R_i^T (T_j - T_i) \big)^\wedge v_{Ri}$$

$$- (v_{Rij}^T \Gamma_{RTij} + v_{Tij}^T \Gamma_{TTij}) R_i^T (v_{Tj} - v_{Ti}) \tag{45}$$

where $D_{ij} = \text{DLog}(R_{ij}^T R_i^T R_j)$. The expressions in Proposition 2 follow from (45) and the definition of gradient.

A Pot of Gold: Rainbows as a Calibration Cue

Scott Workman, Radu Paul Mihail, and Nathan Jacobs

Department of Computer Science
University of Kentucky, USA
{scott,mihail,jacobs}@cs.uky.edu

Abstract. Rainbows are a natural cue for calibrating outdoor imagery. While ephemeral, they provide unique calibration cues because they are centered exactly opposite the sun and have an outer radius of 42 degrees. In this work, we define the geometry of a rainbow and describe minimal sets of constraints that are sufficient for estimating camera calibration. We present both semi-automatic and fully automatic methods to calibrate a camera using an image of a rainbow. To demonstrate our methods, we have collected a large database of rainbow images and use these to evaluate calibration accuracy and to create an empirical model of rainbow appearance. We show how this model can be used to edit rainbow appearance in natural images and how rainbow geometry, in conjunction with a horizon line and capture time, provides an estimate of camera location. While we focus on rainbows, many of the geometric properties and algorithms we present also apply to other solar-refractive phenomena, such as parhelion, often called sun dogs, and the 22 degree solar halo.

1 Introduction

Understanding natural outdoor scenes is challenging because a large number of physical factors affect the imaging process. However, these same factors provide a variety of cues for estimating camera calibration and understanding scene structure. For example, image haze is a strong cue for inferring scene models [7], as are cloud shadows from a partly cloudy day [8], and the motion of shadows is a cue for camera calibration [34]. We explore another natural cue, the rainbow. Rainbows are a fascinating atmospheric effect—in addition to having strong symbolic meaning, they also have interesting geometric properties.

In particular, the location of a rainbow is exactly constrained by the relative geometry of the sun and the viewer. A rainbow is always centered around the antisolar point (the point exactly opposite the sun), and the outer radius of the rainbow is about 42° from the line connecting the viewer's eye to the antisolar point. In Figure 1, the projection of the antisolar point is visible as the shadow of the photographer's head. These strong geometric constraints make the rainbow a powerful calibration object.

In this paper, we explore these constraints both theoretically and practically. First, we characterize the minimal set of constraints necessary to capture the relative viewing geometry of the camera and the sun in both calibrated and

D. Fleet et al. (Eds.): ECCV 2014, Part V, LNCS 8693, pp. 820–835, 2014.

Fig. 1. The rainbow is an ephemeral, but well-defined, geometric object that can be used to perform camera calibration and provides constraints on camera location. The figure above shows the final result of our calibration method, with the image of the antisolar point (yellow circle) and two color bands (red and blue) on the primary rainbow. ("The Double Alaskan Rainbow" by Eric Rolph).

uncalibrated cases. Second, we introduce methods for estimating this geometry from an image of a rainbow, including an image-based refinement technique. Finally, we evaluate the ability of these methods to calibrate a large dataset of real-world images and present several use-cases: a data-driven approach to rainbow appearance modeling, rainbow editing and geolocation estimation.

From a practical standpoint, single-image calibration "in the wild" has become an important vision problem. Many cues have been proposed because not every scene has, for example, orthogonal vanishing points [3] or coplanar circles [4]. Rainbows and similar solar-refractive phenomena are an important new cue for this problem. While rainbows are rare, there are numerous rainbow pictures and many webcams will eventually view a rainbow. Rainbows have advantages for calibration: they are one of the few calibration cues suitable for "mostly sky" webcams, are easier to localize than the sun (which results in a large oversaturated image region), give strong constraints on the focal length and sun position from a single image, and have more distinctive appearance than sky color gradients.

We focus on rainbows but our geometric framework and analysis applies to other solar-refractive phenomena, e.g., sun dogs and halos, and gives a foundation for future work in using webcams to estimate atmospheric conditions using such phenomena.

1.1   Related Work

Our work introduces a new cue that provides constraints on intrinsic and extrinsic camera calibration. Typical approaches to intrinsic camera calibration rely on either reference objects, such as coplanar circles [4], camera motions, such as camera rotation [33], or both [35]. Extrinsic calibration approaches rely on matching to known, static scene elements [19]. However, when such objects do not exist, and the camera is in an unpopulated area without reference imagery, the problem is more challenging.

Recent interest in calibrating Internet imagery has led to the need for new techniques for intrinsic and extrinsic camera calibration. Much of this work has focused on problems associated with calibrating widely distributed cameras, such as webcams. In this domain, clear-sky appearance has been used to estimate orientation, focal length and camera location [11,16,14,17]. Other work has explored the use of video from cloudy days for estimating focal length and absolute orientation [8,9]. In addition, photometric and shadowing cues have been used for geolocalization and calibration [20,12,13,10,28]. Our work is most closely related to work on calibration and localization from sky appearance, with the important differences being that rainbows provide much stronger, single-frame constraints on the focal length and have very consistent color properties.

Methods for outdoor appearance modeling are used for applications ranging from compression to scene understanding. The main focus is on modeling the effect of sun motion and weather conditions on scene appearance. Sunkavalli et al. [31] build a factored representation that directly models sun motion and shadows. Subsequent work in this area has sought to extract deeper scene information, such as surface material properties [30]. More recently, the focus has shifted to estimating 3D scene models using photometric cues [1,2]. While most work has focused on static scene elements, there has also been significant research in building models of sky appearance. Lalonde et al. propose to use webcam image sequences to estimate global lighting models [15] for object insertion. Shen et al. [29] estimate local weather conditions. Peng and Chen [24] propose a random field model to estimate per-pixel sky cloudiness. We extend this line of research by including the geometry and appearance of rainbows.

2   Rainbow Image Formation

We briefly describe the physical process which leads to rainbows and the geometric relationship between the camera calibration, sun position and the image location of the rainbow.

2.1   Physical Rainbow Formation

We present the basic aspects of the physical process that creates rainbows, see [23] for additional details. Rainbows are an atmospheric phenomenon induced by the interplay of light and water droplets. Typically, rainbows begin with a passing rain shower leaving behind water droplets suspended in the air. In some light paths through a droplet, the ray refracts upon entering, undergoes an internal reflection, and refracts again upon exiting. These light paths generate a rainbow. The amount that a ray of light bends is a function of its wavelength. For example, red light (longer wavelength) bends slightly less than blue and violet.

The dispersion of light inside water droplets separates light into its component colors, resulting in a spectrum of light appearing in the sky.

The location of a rainbow depends entirely on the sun position. From the point of view of the observer, the outside of the rainbow (red) is at roughly a 42° angle relative to the antisolar point, the point directly opposite the sun. As we decrease the angular distance from 42°, the colors gradually change from red to violet. The rays from the rainbow to the observer form a conical surface (see Figure 2). While the precise relationship between angle and color depends somewhat on atmospheric scattering, particularly the size and shape of the water droplets [18], we assume spherical drops and use reference angles as computed in [27] (e.g. red = 42.3° and violet = 40.4°).

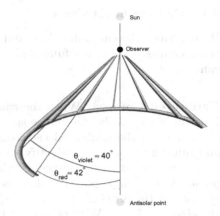

Fig. 2. Rainbows are visual phenomena with relatively simple geometric properties that result from the refraction of sunlight inside of millions of water droplets

2.2 Geometry of Rainbow Images

We now define the relationship between the image of the antisolar point (IAP) and a rainbow point with known color. Consider a world point, $P = [X, Y, Z]^{\mathsf{T}}$, that projects to an image location, $\lambda p = [\lambda u, \lambda v, \lambda]^{\mathsf{T}} = \mathbf{K}[\mathbf{R} \mid \mathbf{t}]P$, with camera intrinsics, $\mathbf{K}$, and extrinsic rotation, $\mathbf{R}$, and translation, $\mathbf{t}$. We assume the camera has zero skew, known principal point, square pixels, and is aligned with the world frame. This results in a simple pinhole camera model, $\lambda p = \mathbf{K}P = diag([f, f, 1])P$, with the focal length, f, as the only unknown.

We define the *absolute angle constraint* which relates the image point on the rainbow, p, and the IAP, s, as follows:

$$p^{\mathsf{T}}\mathbf{K}^{-\mathsf{T}}\mathbf{K}^{-1}s = \|\mathbf{K}^{-1}p\| \|\mathbf{K}^{-1}s\| \cos(\theta_p) \tag{1}$$

where, θ_p, is the angle between the rainbow ray, $\mathbf{K}^{-1}p$, and the antisolar point, $\mathbf{K}^{-1}s$. In practice, the camera calibration, $\mathbf{K}$, and the projection of the antisolar point, s, are unknown and we estimate θ_p from image data.

3 Rainbow to Calibration and Sun Position

The image of a rainbow provides strong constraints on the calibration of the camera and the position of the sun. We begin with an analysis of the constraints in different settings and then describe several alternative calibration methods that build upon them.

3.1   Constraint Analysis

We describe inherent ambiguities and minimally sufficient sets of constraints for two scenarios: one with a fully calibrated camera and one with an uncalibrated camera.

Calibrated Camera. When the camera calibration matrix, K, is known, the location of the rainbow in image space is entirely dependent on the IAP, s. We show that, in the calibrated case, three points at known angles are necessary and sufficient to uniquely identify s.

Consider a set of image points with known angles relative to the antisolar point. With a single point, p, there is a circle of possible solutions, on the view sphere, for the antisolar point, $K^{-1}s$, which make the required angle, θ_p, with the pixel ray, $K^{-1}p$. With two distinct points at known angles, there are at most two solutions where the respective circles intersect. Intuitively, this is because the image of the rainbow could be "bent" in two different directions. Therefore, three distinct points at known angles are necessary to uniquely estimate the antisolar point. This minimal set of constraints is visualized in Figure 3. It shows that, in the ideal case, the circle of possible solutions for each point all intersect at a single location, the antisolar point.

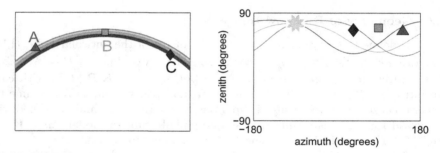

Fig. 3. Absolute Angle Constraint: (left) A synthetic rainbow image (FOV = 60°) with image points annotated on different color bands. (right) For each annotated point there is a circle on the view sphere where the antisolar point could be. In the calibrated case, three points at known angles are necessary to solve for an unambiguous antisolar point.

Given these constraints, numerous algorithms could be used to estimate the antisolar point, and hence the sun position, using three or more image constraints. We have developed analytic methods and nonlinear optimization methods, but we omit them here and instead focus on the uncalibrated case.

Uncalibrated Camera. We now consider the case of an uncalibrated camera in which both the IAP, s, and the focal length, f, are unknown. We initially focus on defining angular constraints and show that at least three points, at two distinct angles relative to the antisolar point, are required to fully constrain a solution for s and f. In the calibrated case, three points at known angles, which are not necessarily distinct, are needed to guarantee a unique solution for the antisolar point. When the focal length is unknown, we find that to eliminate an ambiguity caused by infinite focal lengths, points must be at two *distinct* angles. This is demonstrated visually in Figure 4.

Given a single point at a known angle, there is a circle of possible solutions on the view sphere, at every possible focal length, that make the required angle with the corresponding pixel ray. With two points at the same angle, there is an interval $[x, \infty)$ of focal lengths where the circles will intersect. At infinite focal length, the pixel rays lie along the optical axis and the circles converge. This shows we need at least two distinct angles to remove infinity as a solution. Therefore, with unknown focal length, the minimal configuration necessary to get an unambiguous solution for f and s is three points and two distinct angles.

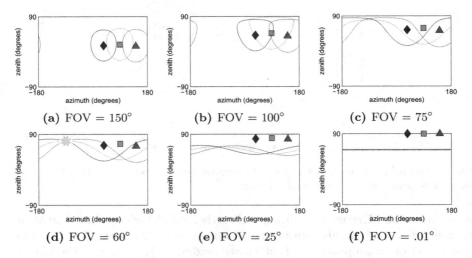

Fig. 4. Absolute Angle Constraint: In the uncalibrated case, the constraints for each annotated point (Figure 3, left) change as the focal length changes. At the correct focal length, all constraints are satisfied at the true antisolar point.

3.2   Estimating Sun Position and Calibration

Three rainbows points with at least two distinct angles are sufficient to guarantee a unique camera calibration solution. We now define several alternative objective functions for solving the calibration problem given the image of a rainbow.

Absolute Angular Error. Given a set of image points, $\{p_i\}$, at known angles, $\{\theta_i\}$, relative to the IAP, s, we formulate the following objective function:

$$\underset{f,s}{\text{argmin}} \sum_{i=1}^{M} \left| \cos^{-1} \left(\frac{p_i^{\mathsf{T}} \mathbf{K}^{-\mathsf{T}} \mathbf{K}^{-1} s}{\|\mathbf{K}^{-1} p_i\| \|\mathbf{K}^{-1} s\|} \right) - \theta_i \right| \qquad (2)$$

derived from the absolute angle constraint (1). We first grid sample 20 focal lengths, f, between 1 and 10 image widths, and for each, optimize over the IAP, s. The minimum error configuration is used to initialize a Nelder-Mead simplex search [22] to estimate the focal length and sun position.

Figure 5 shows the shape of this objective function with different numbers of known points and distinct angles. As described in Section 3.1, three points and two distinct angles is the minimal configuration necessary to ensure a unique global minima.

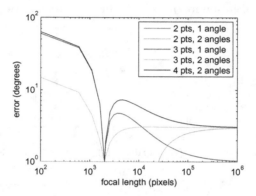

Fig. 5. The solution space of the absolute angular error objective function (2) as the number of points and distinct angles is varied

Absolute Pixel Error. In addition to directly minimizing error based on angular constraints, we can also optimize over image-space distances. Consider once again a set of image points, $\{p_i\}$, at known angles, $\{\theta_i\}$, relative to the IAP, s. We define the following optimization problem:

$$\underset{f,s,\{\tilde{p}_i\}}{\text{argmin}} \sum_i \|p_i - \tilde{p}_i\|^2 \qquad (3)$$

where $\tilde{p}_i$ is the projection of the image point, p_i, onto the rainbow and where the IAP, s, and the projection of p_i onto the estimated rainbow, $\tilde{p}_i$, are constrained by (1). We use Nelder-Mead simplex search [22] to estimate the focal length and sun position. We initialize the optimization by fitting a circle, with radius, r, and center, c, to the points: $f_0 = r/\tan(41°)$, $s_0 = c$, and $\{\tilde{p}_i\}_0 = \{p_i\}$.

As compared to the angular error method, this approach has the advantage of functioning correctly with image points at a single fixed angle, it does not have a trivial solution at $f = \infty$ and the objective function more accurately models typical user errors in clicking points.

3.3   Automatic Calibration Refinement

Since it can sometimes be difficult to identify the precise angle for a particular point on a rainbow, we propose a method to automatically refine manual calibration estimates by maximizing the correlation between the observed rainbow and the expected appearance of a rainbow.

We first estimate the expected appearance of a rainbow from a set of rainbow images with known focal length, f, and IAP, s. For each image, we compute the angle, θ_p, relative to s for each pixel p using (1):

$$\theta_p = cos^{-1}\left(\frac{p^{\mathsf{T}}\mathbf{K}^{-\mathsf{T}}\mathbf{K}^{-1}s}{\|\mathbf{K}^{-1}p\|\|\mathbf{K}^{-1}s\|}\right). \tag{4}$$

We define a rainbow signature as the average color change in the L*a*b* color space for a given antisolar angle, θ, as we move radially away from the IAP. We use the radial derivative because it is much less dependent on the scene behind the rainbow than the raw intensity. We construct a rainbow signature by quantizing θ (we use 200 bins between $[38°, 44°]$) and averaging the radial image gradients across the image regions that contain a rainbow. To model the expected appearance of a rainbow, we average the signatures for each image in our dataset and obtain an average rainbow signature, $E[\frac{\partial L}{\partial \theta}]$. To reduce blurring in the rainbow signature due to imperfect manual calibration, we sequentially align individual signatures [5] to the average signature until convergence.

Given this average rainbow signature and a new unseen rainbow, we refine our estimate of the focal length and the IAP by maximizing the average correlation between the signature of each radial line and the average signature using Nelder-Mead simplex search [22]. In practice, directly optimizing over the focal length and the IAP failed to converge to a globally optimal solution due to coupling between the parameters. To reduce this coupling, we reparameterize the problem by replacing the IAP, s, by a point on the rainbow at 41 degrees, on the line from the sun position to the principal point. The practical result is that the focal length can change without requiring a change in the sun position to keep the rainbow nearby in roughly the same image location. This small change significantly improved our automatic refinement results.

3.4   Fully Automatic Calibration

We describe a discriminative approach to rainbow localization and camera calibration that eliminates the need for manually clicking rainbow points. This is challenging because rainbows are transparent, often highly transparent, and their appearance varies due to atmospheric conditions [21], camera optics, CCD sensor properties and software post-processing.

For an uncalibrated rainbow image, we first use random forest regression to estimate two per-pixel labels: the likelihood that the pixel contains a rainbow and the most likely angle the backprojected pixel ray makes with the antisolar point. We use a 7×7 HSV patch and the eigenvalues and first eigenvector of the 2D

Fig. 6. Rainbow Localization: (left) input rainbow image, (middle) probability of rainbow pixel, and (right) predicted antisolar angle with red = 42° and blue = 40°

structure tensor of the hue channel for each pixel as low-level features. We build a training set by manually calibrating a set of images, assigning a label of rainbow or not (manually filtering non-rainbow pixels between 40 and 42 degrees), and computing the antisolar angle for each pixel using (4). An example image and corresponding per-pixel labels can be seen in Figure 6.

Using the per-pixel predictions, our approach is as follows: 1) select the most probable rainbow pixels (top 5 %, selected empirically to filter out false positives), 2) randomly sample three points and use the optimization from Section 3.2, assuming the estimated antisolar angle is correct, to get an estimate of sun direction and focal length, 3) use our image-based refinement technique from Section 3.3. We repeat this process multiple times and use the configuration with lowest error as the final calibration.

4 Applications

We use the geometric properties and algorithms we derived for several applications.

4.1 Calibration of Internet Imagery

We demonstrate the effectiveness of our calibration approaches on a dataset of 90 images we collected from a popular photo sharing site (http://flickr.com). We only include images from the iPhone 4, a popular camera phone, because it has a fixed focal length and has been used to capture and share many rainbow images. This is a realistic and challenging dataset containing many small, often faint rainbows, some barely visible (see Figure 7 for sample images). The dataset, including the results of our methods on all images, is freely available online (http://cs.uky.edu/~scott/projects/rainbows).

For each image, we manually click points along different color bands and estimate the calibration parameters using the optimization methods from Section 3.2. On average, we annotate 20 points per image (max 39, min 8, $\sigma = 8.4$) on two color bands. See Figure 7 for the results of this experiment, shown in terms of field of view for easier interpretation. We find that the absolute angular error approach gives more accurate results on some images, but the absolute

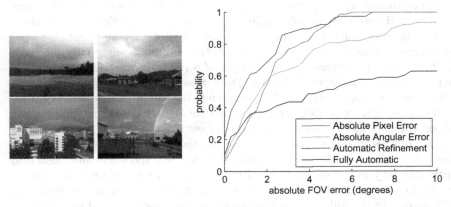

Fig. 7. (left) Example images from our rainbow image dataset. (right) The distribution of errors for various calibration approaches. The method based on pixel error produces fewer outliers. The blue curve shows the result of applying our refinement technique to the output of the pixel error method.

pixel error is more robust. The figure also shows that our image-based refinement technique (Section 3.3), when applied on the output of the absolute pixel error method, improves the calibration estimates relative to calibration based on manual clicks alone. Our fully automatic method (Section 3.4), trained using approximately 300 other rainbow images from Flickr (20 trees, 32 iterations), performs better than the fully manual approaches on some images, but fails dramatically on others. This highlights the difficulty of automatically labeling rainbow pixels in our challenging dataset.

Our implementation, running on a standard desktop PC, takes on average less than a second to perform manual calibration, and 30 seconds for refinement, for a single image.

4.2   Data-Driven Rainbow Appearance Modeling

We use the images in our dataset to construct a rainbow appearance model for the primary rainbow. To our knowledge this is the first attempt to build such a model in a data-driven manner. Previous work has focused on physics-based models [27]. These approaches, while very successful at rendering extreme rainbows, fail to capture the relative distribution of typical rainbow appearance. We show that a data-driven approach can capture this typical appearance, and, as we show in the following section, can be used to exaggerate or diminish the appearance of real rainbows.

We build upon our approach, described in Section 3.3, for estimating the expected rainbow appearance from color changes relative to the antisolar point. Instead of an average image, we estimate a linear basis which captures typical rainbow signature variation. To build this model, we collect rainbow signatures,

$\frac{\partial L}{\partial \theta}$, from all images in our dataset. We use the result of our automatic refinement method to estimate the antisolar point and focal length. In Figure 8, we show the marginal distribution of radial gradients, $P(\frac{\partial L}{\partial \theta}|\theta)$, by aggregating radial color derivatives for all radial lines that contain rainbows (manually filtered). This shows the characteristic color changes of a rainbow overlaid with rainbow signatures from two different images. From these we can see that individual rainbows vary in saturation and intensity and that these changes covary from angle to angle. This motivates the use of a Probabilistic Principal Component Analysis (PPCA) model [32] to describe rainbow signatures.

For all images in our dataset, we compute the rainbow signature from our refined calibration estimates, vectorize these signatures and aggregate them into a matrix. From this, we estimate the PPCA decomposition of rainbow appearance. In Figure 8, we show ten rainbow images randomly sampled from our PPCA model. In the following section we show one possible use of this rainbow appearance model.

4.3   Rainbow Editing

We use a gradient-domain editing approach [25], coupled with our PPCA-based rainbow color model, to exaggerate or diminish rainbows in images. We first calibrate the camera then compute the radial and tangential image gradients. For each radial line, we estimate the parameters of the PPCA model that best describe the color derivatives and then subtract these changes from the radial derivatives. We then solve the Poisson equations to find the image that best fits the updated derivatives. Figure 9 shows several examples of rainbows we attempted to edit, including one failure case due to poor initial calibration. A similar technique could be used to add a rainbow to an image without one, given the sun position, calibration, a soft matte and rainbow appearance parameters.

4.4   Video Geolocalization

We show how to estimate the geolocation of a static camera from a video containing a rainbow. We build on an existing algorithm [26] that computes sun position (zenith/azimuth angle) for a given time and location. Our approach is similar to previous work on sun-based localization [6] which is founded upon the relationship between time, sun position and geolocation. Unlike this previous work, our method does not require extensive pre-calibration of the camera. All we need for our method is the image of a rainbow, the capture time of the video, and an estimate of the horizon line.

Given an image, we use our calibration methods to solve for the focal length, f, and IAP, s. We then compute the sun direction, $S = -\mathbf{R}_{\phi\psi}^{-1}\mathbf{K}^{-1}s$, where $\mathbf{K} = diag([f, f, 1])$ and $\mathbf{R}_{\phi\psi}$ is a rotation matrix that encapsulates camera roll and tilt and is computed directly from the horizon line. Solving for this rotation allows us to compute the solar zenith angle of S relative to the world coordinate system. To estimate the geolocation, we first compute the true sun position for the image capture time [26] on a dense grid of possible geolocations. For each

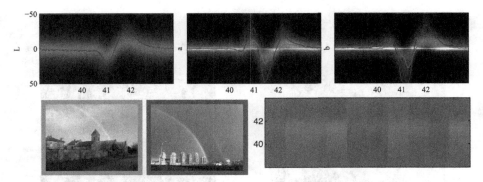

Fig. 8. (top) Conditional color derivative distributions for the L*a*b* color space. (bottom, left) Two rainbow images with rainbow signatures that correspond to two lines in the distribution plots. The green (red) line is the rainbow signature of the left (right) image. (bottom, right) Ten images randomly sampled from our empirical rainbow appearance model overlaid on a blue background image.

Fig. 9. Rainbow image manipulation. Several examples of editing an original image (left), by exaggerating (middle) and diminishing (right) the rainbow using our empirical rainbow appearance model. Poor results occur when we have suboptimal initial calibration (bottom)

location, we assign a score that reflects how close the image-based estimate of the sun zenith angle, z_{est}, is to the true zenith angle, z, for that location. We use the absolute difference between these values, $|z - z_{est}|$, as our score. We average this score across multiple images from the same video and choose the geolocation with the minimum value.

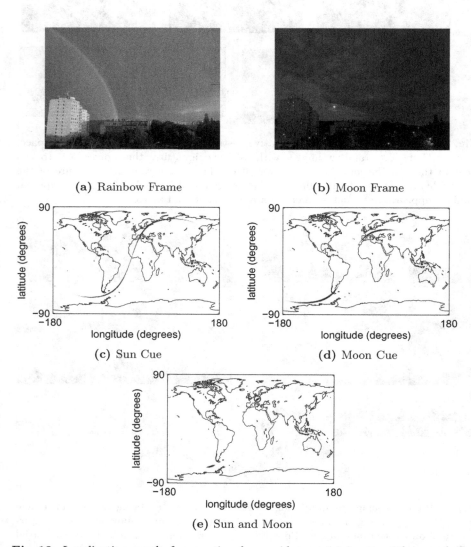

(a) Rainbow Frame   (b) Moon Frame

(c) Sun Cue   (d) Moon Cue

(e) Sun and Moon

Fig. 10. Localization result from a time-lapse video containing a rainbow and the moon. (a-d) Examples of single frame localization scores. (e) The final localization result obtained by combining scores from individual frames. (Video courtesy of Martin Setvak)

In Figure 10, we show several localization score maps generated from a time-lapse video, captured in the Czech Republic, that contains both a rainbow and the moon (which yields constraints on geolocation that are very similar to those provided by the sun). In the video, the rainbow is visible for only fourteen minutes and the moon for thirty. We sample four frames of each, using our automatic refinement technique to estimate the focal length and antisolar point, and hand label the centroid of the moon and the horizon line. Since the moon is in the frame for longer, it provides stronger constraints on location, but it requires the focal length we estimated from the rainbow to interpret. By combining the localization scores from all frames for both cues, we get a final localization result that clearly highlights the true camera location. Geolocating outdoor cameras is challenging and often requires combining multiple cues. To our knowledge, this is the first work on using rainbows (and potentially other solar-refractive phenomena) for camera localization.

5 Conclusion

We derive constraints and demonstrate methods that allow rainbows to be used for camera geolocalization, calibration and rainbow-specific image editing. These methods exploit the strong geometric cues that rainbows offer through the physics of their formation. This adds to a growing body of work termed "lucky imaging" that exploits occasional and transient atmospheric effects to simplify various image analysis challenges.

Acknowledgments. We gratefully acknowledge the inspiration, support and encouragement of Robert Pless. This research was supported by DARPA CSSG D11AP00255.

References

1. Abrams, A., Hawley, C., Pless, R.: Heliometric stereo: Shape from sun position. In: Fitzgibbon, A., Lazebnik, S., Perona, P., Sato, Y., Schmid, C. (eds.) ECCV 2012, Part II. LNCS, vol. 7573, pp. 357–370. Springer, Heidelberg (2012)
2. Ackermann, J., Langguth, F., Fuhrmann, S., Goesele, M.: Photometric stereo for outdoor webcams. In: IEEE Conference on Computer Vision and Pattern Recognition (2012)
3. Caprile, B., Torre, V.: Using vanishing points for camera calibration. International Journal of Computer Vision (1990)
4. Chen, Q.-a., Wu, H., Wada, T.: Camera calibration with two arbitrary coplanar circles. In: Pajdla, T., Matas, J(G.) (eds.) ECCV 2004. LNCS, vol. 3023, pp. 521–532. Springer, Heidelberg (2004)
5. Cox, M., Sridharan, S., Lucey, S., Cohn, J.: Least squares congealing for unsupervised alignment of images. In: IEEE Conference on Computer Vision and Pattern Recognition (2008)
6. Cozman, F., Krotkov, E.: Robot localization using a computer vision sextant. In: International Conference on Robotics and Automation (1995)

7. He, K., Sun, J., Tang, X.: Single image haze removal using dark channel prior. IEEE Transactions on Pattern Analysis and Machine Intelligence (2011)

8. Jacobs, N., Bies, B., Pless, R.: Using cloud shadows to infer scene structure and camera calibration. In: IEEE Conference on Computer Vision and Pattern Recognition (2010)

9. Jacobs, N., Islam, M., Workman, S.: Cloud motion as a calibration cue. In: IEEE Conference on Computer Vision and Pattern Recognition (2013)

10. Jacobs, N., Miskell, K., Pless, R.: Webcam geo-localization using aggregate light levels. In: IEEE Workshop on Applications of Computer Vision (2011)

11. Jacobs, N., Roman, N., Pless, R.: Toward fully automatic geo-location and geo-orientation of static outdoor cameras. In: IEEE Workshop on Applications of Computer Vision (2008)

12. Jacobs, N., Satkin, S., Roman, N., Speyer, R., Pless, R.: Geolocating static cameras. In: IEEE International Conference on Computer Vision (2007)

13. Junejo, I.N., Foroosh, H.: Estimating geo-temporal location of stationary cameras using shadow trajectories. In: Forsyth, D., Torr, P., Zisserman, A. (eds.) ECCV 2008, Part I. LNCS, vol. 5302, pp. 318–331. Springer, Heidelberg (2008)

14. Lalonde, J.-F., Narasimhan, S.G., Efros, A.A.: What does the sky tell us about the camera? In: Forsyth, D., Torr, P., Zisserman, A. (eds.) ECCV 2008, Part IV. LNCS, vol. 5305, pp. 354–367. Springer, Heidelberg (2008)

15. Lalonde, J.F., Efros, A.A., Narasimhan, S.G.: Webcam clip art: Appearance and illuminant transfer from time-lapse sequences. ACM Transactions on Graphics (2009)

16. Lalonde, J.F., Narasimhan, S.G., Efros, A.A.: Camera parameters estimation from hand-labelled sun positions in image sequences. Tech. rep., CMU Robotics Institute (2008)

17. Lalonde, J.F., Narasimhan, S.G., Efros, A.A.: What do the sun and the sky tell us about the camera? International Journal of Computer Vision (2010)

18. Lee, R.L.: Mie theory, airy theory, and the natural rainbow. Applied Optics (1998)

19. Li, Y., Snavely, N., Huttenlocher, D., Fua, P.: Worldwide pose estimation using 3D point clouds. In: Fitzgibbon, A., Lazebnik, S., Perona, P., Sato, Y., Schmid, C. (eds.) ECCV 2012, Part I. LNCS, vol. 7572, pp. 15–29. Springer, Heidelberg (2012)

20. Lu, F., Cao, X., Shen, Y., Foroosh, H.: Camera calibration from two shadow trajectories. In: International Conference on Pattern Recognition (2006)

21. McCartney, E.J., Hall, F.F.: Optics of the atmosphere: Scattering by molecules and particles. Physics Today (1977)

22. Nelder, J.A., Mead, R.: A simplex method for function minimization. The Computer Journal (1965)

23. Nussenzveig, H.M.: The theory of the rainbow. Scientific American (1977)

24. Peng, K.C., Chen, T.: Incorporating cloud distribution in sky representation. In: IEEE International Conference on Computer Vision (2013)

25. Pérez, P., Gangnet, M., Blake, A.: Poisson image editing. ACM Transactions on Graphics, TOG (2003)

26. Reda, I., Andreas, A.: Solar position algorithm for solar radiation applications. Solar energy (2004)

27. Sadeghi, I., Munoz, A., Laven, P., Jarosz, W., Seron, F., Gutierrez, D., Jensen, H.W.: Physically-based simulation of rainbows. ACM Press, New York (2012)

28. Sandnes, F.E.: Determining the geographical location of image scenes based on object shadow lengths. Journal of Signal Processing Systems (2011)

29. Shen, L., Tan, P.: Photometric stereo and weather estimation using internet images. In: IEEE Conference on Computer Vision and Pattern Recognition (2009)

30. Sunkavalli, K., Romeiro, F., Matusik, W., Zickler, T., Pfister, H.: What do color changes reveal about an outdoor scene? In: IEEE Conference on Computer Vision and Pattern Recognition (2008)
31. Sunkavalli, K., Matusik, W., Pfister, H., Rusinkiewicz, S.: Factored time-lapse video. ACM Transactions on Graphics, SIGGRAPH (2007)
32. Tipping, M.E., Bishop, C.M.: Probabilistic principal component analysis. Journal of the Royal Statistical Society: Series B (Statistical Methodology) (1999)
33. Wang, L., Kang, S.B., Shum, H.Y., Xu, G.: Error analysis of pure rotation-based self-calibration. IEEE Transactions on Pattern Analysis and Machine Intelligence (2004)
34. Wu, L., Cao, X., Foroosh, H.: Camera calibration and geo-location estimation from two shadow trajectories. Computer Vision and Image Understanding (2010)
35. Zhang, Z.: A flexible new technique for camera calibration. IEEE Transactions on Pattern Analysis and Machine Intelligence (2000)

Let There Be Color!
Large-Scale Texturing of 3D Reconstructions

Michael Waechter, Nils Moehrle, and Michael Goesele

TU Darmstadt, Germany

Abstract. 3D reconstruction pipelines using structure-from-motion and multi-view stereo techniques are today able to reconstruct impressive, large-scale geometry models from images but do not yield textured results. Current texture creation methods are unable to handle the complexity and scale of these models. We therefore present the first comprehensive texturing framework for large-scale, real-world 3D reconstructions. Our method addresses most challenges occurring in such reconstructions: the large number of input images, their drastically varying properties such as image scale, (out-of-focus) blur, exposure variation, and occluders (*e.g.*, moving plants or pedestrians). Using the proposed technique, we are able to texture datasets that are several orders of magnitude larger and far more challenging than shown in related work.

1 Introduction

In the last decade, 3D reconstruction from images has made tremendous progress. Camera calibration is now possible even on Internet photo collections [20] and for city scale datasets [1]. There is a wealth of dense multi-view stereo reconstruction algorithms, some also scaling to city level [7,8]. Realism is strongly increasing: Most recently Shan *et al.* [18] presented large reconstructions which are hard to distinguish from the input images if rendered at low resolution. Looking at the output of state of the art reconstruction algorithms one notices, however, that color information is still encoded as per-vertex color and therefore coupled to mesh resolution. An important building block to make the reconstructed models a convincing experience for end users while keeping their size manageable is still missing: texture. Although textured models are common in the computer graphics context, texturing 3D reconstructions from images is very challenging due to illumination and exposure changes, non-rigid scene parts, unreconstructed occluding objects and image scales that may vary by several orders of magnitudes between close-up views and distant overview images.

So far, texture acquisition has not attracted nearly as much attention as geometry acquisition: Current benchmarks such as the Middlebury multi-view stereo benchmark [17] focus only on geometry and ignore appearance aspects. Furukawa *et al.* [8] produce and render point clouds with very limited resolution, which is especially apparent in close-ups. To texture the reconstructed geometry Frahm *et al.* [7] use the mean of all images that observe it which yields insufficient visual fidelity. Shan *et al.* [18] perform impressive work on estimating

D. Fleet et al. (Eds.): ECCV 2014, Part V, LNCS 8693, pp. 836–850, 2014.

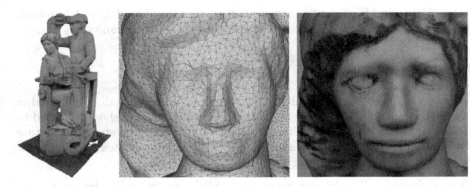

Fig. 1. *Left to right:* Automatically textured model reconstructed from a set of images, mesh close-up, and the same mesh rendered with texture

lighting parameters per input image and per-vertex reflectance parameters. Still, they use per-vertex colors and are therefore limited to the mesh resolution. Our texturing abilities seem to be lagging behind those of geometry reconstruction.

While there exists a significant body of work on texturing (Section 2 gives a detailed review) most authors focus on small, controlled datasets where the above challenges do not need to be taken into account. Prominent exceptions handle only specialized cases such as architectural scenes: Garcia-Dorado *et al.* [10] reconstruct and texture entire cities, but their method is specialized to the city setting as it uses a 2.5D scene representation (building outlines plus estimated elevation maps) and a sparse image set where each mesh face is visible in very few views. Also, they are restricted to regular block city structures with planar surfaces and treat buildings, ground, and building-ground transitions differently during texturing. Sinha *et al.* [19] texture large 3D models with planar surfaces (*i.e.*, buildings) that have been created interactively using cues from structure-from-motion on the input images. Since they only consider this planar case, they can optimize each surface independently. In addition, they rely on user interaction to mark occluding objects (*e.g.*, trees) in order to ignore them during texturing. Similarly, Tan *et al.* [22] propose an interactive texture mapping approach for building façades. Stamos and Allen [21] operate on geometry data acquired with time-of-flight scanners and therefore need to solve a different set of problems including the integration of range and image data.

We argue that texture reconstruction is vitally important for creating realistic models without increasing their geometric complexity. It should ideally be fully automatic even for large-scale, real-world datasets. This is challenging due to the properties of the input images as well as unavoidable imperfections in the reconstructed geometry. Finally, a practical method should be efficient enough to handle even large models in a reasonable time frame. In this paper we therefore present the first unified texturing approach that handles large, realistic datasets reconstructed from images with a structure-from-motion plus multi-view stereo pipeline. Our method fully automatically accounts for typical challenges inherent in this setting and is efficient enough to texture real-world models with hundreds of input images and tens of millions of triangles within less than two hours.

2   Related Work

Texturing a 3D model from multiple registered images is typically performed in a two step approach: First, one needs to select which view(s) should be used to texture each face yielding a preliminary texture. In the second step, this texture is optimized for consistency to avoid seams between adjacent texture patches.

View Selection. The literature can be divided into two main classes: Several approaches select and blend multiple views per face to achieve a consistent texture across patch borders [5,13]. In contrast, many others texture each face with exactly one view [9,10,15,23]. Sinha et al. [19] also select one view, but per texel instead of per face. Some authors [2,6] propose hybrid approaches that generally select a single view per face but blend close to texture patch borders.

Blending images causes problems in a multi-view stereo setting: First, if camera parameters or the reconstructed geometry are slightly inaccurate, texture patches may be misaligned at their borders, produce ghosting, and result in strongly visible seams. This occurs also if the geometric model has a relatively low resolution and does not perfectly represent the true object geometry. Second, in realistic multi-view stereo datasets we often observe a strong difference in image scale: The same face may cover less than one pixel in one view and several thousand in another. If these views are blended, distant views blur out details from close-ups. This can be alleviated by weighting the images to be blended [5] or by blending in frequency space [2,6], but either way blending entails a quality loss because the images are resampled into a common coordinate frame.

Callieri et al. [5] compute weights for blending as a product of masks indicating the suitability of input image pixels for texturing with respect to angle, proximity to the model, and proximity to depth discontinuities. They do however not compute real textures but suggest the use of vertex colors in combination with mesh subdivision. This contradicts the purpose of textures (high resolution at low data cost) and is not feasible for large datasets or high-resolution images. Similarly, Grammatikopoulos et al. [13] blend pixels based on angle and proximity to the model. A view-dependent texturing approach that also blends views is Buehler et al.'s Lumigraph [4]. In contrast to the Lumigraph we construct a global textured model and abstain from blending.

Lempitsky and Ivanov [15] select a single view per face based on a pairwise Markov random field. Their data term judges the quality of views for texturing while their smoothness term models the severity of seams between texture patches. Based on this Allène et al. [2] and Gal et al. [9] proposed data terms that incorporate additional effects compared to the basic data term. Since these methods form the base for our technique, we describe them in Section 3.

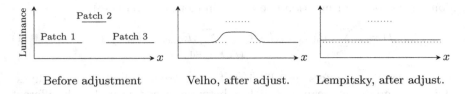

Before adjustment   Velho, after adjust.   Lempitsky, after adjust.

Fig. 2. Color adjustment (here in 1D). *Left:* Patch 2 is lighter than Patch 1 and 3, *e.g.* due to different exposure. *Center:* Velho and Sossai [23] let the luminance transition smoothly towards the seam's mean. *Right:* Lempitsky and Ivanov [15] adjust globally.

Color Adjustment. After view selection the resulting texture patches may have strong color discontinuities due to exposure and illumination differences or even different camera response curves. Thus, adjacent texture patches need to be photometrically adjusted so that their seams become less noticeable.

This can be done either locally or globally. Velho and Sossai [23] (Figure 2 (center)) adjust locally by setting the color at a seam to the mean of the left and right patch. They then use heat diffusion to achieve a smooth color transition towards this mean, which noticeably lightens Patches 1 and 3 at their borders. In contrast, Lempitsky and Ivanov [15] compute globally optimal luminance correction terms that are added to the vertex luminances subject to two intuitive constraints: After adjustment luminance differences at seams should be small and the derivative of adjustments within a texture patch should be small. This allows for a correction where Patch 2 is adjusted to the same level as Patch 1 and 3 (Figure 2 (right)) without visible meso- or large-scale luminance changes.

3   Assumptions and Base Method

Our method takes as input a set of (typically several hundred) images of a scene that were registered using structure-from-motion [1,20]. Based on this the scene geometry is reconstructed using any current multi-view stereo technique (*e.g.*, [7,8]) and further post-processed yielding a good (but not necessarily perfect) quality triangular mesh. This setting ensures that the images are registered against the 3D reconstruction but also yields some inherent challenges: The structure-from-motion camera parameters may not be perfectly accurate and the reconstructed geometry may not represent the underlying scene perfectly. Furthermore, the input images may exhibit strong illumination, exposure, and scale differences and contain unreconstructed occluders such as pedestrians.

We now give an overview over how Lempitsky and Ivanov [15] and some related algorithms work since our approach is based on their work. Section 4 describes the key changes made in our approach to handle the above challenges.

The initial step in the pipeline is to determine the visibility of faces in the input images. Lempitsky and Ivanov then compute a labeling l that assigns a view l_i to be used as texture for each mesh face F_i using a pairwise Markov random field energy formulation (we use a simpler notation here):

$$E(l) = \sum_{F_i \in \text{Faces}} E_{\text{data}}(F_i, l_i) + \sum_{(F_i, F_j) \in \text{Edges}} E_{\text{smooth}}(F_i, F_j, l_i, l_j) \qquad (1)$$

The data term E_{data} prefers "good" views for texturing a face. The smoothness term E_{smooth} minimizes seam (*i.e.*, edges between faces textured with different images) visibility. $E(l)$ is minimized with graph cuts and alpha expansion [3].

As data term the base method uses the angle between viewing direction and face normal. This is, however, insufficient for our datasets as it chooses images regardless of their proximity to the object, their resolution or their out-of-focus blur. Allène *et al.* [2] project a face into a view and use the projection's size as data term. This accounts for view proximity, angle and image resolution. Similar to this are the Lumigraph's [4] view blending weights, which account for the very same effects. However, neither Allène nor the Lumigraph account for out-of-focus blur: In a close-up the faces closest to the camera have a large projection area and are preferred by Allène's data term or the Lumigraph weights but they may not be in focus and lead to a blurry texture. Thus, Gal *et al.* [9] use the gradient magnitude of the image integrated over the face's projection. This term is large if the projection area is large (close, orthogonal images with a high resolution) or the gradient magnitude is large (in-focus images).

Gal *et al.* also introduce two additional degrees of freedom into the data term: They allow images to be translated by up to 64 pixels in x- or y-direction to minimize seam visibility. While this may improve the alignment of neighboring patches, we abstain from this because it only considers seam visibility and does not explain the input data. In a rendering of such a model a texture patch would have an offset compared to its source image. Also, these additional degrees of freedom may increase the computational complexity such that the optimization becomes infeasible for realistic dataset sizes.

Lempitsky and Ivanov's smoothness term is the difference between the texture to a seam's left and right side integrated over the seam. This should prefer seams in regions where cameras are accurately registered or where misalignments are unnoticeable because the texture is smooth. We found, that computation of the seam error integrals is a computational bottleneck and cannot be precomputed due to the prohibitively large number of combinations. Furthermore, it favors distant or low-resolution views since a blurry texture produces smaller seam errors, an issue that does not occur in their datasets.

After obtaining a labeling from minimizing Equation 1, the patch colors are adjusted as follows: First, it must be ensured that each mesh vertex belongs to exactly one texture patch. Therefore each vertex on a seam is duplicated into two vertices: Vertex v_{left} belonging to the patch to the left and v_{right} belonging to the patch to the right of the seam.[1] Now each vertex v has a unique color f_v before adjustment. Then, an additive correction g_v is computed for each vertex,

---

[1] In the following, we only consider the case where seam vertices belong to $n = 2$ patches. For $n > 2$ we create n copies of the vertex and optimize all pairs of those copies jointly, yielding a correction factor per vertex and patch.

by minimizing the following expression (we use a simpler notation for clarity):

$$\underset{\mathbf{g}}{\text{argmin}} \underbrace{\sum_{\substack{v \text{ (split into} \\ v_{\text{left}} \text{ and } v_{\text{right}}) \\ \text{lies on a seam}}} \left(f_{v_{\text{left}}} + g_{v_{\text{left}}} - (f_{v_{\text{right}}} + g_{v_{\text{right}}})\right)^2}_{} + \frac{1}{\lambda} \underbrace{\sum_{\substack{v_i, v_j \text{ are ad-} \\ \text{jacent and in} \\ \text{the same patch}}} \left(g_{v_i} - g_{v_j}\right)^2}_{} \quad (2)$$

The first term ensures that the adjusted color to a seam's left ($f_{v_{\text{left}}} + g_{v_{\text{left}}}$) and its right ($f_{v_{\text{right}}} + g_{v_{\text{right}}}$) are as similar as possible. The second term minimizes adjustment differences between adjacent vertices within the same texture patch. This favors adjustments that are as gradual as possible within a texture patch. After finding optimal g_v for all vertices the corrections for each texel are interpolated from the g_v of its surrounding vertices using barycentric coordinates. Finally, the corrections are added to the input images, the texture patches are packed into texture atlases, and texture coordinates are attached to the vertices.

4   Large-Scale Texturing Approach

Following the base method we now explain our approach, focusing on the key novel aspects introduced to handle the challenges of realistic 3D reconstructions.

4.1   Preprocessing

We determine face visibility for all combinations of views and faces by first performing back face and view frustum culling, before actually checking for occlusions. For the latter we employ a standard library [11] to compute intersections between the input model and viewing rays from the camera center to the triangle under question. This is more accurate than using rendering as, *e.g.*, done by Callieri *et al.* [5], and has no relevant negative impact on performance. We then precompute the data terms for Equation 1 for all remaining face-view combinations since they are used multiple times during optimization, remain constant, and fit into memory (the table has $\mathcal{O}(\#\text{faces} \cdot \#\text{views})$ entries and is very sparse).

4.2   View Selection

Our view selection follows the structure of the base algorithm, *i.e.*, we obtain a labeling such as the one in Figure 3 (left) by optimizing Equation 1 with graph cuts and alpha expansion [3]. We, however, replace the base algorithm's data and smoothness terms and augment the data term with a photo-consistency check.

Data Term. For the reasons described in Section 3 we choose Gal *et al.*'s [9] data term $E_{\text{data}} = -\int_{\phi(F_i, l_i)} \|\nabla(I_{l_i}(p))\|_2 \, dp$. We compute the gradient magnitude $\|\nabla(I_{l_i})\|_2$ of the image into which face F_i is projected with a Sobel operator and sum over all pixels of the gradient magnitude image within F_i's projection $\phi(F_i, l_i)$. If the projection contains less than one pixel we sample the gradient magnitude at the projection's centroid and multiply it with the projection area.

The data term's preference for large gradient magnitudes entails an important problem that Gal *et al.* do not account for because it does not occur in their controlled datasets: If a view contains an occluder such as a pedestrian that has not been reconstructed and can thus not be detected by the visibility check, this view should not be chosen for texturing the faces behind that occluder. Unfortunately this happens frequently with the gradient magnitude term (*e.g.* in Figure 9) because occluders such as pedestrians or leaves often feature a larger gradient magnitude than their background, *e.g.*, a relatively uniform wall. We therefore introduce an additional step to ensure photo-consistency of the texture.

Photo-Consistency Check. We assume that for a specific face the majority of views see the correct color. A minority may see wrong colors (*i.e.*, an occluder) and those are much less correlated. Based on this assumption Sinha *et al.* [19] and Grammatikopoulos *et al.* [13] use mean or median colors to reject inconsistent views. This is not sufficient, as we show in Section 5. Instead we use a slightly modified mean-shift algorithm consisting of the following steps:

1. Compute the face projection's mean color c_i for each view i in which the face is visible.
2. Declare all views seeing the face as inliers.
3. Compute mean μ and covariance matrix Σ of all inliers' mean color c_i.
4. Evaluate a multi-variate Gaussian function $\exp\left(-\frac{1}{2}(c_i - \mu)^\mathsf{T} \Sigma^{-1}(c_i - \mu)\right)$ for each view in which the face is visible.
5. Clear the inlier list and insert all views whose function value is above a threshold (we use $6 \cdot 10^{-3}$).
6. Repeat 3.–5. for 10 iterations or until all entries of Σ drop below 10^{-5}, the inversion of Σ becomes unstable, or the number of inliers drops below 4.

We obtain a list of photo-consistent views for each face and multiply a penalty on all other views' data terms to prevent their selection.

Note, that using the median instead of the mean does not work on very small query sets because for 3D vectors the marginal median is usually not a member of the query set so that too many views are purged. Not shifting the mean does not work in practice because the initial mean is often quite far away from the inliers' mean (see Section 5 for an example). Sinha *et al.* [19] therefore additionally allow the user to interactively mark regions that should not be used for texturing, a step which we explicitly want to avoid.

Smoothness Term. As discussed above, Lempitsky and Ivanov's smoothness term is a major performance bottleneck and counteracts our data term's preference for close-up views. We propose a smoothness term based on the Potts model: $E_{\mathrm{smooth}} = [l_i \neq l_j]$ ($[\cdot]$ is the Iverson bracket). This also prefers compact patches without favoring distant views and is extremely fast to compute.

4.3 Color Adjustment

Models obtained from the view selection phase (*e.g.*, Figure 3 (right)) contain many color discontinuities between patches. These need to be adjusted to minimize seam visibility. We use an improved version of the base method's global adjustment, followed by a local adjustment with Poisson editing [16].

Global Adjustment. A serious problem with Lempitsky and Ivanov's color adjustment is that $f_{v_{\text{left}}}$ and $f_{v_{\text{right}}}$ in Equation 2 are only evaluated at a single location: the vertex v's projection into the two images adjacent to the seam. If there are even small registration errors (which there always are),

Fig. 3. *Left:* A mesh's labeling. Each color represents a different label, *i.e.* input image. *Right:* The textured result with visible luminance differences between patches.

both projections do not correspond to exactly the same spot on the real object. Also, if both images have a different scale the looked up pixels span a different footprint in 3D. This may be irrelevant in controlled lab datasets, but in realistic multi-view stereo datasets the lookups from effectively different points or footprints mislead the global adjustment and produce artifacts.

Color Lookup Support Region. We alleviate this problem by not only looking up a vertex' color value at the vertex projection but along all adjacent seam edges, as illustrated by Figure 4: Vertex v_1 is on the seam between the red and the blue patch. We evaluate its color in the red patch, $f_{v_1,\text{red}}$, by averaging color samples from the red image along the two edges $\overline{v_0 v_1}$ and $\overline{v_1 v_2}$. On each edge we draw twice as many samples as the edge length in pixels. When averaging the samples we weight them according to Figure 4 (right): The sample weight is 1 on v_1 and decreases linearly with a sample's distance to v_1. (The reasoning behind this is that after optimization of Equation 2 the computed correction $g_{v_1,\text{red}}$ is applied to the texels using barycentric coordinates. Along the seam the barycentric coordinates form the transition from 1 to 0.) We obtain average colors for

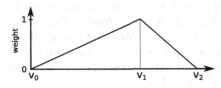

Fig. 4. *Left:* A mesh. Vertex v_1 is adjacent to both texture patches (red and blue). Its color is looked up as a weighted average over samples on the edges $\overline{v_0 v_1}$ and $\overline{v_1 v_2}$. *Right:* Sample weights transition from 1 to 0 as distance to v_1 grows.

the edges $\overline{v_0 v_1}$ and $\overline{v_1 v_2}$, which we average weighted with the edge lengths to obtain $f_{v_{1,\text{red}}}$. Similarly we obtain $f_{v_{1,\text{blue}}}$ and insert both into Equation 2.

For optimization, Equation 2 can now be written in matrix form as

$$\|\mathbf{Ag} - \mathbf{f}\|_2^2 + \|\mathbf{\Gamma g}\|_2^2 = \mathbf{g}^{\mathsf{T}}(\mathbf{A}^{\mathsf{T}}\mathbf{A} + \mathbf{\Gamma}^{\mathsf{T}}\mathbf{\Gamma})\mathbf{g} - 2\mathbf{f}^{\mathsf{T}}\mathbf{Ag} + \mathbf{f}^{\mathsf{T}}\mathbf{f} \qquad (3)$$

$\mathbf{f}$ is a vector with the stacked $f_{v_{\text{left}}} - f_{v_{\text{right}}}$ from Equation 2. $\mathbf{A}$ and $\mathbf{\Gamma}$ are sparse matrices containing ± 1 entries to pick the correct $g_{v_{\text{left}}}$, $g_{v_{\text{right}}}$, g_{v_i} and g_{v_j} from $\mathbf{g}$. Equation 3 is a quadratic form in $\mathbf{g}$ and $\mathbf{A}^{\mathsf{T}}\mathbf{A} + \mathbf{\Gamma}^{\mathsf{T}}\mathbf{\Gamma}$ is very sparse, symmetric, and positive semidefinite (because $\forall \mathbf{z}$: $\mathbf{z}^{\mathsf{T}}(\mathbf{A}^{\mathsf{T}}\mathbf{A} + \mathbf{\Gamma}^{\mathsf{T}}\mathbf{\Gamma})\mathbf{z} = \|\mathbf{Az}\|_2^2 + \|\mathbf{\Gamma z}\|_2^2 \geq 0$). We minimize it with respect to $\mathbf{g}$ with Eigen's [14] conjugate gradient (CG) implementation and stop CG when $\|\mathbf{r}\|_2 / \|\mathbf{A}^{\mathsf{T}}\mathbf{f}\|_2 < 10^{-5}$ ($\mathbf{r}$ is the residual), which typically requires < 200 iterations even for large datasets. Due to automatic white balancing, different camera response curves and different light colors (noon vs. sunset vs. artificial light) between images it is not sufficient to only optimize the luminance channel. We thus optimize all three channels in parallel.

Poisson Editing. Even with the above support regions Lempitsky and Ivanov's global adjustment does not eliminate all visible seams, see an example in Figure 11 (bottom row, center). Thus, subsequent to global adjustment we additionally perform local Poisson image editing [16]. Gal *et al.* [9] do this as well, but in a way that makes the computation prohibitively expensive: They Poisson edit complete texture patches, which results in huge linear systems (with $> 10^7$ variables for the largest patches in our datasets).

We thus restrict the Poisson editing of a patch to a 20 pixel wide border strip (shown in light blue in Figure 5). We use this strip's outer rim (Fig. 5, dark blue) and inner rim (Fig. 5, red) as Poisson equation boundary conditions: We fix each outer rim pixel's value to the mean of the pixel's color in the image assigned to the patch and the image assigned to the neighboring patch. Each inner rim pixel's value is fixed to its current color. If the patch is too small, we omit the inner rim. The Poisson equation's guidance field is the strip's Laplacian.

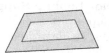

Fig. 5. A texture patch has a border strip (light blue) with an outer (dark blue) and inner rim (red)

For all patches we solve the resulting linear systems in parallel with Eigen's [14] SparseLU factorization. For each patch we only compute the factorization once and reuse it for all color channels because the system's matrix stays the same. Adjusting only strips is considerably more time and memory efficient than adjusting whole patches. Note, that this local adjustment is a much weaker form of the case shown in Figure 2 (center) because patch colors have been adjusted globally beforehand. Also note, that we do not mix two images' Laplacians and therefore still avoid blending.

dataset	# views	# mesh faces	image resolution
Statue	334	4.9 million	5616×3744
City Wall	561	8.2 million	2000×1500
Castle Ruin	287	20.3 million	5616×3744

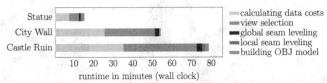

Fig. 6. Summary of the three datasets used in the evaluation and runtime of the individual parts of the algorithm

5 Evaluation

We now evaluate the proposed approach using three datasets (Statue, City Wall, Castle Ruin) of varying complexity, see Figure 6 for a summary of their properties. Even our largest dataset (Castle Ruin, Figure 7) can be textured within less than 80 min on a modern machine with two 8 core Xeon E5-2650v2 CPUs and 128 GB of memory. Main computational bottlenecks are the data cost computation whose complexity is linear in the number of views and the number of pixels per view, and the graph cut-based view selection which is linear in the number of mesh faces and the number of views. When altering the above datasets properties, *e.g.*, by simplifying the mesh, we found that the theoretical complexities fit closely in practice. The data term computation is already fully parallelized but the graph cut cannot be parallelized easily due to the graph's irregular structure. Still, this is in stark contrast to other methods which may yield theoretically optimal results while requiring a tremendous amount of computation. *E.g.*, Goldluecke *et al.* compute for several hours (partially on the GPU) to texture small models with 36 views within a super-resolution framework [12].

In the following sections, we evaluate the individual components of our approach and compare them to related work.

Data Term and Photo-Consistency Check. As argued previously, the data term must take the content of the candidate images and not only their geometric configuration into account. Allène *et al.*'s data term [2] computes a face's projection area and thus selects the image in the center of Figure 8 for texturing the statue's arm, even though this image is not focused on the arm but on its background. Gal *et al.*'s data term [9] favors instead large gradient magnitudes and large projection areas. It thus uses a different image for the arm, yielding a much crisper result as shown in Figure 8 (right).

A failure case of Gal's data term are datasets with little surface texture detail. For example the Middlebury Dino [17] is based on a uniform white plaster statue, all views have the same distance to the scene center and out-of-focus blur is not an issue. Thus, Gal's data term accounts for effects that do not occur in this

Fig. 7. Some texturing results of the Castle Ruin dataset

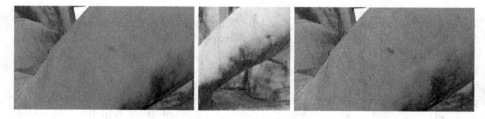

Fig. 8. *Left:* Statue's arm textured with Allène's [2] data term. *Center:* Detail from the image used for texturing the arm in the left image, exhibiting out-of-focus blur. *Right:* The arm textured with Gal's [9] data term. (Best viewed on screen.)

dataset. We found that the data term instead overfits to artifacts such as shadows and the color adjustment is incapable of fixing the resulting artifacts.

Another drawback of Gal's data term is, that it frequently uses occluders to texture the background (as shown in Figure 9 (top right)) if the occluder contains more high-frequency image content than the correct texture.

In Figure 9 (bottom left) we show the photo-consistency check at work for one exemplary face. This face has many outliers (red), *i.e.* views seeing an occluder instead of the correct face content. The gray ellipse marks all views that our check classifies as inliers. Only one view is misclassified. Note the black path taken by the shifted mean: The starting point on the path's bottom left is the algorithm's initial mean. Sinha *et al.* [19] and Grammatikopoulos *et al.* [13] use it without iterating in mean-shift fashion. It is, however, far off from the true inlier mean and if we used a fixed window around it many views would be misclassified. If we used all views' covariance matrix instead of a fixed window all views except for the bottommost data point would be classified as inliers. Our approach only misclassifies the one outlier closest to the inlier set and is able to remove the pedestrian (see Figure 9 (bottom right)).

Our proposed photo-consistency check may fail, *e.g.* if a face is seen by very few views. In this case there is little image evidence for what is an inlier or an

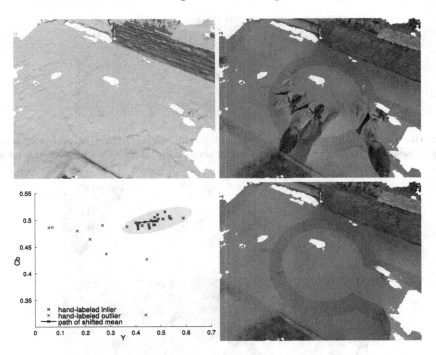

Fig. 9. *Top left:* Input mesh. *Top right:* Pedestrian used as texture for the ground. *Bottom left:* Photo-consistency check visualization for a single face. Red and blue crosses are the face's mean color (here we show only the Y and C_b component) in different images. *Bottom right:* Mesh textured with photo-consistency check.

outlier and the classification becomes inaccurate. However, in our experience this is often fixed by the view selection's smoothness term: If view X is erroneously classified as outlier for face A, but not for face B, it may still be optimal to choose it for texturing both A and B if the data penalty for face A is smaller than the avoided smoothness penalty between A and B. This can also fail, especially in border cases where there are not enough neighbor faces that impose a smoothness penalty, such as in the bottom right corner of the bottom right image in Figure 9.

Smoothness Term. Lempitsky and Ivanov use the error on a seam integrated along the seam as smoothness term for the view selection. The result is a model where blurry texture patches selected from distant views occur frequently since they make seams less noticeable (see Figure 10 (left)). Using the Potts model instead yields a considerably sharper result (see Figure 10 (right)).

Color Adjustment. The global color adjustment used in the base method [15] operates on a per-vertex base. It fails if a seam pixel does not project onto the same 3D position in the images on both sides of its seam. This can occur for various reasons: Camera misalignment, 3D reconstruction inaccuracies or a different 3D footprint size of the looked up pixels if the projected resolution differs

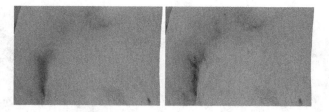

Fig. 10. *Left:* Statue's shoulder with Lempitsky and Ivanov's smoothness term. *Right:* Resulting model with the Potts model smoothness term. (Best viewed on screen.)

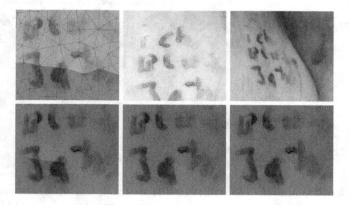

Fig. 11. *Top row:* Unadjusted mesh with wireframe, detail of input image used for upper patch, and detail of input image used for lower patch. *Bottom row:* Artifact from global color adjustment caused by texture misalignment, result of global adjustment with support region, and result after Poisson editing.

Fig. 12. *Top row:* One of the input images. *Bottom row:* Reconstructed City Wall color adjusted without support region and without Poisson editing, and the same reconstruction adjusted with support region and Poisson editing. (Best viewed on screen.)

in both images. In Figure 11 (top left) the vertex on the right side of the letter 'J' projects into the letter itself to the seam's top and into the lighter background to the seam's bottom. The result after global adjustment (bottom left) exhibits a strong color artifact. We alleviate this using support regions during sampling (bottom center). The remaining visible seams are fixed with Poisson editing as shown in Figure 11 (bottom right). Poisson editing does obviously not correct texture alignment problems but disguises most seams well so that they are virtually invisible unless the model is inspected from a very close distance.

These color adjustment problems in Lempitsky and Ivanov's method occur frequently when mesh resolution is much lower than image resolution (which is the key application of texturing). Vertex projections' colors are in this case much less representative for the vertices' surroundings. Figure 12 shows such an example: The result without support region and Poisson editing (bottom left) exhibits several strong color artifacts (white arrows) when compared to a photograph of the area (top). The result with support region and Poisson editing (bottom right) significantly improves quality.

6   Conclusions and Future Work

Applying textures to reconstructed models is one of the keys to realism. Surprisingly, this topic has been neglected in recent years and the state of the art is still to reconstruct models with per-vertex colors. We therefore presented the first comprehensive texturing framework for large 3D reconstructions with registered images. Based on existing work, we make several key changes that have a large impact: Large-scale, real-world geometry reconstructions can now be enriched with high-quality textures which will significantly increase the realism of reconstructed models. Typical effects occurring frequently in these datasets, namely inaccurate camera parameters and geometry, lighting and exposure variation, image scale variation, out-of-focus blur and unreconstructed occluders are handled automatically and efficiently. In fact, we can texture meshes with more than 20 million faces using close to 300 images in less than 80 minutes.

Avenues for future work include improving the efficiency of our approach and accelerating the computational bottlenecks. In addition, we plan to parallelize on a coarser scale to texture huge scenes on a compute cluster in the spirit of Agarwal et al.'s [1] structure-from-motion system.

Acknowledgements. We are grateful for financial support by the Intel Visual Computing Institute through the project *RealityScan*. Also, we thank Victor Lempitsky and Denis Ivanov for providing the code for their paper.

Source Code. This project's source code can be downloaded from the project web page www.gris.informatik.tu-darmstadt.de/projects/mvs-texturing.

References

1. Agarwal, S., Snavely, N., Simon, I., Seitz, S.M., Szeliski, R.: Building Rome in a day. In: ICCV (2009)

2. Allène, C., Pons, J.P., Keriven, R.: Seamless image-based texture atlases using multi-band blending. In: ICPR (2008)
3. Boykov, Y., Veksler, O., Zabih, R.: Fast approximate energy minimization via graph cuts. PAMI 23 (2001)
4. Buehler, C., Bosse, M., McMillan, L., Gortler, S., Cohen, M.: Unstructured lumigraph rendering. In: SIGGRAPH (2001)
5. Callieri, M., Cignoni, P., Corsini, M., Scopigno, R.: Masked photo blending: Mapping dense photographic dataset on high-resolution sampled 3D models. Computers & Graphics 32 (2008)
6. Chen, Z., Zhou, J., Chen, Y., Wang, G.: 3D texture mapping in multi-view reconstruction. In: Bebis, G., Boyle, R., Parvin, B., Koracin, D., Fowlkes, C., Wang, S., Choi, M.-H., Mantler, S., Schulze, J., Acevedo, D., Mueller, K., Papka, M. (eds.) ISVC 2012, Part I. LNCS, vol. 7431, pp. 359–371. Springer, Heidelberg (2012)
7. Frahm, J.-M., Fite-Georgel, P., Gallup, D., Johnson, T., Raguram, R., Wu, C., Jen, Y.-H., Dunn, E., Clipp, B., Lazebnik, S., Pollefeys, M.: Building rome on a cloudless day. In: Daniilidis, K., Maragos, P., Paragios, N. (eds.) ECCV 2010, Part IV. LNCS, vol. 6314, pp. 368–381. Springer, Heidelberg (2010)
8. Furukawa, Y., Curless, B., Seitz, S.M., Szeliski, R.: Towards Internet-scale multi-view stereo. In: CVPR (2010)
9. Gal, R., Wexler, Y., Ofek, E., Hoppe, H., Cohen-Or, D.: Seamless montage for texturing models. Computer Graphics Forum 29 (2010)
10. Garcia-Dorado, I., Demir, I., Aliaga, D.G.: Automatic urban modeling using volumetric reconstruction with surface graph cuts. Computers & Graphics 37 (2013)
11. Geva, A.: ColDet 3D collision detection, http://sourceforge.net/projects/coldet
12. Goldluecke, B., Aubry, M., Kolev, K., Cremers, D.: A super-resolution framework for high-accuracy multiview reconstruction. IJCV (2013)
13. Grammatikopoulos, L., Kalisperakis, I., Karras, G., Petsa, E.: Automatic multi-view texture mapping of 3D surface projections. In: 3D-ARCH (2007)
14. Guennebaud, G., Jacob, B., et al.: Eigen v3 (2010), http://eigen.tuxfamily.org
15. Lempitsky, V., Ivanov, D.: Seamless mosaicing of image-based texture maps. In: CVPR (2007)
16. Pérez, P., Gangnet, M., Blake, A.: Poisson image editing. ACM Transactions on Graphics 22(3) (2003)
17. Seitz, S.M., Curless, B., Diebel, J., Scharstein, D., Szeliski, R.: A comparison and evaluation of multi-view stereo reconstruction algorithms. In: CVPR (2006)
18. Shan, Q., Adams, R., Curless, B., Furukawa, Y., Seitz, S.M.: The visual Turing test for scene reconstruction. In: 3DV (2013)
19. Sinha, S.N., Steedly, D., Szeliski, R., Agrawala, M., Pollefeys, M.: Interactive 3D architectural modeling from unordered photo collections. In: SIGGRAPH Asia (2008)
20. Snavely, N., Seitz, S.M., Szeliski, R.: Photo tourism: Exploring photo collections in 3D. In: SIGGRAPH (2006)
21. Stamos, I., Allen, P.K.: Geometry and texture recovery of scenes of large scale. Computer Vision and Image Understanding 88(2) (2002)
22. Tan, Y.K.A., Kwoh, L.K., Ong, S.H.: Large scale texture mapping of building facades. The International Archives of the Photogrammetry, Remote Sensing and Spatial Information Sciences 37 (2008)
23. Velho, L., Sossai Jr., J.: Projective texture atlas construction for 3D photography. The Visual Computer 23 (2007)

Author Index

Printed in the United States
By Bookmasters